Electronic Commerce 2008

A Managerial Perspective

Electronic Commerce 2008

A Managerial Perspective

Efraim Turban
University of Hawaii

David King
JDA Software Group, Inc.

Judy McKay
Swinburne University, Australia

Peter Marshall
University of Tasmania, Australia

Jae Lee
Korea Advanced Institute of Science and Technology

Dennis Viehland
Massey University, New Zealand

with contributions by

Linda Volonino
Canisius College

Christy Cheung
Hong Kong Baptist University

Linda Lai
Macau Polytechnic Institute of China

Carol Pollard
Appalachian State University

PEARSON
Prentice Hall

Upper Saddle River, NJ 07458

AVP/Executive Editor: Bob Horan
Product Development Manager: Ashley Santora
Assistant Editor: Kelly Loftus
Editorial Assistant: Christine Ietto
Marketing Manager: Jodi Bassett
Marketing Assistant: Ian Gold
Senior Managing Editor: Judy Leale
Associate Managing Editor: Renata Butera
Project Manager, Production: Carol Samet
Permissions Coordinator: Charles Morris
Manufacturing Buyer: Michelle Klein
Design/Composition Manager: Christy Mahon
Art Director: Suzanne Duda
Interior Design: Jill Little
Cover Design: Pat Smythe
Cover Illustration: John Bleck
Composition: Integra Software Services Pvt. Ltd.
Full-Service Project Management: BookMasters, Inc. /Sharon Anderson
Printer/Binder: Courier/Kendallville
Typeface: 10.25/12 ACaslon Regular

Credits and acknowledgments borrowed from other sources and reproduced, with permission, in this textbook appear on appropriate page within text.

Pearson Education LTD.
Pearson Education Singapore, Pte. Ltd
Pearson Education, Canada, Ltd
Pearson Education–Japan

Pearson Education Australia PTY, Limited
Pearson Education North Asia Ltd
Pearson Educación de Mexico, S.A. de C.V.
Pearson Education Malaysia, Pte. Ltd.

10 9 8 7 6 5 4 3 2 1
ISBN-13: 978-0-13-224331-5
ISBN-10:   0-13-224331-8

Dedicated to all those who are interested
in learning about electronic commerce.

Contents in Brief

www.prenhall.com/turban

Contents

CHAPTER 2 E-MARKETPLACES: STRUCTURES, MECHANISMS, ECONOMICS, AND IMPACTS 42

Part 2 Internet Consumer Retailing   90

CHAPTER 3 RETAILING IN ELECTRONIC COMMERCE: PRODUCTS AND SERVICES

Part 4 Other EC Models and Applications   363

Part 5 EC Support Services   471

CHAPTER 17 **LEGAL, ETHICAL, AND COMPLIANCE ISSUES IN EC . . . 771**

Online Chapter

Part 7 Application Development

Online Chapters

Online Appendices

Technical Appendices

Online Tutorials

Entering the third millennium, we are experiencing one of the most important changes to our daily lives—the move to an Internet-based society. According to the *Computer Industry Almanac*, the number of Internet users worldwide topped 1 billion in 2005 (*Computer Industry Almanac* 2006), and that number is expected to reach 2 billion by 2011 primarily due to the use of cell phones used to access the Internet, as well as the advent of less expensive computers ($100 or less). Internet World Stats (internetworldstats.com) reported in January 2007 that almost 70 percent of the U.S. population (over 232 million) surf the Internet. More interesting is the fact that over 90 percent of people between the ages of 5 and 17 surf the Internet on a regular basis. It is clear that these percentages will continue to increase, and similar trends exist in most other countries. As a result, much has changed at home, school, work, and in the government—and even in our leisure activities. Some of these changes are spreading around the globe. Others are just beginning in some countries. One of the most significant changes is in how we conduct business, especially in how we manage marketplaces and trading. For example, the senior author of this book pays all his bills online, trades stock online, buys airline and event tickets online, buys books online, and purchased his computer, printer, and memory sticks online, to cite just a few examples.

Electronic commerce (EC) describes the manner in which transactions take place over networks, mostly the Internet. It is the process of electronically buying and selling goods, services, and information. Certain EC applications, such as buying and selling stocks and airline tickets on the Internet, are growing very rapidly, exceeding non–Internet trades. But EC is not just about buying and selling; it also is about electronically communicating, collaborating, and discovering information (sometimes referred to as *e-business*). It is about e-learning, e-government, social networks, and much more. EC will have an impact on a significant portion of the world, affecting businesses, professions, and, of course, people.

The impact of EC is not just in the creation of Web-based businesses. It is the building of a new industrial order. Such a revolution brings a myriad of opportunities, as well as risks. Bill Gates is aware of this, and the company he founded, Microsoft, is continually developing new Internet and EC products and services. Yet Gates has stated that Microsoft is always 2 years away from failure—that somewhere out there is an unknown competitor who could render its business model obsolete (Heller 2005). Bill Gates knows that competition today is not among products or services, but among business models. What is true for Microsoft is true for just about every other company. The hottest and most dangerous new business models out there are on the Web.

The years between 2005 and 2007 have been characterized by the emergence of Web 2.0, which expanded the boundaries of e-commerce from trading, information search, and collaboration with a business orientation, to personal life support, and then back to business, because companies are now adopting social computing technologies that were designed for individual use (such as blogs, wikis, file sharing, and social networks) to increase the effectiveness and efficiency of their operations.

Forrester Research reports that the easy connections that social computing has given us have made a major impact not only on the social structure that exists outside of the business world, but also on the global economy. Because of the pervasiveness of social computing, Forrester suggests that individuals take information from each other more often, rather than from institutional sources, such as mainstream media outlets and corporations. For a company to survive, Forrester suggests that its marketing initiatives must fundamentally change from a top-down information flow to one where communities and social computing initiatives are part of its products and services (reported by Blancharski 2006).

In revising *E-Commerce 2006* to *E-Commerce 2008*, we paid great attention to these developments. The reason is that the so-called social computing is changing not only our lives and the way we do business, but also the field of e-commerce itself.

The purpose of this book is to describe what EC is—how it is being conducted and managed—as well as to assess its major opportunities, limitations, issues, and risks, all in the social-computing business environment. It is written from a managerial perspective. Because EC is an interdisciplinary topic, it should be of interest to managers and professional people in any functional area of business in all industries. People in government, education, health services, and other areas also will benefit from learning about EC.

Today, EC and e-business are going through a period of consolidation in which enthusiasm for new technologies and ideas is accompanied by careful attention to strategy, implementation, and profitability. Most of all, people recognize that e-business has three parts; it is not just about technology, it is also about commerce and people.

This book is written by experienced authors who share academic as well as real-world practices. It is a comprehensive text that can be used in one-semester or two-semester courses. It also can be used to supplement a text on Internet fundamentals, management information systems (MIS), or marketing.

FEATURES OF THIS BOOK

Several features are unique to this book:

Managerial Orientation

Electronic commerce can be approached from two major aspects: technological and managerial. This text uses the second approach. Most of the presentations are about EC applications and implementation. However, we do recognize the importance of the technology; therefore, we present the essentials of security in Chapter 11 and the essentials of infrastructure and system development in Chapter 19, which is located on the book's Web site (prenhall.com/turban). We also provide some detailed technology material in the files, appendices, and tutorials on the book's Web site. Managerial issues are provided at the end of each chapter.

Real-World Orientation

Extensive, vivid examples from large corporations, small businesses, and government and nonprofit agencies from all over the world make concepts come alive. These examples show students the capabilities of EC, its cost and justification, and the innovative ways real corporations are using EC in their operations. Examples cover both large and small (SME) companies.

Solid Theoretical Background and Research Suggestions

Throughout the book, we present the theoretical foundations necessary for understanding EC, ranging from consumer behavior to the economic theory of competition. Furthermore, we provide Web site resources, many exercises, and extensive references to supplement the theoretical presentations. At the end of each chapter, we provide suggested research topics. Online, we provide a research appendix with an extensive topic-by-topic bibliography.

Most Current Cutting-Edge Topics

The book presents the most current topics relating to EC, as evidenced by the many 2005 to 2007 citations. Topics such as social networking, e-learning, e-government, e-strategy, Web-based supply chain systems, collaborative commerce, mobile commerce, and EC economics are presented from the theoretical point of view as well as from the application side.

Integrated Systems

In contrast to other books that highlight isolated Internet-based systems, we emphasize those systems that support the enterprise and supply chain management. Intra- and interorganizational systems are highlighted as are the latest innovations in global EC and in Web-based applications.

Global Perspective

The importance of global competition, partnerships, and trade is increasing rapidly. EC facilitates export and import, the management of multinational companies, and electronic trading around the globe. International examples are provided throughout the book.

Interdisciplinary Approach

E-commerce is interdisciplinary, and we illustrate this throughout the book. Major EC-related disciplines include accounting, finance, information systems, marketing, management, operations management, and human resources management. In addition, some nonbusiness disciplines are related, especially public administration, computer science, engineering, psychology, political science, and law. Finally, economics plays a major role in the understanding of EC.

EC Failures and Lessons Learned

In addition to EC success stories, we also present EC failures, and, where possible, analyze the causes of those failures with lessons learned.

Online Support

Over 150 files are available online to supplement text material. These include files on generic topics, such as data mining and intranets; cases; technically oriented text; and much more.

User-Friendliness

While covering all major EC topics, this book is clear, simple, and well organized. It provides all the basic definitions of terms as well as logical conceptual support. Furthermore, the book is easy to understand and is full of interesting real-world examples and "war stories" that keep readers' interest at a high level. Relevant review questions are provided at the end of each section so the reader can pause to review and digest the new material.

WHAT'S NEW IN THIS EDITION?

The following are the major changes in this edition:

- **New coauthors.** We welcome Judy McKay (Swinburne University, Australia) and Peter Marshall (Tasmania University, Australia) who bring expertise in several e-business areas. They are coauthors of *Strategic Management of e-Business*, published by John Wiley & Sons in 2004.
- **New chapter.** A new chapter on social networks and industry disruptors (Chapter 18) examines the most cutting-edge technologies and includes case studies of some of the industry players and leaders.

- **Cross-reference table.** This table, provided later in this preface, relates the various sections of Chapter 18 to specific chapters throughout the book.
- **Chapters with major changes.** Major changes have been made to the following chapters:
  - Chapter 1 now includes social networks, new business models, and other leading-edge topics.
  - Chapter 4 includes new coverage of advertising models and strategies.
  - Chapter 7 includes the addition of several challenging innovations demonstrated in new cases.
  - Chapter 11 has been completely rewritten, shifting from a generic view of security to an e-commerce orientation.
  - Chapter 13 includes the addition of major innovations in e-supply chains and e-supply chain strategies.
  - Chapter 14 has significantly upgraded the concepts of business planning, e-strategy, and business models. For more on business models and business planning, see the new Appendices B and C on the book's Web site.
  - Chapter 17 has been completely rewritten to include the legal issues of social networks and other innovative Web sites. The privacy issues have been expanded with an e-commerce orientation.
- **Chapters with less significant changes.** All data in the chapters were updated. About 25 percent of all cases have been replaced. About 20 percent of all end-of-chapter material has been updated and/or expanded. Managerial issues and research topics were updated, as well as figures and tables. Duplications were eliminated and explanations of exhibits have been made more understandable. New topics were added in many of the sections to reflect the Web 2.0 revolution.
- **New online appendices.** Two appendices were added on the book's Web site:
  - Appendix B: Structure and Components of E-Commerce Business Models
  - Appendix C: E-Business Planning and Analysis Framework
- **Online files.** The online files were updated and reorganized. Many new files have been added.

ORGANIZATION OF THE BOOK

The book is divided into 18 chapters grouped into 6 parts. One additional chapter (19), a research appendix, two regular appendices, three technology appendices, and two tutorials are available as online supplements.

PART 1—INTRODUCTION TO EC

In Part 1, we provide an overview of today's business environment as well as the fundamentals of EC and some of its terminology (Chapter 1) and a discussion of electronic markets and their mechanisms and impacts (Chapter 2).

PART 2—INTERNET CONSUMER RETAILING

In Part 2, we describe EC B2C applications in two chapters. Chapter 3 addresses e-tailing and electronic service industries (e.g., travel, e-banking). Chapter 4 deals with consumer behavior online, market research, and online advertising.

PART 3—BUSINESS-TO-BUSINESS E-COMMERCE

In Part 3, we examine the one-to-many B2B models (Chapter 5), including auctions, and the many-to-many models (Chapter 6), including exchanges. Chapter 7 describes the e-supply chain, intrabusiness EC, and collaborative commerce. An online appendix

- Self-Study Quizzes, by Jon Outland, which include multiple-choice, true-false, and essay questions for each chapter. Each question includes a hint and coaching tip for students' reference. Students receive automatic feedback after submitting each quiz.
- All of the Internet Exercises from the end of each chapter in the text are provided on the Web site for convenient student use.

Materials for Your Online Course

Prentice Hall supports adopters using online courses by providing files ready for upload into both WebCT and BlackBoard course management systems for our testing, quizzing, and other supplements. Please contact your local Prentice Hall representative or mis_service@prenhall.com for further information on your particular course.

ACKNOWLEDGMENTS

Many individuals helped us create this text. Faculty feedback was solicited via reviews and through individual interviews. We are grateful to the following faculty for their contributions.

CONTENT CONTRIBUTORS

The following individuals contributed material for this edition:

- Linda Volonino of Canisius College updated Chapters 11 and 17.
- Linda Lai of the Macau Polytechnic Institute of China updated Chapter 8.
- Carol Pollard of Appalachian State University updated Chapter 19, available on the book's Web site.
- Christy Cheung of Hong Kong Baptist University contributed material to Chapter 4 and helped in updating several other chapters.
- Rajiv Kohli of the College of William and Mary contributed Chapter 14 on the economics of e-commerce in *Electronic Commerce 2006*.
- Merrill Warkentin of Mississippi State University contributed to Chapter 3. Merrill is a coauthor of our *Electronic Commerce 2002*.

REVIEWERS

We wish to thank the faculty who participated in reviews of this text and our other EC titles.

David Ambrosini, Cabrillo College

Timothy Ay, Villanova University

Deborah Ballou, University of Notre Dame

Christine Barnes, Lakeland Community College

Martin Barriff, Illinois Institute of Technology

Sandy Bobzien, Presentation College

Stefan Brandle, Taylor University

Joseph Brooks, University of Hawaii

Bruce Brorson, University of Minnesota

Clifford Brozo, Monroe College– New Rochelle

Stanley Buchin, Boston University

John Bugado, National University

Ernest Capozzolli, Troy State University

Mark Cecchini, University of Florida

Sandy Claws, Northern University

Jack Cook, State University of New York at Geneseo

Larry Corman, Fort Lewis College

Mary Culnan, Georgetown University

Chet Cunningham, Madisonville Community College

Roland Eicheleberger, Baylor University

Ted Ferretti, Northeastern University

Colin Fukai, Gonzaga University

Vickie Fullmer, Webster University

Dennis Galletta, University of Pittsburgh

Ken Griggs, California Polytechnic University

Varun Grover, University of South Carolina

Tom Gruen, University of Colorado at Colorado Springs

Norman Hahn, Thomas Nelson Community College

Harry Harmon, University of Central Missouri

James Henson, Barry University

Sadie Herbert, Mississippi Gulf Coast Community College

James Hogue, Wayland Baptist University

Brian Howland, Boston University

Chang Hsieh, University of Southern Mississippi

Paul Hu, University of Utah

Jin H. Im, Sacred Heart University

Jeffrey Johnson, Utah State University

Kenneth H. Johnson, Illinois Institute of Technology

Robert Johnson, University of Connecticut

Morgan Jones, University of North Carolina

Charles Kelley, California Baptist University

Douglas Kline, Sam Houston State University

Mary Beth Klinger, College of Southern Maryland

Tanvi Kothari, Temple University

Joanne Kuzma, St. Petersburg College

Charles Lange, DeVry University

Chunlei Liu, Troy State University

Byungtae Lee, University of Illinois at Chicago

Lakshmi Lyer, University of North Carolina

Joseph Maggi, Technical College of the Lowcountry

Ross Malaga, Montclair State University

Steve Mann, Humphreys College

Michael McLeod, East Carolina University

Susan McNamara, Northeastern University

Mohon Menon, University of South Alabama

Stephanie Miller, University of Georgia

Ajay Mishra, State University of New York at Binghamton

Bud Mishra, New York University

Robert Moore, Mississippi State University

Lawerence Muller, LaGuardia Community College, CUNY

Suzy Murray, Piedmont Technical College

William Nance, San Jose State University

Lewis Neisner, University of Maryland

Katherine A. Olson, Northern Virginia Community College

Robert Oullette, University of Maryland University College

Somendra Pant, Clarkson University

Wayne Pauli, Dakota State University

Craig Peterson, Utah State University

Sarah Pettitt, Champlain College

Dien D. Phan, University of Vermont

H.R. Rao, State University of New York at Buffalo

Catherine M. Roche, Rockland Community College

Jorge Romero, Towson University

Greg Rose, California State University at Chico

Linda Salchenberger, Loyola University of Chicago

George Schell, University of North Carolina at Wilmington

Sri Sharma, Oakland University

Seungjae Shin, Mississippi State University–Meridian

Sumit Sircar, University of Texas at Arlington

Hongjun Song, University of Memphis

Kan Sugandh, DeVry Institute of Technology

John Thacher, Gwinnett Technical College

Goran Trajkovski, Towson University

Dothang Truong, Fayetteville State University

Linda Volonino, Canisius College

Andrea Wachter, Point Park University

Ken Williamson, James Madison University

John Windsor, University of North Texas

Gregory Wood, Canisius College

Walter Wymer, Christopher Newport University

James Zemanek, East Carolina University

Several individuals helped us with the administrative work. Special mention goes to Christy Cheung of Hong Kong Baptist University who helped with editing, drawing figures, verifying URLs, and more. We also thank the many students of San Yet–Sun University in Taiwan for their help in searches and diagramming. We thank Daphne Turban, Sarah Miller, and all these people for their dedication and superb performance shown throughout the project.

We also recognize the various organizations and corporations that provided us with permissions to reproduce material. Special thanks go to Dion Hinchcliffe for allowing us to use his figures. Grateful thanks are also given to Jennifer C. Keem for legal research and Richard P. Volonino, search engine marketing research.

Thanks also to the Prentice Hall team that helped us from the inception of the project to its completion under the leadership of Executive Editor Bob Horan. The dedicated staff includes Editorial Project Managers Ana Jankowski and Ashley Santora, Editorial Assistant Kelly Loftus, Production Managers Carol Samet and Renata Butera, Art Directors Christy Mahon and Suzanne Duda, and Media Project Manager Ashley Lulling.

Last, but not least, we thank Judy Lang, who as coordinator and problem solver, contributed innovative ideas and provided the necessary editing.

REFERENCES

Blacharski, D. "How Social Computing is Changing the World." *ITWorld.com*, February 27, 2006. itworld.com/Tech/2987/nls_itinsights_social_060301 (accessed February 2007).

Computer Industry Almanac. "Worldwide Internet Users Top 1 Billion in 2005." January 4, 2006. c-i-a.com/pr0106.htm (accessed February 2007).

Heller, R. "Strengths and Weaknesses: Assess the Strengths and Weaknesses of Your Business, as Well as the Opportunities and Threats, with SWOT Analysis." *Thinking Managers*, 2005.

Internet World Stats. "Internet Usage Statistics: The Big Picture." January 11, 2007. internetworldstats.com/stats.htm (accessed February 2007)

CHAPTER 1

OVERVIEW OF ELECTRONIC COMMERCE

Content

Dell—Using E-Commerce for Success

Learning Objectives

Upon completion of this chapter, you will be able to:

1. Define electronic commerce (EC) and describe its various categories.

2. Describe and discuss the content and framework of EC.

3. Describe the major types of EC transactions.

4. Describe the digital revolution as a driver of EC.

5. Describe the business environment as a driver of EC.

6. Describe some EC business models.

7. Describe the benefits of EC to organizations, consumers, and society.

8. Describe the limitations of EC.

9. Describe the contribution of EC to organizations responding to environmental pressures.

10. Describe online social and business networks.

DELL—USING E-COMMERCE FOR SUCCESS

The Problem/Opportunity

Founded in 1985 by Michael Dell, Dell Computer Corp. (now known as Dell) was the first company to offer personal computers (PCs) via mail order. Dell designed its own PC system (with an Intel 8088 processor running at 8 MHz) and allowed customers to configure their own customized systems using the build-to-order concept (see Chapter 2, Appendix 2A). This concept was, and is still, Dell's cornerstone *business model*. By 1993, Dell had become one of the top five computer makers worldwide, threatening Compaq, which started a price war. At that time, Dell was taking orders by fax and snail mail and losing money. Losses reached over $100 million by 1994. The company was in trouble.

The Solution
DIRECT MARKETING ONLINE

The commercialization of the Internet in the early 1990s and the introduction of the World Wide Web in 1993 provided Dell with an *opportunity* to expand rapidly. Dell implemented aggressive online order-taking and opened subsidiaries in Europe and Asia. Dell also started to offer additional products on its Web site. This enabled Dell to batter Compaq, and in 2000 Dell became number one in worldwide PC shipments. At that time, Internet sales topped $50 million per day (about $18 billion per year). Today, Dell (*dell.com*) sells about $60 billion a year in computer-related products online, from network switches to printers, employing over 63,000 people.

Direct online marketing is Dell's major electronic commerce (EC) activity. Dell sells to the following groups:

- Individuals for their homes and home offices
- Small businesses (up to 200 employees)
- Medium and large businesses (over 200 employees)
- Government, education, and health-care organizations

Sales to the first group are classified as *business-to-consumer (B2C)*. Sales to the other three groups are classified as *business-to-business (B2B)*. Consumers shop at *dell.com* using an electronic catalog. The sales are completed using mechanisms described in Chapters 2 and 3.

In addition, Dell sells refurbished Dell computers and other products in electronic auctions at *dellauction.com*. As will be discussed in Chapters 2 and 10, online auctions are an important sales channel. In 2006, Dell opened physical stores, mainly in reaction to customer demands.

Business-to-Business EC. Most of Dell's sales are to businesses. Whereas B2C sales are facilitated by standard shopping aids (e.g., catalogs, shopping carts, credit card payments; see Chapters 2 and 3), B2B customers obtain additional help from Dell. Dell provides each of its nearly 100,000 business customers with Premier Dell service.

For example, British Airways (BA) considers Dell to be a strategic supplier. Dell provides notebooks and desktops to 25,000 BA users. Dell offers two e-procurement services to BA purchasing agents. The more basic service, Premier Dell, allows BA (and other businesses) to browse, buy, and track orders on a Dell Web site customized for the user's requirements. The site enables authorized users to select preconfigured PCs for their business unit or department. A more advanced version, Premier B2B, supports e-procurement systems such as Ariba and Commerce One. This provides automatic requisition and order fulfillment once an authorized user has chosen to buy a PC from Dell. BA has placed the e-procurement tools on its E-Working intranet. This allows authorized staff to purchase PCs through a portal that connects directly into Dell's systems.

In addition to supporting its business customers with e-procurement tools, Dell also is using EC in its own procurement. Dell developed an e-procurement model that it shares with its business partners, such as BA. One aspect of this model is the use of electronic tendering to conduct bids (see Chapter 5). Dell uses electronic tendering when it buys the components for its products.

In 2000, Dell created a B2B exchange at *dell.b2b.com*. This venture was a failure, like most other exchanges (see Chapter 6). As a result, Dell's B2B activities (in addition to direct sales and e-procurement) were shifted to collaborative commerce.

E-Collaboration. Dell has many business partners with whom it needs to communicate and collaborate. For example, Dell uses shippers, such as UPS and FedEx, to deliver its computers to individuals. It also uses third-party logistics companies to collect, maintain, and deliver components from its suppliers, and it has many other partners. As we will see in Chapter 7, Dell is using Web Services, an EC technology, to facilitate communication and reduce inventories. Web Services facilitate B2B integration. Integration efforts began in 2000 with other technologies when Dell encouraged its customers to buy online. The B2B integration offer combines Dell PowerEdge servers based on Intel architecture and webMethods B2B integration software to link customers' existing ERP (enterprise resource planning) or procurement systems directly with Dell and other trading partners. In addition, Dell can provide e-procurement applications and consulting services. Dell also educates customers in its technologies and offers suggestions on how to use them. This is particularly true for emerging technologies such as wireless.

Finally, Dell has a superb communication system with its over 15,000 service providers around the globe.

E-Customer Service. Dell uses a number of different tools to provide superb customer service around the clock. To leverage customer relationship management (CRM)—a customer service approach that is customer centered for lasting relationships—Dell provides a virtual help desk for self-diagnosis and service as well as direct access to technical support data. In addition, a phone-based help desk is open 24/7. Customers can also arrange for a live chat with a customer care agent. Product support includes troubleshooting, user guides, upgrades, downloads, news and press releases, FAQs, order status information, a "my account" page, a community forum (to exchange ideas, information, and experiences), bulletin boards and other customer-to-customer interaction features, training books (at a discount), and much more. Dell also offers educational programs at *learn.dell.com*.

Dell keeps a large customer database. Using data mining tools, it learns a great deal about its customers and attempts to make them happy. The database is used to improve marketing as well.

Intrabusiness EC. To support its build-to-order capabilities, significantly improve its demand-planning and factory-execution accuracy, reduce order-to-delivery time, and enhance customer service, Dell partnered with Accenture to create a new, high-performance supply chain planning solution. Now in place in Dell's plants around the world, the program, which paid for itself five times over during the first 12 months of operation, enables Dell to adapt more quickly to rapidly changing technologies and the business environment, maintaining its position as a high-performance business. Dell also has automated its factory scheduling, demand-planning capabilities, and inventory management using information technology and e-supply chain models.

Affiliate Program. Dell provides affiliate partners the opportunity to link from their Web sites to Dell.com. Dell pays 2 to 4 percent on any qualified sale made from clicking on Dell's link at the partners' sites (referring buyers).

The Results

Dell has been one of *Fortune*'s top five "Most Admired" companies since 1999, and it continuously advances in the rankings of the *Fortune* 500 and the *Fortune* Global 500. Dell has over 100 country-oriented Web sites, and profits are nearing $4 billion a year. If you had invested $10,000 in Dell's initial public offering (IPO) in 1987, you would be a millionaire just from that investment.

Dell actively supports EC research at the University of Texas in Austin (Dell's headquarters also are in Austin). It also contributes heavily to charity. Dell has partnered with the National Cristina Foundation (NCF) to provide computer technology to people with disabilities, students at risk, and economically disadvantaged persons. Paired with the company's recycling program, used computers are refurbished and then distributed through NCF. Through Dell's TechKnow Program, the company donates computers to urban middle schools. The students learn about computers by taking them apart and reassembling them, loading software, setting up and running printers, upgrading hardware, diagnosing and correcting basic hardware problems, and using the Internet. Upon completion of the program, students take home the computers they build and receive a year of free Internet access. Dell also awards grants each year to governmental and educational institutions to organize, promote, stage, and recycle computer equipment in a free "No Computer Should Go to Waste" collection event in their communities. Refurbished machines are dispersed through local charities.

In 2006, Dell opened physical stores to match its competitors and customer demands. Still, over 95 percent of its business is online and through mail orders. It also launched a blog called Direct2Dell (*direct2dell.com*). Dell also is expanding its business not only in the computer industry but also in consumer electronics. It is clearly an example of EC success.

Sources: Compiled from Kraemer and Dedrick (2001), Electronic Industry Alliance (2004), Wolfson (2005), Dell Recycling (2006), National Cristina Foundation (2006), and *dell.com* and *dellauction.com* (accessed August 2006).

WHAT WE CAN LEARN . . .

Dell exemplifies the major EC business models. First, it pioneered the direct-marketing model for PCs, and then it moved online. Furthermore, Dell supplemented its direct marketing with the build-to-order model on a large scale (mass customization). In doing so, Dell benefited from the elimination of intermediation with the first model and from extremely low inventories and superb cash flow from the second model. To meet the large demand for its quality products, Dell introduced other EC models, notably e-procurement for improving the purchasing of components, collaborative commerce with its partners, and intrabusiness EC for improving its internal operations. Finally, Dell uses e-CRM (CRM done online; see Chapter 13 for details) with its customers. By successfully using e-commerce models, Dell became a world-class company, triumphing over all of its competitors. Dell's EC business models have become classics and best practices and are followed today by many other manufacturers, notably automakers.

This chapter defines EC and lists the types of transactions that are executed in it. Various EC models and the benefits and limitations of EC also will be examined. Finally, a visual preview of the book's chapters will be provided.

1.1 ELECTRONIC COMMERCE: DEFINITIONS AND CONCEPTS

Let's begin by looking at what the management guru Peter Drucker has to say about EC:

The truly revolutionary impact of the Internet Revolution is just beginning to be felt. But it is not "information" that fuels this impact. It is not "artificial intelligence." It is not the effect of computers and data processing on decision making, policymaking, or strategy. It is something that practically no one foresaw or, indeed even talked about 10 or 15 years ago; e-commerce—that is, the explosive emergence of the Internet as a major, perhaps eventually the major, worldwide distribution channel for goods, for services, and, surprisingly, for managerial and professional jobs. This is profoundly changing economics, markets and industry structure, products and services and their flow; consumer segmentation, consumer values and consumer behavior; jobs and labor markets. But the impact may be even greater on societies and politics, and above all, on the way we see the world and ourselves in it. (Drucker 2002, pp. 3–4)

DEFINING ELECTRONIC COMMERCE

electronic commerce (EC)
The process of buying, selling, or exchanging products, services, or information via computer networks.

Electronic commerce (EC) is the process of buying, selling, transferring, or exchanging products, services, and/or information via computer networks, including the Internet. EC can also be defined from the following perspectives:

▶ **Business process.** From a business process perspective, EC is doing business electronically by completing business processes over electronic networks, thereby substituting information for physical business processes (Weill and Vitale 2001, p. 13).

▶ **Service.** From a service perspective, EC is a tool that addresses the desire of governments, firms, consumers, and management to cut service costs while improving the quality of customer service and increasing the speed of service delivery.

▶ **Learning.** From a learning perspective, EC is an enabler of online training and education in schools, universities, and other organizations, including businesses.

▶ **Collaborative.** From a collaborative perspective, EC is the framework for inter- and intraorganizational collaboration.

▶ **Community.** From a community perspective, EC provides a gathering place for community members to learn, transact, and collaborate. The most popular type of community is *social networks,* such as MySpace.

EC is often confused with e-business.

DEFINING E-BUSINESS

e-business
A broader definition of EC that includes not just the buying and selling of goods and services, but also servicing customers, collaborating with business partners, and conducting electronic transactions within an organization.

Some people view the term *commerce* only as describing transactions conducted between business partners. If this definition of commerce is used, the term *electronic commerce* would be fairly narrow. Thus, many use the term *e-business* instead. **E-business** refers to a broader definition of EC, not just the buying and selling of goods and services but also servicing customers, collaborating with business partners, conducting e-learning, and conducting electronic transactions *within* an organization. According to McKay and Marshall (2004), e-business is the use of the Internet and other information technologies to support commerce and improve business performance. However, some view e-business as comprising those activities that do not involve buying or selling over the Internet, such as collaboration and intrabusiness activities (online activities between and within businesses); that is, it is a complement of e-commerce. In this book, we use the broadest meaning of electronic commerce, which is basically equivalent to e-business. The two terms will be used interchangeably throughout the text.

PURE VERSUS PARTIAL EC

EC can take several forms depending on the *degree of digitization* (the transformation from physical to digital) of (1) the *product* (service) sold, (2) the *process* (e.g., ordering, payment, fulfillment), and (3) the *delivery method.* Choi et al. (1997) created a framework, shown in

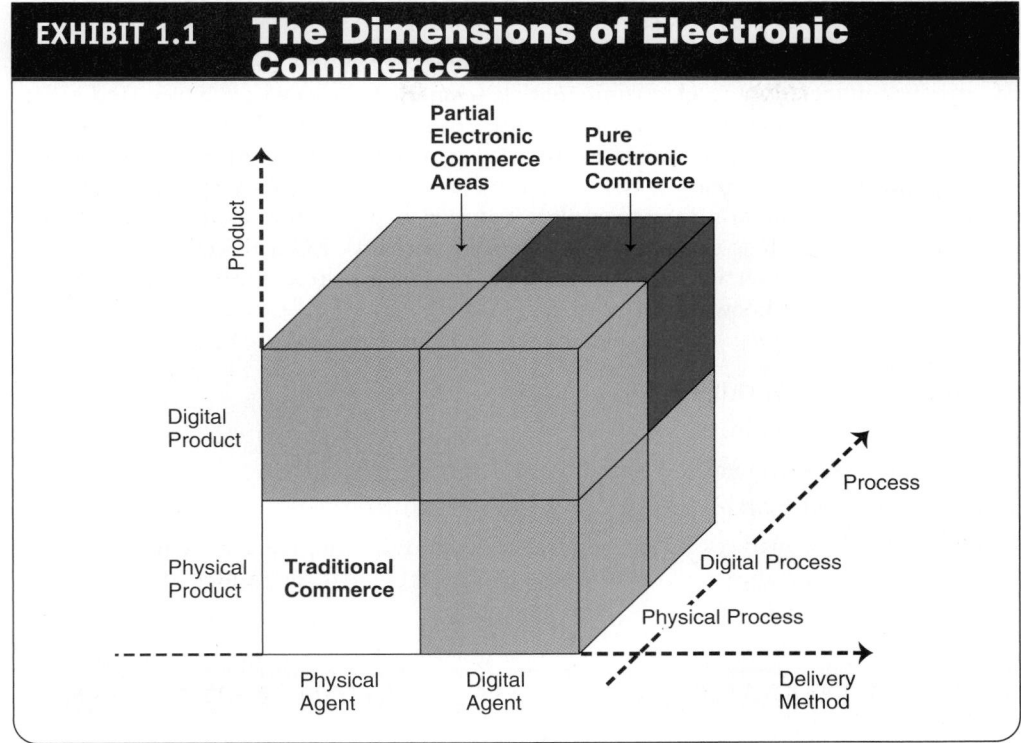

EXHIBIT 1.1   The Dimensions of Electronic Commerce

Source: Based on Whinston, A.B., Stahl, D.O., and Choi, S. *The Economics of Electronic Commerce*. Indianapolis, IN: Macmillan Technical Publishing, 1997. Used with permission.

Exhibit 1.1, which explains the possible configurations of these three dimensions. A product may be physical or digital, the process may be physical or digital, and the delivery method may be physical or digital. These alternatives create eight cubes, each of which has three dimensions. In traditional commerce, all three dimensions of the cube are physical (lower-left cube); in pure EC, all dimensions are digital (upper-right cube). All other cubes include a mix of digital and physical dimensions.

If there is at least one digital dimension, we consider the situation EC, but only *partial EC*. For example, purchasing a computer from Dell's Web site or a book from Amazon.com is partial EC because the merchandise is physically delivered. However, buying an e-book from Amazon.com or a software product from Buy.com is *pure EC* because the product, payment, and delivery to the buyer are all digital.

EC Organizations. Purely physical organizations (companies) are referred to as **brick-and-mortar (old-economy) organizations**, whereas companies that are engaged only in EC are considered **virtual** or **pure-play organizations**. **Click-and-mortar (or click-and-brick) organizations** are those that conduct some EC activities, usually as an additional marketing channel. Gradually, many brick-and-mortar companies are changing to click-and-mortar ones (e.g., Wal-Mart online and Marks & Spencer, see Online File W1.1).

INTERNET VERSUS NON-INTERNET EC

Most EC is done over the Internet, but EC also can be conducted on private networks, such as *value-added networks* (VANs; networks that add communications services to existing common carriers), on *local area networks* (LANs) using intranets, or even on a single computerized machine. For example, buying food from a vending machine where you pay with a smart card or a cell phone can be viewed as an EC activity.

An example of non-Internet EC would be field employees (such as sales reps) who are equipped with mobile handwriting-recognition computers so they can write their notes in the field immediately after a sales call. (For a more in-depth example, see the Maybelline Case at Online File W1.2.)

brick-and-mortar (old-economy) organizations
Old-economy organizations (corporations) that perform their primary business off-line, selling physical products by means of physical agents.

virtual (pure-play) organizations
Organizations that conduct their business activities solely online.

click-and-mortar (click-and-brick) organizations
Organizations that conduct some e-commerce activities, usually as an additional marketing channel.

ELECTRONIC MARKETS AND INTERORGANIZATIONAL AND INTRAORGANIZATIONAL INFORMATION SYSTEMS

EC can be conducted in an **electronic market (e-marketplace)** where buyers and sellers meet online to exchange goods, services, money, or information. Electronic markets may be supplemented by interorganizational or intraorganizational information systems. **Interorganizational information systems (IOSs)** are those where only routine transaction processing and information flow take place between two or more organizations using a standard protocol, such as electronic data interchange (EDI). EC activities that take place *within* individual organizations are facilitated by **intraorganizational information systems**. These systems also are known as *intrabusiness EC*.

Section 1.1 ▶ REVIEW QUESTIONS

1. Define EC and e-business.
2. Distinguish between pure and partial EC.
3. Define click-and-mortar and pure play organizations.
4. Define electronic markets, IOSs, and intraorganizational information systems.
5. Describe non-Internet EC.

1.2 THE EC FRAMEWORK, CLASSIFICATION, AND CONTENT

Although some people still use a stand-alone computer exclusively, the vast majority of people use computers connected to a global networked environment known as the *Internet*, or to its counterpart within organizations, an intranet. An **intranet** is a corporate or government network that uses Internet tools, such as Web browsers, and Internet protocols. Another computer environment is an **extranet**, a network that uses the Internet to link multiple intranets.

The opening case illustrates a new way of conducting business—electronically, using the Internet, intranet, and private networks. The case demonstrates several ways that businesses can use EC to improve the bottom line. Dell is not the only company that has moved its business online. Thousands of other companies, from retailers (e.g., see Online File W1.1, Marks & Spencer) to hospitals, are moving in this direction. In general, selling and buying electronically can be either *business-to-consumer (B2C)* or *business-to-business (B2B)*. In B2C, online transactions are made between businesses and individual consumers, such as when a person purchases a computer at dell.com. In B2B, businesses make online transactions with other businesses, such as when Dell electronically buys components from its suppliers. Dell also *collaborates* electronically with its partners and provides customer service online (e-CRM). Several other types of EC will be described soon.

EC is not yet a significant global economic force (less than 5 percent of all transactions in most industries). However, some predict that it could become globally significant within 10 to 20 years (Drucker 2002). Networked computing is the infrastructure for EC, and it is rapidly emerging as the standard computing environment for business, home, and government applications. *Networked computing* connects multiple computers and other electronic devices that are located in several different locations by telecommunications networks, including *wireless* ones. This connection allows users to access information stored in several different physical locations and to communicate and collaborate with people separated by great geographic distances and/or by time.

AN EC FRAMEWORK

The EC field is a diverse one, involving many activities, organizational units, and technologies (e.g., see Khosrow-Pour 2006). Therefore, a framework that describes its content is useful. Exhibit 1.2 introduces one such framework.

---

electronic market (e-marketplace)

An online marketplace where buyers and sellers meet to exchange goods, services, money, or information.

interorganizational information systems (IOSs)

Communications systems that allow routine transaction processing and information flow between two or more organizations.

intraorganizational information systems

Communication systems that enable e-commerce activities to go on within individual organizations.

intranet

An internal corporate or government network that uses Internet tools, such as Web browsers, and Internet protocols.

extranet

A network that uses the Internet to link multiple intranets.

EXHIBIT 1.2   A Framework for Electronic Commerce

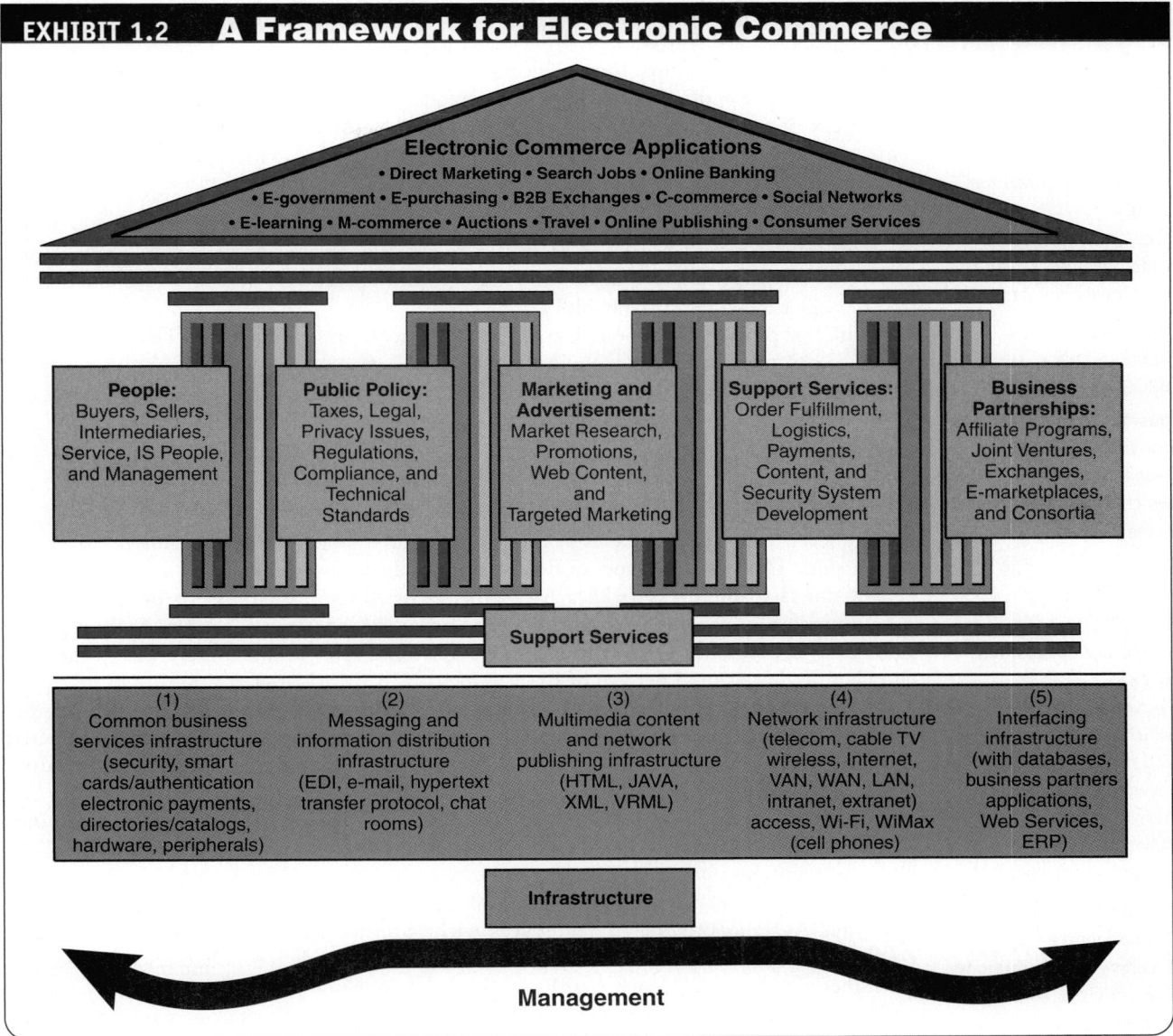

Electronic Commerce Applications
• Direct Marketing • Search Jobs • Online Banking
• E-government • E-purchasing • B2B Exchanges • C-commerce • Social Networks
• E-learning • M-commerce • Auctions • Travel • Online Publishing • Consumer Services

People:
Buyers, Sellers, Intermediaries, Service, IS People, and Management

Public Policy:
Taxes, Legal, Privacy Issues, Regulations, Compliance, and Technical Standards

Marketing and Advertisement:
Market Research, Promotions, Web Content, and Targeted Marketing

Support Services:
Order Fulfillment, Logistics, Payments, Content, and Security System Development

Business Partnerships:
Affiliate Programs, Joint Ventures, Exchanges, E-marketplaces, and Consortia

Support Services

(1)
Common business services infrastructure (security, smart cards/authentication electronic payments, directories/catalogs, hardware, peripherals)

(2)
Messaging and information distribution infrastructure (EDI, e-mail, hypertext transfer protocol, chat rooms)

(3)
Multimedia content and network publishing infrastructure (HTML, JAVA, XML, VRML)

(4)
Network infrastructure (telecom, cable TV wireless, Internet, VAN, WAN, LAN, intranet, extranet) access, Wi-Fi, WiMax (cell phones)

(5)
Interfacing infrastructure (with databases, business partners applications, Web Services, ERP)

Infrastructure

Management

As can be seen in the exhibit, there are many EC applications (top of exhibit), some of which were illustrated in the opening case about Dell; others will be shown throughout the book (see also Papazoglou and Ribbers 2006; Lee et al. 2006; and Jelassi and Enders 2005). To execute these applications, companies need the right information, infrastructure, and support services. Exhibit 1.2 shows that EC applications are supported by infrastructure and by the following five support areas:

▶ **People**. Sellers, buyers, intermediaries, information systems specialists, other employees, and any other participants comprise an important support area.

▶ **Public policy**. Legal and other policy and regulatory issues, such as privacy protection and taxation, which are determined by governments. Included as part of public policy is the issue of technical standards, which are established by government or industry-mandated policy-making groups. Compliance with the regulations is an important issue.

▶ **Marketing and advertisement.** Like any other business, EC usually requires the support of marketing and advertising. This is especially important in B2C online transactions, in which the buyers and sellers usually do not know each other.

**business-to-business
(B2B)**

E-commerce model in
which all of the partici-
pants are businesses or
other organizations.

**business-to-consumer
(B2C)**

E-commerce model in
which businesses sell to
individual shoppers.

e-tailing

Online retailing, usually
B2C.

**business-to-business-to-
consumer (B2B2C)**

E-commerce model in
which a business provides
some product or service
to a client business that
maintains its own
customers.

**consumer-to-business
(C2B)**

E-commerce model in
which individuals use the
Internet to sell products or
services to organizations
or individuals who seek
sellers to bid on products
or services they need.

**mobile commerce
(m-commerce)**

E-commerce transactions
and activities conducted
in a wireless environment.

**location-based
commerce (l-commerce)**

M-commerce transactions
targeted to individuals in
specific locations, at
specific times.

intrabusiness EC

E-commerce category that
includes all internal
organizational activities
that involve the exchange
of goods, services, or
information among various
units and individuals in an
organization.

▶ **Support services**. Many services are needed to support EC. These range from content
creation to payments to order delivery.

▶ **Business partnerships**. Joint ventures, exchanges, and business partnerships of various
types are common in EC. These occur frequently throughout the *supply chain* (i.e., the
interactions between a company and its suppliers, customers, and other partners).

The infrastructure for EC is shown at the bottom of Exhibit 1.2. *Infrastructure* describes
the hardware, software, and networks used in EC. All of these components require good
management practices. This means that companies need to plan, organize, motivate, devise
strategy, and restructure processes, as needed, to optimize the business use of EC models and
strategies. Management also deals with strategic and operational decisions (see Chapter 14
and examples throughout the book).

This text provides details on most of the components of the framework. The infrastructure
of EC is described in online Technical Appendices A through C on the book's Web site (in
Online Files) and in online Chapter 19.

CLASSIFICATION OF EC BY THE NATURE OF THE TRANSACTIONS OR INTERACTIONS

A common classification of EC is by the nature of the transactions or the relationship among
participants. The following types of EC are commonly distinguished.

Business-to-Business (B2B). All of the participants in **business-to-business (B2B)**
e-commerce are either businesses or other organizations (see Chapters 5 through 7).
For example, several of Dell's and Marks & Spencer's applications involve B2B with their
suppliers. Today, over 85 percent of EC volume is B2B (Mockler et al. 2006).

Business-to-Consumer (B2C). **Business-to-consumer (B2C)** EC includes retail transactions of products or services from businesses to individual shoppers. The typical shopper at
Dell online or at Amazon.com is a *consumer* or *customer*. This EC type is also called **e-tailing**
(see Chapter 3).

Business-to-Business-to-Consumer (B2B2C). In **business-to-business-to-consumer
(B2B2C)** EC, a business provides some product or service to a client business. The client
business maintains its own customers, who may be its own employees, to whom the product
or service is provided without adding any value to it. One example of B2B2C is a company
that pays AOL to provide its employees with Internet access rather than having each
employee pay an access fee directly to AOL. Another example is wholesaler-to-retailer-to-
consumer merchandising, such as airlines and travel units that provide travel services, such as
airline tickets and hotel rooms, to business partners, such as travel agencies, who then sell the
services to customers. As a final example, Godiva (see Case 1.1) sells chocolates directly to
business customers. Those businesses may then give the chocolates as gifts to employees or to
other businesses. Godiva may mail the chocolate directly to the recipient (with complements
of . . .). An interesting example of B2B2C can be found in wishlist.com.au. The term B2B
frequently includes B2B2C as well.

Consumer-to-Business (C2B). The **consumer-to-business (C2B)** category includes
individuals who use the Internet to sell products or services to organizations and individuals
who seek sellers to bid on products or services (see Chapter 10). Priceline.com is a well-
known organizer of C2B transactions.

Mobile Commerce. EC transactions and activities conducted in full or in part in a
wireless environment are referred to as **mobile commerce**, or **m-commerce** (see Chapter 9).
For example, people can use Internet-enabled cell phones to do their banking or order a
book from Amazon.com. Many m-commerce applications involve mobile devices. Some
people define m-commerce as those transactions conducted when people are away from
their home or office; such transactions can be done both on wireless or wireline systems.
(See the Maybelline case at Online File W1.2.) If such transactions are targeted to individuals in specific locations, at specific times, they are referred to as **location-based commerce**,
or **l-commerce**.

Intrabusiness EC. The **intrabusiness EC** category includes all internal organizational
activities that involve the exchange of goods, services, or information among various units

---

CASE 1.1
EC Application
BUY CHOCOLATE ONLINE? TRY GODIVA.COM

The Business Opportunity
The demand for high-quality chocolate has been increasing rapidly since the early 1990s. Several local and global companies are competing in this market. Godiva Chocolatier is a well-known international company based in New York whose stores can be found in hundreds of malls worldwide. The company was looking for ways to increase its sales, and after rejecting the use of a CD-ROM catalog, it had the courage to try online sales as early as 1994. The company was a pioneering click-and-mortar e-business that exploited an opportunity years before its competitors.

The Project
Teaming with Fry Multimedia (an e-commerce pioneer), Godiva.com (*godiva.com*) was created as a division of Godiva Chocolatier. The objective was to sell online both to individuals and to businesses. Since its online beginnings in 1994, the Godiva.com story parallels the dynamic growth of e-commerce. Godiva.com went through difficult times—testing e-commerce technologies as they appeared; failing at times, but maintaining its commitment to online selling; and, finally, becoming the fastest-growing division of Godiva, outpacing projections. Godiva.com embodies a true success story. Here we present some of the milestones encountered.

The major driving factors in 1994 were Internet *user groups* of chocolate lovers, who were talking about Godiva and to whom the company hoped to sell its product online. Like other pioneers, Godiva had to build its Web site from scratch without EC-building tools. A partnership was made with *Chocolatier Magazine*, allowing Godiva.com to showcase articles and recipes from the magazine on its site in exchange for providing an online magazine subscription form for e-shoppers. The recognition of the importance of relevant content was correct, as was the need for fresh content. The delivery of games and puzzles, which was considered necessary to attract people to EC sites, was found to be a failure. People were coming to learn about chocolate and Godiva and to buy—not to play games. Another concept that failed was the attempt to make the Web site look like the physical store. It was found that different marketing channels should look different from one another.

Godiva.com is a user-friendly place to shop. Its major features include electronic catalogs, some of which are constructed for special occasions (e.g., Mother's Day and Father's Day); a store locator (how to find the nearest physical store and events at stores close to you); a shopping cart to make it easy to collect items to buy; a gift selector and a gift finder; custom photographs of the products; a search engine by product, price, and other criteria; instructions on how to shop online (take the tour); a chocolate guide that shows you exactly what is inside each box; a place to click for live assistance or for a paper catalog; and the ability to create an address list for shipping gifts to friends or employees. The site also features "My Account," a personalized place where customers can access their order history, account, order status, and so on; general content about chocolate (and recipes); and tools for making shipping and payment arrangements.

Godiva.com sells both to individuals and to corporations. For corporations, incentive programs are offered, including address lists of employees or customers to whom the chocolate is to be sent—an example of the B2B2C EC model.

Godiva.com continues to add features to stay ahead of the competition. The site is now accessible using wireless technologies. For example, the store locator is available to wireless phone users, and Palm Pilot users can download mailing lists.

The Results
Godiva.com's online sales have been growing at a double-digit rate every year, outpacing the company's "old economy" divisions as well as the online stores of competitors.

Sources: Compiled from Reda (2004) and from *godiva.com* (accessed September 2006).

Questions
1. Identify the B2B and B2C transactions in this case.
2. Why did Godiva decide to sell online?
3. List the EC drivers in this case.
4. Visit *godiva.com*. How user-friendly is the site?
5. Describe B2B2C at Godiva.

---

and individuals in that organization. Activities can range from selling corporate products to one's employees to online training and collaborative design efforts (see Chapter 7). Intrabusiness EC is usually performed over intranets and/or *corporate portals* (gateways to the Web).

Business-to-Employees (B2E). The **business-to-employees (B2E)** category is a subset of the intrabusiness category in which the organization delivers services, information, or products to individual employees, as Maybelline is doing (see Online File W1.2). A major category of employees is *mobile employees*, such as field representatives. EC support to such employees is also called *B2ME (business-to-mobile employees)*.

business-to-employees (B2E)
E-commerce model in which an organization delivers services, information, or products to its individual employees.

collaborative commerce (c-commerce)
E-commerce model in which individuals or groups communicate or collaborate online.

consumer-to-consumer (C2C)
E-commerce model in which consumers sell directly to other consumers.

peer-to-peer
Technology that enables networked peer computers to share data and processing with each other directly; can be used in C2C, B2B, and B2C e-commerce.

e-learning
The online delivery of information for purposes of training or education.

e-government
E-commerce model in which a government entity buys or provides goods, services, or information from or to businesses or individual citizens.

exchange
A public electronic market with many buyers and sellers.

exchange-to-exchange (E2E)
E-commerce model in which electronic exchanges formally connect to one another for the purpose of exchanging information.

Collaborative Commerce. When individuals or groups communicate or collaborate online, they may be engaged in **collaborative commerce**, or **c-commerce** (see Chapter 7). For example, business partners in different locations may design a product together (see Boeing, Case 1.2), using screen-sharing; manage inventory online, as in the Dell case; or jointly forecast product demand, as Marks & Spencer does with its suppliers (Online File W1.1).

Consumer-to-Consumer (C2C). In the **consumer-to-consumer (C2C)** category (see Chapter 8), consumers transact directly with other consumers. Examples of C2C include individuals selling residential property, cars, and so on in online classified ads (e.g., see the Case on Craigslist in Chapter 2). The advertisement of personal services over the Internet and the selling of knowledge and expertise online are other examples of C2C. In addition, many auction sites allow individuals to place items up for auction.

Peer-to-Peer Applications. **Peer-to-peer (P2P)** technology can be used in C2C, B2B, and B2C (see Chapter 8). This technology enables networked peer computers to share data files and processing with each other directly. For example, in a C2C peer application, people can exchange (swap) music, videos, software, and other digitizable goods electronically.

E-Learning. In **e-learning**, training or formal education is provided online (see Chapter 8). E-learning is used heavily by organizations for training and retraining employees (called *e-training*). It is also practiced at virtual universities.

E-Government. In **e-government** EC, a government entity buys or provides goods, services, or information from or to businesses (G2B) or from or to individual citizens (G2C) (see Chapter 8). An example of an e-government initiative is provided in Online File W1.3.

Exchange-to-Exchange (E2E). An **exchange** describes a *public electronic market* with many buyers and sellers (see Chapter 6). As B2B exchanges proliferate, it is logical for exchanges to connect to one another. **Exchange-to-exchange (E2E)** EC is a formal system that connects two or more exchanges.

Nonbusiness EC. An increased number of nonbusiness institutions, such as academic institutions, nonprofit organizations, religious organizations, social organizations, and government agencies, are using EC to reduce their expenses or to improve their general operations and customer service. (Note that in the previous categories one can usually replace the word *business* with *organization*.)

Many examples of the various types of EC transactions will be presented throughout this book.

A BRIEF HISTORY OF EC

EC applications were first developed in the early 1970s with innovations such as *electronic funds transfer* (EFT) (see Chapter 12), whereby funds could be routed electronically from one organization to another. However, the use of these applications was limited to large corporations, financial institutions, and a few other daring businesses. Then came *electronic data interchange* (EDI), a technology used to electronically transfer routine documents, which expanded electronic transfers from financial transactions to other types of transaction processing (see Chapter 5 for more on EDI). EDI enlarged the pool of participating companies from financial institutions to manufacturers, retailers, services, and many other types of businesses. Such systems were called *interorganizational system* (IOS) applications, and their strategic value to businesses has been widely recognized. More new EC applications followed, ranging from travel reservation systems to stock trading.

The Internet began life as an experiment by the U.S. government in 1969, and its initial users were a largely technical audience of government agencies and academic researchers and scientists. When the Internet became commercialized and users began flocking to participate in the World Wide Web in the early 1990s, the term *electronic commerce* was coined. EC applications rapidly expanded. A large number of so-called *dot-coms*, or *Internet start-ups*, also appeared (see Cassidy 2002). One reason for this rapid expansion was the development of new networks, protocols, and EC software. The other reason was the increase in competition and other business pressures (see discussion in Section 1.4).

Since 1995, Internet users have witnessed the development of many innovative applications, ranging from online direct sales to e-learning experiences. Almost every

CASE 1.2
EC Application

BOEING CHANGES THE NATURE OF ITS BUSINESS WITH GLOBAL COLLABORATION

Boeing, the $55 billion Chicago-based aerospace company, has been a major player in the global economy for almost a century. But now the company is undertaking a far-reaching transformation as it uses cutting-edge materials and electronics and high-level technology for the design and assembly process of its new passenger plane—the Boeing 787. The new plane, nicknamed the "Dreamliner," is Boeing's bid for market leadership in competition with Airbus. The new midsize passenger jet will have an outer shell and about half of its parts made of carbon-fiber-reinforced plastic, which will make it lighter and give it better fuel economy. In January 2006, the company had 291 firm orders and 88 commitments from 27 airlines for the new 787, which will seat from 250 to 330 passengers in varying configurations. The list price is about $150 million per plane.

The previous state of the art in aviation manufacturing was to have global partners work from a common blueprint to produce parts—actually, whole sections of the airplane—that were then physically shipped to a Boeing assembly plant near Seattle to see if they fit together. Prior to the 787, wood mock-ups of planes would be constructed to see if parts built by partners around the world would really fit together. When the process failed, the cost in time and production was extreme.

Boeing's shift goes beyond making planes faster and cheaper. The new business model takes Boeing from manufacturer to a high-end technology systems integrator. In 2004, Boeing's IT systems people were consolidated into the Boeing Technology Group. Now parts are designed from concept to production concurrently by partners (including companies in Japan, Russia, and Italy) and "assembled" in a computer model maintained by Boeing outside its corporate firewall. Boeing's role is integrator and interface to the airlines, while the partners take responsibility for the major pieces, including their design. Boeing still takes the hit if the planes fail and deliveries are late, but the actual cost of development and manufacturing is spread across its network of *collaborators*. At the same time, building such global relationships may help the company sell its planes overseas. The biggest savings are in the time saved through the online collaboration process (from 33 to 50 percent), creating a huge competitive advantage.

Collaboration is a necessity for Boeing for several reasons. Airplanes are huge and enormously complex. Politically, sales of a "global product" are enhanced when people in other countries are building parts of the airplane. Companies in these countries may then buy from Boeing. Basic collaboration is done through information-flow tools such as Microsoft Office and SharePoint. Boeing and partners are using Dassault Systemes 3D and Product Lifecycle Management solutions.

Other IT tools used are a product suite from Exostar LLC, with which Boeing can share two-dimensional drawings, conduct forward and reverse auctions, and respond to RFPs,

and an application called Catia. The plane is designed at Global Collaboration Environment, a special online site maintained by Boeing.

Three levels of collaboration are facilitated between teams and companies. In the first level—*design collaboration*—all parties involved log in and make their changes electronically in the blueprints, and the team works together. Quality is improved because the computer finds the mistakes. The next level involves *suppliers working with their supply chains*. The third level is *real-time collaboration* that involves a considerable amount of product lifecycle management across multiple countries enabled by technology that differentiates Boeing's new model from the previous kinds of global relationships. Boeing also uses the new partnership to solicit ideas of how to improve designs, integration, and so on. This results in cost-cutting.

Boeing maintains 10 multimedia rooms at its Everett, Washington, complex for the use of collaboration teams. These are open 365 days a year, 24 hours a day. A visualization application developed by Boeing allows the teams to do real-time design reviews of complex geometry without any lag time as the models load. Meetings are conducted in English, with sidebar conversations, as needed, in a team member's native language. Collaborative design also speeds the design process, helping Boeing to avoid expensive penalties from its customers if the plane is not delivered on time, and it gives the company more flexibility in simultaneously designing multiple versions of the 787 that are part of its wide-ranging appeal in the marketplace.

Finished designs are stored in another Dassault product, Enovia, which is also maintained by Boeing. This has become an enormous data-management task. The issue of security has also been a concern; however, security technology has developed to the point that the security of the information is assured.

Collaboration across cultures and time zones can raise a host of issues about the way people work together. The adjustment of management practices to the networked, team-oriented approach is important to consider when redesigning human resources practices to meet virtual resource needs and when developing a custom-tailored collaboration platform.

Sources: Compiled from Cone (2006), *Workforce-Performance* (2006), and Berstein (2006).

Questions

1. Describe online collaboration and its benefits to Boeing.
2. List the levels of collaboration and the parties involved.
3. How does technology facilitate collaboration?

medium- and large-sized organization in the world now has a Web site, and most large U.S. corporations have comprehensive portals through which employees, business partners, and the public can access corporate information. Many of these sites contain tens of thousand of pages and links. In 1999, the emphasis of EC shifted from B2C to B2B, and in 2001 from B2B to B2E, c-commerce, e-government, e-learning, and m-commerce (see Ariguzo et al. 2006). In 2005, social networks started to receive quite a bit of attention, as did l-commerce and wireless applications. Given the nature of technology and the Internet, EC will undoubtedly continue to shift and change. More and more EC successes are emerging (see Athitakis 2003 and Mullaney 2004). For a comprehensive ready-reference guide to EC including statistics, trends, and in-depth profiles of over 400 companies, see Plunkett (2006) and en.wikipedia.org/wiki/E-commerce.

THE INTERDISCIPLINARY NATURE OF EC

Because EC is a new field, it is just now developing its theoretical and scientific foundations. From just a brief overview of the EC framework and classification, you can probably see that EC is related to several different disciplines. The major EC disciplines include the following: *computer science, marketing, consumer behavior, finance, economics, management information systems, accounting, management, human resource management, business law, robotics, public administration,* and *engineering.*

The Google Revolution

During its early years, EC was impacted by companies such as Amazon.com (Chapter 3), eBay (Chapter 10), AOL, and Yahoo! (Chapter 18). However, since 2001 no other company has had more of an impact on EC than Google. As will be seen in Chapter 4, Google related Web searches to targeted advertisements much better than companies such as DoubleClick did. Today, Google is much more than just a search engine; it employs several innovative EC models, is involved in many EC joint ventures, and impacts both organizational activities and individual lives, as described in the Real-World Application Cases at the end of this chapter, Chapter 4, Chapter 18, and Online Chapter 19.

EC Failures

Starting in 1999, a large number of EC companies, especially e-tailing and B2B ones, began to fail (see disobey.com/ghostsites; Carton 2002; and Kaplan 2002). Well-known B2C failures include eToys, Xpeditor, MarchFirst, Drkoop.com, Webvan.com, and Boo.com. Well-known B2B failures include Chemdex.com, Ventro.com, and Verticalnet.com. (Incidentally, the history of these pioneering companies is documented in The Business Plan Archive [businessplanarchive.org] by David Kirch; see also Mark 2004.) A survey by Strategic Direction (2005) found that 62 percent of dot-coms lacked financial skills and 50 percent had little experience with marketing. Similarly, many companies failed to ensure they had the inventory and distribution setup to meet initial demand. The reasons for these and other EC failures are discussed in detail in Hwang and Stewart (2006) and in Chapters 3, 6, and 14.

Does the large number of failures mean that EC's days are numbered? Absolutely not! First, the dot-com failure rate is declining sharply (Rovenpor 2003). Second, the EC field is basically experiencing consolidation as companies test different business models and organizational structures. Third, most pure EC companies, including giants such as Amazon.com, *are* expanding operations and generating increasing sales.

EC Successes

The last few years have seen the rise of extremely successful virtual EC companies such as eBay, Google, Yahoo!, VeriSign, AOL, and E-Trade. Click-and-mortar companies such as Cisco, Wal-Mart online, General Electric, IBM, Intel, and Schwab also have seen great success (see Papazoglou and Ribbers 2006; Mullaney 2004; Lee et al. 2006; and Jelassi and Enders 2005). Additional success stories include start-ups such as Alloy.com (a young-adults-oriented portal), Bluenile.com, FTD.com, Expedia.com, and Campusfood.com (see Online File W1.4).

For more on the history of e-commerce, see Tian and Stewart (2006).

THE FUTURE OF EC

In 1996, Forrester Research (forrester.com), a major EC-industry analyst, predicted that B2C would be a $6.6 billion business by 2000, up from $518 million in 1996 (Tewksbury 1998). In 1998, B2C sales in the United States were already about $43 billion, or 1 percent of total retail sales (Greenberg 2004). Today's predictions about the future size of EC, provided by respected analysts such as AMR Research, Jupiter Media, Emarketer.com, and Forrester, vary. For example, 2006 global online shopping and B2B transactions are estimated to be about $7 trillion (Tian and Stewart 2006). According to Jupiter Media (2006), online retail spending will increase from $81 billion in 2005 to $95 billion in 2006, growing to $144 billion in 2010. By 2010, 71 percent of online users will use the Internet to shop, compared to 65 percent in 2005, and the Internet will influence nearly half of total retail sales, compared to just 27 percent in 2005. According to Forrester Research (2006), online sales reached $176 billion in 2005 and were expected to grow to $211 billion in 2006. Excluding travel, online sales account for nearly 5 percent of the U.S. retail market (vs. less than 2 percent in 2000). The number of Internet users worldwide was estimated at 700 million in mid-2006 (Mann 2006). Experts predict that as many as 50 percent of all Internet users will shop online by that time. EC growth will come not only from B2C but also from B2B and from newer applications such as e-government, e-learning, B2E, and c-commerce. Overall, the growth of the field will continue to be strong into the foreseeable future. Despite the failures of individual companies and initiatives, the total volume of EC is growing by 15 to 25 percent every year; as Lashinsky (2006) and Savitz (2005) said: "The Boom is Back."

Abramson (2005) thinks that the next phase of the new economy will be shaped by public policy decisions to create the necessary technology infrastructure and by entrepreneurs responding to that environment. The key variable is intellectual property rights.

Web 2.0

The term **Web 2.0** was coined by O'Reilly Media in 2004 to refer to a supposed second-generation of Internet-based services that let people collaborate and share information online in perceived new ways—such as social networking sites, wikis, communication tools, and folksonomies. O'Reilly Media, in collaboration with MediaLive International, used the phrase as a title for a series of conferences. Since then, it has become a popular, if ill-defined and often criticized, buzzword in the technical and marketing communities.

O'Reilly (2005) provides the following examples to illustrate the differences between Web 2.0 and the previous generation, referred to as Web 1.0.

Web 2.0
The second-generation of Internet-based services that let people collaborate and share information online in perceived new ways—such as social networking sites, wikis, communication tools, and folksonomies.

Web 1.0		Web 2.0
DoubleClick	—>	Google AdSense
Ofoto	—>	Flickr
Akamai	—>	BitTorrent
mp3.com	—>	Napster
Britannica Online	—>	Wikipedia
personal Web sites	—>	blogging
Evite	—>	upcoming.org and EVDB
domain name speculation	—>	search engine optimization
page views	—>	cost per click
screen scraping	—>	Web services
publishing	—>	participation
content management systems	—>	wikis
directories (taxonomy)	—>	tagging ("folksonomy")
stickiness	—>	syndication

He also provided a road map (see O'Reilly 2005), which later was expanded by Angermeier (see Exhibit 1.3).

EXHIBIT 1.3   Mind Map of Web 2.0

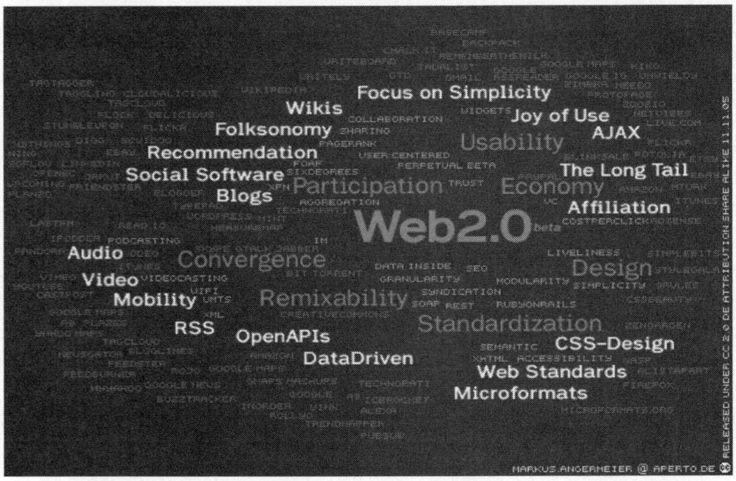

Source: Angermeier, M. "The Huge Cloud Lense Web 2.0." Kosmar.de, November 11, 2005. *kosmar.de/archives/2005/11/11/the-huge-cloud-lens-bubble-map-web20/* (accessed September 2006). Reprinted by permission of Markus Angermeier.

Schonfeld (2006a) believes a major characteristic of Web 2.0 is the global spread of innovative Web sites. As soon as a successful idea is deployed as a Web site in one country, similar sites appear around the globe. He presents 23 Web 2.0 type sites in 10 countries.

Section 1.2 ▶ REVIEW QUESTIONS

1. List the major components of the EC framework.
2. List the major transactional types of EC.
3. Describe the major landmarks in EC history.
4. List some EC successes and failures.

Now that you are familiar with the concepts of EC, let's see what drives it (Sections 1.3 and 1.4).

1.3 THE DIGITAL REVOLUTION DRIVES E-COMMERCE

The major driver of EC is the digital revolution.

THE DIGITAL REVOLUTION AND ECONOMY

The digital revolution is upon us. We see it every day at home and work, in businesses, schools, and hospitals, on roads, and even in wars. One of its major aspects is the digital economy.

The Digital Economy

digital economy
An economy that is based on digital technologies, including digital communication networks, computers, software, and other related information technologies; also called the Internet economy, the new economy, or the Web economy.

The **digital economy** refers to an economy that is based on digital technologies, including digital communication networks (the Internet, intranets, extranets, and VANs), computers, software, and other related information technologies. The digital economy is sometimes called the *Internet economy*, the *new economy*, or the *Web economy*. In this new economy, digital networking and communications infrastructures provide a global platform over which people and organizations interact, communicate, collaborate, and search for information. According to Sharma (2006) and Choi and Whinston (2000), this platform displays the following characteristics:

▶ A vast array of digitizable products—databases, news and information, books, magazines, TV and radio programming, movies, electronic games, musical CDs, and software—are delivered over a digital infrastructure anytime, anywhere in the world.

▶ Consumers and firms conduct financial transactions digitally through digital currencies or financial tokens that are carried via networked computers and mobile devices.

- Microprocessors and networking capabilities are embedded in physical goods such as home appliances and automobiles.
- Information is transformed into a commodity.
- Knowledge is codified.
- Work and production are organized in new and innovative ways.

The term *digital economy* also refers to the convergence of computing and communications technologies on the Internet and other networks and the resulting flow of information and technology that is stimulating EC and vast organizational changes. This convergence enables all types of information (data, audio, video, etc.) to be stored, processed, and transmitted over networks to many destinations worldwide (see also Sharma 2006; Kehal and Singh 2004; and Turban et al. 2007).

The digital economy is creating an economic revolution (see Chapter 15 and Chen 2004), which, according to the *Emerging Digital Economy II* (U.S. Department of Commerce 1999), was evidenced by unprecedented economic performance and the longest period of uninterrupted economic expansion in U.S. history (1991–2000), combined with low inflation. Because of the growth of the Internet and its usage, hardware advances (e.g., PCs, cell phones), progress in communications capabilities (e.g., VoIP, worldwide broadband adoption), advanced usage of digital media (e.g., Internet video, blogs, and wikis), and IT spending for better productivity, the future of the digital economy is looking good (Lenard and Britton 2006)

The digital revolution accelerates EC mainly by providing competitive advantage to organizations.

The digital revolution enables many innovations, some of which are listed in Insights and Additions 1.1. Many, many other innovations characterize the digital revolution, and new ones appear daily.

Exhibit 1.4 describes the major characteristics of the digital economy.

The digital revolution drives EC by providing the necessary technologies, as well as by creating major changes in the business environment, as described in the next section.

Section 1.3 ▶ REVIEW QUESTIONS

1. Define the digital economy.
2. List the characteristics of the digital economy (per Choi and Whinston 2000 and Exhibit 1.4).

EXHIBIT 1.4   Some Characteristics of the Digital Revolution

Area	Description
Globalization	Global communication and collaboration; global electronic marketplaces.
Digital system	From TV to telephones and instrumentation, analog systems are being converted to digital ones.
Speed	A move to real-time transactions, thanks to digitized documents, products, and services. Many business processes are expedited by 90 percent or more.
Information overload	Although the amount of information generated is accelerating, intelligent search tools can help users find what they need.
Markets	Markets are moving online. Physical marketplaces are being replaced by electronic markets; new markets are being created, increasing competition.
Digitization	Music, books, pictures, and more (see Chapter 2) are digitized for fast and inexpensive distribution.
Business models and processes	New and improved business models and processes provide opportunities to new companies and industries. Cyberintermediation and no intermediation are on the rise.
Innovation	Digital and Internet-based innovations continue at a rapid pace. More patents are being granted than ever before.
Obsolescence	The fast pace of innovation creates a high rate of obsolescence.
Opportunities	Opportunities abound in almost all aspects of life and operations.
Fraud	Criminals employ a slew of innovative schemes on the Internet. Cybercons are everywhere.
Wars	Conventional wars are changing to cyberwars.
Organizations	Organizations are moving to digital enterprises.

Insights and Additions 1.1 Interesting and Unique Applications of EC

▶ According to Farivar (2004), VIP patrons of the Baja Beach Club in Barcelona, Spain, can have radio frequency identification (RFID) chips, which are the size of a grain of rice, implanted into their upper arms, allowing them to charge drinks to a bar tab when they raise their arm toward the RFID reader. An RFID is a tiny tag that contains a processor and antenna; it can communicate wirelessly with a detecting unit in a reader over a short distance (see Lebbecke 2006 and Chapters 7 and 9). "You don't call someone crazy for getting a tattoo," says Conrad Chase, director of Baja Beach Clubs international. "Why would they be crazy for getting this?"

▶ Pearson Education, Inc., the publisher of this book, in collaboration with O'Reilly & Associates, offers professors reasonably priced, customized textbooks for their classes by compiling material from thousands of Pearson's publications and the instructors' own materials. The customized books are either electronic (Chapter 8) or more expensive hard copies.

▶ In Japan, a person can wave a Casio watch over a scanner to purchase products from a vending machine, pay for food in a cafeteria, or pay for gasoline.

▶ Dryers and washers in college dorms are hooked to the Web. Students can punch a code into their cell phones or sign in at *esuds.net* and check the availability of laundry machines. Furthermore, they can pay with their student ID or with a credit card and receive e-mail alerts when their wash and dry cycles are complete. Once in the laundry room, a student activates the system by swiping a student ID card or keying in a PIN number. The system automatically injects premeasured amounts of detergent and fabric softener, at the right cycle time.

▶ More than 50 percent of all airline tickets sold in the United States are electronic tickets. It costs more to purchase a ticket from a local travel agent or by phone directly from the airline. In some airports, travelers can get their boarding passes from a machine. Most airlines allow travelers to print their boarding passes from home.

▶ In January 2004, NASA's Web site received more than 6.5 billion hits in a few days—the biggest Internet government event to date—because people were interested in viewing the Mars Exploration Rover's landing on Mars.

▶ Several banks in Japan issue smart cards that can be used only by their owners. When using the cards, the palm vein of the owner's hand is compared with a prestored template of the vein stored on the smart card. When the owner inserts the card into ATM or vendors' card readers that are equipped with the system, it will dispense the card owner's money. The police are alerted if anyone other than the card's owner tries to use it.

▶ Jacobi Medical Center in New York tracks the whereabouts of patients in the hospital. Each patient has an RFID in a plastic band strapped to the wrist. Each time a patient passes an RFID reader, the patient's location is transmitted in real time to the responsible staff member. The RFID is linked to the hospital's computer network, connecting the patient's records to labs, billing, and the pharmacy.

▶ To find adoptive parents for himself and a baby sister after both parents died of cancer, a Chinese boy in Zhengzhou, China, created a special Web site that described the children and showed photos. Within a short time, dozens of people from many countries expressed an interest (*Zhengzhou Evening News* [in Chinese], September 27, 2004).

▶ CompUSA offers an ATM-like service that dispenses software like candy from a vending machine. An ATM-like device with a touch screen lets CompUSA consumers shop for software by choosing an operating system and selecting from categories such as business, education, and games. The consumer is presented with a list of titles and descriptions and prices. Once the consumer picks a title, an order ticket is printed. The consumer then presents the order ticket to a sales rep and pays for the software. The rep then enters information into a second machine, called an order-fulfillment station. It burns the software onto a CD. The sales rep packages the CD and instructions in a box.

▶ According to *People's Daily Online* from China (2006), distressed parents have created a blog to track down their missing 24-year-old son (*blog.sina.com.cn/m/xunzi*). The blog is linked to some celebrity blogs to get more attention.

▶ Using his blog site (*oneredpaperclip.blogspot.com*), Kyle MacDonald of Canada was able to trade a red paper clip into a three-bedroom house. He started by advertising in the barter section of Craigslist.com that he wanted something bigger or better for one red paper clip. In the first iteration, he received a fish-shaped pen, and he posted on Craigslist again and again. Following many iterations and publicity on TV, he finally, after one year, received a house (see Chapter 10 for details).

▶ Camera-equipped cell phones are used in Finland as health and fitness advisors. A supermarket shopper using the technology can snap an image of the bar code on a packet of food. The phone forwards the code number to a central computer, which sends back information on the item's ingredients and nutritional value. The computer also calculates how much exercise the shopper will have to do to burn off the calories based on the shopper's height, weight, age, and other factors.

1.4 THE BUSINESS ENVIRONMENT DRIVES EC

Economic, legal, societal, and technological factors have created a highly competitive *business environment* in which customers are becoming more powerful. These environmental factors can change quickly, vigorously, and sometimes in an unpredictable manner. Companies need to react quickly to both the problems and the opportunities resulting from this new business environment. Because the pace of change and the level of uncertainty are expected to accelerate, organizations are operating under increasing pressures to produce more products, faster, and with fewer resources.

According to Huber (2004), the new business environment is a result of advances in science occurring at an accelerated rate. These advances create scientific knowledge that feeds on itself, resulting in more and more technology. The rapid growth in technology results in a large variety of more complex systems. As a result, the business environment has the following characteristics: a more turbulent environment, with more business problems and opportunities; stronger competition; the need for organizations to make decisions more frequently, either by expediting the decision process or by having more decision makers; a larger scope for decisions because more factors (market, competition, political issues, and global environment) need to be considered; and more information and/or knowledge is needed for making decisions.

THE BUSINESS ENVIRONMENT

Most people, sports teams, and organizations are trying to improve their *performance*. For some, it is a challenge; for others, it is a requirement for survival. Yet, for some it is the key to improved life, profitability, or reputation.

Most organizations measure their performance periodically, comparing it to some metrics and to the organization's mission, objectives, and plans. Unfortunately, in business, performance often depends not only on what you do but also on what others are doing, as well as on forces of nature. In the business world, we refer to such events, in totality, as the *business environment*. Such an environment may create significant pressures that can impact performance in uncontrollable, or sometimes even in unpredictable, ways.

The Business Environment Impact Model

The model shown in Exhibit 1.5 illustrates how the business environment (left) creates problems and opportunities that drive what organizations are doing in their business processes (the "our company" box). Other drivers are the organization's mission, goals, strategy, and plans. Business processes include competencies, activities, and responses to the environmental pressures that result in problems, constraints, and opportunities (what we term *critical response activities* or *solutions*). Organizational activities in business processes result in measurable

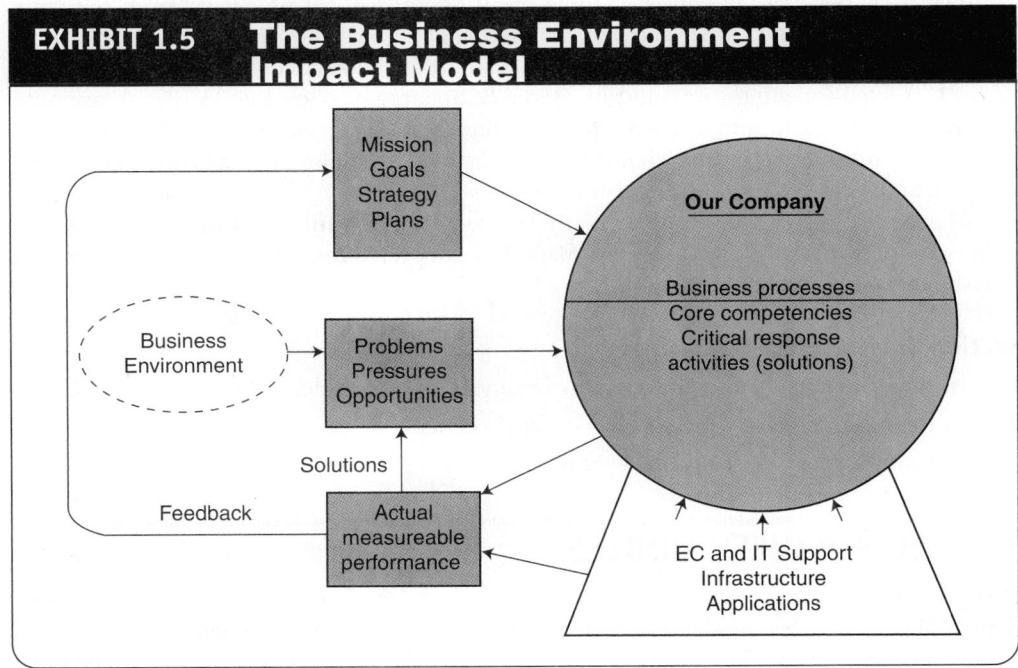

EXHIBIT 1.5 The Business Environment Impact Model

EXHIBIT 1.6   Major Business Pressures

Market and Economic Pressures	Societal Pressures	Technological Pressures
Strong competition	Changing nature of workforce	Increasing innovations and new technologies
Global economy	Government deregulation, leading to more competition	Rapid technological obsolescence
Regional trade agreements (e.g., NAFTA)	Compliance (e.g., Sarbanes-Oxley Act)	Increases in information overload
Extremely low labor cost in some countries	Shrinking government subsidies	Rapid decline in technology cost versus labor cost
Frequent and significant changes in markets	Increased importance of ethical and legal issues	
Increased power of consumers	Increased social responsibility of organizations	
	Rapid political changes	

performance, which provides the solution to problems/opportunities, as well as feedback on the mission, strategy, and plans.

Notice that in the figure EC and IT provide support to organizations' activities and to actual performance, countering business pressures. We will demonstrate this throughout the book. Now, let's examine the two major components of the model: business pressures and organizational responses.

Business Pressures

In this text, business pressures are divided into the following categories: market (economic), societal, and technological. The main types of business pressures in each category are listed in Exhibit 1.6.

Organizational Response Strategies

How can organizations operate in such an environment? How can they deal with the threats and the opportunities? To begin with, many traditional strategies are still useful in today's environment. However, because some traditional response activities may *not* work in today's turbulent and competitive business environment, many of the old solutions need to be modified, supplemented, or discarded. Alternatively, new responses can be devised. Critical response activities can take place in some or all organizational processes, from the daily processing of payroll and order entry to strategic activities such as the acquisition of a company. Responses can also occur in the supply chain, as demonstrated by the cases of Boeing (Case 1.2), Dell (opening case), and in Marks & Spencer (Online File W1.1). A response activity can be a reaction to a specific pressure already in existence, or it can be an initiative that will defend an organization against future pressures. It can also be an activity that exploits an opportunity created by changing conditions.

Many response activities can be greatly facilitated by EC. In some cases, EC is the *only* solution to these business pressures. The major EC-supported response activities are provided in Exhibit 1.7 and in Online File W1.5.

Section 1.4 ▸ REVIEW QUESTIONS

1. List the components of the business environment impact model and explain the model.
2. List the major factors in today's business environment.
3. List some of the major response activities taken by organizations.

business model
A method of doing business by which a company can generate revenue to sustain itself.

1.5 EC BUSINESS MODELS

One of the major characteristics of EC is that it enables the creation of new business models (see Rappa 2006). A **business model** is a method of doing business by which a company can generate revenue to sustain itself. The model also spells out where the company is positioned in the value

EXHIBIT 1.7   Innovative Organizational Responses

Response Strategy	Descriptions
Strategic systems	Improve strategic advantage in industry.
Agile systems	Increase ability to adapt to changes and flexibility.
Continuous improvements and business process management	Using enterprise systems improve business processes. Introduce e-procurement.
Customer relationship management	Introduce programs to improve customers relationships using the Internet and EC models (see Online File W1.6).
Business alliances and Partner Relationship Management (PRM)	Create joint ventures, partnerships, e-collaboration, virtual corporationsand others for win-win situations (even with competitors). (See Boeing Case 1.3).
Electronic markets	Use both private and public electronic market to increase efficiency and effectiveness.
Cycle time reduction	Increase speed of operation and reduce time-to-market (see Online File W1.7).
Empowering employees, especially at the frontline (interacting with customers, partners)	Provide employees with computerized decision aids so they can make quick decisions on their own. (See Davenport 2006).
Supply chain improvements	Reduce problems along the supply chain, expedite flows, reduce inventories.
Mass customization in a build-to-order system	Produce customized products (services), rapidly at reasonable cost to many, many customers (mass) as Dell does. See Appendix 2A.
Intrabusiness use of automation	Many intrabusiness activities, from sales force automation to inventory management can be improved with e-commerce and m-commerce.
Knowledge management	Appropriate creation, storage, and dissemination of knowledge using electronic systems, increases productivity, agility, and competitiveness.
Customer selection, loyalty, and service	Identify customers with the greatest profit potential; increase likelihood that they will want the product or service offering; retain their loyalty.
Human capital	Select the best employees for particular tasks or jobs, at particular compensation levels.
Product and service quality	Detect quality problems early and minimize them.
Financial performance	Better understand the drivers of financial performance and the effects of nonfinancial factors.
Research and development	Improve quality, efficacy, and where applicable, safety of products and services.

chain—that is, by what activities the company adds value to the product or service it supplies. (The *value chain* is the series of value-adding activities that an organization performs to achieve its goals, such as making profit, at various stages of the production process.) Some models are very simple. For example, Wal-Mart buys merchandise, sells it, and generates a profit. In contrast, a TV station provides free broadcasting to its viewers. The station's survival depends on a complex model involving advertisers and content providers. Public Internet portals, such as Yahoo!, also use a complex business model. One company may have several business models.

Business models are a subset of a business plan or a business case. These concepts frequently are confused. (In other words, some equate a *business model* with a *business plan*.) However, as Chapters 14 and 16 explain, business plans (Appendix 16A) and cases differ from business models (also see Preissl et al. 2004; Lee et al. 2006; and Currie 2004).

THE STRUCTURE OF BUSINESS MODELS

Several different EC business models are possible, depending on the company, the industry, and so on. Weill and Vitale (2001) developed a framework for evaluating the viability of e-business initiatives. According to this methodology, eight elementary, or "atomic," e-business models can be combined in different ways to create operational e-business initiatives. The eight atomic business models are *direct marketing, intermediary, content provider, full-service provider, shared infrastructure, value net integrator, virtual community,* and *consolidator of services* for large organizations. For example, the Amazon.com business model combines direct marketing, the intermediary role, virtual community, and content provider. Each atomic model can be described by four characteristics: strategic objectives, sources of revenue, critical success factors, and core competencies required. However, all business models share common elements.

According to McKay and Marshall (2004), a comprehensive business model is composed of the following six elements:

- A description of the *customers* to be served and the company's relationships with these customers, including what constitutes value from the customers' perspective (*customers' value proposition*)
- A description of all *products* and *services* the business will offer
- A description of the *business process* required to make and deliver the products and services
- A list of the *resources* required and the identification of which ones are available, which will be developed in house, and which will need to be acquired
- A description of the organization's *supply chain,* including *suppliers* and other *business partners*
- A description of the revenues expected (*revenue model*), anticipated costs, sources of financing, and estimated profitability (*financial viability*)

Models also include a *value proposition,* which is an analysis of the benefits of using the specific model (tangible and intangible), including the customers' value proposition cited earlier.

A detailed discussion of and examples of business models and their relationship to business plans is presented in Chapter 16. For a list of components and key issues of EC business models, see Lee et al. (2006).

This chapter presents two of the elements that are needed to understand the material in Chapters 2 through 15: revenue models and value propositions.

---

revenue model
Description of how the company or an EC project will earn revenue.

Revenue Models

A **revenue model** outlines how the organization or the EC project will generate revenue. For example, the revenue model for Godiva's online EC initiative shows revenue from online sales. The major revenue models are:

- **Sales.** Companies generate revenue from selling merchandise or services over their Web sites. An example is when Wal-Mart, Amazon.com, or Godiva sells a product online.
- **Transaction fees.** A company receives a commission based on the volume of transactions made. For example, when a homeowner sells a house, he typically pays a transaction fee to the broker. The higher the value of the sale, the higher the total transaction fee. Alternatively, transaction fees can be levied *per transaction.* With online stock trades, for example, there is usually a fixed fee per trade, regardless of the volume.
- **Subscription fees.** Customers pay a fixed amount, usually monthly, to get some type of service. An example would be the access fee for AOL. Thus, AOL's primary revenue model is subscription (fixed monthly payments).
- **Advertising fees.** Companies charge others for allowing them to place a banner on their sites. This is how Google has made its fortune. (See Chapter 4 and the Real-World Application Case at the end of this chapter.
- **Affiliate fees.** Companies receive commissions for referring customers to others' Web sites.
- **Other revenue sources.** Some companies allow people to play games for a fee or to watch a sports competition in real time for a fee (e.g., see *espn.go.com*). Another revenue source is licensing fees (e.g., *datadirect-technologies.com*). Licensing fees can be assessed as an annual fee or a per usage fee. Microsoft takes fees from each workstation that uses Windows NT, for example.

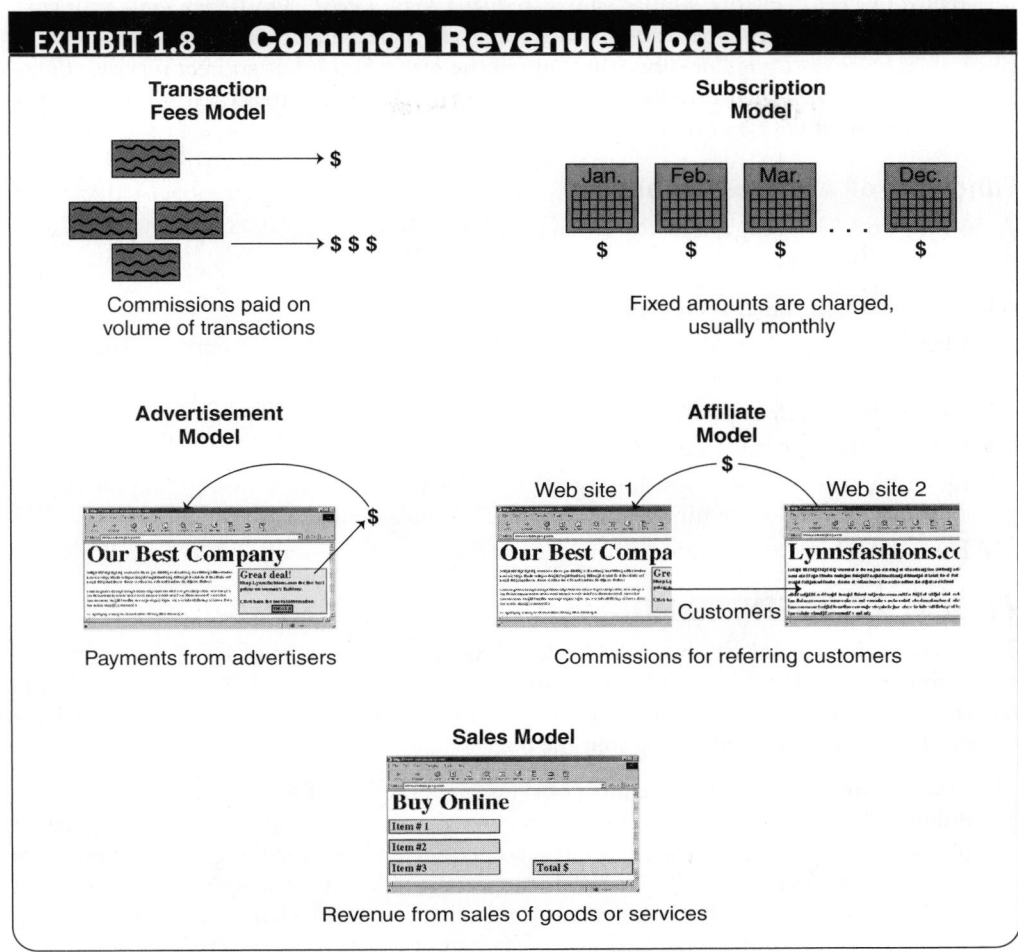

EXHIBIT 1.8   Common Revenue Models

Transaction Fees Model

Commissions paid on volume of transactions

Subscription Model

Jan. Feb. Mar. . . . Dec.

Fixed amounts are charged, usually monthly

Advertisement Model

Our Best Company

Great deal!

Payments from advertisers

Affiliate Model

Web site 1   Web site 2

Our Best Compa   Lynnsfashions.co

Customers

Commissions for referring customers

Sales Model

Buy Online

Item # 1
Item #2
Item #3   Total $

Revenue from sales of goods or services

A company uses its *revenue model* to describe how it will generate revenue and its *business model* to describe the *process* it will use to do so. Exhibit 1.8 summarizes five common revenue models. For example, Godiva's online revenue model shows that customers can order products online. The customers can pick up the merchandise at a Godiva store or, for an extra charge, have it shipped to their homes. The revenue comes from sales, which take place both off-line and online.

The revenue model can be part of the value proposition or it may complement it.

Value Proposition

Business models also include a value-proposition statement. A **value proposition** refers to the benefits, including the intangible, nonquantitative ones, that a company can derive from using the model. In B2C EC, for example, a value proposition defines how a company's product or service fulfills the needs of customers. The value proposition is an important part of the marketing plan of any product or service.

Specifically, how do e-marketplaces create value? Amit and Zott (2001) identify four sets of values that are created by e-business: search and transaction cost-efficiency, complementarities, lock-in, and novelty. *Search and transaction cost-efficiency* enables faster and more informed decision making, wider product and service selection, and greater economies of scale—cost savings per unit as greater quantities are produced and sold (e.g., through demand and supply aggregation for small buyers and sellers). *Complementarities* involve bundling some goods and services together to provide more value than from offering them separately. *Lock-in* is attributable to the high switching cost that ties customers to particular suppliers. *Novelty* creates value through innovative ways for structuring transactions, connecting partners, and fostering new markets.

value proposition
The benefits a company can derive from using EC.

Bakos (1991) identifies similar values: reduced search cost, significant switching cost, economies of scale and scope, and network externality (i.e., the tendency for consumers to place more value on a good or service as more of the market uses that good or service). Bakos regards *search cost reduction* as the attribute most specific to e-marketplaces. It is the subject of analysis in many studies on e-marketplaces.

Functions of a Business Model

According to Chesbrough and Rosenbloom (2002), business models have the following functions or objectives:

▶ Articulate a customer value proposition.

▶ Identify a market segment (*who* will use the technology for *what* purpose; specify the revenue-generation process).

▶ Define the venture's specific value chain structure.

▶ Estimate the cost structure and profit potential.

▶ Describe the venture's positioning within the value network linking suppliers and customers (includes identification of potential complementors and competitors).

▶ Formulate the venture's competitive strategy.

TYPICAL EC BUSINESS MODELS

There are many types of EC business models. Examples and details of EC business models can be found throughout this text (and also in Rappa 2006; Currie 2004; Rossi et al. 2003; and Afuah and Tucci 2003). The following list describes some of the most common or visible models. Details are provided throughout the text.

1. **Online direct marketing.** The most obvious model is that of selling products or services online. Sales may be from a manufacturer to a customer, eliminating intermediaries or physical stores (e.g., Godiva), or from retailers to consumers, making distribution more efficient (e.g., Wal-Mart). This model is especially efficient for digitizable products and services (those that can be delivered electronically). This model has several variations (see Chapters 3 and 5). It is practiced in B2C (where it is called *e-tailing*) and in some B2B types of EC.

2. **Electronic tendering systems.** Large organizational buyers, private or public, usually make large-volume or large-value purchases through a **tendering (bidding) system**, also known as a *reverse auction*. Such tendering can be done online, saving time and money. Pioneered by General Electric Corp., e-tendering systems are gaining popularity. Indeed, several government agencies mandate that most of their procurement must be done through e-tendering (see Chapter 5).

3. **Name your own price.** Pioneered by Priceline.com, the **name-your-own-price model** allows buyers to set the price they are willing to pay for a specific product or service. Priceline.com will try to match a customer's request with a supplier willing to sell the product or service at that price. This model is also known as a *demand-collection model* (see Chapter 10).

4. **Find the best price.** According to this model, also known as a *search engine model* (see Bandyopadhyay 2001), a customer specifies a need and then an intermediate company, such as Hotwire.com, matches the customer's need against a database, locates the lowest price, and submits it to the consumer. The potential buyer then has 30 to 60 minutes to accept or reject the offer. A variation of this model is available for purchasing insurance: A consumer can submit a request for insurance to Insweb.com and receive several quotes. Many companies employ similar models to find the lowest price. For example, consumers can go to eloan.com to find the best interest rate for auto or home loans. A well-known company in this area is Shopping.com, which is described with similar companies in Chapter 3.

5. **Affiliate marketing. Affiliate marketing** is an arrangement whereby a marketing partner (a business, an organization, or even an individual) refers consumers to a selling company's Web site (see Chapter 4). The referral is done by placing a banner ad or the logo of the

tendering (bidding) system
Model in which a buyer requests would-be sellers to submit bids; the lowest bidder wins.

name-your-own-price model
Model in which a buyer sets the price he or she is willing to pay and invites sellers to supply the good or service at that price.

affiliate marketing
An arrangement whereby a marketing partner (a business, an organization, or even an individual) refers consumers to the selling company's Web site.

selling company on the affiliated company's Web site. Whenever a customer who was referred to the selling company's Web site makes a purchase there, the affiliated partner receives a commission (which may range from 3 to 15 percent) of the purchase price. In other words, by using affiliate marketing, a selling company creates a *virtual commissioned sales force*. Pioneered by CDNow (see Hoffman and Novak 2000), the concept is now employed by thousands of retailers and manufacturers. For example, Amazon.com has over 1,000,000 affiliates, and even tiny Cattoys.com offers individuals and organizations the opportunity to put its logo and link on their Web sites to generate commissions.

6. **Viral marketing.** According to the **viral marketing** model (see Chapter 4), an organization can increase brand awareness or even generate sales by inducing people to send messages to other people or to recruit friends to join certain programs. It is basically Web-based word-of-mouth marketing.

7. **Group purchasing.** In the off-line world of commerce, discounts are usually available for purchasing large quantities. So, too, EC has spawned the concept of *demand aggregation*, wherein a third party finds individuals or **SMEs (small-to-medium enterprises)**, aggregates their small orders to attain a large quantity, and then negotiates (or conducts a tender) for the best deal. Thus, using the concept of **group purchasing**, a small business, or even an individual, can get a discount. This model, also known as the *volume-buying model*, is described in Chapter 5. One leading aggregator is Letsbuyit.com (see also Krishnan and Ravi 2003) Online purchasing groups are also called **e-co-ops**.

8. **Online auctions.** Almost everyone has heard of eBay, the world's largest online auction site. Several hundred other companies, including Amazon.com and Yahoo!, also conduct online auctions. In the most popular type of auction, online shoppers make consecutive bids for various goods and services, and the highest bidders get the items auctioned. E-auctions come in different shapes (Chapters 2 and 10) and use different models. For example, eBay is using about 40,000 "assistants" in a model where the assistants perform the order fulfillments (see Chapter 2).

9. **Product and service customization.** With **customization**, a product or service is created according to the buyer's specifications. Customization is not a new model, but what *is* new is the ability to quickly configure customized products online for consumers at costs not much higher than their noncustomized counterparts (see Chapters 3 and 5). Dell is a good example of a company that customizes PCs for its customers.

    Many other companies are following Dell's lead: The automobile industry is customizing its products and expects to save billions of dollars in inventory reduction alone every year by producing made-to-order cars (see Li and Du 2004). Mattel's My Design lets fashion-doll fans custom-build a friend for Barbie at Mattel's Web site; the doll's image is displayed on the screen before the person places an order. Nike allows customers to customize shoes, which can be delivered in a week. Lego.com allows customers to configure several of their toys. Finally, De Beers allows customers to design their own engagement rings.

    Configuring the details of the customized products, including the final design, ordering, and paying for the products, is done online. Also known as *build-to-order*, customization can be done on a large scale, in which case it is called *mass customization*. For a historical discussion of the development of the idea of mass customization, see Appendix 2A at the end of Chapter 2.

10. **Electronic marketplaces and exchanges.** Electronic marketplaces existed in isolated applications for decades (e.g., stock and commodities exchanges). But as of 1996, hundreds of e-marketplaces have introduced new efficiencies to the trading process. If they are well organized and managed, e-marketplaces can provide significant benefits to both buyers and sellers. Of special interest are *vertical* marketplaces, which concentrate on one industry (e.g., GNX.com for the retail industry and Chemconnect.com for the chemical industry).

11. **Information brokers (informediaries).** Information brokers (see Chapters 3 through 8) provide privacy, trust, matching, search, content, and other services (e.g., Bizrate.com, Froogle.com).

viral marketing
Word-of-mouth marketing in which customers promote a product or service to friends or other people.

SMEs
Small-to-medium enterprises.

group purchasing
Quantity (aggregated) purchasing that enables groups of purchasers to obtain a discount price on the products purchased.

e-co-ops
Another name for online group purchasing organizations.

customization
Creation of a product or service according to the buyer's specifications.

12. **Bartering.** Companies use bartering (see Chapters 2 and 10) to exchange surpluses they do not need for things that they do need. A market maker (e.g., Web-barter.com or Tradeaway.com) arranges such exchanges.

13. **Deep discounting.** Companies such as Half.com offer products and services at deep discounts, as much as 50 percent off the retail price (see Chapter 3).

14. **Membership.** A popular off-line model, in which only members get a discount, also is being offered online (e.g., Netmarket.com and NYTimes.com) (for details, see Bandyopadhyay 2001).

15. **Value-chain integrators.** This model offers services that aggregate information-rich products into a more complete package for customers, thus adding value. For example, Carpoint.com provides several car-buying–related services, such as financing and insurance.

16. **Value-chain service providers.** These providers specialize in a supply chain function such as logistics (UPS.com) or payments (PayPal.com, now part of eBay) (see Chapters 7, 12, and 13).

17. **Supply chain improvers.** One of the major contributions of EC is in the creation of new models that change or improve supply chain management, as shown in the opening case about Dell. Most interesting is the conversion of a *linear* supply chain, which can be slow, expensive, and error prone, into a *hub*.

18. **Social networks, communities, and blogging.** Many companies are developing commercial benefits from social networks (see Section 1.7), communities, and blogging (e.g., for paid advertising or as a sales channel).

19. **Direct sale by manufacturers.** According to this model, the manufacturer eliminates all intermediaries, selling directly to customers.

20. **Negotiation.** The Internet offers negotiation capabilities between individuals (e.g., Ioffer.com) or between companies (e.g., in exchanges, Chapter 6). Negotiation can also be facilitated by intelligent agents. See Online Appendix C.

To succeed in the fast-moving marketplace, business and revenue models must change with changing market conditions. A good example is Amazon.com, which moved from selling only books to becoming a huge online store for products and services. Amazon.com also added auctions as a marketing channel. In addition, it provides order-fulfillment services as a subcontractor to others, and much more.

Any of the business models presented in this section can be used alone or in combination with each other or with traditional business models. One company may use several different business models. The models can be used for B2C, B2B, and other forms of EC. Although some of the models are limited to B2C or B2B, others can be used in several types of transactions, as will be illustrated throughout the text.

Section 1.5 ▶ REVIEW QUESTIONS

1. Define the following: business plan, business case, and business model.
2. Describe a revenue model and a value proposition.
3. Describe the following business models: name your own price, affiliate marketing, viral marketing, and product customization.
4. Identify business models related to buying and those related to selling.

1.6   BENEFITS AND LIMITATIONS OF EC

Few innovations in human history encompass as many benefits as EC does. The global nature of the technology, the opportunity to reach hundreds of millions of people, its interactive nature, the variety of possibilities for its use, and the resourcefulness and rapid growth of its supporting infrastructures, especially the Web, result in many potential benefits to organizations, individuals, and society. These benefits are just starting to materialize, but they will increase significantly as EC expands. It is not surprising that some maintain that the EC revolution is as profound as the change that accompanied the Industrial Revolution (Drucker 2002).

THE BENEFITS OF EC

EC provides benefits to organizations, individual customers, and society. These benefits are summarized in Exhibit 1.9. An example of how EC technologies assist homeland security can be found in Insights and Additions 1.2. More details are shown in Online File W1.8.

Facilitating Problem Solving

One of the major benefits of EC is its ability to solve complex problems that have remained unsolved for generations. Such problems may require several EC and IT tools. Problems exist in small organizations and large ones, as well as in cities and even countries.

EXHIBIT 1.9   Benefits of E-Commerce

Benefit	Description
Benefits to Organizations	
Global reach	Locating customers and/or suppliers worldwide, at reasonable cost and fast.
Cost reduction	Lower cost of information processing, storage, distribution (see examples at Online File W1.9).
Supply chain improvements	Reduce delays, inventories, and cost.
Business always open	Open 24/7/365; no overtime or other cost.
Customization/personalization	Make it to consumers' wish, fast and at reasonable cost.
Sellers specialization (niche market)	Seller can specialize in a narrow field (e.g., dog toys), yet make money.
Ability to innovate, use new business models	Facilitate innovation and enable unique business models.
Rapid time-to-market and increased speed	Expedite processes; higher speed and productivity.
Lower communication cost	The Internet is cheaper then VAN private lines.
Efficient procurement	Saves time and reduces cost by enabling e-procurement.
Improved customer service and relationship	Direct interaction with customers, better CRM.
Fewer permits and less tax	May need fewer permits and be able to avoid sales tax.
Up-to-date company material	All distributed material is up-to-date.
Help SME to compete	EC may help small companies to compete against large ones by using special business models.
Lower inventories	Using customization inventories can be minimized.
Lower cost of distributing digitalizable product	Delivery online can be 90 percent cheaper.
Benefits to consumers	
Ubiquity	Can shop any time from any place.
More products/services	Large selection to choose from (vendor, products, styles).
Customized products/services	Can customize many products and/or services.
Cheaper products/services	Can compare and shop for lowest prices.
Instant delivery	Digitized products can be downloaded immediately upon payment.
Information availability	Easy finding what you need, with details, demos, etc.
Convenient auction participation	Do auctions any time and from any place.
No sales tax	Sometimes.
Enable telecommuting	Can work or study at home.
Electronic socialization	Can socialize online in communities yet be at home.
Find unique items	Using online auctions, collectible items can be found.
Benefits to Society	
Enable telecommuting	Facilitate work at home; less traffic, pollution.
More public services	Make education, health, etc., available for more people. Rural area can share benefits; more services for the poor.
Improved homeland security	Facilitate home security (see Insights and Additions 1.2).
Increased standard of living	Can buy more and cheaper goods/services.
Close the digital divide	Allow people in developing countries and rural areas to accept more services and purchase what they really like.

Insights and Additions 1.2   Enhancing Homeland Security Electronically

The U.S. Department of Homeland Security (DHS) must determine which preexisting applications and data can help the organization meet its goals; migrate data to a secure, usable, state-of-the-art framework; and integrate the disparate networks and data standards of 22 federal agencies, with 170,000 employees, that merged to form the DHS. The real problem is that federal agencies have historically operated autonomously, and their IT systems were not designed to interoperate with one another. Essentially, the DHS needs to link large and complex silos of data together.

Major problems have occurred because each agency has its own set of business rules that dictate how data are described, collected, and accessed. Some of the data are unstructured and not organized in relational databases, and they cannot be easily manipulated and analyzed. Commercial applications, mostly data warehouse and data-mart technologies, are being used for the major integration activities. Informatica, one of several software vendors working with the DHS, has developed data integration solutions that will enable the DHS to combine disparate systems to make information more widely accessible throughout the organization (see *informatica.com*).

The new DHS system will have information-analysis and infrastructure-protection components. The DHS not only has to make sense of a huge mountain of intelligence gathered from disparate sources, but then it must get that information to the people who can most effectively act on it. Many of these people are outside the federal government.

Sources: Compiled from Foley (2003), Peters (2003), and Thibodeau (2003).

THE LIMITATIONS AND BARRIERS OF EC

Barriers to EC can be classified as either technological or nontechnological. The major barriers are summarized in Exhibit 1.10.

According to a 2006 study (Harmonyhollow.net 2006), the major barriers to EC are (1) resistance to new technology, (2) implementation difficulties, (3) security concerns, (4) lack of technology skills, (5) lack of potential customers, and (6) cost. Van Toorn et al. (2006) believe that the barriers are sectoral barriers (e.g., government, private sector, international organizations), internal barriers (e.g., security, lack of technical knowledge, and lack of time and resources), and external barriers (e.g., lack of government support). Van Toorn et al. (2006) also list the top barriers with regards to global EC, cultural differences, organizational differences, incompatible B2B interfaces, international trade barriers, and lack of standards.

EXHIBIT 1.10   Limitations of Electronic Commerce

Technological Limitations	Nontechnological Limitations
Lack of universal standards for quality, security, and reliability.	Security and privacy concerns deter customers from buying.
The telecommunications bandwidth is insufficient, especially for m-commerce.	Lack of trust in EC and in unknown sellers hinders buying.
Software development tools are still evolving.	People do not yet sufficiently trust paperless, faceless transactions.
It is difficult to integrate Internet and EC software with some existing (especially legacy) applications and databases.	Many legal and public policy issues, including taxation, have not yet been resolved or are not clear.
Special Web servers are needed in addition to the network servers, which add to the cost of EC.	National and international government regulations sometimes get in the way.
Internet accessibility is still expensive and/or inconvenient.	It is difficult to measure some of the benefits of EC, such as online advertising. Mature measurement methodologies are not yet available.
Order fulfillment of large-scale B2C requires special automated warehouses.	Some customers like to feel and touch products. Also, customers are resistant to the change from shopping at a brick-and-mortar store to a virtual store.
	People do not yet sufficiently trust paperless, faceless transactions.
	In many cases, the number of sellers and buyers that are needed for profitable EC operations is insufficient.
	Online fraud is increasing.
	It is difficult to obtain venture capital due to the failure of many dot-coms.

Despite these barriers, EC is expanding rapidly. For example, the number of people in the United States who buy and sell stocks electronically increased from 300,000 at the beginning of 1996 to over 25 million by the spring of 2002 (Emarketer.com 2002). In Korea, about 60 percent of all stock market transactions took place over the Internet in the summer of 2004, versus 2 percent in 1998 (*Seoul Digital City* 2004). According to IDC Research (2000), the number of online brokerage customers worldwide will reach 122.3 million in 2004, compared with 76.7 million in 2002 (as reported by Plunkett Research 2004). As experience accumulates and technology improves, the cost-benefit ratio of EC will increase, resulting in greater rates of EC adoption.

The benefits presented here may not be convincing enough reasons for a business to implement EC. Much more compelling, perhaps, are the omnipresence of the digital revolution and the influence of EC on the business environment, as described in Sections 1.3 and 1.4.

Section 1.6 ❱ REVIEW QUESTIONS

1. Describe some EC benefits to organizations, individuals, and society.
2. List the major technological and nontechnological barriers to EC.
3. Describe some contributions of EC to homeland security.

1.7 SOCIAL AND BUSINESS NETWORKS

The most interesting e-commerce application in recent years has been the emergence of social and business networks. Originating from online communities (Chapter 17), these networks are growing rapidly and providing many new EC initiatives.

SOCIAL NETWORKS

Social networks are Web sites that connect people with specified interests by providing free services, such as photo presentation, e-mail, blogging, and so on. The transactions in social networks are mostly people-to-people. But as we will see in Chapters 17 and 18 (Case 18.1), corporations are starting to have an interest in this EC feature (e.g., see linkedin.com, a network that connects businesses by industry, functions, geography, and areas of interest.

According to Lashinsky (2006) and Schonfeld (2006b), the action today is with the following social networks:

social networks
Web sites that connect people with specified interests by providing free services such as photo presentation, e-mail, blogging, etc.

- ❱ Facebook.com—facilitates socialization by students
- ❱ Gawker.com—features snarky gossip and celebrity stalking
- ❱ YouTube.com and Metcafe.com—users can upload and view videoclips
- ❱ Flickr.com—users share photos
- ❱ Friendster.com—provides a platform to find friends and make contacts
- ❱ Myheritage.com—face recognition in genealogy; recognizes faces in different stages of peoples' lives
- ❱ Cyworld.rate.com—Asia's largest social network
- ❱ Habbohotel.com—Entertaining country-specific sites (18) for kids and adults
- ❱ MySpace.com—The most visited social network (see Case 1.3)
- ❱ YUB.com—A social network for discount shoppers

Business-Oriented Networks

Business-oriented networks are social networks whose primary objective is to facilitate business. For example, YUB.com is a network of shoppers looking for discounts and bargains. Another example is Craigslist.com, the super site for classified ads that offers many social-oriented features (see Case 2.4 in Chapter 2). Yet, its major objective is to help people find accommodations, barter items, or conduct other business-oriented activities. Many B2B portals offer community services for thousands of members.

CASE 1.3

EC Application

MYSPACE: THE WORLD'S MOST POPULAR SOCIAL NETWORKING WEB SITE

MySpace is an interactive social network of user-submitted blogs, profiles, groups, photos, MP3s, videos and an internal e-mail system. It has become an increasingly influential part of contemporary pop culture. The site claims to have over 100 million members (the world's fourth most popular English-language Web site) and draws 500,000 new members each week.

MySpace is also used by some independent musicians and filmmakers who upload songs and short films on their profiles. These songs and films can also be embedded in other profiles, an interconnectedness that adds to MySpace's appeal.

Contents of a MySpace Profile

Each member's profile contains two "blurbs": "About Me" and "Who I'd Like to Meet." Profiles also can contain optional sections about personal features such as marital status, physical appearance, and income. Profiles also contain a blog with standard fields for content, emotion, and media. MySpace also supports uploading images and videos.

Users can choose a certain number of friends to be displayed on their profile in the "Top Friends" area. In 2006, MySpace allowed up to 24 friends to be displayed. The "Comments" area allows the user's friends to leave comments. MySpace users can delete comments or require all comments to be approved before posting. The site gives users some flexibility to modify their user pages, or "MySpace editors" are available to help.

MySpace Celebrities

MySpace has led to the emergence of MySpace celebrities, popular individuals who have attracted hundreds of thousands of "friends," leading to coverage in other media. Some of these individuals have remained only Internet celebrities, others have been able to jump to television, magazines, and radio.

Major Issues Surrounding MySpace

The following are several major issues surrounding MySpace use.

Accessibility

Sometimes there are accessibility problems on users' profiles, because the site is set up so that anyone can customize the layout and colors of their profile page with virtually no restrictions. Poorly constructed MySpace profiles may freeze up Web browsers. Also, new features, such as song and video sharing through streaming media and the huge number of MySpace users joining daily means that more users are online for longer periods; this increase in usage slows down the MySpace servers at peak times.

Restricting Access

Many schools and public libraries in the United States and the United Kingdom have begun to restrict access to MySpace because it has become "such a haven for student gossip and malicious comments" and because MySpace was consuming up to 40 percent of the daily Internet bandwidth, impeding delivery of Web-based courses. Regular administrative functions may also be slowed down, making the normal running of universities difficult.

Potential Damage to Students

The *Chicago Tribune*'s RedEye printed an article concerning MySpace and an individual's search for employment. The author argued that young college graduates compromise their chances of starting careers because of the content they post on their accounts. An employer may not hire a highly qualified candidate because the candidate maintains an account that suggests overly exuberant behavior.

Security and Safety

MySpace allows registering users to be as young as 14. Profiles of users with ages set to 14 to 15 years are automatically private. Users whose ages are set at 16 or over do have the option to restrict their profiles, as well as the option of merely allowing certain personal data to be restricted to people other than those on their "friends list." The full profiles of users under age 18 are restricted to direct MySpace friends only.

Globalization and Competition

In 2006, News Corporation took MySpace to China where it is spreading rapidly (in Chinese, of course). In Korea, a competitor, Cyworld, launched a U.S. version in 2006 (see Schonfeld 2006b and Chapter 18).

Other Issues

Other issues affecting MySpace are musicians' rights and the user agreement, social and cultural issues, and legal issues. These and other issues are discussed in Chapter 18.

Revenue Model and Competition

When News Corporation purchased MySpace in July 2005 for $580 million, many questioned the wisdom of paying so much for a site with no income and questionable advertisement revenue sources. However, in August 2006 Google paid MySpace almost the entire purchase sum for allowing Google to place its search and advertising on MySpace pages. This is helpful to MySpace, too, because now its users do not have to leave the site to conduct a Google search.

As of 2006, MySpace's major competitors were Xanga, Wayn, Reunion, Friendster, and Facebook. See Chapter 18 for details.

Sources: Compiled from Miller (2005), Sellers (2006), and en.wikipedia.org/wiki/MySpace (accessed August 2006).

Questions

1. Why does MySpace attract so many visitors?
2. List the major issues faced by the company.
3. What are the benefits to MySpace and Google from their collaboration?

Carnival Cruise Lines is sponsoring a social networking site (carnivalconnections.com) to attract cruise fans. Visitors can use the site to exchange opinions, organize groups for trips, and much more. It cost the company $300,000 to set up the site, but Carnival anticipates that the cost will be covered by increased business. For details, see Fass (2006).

One of the most interesting emerging business-social networks is Xing.com (xing.com).

Example: Xing.com

Originating in Germany, Xing.com is a business network that attracts millions of executives, sales representatives, and job seekers from many countries, mostly in Europe. The site offers secure services in 16 languages. Users can use the site to:

▶ Establish new business contacts.
▶ Systematically expand their networks.
▶ Easily manage their contacts.
▶ Market themselves in a professional business context.
▶ Identify experts and receive advice on any topic.
▶ Organize meetings and events.
▶ Manage contacts from anywhere.
▶ Control the level of privacy and ensure that their personal data are protected.

For additional details, take the site's "Guided Tour." Services also are available for mobile device users.

Revenue Models of Social and Business Networks

Most of the social-networking sites expect to earn revenue from advertising (as MySpace does with Google). In contrast, business-oriented networks may collect registration fees or even transaction fees. Due to the huge number of members, fees can be minimal. Recruiters, for example, already use the social networks to find people whom other people know. This enables a warm call by the recruiter ("Hi, your friend Mr. Z suggested we contact you.). For details on how recruiters use social networks, see Totty (2006). How many of these networks will survive is not known, but some already have been sold for hundreds of millions of dollars (e.g., Google paid $1.65 billion for YouTube in 2006).

Section 1.7 ▶ REVIEW QUESTIONS

1. What is a social network? Identify major features offered by social networks.
2. Describe MySpace. Why is it so popular?
3. What are some major issues faced by social network sites?
4. What is a business-oriented network?
5. Describe Xing.com and list five of its major benefits.

1.8 THE DIGITAL ENTERPRISE

The task facing each organization is how to put together the components that will enable it to transform itself within the digital economy and gain competitive advantage by using EC. The first step is to put in the right infrastructure—connective networks—upon which applications can be structured. The second step is to create (or transform) to the *digital enterprise*.

THE DIGITAL ENTERPRISE

The term *digital enterprise* has a number of definitions. It usually refers to an enterprise such as Dell, which uses computers and information systems to automate most of its business processes. Davis (2005) believes that the **digital enterprise** is a new business model that uses IT in a fundamental way to accomplish one or more of three basic objectives: reach and engage

digital enterprise
A new business model that uses IT in a fundamental way to accomplish one or more of three basic objectives: reach and engage customers more effectively, boost employee productivity, and improve operating efficiency. It uses converged communication and computing technology in a way that improves business processes.

EXHIBIT 1.11 The Digital Versus Brick-and-Mortar Company

Brick-and-Mortar Organizations	Digital Organizations
Selling in physical stores	Selling online
Selling tangible goods	Selling digital goods as well
Internal inventory/production planning	Online collaborative inventory forecasting
Paper catalogs	Smart electronic catalogs
Physical marketplace	Marketplace (electronic)
Use of telephone, fax, VANs, and traditional EDI	Use of the Internet and extranets
Physical and limited auctions	Online auctions, everywhere, any time
Broker-based services, transactions	Electronic infomediaries, value-added services
Paper-based billing	Electronic billing
Paper-based tendering	Electronic tendering (reverse auctions)
Push production, starting with demand forecast	Pull production, starting with an order
Mass production (standard products)	Mass customization, build-to-order
Physical-based commission marketing	Affiliated, virtual marketing
Word-of-mouth, slow and limited advertisement	Explosive viral marketing
Linear supply chains	Hub-based supply chains
Large amount of capital needed for mass production	Less capital needed for build-to-order; payments can flow in before production starts
Large fixed cost required for plant operation	Small fixed cost required for plant operation
Customers' value proposition is frequently a mismatch (cost > value)	Perfect match of customers' value proposition (cost = value)

customers more effectively, boost employee productivity, and improve operating efficiency. It uses converged communication and computing technology in a way that improves business processes. The major characteristics of the digital enterprise are illustrated in Exhibit 1.11, where they are compared with those of a traditional enterprise.

The digital enterprise shifts the focus from managing individual information resources—devices, applications, and datasets—*to orchestrating the services and workflows* that define the business and ultimately deliver value to customers and end users.

A digital enterprise uses networks of computers to electronically connect:

 ▶ All its internal parts via an *intranet*, which is the counterpart of the Internet.
 ▶ All its business partners via the *Internet*, or via a secured Internet, called an *extranet*, or via value-added private communication lines.

corporate portal
A major gateway through which employees, business partners, and the public can enter a corporate Web site.

The vast majority of EC is done on computers connected to these networks. Many companies employ a **corporate portal**, which is a gateway for customers, employees, and partners to reach corporate information and to communicate with the company. For additional details, see Tatnall (2006) and Chapter 7.

The major concern of many companies today is how to transform themselves to take part in the digital economy, where e-business is the norm. For example, Harrington (2006) describes why and how, as a CEO, he transformed the Thomson Corp. from a traditional $8 billion publishing business into an electronic information services provider and publisher for professionals in targeted markets. In 5 years, revenue increased over 20 percent and profit increased by more than 65 percent. For more on transformation to the digital economy, see Chapter 16. If the transformation is successful, many companies will reach the status of our hypothetical company shown in Exhibit 1.12, which uses the Internet, intranets, and extranets in an integrated manner to conduct various EC activities.

It may take 5 to 10 years for companies to become fully digitized like the hypothetical Toys, Inc. Major companies, such as Schwab, IBM, Intel, and General Electric, are moving rapidly toward such a state.

EXHIBIT 1.12 A Digital Enterprise: How a Company Uses the Internet, Intranets, and Extranets

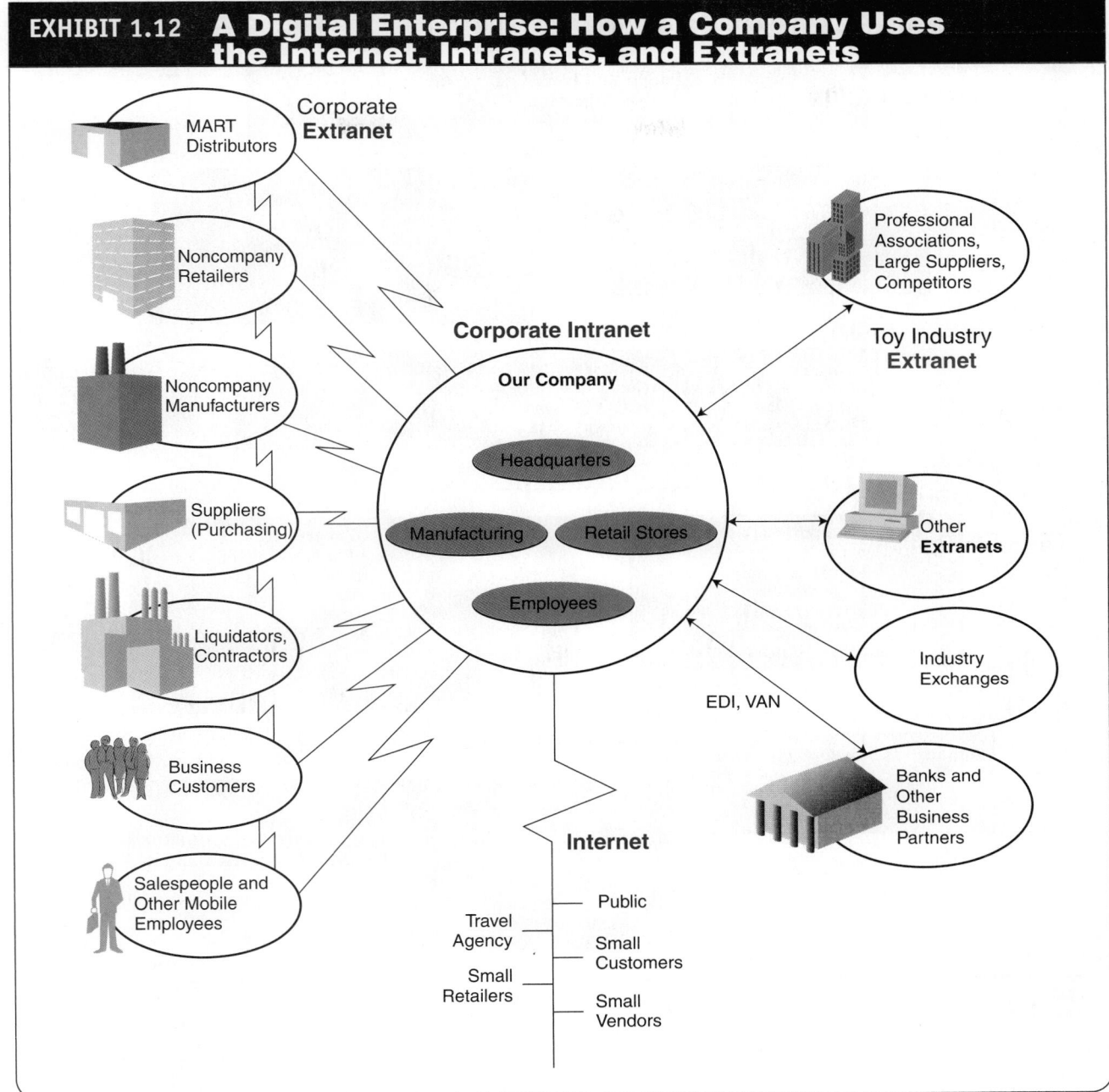

Section 1.8 ▶ REVIEW QUESTIONS

1. Define a digital enterprise.
2. Define intranets and extranets.
3. What is a corporate portal?
4. Identify EC transaction models (e.g., B2B) in Exhibit 1.11.

1.9 OVERVIEW OF THIS BOOK

This book is composed of 18 chapters grouped into 6 parts, as shown in Exhibit 1.13. Additional content is available online at the book's Web site. The Web site provides a seventh part, one additional chapter, a tutorial, an appendix on EC research, three technical appendices, and online supplemental material for each chapter.

EXHIBIT 1.13 Plan of the Book

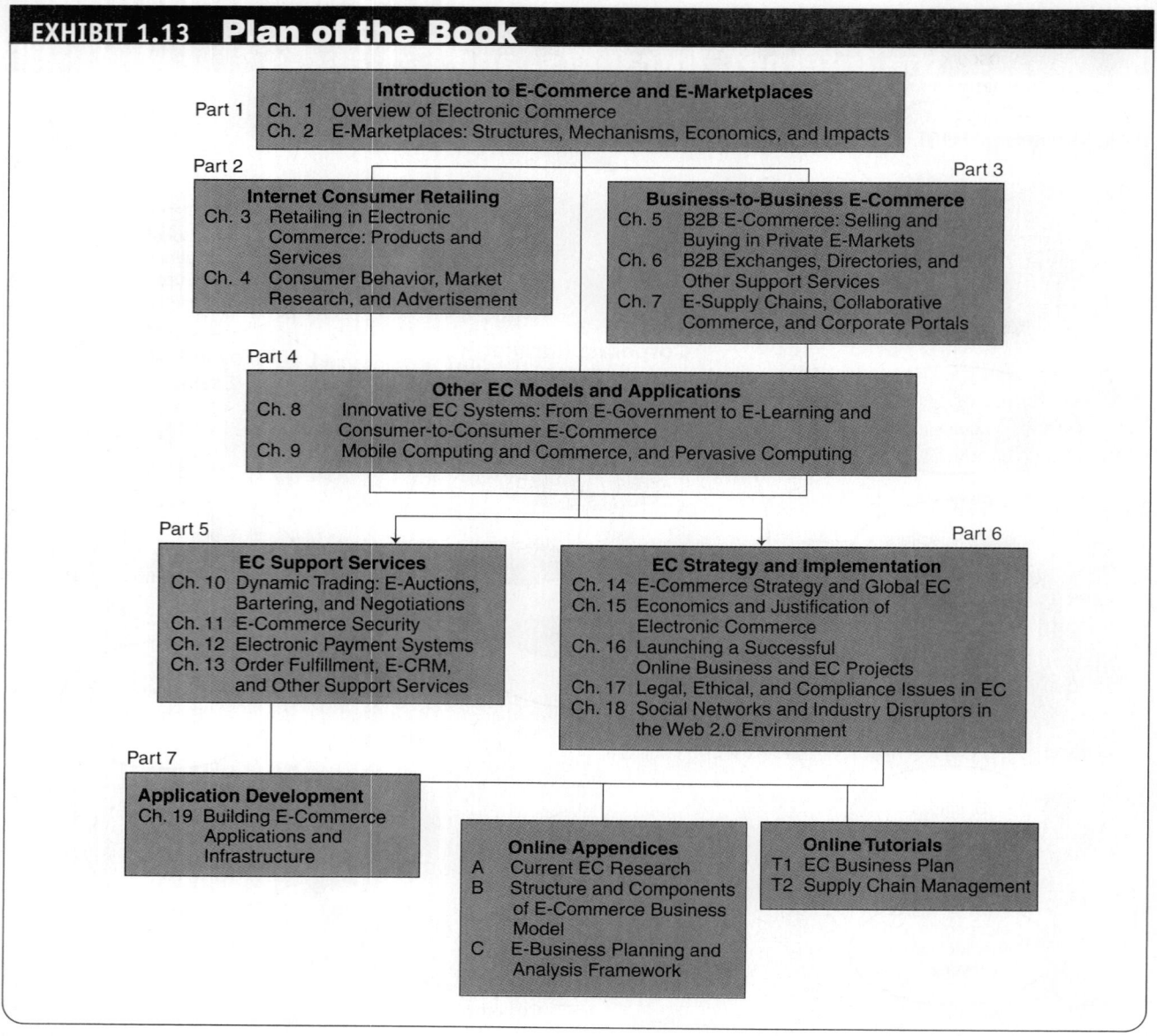

The specific parts and chapters of this textbook are as follows.

PART 1: INTRODUCTION TO E-COMMERCE AND E-MARKETPLACES

This section of the book includes an overview of EC and its content, benefits, limitations, and drivers, which are presented in Chapter 1. Chapter 2 presents electronic markets and their mechanisms, such as electronic catalogs and auctions. Chapter 2 also includes a discussion of the impacts of EC on industries and companies.

PART 2: INTERNET CONSUMER RETAILING

This section includes two chapters. Chapter 3 describes e-tailing (B2C), including some of its most innovative applications for selling products online. It also describes the delivery of services, such as online banking, travel, and insurance. Chapter 4 explains consumer behavior in cyberspace, online market research, and Internet advertising.

PART 3: BUSINESS-TO-BUSINESS E-COMMERCE

Part 3 is composed of three chapters. In Chapter 5, we introduce B2B EC and describe primarily company-centric models (one buyer—many sellers, one seller—many buyers). Electronic exchanges (many buyers and many sellers) are described in Chapter 6. Chapter 7 deals with e-supply chain topics, c-commerce, and corporate portals.

PART 4: OTHER EC MODELS AND APPLICATIONS

Several other EC models and applications are presented in Part 4. E-government, e-learning, C2C, and knowledge management are the major subjects of Chapter 8. In Chapter 9, we introduce the topics of m-commerce and pervasive computing.

PART 5: EC SUPPORT SERVICES

Part 5 examines issues involving the support services needed for EC applications. Chapter 10 describes the use of e-auctions to conduct EC. Chapter 11 delves into EC security. Of the many diverse Web support activities, we concentrate on three: payments (Chapter 12), order fulfillment (Chapter 13), and CRM (Chapter 13).

PART 6: EC STRATEGY AND IMPLEMENTATION

Part 6 includes five chapters on EC strategy and implementation. Chapter 14 deals with e-strategy and planning, including going global and the impact of EC on small businesses. Chapter 15 deals with the economics of EC. Chapter 16 deals with creating, operating, and maintaining an Internet company. It also deals with initiating EC initiatives and creating EC content. Chapter 17 provides an examination of legal and societal issues in EC. Finally, Chapter 18 is a study of the new trends of social networking and industry disruptors in the Web 2.0 environment.

ONLINE PART 7: APPLICATION DEVELOPMENT

One additional complete chapter is available online at the book's Web site (prenhall.com/turban). Chapter 19 addresses EC application development processes and methods, including the emerging topics of software as a service, Web Services, and service-oriented architecture (SOA).

ONLINE TUTORIAL

Two tutorials are available at the book's Web site (prenhall.com/turban):

- Tutorial T1: Business Plan
- Tutorial T2: Supply Chain

ONLINE APPENDICES

Four appendices are available on the book's Web site (prenhall.com/turban). Three of these we call *Technical Appendices* because of the technical nature of their content. The online appendices are:

A Current EC Research
B Structure and Components of E-Commerce Business Model
C E-Business Planning and Analysis Framework

Technical Appendices:

- Appendix A: Infrastructure for Electronic Commerce
- Appendix B: Web Page Design and Creation
- Appendix C: Software (Intelligent) Agents

ONLINE SUPPLEMENTS

A large number of Online Files organized by chapter number support the content of each chapter.

MANAGERIAL ISSUES

Many managerial issues are related to EC. These issues are discussed throughout the book and also are summarized in a separate section (like this one) near the end of each chapter. Some managerial issues related to this introductory chapter are as follows.

1. **Is it real?** For those not involved in EC, the first question that comes to mind is, "Is it real?" We believe that the answer is an emphatic "yes." Just ask anyone who has banked from home, purchased company stocks online, or bought a book from Amazon.com. Randy Mott, Wal-Mart's Chief Information Officer (CIO), gives an interesting tip for organizations and managers: "Start EC as soon as possible; it is too dangerous to wait." Jack Welch, former Chief Executive Officer (CEO) of General Electric, has commented, "Any company, old or new, that doesn't see this technology literally as important as breathing could be on its last breath" (McGee 2000).

2. **Why is B2B e-commerce so attractive?** B2B EC is attractive for several reasons. First, some B2B models are easier to implement than traditional off-line models. In contrast, B2C has several major problems, ranging from channel conflict with existing distributors to lack of a critical mass of buyers. Also, the value of transactions is larger in B2B, and the potential savings are larger and easier to justify. Rather than waiting for B2C problems to be worked out, many companies can start B2B by simply buying from existing online stores or selling electronically by joining existing marketplaces or an auction house. The problem is determining where to buy or sell.

3. **There are so many EC failures—how can one avoid them?** Beginning in early 2000, the news was awash with stories about the failure of many EC projects within companies as well as the failure of many dot-coms. Industry consolidation often occurs after a "gold rush." About 100 years ago, hundreds of companies tried to manufacture cars, following Ford's success in the United States; only three survived. The important thing is to learn from the successes and failures of others. For lessons that can be learned from EC successes and failures, see Chapters 3, 6, and 16.

4. **How do we transform our organization into a digital one?** Once a company determines its strategy and decides to move to EC, it is necessary to plan how to implement the strategy. This process is shown in Chapters 14 and 16. It is also discussed by Davenport et al. (2004) and at digitalenterprise.org.

5. **How should we evaluate the magnitude of business pressures and technological advancement?** A good approach is to solicit the expertise of research institutions, such as Gartner or Forrester Research, which specialize in EC. Otherwise, by the time you determine what is going on, it may be too late. The consulting arms of big certified public accounting companies may be of help too. (PricewaterhouseCoopers, Accenture, and others provide considerable EC information on their Web sites.) It is especially important for management to know what is going on in its own industry.

6. **How can we exploit social/business networking?** There are major possibilities here. Some companies even open their own social networks. Advertising is probably the first thing to consider. Recruiting can be a promising avenue as well. Offering discounted products and services should also be considered. Finally, sponsoring a site may be rewarding as well.

7. **What should be my company's strategy toward EC?** A company can choose one of three basic strategies: lead, wait, or experiment. This issue is revisited in Chapter 14, together with related issues such as the cost-benefit trade-offs of EC, integrating EC into the business, outsourcing, going global, and how SMEs can use EC. Another strategic issue is the prioritization of the many initiatives and applications available to a company.

8. **What are the top challenges of EC?** The top 10 *technical* issues for EC (in order of their importance) are security, adequate infrastructure, data access, back-end systems integration, sufficient bandwidth, network connectivity, up time, data warehousing and mining, scalability, and content distribution. The top 10 *managerial* issues for EC are budgets, project deadlines, keeping up with technology, privacy issues, the high cost of capital expenditures, unrealistic management expectations, training, reaching new customers, improving customer ordering services, and finding qualified EC employees. Most of these issues are discussed throughout this book.

RESEARCH TOPICS

Here are some suggested research topics related to this chapter. For details, references, and additional topics, refer to the Online Appendix A "Current EC Research."

1. **The EC Life Cycle**
   - Examine the evolution of EC with the view of stage theory.
   - Conduct an empirical study of the EC evolution stages of an industry in a given country and compare it with EC stages in other countries.
   - Where is EC going? Find and analyze future trends.
   - Research the impact of EC adoption on the market value of firms.
   - Examine the benefits of e-marketplaces by industry and by product type.
   - Study the roles of e-marketplaces as coordinators among partners and as an unbiased open-to-all third-party platform.
   - Determine if traditional personal roles can be moved to e-marketplaces.

2. **The Potential and the Limitations of EC Penetration at the Macro Level**
   - Does the nature of an industry impact the potential for EC penetration?
   - Examine, compare, and analyze the level of EC penetration in different countries.
   - Conduct a cross-country and cross-product/service comparative survey to explore differences in EC penetration.
   - Identify generic factors that deter EC penetration and develop a strategy to eliminate such hurdles.

3. **Synergy of EC with Traditional Commerce**
   - Study the optimal and synergetic design of EC, including both online activities and the physical process.
   - Examine synergies between electronic retailing and traditional retailing.
   - Examine synergies between traditional logistic services and electronic services.

4. **E-Business Models**
   - Determine the relationship between a model's success and the characteristics of organizations using it.
   - Examine the proliferation of social networks and describe their impact on EC.
   - How can the best models for a specific situation be identified?
   - Why do some EC models fail?
   - For EC resources, see Online File W1.10.

SUMMARY

In this chapter, you learned about the following EC issues as they relate to the learning objectives.

1. **Definition of EC and description of its various categories.** EC involves conducting transactions electronically. Its major categories are pure versus partial EC, Internet-based versus non-Internet based, and electronic markets versus interorganizational systems.

2. **The content and framework of EC.** The applications of EC, and there are many, are based on infrastructures and are supported by people; public policy and technical standards; marketing and advertising; support services, such as logistics, security, and payment services; and business partners—all tied together by management.

3. **The major types of EC transactions.** The major types of EC transactions are B2B, B2C, C2C, m-commerce, intrabusiness commerce, B2E, c-commerce, e-government, and e-learning.

4. **The role of the digital revolution.** EC is a major product of the digital and technological revolution, which enables companies to simultaneously increase both growth and profits. This revolution enables digitization of products, services, and information.

5. **The role of the business environment as an EC driver.** The business environment is changing rapidly due to technological breakthroughs, globalization, societal changes, deregulations, and more. The changing business environment forces organizations to respond. Traditional responses may not be sufficient because of the magnitude of the pressures and the pace of the changes involved. Therefore, organizations must frequently innovate and reengineer their operations. In many cases, EC is the major facilitator of such organizational responses.

---

6. **The major EC business models.** The major EC business models include online direct marketing, electronic tendering systems, name-your-own-price, affiliate marketing, viral marketing, group purchasing, online auctions, mass customization (make-to-order), electronic exchanges, supply chain improvers, finding the best price, value-chain integration, value-chain providers, information brokers, bartering, deep discounting, and membership.

7. **Benefits of EC to organizations, consumers, and society.** EC offers numerous benefits. Because these benefits are substantial, it looks as though EC is here to stay and cannot be ignored.

8. **Barriers to EC.** The barriers to EC can be categorized as technological and nontechnological. As time passes and network capacity, security, and accessibility continue to improve through technological innovations, the barriers posed by technological limitations will continue to diminish. Nontechnological barriers also will diminish over time, but some, especially the behavioral ones, may persist for many years in some organizations, cultures, or countries.

9. **Contribution to organizations responding to environmental changes.** EC provides strategic advantage so organizations can compete better. Also, organizations can go into remote and global markets for both selling and buying at better prices. Organizations can speed time-to-market to gain competitive advantage. They can improve the internal and external supply chain as well as increase collaboration. Finally, they can better comply with government regulations.

10. **Social and business Online Networks.** Social and business networks attract huge numbers of visitors. Many of the visitors are young future EC customers. Therefore, advertisers are willing to spend money on advertising, either to an entire group or to individuals (e.g., using Google's technology). Already among the most visited sites, they offer many innovative applications as well.

KEY TERMS

Affiliate marketing	22	Digital economy	14	Intraorganizational information systems	6
Brick-and-mortar (old-economy) organizations	5	Digital enterprise	29	Location-based commerce (l-commerce)	8
Business model	18	E-business	4		
Business-to-business (B2B)	8	E-co-ops	23	Mobile commerce (m-commerce)	8
Business-to-business-to-consumer (B2B2C)	8	E-government	10	Name-your-own-price model	22
		E-learning	10		
Business-to-consumer (B2C)	8	E-tailing	8	Peer-to-peer (P2P)	10
Business-to-employees (B2E)	9	Electronic commerce (EC)	4	Revenue model	20
Click-and-mortar (click-and-brick) organizations	5	Electronic market (e-marketplace)	6	SMEs	23
		Exchange (electronic)	10	Social networks	27
Collaborative commerce (c-commerce)	10	Exchange-to-exchange (E2E)	10	Tendering (bidding) system	22
		Extranet	6	Value proposition	21
Consumer-to-business (C2B)	8	Group purchasing	23	Viral marketing	23
Consumer-to-consumer (C2C)	10	Interorganizational information systems (IOSs)	6	Virtual (pure-play) organizations	5
Corporate portal	30	Intrabusiness EC	8		
Customization	23	Intranet	6	Web 2.0	13

QUESTIONS FOR DISCUSSION

1. Compare brick-and-mortar and click-and-mortar organizations.
2. Why is buying with a smart card from a vending machine considered EC?
3. Why is e-learning considered EC?
4. Why is it said that EC is a catalyst for fundamental changes in organizations?
5. How does EC facilitate customization of products and services?
6. Discuss the relationships among the various components of a business model.
7. Explain how EC can reduce cycle time, improve employees' empowerment, and facilitate customer support.

8. Compare and contrast viral marketing with affiliate marketing.

9. Explain how EC is related to supply chain management.

10. Discuss the contribution of EC technologies to homeland security.

11. Carefully examine the nontechnological limitations of EC. Which are company dependent and which are generic?

12. Which of the EC limitations do you think will be more easily overcome—the technological or the nontechnological limitations? Why?

13. Why are social networks, such as MySpace, considered EC?

14. Would you consider eDiets.com to be a social network? Why or why not?

INTERNET EXERCISES

1. Visit **bigboxx.com** and identify the services the company provides to its customers. What type of EC is this? What business model(s) does Bigboxx use?

2. Visit Amazon.com's site (**amazon.com**) and locate recent information in the following areas:

   a. Find the five top-selling books on EC.

   b. Find a review of one of these books.

   c. Review the customer services you can get from Amazon.com and describe the benefits you receive from shopping there.

   d. Review the products directory.

3. Visit **priceline.com** and identify the various business models used by Priceline.com.

4. Go to **ups.com** and find information about recent EC projects that are related to logistics and supply chain management. How is UPS using wireless services?

5. Go to **nike.com** and design your own shoes. Next visit **office.microsoft.com** and create your own business card. Finally, enter **jaguar.com** and configure the car of your dreams. What are the advantages of each activity? The disadvantages?

6. Visit **chemconnect.com**. What kind of EC does this site represent? What benefits can it provide to buyers? To sellers?

7. It is time to sell or buy on an online auction. You can try **ebay.com**, **auction.yahoo.com**, or an auction site of your choice. You can participate in an auction in almost any country. Prepare a short report describing your experiences.

8. Try to save on your next purchase. Visit **letsbuyit.com** and **buyerzone.com**. Which site do you prefer? Why?

9. Enter **espn.go.com** and identify and list all of the revenue sources on the site.

10. Enter **eDiets.com**. Find the personalized programs. Explain their benefits. Also, identify eDiets' revenue model.

11. Enter **philatino.com** and **statusint.com**. Identify the business model(s) and revenue models they use.

12. Enter **lowes.com**. View the "design it" online feature and the animated "How Tos." Examine the Project Calculators and Gift Advisor features. Relate these to the business models and other EC features of this chapter.

TEAM ASSIGNMENTS AND ROLE PLAYING

1. Visit **smallbusiness.yahoo.com** and **google.com** and find 15 EC success stories. For each, identify the types of EC transactions and the business model used.

2. Each team will research two EC success stories. Members of the group should examine companies that operate solely online and some that extensively utilize a click-and-mortar strategy. Each team should identify the critical success factors for their companies and present a report to the other teams.

3. Each team member studies three social networks (see **wikipedia.org** for a list). Then the team makes a presentation on the features of the companies, the revenue models, the unique characteristics, and the IT support.

4. Enter the customer video library at **citrix.com**. Each team member reviews an EC-related case. Relate each case to the nature of EC transaction and to the business model used.

Real-World Case

GOOGLE IS CHANGING EVERYTHING

Introduction

Of all the companies associated with EC, probably no other company has impacted our work and life as much as Google has. More than that, according to Carr (2006), Google's unconventional IT and EC management strategy is both effective and efficient, and it offers a glimpse into how organizations might deploy technology in the future. Google runs on close to 500,000 servers. Google has grown more quickly than any other EC company, and it started to generate profit faster than most start-ups. By 2005, its revenue had reached $6 billion and its net profit $1.46 billion (estimates for 2006 are $9 billion and $2 billion, respectively).

Google is known primarily for its search engine and its related targeted-advertising tools. Google delivers its advertisers far more revenue per click in search results than its competitors (mainly Microsoft and Yahoo!) do. In Chapter 4, we will explain Google's ad-matching strategy. However, Google is doing many other things. Let's examine some of Google's many activities.

A Glimpse at Google's Activities

Google's goal is to deliver technologies to organize the world's information and make it universally accessible and useful. For example, Google is trying to reinvent the spreadsheet as a Web-based application that makes it simple for users to input and share data. Google Spreadsheet is a free Web-based application that can be shared with up to 10 users simultaneously, overcoming a key limitation of Microsoft's Excel. Google chose spreadsheets because that is what most people use to organize information; most individual users do not create databases. Google Spreadsheet, which can import or export data from Excel's .xls format or the open Comma Separated Value (.csv) format, is aimed at small work teams in social situations or small businesses, but not big enterprises.

The program is designed to help people organize their own information and make it more easily accessible to others via the Web. Data in the spreadsheets are saved automatically with each user action over the Web onto Google computer servers. Users can sort data and take advantage of 200 functions and common spreadsheet formulas for doing basic calculations. Google Spreadsheet is one of several user productivity applications that Google has been testing, including the Writely word processing application it acquired in 2006 and its internally developed Google Calendar.

Google is currently studying how much demand there is for Google Spreadsheet to work with Google Base, an online database service that allows Google users to post various types of information online. Google Base is viewed by analysts as a stepping stone into classified e-advertising, an e-commerce activity, by helping users feature relevant information on Google's main search index, its Froogle shopping comparison tool (*froogle.google.com*), and Google Local search (*local.google.com*).

In 2006, Google expanded into the software business, offering Google Office (initially free, to compete with Microsoft). Also, Google offers a set of Web programs (e.g., for e-mail, communications, and scheduling). Other offerings are Google Calendar, Google Earth, Google Maps, and Google Mini, just to name a few. For more on Google products, visit *google.com/intl/en/options*.

Enterprise Search

An enterprise search identifies and enables specific content across the enterprise to be indexed, searched, and displayed to authorized users. Google has partnered with BearingPoint, an IT consulting firm, to supply enterprise search capabilities. BearingPoint has experience in extending Google to provide search services to specific industries. A crucial enterprise search issue is programming search engines to crawl through all the various data sources at a company and index their contents.

Enterprise searches can be integrated with other applications to improve performance. For example, Cognos Go! Search Service is a BI (business intelligence) search utility. It offers a familiar search interface for accessing strategic enterprise information, such as reports, metrics, analyses, and business events, that answer critical business questions with a simple keyword search. Oracle offers a search engine for enterprise systems, such as ERP and CRM.

Example

Kaiser Permanente (*kaiserpermanente.org*), America's largest nonprofit health maintenance organization (HMO), has almost 9 million members. The amount of available medical knowledge doubles about every 7 years, so keeping up with new knowledge is an important aspect of good caregiving by HMOs.

When Kaiser Permanente developed a clinical-knowledge corporate portal for its 50,000 doctors, nurses, and other caregivers, enterprise search was a part of the plan. The Permanente Knowledge Connection, available from anywhere in the Kaiser wide area network, gives medical staff access to diagnostic information, best practices, publications, educational material, and other clinical resources. The portal's resources are distributed across the entire United States. Putting the right information quickly and easily into caregivers' hands is essential to the clinical portal's success.

Kaiser turned to the Google Search Appliance, which enabled the HMO to index 150,000 documents across the Kaiser network. Clinicians now search the site in situations that range from leisurely research to urgent care, from the exam room to the emergency room. Doctors and nurses use the search engine to help them reach diagnoses and specify treatments, check the side effects of new medications, and consult clinical research studies and other medical publications. Google's spell-checking capability is especially useful in the medical profession: Doctors' handwriting can be problematic and pharmaceutical product names are difficult.

Sources: Compiled from Carr (2006), Brown (2006), and Hicks (2004).

Questions

1. Use Google to conduct a search. What advertisements appear next to the search results?
2. What is Google trying to do with spreadsheets?
3. What is an enterprise search?
4. Identify potential revenue models in Googler's activities described here and on its Web site.
5. How do Google's services benefit a company such as Kaiser?

REFERENCES

Abramson, B. *Digital Phoenix: Why the Information Economy Collapsed and How it Will Rise Again.* Boston: MIT Press, 2005.

Afuah, A., and C. L. Tucci. *Internet Business Models and Strategies,* 2d ed. New York: McGraw-Hill, 2003.

Amit, R., and C. Zott. "Value Creation in E-Business." *Strategic Management Journal* 22, no. 6 (2001).

Angermeier, M. "The Huge Cloud Lens Web 2.0." *Kosmar.de,* November 11, 2005. **kosmar.de/archives/2005/11/11/the-huge-cloud-lens-bubble-map-web20** (accessed March 2007).

Ariguzo, G. C., E. G. Mallach, and D. S. White. "The First Decade of E-Commerce." *International Journal of Business Information Systems,* 2, no. 3 (2006).

Athitakis, M. "How to Make Money on the Net." *Business 2.0,* May 2003.

Bakos, J. J. "A Strategic Analysis of Electronic Marketplaces." *MIS Quarterly* 15, no. 3 (1991).

Bandyopadhyay, S. "A Critical Review of Pricing Strategies for Online Business Model." *Quarterly Journal of Electronic Commerce* 2, no. 1 (2001).

Berstein, M. "Boeing Shrinks Supply Chain to Facilitate Risk Sharing." *World Trade,* April 1, 2006.

Brown, M. C. "Hacking Google Maps." *ExtremeTech.com,* August 31, 2006. **extremetech.com/article2/0,1558,2011239,00.asp** (accessed September 2006).

Carr, D. F. "How Google Works." *Baseline,* July 2006.

Carton, S. *The Dot.Bomb Survival Guide.* New York: McGraw-Hill, 2002.

Cassidy, J. *Dot.com: The Greatest Story Ever Sold.* New York: Harper Collins Publication, 2002.

Chen, S. *Strategic Management of E-Business,* 2d ed. Chichester, England: John Wiley & Sons, 2004.

Chesbrough, H., and R. Rosenbloom. "The Role of the Business Model: Evidence from Xerox Corp." *Industrial and Corporate Change* 11, no. 3 (2002).

Choi, S. Y., and A. B. Whinston. *The Internet Economy, Technology, and Practice.* Austin, TX: Smartecon.com, 2000.

Choi, S. Y., A. B. Whinston, and D. O. Stahl. *The Economics of Electronic Commerce.* Indianapolis, IN: Macmillan Technical Pub, 1997.

Cone, E. "Flying in Formation." *Cioinsights.com,* March 2006.

Currie, W. *Value Creation from E-Business Models.* Burlington, MA: Butterworth-Heinemann, 2004.

Davenport, T., J. Harris, and S. Cantrell. "Enterprise Systems and Ongoing Process Change." *Business Process Management Journal.* (February 2004).

Davenport, T. H. "Competing on Analytics." *Harvard Business Review* (January 2006).

Davis, J. E. "Toward the Digital Enterprise." White paper, Intel Corporation, 2005. **intel.com/it/digitalenterprise** (accessed April 2006).

Dell Recycling. **dell.com/recycling** (accessed September 2006).

Drucker, P. *Managing in the Next Society.* New York: Truman Talley Books, 2002.

Electronic Industry Alliance. "Dell Recycling Grant Program Names 20 Recipients for Fall 2004." *Eiae.org,* August 31, 2004. **eiae.org/whatsnew/news.cfm?ID=110** (accessed February 2005).

Emarketer.com. "Online Purchases in the U.S., by Category, 2002." **emarketer.com,** June 26, 2002 (accessed April 2004).

Farivar, C. "New Ways to Pay." *Business 2.0,* July 1, 2004.

Fass, A. "TheirSpace.com." *RedOrbit.com,* April 25, 2006. **redorbit.com/news/technology/481499/theirspacecom/index.html?source=r_technology** (accessed November 2006).

Foley, J. "Data Debate." *Information Week,* May 19, 2003.

Forrester Research. "Retail First Look," *Forrester.com,* June 1, 2006. **forrester.com/FirstLook/Vertical/Issue/0,6454,600,00.html** (accessed September 2006).

Greenberg, P. *CRM at the Speed of Light: Capturing and Keeping Customers in Internet Real Time,* 3d ed. New York: McGraw-Hill, 2004.

Harmonyhollow.net, "What Are The Barriers of Implementing E-Commerce Solutions?" 2006. **harmonyhollow.net/webmaster-resources/ecommerce/15604.php** (accessed August 2006).

Harrington, R. "The Transformer" (an e-mail interview with *Baseline's* editor-in-chief, J. McCormic). *Baseline,* April 2006.

Hicks, M. "Google's Next Step: Banner Ads," *eWeek.com,* May 13, 2004. **eweek.com/article2/0,1895,1592027,00.asp** (accessed September 2006).

Hoffman, K. L., and T. P. Novak. "How to Acquire Customers on the Web." *Harvard Business Review* (May–June 2000).

Huber, G. *The Necessary Nature of Future Firms.* San Francisco: Sage Publications, 2004.

Hwang, H. S., and C. Stewart. "Lessons from Dot-Com Boom and Bust," in Khosrow-Pour (2006).

Jelassi, T., and A. Enders. *Strategies for e-Business.* Harlow, England: FT, Prentice Hall, 2005.

Jonietz, E. "Traffic Avoidance." *Technology Review* (December 2005–January 2006).

Jupiter Media. "Jupiter Research Forecasts Online Retail Spending Will Reach $144 Billion in 2010, a CAGR of 12% from 2005." February 6, 2006. **jupitermedia.com/corporate/releases/06.02.06-newjupresearch.html** (accessed September 2006).

Kaplan, P. J. *F'd Companies: Spectacular Dot.com Flameouts.* New York: Simon and Schuster, 2002.

Kehal, H. S., and V. P. Singh. *Digital Economy: Impacts, Influences, and Challenges.* Hershey, PA: Idea Group Publishing, 2004.

Khosrow-Pour, M. (ed.) *Encyclopedia of E-Commerce, E-Government, and Mobile Commerce,* Hershey, PA: Idea Group Reference, 2006.

Kraemer, K., and J. Dedrick. "Dell Computer: Using E-Commerce to Support a Virtual Company," a special report, June 2001, available in M. Rappa, "Case Study: Dell Computer." **digitalenterprise.org/cases/dell.html** (accessed September 2006).

Krishnan, S. A., and A. Ravi. "Group Buying on the Web: A Comparison of Price-Discovery Mechanisms." *INFORMS,* November 2003.

Lashinsky, A. "The Boom is Back." *Fortune,* May 1, 2006.

Lebbecke, C. "RFID in the Retail Supply Chain," in Khosrow-Pour (2006).

Lenard, T. M., and D. B. Britton. "The Digital Economy Factbook," 8th ed. The Progress and Freedom Foundation, 2006. **pff.org/issues-pubs/books/factbook_2006.pdf** (accessed March 2007).

Lee, C. S., Y. G. Chen, and Y.-H. Fan. "Structure and Components of E-commerce Business Model," in Khosrow-Pour 2006.

Li, E. Y., and T. C. Du. *Advances in Electronic Business,* vol. 1. Hershey, PA: Idea Group Publishing, 2004.

Mann, J. TechSpot.com, May 5, 2006. **techspot.com/news/21504-700-million-internet-users-says-comscore-networks.html** (accessed September 2006).

Mark, K. "Wanted: Digital History." *Internetnews.com,* October 2004. **internetnews.com/bus-news/article.php/3425681** (accessed February 2005).

McGee, M. K. "Chiefs of the Year: Internet Call to Arms." *Information Week,* November 27, 2000.

McKay, J., and P. Marshall. *Strategic Management of E-Business.* Milton, Qld., Australia: John Wiley and Sons, 2004.

Miller, J. L. "No Place Like MySpace," *Webpronews.com,* October 11, 2005. **webpronews.com/insiderreports/marketinginsider/wpn-50-20051011NoPlace-LikeMySpace.html** (accessed September 2006).

Mockler, R. J., et al. "B2B E-Business," in Khosrow-Pour (2006).

Mullaney, T. J. "E-Biz Strikes Again!" *BusinessWeek,* May 10, 2004.

National Cristina Foundation. **cristina.org/dsf/dell.ncf** (accessed September 2006).

O'Reilly, T. "What is Web 2.0?" *OReillynet.com,* September 30, 2006. **oreillynet.com/pub/a/oreilly/tim/news/2005/09/30/what-is-web-20.html** (accessed September 2006).

Papazoglou, M. P., and P. M. A. Ribbers. *e-Business: Organizational and Technical Foundations.* West Sussex, England: Wiley 2006.

People's Daily Online (China). "Distressed Parents Create Blog to Track Down Missing Son." **english.people.com.cn/200608/01/eng20060801_288726.html** (accessed September 2006).

Peters, K. M. "Homeland Security Hurdles." *Government Executive,* February 2003.

Plunkett, J. W. *Plunkett's E-Commerce and Internet Business Almanac 2006,* Houston, TX: Plunkett Research, Ltd., February 2006.

Plunkett Research. "State of Online Financial Services." 2004. **plunkettresearch.com/finance/financial_overview.htm#6** (no longer available online).

Preissl, B., et al. (eds.). *E-Life After the Dotcom Bust.* Heidelberg, Germany: Physica-Verlag, 2004.

Rappa, M. "Business Models on the Web," *Digitalenterprise.org,* 2006, **digitalenterprise.org/models/models.html** (accessed August 2006).

Reda, S. "Godiva.com's Story Parallels Dynamic Growth of E-Commerce." *Stores,* February 2004.

Rossi, M., T. Saarinen, and V. K. Tuunainen. "New Business Models for Electronic Commerce." *Data Base* (Spring 2003).

Rovenpor, J. "Explaining the E-Commerce Shakeout: Why Did So Many Internet-Based Businesses Fail?" *e-Service Journal,* Fall 2003.

Savitz, E. "Look Who's Storming the Net," *SmartMoney,* June 2005.

Schonfeld, E. "Web 2.0 Around the World," *Business 2.0,* August 2006a.

Schonfeld, E. "Cyworld Attacks!" *Business 2.0*, August 2006b.

Sellers, P. "MySpace Cowboys." *Fortune*, September 4, 2006.

Seoul Digital City. "E-Commerce In Korea: Myths, Facts," April 28, 2004. **urban.blogs.com/seoul/2004/04/ecommerce_in_ko.html** (accessed September 2006).

Sharma, S. K. "E-Commerce in the Digital Economy," in Khosrow-Pour (2006).

Strategic Direction. "DotCom Boom and Bust: The Secrets of E-Commerce Failure and Success," *Strategic Direction*, February 2005.

Tatnall, A. "Web Portal Gateways," in Khosrow-Pour, (2006).

Tewksbury, R. B. "Is the Internet Heading for a Cache Crunch?" On the Internet, January/February 1998. **isoc.org/oti/articles/0198/tewksbury.html** (accessed March 2007).

Thibodeau, P. "DHS Sets Timeline for IT Integration." *Computer World*, June 16, 2003.

Tian, Y., and C. Stewart. "History of E-Commerce," in Khosrow-Pour (2006).

Totty, M. "New Tools Emerge for Frazzled Recruiters." *Wall Street Journal*, October 23, 2006.

Turban, E., et al. *Information Technology for Management*, 6th ed. New York: John Wiley & Sons, 2007.

U.S. Department of Commerce. "The Emerging Digital Economy II." June 1999. **esa.doc.gov/reports/EDE2report.pdf** (no longer available online).

Van Toorn, C., D. Bunker, K. Yee, and S. Smith. "The Barriers to the Adoption of E-Commerce by Micro Businesses, Small Businesses and Medium Enterprises," Sixth International Conference on Knowledge, Culture, and Change in Organisations, Prato, Tuscany, Italy, July 11–14, 2006.

Weill, P., and M. R. Vitale. *Place to Space: Migrating to eBusiness Models.* Boston: Harvard Business School Press, 2001.

Wolfson, H. "Dell Provides Computers for Students to Take Apart." *Al.com*, January 26, 2005. **al.com/news/birminghamnews/east.ssf?/base/community/1106735278260730.xml** (accessed February 2005).

Workforce-Performance. "Boeing 787 Global Design Team Benefits from Collaboration Solution Incorporating Simulation," *Workforce-Performance*, May 22, 2006, **workforce-performancenewsline.com/News/05–22–06a.html** (accessed August 2006).

Zhengzhou Evening News (in Chinese), September 27, 2004.

E-MARKETPLACES: STRUCTURES, MECHANISMS, ECONOMICS, AND IMPACTS

Learning Objectives

Upon completion of this chapter, you will be able to:

1. Define e-marketplaces and list their components.
2. List the major types of e-marketplaces and describe their features.
3. Describe the various types of EC intermediaries and their roles.
4. Describe electronic catalogs, shopping carts, and search engines.
5. Describe the major types of auctions and list their characteristics.
6. Discuss the benefits, limitations, and impacts of auctions.
7. Describe bartering and negotiating online.
8. Define m-commerce and explain its role as a market mechanism.
9. Discuss competition in the digital economy.
10. Describe the impact of e-marketplaces on organizations and industries.

Content

How Blue Nile Inc. Is Changing the Jewelry Industry

2.1 E-Marketplaces
2.2 Types of E-Marketplaces: From Storefronts to Portals
2.3 Transactions, Intermediation, and Processes in E-Commerce
2.4 Electronic Catalogs and Other Market Mechanisms
2.5 Auctions as EC Market Mechanisms
2.6 Bartering and Negotiating Online
2.7 E-Commerce in the Wireless Environment: M-Commerce and L-Commerce
2.8 Competition in the Digital Economy and Its Impact on Industries
2.9 Impacts of EC on Business Processes and Organizations

Managerial Issues

Real-World Case: Wal-Mart Leads RFID Adoption

Appendix 2A: Build-to-Order Production

HOW BLUE NILE INC. IS CHANGING THE JEWELRY INDUSTRY

Blue Nile Inc. (*bluenile.com*), a pure-play online e-tailer that specializes in diamonds and jewelry, capitalized on online diamond sales as a dot-com start-up in 1999. The company provides a textbook case of how EC fundamentally undercuts the traditional way of doing business.

The Opportunity

Using the B2C EC model—knocking out expensive stores and intermediaries and then slashing prices (up to 35 percent less than rivals to gain market share), Blue Nile captured a high market share in a short time, inducing more and more people to buy online and making a sizable profit.

How did the start-up defy conventional wisdom that diamonds could not be sold online? Basically, Blue Nile offers a huge selection of diamonds and more information on diamonds than a jewelry expert offers in a physical store. It features educational guides in plain English and provides independent (and trusted) quality ratings for every stone. A customer can look over a rating scale for cut, clarity, color, and so on and then conduct a price comparison with Diamond.com (*diamond.com*) and other online stores. Most important is the 30-day money-back guarantee (now an online industry standard). This provides customers a comfort level against fraud and gives Blue Nile a competitive edge against stores that take the stones back but charge a fee to do so.

The Results

Blue Nile sales reached $129 million in 2003 (a 79 percent increase over 2002), with a net income of $27 million. In 2006, sales exceeded $210 million (40 percent annual growth). The company became the eighth-largest specialty jewelry company in the United States and went public in 2004 (one of the most successful IPOs of 2004).

To sell $210 million in jewelry, a traditional retail chain needs 200 stores and close to 1,800 employees. Blue Nile does it with one 10,000-square-foot warehouse and 115 staffers. The company also bypasses the industry's tangled supply chain, in which a diamond can pass through five or more middlemen before reaching a retailer. Blue Nile deals directly with original suppliers, such as Thaigem.com (*thaigem.com*; see Online File W2.5).

This is one reason why in the United States some 465 small jewelry stores closed in 2003 alone. The survivors specialize in custom-crafted pieces. Large rivals try to fight back, streamlining the supply chain, emphasizing customer service, and even trying to sell some products online.

The future seems to be clear, as summarized by Roger Thompson, a small jeweler in Lambertville, New Jersey, who said, "Anyone with half a brain, who wants a diamond engagement ring will go to the Internet." So, he stopped selling diamonds. In the meantime, grooms make proposals with Blue Nile rings, saving $3,000 to $5,000.

Sources: Adapted from Mullaney (2004), BusinessWeek Online (2006), and *bluenile.com* (accessed December 2006).

WHAT CAN WE LEARN . . .

Blue Nile is a pure-play online store (a *storefront*) that uses electronic catalogs, virtual shopping carts, and superb customer service to sell diamonds and jewelry. Storefronts, carts, and catalogs are the major mechanisms for selling online, and they are described here and in Chapter 16. This case also shows the impact of online sales on an industry. Because of low operating costs and global reach, Blue Nile and other online jewelers quickly conquered an impressive market share, driving hundreds of small traditional jewelry retailers out of business. This competitive impact and other impacts of EC are discussed in this chapter.

2.1 E-MARKETPLACES

According to Bakos (1998), electronic markets play a central role in the economy, facilitating the exchange of information, goods, services, and payments. In the process, they create economic value for buyers, sellers, market intermediaries, and for society at large.

Markets (electronic or otherwise) have three main functions: (1) matching buyers and sellers; (2) facilitating the exchange of information, goods, services, and payments associated with market transactions; and (3) providing an institutional infrastructure, such as a legal and regulatory framework that enables the efficient functioning of the market (see Zwass 2003 for details).

ELECTRONIC MARKETS

e-marketplace

An online market, usually B2B, in which buyers and sellers exchange goods or services; the three types of e-marketplaces are private, public, and consortia.

The major place for conducting EC transactions is the electronic market (e-market). An **e-marketplace** is a virtual marketplace in which sellers and buyers meet and conduct different types of transactions. Customers exchange these goods and services for money (or other goods and services if bartering is used). The functions of an e-market are the same as that of a physical marketplace; however, computerized systems tend to make markets much more efficient by providing more updated information to buyers and sellers.

In recent years, markets have seen a dramatic increase in the use of IT and EC (Turban et al. 2007). EC has increased market efficiencies by expediting or improving the functions listed in Exhibit 2.1. Furthermore, EC has been able to significantly decrease the cost of executing these functions.

The emergence of *electronic marketplaces* (also called *e-marketplaces* or *marketspaces*), especially Internet-based ones, changed several of the processes used in trading and supply chains. These changes, driven by technology, resulted in:

▶ Greater information richness of the transactional and relational environment

▶ Lower information search costs for buyers

▶ Diminished information asymmetry between sellers and buyers

▶ Greater temporal separation between time of purchase and time of possession of physical products purchased in the e-marketplace

▶ Greater temporal proximity between time of purchase and time of possession of digital products purchased in the e-marketplace

▶ The ability of buyers and sellers to be in different locations

EXHIBIT 2.1   Functions of a Market

Matching of Buyers and Sellers	Facilitation of Transactions	Institutional Infrastructure

• Determination of product offerings
   Product features offered by sellers
   Aggregation of different products
• Search (of buyers for sellers and of sellers for buyers)
   Price and product information
   Organizing bids and bartering
   Matching seller offerings with
    buyer preferences
• Price discovery
   Process and outcome in
    determination of prices
   Enabling price comparisons
• Others
   Providing sales leads
	• Logistics
	   Delivery of information, goods,
	    or services to buyers
	• Settlement
	   Transfer of payments to sellers
	• Trust
	   Credit system, reputations, rating
	    agencies such as *Consumer Reports*
	    and the BBB, special escrow and
	    online trust agencies
	• Communication
	   Posting buyers' requests
		• Legal
		   Commercial code, contract law,
		    dispute resolution, intellectual
		    property protection
		   Export and import law
		• Regulatory
		   Rules and regulations, monitoring,
		    enforcement
		• Discovery
		   Provides market information
		    (e.g., about competition,
		    government regulations)

Sources: Compiled from Bakos (1998) and from E-Market Services (2006).

EC leverages IT with increased effectiveness and lower transaction and distribution costs, leading to more efficient, "friction-free" markets. An example of such efficiency is the Blue Nile case. For more on e-marketplaces, see Li and Du (2005) and Varadarajan and Yadav (2002).

E-MARKETPLACE COMPONENTS AND PARTICIPANTS

A **marketspace** includes electronic transactions that bring about a new distribution of goods and services. The major components and players in a marketspace are customers, sellers, goods and services (physical or digital), infrastructure, a front end, a back end, intermediaries and other business partners, and support services. A brief description of each follows:

▶ **Customers.** The 1.6 billion people worldwide who surf the Web are potential buyers of the goods and services offered or advertised on the Internet. These consumers are looking for bargains, customized items, collectors' items, entertainment, socialization, and more. They are in the driver's seat. They can search for detailed information, compare, bid, and sometimes negotiate. Organizations are the largest consumers, accounting for more than 85 percent of EC activities.

▶ **Sellers.** Millions of storefronts are on the Web, advertising and offering a huge variety of items. These stores are owned by companies, government agencies, or individuals. Every day it is possible to find new offerings of products and services. Sellers can sell direct from their Web sites or from e-marketplaces.

▶ **Products and services.** One of the major differences between the marketplace and the marketspace is the possible digitization of products and services in a marketspace. Although both types of markets can sell physical products, the marketspace also can sell **digital products**, which are goods that can be transformed to digital format and instantly delivered over the Internet. In addition to digitization of software and music, it is possible to digitize dozens of other products and services, as shown in Online File W2.1. Digital products have different cost curves than those of regular products. In digitization, most of the costs are fixed, and variable costs are very low. Thus, profit will increase very rapidly as volume increases, once the fixed costs are paid for.

▶ **Infrastructure.** The marketspace infrastructure includes electronic networks, hardware, software, and more. (EC infrastructure is presented in Chapter 1; also see Online Chapter 19.)

▶ **Front end.** Customers interact with a marketspace via a **front end**. The components of the front end can include the *seller's portal*, electronic catalogs, a shopping cart, a search engine, an auction engine, and a payment gateway. (For details, see Beynon-Davies 2004.)

▶ **Back end.** All the activities that are related to order aggregation and fulfillment, inventory management, purchasing from suppliers, accounting and finance, insurance, payment processing, packaging, and delivery are done in what is termed the **back end** of the business. (For details, see Beynon-Davies 2004.)

▶ **Intermediaries.** In marketing, an **intermediary** is typically a third party that operates between sellers and buyers. Intermediaries of all kinds offer their services on the Web. The role of these electronic intermediaries (as will be seen throughout the text and especially in Chapters 3, 5, and 10) is frequently different from that of regular intermediaries (such as wholesalers). For example, online intermediaries create and manage the online markets. They help match buyers and sellers, provide some infrastructure services, and help customers and/or sellers to institute and complete transactions. They also support the vast number of transactions that exist in providing services, as demonstrated in the WebMD case (Case 2.1). Most of these online intermediaries operate as computerized systems.

▶ **Other business partners.** In addition to intermediaries, several types of partners, such as shippers, use the Internet to collaborate, mostly along the supply chain.

▶ **Support services.** Many different support services are available, ranging from certification and escrow services (to ensure security) to content providers.

marketspace
A marketplace in which sellers and buyers exchange goods and services for money (or for other goods and services) but do so electronically.

digital products
Goods that can be transformed to digital format and delivered over the Internet.

front end
The portion of an e-seller's business processes through which customers interact, including the seller's portal, electronic catalogs, a shopping cart, a search engine, and a payment gateway.

back end
The activities that support online order fulfillment, inventory management, purchasing from suppliers, payment processing, packaging, and delivery.

intermediary
A third party that operates between sellers and buyers.

CASE 2.1
EC Application
WEBMD

WebMD is the largest medical services company in the United States. Although the company is known mainly for its consumer portal, *webmd.com*, the most visited medical-related Web site, its core business is being an e-intermediary.

The health-care industry is huge (close to $2 trillion per year, the largest in terms of GNP). Almost $600 billion is spent just on administrative expenses. The government (federal and state) provides large amounts of money to health-care providers (e.g., physicians, hospitals, drug companies), and it attempts to control costs. A major instrument for cost control is the Health Insurance Portability and Accountability Act of 1996 (HIPAA), which requires digital medical records and standardized documents for the health-care industry. WebMD is attempting to capitalize on this legislation by providing computer-related services to both the providers and purchasers (government, insurance companies, HMOs) of services, mainly in terms of standardized electronic transactions. The company provides services to health-care providers, vendors, customers, and government entities.

WebMD's major objective is to reduce costs for the participants by facilitating electronic communication and collaboration because paper-based transactions are 20 to 30 times more expensive than electronic ones. It also seeks to speed cycle time.

WebMD operates via several separate, but electronically linked, divisions:

▶ **WebMD Envoy.** This division (now a subsidiary of Emdeon) is the leading clearinghouse for real-time transactions (over $2.5 billion a year) among over 300,000 medical and dental providers, 600 hospitals, 650 software vendors, 36,000 pharmacies and laboratories, and 1,200 government and commercial health agencies. Transactions are secure; large customers use EDI (Chapter 5), and others use the Internet. The system handles all types of transactions, from clinical data to billing.

▶ **WebMD Practice Services.** This division provides software and programs that help physicians and other providers manage their businesses. Hundreds of different applications are available (this service is referred to as Intergy EHR). Some provide access to patient information, whereas others retrieve medical knowledge. Practice Services is a leading provider of payment and transaction services at the vanguard of bringing innovative practice management solutions to the rapidly changing health-care industry.

▶ **WebMD Health.** This information gateway has portals for both consumers and professionals. For consumers, information is provided about wellness, diseases, and treatments. For professionals (physicians, nurses, medical technicians,

etc.), the Medscape portal provides medical news, medical education, research-related information, and more.

▶ **Porex.** The medical product unit manufactures and sells specialty medical products.

Of the many services available on the portal, notable are:

▶ **News Center.** Provides the latest in health news.

▶ **A-Z Guides.** Provides guides on topics ranging from medical tests to prescription drugs to common symptoms.

▶ **Health Search.** An enhanced search tool that enables users to find the information they need, quickly and completely.

▶ **WebMD.** Videos are offered on a number of health-related topics.

▶ **Family and Pregnancy.** Provides valuable information for parents, future parents, grandmothers and grandfathers, and caregivers.

▶ **Blogs for Experts.** Blogs devoted to specific topics within an industry.

▶ **Blogs for Readers.** Blogs on multiple topics made available to any and all who are interested.

According to O'Buyonge and Chen (2006), the success of WebMD is a result of the proper value proposition in its business model. Most important are the value-added services provided to health-care providers, insurers, and other B2B participants.

WebMD's future as an intermediary is not clear. On the one hand, disintermediation is possible due to the fact that the largest customers may develop their own B2B connections. On the other hand, the need to comply with HIPAA may facilitate the role of WebMD, especially for small- and medium-sized health-care participants.

Sources: Compiled from Southwick (2004), *webmd.com* (accessed September 2006), and *webmd.com* (accessed September 2006).

Questions

1. Visit *webmd.com* to learn more about the types of intermediation it provides. Write a report based on your findings.

2. What kinds of reintermediation do you foresee for the company?

3. WebMD Health does not bring in much revenue. Should the company close it? Why or why not?

4. What impact can WebMD have on the health-care industry? (Use the chapter's framework in your answer.)

Section 2.1 ▶ REVIEW QUESTIONS

1. What is the difference between a physical marketplace and an e-marketplace (marketspace)?
2. List the components of a marketspace.
3. Define a digital product and provide five examples.

2.2 TYPES OF E-MARKETPLACES: FROM STOREFRONTS TO PORTALS

There are several types of e-marketplaces. The major B2C e-marketplaces are *storefronts* and *Internet malls*. B2B e-marketplaces include private *sell-side* e-marketplaces, *buy-side* e-marketplaces, and *exchanges*. Let's elaborate on these, as well as on the gateways to e-marketplaces—portals.

ELECTRONIC STOREFRONTS

An electronic or Web **storefront** refers to a single company's Web site where products and services are sold. It is an electronic store. The storefront may belong to a manufacturer (e.g., geappliances.com and dell.com), to a retailer (e.g., walmart.com and wishlist.com.au), to individuals selling from home, or to another type of business. Note that companies that sell services (such as insurance) may refer to their storefronts as *portals*. An example of a service-related portal is a hotel reservation system, as shown in Online File W2.2.

A storefront includes several mechanisms that are necessary for conducting the sale (see also Chapter 16). The most common mechanisms are an *electronic catalog;* a *search engine* that helps the consumer find products in the catalog; an *electronic cart* for holding items until checkout; *e-auction facilities;* a *payment gateway* where payment arrangements can be made; a *shipment court* where shipping arrangements are made; and *customer services,* including product and warranty information. The first three mechanisms are described in Section 2.4; e-auctions are described in Section 2.5 and in Chapter 10; payment mechanisms are described in Chapter 12; and shipments are discussed in Chapter 13. Customer services, which can be fairly elaborate, are covered throughout the book and especially in Chapter 13 (see CRM).

storefront
A single company's Web site where products or services are sold.

ELECTRONIC MALLS

In addition to shopping at individual storefronts, consumers can shop in electronic malls (e-malls). Similar to malls in the physical world, an **e-mall (online mall)** is an online shopping location where many stores are located. For example, Hawaii.com (hawaii.com) is an e-mall that aggregates Hawaiian products and stores. It contains a directory of product categories and the stores in each category. When a consumer indicates the category he or she is interested in, the consumer is transferred to the appropriate independent *storefront.* This kind of a mall does not provide any shared services. It is merely a directory. Other malls do provide shared services (e.g., choicemall.com). Some malls are actually large click-and-mortar retailers; others are virtual retailers (e.g., buy.com).

e-mall (online mall)
An online shopping center where many online stores are located.

Visualization and Virtual Realty in Shopping Malls

To attract users to shopping malls, vendors use rich media, including virtual reality (VR). Lepouras and Vassilakis (2006) proposed an architecture for a VR Mall (see Exhibit 2.2). The major task of VR is to relate the content via digital representation to the potential buyers.

TYPES OF STORES AND MALLS

Stores and malls are of several different types:

▶ **General stores/malls.** These are large marketspaces that sell all types of products. Examples are amazon.com, choicemall.com, shop4.vcomshop.com, spree.com, and the major public portals (yahoo.com, aol.com, and msn.com). All major department and discount stores also fall into this category.

▶ **Specialized stores/malls.** These sell only one or a few types of products, such as books, flowers, wine, cars, or pet toys. Amazon.com started as a specialized e-bookstore but today is a generalized store. 1800flowers.com sells flowers and related gifts; fashionmall.com/beautyjungle specializes in beauty products, tips, and trends; and cattoys.com sells cat toys.

▶ **Regional versus global stores.** Some stores, such as e-grocers or sellers of heavy furniture, serve customers that live nearby. For example, parknshop.com serves the Hong

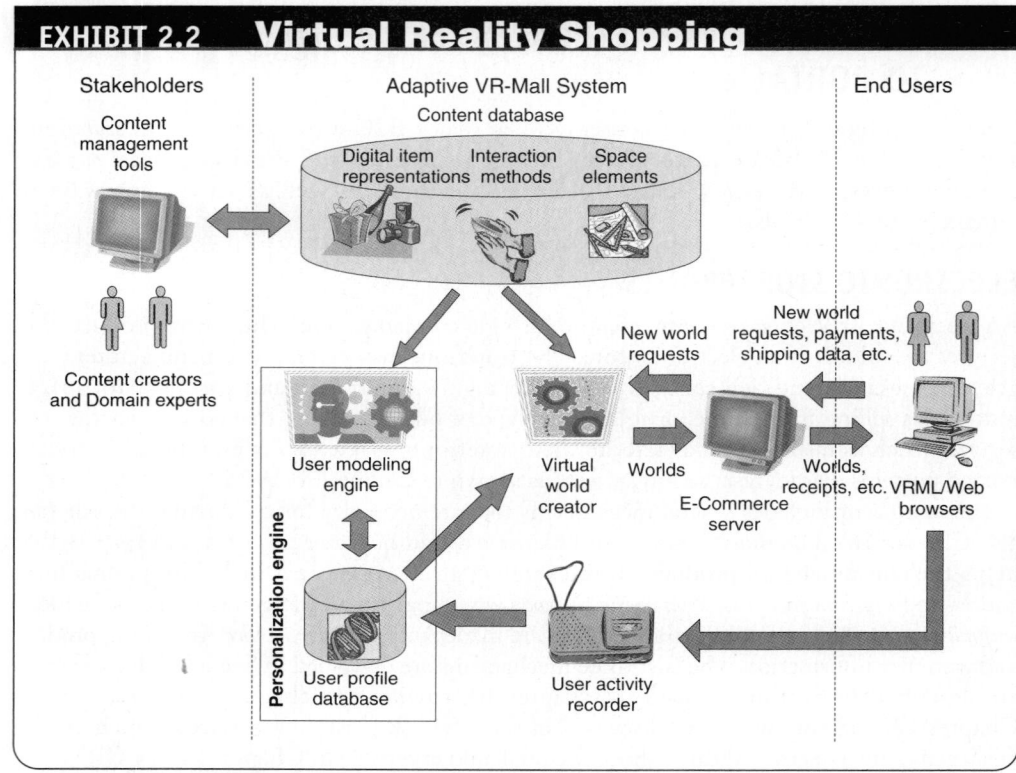

EXHIBIT 2.2 Virtual Reality Shopping

Source: Lepouras, G., and C. Vassilakis. "Adaptive Virtual Reality Shopping Malls," in *Khosrow-Pour, 2006.*

Kong community; it will not deliver groceries to New York. However, some local stores will sell to customers in other countries if the customer will pay the shipping, insurance, and other costs (e.g., see hothothot.com).

▶ **Pure-play online organizations versus click-and-mortar stores.** Stores may be pure online (i.e., virtual or pure-play) organizations, such as Blue Nile, Amazon.com, Buy.com, or Cattoys.com. They do not have physical stores. Others are physical (i.e., *brick-and-mortar*) stores that also sell online (e.g., Wal-Mart with walmart.com, 1–800-Flowers.com with 1800flowers.com, and Woolworths with woolworths.com.au). This second category is called *click-and-mortar*. Both categories will be described further in Chapter 3.

TYPES OF E-MARKETPLACES

In general conversation, the distinction between a mall and a marketplace is not always clear. In the physical world, malls are often viewed as collections of stores (i.e., shopping centers) where the stores are isolated from each other and prices are generally fixed. In contrast, marketplaces, some of which are located outdoors, are often viewed as places where many vendors compete and shoppers look for bargains and are expected to negotiate prices.

On the Web, the term *marketplace* has a different and distinct meaning. If individual customers want to negotiate prices, they may be able to do so in some storefronts or malls. However, the term *e-marketplace* usually implies B2B, not B2C. We distinguish two types of e-marketplaces: private and public.

Private E-Marketplaces

Private e-marketplaces are those owned and operated by a single company (see Chapter 5). As can be seen in the Raffles Hotel case (Online File W2.2), private markets are either sell-side or buy-side. In a **sell-side e-marketplace**, a company, for example, Cisco, will sell either standard or customized products to qualified companies; this type of selling is considered to be *one-to-many*. It is similar to a B2C storefront. In a **buy-side e-marketplace**, a company purchases from many suppliers; this type of purchasing is considered to be *many-to-one*. For

private e-marketplaces
Online markets owned by a single company; may be either sell-side and/or buy-side e-marketplaces.

sell-side e-marketplace
A private e-marketplace in which one company sells either standard and/or customized products to qualified companies.

buy-side e-marketplace
A private e-marketplace in which one company makes purchases from invited suppliers.

example, Raffles Hotel buys its supplies from approved vendors that come to its market. Private marketplaces are frequently open only to selected members and are not publicly regulated. We will return to the topic of private e-marketplaces in Chapter 5.

Public E-Marketplaces

Public e-marketplaces are B2B markets. They often are owned by a third party (not a seller or a buyer) or by a group of buying or selling companies (a consortium), and they serve many sellers and many buyers. These markets also are known as *exchanges* (e.g., a stock exchange). They are open to the public and are regulated by the government or the exchange's owners. An example of a public marketplace, NTE.net, is provided in Online File W2.3. Public e-marketplaces are presented in detail in Chapter 6.

public e-marketplaces
B2B marketplaces, usually owned and/or managed by an independent third party, that include many sellers and many buyers; also known as *exchanges*.

INFORMATION PORTALS

A portal is a mechanism that is used in e-marketplaces, e-stores, and other types of EC (e.g., in intrabusiness, e-learning, etc.). With the growing use of intranets and the Internet, many organizations encounter information overload at a number of different levels. Information is scattered across numerous documents, e-mail messages, and databases at different locations and in disparate systems. Finding relevant and accurate information is often time-consuming and requires access to multiple systems.

As a consequence, organizations lose a lot of productive employee time. One solution to this problem is the use of *portals*. A portal is an information gateway. It attempts to address information overload by enabling people to search and access relevant information from disparate IT systems and the Internet, using advanced search and indexing techniques (such as Google's desktop), in an intranet-based environment. An **information portal** is a single point of access through a Web browser to critical business information located inside and outside of an organization. Many information portals can be personalized for the users.

information portal
A single point of access through a Web browser to business information inside and/or outside an organization.

Types of Portals

Portals appear under many descriptions and shapes. One way to distinguish among them is to look at their content, which can vary from narrow to broad, and their community or audience, which also can vary. The following are the major types of portals:

> ▶ **Commercial (public) portals.** These portals offer content for diverse communities and are the most popular portals on the Internet. Although they can be customized by the user, they are still intended for broad audiences and offer fairly routine content, some in real time (e.g., a stock ticker and news about a few preselected items). Examples of such sites are yahoo.com, aol.com, and msn.com.
>
> ▶ **Corporate portals.** Corporate portals provide organized access to rich content within relatively narrow corporate and partners' communities. They also are known as *enterprise portals* or *enterprise information portals*. Corporate portals appear in different forms and are described in detail in Chapter 7.
>
> ▶ **Publishing portals.** These portals are intended for communities with specific interests. These portals involve relatively little customization of content, but they provide extensive online search features and some interactive capabilities. Examples of such sites are techweb.com and zdnet.com.
>
> ▶ **Personal portals.** These target specific filtered information for individuals. They offer relatively narrow content and are typically very personalized, effectively having an audience of one.
>
> ▶ **Mobile portals.** Mobile portals are portals that are accessible from mobile devices (see Chapter 9 for details). Although most of the other portals mentioned here are PC based, increasing numbers of portals are accessible via mobile devices. One example of such a mobile portal is i-mode, which is described in Section 2.7.
>
> ▶ **Voice portals.** Voice portals are Web sites, usually portals, with audio interfaces. This means that they can be accessed by a standard telephone or a cell

mobile portal
A portal accessible via a mobile device.

voice portal
A portal accessed by telephone or cell phone.

phone. AOLbyPhone is an example of a service that allows users to retrieve e-mail, news, and other content from AOL via telephone. It uses both speech recognition and text-to-speech technologies. Companies such as Tellme.com (tellme.com) and BeVocal (bevocal.com) offer access to the Internet from telephones and tools to build voice portals. Voice portals are especially popular for 1–800 numbers (Enterprise 800 numbers) that provide self-service to customers with information available in Internet databases (e.g., find flight status at delta.com).

▶ **Knowledge portals.** Knowledge portals enable access to knowledge by knowledge workers and facilitate collaboration (see Chapter 7).

Agent-Based E-Marketplaces

E-marketplaces, especially for B2B and mega B2C (such as Amazon.com) may be plagued by information overload. To overcome the problem, Guan (2006) suggests using intelligent (or software) agents. As we will see in Chapter 3, software agents already provide comparisons (e.g., froogle.com, comparefare.com). Various search engines can help explore catalogs, and monitoring agents watch auctions. But today's state of the art is still limited (see Appendix C). Guan (2006) explores a more autonomous system called a *virtual marketplace* that is composed of a control center, a business center, and a financial center. Each center has its own database and agent (e.g., negotiating agents). The seller and buyer agents can interact in the fully automated market (see Exhibit 2.3).

EXHIBIT 2.3 Agent-Based E-Marketplace

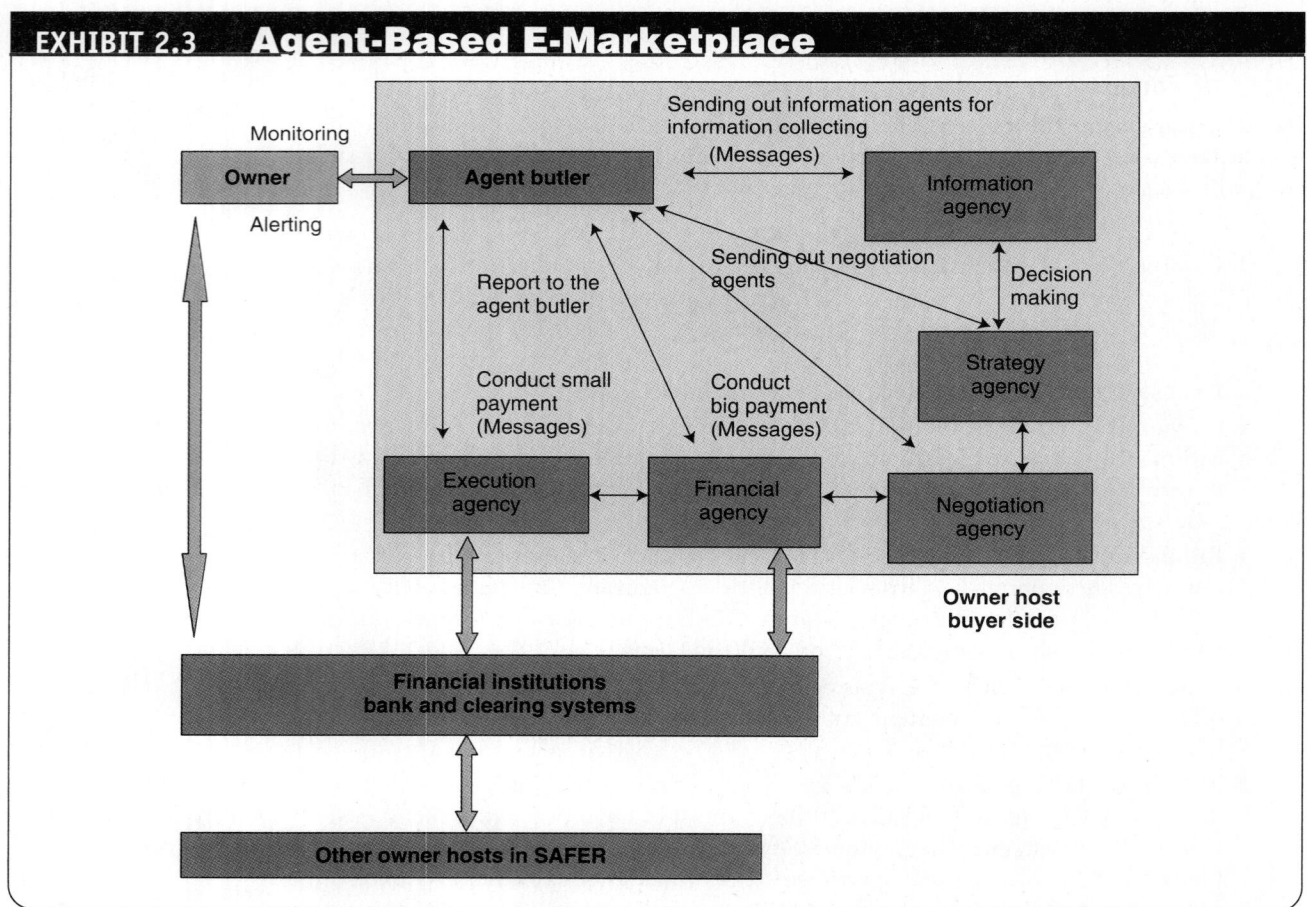

Source: Guan, S. U. "E-Commerce Agents and Payment Systems," in *Khosrow-Pour,* 2006.

Section 2.2 ▶ REVIEW QUESTIONS

1. Describe electronic storefronts and e-malls.
2. List the various types of stores and e-malls.
3. Differentiate between private and public e-marketplaces.
4. What are information portals? List the major types.
5. Describe agent-based e-marketplaces.

2.3 TRANSACTIONS, INTERMEDIATION, AND PROCESSES IN E-COMMERCE

Now that we are familiar with marketplaces, their types, components, and participants, let's look at what is going on in these markets.

SELLERS, BUYERS, AND TRANSACTIONS

The major EC activity is electronic trading. Typically, a seller (retailer, wholesaler, or manufacturer) sells to customers. The seller itself buys from suppliers: either raw material (as a manufacturer) or finished goods (as a retailer). This process is illustrated in Exhibit 2.4.

The selling company is shown in the center of the figure, marked as "our company." Internally, processes in the different functional areas are supported by enterprise software, such as ERP and B2E activities. The customers can be individuals (B2C), businesses (B2B), or government agencies (B2G). The customers place orders, and the seller fulfills them.

Our company buys materials, products, and so on from suppliers, distributors (B2B), or from the government (G2B) in a process called *e-procurement*. Sometimes intermediaries are involved in this process.

THE ROLES AND VALUE OF INTERMEDIARIES IN E-MARKETPLACES

Intermediaries (brokers) play an important role in commerce by providing value-added activities and services to buyers and sellers. There are many types of intermediaries. The most well-known intermediaries in the physical world are wholesalers and retailers. In cyberspace, there are, in addition, intermediaries that provide and/or control information flow. These electronic intermediaries are known as **infomediaries**. The information flows to and from buyers and sellers via infomediaries, as shown in Online File W2.4. Frequently, intermediaries aggregate information and sell it to others (see "syndication" in Chapter 16).

According to Wikipedia (2006a), online intermediaries are companies that facilitate transactions between buyers and sellers and receive a percentage of the transaction's value.

infomediaries
Electronic intermediaries that provide and/or control information flow in cyberspace, often aggregating information and selling it to others.

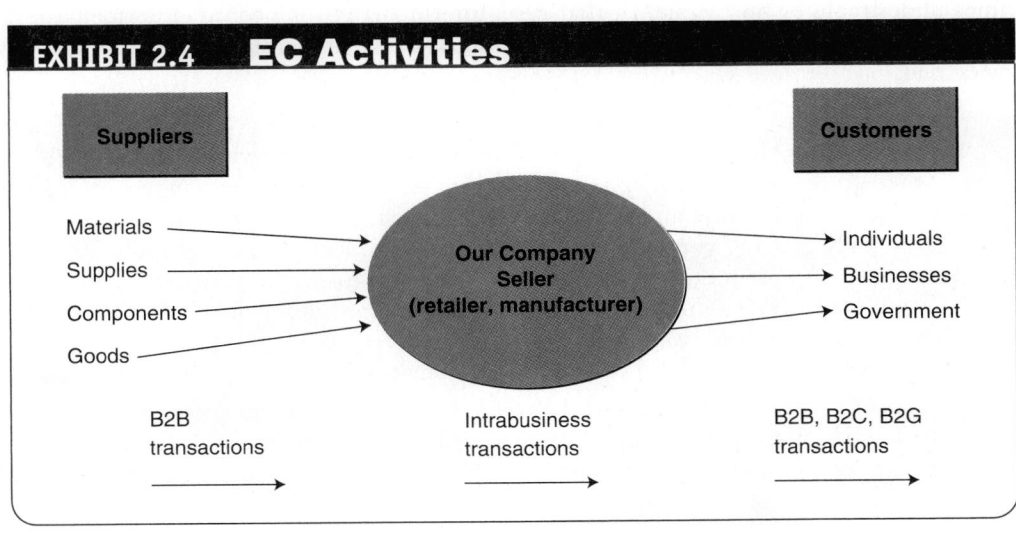

EXHIBIT 2.4   EC Activities

These firms make up the largest group of B2C companies today. The two types of online intermediaries are brokers and infomediaries.

Brokers

A *broker* is a company that facilitates transactions between buyers and sellers. The following are different types of brokers:

- **Buy/sell fulfillment.** A corporation that helps consumers place buy and sell orders (e.g., eTrade).
- **Virtual mall.** A company that helps consumers buy from a variety of stores (e.g., Yahoo! Stores).
- **Metamediary.** A firm that offers customers access to a variety of stores and provides them with transaction services, such as financial services (e.g., Amazon zShops).
- **Bounty.** An intermediary that will locate a person, place, or idea for a fee (e.g., BountyQuest (now defunct).
- **Search agent.** A company that helps consumers compare different stores (e.g., Shopping.com).
- **Shopping facilitator.** A company that helps consumers use online shops by providing currency conversion, language translation, payment features, and delivery solutions, and potentially a user-customized interface, (e.g., MyOrbital.com).

Infomediaries

Web sites that gather and organize large amounts of data and act as intermediaries between those who want the information and those who supply the information are called *infomediaries* (Webopedia 2006). There are two types of infomediaries:

- The first type offers consumers a place to gather information about specific products and companies before they make purchasing decisions. It is a third-party provider of unbiased information; it does not promote or try to sell specific products in preference over other products or act on behalf of any vendors (e.g., Autobytel.com and BizRate.com).
- The second type is not necessarily Web-based. It provides vendors with consumer information that will help the vendor develop and market products. The infomediary collects the personal information from the buyers and markets that data to businesses. The advantage of this approach is that consumer privacy is protected and some infomediaries offer consumers a percentage of the brokerage deals.

Producers and consumers may interact directly in an e-marketplace: Producers provide information to customers, who then select from among the available products. In general, producers set prices; sometimes prices are negotiated. However, direct interactions are sometimes undesirable or unfeasible. In that case, intermediation is needed. Intermediaries, whether human or electronic, can address the following five important limitations of *direct interaction*:

1. **Search costs.** It may be expensive for providers and consumers to find each other. In electronic marketplaces, thousands of products are exchanged among thousands of vendors and millions of consumers. Producers may have trouble accurately gauging consumer demand for new products; many desirable items may never be produced simply because no one recognizes the demand for them. Some intermediaries maintain databases of customer preferences, and they can predict demand and *reduce search costs* by selectively routing information from providers to consumers and by *matching* customers with products and/or services.

2. **Lack of privacy.** Either the buyer or seller may wish to remain anonymous or at least protect some information relevant to a trade. Intermediaries can relay messages and make pricing and allocation decisions without revealing the identity of one or both parties.

3. **Incomplete information.** The buyer may need more information than the seller is able or willing to provide, such as information about product quality, competing products, or customer satisfaction. An intermediary can gather product information from sources other than the product provider, including independent evaluators and other customers. Many third-party Web sites provide such information (e.g., *bizrate.com*, *mysimon.com*, and *consumerguide.com*).

4. **Contract risk.** A consumer may refuse to pay after receiving a product, or a producer may provide inferior products or give inadequate postpurchase service. Intermediaries have a number of tools to reduce such risks. First, the broker can disseminate information about the past behavior of providers and consumers. The threat of publicizing bad behavior or removing a seal of approval may encourage both producers and consumers to meet the broker's standard for fair dealing. Or the broker may accept responsibility for the behavior of parties in transactions it arranges and act as a "policeman" on its own. Third, the broker can provide insurance against bad behavior. The credit card industry uses all three approaches to reduce providers' and consumers' exposure to risk.

In the online auction arena or when you buy expensive items or buy from an unknown seller, some companies act as *escrow agencies*, accepting and holding payment from the buyer while the seller completes delivery of the product or service to the escrow agency. Then, if the product is satisfactory, the agency releases payment to the seller and the product to the buyer.

5. **Pricing inefficiencies.** By jockeying to secure a desirable price for a product, providers and consumers may miss opportunities for mutually desirable trades. This is particularly likely in negotiations over unique or custom products, such as houses, and in markets for information products and other public goods where freeloading is a problem. Intermediaries can use pricing mechanisms that induce just the appropriate trades; for example, dealing with an imbalance of buy and sell orders in stock markets.

For a study on how different strategies of intermediation affect the efficiency of electronic markets, see Yarom et al. (2003).

E-Distributors in B2B

A special type of intermediary in e-commerce is the B2B **e-distributor**. These intermediaries connect manufacturers with business buyers (customers), such as retailers (or resellers in the computer industry). E-distributors basically aggregate the catalogs or the product information from many manufacturers, sometimes thousands of them, in one place—the intermediary's Web site. An example is W. W. Grainger (see Chapter 5 for details).

e-distributor
An e-commerce intermediary that connects manufacturers with business buyers (customers) by aggregating the catalogs of many manufacturers in one place—the intermediary's Web site.

DISINTERMEDIATION AND REINTERMEDIATION

Intermediaries are agents that mediate between sellers and buyers. Usually, they provide two types of services: (1) They provide relevant information about demand, supply, prices, and requirements and, in doing so, help match sellers and buyers. (2) They offer value-added services such as transfer of products, escrow, payment arrangements, consulting, or assistance in finding a business partner. In general, the first type of service can be fully automated and thus is likely to be assumed by e-marketplaces, infomediaries, and portals that provide free or low-commission services. The second type requires expertise, such as knowledge of the industry, the products, and technological trends, and it can only be partially automated.

Intermediaries that provide only (or mainly) the first type of service may be eliminated; a phenomena called **disintermediation**. An example is the airline industry and its push for buying electronic tickets directly from the airlines. As of 2004, most airlines require customers to pay $5 per ticket or more if they buy a ticket from an agent, which is equivalent to the agent's commission. This is resulting in the disintermediation of travel agents from the

disintermediation
Elimination of intermediaries between sellers and buyers.

purchasing process. In another example, discount stockbrokers that only execute trades manually are disappearing. However, brokers who manage electronic intermediation are not only surviving but may actually be prospering (e.g., E-Trade). This phenomenon, in which disintermediated entities or newcomers take on new intermediary roles, is called **reintermediation** (see Chapters 3, 6, and 14).

Disintermediation is more likely to occur in supply chains involving several intermediaries, as illustrated in the opening case. Online File W2.5 illustrates an intermediary that does both B2C and B2B.

reintermediation
Establishment of new intermediary roles for traditional intermediaries that have been disintermediated, or for newcomers.

THE PURCHASING PROCESS

Customers buy goods online in different modes. The most common mode is purchasing from catalogs at fixed prices. Sometimes prices may be negotiated or discounted. Another mode is *dynamic pricing*, which refers to nonfixed prices, such as those in *auctions* or stock (commodity) markets. The buyer uses the process illustrated in Exhibit 2.5

The process starts with logging into a seller's site, registering (if needed), and entering into an online catalog or the buyer's "my account." E-catalogs can be very large, so a search

EXHIBIT 2.5   Buying Process in E-Market

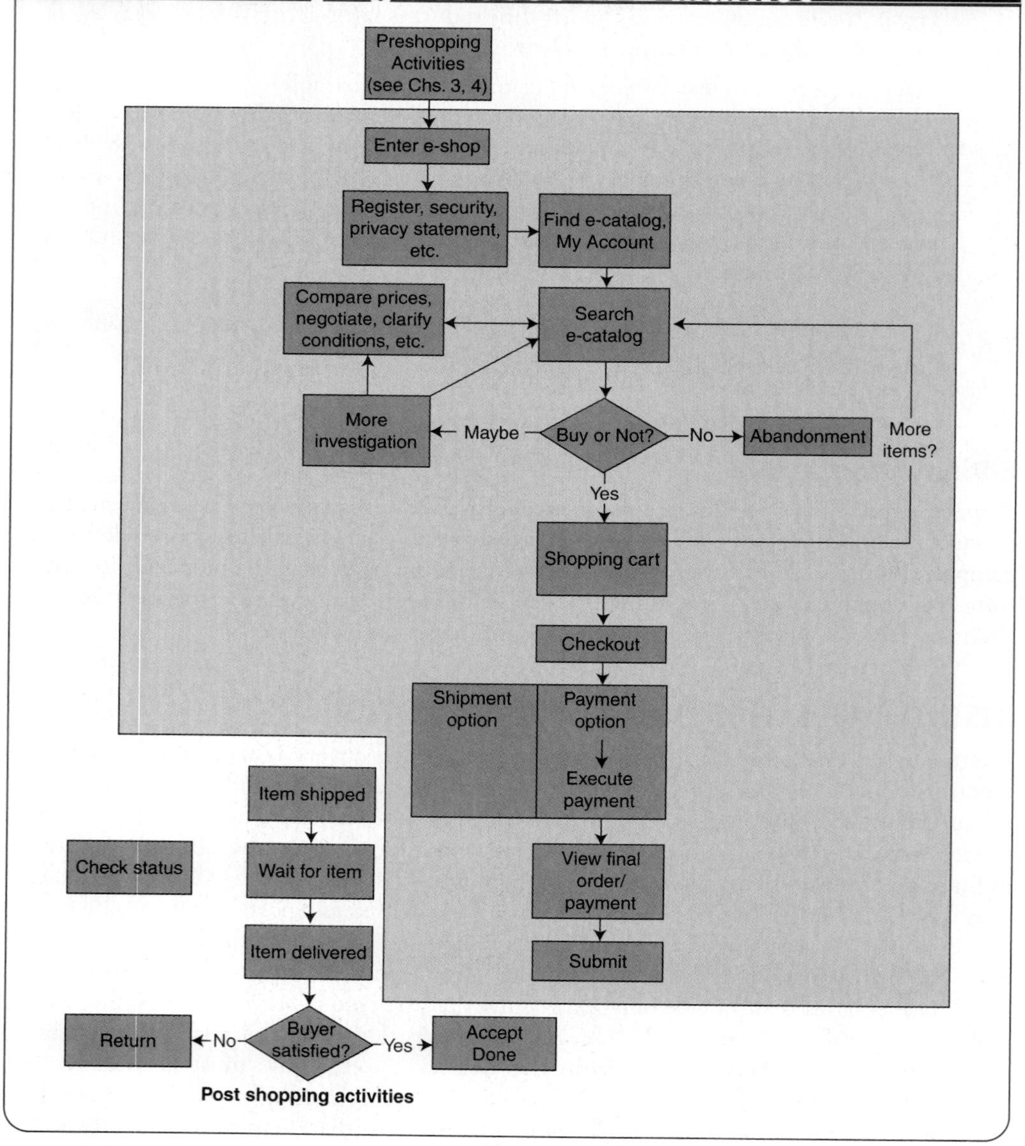

```
                        Preshopping
                         Activities
                        (see Chs. 3, 4)
                              │
                              ▼
                        Enter e-shop
                              │
                              ▼
              Register, security,        Find e-catalog,
              privacy statement,   ───▶   My Account
                   etc.                        │
                    │                          ▼
         Compare prices,               ┌──▶ Search
         negotiate, clarify   ◀────────┤    e-catalog ◀──────────┐
         conditions, etc.              │        │                │
                    ▲                  │        ▼                │
                    │                  │                         │
                More                   │                     More
             investigation ◀─ Maybe ─◀ Buy or Not? ─No─▶ Abandonment  items?
                              └────────    │
                                          Yes
                                           │
                                           ▼
                                    Shopping cart ◀────────────────┘
                                           │
                                           ▼
                                       Checkout
                                           │
                          Shipment      Payment
                           option        option
                                           │
               Item shipped             Execute
                                        payment
            Check status   Wait for item    │
                                           ▼
               Item delivered         View final
                    │                 order/
                    ▼                 payment
                                           │
              Return ◀─No─ Buyer ─Yes─▶ Accept  Submit
                          satisfied?       Done

                  Post shopping activities
```

mechanism may be needed. Also, the buyer needs to compare prices. Some sellers (e.g., American Airlines) will provide comparisons with competing vendors. Otherwise, the buyer may need to leave the site or do the comparison *before* entering into the specific seller's store. If not satisfied, the buyer will abandon the site. If satisfied, the buyer will select the item and place it in a *shopping cart*. The buyer may return to the catalog to choose more items. Each selected item is placed in the shopping cart. When shopping is completed, the buyer goes to a checkout page where a shipment option is selected from a menu. Also, a payment option may be available. For example, newegg.com lets you pay by credit card, PayPal, after billing, in installments, and so on. After checking all details for accuracy, the buyer *submits* the order.

In the remainder of this chapter, we will describe the major mechanisms that support this process.

Section 2.3 ▶ REVIEW QUESTIONS

1. Describe the transaction process between a seller and its customers and suppliers.
2. List the roles of intermediaries in e-markets.
3. Describe e-distributors.
4. What are disintermediation and reintermediation?
5. Describe the purchasing process.

2.4 ELECTRONIC CATALOGS AND OTHER MARKET MECHANISMS

To enable selling online, a Web site usually needs *EC merchant server software* (see Chapter 16 and Online Chapter 19). The basic functionality offered by such software includes electronic catalogs, search engines, and shopping carts.

ELECTRONIC CATALOGS

Catalogs have been printed on paper for generations. Recently, electronic catalogs on CD-ROM and the Internet have gained popularity. **Electronic catalogs** consist of a product database, directory and search capabilities, and a presentation function. They are the backbone of most e-commerce sales sites. For merchants, the objective of electronic catalogs is to advertise and promote products and services. For the customer, the purpose of such catalogs is to locate information on products and services. Electronic catalogs can be searched quickly with the help of search engines, and they can be interactive (Cox and Koelzer 2006). For example, *Change My Image* from Infinisys (infinisys.co.jp) allows you to insert your photo and then change the hairstyle and color. Electronic catalogs can be very large; for example, the Library of Congress Web catalog (catalog.loc.gov) contains millions of records.

electronic catalogs
The presentation of product information in an electronic form; the backbone of most e-selling sites.

The majority of early online catalogs were replications of text and pictures from printed catalogs. However, online catalogs have evolved to become more dynamic, customized, and integrated with selling and buying procedures. As online catalogs have become more integrated with shopping carts, order taking, and payment, the tools for building them are being integrated with merchant suites and Web hosting (e.g., see smallbusiness.yahoo.com/merchant).

Electronic catalogs can be classified according to three dimensions:

1. **The dynamics of the information presentation.** Catalogs may be static or dynamic. In *static catalogs*, information is presented in text and static pictures. In *dynamic catalogs*, information is presented in motion pictures or animation, possibly with supplemental sound. Dynamic catalogs can be real time, changing frequently, such as with prices of stocks (and commodities) on stock exchange tickers.
2. **The degree of customization.** Catalogs may be standard or customized. In *standard catalogs*, merchants offer the same catalog to any customer. In *customized catalogs*, content, pricing, and display are tailored to the characteristics of specific customers.

3. **Integration with business processes.** Catalogs can be classified according to the degree of integration with the following business processes or features: order taking and fulfillment; electronic payment systems; intranet workflow software and systems; inventory and accounting systems; suppliers' or customers' extranets; and paper catalogs. For example, when a customer places an order at amazon.com, the order is transferred automatically to a computerized inventory-availability check. Many sellers advise you on the availability of items and delivery dates.

Although used occasionally in B2C commerce, *customized catalogs* are especially useful in B2B e-commerce. For example, e-catalogs can show only the items that the employees in a specific organization are allowed to purchase and can exclude items the buying company's managers do not want their employees to see or to buy. E-catalogs can be customized to show the same item to different customers at different prices, reflecting discounts or purchase-contract agreements. They can even show the buyer's ID number for the item, model, or *stock-keeping unit* (SKU) number, rather than the seller's ID numbers. Extranets, in particular, can deliver customized catalogs to different business customers.

For a comprehensive discussion of online catalogs, see Bauknecht et al. (2002), jcmax.com/advantages.html, and purchasing.about.com.

Online Catalogs Versus Paper Catalogs

The advantages and disadvantages of online catalogs are contrasted with those of paper catalogs in Exhibit 2.6. Although online catalogs have significant advantages, such as ease of updating; the ability to be integrated with the purchasing process; coverage of a wide spectrum of products, interactivity; customization; and strong search capabilities, they do have disadvantages and limitations. To begin with, customers need computers and Internet access to view online catalogs. However, as computers and Internet access are spreading

EXHIBIT 2.6	Comparison of Online Catalogs with Paper Catalogs	
Type	**Advantages**	**Disadvantages**
Paper catalogs	• Easy to create without high technology • Reader is able to look at the catalog without computer system • More portable than electronic	• Difficult to update changed product information promptly • Only a limited number of products can be catalog displayed • Limited information through photographs and textual description is available • No possibility for advanced multimedia such as animation and voice
Online catalogs	• Easy to update product information • Able to integrate with the purchasing process • Good search and comparison capabilities • Able to provide timely, up-to-date product information • Provision for globally broad range of product information • Possibility of adding on voice and animated pictures • Long-term cost savings • Easy to customize • More comparative shopping • Ease of connecting order processing, inventory processing, and payment processing to the system	• Difficult to develop catalogs, large fixed cost • There is a need for customer skill to deal with computers and browsers

rapidly, a large number of paper catalogs will be supplemented by, if not actually replaced by, electronic ones. However, considering the fact that printed newspapers and magazines have not diminished due to online ones, paper catalogs probably will not disappear soon. There seems to be room for both media, at least in the near future. However, in B2B paper catalogs may disappear more quickly.

A representative tool for building online catalogs is Microsoft's Commerce Server 2006—a .NET tool for creating Web sites. RadioShack (Radioshack.com) builds and maintains electronic catalogs based on its customers' paper catalogs. The service includes search capabilities, the ability to feature large numbers of products, enhanced viewing capabilities, and ongoing support.

Customized Catalogs

A *customized catalog* is a catalog assembled specifically for a company, usually a customer of the catalog owner. It also can be tailored to loyal individual shoppers or to a segment of shoppers (e.g., frequent buyers). There are two approaches to creating customized catalogs.

The first approach is to let the customers identify the parts of interest to them from the total catalog, as is done by software products such as QuickSilver from Broadvision (broadvision.com). Then customers do not have to deal with items that are irrelevant to them. Such software allows the creation of catalogs with branded value-added capabilities that make it easy for customers to find the products they want to purchase, locate the information they need, and quickly configure their order.

The second approach is to let the system automatically identify customer characteristics based on the customer's transaction records. However, to generalize the relationship between the customer and items of interest, data-mining technology (Chapter 4) may be needed. This second approach can be combined with the first one.

As an example of the second approach, consider the following scenario, which uses Oracle's 9i server: Joe Smith logs on to the Acme Shopping site, where he has the option to register as an account customer and record his preferences in terms of address details, interest areas, and preferred method of payment. Acme Shopping offers a wide range of products, including electronics, clothing, books, and sporting goods. Joe is interested only in clothing and electronics. He is neither a sportsman nor a great book lover. Joe also has some very distinct hobby areas—one is photography.

After Joe has recorded his preferences, each time he returns to Acme's electronic store the first page will show him only the clothing and electronics departments. Furthermore, when Joe goes into the electronics department, he sees only products related to photography—cameras and accessories. Some of the products are out of Joe's price range, so Joe can refine his preferences further to indicate that he is interested only in electronics that relate to photography and cost $300 or less. Such *personalization* gives consumers a value-added experience and adds to their reasons for revisiting the site, thus building brand loyalty to that Internet store.

Against the backdrop of intense competition for Web time, personalization provides a valuable way to match consumers with the products and information in which they are most interested as quickly and painlessly as possible. An example of how corporations customize their catalogs for corporate clients is provided in Online File W2.6.

Implementing E-Catalogs

Implementing e-catalogs on a small scale is fairly simple (see Chapter 16). However, transforming a large-scale catalog to an e-catalog is not an easy task because it is necessary to create a matching customer support system. See Schmitz et al. (2005) for a discussion of the topic, examples of successes and failures, and suggestions for implementation. Large online catalogs need a search engine.

SEARCH ENGINES AND INTELLIGENT AGENTS

A **search engine** is a computer program that can access databases of Internet resources, search for specific information or keywords, and report the results. For example, customers tend to ask for product information (e.g., requests for product information or pricing) in the

search engine
A computer program that can access databases of Internet resources, search for specific information or keywords, and report the results.

same general manner. This type of request is repetitive, and answering such requests is costly when done by a human. Search engines deliver answers economically and efficiently by matching, for example, questions with FAQ (frequently asked question) templates, which respond with "canned" answers.

Google, AltaVista, and Lycos are popular search engines. Portals such as AOL, Yahoo!, and MSN have their own search engines. Special search engines organized to answer certain questions or search in specified areas, include Ask.com, Northern Light, Mama, and Looksmart. Thousands of different public search engines are available (see searchengineguide.com). In addition, hundreds of companies have search engines on their portals or storefronts. A search engine for online catalogs is Endeca InFront (from endeca.com).

software (intelligent) agent
Software that can perform routine tasks that require intelligence.

Unlike a search engine, a **software (intelligent) agent** can do more than just "search and match." It has capabilities that can be used to perform routine tasks that require intelligence. For example, it can monitor movements on a Web site to check whether a customer seems lost or ventures into areas that may not fit the customer's profile. If it detects such confusion, the agent can notify the customer and provide assistance. Software agents can be used in e-commerce to support tasks such as comparing prices, interpreting information, monitoring activities, and working as an assistant. Users can even chat or collaborate with agents.

Users use both search engines and intelligent agents in e-commerce. If customers are inside a storefront or an e-mall, they can use the search engine to find a product or a service. They can also use Web search engines, such as Google, to find general information about a product or service. Finally, they can use software agents that make comparisons (e.g., mysimon.com or froogle.com) and conduct other tasks. The essentials of software agents are provided in Online Technical Appendix C. Applications of software agents are described in several chapters, especially in Chapters 3 through 7. For more on search engines see Chapter 18.

SHOPPING CARTS

electronic shopping cart
An order-processing technology that allows customers to accumulate items they wish to buy while they continue to shop.

An **electronic shopping cart** is an order-processing technology that allows customers to accumulate items they wish to buy while they continue to shop. In this respect, it is similar to a shopping cart in the physical world. The software program of an electronic shopping cart allows customers to select items, review what has been selected, make changes, and then finalize the list. Clicking on "buy" will trigger the actual purchase.

Shopping carts for B2C are fairly simple (visit amazon.com to see an example), but for B2B a shopping cart may be more complex. A B2B shopping cart could enable a business customer to shop at several sites while keeping the cart on the buyer's Web site to integrate it with the buyer's e-procurement system. A special B2B cart was proposed for this purpose by Lim and Lee (2003) where, in addition to the cart offered at the seller's site, there is a buyers' cart ("b-cart") that resides on the buyers' sites and is sponsored by the participating sellers.

Shopping-cart software is sold or provided for free as an independent component (e.g., monstercommerce.com and easycart.com). It also is embedded in merchants' servers, such as smallbusiness.yahoo.com/merchant. Free online shopping carts (trials and demos) are available at volusion.com and gomerchant.com.

For more on shopping carts, see Chapter 16 and Online Chapter 19.

Product Configuration

A key characteristic of EC is the self-customization of products and services, as done by Dell. Manufacturers need to produce the customized products in an economic way so that the price of the products will be competitive. *Product configuration* systems support the acquisition of the customer requirements while automating the order-taking process, and they allow customers to configure their products by specifying their technical requirements.

Sophisticated product configuration systems use artificial intelligence (AI) tools because they need to support the interaction with the customers and understand their needs. For an overview, see Blecker (2006a).

Section 2.4 ▶ REVIEW QUESTIONS

1. List the dimensions by which electronic catalogs can be classified.
2. List the benefits of electronic catalogs.
3. Explain how customized catalogs are created and used.
4. Compare search engines with software agents.
5. Describe an electronic shopping cart.

2.5 AUCTIONS AS EC MARKET MECHANISMS

One of the most interesting market mechanisms in e-commerce is electronic auctions (Nissanoff 2006). They are used in B2C, B2B, C2C, G2B, G2C, and more.

DEFINITION AND CHARACTERISTICS

An **auction** is a market mechanism that uses a competitive process by which a seller solicits consecutive bids from buyers (forward auctions) or a buyer solicits bids from sellers (reverse auctions). Prices are determined dynamically by the bids. A wide variety of online markets qualify as auctions using this definition. Auctions, an established method of commerce for generations, deal with products and services for which conventional marketing channels are ineffective or inefficient, and they ensure prudent execution of sales. For example, auctions can expedite the disposal of items that need to be liquidated or sold quickly. Rare coins and other collectibles are frequently sold in auctions.

There are several types of auctions, each with its own motives and procedures. (For details, see Chapter 10.) Auctions can be done *online* or *offline*. They can be conducted in *public* auction sites, such as at eBay. They also can be done by invitation to *private* auctions.

This section presents the essential information about auctions that is necessary for understanding related material in Chapters 3 through 6. See also Saarinen et al. (2006) and Bajari and Hortacsu (2004) for e-auction information.

auction
A competitive process in which a seller solicits consecutive bids from buyers (forward auctions) or a buyer solicits bids from sellers (backward auctions). Prices are determined dynamically by the bids.

TRADITIONAL AUCTIONS VERSUS E-AUCTIONS

Traditional, physical auctions are still very popular. However, the volume traded on e-auctions is significantly larger and continues to increase.

Limitations of Traditional Offline Auctions

Traditional offline auctions, regardless of their type, have the following limitations: They generally last only a few minutes, or even seconds, for each item sold. This rapid process may give potential buyers little time to make a decision, so they may decide not to bid. Therefore, sellers may not get the highest possible price; bidders may not get what they really want, or they may pay too much for the item. Also, in many cases the bidders do not have much time to examine the goods. Bidders have difficulty learning about auctions and cannot compare what is offered at each location. Bidders must usually be physically present at auctions; thus, many potential bidders are excluded.

Similarly, it may be difficult for sellers to move goods to an auction site. Commissions are fairly high because a location must be rented, the auction needs to be advertised, and an auctioneer and other employees need to be paid. Electronic auctioning removes these deficiencies.

Electronic Auctions

The Internet provides an infrastructure for executing auctions electronically at lower cost, with a wide array of support services and with many more sellers and buyers. Individual consumers and corporations both can participate in this rapidly growing and very convenient form of e-commerce. Forrester Research projects that the Internet auction industry will reach $65.2 billion in sales by 2010 (123jump.com 2006).

Electronic auctions (e-auctions) are similar to offline auctions except that they are done online. E-auctions have been in existence since the 1980s over LANs (e.g., flowers; see

electronic auction (e-auction)
Auctions conducted online.

CASE 2.2
EC Application
INNOVATIVE AUCTIONS

The following are some examples of innovative implementations of e-auctions:

▶ Every year, Warren Buffett, the famous U.S. stock investor and investment guru, invites a group of eight people to lunch with him. The eight pay big money for the pleasure. The money is donated to the needy in San Francisco. In the past, Buffett charged $30,000 per group. As of July 2003, Buffett places the invitation on an online auction (eBay). In 2003, bidders pushed the bid from $30,000 to $250,100. The winning bid in 2006 was $620,100. One of the winners commented that he was willing to pay whatever was needed so that he could express to Buffett his appreciation for investment guidance. Before the auction, he had no chance to be invited.

▶ A Harley-Davidson motorcycle autographed by celebrities and offered by talk-show host Jay Leno fetched $800,100 on eBay to benefit tsunami victims.

▶ Richard Dan operates an eBay store in Maui, Hawaii, called Safedeal (see trading assistants list on *ebay.com*). Initially he was selling unclaimed items from his pawnbroker business. Now he is also one of eBay's 40,000 "trading assistants." Web Auction Hawaii and other trading assistants handle advertisements, auction listings, appraisals, descriptions, authentication, payments, shipments, insurance, and more. Dan also advises sellers as to which eBay category is the best for their particular item. Dan is helping nonprofit organizations, estate administrators, and others to sell just about anything, including the four mules he helped sell in September 2004. Dan's basic charge is $25 per item plus a 25 percent commission. (Dan only handles items with an expected price of over $200.)

Questions

1. Why is Warren Buffett so successful with his auctions?
2. You can place your item for sale on eBay without a trading assistant and save on the commission. Why do people use Dan's services?
3. What are the advantages of fundraising via auctions?

Saarinen et al. 2006) and were started on the Internet in 1995. Host sites on the Internet serve as brokers, offering services for sellers to post their goods for sale and allowing buyers to bid on those items.

Major online auctions, such as eBay, offer consumer products, electronic parts, artwork, vacation packages, airline tickets, and collectibles, as well as excess supplies and inventories being auctioned off by B2B marketers. Another type of B2B online auction is increasingly used to trade special types of commodities, such as electricity transmission capacities and gas and energy options. Furthermore, conventional business practices that traditionally have relied on contracts and fixed prices are increasingly being converted into auctions with bidding for online procurements (e.g., Raffles Hotel, Online File W2.2).

Of course, many consumer goods are not suitable for auctions, and for these items conventional selling—such as posted-price retailing—is more than adequate. Yet the flexibility offered by online auction trading offers innovative market processes for many other goods. For example, instead of searching for products and vendors by visiting sellers' Web sites, a buyer may solicit offers from all potential sellers. Such a buying mechanism is so innovative that it has the potential to be used in almost all types of consumer goods auctions (as will be shown later when reverse auctions and "name-your-own-price" auctions are discussed). Some examples of innovative auctions are provided in Case 2.2.

DYNAMIC PRICING AND TYPES OF AUCTIONS

dynamic pricing
Prices that change based on supply and demand relationships at any given time.

A major characteristic of auctions is that they are based on dynamic pricing. **Dynamic pricing** refers to prices that are not fixed but that are allowed to fluctuate as supply and demand in a market change. In contrast, catalog prices are fixed, as are prices in department stores, supermarkets, and many electronic storefronts.

Dynamic pricing appears in several forms. Perhaps the oldest forms are negotiation and bargaining, which have been practiced for many generations in open-air markets. It is customary to classify dynamic pricing into four major categories based on how many buyers and sellers are involved. These four categories are outlined in the following text and are discussed more fully in Chapter 10.

One Buyer, One Seller

In this configuration, one can use negotiation, bargaining, or bartering. The resulting price will be determined by each party's bargaining power, supply and demand in the item's market, and (possibly) business environment factors.

One Seller, Many Potential Buyers

In this configuration, the seller uses a **forward auction**, an auction in which a seller entertains bids from multiple buyers. (Because forward auctions are the most common and traditional form, they often are simply called *auctions*.) The four major types of forward auctions are *English* and *Yankee* auctions, in which bidding prices increase as the auction progresses, and *Dutch* and *free-fall* auctions, in which bidding prices decline as the auction progresses. Each of these can be used for either liquidation or for market efficiency (see Chapter 10 and Gallaugher 2002).

One Buyer, Many Potential Sellers

Two popular types of auctions in which there is one buyer and many potential sellers are reverse auctions (tendering) and "name-your-own-price" auctions.

Reverse Auctions. When there is one buyer and many potential sellers, a **reverse auction** (also called a **bidding** or **tendering system**) is in place. In a reverse auction, the buyer places an item he or she wants to buy for bid (or *tender*) on a *request for quote* (RFQ) system. Potential suppliers bid on the item, reducing the price sequentially (see Exhibit 2.7). In electronic bidding in a reverse auction, several rounds of bidding may take place until the bidders do not reduce the price further. The winner is the one with the lowest bid (assuming that only price is considered). Reverse auctions are primarily a B2B or G2B mechanism. (For further discussion and examples, see Chapter 5.)

The Name-Your-Own-Price Model. Priceline.com pioneered the **"name-your-own-price" model**. In this model, a would-be buyer specifies the price (and other terms) that he or she is willing to pay to any willing and able seller. For example, Priceline.com presents consumers' requests to sellers, who fill as much of the guaranteed demand as they wish at prices and terms requested by buyers. Alternately, Priceline.com searches its own database that contains vendors' lowest prices and tries to match supply against requests. Priceline.com asks customers to guarantee acceptance of the offer if it is at or below the requested price by giving a credit card number. This is basically a C2B model, although some businesses use it too (see Chapter 10 for details.)

forward auction
An auction in which a seller entertains bids from buyers. Bidders increase price sequentially.

reverse auction (bidding or tendering system)
Auction in which the buyer places an item for bid (*tender*) on a request for quote (RFQ) system, potential suppliers bid on the job, with the price reducing sequentially, and the lowest bid wins; primarily a B2B or G2B mechanism.

"name-your-own-price" model
Auction model in which a would-be buyer specifies the price (and other terms) he or she is willing to pay to any willing and able seller. It is a C2B model that was pioneered by Priceline.com.

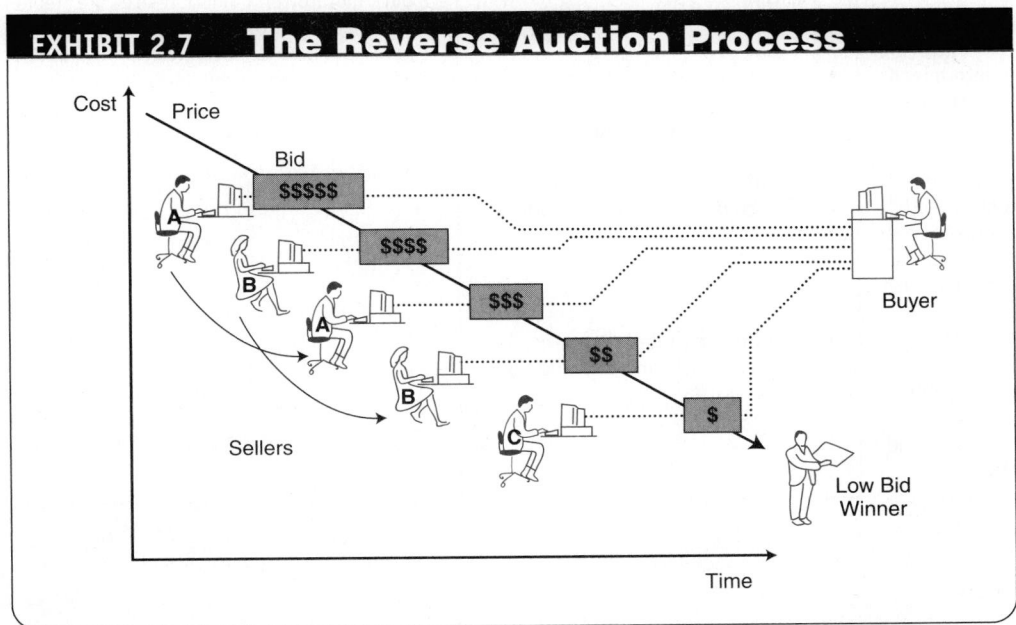

EXHIBIT 2.7   The Reverse Auction Process

Many Sellers, Many Buyers

When there are many sellers and many buyers, buyers and their bidding prices are matched with sellers and their asking prices based on the quantities on both sides. Stocks and commodities markets are typical examples of this configuration. Buyers and sellers may be individuals or businesses. Such an auction is called a **double auction** (see Chapter 10 for details).

double auction
Auctions in which multiple buyers and their bidding prices are matched with multiple sellers and their asking prices, considering the quantities on both sides.

BENEFITS, LIMITATIONS, AND IMPACTS OF E-AUCTIONS

E-auctions are becoming important selling and buying channels for many companies and individuals. E-auctions enable buyers to access goods and services anywhere auctions are conducted. Moreover, almost perfect market information is available about prices, products, current supply and demand, and so on. These characteristics provide benefits to all.

Benefits of E-Auctions

According to Nissanoff (2006), the auction culture will revolutionize the way customers buy, sell, and obtain what they want. A listing of the benefits of e-auctions to sellers, buyers, and e-auctioneers is provided in Insights and Additions 2.1.

Limitations of E-Auctions

E-auctions have several limitations. The most significant limitations are minimal security, the possibility of fraud, and limited participation.

Minimal Security. Some of the C2C auctions conducted on the Internet are not secure because they are done in an unencrypted environment. This means that credit card numbers could be stolen during the payment process. Payment methods such as PayPal (paypal.com)

Insights and Additions 2.1 Benefits of E-Auctions

Benefits to Sellers	Benefits to Buyers	Benefits to E-Auctioneers
• Increased revenues from broadening bidder base and shortening cycle time.	• Opportunities to find unique items and collectibles.	• Higher repeat purchases. Jupiter Research (*jupiterresearch.com*) found that auction sites, such as eBay, tend to garner higher repeat-purchase rates than the top B2C sites, such as Amazon.com.
• Opportunity to bargain instead of selling at a fixed price.	• Entertainment. Participation in e-auctions can be entertaining and exciting.	• High "stickiness" to the Web site (the tendency of customers to stay at sites longer and come back more often). Auction sites are frequently "stickier" than fixed-priced sites. Stickier sites generate more ad revenue for the e-auctioneer.
• Optimal price setting determined by the market (more buyers, more information).	• Convenience. Buyers can bid from anywhere, even with a cell phone; they do not have to travel to an auction place.	• Easy expansion of the auction business.
• Sellers can gain more customer dollars by offering items directly (saves on the commission to intermediaries; also, physical auctions are very expensive compared with e-auctions).	• Anonymity. With the help of a third party, buyers can remain anonymous.	
• Can liquidate large quantities quickly.	• Possibility of finding bargains, for both individuals and organizations.	
• Improved customer relationship and loyalty (in the case of specialized B2B auction sites and electronic exchanges).		

can be used to solve the payment problem (see Chapter 12). In addition, some B2B auctions are conducted over highly secure private lines.

Possibility of Fraud. Auction items are in many cases unique, used, or antique. Because the buyer cannot see the items, the buyer may get defective products. Also, buyers can commit fraud by receiving goods or services without paying for them. Thus, the fraud rate on e-auctions is relatively high. For a discussion of e-auction fraud and fraud prevention, see Chapter 10.

Limited Participation. Some auctions are by invitation only; others are open to dealers only. Limited participation may be a disadvantage to sellers, who usually benefit from as large a pool of buyers as possible.

Impacts of Auctions

Because the trade objects and contexts for auctions are very diverse, the rationale behind auctions and the motives of the different participants for setting up auctions are quite different. The following are some representative impacts of e-auctions.

Auctions as a Coordination Mechanism. Auctions are used increasingly as an efficient coordination mechanism for establishing a price equilibrium. An example is auctions for the allocation of telecommunications bandwidth.

Auctions as a Social Mechanism to Determine a Price. For objects that are not traded in traditional markets, such as unique or rare items, or for items that may be offered randomly or at long intervals, an auction creates a marketplace that attracts potential buyers, and often experts. By offering many of these special items at a single place and time and by attracting considerable attention, auctions provide the requisite exposure of purchase and sale orders, and hence liquidity of the market in which an optimal price can be determined. Typical examples are auctions of fine arts or rare items, as well as auctions of communications frequencies, Web banners, and advertising space. For example, wine collectors can find a global wine auction at winebid.com.

Auctions as a Highly Visible Distribution Mechanism. Some auctions deal with special offers. In this case, a supplier typically auctions off a limited number of items, using the auction primarily as a mechanism to gain attention and to attract those customers who are bargain hunters or who have a preference for the gambling dimension of the auction process. The airline seat auctions by Cathay Pacific, American Airlines, and Lufthansa fall into this category (see Saarinen et al. 2006).

Auctions as an EC Component. Auctions can stand alone, or they may be combined with other e-commerce activities. An example of the latter is the combination of *group purchasing* with reverse auctions, as described in Online File W2.7.

Section 2.5 ▶ REVIEW QUESTIONS

1. Define auctions and describe how they work.
2. Describe the benefits of electronic auctions over traditional (offline) auctions.
3. List the four types of auctions.
4. Distinguish between forward and reverse auctions.
5. Describe the "name-your-own-price" auction model.
6. List the major benefits of auctions to buyers, sellers, and auctioneers.
7. What are the major limitations of auctions?
8. List the major impacts of auctions on markets.

2.6 BARTERING AND NEGOTIATING ONLINE

Two emerging mechanisms are gaining popularity (as can be seen in Chapter 10) in EC: e-bartering and e-negotiation.

ONLINE BARTERING

Bartering, the exchange of goods and services, is the oldest method of trade. Today, it is done primarily between organizations. The problem with bartering is that it is difficult to find trading partners. Businesses and individuals may use classified ads to advertise what they

bartering
The exchange of goods or services.

need and what they offer, but they still may not be able to find what they want. Intermediaries may be helpful, but they are expensive (20 to 30 percent commission) and very slow.

e-bartering (electronic bartering)
Bartering conducted online, usually in a bartering exchange.

E-bartering (electronic bartering)—bartering conducted online—can improve the matching process by attracting more partners to the barter. In addition, matching can be done faster, and as a result, better matches can be found. Items that are frequently bartered online include office space, storage, and factory space; idle facilities; and labor, products, and banner ads. (Note that e-bartering may have tax implications that need to be considered.)

bartering exchange
A marketplace in which an intermediary arranges barter transactions.

E-bartering is usually done in a **bartering exchange**, a marketplace in which an intermediary arranges the transactions. These exchanges can be very effective. Representative bartering Web sites include allbusiness.com, intagio.com, and barterdepot.com. The process works like this: First, the company tells the bartering exchange what it wants to offer. The exchange then assesses the value of the company's products or services and offers it certain "points" or "bartering dollars." The company can use the "points" to buy the things it needs from a participating member in the exchange.

Bartering sites must be financially secure. Otherwise users may not have a chance to use the points they accumulate. (For further details see virtualbarter.net and barternews.com).

ONLINE NEGOTIATING

Dynamic prices also can be determined by *negotiation*. Negotiated pricing commonly is used for expensive or specialized products. Negotiated prices also are popular when large quantities are purchased. Much like auctions, negotiated prices result from interactions and bargaining among sellers and buyers. However, in contrast with auctions, negotiation also deals with nonpricing terms, such as the payment method and credit. Negotiation is a well-known process in the offline world (e.g., in real estate, automobile purchases, and contract work). In addition, in cases where there is no standard service or product to speak of, some digital products and services can be personalized and "bundled" at a standard price. Preferences for these bundled services differ among consumers, and thus they are frequently negotiated. More discussions on electronic negotiations can be found in Bichler et al. (2003). A simple P2P negotiation can be seen in ioffer.com (see Chapter 10). For more on negotiation in P2P money lending see the ZOPA and Prosper cases in Chapter 18.

mobile computing
Use of portable devices, including smart cell phones, usually in a wireless environment. It permits real-time access to information, applications, and tools that, until recently, were accessible only from a desktop computer.

According to Choi and Whinston (2000), *online (electronic) negotiation* is easier than offline negotiation. Due to customization and bundling of products and services, it often is necessary to negotiate both prices and terms for online sales. E-markets allow such online negotiations to be conducted virtually for all products and services. Three factors may facilitate online negotiation: (1) the products and services that are bundled and customized, (2) the computer technology that facilitates the negotiation process, and (3) the software (intelligent) agents that perform searches and comparisons, thereby providing quality customer service and a base from which prices can be negotiated.

Section 2.6 ▶ REVIEW QUESTIONS

1. Define bartering and describe the advantages of e-bartering.
2. Explain the role of online negotiation in EC.

mobile commerce (m-commerce)
E-commerce conducted via wireless devices.

2.7 E-COMMERCE IN THE WIRELESS ENVIRONMENT: M-COMMERCE AND L-COMMERCE

m-business
The broadest definition of m-commerce, in which e-business is conducted in a wireless environment.

The widespread adoption of wireless and mobile networks, devices (smart cell phones, PDAs, etc.), and *middleware* (software that links application modules from different computer languages and platforms) is creating exciting new opportunities. These new technologies are making **mobile computing** possible. These technologies permit *real-time* access to information, applications, and tools that, until recently, were accessible only from a desktop computer. **Mobile commerce (m-commerce)** refers to the conduct of e-commerce via wireless devices or from portable devices (see the Maybelline case in Online File W1.2). It is also sometimes called **m-business**, when reference is made to its broadest definition, in which the e-business environment is wireless (Deans 2005; Sadeh 2002).

THE MOBILITY REVOLUTION

Around the world, enterprises are adopting mobilized computing technologies at a tremendous rate. They are using wireless hardware and applications for untethered computing. The productivity gains available with mobilized technology continue to expand as the price of the technology continues to drop. And in the case of mobility, the technology revolutionizes the way that people work.

Organizations are embracing mobilized computing technologies for several reasons:

▶ It improves the productivity of workers in the field.
▶ Wireless telecom support for mobility is growing quickly.
▶ More applications can run both online and offline.
▶ The prices of notebook computers, wireless handhelds, and smart phones continue to fall as their capabilities increase.

Although mobility makes employees in all types of jobs more productive, one of the biggest areas of opportunity lies with field service personnel. An estimated 350 million field service workers around the world are carrying clipboards and notepads. Only about 30 percent of these workers are computerized. Therefore, the potential for productivity gains is huge.

Example: BNSF Railway Co.

BNSF Railway Co., which operates one of the largest railroad networks in North America, gave key field maintenance workers notebooks with Intel Centrino mobile technology and equipped them with mobilized engineering applications to manage and track repairs, access electronic work orders and technical manuals, submit reports, and plan maintenance activities. In the past, engineers could only handle these tasks by driving back and forth to the regional office, which could be many miles away from the day's work site.

With the new mobilized technology, field service workers can now access BNSF's maintenance and engineering systems from anywhere in their field territory. They can file reports, monitor maintenance activities, and better identify and resolve problems. All of this results in smoother, more efficient railroad operations (Intel 2005).

There is a reason for the strong interest in the topic of mobile commerce. According to a study conducted by Telecom Trends International (2004), the number of m-commerce users was 94.9 million in 2003 and will grow to 1.67 billion in 2008. In addition, revenues from m-commerce will grow globally from $6.86 billion in 2003 to over $554.37 billion in 2008. Some facts and projections regarding m-commerce are provided in Online File W2.8.

Mobile devices can be connected to the Internet, allowing users to conduct transactions from anywhere. The Gartner Group estimated that at least 40 percent of all B2C transactions, totaling over $200 billion by 2005, will be initiated from smart wireless devices (Telus Mobility 2002). Others predict much higher figures, believing that mobile devices will soon overtake PCs as the predominant Internet access device, creating a global market of over 500 million subscribers. However, others predict a much slower adoption rate (see Chapter 9).

THE PROMISE OF M-COMMERCE

Since 1999, m-commerce has become one of the hottest topics in IT in general and in EC in particular. Mobility significantly changes the manner in which people and trading partners interact, communicate, and collaborate. Mobile applications are expected to change the way we live, play, are entertained, and do business. Much of the Internet culture, which is currently PC based, may change based on mobile devices. As a result, m-commerce creates new business models for EC, notably location-based applications.

Location-Based Commerce (LBC) and Pervasive Computing

Location-based commerce (LBC) is an m-commerce application targeted to a customer whose preferences and needs and location (e.g., using GPS) are known in real time. Given this information, a merchant could send an MSM message such as, "you are near our Italian restaurant, please enter (address) and get a 10 percent discount." For more on LBC applications, see Chapter 9 and en.wikipedia.org/wiki/Mobile-Commerce.

location-based commerce (LBC)
An m-commerce application targeted to a customer whose location, preferences, and needs are known in real time.

An emerging area in m-commerce is *pervasive computing* (see Chapter 9). One of its promising applications is the use of RFID to improve the supply chain (see the Real-World Case on Wal-Mart at the end of this chapter).

M-Commerce Adoption

Although there are currently many hurdles to the widespread adoption of m-commerce, it is clear that many of these will be reduced or eliminated in the future. Many companies are already shifting their strategy to the mobile world. Many large corporations with huge marketing presence—Microsoft, IBM, Intel, Sony, Google, AT&T, TimeWarner, to name a few—are transforming their businesses to include m-commerce–based products and services. Nokia emerged as a world-class company not just because it sells more cell phones than anyone else but also because it has become the major player in the mobile economy. Similarly, major telecommunications companies, from Verizon to Vodafone, are shifting their strategies to wireless products and services. In the United States, General Motors produced 1.4 million vehicles equipped with in-vehicle safety and communications systems in 2004 and equipped 2.2 million 2005 models. The company plans to double production of OnStar-equipped vehicles for the model year 2006 (Onstar.com 2004). DoCoMo, the world's largest mobile portal (nttdocomo.com; see Vision 2010), is investing billions of dollars to expand its services to other countries via its i-mode Global. Finally, in Europe alone over 200 companies offer mobile portal services.

I-MODE: A SUCCESSFUL MOBILE PORTAL

To illustrate the potential spread of m-commerce, let's examine DoCoMo's i-mode, the pioneering wireless service that took Japan by storm in 1999 and 2000. With a few clicks on a handset, i-mode users can conduct a large variety of m-commerce activities, ranging from online stock trading and banking to purchasing travel tickets and booking karaoke rooms. Users can also use i-mode to send and receive color images. Launched in February 1999, i-mode went international in 2000 and had over 15 million users by the end of that year and 51.8 million by June 2006, including 5 million outside Japan (Wikipedia.com 2006b). The following are some interesting i-mode applications:

- **Shopping guides.** The addresses and telephone numbers of shops in the major shopping malls in Tokyo and other Japanese cities are provided with a supporting search engine. Consumers can locate information about best-selling books and then buy them. Users can purchase music online to enjoy anywhere.

- **Maps and transportation.** Digital maps show detailed guides of local routes and stops of the major public transportation systems in all major Japanese cities. Users can access train and bus timetables, guides to shopping areas, and automatic notification of train delays.

- **Ticketing.** Airline tickets, events, and entertainment tickets can be purchased online.

- **News and reports.** Fast access to global news, local updated traffic conditions, the air pollution index, and weather reports are provided continuously.

- **Personalized movie service.** Updates on the latest movies with related information, such as casting and show times, are provided. Also, subscribers can search for their own favorite movies by entering the name of the movie or the name of the movie theater.

- **Entertainment.** Up-to-date personalized entertainment, such as favorite games, can be searched for and accessed easily. Online "chatting" also is provided, and users can send or receive photos. Also, users can subscribe to receive Tamagotchi's characters each day for only $1 a month. These virtual pets (the translation of their Japanese name means "cute little eggs") exhibit intelligent behavior; for example, a Tamagotchi cat will purr if you pet it but "bite" if it is hungry.

- **Dining and reservations.** The exact location of a selected participating restaurant is shown on a digital map. Subscribers also can find restaurants that offer meals in a particular price range. Reservations can be made online. Discount coupons also are available online.

- **Additional services.** Additional services, such as banking, stock trading, telephone directory searches, dictionary services, and horoscopes, are available.

CASE 2.3
EC Application
WIRELESS PEPSI INCREASES PRODUCTIVITY

The Pepsi Bottling Group (PBG; *pbg.com*), the largest manufacturer, seller, and distributor of Pepsi-Cola, has the mountainous job of stocking and maintaining its Pepsi vending machines as well as completing huge amounts of paperwork and searching for parts and equipment to fix these machines. Any time drinks in one of the tens of thousands of machines is out of stock or a machine is not functioning the company loses revenue and profits.

In 2002, the company began to equip its service technicians with handheld devices hooked into a wireless wide area network (WWAN). The handheld is the Melard Sidearm (from Melard Technologies, *melard.com*), and it is designed to work with many wireless platforms. iAnywhere (from Sybase, Inc., *sybase.com*) provides the mobile database application that allows wireless communications around the United States in real time. The database includes the repair parts inventory available on each service truck, so dispatchers know whom to send for maintenance and where the trucks are at any given moment. It also has a back-office system that maintains the overall inventory. The company is also able to locate the whereabouts of each truck in real time, using global positioning systems (GPS). This makes scheduling and dispatching more effective.

In the summer of 2002, only about 700 technicians used the wireless system, but already the company was saving $7 million per year. Each of these technicians was able to handle one more call each day than previously. PBG had provided the wireless capability to thousands of technicians by 2006.

Sources: Compiled from Rhey (2002) and from *pbg.com* (accessed August 2006).

Questions

1. What are the capabilities of the handheld devices used by the PBG technicians?

2. How do the handhelds relate to databases and dispatching?

3. This case deals with vending machine maintenance. In what ways, if any, could wireless technologies help with stocking the machines?

These applications are for individual users and are provided via a mobile portal. An even greater number of applications are available in the B2B area and in the intrabusiness area, as illustrated in Case 2.3. For more complete coverage of m-business applications, see Chapter 9, Shi (2004), Deans (2005), and Dekleva (2004).

Section 2.7 ❱ REVIEW QUESTIONS

1. Define mobile computing and m-commerce.
2. How does m-commerce differ from EC?
3. Define location-based commerce.
4. What are some of the major services provided by i-mode?

2.8 COMPETITION IN THE DIGITAL ECONOMY AND ITS IMPACT ON INDUSTRIES

One of the major economic impacts of EC is its contribution to competitive advantage, as will be shown next.

THE INTERNET ECOSYSTEM

The prevailing model of competition in the Internet economy is more like a web of inter-relationships than the hierarchical command-and-control model of the industrial economy. Because of these interrelationships, the business model of the Internet economy has been called the **Internet ecosystem**. Just like an ecosystem in nature, the activities in the Internet economy are self-organizing: The process of *natural selection* takes place around company profits and value to customers.

Internet ecosystem
The business model of the Internet economy.

The Internet economy has low barriers to entry, and so it is expanding rapidly. As the Internet ecosystem evolves both technologically and in population, it will be even easier and likelier for countries, companies, and individuals to participate in the Internet economy. Already, a $1 trillion technical infrastructure is in place, ready and available for anyone to use at any time—free of charge. New ideas and ways of doing things can come from anywhere at any time in the Internet economy. Some of the old rules of competition no longer apply.

Competitive Factors

EC competition is very intense because online transactions enable the following:

▶ **Lower search costs for buyers.** E-markets reduce the cost of searching for product information (e.g., sellers, models, prices, etc.), frequently to zero. This can significantly impact competition, enabling customers to find cheaper (or better) products and forcing sellers, in turn, to reduce prices and/or improve customer service. Sellers that provide information to buyers can exploit the Internet to gain a considerably larger market share. For example, according to Tsai (2004) Wal-Mart and Walgreens are developing intelligent search tools that are expected to increase online sales on their sites by 25 to 50 percent.

▶ **Speedy comparisons.** Not only can customers find inexpensive products online, but they also can find them quickly. For example, a customer does not have to go to several bookstores to find the best price for a particular book. Using shopping search engines such as allbookstores.com, bestwebbuys.com/books, or shopping.com for consumer products, customers can find what they want and compare prices. Companies that sell online and provide information to search engines will gain a competitive advantage.

▶ **Lower prices.** Buy.com, Half.com, and other companies can offer low prices due to their low costs of operation (no physical facilities, minimum inventories, etc.). If volume is large enough, prices can be reduced by 40 percent or more (see the Blue Nile case at the beginning of the chapter).

▶ **Customer service.** Amazon.com and Dell, for example, provide superior customer service. As will be shown in Chapters 3 and 13, such service is an extremely important competitive factor.

▶ **Barriers to entry are reduced.** Setting up a Web site is relatively easy and inexpensive, and doing so reduces the need for a sales force and brick-and-mortar stores. Companies have to view this as both a threat (e.g., Where will our next competitor come from?) and as an opportunity (e.g., Can we use our core competencies in new areas of business?).

▶ **Virtual partnerships multiply.** With access to a World Wide Web of expertise and the ability to share production and sales information easily, the ability of a firm to create a virtual team to exploit an EC opportunity increases dramatically (recall the Boeing case, Chapter 1.) The Internet is especially good at reducing interaction costs, the time and money expended when people and companies exchange goods, services, and ideas (e.g., meetings, sales presentations, telephone calls).

▶ **Market niches abound.** The market-niche strategy is as old as the study of competitive advantage. What has changed is that without the limits imposed by physical storefronts, the number of business opportunities is as large as the Web. The challenge strategists face is to discover and reap the benefits from profitable niches before the competition does so.

▶ **Differentiation and personalization. Differentiation** involves providing a product or service that is not available elsewhere. For example, Amazon.com differentiates itself from other book retailers by providing customers with information that is not available in a physical bookstore, such as communication with authors, almost real-time book reviews, and book recommendations. An example of personalization is the Bombay Sapphire case (Online File W2.9).

In addition, EC provides for personalization or customization of products and services. **Personalization** refers to the ability to tailor a product, service, or Web content to specific user preferences (see Chapter 18). For example, Amazon.com notifies customers by e-mail when new books on their favorite subjects or by their favorite authors are published. Several sites will track news or stock prices based on the consumer's preferences. For example, Google will e-mail all news regarding certain topics (e.g., Chinese stocks and companies) to

differentiation
Providing a product or service that is unique.

personalization
The ability to tailor a product, service, or Web content to specific user preferences.

a user. The aim of personalization is to increase the usability of complex information by customizing the presentation, making the user interface more intuitive and easier to understand, and reducing information overload by tailoring content and navigation. For personalization techniques, see Anke and Sundaram (2006).

Example: Amazon.com

Amazon.com's catalog includes several million items. Amazon.com provides easy navigation, but it provides personalization as well. For example, when a customer looks up a book on a certain topic, it recommends popular books on the same topic ("customers who bought this book also bought . . ."). In addition, it recommends five authors in the customer's area of interest. Recommendations appear several times. Amazon.com also bundles a similar book with the book the customer is interested in for a large discount. For details, see the opening case in Chapter 3.

Consumers like differentiation and personalization and are frequently willing to pay more for them. Differentiation reduces the substitutability between products, benefiting sellers who use this strategy. Also, price cutting in differentiated markets does not impact market share very much: Many customers are willing to pay a bit more for personalized products or services.

Certain other competitive factors have become less important as a result of EC. For example, the size of a company may no longer be a significant competitive advantage (as will be shown later). Similarly, location (geographical distance from the consumer) now plays a less significant role, and language is becoming less important as translation programs remove some language barriers (see Chapters 14 and 16). Finally, digital products are not subject to normal wear and tear, although some become obsolete.

All in all, EC supports efficient markets and could result in almost perfect competition. In such markets, a *commodity* (an undifferentiated product) is produced when the consumer's willingness to pay equals the marginal cost of producing the commodity and neither sellers nor buyers can influence supply or demand conditions individually. The following are necessary for *perfect competition*:

- Many buyers and sellers must be able to enter the market at little or no entry cost (no barriers to entry).
- Large buyers or sellers are *not able* to individually influence the market.
- The products must be homogeneous (commodities). (For customized products, therefore, there is no perfect competition.)
- Buyers and sellers must have comprehensive information about the products and about the market participants' demands, supplies, and conditions.

EC could provide, or come close to providing, these conditions. It is interesting to note that the ease of finding information benefits both buyers (finding information about products, vendors, prices, etc.) and sellers (finding information about customer demands, competitors, etc.).

It can be said that competition between companies is being replaced by competition between *networks*. The company with better communication networks, online advertising capabilities, and relationships with other Web companies (e.g., having an affiliation with Amazon.com) has a strategic advantage. It can also be said that competition is now mostly between *business models*. The company with the better business model will win.

Porter's Competitive Analysis in an Industry

Porter's (2001) **competitive forces model** identifies five major forces of competition that determine an industry's structural attractiveness. These forces, in combination, determine how the economic value created in an industry is divided among the players in the industry. Such an industry analysis helps companies develop their competitive strategy.

Because the five forces are affected by both the Internet and e-commerce, it is interesting to examine how the Internet influences the industry structure portrayed by Porter's model. Porter divided the impacts of the Internet into either positive or negative for the industry. As shown in Exhibit 2.8, most of the impacts are negative (marked by a minus sign). Of course, there are variations and exceptions to the impacts shown in the illustration, depending on the industry, its location, and its size. A negative impact means that competition will intensify in

competitive forces model
Model devised by Porter that says that five major forces of competition determine industry structure and how economic value is divided among the industry players in an industry; analysis of these forces helps companies develop their competitive strategy.

EXHIBIT 2.8 **Porter's Competitive Forces Model: How the Internet Influences Industry Structure**

Threat of substitute products or services

(+) By making the overall industry more efficient, the Internet can expand the size of the market

(−) The proliferation of Internet approaches creates new substitution threats

Bargaining power of suppliers

Rivalry among existing competitors

Buyers

| Bargaining power of channels | Bargaining power of end users |

(−) Procurement using the Internet tends to raise bargaining power over suppliers, though it can also give suppliers access to more customers

(−) The Internet provides a channel for suppliers to reach end users, reducing the leverage of intervening companies

(−) Internet procurement and digital markets tend to give all companies equal access to suppliers, and gravitate procurements to standardized products that reduce differentiation

(−) Reduced barriers to entry and the proliferation of competitors downstream shifts power to suppliers

(−) Reduces differences among competitors as offerings are difficult to keep proprietary

(−) Migrates competition to price

(−) Widens the geographic market, increasing the number of competitors

(−) Lowers variable cost relative to fixed cost, increasing pressures for price discounting

(+) Eliminates powerful channels or improves bargaining power over traditional channels

(−) Shifts bargaining power to end consumers

(−) Reduces switching costs

Barriers to entry

(−) Reduces barriers to entry such as the need for a sales force, access to channels, and physical assets; anything that Internet technology eliminates or makes easier to do reduces barriers to entry

(−) Internet applications are difficult to keep proprietary from new entrants

(−) A flood of new entrants has come into many industries

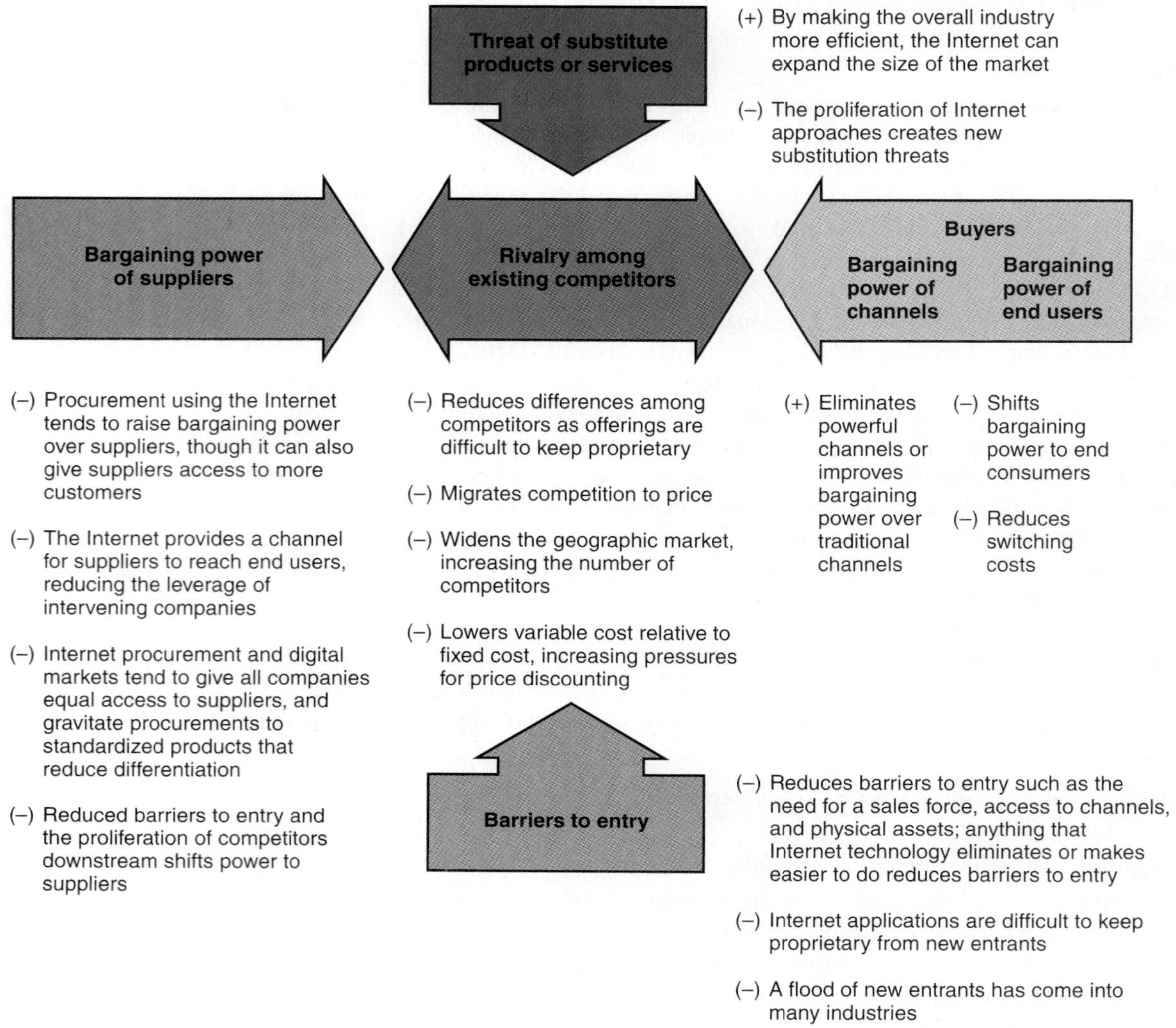

Source: "Porter's Competitive Forces Model: How the Internet Influences Industry Structure" from "Strategy and the Internet," by M. E. Porter, March 2001 © 2001 by the Harvard Business School Publishing Corp. *Harvard Business Review.* Reprinted by permission.

most industries as the Internet is introduced, causing difficulties to a competing company. Because the strength of each of the five forces varies considerably from industry to industry, it would be a mistake to draw general conclusions about the impact of the Internet on long-term industry profitability; each industry is affected in different ways. Nevertheless, an examination of a wide range of industries in which the Internet is playing a role reveals some clear trends, as summarized in Exhibit 2.8. The Internet can also boost an industry's efficiency in various ways, expanding the overall size of the market by improving its position relative to traditional substitutes. Thus, the Internet means stronger competition. This competition, which is especially strong for commodity-type products (e.g., toys, books, CDs), was a major contributor to the collapse of many dot-com companies in 2000 to 2001. To survive and prosper in such an environment, a company needs to use innovative strategies.

Examples of how e-commerce is changing entire industries are financial services, especially stock trading, cyberbanking, and e-mortgages. Zopa. com (Chapter 3) may change money lending by moving it from banks to a person-to-person level. Obviously, retailing is changing, and so are travel, entertainment, and more. An emerging change is in classified ads, as demonstrated in Case 2.4.

CASE 2.4
EC Application
CRAIGSLIST: THE ULTIMATE ONLINE CLASSIFIED SITE

If you want to find (or offer) a job, housing, goods and services, social activities, and much more in over 300 cities in more than 50 countries worldwide for free, go to *craigslist.org*. The site has much more information than you will find in all the newspapers in the individual cities. For example, more than 500,000 new jobs are listed from the more than 10 million new classified ads received by Craigslist every month. Craig Newmark, the founder of Craigslist, has said that everything is for sale on the site except the site itself. Although many other sites offer free classifieds, no other site even comes close to Craigslist.

In addition, Craigslist features 80 topical discussion forums with more than 40 million user postings. No wonder that Craigslist has over 4 billion page views per month, making it the seventh most visited site in the English language. Craigslist is considered by many as one of the few Web sites that could change the world because it is simply a free notice-board with more than four billion readers (Naughton 2006).

Users cite the following reasons for the popularity of Craigslist:

▶ It gives people a voice.
▶ It promotes a sense of trust, even intimacy.
▶ Its consistency and down-to-earth values.
▶ Its simplicity.
▶ Its social networking capabilities.

As an example of the site's effectiveness, we provide the personal experience of one of the authors who needed to rent his condo in Los Angeles. The usual process would take 2 to 4 weeks and $400 to $700 in newspaper ads plus the local

online for rent services to get the condo rented. With Craigslist, it took less than a week at no cost. As more people discover Craigslist, the traditional newspaper-based classified ad industry will probably be the loser; ad rates may become lower, and fewer ads will be printed.

eBay owns 25 percent of Craigslist. Craigslist charges for "help wanted" ads and apartment broker listings in some larger cities. In addition, Craigslist may charge ad placers, especially when an ad has rich media features. Classified advertising is Craigslist's real money-making feature. According to Copeland (2006), offline classifieds generate $27 billion in annual profits, and online classifieds could quadruple that amount in four years. Both Google and Microsoft are attempting to control this market. So, it is likely that Craigslist.org will be purchased soon.

Sources: Compiled from *craigslist.org* (accessed October 2006), Brandon (2006), Naughton (2006), Copeland (2006), and *Time* (2006).

Questions

1. Identify the business model used by Craigslist.
2. Visit *craigslist.org* and identify the social network and business network elements.
3. Why is Craigslist considered a site that "changes the world"?
4. What do you like about the site? What do you dislike about it?

IMPACT ON WHOLE INDUSTRIES

In addition to its impact on functional areas and organizations, EC is reshaping entire industries. In addition to impacting internal competition, major changes are taking place in the way that business is done. For example, the travel and hospitality industry is going through a major transition (see Case 18.2 in Chapter 18). The health-care industry is also undergoing dramatic changes. Suomi (2006) identifies the following major emerging changes in the health-care industry:

▶ Patient self-care is growing rapidly.
▶ The amount of free medical information is exploding (e.g., WebMd.com).
▶ Patient empowerment is gaining importance (more information, more choices).
▶ Increasing electronic interaction among patients, hospitals, pharmacies, etc.
▶ Increasing digital hospital and other health-care facilities.
▶ Data collected about patients is growing in amount and quality.
▶ Easy and shared access to patient data.
▶ Elder care and special types of care are improving significantly due to wireless systems.
▶ Increasing need to protect patient privacy and contain cost.

Therefore, the industry will change. For example, home care may increase and more specialty hospitals may emerge.

Section 2.8 ❯ REVIEW QUESTIONS

1. Why is competition so intense online?
2. Describe Porter's competitive forces model as it applies to the Internet and EC.
3. Describe the impact of competition on whole industries.

2.9 IMPACTS OF EC ON BUSINESS PROCESSES AND ORGANIZATIONS

Little statistical data or empirical research on the full impact of EC is available because of the relative newness of the field. Therefore, the discussion in this section is based primarily on experts' opinions, logic, and some actual data.

Existing and emerging Web technologies are offering organizations unprecedented opportunities to rethink strategic business models, processes, and relationships. Feeny (2001) called these *e-opportunities*, dividing them into three categories: e-marketing (Web-based initiatives that improve the marketing of existing products), e-operations (Web-based initiatives that improve the creation of existing products), and e-services (Web-based initiatives that improve customer services). Zwass (2003) also addressed the opportunities of e-marketplaces: the creation of virtual marketplaces with desired rules, flexible pricing (including price discovery), multichannel marketplaces (including bricks-and-clicks), customization, and new business models.

The discussion here is also based in part on the work of Bloch et al. (1996), who approached the impact of e-marketplaces on organizations from a value-added point of view. Their model, which is shown in Exhibit 2.9, divides the impact of e-marketplaces into three

EXHIBIT 2.9   The Analysis-of-Impacts Framework

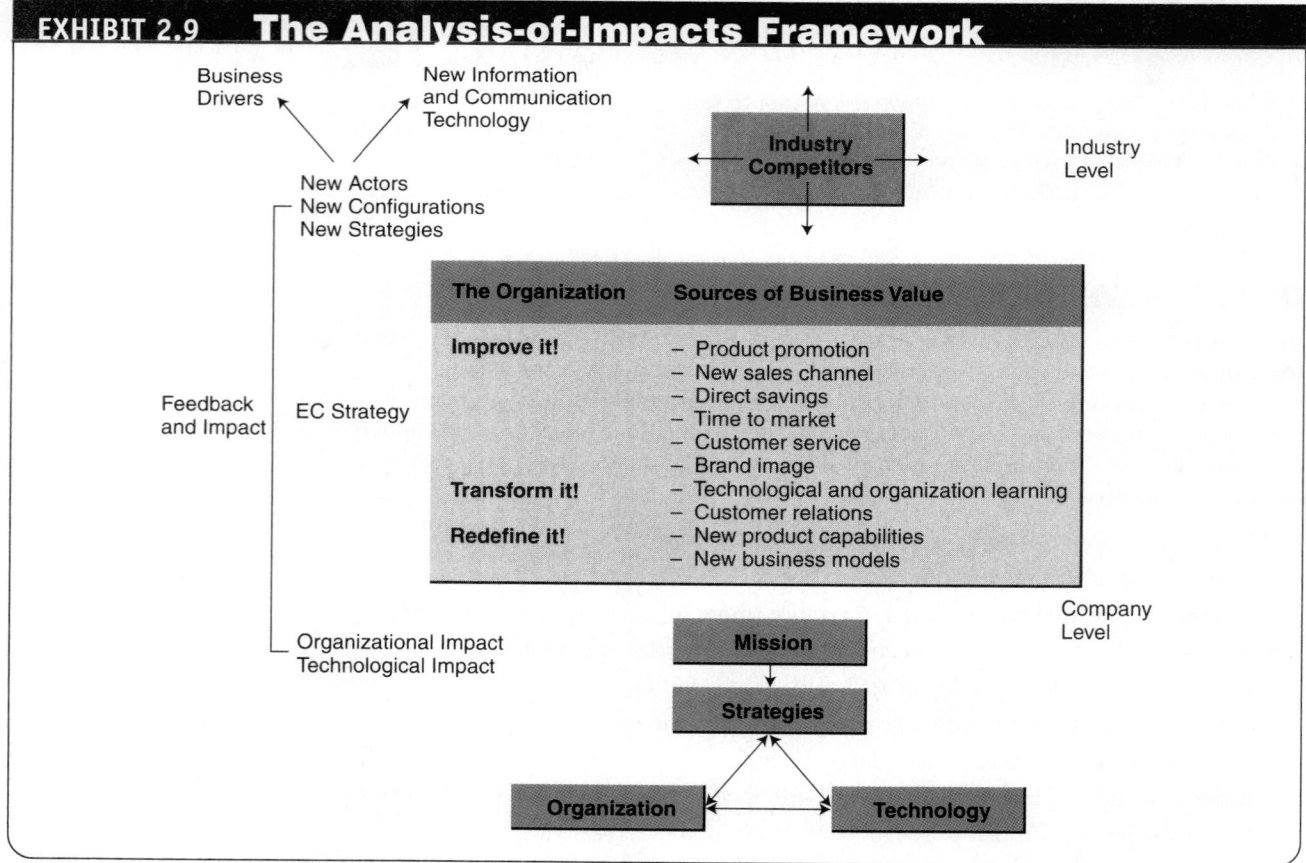

Source: Bloch, M., Y. Pigneur, and A. Segev. "Leveraging Electronic Commerce for Competitive Advantage: A Business Value Framework." *Proceedings of the Ninth International Conference on EDI-IOS*, Bled, Slovenia, June 1996. Reprinted by permission of Yves Pigneur.

major categories: improving direct marketing, transforming organizations, and redefining organizations. This section examines each of these impacts.

IMPROVING MARKETING AND SALES

Traditional *direct marketing* is done by mail order (catalogs) and telephone (telemarketing). According to the Direct Marketing Association, actual sales generated by direct mail totaled $747.6 billion in 2004, and are expected to increase to $954.7 billion by 2007 (Radio Advertising Bureau 2005). This figure is small, but growing rapidly (about 15 percent in 2005).

Bloch et al. (1996), Kioses et al. (2006), and Singh (2006) describe the following impacts of e-marketplaces on B2C direct marketing:

▶ **Product promotion.** The existence of e-marketplaces has increased the promotion of products and services through direct marketing. Contact with customers has become more information rich and interactive.

▶ **New sales channel.** Because of the direct reach to customers and the bidirectional nature of communications in EC, a new distribution channel for existing products has been created.

▶ **Direct savings.** The cost of delivering information to customers over the Internet results in substantial savings to senders of messages. Major savings are realized in delivering digitized products (such as music and software) rather than physical ones.

▶ **Reduced cycle time.** The delivery time of digitized products and services can be reduced to seconds. Also, the administrative work related to physical delivery, especially across international borders, can be reduced significantly, cutting the cycle time by more than 90 percent. One example of this is TradeNet in Singapore, which reduced the administrative time of port-related transactions from days to minutes. Cycle time can be reduced through improvements along the supply chain (e.g., by using RFID).

▶ **Improved customer service.** Customer service can be greatly enhanced by enabling customers to find detailed information online. For example, FedEx and other shippers allow customers to trace the status of their packages. Also, autoresponders (see Chapter 13) can answer standard e-mail questions in seconds. Finally, human experts' services can be expedited using help-desk software.

▶ **Brand or corporate image.** On the Web, newcomers can establish corporate images very quickly. What Amazon.com did in just 3 years took traditional companies generations to achieve. A good corporate image facilitates trust, which is necessary for direct sales. Traditional companies such as Intel, Disney, and Wal-Mart use their Web activities to affirm their corporate identity and brand image. Online File W2.9 demonstrates how one company uses personalization to bolster its image.

▶ **Customization.** EC enables customization of products and services. Buying in a store or ordering from a television advertisement usually limits customers to a supply of standard products. Dell is the classic example of customization success. Today, customers can configure not only computers but also cars, jewelry, shoes, clothes, gifts, and hundreds of other products and services. If done properly, a company can achieve mass customization that provides a competitive advantage and increases the overall demand for certain products and services. Customization is changing marketing and sales activities both in B2C and in B2B.

▶ **Advertising.** With direct marketing and customization comes one-to-one, or direct, advertising, which can be much more effective than mass advertising. Direct advertising creates a fundamental change in the manner in which advertising is conducted, not only for online transactions but also for products and services that are ordered and shipped in traditional ways. As will be shown in Chapter 4, the entire concept of advertising is going through a fundamental change due to EC.

> ▶ **Ordering systems.** Taking orders from customers can be drastically improved if it is done online, reducing both processing time and mistakes. Electronic orders can be quickly routed to the appropriate order-processing site. This process reduces expenses and also saves time, freeing salespeople to develop marketing plans.
>
> ▶ **Market operations.** Direct e-marketing is changing traditional markets. Some physical markets may disappear, as will the need to make deliveries of goods to intermediaries in the marketplace. In an e-marketspace, goods are delivered directly to buyers upon completion of the purchase, making markets much more efficient and saving the cost of the shipment into and from the brick-and-mortar store.
>
> ▶ **Accessibility.** The ability to access a market anytime from any place (especially with wireless devices) enhances direct e-marketing.

For digital products—software, music, and information—the changes brought by e-markets will be dramatic. Already, small but powerful software packages are delivered over the Internet. The ability to deliver digitized products electronically affects (eliminates) packaging and greatly reduces the need for specialized distribution models.

New sales models such as shareware, freeware, and pay-as-you-use are emerging. Although these models currently exist only within particular sectors, such as the software and publishing industries, they will eventually pervade other sectors.

Another way to view the impact of e-marketplaces on marketing is provided by Wind (2001). Kioses et al. (2006) summarize the changes in marketing. These changes are listed in Exhibit 2.10.

EXHIBIT 2.10 The Changing Face of Marketing

	Old Model—Mass and Segmented Marketing	New Model—One-to-One and Customization
Relationships with customers	Customer is a passive participant in the exchange	Customer is an active coproducer. Target marketing is to individuals
Customer needs	Articulated	Articulated and unarticulated
Segmentation	Mass market and target segments	Segments looking for customized solutions and segmented targets. One-to-one targets
Product and service offerings	Line extensions and modification	Customized products, services, and marketing
New product development	Marketing and R&D drive new product development	R&D focuses on developing the platforms that allow consumers to customize based on customer inputs
Pricing	Fixed prices and discounting	Customer influencing pricing (e.g., Priceline.com; auctions); value-based pricing models, e-auctions, e-negotiations (i-offer)
Communication	Advertising and PR	Integrated, interactive, and customized marketing communication, education, and entertainment
Distribution	Traditional retailing and direct marketing	Direct (online) distribution and rise of third-party logistics services
Branding	Traditional branding and cobranding	The customer's name as the brand (e.g., My Brand or Brand 4 ME)
Basis of competitive advantage	Marketing power	Marketing finesse and "capturing" the customer as "partner" while integrating marketing, operations, R&D, and information
Communities	Discount to members in physical communities	Discounts to members of e-communities

Sources: Compiled from Wind (2001), Kioses et al. (2006), and Singh (2006).

All of these impacts of e-markets on direct marketing provide companies, in some cases, with a competitive advantage over those that use only traditional direct-sales methods, as vividly illustrated in the Blue Nile case. Furthermore, because the competitive advantage is so large, e-markets are likely to replace many nondirect marketing channels. Some people predict the "fall of the shopping mall," and many retail stores and brokers of services (e.g., stocks, real estate, and insurance) are labeled by some as soon-to-be-endangered species.

TRANSFORMING ORGANIZATIONS

A second impact of e-marketplaces is the transformation of organizations. Here, we look at two key topics: organizational learning and the nature of work.

Technology and Organizational Learning

Rapid progress in EC will force a Darwinian struggle: To survive, companies will have to learn and adapt quickly to the new technologies. This struggle will offer them an opportunity to experiment with new products, services, and business models, which may lead to strategic and structural changes. These changes may transform the way in which business is done. We believe that as EC progresses, it will have a large and durable impact on the strategies of many organizations (see the Rosenbluth [now part of American Express] case, Online File W2.10).

Thus, new technologies will require new organizational structures and approaches. For instance, the structure of the organizational unit dealing with e-marketspaces might be different from the conventional sales and marketing departments. Specifically, a company's e-commerce unit might report directly to the chief information officer (CIO) rather than to the sales and marketing vice president. To be more flexible and responsive to the market, new processes must be put in place. For a while, new measurements of success may be needed. For example, the measures—called *metrics*—used to gauge success of an EC project in its early stages might need to be different from the traditional revenue–expenses framework (see Chapters 14 and 15). However, in the long run, as many dot-coms have found out, no business can escape the traditional revenue–expenses framework.

In summary, corporate change must be planned and managed. Before getting it right, organizations may have to struggle with different experiments and learn from their mistakes.

The Changing Nature of Work

The nature of some work and employment will be restructured in the Digital Age; it is already happening before our eyes. For example, driven by increased competition in the global marketplace, firms are reducing the number of employees down to a core of essential staff and *outsourcing* whatever work they can to countries where wages are significantly lower. The upheaval brought on by these changes is creating new opportunities and new risks and is forcing people to think in new ways about jobs, careers, and salaries.

Digital Age workers will have to be very flexible. Few will have truly secure jobs in the traditional sense, and many will have to be willing and able to constantly learn, adapt, make decisions, and stand by them. Many will work from home.

The Digital Age company will have to view its core of essential workers as its most valuable asset. It will have to constantly nurture and empower them and provide them with every means possible to expand their knowledge and skill base (see Drucker 2002).

REDEFINING ORGANIZATIONS

The following are some of the ways in which e-markets redefine organizations.

New and Improved Product Capabilities

E-markets allow for new products to be created and for existing products to be customized in innovative ways. Such changes may redefine organizations' missions and the manner in which they operate. Customer profiles, as well as data on customer preferences, can be used as a source of information for improving products or designing new ones.

Mass customization, as described earlier, enables manufacturers to create specific products for each customer, based on the customer's exact needs (see Appendix 2A on build-to-order

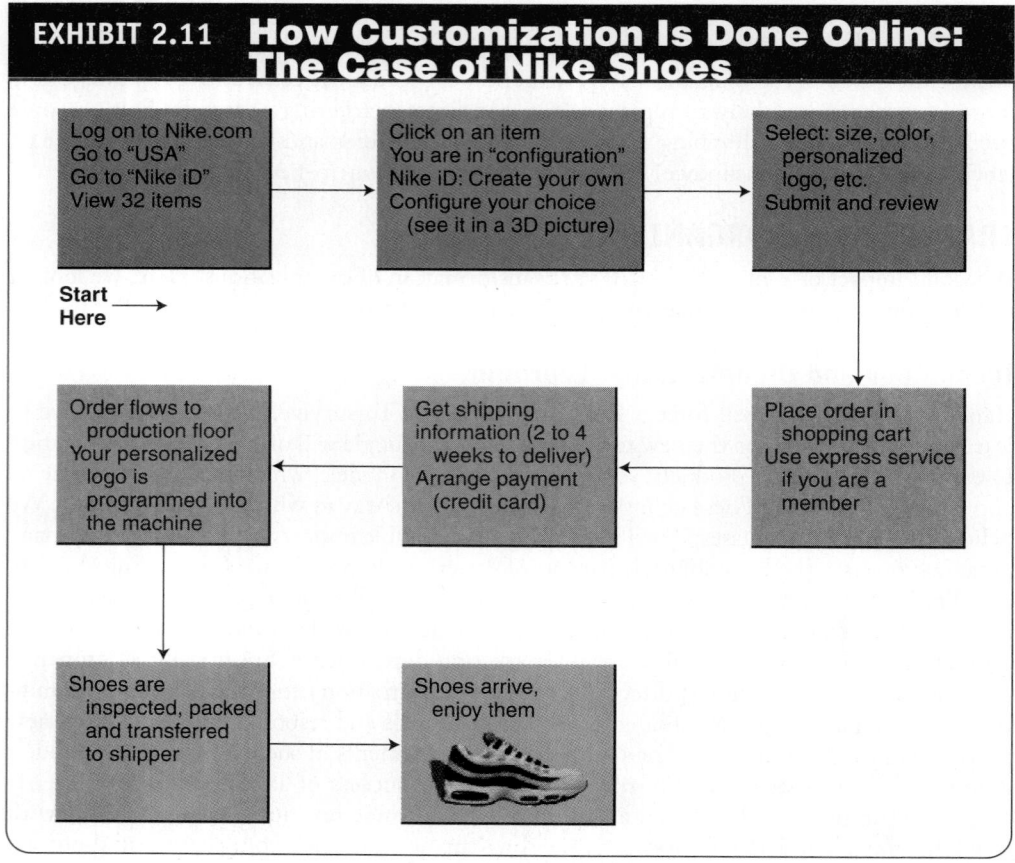

EXHIBIT 2.11   How Customization Is Done Online: The Case of Nike Shoes

at the end of this chapter). For example, Motorola gathers customer needs for a pager or a cellular phone, transmits the customer's specifications electronically to the manufacturing plant where the device is manufactured, and then sends the finished product to the customer within a day. Dell and General Motors use the same approach in building their products. Customers can use the Web to design or configure products for themselves. For example, customers can use the Web to design T-shirts, furniture, cars, jewelry, Nike shoes, and even a Swatch watch. With the use of mass-customization methods, the cost of customized products is at or slightly above the comparable retail price of standard products. Exhibit 2.11 shows how customers can order customized Nike shoes.

New Industry Order and Business Models

E-markets affect not only individual companies and their products, but also entire industries (e.g., airlines are moving to electronic ticketing and stocks are moving to online trading). The wide availability of information and its direct distribution to consumers will lead to the use of new business models (e.g., the name-your-own-price model of Priceline.com).

Improving the Supply Chain

One of the major benefits of e-markets is the potential improvement in supply chains. A major change is the creation of a hub-based chain, as shown in Exhibit 2.12 (in comparison with a traditional supply chain—upper part of the exhibit), and in Chapter 7.

Self-Service. One of the major changes in the supply chain is to transfer some activities to customers and/or employees through self-service. This strategy is used extensively in call centers (e.g., track your package at UPS or FedEx), with self-configuration of products (e.g., Dell, Nike), by having customers use FAQs, and by allowing employees to update personal

EXHIBIT 2.12 Changes in the Supply Chain

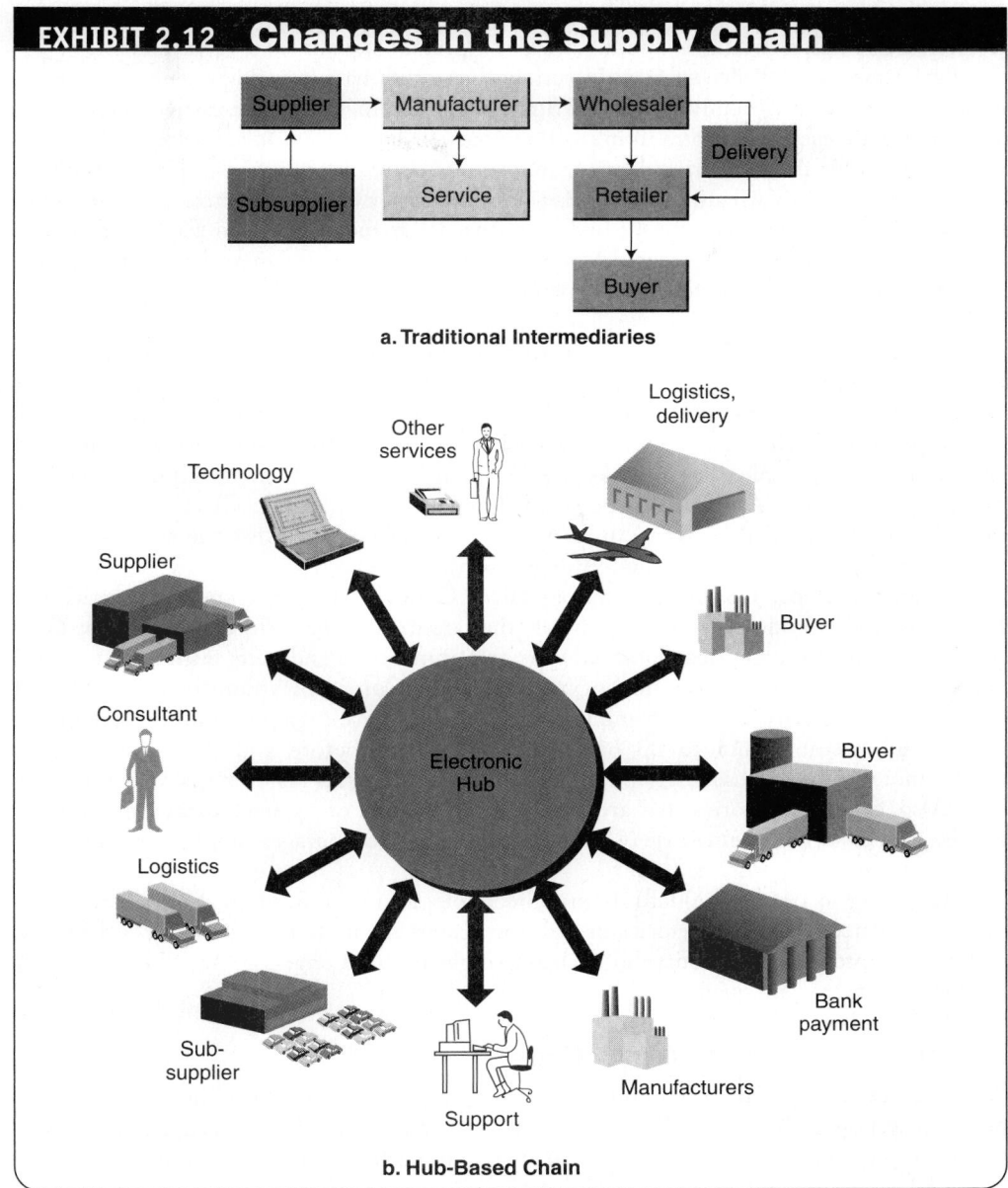

a. Traditional Intermediaries

b. Hub-Based Chain

data online. Shifting activities to others in the supply chain saves money and increases data accuracy and accountability.

Impacts on Manufacturing

EC is changing manufacturing systems from mass production lines to demand-driven, just-in-time manufacturing (see Blecker et al. 2005). These new production systems are integrated with finance, marketing, and other functional systems, as well as with business partners and customers. Using Web-based ERP systems (supported by software such as SAP R/3), companies can direct customer orders to designers and/or to the production floor within seconds (Norris 2005). Production cycle time can be cut by 50 percent or more in many cases, even if production is done in a different country from where the designers and engineers are located. (Recall the Boeing Case, Chapter 1.)

Build-to-Order Manufacturing. Build-to-order (pull system) is a manufacturing process that starts with an order (usually customized). Once the order is paid for, the vendor starts to fulfill it. This changes not only production planning and control but also the entire supply chain and payment cycle. For example, manufacturing or assembly starts only after an

build-to-order (pull system)
A manufacturing process that starts with an order (usually customized). Once the order is paid for, the vendor starts to fulfill it.

order is received. For more on build-to-order production, see Appendix 2A at the end of this chapter. One implementation of build-to-order is presented next.

Real-Time Demand-Driven Manufacturing. Successful manufacturing organizations must respond quickly and efficiently to demand. Strategies and techniques of the past no longer work, and it is a challenge to transform from the traditional, inventory-centric model to a more profitable and flexible demand-driven enterprise. *Demand-driven manufacturing* (DDM) provides customers with exactly what they want, when and where they want it. Effective communication between the supply chain and the factory floor is needed to make it happen. Partnerships must be focused on reducing costs through shared quality goals, shared design responsibility, on-time deliveries, and continuous performance reviews. An explanation of the DDM process is provided in Online File W2.11.

Virtual Manufacturing. An interesting organizational concept is that of *virtual manufacturing*—the ability to run multiple manufacturing plants as though they were at one location. A single company controls the entire manufacturing process, from the supply of components to shipment, while making it completely transparent to customers and employees. For example, Cisco works with 34 plants globally, 32 of which are owned by other companies. Each of Cisco's products will look exactly alike, regardless of where it was manufactured. Up-to-the-minute information sharing is critical for the success of this mass-customization approach (Blecker et al. 2005).

Assembly Lines. Companies such as IBM, General Motors, General Electric, and Boeing assemble products from components that are manufactured in many different locations, even different countries. Subassemblers gather materials and parts from their vendors, and they may use one or more tiers of manufacturers. Communication, collaboration, and coordination are critical in such multitier systems. Using electronic bidding, assemblers acquire subassemblies 15 to 20 percent cheaper than before and 80 percent faster. Furthermore, such systems are flexible and adaptable, allowing for fast changes with minimum cost. Also, costly inventories that are part of mass-production systems can be minimized. Finally, as seen in the Boeing case (Chapter 1), the system encourages suppliers to contribute innovative ideas.

According to Blecker (2006b), Internet technologies in the future will impact the shop floors in isolated islands of factories in real time. Internal communication and collaboration systems will interconnect automation, such as a single machine, or an assembly line, increasing productivity, speed, and quality.

Impacts on Finance and Accounting

E-markets require special finance and accounting systems. Most notable of these are electronic payment systems (Chapter 12). Traditional payment systems may be ineffective or inefficient for electronic trade. The use of new payment systems such as electronic cash is complicated because legal issues and agreements on international standards are involved. Nevertheless, electronic cash is certain to come soon, and it will change how payments are made. It could also change consumers' financial lives and shake the foundations of financial systems.

Executing an electronic order triggers an action in what is called the *back office*. Back-office transactions include buyers' credit checks, product availability checks, order confirmations, changes in accounts payable, receivables, billing, and much more. These activities must be efficient, synchronized, and fast so that the electronic trade will not be slowed down. An example of this is online stock trading. In most cases, orders are executed in less than 1 second, and the trader can find an online confirmation of the trade immediately.

One of the most innovative concepts in accounting and finance is the "virtual close," which would allow companies to close their accounting records, or "books," within a day. This Cisco Systems project is described in Online File W2.12. For more on impacts of EC on the financial services industry, see Malhotra and Malhotra (2006).

Impact on Human Resources Management and Training

EC is changing how people are recruited (see Chapter 3), evaluated, promoted, and developed. EC also is changing the way training and education are offered to employees. Online distance learning is exploding, providing opportunities that never existed in the past. Companies are cutting training costs by 50 percent or more, and virtual courses and programs are mushrooming (see Chapter 8).

New e-learning systems offer two-way video, on-the-fly interaction, and application sharing. Such systems provide for interactive remote instruction systems, which link sites over a high-speed intranet. At the same time, corporations are finding that e-learning may be their ticket to survival as changing environments, new technologies, and continuously changing procedures make it necessary for employees to be trained and retrained constantly, a process known as e-Human Resources (Ensher et al. 2002). EC systems are revolutionizing human resources (HR) operations (see Online File W2.13).

Section 2.9 ▶ REVIEW QUESTIONS

1. List the major parts of Bloch et al.'s model.
2. Describe how EC improves direct marketing.
3. Describe how EC transforms organizations.
4. Describe how EC redefines organizations.
5. Describe the concept of build-to-order (customization).
6. Describe the concept of the virtual close (described in Online File W2.12)

MANAGERIAL ISSUES

Some managerial issues related to this chapter are as follows.

1. **What about intermediaries?** Many EC applications will change the role of intermediaries. This may create a conflict between a company and its distributors. It may also create opportunities. In many cases, distributors will need to change their roles. This is a sensitive issue that needs to be planned for during the transformation to the e-business plan.

2. **Should we auction?** A major strategic issue is whether to use auctions as a sales channel. Auctions do have some limitations, and forward auctions may create conflicts with other distribution channels. If a company decides to use auctions, it needs to select auction mechanisms and determine a pricing strategy. These decisions determine the success of the auction and the ability to attract and retain visitors on the site. Auctions also require support services. Decisions about how to provide these services and to what extent to use business partners are critical to the success of high-volume auctions.

3. **Should we barter?** Bartering can be an interesting strategy, especially for companies that lack cash, need special material or machinery, and have surplus resources. However, the valuation of what is bought or sold may be hard to determine, and the tax implications in some countries are not clear.

4. **What m-commerce opportunities are available?** A company should develop an m-commerce strategy if it is likely to be impacted by m-commerce. The opportunities presented by m-commerce are enormous, but so are the risks. However, doing nothing may be even riskier. For further discussion, see Lei (2006) and Sadeh (2002).

5. **How do we compete in the digital economy?** Although the basic theories of competition are unchanged, the rules are different. Of special interest are digital products and services, whose variable costs are very low. Competition involves both old-economy and new-economy companies. The speed of changes in competitive forces can be rapid, and the impact of new business models can be devastating. As Bill Gates once said, "Competition is not among companies, but among business models" (Financial Analysts Meeting 1998).

6. **What organizational changes will be needed?** Companies should expect organizational changes in all functional areas once e-commerce reaches momentum. At a minimum, purchasing will be done differently in many organizations. Introducing models such as forward auctions and affiliate programs may also have a major impact on business operations. Finally, the trends toward build-to-order and demand-driven manufacturing will continue to expand.

RESEARCH TOPICS

Some EC research issues related to this chapter follow. For details, references, and additional topics, refer to the Online Appendix A "Current EC Research."

1. **Benefits and Issues of E-Marketplaces**
   - Analyze the benefits of e-marketplaces by industry, product, and e-market type.
   - What is the role of e-marketplaces in facilitating coordination with partners and intermediaries?
   - Summarize and compare typical empirical EC studies and outline potential new EC studies.
   - Research privacy considerations in e-marketplaces.

2. **The Roles of Intermediaries in E-Marketplaces**
   - Examine the traditional roles of intermediaries and their roles in e-marketplaces (reintermediation).
   - Investigate how intermediation affects competition and customer service.
   - Analyze disintermediation and reintermediation in e-marketplaces.

3. **Electronic Catalogs**
   - What are the benefits of intelligent catalog-search tools to buyers? What methods are used for search?
   - From the buyer's point of view, what are the benefits of customized, aggregated catalogs?
   - How accurate is dynamic customer profiling?
   - Research search agents for electronic catalogs.

4. **Auctions and Negotiation as B2B EC Mechanisms**
   - Investigate the reasons for the success of online auctions (success factors).
   - Examine how businesses use auctions, especially reverse ones, as a business strategy.
   - Research different aspects of online negotiation (e.g., the role of intelligent agents).

5. **The Impact of EC**
   - Research the impact of EC on organizations, functional departments, competition, market structures, and business processes.
   - Use surveys and statistics to compare the impact of EC on different countries and industries.

6. **Mobile Computing and Commerce**
   - Use theoretical models, frameworks, and surveys to compare and contrast m-commerce and e-commerce.
   - Examine how wireline and wireless technologies are related (complementation, substitution, facilitation).
   - Investigate the adaptation of new m-commerce technologies, such as RFID.

7. **Build-to-Order Manufacturing and Assembly**
   - Investigate the implementation strategy of EC and its relationship to mass customization from different angles (e.g., by industry, by product type).
   - Examine the design of information systems used to facilitate build-to-order.
   - Examine the adaptation of DDM in different industries.

8. **Agent-Based E-Marketplaces**
   - Discuss creation of protocols for agent-based EC.
   - Will people use EC intelligent agents? Is there a limit to what autonomous agents can do in EC?
   - Research the integration of Agent Communication Language (ACL), EDI, and B2B protocols.
   - How are agents incorporated into Web Services?
   - How do agents extract knowledge from Web pages?
   - Describe the Semantic Web with eXtensible Rule Markup Language (XRML) framework.
   - Describe design of market mechanisms and experimental simulation of their performances.
   - Examine agents in context-aware ubiquitous environments: architectures and applications.

9. **The Effect of EC on Organizational Structures**
   - How has EC changed the organizational structure of firms?
   - How has EC affected procurement and sales departments?
   - What kinds of internal processes can be outsourced?
   - Examine the transformation process and issues involved in changing to a digital enterprise.

SUMMARY

In this chapter you learned about the following EC issues as they relate to the learning objectives.

1. **E-marketplaces and their components.** A marketspace, or e-marketplace, is a virtual market that does not suffer from limitations of space, time, or borders. As such, it can be very effective. Its major components include customers, sellers, products (some digital), infrastructure, front-end processes, back-end activities, electronic intermediaries, other business partners, and support services.

2. **The role of intermediaries.** The role of intermediaries will change as e-markets develop; some will be eliminated (disintermediation), others will change their roles and prosper (reintermediation). In the B2B area, for example, e-distributors connect manufacturers with buyers by aggregating electronic catalogs of many suppliers. New value-added services that range from content creation to syndication are mushrooming.

3. **The major types of e-marketplaces.** In the B2C area, there are storefronts and e-malls. In the B2B area, there are private and public e-marketplaces, which may be vertical (within one industry) or horizontal (across different industries). Different types of portals provide access to e-marketplaces.

4. **Electronic catalogs, search engines, and shopping carts.** The major mechanisms in e-markets are electronic catalogs, search engines, software (intelligent) agents, and electronic shopping carts. These mechanisms facilitate EC by providing a user-friendly shopping environment.

5. **Types of auctions and their characteristics.** In forward auctions, bids from buyers are placed sequentially, either in increasing (English and Yankee) mode or in decreasing (Dutch and free-fall) mode. In reverse auctions, buyers place an RFQ and suppliers submit offers in one or several rounds. In "name-your-own-price" auctions, buyers specify how much they are willing to pay for a product or service and an intermediary tries to find a supplier to fulfill the request.

6. **The benefits and limitations of auctions.** The major benefits for sellers are the ability to reach many buyers, to sell quickly, and to save on commissions to intermediaries. Buyers have a chance to obtain bargains and collectibles while shopping from their homes. The major limitation is the possibility of fraud.

7. **Bartering and negotiating.** Electronic bartering can greatly facilitate the swapping of goods and services among organizations, thanks to improved search and matching capabilities, which is done in bartering exchanges. Software agents can facilitate online negotiation.

8. **The role of m-commerce.** Mobile commerce is emerging as a phenomenon that can provide Internet access to millions of people. It also creates new location-related applications.

9. **Competition in the digital economy.** Competition in online markets is very intense due to the increased power of buyers, the ability to find the lowest price, and the ease of switching to another vendor. Global competition has increased as well.

10. **The impact of e-markets on organizations.** All functional areas of an organization are affected by e-markets. Broadly, e-markets improve direct marketing and transform and redefine organizations. Direct marketing (manufacturers to customers) and one-to-one marketing and advertising are becoming the norm, and mass customization and personalization are taking off. Production is moving to a build-to-order model, changing supply chain relationships and reducing cycle time. Virtual manufacturing is also on the rise. Financial systems are becoming more efficient as they become networked with other business functions, and the human resources activities of recruiting, evaluation, and training are being managed more efficiently due to employees' interactions with machines.

KEY TERMS

Auction	59	Disintermediation	53	Electronic shopping cart	58
Back end	45	Double auction	62	Forward auction	61
Bartering	63	Dynamic pricing	60	Front end	45
Bartering exchange	64	E-bartering (electronic bartering)	64	Infomediaries	51
Build-to-order (pull system)	77	E-distributor	53	Information portal	49
Buy-side e-marketplace	48	E-mall (online mall)	47	Intermediary	45
Competitive forces model	69	E-marketplace	44	Internet ecosystem	67
Differentiation	68	Electronic auction (e-auction)	59	Location-based commerce (LBC)	65
Digital products	45	Electronic catalog	55	M-business	64

QUESTIONS FOR DISCUSSION

1. Compare marketplaces with marketspaces. What are the advantages and limitations of each?
2. Compare and contrast competition in traditional markets with that in digital markets.
3. Explain why sell-side and buy-side marketplaces in the same company are usually separated, whereas in an exchange they are combined.
4. Discuss the need for portals in EC.
5. Discuss the advantages of dynamic pricing over fixed pricing. What are the potential disadvantages of dynamic pricing?
6. The "name-your-own-price" model is considered a reverse auction. However, this model does not include RFQs or consecutive bidding. Why is it called a reverse auction?
7. Discuss the advantages of m-commerce over e-commerce.
8. Discuss the relationship of DDM with build-to-order.

INTERNET EXERCISES

1. Visit **bluenile.com**, **diamond.com**, and **jewelry exchange.com**. Compare the sites. Comment on the similarities and the differences.
2. Go to **cisco.com**, **google.com**, and **cio.com** and locate information about the status of the "virtual close." Write a report based on your findings.
3. Visit **ticketmaster.com**, **ticketonline.com**, and other sites that sell event tickets online. Assess the competition in online ticket sales. What services do the different sites provide?
4. Examine how bartering is conducted online at **tradeaway.com**, **buyersbag.com**, **u-exchange.com**, and **intagio.com**. Compare the functionalities and ease of use of these sites.
5. Enter **pages.ebay.com/wireless/** and investigate the use of "anywhere wireless." Review the wireless devices and find out how they work.
6. Enter **mfgquote.com** and review the process by which buyers can send RFQs to merchants of their choice. Evaluate all of the online services provided by the company. Write a report based on your findings.
7. Enter **bloomsburgcarpet.com**. Explain how the site solves the problem of sending carpet sample books to representatives all over the country. What are the special features of the electronic catalogs here? (*Hint:* It might be useful to read Kapp 2001.)
8. Enter **respond.com** and send a request for a product or a service. Once you receive replies, select the best deal. You have no obligation to buy. Write a short report based on your experience.
9. Enter **onstar.com** and review its services. Comment on the usability of each service.
10. Enter **yahoo.com** and find what personalization methods it uses.
11. Enter Timberland Boot Studio (**timberland.com**) and design a pair of boots. Compare it to building your own sneakers at **nike.com**.

TEAM ASSIGNMENTS AND ROLE PLAYING

1. Have several teams each review Porter's (2001) and Bako's (1998) articles. Each team member will research one of the issues raised in the papers (e.g., competition, disintermediation, and Internet impacts) in light of recent developments in the economy and the e-commerce field.

2. Reread the opening case and discuss the following:

   a. Discuss the key success factors for Blue Nile.

   b. Amazon.com makes only a 15 percent margin on the products it sells. This enables Amazon.com to sell diamond earrings for $1,000 (traditional jewelers charge $1,700 for the same). Do you think that Amazon.com will succeed in selling this type of jewelry as Blue Nile did in selling expensive engagement rings?

   c. Competition between Blue Nile and Amazon.com will continue to increase. In your opinion, which one will win (visit their Web sites and see how they sell jewelry).

   d. Why is "commoditization" so important in the diamond business?

   e. Compare the following three sites: **diamond.com**, **ice.com**, and **bluenile.com**.

   f. Follow the performance of Blue Nile's stock since 2003 (symbol: NILE).

Real-World Case

WAL-MART LEADS RFID ADOPTION

In the first week of April 2004, Wal-Mart (*walmart.com*) launched its first live test of RFID tracing technology. Using one distribution center and seven stores, 21 products from participating vendors were used in the pilot test.

In the pilot application, passive RFID chips with small antennae were attached to cases and pallets. When passed near an RFID "reader," the chip activated, and its unique product identifier code was transmitted back to an inventory control system. Cases and pallets containing the 21 products featuring RFID tags were delivered to the distribution center in Sanger, Texas, where RFID readers installed at the dock doors notified both shippers and Wal-Mart what products had entered the Wal-Mart distribution center and where the products were stored. RFID readers were also installed in other places, such as conveyor belts, so that each marked case could be tracked. The readers used by Wal-Mart have an average range of 15 feet. (See Chapter 7 for more on how RFID works.)

Wal-Mart set a January 2005 target for its top 100 suppliers to place RFID tags on cases and pallets destined for Wal-Mart stores. Wal-Mart believed that the implementation of the pilot scheme will pave the way for achieving this goal. According to Linda Dillman, CIO at Walmart, the company's RFID strategy was a success in that by the end of January the required RFID systems were in place and many of Wal-Mart's suppliers were collecting data on the delivery of their products (IDTechEX 2005). The system is expected to improve flows along the supply chain, reduce theft, increase sales, reduce inventory costs (by eliminating both overstocking and understocking), and provide visibility and accuracy throughout Wal-Mart's supply chain. By January 2007, Wal-Mart expects 630 suppliers to be on the system (nearly doubling the 330 in January 2006).

Although some of Wal-Mart's suppliers have been late in implementing the system, it is clear that if the pilot is successful (and so far it is) RFID will become an industry standard. After all, nearly $70 billion is lost in the retail sector in the United States every year due to products getting lost in the supply chain or being stored in wrong places.

In addition to requiring RFID from its suppliers, Wal-Mart is installing the technology internally. According to Scherago (2006), more than 2,000 Wal-Mart stores were RFID-enabled with gate readers and hand-helds at loading docs, the entrance, stockrooms, and the sales floor by the end of 2006.

The next step in Wal-Mart's pilot is to mark each individual item with a tag. This plan raises a possible privacy issue: What if the tags are not removed from the products? People fear that they will be tracked after leaving the store. Wal-Mart also can use RFIDs for many other applications. For example, it could attach tags to shoppers' children, so if they are lost in the megastore they could be tracked in seconds.

Retailers such as Wal-Mart believe that the widespread implementation of RFID technology marks a revolutionary change in supply chain management, much as the introduction of bar codes was seen as revolutionary two decades ago.

The RFID initiative is an integral part of improving the company's supply chain (Scherago 2006). The RFID along with a new EDI will improve the collaboration with the suppliers and help reduce inventories. According to Ferguson (2006), Wal-Mart's new CIO has said that he will stand behind the RFID technology.

Sources: Condensed from Lundquist (2003), *BusinessWeek* Online (2004), IDTechEX (2005), Ferguson (2006), Scherago (2006), and Kaiser (2004).

Questions

1. Assuming that the cost of RFID is low (less than $0.05 per item), what advantages can you see for tagging individual items in each store? Is it necessary to do so?
2. Find some information regarding the advantages of RFIDs over regular bar codes.
3. Is this an e-business application? Why or why not? If it is, what business model is being used?
4. What are some of the business pressures driving the use of RFID in retailing?

REFERENCES

123jump.com. "Bidz.com" March 17, 2006. **123jump.com/ipo/ipo_view/BIDZ/Bidz.com?PHPSESSID=5a408d8210836e2ca9569498a39682b5** (accessed August 2006).

Anke, J., and D. Sundaram. "Personalization Techniques and Their Application," in Khosrow-Pour (2006).

Bajari, P., and A. Hortacsu. "Economic Insights from Internet Auctions." *Journal of Economic Literature* (June 2004).

Bakos, Y. "The Emerging Role of Electronic Marketplaces on the Internet." *Communications of the ACM* (August 1998).

Bauknecht, K., et al. *E-Commerce and Web Technologies.* New York: Springer, 2002.

Beynon-Davies, P. *@-business.* New York: Palgrave-Macmillan, 2004.

Bichler, M., G. Kersten, and C. Weinhardt. "Electronic Negotiations: Foundations, Systems and Experiments." *Introduction to the Special Issue of Group Decision and Negotiation,* 12 (May–December 2003).

Blecker, T., et al. *Information and Management Systems for Product Customization.* New York: Springer, 2005.

Blecker, T. "Product Configuration Systems," in Khosrow-Pour (2006a).

Blecker, T. "Internet Technologies in Factory Automation," in Khosrow-Pour (2006b).

Bloch, M., Y. Pigneur, and A. Segev. "Leveraging Electronic Commerce for Competitive Advantage: A Business Value Framework." *Proceedings of the Ninth International Conference on EDI-IOS,* June 1996, Bled, Slovenia.

Bluenile.com. "Blue Nile Launches New Interactive Diamond Search." March 27, 2006. **bluenile.com/pressreleases/03_27_2006.asp** (accessed September 2006).

Brandon, E. "Finding an Apartment on Craigslist: Five Tips." *U.S. News and World Report,* July 10, 2006.

BusinessWeek Online. "Business Week's Hot Growth Companies: Blue Nile," 2006. **businessweek.com/hot_growth/2006/company/10.htm** (accessed August 2006).

BusinessWeek Online. "Talking RFID with Wal-Mart's CIO." *BusinessWeek* Online, February 4, 2004. **businessweek.com/technology/content/feb2004/tc2004024_3168_tc165.htm** (accessed February 2005).

Choi, S. Y., and A. B. Whinston. *The Internet Economy: Technology and Practice.* Austin, TX: Smartecon Publishing, 2000.

Copeland, M. V. "The Big Guns' Next Target: eBay." *CNNMoney.com,* January 31, 2006. **money.cnn.com/magazines/business2/business2_archive/2006/01/01/8368106/index.htm** (accessed November 2006).

Cox, B. G., and W. Koelzer. *Internet Marketing: Strategy, Implementation, and Practice,* 3d ed. Upper Saddle River, NJ: Prentice Hall, 2006.

Craigslist.org. "Craigslist Fact Sheet." 2006. **craigslist.org/about/pr/factsheet.html** (accessed November 2006).

Deans, P. C. *E-Commerce and M-Commerce Technologies.* Hershey, PA: Idea Group, Inc., 2005.

Dekleva, S. "M-Business: Economy Driver or a Mess?" *Communications of the AIS* (February 2004).

Drucker, P. *Managing in the Next Society.* New York: Truman Talley Books, 2002.

E-Market Services. (2006). "Why Use E-Markets?" *E-marketservices.com.* **emarketservices.com/templates/Page_434.aspx** (accessed August 2006).

Ensher, E. A., E. Grant-Vallone, and T. R. Nielson. "Tales from the Hiring Line." *Organizational Dynamics* (October–December 2002).

Feeny, D. "Making Business Sense of the E-Opportunity." *MIT Sloan Management Review* (Winter 2001).

Ferguson, R. B. "Wal-Mart's New CIO Says He'll Back RFID." *eWeek*, August 13, 2006. **eweek.com/article2/0,1759,1949396,00.asp?kc=EWRSS03119TX1K0000 594** (accessed November 2006).

Financial Analysts Meeting, Seattle, Washington, July 23, 1998.

Gallaugher, J. M. "E-Commerce and the Undulating Distribution Channel." *Communications of the ACM* (July 2002).

Guan, S. U. "E-Commerce Agents and Payment Systems," in Khosrow-Pour (2006).

IDTechEX. "RFID Progress at Wal-Mart." October 1, 2005. **idtechex.com/products/en/articles/00000161.asp** (accessed August 2007).

Intel. "BNSF: Intel® Centrino™ Mobile Technology-Based Notebook Usage Drives Efficiencies, Cost Savings at Leading Railroad." June 2005. **intel.com/cd/00/00/22/34/223434_223434.pdf** (accessed March 2007).

Kaiser, E. "Wal-Mart Starts RFID Test." *Forbes.com*, April 30, 2004. **forbes.com/home/newswire/2004/04/30/rtr1355059.html** (accessed February 2005).

Kapp, K. "A Framework for Successful E-technology Implementation: Understand, Simplify, Automate." *Journal of Organizational Excellence* (Winter 2001).

Khosrow-Pour, M. (ed.). *Encyclopedia of E-Commerce, E-Government, and Mobile Commerce.* Hershey, PA: Idea Group Reference, 2006.

Kioses, E., K. Pramatari, and G. Doukidis. "Factors Affecting Perceived Impact of E-Marketplaces." *Proceedings of the 19th Bled eConference,* Bled, Slovenia, June 5–7, 2006.

Lei, P. "M-Commerce Opportunities," in Khosrow-Pour (2006).

Lepouras, G., and C. Vassilakis. "Adaptive Virtual Reality Shopping Malls," in Khosrow-Pour (2006).

Li, E. Y., and T. C. Du. *Advances in Electronic Business, Volume 1.* Hershey, PA: Idea Group Publishing, 2004.

Lim, G. G., and J. K. Lee. "Buyer Carts for B2B EC: The B-Cart Approach." *Organizational Computing and Electronic Commerce* (July–September 2003).

Lundquist, E. "Wal-Mart Gets It Right." *E-Week*, July 14, 2003.

Malhotra, R., and D. K. Malhotra, "The Impact of Internet and E-Commerce on the Evolving Business Models in the Financial Services Industry," *International Journal of Electronic Business*, 4, no. 1 (2006).

Microsoft Corp. "RadioShack.ca Increases Customer Satisfaction While Decreasing Management Time and Cost with Commerce Server 2002." *Microsoft.com*, July 1, 2002. **microsoft.com/resources/casestudies/CaseStudy.asp?CaseStudyID=13381** (accessed February 2005).

Mullaney, T. J. "E-Biz Strikes Again!" *BusinessWeek*, May 10, 2004. **businessweek.com/magazine/content/04_19/b3882601.htm** (accessed September 2006).

Naughton, J. "Web Sites That Changed the World." *The Hindu*, August 14, 2006. **hindu.com/holnus/008200608141150.htm** (accessed November 2006).

Nissanoff, D. *Future Shop: How the New Auction Culture Will Revolutionize the Way We Buy, Sell, and Get Things We Really Want.* New York: The Penguin Press, 2006.

Norris, G. *E-Business & ERP: Transforming the Enterprise with E-Business & ERP: Rapid Implementation and Project Planning Set.* New York: John Wiley & Sons, 2005.

O'Buyonge, A. A., and L. Chen. "E-Health Dot-Coms' Critical Success Factors," in Khosrow-Pour (2006).

OnStar. "GM to Double Production of OnStar-Equipped Vehicles: Customer Demand Prompts GM Decision." September 21, 2004. **onstar.internetpressroom.com/prr_releases_detail.cfm?id=297** (accessed February 2005). **pbg.com** (accessed November 2004).

Porter, M. E. "Strategy and the Internet." *Harvard Business Review* (March 2001).

Radio Advertising Bureau. "Direct Advertising." 2005. **rab.com/public/media/detail.cfm?id=7** (accessed March 2007).

Rhey, E. "Pepsi Refreshes, Wirelessly." *PC Magazine*, September 17, 2002.

Saarinen, T., M. Tinnild, and A. Tseng (eds.). *Managing Business in a Multi-Channel World.* Hershey, PA: Idea Group, Inc., 2006.

Sadeh, N. *Mobile Commerce: New Technologies, Services and Business Models.* New York: John Wiley & Sons, April 2002.

Scherago, D. "Wal-Smart." *Retail Technology Quarterly*, January 2006.

Schmitz, V., J. Leukel, F. D. Dorloff. "Do E-Catalog Standards Support Advanced Processes in B2B E-Commerce?" *Proceedings of the 38th Hawaii International Conference on System Sciences*, Big Island, Hawaii, January 3–6, 2005.

Shi, N. (ed.). *Mobile Commerce Applications.* Hershey, PA: The Idea Group Inc., 2004.

Singh, A. M. "Evolution of Marketing to E-Marketing," in Khosrow-Pour (2006).

Southwick, K. (2004). "Diagnosing WebMD: Ultimate Dot-Com Survivor Faces New Challenges." *CNetNews.com*, May 11, 2004. **news.com.com/Diagnosing+WebMD/2009–1017_3–5208510.html** (accessed September 2006).

Suomi, R. "Governing Health Care with IT," in Khosrow-Pour (2006).

Telecom Trends International. "Mobile Commerce Takes-Off: Market Trends and Forecasts." **telecomtrends.net/pr_MIIS-1.htm** (accessed November 2004).

Telus Mobility. "Wireless Security Primer." *Telus Mobility*, August 2002. **telusmobility.com/pdf/business_solutions/security_primer.pdf** (accessed November 2004).

Time Magazine. "50 Coolest Web Sites 2006." *Time Magazine*, August 23, 2006.

Tsai, M. "Online Retailers See Improved Site Search as Sales Tool." *Dow Jones Newswires*, August 20, 2004.

Turban, E., et al. *Information Technology for Management*, 6th ed. New Jersey: Wiley, 2007.

Varadarajan, P. R., and M. S. Yadav. "Marketing Strategy and the Internet: An Organizing Framework." *Academy of Marketing Science*, 30, no. 4 (Fall 2002).

Webopedia. "Infomediary." 2006. **webopedia.com/TERM/I/infomediary.html** (accessed November 2006).

Wikipedia. "Business-to-Consumer Electronic Commerce." 2006a. **en.wikipedia.org/wiki/Business-to-consumer_electronic_commerce** (accessed November 2006).

Wikipedia, "i-Mode." 2006b. **en.wikipedia.org/wiki/I-mode** (accessed August 2006).

Wind, Y. "The Challenge of Customization in Financial Services." *Communications of the ACM* (2001).

Yarom, I., C. V. Goldman, and J. S. Rosenschein. "The Role of Middle-Agents in Electronic Commerce." *IEEE Intelligent Systems* (November–December 2003).

Zwass, V. "Electronic Commerce and Organizational Innovation: Aspects and Opportunities." *International Journal of Electronic Commerce*, 7, no. 3 (2003).

BUILD-TO-ORDER PRODUCTION

The concept of *build-to-order* means that a firm starts to make a product or service only after an order for it is placed. It is also known as *demand-driven manufacturing (DDM), customization, personalization,* and *pull technology.* This concept is as old as commerce itself and was the only method of production until the Industrial Revolution. According to this concept, if a person needs a pair of shoes, he or she goes to a shoemaker, who takes the person's measurements. The person negotiates quality, style, and price and pays a down payment. The shoemaker buys the materials and makes a customized product for the customer. Customized products are expensive, and it takes a long time to finish them. The Industrial Revolution introduced a new way of thinking about production.

The Industrial Revolution started with the concept of dividing work into small parts. Such *division of labor* makes the work simpler, requiring less training for employees. It also allows for *specialization.* Different employees become experts in executing certain tasks. Because the work segments are simpler, it is easier to *automate* them. As machines were invented to make products, the concept of *build-to-market* developed. To implement build-to-market, it was necessary to design standard products, produce them, store them, and then sell them.

The creation of standard products by automation drove prices down, and demand accelerated. The solution to the problem of increased demand was *mass production*. In mass production, a company produces large amounts of standard products at a very low cost and then "pushes" them to consumers. Thus began the need for sales and marketing organizations. Specialized sales forces resulted in increased competition and the desire to sell in wider, and more remote, markets. This model also required the creation of large factories and specialized departments such as accounting and personnel to manage the activities in the factories. With mass production, factory workers personally did not know the customers and frequently did not care about customers' needs or product quality. However, the products were inexpensive and good enough to fuel demand, and thus the concept became a dominant one. Mass production also required inventory systems at various places in the supply chain, which were based on forecasted demand. If the forecasted demand was wrong, the inventories were incorrect. Thus, companies were always trying to achieve the right balance between not having enough inventory to meet demand and having too much inventory on hand.

As society became more affluent, the demand for customized products increased. Manufacturers had to meet the demand for customized products to satisfy customers. As long as the demand for customized product was small, it could be met. Cars, for example, have long been produced using this model. Customers were asked to pay a premium for customization and wait a long time to receive the customized product, and they were willing to do so. Note that the process starts with *product configuration* (Blecker 2006); namely, the customer decides what the product is going to look like, what operations it will perform, and what capabilities it will have (e.g., the *functionalities* in Dell).

Slowly, the demand for customized products and services increased. Burger King introduced the concept of "having it your way," and manufacturers sought ways to provide customized products in large quantities, which is the essence of *mass customization*, as pioneered by Dell. Such solutions were usually enhanced by some kind of information technology. The introduction of customized personal computers (PCs) by Dell was so successful that many other industries wanted to try mass customization.

EC can facilitate customization, even mass customization. In many cases, EC is doing it via personalization (Anke and Sundaram 2006). To understand how companies can use EC for customization, let's first compare mass production, also known as a *push system*, and mass customization, also known as a *pull system*, as shown in Exhibit 2A.1.

Notice that one important area in the supply chain is order taking. Using EC, a customer can self-configure the desired product online. The order is received in seconds. Once the order is verified and payment arranged, the order is sent electronically to the production floor. This saves time and money. For complex products, customers may collaborate in real time with the manufacturer's designers, as is done at Cisco Systems. Again, time and money are saved and errors are reduced due to better communication and collaboration. Other contributions of EC are that the customers' needs are visible to all partners in the order fulfillment chain (fewer delays, faster response time), inventories are reduced due to rapid communication, and digitizable products and services can be delivered electronically.

A key issue in mass customization is knowing what the customers want. In many cases, the seller can simply ask the customer to configure the product or service. In other cases, the seller tries to predict what the customer wants. EC is very helpful in this area due to the use of online market research methods such as collaborative filtering (see Chapter 4 and Holweg and Pil 2001). Using collaborative filtering,

EXHIBIT 2A.1   Push Versus Pull Production Systems

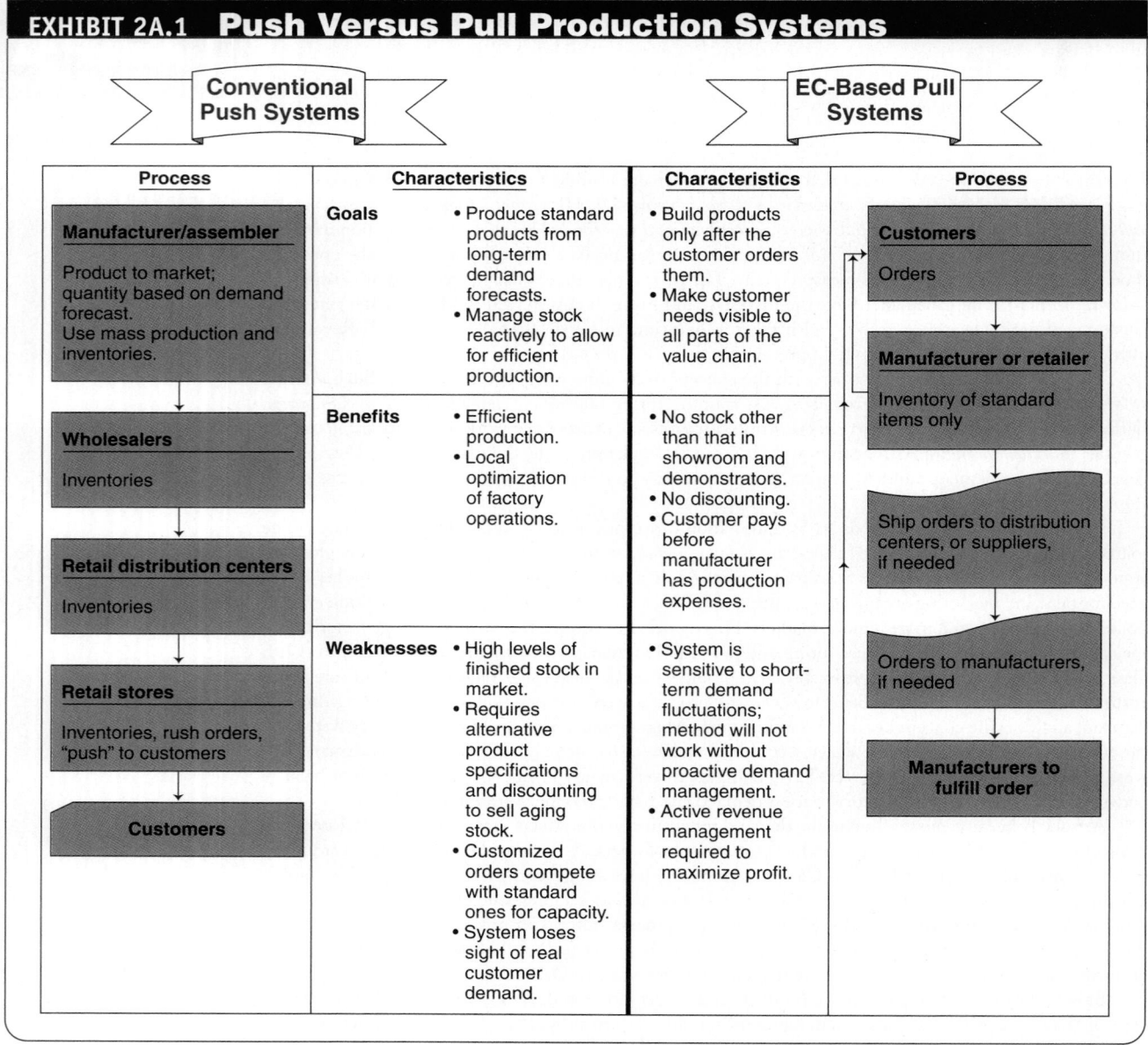

a company can discover what each customer wants without asking the customer directly. Such market research is accomplished more cheaply by a machine than by human researchers.

From the production point of view, EC also can enable mass customization. In the factory, for example, IT in general and e-commerce in particular can help in expediting the production changeover from one item to another. Also, because most mass production is based on the assembly of standard components, EC can help a company create the production process for a product in minutes and identify needed components and their location. Furthermore, a production schedule can be generated automatically, and needed resources can be deployed, including money. This is why many industries, and particularly the auto manufacturers, are planning to move to build-to-order using EC. By doing so, they are expecting huge cost reductions, shorter order-to-delivery times, and lower inventory costs.

Mass customization on a large scale is not easy to attain (Zipkin 2001; Warschat et al. 2005), but if performed properly, it may become the dominant model in many industries.

REFERENCES

Anke, J., and D. Sundaram. "Personalization Techniques and Their Application," in Khosrow-Pour (2006).

Blecker, T. "Product Configuration Systems," in Khosrow-Pour (2006).

Holweg, M., and F. Pil. "Successful Build-to-Order Strategies Start with the Customer." *MIT Sloan Management Journal* 43, no. 1 (2001).

Khosrow-Pour, M. (ed.). Encyclopedia of E-Commerce, E-Government, and Mobile Commerce. Hershey, PA: Idea Group Reference, 2006.

Warschat, J., M. Kurumluoglu, and R. Nostdal. "Enabling IT for Mass Customization." *International Journal of Mass Customization,* 1, nos. 2–3 (2005).

Zipkin, P. "The Limits of Mass Customization." *MIT Sloan Management Review* (Spring 2001).

RETAILING IN ELECTRONIC COMMERCE: PRODUCTS AND SERVICES

Learning Objectives

Upon completion of this chapter, you will be able to:

1. Describe electronic retailing (e-tailing) and its characteristics.

2. Define and describe the primary e-tailing business models.

3. Describe how online travel and tourism services operate and their impact on the industry.

4. Discuss the online employment market, including its participants, benefits, and limitations.

5. Describe online real estate services.

6. Discuss online stock-trading services.

7. Discuss cyberbanking and online personal finance.

8. Describe on-demand delivery by e-grocers.

9. Describe the delivery of digital products and online entertainment.

10. Discuss various e-tail consumer aids, including comparison-shopping aids.

11. Identify the critical success factors and failure avoidance tactics for direct online marketing and e-tailing.

12. Describe reintermediation, channel conflict, and personalization in e-tailing.

Content

Amazon.com: Taking E-Tailing to the Next Level

AMAZON.COM: TAKING E-TAILING TO THE NEXT LEVEL

The Opportunity

It was not a business problem but an opportunity that faced entrepreneur Jeff Bezos: He saw the huge potential for retail sales over the Internet and selected books as the most logical product for e-tailing. In July 1995, Bezos started Amazon.com, an e-tailing pioneer, offering books via an electronic catalog from its Web site (*amazon.com*).

Over the years, the company has recognized that it must continually enhance its business models and electronic store by expanding product selection, improving the customer's experience, and adding services and alliances. Also, the company recognized the importance of order fulfillment and warehousing. It invested hundreds of millions of dollars in building physical warehouses designed for shipping small packages to hundreds of thousands of customers. Amazon.com's challenge was, and remains, how to succeed where many have failed—namely, how to compete in selling consumer products online, showing profit and a reasonable rate of return on the huge investment it has made.

Reaching Out to Customers

In addition to its initial electronic bookstore, Amazon.com has expanded its offerings to a vast array of products and services (see figure), segmented into three broad categories: media (books, music, DVDs, videos, software, computer games, rentals, etc.); electronics and other merchandise (electronics, office supplies, photography, toys, pet supplies, clothing, homewares, jewelry, health, gourmet groceries, etc.); and other (nonretail activities such as Web services, Amazon Enterprise Solutions, cobranded credit cards, etc.). Key features of the Amazon.com superstore are easy browsing, searching, and ordering; useful product information, reviews, recommendations, and personalization; broad selection; low prices; secure payment systems; and efficient order fulfillment.

The Amazon.com Web site has a number of features that make the online shopping experience more enjoyable. Its "Gift Ideas" section features seasonally appropriate gift ideas and services. Through its "E-Cards" section, customers can send free animated electronic greeting cards to friends and family. AmazonConnect allows customers to select their favorite authors, read about them, and then receive e-mails from those authors. A recent foray into digital content, Amazon Fishbowl, is a weekly 30-minute online Web show, hosted by Bill Maher, featuring interviews with authors, entertainers, movie stars, musicians, and the like. Ads featuring products relating to the guests are shown alongside the video window, thus enabling Amazon to further showcase and promote books, music, and videos, which still comprise the majority of Amazon's online sales.

The Vast Range of Products and Services at Amazon

Amazon.com also offers various marketplace services. Amazon Auctions hosts and operates auctions on behalf of individuals and small businesses throughout the world. The Shops service hosts electronic storefronts for a monthly fee, offering small businesses the opportunity to have customized storefronts supported by the richness of Amazon.com's order-fulfillment processing. Customers can use Web-enabled cell phones, PDAs, or Pocket PCs to access Amazon.com and shop anywhere, anytime. Amazon.com also can be accessed via AT&T's #121 voice service.

Amazon.com is recognized as an online leader in creating sales through customer intimacy and customer relationship management (CRM) which are cultivated by informative marketing front ends and one-to-one advertisements. For example, to support CRM Amazon.com provides details of movie screenings in selected areas. In addition, sales are supported by highly automated, efficient back-end systems. When a customer makes a return visit to Amazon.com, a cookie file (see Chapter 4) identifies the user and says, for example, "Welcome back, Sarah Shopper," and then proceeds to recommend new books from the same genre of previous customer purchases and a range of other items. The company tracks customer purchase histories and sends purchase recommendations via e-mail to cultivate repeat buyers. It also provides detailed product descriptions and ratings to help consumers make informed purchase decisions. These efforts usually result in satisfactory shopping experiences and encourage customers to return. The site has an efficient search engine and other shopping aids. Amazon.com has a superb warehousing system. This system, which is described in Chapter 13, gives the company an advantage over the competition.

Customers can personalize their accounts and manage orders online with the patented "1-Click" order feature. This personalized service includes an *electronic wallet* (see Chapter 12), which enables shoppers to place an order in a secure manner without the need to enter their address, credit card number, and other information each time they shop. 1-Click also allows customers to view their order status, cancel or combine orders that have not yet entered the shipping process, edit the shipping options and addresses on unshipped orders, modify the payment method for unshipped orders, and more.

In 1997, Amazon.com started an extensive associates program. By 2006, the company had more than 2 million partners worldwide that refer customers to Amazon.com. Amazon.com pays a 4 to 10 percent commission on any resulting sale. Starting in 2000, Amazon.com has undertaken alliances with major "trusted partners" that provide knowledgeable entry into new markets. For example, Amazon.com's alliance with Carsdirect.com allows it to sell cars online. Clicking "Photo Services" on the Amazon.com Web site takes the visitor to a site Amazon.com operates jointly with Shutterfly; clicking on "Office Supplies" allows customers either to select from Amazon's office supplies or to browse those of Office Depot; clicking on "Health and Personal Care" allows customers to benefit from great deals offered by Weight Watchers. In yet another extension of its services, in September 2001 Amazon signed an agreement with Borders Group Inc., providing Amazon.com's users with the option of picking up books, CDs, and other merchandise at Borders' physical bookstores (In-Store pickup). Amazon.com also is becoming a Web fulfillment contractor for national chains such as Target and Circuit City. Amazon.com also has its own search engine, called A9.com (*a9.com*), and offers a range of Web services to developers (Amazon Web Services).

The Results

Amazon.com maintained its position as the number one e-tailer in 2006, generating revenues of $8.5 billion in 2005, with a net profit of $359 million for the same period. Annual sales for Amazon.com have trended upward, driven largely by product diversification and its international presence. This pioneer e-tailer now offers over 17 million book, music, and DVD/video titles to some 20 million customers. Amazon.com also offers several features for international customers, including over 1 million Japanese-language titles.

In January 2002, Amazon.com declared its *first* profit—for the 2001 fourth quarter. Since then, the company has maintained profitability. However, the company's financial success is by no means assured. Despite increasing a sales and net profits, in percentage terms, Amazon has seen a drop in profitability in 2006, attributed to huge spending on further developing its technology infrastructure and its investment in the Amazon Prime discount shipping program. Like all businesses—and especially e-tailing ones—Amazon.com, the king of e-tailers, which has shown all others the potential of B2C EC, will continue to walk the fine line of profitability, at least in the short run.

Sources: Compiled from *BusinessWire* (2006), *CNNMoney.com* (2006a), Parker (2006), and *Internetretailer.com* (2006a).

WHAT WE CAN LEARN . . .

The case of Amazon.com, the most recognized e-tailer in the world, demonstrates some of the features and managerial issues related to e-tailing. It demonstrates the evolution of e-tailing, some of the problems encountered by e-tailers, and the solutions employed by Amazon.com to expand its business. It is also indicative of a key trend in Internet retailing: that the biggest online retailers are still growing and becoming more dominant, with the top 100 e-retailers accounting for 54.5 percent ($59.6 billion) of all online sales in 2005 (Brohan 2006). However, some experts argue that online retailers will need to better understand customer behaviors and preferences if they are to achieve a better convergence between technological capability and customer desires (*Internetretailer.com* 2006b). In this chapter, we will look at the delivery of both products and services online to individual customers. We also will discuss e-tailing successes and failures.

3.1 INTERNET MARKETING AND ELECTRONIC RETAILING

The Amazon.com case illustrates how commerce can be conducted on the Internet. Indeed, the amount and percentage of goods and services sold on the Internet is increasing rapidly, despite the failure of many dot-com companies. According to data from eMarketer (cited by Grau 2005), approximately three in four Internet users age 14 and over shop online and/or research offline sales online. With estimates of 175 to 180 million Internet users in the United States, this suggests that in 2006 there were approximately 118 million online shoppers (Grau 2005). However, as the number of Internet users reaches saturation, the rate of increase of online shoppers will slow. One of the challenges for electronic retailers, therefore, is to increase the amount spent online. As discussed in Chapters 1 and 2, companies have many reasons to market and sell their goods and services online. Innovative marketing strategies and a deep understanding of online consumer behavior and preferences will be required for sustained success in a competitive online environment.

This chapter presents an overview of Internet retailing, its diversity, prospects, and limitations. (For more detailed analysis, see Cox and Koelzer 2004 and Kimiloglu 2004.) Retailing, especially when conducted in a new medium, must be supported by an understanding of consumer buying behavior, market research, and advertising, topics that will be presented in Chapter 4. Let's begin our discussion of EC products and services with an overview of electronic retailing.

OVERVIEW OF ELECTRONIC RETAILING

A retailer is a sales *intermediary*, a seller that operates between manufacturers and customers. Even though many manufacturers sell directly to consumers, they supplement their sales through wholesalers and retailers (a *multichannel approach*). In the physical world, retailing is done in stores (or factory outlets) that customers must visit in order to make a purchase. Companies that produce a large number of products, such as Procter & Gamble, must use retailers for efficient distribution. However, even if a company sells only a relatively few products (e.g., Kodak), it still may need retailers to reach a large number of customers.

Catalog sales offer companies and customers a relief from the constraints of space and time: Catalogs free a retailer from the need for a physical store from which to distribute products, and customers can browse catalogs on their own time. With the ubiquity of the Internet, the next logical step was for retailing to move online. Retailing conducted over the Internet is called **electronic retailing**, or e-tailing, and those who conduct retail business online are called **e-tailers**. E-tailing also can be conducted through auctions. E-tailing makes it easier for a manufacturer to sell directly to the customer, cutting out the intermediary (e.g., Dell and Godiva in Chapter 1). This chapter examines the various types of e-tailing and related issues.

electronic retailing (e-tailing)
Retailing conducted online, over the Internet.

e-tailers
Retailers who sell over the Internet.

The concept of retailing and e-tailing implies sales of goods and/or services to *individual customers*—that is, B2C EC. However, the distinction between B2C and B2B EC is not always clear. For example, Amazon.com sells books mostly to individuals (B2C), but it also sells to corporations (B2B). Amazon.com's chief rival in selling books online, Barnes & Noble (barnesandnoble.com), has a special division that caters only to business customers. Wal-Mart (walmart.com) sells to both individuals and businesses (via Sam's Club). Dell sells its computers to both consumers and businesses from dell.com, Staples sells to both markets at staples.com, and insurance sites sell to both individuals and corporations.

SIZE AND GROWTH OF THE B2C MARKET

The statistics for the volume of B2C EC sales, including forecasts for future sales, come from many sources. Reported amounts of online sales *deviate substantially* based on how the numbers are derived, and thus it is often difficult to obtain a consistent and coherent picture of the growth of EC. Some of the variation stems from the use of different definitions and classifications of EC. For example, when tallying financial data some analysts include the investment costs in Internet infrastructure, whereas others include only the value of the actual transactions conducted via the Internet. Another issue is how the items for sale are categorized. Some sources combine certain products and services; others do not. Some sources include online

---

EXHIBIT 3.1   Representative Sources of EC Statistics

AM Research (*amresearch.com*)
BizRate (*bizrate.com*)
Business 2.0 (*business2.com*)
ClickZ Network (*clickz.com*)
Fulcrum Velocity Analytics (*cyberdialogue.com*)
DoubleClick (*doubleclick.com*)
Ecommerce Info Center (*ecominfocenter.com*)
Forrester Research (*forrester.com*)
Gartner (*gartner.com*)
Gomez (*gomez.com*)
IDe (*ide.com*)
JupiterResearch (*jupiterresearch.com*)
Lionbridge (*lionbridge.com*)
Nielsen//Netratings (*nielsen-netratings.com*)
Shop.org (*shop.org*)
StatMarket (*websidestory.com*)
Yankee Group (*yankeegroup.com*)
U.S. Census Bureau (*census.gov/estats*)

---

travel sales in the data for EC retail; others do not. Sometimes different time periods are used in the measurement. When reading data about B2C EC sales, therefore, it is very important that care is taken in interpreting the figures.

The sites listed in Exhibit 3.1 provide statistics on e-tailing as well as on other Internet and EC activities. Typical statistics used in describing e-tailing and consumer behavior include Internet usage by demographic (online sales by age, gender, country, etc.); online sales by item; online sales by vendor; and buying patterns online.

The following are some general statistics about online sales. Data from the U.S. Census Bureau (2006a) suggest that B2C EC grew by some 25.2 percent in 2004 to $71 billion, with estimates of further increases to $88 billion in 2005, an increase of 23.9 percent. This 2005 figure, however, although large in dollar terms and representing extraordinary growth over the past decade, still sees B2C EC sales as representing only about 2.4 percent of total retail sales in the United States. Preliminary data for the first quarter, 2006, show the EC retail figure increased to approximately 2.7 percent of total retail. Data from the U.S. Census Bureau do not include online travel. When travel is included in the data, B2C sales total fall in the range of $165 billion, as estimated by Forrester (Mulpuru 2006), to $176.4 billion, as estimated by ClickZ.com (Burns 2006a). Both these figures suggest that B2C sales continue to grow in excess of 20 percent per annum, with expectations of total sales of $211.4 billion for 2006, with some estimates suggesting that by the end of 2006 online sales could represent 4 percent of total retail sales (*Internetretailer.com* 2006b). This is compared against growth rates of approximately 8.1 percent in total retail sales in the United States (U.S. Census Bureau 2006b). Forrester expects this extraordinary growth rate to continue long term, with estimates of total B2C sales of approximately $329 billion by 2010 (Johnson 2005). Also, profitability is up, and marketing costs per order are declining.

The year 2006, however, could mark an important milestone for B2C EC, with expectations that online retail will surpass $100 billion for the first time (*Internetretailer.com* 2006b).

WHAT SELLS WELL ON THE INTERNET

With approximately 118 million shoppers online in the United States in 2005, e-tailers appreciate the need to provide excellent choice and service to an ever-increasing cohort of potential customers. Hundreds of thousands of items are available on the Web from numerous vendors. The following categories are all selling well online.

Travel

Online travel sales are the largest category of online retail, with estimates of $73.4 billion in sales forecast in 2006 (Burns 2006a). Expedia and Travelocity are major players in this category. Typically, online travel agents offer a range of services, including travel booking, hotel reservations, car rentals, and vacation packages.

Computer Hardware and Software

Dell and Gateway are the major online vendors of computer hardware and software. This industry will see more than $16.8 billion in sales in 2006. People buy lots of hardware and software online; for example, the computer used in preparing this book, together with Microsoft Office and other software, was purchased at Dell. Computer hardware and software is the largest category of products sold online, excluding travel, and is predicted to be the first nontravel category to sell the majority of its goods and services online (54.5 percent by 2010) (*CRMToday* 2006). Computer software is selling particularly well, with an increase in sales of 39 percent in 2006 (*Internetretailer.com* 2006b).

Consumer Electronics

According to the U.S. Census Bureau (2006b), 59 percent of consumer electronics are now sold online, with estimates of up to $4.8 billion in sales online in 2005. Digital cameras, printers, scanners, and wireless devices (including PDAs and cell phones) are just some of the consumer electronics bought online. However, some suggest that consumer electronics will not enjoy quite the same degree of success in online sales as computers, for example, at least in the short term. This is because with some consumer electronics, particularly new products, consumers still express a strong preference to see, touch, and feel before buying. For example, Gateway (gateway.com) has become a leader in sales of plasma screens: Its online presence allows customers to research many brands before buying, and then customers can visit Gateway retail stores to see the screen quality and other features before purchasing. Gateway customers are able to complete the purchase either in-store or online (Baker 2004).

Office Supplies

Gaining accurate data as to the B2C sales of office supplies is sometimes difficult because there is little agreement on what exactly is included in this figure. For example, sales of office supplies at officedepot.com, up 10 percent in 2004, were estimated to be about $13.6 billion (*Internetretailer.com* 2005). However, the U.S. Census Bureau estimates that online sales of office supplies and equipment were about $4 billion in 2004, a substantially lower figure. However, both B2C and B2B sales of office supplies are increasing rapidly, all over the world, as companies increasingly use the Internet to place orders for stationery and the like. In 2006, for example, sales of office supplies were estimated to grow by 54 percent, well ahead of the average for nontravel retail of 25 percent (*Internetretailer.com* 2006b).

Sport and Fitness Goods

Sporting goods sell very well on the Internet. However, it is difficult to measure the exact amount of sales because only a few e-tailers sell sporting goods exclusively online (e.g., fogdog.com). However, experts expected that online sales in the sports and fitness category would increase by 38 percent in 2006 (*Internetretailer.com* 2006b).

Books and Music

Amazon.com and Barnesandnoble.com are the major sellers of books (Amazon.com alone sold approximately $8.5 billion worth of goods, about two-thirds of them books and music, in 2005). However, hundreds of other e-tailers sell books on the Internet, especially specialized books (e.g., technical books, children's books).

Toys

Total retail sales of toys (both traditional and online) dropped by about 4 percent in 2005. However, the proportion of sales of toys sold online increased to about 6 percent in 2005. (Direct Marketing Association 2006). However, there are reports of pleasing growth again in

2006, with sales of toys online continuing to grow ahead of the average, with estimates of an approximately 33 percent increase in 2006 (*Internetretailer.com* 2006b).

Health and Beauty

A large variety of health and beauty products—from vitamins to cosmetics and fragrances—are sold online by most large retailers and by specialty stores. Health and beauty products are one of the fastest-growing categories in terms of online sales, with $800 million in sales of cosmetics and fragrances predicted for 2006 (Burns 2006a). Some forecasts suggest that sales of these items will more than double by 2010 (*CRMToday* 2006).

Entertainment

This is another area where dozens of products, ranging from tickets to events (e.g., ticketmaster.com) to paid fantasy games (see Section 3.8), are embraced by millions of shoppers worldwide. Growth in online sales of event tickets alone is estimated to be growing by approximately 26 percent per year (Burns 2006b). Online event tickets sales reached $3.8 billion in 2005, representing 18.5 percent of total sales (*Infoplease.com* 2006a).

Apparel and Clothing

With the possibility of buying customized shirts, pants, and even shoes, the online sale of apparel also is growing. In 2005, online sales of apparel represented about 5.9 percent of total retail sales in this category (*CRMToday* 2006), with sales of $13.8 billion anticipated for 2006 (*Retailbulletin.com* 2006). This suggests that customers are feeling increasingly comfortable with online purchases, buoyed by guaranteed returns policies and improving features on fitting clothing without first trying it on.

Jewelry

Online sales of jewelry are booming, with online sales rising approximately 27 percent in 2005 to about $172 billion (Burns 2006b; *Marketing.gold.org* 2005). With claims of prices about 40 percent less than would be paid in traditional stores, the trend toward online jewelry sales is likely to continue. Some experts suggest that by 2010 14 percent of all jewelry sales will be online, up from about 5 percent currently (IC-Agency 2005). The largest online jewelry store, Blue Nile, has grown very rapidly and was ranked as the tenth fastest growing company by *BusinessWeek* in 2006 (*BusinessWeek.com* 2006). In addition to the attractive prices, shoppers are benefiting from the huge range of stocked items, certified quality diamonds, detailed information to help educate shoppers about buying diamonds and precious stones, and solid guarantees of returns. Initially it was men who flocked to online jewelry stores, but increasing numbers of women are using the Web to research, comparison shop, and buy.

Cars

The sale of cars over the Internet is just beginning (people still like to "kick the tires"), but could be one of the top sellers on the Internet in the near future. Already, car manufacturers, retailers, and intermediaries that provide related services, both click-and-mortar and pure-play companies, are participating. The business is a multibillion dollar one, involving new and used cars, fleets or rental car companies, and auto parts; the market includes B2B, B2C, C2C, and G2B. Customers like the build-to-order capabilities, but even selling used cars online has advantages and is increasing rapidly. Auctions of antique, used, or new cars are very popular, too. Support services such as financing, warranties, and insurance also are selling well online. Yamada (2004) studies how automobile dealer portals help vehicle makers cut costs and boost profits.

Services

Sales in service industries, especially travel, stock trading, electronic banking, real estate, and insurance, are increasing—more than doubling every year in some cases. According to Bonne (2004), one popular EC activity is online banking and bill paying, which is used by 44 percent of all U.S. Internet users. Eighty-seven percent buy tickets including airline, train, and bus online. Services online are discussed in detail in Sections 3.3 through 3.6.

Pet Supplies

Pet supplies is a new category in the top-seller list, with reports of $700 million in online sales in 2005, 3.2 percent of total spending on pets (*Infoplease.com* 2006a), and forecasts for rapid increases in spending (Pet Product News International 2006). As family pets become more and more integrated as a member of the family, online spending on toys, edible treats, food, pet accessories, and veterinary products and services is soaring.

Others

Many other products, ranging from prescription drugs (see Online File W3.1) to custom-made shoes are offered on the Internet. As more and more retailers sell online, virtually every item that is available in a physical store may be sold online as well. Many of these items are specialized or niche products. The Internet offers an open and global market to shops that are trying to sell specialized products they would not be able to market in any other way (e.g., antique Coca-Cola bottles at antiquebottles.com and tea tree oil at iherb.com).

Some Trends in B2C

Some important trends in B2C EC need to be noted at this point. First, many offline transactions are now heavily influenced by research conducted online, with approximately 85 percent of online shoppers now reporting that they used the Internet to research and influence their offline shopping choices (*Jupitermedia.com* 2006). Furthermore, it is estimated that by 2010, the Internet will influence approximately 50 percent of all retail sales, a significant increase over just 27 percent of all sales in 2005 (*Jupitermedia.com* 2006). Thus, multichannel retailers, those that have a physical presence and an online presence, seem destined to be the winners. They support the convenience of online research and sales, offer excellent order fulfillment and delivery if the sale is completed online, and enable customers to touch and feel and try on an item in a physical store. The need and opportunity to integrate offerings across all channels and to seek incentives for cross-channel sales is seen as an important development into the future (Mulpuru 2006). This becomes extremely important as the numbers of online shoppers reaches saturation, and successful e-tailers will be those who are able to increase the spending of existing buyers rather than purely focusing on attracting new buyers (*Jupitermedia.com* 2006).

Another trend in B2C is the use of rich media in online advertising. For example, virtual reality is used in an online mall (Lepouras and Vassilakis 2006). Scene7.com is a leading vendor in the area. Finally, the use of cell phones to shop online is increasing rapidly. For example, in Japan about 25 percent of all B2C is done from cell phones (see Insights and Additions 3.1).

Insights and Additions 3.1   Mobile B2C Shopping in Japan

Although EC in Japan is only 20 percent of that in the United States, m-commerce in Japan is growing exponentially and now represents the largest amount of m-commerce sales in the world. Over 60 million Japanese are buying over their cell phones while riding the trains, even buying their train tickets. Such shopping is popular with busy single parents, executives, and teenagers (who are doing over 80 percent of their EC shopping from cell phones). Cell phones allow direct communication with consumers; they are the ultimate one-to-one channel (see Chapter 4).

Traditional retailers in Japan, such as 7-Eleven and I Holding Company, have been losing millions of customers to Web shopping companies such as Rakuten Inc. A group of convenience stores and 7-Eleven Japan Co. have set up

7dream.com, offering online services for music, travel, tickets, gifts, and other goods to its 8,000 7-Eleven stores in Japan. Meanwhile pure m-commerce operators such as Xavel Inc. (*xavel.com*) are growing rapidly, forcing traditional retailers such as Marui department stores to expand their e-commerce to include m-commerce.

A major contributor to the success of m-commerce is the spread of 3G high-speed mobile phone services that are offered on a flat-fee (e.g., monthly) basis. According to the Daiwa Institute of Research (reported by Izumi 2006), impulse shopping accounts for most of the purchases that are done on mobile phones, but only if the users are on flat-fee-based service.

Sources: Compiled from Izumi (2006) and PBS.org (2006).

CHARACTERISTICS OF SUCCESSFUL E-TAILING

Many of the same basic principles that apply to retail success also apply to e-tail success. Sound business thinking, visionary leadership, thorough competitive analysis and financial analysis, and the articulation of a well–thought-out EC strategy are essential. So, too, is ensuring appropriate infrastructure, particularly a stable and scalable technology infrastructure to support the online and physical aspects of EC business operations. Newly required capabilities (e.g., capabilities in logistics and distribution) may need to be obtained through external strategic alliances. Offering quality merchandise at good prices, coupled with excellent service, and cross-channel coordination and integration in which customers can almost seamlessly operate between the online and physical environments of a business are also important elements in successful e-tailing. In a sense, the online and traditional channels are not very different. However, e-tailers can offer expanded consumer services not offered by traditional retailers. For a comparison of e-tailing and retailing, see Exhibit 3.2.

With all else being equal in the online environment, goods with the following characteristics are expected to facilitate higher sales volumes:

- High brand recognition (e.g., Lands' End, Dell, Sony)
- A guarantee provided by highly reliable or well-known vendors (e.g., Dell, L.L. Bean)
- Digitized format (e.g., software, music, or videos)
- Relatively inexpensive items (e.g., office supplies, vitamins)
- Frequently purchased items (e.g., groceries, prescription drugs)

EXHIBIT 3.2 Retailing Versus E-Tailing

	Retailers	E-Tailers
Physical expansion (when revenue increases as the number of visitors grows)	• Expansion of retailing platform to include more locations and space	• Expansion of e-commerce platform to include increased server capacity and distribution facilities
Physical expansion (when revenue does not increase as the number of visitors grows)	• May not need physical expansion • Expand marketing effort to turn "window shoppers" into effective shoppers	• May still need physical expansion to provide sustainable services • Expand marketing to turn "pane shoppers" into effective shoppers
Technology	• Sales automation technologies such as POS systems	• Front-end technologies benefit from browsing • Back-end technologies • "Information" technologies
Customer relations	• More stable due to nonanonymous contacts • More tolerable of disputes due to visibility • "Physical" relationships	• Less stable due to anonymous contacts • More intolerant of disputes due to invisibility • "Logical" relationships
Cognitive shopping overhead	• Lower cognitive shopping overhead due to easy-to-establish mutual trust	• Higher cognitive shopping overhead due to hard-to-establish mutual trust
Competition	• Local competition • Fewer competitors	• Global competition • More competitors
Customer base	• Local area customers • No anonymity • Fewer resources needed to increase customer loyalty • Customers remain loyal for future purchases	• Wide area customers • Anonymity • More resources needed to increase customer loyalty • Customers shift loyalty

Sources: Compiled from Lee and Brandyberry (2003) and *NDP.com* (2001).

▶ Commodities with standard specifications (e.g., books, CDs, airline tickets), making physical inspection unimportant

▶ Well-known packaged items that cannot be opened even in a traditional store (e.g., foods, chocolates, vitamins)

The next section examines business models that have proved successful in e-tailing.

Section 3.1 ▶ REVIEW QUESTIONS

1. Describe the nature of B2C EC.
2. What sells well in B2C?
3. What are the characteristics of high-volume products and services?
4. Describe the major trends in B2C.

3.2 E-TAILING BUSINESS MODELS

In order to better understand e-tailing, let's look at it from the point of view of a retailer or a manufacturer that sells to individual consumers. The seller has its own organization and must also buy goods and services from others, usually businesses (B2B in Exhibit 3.3). As also shown in Exhibit 3.3, e-tailing, which is basically B2C (right side of the exhibit), is done between the seller (a retailer or a manufacturer) and the buyer. The exhibit shows other EC transactions and related activities because they may impact e-tailing. In this section, we will look at the various B2C models and their classifications

CLASSIFICATION BY DISTRIBUTION CHANNEL

A business model is a description of how an organization intends to generate revenue through its business operations. More specifically, it is an analysis of the organization's customers and, from that, a discussion of how that organization will achieve profitability and sustainability by delivering goods and services (value) to those customers (McKay and

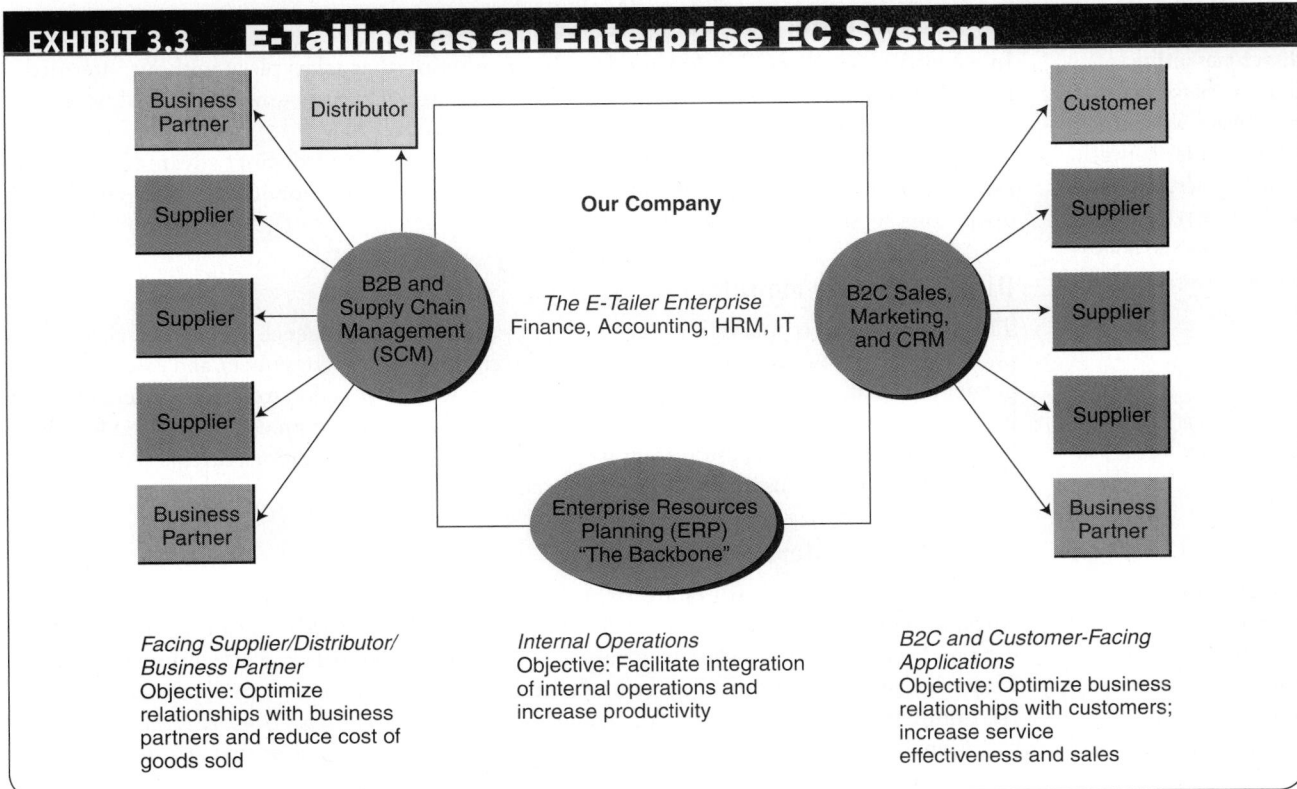

EXHIBIT 3.3   E-Tailing as an Enterprise EC System

Facing Supplier/Distributor/Business Partner
Objective: Optimize relationships with business partners and reduce cost of goods sold

Internal Operations
Objective: Facilitate integration of internal operations and increase productivity

B2C and Customer-Facing Applications
Objective: Optimize business relationships with customers; increase service effectiveness and sales

Marshall 2004). E-tailing business models can be classified in several ways. For example, some classify e-tailers by the scope of items handled (general purpose versus specialty e-tailing) or by the scope of the sales region covered (global versus regional), whereas others use classification by revenue models (see Chapter 1). Here we will classify the models by the distribution channel used, distinguishing five categories:

1. **Mail-order retailers that go online.** Most traditional mail-order retailers, such as QVC, Sharper Image, and Lands' End, simply added another distribution channel—the Internet. Several of these retailers also operate physical stores, but their main distribution channel is direct marketing.

2. **Direct marketing from manufacturers.** Manufacturers, such as Dell, Nike, Lego, Godiva (Chapter 1), and Sony, market directly online from company sites to individual customers. Most of these manufacturers are click-and-mortar, also selling in their own physical stores or via retailers. However, the manufacturer may be a pure-play company (e.g., Dell).

3. **Pure-play e-tailers.** These e-tailers do not have physical stores, only an online sales presence. Amazon.com is an example of a pure-play e-tailer.

4. **Click-and-mortar retailers.** These are of two sorts, depending on how the businesses were originally founded. Originally, click-and-mortar referred to traditional businesses that developed Web sites to support their business activities in some way (e.g., walmart.com, homedepot.com, and sharperimage.com). For details, see Bahn (2006). However, we are now seeing the reverse trend. A small number of successful e-tailers are now creating physical storefronts, leveraging the brand power of the online environment to support more traditional trading activities via stores. For example, Expedia.com, one of the largest online travel companies in the world, has opened physical stores. Dell, a pioneer of e-tailing and one of the largest sellers of computers online, has also opened physical stores.

5. **Internet (online) malls.** As described in Chapter 2, these malls include large numbers of independent storefronts.

We'll look at each of these categories of distribution channels in the pages that follow.

Direct Marketing by Mail-Order Companies

direct marketing
Broadly, marketing that takes place without intermediaries between manufacturers and buyers; in the context of this book, marketing done online between any seller and buyer.

In a broad sense, **direct marketing** describes marketing that takes place without intermediaries. Direct marketers take orders directly from consumers, bypassing traditional wholesale or retail distribution.

Firms with established, mature mail-order businesses have a distinct advantage in online sales, given their existing payment processing, inventory management, and order-fulfillment operations, as shown in Case 3.1.

Direct Sales by Manufacturers

The parties in direct marketing have a great opportunity to influence each other. Sellers can understand their markets better because of the direct connection to consumers, and consumers gain greater information about the products through their direct connection to the manufacturers. Dell is primarily using direct marketing combined with a build-to-order approach (see Appendix 2A for more on build-to-order), customizing its products. Insights and Additions 3.2 (p. 102) describes the process by which customers can configure and order cars online.

Pure-Play E-Tailers

virtual (pure-play) e-tailers
Firms that sell directly to consumers over the Internet without maintaining a physical sales channel.

Virtual (pure-play) e-tailers are firms that sell directly to consumers over the Internet without maintaining a physical sales channel. Amazon.com is a prime example of this type of e-tailer. Virtual e-tailers have the advantage of low overhead costs and streamlined processes. However, one drawback can be a lack of established infrastructure (or back office) to support the online front-office activities. Virtual e-tailers may be *general purpose* or *specialized*.

General e-tailers, such as Amazon.com (see the opening case of this chapter), selling a vast range of goods and services online capitalize on the Internet to offer such variety to a

CASE 3.1
EC Application

LITTLEWOODS SHOP DIRECT GROUP: FROM MAIL-ORDER CATALOGUE TO HIGH STREET TO THE WEB

Littlewoods Shop Direct Group (LSDG) boasts a long, proud tradition. It can trace its origins to 1923, when it was originally owned by the Moores family in Liverpool in northwest England and made money by allowing customers to wager on the results of soccer matches. Inspired by the success of flourishing companies in the United States, such as Sears Roebuck, Littlewoods entered the catalogue retail business in 1932. Such was the success of this early catalogue business that the family decided to expand the business and open High Street department stores, with the first store opening in 1937 in Blackpool, England. However, the catalogue business flourished in the United Kingdom, and by the 1990s Littlewoods controlled 28 percent of the $7 billion mail-order business.

Facing pressure from other established retail chains, and with the growing penetration of the Internet and online retail, in 2005 a decision was taken to sell off all High Street stores and to refocus the organization on reestablishing its preeminence in the home-shopping arena. The last Littlewoods stores disappeared in March 2006. Through a series of acquisitions & mergers, Littlewoods was merged with Shop Direct to form Littlewoods Shop Direct Group (LSDG), the largest mail-order shopping business in the United Kingdom. Annual sales for LSDG in 2005 were $5.5 billion, with profits of $164 million. LSDG is now ranked as Britain's eighth top-performing private company.

LSDG has implemented its vision of being "the natural choice" for customers who shop from home through investment in a network of sorting centers, depots and distribution centers, customer contact centers, warehousing and returns facilities, document management and data services centers, and a sourcing facility. LSDG continues to distribute its catalogue, mailing over 9 million "books," each one 200 pages long and containing more than 70,000 items from a variety of categories, including brand name apparel, accessories and footwear, home and garden, sport and leisure, appliances and electronics, and toys and gifts. With online sales becoming an increasing part of the LSDG business, the entire catalogue is now available online. Because of investment in order fulfillment capabilities, the B2C

sales are supported by low-cost delivery services to residential addresses within 48 hours, with no signature required, overcoming the problem of failed deliveries if customers are not at home.

LSDG offers its customers a range of services. Customers can access a range of credit cards, financial services, insurance, and warranty products. Online shoppers can request a catalogue be sent to them or they can phone LSDG's customer contact centers for personal assistance with their requirements. The LSDG Web site contains detailed information for the customer, including specific sizing, instructions on how to take measurements, fabric information, and close-up photos to show special detail on garments. Customers also can track the status of their orders and any returned goods. The Web site offers detailed instructions on how to navigate the LSDG Web site, recognizing the range of abilities that might be enticed to shop online and migrate from the traditional catalogue. All indicators, suggest that the move from the catalogue to the Web is well underway.

Sources: Complied from *Thecatalogshop.co.uk* (2006), *littlewoods.co.uk* (accessed November 2006), and en.wikipedia.org/wiki/Littlewoods_Shop_Direct_Group (accessed August 2006).

Questions

1. In rolling back from department store outlets and relying on catalogue and online shopping, Littlewoods is adopting a different strategy from other leading online and direct mail companies, such as Lands' End. Discuss the advantages and disadvantages of Littlewoods' approach.

2. If Littlewoods is to remain a successful catalogue and online retailer, what factors do you believe will be essential to its success? What will Littlewoods have to do to survive and prosper in this competitive market space?

3. Use the Littlewoods' site to select a gift purchase and some garments for yourself. Try the same thing with other online retailers. Compare the experiences.

very diverse group of customers geographically without the need to maintain a large physical retail (storefront) network.

Specialty e-tailers can operate in a very narrow market, as does Cattoys.com (cattoys.com), described in Online File W3.2, or Rugman.com (rugman.com), which specializes in offering more than 12,000 Oriental and Persian rugs online. Such specialized businesses would find it difficult to survive in the physical world because they would not have enough customers and could not hold the variety of stock.

Insights and Additions 3.2   Selling Cars Online: Build to Order

The world's automobile manufacturers are complex enterprises with thousands of suppliers and millions of customers. Their traditional channel for distributing cars has been the automobile dealer, who orders cars and then sells them from the lot. When a customer wants a particular feature or color ("options"), the customer may have to wait weeks or months until the "pipeline" of vehicles has that particular car on the production line.

In the traditional system, the manufacturers conduct market research in order to estimate which features and options will sell well, and then they make the cars they wish to sell. In some cases, certain cars are ultimately sold from stock at a loss when the market exhibits insufficient demand for a particular vehicle. The carmakers have long operated under this "build-to-stock" environment, building cars that are carried as inventory during the outbound logistics process (ships, trucks, trains, and dealers' lots). General Motors (GM) estimates that it holds as much as $40-billion worth of unsold vehicles in its distribution channels. Other automakers hold large amounts as well.

Ford and GM, along with other automakers around the world, have announced plans to implement a build-to-order program, much like the Dell approach to building computers. These auto giants intend to transform themselves from build-to-stock companies to build-to-order companies, thereby cutting inventory requirements in half, while at the same time giving customers the vehicle they want in a short period (e.g., one to two weeks). However, according to Weiner (2006) this transformation has so far been "doomed to failure by rigid production processes, inflexible product structures, the lack of integrated logistics processes, and inadequate networking of manufacturers, suppliers and customers." Only when a network of suppliers producing standard modules for cars using standardized processes and IT systems will the dream of a truly agile and responsive supply chain delivering build-to-customer-order capability be realized.

As an example of this trend toward build-to-order mass customization in the new car market, Jaguar car buyers can build a dream car online. On Jaguar's Web site (*jaguar.com*), consumers are able to custom configure their car's features and components, see it online, price it, and have it delivered to a nearby dealer. Using a virtual car on the Web site, customers can view in real time more than 1,250 possible exterior combinations out of several million, rotate the image 360 degrees, and see the price updated automatically with each selection of trim or accessories. After storing the car in a virtual garage, the customer can decide on the purchase and select a dealer at which to pick up the completed car. (Thus, conflicts with the established dealer network channel are avoided.) The Web site helps primarily with the research process—it is not a fully transactional site. The configuration, however, can be transmitted to the production floor, thereby reducing delivery time and contributing to increased customer satisfaction. Similar configuration systems are available from all the major car manufacturers. Customers can electronically track the progress of the car, including visualization of the production process in the factory. Another similarly impressive Web site with similar functionality is *hummer.com*.

Sources: Compiled from Agrawal et al. (2001), Gapper (2004), *jaguar.com* (accessed September 2006), *hummer.com* (accessed September 2006), Voigt et al. (2006), Weiner (2006), and *Knowledge@Wharton* (2005).

Click-and-Mortar Retailers

click-and-mortar retailers
Brick-and-mortar retailers that offer a transactional Web site from which to conduct business.

A **click-and-mortar retailer** is a combination of both the brick-and-mortar retailer and an online transactional Web site. Many click-and-mortar retailers started life as a traditional storefront with a physical retail presence only and over time adopted an online transactional capability as well (brick only to brick-and-click). Another type of click-and-mortar business is those that started their business online and then expanded to physical storefronts as well (click only to click-and-brick).

brick-and-mortar retailers
Retailers who do business in the non-Internet, physical world in traditional brick-and-mortar stores.

Brick-and-mortar retailers conduct business in the physical world, in traditional brick-and-mortar stores. Traditional retailing frequently involves a single distribution channel, the physical store. In some cases, traditional sellers also may operate a mail-order business.

multichannel business model
A business model where a company sells in multiple marketing channels simultaneously (e.g., both physical and online stores).

In today's digital economy, click-and-mortar retailers sell via stores, through voice phone calls to human operators, over the Internet through interactive Web sites, and by mobile devices. A firm that operates both physical stores and an online e-tail site is said to be a click-and-mortar business selling in a **multichannel business model** (see Reda 2002). Examples of brick only to brick-and-click would be department stores, such as Macy's (macys.com), Sears (sears.com), or Nordstrom (nordstrom.com), as well as discount stores, such as Wal-Mart (walmart.com) and Target (target.com). It also includes supermarkets and all other types of retailing.

Expedia in the travel industry and Dell in the computer industry are examples of companies moving from click only to click-and-brick. For many years, some catalogue companies, such as Argos in the United Kingdom, have had storefronts but these served to display catalogs, to offer advice, and to accept orders and payments for goods, which were then delivered via the usual catalog delivery modes. This is precisely the approach Dell has adopted in opening its physical stores in Dallas and New York. Dell has for some time operated kiosks in shopping malls in the United States, but the physical stores add a new dimension to their move to click-and-mortar. Various models of computers are on display in the stores, and Dell staff are available to offer advice and support and to assist customers in personalizing their purchases. However, the stores hold no inventory, so interested customers must still place their orders online from within these stores, assisted by Dell staff. The difference from the Web site is that customers are able to touch and feel and compare different Dell models before buying. Dell has not really altered its direct-to-customer model because the physical stores do not currently have the capability to transact directly (*Ebcenter.org* 2006).

Although there may be practical advantages to being a virtual seller, such as lower overhead costs, it has many drawbacks and barriers, which are described later. Therefore, many experts suggest that the ultimate winners in many market segments will be the companies that are able to leverage the best of both worlds using the click-and-mortar approach.

Retailing in Online Malls

Online malls, as described in Chapter 2, are of two types: referring directories and malls with shared services (see Cox and Koelzer 2004).

Referring Directories. This type of mall is basically a directory organized by product type. Catalog listings or banner ads at the mall site advertise the products or stores. When users click on the product and/or a specific store, they are transferred to the storefront of the seller, where they then complete the transaction. An example of a directory is hawaii.com/marketplace. The stores listed in a directory either collectively own the site, or they pay a subscription fee or a commission to the third party (e.g., a portal) that advertises their logos. This type of e-tailing is basically a kind of affiliate marketing. Other examples of referring directories can be found at insurancefinder.com and bedandbreakfast.com.

Malls with Shared Services. In online malls with shared services, a consumer can find a product, order and pay for it, and arrange for shipment. The hosting mall provides these services, but they usually are executed by each store independently. (To see the variety of services provided, consult smallbusiness.yahoo.com.) The buyer must repeat the process in each store visited in the mall, but it is basically the same process. The storefront owners pay rent and/or transaction fees to the owner. Both manufacturers and retailers sell in such malls. Yahoo! provides a rich example of this type of shared-services mall. When a user goes to Yahoo!, clicks on "shopping," then "all categories," "pets," "dogs," and then "dog toys," for example, a large range of dog toys, sourced from many different e-tailers, is displayed for shoppers. You can see the name of the company selling the item, the price and availability, and so on. In addition, when two e-tailers supply the same product, users are provided with a comparison of the price at each of those stores. Alternatively, users can go directly to one of the vendors' sites; in this case, users will not know that they are in the Yahoo! environment until the check-out process. Other malls with shared services are firststopshops.com and shopping.msn.com.

Ideally, the customer would like to go to different stores in the same mall, use one shopping cart, and pay only once. This arrangement is possible in Yahoo! stores (smallbusiness.yahoo.com/ecommerce).

OTHER B2C MODELS AND SPECIAL RETAILING

Several other business models are used in B2C. They are discussed in various places throughout the book. Some of these models also are used in B2B, B2B2C, G2B, and other types of EC. A summary of these other models is provided in Exhibit 3.4.

Representative Special B2C Services

Of the many other B2C services, four examples that deliver physical products, digital products, and digital services are discussed.

EXHIBIT 3.4   Other B2C Business Models

Model Name	Description	Location in Book
Transaction brokers	Electronically mediate between buyers and sellers. Popular in services, the travel industry, the job market, stock trading, and insurance.	Chapters 3,9
Information portals	Besides information, most portals provide links to merchants, for which they are paid a commission (affiliate marketing). Some provide hosting and software (e.g., *store.yahoo.com*), some also sell.	Chapters 3,6
Community portal	Combines community services with selling or affiliate marketing (e.g., *virtualcommunities.start4all.com*).	Chapter 17
Content creators or disseminators	Provide content to the masses (news, stock data). Also participate in the syndication chain (e.g., *espn.com, reuters.com, cnn.com*).	Chapters 2,16
Viral marketing	Use e-mail or SMS to advertise. Also can sell direct or via affiliates (e.g., *blueskyfrog.com*).	Chapters 4,9
Market makers	Create and manage many-to-many markets (e.g., *chemconnect.com*); also auction sites (e.g., *ebay.com, dellauction.com*). Aggregate buyers and/or sellers (e.g., *ingrammicro.com*).	Chapters 6,7
Make(build)-to-order	Manufacturers that customize their products and services via online orders (e.g., *dell.com, nike.com, jaguar.com*).	Chapters 2,3,4
B2B2C	Manufacturer sells to a business but delivers to individual customers (*godiva.com*).	Chapters 2,3
Service providers	Offer online payments, order fulfillment (delivery), and security (e.g., *paypal.com, escrow.com*).	Chapters 3,12,13

Postal Services. One of the early applications of EC was online postal services with pioneering sites such as estamp.com (now stamps.com). Today, Internet postage services are available in dozens of countries and on a variety of sites. For example, in China customers can go to the post office and use computers that offer online services to make remittances to sellers. (In China, the use of credit cards is very limited.) Another example of postal services is Postage by Phone (pb.com), offered by Pitney Bowes. It offers highly secure and reliable functions, such as printing postage, as well as flexibility and convenience. The entire mailing process is done online or via a telephone.

The U.S. Postal Service offers a system that enables customers to purchase and print postage around the clock, weigh packages up to 4.4 pounds, and prepare first class, priority, express, and international mail. Meters can be leased from commercial manufacturers in cooperation with the U.S. Postal Service that allow customers to download postage directly into their machines and then print it as they need it. Customers can store frequent mailing addresses, print exact postage, track postage use, and more. The hardware is small enough to fit in the palm of a hand.

Services and Products for Adults. Selling virtual sex on the Internet is probably the most profitable B2C model, with estimates that Internet pornography generates about $2.5 billion per year. In 2006, 4.2 million pornographic Web sites existed, representing 12 percent of total Web sites. They contained 372 million pages of pornographic materials and services. Each day 68 million pornographic search engine requests are made, approximately 25 percent of all search engine requests. Eight percent of all e-mails are now said to contain pornographic material, with the average Internet user receiving 4.5 pornographic e-mails per day. Each year, 72 million users visit pornographic Web sites (Ropelato 2006). With little or no advertising effort to attract viewers, many of these sites are making good money. According to reports by market research firms that monitor the industry, such as Forrester, IDC, DataMonitor, Jupiter Media, and NetRating, viewers eagerly pay substantial subscription fees to view adult sites. One reason is that many customers may be hesitant to make a purchase at a local physical store but are comfortable making such purchases online because of the privacy afforded by such sites.

The sites also use innovative streaming video to attract customers. Adult entertainment sites also are well versed in the art of up-selling and cross-selling (e.g., adultshop.com). Many sites also collect fees from advertisers. Finally, adult entertainment sites cut costs by using banner exchanges, joint ventures, and affiliate programs.

A major problem for these sites is their ability to work within the regulatory framework of the local environment. Also, competition is strong; as with any other successful business model, newcomers are continuously trying their luck. Increased competition drives down prices, and many porn sites may go out of business.

Wedding Channels. Weddings are big business. In the United States, 2.2 million weddings took place in 2006, with an average cost of $26,400 (*Theweddingreport.com* 2006). Seventy-seven percent of couples will use the Internet to plan some aspect of their wedding online, with about 13 percent making purchases for their wedding online. The online wedding industry is thus worth about $7.9 billion per year in the United States alone (*Theweddingreport.com* 2006). Each year, brides-to-be use TheKnot.com (theknot.com), the largest online wedding site, to plan their weddings. Approximately 2.1 million unique visitors per month visit The Knot, and 3,600 new members sign up each day to receive information on wedding-related products and services. A "Knot Box" with insert folders is sent to users by regular mail. Each insert is linked to a corresponding page on theknot.com. Advertisers underwrite the mail campaign. The Web site provides brides with information and help in planning the wedding and selecting vendors. Orders can be placed by phone or online (although not all products can be ordered online). The WeddingChannel (weddingchannel.com) offers similar features. SelltheBride (sellthebride.com) offers advice and consultancy services to organizations planning to sell a variety of goods and services to prospective brides and grooms.

Gift Registries. The U.S. bridal industry is estimated to have annual revenues of $72 billion. The gift-registry part of the industry—where the lucky couple lists what presents they hope their guests will buy for them—is estimated to be about $19 billion (*TheKnot.com* 2006). Gift registries also are used by people buying gifts for other occasions (anniversaries, birthdays, graduations, etc.).

From an IT point of view, a gift registry is a relatively complex set of database and supply chain interactions. Usually the gift registry is done jointly between the gift registry company and a department store (e.g., macys.com). The database has to present a secure environment to the person who is registering. That information is then displayed to those who are buying the gifts. When a specific gift is selected, it is removed from the list before anyone else orders the same thing. Meanwhile, the database has to interact with the selling company's inventory lists, showing what's in stock and, in the best of all possible worlds, alerting buyers and registrants when items are backordered.

Selling physical products online requires their physical delivery. In contrast, selling services online usually involves online delivery. Therefore, the potential savings are very large, and online services are very popular. The following sections describe the delivery of services online.

Section 3.2 ▶ REVIEW QUESTIONS

1. List the B2C distribution channel models.
2. Describe how mail-order houses are going online.
3. Describe the direct marketing model used by manufacturers.
4. Describe virtual e-tailing.
5. Describe the click-and-mortar approach.
6. Describe e-malls.
7. Describe online wedding and gift services.

3.3 TRAVEL AND TOURISM SERVICES ONLINE

Online travel bookings and associated travel services are one of the most successful e-commerce implementations, with estimates of sales of $73.4 billion in 2006 (Burns 2006a), approaching 30 percent of the total travel spending (*Omniture.com* 2006). This is expected to increase to

34 percent of total travel spending by 2010, valued at about $104 billion (*Omniture.com* 2006). The number of travelers using the Internet to plan and book trips is still growing significantly, with some 79 million Americans using the Internet to research travel options and destination information in 2005. Of interest is that now 82 percent of those who do this research online also convert to booking their travel online. They most often purchase airline tickets, accommodation, and car rentals online, but future growth is expected in associated events such as cultural event tickets, theme/amusement park tickets, and tickets for sporting events (*Tia.org* 2005). The most popular types of Web sites are online travel agencies (such as Expedia, Travelocity, and Priceline), search engine Web sites (such as Google, Yahoo!), and company-owned Web sites for airlines, hotels, and the like (*Tia.org* 2005). This outstanding performance is underpinned by increased Web traffic of more than 10 percent to major travel sites, higher conversion of visitors to sales, and increased average value per sale, all suggesting that people are becoming more confident and trusting of booking travel related services online (*Internetretailer.com* 2006c).

Some major travel-related Web sites are expedia.com, travelocity.com, zuji.com (now owned by Travelocity but operating separately), webjet.com.au, orbitz.com, travelzoo.com, asiatravel.com, hotwire.com, travelweb.com, ebookers.com, eurovacations.com, and priceline.com. Online travel services also are provided by all major airlines (e.g. britishairways.com), vacation services (e.g., blue-hawaii.com), large conventional travel agencies, trains (e.g., amtrak.com), car rental agencies (e.g., autoeurope.com), hotels (e.g., marriott.com), commercial portals, and tour companies (e.g., atlastravelweb.com). Publishers of travel guides such as Fodors and Lonely Planet provide considerable amounts of travel-related information on their Web sites (fodors.com and lonelyplanet.com), as well as selling travel services there. The online ticket consolidator ebookers.com and the travel information broker tiscover.com are linking up to create a comprehensive online travel resource.

The revenue models of online travel services include direct revenues (commissions), revenue from advertising, lead-generation payments, consultancy fees, subscription or membership fees, revenue-sharing fees, and more. With such rapid growth and success, the travel industry seems to have matured beyond initial concerns such as trust, loyalty, and brand image. However, competition among online travel e-tailers is fierce, with low margins, little customer loyalty, and increasing commoditization of products and services. Thus, guaranteed best rates and various loyalty programs are likely to be popular ways of affecting customer behavior.

Three important trends will drive further changes in the online travel industry. First, online travel agents may try to differentiate themselves through customer-service messaging and other related services, presenting themselves as adding value to the customer. Second, the number of travel meta search facilities, or "travel bots"—online sites or services that search through a range of related sites to find the best price or compare the value of travel products for a consumer—is likely to increase (*Hedna.org* 2005). Third, online travel companies are likely to increasingly use the growing phenomenon of social networking sites (such as myspace.com) to provide content to would-be travelers and also use these sites to study the behavior of potential customers (*Omniture.com* 2006).

SERVICES PROVIDED

Virtual travel agencies offer almost all of the services delivered by conventional travel agencies, from providing general information to reserving and purchasing tickets, accommodations, and entertainment. In addition, they often provide services that most conventional travel agencies do not offer, such as travel tips provided by people who have experienced certain situations (e.g., a visa problem), electronic travel magazines, fare comparisons, city guides, currency conversion calculators, fare tracking (free e-mail alerts on low fares to and from a city and favorite destinations), worldwide business and place locators, an outlet for travel accessories and books, experts' opinions, major international and travel news, detailed driving maps and directions within the United States and several other countries (see infohub.com), chat rooms and bulletin boards, and frequent-flier deals. In addition, some offer several other innovative services, such as online travel auctions.

SPECIAL SERVICES

Many online travel services offer travel bargains. Consumers can go to special sites, such as those offering stand-by tickets, to find bargain fares. Lastminute.com (lastminute.com) offers very low airfares and discounted accommodation prices to fill otherwise-empty seats and hotel rooms. Last-minute trips also can be booked on americanexpress.com, sometimes at a steep discount. Travelzoo.com (travelzoo.com) and hotwire.com offer deep travel discounts. Special vacation destinations can be found at priceline.com, tictactravel.com, stayfinder.com, and greatrentals.com. Flights.com (flights.com) offers cheap tickets and also Eurail passes. Travelers can access cybercaptive.com for a list of thousands of Internet cafes around the world. Similar information is available via many portals, such as Yahoo! and MSN.

Also of interest are sites that offer medical advice and services for travelers. This type of information is available from the World Health Organization (who.int), governments (e.g., cdc.gov/travel), and private organizations (e.g., tripprep.com, medicalert.org, and webmd.com).

Wireless Services

Several airlines (e.g., Cathay Pacific, Delta, and Qantas) allow customers with cell phones with Internet access to check their flight status, update frequent flyer miles, and book flights. Singapore Airlines offers customers global flight alerts via short message service (SMS). Users register the flight for which they want to receive an alert at singaporeair.com and specify when they wish to receive the alert and provide their phone number. British Air offers a broadband Internet connection for passengers on board (initially for first and business classes). Qantas (qantas.com.au) has announced that as of early 2007 customers will be able to send and receive in-flight e-mails, SMS, and calls via their own mobile phones and personal electronic devices, such as Blackberries. Although technological advances now allow communication devices to be used safely in-flight, Qantas is still working on protocols regarding the use of mobile phones during flights (*Qantas.com.au* 2006).

Direct Marketing

Airlines sell electronic tickets over the Internet. When customers purchase electronic tickets online (or by phone), all they have to do is print the boarding pass from their computer's printer or upon arrival at the airport enter their credit card at an *electronic kiosk* to get a boarding pass. Alternatively, travelers can get a boarding pass at the ticket counter.

Using direct marketing techniques, airlines are able to build customer profiles and target specific customers with tailored offers. Many airlines offer "specials" or "cyber offers" on their Web sites (e.g., cathaypacific.com). Airlines such as Scandinavian Airlines offer booking, seat selection, Web check-in, automated flight status service, frequent-flyer programs, personalized services, and more (see sas.se).

Alliances and Consortia

Airlines and other travel companies are creating alliances to increase sales or reduce purchasing costs. For example, some consortia aggregate only fares purchased over the Internet. Several alliances exist in Europe, the United States, and Asia. For example, zuji.com is a travel portal dedicated to Asia-Pacific travelers. It is a consortium of regional airlines, Travelocity, some hotel chains, and car-rental providers. It specializes in tour packages in the region. The company also has a booking engine for travel agents, enabling them to store their customers' e-mail addresses (a B2B2C service).

BENEFITS AND LIMITATIONS OF ONLINE TRAVEL SERVICES

The benefits of online travel services to travelers are enormous. The amount of free information is tremendous, and it is accessible at any time from any place. Substantial discounts can be found, especially for those who have time and patience to search for them. Providers of travel services also benefit: Airlines, hotels, and cruise lines are selling otherwise-empty spaces. Also, direct selling saves the provider's commission and its processing.

Online travel services do have some limitations. First, many people do not use the Internet. Second, the amount of time and the difficulty of using virtual travel agencies may be significant, especially for complex trips and for inexperienced Internet surfers. Finally, complex trips or those that require stopovers may not be available online because they require specialized knowledge and arrangements, which may be better done by a knowledgeable, human travel agent. Therefore, the need for travel agents as intermediaries remains, at least for the immediate future. However, as will be discussed later, intelligent agents may lessen some of these limitations, further reducing the reliance on travel agents.

CORPORATE TRAVEL

The corporate travel market is huge and has been growing rapidly in recent years. Corporations can use all of the travel services mentioned earlier. However, many large corporations receive additional services from large travel agencies. To reduce corporate travel costs, companies can make arrangements that enable employees to plan and book their own trips. Using online optimization tools provided by travel companies, such as those offered by American Express (americanexpress.com) (see Online File W2.10), companies can try to reduce travel costs even further. Travel authorization software that checks availability of funds and compliance with corporate guidelines is usually provided by travel companies such as American Express. Another vendor in the corporate travel market is Amadeus Global Travel Distribution (amadeus.com), via e-Travel (e-travel.com), which provides marketing, distribution, and IT services to automate and manage online booking. Expedia Inc. (expedia.com), Travelocity (travelocity.com), and Orbitz (orbitz.com) also offer software tools for corporate planning and booking.

An example of how a major corporation uses online corporate travel services is described in Online File W3.3. For further discussion, see B2B travel in Chapter 5.

IMPACT OF EC ON THE TRAVEL INDUSTRY

It was not uncommon in the mid-late 1990s for people to forecast the demise of travel agents, arguing that all travel agency services would be replaced by the rise of travel superstores on the Internet (e.g., see Bloch and Segev 1997). Others suggested that only the value-added activities of travel agencies that could not be automated would be performed by travel organizations that would serve certain targeted markets and customers (also see Van der Heijden 1996). Travel superstores, providing many products, services, and entertainment, may enter the industry, as well as innovative individuals operating as travel agents and undertaking some aspects of service tasks from their homes. The *Economist* (2004) analyzed the travel industry and predicted that most travel bookings are likely to move online within a decade. So what is happening in the travel industry online?

The Internet has had a large impact on the role travel agents, with estimates of more than 33 percent of agents having disappeared (NCECIC 2001). This has occurred through direct impacts, with customers increasingly using the Internet to make bookings. It has also occurred somewhat indirectly, with airlines and hotel chains, for example, encouraging customers to book direct or through online wholesalers, bypassing travel agents. However, others argue that travel agents will become the "leisure consultants" of the future, gaining an advantage through their overall knowledge of the industry and their independent advice. In these cases, both a physical and virtual presence are seen as essential, and investing in content (information, travel advice, and the like) is seen as an absolute requirement for success in this competitive market (Atkinson 2005).

At the same time that the Internet may be contributing to a sharp reduction in the number of travel agents, it has also driven the rise of intermediaries. It is now possible to find a number of third-party online sellers and portals, many providing price comparisons and a range of other value-adding services for the consumer. Major companies, such as Expedia and Orbitz, provide excellent service via their Web sites and search through their own extensive databases and networks to offer attractive deals and packages to customers. Rapid growth of late, however, has occurred in the use of travel search engines, or travel bots.

INTELLIGENT AGENTS IN TRAVEL SERVICES

EC will play an even greater role in the travel industry in the future. One area that is currently gaining prominence is that of the travel meta-search engine, or travel bot (*Hedna.org* 2005). Leading examples of such sites are Sidestep (**sidestep.com**), Kayak (**kayak.com**), and Mobissimo (**mobissimo.com**). These sites are all able to search across multiple other travel sites simultaneously, making it much easier for consumers to source information, compare prices, and locate the very best deals to suit their requirements. Mobissimo, for example, searches across 169 sites directly; an inquiry to Kayak about flights will see it searching through more than 120 sites related to airline flight availability. In addition to the usual flights, accommodations, and car rentals, Sidestep searches across events and activities by city, provides detailed travel guides, and features a forum for customers to ask advice and questions of other interested travelers. This makes booking travel and holidays a lot simpler than using many different travel agent sites at once. See Insights and Additions 3.3.

Another promising area is the use of software (intelligent) agents. The agents emulate the work and behavior of human agents in executing organizational processes, such as travel authorization, planning (Camacho et al. 2001), or decision making (Milidiu et al. 2003). Each agent is capable of acting autonomously, cooperatively, or collectively to achieve the stated goal (see Online Technical Appendix C). The system increases organizational productivity by carrying out several tedious watchdog activities, thereby freeing humans to work on more challenging and creative tasks.

Intelligent agents could also be involved in buyer–seller negotiations, as illustrated in the following scenario: You want to take a vacation in Hawaii. First you called a regular travel agent who gave you the impression he was too busy to help you. Finally, he gave you a travel plan and a price that you do not like. A friend suggested that you use a software agent instead. Here is how the process works: First you enter your desired travel destination, dates, available budget, special requirements, and desired entertainment to your online agent

Insights and Additions 3.3   Travel Bots Make Online Travel Purchases Easier

As the Internet grows and an increasing number of organizations strive to attract consumers to their sites, it can be almost overwhelming for consumers to conveniently locate required goods and services at attractive prices. In the travel space, for example, a number of large, reputable, successful companies are online, all vying for the consumer dollar, and all offering a range of attractively bundled services for consumers. In addition to these travel companies, a number of travel search engines purport to search through travel sites. For the consumer, having to go from Web site to Web site or from search engine to search engine can be time consuming and tedious. The travel bot is one innovation that aims to alleviate some of that tedium.

Travel bots are meta-search engines that search a range of related sites or search engines, seeking the best product or service for a particular consumer (*Hedna.org* 2005). Using travel bots, prospective travelers can elect a very broad or much more specific search without moving from one site to another. These meta-search engines search airline, hotel, and other travel sites seeking a good price or a package of value to the consumer. Kayak has recently announced KayakMobile, which will enable consumers with Internet-enabled mobile phones to access Kayak's service via the phone's browser.

Generally speaking, meta-search engines make money not through charging fees to the customers as they direct the customer to a specific airline or hotel site (for example) to complete their booking, but rather through paid advertisements, clickthroughs on advertisements, and kickbacks from the airlines and hotels (*Consumersearch.com* 2005). Their business models are not dissimilar to that of Google.

These meta engines do not have the same market power as the large travel sites, such as Expedia and Travelocity, but growth rates in excess of 300 percent are predicted for 2005–2006. No doubt both the dedicated travel sites and the meta-search engines will play different roles into the future, and hence will work in complementary ways. Travel sites are supposedly better equipped to deal with searching for packages and offer more flexibility. However, if you know exactly when you want to travel and where, then the meta-search engines are often able to secure the best deal.

Sources: Complied from *Consumersearch.com* (2005), *kayak.com* (accessed November 2006), *sidestep.com* (accessed November 2006), and *Hedna.org* (2005).

residing on your computer. The software agent then "shops around," entering the Internet and communicating electronically with the databases of airlines, hotels, and other vendors. The agent attempts to match your requirements against what is available, sometimes negotiating with the vendors' agents. These agents may activate other agents to make special arrangements, cooperate with each other, activate multimedia presentations, or make special inquiries. Within minutes the software agent returns to you with suitable alternatives. You have a few questions, and you want modifications. No problem. Within a few minutes, the agent will provide replies. Then it is a done deal. No waiting for busy telephone operators, and no human errors. Once you approve the deal, the intelligent agent will make the reservations, arrange for payments, and even report to you about any unforeseen delays in your departure. How do you communicate with your software agent? By voice, of course. This scenario is not as far off as it may seem. Such a scenario may be possible by 2008.

Section 3.3 ▶ REVIEW QUESTIONS

1. What travel services are available online that are not available offline?
2. List the benefits of online travel services to travelers and to service providers.
3. What role do software (intelligent) agents have in online travel services? What future applications may be possible?

3.4 EMPLOYMENT PLACEMENT AND THE JOB MARKET ONLINE

The job market is very volatile, and supply and demand are frequently unbalanced. Traditionally, job matching has been done in several ways, ranging from ads in classified sections of newspapers to the use of corporate recruiters, commercial employment agencies, and headhunting companies. The job market has now also moved online. The online job market connects individuals who are looking for a job with employers who are looking for employees with specific skills. It is a very popular approach, and, increasingly, both job seekers and prospective employers are turning away from traditional print-based advertising and recruitment methods in preference of online advertisements and recruitment activities. In addition to online job ads and placement services available through specialized Web sites (such as careerbuilder.com), larger companies are increasingly building career portals on their corporate Web sites as a way of trimming recruitment costs and reducing the time to fill vacancies (Cox 2006). Advantages of the online job market over the traditional one are listed in Exhibit 3.5.

EXHIBIT 3.5 Traditional Versus Online Job Markets

Characteristic	Traditional Job Market	Online Job Market
Cost	Expensive, especially in prime space	Can be very inexpensive
Life cycle	Short	Long
Place	Usually local and limited if global	Global
Context updating	Can be complex, expensive	Fast, simple, inexpensive
Space for details	Limited	Large
Ease of search by applicant	Difficult, especially for out-of-town applicants	Quick and easy
Ability of employers to find applicants	May be very difficult, especially for out-of-town applicants	Easy
Matching of supply and demand	Difficult	Easy
Reliability	Hard copy material is easily lost or misplaced	High
Communication speed between employees and employers	Can be slow	Fast
Ability of employees to compare jobs	Limited	Easy, fast

THE INTERNET JOB MARKET

The Internet offers a rich environment for job seekers and for companies searching for hard-to-find employees. Nearly all *Fortune* 500 companies now use the Internet for some of their recruitment requirements, and studies reveal that online resources are now the most popular way to find suitably qualified applicants for job vacancies (*Careerbuilder.com* 2006). Online job recruitment revenues and volume overtook print ad classifieds at the end of 2005 (Cox 2006), and in 2006 were estimated to reach $2.3 billion (*Careerbuilder.com* 2006). The U.S. market is dominated by three major players: Monster, Careerbuilder, and Yahoo! HotJobs, which together comprise about 55 percent of the market. In Australia, the leading site is seek.com.au. Revenue from online job advertising is growing quickly, and is expected to reach $16 billion in 2008, up from approximately $10 billion in 2006 (*Marketresearch.com* 2005). In the United Kingdom, there is also evidence of rapid uptake of online recruitment services. For example, totaljobs.com receives about 740,000 job applications per month, or one every 3.5 seconds, a 143 percent increase in 12 months, for the approximately 100,000 job vacancies it carries at any one time (*Onrec.com* 2006).

The following parties use the Internet job market:

▶ **Job seekers.** Job seekers can reply to employment ads. Or, they can take the initiative and place their resumes on their own homepages or on others' Web sites, send messages to members of newsgroups asking for referrals, and use the sites of recruiting firms, such as careerbuilder.com, Yahoo! HotJobs (hotjobs.yahoo.com), and monster.com. For entry-level jobs and internships for newly minted graduates, job seekers can go to company.monster.com/jobs. Job seekers can also assess their market value in different U.S. cities at wageweb.com and use the Web to compare salaries and conditions, obtain information about employers, and get career advice. Passive job seekers, those just keeping an eye on opportunities, are using this medium, as well as those actively seeking new employment.

▶ **Employers seeking employees.** Many organizations, including public institutions, advertise openings on their Web sites. Others advertise job openings on popular public portals, online newspapers, bulletin boards, and with recruiting firms. Employers can conduct interviews and administer interactive intelligence, skills, and psychological tests on the Web. Some employers, such as Home Depot, have kiosks in some of their stores on which they post job openings and allow applicants to complete an application electronically.

▶ **Job agencies.** Hundreds of job agencies are active on the Web. They use their own Web pages to post available job descriptions and advertise their services in e-mails and at other Web sites. Job agencies and/or employers use newsgroups, online forums, bulletin boards, Internet commercial resume services, and portals such as Yahoo! HotJobs and AOL. Most portals are free; others, such as marketing.theladders.com, charge membership fees but offer many services.

▶ **Government agencies and institutions.** Many government agencies advertise openings for government positions on their Web sites and on other sites; some are required by law to do so. In addition, some government agencies use the Internet to help job seekers find jobs elsewhere, as is done in Hong Kong and the Philippines (see Online File W3.4). An initiative by the Australian Government, Jobsearch (jobsearch.gov.au), the largest free job board in the country, offers free advertising to employers. It claims the largest candidate database in Australia and has over 1 million visitors per month, with an average of 75,000 jobs on offer at any one time. It links this online presence to an Australia-wide network of touch-screen kiosks. Employers are notified when a candidate's resume matches an advertised job (*Jobsearch.gov.au* 2006).

A Consortium of Large Employers and College Careers Advisors

Most large employers, such as GE, IBM, and Xerox, spend hundreds of thousands of dollars annually on commissions to online job companies and on recruitment activities. For colleges, an important performance metric is the employability of their graduates; hence, providing career advice and services is an important part of campus life. To save money, a number of leading companies joined a nonprofit consortium that created a career portal called jobcentral.com. The National Association of Colleges and Employers created other sites (nacelink.com), a national job posting and college recruiting system, and JobWeb (jobweb.com), a Web site of career development and job-search information for college students and recent college graduates. These nonprofit associations have now merged to form JobCentral to provide people at all levels timely information about careers and employment opportunities nationwide (*JobCentral.com* 2006). The site is used primarily to catalog job postings from the sites of the member employers. It also provides a rich resource of information about occupations, career development, relocation information, and the like. Having the job postings of a number of large employers in one place makes it easy for job searchers to explore available openings.

Global Online Portals

The Internet is very helpful for anyone looking for a job in another country. An interesting global portal for Europe is described in Online File W3.5. An interesting global site for placing/finding jobs in different countries is xing.com (see Internet Exercise 15).

BENEFITS AND LIMITATIONS OF THE ELECTRONIC JOB MARKET

As indicated earlier, the electronic job market offers a variety of benefits for both job seekers and employers. These major advantages are shown in Exhibit 3.6.

Probably the biggest limitation of the online job market is the fact that some people do not use and do not have access to the Internet, although this problem has declined substantially. Nonetheless, the potential for an ever-increasing gap between those with skills and access to the Internet and those without is of concern. To overcome this problem, companies may use both traditional advertising approaches and the Internet. However, the trend is clear: Over time, more and more of the job market will be on the Internet. One solution to the problem of limited access is the use of Internet kiosks, as described in Online File W3.4 and as used by companies such as Home Depot.

EXHIBIT 3.6   Advantages of the Electronic Job Market for Job Seekers Employers

Advantages for Job Seekers	Advantages for Employers
• Can find information on a large number of jobs worldwide	• Can advertise to large numbers of job seekers
• Can communicate quickly with potential employers	• Can save on advertisement costs
• Can market themselves directly to potential employers (e.g., *quintcareers.com*)	• Can reduce application-processing costs by using electronic application forms
• Can write and post resumes for large-volume distribution (e.g., Personal Search Agent at *careerbuilder.com, brassring.com*)	• Can provide greater equal opportunity for job seekers
• Can search for jobs quickly from any location	• Increased chance of finding highly skilled employees
• Can obtain several support services at no cost (e.g., *hotjobs.yahoo.com* and *monster.com* provide free career-planning services)	• Can describe positions in great detail
• Can assess their market value (e.g., *wageweb.com* and *rileyguide.org*; look for salary surveys)	• Can conduct interviews online (using video teleconferencing)
• Can learn how to use their voice effectively in an interview (*greatvoice.com*)	• Can arrange for testing online
• Can access newsgroups that are dedicated to finding jobs (and keeping them)	• Can view salary surveys for recruiting strategies

Interestingly, the reverse of lack of access is also a major limitation of online recruiting. Many companies find that they are flooded with applicants when they advertise online, most of whom are not really suited to the position advertised. Screening all these applications can be a time-consuming and costly process. However, the use of intelligent agents (see the next section) offers a solution to this problem for many organizations.

Security and privacy may be another limitation. For one thing, resumes and other online communications are usually not encrypted, so one's job-seeking activities may not be secure, and thus confidentiality and data protection cannot be guaranteed. For another, it is possible that someone at a job seeker's current place of employment (possibly even his or her boss) may find out that that person is job hunting. The electronic job market may also create high turnover costs for employers by accelerating employees' movement to better jobs. Finally, finding candidates online is more complicated than most people think, mostly due to the large number of resumes available online. Many prospective employers are struggling with large numbers of unsuitable applicants and find that key word searches on some selection criteria may not be sufficient to screen out unsuitable applicants while ensuring all desirable applicants are processed appropriately. Some employers are complaining of receiving spam e-mails with regards to jobs. Some sites offer prescreening of candidates (e.g., monstertrak.monster.com), which may alleviate this problem.

INTELLIGENT AGENTS IN THE ELECTRONIC JOB MARKET

The large number of available jobs and resumes online makes it difficult both for employers and employees to search the Internet for useful information. Intelligent agents can solve this problem by matching resumes with open positions. Exhibit 3.7 shows how three intelligent agents in the online job market work for both job seekers and recruiters.

Intelligent Agents for Job Seekers

Many online recruitment sites are now employing intelligent agents to support both job seekers and employees. For example at CareerShop.com (careershop.com) and NowHiring.com (nowhiring.com), job seekers are offered a free service that uses intelligent agents to periodically search the Internet's top job sites and databases for job postings based

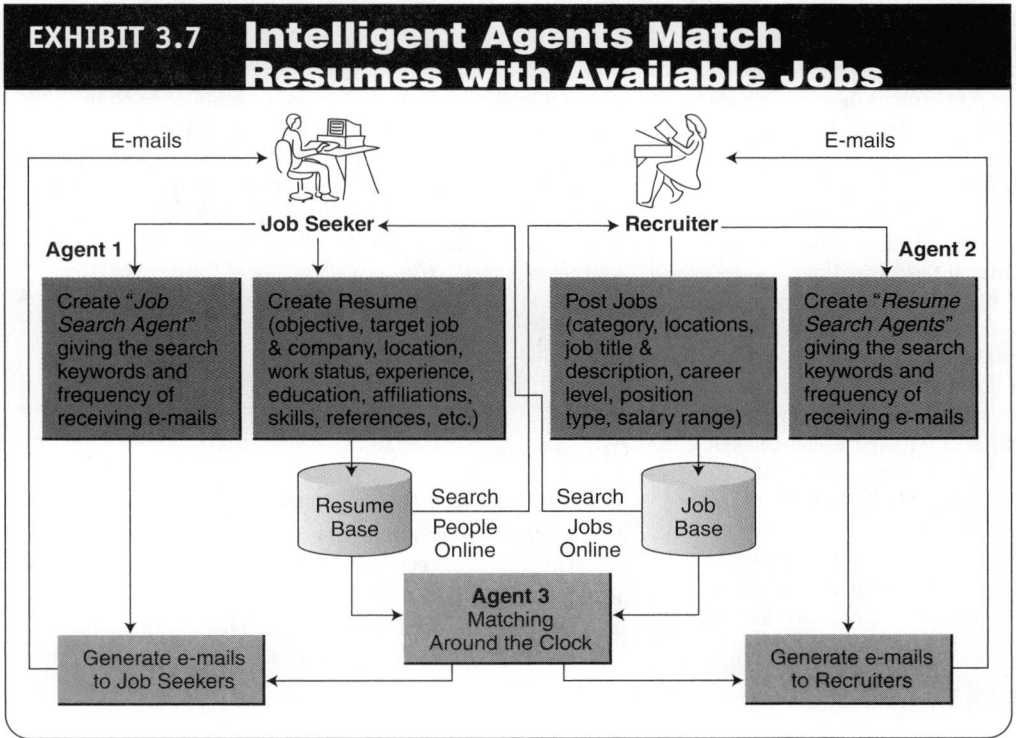

EXHIBIT 3.7 Intelligent Agents Match Resumes with Available Jobs

on users' profiles. Basically, these intelligent agents work by periodically searching through a vast set of online job advertisements. Users receive an e-mail whenever a suitable match is made between their resume for U. S. Market and the advertised positions (e.g., Personal Search Agent at careerbuilder.com and the Personal Job Shopper at careershop.com). This saves the users a tremendous amount of time. For technology jobs, try dice.com.

Intelligent Agents for Employers

Employers may be flooded by hundreds of thousands of applications. Various software tools are available to help recruiters deal with all these applications in a time- and cost-effective manner (see Case 3.2).

A special search engine powered by an intelligent agent can help employers find resumes that match specific job descriptions. There are many such tools available now, and these are employed by a number of the major e-recruitment sites. Typically these tools (such as Autohire used by CareerShop) allow the prospective employer to source suitable applicants through matching key selection criteria against candidates' resumes, screen candidates, rank suitable

---

CASE 3.2
EC Application

USING INTELLIGENT SOFTWARE AND SOCIAL NETWORKING TO IMPROVE RECRUITING PROCESSES

The Internet has made advertising and applying for jobs online a much simpler process. However, sometimes with simplicity comes complexity. The challenge now for some large companies is how to cost-effectively manage the online recruiting process because online ads are attracting large numbers of applicants. For example, Infosys now receives in excess of 1 million job applications each year to fill about 9,000 positions. It might sound like a good problem to have too many applicants, but companies are finding that there is often a poor match between the skills and attributes they require and the many hundreds of applications received. Thus, despite attracting a lot of applicants, they often still suffer from a shortage of good applications. Furthermore, how can a company be sure it is accessing and attracting the very best talent in a particular field? Some interesting new developments are changing the way companies may address these issues.

Trovix offers a service to companies based on its award-winning HR software, which uses embedded intelligence to help manage the entire recruitment process. Trovix argues that its tools Trovix Recruit and Trovix Intelligent Search can emulate human decision makers and assess a candidate's amount, depth, relevance and recency of work experience, education, and the like. The software presents in rank order the best candidates to fit an advertised position. Other features enable tracking of applicants, reporting, and communications. A number of institutions are using this service, including Stanford University, which needs to fill thousands of positions each year. Trend Micro adopted Trovix and was able to screen 700 applicants and list the top 10 in about 20 minutes. The accuracy is probably no better than manual processing, but the software can screen applicants in a much shorter period of time.

A slightly more personal approach is available through some of the social networking sites, which offer support for companies to locate the best talent for a particular position. Sites such as Jobster (*jobster.com*) and LinkedIn (*linkedin*.com) rely more on a networking approach. Jobs posted on Jobster, for example, are linked to other job sites, to blogs, to user groups, to university alumni sites, and so on. People who are part of the social network are encouraged to recommend others who might be suited to a particular job, irrespective of whether they are actively seeking new work. In this way, a company looking to recruit the best talent has its job advertised much more widely and may benefit from word-of-mouth recommendations and referrals. For example, LinkedIn offers prospective employers a network of more than 8 million people across 130 industries, meaning much larger exposure for job vacancies and a much larger talent pool to seek referrals from. Sites such as Jobster can also track where applicants come from, helping companies adopt better recruitment strategies and thus achieve better returns from their investments in seeking the best staff.

Sources: Compiled from McKay (2004), Totty (2006), *Ere.net* (2006), *trovix.com* (accessed November 2006), *jobster.com* (accessed November 2006), and *LinkedIn.com* (2006).

Questions

1. What are some of the challenges of online recruitment?
2. How can intelligent recruitment software and Internet technologies support and improve an organization's search for new talent?
3. What role can social networking approaches to recruitment play? Are there any disadvantages or risks involved in such approaches?

candidates according to their level of expertise, and manage candidate information and communications more effectively throughout the hiring process through a tracking capability. These intelligent agents effectively help to manage some of the limitations of e-recruitment so that employers see online recruiting as a viable alternative for their organization.

Section 3.4 ▶ REVIEW QUESTIONS

1. What are the driving forces of the electronic job market?

2. What are the major advantages of the electronic job market to the candidate? To employers?

3. Describe the role of intelligent agents in the electronic job market.

3.5 REAL ESTATE, INSURANCE, AND STOCK TRADING ONLINE

Online financial services are exploding on the Internet and are being embraced by customers (Verma et al. 2004). According to Dandapani (2004), online financial services essentially altered the industry landscape. Sainsbury's Bank estimated that around 3 million people would take out a financial product, such as a credit card or insurance, online during 2004, 31 percent more than during 2003. The major financial services are presented in this and the following section.

REAL ESTATE ONLINE

The increasing presence and realization of e-commerce possibilities and opportunities in the real estate business is creating a momentum and a readiness for change and slowly adding pressure to transform the old ways of doing things in this previously stable and conservative business. Changes are reaching a tipping point, beyond which the nature of the real estate business will be altered. The changes have been some time in coming, but after a long period of quantitative changes experts are beginning to see some fundamental qualitative changes in the industry (Borrell Associates 2006; Knox 2006; Kaye 2006).

To get some idea of the changes, consider the following statistics. In 2001, when total real estate advertising spending was $11 billion, online real estate advertising spending was $395 million, or 3.5 percent of the total. In 2006, when total advertising spending in real estate was approximately the same, at $11.5 billion, online spending had grown to $2 billion, or 17.7 percent of the total. By 2010, when online spending is predicted to pass $3 billion, online spending is forecast to surpass newspaper print advertising in terms of market share (Borrell Associates 2006). The presence of such large-scale Internet-based advertising has led to much better informed consumers. This, in turn, has led to downward pressure on real estate agents' commissions, as well as causing well-informed consumers to ask what value the realtor is adding. In 2006, commissions were reported to be down to an average of 5.1 percent, compared to the long-standing average of 6 percent (Knox 2006).

The increase in Internet real estate advertising is understandably influencing buying behavior. Studies by the National Association of Realtors (NAR) have shown that over 77 percent of real estate buyers begin their searches for properties on the Internet. Further, 24 percent of buyers eventually choose a home they first identified online (Mullaney 2004).

In the face of such increases in consumer knowledge and control of the early parts of the identification and purchase of properties, some U.S. realtors have tried to restrict public access to some of the databases of properties, such as the local Multiple Listing Services. In many localities, local brokers have tried to restrict access to such databases to members of a professional association, such as the NAR. Such behavior has been the subject of a lawsuit filed in September 2005 by the U.S. Department of Justice, which charges that the NAR's restrictive Multiple Listing Services' policies unlawfully restrict competition (McCullagh 2006).

In summary, e-commerce and the Internet are slowly but surely having an ever-increasing impact on the real estate industry. As in many areas of business, the early predictions of Internet-enabled change seem to be finally coming to pass, although perhaps in a less black-and-white fashion than early predictions led us to believe. For example, despite the changes that are beginning to emerge, real estate agents have not been disintermediated. Homebuyers today tend to use both real estate agents and the Internet. In fact, in 2006 81 percent of homebuyers who used the Internet to look for a property also used a real estate agent (Knox 2006). Thus, despite the fact that the Internet is shaking up the real estate industry, the emerging pattern is more complex than the simple disintermediation of agents.

REAL ESTATE APPLICATIONS

The real estate industry is projected as one of the six industries to be changed by EC soon (Mullaney 2004). Some real estate applications and services, with their representative URLs, are shown in the following list. More applications and services are sure to proliferate in the coming years.

- Advice to consumers on buying or selling a home is available at assist2sell.com.
- The International Real Estate Directory and News (ired.com) is a comprehensive real estate Web site.
- Commercial real estate listings can be found at starboardnet.com.
- Listings of residential real estate in multiple databases can be viewed at homegain.com, justlisted.com, and realestate.yahoo.com.
- The National Association of Realtors (realtor.com) has links to house listings in all major cities. Also see move.com and homes.com.
- Maps are available on mapquest.com and realestate.yahoo.com.
- Information on current mortgage rates is available at bankrate.com, eloan.com, and quickenloans.com.
- Mortgage brokers can pass loan applications over the Internet and receive bids from lenders who want to issue mortgages (e.g., eloan.com).
- Online lenders, such as arcsystems.com, can tentatively approve loans online.
- To automate the closing of real estate transactions, which are notorious for the paperwork involved, see Broker Backoffice from realtystar.com.
- Property management companies (residential, commercial, and industrial) are using the Internet for many applications, ranging from security to communication with tenants. For an example, see superhome.net in Hong Kong.
- Sites for home sellers such as owners.com provide a place for those who want to sell their homes privately, without using a real estate agent.
- Decided not to buy? Rental properties are listed on homestore.net. Several services are available, including a virtual walk-through of some listings.

In general, online real estate is supporting rather than replacing existing agents. Due to the complexity of the process, real estate agents are still charging high commissions. However, several Web sites have started to offer services at lower commissions (e.g., see assist2sell.com), some at 1 percent instead of 6 percent (see discounted brokers at ziprealty.com and foxtons.com).

Real Estate Mortgages

Large numbers of companies compete in the residential mortgage market. Several online companies are active in this area (e.g., see lendingtree.com and eloan.com). Many sites offer loan calculators (e.g., eloan.com and quickenloans.com). Mortgage brokers can pass loan applications over the Internet and receive bids from lenders that want to issue mortgages. Priceline.com (priceline.com) offers its "name your own price" model for obtaining residential loans. In another case, a Singaporean company aggregates loan seekers and then places the package for bid on the Internet. Some institutions approve loans online in 10 minutes and settle in 5 days (e.g., homeside.com.au). Large numbers of independent brokers are active on the Internet, sending unsolicited e-mails to millions of people in the United States, promising low rates for refinancing and new home loans (an activity that some recipients see as *spamming*).

INSURANCE ONLINE

Although the uptake of EC in the insurance industry is relatively slow in some countries, such as New Zealand (Yao 2004), an increasing number of companies use the Internet to offer standard insurance policies, such as auto, home, life, or health, at a substantial discount. Furthermore, third-party aggregators offer free comparisons of available policies. Several large insurance and risk-management companies offer comprehensive insurance contracts online. Although many people do not trust the faceless insurance agent, others are eager to take advantage of the reduced premiums. For example, a visit to insurance.com will show a variety of different policies. At answerfinancial.com customers and businesses can compare car insurance offerings and then make a purchase online. At travel-insurance-online.com, customers can book travel insurance. Some other popular insurance sites include insweb.com, and insurance.com. Many insurance companies use a dual strategy (MacSweeney 2000), keeping human agents but also selling online. Like the real estate brokers, insurance brokers send unsolicited e-mails to millions of people.

ONLINE STOCK TRADING

In the late 1990s, online trading was an exciting innovation in the financial services industry. However, the dot-com crash and increasing competition saw consolidation, cost-cutting, and price reduction become the order of the day (*CNNMoney.com* 2006b; Regan 2005a; Regan 2005b). Major consolidations, involving billions of dollars in total, took place in 2005, with Ameritrade acquiring TD Waterhouse and E-Trade acquiring BrownCo, Harris Direct, and Kobren Insight Management (Regan 2005a; Regan 2005b; Regan 2005c). Regarding the cost of trading, *CNNMoney.com* reported in 2006 that fees are now as low as $1 to $3 per trade. For example, Genesis Securities, through its new unit SogoInvest, offers investors 15 free trades a month for a $15 a month fee with no account minimum required. Investors unwilling to pay the monthly fee can still conduct trades for $3 each (*CNNMoney.com* 2006b).

Today, the majority of stock trading is carried out via the Internet, with 12 brokerage firms handling 75 percent of online trades (Cropper 2004). The top three brokerage firms after the 2005 mergers are Ameritrade, Charles Schwab, and E-Trade (Regan 2005a).

The commission for an online trade is between $1 and $19, compared with an average fee of $100 from a full-service broker and $25 from a discount broker. With online trading, there are no busy telephone lines, and the chance for error is small because there is no oral communication in a frequently noisy environment. Orders can be placed from anywhere, at any time, day or night, and there is no biased broker to push a sale. Furthermore, investors can find a considerable amount of free information about specific companies or mutual funds.

Several discount brokerage houses initiated extensive online stock trading, notably Charles Schwab in 1995. Full-service brokerage companies such as Merrill Lynch followed in 1998–1999. By 2002, most brokerage firms in the United States offered online trading, and the volume of trading has increased significantly in the last 5 years. In 2002, Charles Schwab opened cybertrader.com, charging only $9.95 per trade.

How does online trading work? Let's say an investor has an account with Schwab. The investor accesses Schwab's Web site (schwab.com), enters an account number and password, and clicks stock trading. Using a menu, the investor enters the details of the order (buy, sell, margin or cash, price limit, or market order). The computer tells the investor the current (real-time) "ask" and "bid" prices, much as a broker would do over the telephone, and the investor can approve or reject the transaction. The flow chart of this process is shown in Exhibit 3.8. However, companies such as Schwab are now also licensed as exchanges. This allows them to match the selling and buying orders of their own customers for many securities in 1 to 2 seconds.

Some well-known companies that offer online trading are E-TRADE, Ameritrade, TD Waterhouse, and Suretrade. E-TRADE offers many finance-related services using multimedia software. It also challenges investors to participate in a simulated investment game.

Of the many brokers online, of special interest are Ameritrade and Datek. These two brokers have now combined as one company (ameritrade.com) and offer customers extremely

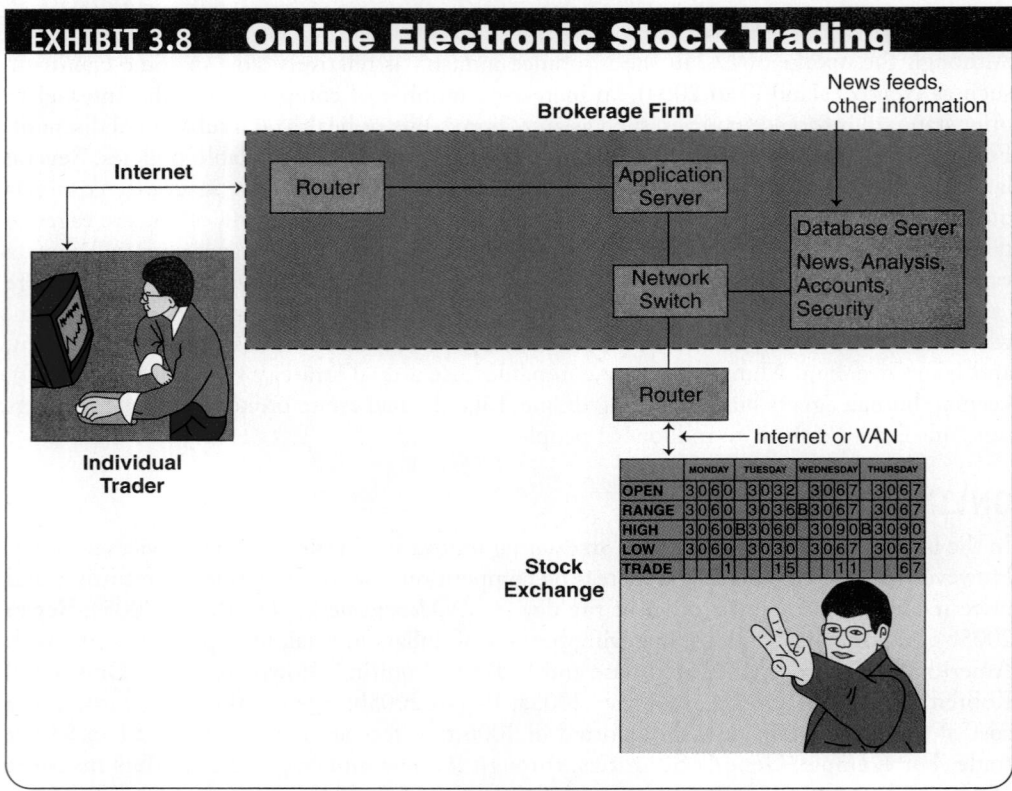

EXHIBIT 3.8   Online Electronic Stock Trading

fast executions or their commission money back. The most innovative collection of online brokerage services is that of E-TRADE. In 1999, E-TRADE broadened its services by starting its own portfolio of mutual funds. E-TRADE is expanding rapidly into several countries, enabling global stock trading. For more on brokerage services provided online, see Adams (2004) and Cropper (2004).

With the rapid pace of adoption of mobile handsets, mobile banking will become more and more popular. Mobile banking services enable users to receive information on their account balances via SMS and to settle payments for bills and purchase stocks (Mallat et al. 2004).

Investment Information

An almost unlimited amount of investment-related information is available online, mostly free of charge (usually in exchange for a registration or for customers only). Here are some examples:

- Current financial news is available at CNN Financial (money.cnn.com). This portal also has large amounts of company information, all free. Similar information is available at Hoover's (hoovers.com) and Bloomberg (bloomberg.com).
- Municipal bond prices are available at bloomberg.com.
- Many tools are available to help investors in the bond market. For example, "how-to-invest manuals," free research reports, and charts and tables of foreign currencies all are available at bloomberg.com.
- A good source of overall market information, with many links to other financial sites, is investorguide.com.
- Free "guru" (expert) advice is available from thestreet.com.
- Stock screening and evaluation tools are available at (marketwatch.multexinvestor.com).
- Articles from the *Journal of the American Association of Individual Investors* can be read at aaii.org.

- Schwab Trader encourages consumers to practice trading strategies, using its StreetSmart Pro (schwabtrader.com).
- The latest on funding and pricing of IPOs is available at premium.hoovers.com/global/ipoc/index.xhtml.
- People can learn about investing at edgarscan.pwcglobal.com, which covers everything from financial ratios to stock analyses.
- Chart lovers will enjoy bigcharts.marketwatch.com. Charts also are available on many other sites.
- Mutual fund evaluation tools and other interesting investment information are available from Morningstar (morningstar.com).
- Earnings estimates and much more are available at thomson.com.
- Almost anything that anyone would need to know about finance and stocks can be found at finance.yahoo.com.
- A comprehensive site that tries to educate, amuse, and enrich is The Motley Fool (fool.com). A portal for individual investors, the site has gained considerable popularity. It acts as a community and is managed by two brothers who also author books and write a nationally syndicated newspaper column.

Most of these services are free. Many other services relating to global investing, portfolio tracking, and investor education also are available. For example, a number of free Web sites allow investors to scan mutual-fund offerings to find a suitable investment sector, country to invest in, and risk profile. For instance, Morningstar (morningstar.com) not only rates mutual funds but also provides a search engine to help users narrow their search. An investor can use the "Fund selector" option and go to "Morningstar category." If the investor wants to invest in, say, Southeast Asia, the investor can find funds operating not only in the United States but also in Hong Kong, Singapore, or Malaysia. Once the investor has picked a market, it can be segmented further by the size of the fund, by return on investment during the last 5 or 10 years, and by other criteria. The investor also can consider the fund's risk level and even the fund manager's tenure. The site has news and chat rooms for each fund. It also lets investors look at the top-10 holdings of most funds. Other evaluation sites similar to Morningstar, such as lipperweb.com, also rank funds by volatility. Investors can get their fund details and charts showing past performance against a relevant index for each fund.

Related Financial Markets

In addition to stocks, online trading is expanding to include commodities, financial derivatives, and more. Futures exchanges around the world are moving to electronic trading. For example, the Chicago Board of Trade, the world's largest futures exchange, is offering full-range electronic trading. Of special interest is mortgage banking online (see mortgagebankers.org).

The Risk of Having an Online Stock Account

The major risk of online trading is security. Although all trading sites require users to have an ID and password, problems may still occur.

In 2004, it was discovered that hackers could steal users' ID numbers and passwords when they use the Windows operating system. The problem has been corrected. Problems of this nature also may occur when conducting online trading or online banking, our next topic.

Section 3.5 ▶ REVIEW QUESTIONS

1. List the major online real estate applications.
2. What are the advantages of online stock tracking?
3. What investment information is available online?
4. What are some of the risks of trading stocks online?

3.6 BANKING AND PERSONAL FINANCE ONLINE

electronic (online) banking or (e-banking)
Various banking activities conducted from home or the road using an Internet connection; also known as cyberbanking, virtual banking, online banking, and home banking.

Online banking, or **electronic banking (e-banking)**, also known as *cyberbanking, virtual banking,* or *home banking,* includes various banking activities conducted via the Internet from home, business, or on the road rather than at a physical bank location. Consumers can use e-banking to check their accounts, pay bills online, secure a loan electronically, and much more.

E-banking saves users time and money. For banks, it offers an inexpensive alternative to branch banking and a chance to enlist remote customers. Many physical banks now offer home banking services, and some use EC as a major competitive strategy. One such U.S. bank is Wells Fargo (wellsfargo.com). In Hong Kong, a leading bank is the Bank of East Asia (hkbea-cyberbanking.com). Many banks offer wireless services (see Chapter 9)

Online banking has in recent years become a mainstream Internet activity. At present it is holding steady, increasing at the same pace as Internet usage. A faster rate of increase in the activity, analysts believe, is being held back by a lack of trust in Internet banking security (Fox and Beier 2006).

An emerging innovation in online banking is peer-to-peer (P2P) online banking. Zopa is a UK Web site offering P2P banking services. People join Zopa as borrowers or lenders. The site has about 90,000 members, and more than $100,000 is being lent every day. The average interest rate on Zopa loans is 7 percent, and uncollectible debts are running at a low 0.05 percent (in mid-2006) (Schonfeld and Borzo 2006).

Pew Internet's December 2005 survey found that 43 percent of all adult Internet users in the United States—63 million adults—were banking online. The users of online banking services were found to be spread across all age groups under the age of 65, with men and women being equally likely to bank online. Those with greater disposable incomes were more likely to bank online, with 55 percent of Internet users living in households with $75,000 or more in annual income saying that they bank online, compared to 29 percent of Internet users living in households with less than $30,000 in annual income (Fox and Beier 2006).

Online banking has not only been embraced in the developed world; it is becoming an enabling feature of business growth in the developing world. For example, online banking in China is increasing rapidly in popularity, especially among China's new educated middle class in the developed cities. Consequently, the overall turnover of online banking activities is also growing rapidly.

The Bank of China and the China Merchants Bank started their online banking service in 1998. These online service offerings were followed by online offerings by China's other major banks and a number of smaller banks. These services have been enthusiastically embraced by China's new business classes. In 2005, 34 million users were using online banking services, and the overall turnover was $260 billion. Also in 2005, 740,000 businesses were using online banking, and the corresponding turnover of enterprise-based online banking reached $9 trillion (Wood 2006).

Banking online is becoming popular even with small businesses. In 2004, about 16 percent of United States' small businesses banked online, versus 3.3 percent in 2001 (Celent 2004). In 2006, the British Bankers' Association reported that 4 out of 10 small businesses in Britain now bank online (Moules 2006).

HOME BANKING CAPABILITIES

Southard and Siau (2004) divide banking applications into the following categories: informational, administrative, transactional, portal, and others (see Exhibit 3.9). They also found that the larger the bank, the more services that were offered. A description of some of the major e-banking capabilities is provided in Online Exhibit W3.1.

Electronic banking offers several of the EC benefits listed in Chapter 1, both to the bank and to its customers, such as expanding the bank's customer base and saving on the cost of paper transactions (Pascoe 2004).

VIRTUAL BANKS

In addition to regular banks' adding online services, *virtual banks* have emerged; these have no physical location but only conduct online transactions. Security First Network Bank

EXHIBIT 3.9   Online Banking Capabilities

Informational	General bank information and history
	Financial education information
	Employment information
	Interest rate quotes
	Financial calculators
	Current bank and local news
Administrative	Account information access
	Open new account online
	Applications for services
	Move all banking online
	Personal finance software applications
Transactional	Account transfer capabilities
	Transfer funds housed at different financial institutions
	Bill-pay services
	Corporate services(e.g., cash management, treasury)
	Online insurance services
	Online brokerage servies
	Real-time funds transfer
	Online trust services
Portal	Links to financial information
	Links to community information
	Links to local business
	Links to nonlocal business (and/or advertisers)
other	Wireless capabilities
	Search function

Sources: Compiled from Southard and Siau (2004) and *Primezone.com* (2006).

(SFNB) was the first such bank to offer secure banking transactions on the Web. Amidst the consolidation that has taken place in the banking industry, SFNB has since been purchased and now is a part of RBC Centura (rbccentura.com). Other representative virtual banks in the United States are NetBank (netbank.com) and First Internet Bank (firstib.com). Virtual banks exist in many other countries (e.g., bankdirect.co.nz). In some countries, virtual banks are involved in stock trading, and some stockbrokers are doing online banking (e.g., see etrade.com). According to Dandapani (2004), 97 percent of the hundreds of pure-play virtual banks failed by 2003 due to lack of financial viability.

A word of caution about virtual banking: Before sending money to any cyberbank, especially those that promise high interest rates for your deposits, make sure that the bank is a legitimate one. Several cases of fraud already have occurred.

One legitimate online banking success is illustrated in Case 3.3.

INTERNATIONAL AND MULTIPLE-CURRENCY BANKING

International banking and the ability to handle trades in multiple currencies are critical for international trading. Although some international retail purchasing can be done by providing a credit card number, other transactions may require international banking support. Examples of such cross-border support include the following:

▶ Tradecard and MasterCard have developed a multiple-currency system for global transactions (see tradecard.com). This system is described in Chapter 12.

▶ Bank of America and most other major banks offer international capital funds, cash management, trades and services, foreign exchange, risk management investments, merchant services, and special services for international traders.

CASE 3.3
EC Application

ING DIRECT: AN ONLINE BANKING SUCCESS STORY

ING was formed in 1991 with the merger of Nationale-Nederlanden, the largest Dutch insurance company, and NMB Postbank Groep, a banking operation offering a range of wholesale and retail financial services. In the 1990s, ING expanded internationally throughout Europe and the United States. In 2005, the company had $734 billion assets under management. It employed 115,300 staff worldwide. In 2006, the company earned $2 billion in third-quarter profits.

Intensive market research in 1996 led ING to plan its first foreign direct or online banking initiative in Canada. ING market researchers saw Canada as a mid-sized and receptive market of potential customers sensitive to the low interest rates and high service charges they were experiencing. The initiative was launched in Canada in 1997 as ING Direct. ING Direct followed an aggressive expansion strategy and by the end of 1999 had successfully launched in Spain, France, Germany, Italy, the United Kingdom, and Australia. By 2000, ING Direct had become Canada's largest online bank. In that year, the Canadian ING Direct team was moved south to build an equally successful direct banking operation in the United States. ING Direct now operates in nine countries worldwide and is planning expansion into Japan, Scandinavia, Switzerland, and Portugal.

ING Direct now has more than 16 million customers in nine countries. By 2006, ING Direct had attracted deposits totaling more than $268 billion and made a pretax profit of $263 million in the second quarter. This makes it the fastest-growing subsidiary for the ING Group.

What factors drove ING Direct's success? ING Direct focused on delivering a limited number of services on which the company could make money. It then delivered value to customers by offering significantly higher interest rates on savings compared to traditional banks. Further, it charged no fees and set no minimum deposits for its customers. Its marketing message was simple and direct: "great rates, no fees, no minimums."

ING Direct's business operations were low cost but effective. The company accepted deposits, sold investment products and several mutual funds, and wrote home mortgages. It did not offer payment services such as checking, face-to-face teller services, or automatic teller machines. Instead, ING Direct encouraged its depositors to utilize their current bank's payment services and switch money back and forth at no cost between their traditional bank and ING Direct. Thus, ING Direct possessed the customer's high-margin

activities, and the customer's traditional bank supported the lower-margin activities. This slight increase in complexity for the customer was worth it for the customers because of ING Direct's high interest rates and low fees.

A further innovation by ING Direct was the establishment of a face-to-face presence via ING Direct "cafes." Coffee, pastries, and advice are available at the cafes, along with the opportunity to access information via online terminals. ING Direct management felt the physical presence of the cafes gave reassurance to prospective customers who felt the need to check out the company in some way. Thus, the cafes helped with publicity and with building trust through personal interaction. However, the company is firm in its resolve not to open branches because it believes this enables them to keep costs low and, hence, remain competitive and attractive through higher interest rates on savings to its customers.

In summary, ING Direct has a successful strategy that allows it to operate in high-margin online banking activities without the expense of a branch network and ATMs, while at the same time relying on traditional banks to provide the low-margin high-expense services. ING Direct's innovativeness underlines the need for traditional banks to determine effective strategies for addressing the opportunities in banking opened up by the Internet.

Sources: Complied from *inggroup.com*, *ingdirect.co.uk*, and *ingdirect.com.au* (all accessed November 2006) and Heskett (2005) and Marketwatch (2006).

Questions

1. What factors have contributed to ING Direct's success to date?

2. Visit *ingdirect.com*. How easy is to establish a new savings account? Do you feel confident that your funds would be safely managed?

3. ING Direct relies on customers maintaining ATM accounts with traditional banks and having its customers transfer money regularly from their ING Direct savings accounts to their ATM accounts. How convenient do you think this would be? Would it inhibit your willingness to bank with ING? How would you assess higher interest rates with ING Direct versus this slight inconvenience?

▶ Fxall.com is a multidealer foreign exchange service that enables faster and cheaper foreign exchange transactions (e.g., see Sales 2002). Special services are being established for stock market traders who need to pay for foreign stocks (e.g., at Charles Schwab). See *Global Finance* (2004) for more information about foreign exchange banks.

ONLINE FINANCIAL TRANSACTION IMPLEMENTATION ISSUES

As one would expect, the implementation of online banking and online stock trading can be interrelated. In many instances, one financial institution offers both services. The following are some implementation issues for online financial transactions. For an in-depth analysis, see Dandapani (2004). For an example, see Xu et al. (2006).

Securing Financial Transactions

Financial transactions for home banking and online trading must be very secure. In Chapter 12, we discuss the details of secure EC payment systems. In Case 3.4, we give an example of how a bank provides security and privacy to its customers.

Access to Banks' Intranets by Outsiders

Many banks provide their large business customers with personalized service by allowing them access to the bank's intranet. For example, Bank of America allows its business customers access to accounts, historical transactions, and other data, including intranet-based decision-support applications, which may be of interest to large business customers. Bank of America also allows its small business customers to apply for loans through its Web site.

Imaging Systems

Several financial institutions (e.g., Bank of America and Citibank) allow customers to view images of all of their incoming checks, invoices, and other related online correspondence. Image access can be simplified with the help of a search engine.

CASE 3.4
EC Application
ONLINE SECURITY AT A BANK

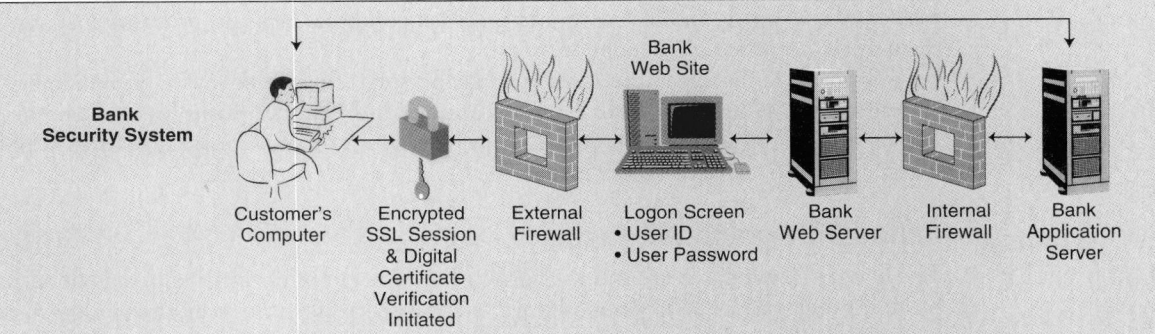

Banks provide extensive security to their customers. The following describes some of the safeguards provided.

Customers accessing the bank system from the outside must go through encryption provided by SSL (Secure Socket Layer) and digital certification verification (see Chapters 11 and 12). The certification process assures users each time they sign on that they are indeed connected to their specific bank. The customer inquiry message then goes through an external firewall. Once the log-on screen is reached, a user ID and a password are required. This information flows through a direct Web server and then goes through an internal firewall to the application server.

The bank maintains accurate information. Corrections are made quickly.

Information is shared among the company's family of partners only for legitimate business purposes. Sharing information with outside companies is done with extreme care.

The bank does not capture information provided by customers when they conduct "what-if" scenarios using the bank's planning tools (to assure privacy). The company does use cookies to learn about its customers; however, customers can control both the collection and use of the information. In addition, the bank provides suggestions on how users can increase security (e.g., "Use a browser with 128-bit encryption.")

Sources: Compiled from various security statements of online bank Web sites, including *Cooperativebank.co.uk* (2006) and *Thestatebank.com* (2006).

Questions

1. Why is security so important for a bank?
2. Why is there a need for two firewalls?
3. Who is protected by the bank's security system—the customer, the bank, or both? Elaborate.
4. What might be the limitations of such a system?

Pricing Online Versus Offline Services

Computer-based banking services are offered free by some banks, whereas others charge $5 to $10 a month. Also, some banks charge fees for individual transactions (e.g., fee per check, per transfer, and so on). Financial institutions must carefully think through the pricing of online and offline services. Pricing issues must take into account the costs of providing the different types of services, the organization's desire to attract new customers, and the prices offered by competitors. For further discussion, see Ericson (2004).

Risks

Online banks, as well as click-and-mortar banks, may carry some risks and problems, especially in international banking. The first risk that most people think of is the risk of hackers getting into their account. In addition, some believe that virtual banks carry *liquidity* risk (the risk of not having sufficient funds to pay obligations as they come due) and could be more susceptible to panic withdrawals. Regulators are grappling with the safeguards that need to be imposed on e-banking.

PERSONAL FINANCE ONLINE

Individuals often combine electronic banking with personal finance and portfolio management. Also, brokerage firms such as Schwab offer personal finance services such as retirement planning. However, vendors of specialized personal finance software offer more diversified services (Tyson 2003). For example, both Intuit's Quicken (Tessler 2004) and Microsoft's Money offer the following capabilities: bill paying and electronic check writing; tracking of bank accounts, expenditures, and credit cards; portfolio management, including reports and capital gains (losses) computations; investment tracking and monitoring of securities; stock quotes and past and current prices of stocks; personal budget organization; record keeping of cash flow and profit and loss computations; tax computations and preparations; and retirement goals, planning, and budgeting.

Although Quicken is the most popular personal finance software, more sophisticated packages such as Prosper (from Ernst & Young) and Captool (captools.com) are available. All of these products are available as independent software programs for use with the Internet or coupled with other services, such as those offered by AOL.

Online Billing and Bill Paying

The era of e-payment is around the corner. The number of checks the U.S. Federal Reserve System processed in 2003 decreased for the fourth consecutive year, dropping 4.7 percent to 15.81 billion checks, while commercial automated clearinghouse (ACH) volume increased 12.1 percent to $95.96 billion in payments (Dernovsek 2004). Many people prefer to pay monthly bills, such as telephone, utilities, rent, credit cards, cable, and so on, online. The recipients of such payments are equally eager to receive money online because online payments are received much more regularly and quickly and have lower processing costs.

The following are representative payment systems:

- **Automatic transfer of mortgage payments.** This method has existed since the late 1980s. Payers authorize their bank to pay the mortgage directly from their bank account.
- **Automatic transfer of funds to pay monthly utility bills.** Since fall 1998, the city of Long Beach has allowed its customers to pay their gas and water bills automatically from their bank accounts. Many other utilities worldwide provide such an option today.
- **Paying bills from online banking accounts.** Payments from one bank account can be made into any other bank account. Many people pay their monthly rent and other bills directly into the payees' bank account.
- **Merchant-to-customer direct billing.** Under this model, a merchant such as American Express posts bills on its Web site, where customers can then view and pay them. (This approach is called presentment and payment; see Chapter 12.) Utilities in many cities allow customers to pay bills on the utilities' Web sites, charging customers up to 20 cents

per transaction, which is less than the price of a stamp. However, this means that customers have to go to many different Web sites to pay all of their bills.

▶ **Using an intermediary for bill consolidation.** In this model, a third party such as Transpoint (from Microsoft, Citibank, and First Data Corporation) consolidates all of a customer's bills at one site and in a standard format. Collecting a commission on each transaction, the intermediary makes it convenient both for the payee and payer to complete transactions. This latest model is of interest to many vendors, including E-TRADE and Intuit.

▶ **Person-to-person direct payment.** An example of this service is PayPal (paypal.com), which enables a person to send funds to another individual over the Internet. A person opens an account with PayPal (now part of eBay) and charges the amount he or she wants to send on a credit card or bank account. PayPal alerts the person to whom the user wants to send the funds by e-mail, and the recipient accesses the account and transfers the funds to his or her credit card or bank account (see Chapter 12). PayPal is being followed in the market by a number of competitors.

▶ **Pay bills at bank kiosks.** As described in Chapter 12, some banks allow customers to pay bills from their account using electronic kiosks outside the bank (usually combined with regular ATMs).

Online billing and bill paying can be classified into B2C, B2B, or C2C. This section has focused largely on B2C services, which help consumers save time and payees save on processing costs. However, large opportunities also exist in B2B services, which can save businesses about 50 percent of billing costs. In Hong Kong, for example, CitiCorp enables automatic payments by linking suppliers, buyers, and banks on one platform.

Taxes

One important area in personal finance is advice about and computation of taxes. Dozens of sites are available to help people in their federal tax preparations. Many sites will help people legally cut their taxes. The following list offers some sites worth checking:

▶ irs.gov: The official Web site of the Internal Revenue Service.
▶ webtax.com: A massive directory of tax-related information, research, and services.
▶ fairmark.com: A tax guide for investors.
▶ moneycentral.msn.com/tax/home.asp: A useful reference and educational site.
▶ quicken.com/taxes: Emphasizes tax planning.
▶ taxcut.com/taxtips/hrblock_tips.html: Offers advice on minimizing taxes.
▶ taxaudit.com: Offers advice on minimizing taxes.
▶ taxprophet.com: Provides tax advice in an entertaining manner.
▶ bankrate.com/brm/itax: Contains informative articles about taxation.
▶ 1040.com: Information about deduction rules.
▶ unclefed.com: Offers advice on audits.

Section 3.6 ▶ REVIEW QUESTIONS

1. List the capabilities of online banking. Which of these capabilities would be most beneficial to you?
2. Discuss some implementation issues of financial services.
3. List the major personal finance services available online.
4. Explain online bill paying.

3.7 ON-DEMAND DELIVERY SERVICES AND E-GROCERS

Most e-tailers use common logistics carriers to deliver products to customers. They may use the postal system within their country or they may use private shippers such as UPS, FedEx, or DHL. Delivery can be made within days or overnight if the customer is willing to pay for the expedited shipment.

e-grocer

A grocer that takes orders online and provides deliveries on a daily or other regular schedule or within a very short period of time.

on-demand delivery service

Express delivery made fairly quickly after an online order is received.

Some e-tailers and direct marketing manufacturers own a fleet of delivery vehicles and incorporate the delivery function into their business plan in order to provide greater value to the consumer. These firms will either provide regular deliveries on a daily or other regular schedule or they will deliver items within very short periods of time, usually 1 hour. They may also provide additional services to increase the value proposition for the buyers. An example is Bigboxx.com (bigboxx.com), presented in Online File W5.1. An online grocer, or **e-grocer**, is a typical example of businesses in this category. Home delivery of food from restaurants is another example. In addition, another class of firms (groceries, office supplies, repair parts, and pharmaceutical products) promise virtually instantaneous or at least same-day delivery of goods to consumers.

Whether the delivery is made by company-owned vehicles or is outsourced to a carrier, an express delivery model is referred to as an **on-demand delivery service**. In such a model, the delivery must be done fairly quickly after an order is received. (For more on this topic, see Chapter 13.) A variation of this model is *same-day delivery*. According to this model, delivery is done faster than "overnight" but slower than the 30 to 60 minutes expected with on-demand delivery. E-grocers often deliver using the same-day delivery model.

THE CASE OF E-GROCERS

The U.S. grocery market is valued at over $808 billion annually (Oo 2006). Approximately 1 percent of Americans, or just over 2 million people, buy groceries online (Riseley 2006). It is a very competitive market, and margins are very thin. Online grocery sales are forecast to reach $6.2 billion in 2006, a 17 percent increase on 2005 (McTaggart 2006). Many e-grocers are click-and-mortar retailers that operate in the countries where they have physical stores, such as Woolworths in Australia (woolworths.com.au) and Albertsons (albertsons.com) in the United States. (For statistics on the grocery industry, see retailindustry.about.com/library.)

All e-grocers offer consumers the ability to order items online and have them delivered to their homes. Some e-grocers offer free regular "unattended" weekly delivery (e.g., to the customer's garage), based on a monthly subscription model. Others offer on-demand deliveries (if the customer is at home) with a surcharge added to the grocery bill and sometimes an additional delivery charge. One e-grocer sells only nonperishable items shipped via common carrier, a model also adopted by Amazon.com with its recent foray into online grocery sales. Many offer additional services, such as dry-cleaning pickup and delivery. Other add-on features include "don't run out" automatic reordering of routine foods or home office supplies, as well as fresh flower delivery, movie rentals, meal planning, recipe tips, multimedia features, and nutritional information.

Today, it is possible to shop for groceries from cell phones, Blackberries, and PDAs (see Chapter 9).

Implementing E-Grocery

An extensive survey conducted by the Consumer Direct Cooperative in 2000 (Cude and Morganosky 2000) pointed to the following groups of potential online grocery shoppers: *Shopping avoiders* are willing to shop online because they dislike going to the grocery store; *necessity users* would do so because they are limited in their ability to shop (e.g., disabled and elderly people, shoppers without cars). *New technologists,* those who are young and comfortable with technology, represent another group of online grocery shoppers. Extremely busy, *time-starved consumers* may be willing to shop online in order to free up time in their schedules. Finally, some consumers gain a sense of self-worth from online shopping and being on the *leading edge* of what may be a new trend.

Online grocery customers are generally repeat customers who order week after week in a tight ongoing relationship with the grocer. The user interaction with the Web site is much more substantial than with other B2C Web sites, and user feedback is more prevalent. Shopping for groceries online is a very sophisticated purchase compared to most EC shopping transactions. For example, online grocery retailers have had to learn how to handle "out of stocks" and order errors effectively, because studies suggest that online grocery shoppers tend to be pickier than those going to supermarkets. Experience suggests that online customers need to be asked upfront whether they want substitutes for goods ordered that are out of stock, and some retailers, such as SimonDelivers, offer a notes function, which allows the online customer to leave messages for the picker of their order (McTaggart 2006).

Around the world, many e-grocers are targeting the busy consumer with the promise of rapid home delivery of groceries. For example, Parknshop (parknshop.com), the largest supermarket chain in Hong Kong, offers a "personal shopping list" that helps customers easily order repetitive items on each visit. (The Web site also uses advertising as an additional source of revenue to make the business model a bit more solid.) The Tesco chain in the United Kingdom (tesco.com) is another successful e-grocer.

So far, online sales are usually not as profitable as sales in physical grocery stores due to very slim margins in the grocery industry, the delivery costs associated with rapid home delivery, and the relatively low volume of online sales. However, this additional channel allows grocers to increase their sales volume and serve customers who are unable to visit their physical stores. In addition, they can increase their brand recognition by maintaining an Internet presence. Furthermore, a move online can be a defensive strategy to avoid pure play e-grocers from stealing some of their market share. However, these retailers can benefit in two important ways. First, for retailers offering a broad range of merchandise, such as Wal-Mart and Amazon.com, the move into selling groceries online can be a way of attracting customers back to their Web sites more often (consumers typically buy groceries much more frequently than they do books, electronics, and the like). Second, the online experience can provide e-grocers with a much more intimate real-time knowledge of customer preferences, wants, and needs and their online shopping behaviors. E-Grocers such as SimonDelivers are now sometimes used by major manufacturers to launch new products before wide-scale release and to test pilot products (McTaggart 2006).

Despite the promise that on-demand delivery seems to hold, virtual e-grocers have had a checkered history. For example, StreamLine.com and ShopLink.com folded in 2000. HomeGrocer.com and Kozmo.com folded in 2001 (see Chapter 13). As of 2006, there are three major e-grocers: peapod.com, freshdirect.com, and simondelivers.com. Their success has been attributed to excellent logistics, a commitment to delivering a good experience for customers, and differentiation (e.g., FreshDirect now specializes in sourcing organic foods, offering prepared meals, and in emphasizing the freshness of its products).

One of the most interesting stories of e-grocers that failed is that of Webvan.com, a company that raised many expectations and was founded in 1999 with a goal of delivering anything (particularly groceries), anytime and anywhere, in an efficient manner. Webvan designed and started to build sophisticated automated warehouses—each the size of seven football fields and equipped with more than 4 miles of conveyor belts (see Steinert-Therlkeld 2000). In 2001, Webvan purchased Homegrocer.com, a smaller rival, but was unable to merge the two companies properly. Furthermore, the company was unable to secure more funds due to the accumulating failures of dot-com companies, which led to a loss of investor confidence. Declining demands due to economic conditions contributed to staggering losses. Finally, Webvan folded in 2001. Overall, it lost more than $1 billion, the largest of any dot-com failure. (For more details, see Online File W3.6.)

A similar company, Groceryworks.com, was purchased by Safeway, a successful click-and-mortar grocer. The results have been quite different from those of Webvan, as detailed in Online File W3.7.

Third-Party Service Providers in the Online Grocery Industry

One of the reasons for the uncertain results for some forays into online grocery was the costs and risks involved in building the appropriate infrastructure, both physical and technical. Third-party service providers and some alliance arrangements are changing the landscape in this regard.

MyWebGrocer.com (mywebgrocer.com) is a provider of technical and online shopping solutions in the supermarket industry. It provides the complete software, hardware, and technical expertise for organizations wishing to sell groceries online. MyWebGrocer typically services existing supermarkets, providing the EC infrastructure they need for a move into online grocery selling together with e-marketing expertise. This has meant that existing grocery chains can leverage their brand, their store locations, and industry knowledge without investing in building technical expertise as well. Customers of MyWebGrocer often see about 10 percent of their sales coming online, meaning that their online investment becomes a profitable additional business channel (McTaggart 2006).

Buy4Now.com (buy4now.com) is an Irish company offering similar expertise. It relies on an in-store picking model, where supermarkets are helped to leverage their existing infrastructure in moving online with relatively small investments. For example, Buy4Now.com teamed with Roche Bros in Boston to help Roche reclaim clientele lost to PeaPod. The in-store picking model allows customers to place their orders up to 3 hours before a delivery slot starts (PeaPod requires an order by 10:00 a.m. for same-day delivery). Not only do customers get this extra convenience, but through the Roche online solution provided by Buy4Now, customers can access 16,000 products online, compared to 9,000 at Peapod (*Buy4now.com* 2006).

Section 3.7 ❯ REVIEW QUESTIONS

1. Explain on-demand delivery service.
2. Describe e-grocers and how they operate.
3. Who are the typical e-grocery shoppers? What services do they require?
4. What are the difficulties in shopping online for groceries?

3.8 ONLINE DELIVERY OF DIGITAL PRODUCTS, ENTERTAINMENT, AND MEDIA

Certain goods, such as software, music, or news stories, may be distributed in a physical form (such as hard copy, CD-ROM, DVD, and newsprint), or they may be digitized and delivered over the Internet. For example, consumers may purchase shrink-wrapped CD-ROMs containing software (along with the owner's manual and a warranty card) or pay for the software at a Web site and immediately download it onto their computers (usually through File Transfer Protocol [FTP], a fast way to download large files).

As described in Chapter 2, products that can be transformed to digital format and delivered over the Internet are called *digital products*. Exhibit 3.10 provides examples of digital products that may be distributed either physically or digitally. Each delivery method has advantages and disadvantages for both sellers and buyers. Customers, for example, may prefer the formats available through physical distribution. They perceive value in holding a physical CD-ROM or music CD as opposed to a downloaded file. In addition, the related packaging of a physical product may be significant. In some cases, customers enjoy the "liner notes" that accompany a music CD. Paper-based software user manuals and other materials also have value and may be preferred over online help features. However, customers may have to wait days for physical products to be delivered.

For sellers, the costs associated with the manufacture, storage, and distribution of physical products (DVDs, CD-ROMs, paper magazines, etc.) can be enormous. Inventory management also becomes a critical cost issue, and so does delivery and distribution. The need for retail intermediaries requires the establishment of relationships with channel partners and revenue-sharing plans. Direct sales of digital content through digital download, however,

EXHIBIT 3.10 Distribution of Digital Versus Physical Products

Type of Product	Physical Distribution	Digital Distribution
Software	Boxed, shrink-wrapped	FTP, direct download, e-mail
Newspapers, magazines	Home delivery, postal mail	Display on Web, "e-zines"
Greeting cards	Retail stores	E-mail, URL link to recipient
Images (e.g., clip-art, graphics)	CD-ROM, magazines	Web site display, downloadable
Movies	DVD, VHS, NTSB, PAL	MPEG3, streaming video, RealNetwork, AVI, QuickTime, etc.
Music	CD, cassette tape	MP3, WAV, RealAudio downloads, wireless devices, iTunes

allow a producer of digital content to bypass the traditional retail channel, thereby reducing overall costs and capturing greater profits. However, retailers are often crucial in creating demand for a product through in-store displays, advertising, and human sales efforts, all of which are lost when the producer disintermediates the traditional channel.

A major revolution in the online entertainment industry occurred when Napster introduced the P2P file-sharing of music (see Online File W3.8). Another major phenomenon in the online delivery of entertainment is YouTube (see Case 3.5).

ONLINE ENTERTAINMENT

Online entertainment is growing rapidly. A survey by Knowledge Networks/Statistical Research Inc. (Castex 2003) shows that online entertainment is already the most popular medium in the United States among young people between the ages of 8 and 17. Thirty-three percent of these respondents prefer to be entertained online, whereas only 26 percent prefer to watch television. There are many kinds of Internet entertainment. It is difficult to precisely categorize them because there tends to be a mixture of entertainment types, delivery modes, and personal taste and choice in deciding whether something is entertainment or not. Some online entertainment can be regarded as interactive, in that the user can interact, often in a somewhat conversational way, with the software and thus change the outcome or shape the direction of the entertainment activity.

The major forms of traditional entertainment are television, film, radio, music, games, reading, and gambling. All of these are now available over the Internet. However, some have

---

CASE 3.5

EC Application

THE YOUTUBE PHENOMENON

YouTube was founded in February 2005 and officially launched its online service in November 2005. In 2006, Google announced its acquisition of YouTube for $1.65 billion in a stock-for-stock transaction.

At the time of the acquisition, YouTube was one of the fastest-growing Web sites in the world, becoming the tenth most popular site on the Web and growing much more rapidly than the much-touted MySpace social networking site. By July 2006, about 100 million video clips were viewed on YouTube daily, and about 65,000 new video clips were uploaded to the site every day. About 20 million people visit the site each month, the predominant age group being 12 to 17 year olds. In a very short time, YouTube has achieved an astounding dominance of the online video market.

YouTube describes itself as a consumer media company. It enables its visitors to upload, view, share, rate, and comment on videos, mostly short clips of less than 10 minutes. Visitors can share their video clips publicly or through private communities and groups who share similar interests. Visitors can also integrate YouTube video clips onto other Web sites. It is a free service, despite its massive bandwidth requirements, with YouTube's revenues coming from advertising dollars.

YouTube prohibits the submission of copyrighted video material and encourages users on the site to be "self-policing" in the sense that they can report material they suspect is copyrighted. Some major filmmakers have submitted requests for YouTube to remove some copyrighted material, but others have adopted more of a policy of engagement

with YouTube, with strategic partnerships seeming more likely than endless litigation at this stage. In addition, YouTube has announced the use of antipiracy software that is designed to detect cheap illegal copies of copyrighted videos. However, there are also concerns that unless the Google–YouTube alliance acts to deal swiftly with copyright concerns, and perhaps offers content owners a share in revenues from uploaded content, the parties may become embroiled in damaging litigation.

The outcome of the acquisition by Google remains to be seen, but it is expected to be a highly innovative partnership, leveraging YouTube's expertise in the media space and Google's expertise in searching and organizing information.

Sources: Compiled from *youtube.com* (accessed November 2006), *Google.com* (2006), *en.wikipedia.org/wiki/YouTube* (accessed November 2006) and Bernoff and Haven (2006).

Questions

1. Describe YouTube's business model. Is it a sustainable model?

2. What complementary capabilities do Google and YouTube offer one another? Could this acquisition prove successful for Google?

3. What legal and ethical issues might YouTube and Google need to be aware of in offering a video-sharing Web site?

become much more popular in the new environment because the capabilities of modern technology mean that the experience can be enhanced for people who enjoy that activity. For example, online games offer multimedia experiences with colorful animations and sound and allow the player to affect the course and outcome of the game.

Examples of Online Entertainment

The following are prominent categories of online entertainment.

- **Web browsing.** This category includes Web sites that require more than the usual user input as part of the process of using the Web site. It is likely that in the future the Web itself will transform into an environment where the user can move through the Web in a virtual reality world. Wikipedia and various blog sites are examples where users can add their own content and views to Web sites.

- **Internet gaming.** This includes all forms of gaming, including arcade gaming, lotteries, casino gaming, promotional incentives, and so on. This is already a substantial market and is growing rapidly. Burns (2006c) reports that the online game market generated $1.1 billion in revenues in 2005 and that this is expected to grow to $4.4 billion by 2010.

- **Fantasy sports games.** According to *eMarketer Daily*, the number of unique visitors to fantasy sports sites exceeds 7.4 million a month (reported by *RealSEO.com* 2004). The major sites are sportline.com and espn.com.

- **Single and multiplayer games.** These include online games in which multiple users log on to a Web site to participate in a game as well as games that require downloading from the Web site and installation on a PC. Examples of such sites include battle.net, games.msn.com, chess.net, and casesladder.com. MMOGs (massively multiplayer online games) in which large numbers of people interact to play a role-playing game where they assume the role of a fictional character via a virtual world worldwide have witnessed dramatic growth. Some of the commercially available games have millions of subscribers, with estimates that such games generate about $350 billion in revenues per year (Burns 2006d).

- **Adult entertainment.** Adult entertainment has exploded onto the Internet. This is one industry that seems certain to find a lucrative home on the Internet. Indeed, adult entertainment has been called the Net's most profitable business model (see Chapter 8).

- **Card games.** These are very popular and some involve gambling. For a discussion, see Chapter 8.

- **Social networking sites.** A range of social networking sites have arisen where like-minded people can share information and viewpoints, publicize events and activities, and generally form a community online. One of the largest of these, MySpace.com was described in Chapter 1 and is featured in Chapter 18.

- **Participatory Web sites.** Participatory Web sites include clubs, user groups, and "infotainment" sites (i.e., a site that provides information on all aspects of a topic and provides mechanisms for the user to interact with other people interested in the topic; for example, a Web site about sports).

- **Reading.** E-books are now published on the Web (see Chapter 8). Web versions of print media, including magazines and newspapers, are now available.

- **Live events.** Sports fans can listen to and/or watch live sporting events on the Internet, sometimes free of charge.

A range of entertainment activities also are available on a number of mobile Internet-enabled devices. For example, in Australia subscribers to the three mobile networks can watch cricket on their mobile phones in real time.

Entertainment-Related Services

The Internet also enables a number of services that support offline entertainment activities:

- **Event ticketing.** The click-and-mortar giant TicketMaster (ticketmaster.com) is the most popular place for getting tickets to many types of offline entertainment. However, tickets also can be obtained from the vendors directly. An example of ticketing in Asia is cityline.com.hk, which offers tickets to events and movie theaters. Tickets also are being sold via cell phone (see Chapter 9).

▶ **Restaurants.** Many restaurants allow online reservations. They are computerizing their reservation systems using software from companies such as OpenTable (opentable.com), one of the leaders in this area. More than 5,000 restaurants have adopted OpenTable online reservation and guest management software. Once a restaurant adopts the software, it becomes part of the OpenTable network, enabling customers to either make a reservation directly with the restaurant online or via the OpenTable.com Web site (*OpenTable.com* 2006). Some restaurants offer deliveries as well. Examples are pizza places and Chinese restaurants. This kind of service is frequently accomplished via cell phones, telephones, or the Internet (e.g., geoexpat.com).

▶ **Information retrieval.** Many portals offer entertainment-related information for retrieval by users. The Internet has quickly become the largest source of information on many topics.

▶ **Retrieval of audio and video entertainment.** Users can download audio, music, video, and movies from Internet servers for non–real-time playback. In 2003, Apple introduced the iPod and iTunes, a service that allows songs to be sold online (100 million were sold the first year). In July 2004, Duke University gave all of its incoming freshmen free iPods. The university arranged a Web site, modeled on iTunes, that allows the downloading of lectures, music, audio, books, and so on. Other companies offer similar services.

DEVELOPMENTS IN THE DELIVERY OF DIGITAL PRODUCTS

An interesting development in music distribution is the availability of CD customization sites (e.g., see angelfire.com). These sites enable consumers to collect their favorite songs from various artists and then create a "personal favorites" compilation CD, which is shipped to the consumer. The CD mastering sites pay royalties to the various artists through established channels.

Another trend is the disintermediation of traditional print media. Several journals and magazines ceased publishing "dead paper" versions and have become strictly online distributors of digital content (e.g., pcai.com), generating revenues through advertising or by online subscriptions. (Some of these transformations were subsequently reversed due to lack of financial success of the online version.) Other prominent publications, including the *Wall Street Journal*, now offer either a paper-only subscription, an online-only subscription (at a lower subscription price), or a dual-mode subscription for consumers who want to access their business news through both methods so that they can use search engines to find archived information or read information not available in the paper version.

Similarly, Egghead Software closed all of its brick-and-mortar stores and became a pure-play software store. In doing so, the company dramatically cut operating costs and streamlined its inventory requirements but lost certain advantages offered by a physical presence. Unfortunately, Egghead.com went out of business due to strong online competition in 2001; its assets were picked up by Amazon.com. As you may recall from Chapter 1, CompUSA is now selling software from kiosks. Hundreds of software companies are selling their products as downloads (e.g., Norton Security from Symantec). Time will tell if digital delivery replaces or enhances traditional delivery methods for various types of digital content.

Section 3.8 ▶ REVIEW QUESTIONS

1. Describe digital goods and their delivery.
2. What are the benefits and the limitations of digital delivery?
3. What are the major forms of online entertainment? Do you think people of different age groups and social classes might be attracted to different types of online entertainment?

3.9   ONLINE PURCHASE-DECISION AIDS

Many sites and tools are available to help consumers with online purchasing decisions. Wal-Mart, for example, equipped its online store with an intelligent search engine. Consumers must decide which product or service to purchase, which site to use for the purchase (a manufacturer site, a general-purpose e-tailer, a niche intermediary, or some other site), and what other services to employ. Some sites offer price comparisons as their primary tool (e.g., pricerunner.com, shopzilla.com, and goodgearguide.com.au); others evaluate services, trust, quality, and other factors. Shopping portals, shopping robots ("shopbots"), business ratings sites, trust verification sites, and other shopping aids also are available.

SHOPPING PORTALS

shopping portals

Gateways to e-storefronts and e-malls; may be comprehensive or niche oriented.

Shopping portals are gateways to storefronts and e-malls. Like any other portal, they may be comprehensive or niche oriented. Comprehensive or general-purpose portals have links to many different sellers and present and evaluate a broad range of products. An example of a comprehensive portal is Ecost.com (ecost.com). Several public portals also offer shopping opportunities and comparison aids. Examples are shopping.com, shopping.yahoo.com, shopping.msn.com, and shopping.aol.com. These all have clear shopping links from the main page of the portal, and they generate revenues by directing consumers to their affiliates' sites. Some of these portals even offer comparison tools to help identify the best price for a particular item. Several of these evaluation companies have purchased shopbots (see the following discussion) or other, smaller shopping aids and incorporated them into their portals.

Shopping portals may also offer specialized niche aids with information and links for purchasers of automobiles, toys, computers, travel, or some other narrow area. Such portals also help customers conduct research. Examples include review.zdnet.com and shopper.cnet.com for computer equipment. The advantage of niche shopping portals is their ability to specialize in a certain line of products and carefully track consumer tastes within a specific and relevant market segment. Some of these portals seek only to collect the referral fee from their affiliation with sites they recommend. Others have no formal relationship with the sellers; instead, they sell banner ad space to advertisers who wish to reach the communities who regularly visit these specialized sites. In other cases, shopping portals act as intermediaries by selling directly to consumers, though this may harm their reputation for independence and objectivity.

SHOPBOTS SOFTWARE AGENTS

shopping robots (shopping agents or shopbots)

Tools that scout the Web on behalf of consumers who specify search criteria.

Savvy Internet shoppers may bookmark their favorite shopping sites, but what if they want to find other stores with good service and policies that sell similar items at lower prices? **Shopping robots** (also called shopping agents or shopbots) are tools that scout the Web for consumers who specify search criteria. Different shopbots use different search methods. For example, MySimon (mysimon.com) searches the Web to find the best prices and availability for thousands of popular items. This is not a simple task. The shopbot may have to evaluate different SKU (stock-keeping unit) numbers for the same item, because each e-tailer may have a different SKU rather than a standardized data-representation code. In addition to price, pricegrabber.com includes product details and features, product reviews from merchants and consumers, and additional information about the store selling the item.

Some agents specialize in certain product categories or niches. For example, consumers can get help shopping for cars at autobytel.com, carsdirect.com, autovantage.com, and autos.msn.com. Zdnet.com searches for information on computers, software, and peripherals. A shopping agent at office.com helps consumers find the best price for office supplies. A shopping agent for books is isbn.nu. In addition, agents such as pricegrabber.com are able to identify customers' preferences. Shopping.com (shopping.com) (now owned by eBay) allows consumers to compare over 1,000 different merchant sites and seeks lower prices on their behalf. Negotiation agents are even available to assist auction bidders (e.g., auctionbid.com) by automating the bid process using the bidder's instructions. For a comparison of shopping bots, refer to Aquino (2005) and Wang (2006).

"Spy" Services

In this context, "spy" services are not the CIA or MI5 (mi5.gov.uk). Rather, they are services that visit Web sites for customers, at their direction, and notify them of their findings. Web surfers and shoppers constantly monitor sites for new information, special sales, ending time of auctions, stock updates, and so on, but visiting the sites to monitor them is time consuming. Several sites will track stock prices or airline special sales and send e-mails accordingly. For example, cnn.com, pcworld.com, and expedia.com will send people personalized alerts. Spectorsoft.com enables users to create a list of "spies" that visit Web sites; the spy sends an e-mail when it finds something of interest. Users can choose predesigned spies or create their own. Special searches are provided by web2mail.com, which responds to e-mail queries. Of special interest is Yahoo! Alerts (alerts.yahoo.com), an index of e-mail alerts for many different things, including job listings, real estate, travel specials, and auctions. Users set up alerts so that they hit their in-boxes periodically or whenever new information is available. The alerts are sent via e-mail and come with commercial ads.

Of course, one of the most effective ways to spy on Internet users is to introduce cookies and spyware in their computers. (See Chapters 4 and 17 for details.)

Wireless Shopping Comparisons

Users of Mysimon.com (all regular services) and AT&T Digital PocketNet service have access to wireless shopping comparisons. Users who are equipped with an AT&T Internet-ready cell phone can find the service on the AT&T main menu; it enables shoppers to compare prices any time from anywhere, including from any physical store.

BUSINESS RATINGS SITES

Many Web sites rate various e-tailers and online products based on multiple criteria. Bizrate.com (bizrate.com), Consumer Reports Online (consumerreports.org), Forrester Research (forrester.com), and Gomez Advisors (gomez.com) are such well-known sites. At Gomez.com, the consumer can actually specify the relative importance of different criteria when comparing online banks, toy sellers, e-grocers, and so on. Bizrate.com organized a network of shoppers that report on various sellers and uses the compiled results in its evaluations. Note that different raters may provide different rankings. Case 3.6 discusses ResellerRatings.com, an interesting example of a business ratings site.

TRUST VERIFICATION SITES

With so many sellers online, many consumers are not sure whom they should trust. A number of companies purport to evaluate and verify the trustworthiness of various e-tailers. One such company is TRUSTe. The TRUSTe seal appears at the bottom of each TRUSTe-approved e-tailer's Web site. E-tailers pay TRUSTe for use of the seal (which they call a "trustmark"). TRUSTe's 1,300-plus members hope that consumers will use the seal as an assurance and as a proxy for actual research into their conduct of business, privacy policy, and personal information protection.

The most comprehensive trust verification sites are VeriSign, BBBOnline, and WebTrust (cpawebtrust.org). VeriSign (verisign.com) tends to be the most widely used. Other sources of trust verification include Secure Assure (secureassure.com), which charges yearly license fees based on a company's annual revenue. In addition, Ernst and Young, the global public accounting firm, has created its own service for auditing e-tailers in order to offer some guarantee of the integrity of their business practices.

OTHER SHOPPING TOOLS

Other digital intermediaries assist buyers or sellers, or both, with the research and purchase processes. For example, escrow services (e.g., escrow.com and fortis-escrow.com) assist buyers and sellers in the exchange of items and money. Because buyers and sellers do not see or know each other, a trusted third party frequently is needed to facilitate the proper exchange of money and goods. Escrow sites may also provide payment-processing support, as well as letters of credit (see Chapter 12).

CASE 3.6
EC Application

RESELLER RATINGS: MAKING ONLINE RETAILERS ACCOUNTABLE TO CUSTOMERS

ResellerRatings (*resellerratings.com*) started life as a one-stop shopping resource for consumers of computer products and electronics, offering site visitors the option of comparing prices of many products across different online vendors. However, its mission was slightly different. ResellerRatings believed that online merchants needed to be accountable to their customers and that customers needed not only to be able to find great products and good prices but also to be sure of the reputability of the merchants they were buying from. However, ResellerRatings also recognized a role of helping merchants to offer better service and experience for their customers by providing them with feedback from customers on their perceptions of the businesses' performance.

For merchants, ResellerRatings offers a free subscription service that includes a point-of-sale exit survey for customers. This survey enables a retailer to elicit feedback from customers on a variety of dimensions, including their perceptions of the range of products and services, the ease of finding goods and placing an order, and their satisfaction with the shopping experience. For a modest premium subscription, the merchant can benefit form additional services, such as receiving e-mail alerts whenever a customer posts a review on the company and placing advertisements on the ResellerRatings Web site.

Customers are encouraged to post reviews of a company, both positive and negative, and to voice their opinion about their experience with a particular retailer. Retailers are given an option to respond to customer concerns, to confirm that a particular transaction and invoice number are legitimate, and to help resolve the customer's concerns. ResellerRatings ensures that the comments posted are legitimate (legitimate customers commenting on genuine transactions and posted once only). Retailers cannot opt out of this system (they cannot request to be removed). ResellerRatings then computes a table of both the best and the worst retailers, based on verified customer feedback and responses to the survey. When using the site for price comparisons, customers can also check that the store with the most attractive deal for the item of interest is also a reputable dealer.

So, how does ResellerRatings make money? What is its business model? How does it sustain itself? Who benefits? The point-of-sale exit survey contains about 40 questions, 6 of which are used to compute its published rating of retailers. The remaining questions are analyzed and sold as market research data to other companies. Essentially, these companies pay for analyzed data so that they can better understand the needs and wishes of online shoppers. In the case of ResellerRatings, customers benefit through increased trust and confidence in a prospective merchant and by having an opportunity to express their concerns about poor service. Merchants benefit by having access to reviews and the opportunity to redress customer concerns. ResellerRatings benefits through its careful analysis of data which is then sold to interested parties.

Source: Compiled from *ResellerRatings.com* (2006).

Questions

1. Discuss your concerns about the trustworthiness of an online retailer. Would using a site such as ResellerRatings.com increase your confidence in shopping online?

2. Discuss the business model of ResellerRatings.com. Compare it to the business model of other ratings sites, such as Bizrate.com.

3. Visit *resellerratings.com* and search for an item. How was it to compare the various offerings?

Other decision aids include communities of consumers who offer advice and opinions on products and e-tailers. One such site is epinions.com, which has searchable recommendations on thousands of products. Pricescan.com is a price comparison engine, and pricegrabber.com is a comparison shopping tool that covers over 1 million products. Onlineshoes.com specializes in all types of shoes, and iwon.com specializes in apparel, health and beauty, and other categories. Other software agents and comparison sites are presented in Exhibit 3.11.

Another shopping tool is a *wallet*—in this case, an *electronic wallet*, which is a program that contains the shopper's information. To expedite online shopping, consumers can use electronic wallets so that they do not need to reenter the information each time they shop. Although sites such as Amazon.com offer their own specialized wallets, Microsoft has a universal wallet in its Passport program (see Chapters 12 and 17 for details).

EXHIBIT 3.11 Representative Shopping Software Agents and Comparison Sites

Agent Classification	Product (URL)	Description
Learning agents	Empirical (*vignette.com*)	Surveys user's reading interests and uses machine learning to find Web pages using neural-network-based collaborative filtering technology.
	Blinkx (*blinkx.com*)	Searches intelligently and constantly for video and audio clips of the user's choice.
Comparison shopping agents	MySimon (*mysimon.com*)	Using VLA (virtual learning agent) technology, shops for the best price from merchants in hundreds of product categories with a real-time interface.
	CompareNet (*comparenet.com*)	Interactive buyer's guide that educates shoppers and allows them to make direct comparisons between brands and products.
	Kelkoo (*kelkoo.co.uk*)	Price comparison on UK Web sites.
AI/Logic-supported approaches	Cnetshopper (*shopper.cnet.com*)	Makes price comparisons.
Computer-related shopping guide	Netbuyer (*shopping.zdnet.co.uk/shopping*)	Supplies sales and marketing solutions to technology companies by delivering information about computer and communications industry trends, product developments, and buyer activity.
Car-related shopping guides	Auto-by-Tel (*autobytel.com*)	A low-cost, no-haggle car-buying system used by leading search engines and online programs such as Excite, NetCenter, Lycos, and AT&T WorldNet Services.
	Trilegiant Corp. (*trilegiant.com*)	The Web's premier savings site for great deals on autos. (Also offers travel, shopping, dining, and other services.)
	CarPoint (*autos.msn.com*)	A one-stop shopping place for searching and purchasing automobiles.
Find lowest prices	PriceScan (*pricescan.com*)	Searches for lowest price for a given product.
	PriceGrabber (*pricegrabber.com*)	Looks for the best deals.
Aggregator portal	Pricing Central (*pricingcentral.com*)	Aggregates information from other shopping agents and search engines. Comparison shopping is done in real time (latest pricing information).
Personalized information	Newsbot (*newsbot.msnbc.msn.com*)	Automatic personalization of business and industry news.
Real-time agents	Kanndu (*kanndu.com*)	Allows users to surf over to a single mobile Internet portal and click around to multiple e-shopping sites to make purchases with only a few keystrokes.
Comparison shopping agents	Shopping.com (*shopping.com*)	Compares prices; saving the consumer time and money by giving key information as the consumer is shopping online.
Evaluation and comparisons	BizRate (*bizrate.com*)	Rates merchants based on real consumer feedback, per product. Comparison of similar products.

Amazon.com's A9 Search Engine

Amazon.com offers a special search tool known as A9.com (a9.com). A9.com is a powerful search engine; it uses Web search and image search results enhanced by Google, Search Inside the Book® results from Amazon.com, reference results from Answers.com, movie results from IMDb, and more.

A9.com remembers information so the user doesn't have to. A user can make notes about any Web page and search them. It offers a new way to store and organize bookmarks. It even recommends new sites and favorite old sites specifically for the user to visit. With the A9 Toolbar installed, the user's Web browsing history will be saved, allowing the user to search through his or her whole history (and clear items the user doesn't want kept). A9.com uses the user's history to recommend new sites, to alert the user of new search results, and to let the user know the last time a particular page was visited.

Answers.com

Finding relevant information is the most important feature of a search tool, followed by getting credible results and doing it quickly. Answers.com (answers.com, formerly GuruNet) was founded in 1999 and aims to provide answers to many of the questions that customers may have. Answers.com is aimed at all people who must locate and deal with all kinds of information as part of their daily routines, including writers, students, educators, marketers, journalists, and other professionals. In addition to revenues raised through advertising, Answers.com sells content to third parties for either a revenue share or usage fee.

Section 3.9 ▶ REVIEW QUESTIONS

1. Define shopping portals and provide two examples.
2. What are shopbots?
3. Explain the role of business and Web site rating and site verification tools in the purchase-decision process.
4. Why are escrow services and electronic wallets useful for online purchases?
5. Describe the role of search engines to support shopping.

3.10   PROBLEMS WITH E-TAILING AND LESSONS LEARNED

There are a number of challenges in creating a successful e-tailing business. A few companies do not even try e-tailing, although these numbers are declining. The reasons that retailers give for not going online include: their product is not appropriate for Web sales, lack of significant opportunity, high cost, technological immaturity, online sales conflict with core business, and the like. Others try e-tailing but do not succeed. E-tailing offers some serious challenges and tremendous risks for those who fail to provide value to the consumer, who fail to establish a profitable business model, or who fail to properly execute the model they establish. The road to e-tail success is littered with dead companies that could not deliver on their promises. The shakeout from mid-2000 to late-2002 caused many companies to fail; others learned and adapted. It is fair to say that the much more balanced, analytical, and sober perspective of late offers a much better appreciation of the issues, challenges, risks, and potential benefits of EC.

Insights and Additions 3.4 provides a sample of failed B2C companies. Some enduring principles can be distilled from the failures, and these "lessons learned" are discussed next. (See Chapter 14 for further discussion.)

WHAT LESSONS CAN BE LEARNED FROM THESE FAILURES?

Painful as failures are, at least they can point out some valuable lessons. The following lessons can be drawn from the B2C dot-com failures in Insights and Additions 3.4 and other cases.

Insights and Additions 3.4   B2C Dot-Com Failures

During 2000–2001, more than 600 dot-coms folded in the United States, and more than 1,000 folded worldwide. Here are some examples. While our understanding of the factors contributing to EC success has improved dramatically, there are still important lessons that can be learned from expensive failures.

Kozmo.com. Kozmo.com initiated a creative idea for on-demand deliveries of movie rentals (and related items) to customer's doors. The first problem was how to return the movies. Drop boxes for the returns were vandalized, volume was insufficient, competitors entered the market, and even an alliance with Starbucks (to host the drop boxes) and a large porn selection did not help. In addition, the company was sued for refusal to deliver to low-income neighborhoods that had high crime rates. The company failed in 2001 after "burning" $250 million. (See Chapter 13 for the full story.)

The lessons from Kozmo are that attending to the supply chain, in this case delivery and return of the goods, is essential. So, too, is understanding the business environment and the potential impact of sociotechnical issues on the viability of the proposed business model. Ensuring adequate cash flows while the company achieves viability is also an important issue with new ventures.

Furniture.com. Selling furniture on the Internet may sound like a great idea. Furniture.com even paid $2.5 million for its domain name. Delivering the furniture was the problem. A number of manufacturers were not able to meet the delivery dates for the most popular items. In addition, many pieces of furniture cannot be delivered by UPS because of their size and weight. The cost of special deliveries was $200 to $300 per shipment, resulting in a loss. The company folded in 2001 after "burning" $75 million. For details, see Wang et al. (2006).

The failure of Furniture.com points to the important lesson of delivery. Typically, online shoppers demand easy delivery options, and any business model needs to figure the cost and viability of arranging delivery. This might suggest that large, heavy items and the like may be difficult to sell directly online unless a cost-effective delivery method is found.

eRegister.com. Registering online for classes via an intermediary may sound interesting to investors, but not to customers. If a person wants to register to take a class at the YMCA or Weight Watchers, why not do it directly? The business model simply did not work, and the company folded in 2001.

The failure of eRegister.com demonstrates the importance of market research to establish the viability of a business idea before huge amounts of money are invested. This is particularly true in EC, where businesses often are venturing into totally unexplored territory.

Go.com. Go.com was a Disney portal site that was formed to manage Disney's Web sites and generate revenue from advertising. The business model did not work. To cover the salaries of its 400 employees, it was necessary for Go.com to sell 2 *billion* paid ad impressions per year. The company was able to sell only 1.6 million impressions. After losing $790 million in write-offs and $50 million in expenses, the site closed in February 2000. No amount of Disney magic helped.

Again, market research to establish viability of the concept is essential. Some sober assessments of sales forecasts might have saved Disney some financial pain in this case.

Pets.com. Pets.com, a Web site devoted to selling pet food, pet toys, and pet supplies, operated in a very competitive market. This market competition forced Pets.com to advertise extensively and to sell goods below cost. The cost of acquiring customers mounted to $240 per new customer. Yet, being one of the early dot-com companies, it was able to buy a rival, Petstore.com, in 2000. After spending $147 million in less than 2 years, Pets.com had a lot of brand recognition but not a real brand. After collapsing, its assets were sold to Petsmart.com (*petsmart.com*), a click-and-mortar pet supplies retailer. At the same time, click-and-mortar Petco.com purchased Petopia.com, another B2C failure in the pet area.

Selling goods below price is a risky strategy and requires careful modeling to demonstrate the viability of this notion beyond the very short term. On top of this, Pets.com also had to raise brand awareness, placing it at a disadvantage to already established brands such as Petsmart. The viability of the business model on which this dot-com idea was based seems to have been flawed.

Sources: Compiled from Kaplan (2002) and Hwang and Stewart (2006).

Don't Ignore Profitability

One fundamental lesson is that each marginal sale should lead to a marginal profit. It has been said that in business, "If it doesn't make cents, it doesn't make sense." The trouble with most virtual e-tailers is that they lose money on every sale as they try to grow to a profitable size and scale.

Many pure-play e-tailers were initially funded by venture capital firms that provided enough financing to get the e-tailers started and growing. However, in many cases the funding ran out before the e-tailer achieved sufficient size and maturity to break even and become self-sufficient. In some cases, the underlying cost and revenue models were not sound—the firms would never be profitable without major changes in their funding sources, revenue model and pricing, and controlled costs. Long-run success requires financial viability. Many firms were also damaged by insufficient attention to cash flows. Thus, revenue growth, cash flows, and sustainable profitability are all vital ingredients in EC success.

Manage New Risk Exposure

The Internet creates new connectivity with customers and offers the opportunity to expand markets. However, it also has the potential to expose a retailer to more sources of risk. Local companies have to contend only with local customers and local regulations, whereas national firms have more constituents with which to interact. Global firms have to contend with numerous cultural, financial, and other perspectives: Will they offend potential customers because of a lack of awareness of other cultures? Global Internet firms also have to manage their exposure to risk from the mosaic of international legal structures, laws, and regulations. For example, they can be sued in other countries for their business practices. (For additional details, see Chapter 14.)

Groups of disgruntled employees or customers can band together to contact the news media, file a class action lawsuit, or launch their own Web site to publicize their concerns. One example of this is ihatewalmart.blogspot.com, where people disaffected by Wal-Mart, have an opportunity to express their concerns online. Blogging and other accessible Web sites make it relatively easy for ordinary people to voice their concerns about the behaviors and policies of government at all levels, businesses, corporations, and the like. When each disgruntled individual tells 50 friends and coworkers about a problem, it may result in a few lost sales; with the Internet, these people can now reach thousands or even millions of potential customers.

Watch the Cost of Branding

Branding has always been considered a key to retail success. Consumers are thought to be more willing to search out products with strong brand recognition, as well as pay a bit more for them. In the relatively early days of e-tailing, it was sometimes argued that brand recognition was the key to success, with the argument that Internet sites such as Amazon.com are putting established brands (e.g., traditional brick-and-mortar booksellers) at risk by creating quick brand recognition. However, this has not necessarily been the case. For one thing, in e-tailing the drive to establish brand recognition quickly often leads to excessive spending. For example, one upstart e-tailer (epidemic.com) spent over 25 percent of its venture capital funding on one 30-second television advertisement during the Super Bowl! The company folded a few months later (Carton and Locke 2001), suggesting that big spending to build brand image does not guarantee success. In other cases, e-tailers offered extravagant promotions and loss-leading offers to drive traffic to their sites and then lost money on every sale. The huge volume of site traffic merely served to increase their losses. The lesson from success stories is that most customers, especially long-term loyal customers, come to a Web site from known and trusted business names, affiliate links, search engines, or personal recommendations—not from Super Bowl ads. Those organizations achieving online success as e-tailers often do so because they have a well-articulated and integrated strategy, visionary leadership, effective supply chains, and information systems and technology platforms that support efficient processes and provide real-time access to relevant, accurate data (irrespective of whether the data are gathered from an online transaction or a traditional in-store transaction) (Epstein 2004; Huang et al. 2005).

Do Not Start with Insufficient Funds

It may seem obvious that a venture will not succeed if it lacks enough funds at the start, but many people are so excited about their business idea that they decide to try anyway. An example of this is the failure of Garden.com. Garden.com was a Web site that provided rich, dynamic gardening content (how to plant bulbs, tips on gardening, an "ask the expert" feature, etc.) and a powerful landscape design tool, which allowed a visitor to lay out an entire garden and then purchase all the necessary materials with one click. Garden.com also hosted various "community" features with discussions about various gardening-related topics. Gardeners are often passionate about their hobby and like to learn more about new plants and gardening techniques. The business idea sounded good. However, the site failed due to the company's inability to raise sufficient venture capital necessary to cover losses until enough business volume was reached.

The Web Site Must Be Effective

Today's savvy Internet shoppers expect Web sites to offer superior technical performance—fast page loads, quick database searches, streamlined graphics, and so forth. Web sites that delay or frustrate consumers will not experience a high sales volume because of a high percentage of abandoned purchases. Online Chapter 19 describes the functionalities that are needed for effective sites.

Keep It Interesting

Web sites without dynamic content will bore returning visitors. Static design is a turnoff. Today, most e-tailers offer valuable tips and information for consumers, who often come back just for that content and may purchase something in the process. L.L. Bean, for example, offers a rich database of information about parks and recreational facilities as well as its buying guides. Visitors who enter the site to find a campground or a weekend event may also purchase a tent or a raincoat.

Although there have been many e-tailing failures (mostly pure-play e-tailers, but some click-and-mortar companies or EC initiatives, too), success stories abound. Many are described throughout this book. The successful case of a floral business is presented in Online File W3.9. In general, although pure-play online retailing is risky and its future is not clear, online retailing is growing very rapidly as a complementary distribution channel to physical stores and mail-order catalogs. In other words, the click-and-mortar model appears to be winning.

SUCCESSFUL CLICK-AND-MORTAR STRATEGIES

Although thousands of companies have evolved their online strategies into mature Web sites with extensive interactive features that add value to the consumer purchase process, many sites remain simple "brochureware" sites with limited interactivity. Many traditional companies are in a transitional stage. Mature transactional systems include features for payment processing, order fulfillment, logistics, inventory management, and a host of other services. In most cases, a company must replicate each of its physical business processes and design many more that can only be performed online. Today's environment includes sophisticated access to order information, shipping information, product information, and more through Web pages, touchtone phones, Web-enabled cellular phones, and PDAs over wireless networks. Faced with all of these variables, the challenges to implementing EC can be daunting.

The real gains for traditional retailers come from leveraging the benefits of their physical presence and the benefits of their online presence. Web sites frequently offer better prices and selection, whereas physical stores offer a trustworthy staff and opportunities for customers to examine items before purchasing. (Physical examination often is critical for clothing and ergonomic devices, for example, but not for commodities, music, or software.) Large, efficient established retailers, such as Wal-Mart (walmart.com), Marks & Spencer (marksandspencer.com), and Nordstrom (nordstrom.com), are able to create the optimum value proposition for their customers by providing a complete offering of services.

A traditional brick-and-mortar store with a mature Web site that uses a click-and-mortar strategy is able to do the following:

- ▶ **Speak with one voice.** A firm can link all of its back-end systems to create an integrated customer experience. Regardless of how a customer interfaces with a company, the information received should be consistent and the service provided should be similar. The online experience should be an extension of the experience encountered in traditional transactions.

▶ **Leverage the multichannels.** The innovative retailer will offer the advantages of each marketing channel to customers from all channels. Whether the purchase is made online or at the store, the customer should benefit from the presence of both channels. For example, customers who purchase from the Web site should be allowed to return items to the physical store (Eddie Bauer's policy). In addition, many physical stores, such as Best Buy, now have in-store terminals for ordering items from the Web site if they are not available in the store. Needless to say, prices should be consistent in both channels to avoid "channel conflict" (discussed in Section 3.11).

▶ **Empower the customer.** The seller needs to create a powerful 24/7 channel for service and information. Through various information technologies, sellers can give customers the opportunity to perform various functions interactively, at any time. Such functions include the ability to find store locations, product information, and inventory availability online. Circuit City's Web site (circuitcity.com), for example, allows customers to receive rich product comparisons between various models of consumer electronics products.

In Online File W3.10, we provide an example of successful transformation to a click-and-mortar at Circuit City.

Section 3.10 ▶ REVIEW QUESTIONS

1. Why are virtual e-tailers usually not profitable?
2. Relate branding to profitability.
3. Why are technical performance and dynamic site content important?
4. What motivates a brick-and-mortar company to sell online?
5. Read Online File W3.9. What customer services are provided by Circuit City on its Web site?

3.11 ISSUES IN E-TAILING

The following are representative issues that need to be addressed when conducting B2C.

DISINTERMEDIATION AND REINTERMEDIATION

In the traditional distribution channel, intermediating layers exist between the manufacturer and consumer, such as wholesalers, distributors, and retailers, as shown in part A of Exhibit 3.12. In some countries, such as Japan, one may find inefficient distribution networks with as many as 10 layers of intermediaries. These extra layers can add as much as a 500 percent markup to a manufacturer's prices.

Intermediaries traditionally have provided trading infrastructure (such as a sales network), and they manage the complexity of matching buyers' and sellers' needs. However, the introduction of EC has resulted in the automation of many tasks provided by intermediaries. Does this mean that travel agents, real estate agents, job agency employees, insurance agents, and other such jobs and businesses will disappear?

disintermediation
The removal of organizations or business process layers responsible for certain intermediary steps in a given supply chain.

Manufacturers can use the Internet to sell directly to customers and provide customer support online. In this sense, the traditional intermediaries are eliminated, or *disintermediated*. **Disintermediation** refers to the removal of organizations or business process layers responsible for certain intermediary steps in a given supply chain. As shown in part B of Exhibit 3.12, the manufacturer can bypass the wholesalers and retailers, selling directly to consumers. Also, e-tailers may drive regular retailers out of business. For a vivid case of such disintermediation, see the Blue Nile case in Chapter 2.

reintermediation
The process whereby intermediaries (either new ones or those that had been disintermediated) take on new intermediary roles.

However, consumers may have problems selecting an online vendor; vendors may have problems delivering to customers; and both may need an escrow service to ensure the transaction. Thus, new online assistance may be needed, and it may be provided by new or by traditional intermediaries. In such cases, the traditional intermediaries fill new roles, providing *added value* and assistance. This process is referred to as **reintermediation**. It is pictured in part C of Exhibit 3.12. Thus, for the intermediary, the Internet offers new ways to reach new customers, new ways to bring value to customers, and perhaps new ways to generate revenues.

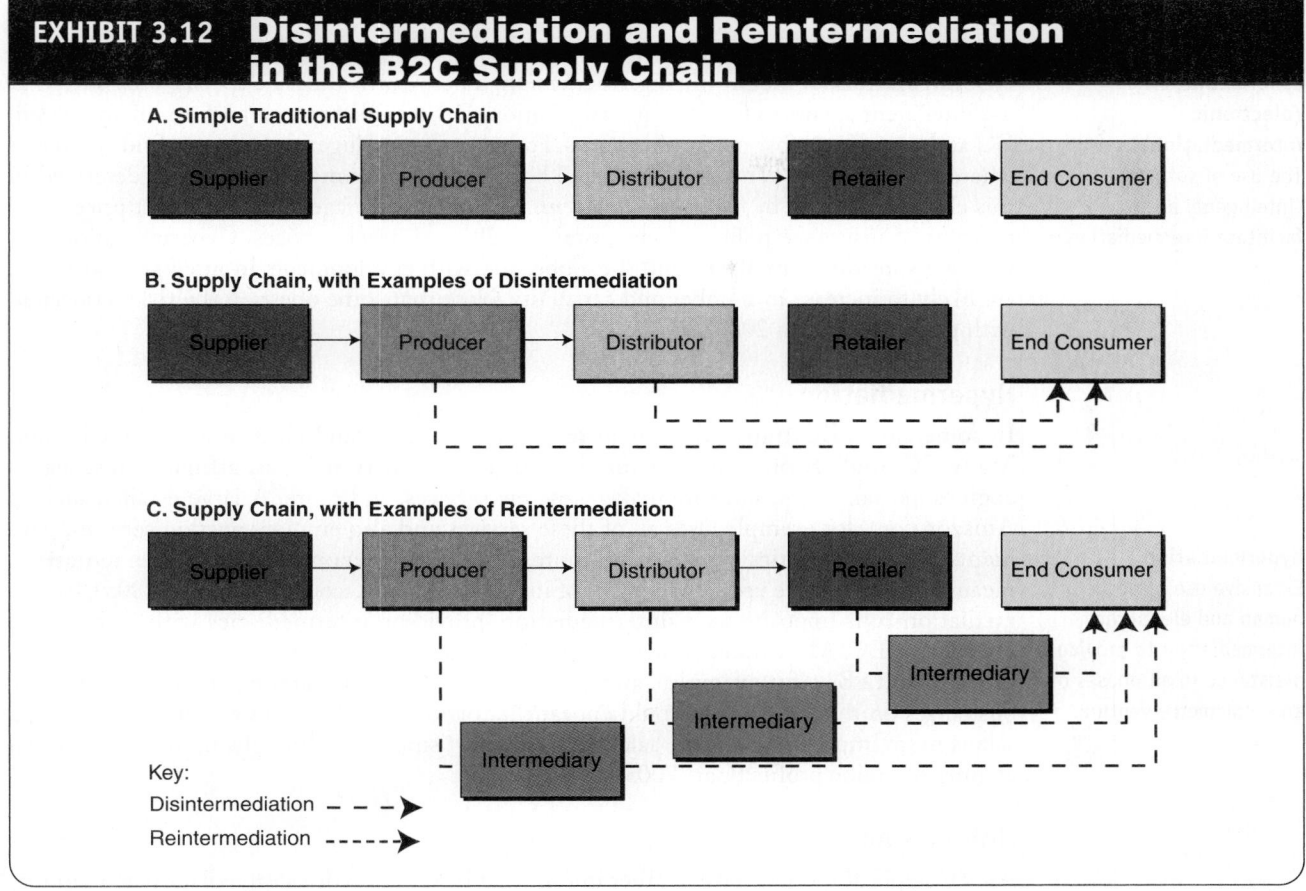

EXHIBIT 3.12   Disintermediation and Reintermediation in the B2C Supply Chain

This chapter has already featured many examples of reintermediation, where comparison shopping sites, ratings sites, and the like, all provide additional services to the consumer to try to build trust, confidence, and facilitate online transactions.

The intermediary's role is shifting to one that emphasizes value-added services, such as assisting customers in comparison shopping from multiple sources, providing total solutions by combining services from several vendors, and providing certifications and trusted third-party control and evaluation systems. For instance, in the world of online new and used car sales, electronic intermediaries assist buyers and/or sellers. These are new *reintermediaries*, intermediaries that have restructured their role in the purchase process.

An example of the new roles of intermediaries are Edmunds (edmunds.com), which gives consumers a vast amount of information about cars, including price comparisons, ratings, the location of cars for sale, and the dealer's true costs; CARFAX (carfax.com), which can research a specific used car and tell the consumer if it has ever been in an accident or had an odometer rollback; and iMotors (imotors.com), which offers members discounts on insurance, gas, and repairs. Additionally, "lead services" direct buyers to member dealers and, in some cases, also offer direct sales of new cars. The leading site in this category is autobytel.com. Others include Amazon.com's partner CarsDirect (carsdirect.com), Autoweb (autoweb.com), and Cars.com (cars.com).

Some reintermediaries are newcomers, rivaling the traditional retail stores (e.g., Blue Nile), whereas others are additional operations established by the traditional retailers or intermediaries, such as Edmunds, that use both the old and the new intermediation methods (like click-and-mortar). Some reintermediaries cooperate with manufacturers or retailers to provide a needed service to the seller or distributor in the online environment. Other reintermediaries are virtual e-tailers that fill a unique niche. Intermediaries such as online retailers and shopping portals can also act as reintermediaries. The evolution and operation of these companies is critical to the success of e-commerce.

Cybermediation

In addition to reintermediation, a completely new role in EC has emerged called **cybermediation**, or **electronic intermediation**. These terms describe special Web sites that use intelligent agents to facilitate intermediation. Cybermediators can perform many roles in EC and can affect most market functions. For example, intelligent agents can find when and where an item that a consumer wants will be auctioned. The matching services described in this chapter are done by *cybermediator agents*. Cybermediator agents also conduct price comparisons of insurance policies, long-distance calls, and other services. Cybermediation services are spreading rapidly around the globe, and with developments in intelligent software, are likely to increase in number and capability. Note that some question the risks associated with this (Shoniregun 2004).

Hypermediation

In some cases, EC transactions require extensive human and electronic intermediation. Many EC applications require content providers, security services, affiliate sites, search engines, portals, ISPs, software makers, escrow services, and more. A large e-tailer, such as Amazon.com, for example, uses all of these services and also employs auction services, payments services, logistics support, and more. This phenomenon is called **hypermediation**, meaning the extensive use of new types of intermediation. According to Carr (2005), hypermediation runs opposite to disintermediation, providing intermediaries with a chance to profit from EC. Most transactions now involve a number of intermediaries (such as Yahoo!, Google, and eBay, for example), and these intermediaries are among the most profitable businesses on the Internet. It would appear that controlling the clicks en route to making a sale is more important than the sale itself, as advertising click-throughs become substantial engines of online profits (Carr 2005).

Unbundling

An EC application may have another impact that is related to disintermediation and reintermediation. Bauer and Colgan (2002) call this impact *unbundling*. According to this concept, old economy processes will be broken into specialized segments that can be delivered by specialized intermediaries. For example, in the financial services industry, buying a stock may be done in five separate segments: information gathering, trade ordering, execution, settlement, and account keeping. As a result of unbundling the processes, the specialized services that are offered can be executed in small segments better, faster, and more efficiently.

CHANNEL CONFLICT

Many traditional retailers establish a new marketing channel when they start selling online. Similarly, some manufacturers have instituted direct marketing initiatives in parallel with their established channels of distribution, such as retailers or dealers. In such cases, channel conflict may occur. **Channel conflict** refers to any situation in which direct competition and/or damage caused by bypassing a former existing channel partner is perceived to have resulted from the introduction of a new, often online, channel. The extent of this conflict varies according to the nature of the industry and characteristics of particular firms, but sometimes, a move to sell online can damage old, valued relationships between trading partners. Channel conflict can also be said to occur when a move to online trading simply moves a company's customers from their traditional stores, for example, to an online environment, thus cannibalizing the sales from the former and potentially negatively impacting the traditional outlets by rendering them less profitable. However, careful management and the adoption of sound strategies can deliver a number of synergies for bricks and mortar e-tailers, especially those associated with encouraging cross-channel cooperation, and exploiting the unique strengths of each channel to maximize the experience for the customer.

DETERMINING THE RIGHT PRICE

Pricing a product or service on the Internet, especially by a click-and-mortar company, is complicated. On the one hand, prices need to be competitive on the Internet. Today's comparison engines will show the consumer the prices at many stores, for almost all commodity products, at almost no cost to the consumer. However, balanced against this is the fact that for some items, transaction costs will decrease, the cost of distribution will decrease, and supply chains may become more efficient and shorter, meaning that e-tailers may be able to compete in the aggressive online market space. On the other hand, prices should be in line with the corporate policy on profitability, and in a click-and-mortar company, in line with the offline channel's pricing strategy. To avoid price conflict, some companies have created independent online subsidiaries.

EC offers companies new opportunities to test prices, segment customers, and adjust to changes in supply and demand. We argue that companies are not taking advantage of these opportunities. Companies can make prices more precise (optimal prices); they can be more adaptable to changes in the environment; and they can be more creative and accurate regarding different prices to different segments. In addition, in one-to-one marketing (Chapter 4) a company can have personalized prices. (For more on pricing strategies as they relate to different business models, see Bandyopadhyay et al. 2001; for use of price optimization tools in retailing, see Parks 2004.)

PERSONALIZATION

One significant characteristic of many online marketing business models is the ability of the seller to create an element of *personalization* for each individual consumer. For example, an e-tailer can use cookie files and other technologies to track the specific browsing and buying behavior of each consumer. With that information, the e-tailer can create a marketing plan tailored to that consumer's pattern by showing items of interest, offering incentives that appeal to that consumer's sense of value, or providing certain services that will attract that consumer back to the Web site. For example, each time an Amazon.com customer returns to the site, Amazon.com suggests titles related to the customer's previous purchasing and browsing behavior. Amazon.com also periodically sends out e-mails alerting customers to specific titles of interest.

The Internet also allows for easy self-configuration ("design it your way"). This creates a large demand for personalized products and services. Manufacturers can meet that demand by using a *mass customization* strategy. As indicated earlier, many companies offer customized products from their Web sites.

Although pure-play e-tailing is risky and its future is unclear, e-tailing is growing rapidly as a complementary distribution channel to traditional stores and catalogs. In other words, the *click-and-mortar model is winning currently and all evidence suggests that this trend will continue.* (See the Real-World Case at the end of the chapter and Online File W3.10.)

FRAUD AND OTHER ILLEGAL ACTIVITIES

A major problem in B2C is the increasing rate of online fraud. This can cause losses to both buyers and sellers. For a more detailed and thorough discussion of online fraud, see the discussion of online fraud in Chapter 17.

HOW TO MAKE CUSTOMERS HAPPY

A critical success factor for B2C is to find what customers want, so the vendor can make them happy. In addition to price, customers want convenience, service, and quality, and they often want to enjoy the experience of online shopping. Merchants can find out what customers want through *market research*, the topic of our next chapter.

Section 3.11 ▶ REVIEW QUESTIONS

1. Define disintermediation.
2. Describe mediation issues, including disintermediation, reintermediation, cybermediation, hypermediation, and unbundling.
3. Describe channel conflict and other conflicts that may appear in e-tailing.
4. Describe price determination in e-tailing.
5. Explain personalization and mass customization opportunities in e-tailing.

MANAGERIAL ISSUES

Some managerial issues related to this chapter are as follows.

1. **What should our strategic position be?** The most important decision for retailers and e-tailers is the overall *strategic position* they establish within their industry. What niche will they fill? What business functions will they execute internally, and which functions will be outsourced? What partners will they use? How will they integrate brick-and-mortar facilities with their online presence? What are their revenue sources in the short and long run, and what are their fixed and marginal costs? An e-business is still a business and must establish solid business practices in the long run in order to ensure profitability and viability. We discuss such issues in Chapters 14 and 16.

2. **Are we financially viable?** The collapse of the dot-com bubble that started in early 2000 provided a wake-up call to many e-tailers. Some returned to business fundamentals, whereas others sought to redefine their business plan in terms of click-and-mortar strategies or alliances with traditional retailers. Because most easy sources of funding have dried up and revenue models are being scrutinized, many e-tailers also are pursuing new partners, and consolidation will continue until there is greater stability within the e-tail segment. Ultimately, there will likely be a smaller number of larger sellers with comprehensive sites and many smaller, specialized niche sites.

3. **How should we introduce wireless shopping?** In some countries (e.g., Japan) shopping from cell phones is very popular (see Chapter 9). However, offering mobile shopping may not be simple or appropriate to all businesses.

4. **Are there international legal issues regarding online recruiting?** Various legal issues must be considered with international online recruiting. For example, online recruitment of people from other countries may involve immigration and legal constraints, and the validity of contracts signed in different countries must be checked by legal experts.

5. **Do we have ethics and privacy guidelines?** Ethical issues are extremely important in an agentless system. In traditional systems, human agents play an important role in assuring the ethical behavior of buyers and sellers. Will online ethics and the rules of etiquette be sufficient to guide behavior on the Internet? Only time will tell. For example, as job-applicant information travels over the Internet, security and privacy become even more important. It is management's job to make sure that information from applicants is secure. Also, e-tailers need to establish guidelines for protecting the privacy of customers who visit their Web sites.

6. **How will intermediaries act in cyberspace?** It will take a few years before the new roles of Internet intermediaries will be stabilized, as well as their fees. Also, the emergence of support services, such as escrow services in global EC, will have an impact on intermediaries and their role.

7. **Should we set up alliances?** Alliances for online initiatives are spreading rapidly. For example, in Hong Kong four banks created a joint online e-bank (to save on capital costs and share the risk). Some online trading brokers are teaming up with banks. Banks are teaming up with telecommunications companies, software companies, and even airlines. Finally, six of the largest music retailers created a joint company (named Echo) to sell music that can be downloaded from the Web (Patsuris 2003). Alliances involving retailers are very popular. However, careful analysis must be done. See Chapters 14 and 16 for more information.

RESEARCH TOPICS

Here are some suggested topics related to this chapter. For details, references, and additional topics, refer to the Online Appendix A "Current EC Research."

1. **Performance Evaluation of Electronic Retailers**
   - Compare the performance of e-tailers with traditional retailers by time, industry, and country.
   - Contrast popular merchandise for e-tailing and physical retailing (what sells well on the Internet and why).

   - Explore the impact of e-tailing on digital content such as music and electronic books.

2. **Pricing Issues in Electronic Channels**
   - Explore the risks versus advantages of differential prices on the Internet.

- Conduct an empirical study of how companies are currently treating differential pricing online.
- Research customers' behavior and their perception of online pricing.
- Research the evolution of pricing strategies in electronic markets.
- Explore the diffusion of price comparison and lowest-price-matching services.
- Research the effect of group purchasing on price discounts.
- Research the effect of using intelligent agents in price reduction.

3. **Channel Conflict and Its Resolution**
- Identify resolution strategies for conflict between online and offline channels.
- Research the theory of power and coalition in conflict resolution.

4. **Online Services and Their Strategies**
- Research consumers' preferences for using online services in comparison with other service-delivery modes.
- Research consumer search behavior for e-tailing.
- Identify the pricing strategy behind bundling digitized products.
- Research security protection strategies for online software distribution of digital products.

5. **Software Agents for Customer Purchase-Decision Aids**
- Research the design of agents used for several of the most time-consuming steps of the buying process.

- Explore the buyer behavior framework in the development of software agents.
- Research human–computer collaboration for purchase decisions.
- Research how next-generation multimedia call centers use software agents.
- Identify appropriate uses of comparison agents.

6. **Internet Banking**
- Explore how banks have reengineered traditional branches after the penetration of electronic channels.
- Analyze the revenue structure of Internet banking services.
- Evaluate the risks of Internet banking and consumer attitudes toward Internet banking.
- Research how banks are using wireless services.

7. **Online Stock Trading**
- Research the application of intelligent agents in online stock trading.
- Examine how traditional branch offices have been restructured following large penetration of the electronic channel.
- Analyze the revenue structure of online brokerage services versus brick-and-mortar ones.
- Explore the use of wireless services.

8. **Customer's Information Processing Provisions and Cost for Online Stock Trading**
- Disintermediation: Where is it really happening and to what extent?
- What can companies do about disintermediation?

SUMMARY

In this chapter, you learned about the following EC issues as they relate to the learning objectives.

1. **The scope of e-tailing.** E-tailing, the online selling of products and services, is growing rapidly. Computers, software, and electronics are the major items sold online. Books, CDs, toys, office supplies, and other standard commodities also sell well. More successful are services sold online, such as airline tickets and travel services, stocks, and insurance.

2. **E-tailing business models.** The major e-tailing business models can be classified by distribution channel— a manufacturer or mail-order company selling direct to consumers, pure-play (virtual) e-tailing, a click-and-mortar strategy with both online and traditional channels, and online malls that provide either referring directories or shared services.

3. **How online travel/tourism services operate.** Most services available through a physical travel agency also are available online. In addition, customers get much more information, much more quickly through online resources. Customers can even receive bids from travel providers. Finally, travelers can compare prices, participate in auctions and chat rooms, and view videos and maps.

4. **The online job market and its benefits.** The online job market is growing rapidly, with thousands and thousands of jobs matched with job seekers each year. The major benefits of online job markets are the ability to reach a large number of job seekers at low cost, to provide detailed information online, to take applications,

and even to conduct tests. Also, using intelligent agents, resumes can be checked and matches made more quickly. Millions of job offers posted on the Internet help job seekers, who also can post their resumes for recruiters.

5. **The electronic real estate market.** The online real estate market is basically supporting rather than replacing existing agents. However, both buyers and sellers can save time and effort in the electronic market. Buyers can purchase distant properties much more easily and in some places have access to less expensive services. Eventually, commissions on regular transactions are expected to decline as a result of the electronic market for real estate, and more sales "by owner" will materialize.

6. **Online trading of stocks and bonds.** One of the fastest growing online businesses is the online trading of securities. It is inexpensive, convenient, and supported by a tremendous amount of financial and advisory information. Trading is very fast and efficient, almost fully automated, and moving toward 24/7 global trading. However, security breaches may occur, so tight protection is a must.

7. **Cyberbanking and personal finance.** Branch banking is on the decline due to less expensive, more convenient online banking. The world is moving toward online banking; today, most routine banking services can be done from home. Banks can reach customers in remote places, and customers can bank with faraway institutions. This makes the financial markets more efficient. Online personal finance applications, such as bill paying, tracking of accounts, and tax preparation, also are very popular.

8. **On-demand delivery service.** On-demand delivery service is needed when items are perishable or when delivering medicine, express documents, or urgently needed supplies. One example of on-demand delivery is e-groceries; these may be ordered online and are shipped or ready for store pickup within 24 hours or less.

9. **Delivery of digital products.** Anything that can be digitized can be successfully delivered online. Delivery of digital products such as music, software, movies, and other entertainment online has been a success. Some print media, such as electronic versions of magazines or electronic books (see Chapter 8), also are having success when digitized and delivered electronically.

10. **Aiding consumer purchase decisions.** Purchase-decision aids include shopping portals, shopbots and comparison agents, business rating sites, trust verification sites, and other tools.

11. **Critical success factors.** Critical success factors for direct online sales to consumers and e-tailing are managing risk properly; using correct business models; creating a profitable, effective, and interesting site; and watching operating costs. Also, sufficient cash flow is critical, as is appropriate customer acquisition.

12. **Disintermediation and reintermediation.** Direct electronic marketing by manufacturers results in disintermediation by removing wholesalers and retailers. However, online reintermediaries provide additional value, such as helping consumers make selections among multiple products and vendors. Traditional retailers may feel threatened or pressured when manufacturers decide to sell online; such direct selling can cause channel conflict. Pricing of online and offline products and services is one issue that always needs to be addressed.

KEY TERMS

Brick-and-mortar retailers	102	E-grocer	126	On-demand delivery service	126
Channel conflict	142	E-tailers	93	Reintermediation	140
Click-and-mortar retailers	102	Electronic (online) banking		Shopping portals	132
Cybermediation (electronic		(e-banking)	120	Shopping robots (shopbots or	
intermediation)	142	Electronic retailing (e-tailing)	93	shopping agents)	132
Direct marketing	100	Hypermediation	142	Virtual (pure-play) e-tailers	100
Disintermediation	140	Multichannel business model	102		

QUESTIONS FOR DISCUSSION

1. When electronic retailing began in the 1990s, everything was an innovation and, by definition, everything was new and exciting. Now, there is more consolidation and less innovation. Discuss the proposition.

2. Comment on the proposition that the earlier analyses and predictions regarding e-tailing by academics, journalists, and other commentators were both hyped and exaggerated and, further, neglected the psychological

and social factors involved in accepting and embracing a new and innovative way of doing business.

3. Comment on the proposition that e-tailing, with a few exceptions, will simply become a part of every retail business operation, thus becoming an ordinary part of retail business rather than a specialist venture of "virtual" firms.

4. What are Amazon.com's critical success factors? Is its decision not to limit its sales to books, music, and movies but to offer a much broader selection of items a good marketing strategy? With the broader selection, do you think the company will dilute its brand or extend the value proposition to its customers?

5. Compare the major e-tail business models.

6. Will direct marketing of automobiles be a successful strategy? How should the dealers' inventory and the automakers' inventory and manufacturing scheduling be coordinated to meet a specific order with a quick due date?

7. Discuss the advantages of established click-and-mortar companies such as Wal-Mart over pure-play e-tailers such as Amazon.com. What are the disadvantages of click-and-brick retailers as compared with pure-play e-tailers?

8. Discuss the various B2C models and their advantages and limitations.

9. Discuss the advantages of shopping aids to the consumer. Should a vendor provide a comparison tool on its site that will show that a competitor is cheaper? Why or why not?

10. Discuss the advantages of a specialized e-tailer, such as Dogtoys.com (dogtoys.com). Can such a store survive in the physical world? Why or why not?

11. Do you agree with the proposition that P2P financial services activities need a regulatory framework for them to become a successful commercial phenomenon? Explain your point of view.

12. Discuss the benefits of build-to-order to buyers and sellers. Are there any disadvantages?

13. Why are online travel services a popular Internet application? Why do so many Web sites provide free travel information?

14. Compare the advantages and disadvantages of online stock trading with offline trading.

15. It is said that the service Zuji.com provides to travel agents will lead to their reintermediation. Discuss.

16. Intelligent agents read resumes that are posted online and forward them to potential employers without the candidates' knowledge. What are the benefits of this use of intelligent agents? Do they violate the privacy of job seekers?

17. Online employment services make it easy to change jobs; therefore, turnover rates may increase. This could result in total higher costs for employers because of increased costs for recruiting and training new employees and the need to pay higher salaries and wages to attract or keep employees. What can companies do to ease this problem?

18. How can brokerage houses offer very low commissions for online stock purchases (as low as $4 per trade, with some even offering no commission for certain trades)? Why would they choose to offer such low commissions? Over the long run, do you expect commissions to increase, stay the same, or continue to decrease? Why?

19. Explain what is meant by the statement, "Intermediaries will become knowledge providers rather than transaction providers.

20. YouTube allows the upload of personal videos. Already some of the videos have caused considerable comment. Some have violent and sexual content that offends some viewers. Others involve content that may compromise the legal rights of the persons involved, such as a situation of a video of what seems to be an overly violent arrest. Comment on the legal and social issues involved, including the issue regarding the responsibilities of the Web site management.

21. Compare the advantages and disadvantages of distributing digitizable products electronically versus physically.

22. How can a sports-related merchant target fantasy game players?

INTERNET EXERCISES

1. Visit the following e-grocers: **stopandshop.com**, **freshdirect.com**, **albertson.com**, and **netgrocer.com**. Compare the products and services offered by each and evaluate their chances for success. Why do you think "unattended delivery" e-grocers, such as Shoplink.com, failed?

2. Many consumer portals offer advice and ratings of products or e-tailers. Identify and examine two separate general-consumer portals that look at other sites and compare prices or other purchase criteria. Try to find and compare prices for a digital camera, a microwave oven, and an MP3 player. Visit

clusty.com. How can this site help you in your shopping? Summarize your experience. Comment on the strong and weak points of such shopping tools.

3. Design a trip to Kerala, India (use **stayfinder.com** to start). Find accommodations, restaurants, health clubs, festival information, and art. Arrange a tour for two people for 7 days. How much will it cost?

4. Almost all auto manufacturers allow consumers to configure their cars online. Visit a major automaker's Web site and configure a car of your choice (e.g., **jaguar.com**). Also visit one electronic intermediary (e.g., **autobytel.com**). After you decide what car you want, examine the payment options and figure your monthly payments. Print your results. How does this process compare with visiting an auto dealer? Do you think you found a better price online? Would you consider buying a car this way?

5. Visit **amazon.com** and identify at least three specific elements of its personalization and customization features. Browse specific books on one particular subject, leave the site, and then go back and revisit the site. What do you see? Are these features likely to encourage you to purchase more books in the future from Amazon.com? Check the 1-Click feature and other shopping aids provided. List the features and discuss how they may lead to increased sales.

6. Use a statistics source (e.g., **shop.org**, **emarketer.com**, or **clickz.com/stats**) and look for recent statistics about the growth of Internet-based consumer-oriented EC in your country and in three other countries. Where is the greatest growth occurring? Which countries have the largest total e-tail sales? Which countries have the highest per-capita participation (i.e., "penetration rate")? What are the forecasts for continued growth in the coming years?

7. Visit **landsend.com** and prepare a customized order for a piece of clothing. Describe the process. Do you think this will result in better-fitting clothing? Do you think this personalization feature will lead to greater sales volume for Lands' End?

8. Make your resume accessible to millions of people. Consult **asktheheadhunter.com** or **careerbuilder.com** for help

rewriting your resume. See **monster.com** for ideas about planning your career. Get prepared for a job interview. Also, use the Web to determine what salary you can get in the city of your choice in the United States.

9. Visit **homeowner.com**, **decisionaide.com**, or a similar site and compute the monthly mortgage payment on a 30-year loan at 7.5 percent fixed interest. Also check current interest rates. Estimate your closing costs on a $200,000 loan. Compare the monthly payments of the fixed rate with that of an adjustable rate for the first year. Finally, compute your total payments if you take the loan for 15 years at the going rate. Compare it with a 30-year mortgage. Comment on the difference.

10. Access the Virtual Trader game at **virtualtrader.co.uk** and register for the Internet stock game. You will be bankrolled with £100,000 in a trading account every month. You also can play investment games at **investorsleague.com**, **fantasystockmarket.com**, and **etrade.com**.

11. Visit **etrade.com** and **boom.com** and find out how you can trade stocks in countries other than the one you live in. Prepare a report based on your findings.

12. Examine the consolidated billing process. Start with **e-billingonline.com** and **intuit.com**. Identify other consolidators in the field. What standard capabilities do they all offer? What capabilities are unique to certain sites?

13. Compare the price of a Sony digital camera at **shopping.com**, **mysimon.com**, **bottomdollar.com**, **bizrate.com**, and **pricescan.com**. Which site locates the best deal? Where do you get the best information?

14. Enter **dice.com** and see how it can assist technically oriented job seekers and employers. Compare the services offered with those at **monster.com**.

15. Enter **xing.com** and identify its job-related offerings. Prepare a list of support activities offered.

16. Compare the "build-your-own" at Nike (**nike.com**) with Timberland's Boot Studio (**timberland.com**).

17. Enter **scene7.com** and review their on-demand rich media offering.

TEAM ASSIGNMENTS AND ROLE PLAYING

1. Each team will investigate the services of two online car-selling sites from the following list (or other sites). When teams have finished, they should bring their research together and discuss their findings.

   a. Buying new cars through an intermediary (**autobytel.com**, **carsdirect.com**, **autoweb.com**, or **amazon.com**)

   b. Buying used cars (**autotrader.com**)

   c. Buying used cars by auto dealers (**manheim.com**)

   d. Automobile ratings sites (**carsdirect.com**, and **fueleconomy.gov**)

   e. Car-buying portals (**thecarportal.com** and **cars.com**)

f. Buying antique cars (**classiccars.com** and **antiquecars.com**)

2. Each team will represent a broker-based area (e.g., real estate, insurance, stocks, job finding). Each team will find a new development that has occurred in the assigned area over the most recent 3 months. Look for the site vendor's announcement and search for more information on the development with **google.com** or another search engine. Examine the business news at **bloomberg.com**. After completing your research, as a team, prepare a report on disintermediation in your assigned area.

3. You can buy books from hundreds of book stores. Have each team examine the prices of the same books at **amazon.com, buy.com, overstock.com**, or another site. Compare the sites' customer support services. Also look at technical book stores, textbook stores, or other specialty stores (each team should look at one type).

4. Each team will examine fantasy games at various sites. Each team should examine the type of game, the rules, and the cost. Play at least one time. Each team should write a report based on its experiences.

5. Team members should examine online and offline record stores. Assess the competition between the two and assess the impact of online music sources on traditional record stores.

Real-World Case

WAL-MART POWERS ONLINE

Wal-Mart (*walmart.com*) is the largest retailer in the world with $312.4 billion in sales for the fiscal year ending January 31, 2006. Altogether, Wal-Mart employs 1.8 million people, 1.3 million in the United States. The company has 3,800 stores in the United States and more than 2,600 in the rest of the world. Each week, 176 million customers visit Wal-Mart stores worldwide, including 127 million in the United States (see *walmartfacts.com*).

Wal-Mart maintains an intense strategic focus on the customer. Its standard company cheer ends with, "Who's number one? The customer." Wal-Mart has also established itself as a master of the retail process by streamlining its supply chain and undercutting competitors with low prices.

Wal-Mart has had an online presence since 1996. However, one problem with its strategy for growing online sales has been the demographics of its primary customer base. Wal-Mart's target demographic is households with $25,000 in annual income, whereas the median income of online consumers is perhaps $60,000. Despite these demographics, online sales (primarily in music, travel, and electronics) through *walmart.com* already account for about 10 percent of Wal-Mart's U.S. sales. Its long-time chief rival, Kmart, Inc., tried to attract its demographic audience to its Web site (*kmart.com*) by offering free Internet access. This appealed to its cost-conscious, lower-income constituency and provided the opportunity for those customers to access the site to conduct purchases. However, this move decreased company profits in the short run and was one of the factors that led Kmart to file for bankruptcy in 2002.

Wal-Mart also has concerns about cannibalizing its in-store sales. Its alliance with AOL is designed to provide cobranded low cost Internet access to dwellers in both very rural and very urban areas, where there are no Wal-Mart stores nearby. The intent is to lure new market segments and thus cancel the effect of cannibalization. Ultimately, a hybrid e-tailer that can offer a combination of huge selection with the click-and-mortar advantages of nearby stores (e.g., merchandise pickup or returns) may prove to be the 800-pound gorilla of online consumer sales.

In 2002, Walmart.com matured, offering order status and tracking, a help desk, a clear return policy and mechanisms, a store locator, and information on special sales and liquidations. Also, community services such as photo sharing are provided.

Wal-Mart only offers some of its merchandise online, but the selection is increasing, including items not available in some or all stores (e.g., spas, mattresses). In 2004, Wal-Mart started selling songs online for 88 cents each, competing with Apple's iTunes. Inexpensive items (e.g., those that sell for less than $5) are not available online. Also in 2004, during a 4-day Thanksgiving special, Wal-Mart began to court more affluent shoppers with new and more expensive items available only online. Products included cashmere sweaters and shiatsu massage chairs. The Web site averaged 8 million visitors each week prior to the promotion.

Wal-Mart had added many new products to its online catalog. International customers can buy Wal-Mart products directly from Wal-Mart (if shipping is available) or from affiliate sites. For example, see ASDA (*asda.co.uk*), a Wal-Mart owned U.K. company.

According to Nielsen/NetRatings, in 2006 Wal-Mart recorded the second-largest increase in Web traffic among the top 10 online shopping and travel sites. Site visits to Walmart.com in July 2006 were 19.5 million, up 27 percent over July 2005. For July 2006, Walmart.com was ranked the fourth top site by Nielsen/NetRatings in terms of the number of visits, following the top three sites of eBay, Amazon.com, and Target (*Internetretailer.com* 2006c).

Sources: Maguire (2002), Bhatnagar (2004), *Internetretailer.com* (2006c), and *walmart.com* (accessed November 2006).

Questions

1. Compare *walmart.com* with *amazon.com*. What features do the sites have in common? Which are unique to Walmart.com? To Amazon.com?

2. Will Wal-Mart become the dominant e-tailer in the world, replacing Amazon.com, or will Amazon.com dominate Wal-Mart online? What factors would contribute to Wal-Mart's success in the online marketplace? What factors would detract from its ability to dominate online sales the way it has been able to dominate physical retail sales in many markets?

3. Check the shopping aids offered at *walmart.com*. Compare them with those at *amazon.com*.

4. What online services can be purchased on Walmart.com?

5. Compare buying a song from Walmart.com versus buying it from Apple's iTunes.

6. Walmart.com sells movies online for a monthly fee. How do similar sellers compare?

7. Visit *walmart.com*, *target.com marksandspencer.com*, and *sears.com*. Identify the common features of their online marketing and at least one unique feature evident at each site. Do these sites have to distinguish themselves primarily in terms of price, product selection, or Web site features?

8. Investigate the options for international customers on the Wal-Mart Web site.

REFERENCES

Adams, J. "Trading: New Tools for CyberTraders." *Bank Technology News*, March 1, 2004.

Agrawal, M., T. V. Kumaresh, and G. A. Mercer. "The False Promise of Mass Customization." *The McKinsey Quarterly* no. 3 (2001).

Aquino, G. "Deal Finders." *PCWorld.com*, October 28, 2005. **pcworld.com/reviews/article/0,aid,122931,00.asp** (accessed November 2006).

Atkinson, W. "Internet Impacts Potential, Current Owners." *Hotel and Motel Management*, June 6, 2005. **hotelmotel.com/hotelmotel/article/articleDetail.jsp?id=164387** (accessed November 2006).

Bahn, D. L. "Clicks and Mortar," in Khosrow-Pour (2006).

Baker, V. L. "Make Online Business Models Work for Consumer Electronics." *Gartner Industry Research*, March 22, 2004, QA-0304-0016.

Bandyopadhyay, S., G. Lin, and Y. Zhong. "A Critical Review of Pricing Strategies for Online Business Models." *Quarterly Journal of Electronic Commerce* 2, no. 1 (2001).

Bauer, C., and J. Colgan. "The Internet as a Driver for Unbundling: A Transaction Perspective from the Stockbroking Industry." *Electronic Markets* 12, no. 2 (2002).

Bernoff, J. and Haven, B. "Commentary: Google-YouTube and the Value of Social Computing." Forrester Research Special to *CNET News.com*, October 10, 2006. **news.com.com/Commentary+Google-YouTube+and+the+value+of+social+computing/2030-1030_3-6124497.html?tag=nl** (accessed November 2006).

Bhatnagar, P. "Walmart.com's Going Upscale." *CNNMoney*, November 18, 2004. **money.cnn.com/2004/11/18/news/fortune500/walmart_online** (accessed November 2006).

Bloch, M., and A. Segev. "The Impact of Electronic Commerce on the Travel Industry." *Proceedings 30th Annual HICSS*, Maui, Hawaii, January 1997.

Bonne, J. "Life's Not the Same without the Net." MSNBC News, August 11, 2004. **msnbc.msn.com/id/566482** (no longer available online).

Borrell Associates. "2006 Update: Online Real Estate Advertising." *Borrellassociates.com*, July 2006. **borrellassociates.com/report.cfm** (accessed September 2006).

Brohan, M. "The Top 500 Guide." Internetretailer.com, June 2006. **www.internetretailer.com/article.asp?id=18747** (accessed April 2007).

Burns, E. "Online Retail Revenues to Reach $200 Billion." *Clickz.com*, June 5, 2006a. **clickz.com/showPage.html?page=3611181** (accessed August 2006).

Burns, E. "Online Retail Sales Grew in 2005." *Clickz.com*, January 5, 2006b. **clickz.com/showPage.html?page=3575456** (accessed August 2006).

Burns, E. "Online Games Market to Hit $4.4 Billion by 2010." *Clickz.com*, August 30, 2006c. **clickz.com/showPage.html?page=3623306l** (accessed September 2006).

Burns, E. "Marketing Opportunities Emerge in Online Gaming Venues," *Clickz.com*, August 1, 2006d. **clickz.com/showPage.html?page=3623035** (accessed September 2006).

Businessweek.com. "Hot Growth Companies: 100 Sizzling Companies to Watch." June 5, 2006, **businessweek.com/hot_growth/2006/index.htm** (accessed September 2006).

BusinessWire "Amazon.com Announces 22% Sales Growth Fueled by Lower Prices, Free Shipping." July 25, 2006. **earningscast.com/amzn-q2-2006-earnings-call** (accessed August 2007).

Buy4now.com. "Buy4Now eTail Solutions." 2006. **buy4now.com/etailsolutions/** (accessed September 2006).

Camacho, D., D. Borrajo, and J. M. Molina. "Intelligent Travel Planning: A MultiAgent Planning System to Solve Web Problems in the e-Tourism Domain." *Autonomous Agents and Multi-Agent Systems*, no. 4 (2001).

Careerbuilder.com. "CareerBuilder.com's Job Forecast: Q3 2006." March 2006. **img.cbdr.com/images/aboutus/pressroom/CB-JobForecast-Q3-2006.pdf** (accessed September 2006).

Carr, N. G. "Hypermediation 2.0." 2005. **roughtype.com/archives/2005/11/hypermediation.php** (accessed October 2006).

Carton, W., and C. Locke. *Dot.Bomb*. New York: McGraw-Hill, 2001.

Castex, S. "Trends and News." *Promotional Products Business*, July 2003. **ppa.org/Legacy/Publications/PPB/sections.asp?section=1&issues=all** (accessed November 2006).

Celent. "Banks Increase Their Focus on Small Businesses." *Celent.com*, November 3, 2004. **celent.com/PressReleases/20041103/SmallBusVendors.htm** (accessed April 2007)

CNNMoney.com. "Amazon, Maher to Swim in 'Fishbowl.'" January 18, 2006a. **money.cnn.com/2006/01/19/news/companies/amazon_maher/index.htm** (accessed August 2006).

CNNMoney.com. "Report: Online Stock Trading Gets Cheaper," July 11, 2006b. **money.cnn.com/2006/07/11/markets/online_stocks/index.htm** (accessed September 2006).

Consumersearch.com. "Full Story—Travel Sites Consumer Report." November 2005. **consumersearch.com/www/Internet/travel-sites/fullstory.html** (accessed November 2006).

Cooperativebank.co.uk. "How We Protect You." 2006. **co-operativebank.co.uk/servlet/Satellite?c=Page&cid=1125470773575&pagename=CoopBank%2FPage%2FtplPageStandard** (accessed November 2006).

Cox, B., and W. Koelzer. *Internet Marketing*, Upper Saddle River, NJ: Prentice Hall, 2004.

Cox, J. "Online Recruitment Increases Exponentially." March 31, 2006. **william.com.au/readingroom/articlePopup.asp?article_id=133** (accessed November 2006).

CRMToday. "Consumers Poised to Spend 50% More Online." May 10, 2006. **crm2day.com/news/crm/118555.php** (accessed August 2006).

Cropper, C. M. "Choosing an Online Broker; Most—But Not All—Brokerage Web Sites Now Slap on a Slew of Fees." *BusinessWeek*, May 17, 2004.

Cude, B. J., and M. A. Morganosky. "Online Grocery Shopping: An Analysis of Current Opportunities and Future Potential." *Consumer Interests*, 46 (2000). **consumerinterests.org/files/public/online.PDF** (accessed November 2006).

Dandapani, K. "Success and Failures in Web-Based Financial Services." *Communications of the ACM* (May 2004).

Dernovsek, D. "The Move to E-payments." *Credit Union Magazine*, August 2004.

Direct Marketing Association. "Toy Sales Fell in 2005, Reports NPD Group; Sales Hit $21.3 Billion Last Year." 2006. **the-dma.org/cgi/dispnewsstand?article=4454+++++** (accessed September 2006).

Ebcenter.org. "Dell Invests in Physical Stores to Reach Customers." Newsletter, June 1–15, 2006. **iese.edu/en/ad/eb-center.junio20061/newsletter/asp#22797** (accessed November 2006).

Economist. "Click to Fly." *The Economist*, May 13, 2004.

Epstein, M. J. "Implementing E-Commerce Strategies: A Guide to Corporate Success After the Dot.Com Bust." Westport, CT: Praeger Publishers, 2004.

Ere.net. "Trovix Makes Good at Stanford University: Premier Educational Institution Turns to Intelligent Search Provider for Recruiting Top Talent." March 8, 2006. **ere.net/newswire/announcement.asp?LISTINGID=%7B66B8732B-C61D-4906-B35F-490AD939DE23%7D** (accessed November 2006).

Ericson, J. "Name Your Price." *Line56*, January 19, 2004.

Fox, S., and J. Beier. "Online Banking 2006: Surfing to the Bank" Pew Internet, June 14, 2006. **pewinternet.org/pdfs/PIP_Online_Banking_2006.pdf** (accessed November 2006).

Gapper, J. "Why Nobody Sells the Car We Really Want." *Financial Times*, June 29, 2004.

Global Finance. "World's Best Foreign Exchange Banks 2004." *Global Finance*, March 2004.

Google.com. "Google to Acquire YouTube for $1.65 Billion in Stock." October 8, 2006. **google.com/press/pressrel/google_youtube.html** (accessed November 2006).

Grau, J. "Defining the Online Shopper." *iMediaConnection.com*, April 22, 2005. **imediaconnection.com/content/5547.asp** (accessed August 2006).

Hedna.org. "Travel Search Engines Redefine Distribution." 2005, Executive White Paper Series. **hedna.org/pdf/**

Executive_Summary_Travel_Search_Engines_ Redefine_Distribution.pdf (accessed September 2006).

Heskett, J. L. "ING Direct." Harvard Business Online, May 17, 2005. **harvardbusinessonline.hbsp.harvard.edu/b01/en/ common/item_detail.jhtml;jsessionid=JT34AWVJK5T WOAKRGWDR5VQBKE0YIISW?id=804167** (accessed November 2006).

Huang, J., Wang, H. and Zhao, C. "E-Commerce Success Factors: Exploratory and Empirical Research on the Chinese Publishing Industry." *Proceedings of the 2005 IEEE International Conference on e-Business Engineering* (ICEBE '05), Beijing, China, October 18–20, 2005.

Hwang, H. S., and C. Stewart. "Lessons from Dot-Com Boom and Bust," in Khosrow-Pour (2006).

IC-Agency. "Selling Luxury Online, or the Emergence of Fashion's New 'Wild West.'" November 3, 2005. **europastar.com/europastar/magazine/article_ display.jsp?vnu_content_id=1001433585** (accessed September 2006).

Infoplease.com. "Online Spending by Product Category 2005." 2006a. **infoplease.com/ipa/A0931603.html** (accessed August 2006).

Infoplease.com. "Online Computer Spending by Kind of Business 2003–2005." 2006b. **infoplease.com/ipa/ A0933517.html** (accessed August 2006).

Infoplease.com. "Online Consumer Spending by Product 2002–2004." 2006c. **infoplease.com/ipa/ A0921857.html** (accessed August 2006).

Internetretailer.com. "Amazon Grows 23% in 2005, but Profits Slide." February 3, 2006a. **internetretailer.com/ dailyNews.asp?id=17513** (accessed August 2006).

Internetretailer.com. "First-Half Online Retail Spending Rises 25% to 46 Billion." August 3, 2006b. **internetretailer. com/printArticle.asp?id=19450** (accessed August 2006).

Internetretailer.com. "Target Posts Largest July Traffic Gain Among Top 10 Shopping Sites." September 1, 2006c. **internetretailer.com/dailyNews.asp?id=19761** (accessed October 2006).

Internetretailer.com. "Office Depot's Web Sales Grew 19.2% in 2004." February 10, 2005. **internetretailer.com/ dailyNews.asp?id=14109** (accessed November 2006).

Izumi, S. "Mobile Commerce Seen as Retailer's Next Big Thing." *The Japan Times*, September 20, 2006.

JobCentral.com. "Welcome to JobCentral." 2006. **jobcentral.com/ aboutus.asp** (accessed September 2006).

Jobsearch.gov.au. "What is Australian JobSearch?" 2006. **jobsearch.gov.au,** (accessed September 2006).

Johnson, C. A. *"U.S. eCommerce: 2005 to 2010."* September 14, 2005. **forrester.com/Research/Document/Excerpt/ 0,7211,37626,00.html** (accessed August 2006).

Jupitermedia.com. "Jupiterresearch Forecasts Online Retail Spending Will Reach $144 Billion in 2010, a CAGR of 12% from 2005," June 6, 2006. **jupitermedia.com/ corporate/releases/06.06.06-newjupresearch.html** (accessed August 2006).

Kaplan, P. J. *The F'd Companies: Spectacular Dot.Com Flameouts.* New York: Simon & Schuster, 2002.

Kaye, K. "Real Estate Ad Shift Continues, but Web Adoption Is Mixed." *ClickZ*, August 31, 2006. **clickz.com/ showPage.html?page=3623309** (accessed October 2006).

Khosrow-Pour, M., (ed.), *Encyclopedia of E-Commerce, E-Government, and Mobile Commerce,* Hershey, PA: Idea Group Reference, 2006.

Kimiloglu, H. "The 'E-Literature': A Framework for Understanding the Accumulated Knowledge about Internet Marketing." *Academy of Marketing Science Review,* June 2004.

Knowledge@Wharton. "Car Trouble: Should We Recall the U.S. Auto Industry?" May 4, 2005. **knowledge. wharton.upenn.edu/article.cfm?articleid=1183,2005** (accessed September 2006).

Knox, N. "It's Always 'OPEN HOUSE' as Real Estate Goes Online." *USA Today*, May 16, 2006.

Lee, S. C., and A. A. Brandyberry, "The E-tailer's Dilemma." *ACM SIGMIS Database*, June 2003.

Lepouras, G., and C. Vassilakis. "Adaptive Virtual Reality Shopping Malls," in Khosrow-Pour (2006).

LinkedIn.com. "LinkedIn's Simple Philosophy: Relationships Matter," 2006. **linkedin.com/static?key= company_info** (accessed November 2006).

MacSweeney, G. "Dual Strategy." *Insurance and Technology*, July 2000.

Maguire, J. "Case Study: Walmart.com." *Internet.com*, November 15, 2002. **ecommerce.internet.com/news/ insights/trends/article/0,,10417_1501651,00.html** (no longer available online).

Mallat, N., M. Rossi, and V. K. Tuunainen. "Mobile banking services." *Communications of the ACM* (May 2004).

Marketing.gold.org. "Online Jewelry Sales Set to Increase," May 25, 2005. **marketing.gold.org/index.php?option= com_headlines&task=viewStory&dhid=8586279& d=25&m=05&y=2005** (accessed September 2006).

MarketResearch.com. "Online Recruitment—US." June 1, 2005. **marketresearch.com/map/prod/1086473.html** (accessed September 2006).

MarketWatch. "ING Direct to Further Expand in US; Considers Entry into Japan." September 27, 2006. **marketwatch.com/news/story/story.aspx?siteid= mktw&guid={D495E563-ED4F-417D-A9F3- CE9AF0FAD77B** (accessed November 2006).

McCullagh, D. "Real Estate's Net Turf War." *CNet News*, July 28, 2006. **news.com.com/Real+estates+Net+turf+war/ 2100-1038_3-6099762.html** (accessed November 2006).

McKay, J. "Where Did Jobs Go? Look in Bangalore." March 21, 2004. **post-gazette.com/pg/04081/ 288539.stm** (accessed November 2006).

McKay, J. and P. Marshall. *Strategic Management of eBusiness.* New York: John Wiley and Sons, 2004.

McTaggart, J. "Online Retailing: E-grocery's reality check." *Progressive Grocer*, August 2006.

Milidiu, R. L., T. Melcop, F. dos S. Liporace, and C. J. Pereira de Lucena. "SIMPLE: A Multi-Agent System for Simultaneous and Related Auctions." *Proceedings of the IEEE/WIC International Conference on Intelligent Agent Technology 2003*, Beijing, China, October 13–16, 2003.

Moules, J. "Online Banking Gains Popularity." *Financial Times*, October 14, 2006.

Mullaney, T. J. "E-Biz Strikes Again." *BusinessWeek*, May 10, 2004.

Mulpuru, S. *2005 U.S. eCommerce: The Year in Review.* *Forrester.com.* **forrester.com/Research/Document/Excerpt/0,7211,38809,00.html** (accessed April 2007).

NCECIC (National Commission to Ensure Consumer Information and Choice in the Airline Industry). News Release, November 13, 2001. **govinfo.library.unt.edu/ncecic/press/Commission_Findings_Final.pdf** (accessed September 2006).

NDP.com press release, July 17, 2001. (no longer available online).

Omniture.com. "Industry Guide: Travel and Hospitality Sites." 2006. **omniture.com/static/378** (accessed April 2007).

Onrec.com. "Totaljobs Audits Application Figures." March 2006. **onrec.com/content2/printit.asp?id=13280** (accessed September 2006).

Oo, P. "Grocery Stores: Trends and Tips." May 5, 2006. **www1.umn.edu/umnnews/Feature_Stories/Grocery_stores3A_trends_and_tips.html** (accessed September 2006).

OpenTable.com. "About OpenTable." 2006. **opentable.com/info/aboutus.aspx** (accessed September 2006).

Parker, P. "Amazon to Develop Online Talk Show." *Clickz.com*, January 19, 2006. **clickz.com/ showPage.html?page=3578551** (accessed November 2006).

Parks, L. "Making Sure the Price Is Right." *Stores*, August 2004.

Pascoe, J. "Put Your Money Where Your Mouse Is." *Smart Computing in Plain English*, March 2004.

Patsuris, P. "Music Chains Raise the Volume on Downloads." *Forbes.com*, January 27, 2003. **forbes.com/2003/01/27/cx_pp_0127music.html** (accessed November 2006).

PBS.org. "B2B Japan." Nightly Business Report, January 9, 2006. **pbs.org/nbr/site/research/educators/060106_04b** (accessed December 2006).

Pet Product News International. "Jump Seen in Online Sales of Pet Products." June 12, 2006. **animalnetwork.com/ppn/details** (accessed November 2006).

Primezone.com "Cash Edge Survey Confirms Consumer Demand for Value Added Online Banking Services, October 12, 2006. **primezone.com/newsroom/news.html?d-106700** (accessed December 2006).

Qantas.com.au. "Qantas to Conduct an Evaluation of New Technology Allowing Customers to Stay Connected Inflight." August 28, 2006. **qantas.com.au/regions/dyn/au/publicaffairs/details?ArticleID=2006/aug06/Q3469** (accessed September 2006).

RealSEO.com. "Sports Can Attract Sales to a Web Site." July 29, 2004. **realseo.com/archives/2004_07.html** (accessed November 2006).

Reda, S. "Online Retail Grows Up." *Stores*, February 2002.

Regan, K. "E*Trade Buys Harrisdirect as Online Brokers Consolidate," *E-Commerce Times*, August 8, 2005a. **ecommercetimes.com/story/45304.html** (accessed September 2006).

Regan, K. "E*Trade Buys BrownCo From JPMorgan for $1.6 Billion." *E-Commerce Times*, September 29, 2005b. **ecommercetimes.com/story/46426.html** (accessed September 2006).

Regan, K. "E*Trade Announces Second Acquisition in Two Days." August 9, 2005c. **ecommercetimes.com/story/45345.html** (accessed November 2006).

ResellerRatings.com. "Open Letter to Resellerratings.com Visitors." 2006. **resellerratings.com/openletter.pl** (accessed September 2006).

Retailbulletin.com. "Survey Predicts U.S. Online Retail Sales to Increase by 20%." **retailbulletin.com/ index. php?page=5&id=8402&cat=news** (accessed August 2006).

Rickards, G. "What's All This about Online Banking?" *MsMoney.com.* **msmoney.com/mm/banking/articles/about_online_banking.htm** (accessed November 2006).

Riseley, M. J. "Findings: Amazon Moves Into Online Grocery Shopping Niche." *Gartner Industry Research*, July 3, 2006.

Ropelato, J. "Internet Pornography Statistics." 2006. **Internet-filter-review.toptenreviews.com/Internet-pornography-statistics.html** (accessed November 2006).

Sales, R. "Electronic FX: Reality or Just a Smoke Screen?" *Wall Street and Technology*, April 2002, 16–17.

Schonfeld, E. and Borzo, J. "Social Networking for Dollars." CNNMoney.com, **http://money.cnn.com/2006/09/15/technology/disruptors_zopa.biz2/index.htm** (accessed April, 2007).

Shoniregun, C. A. "Is Cybermediation Really the Future or Risk?" *International Journal of Electronic Business*, 2, no. 6 2004.

Southard, P., and K. Siau. "A Survey of Online E-Banking Retail Initiatives." *Communications of the ACM* (October 2004).

Steinert-Therlkeld, T. "GroceryWorks: The Low Touch Alternative." *Interactive Week*, January 31, 2000.

Tessler, F. N. "Online Banking Made Easy." *Macworld* 21, no. 8 (August 2004).

Thecatalogshop.co.uk. "Littlewoods Catalogue Home Shopping: 7 Decades of Mail Order Shopping in Britain." 2006. **thecatalogueshop.co.uk** (accessed August 2006).

Theknot.com. "Bridal Industry Statistics." 2006. **theknot.com/au_industrystats.shtml** (accessed November 2006).

Thestatebank.com. "Security Information." 2006. **thestatebank.com/security.htm** (accessed November 2006).

Theweddingreport.com. "The Wedding Report." 2006. **theweddingreport.com** (accessed November 2006).

Tia.org. "Executive Summaries—E-Travel Consumers: How They Plan and Buy Leisure Travel Online." 2005. **tia.org/researchpubs/executive_summaries_e_travel.html** (accessed December 2006).

Totty, M. "Career Journal: Recruiters Try New Tools to Find the Best Candidates—Services Analyze, Rank Online Resumes, Saving Valuable Time." *The Wall Street Journal Asia*, October 24, 2006. **awsj.com.hk/factiva-ns** (accessed November 2006).

Tyson, E. *Personal Finance for Dummies*, 4th ed. New York: John Wiley and Sons, 2003.

U.S. Census Bureau. "Quarterly Retail E-Commerce Sales First Quarter 2006." May 18, 2006a. **census.gov/mrts/www/data/html/06Q1.html** (accessed August 2006).

U.S. Census Bureau. "E-Stats." May 25, 2006b. **census.gov/estats** (accessed August 2006).

Van der Heijden, J. G. M. "The Changing Value of Travel Agents in Tourism Networks: Towards a Network Design Perspective." In Stefan Klein, et al. (eds.), *Information and Communication Technologies in Tourism*, pages 151–159. New York: Springer-Verlag, 1996.

Verma, R., Z. Iqbal, and G. Plaschka. "Understanding Choices in E-Financial Services." *California Management Review* (Summer 2004).

Voigt, K., M. Saatman, and S. Schorr. "Flexibility-Cost Oriented Management of New Car Orders in the Automotive Industry." *Proceedings of the Fourth International Annual Symposium on Supply Chain Management*. Toronto, Canada, October 4–6, 2006.

Wang, F. "E-Shoppers' Perception of Web-Based Decision Aid," in Khosrow-Pour (2006).

Wang, J., Y. Ding, and D. Straub. "Failure of Furniture.com," in Khosrow-Pour (2006).

Weiner, M. (2006) "The 5-Day Car: Ordered on Monday—Delivered on Friday." February 28, 2006. **fraunhofer.de/fhg/Images/magazine_2–2006_28_tcm6–64704.pdf** (accessed September 2006).

Wood, L. "Research and Markets: The Number of Enterprise Online Bankers Reaches 34 Million & the Overall Turnover Surpassed RMB 2 Trillion in China." *M2 Presswire*, November 6, 2006.

Xu, M. X., S. Wilkes, and M. H. Shah. "E-Banking Application and Issues in Abbey National PLC," in Khosrow-Pour (2006).

Yamada, K. "Let's Make a Deal." *Portals Magazine*, June 1, 2004. **portalsmag.com/print/default.asp?ArticleID=5761** (accessed November 2006).

Yao, J. T. "Ecommerce Adoption of Insurance Companies in New Zealand." *Journal of Electronic Commerce Research* 5, no. 1 (2004).

CHAPTER 4

CONSUMER BEHAVIOR, MARKET RESEARCH, AND ADVERTISEMENT

Content

Learning Objectives

Upon completion of this chapter, you will be able to:

1. Describe the factors that influence consumer behavior online.

2. Understand the decision-making process of consumer purchasing online.

3. Describe how companies are building one-to-one relationships with customers.

4. Explain how personalization is accomplished online.

5. Discuss the issues of e-loyalty and e-trust in EC.

6. Describe consumer market research in EC.

7. Describe Internet marketing in B2B, including organizational buyer behavior.

8. Describe the objectives of Web advertising and its characteristics.

9. Describe the major advertising methods used on the Web.

10. Describe various online advertising strategies and types of promotions.

11. Describe permission marketing, ad management, localization, and other advertising-related issues.

12. Understand the role of intelligent agents in consumer issues and advertising applications.

NETFLIX INCREASES SALES USING DVD RECOMMENDATIONS AND ADVERTISEMENTS

Netflix (*netflix.com*) is the world's largest online movie rental subscription company. The company has more than 14,200 employees and over 5.2 million subscribers. It offers more than 65,000 titles in over 200 categories and more than 42 million DVDs. A typical neighborhood movie store generally has fewer than 3,000 titles and has multiple copies of only a fraction of them. Netflix distributes 1 million DVDs each day.

The Problem

Because of the large number of titles available on DVD, customers often had difficulty determining which ones they would like to watch. In most cases, they picked up the most popular titles, which meant that Netflix had to maintain more and more copies of the same title. In addition, some unpopular titles were not renting well, even though they matched certain customers' preferences. For Netflix, matching titles with customers and maintaining the right level of inventory is critical.

A second major problem facing Netflix is the competitive nature of the movie rental business. Netflix competes against Blockbuster and other rental companies, as well as against companies offering downloads of movies and videos.

The Solution

Netflix reacted successfully to the first problem by offering a recommendation service called CineMatch. This software agent uses data mining tools to sift through a database of over 1 billion film ratings (which is growing rapidly), as well as through customers' rental histories. Using proprietary formulas, CineMatch recommends rentals to individuals. It is a personalized service, similar to the one offered by Amazon.com that recommends books to customers. The recommendation is accomplished by comparing an individual's likes, dislikes, and preferences against people with similar tastes using a variant of collaborative filtering (described later in this chapter). (Both Blockbuster and Walmart.com are emulating its model.) With the recommendation system, Netflix does not automatically deliver the DVDs; instead, it tells subscribers which ones they will probably like. CineMatch is like the geeky clerk at a small movie store who sets aside titles he knows you will like and tells you to return them whenever.

Netflix subscribers can also invite one another to become "friends" and make movie recommendations to each other, peek at one another's rental lists, and see how other subscribers have rated other movies using a social network called FriendsSM. All these personalized functions make the online rental store very customer-friendly.

To improve CineMatch's accuracy, in October 2006 Netflix began a contest offering $1 million to the first person or team to write a program that would increase the prediction accuracy of CineMatch by 10 percent. The company understands that this will take quite some time; therefore, it is offering a $50,000 Progress Prize each year the contest runs. This prize goes to the team whose solution shows the most improvement over the previous year's accuracy bar (see *netflixprize.com*).

Netflix is advertising extensively on the Web using several methods. For example, to promote its brand, Netflix has placed static banner ads on the Yahoo!, MSN, and AOL Web sites, as well as a number of other sites. Search engine advertisement is also being used (discussed later in this chapter). It also has an affiliate program. Netflix uses almost all online advertising techniques, especially permission e-mail, blogs, social networking, classifieds, Really Simple Syndication (RSS), and more.

Starting September 13, 2006, Netflix launched a 5-week trivia sweepstakes program with *USA Weekend* magazine. Trivia questions were published each week in *USA Weekend*, directing its 50 million readers to *netflix.com/usaweekend* to enter the sweepstakes and qualify to win weekly prizes. Prizes ranged from $250 to $4,000 and cost the company over $140 million.

The Results

As a result of implementing its CineMatch system, Netflix has seen very fast growth in sales and membership. The benefits of CineMatch include the following:

- *Effective recommendations.* According to Netflix (2006) members select 70 percent of their movies based on CineMatch's recommendations.
- *Increased customer satisfaction and loyalty.* The movies recommended generate more satisfaction than the ones customers choose from the new releases page. As a result, between 70 and 80 percent of Netflix rentals come from the company's back catalog of 38,000 films rather than recent releases. It increases customer loyalty to the site and satisfaction for over 90 percent of the customers.
- *Broadened title coverage.* Renters expand their taste. Seventy percent of the movies Netflix customers rent are recommended to them on the site; 80 percent of rental activity comes from 2,000 titles. This decreases demand for popular new releases, which is good for Netflix, whose revenue-sharing agreements require larger payouts for newly released films.

One example is *Control Room*, a documentary about Arab television outlet Al Jazeera. Netflix has a 12 percent share of the movie rental market, and you would expect its share of the rentals for *Control Room* to be in the same range. But Netflix accounted for 34 percent of the title's rental activity in the United States the week it was released on DVD. The difference is primarily due to Netflix's recommendation tools.

- *Better understanding of customer preference*. Netflix's recommendation system collects more than 2 million ratings forms from subscribers daily to add to its huge database of users' likes and dislikes.

- *Fast membership growth*. Netflix found that the most reliable prediction for how much a customer will like a

movie is what the customer thought of other movies. The company credits the system's ability to make automated, yet accurate, recommendations as a major factor in its growth from 600,000 subscribers in 2002 to nearly 5 million in mid-2006.

CineMatch has become the company's core competence. Netflix's future relies heavily on CineMatch's making accurate recommendations and subscribers' accepting them, which is why the company strives to increase its accuracy.

Sources: Compiled from Flynn (2006), Null (2003), and *Netflix.com* (2006).

WHAT WE CAN LEARN . . .

This case illustrates the use of intelligent agents (Appendix C) in movie recommendation system software. Netflix's CineMatch is designed to increase sales and customer satisfaction and loyalty. The case also identifies some of the most popular advertising methods used in EC. These topics are the subject of Chapter 4.

4.1 LEARNING ABOUT CONSUMER BEHAVIOR ONLINE

Companies are operating in an increasingly competitive environment. Therefore, they treat customers like royalty as they try to lure them to buy their goods and services. Finding and retaining customers is a major critical success factor for most businesses, both offline and online. One of the keys to building effective customer relationships is an understanding of consumer behavior online. For an overview, see Markellou et al. (2006).

A MODEL OF CONSUMER BEHAVIOR ONLINE

For decades, market researchers have tried to understand consumer behavior, and they have summarized their findings in various models. The purpose of a consumer behavior model is to help vendors understand how a consumer makes a purchasing decision. If a firm understands the decision process, it may be able to influence the buyer's decision, for example, through advertising or special promotions.

Exhibit 4.1 shows the basics of a consumer behavior model in the EC environment. The model is composed of the following parts:

- *Independent* (or uncontrollable) *variables,* which are shown at the top of Exhibit 4.1, can be categorized as *personal characteristics* and *environmental characteristics.*

- *Intervening* (or moderating) *variables* are variables within the vendors' control. They are divided into *market stimuli* and *EC systems.*

- The *decision-making process,* which is shown in the center of the exhibit, is influenced by the independent and intervening variables. This process ends with the buyers' decisions (shown on the right) resulting from the decision-making process.

- The *dependent variables* describe types of decisions made by buyers.

Exhibit 4.1 identifies some of the variables in each category. This chapter examines the following model-related issues: the decision process, seller–customer-relationship building, and customer service. Discussions of other issues can be found in Internet marketing books, such as Cox and Koelzer (2004). For other aspects, see Efendioglu (2006) and Bridges et al. (2006).

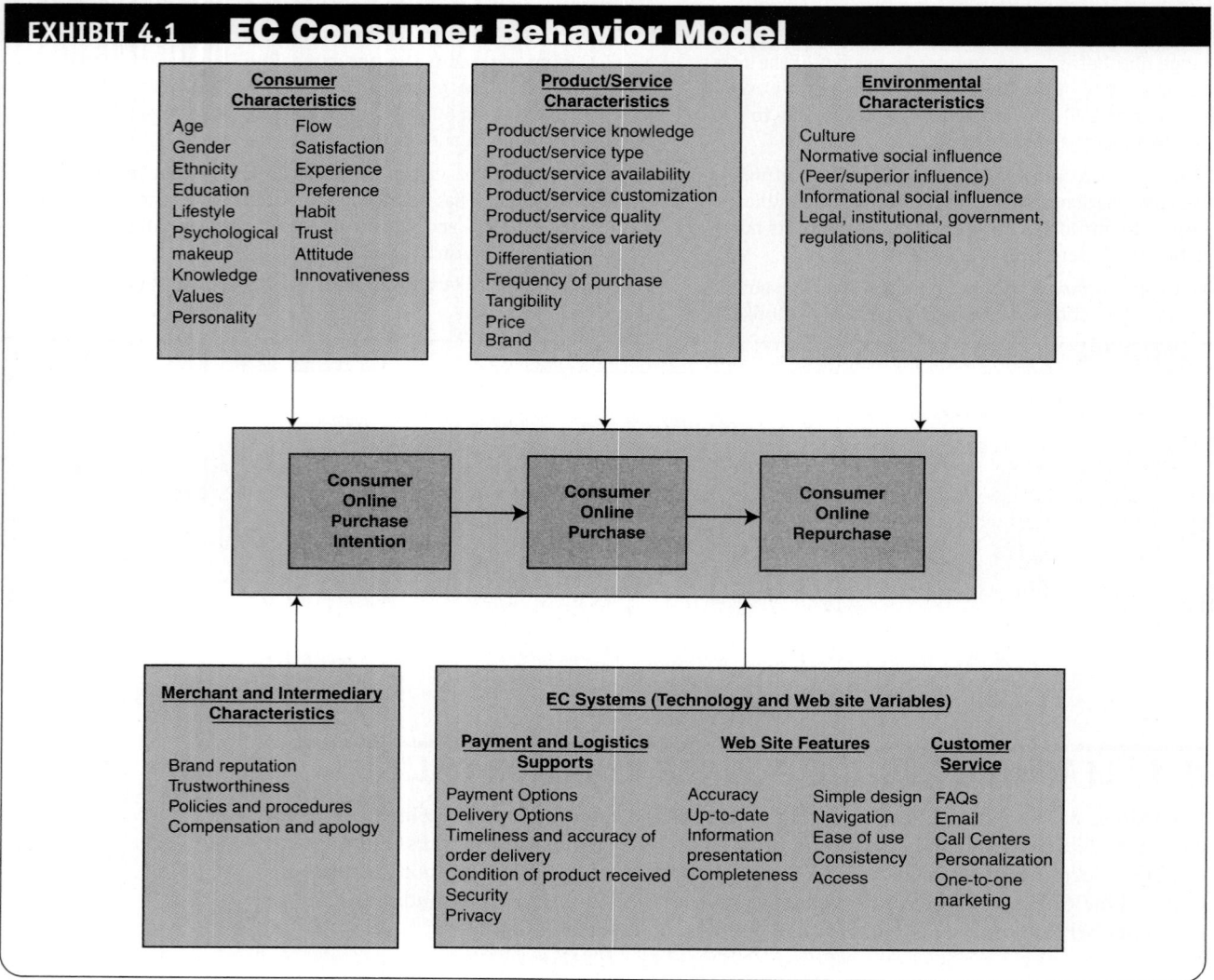

EXHIBIT 4.1   EC Consumer Behavior Model

Before examining the consumer behavior model's variables, let's examine who the EC consumers are. Online consumers can be divided into two types: *individual consumers*, who get much of the media attention, and *organizational buyers*, who do most of the actual shopping in cyberspace in terms of dollar volume of sales. Organizational buyers include governments, private corporations, resellers, and public organizations. Purchases by organizational buyers are generally used to create other products (services) by adding value to the products. Also, organizational buyers may purchase products for resale without any further modifications. We will briefly discuss organizational purchasing in Section 4.5 and describe it in detail in Chapter 5 (e-procurement).

The Independent Variables

Two types of independent variables are distinguished: personal characteristics and environmental variables.

Personal Characteristics. Personal characteristics, which are shown in the top-left portion of Exhibit 4.1, refer to demographic factors, internal individual factors, and behavioral characteristics (Cheung et al. 2005a). Several Web sites provide information on customer buying habits online (e.g., emarketer.com, clickz.com, and comscore.com). The major demographics that such sites track are gender, age, marital status, educational level, ethnicity, occupation, and household income, which can be correlated with Internet usage and EC data. A survey on the trend of global Internet shopping (Crampton 2005) revealed that the gender of online shoppers is roughly balanced. However, when it comes to certain products and services, the differences are significant. In some countries (including China, Sweden, and Austria), more women than men are making their purchases online. Exhibit 3.1 (p. 94) provides the major sources and types of these and other Internet and EC statistics.

It is interesting to note that consumers often browse online stores even if they do not intend to buy. Sixty-eight percent reported that they browse online more than in the past. However, 67 percent of consumers abandoned their shopping carts because of the lack of satisfactory product information (Burns 2006). Internet statistics not only provide us with the information about what people buy but also why they *do not* buy. The two most-cited reasons for *not* making purchases are shipping charges (51 percent) and the difficulty in judging the quality of the product (44 percent). About 32 percent of users do not make purchases because they cannot return items easily. Twenty-four percent are worried about credit card safety. An additional 23 percent of users do not purchase online because they cannot ask questions; 16 percent say they do not buy when it takes too long to download the screen; 15 percent are concerned about delivery time; and 10 percent enjoy shopping offline. However, only 1.9 percent of online consumers have actually had an unfavorable experience (the least-cited reason for not making more purchases on the Web). (Note: People were asked to cite the three most important reasons; thus, the answers total to more than 100 percent.) According to Forrester Research (Temkin 2002), psychological variables are another personal characteristic studied by marketers. Such variables include personality and lifestyle characteristics. These variables are briefly mentioned in several places throughout the text. The reader who is interested in the impact of lifestyles differences on online shopping should see Wang et al. (2006).

Environmental Variables. As shown in the box in the top-right portion of the figure, *environmental variables* can be grouped into the following categories:

▶ **Social variables.** These variables play an important role in EC purchasing. People are influenced by family members, friends, co-workers, and "what's in fashion this year." For more discussions on the role of social factors (e.g., informational social influence, customer endorsement strategies, word-of-mouth) in Internet shopping, see Lee et al. (2006) and Lim et al. (2006). Of special importance in EC are *Internet communities* (see Chapter 17) and *discussion groups*, in which people communicate via chat rooms, electronic bulletin boards, and newsgroups. These topics are discussed in various places in the text.

▶ **Cultural/community variables.** It makes a big difference in what people buy if a consumer lives near Silicon Valley in California or in the mountains in Nepal. Chinese shoppers differ from French shoppers, and rural shoppers differ from urban ones. For further discussion of the impact of cultural variables, see Witkowski (2005).

▶ **Other environmental variables.** These include things such as the available information, government regulations, legal constraints, and situational factors.

The Intervening (Moderating) Variables

The intervening (moderating) variables are those that can be controlled by vendors. As in the offline environment, these include pricing, advertising and promotions, and branding (the products themselves and their quality). The physical environment (e.g., display in stores), logistics support, technical support, and customer services also are important. Customer service is described in this chapter; the other intervening variables (e.g., logistics and technical support) will be described in various chapters of the book.

The Dependent Variables: The Buying Decisions

With the dependent variables, the customer is making several decisions, such as "To buy or not to buy?" "What to buy?" and "Where, when, and how much to buy?" These decisions *depend* on the independent and intervening variables. The objective of learning about customers and conducting market research is to know enough so that the vendors who provide some of the market stimuli and/or control the EC systems can make decisions on the intervening variables.

The structure of the consumer behavior model in Exhibit 4.1 is a simplified version of what actually goes on in the decision-making process. In reality, consumer decision making can be complicated, especially when new products or procedures need to be purchased.

A Process Model

Online consumer behavior also can be studied from a process point of view. Markellou et al. (2006) suggested such a model composed of 13 steps of what customers are doing (e.g., intention to buy, decision to buy, and so forth). This model can be useful in the design of storefronts and shopping aids.

Section 4.1 ▶ REVIEW QUESTIONS

1. Describe the major components and structure of the consumer online purchasing behavior model.
2. List some major personal characteristics that influence consumer behavior.
3. List the major environmental variables of the purchasing environment.
4. List and describe the major vendor-controlled variables.
5. Define the process model of consumer behavior online.

4.2 THE CONSUMER DECISION-MAKING PROCESS

Returning to the central part of Exhibit 4.1, where consumers make purchasing decisions, let's clarify the roles people play in the decision-making process. The major roles are as follows (Kotler and Armstrong 2006; Armstrong and Kotler 2007):

▶ **Initiator.** The person who first suggests or thinks of the idea of buying a particular product or service.
▶ **Influencer.** A person whose advice or view carries some weight in making a final purchasing decision.
▶ **Decider.** The person who ultimately makes a buying decision or any part of it—whether to buy, what to buy, how to buy, or where to buy.
▶ **Buyer.** The person who makes an actual purchase.
▶ **User.** The person who consumes or uses a product or service.

If one individual plays all of these roles, the marketer needs to understand and target that individual. When more than one individual plays these different roles, it becomes more difficult to properly target advertising and marketing efforts. How marketers deal with the issue of multiple people in decision-making roles is beyond the scope of this book.

Several models have been developed in an effort to describe the details of the decision-making process that lead up to and culminate in a purchase. These models provide a framework for learning about the process in order to predict, improve, or influence consumer decisions. Here we introduce three relevant models.

A GENERIC PURCHASING-DECISION MODEL

A general purchasing-decision model consists of five major phases (Kotler 2005). In each phase, we can distinguish several activities and, in some, one or more decisions. The five phases are (1) need identification, (2) information search, (3) evaluation of alternatives, (4) purchase and delivery, and (5) postpurchase behavior Although these phases offer a general guide to the consumer decision-making process, one should not assume that every consumer's decision-making process will necessarily proceed in this order. In fact, some consumers may proceed to a point and then revert back to a previous phase, or they may skip a phase altogether.

The first phase, *need identification*, occurs when a consumer is faced with an imbalance between the actual and the desired states of a need. A marketer's goal is to get the consumer to recognize such imbalance and then convince the consumer that the product or service the seller offers will fill this gap.

After identifying the need, the consumer *searches for information* (phase 2) on the various alternatives available to satisfy the need. Here, we differentiate between two decisions: what product to buy **product brokering**) and from whom to buy it (**merchant brokering**) (see Guan 2006). These two decisions can be separate or combined. In the consumer's search for information, catalogs, advertising, promotions, and reference groups influence decision making. During this phase, online product search and comparison engines, such as can be found at shopping.com, buyersindex.com, and mysimon.com, can be very helpful.

The consumer's information search will eventually generate a smaller set of preferred alternatives. From this set, the would-be buyer will further *evaluate the alternatives* (phase 3) and, if possible, negotiate terms. In this phase, a consumer will use the collected information to develop a set of criteria. These criteria will help the consumer evaluate and compare alternatives. In phase 4, the consumer will make the *purchasing decision*, arrange payment and delivery, purchase warranties, and so on.

The final phase is a *postpurchase* phase (phase 5), which consists of customer service and evaluation of the usefulness of the product (e.g., "This product is really great!" or "We really received good service when we had problems").

In addition, repeat site visits and repeat purchases can be included in the model as decision activities.

product brokering
Deciding what product to buy.

merchant brokering
Deciding from whom (from what merchant) to buy a product.

A CUSTOMER DECISION MODEL IN WEB PURCHASING

The preceding generic purchasing-decision model was widely used in research on consumer-based EC (Cheung et al. 2003). O'Keefe and McEachern (1998) built a framework for a Web purchasing model. As shown in Exhibit 4.2, each of the phases of the purchasing model can be supported by both Consumer Decision Support System (CDSS) facilities and Internet and Web facilities. The CDSS facilities support the specific decisions in the process.

EXHIBIT 4.2   Purchase Decision-Making Process and Support System

Steps in the Decision-Making Process	CDSS Support Facilities	Generic Internet and Web Support Facilities
Need recognition	Agents and event notification	Banner advertising on Web sites URL on physical material Discussions in newsgroups
Information search	Virtual catalogs Structured interaction and question/answer sessions Links to (and guidance on) external soures	Web directories and classifiers Internal search on Web site External search engines Focused directories and information brokers
Evaluation, negotiation, selection	FAQs and other summaries Samples and trials Models that evaluate consumer behavior Pointers to and information about existing customers	Discussions in newsgroups Cross-site comparisons Generic models
Purchase, payment, and delivery	Ordering of product or service Arrangement of delivery	Electronic cash and virtual banking Logistics providers and package tracking
After-purchase service and evaluation	Customer support via e-mail and newsgroups	Discussions in newsgroups

Source: O'Keefe, R. M., and T. McEachern (1998).

Generic EC technologies provide the necessary mechanisms as well as enhance communication and collaboration. Specific implementation of this framework and explanation of some of the terms are provided throughout this chapter and the entire text.

Others have developed similar models (e.g., see Jiang et al. 2005). The point here is that the planner of B2C marketing needs to consider the Web purchasing models in order to better influence the customer's decision making (e.g., by effective one-to-one advertising and marketing).

ONLINE BUYER DECISION SUPPORT MODEL

Silverman et al. (2001) developed a model for a Web site that supports buyer decision making and searching. This model revises the generic model by describing the purchasing framework that is shown in Online File W4.1. The model is divided into three parts. The first is based on Miles et al. (2000), and it includes three stages of buyer behavior (see top of exhibit): identify and manage buying criteria, search for products and merchants, and compare alternatives. Below these activities are seven boxes with decision support system (DSS) design options (such as product representation), the options to support searching, and the options to compare alternatives.

The second part of the model (on the right), which is based on Guttman et al. (1998), has three boxes: price, shipping, and finance. These become relevant when alternatives are compared. The third part, at the bottom of the exhibit, is composed of three boxes. The model demonstrates the flow of data and the decisions that support EC.

OTHER MODELS

Several other purchasing-decision models have been proposed. Some are referenced in the Online Research Appendix "Current EC Research." Of special interest is a model proposed by Chaudhury et al. (2001). In this model, the buying decision is influenced by how much time is available and the locale (space) where the purchasing is done. In this context, *space* is the equivalent to shelf space in a physical store—namely how well a product is presented online and where it is presented on the Web site. Space also can refer to whether products are sold via wireline or wireless devices. The model distinguishes four scenarios: "less time and more space," "more time and less space," "more time and more space," and "less time and less space." For example, the space on a small banner ad is more limited than the space on a large pop-up ad. For each scenario, the vendors can develop different Web sites.

Section 4.2 ▶ REVIEW QUESTIONS

1. List the roles people play in purchasing.
2. List the five stages in the generic purchasing-decision model.
3. Describe the Web-based purchasing-decision model.
4. Describe the structure of the online buyer decision support model.

4.3 MASS MARKETING, MARKET SEGMENTATION, AND ONE-TO-ONE MARKETING

one-to-one marketing
Marketing that treats each customer in a unique way.

One of the greatest benefits of EC is its ability to match products and services with individual consumers. Such a match is a part of **one-to-one marketing**, which treats each customer in a unique way to fit marketing and advertising with the customer's profile and needs. Let's first see how the one-to-one approach evolved from the traditional marketing approaches.

FROM MASS MARKETING TO ONE-TO-ONE MARKETING

Three basic approaches are used in marketing and advertising: mass marketing, market segmentation, and one-to-one.

Mass Marketing

Marketing efforts traditionally were targeted to everyone (the "masses"). For example, using a newspaper or TV ad usually means one-way, interpersonal communication to whomever sees it. Such an effort may be effective for brand recognition or for introducing a new product or service. It can be conducted on the Internet as well.

In 2005, Ford Motor Company unveiled a *roadblock* approach on the Internet to promote its F-150 truck. (A "roadblock" refers to running a commercial on all major TV channels at exactly the same time, so viewers cannot switch channels to escape the commercial.) On the day of the launch, Ford placed static banner ads for 24 hours on the three leading Internet portals—AOL, MSN, and Yahoo!—introducing a 3-month campaign. Some 50 million Web surfers saw Ford's banner. Millions of them clicked on the banner, pouring onto Ford's Web site at a rate that reached 3,000 per second. Ford claimed that the traffic led to a 6 percent increase in sales over the first 3 months of the campaign. For details, see Baker (2004).

Although mass marketing may be effective in many cases, it is not good in all cases. As a matter of fact, it can be a waste. Oftentimes *targeted marketing*—marketing and advertising efforts targeted to groups (market segmentation) or to individuals (one-to-one)—is a better approach.

Market Segmentation

As consumers began purchasing and using products online, more data became available about them. Data analysts began associating products with the customers who were buying them. And it was through these analysis activities that companies began to understand that their customer data could be valuable.

Market segmentation refers to the practice of promoting a product or service to a subset of customers or prospects. We will explain how market segmentation is done in Section 4.4.

Modern companies assign a variety of segments to their customers, often dynamically defining segments and temporarily regrouping customers for specific campaigns. By segmenting customers, companies could begin more specialized communications about their products. Much of this relies on the company's understanding its business strategies to the extent that they know their most desirable segments. For instance, if a bank has set its sites on deriving most of its profits from fee-income products offered in its investment services line of business, customers for this bank will likely have different preferences and characteristics from those opening only savings accounts. Segmenting customers based on their preferred line of business or desired product features can reveal interesting facts about their different preferences and behaviors.

A simple way to segment online is to go to a specialized site or portal and advertise to its visitors. For example, by going to ivillage.com, you reach mostly women. Advertising in Internet communities and social networks usually provides you with market segmentation. Increasingly, advertising is being placed on social networking sites (e.g., myspace.com, facebook.com, bebo.com, friendster.com, spaces.live.com, 360.yahoo.com, xanga.com). U.S. spending on social network advertising is expected to rise to $865 million in 2007 and $2.15 billion in 2010 (*eMarketer.com* 2006). Some Weblogs that focus on specific niches (e.g., paidcontent.org, fark.com) have received a generous amount of dollars from advertisers (Sloan and Kaihla 2006).

One advantage of market segmentation is that advertising and marketing efforts match the segments better than the "mass," providing a better response rate. Also, the expense of reaching the segments is lower, and marketing efforts can be faster (e.g., e-mails are sent to fewer people, or banner ads are placed on fewer Web sites). The Internet enables more effective market segmentation (see Section 4.4), but it enables an even better approach, that of true *relationship marketing*, or one-to-one.

market segmentation
The process of dividing a consumer market into logical groups for conducting marketing research and analyzing personal information.

Relationship and One-To-One Marketing

Instead of selling a single product to as many customers as possible, marketers are trying to sell as many products as possible to one customer—over a long period of time and across different product lines. To do this, marketers need to concentrate on building unique relationships with individual customers on a *one-to-one* basis. *Relationship marketing* is a way for

EXHIBIT 4.3   From Mass Marketing to Segmentation, to One-to-One

Factor	Mass Marketing	Market Segmentation	Relationship Marketing (One-to-One)
Interactions	Usually none, or one-way	Usually none, or with a sample	Active, two-way
Focus	Product	Group (segment)	Customer-focused (one)
Recipient	Anonymous	Segment profiles	Individuals
Campaigns	Few	More	Many
Reach	Wide	Smaller	One at a time
Market Research	Macro in nature	Based on segment analysis or demographics	Based on detailed customer behaviors and profiles

Source: Drawn by E. Turban.

marketing departments to get to know their customers more intimately by understanding their preferences and thus increasing the odds of retaining them.

One-to-one means not only communicating with customers as individuals, but possibly developing custom products and tailored messages based on the customer's spoken and unspoken needs. It relies on a two-way dialog between a company and its customers in order to foster a true relationship and allows customers to truly express the desires that the company can help fulfill. It relies as heavily on the customer's experience of the company as it does on the specific marketing messages the customer receives. The major characteristics of one-to-one marketing as compared to mass marketing and market segmentation are illustrated in Exhibit 4.3.

HOW ONE-TO-ONE RELATIONSHIPS ARE PRACTICED

Although some companies have had one-to-one marketing programs for years, it may be much more beneficial to institute a corporate-wide policy of building one-to-one relationships around the Web. This can be done in several ways. For example, Gartner Inc., an IT consulting company, proposed what it calls "the new marketing cycle of relationship building" (see Marcus 2001). This proposal, illustrated in Exhibit 4.4, views relationships as a two-way street: The process can start at any point in the cycle. Usually, though, it starts with "Customer receives marketing exposure" (at the top of the figure). The customer then decides how to respond to the marketing exposure (e.g., whether to buy the product online or offline; if online, whether to buy as individual or to use group purchasing). When a sale is made, customer information is collected (lower-right corner) and then placed in a database. Then, a customer's profile is developed, and the so-called *four P's* of marketing (product, place, price, and promotion) are generated on a one-to-one basis. Based on this individualized profile, appropriate advertisements are prepared that will hopefully lead to another purchase by the customer. Once a purchase is made, the detailed transaction is added to the database, and the cycle is repeated. All of this can, and should, be done in the Web environment.

One of the benefits of doing business over the Internet is that it enables companies to better communicate with customers and better understand customers' needs and buying habits. These improvements, in turn, enable companies to enhance and frequently customize their

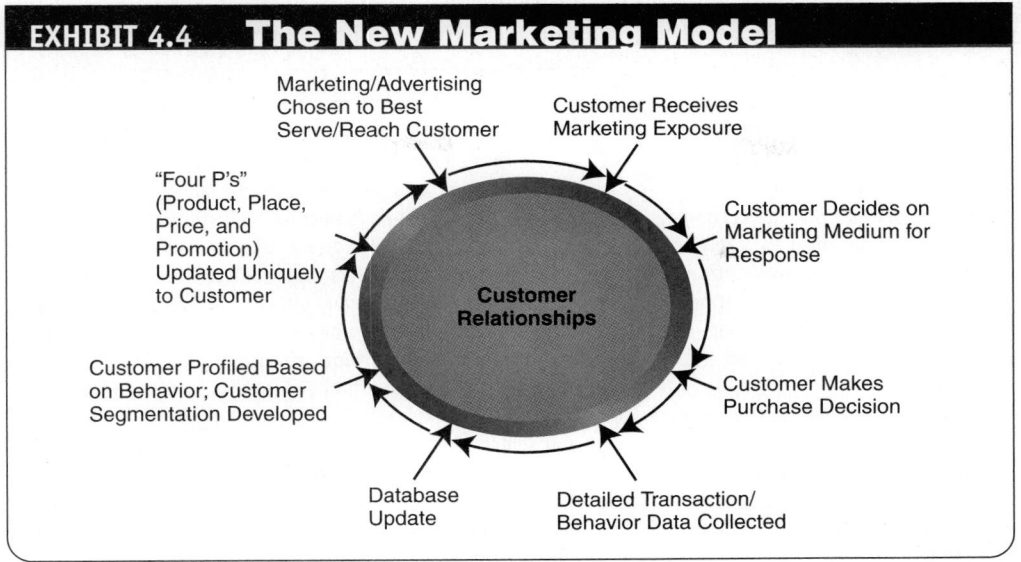

EXHIBIT 4.4   The New Marketing Model

Source: Nelson, S. "The New Marketing Relationship Model," Gartner, Inc., July 22, 1996. © Gartner, Inc. Used with permission.

future marketing efforts. For example, Amazon.com can e-mail customers announcements of the availability of books in their areas of interest as soon as they are published; Expedia.com will ask consumers where they like to fly and then e-mail them information about special discounts to their desired destination. Details on these key concepts are discussed in Section 4.4.

Section 4.3 ▶ REVIEW QUESTIONS

1. Define mass marketing.
2. Define market segmentation.
3. Define one-to-one marketing.
4. Describe the marketing relationship process.

4.4 PERSONALIZATION, LOYALTY, SATISFACTION, AND TRUST IN EC

Internet marketing facilitates the use of market segmentation and one-to-one marketing. Here we will address several key issues related to one-to-one marketing: personalization, collaborative filtering, customer loyalty, permission marketing (Section 4.9), and trust. For details on these and other issues related to implementing EC-based one-to-one marketing, see Kalyanam and Zweben (2005). For discussion of how one-to-one marketing is related to CRM, see Chapter 13.

PERSONALIZATION IN E-COMMERCE

Personalization refers to the matching of services, products, and advertising content to individuals and their preferences. The matching process is based on what a company knows about the individual user. This knowledge is usually referred to as a **user profile**. The user profile defines customer preferences, behaviors, and demographics. Profiles can be generated in several ways. The major strategies used to compile user profiles include the following:

▶ **Solicit information directly from the user.** This is usually done by asking the user to fill in a questionnaire or by conducting an interview with the user.

▶ **Observe what people are doing online.** A common way to observe what people are doing online is through use of a **cookie**—a data file that is stored on the user's hard drive, frequently without disclosure or the user's consent. Sent by a remote Web server over the Internet, the information stored will surface when the user's browser again

personalization
The matching of services, products, and advertising content with individual consumers and their preferences.

user profile
The requirements, preferences, behaviors, and demographic traits of a particular customer.

cookie
A data file that is placed on a user's hard drive by a remote Web server, frequently without disclosure or the user's consent, that collects information about the user's activities at a site.

Insights and Additions 4.1 Cookies in E-Commerce

Are cookies bad or good? The answer is "both." When users revisit Amazon.com or other sites, they are greeted by their first name. How does Amazon.com know a user's identity? Through the use of cookies! Vendors can provide consumers with considerable personalized information if they use cookies that signal a consumer's return to a site. A variation of cookies is known as *e-sugging* ("SUG-ing," from "selling under the guise of research"). For example, consumers who visit travel sites may get more and more unsolicited travel-related e-mails and pop-up ads.

Cookies can provide a wealth of information to marketers, which then can be used to target ads to consumers. Thus, marketers get higher rates of "click-throughs," and customers can view the most relevant information. Cookies can also prevent repetitive ads because vendors can arrange for a consumer not to see the same ad twice. Finally, advanced data mining

companies, such as NCR and Sift, can analyze information in cookie files so companies can better meet the customers' needs.

However, some people object to cookies because they do not like the idea that "someone" is watching their activity on the Internet. Users who do not like cookies can disable them. However, some consumers may want to keep the friendly cookies. For example, many sites recognize a person as a subscriber so that they do not need to reregister. Netscape 6 and higher allows users to block third-party cookies. Internet Explorer (IE) 6.09 and higher also gives users control over third-party cookies. (Go to "Internet Options" under "Tools" and select "Private tab," click "Advanced," and put a check mark next to "Override automatic cookie handling." Then, direct IE to accept first-party cookies.) See *wikipedia.org* and *pcworld.com/resource/browse/0,cat,1384,sortIdx,1,00.asp* for more on cookies.

accesses the specific Web server, and the cookie will collect information about the user's activities at the site (see cookiecentral.com). The use of cookies is one of the most controversial issues in EC, as discussed in Insights and Additions 4.1. Other tools, such as spyware and Web bugs, are described in Section 4.5. For an overview of personalization in EC, see Chan (2005) and Anke and Sundaram (2006).

▶ **Build from previous purchase patterns.** For example, Amazon.com builds customer profiles to recommend books, CDs, and other products, based on what customers have purchased before, rather than asking customers, using cookies, or doing market research.

▶ **Perform marketing research.** Firms can research the market using tools described in Section 4.5 and in the Netflix case at the beginning of the chapter.

▶ **Make inferences.** Infer from information provided by customers on other issues or by analyzing similar customers. (See collaborative filtering in Section 4.5 and the Netflix case.)

Once a customer profile is constructed, a company matches the profile with a database of products, services, or ads. Manual matching is time consuming and expensive; therefore, the matching process is usually done by software agents. One-to-one matching can be applied through several different methods. One well-known method is *collaborative filtering* (Section 4.5).

Chellappa and Sin (2005) highlighted the values of online personalization to consumers. For example, some stores send an instant alert to their customers' handheld devices and notify them when prices of particular stocks in their "watch list" drop to a predefined level or when an auction comes to a close. Some stores also allow users to personalize Web site attributes, such as the site's color or the greeting name. However, privacy and trust issues remain a limiting factor for personalization (Cone 2005).

According to Sackmann et al. (2006), the Internet offers online retailers different ways to tailor services to their customers, including:

▶ *Personalized services*. Services built on a one-to-one communication channel requiring personal data from customers.

▶ *Individual services*. Recommendation services built on the sequence of clicks, page requests, or items that have been added to the shopping cart. This approach improves the shopping experience while also maintaining consumer anonymity.

▶ *Universal services*. Consumers use the product search function or read customer reviews. This approach does not require personal or context data.

These services are a form of personalization because a single customer can choose a service that meets his or her needs at any particular time. All three types of personalization strategies will help build customer relationships, increase customer satisfaction, generate a lock-in situation, and realize greater product or service turnover.

CUSTOMER LOYALTY

One of the major objectives of one-to-one B2C marketing, as well as B2B marketing, is to increase customer loyalty (recall the Netflix case). *Customer loyalty* refers to "a deep commitment to rebuy or repatronize a preferred product/service consistently in the future, thereby causing repetitive same-brand or same brand-set purchasing, despite situational influences and marketing efforts having the potential to cause switching behavior" (Oliver 1999, p. 34).

Attracting and retaining loyal customers remains the most important issue for any selling company, including e-tailers. Increased customer loyalty can bring cost savings to a company in various ways: lower marketing and advertising costs, lower transaction costs, lower customer turnover expenses, lower failure costs such as warranty claims, and so on. Customer loyalty also strengthens a company's market position because loyal customers are kept away from the competition. In addition, customer loyalty can lead to enhanced resistance to competitors, a decrease in price sensitivity, and an increase in favorable word-of-mouth (Balabanis et al., 2006).

Loyalty programs were introduced over 100 years ago and are widely used among airlines, hotel chains, and credit-card companies. But now, loyalty programs have been expanded to all kinds of businesses. Octopus Hong Kong (octopuscards.com), a stored-value card operator, launched a reward program for consumers aimed at increasing card usage across Hong Kong. Reward points are gained by purchasing at a number of leading merchants across the territory, including Wellcome, Watsons, UA Cinemas, and McDonalds. Each Octopus card can store up to 1,000 rewards points, which can be redeemed on the next purchase. FANCL (fancl.com), a Japanese cosmetics and health-care company, offers the "FANCL point program" where consumers earn FANCL points that are saved for gift redemption. Maxwell House Coffee has its own program where consumers earn "House Points" with each can of coffee they buy and redeem for gift awards.

However, the introduction of Internet technologies has the potential to undermine brands and discourage customer loyalty. The customers' ability to shop, compare, and switch to different vendors becomes easier, faster, and less expensive given the aid of search engines and other technologies. Further, customers are less loyal to the brand because they want to take advantage of special offers and promotions, as well as to try on new things (*New Media Age* 2006).

The introduction of EC decreases loyalty in general because customers' ability to shop, compare, and switch to different vendors becomes easier, faster, and less expensive given the aid of search engines and other technologies. However, companies have found that loyal customers end up buying more when they have a Web site to shop from. For example, W. W. Grainger, a large industrial-supply company, found that loyal B2B customers increased their purchases substantially when they began using Grainger's Web site (grainger.com). (See Grainger, Inc. [1998] for more information.) Also, loyal customers may refer other customers to a site. Every company's goal is to increase customer loyalty. The Web offers ample opportunities to do so.

E-Loyalty

E-loyalty refers to a customer's loyalty to an e-tailer or a manufacturer that sells directly online or to loyalty programs delivered online or supported electronically. Customer acquisition and retention is a critical success factor in e-tailing. The expense of acquiring a new customer can be over $100; even for Amazon.com, which has a huge reach, it is more than $15. In contrast, the cost of maintaining an existing customer at Amazon.com is $2 to $4.

Companies can foster e-loyalty by learning about their customers' needs, interacting with customers, and providing superb customer service. A major source of information about e-loyalty is e-loyaltyresource.com. One of its major services is an online journal, the *e-Loyalty Resource Newsletter*, which offers numerous articles describing the relationships among e-loyalty, customer service, personalization, CRM, and Web-based tools. Another source of

e-loyalty
Customer loyalty to an e-tailer or loyalty programs delivered online or supported electronically.

information is colloquy.com, which concentrates on loyalty marketing. Comprehensive reviews of the use of the Web and the Internet to foster e-loyalty are provided by Harris and Goode (2004) and Yeo and Chiam (2006).

One of the most publicized computer-based loyalty programs is the one used by Harrah's, the largest casino chain in the world. The casino industry is extremely competitive, with more and more gambling channels and new physical casinos opening to the public. Standing out from the competition is becoming an increasingly enormous challenge. All casinos employ basic loyalty programs. They record the money spent in the machines, tables, restaurants, and so forth by each player and provide awards to frequent gamblers (e.g., a free night's stay in their hotels). Using data mining and business intelligence, Harrah's was able to learn more accurately about its customers and offer them the rewards on a one-to-one basis the players really like.

Lately, Harrah's moved one step farther in order to increase its understanding of its customers and their loyalty by moving to a real-time rewards system (Evans 2006; *Cognos.com* 2006; *SAS.com* 2006). For example, if the casino knows who is playing on each slot machine and the birthdays of each player, it can arrange for a manager to come to the player with a birthday cake and a gift while on the casino floor. And each player may prefer a different gift. Using a teradata data warehouse as well as SAS and Cognos software, an analysis of millions of customers becomes feasible and economical. This enables Harrah's to deliver the best in one-to-one marketing and to do it in real time. Customers feel that the company knows them and their needs, so they keep coming back.

According to Floh and Treiblmaier (2006), satisfaction and trust are the two most important factors in determining customer e-loyalty. More discussion on satisfaction and trust can be found in the following sections. In addition, e-loyalty is a major barrier that customers must cross when deciding to exit to a competitor. See Online File W4.2 at the book's Web site for more on customer exit barriers.

SATISFACTION IN EC

Given the changing dynamics of the global marketplace and the increasingly intense competition, delivering world-class customer online experience becomes a differentiating strategy. Satisfaction is one of the most important consumer reactions in the B2C online environment. Maintaining customer satisfaction in the online shopping experience is as important as the high level of satisfaction associated with several key outcomes (e.g., repeat purchase, positive word-of-mouth, and so on). Eighty percent of highly satisfied online consumers would shop again within 2 months, and 90 percent would recommend Internet retailers to others. However, 87 percent of dissatisfied consumers would permanently leave their Internet retailers without any complaints (Cheung and Lee 2005b).

Satisfaction has received an enormous amount of attention in studies of consumer-based EC. ForeSee Results, an online customer satisfaction measurement company, developed the American Customer Satisfaction Index (ACSI) (theasci.org) for measuring customer satisfaction with EC. In the fourth quarter of 2005, the ACSI for e-commerce category had increased 1.3 percent over the previous quarter to an aggregate score of 79.6 on a 100-point scale (Tode 2006), below its all-time high of 80.8 in 2003. The Customer Respect Group (customerrespect.com) also provides an index to measure the customer's online experience. The Customer Respect Index (CRI) includes the following components: simplicity, responsiveness, transparency, principles, attitude, and privacy.

Researchers have proposed several models to explain the formation of satisfaction with online shopping. For example, Cheung and Lee (2005a) proposed a framework for consumer satisfaction with Internet shopping by correlating the end-user satisfaction perspective with the service quality viewpoint. The framework has been updated and is shown in Exhibit 4.5.

The ability to predict consumer satisfaction can be useful in designing Web sites as well as advertising and marketing strategies. Shih and Fang (2006) developed a predictive model of customer satisfaction. However, Web site designers should also pay attention to the nature of Web site features. Different features have different impacts on customer (dis)satisfaction. If certain Web site features, such as reliability of content, loading speed, and usefulness, fail to perform properly, customer satisfaction will drop dramatically. In contrast, if features such

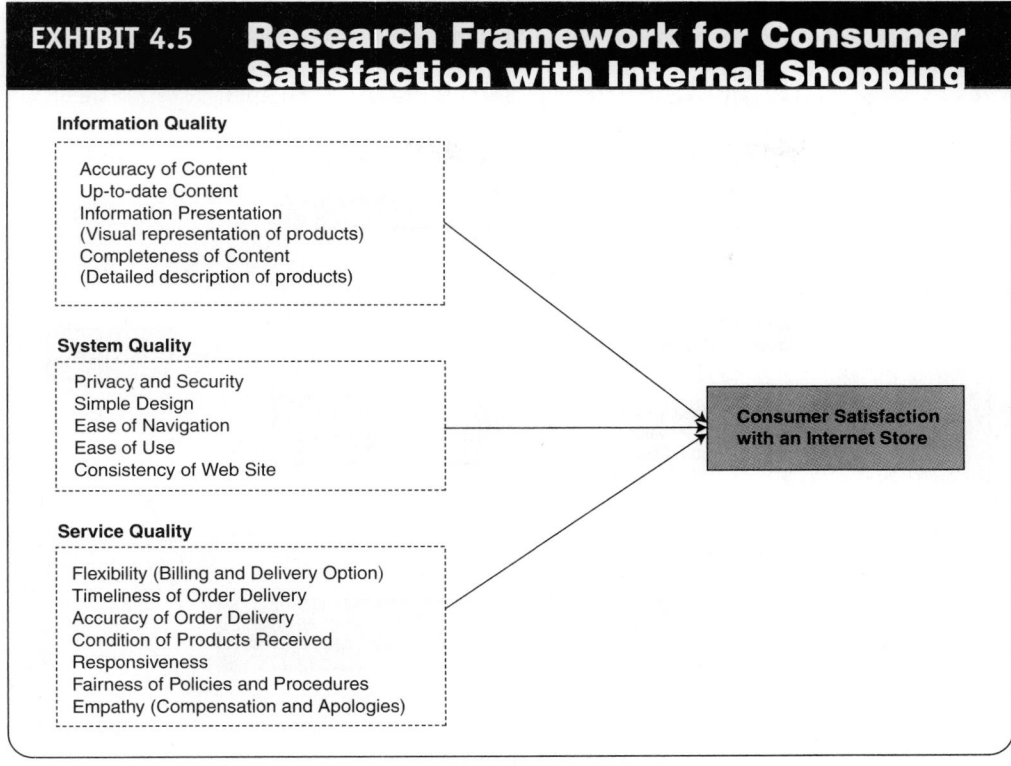

EXHIBIT 4.5   Research Framework for Consumer Satisfaction with Internal Shopping

Information Quality

Accuracy of Content
Up-to-date Content
Information Presentation
(Visual representation of products)
Completeness of Content
(Detailed description of products)

System Quality

Privacy and Security
Simple Design
Ease of Navigation
Ease of Use
Consistency of Web Site

Service Quality

Flexibility (Billing and Delivery Option)
Timeliness of Order Delivery
Accuracy of Order Delivery
Condition of Products Received
Responsiveness
Fairness of Policies and Procedures
Empathy (Compensation and Apologies)

Consumer Satisfaction with an Internet Store

as those that make the usage enjoyable, entertaining, and fun perform well, they will surprise customers and result in a radical jump in customer satisfaction. The discussion of these two types of features on Web site satisfaction can be found in Cheung and Lee (2005b).

More discussion on EC satisfaction can be found in Collier and Bienstock (2006) and Massad et al. (2006).

TRUST IN EC

Trust is the psychological status of depending on another person or organization to achieve a planned goal. When people trust each other, they have confidence that as transaction partners they will keep their promises. However, both parties in a transaction assume some risk. In the electronic marketplace, sellers and buyers do not meet face to face. The buyer can see a picture of the product but not the product itself. Promises of quality and delivery can be easily made—but will they be kept? To deal with these issues, EC vendors need to establish high levels of trust with current and potential customers. Trust is particularly important in global EC transactions due to the difficulty of taking legal action in cases of a dispute or fraud and the potential for conflicts caused by differences in culture and business environments.

In addition to sellers and buyers trusting each other, both must have trust in the EC computing environment and in the EC infrastructure. If people do not trust the security of the EC infrastructure, they will not feel comfortable about using credit cards to make EC purchases.

trust
The psychological status of willingness to depend on another person or organization.

EC Trust Models

Several models have been put forth to explain the EC–trust relationship. For example, Lee and Turban (2001) examined the various aspects of EC trust and developed the model shown in Exhibit 4.6. According to this model, the level of trust is determined by numerous variables (factors) shown on the left side and in the middle of the figure. The exhibit illustrates the complexity of trust relationships, especially in B2C EC. Paravastu and Gefen (2006) distinguished between initial and ongoing trust and developed a model accordingly. Oermann and Dittmann (2006) looked at trust specifically in e-technologies.

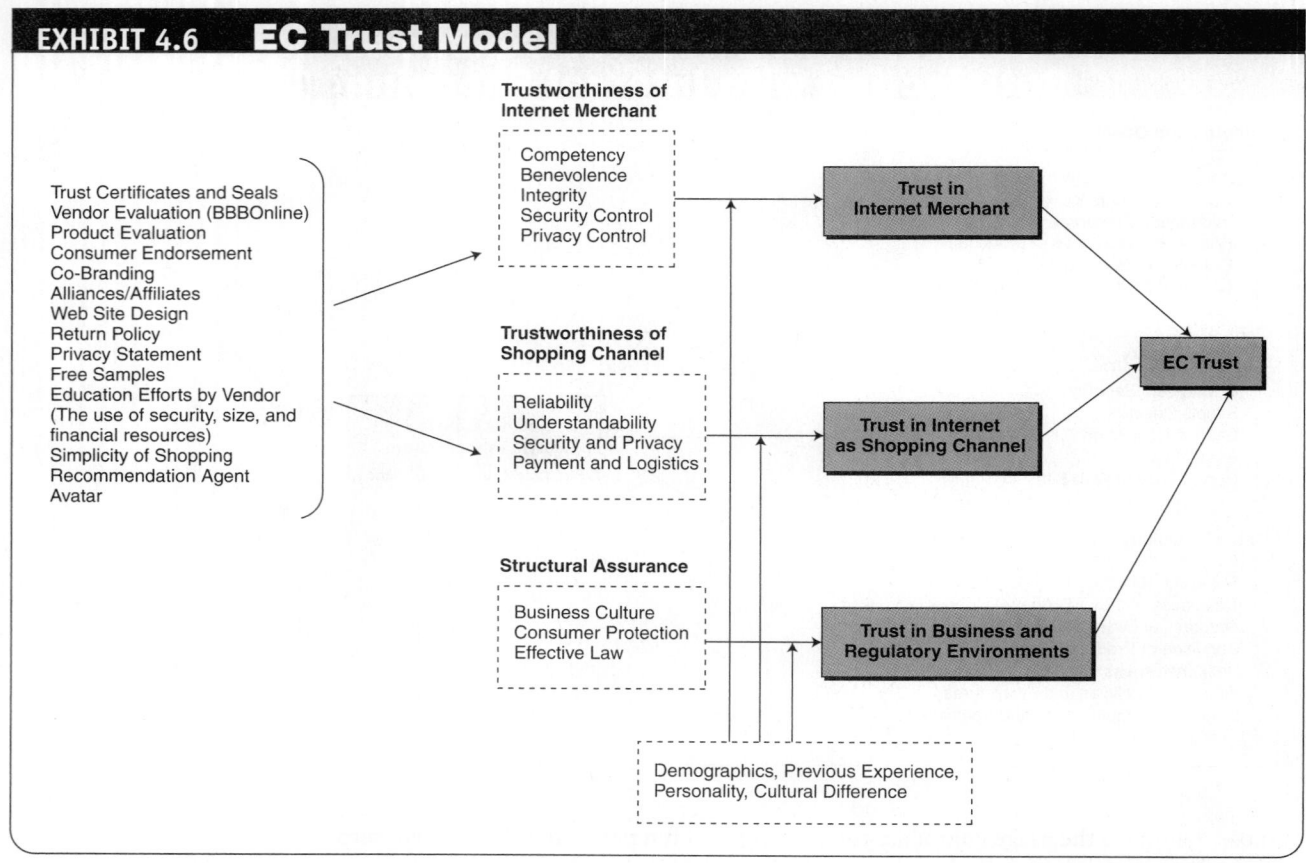

EXHIBIT 4.6   EC Trust Model

Most of the research on trust has examined individuals and B2C. Ratnasingam (2005) has investigated the trust issue in B2B.

How to Increase Trust in EC

Consumer trust is fundamental to successful online retailing. Urban et al. (2000) advocated that trust is the currency of the Internet. The following are several guidelines for building consumer trust in EC (Cheung and Lee 2006, Jeanson and Ingham 2006).

Affiliate with an Objective Third Party. This approach aims at building consumer trust by affiliating with trusted third parties. Internet stores can put hypertext links on their Web sites to other trusted targets, including reputable companies or well-known portals. These reputable companies are able to transfer brand equity to the Internet stores because companies with brand names induce trust. Internet stores can also use the third-party seals of approval such as TRUSTe (truste.com) and BBBOnLine (bbbonline.org) (the online version of the Better Business Bureau). Escrow providers and reputation finders (e.g., cyberalert.com and cymfony.com) also are useful. These agencies provide business-critical intelligence on how brands are being used on the Internet as well as research about spying on businesses.

Working against EC trust are stories of a considerable amount of fraud on the Internet, especially when unknown parties are involved. In Chapters 11 and 17, we describe measures to reduce fraud and increase trust.

Establish Trustworthiness. Trustworthiness can be achieved through three key elements: integrity, competence, and security. Integrity conveys an overall sense of the ability of the Internet store to build an image of strong justice and fulfill all of the promises that have been made to the customers (i.e., offering a money-back guarantee with the products and clearly stating the guarantee policy on the Web site). Another indicator of trustworthiness is an Internet store's competence. Stores can promote the perception of competence by delivering a professional Web site. A professional appearance should include the basic features that facilitate navigation, including correct grammar and spelling, full and accurate information, and good use of graphic design. The Web site should include some advanced features that provide support to users, such as an internal search engine, quick order ability, order tracking, and an online chat room. Finally, EC security mechanisms can help solidify trust. Dell was the first PC manufacturer to launch an online secure shopping guarantee to online shoppers making purchases at its Web site.

In summary, the Internet offers a new way to conduct business. At this stage, rules and conventions are still evolving. Many of the things adapted from traditional business need further evaluation to fit the online environment. For example, security must be able to safeguard against increasingly malicious attacks. Trust-transference programs through portal affiliation, seal of approval programs, online shopping communities, customer endorsements, and the like are needed. Finally, a global regulatory environment must be established to induce trust in the online environment.

For a more comprehensive treatment of EC trust, see Jeanson and Ingham (2006) and Hoffman et al. (2006).

Section 4.4 ❱ REVIEW QUESTIONS

1. Explain how personalization (matching people with goods/services) is done.
2. Define loyalty and describe e-loyalty.
3. Describe the issue of trust in EC and how to increase it.
4. What influences consumer satisfaction online? Why do companies need to monitor it?
5. How can trust be increased in EC?

4.5 MARKET RESEARCH FOR EC

The goal of market research is to find information and knowledge that describe the relationships among consumers, products, marketing methods, and marketers. Its aim is to discover marketing opportunities and issues, to establish marketing plans, to better understand the purchasing process, and to evaluate marketing performance. On the Web, the objective is to turn browsers into buyers. Market research includes gathering information about topics such as the economy, industry, firms, products, pricing, distribution, competition, promotion, and consumer purchasing behavior. Here we focus on the latter. In Chapter 14, we will look at some other market research topics: the need to research the market, the competition, the technology, the business environment, and much more.

Businesses, educational institutions, and governments use various tools to conduct consumer market research both *offline* and *online*. The major ones that are used in e-commerce are described later in this section.

METHODS FOR CONDUCTING MARKET RESEARCH ONLINE

EC market research can be conducted through conventional methods, or it can be done with the assistance of the Internet. Although telephone or shopping mall surveys will continue, interest in Internet research methods is on the rise. Market research that uses the Internet frequently is faster and more efficient and allows the researcher to access a more geographically diverse audience than those found in offline surveys (see FAQs at casro.org and accutips.com). Also, on the Web market researchers can conduct a very large study much more cheaply than with other methods. The larger the sample size, the larger the accuracy and the predictive capabilities of the results. Telephone surveys can cost as much as $50 per respondent. This may be too expensive for a small company that needs several hundred respondents. An online survey will cost a fraction of a similarly sized telephone survey and can expedite research considerably, as shown in Case 4.1. Hewson et al. (2003) provide a comprehensive review of online market research technologies, methods, tools, and issues, including ethical ones. As you may recall, marketers concentrate on market segmentation and one-to-one. Let's see how this is accomplished.

CASE 4.1
EC Application
INTERNET MARKET RESEARCH EXPEDITES TIME-TO-MARKET AT PROCTER & GAMBLE

For decades, Procter & Gamble (P&G) and Colgate-Palmolive have been competitors in the market for personal care products. Developing a major new product from concept to market launch used to take over 5 years. First, a concept test was conducted: The companies sent product photos and descriptions to potential customers, asking whether they might buy the product. If the feedback was negative, they tried to improve the product concept and then repeated previous tasks. Once positive response was achieved, sample products were mailed out, and the customers were asked to fill out detailed questionnaires. When customers' responses met the companies' internal hurdles, the companies would start with mass TV advertising.

However, thanks to the Internet, it took P&G only 3 and one-half years to get Whitestrips, the teeth-brightening product, onto the market and to a sales level of $200 million a year—considerably quicker than other oral care products. In September 2000, P&G threw out the old marketing test model and instead introduced Whitestrips on the Internet, offering the product for sale on P&G's Web site. The company spent several months studying who was coming to the site and buying the product and collecting responses to online questionnaires, which was much faster than the old mail-outs.

The online research, which was facilitated by data mining conducted on P&G's huge historical data (stored in a data warehouse) and the new Internet data, revealed the most enthusiastic groups. These included teenage girls, brides-to-be, and young Hispanic Americans. Immediately, the company started to target these segments with appropriate advertising. The Internet created a product awareness of 35 percent, even before any shipments were made to stores. This buzz created a huge demand for the product by the time it hit the shelves.

In 2006, P&G began using on-demand solutions from RightNow Technologies (rightnow.com) including survey tools that execute opinion polls among selected segments of consumers who have opted into the company's market research programs.

From these experiences, P&G learned important lessons about flexible and creative ways to approach product innovation and marketing. The whole process of studying the product concept, segmenting the market, and expediting product development has been revolutionized.

Sources: Compiled from TMCnet (2006), Buckley (2002), and *pg.com* (accessed December 2006).

Questions

1. How did P&G reduce time-to-market?
2. What was data mining used for?
3. What research methods were used?

What Are Marketers Looking for in EC Market Research?

By looking at a personal profile that includes observed behaviors on the Web, it is possible for marketers to explain and predict online buying behavior. For example, companies want to know why some customers are online shoppers whereas others are not (see Limayem et al. 2004). Major factors that are used for prediction are (in descending order of importance): product information requested, number of related e-mails, number of orders made, products/services ordered, and gender.

Typical questions that online market research attempts to answer are: What are the purchase patterns for individuals and groups (market segmentation)? What factors encourage online purchasing? How can we identify those who are real buyers from those who are just browsing? How does an individual navigate—does the consumer check information first or do they go directly to ordering? What is the optimal Web page design? Knowing the answers to questions such as these helps a vendor to advertise properly, to price items, to design the Web site, and to provide appropriate customer service. Online market research can provide such data about individuals, about groups, and even about the entire Internet.

Internet-based market research is often done in an interactive manner, allowing personal contact with customers, and it provides marketing organizations with a greater ability to understand the customer, the market, and the competition. For example, it can identify early shifts in product and customer trends, enabling marketers to identify products and marketing opportunities and to develop those products that customers really want to buy. It also tells management when a product or a service is no longer popular. To learn more about market research on the Web, see the tutorials at webmonkey.com.

The following discussion describes some online market research methods.

Market Segmentation Research

Because EC also has to identify an appropriate customer group for specific products and services, it is important first to understand how groups of consumers are classified. This classification is called *market segmentation*.

For years, companies used direct mail to contact customers. However, they frequently did so regardless of whether the products or services were appropriate for the specific individuals on the company's mailing list. For example, ABC Company sends out four mailings of 1,000,000 pieces each year. The cost of the direct mailings is $1.25 per customer, and only 1 percent respond. This means the cost per responding customer is $125. Obviously, this type of direct marketing usually is not cost-effective.

Markets can be segmented to increase the percentage of responses and to formulate effective marketing strategies that appeal to specific consumer groups. Market segmentation is the process of dividing a consumer market into logical groups for conducting marketing research, advertising, and sales. A consumer market can be segmented in several ways, for example, by geography, demographics, psychographics, and benefits sought, as shown in Exhibit 4.7. For a description, see Chan (2005).

A company can separate even millions of customers into smaller segments and tailor its campaigns to each of those segments. Brengman et al. (2005) segmented Internet shoppers based on their Web-usage–related lifestyle, themes of Internet usage, Internet attitude, and psychographic and demographic characteristics. They identified four online shopping segments (tentative shoppers, suspicious learners, shopping lovers, and business users) and four online nonshopping segments (fearful browsers, positive technology muddlers, negative technology muddlers, and adventurous browsers). By isolating and identifying combinations of attributes that make markets, prospects, and customers unique, marketers use strategies developed to appeal to targeted segments. One segment that is being targeted is the so-called *Internet generation,* or *NetGen*, the generation that has been raised with the power of the Internet. Internet marketing and advertising is more appropriate to the NetGen than traditional advertising (*Mirror99.com* 2006).

Market segmentation is done with the aid of tools such as data modeling (Oh et al. 2003) and data warehousing. Using data mining (Gregg and Walczak 2006) and Web mining (see Online File W4.3), businesses can look at consumer buying patterns to slice segments even finer. This is not an easy process, and it requires considerable resources and computer support. Most of the market segmentation success stories involve large companies. For example, Royal Bank of Canada segments its 10 million customers at least once a month to determine credit risk, profitability, and so on. This market segmentation has been very successful: The response to Royal Bank of Canada advertising campaigns has increased from 3 to 30 percent (Gold 2001). Market segmentation can be very effective in

EXHIBIT 4.7	Consumer Market Segmentation in the United States (A Partial List)
Market Segmentation	**Bases/Descriptors**
Geographic	Region; size of city, county, or Standard Metropolitan Statistical Area (SMSA); population density; climate; language
Demographic	Age, occupation, gender, education, family size, religion, race, income, nationality, urban (or suburban or rural)
Psychograhic (lifestyle)	Social class, lifestyle, personality, activities, VALS typology (see *sric-bi.com/VALS/presurvey.shtml*)
Cognitive, affective, behavioral	Attitudes, benefits sought, loyalty status, readiness stage, usage rate, perceived risk, user status, innovativeness, usage situation, involvement, Internet shopping experience
Profitability	Valued customers are placed in a special category
Risk score	Low risk customers are in a special category

the Web environment, especially when used with appropriate statistical tools. For more on market segmentation surveys, see sric-bi.com/VALS/presurvey.shtml.

Market Research for One-to-One

A considerable amount of market research is done in support of the one-to-one marketing approach. The major one-to-one marketing approaches are:

▶ Direct solicitation of information (surveys, focus groups)
▶ Observing what customers are doing on the Web
▶ Collaborative filtering

Online research methods range from one-to-one communication with specific customers, usually by e-mail, to moderated focus groups conducted in chat rooms, to questionnaires placed on Web sites, to tracking of customers' movements on the Web. Professional pollsters and marketing research companies frequently conduct online voting polls (e.g., see cnn.com and acnielsen.com). For an overview of online market research methods, see Hewson et al. (2003). A typical Internet-based market research process is shown in Exhibit 4.8.

With the high Internet penetration rate, there has been a tremendous increase in the number of published articles on online survey research. Online survey research has numerous advantages, including lower overall preparation and administration costs, greater speed in survey distribution and collection, fewer response errors, more complete responses, easier follow-up, and more flexibility in the questionnaire design. Despite all of these benefits, online surveys also have some potential weaknesses, including lack of anonymity and data privacy and security, technological variation of the potential respondents, and being impersonal. However, according to surveys conducted by the Georgia Institute of Technology

---

EXHIBIT 4.8   Online Market Research Process

Steps in Collecting Market Research Data
1. Define the research issue and the target market.
2. Identify newsgroups and Internet communities to study.
3. Identify specific topics for discussion.
4. Subscribe to the pertinent groups; register in communities.
5. Search discussion group topic and content lists to find the target market.
6. Search e-mail discussion group lists.
7. Subscribe to filtering services that monitor groups.
8. Read FAQs and other instructions.
9. Visit chat rooms.

Content of the Research Instrument
1. Post strategic queries to groups.
2. Post surveys on a Web site.
3. Offer rewards for participation.
4. Post strategic queries on a Web site.
5. Post relevant content to groups, with a pointer to a Web site survey.
6. Post a detailed survey in special e-mail questionnaires.
7. Create a chat room and try to build a community of consumers.

Target Audience of the Study
1. Compare audience with the target population.
2. Determine editorial focus.
3. Determine content.
4. Determine what Web services to create for each type of audience.

Sources: Compiled from Vassos (1996) and Moisander and Valtomen (2006).

(1998), more than 40 percent of the information people place on such questionnaires is incorrect. Appropriate design of Web questionnaires and incentives for truthful completion are critical for the validity of the results (Birnbaum 2004).

Implementing Web-Based Surveys. Web-based surveys are becoming popular with companies and researchers. For example, Mazda North America used a Web-based survey to help design its Miata line. Web surveys may be passive (a fill-in questionnaire) or interactive (respondents download the questionnaires, add comments, ask questions, and discuss issues). For more information and additional software tools, see supersurvey.com, surveymonkey.com, websurveyor.com, and clearlearning.com. For an introduction on how to conduct Web-based surveys, see Faught et al. (2004).

A major provider of online surveys is Zoomerang (zoomerang.com). At Zoomerang, users can select survey templates, edit them, and send them to preselected recipients. The basic service is free. For an evaluation of leading Web survey software, see Chen (2004).

Online Focus Groups. Several research firms create panels of qualified Web regulars to participate in online focus groups. For example, NPD's panel (npd.com) consists of 15,000 consumers recruited online and verified by telephone; Greenfield Online (greenfieldonline.com) picks users from its own database and then calls them periodically to verify that they are who they say they are. Another online research firm, Research Connections (researchconnections.com), recruits participants in advance by telephone and takes the time to help them connect to the Internet, if necessary. Use of preselected focus group participants helps to overcome some of the problems (e.g., small sample size and partial responses) that sometimes limit the effectiveness of Web-based surveys.

Hearing Directly from Customers. Instead of using focus groups, which are costly and possibly slow, customers can be asked directly what they think about a product or service. Westcott (2006) advocates the need to listen to customers. Toymaker Lego used a market-research vendor to establish a survey on an electronic bulletin board where millions of visitors read each other's comments and share opinions about Lego toys. The research vendor analyzed the responses daily and submitted the information to Lego. Netflix is using this approach extensively by inducing customers to report their likes and dislikes as described earlier in this chapter. In addition, companies can use chat rooms, newsgroups, blogs, wikis, podcasts, and electronic consumer forums to interact with consumers.

Software tools that can be used to hear directly from customers include Brand Advocacy Insights (used by Lego) from Informative, Inc. (informative.com), Betasphere (voc-online.com), InsightExpress (insightexpress.com), and Survey.com (survey.com).

Observing Customers

To avoid some of the problems of online surveys, especially the giving of false information, some marketers choose to learn about customers by observing their behavior rather than by asking them questions. Many marketers keep track of consumers' Web movements using methods such as transaction logs (log files) or cookie files.

Transaction Logs. A **transaction log** records user activities at a company's Web site. A transaction log is created by a *log file*, which is a file that lists actions that have occurred. With log file analysis tools, it is possible to get a good idea of where visitors are coming from, how often they return, and how they navigate through a site (Cyr et al. 2005; Jansen and Spink 2006). The transaction-log approach is especially useful if the visitors' names are known (e.g., when they have registered with the site). In addition, data from the shopping-cart database can be combined with information in the transaction log.

transaction log
A record of user activities at a company's Web site.

Note that as customers move from site to site, they establish their **clickstream behavior,** a pattern of their movements on the Internet, which can be seen in their transaction logs. Both ISPs and individual Web sites are capable of tracking a user's clickstream.

clickstream behavior
Customer movements on the Internet.

An example of the use of transaction logs is Internet Profile Corporation (IPC) (ipro.com), which collects data from a company's client/server logs and provides the company with periodic reports that include demographic data such as where customers come from or how many customers have gone straight from the homepage to placing an order. IPC also translates the Internet domain names of visitors into real company names. This way, a company knows where its customers are coming from.

Web bugs

Tiny graphics files
embedded in e-mail mes-
sages and in Web sites that
transmit information about
users and their movements
to a Web server.

spyware

Software that gathers
user information over an
Internet connection with-
out the user's knowledge.

clickstream data

Data that occur inside
the Web environment;
they provide a trail of
the user's activities
(the user's clickstream
behavior) in the Web site.

Cookies, Web Bugs, and Spyware. Cookies and Web bugs can be used to supplement transaction-log methods. As discussed earlier, cookies allow a Web site to store data on the user's PC; when the customer returns to the site, the cookies can be used to find what the customer did in the past. Cookies are frequently combined with **Web bugs,** tiny graphics files embedded in e-mail messages and on Web sites. Web bugs transmit information about the user and his or her movements to a monitoring site.

Spyware is software that gathers user information through an Internet connection without the user's knowledge (Stafford and Urbaczewski 2004). Originally designed to allow freeware authors to make money on their products, spyware applications are typically bundled together with freeware for download onto users' machines. Many users do not realize that they are downloading spyware with the freeware. Sometimes the freeware provider may indicate that other programs will be loaded onto the user's computer in the licensing agreement (e.g., "may include software that occasionally notifies users of important news"). Spyware stays on the user's hard drive and continually tracks the user's actions, periodically sending information on the user's activities to the owner of the spyware. It typically is used to gather information for advertising purposes. Users cannot control what data are sent via the spyware, and unless they use special tools they often cannot uninstall the spyware, even if the software it was bundled with is removed from the system. Effective tools for fighting spyware include Ad-aware (lavasoftusa.com/software/adaware), Spykiller (spykiller.com), and Webwasher Spyware from Secure Computing (securecomputing.com). For more on spyware and banners, see Online File W4.4.

Representative vendors that provide tools for tracking customers' movements are Tealeaf Technology, Inc. (tealeaf.com, log files), Acxiom Corp. (acxiom.com, data warehousing), and Stat Counter (statcounter.com, real-time tracking).

The use of cookies and Web bugs is controversial. Many believe that they invade the customer's privacy (see privacyfoundation.org). Tracking customers' activities *without their knowledge or permission* may be unethical or even illegal.

Analysis of B2C Clickstream Data. Large and ever-increasing amounts of B2C data can be collected on consumers, products, and so on. Such data come from several sources: internal data (e.g., sales data, payroll data, etc.), external data (e.g., government and industry reports), and clickstream data. **Clickstream data** are data generated in the Web environment; they provide a trail of a user's activities (the user's clickstream behavior) in a Web site (Park and Fader 2004). These data include a record of the user's browsing patterns: every Web site and every page of every Web site the user visits, how long the user remains on a page or site, in what order the pages were visited, and even the e-mail addresses of mail that the user sends and receives. By analyzing clickstream data, a firm can find out, for example, which promotions are effective and which population segments are interested in specific products.

According to Inmon (2001), B2C clickstream data can reveal information such as the following:

- What goods the customer has looked at
- What goods the customer has purchased
- What goods the customer examined but did not purchase
- What items the customer bought in conjunction with other items
- What items the customer looked at in conjunction with other items but did not purchase
- Which ads and promotions were effective and which were not
- Which ads generate a lot of attention but few sales
- Whether certain products are too hard to find and/or too expensive
- Whether there is a substitute product that the customer finds first
- Whether there are too many products for the customer to wade through
- Whether certain products are not being promoted
- Whether the products have adequate descriptions

Several companies offer tools that enable such an analysis. For example, WebTrends 7 features several advanced tools for analyzing clickstream data (e.g., see webtrends.com).

In addition, clickstream data can be maintained in a clickstream data warehouse for further analysis (see Sweiger et al. 2002). Despite storing many terabytes of clickstream data and investing heavily in Web analytic tools, very few companies understand how to use the data effectively (Sen et al. 2006).

Web Analytics and Mining. Web analytics services and software have grown beyond simply reporting which page was clicked and how long a visitor stayed there. They now offer more advanced functions that retailers are finding indispensable. For example, options from Coremetrics Inc. (coremetrics.com) and others are enabling retailers to make site adjustments on the fly, manage online marketing campaigns and e-commerce initiatives, and track customer satisfaction. Also, if a company redesigns its Web site it can gain almost-instant feedback on how the new site is performing. Web analytics can be done on a customer-by-customer or prospect-by-prospect basis, helping marketers decide which products to promote and merchandisers achieve a better understanding of the nature of demand. For tutorials on data mining and Web mining, see autonlab.org/tutorials.

Web mining refers to the use of data mining techniques for discovering and extracting information from Web documents. Web mining explores both *Web content* and *Web usage*. The usage analysis is derived from clickstream data. According to Gregg and Walczak (2006), Web mining has the potential to dramatically change the way we access and use the information available on the Web.

> **Web mining**
> Data mining techniques for discovering and extracting information from Web documents. Web mining explores both *Web content* and *Web usage*.

Collaborative Filtering

Once a company knows a consumer's preferences (e.g., music, movie, or book preferences), it would be useful if the company could predict, without asking the customer directly, what other products or services this consumer might enjoy. One way to do this is through **collaborative filtering,** which uses customer data to infer customer interest in other products or services. This prediction is based on special formulas derived from behavioral sciences. For more on the methods and formulas used to execute collaborative filtering, see Wang et al. (2005) and Chen and McLeod (2006). The prediction also can be based on what marketers know about other customers with similar profiles. One of the pioneering filtering systems was Firefly (now embedded in Microsoft's Passport System). Many personalization systems (recall the Netflix case) are based on collaborative filtering (e.g., backflip.com and choicestream.com).

The following are some variations of collaborative filtering:

> **collaborative filtering**
> A market research and personalization method that uses customer data to predict, based on formulas derived from behavioral sciences, what other products or services a customer may enjoy; predictions can be extended to other customers with similar profiles.

- ▶ **Rule-based filtering.** A company asks consumers a series of yes/no or multiple-choice questions. The questions may range from personal information to the specific information the customer is looking for on a specific Web site. Certain behavioral patterns are predicted using the collected information. From this information, the collaborative filtering system derives behavioral and demographic rules such as, "If customer age is greater than 35, and customer income is above $100,000, show Jeep Cherokee ad. Otherwise, show Mazda Protégé ad."
- ▶ **Content-based filtering.** With this technique, vendors ask users to specify certain favorite products. Based on these user preferences, the vendor's system will recommend additional products to the user. This technique is fairly complex, because mapping among different product categories must be completed in advance.
- ▶ **Activity-based filtering.** Filtering rules can also be built by watching the user's activities on the Web.

For more about personalization and filtering, see knowledgestorm.com.

Legal and Ethical Issues in Collaborative Filtering. Information often is collected from users without their knowledge or permission. This raises several ethical and legal questions, including invasion-of-privacy issues (see Chen and McLeod 2006). Several vendors offer *permission-based* personalization tools. With these, companies request the customer's permission to receive questionnaires and ads (e.g., see knowledgestorm.com). See Chapter 17 for more on privacy issues and Section 4.8 for information on permission marketing.

LIMITATIONS OF ONLINE MARKET RESEARCH AND HOW TO OVERCOME THEM

One problem with online market research is that too much data may be available. To use data properly, one needs to organize, edit, condense, and summarize it. However, such a task may be expensive and time consuming. The solution to this problem is to automate the process by using data warehousing and data mining. The essentials of this process, known as *business intelligence*, are provided in Online File W4.3 and Turban et al. (2007).

Some of the limitations of online research methods are accuracy of responses, loss of respondents because of equipment problems, and the ethics and legality of Web tracking. In addition, focus group responses can lose something in the translation from an in-person group to an online group. A researcher may get people online to talk to each other and play off of each other's comments, but eye contact and body language are two interactions of traditional focus group research that are lost in the online world. However, just as it hinders the two-way assessment of visual cues, Web research can actually offer some participants the anonymity necessary to elicit an unguarded response. Finally, a major limitation of online market research is the difficulty in obtaining truly representative samples.

Concerns have been expressed over the potential lack of representativeness in samples of online users. Online shoppers tend to be wealthy, employed, and well educated. Although this may be a desirable audience for some products and services, the research results may not be extendable to other markets. Although the Web-user demographic is rapidly diversifying, it is still skewed toward certain population groups, such as those with convenient Internet access (at home or work). Another important issue concerns the lack of clear understanding of the online communication process and how online respondents think and interact in cyberspace.

It is important for a company to identify the intended target audience or demographic so that the right kind of sampling can be performed. Web-based surveys typically have a lower response rate than e-mail surveys, and there is no respondent control for public surveys. If target respondents are allowed to be anonymous, it may encourage them to be more truthful in their opinions. However, anonymity may result in the loss of valuable information about the demographics and characteristics of the respondents. Finally, there are still concerns about the security of the information transmitted, which also may have an impact on the respondents' truthfulness.

To overcome some of the limitations of online market research, companies can outsource their market research needs. Only large companies have specialized market research departments. Most other companies use third-party research companies, such as AC Nielsen.

BIOMETRIC MARKETING

One problem with Web analytics, Web mining, clickstream data, and so on is that we observe and follow a *computer*, not knowing who is actually moving the mouse. Many households have several users; thus, the data collected may not represent any one person's preferences (unless of course, we are sure that there is one and only one user, as in the case of smart cell phones). A potential solution is suggested by Pons (2006) in the form of *biometric marketing*.

biometrics
An individual's unique physical or behavioral characteristics that can be used to identify an individual precisely (e.g., fingerprints).

A **biometric** is one of an individual's unique physical or behavioral characteristics that can be used to identify an individual precisely (e.g., fingerprints; see list in Chapter 11). By applying the technology to computer users, we can improve both security and learn about the user's profile precisely. The question is how to do it? Indeed, there are programs by which users identify themselves to the computer by biometrics, and these are spreading rapidly. To utilize the technology for marketing involves social and legal acceptability. For these reasons, advertisers are using methods that target individuals without knowing their profiles. An example is search engine-based methods such as *Adwords* used by Google (see Section 4.6).

Some researchers are wildly optimistic about the prospects for market research on the Internet; others are more cautious.

1. Describe the objectives of market research.
2. Define and describe market segmentation.
3. Describe how market research is done online and the major market research methods.
4. Describe the role of Web logs and clickstream data.
5. Describe how biometrics and cell phones can improve market research and advertising.
6. Relate cookies, Web bugs, and spyware to market research.
7. Describe the limitations of online market research.

4.6 INTERNET MARKETING IN B2B

B2B marketing is completely different from B2C marketing, which was introduced in Chapter 3 and in Sections 4.1 through 4.4. Major differences also exist between B2B and B2C with respect to the nature of demand and supply and the trading process. Here we discuss the corporate purchaser's buying behavior and the marketing and advertising methods used in B2B. More discussion is provided in Chapters 5 through 7.

ORGANIZATIONAL BUYER BEHAVIOR

Organizations buy large quantities of *direct materials* that they consume or use in the production of goods and services and in the company's operations. They also buy *indirect materials*, such as PCs, delivery trucks, and office supplies, to support their production and operations processes.

Although the number of organizational buyers is much smaller than the number of individual consumers, their transaction volumes are far larger, and the terms of negotiations and purchasing are more complex. In addition, the purchasing process itself, as will be seen in Chapter 5, usually is more complex than the purchasing process of an individual customer. Also, the organization's buyer may be a group. In fact, decisions to purchase expensive items are usually decided by a group. Therefore, factors that affect individual consumer behavior and organizational buying behavior are quite different (e.g., see Bridges et al. 2006).

A Behavioral Model of Organizational Buyers

The behavior of an organizational buyer can be described by a model similar to that of an individual buyer, which was shown in Exhibit 4.1. A behavioral model for organizational buyers is shown in Exhibit 4.9. Compare the two models. Note that some independent variables differ; for example, in the organizational model, the family and Internet communities may have no influence. Also, an *organizational influences module* is added to the B2B model. This module includes the organization's purchasing guidelines and constraints (e.g., contracts with certain suppliers) and the purchasing system used. Also, interpersonal influences, such as authority, are added. Finally, the possibility of group decision making must be considered. For a detailed discussion of organizational buyers, see Armstrong and Kotler (2007). For information on Internet procurement by purchasing agents, see Martin and Hafer (2002).

THE MARKETING AND ADVERTISING PROCESSES IN B2B

The marketing and advertising processes for businesses differ considerably from those used for selling to individual consumers. For example, traditional (offline) B2B marketers use methods such as trade shows, advertisements in industry magazines, paper catalogs, and salespeople who call on existing customers and potential buyers.

In the digital world, these approaches may not be effective, feasible, or economical. Therefore, organizations use a variety of online methods to reach business customers. Popular methods include online directory services, matching services, the marketing and advertising services of exchanges (Chapter 6), cobranding or alliances, affiliate programs, online marketing services (e.g., see digitalcement.com), or e-communities (see Chapter 17 and b2bcommunities.com). Several of these methods are discussed next.

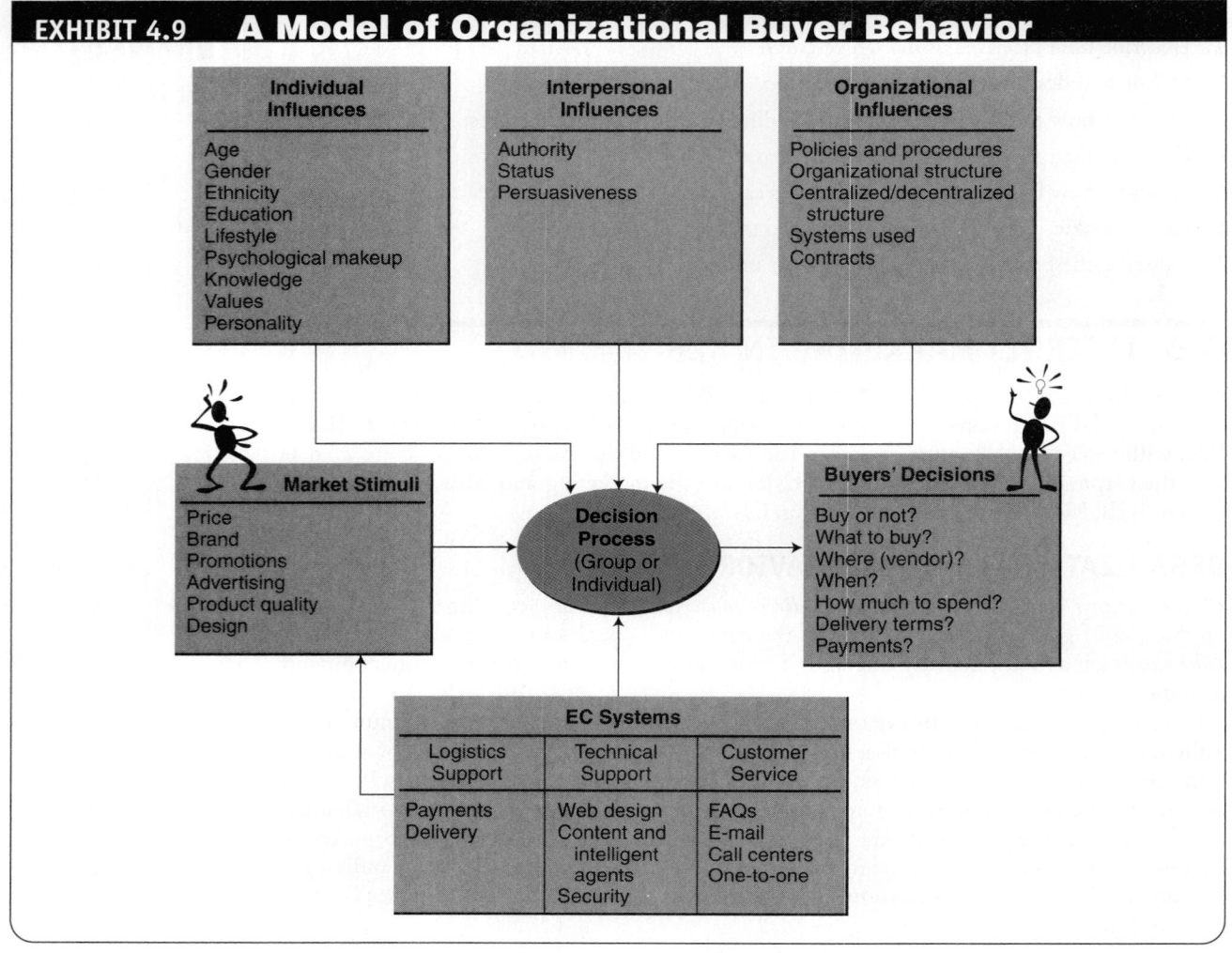

EXHIBIT 4.9   A Model of Organizational Buyer Behavior

METHODS FOR B2B ONLINE MARKETING

When a B2C niche e-tailer seeks to attract its audience of skiers, musicians, or cosmetic customers, it may advertise in traditional media targeted to those audiences, such as magazines or television shows. The same is true in B2B when trade magazines and directories are used. But when a B2B vendor wants to grow by adding new customers or products, it may not have a reliable, known advertising channel. How can it reach new customers?

Targeting Customers

A B2B company, whether a provider of goods or services, an operator of a trading exchange, or a provider of digital real-time services, can contact all of its targeted customers individually when they are part of a well-defined group. For example, to attract companies to an exchange for auto supplies, one might use information from industry trade association records or industry magazines to identify potential customers.

Another method of bringing new customers to a B2B site is through an affiliation service, which operates just as a B2C affiliate program does. A company pays a small commission every time the affiliate company "drives traffic" to its site. For more on online B2B marketing, see Harrison-Walker and Neeley (2004) and b2bmarketingtrends.com.

An important part of any marketing effort is advertising. Several of the advertising methods that will be presented later in this chapter are applicable both to B2C and B2B. For example, an *ad server network provider*, such as DoubleClick (doubleclick.com), can be used to target customers in B2B2C EC.

Electronic Wholesalers

One of the interesting B2B ventures is the e-wholesaler. Like click-and-mortar e-tailer Sam's Club, this kind of intermediary sells directly to businesses but does so exclusively online. An example is Bigboxx.com, described in Online File W5.1.

Other B2B Marketing Services

Several other B2B marketing services exist. Here are several examples:

▶ **Digital Cement.** This firm provides corporate marketing portals. In essence, it provides content tailored to the client's customer base. Digital Cement (digitalcement.com) advocates a private-label content approach versus partnering with a branded dot-com that will give a company content for free but may also take away its customers.

▶ **National Systems.** This company (nationalsystems.com) will track what is going on in a particular industry. It then generates competitive intelligence on pricing, product mix, promotions, and ad content and provides the client company with tailored marketing and advertising services.

▶ **BusinessTown.** This firm (businesstown.com) provides information and services to small businesses, including startups. It includes a directory of businesses in over 20 industries, information on functional areas (accounting, finance, legal, marketing), and business-planning advice. Although much of its offerings deal with intrabusiness and B2C EC, it offers several directories and information sources relevant to B2B.

AFFILIATE PROGRAMS, INFOMEDIARIES, AND DATA MINING

Many more methods and approaches can be used in B2B marketing and advertising (e.g., see Oliva 2004). Here we examine three popular methods: affiliate programs, infomediaries, and online data mining services.

Affiliate Programs

B2C affiliation services were introduced in Chapter 1. There are several types of affiliate programs. With the simplest type, which is used extensively in B2C EC, an affiliate puts a banner of another vendor, such as Amazon.com, on its site. When a consumer clicks the vendor's banner, the consumer is taken to that vendor's Web site, and a commission is paid to the affiliate if the customer makes a purchase. Examples include the Netflix case and Internet Exercise 16. The same method works for B2B.

With B2B, additional types of affiliate programs are possible. Schaeffer Research (schaeffersresearch.com), for example, offers financial institutions a *content* alliance program in which content is exchanged so that all obtain some free content. For more on B2B affiliate programs, see en.wikipedia.org/wiki/Affiliate_marketing.

Infomediaries and Online Data Mining Services

Marketing managers must understand current shopping behaviors in order to effectively advertise to customers in the future. Traditional B2C retailers evaluate point-of-sale (POS) data (e.g., grocery scanner data) and other available data to generate valuable marketing information. In today's online environment, more relevant information is available than ever before. However, the potential of the information can only be realized if the clickstream data can be analyzed and mined to produce constructive knowledge that can be used to improve services and marketing efforts. A new intermediary is emerging to provide such services to Web site owners who do not have the specialized knowledge and systems to perform such data mining on their own. As described in Chapter 2, these B2C and B2B intermediaries are called *infomediaries*.

Infomediaries start by processing existing information until new, useful information is extracted from it. This new information is sold to B2B customers or exchanged for more information, which is manipulated yet again, until even more valuable information can be extracted. B2B vendors use the information from infomediaries to identify likely buyers with much greater precision than ever before—leading to increased sales and drastically reduced marketing expenses. Representative infomediaries and data mining specialists are SAS

Institute (sas.com), Unica NetTracker (unica.com), WebTrends (webtrends.com), NetIntellect (available from bizdesign.com), and SurfReport from netrics.com. For a discussion of data mining and an example of its use in B2B, see Online File W4.3. For how data mining unveils promotion opportunities, see Amato-McCoy (2006).

One of the major objectives of market research is to provide tactics and strategies for EC advertisement, the topic of Section 4.7.

Section 4.6 ▶ REVIEW QUESTIONS

1. Distinguish between organizational buyers and individual consumers.
2. Describe B2B marketing and advertising methods.
3. Explain how affiliate programs and data mining work in B2B.

4.7 WEB ADVERTISING

Advertising on the Web by all types of organizations plays an extremely important role in e-commerce. Blacharski (2005) reports that Internet advertisers are growing very rapidly and companies are changing their advertisement strategies, which gives them a competitive edge. According to Delaney (2006), Internet advertising is growing by about 20 percent annually and was $12 billion in 2005.

OVERVIEW OF WEB ADVERTISING

Advertising is an attempt to disseminate information in order to affect buyer–seller transactions. In *traditional* marketing, advertising was impersonal, one-way mass communication that was paid for by sponsors. Telemarketing and direct mail ads were attempts to personalize advertising to make it more effective. These *direct marketing* approaches worked fairly well but were expensive and slow and seldom truly one-to-one interactive. For example, say a direct mail campaign costs about $1 per person and has a response rate of only 1 to 3 percent. This makes the cost per responding person in the range of $33 to $100. Such an expense can be justified only for high-ticket items (e.g., cars).

One of the problems with direct mail advertising was that the advertisers knew very little about the recipients. Market segmentation by various characteristics (e.g., age, income, gender) helped a bit but did not solve the problem. The Internet introduced the concept of **interactive marketing,** which has enabled marketers and advertisers to interact directly with customers. In interactive marketing, a consumer can click an ad to obtain more information or send an e-mail to ask a question. Besides the two-way communication and e-mail capabilities provided by the Internet, vendors also can target specific groups and individuals on which they want to spend their advertising dollars. The Internet enables truly one-to-one advertising. A comparison of mass advertising, direct mail advertising, and interactive online advertising is shown in Online File W4.5.

In 2006, organizations looking to grow and gain more business are turning to the experts who market to the Net Generation to create campaigns that drive leads to their company. Many Internet users contribute to these campaigns everyday without realizing it. For example, a simple Google search for a mortgage rate quote and a visit to a site where a request for the quote is made generates a lead. The company receives a quantitative result from an advertising campaign (*Mirror99.com* 2006).

Companies use Internet advertising as *one* of their advertising channels. At the same time, they also may use TV, newspapers, or other traditional channels. In this respect, the Web competes on a budget with the other channels. The two major business models for advertising online are (1) using the Web as a channel to advertise a firm's own products and services and (2) making a firm's site a public portal site and using captive audiences to advertise products offered by other firms. For example, the audience might come to a P&G Web site to learn about Tide, but they might also get additional ads for products made by companies other than P&G.

This chapter deals with Internet advertising in general. For additional resources on Internet advertising, see adage.com and webmonkey.com.

interactive marketing
Online marketing, facilitated by the Internet, by which marketers and advertisers can interact directly with customers and consumers can interact with advertisers/vendors.

EXHIBIT 4.10 The Advertising Cycle

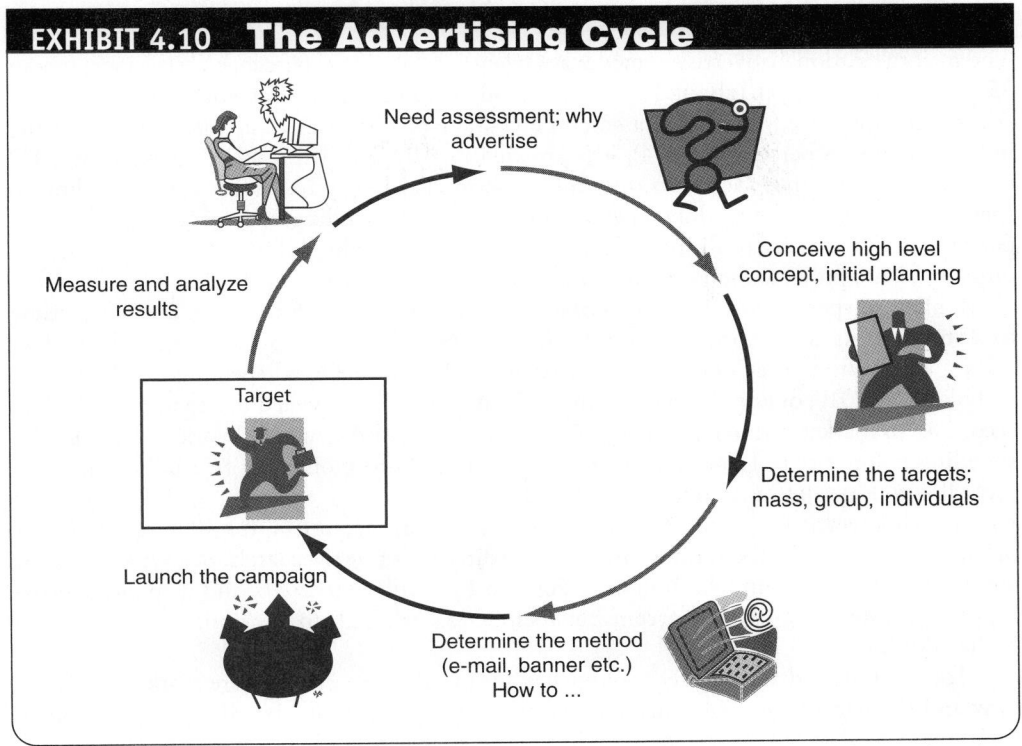

Need assessment; why advertise

Conceive high level concept, initial planning

Determine the targets; mass, group, individuals

Determine the method (e-mail, banner etc.) How to ...

Launch the campaign

Target

Measure and analyze results

ad views
The number of times users call up a page that has a banner on it during a specific period; known as *impressions* or *page views*.

button
A *button* is a small banner that is linked to a Web site. It may contain downloadable software.

page
A *page* is an HTML (Hypertext Markup Language) document that may contain text, images, and other online elements, such as Java applets and multimedia files. It may be generated statically or dynamically.

click (click-through or ad click)
A count made each time a visitor clicks on an advertising banner to access the advertiser's Web site.

CPM (cost per thousand impressions)
The fee an advertiser pays for each 1,000 times a page with a banner ad is shown.

conversion rate
The percentage of clickers who actually make a purchase.

click-through rate
The percentage of visitors who are exposed to a banner ad and click on it.

click-through ratio
The ratio between the number of clicks on a banner ad and the number of times it is seen by viewers; measures the success of a banner in attracting visitors to click on the ad.

hit
A request for data from a Web page or file.

The Advertising Cycle

With *closed-loop campaign management*, companies are treating advertisement as a cyclical process, as shown in Exhibit 4.10. The cyclical process entails carefully planning a campaign to determine who the target is and how to reach that consumer. Analyzing the campaign after its completion assists a company in understanding the campaign's success and why it succeeded. This new knowledge is then used when planning future campaigns.

Before we describe the various steps of the cycle as it is implemented in Web advertising, let's learn some basic advertising technology.

SOME INTERNET ADVERTISING TERMINOLOGY

The following list of terms and marginal glossary will be of use as you read about Web advertising.

▶ Ad views
▶ Button
▶ Page
▶ Click (click-through or ad click)
▶ CPM
▶ Conversion rate
▶ Click-through rate (or ratio)
▶ Hit
▶ Visit
▶ Unique visit
▶ Stickiness

visit
A series of requests during one navigation of a Web site; a pause of a certain length of time ends a visit.

unique visits
A count of the number of visitors entering a site, regardless of how many pages are viewed per visit.

stickiness
Characteristic that influences the average length of time a visitor stays in a site.

WHY INTERNET ADVERTISING?

The major traditional advertising media are television (about 36 percent), newspapers (about 35 percent), magazines (about 14 percent), and radio (about 10 percent) (Boswell 2002). Although Internet advertising is a small percentage of the $120-billion-a-year advertising industry (about 8 percent in 2004), it is growing rapidly and will reach 17 percent by 2007 (Lewin 2004). By most accounts, the online-ad market barely has been tapped. Online ad spending, which represents only 5 percent of total media spending, is projected to grow 24.4 percent in 2007, whereas all media, including television, radio, billboards, newspapers and direct mail, are projected to grow only 4.2 percent (Mills 2006).

Online ad spending in the United States rose to a record $12.5 billion in 2005, according to a study released in April 2006 by the Interactive Advertising Bureau and independent auditor PricewaterhouseCoopers. In the first six months of 2006, ad spending reached about $8 billion. By 2010, online ad spending in the United States is expected to rise to $23.5 billion, according to market research and consulting firm Parks and Associates. Worldwide, online ad spending is forecast to grow from $19.5 billion in 2005 to more than $55 billion in 2010, according to Piper Jaffray (reported by Mills 2006).

Search advertising is by far the most lucrative area, accounting for 40 percent of total online ad spending in the United States, according to JupiterResearch. Search advertising is expected to grow from $4.2 billion in 2005 to $7.5 billion in 2010, and display advertising is forecasted to grow 10 percent between 2005 and 2010 to $7.5 billion (reported by Mills 2006).

Today, online-advertising technology has advanced to the point where marketers can see how and if their ads result in increased sales, even for target ads based on demographics, location, and other factors. Such analysis of offline advertising is not nearly as fast, easy, or inexpensive.

Companies advertise on the Internet for several reasons. To begin with, television viewers are migrating to the Internet. The UCLA Center for Communication Policy (2004) found that Internet users are spending time online that they previously spent viewing television. Worldwide, Internet users are spending significantly less time watching television and more time using the Internet at home. This trend will continue, especially as Internet-enabled cell phones become commonplace. In addition, many Internet users are well educated and have high incomes. These Internet surfers are a desired target for advertisers.

According to Hallerman (2006), the major advantages of using the Internet over mass advertising are the precise targeting, interactivity, rich media (grabs attention), cost reduction, and customer acquisition.

Advertisers are limited (by cost and space) in the amount of information they can gather about the television and print ads they place. Advertisers are not able to track the number of people who actually view an ad in a print publication or on TV. Print ads cannot be rotated when a person opens the same page multiple times. Print and television ads cannot be filtered only to female readers who earn over $50,000, own a home, and work in a university. Of the people who do look at the ad, the advertiser cannot even record the length of time they spent looking at it. The only piece of hard data available for traditional advertising is the total number of print copies sold or the estimated viewing audience of the TV program. Everything else is guesswork.

Much more information and feedback is possible with Internet advertising. Special tracking and ad management programs enable online advertisers to do all of the things mentioned here and more (see Sections 4.8 and 4.9).

Meeker (1997) examined the length of time it took for each ad medium to reach the first 50 million U.S. users. Meeker found that it took radio 38 years, television 13 years, and cable television 10 years to reach 50 million viewers. Remarkably, it took only about 5 years for the Internet to reach 50 million users! According to these statistics, the Internet is the fastest-growing communication medium by far. Worldwide, the number of Internet users surpassed 1 billion in 2005; the 2 billion Internet users milestone is expected in 2011 (*Computer Industry Almanac* 2006). Of course, advertisers are interested in a medium with such potential reach, both locally and globally.

Other reasons why Web advertising is growing rapidly include:

- **Cost.** Online ads are sometimes cheaper than those in other media. In addition, ads can be updated at any time with minimal cost.
- **Richness of format.** Web ads can effectively use the convergence of text, audio, graphics, and animation. In addition, games, entertainment, and promotions can be easily combined in online advertisements. Also, services such as MySimon.com enable customers to compare prices and, using PDA or cell phone, do it at any time from anywhere.
- **Personalization.** Web ads can be interactive and targeted to specific interest groups and/or individuals; the Web is a much more focused medium.
- **Timeliness.** Internet ads can be fresh and up-to-the-minute.
- **Location-basis.** Using wireless technology and GPS, Web advertising can be location based; Internet ads can be sent to consumers whenever they are in a specific time and location (e.g., near a restaurant or a theater).
- **Linking.** It is easy to link from an online ad to a storefront—one click does it.
- **Digital branding.** Even the most price-conscious online shoppers are willing to pay premiums for brands they trust. These brands may be click-and-mortar brands (e.g., P&G), or dot-coms such as Amazon.com. British Airways places many Internet banner ads. However, these ads are not for clicking on to buy; they are all about branding, that is, establishing British Airways as a brand.

As of 1998, these factors began to convince large consumer-products companies, such as P&G, to shift an increasing share of their advertising dollars away from traditional media to Web advertising.

Of course, each advertising medium, including the Internet, has its advantages and limitations. Online File W4.6 compares the advantages and limitations of Internet advertising against traditional advertising media. For a comprehensive comparison of the effectiveness of Internet ads versus traditional methods, see Yoon and Kim (2001). Moreover, Chang and Thorson (2004) found that television–Web synergy can help attract more attention than either medium on its own. *New Media Age* (2003) found that a TV campaign increases brand awareness by 27 percent, whereas a combined TV and online campaign increases it by 45 percent. A TV campaign increases intent to purchase by 2 percent, whereas a combined TV and online campaign increases it by 12 percent.

ADVERTISING NETWORKS

One of the major advantages of Internet advertising is the ability to customize ads to fit individual viewers. Specialized firms have sprung up to offer this service to companies that wish to locate customers through targeted advertising. Called **advertising networks** (or *ad server networks*), these firms offer special services such as brokering banner ads for sale, bringing together online advertisers and providers of online ad space, and helping target ads to consumers who are presumed to be interested in categories of advertisements based on technology-based consumer profiling. DoubleClick is a premier company in this area. DoubleClick created an advertising network for 1,500 companies. It prepares thousands of ads for its clients every week, following the process shown in Online File W4.7.

advertising networks Specialized firms that offer customized Web advertising, such as brokering ads and targeting ads to select groups of consumers.

One-to-one targeted advertising and marketing may be expensive, but it can be very rewarding. According to Taylor (1997), for example, successful targeted online ads proved very effective for selling Lexus cars, at a cost of $169 per car sold. Targeting ads to groups based on market segmentation rather than to individuals also can be very cost-effective, depending on the advertising method used.

Section 4.7 ▶ REVIEW QUESTIONS

1. Define Web advertising and the major terms associated with it.
2. Describe the reasons for the growth in Web advertising.
3. List the major characteristics of Web advertising.
4. Explain the role of ad networks in Web advertising.

4.8   ONLINE ADVERTISING METHODS

A large number of online advertising methods exist. The major ones are covered in this section.

BANNERS

A **banner** is a graphic display that is used for advertising on a Web page. The size of the banner is usually 5 to 6.25 inches in length, 0.5 to 1 inch in width, and is measured in pixels. A banner ad is linked to an advertiser's Web page. When users "click" the banner, they are transferred to the advertiser's site. Advertisers go to great lengths to design a banner that catches consumers' attention. Banners often include video clips and sound. Banner advertising including pop-up banners is the most commonly used form of advertising on the Internet.

There are several types of banners. **Keyword banners** appear when a predetermined word is queried from a search engine. They are effective for companies that want to narrow their target audience. **Random banners** appear randomly, not as a result of some action by the viewer. Companies that want to introduce new products (e.g., a new movie or CD) or promote their brand use random banners. *Static banners* are always on the Web page. Finally, *pop-up banners* appear when least expected, as will be described later.

If an advertiser knows something about a visitor, such as the visitor's user profile, it is possible to *match* a specific banner with that visitor. Obviously, such targeted, personalized banners are usually most effective.

In the near future, banner ads will greet people by name and offer travel deals to their favorite destinations. Such personalized banners are being developed, for example, by dotomi.com. It delivers ads to consumers who opt in to its system. Initial results show a 14 percent click-through rate versus 3 to 5 percent with nonpersonalized ads.

Benefits and Limitations of Banner Ads

The major benefit of banner ads is that by clicking on them users are transferred to an advertiser's site, frequently directly to the shopping page of that site. Another advantage of using banners is the ability to customize them for individual surfers or a market segment of surfers. Also, viewing of banners is fairly high, because in many cases customers are forced to see banner ads while waiting for a page to load or before they can get the free information or entertainment that they want to see (a strategy called *forced advertising*). Finally, banners may include attention-grabbing multimedia.

The major disadvantage of banners is their cost. If a company demands a successful marketing campaign, it will need to allocate a large percentage of its advertising budget to place banners on high-volume Web sites. Another drawback is that a limited amount of information can be placed on the banner. Hence, advertisers need to think of a creative but short message to attract viewers.

However, it seems that viewers have become somewhat immune to banners and simply do not notice them as they once did. The *click-through ratio*, which measures the success of a banner in attracting visitors to click it, has been declining over time. For example, if a page receives 1,000 views and the banner is clicked on 30 times, the click ratio is 3 percent. The University of Michigan found the average click ratio was 3 percent in the mid-1990s. According to *eMarketer* (2004), it was less than 0.8 percent in late 2004, but is slowly increasing again.

Because of these drawbacks, it is important to decide *where* on the screen to place banners. For example, a study of Web ads conducted by the University of Michigan found that ads placed in the lower-right-hand corner of the screen, next to the scrollbar, generate a 228 percent higher click-through rate than ads at the top of the page (Doyle et al. 1997). The study also found that ads placed one-third of the way down the page and centered increased click-through 77 percent over ads at the top of the page, where ads are frequently positioned. For this reason, the price of the banner may depend on where it is located on the screen. Though frequency can help generate brand awareness, overplayed advertisements can become irritating. At the end of the day, the creativity of the ad designer is the key to winning

---

banner
On a Web page, a graphic advertising display linked to the advertiser's Web page.

keyword banners
Banner ads that appear when a predetermined word is queried from a search engine.

random banners
Banner ads that appear at random, not as the result of the user's action.

or losing the consumer (*New Media Age* 2004). For more on the efficient use of banner ads, see Amiri and Menon (2003) and Online File W4.8.

Banner Swapping and Banner Exchanges

Banner swapping means that company A agrees to display a banner of company B in exchange for company B's displaying company A's banner. This is probably the least expensive form of banner advertising, but it is difficult to arrange. A company must locate a site that will generate a sufficient amount of relevant traffic. Then, the company must contact the owner/Webmaster of the site and inquire if the company would be interested in a reciprocal banner swap. Because individual swaps are difficult to arrange, many companies use banner exchanges.

Banner exchanges are markets where companies can trade or exchange placement of banner ads on each other's Web sites. A multicompany banner match may be easier to arrange than a two-company swap. For example, company A can display B's banner effectively, but B cannot display A's banner optimally. However, B can display C's banner, and C can display A's banner. Such bartering may involve many companies. Banner-exchange organizers arrange the trading, which works much like an offline bartering exchange. Firms that are willing to display others' banners join the exchange. Each time a participant displays a banner for one of the exchange's other members, it receives a credit. After a participant has "earned" enough credits, its own banner is displayed on a suitable member's site. Most exchanges offer members the opportunity to purchase additional display credits.

Examples of exchanges are linkswap.co.uk, click4click.com, unitedbanners.com, exchange-it.com, and microsoft.com/smallbusiness. For auctions related to banners, see thefreeauction.com/exchange.

Banner exchanges are not without their disadvantages. To begin with, some charge fees, charging members either money or ad space, or both. Second, some banner exchanges will not allow certain types of banners. In addition, tax issues may arise for companies that barter their banners.

banner swapping
An agreement between two companies to each display the other's banner ad on its Web site.

banner exchanges
Markets in which companies can trade or exchange placement of banner ads on each other's Web sites.

POP-UP AND SIMILAR ADS

One of the most annoying phenomena in Web surfing is the increased use of pop-up, pop-under, and similar ads. A **pop-up ad,** also known as *ad spawning*, is the automatic launching of new browser windows with an ad when a visitor enters or exits a site, on a delay (see interstitials), or on other triggers. A pop-up ad appears in front of the active window. A **pop-under ad** is an ad that appears underneath (in back of) the current browser window; when users close the active window, they see the ad. (A number of pop-under exchanges function much like banner exchanges.) Pop-ups cover the user's current screen and may be difficult to close. Pop-up and pop-under ads are controversial: Many users strongly object to this advertising method, which they consider intrusive (see Chapter 17). In 2004, the Pop-Up Task Force of the Interactive Advertising Bureau embarked on a study to understand the main challenges of online rich media advertising. (For more details, see iab.net/standards/popup/index.asp.)

Several related tactics, some of which are very aggressive, are used by advertisers, and their use is increasing. See Online File W4.9. Some of these tactics are accompanied by music, voice, and other rich multimedia.

pop-up ad
An ad that appears in a separate window before, after, or during Internet surfing or when reading e-mail.

pop-under ad
An ad that appears underneath the current browser window, so when the user closes the active window the ad is still on the screen.

Interstitials

An **interstitial,** a type of pop-up ad, is a page or box that appears after a user clicks a link. These ads remain while content is loading. (The word *interstitial* comes from *interstice*, which means "a small space between things.") An interstitial may be an initial Web page or a portion of one that is used to capture the user's attention for a short time, either as a promotion or a lead-in to the site's homepage or to advertise a product or a service. They pop onto the PC screen, much like a TV commercial.

interstitial
An initial Web page or a portion of it that is used to capture the user's attention for a short time while other content is loading.

How to Deal with Unsolicited Pop-Ups, Pop-Unders, and Interstitials

If viewers do not want to see these ads, they can remove them by simply closing them or by installing software to block them. Several software packages are available on the market to assist users in blocking these types of ads. Protection against pop-ups is offered by ISPs (e.g., AOL), by software security vendors (e.g., STOPzilla at stopzilla.com and Pop-up Stopper from panicware.com), and by portals (e.g., Yahoo!, Google). In summer 2004, Microsoft introduced a built-in blocker in Internet Explorer. Also, legal attempts have been made to control pop-ups because they are basically a form of spam (see Chapter 17).

E-MAIL ADVERTISING

A popular way to advertise on the Internet is to send company or product information to people or companies listed in mailing lists via e-mail. E-mail messages may be combined with brief audio or video clips promoting a product and provide on-screen links that users can click to make a purchase. The Direct Marketing Association reports that e-mail has the second highest return on investment (ROI) index for direct response marketing (reported by *Firstfold.com* 2006).

DoubleClick (2004) found that e-mail continues to enjoy popularity among consumers and that there is an increasing acknowledgment of e-mail as a legitimate and relied-upon marketing channel. However, an Atlantic Media Company (2006) trend analysis suggests that the growth of e-mail advertising is slowing, growing from 8 percent in 2005 to 11 percent in 2006, and forecasting that it will only be 13 percent in 2010. In contrast, rich media advertising will increase from 11 percent in 2005 to 13 percent in 2006 and 18 percent in 2010.

The advantages of e-mail advertising are its low cost and the ability to reach a wide variety of targeted audiences. Also, e-mail is an *interactive* medium, and it can combine advertising and customer service. It can include a direct link to any URL, so it acts like a banner. A 2004 study by Interactive Prospect Targeting (IPT) found that 32 percent of consumers picked e-mail as the most effective marketing communication channel. IPT also found that consumers are more likely to respond to e-mail messages related to discounts or special sales. Most companies have a database of customers to whom they can send e-mail messages. However, using e-mail to send ads (sometimes floods of ads) without the receivers' permission is considered *spamming*.

Undoubtedly, the quantity of e-mail that consumers receive is exploding. In light of this, marketers employing e-mail must take a long-term view and work toward motivating consumers to continue to read the messages they receive. As the volume of e-mail increases, consumers' tendency to screen and block messages will rise as well. Most e-mail services (e.g., see hotmail.com) permit users to block messages from specific sources.

A list of e-mail addresses can be a very powerful tool with which a company can target a group of people it knows something about. For information on how to create a mailing list, consult groups.yahoo.com (the service is free) or topica.com.

E-mail also can be sent to PDA devices and to mobile phones. Mobile phones offer advertisers a real chance to advertise interactively and on a one-to-one basis with consumers, anytime, any place. In the future, e-mail ads will be targeted to individuals based not only on their user profiles but also on their physical location at any point in time. See Chapter 9 for a description of this concept, known as *l-commerce*.

E-Mail Advertising Management

Although sending e-mail ads sounds simple, it is not. Preparing mailing lists, deciding on content, and measuring the results are some of the activities that are part of e-mail advertising management. One important area is getting reliable mailing lists. Companies such as Worldata.com can help supply lists for both B2C and B2B EC. Worldata.com also provides ad management services. (See the demo of the e-mail tracking system at worldata.com.)

Given the new e-marketing technologies, consumer frustration over spam, and new regulations, marketers should reevaluate how their e-mail advertisements are created, deployed, and measured. The Peppers and Rogers Group (2004) suggests four guidelines that marketers should consider to leverage customer insights throughout the e-mail marketing campaign lifecycle: (1) thinking about customer experience, (2) making privacy protection a part of their brand promise, (3) ensuring their recipients know about their privacy protection, and (4) measuring impact. By applying these guidelines, companies can enhance customer experiences and create long-term and loyal relationships. More guidelines are offered by Chase (2006) and Mordkovich and Mordkovich (2005).

E-mail Hoaxes. E-mail hoaxes are very popular; some of them have been going on for years (e.g., Neiman Marcus's cookie recipe, the Nigerian treasure, the Koran and the Iraq invasion). Some of these are scams. For details, see ftc.gov and Fleita (2003).

Fraud. Fraud also is a danger. For example, a person may get an e-mail stating that his or her credit card number is invalid or that his or her AOL service or newspaper delivery will be terminated unless another credit card number is sent as a reply to the e-mail. For protection against such hoaxes, see scambusters.org.

E-Mail Advertising Methods and Successes

E-mail advertising can be done in a number of different ways (see McDougall and Malykhina 2006 and Chase 2004), as shown in Online File W4.10.

NEWSPAPER-LIKE AND CLASSIFIED ADS

In 2001, the Internet Advertising Bureau, an industry trade group, adopted five standard ad sizes for the Internet. These standardized ads are larger and more noticeable than banner ads. They look like the ads in a newspaper or magazine, so advertisers like them. Tests found that users read these ads four times more frequently than banners (Tedeschi 2001). The ads appear on Web sites in columns or boxes. One of the most popular of the standardized ads is a full-column-deep ad called a *skyscraper ad.* Publishers, such as the *New York Times* (nytimes.com), publish these standardized ads, sometimes as many as four on one Web page. Some of these ads are interactive; users can click on a link inside the ad for more information about a product or service. These sizes also are used in pop-up ads, in fixed banners, or in classified ads. (To find out how much an Internet ad currently costs, see webhq/ webconnect.com.au.)

Classified Ads

Another newspaper-like ad is the *classified* ad. These ads can be found on special sites (e.g., craigslist.org, infospace.com), as well as on online newspapers, exchanges, portals, and so on. In many cases, posting regular-size classified ads is free, but placing them in a larger size or with some noticeable features is done for a fee. For examples, see traderonline.com and advertising.msn.com. For the capabilities and effectiveness of Craigslist.org see Case 2.4 (Chapter 2).

SEARCH ENGINE ADVERTISEMENT

Most search engines allow companies to submit their Internet addresses, called URLs (Universal Resource Locators), for free so that these URLs can be searched electronically. Search engine spiders crawl through each site, indexing its content and links. The site is then included in future searches. Because there are several thousand search engines, advertisers who use this method should register URLs with as many search engines as possible. In some cases, URLs may be searched even if they are not submitted. For details, see Chase (2006).

The major advantage of using URLs as an advertising tool is that it is *free*. Anyone can submit a URL to a search engine and be listed. By using URLs, it is likely that searchers for a company's products will receive a list of sites that mention the products, including the company's own site. Search engine advertisement has become the most popular online advertising method, mainly thanks to Google (see Chapter 18).

However, the URL method has several drawbacks. The major one has to do with location: The chance that a specific site will be placed at the top of a search engine's display list (say, in the first 10 sites) is very slim. Furthermore, even if a company's URL makes it to the top, others can quickly displace the URL from the top slot. Second, different search engines index their listings differently; therefore, it is difficult to make the top of several lists. The searcher may have the correct keywords, but if the search engine indexed the site listing using the "title" or "content description" in the meta tag, then the effort could be fruitless. A *meta tag* is a coding statement (in HTML) that describes the content of a Web page and is used by search engines to index content so it can be found.

Improving a Company's Search-Engine Ranking (Optimization)

By simply adding, removing, or changing a few sentences, a Web designer may alter the way a search engine's spider ranks its findings (see Kent 2006) and, therefore, improve a company's ranking on the search engine's list. Several companies have services that *optimize* Web content so that a site has a better chance of being discovered by a search engine (e.g., googleresources.com/google-keyword-resources/keywordcount.html or Web Position from WebTrends webtrends.com). More tips for improving a site's listing in various search engines can be found at searchenginewatch.com. For further details see Chapter 16.

Another way to improve the search-engine ranking is via link partnerships. For example, tucsonproperties.net, a real estate company, contacts other real estate companies and proposes placing links on each other's Web sites. The more links made, the higher the ranking may be. For more on search engine marketing, see Mordkovich and Mordkovich (2005).

Paid Search-Engine Inclusion

Several search engines charge fees for including URLs at or near the top of the search results. For example, Google and Overture charge firms for "sponsor matching." The more the company pays, the closer it will be to the top of the sponsor's list. Overture works with several search engines.

Others advertise to members of Internet communities (Chapter 17). Community sites, such as Geocities.com, offer targeted advertising opportunities, and vendors usually offer discounts to members on the advertised products. Ads also link users to other sites that might be of interest to community members. Advertisers also use online fantasy sports (e.g., available at Yahoo!) to send ads to the specific sport fans (e.g., National Football League [NFL] and Major League Baseball [MLB]). According to *eMarketer.com*, online fantasy sports attract millions of visitors every month (reported by Nucifera 2004).

ASSOCIATED AD DISPLAY

associated ad display (text links)
An advertising strategy that displays a banner ad related to a key term entered in a search engine.

Sometimes it is possible to associate the content of a Web page with a related ad. Suppose a person is interested in finding material on e-loyalty. If she uses Yahoo! to search for "e-loyalty," she will receive a list of sources and a banner ad with "sponsor results." Banner ads may appear when she clicks on the top sites that deal with e-loyalty. This strategy of displaying a banner ad related to a term entered in a search engine is called **associated ad display** or text links. For example, when using MapQuest (mapquest.com), which provides maps and driving directions, the user will receive the results and related sponsored links. This is an early search engine advertisement method that preceded Google's AdWord.

Companies usually implement the associated ad display strategy through their *affiliate programs*, as is done by Yahoo! A unique approach is that implemented by Google.

Google—The Online Advertising King

No other EC company can match the success of Google and its meteoric rise. Google is considered by many to be not only changing the Internet but also the world. Google is using several varieties of search engine advertising methods that are generating billions of dollars in revenue and profits (see Chapters 14 and 18). In Insights and Additions 4.2, we describe two of these methods.

ADVERTISING IN CHAT ROOMS, BLOGS, AND SOCIAL NETWORKS

A chat room can be used to build a community, promote a political or environmental cause, support people with medical problems, or enable hobbyists to share their interest. It can be used for advertising as well (e.g., see Gelb and Sundaram 2002).

Vendors frequently sponsor chat rooms. The sponsoring vendor places a chat link on its site, and the chat vendor does the rest (e.g., talkcity.com), including placing the advertising

Insights and Additions 4.2 Google's Advertisement Methods

Google uses several methods to perform online advertisements. The major methods are AdWords and AdSense.

AdWords

AdWords is a self-service *ad server* that uses *relevance-ranking algorithms* similar to the ones that make the search engine so effective. Advertisers tell Google how much they want to spend and then "buy" pertinent keywords. When Web surfers type in a term that matches the advertiser's keyword, the advertiser is listed in a banner near the search results with the heading "Sponsored Links." Each time a user clicks the advertiser's banner ad, Google subtracts the cost-per-click for the advertiser's prepaid account; when the account's daily ad budget is depleted, Google stops displaying the ad. For details, see Goodman (2006).

The system is easy to use and remarkably effective. The click-through rate is about 15 percent, which is more than 10 times the rate of the average banner ad. According to industry experts, many Google advertisers have experienced a 20 to 25 percent increase in online sales.

Each time a visitor clicks on an ad (which takes the visitor to the advertiser's site) the site owner shares the commission paid by the advertiser with Google. The advertisers also participate in the AdWords program.

Despite its success, AdWords by itself does not provide the best one-to-one targeting. This may be achieved in many cases through a complementary program—AdSense.

AdSense

Google's *AdSense* is an *affiliate program* in which Google offers Web site owners a chance to earn a commission for their willingness to place ads of other advertisers on their sites. AdSense automatically delivers an advertiser's text and image ads that are precisely matched to each affiliate site. This is a major improvement over matching individuals based on their preferences, which is less accurate in many cases and much more expensive. The matching (called *contextual matching*) is based on a proprietary algorithm (Google filed for over 60 patents on these and other innovations). The key is the quality and appearance of both the pages and the ads, as well as the popularity of the site. Google even provides affiliates with analytics that help convert visitors to customers.

Example

AdSense uses Google's relevance-scoring algorithms to find the best match of an ad to a surfer by analyzing the content of the Web pages of the affiliates' sites and advertisers' keywords. Upon clicking a banner ad, which includes a short sentence describing the advertiser's product (service), the user is transferred to the advertiser's site. All this is done automatically.

In the example shown, the company Namedog.com is the affiliate (site owner). It agrees to allow Google to place banners of its clients (e.g., Petsmart.com) on the company's site (see attached figure).

Source: *google.com/services/adsense_tour*

For an example of a site using AdSense, see *rtcmagazine.com*. Hundreds of thousands participate in the affiliate program.

Google's success is attributed to the quality of the matches, the large number of advertisers in its network, the ability to use ads in many languages, and the ability to understand the content of Web sites. Any characteristics and demographics of the visitors that Google knows are considered in the match. This is also true of Google's competitors (e.g., MSN, with its AdCenter methodology). Yahoo! and eBay offer similar programs (e.g., see eBay AdContex and Yahoo's Content Match). The closer the match, the less intrusive the ad is to the visitor, and the better the chance of the visitor's clicking on the ad.

Sources: Compiled from *adwords.google.com/select*, *google.com/adsense, en.wikipedia.org/wiki/AdSense* (all sites accessed October 2006), Chase (2006), and Goodman (2006).

that pays for the session. The advertising in a chat room merges with the activity in the room, and the user is conscious of what is being presented.

The main difference between an advertisement that appears on a static Web page and one that comes through a chat room is that the latter allows advertisers to cycle through messages and target the chatters again and again. Also, advertising can become more thematic in a chat room. An advertiser can start with one message and build upon it to a climax, just as an author does with a good story. For example, a toymaker may have a chat room dedicated to electronic toys. The advertiser can use the chat room to post a query such as, "Can anyone tell me about the new Electoy R3D3?" In addition, a company can go to competitors' chat rooms and observe the conversations there.

Chat rooms also are used as one-to-one connections between a company and its customers. For example, Mattel (mattel.com) sells about one-third of its Barbie dolls to collectors. These collectors use the chat room to make comments or ask questions that are then answered by Mattel's staff.

As described in Chapter 1, advertisers are using social networks to deliver messages to the network's members. Google and MySpace have an agreement on revenue sharing when MySpace members click on Google's ads. Google purchased YouTube for the same reason. Popular blogs contain ads that are based on the bloggers' being affiliates of advertisers. For further details see Chapter 18.

OTHER FORMS OF ADVERTISING

Online advertising can be done in several other ways, ranging from ads in newsgroups to ads in computer kiosks. Advertising on *Internet radio* is just beginning, and soon advertising on *Internet television* will commence. In November 2004, Amazon.com launched a series of short films for the holiday season that promoted items that customers could purchase. (BMW promotes its cars with short films as well.) According to Wang (2004), marketers are beginning to use online videos in B2B. *eMarketer* (2004) reports that video ads are increasing more than 50 percent each year, topping $120 million in revenue in 2004. Innovative ad methods online have no limit. For example, one innovative method is auctions where the winner is the lowest bidder (see Petrecca 2006 and Chapter 10). Another innovation is presented in Insights and Additions 4.3.

advertorial
An advertisement "disguised" to look like editorial content or general information.

Some marketers use **advertorials**. An advertorial looks like editorial content or general information, but it is really an advertisement. This form of advertisement is also used in newspapers.

In addition, a site's *domain name* may be used for brand recognition. This is why some companies pay millions of dollars to keep certain domain names under their control (see alldomains.com) or to buy popular names (e.g., tom.com was purchased for $8 million).

Insights and Additions 4.3 Innovation in Targeted Ads

Google, Value Click, 24/7 Real Media, Yahoo!, MSN, and more are competing in the targeted ad market. The winner, so far, is Google. However, according to Schonfeld and Borzo (2006), this situation may soon change. The reason is that the tools used for targeting segments of the population look at text advertisements. However, display ads are on the rise. A new company, BlueLithium (*bluelithium.com*) has developed a method by which it can build a profile of a user's clickstream. The more sites a user visits, the larger that user's surfing history becomes, and the more BlueLithium knows about the user. The profile includes what sites the user visits, what ads the user clicks on, and what ads other people with similar clickstreams have

clicked. This method concentrates on banner ads, not on key words. Having over 100 million clickstream histories (in October 2006), the company can direct any kind of ads to a user, including video clips.

As with similar tracking methods, this method observes a computer, not knowing if one or several users are involved. Privacy issues must also be dealt with. Regardless of these limitations, the company is doing extremely well, generating profit within 3 months of operations and expecting to gross over $100 million by the end of 2007.

Sources: Schonfeld and Borzo (2006) and *bluelithium.com* (accessed November 2006).

Known as domainers, some individuals buy thousands of names and then run ads on them with Google, charging advertisers (see Sloan 2005 for details). By the end of 2006, the use of video clips in online ads was increasing. For example, see qvc.com (featured products), edmunds.com (cars), and so on. For details, see Ossinger (2006).

Finally, as will be shown in Chapter 9, advertising on cell phones and other mobile devices is expected to increase rapidly.

Advertising in Newsletters

Free newsletters are abundant; in e-commerce there are many. An example is *Ecommerce Times*. This informative newsletter (ecommercetimes.com) solicits ads from companies (see "How to Advertise"). Ads are usually short, and they have a link to details. They are properly marked as "Advertisement."

Posting Press Releases Online

Millions of people visit popular portals such as Yahoo!, MSN, AOL, or Google every day looking for news. Thus, it makes sense to try to reach an audience through such sites. Indeed, Southwest Airlines was successful in selling $1.5 million in tickets by posting four press releases online. However, it is not as simple as it sounds. For a discussion of how to place online press releases, see the case study at *Marketingsherpa.com* (2004).

Advergaming

Advergaming is the practice of using games, particularly computer games, to advertise or promote a product, an organization, or a viewpoint. Advergaming normally falls into one of three categories:

▶ A company provides interactive games on its Web site in the hope that potential customers will be drawn to the game and spend more time on the Web site or simply become more product (or brand) aware. The games themselves usually feature the company's products prominently. Examples are intel.co.uk/itgame and clearahill.com.

▶ Games are published in the usual way, but they require players to investigate further. The subjects may be commercial, political, or educational. Examples include *America's Army* (americasarmy.com/downloads), intended to boost recruitment for the United States Army, and pepsiman.com.

▶ With some games, advertising appears within the actual game. This is similar to subtle advertising in films, whereby the advertising content is within the "world" of the movie or game. An example is cashsprint.com, which puts advertising logos directly on the player's racing vehicle and around the racetrack.

advergaming
The practice of using computer games to advertise a product, an organization, or a viewpoint.

With the growth of the Internet, advergames have proliferated, often becoming the most visited aspect of brand Web sites and becoming an integrated part of brand media planning in an increasingly fractured media environment. LifeSavers started a game site called Candystand that has blossomed to a portal for many different advergames; at its peak it was averaging more than four to five million unique visitors a month (Graham 2005).

Advergames promote repeat traffic to Web sites and reinforce brands in compelling ways. Users choose to register to be eligible for prizes that can help marketers collect customer data. Gamers may invite their friends to participate, which could assist promotion from word-of-mouth or viral marketing. For further discussion, see en.wikipedia.org/wiki/Advergaming, adverblog.com, and Gurau (2006).

Section 4.8 ▶ REVIEW QUESTIONS

1. Define banner ads and describe their benefits and limitations.
2. Describe banner swapping and banner exchanges.
3. Describe the issues surrounding pop-ups and similar ads.
4. Explain how e-mail is used for advertising.
5. Describe advertising via classified ads.

6. Discuss advertising via URLs and in chat rooms.

7. Discuss advertising in blogs and social networks.

8. Describe the search engine ad strategy.

9. Describe Google's AdWord and AdSense.

10. Define advergaming and describe how it works.

4.9 ADVERTISING STRATEGIES AND PROMOTIONS ONLINE

Several advertising strategies can be used over the Internet. In this section, we will present the major strategies used.

AFFILIATE MARKETING AND ADVERTISING

affiliate marketing
A marketing arrangement by which an organization refers consumers to the selling company's Web site.

In Chapters 1 through 3, we introduced the concept of **affiliate marketing,** the revenue model by which an organization refers consumers to the selling company's Web site. Affiliate marketing is used mainly as a revenue source for the referring organization and as a marketing tool for sellers. However, the fact that the selling company's logo is placed on many other Web sites is free advertising as well. Consider Amazon.com, whose logo can be seen on about 1 million affiliate sites! For a comprehensive directory of affiliate programs, see cashpile.com. In addition, Hoffman and Novak (2000) provide an example of how CDNow (a subsidiary of Amazon.com) and Amazon.com both are pioneers in the "get paid to view" or "listen to" commercials used in affiliate marketing.

ADS AS A COMMODITY

With the *ads-as-a-commodity* approach, people are paid for time spent viewing an ad. This approach is used at mypoints.com, clickrewards.com, and others. At Mypoints.com, interested consumers read ads in exchange for payment from the advertisers. Consumers fill out data on personal interests, and then they receive targeted banners based on their personal profiles. Each banner is labeled with the amount of payment that will be paid if the consumer reads the ad. If interested, the consumer clicks the banner to read it, and after passing some tests as to its content, is paid for the effort. Readers can sort and choose what they read, and the advertisers can vary the payments to reflect the frequency and desirability of the readers. Payments may be cash (e.g., $0.50 per banner) or product discounts. This method is used with smart phones, too (Chapter 9). For further details, see en.wikipedia.org/wiki/Online_advertising#Payment_conventions.

VIRAL MARKETING

viral marketing
Word-of-mouth marketing by which customers promote a product or service by telling others about it.

Viral marketing or advertising refers to *word-of-mouth* marketing in which customers promote a product or service by telling others about it. This can be done by e-mails, in conversations facilitated in chat rooms, by posting messages in newsgroups, and in electronic consumer forums. Having people forward messages to friends, asking them, for example, to "check out this product," is an example of viral marketing. This marketing approach has been used for generations, but now its speed and reach are multiplied by the Internet. This ad model can be used to build brand awareness at a minimal cost (*MoreBusiness.com* 2007), because the people who pass on the messages are paid very little or nothing for their efforts.

Viral marketing has long been a favorite strategy of online advertisers pushing youth-oriented products. For example, advertisers might distribute, embedded within a sponsor's e-mail, a small game program that is easy to forward. By releasing a few thousand copies of the game to some consumers, vendors hope to reach hundreds of thousands of others. Viral marketing also was used by the founder of Hotmail, a free e-mail service that grew from zero to 12 million subscribers in its 18 initial months and to over 50 million in about 4 years. Each e-mail sent via Hotmail carries an invitation for free Hotmail service. Also known as *advocacy marketing,* this innovative approach, if properly used, can be effective, efficient, and relatively inexpensive. For further details, see en.wikipedia.org/wiki/Viral_marketing#Types_of_viral_campaigns. Goldsmith (2006) investigated the word-of-mouth process and its relationship to social communication.

One of the downsides of this strategy is that several e-mail hoaxes have been spread this way (see Fleitas 2003). Another danger of viral advertising is that a destructive virus can be added to an innocent advertisement-related game or message. For viral marketing in social networks see Chapter 18.

CUSTOMIZING ADS

The Internet has too much information for customers to view. Filtering irrelevant information by providing consumers with customized ads can reduce this information overload. BroadVision (broadvision.com) provides a customized ad service platform called BroadVision eMarketing. The heart of eMarketing is a customer database, which includes registration data and information gleaned from site visits. The companies that advertise via One-to-One use the database to send customized ads to consumers. Using this feature, a marketing manager can customize display ads based on users' profiles. The product also provides market segmentation.

Another model of personalization can be found in **Webcasting,** a free Internet news service that broadcasts personalized news and information as well as e-seminars (Chapter 8). Users sign into the Webcasting system and select the information they would like to receive, such as sports, news, headlines, stock quotes, or desired product promotions. The users receive the requested information along with personalized ads based on their expressed interests and general ads based on their profile.

Webcasting
A free Internet news service that broadcasts personalized news and information, including seminars, in categories selected by the user.

ONLINE EVENTS, PROMOTIONS, AND ATTRACTIONS

In the winter of 1994, the term *EC* was hardly known, and people were just starting to discover the Internet. One company, DealerNet, which was selling new and used cars from physical lots, demonstrated a new way of doing business: It started a virtual car showroom on the Internet. It let people "visit" dozens of dealerships and compare prices and features. At the time, this was a revolutionary way of selling cars. To get people's attention, DealerNet gave away a car over the Internet.

This promotion, unique at the time, received a lot of offline media attention and was a total success. Today, such promotions are regular events on thousands of Web sites. Contests, quizzes, coupons (see coolsavings.com), and giveaways designed to attract visitors are as much a part of online marketing as they are of offline commerce (see Clow and Baack 2004; Sonal and Preeta 2005). Some innovative ideas used to encourage people to pay attention to online advertising are provided in Online File W4.11.

Live Web Events

Live Web events (concerts, shows, interviews, debates, videos), if properly done, can generate tremendous public excitement and bring huge crowds to a Web site. According to Akamai Technologies, Inc. (2000a), the best practices for successful live Web events are:

- Carefully planning content, audience, interactivity level, preproduction, and schedule
- Executing the production with rich media if possible
- Conducting appropriate promotion via e-mails, affinity sites, and streaming media directories, as well as conducting proper offline and online advertisement
- Preparing for quality delivery
- Capturing data and analyzing audience response so that improvements can be made

Admediation

Conducting promotions, especially large-scale ones, may require the help of vendors who specialize in promotions, such as those listed in Online File W4.11. Gopal et al. (2005) researched this area and developed a model that shows the role of such third-party vendors (such as Mypoints.com), which they call **admediaries**. Their initial model is shown in Exhibit 4.11. The exhibit concentrates on e-mail and shows the role of the admediaries (in the box between the customers and sellers).

admediaries
Third-party vendors that conduct promotions, especially large-scale ones.

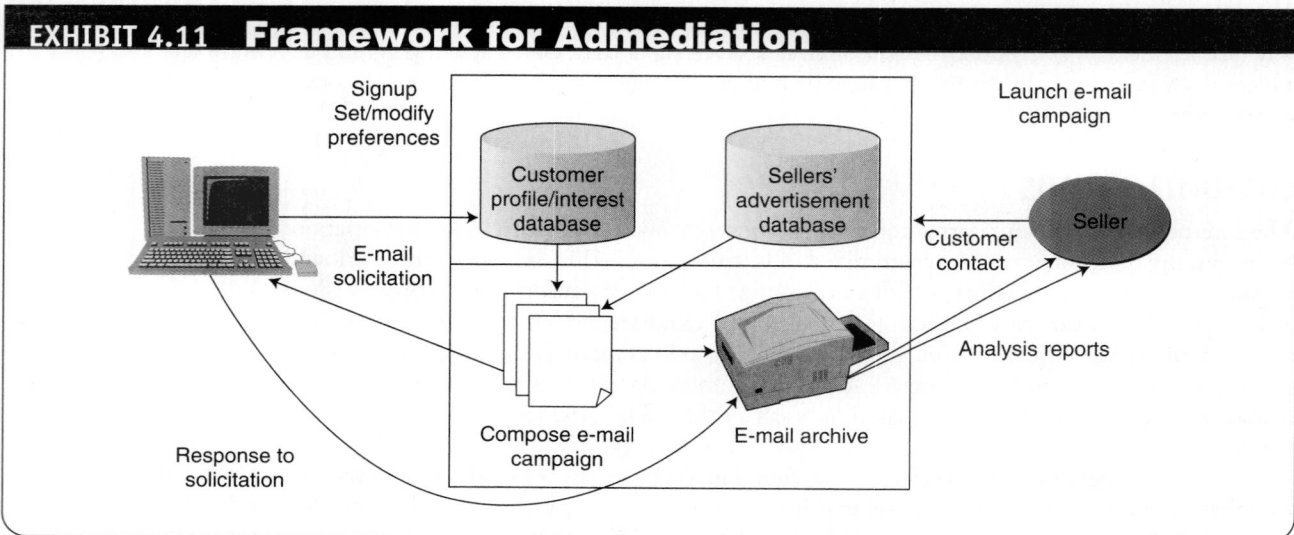

EXHIBIT 4.11 Framework for Admediation

Source: Gopal, R. D., et al. "Admediation: New Horizons in Effective Email Advertising." *The Communications of the ACM.* ©2001 ACM Inc. Used with permission.

Running promotions on the Internet is similar to running offline promotions. According to Clow and Baack (2004), some of the major considerations when implementing an online ad campaign include the following:

- The target audience needs to be clearly understood and should be online surfers.
- The traffic to the site should be estimated, and a powerful enough server must be prepared to handle the expected traffic volume.
- Assuming that the promotion is successful, what will the result be? This assessment is needed to evaluate the budget and promotion strategy.
- Consider cobranding; many promotions succeed because they bring together two or more powerful partners.

For more information about promotions and ad strategies, see Clow and Baack (2004).

 Companies combine several advertising methods as a result of market research. And if they have several Web sites, they may use different methods on each site. For example, P&G is experimenting with several methods to increase brand recognition (see Online File W4.12).

Selling Space by Pixels

Million Dollar Homepage (milliondollarhomepage.com), was created by 21-year-old student Alex Tew in the U.K. The Web site sold advertising space on a one-page grid, much as real estate is sold, displaying a total of one million pixels at $1 per pixel. The site was launched in August 2005 and sold out by January 13, 2006. Within a short time, people started to sell pixels in other countries (i.e., milliondollarhomepage.com.au, one of several Australian sites). Also, people who bought pixels at $1 each were selling them at higher prices through auctions. This is an innovative way of owning space because once you buy it, it's there forever.

MillionDollarHomepage.com has been subjected to a distributed denial-of-service (DDoS) attack by malicious hackers who have caused the site to be extremely slow loading or completely unavailable for a few days. Blackmailers at first asked for $5,000 to avert an attack on the site. The DDoS attack was launched after Tew declined to pay, and the hackers then demanded $50,000 to stop it. A further refusal to pay prompted the attackers to deface the site, replacing the regular page with a message stating: "don't come back you sly dog!" For details see Sanders (2006).

Section 4.9 ▶ REVIEW QUESTIONS

1. Discuss the process and value of affiliate marketing.
2. How does the ads-as-a-commodity strategy work?

3. Describe viral marketing.
4. How are ads customized?
5. List some typical Internet promotions.
6. Define admediaries and describe their roles.

4.10 SPECIAL ADVERTISING TOPICS

The following are major representative topics related to Internet advertisement.

PERMISSION ADVERTISING

One of the major issues of one-to-one advertising is the flooding of users with unwanted (junk) e-mail, banners, pop-ups, and so on. One of the authors of this book experienced a flood of X-rated ads. Each time such an ad arrived, he blocked receipt of further ads from this source. That helped for a day or two, but then the same ads arrived from another e-mail address. His e-mail service provider, Hotmail (hotmail.com), was very helpful in providing several options to minimize this problem. Most e-mail providers can place software agents to identify and block such junk mail. This problem, the flooding of users with unsolicited e-mails, is called **spamming** (see Chapter 17). Spamming typically upsets consumers and may keep useful advertising from reaching them.

> **spamming**
> Using e-mail to send unwanted ads (sometimes floods of ads).

One solution used by advertisers is **permission advertising (permission marketing,** or the *opt-in approach*), in which users register with vendors and *agree* to accept advertising (see returnpath.net). For example, the authors of this book agreed to receive a large number of e-commerce newsletters (known as "opt-in"), knowing that some would include ads. This way we can keep abreast of what is happening in the field. We also agree to accept e-mail from research companies, newspapers, travel agencies, and more. These vendors push, for free, very valuable information to us. The accompanying ads pay for such services. One way to conduct permission advertisement is to provide incentives, as discussed in Section 4.8. Note that Netflix asks permission to send users recommendations, but it does not ask whether it can use historical purchasing data to create them (see Team Assignment 5).

> **permission advertising (permission marketing)**
> Advertising (marketing) strategy in which customers agree to accept advertising and marketing materials (known as "opt-in").

ADVERTISEMENT AS A REVENUE MODEL

Many of the dot-com failures in 2000 to 2002 were caused by a revenue model that contained advertising income as the major or only revenue source. Many small portals failed, but several large ones are dominating the field: Google, AOL, Yahoo!, and MSN. However, even these heavy-traffic sites only started to show a significant profit in 2004. Too many Web sites are competing for advertising money. Almost all portals are adding other sources of revenue.

However, if careful, a small site can survive by concentrating on a niche area. For example, playfootball.com is doing well. It pulls millions of dollars in advertising and sponsorship by concentrating on NFL fans. The site provides comprehensive and interactive content, attracting millions of visitors. For more on ad payments, see Wikipedia (2006c).

MEASURING ONLINE ADVERTISING'S EFFECTIVENESS

One managerial issue is how to measure the effectiveness of online advertisement. A related topic is how to charge for ads. These two topics are presented as a complete section in Online File W4.13. For a special report on the topic, see Blanford (2004).

AD MANAGEMENT

The activities involved in Web advertising, which range from tracking viewers to rotating ads, require a special methodology and software known as **ad management** software. Ad management software lets an advertiser send very specific ads on a schedule and target ads to certain population segments, which can be very small. For example, an advertiser can send an ad to all male residents of Los Angeles County between the ages of 26 and 39 whose income level is above $30,000. The advertiser can even refine the segment further by using ethnic origin, type of employment, or whether recipients own their home.

> **ad management**
> Methodology and software that enable organizations to perform a variety of activities involved in Web advertising (e.g., tracking viewers, rotating ads).

When selecting ad management software, a company should look for the following features, which will optimize their ability to advertise online:

- **The ability to match ads with specific content.** Being able to match ads with Web content would allow an advertiser, for example, to run an ad from a car company in an article about the Indy 500.
- **Tracking.** Of course, the advertiser will need to deliver detailed metrics (performance measures) to its customers, showing impression rates, click-through rates, and other metrics. Tracking of viewing activity is essential in providing such metrics.
- **Rotation.** Advertisers may want to rotate different ads in the same space.
- **Spacing impressions.** If an advertiser buys a given number of impressions over a period of time, the software should be able to adjust the delivery schedule so that they are spread out evenly.

A variety of ad management software packages are available, including some from application service providers (ASPs) and some freeware. A comprehensive package is AdManager from accipiter.com, which delivers all of the features just discussed (see also their AdTraffick and AdMarket).

One topic in ad management is *campaign management*; that is, management of an entire marketing and advertising campaign. Campaign management tools fall into two categories: those that are folded into CRM (customer relationship management), which consist mainly of marketing automation, and those that are targeted, stand-alone campaign management products. Companies such as DoubleClick provide partial management. More comprehensive management is provided by Atlas DMT's Digital Marketing suite (see accipiter.com/products/admanager.php).

Another topic in ad management is measuring the *effectiveness* of Web advertising, which was discussed earlier. Yet another is localization.

LOCALIZATION

localization

The process of converting media products developed in one environment (e.g., country) to a form culturally and linguistically acceptable in countries outside the original target market.

Localization is the process of converting media products developed in one environment (e.g., a country) to a form culturally and linguistically acceptable outside the original target market. It is usually done by a set of *internationalization* guidelines. Web-page translation (Chapters 14 and 17) is just one aspect of internationalization. However, several other aspects also are important. For example, a U.S. jewelry manufacturer that displayed its products on a white background was astonished to find that this display might not appeal to customers in some countries where a blue background is preferred.

If a company aims at the global market (and there are millions of potential customers out there), it must make an effort to localize its Web pages. This may not be a simple task because of the following factors:

- Many countries use English, but the English used may differ in terminology, spelling, and culture (e.g., United States versus United Kingdom versus Australia).
- Some languages use accented characters. If text includes an accented character, the accent will disappear when converted into English, which may result in an incorrect translation.
- Hard-coded text and fonts cannot be changed, so they remain in their original format in the translated material.
- Graphics and icons look different to viewers in different countries. For example, a U.S. mailbox resembles a European trashcan.
- When translating into Asian languages, significant cultural issues must be addressed, for example, how to address older adults in a culturally correct manner.
- Dates that are written mm/dd/yy (e.g., June 8, 2007) in the United States are written dd/mm/yy (e.g., 8 June 2007) in many other countries. Therefore, "6/8" would have two meanings (June 8 or August 6), depending on the location of the writer.
- Consistent translation over several documents can be very difficult to achieve. (For free translation in six languages, see freetranslation.com.)

For variables involved in localization, see Online File W4.14.

Automatic Versus Manual Web Page Translation

Certain localization difficulties result in a need for experienced human translators, who are rare, expensive, and slow. Therefore, companies are using automatic translation software, at least as an initial step to expedite the work of human translators. (See Chapter 14 for further discussion and references.)

Using Internet Radio for Localization

Internet radio Web sites provide music, talk, and other entertainment, both live and stored, from a variety of radio stations (*PCMag.com* 2006). The big advantage of Internet radio is that there are few limits on the type or number of programs it can offer, as compared with traditional radio stations. It is especially useful in presenting programming for local communities. For example, KISSFM (kiisfm.com) is a Los Angeles site that features music from up-and-coming L.A. bands, live concerts, interviews with movie stars, and so forth. About 40 percent of the site's traffic comes from listeners in California, and the rest from listeners around the world. The company that powers the KISSFM Web site also operates sites focused on country music, Latin music, and so forth. Advertisers can reach fairly narrow audience segments by advertising on a particular Internet radio site.

Internet radio
A Web site that provides music, talk, and other entertainment, both live and stored, from a variety of radio stations.

WIRELESS ADVERTISING

As will be seen in Chapter 9, the number of applications of m-commerce in marketing and advertising is growing rapidly, with advertising on cell phones and PDAs on the rise. One area is that of *pervasive computing*— the idea that computer chips can be embedded in almost any device (clothing, tools, appliances, homes, and so on), and then the device can be connected to a network of other devices. An interesting application of this is digital ads atop 12,000 taxis in various U.S. cities. The ads also include public service announcements. The technology comes from Vert Inc. (vert.net).

Vert displays live content and advertising messages very effectively by targeting specific zip codes, neighborhoods, and individual city blocks. Ads can be scheduled for specific times during the day (e.g., promote coffee during the morning commute). Ads are beamed to Vert-equipped taxis like a cell phone signal. GPS satellites pinpoint where the cab is traveling, allowing ads to change from block to block (*Vert.net* 2006). For further discussion, see Patrick (2005).

As advertisers look for the best business model, 2006 was a year of experimentation for the emerging mobile advertising market. Between 2006 and 2011, we will see a change by major brands from simple SMS mobile marketing to more classy multimedia advertising. By the end of 2007, brands will know what works, and mobile advertising will become ordinary by 2008. From 2005, when the emerging market garnered $255 million in the United States and Europe, mobile marketing and advertising in these two geographical areas will grow to exceed $1 billion in 2009 (reported by Anywhere You Go 2006).

VERT Intelligent Displays: Advertising Used Atop Taxi Cabs

Source: Courtesy of Vert Incorporated.

AD CONTENT

The content of ads is extremely important, and companies use ad agencies to help in content creation for the Web just as they do for other advertising media. A major player in this area is Akamai Technologies, Inc. (akamai.com). In a white paper (Akamai Technologies, Inc. 2000b), the company points out how the right content can drive traffic to a site. Akamai also describes how to evaluate third-party vendors and determine what content-related services are important.

Content is especially important to increase *stickiness*. Customers are expensive to acquire; therefore, it is important that they remain at a site, read its content carefully, and eventually make a purchase. The writing of the advertising content itself is, of course, important (see adcopywriting.com and Chapter 16.) Finding a good ad agency to write content and shape the advertising message is one of the key factors in any advertising campaign, online or offline. Yet, matching ad agencies and advertising clients can be complex. AgencyFinder (agencyfinder.com) maintains a huge database that can be tapped for a perfect match.

Section 4.10 ▶ REVIEW QUESTIONS

1. Describe permission advertising.
2. What is localization? What are the major issues in localizing Web pages?
3. How is wireless advertising practiced?
4. What is the importance of ad content?

4.11 SOFTWARE AGENTS IN MARKETING AND ADVERTISING APPLICATIONS

As the volume of customers, products, vendors, and information increases, it becomes uneconomical, or even impossible, for customers to consider all relevant information and to manually match their interests with available products and services. The practical solution to handling such information overload is to use software (intelligent) agents. In Chapter 3, we demonstrated how intelligent agents help online shoppers find and compare products, resulting in significant time savings.

In this section, we will concentrate on how software agents can assist customers in the online purchasing decision-making process as well as in advertisement. Depending on their level of intelligence, agents can do many things (see Greenwald et al. 2003 and Online Technical Appendix C).

A FRAMEWORK FOR CLASSIFYING EC AGENTS

Exhibit 4.2 detailed the customer's purchase decision-making process. A logical way to classify EC agents is by relating them to this decision-making process (in a slightly expanded form), as shown in Exhibit 4.12. In the decision-making model in Exhibit 4.12, the second step was information search. Because of the vast quantity of information that software (intelligent) agents can sift through, the step has been split here into two types of agents: those that first answer the question, "What to buy?" and those that answer the next question, "From whom?" Let's see how agents support each of the phases of the decision-making process.

Agents That Support Need Identification (What to Buy)

Agents can help buyers recognize their need for products or services by providing product information and stimuli. For example, Expedia notifies customers about low airfares to a customer's desired destination whenever they become available.

Several commercial agents can facilitate need recognition directly or indirectly. For example, FindGift (findgift.com).com asks customers questions about the person for whom they are buying a gift and helps them hunt down the perfect gift.

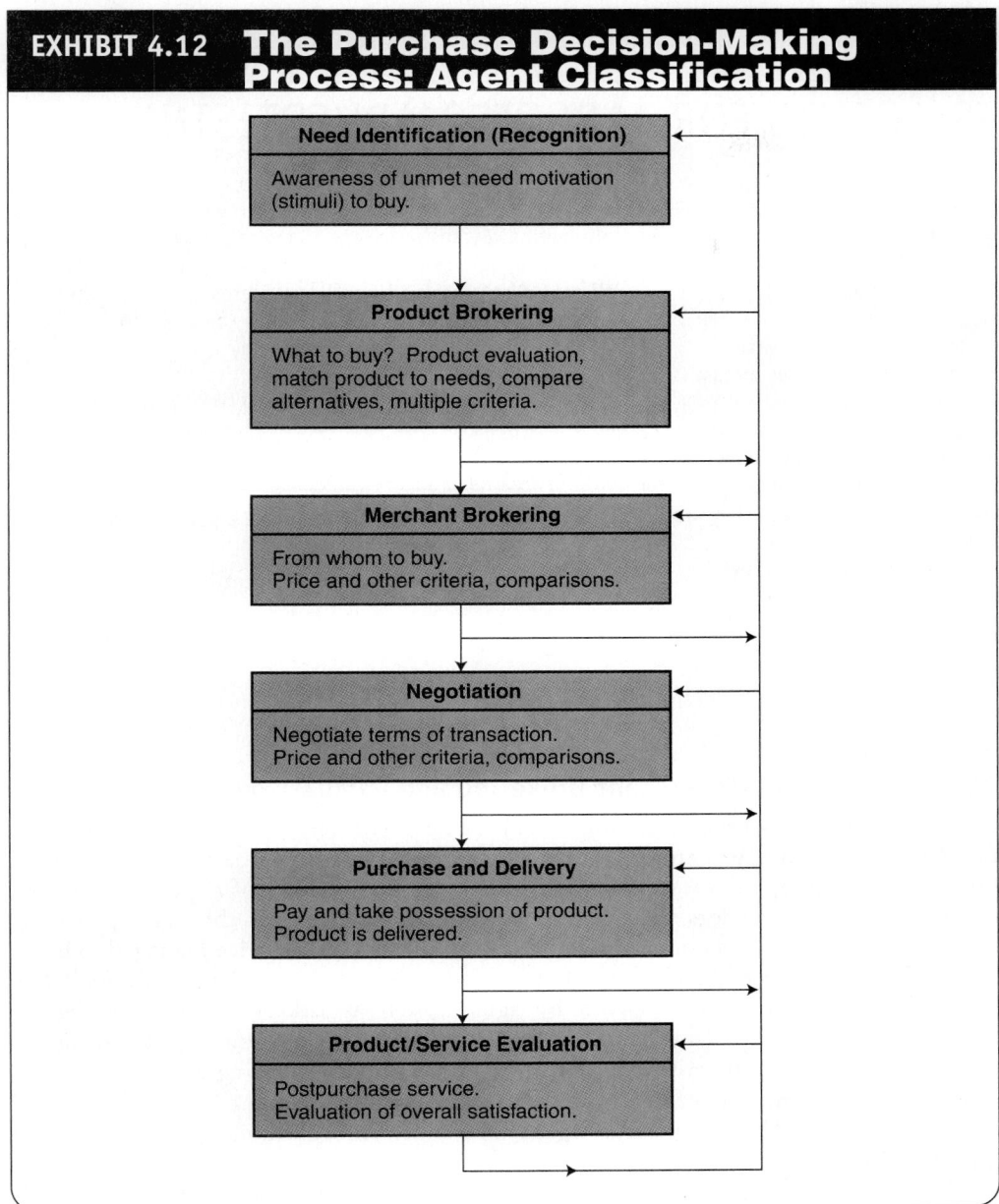

EXHIBIT 4.12 The Purchase Decision-Making Process: Agent Classification

Agents That Support Product Brokering (From Whom to Buy)

Once a need is established, customers search for a product (or service) that will satisfy the need. Several agents are available to assist customers with this task. The comparison agents cited in Chapter 3 belong in this category. An example of how these agents are used in advertising is provided in Case 4.2.

Some agents can match people that have similar interest profiles. Even more ambitious agents try to predict which brands of computers, cars, and other goods will appeal to customers based on market segmentation preferences in a variety of different product categories, such as wine, music, or breakfast cereal. (See the earlier discussion on *collaborative filtering*.) For a discussion on agents that do both product and merchant brokering, see He and Leung (2002). Guan (2006) describes how agents support product brokering.

CASE 4.2
EC Application

FUJITSU USES AGENTS FOR TARGETED ADVERTISING IN JAPAN

Fujitsu (*fujitsu.com*) is a Japanese-based global provider of Internet-focused information technology solutions. Since the end of 1996, Fujitsu has been using an agent-based technology called the Interactive Marketing Interface (iMi). The system allows advertisers to interact directly with specific segments of the consumer market through the use of software agents, while ensuring that consumers remain anonymous to advertisers. Consumers submit a personal profile to iMi, indicating such characteristics as product categories of interests, hobbies, travel habits, and the maximum number of e-mail messages per week that they are willing to receive. In turn, customers receive product announcements, advertisements, and marketing surveys by e-mail from advertisers based on their personal profile

information. By answering the marketing surveys or acknowledging receipt of advertisements, consumers earn iMi points, redeemable for gift certificates and phone cards. Many other companies in Japan (e.g., *nifty.com* and *lifemedia.co.jp*) also use this technology.

Source: Compiled from *fujitsu.com* (accessed March 2007).

Questions

1. Why would customers agree to have a personal profile built on them?
2. What is the role of the software agent in this case?

Agents That Support Merchant Brokering and Comparisons

Once a consumer has a specific product in mind, he or she needs to find a place to buy it. BargainFinder (from Accenture) was the pioneering agent in this category. When used for online CD shopping, for example, this agent queried the price of a specific CD from a number of online vendors and returned a list of prices. However, this system encountered problems because vendors who did not want to compete on price managed to block out the agent's requests. (Today's version is at cdrom-guide.com, "Bargain finder") The blocking problem has been solved by agents such as Inktomi Shopping Agent, Froogle.com, My Simon (mysimon.com), and Junglee (of Amazon.com). These agents originate the requests from whatever computer the user is accessing at the time. This way, vendors have no way of determining whether the request comes direct from a real customer or from the comparison agent. For more information, see Boudriga and Obaidat (2004).

Fraud is of major concern to buyers because buyers cannot see the products or the sellers (see Chapter 17). Several vendors offer agent-based fraud detection systems. One such system is Risk Suite (fairisaac.com). It is based on pattern recognition driven by neural computing. Other products from Fairisaac are FICO Risk Score and VeriComp Fraud Managers.

Comparison Agents. Part of the merchant-brokering process is determining price and other purchase criteria. Large numbers of agents enable consumers to perform all kinds of comparisons, as was shown in Chapter 3. Here are some additional examples:

- Allbookstores.com and bestbookbuys.com are two of several agents that help consumers find the lowest prices of books available online.
- Bottomdollar.com, compare.net, shopper.com, roboshopper.com, and bargainvillage.com are examples of agents (out of several dozen) that suggest brands and compare prices once consumers specify what they want to buy.
- Pricescan.com guides consumers to the best prices on thousands of computer hardware and software products.
- Buyerzone.com is a B2B portal at which businesses can find the best prices on many products and services.

Agents That Support Buyer–Seller Negotiation

The traditional concept of "market" implies negotiation, mostly about price. Whereas many large retail stores engage in fixed-price selling, many small retail stores and many markets use negotiation extensively. In several cultures (e.g., Chinese), negotiation is very common. In many B2B transactions, negotiation is common, too. The benefit of dynamically negotiating a price is that the pricing decision is shifted from the seller to the marketplace. In a fixed-price situation, if the seller fixes a price that is too high, sales volume will suffer. If the price is set too low, profits will be lower.

Negotiations, however, are time consuming and often disliked by individual customers who cannot negotiate properly because they lack information about the marketplace and prices or because they do not know how to negotiate. Many vendors do not like to negotiate either. Therefore, electronic support of negotiation can be extremely useful.

Agents can negotiate in pairs, or one agent can negotiate for a buyer with several sellers' agents. In the latter case, the contact is done with each seller's agent individually, and the buyer's agent can conduct comparisons. Also, customers can negotiate with sellers' agents. One system automates the bargaining on a seller's side. The system can bargain with customers based on their bargaining behavior. For example, if the customer starts very low, the system helps the seller know how to respond. For details, see Sim (2006), Wang et al. (2005), and Chapter 5 (for B2B).

Agents That Support Purchase and Delivery

Agents are used extensively during the actual purchase, often arranging payment and delivery. For example, if a customer makes a mistake when completing an electronic order form, an agent will point it out immediately. When a customer buys stocks, for example, the pricing agent will tell the customer when a stock they want to buy on margin is not marginable or when the customer does not have sufficient funds. Similarly, delivery options are posted by agents at Amazon.com and other e-tailers, and the total cost of the transaction is calculated in real time.

Agents That Support After-Sale Service and Evaluation

Agents also can be used to facilitate after-sale service. For example, the automatic e-mail answering agents described in Chapter 13 usually are effective in answering customer queries. A non-Internet-based agent can monitor automobile usage and notify owners when it is time to take their car in for periodic maintenance. Agents that facilitate feedback from customers also are useful.

CHARACTER-BASED ANIMATED INTERACTIVE AGENTS

Several agents enhance customer service by interacting with customers via animated characters. Similar agents are used to facilitate advertising. Animated characters are software agents with personalities. They are versatile and employ friendly front ends to communicate with users. They are not necessarily intelligent. These animated agents also are called *avatars*. **Avatars** are animated computer representations of humanlike movements and behaviors in a computer-generated three-dimensional world. Advanced avatars can "speak" and exhibit behaviors such as gestures and facial expressions. They can be fully automated to act like robots. The purpose of avatars is to introduce believable emotions so that the agents gain credibility with users. Insights and Additions 4.4 describes the use of avatars at a virtual mall in Korea.

Avatars are considered a part of **social computing,** an approach aimed at making the human–computer interface more natural (Castronova 2004). Studies conducted by Extempo Systems (Extempo Systems, Inc. 1999) showed that interactive characters can improve customer satisfaction and retention by offering personalized, one-to-one service. They also can help companies get to know their customers and support advertising. For more on avatars, see Rehm and Andre (2005).

avatars
Animated computer characters that exhibit humanlike movements and behaviors.

social computing
An approach aimed at making the human–computer interface more natural.

Insights and Additions 4.4 Brand Names at a Korean Virtual Mall

Avatars are big business in South Korea. Internet users express themselves by putting clothes, shoes, and accessories on their avatars. The clothes are really pixels on the computer screen designed for avatars that represent the users and are moved around a virtual chat room. Clothing the avatars in attire bought in virtual malls is part of the fun. Sayclub, operated by NeoWiz, was the first to introduce avatar services there in 2000. The company had more than 15 million members in 2002, who spent a total of $1.6 million a month on their avatars, dressing them in the over 30,000 outfits from the virtual shopping mall (*saymall.sayclub.com*).

"It is an unusual strategy, but avatars can be very effective marketing tools," says Chung Jae Hyung, chief executive officer at DKIMS Communications, an online marketing agency. "They are so popular with young people these days that they can get you a lot of exposure very quickly. An avatar is a given; just like everyone has a cell phone, everyone has an avatar," says Chung. Samsung Economic Research Institute estimates that the avatar industry generated $16 million in revenue in 2001 (Yoon 2002). By 2006, according to private communications with Samsung researchers, the estimate grew to $30 million.

As competition grew from the top portals, such as Yahoo!, Sayclub responded by offering more items, including hair dyes, accessories, and brands. "We needed something to differentiate ourselves and improve our brand image," says Chang Hyun Guk, manager of the business-planning team at Sayclub. "The best way to do that was to bring real-life brands to our virtual mall." Therefore, to improve its own brand image, Sayclub sought to offer well-known consumer brands as products one could buy for one's

avatar from the Sayclub site. In addition to improving the Sayclub brand, these products would generate money from additional sales.

However, convincing top brands to go virtual was not easy. For example, because Mattel, the maker of Barbie, did not have any idea what the avatar market was all about, it needed to be educated before it would sign a licensing agreement allowing outfits from the Barbie Fashion Avenue line of doll dresses to be "avatarized" for a percentage of total sales. Numerous Barbie outfits have gone on sale at prices ranging from $4 to $5.35. That may not sound like much, but as of June 2002, avatar outfits made up almost 15 percent of Barbie's licensing business in Korea. By exposing Sayclub's users (mostly people in their teens and 20s) to Barbie paraphernalia, Mattel has been able to extend her popularity beyond children the ages of 8 or 9. Jisun Lee, a 23-year-old student, had not owned anything "Barbie" in over a decade but spent more than $85 in 2002 dressing her avatar in Barbie outfits.

During the Korean World Cup games in June 2002, Sayclub formed a partnership with Nike Korea and introduced avatars based on real images of Korean soccer players. They provided various soccer-related avatar items, including uniforms and Nike products. Sayclub granted uniform numbers of national soccer players to all users who bought Nike soccer items, including soccer player avatars or national team uniforms. They also gave away gifts to users with uniform numbers (selected by lottery) if the players their avatars represented scored during the games.

Sources: Compiled from Yoon (2002), *sayclub.com* (accessed November 2006), and *neowiz.com* (accessed November 2006).

Chatterbots

chatterbots
Animation characters that can talk (chat).

A special category of animated characters is characters that can chat, known as **chatterbots**. A chatterbot is a program that attempts to simulate a conversation, with the aim of at least temporarily fooling a customer into thinking they are conversing with a human. The concept started with Eliza, created by Joseph Weizenbaum at MIT in 1957. In his program, users conversed with a psychoanalyst. Today's version is very powerful (try simonlaven.com/eliza.htm; the program can be downloaded for free). The major differences are that today the programs are on the Web and they include a static or moving character. The technology is based on *natural language programming* (NLP), an applied artificial intelligence program that can recognize typed or spoken key words and short sentences.

A major use of character-based interactive agents is in customer service and CRM. The following sites offer demos and the opportunity to converse with virtual representatives:

▸ Artificial-life.com. This site offers CRM and other agents. The site can be accessed by cell phones as well as traditional Web connections. (In Chapter 13, we illustrate the use of CRM agents; see Exhibit 13.7.) This company offers e-learning applications, too.

▶ Verity.com. This site offers "Virtual Response," which acts as a "v-rep" (virtual representative) that can answer customer questions and provide potential solutions.

▶ Zabaware.com. This site provides desktop assistance for answering customers' queries.

For an inventory of chatterbots and other resources, visit Simon Laven's site (simonlaven.com).

Chatterbots can do many things to enhance customer service, such as greeting a consumers when they enter a site or giving the consumer a guided tour of the site. For example, consider the following chatterbot agents: "Ed, Harmony, and Nina" are virtual guides that help visitors who wish to learn more about products and tools available at extempo.com (which specializes in avatars). "Arthur bot" helps people build their own chatterbots at ai-buddy.com For additional information on interactive characters, see Agent Interactive (2006), microsoft.com/msagent, and artificial-life.com. Rehm and Andre (2005) studied communication behaviors of humans and whether these behaviors differed when conversing with an agent as opposed to talking with other humans.

OTHER EC AGENTS

Other agents support consumer behavior, customer service, and advertising activities. For example, Resumix (see Chapter 3) is an application that wanders the Web looking for Web pages containing resume information. If it identifies a page as being a resume, it tries to extract pertinent information from the page, such as the person's e-mail address, phone number, skill description, and location. The resulting database is used to connect job seekers with recruiters. For current lists of various EC agents, see botspot.com and agents.umbc.edu (see the "Agents 101" tutorial). For a comprehensive guide to EC agents, see Iyer and Pazgal (2003). For more information these EC agents and others, see Online File W4.15.

Section 4.11 ▶ REVIEW QUESTIONS

1. List the major types of software (intelligent) agents used in customer-related and advertising applications.

2. What role do software agents play in *need identification*?

3. How do software agents support *product brokering* and *merchant brokering*?

4. What are avatars and chatterbots? Why are they used on Web sites?

MANAGERIAL ISSUES

Some managerial issues related to this chapter are as follows.

1. **Do we understand our customers?** Understanding customers, specifically what they need and how to respond to those needs, is the most critical part of consumer-centered marketing. To excel, companies need to satisfy and retain customers, and management must monitor the entire process of marketing, sales, maintenance, and follow-up service.

2. **Should we use intelligent agents?** Any company engaged in EC must examine the possibility of using intelligent agents to enhance customer service, and possibly to support market research and match ads with consumers. Commercial agents are available on the market at a reasonable cost. For heavy usage, companies may develop customized agents.

3. **Who will conduct the market research?** B2C requires extensive market research. This research is not easy to do, nor is it inexpensive. Deciding whether to outsource to a market research firm or maintain an in-house market research staff is a major management issue.

4. **Are customers satisfied with our Web site?** This is a key question, and it can be answered in several ways. Many vendors are available to assist you; some provide free software. For discussion on how to improve customer satisfaction, see webhelp.com and e-usatisfy.co.uk. For Web site improvements, see futurenowinc.com.

5. **Can we use B2C marketing methods and research in B2B?** Some methods can be used with adjustments; others cannot. B2B marketing and marketing research require special methods.

6. **How do we decide where to advertise?** Web advertising is a complex undertaking, and outsourcing its management should seriously be considered for large-scale ads. Some outsourcers specialize in certain industries (e.g., ebizautos.com for auto dealers). Companies should examine the adage.com site, which contains an index of Web sites, their advertising rates, and reported traffic counts, before selecting a site on which to advertise. Companies also should consult third-party audits.

7. **What is our commitment to Web advertising, and how will we coordinate Web and traditional advertising?** Once a company has committed to advertising on the Web, it must remember that a successful program is multifaceted. It requires input and vision from marketing, cooperation from the legal department, and strong technical leadership from the corporate information systems (IS) department. A successful Web advertising program also requires coordination with non-Internet advertising and top management support.

8. **Should we integrate our Internet and non-Internet marketing campaigns?** Many companies are integrating their TV and Internet marketing campaigns. For example, a company's TV or newspaper ads direct the viewers/readers to the Web site, where short videos and sound ads, known as *rich media*, are used. With click-through ratios of banner ads down to less than 0.5 percent at many sites, innovations such as the integration of offline and online marketing are certainly needed to increase click-throughs.

9. **What ethical issues should we consider?** Several ethical issues relate to online advertising. One issue that receives a great deal of attention is spamming (Chapter 17). Another issue is the selling of mailing lists and customer information. Some people believe not only that a company needs the consent of the customers before selling a list, but also that the company should share with customers the profits derived from the sale of such lists. Using cookies without an individual's consent is considered by many to be an ethical issue. The negative impacts of advertising need to be considered (see Gao et al. 2006).

10. **Are any metrics available to guide advertisers?** A large amount of information has been developed to guide advertisers as to where to advertise, how to design ads, and so on. Specific metrics may be used to assess the effectiveness of advertising and to calculate the ROI from an organization's online advertising campaign.

11. **Which Internet marketing/advertising channel to use?** An increasing number of online methods are available from which to choose. These include banners, search engines, blogging, social networks, and more. Angel (2006) proposed a methodology to assess these alternatives with a matrix for selection and implementation.

RESEARCH TOPICS

Here are some suggested topics related to this chapter. For details, references, and additional topics, refer to the Online Appendix A "Current EC Research."

1. **Online Consumer Behavior Models**
   - Key drivers and behavioral factors of online purchasing
   - Consumers' attitude toward Internet shopping in comparison with other channels
   - Potential and status of penetration in online purchasing by product (service) types
   - Stage theory of online purchasing by country
   - Impact of broadband penetration of consumer purchasing online
   - Consumer reaction to mobile ads

2. **Factors Influencing the Online Purchases**
   - Product and service types
   - Price and quality level of products
   - Consumer attitudes about shopping online
   - Shoppers' online experience
   - Gender, age, and occupation
   - Online services and privacy concerns
   - Behavior related to the acceptance of new technology
   - Country and cultural differences

- Behavior regarding time to delivery
- Brand effect and trust
- Sociological factors concerning consumer and product characteristics
- Perception of decision aids

3. **Online Customers Trust and Loyalty**
   - Role and importance of trust on EC
   - Trust requirement and previous experiences regarding trust in e-business
   - Impact of trust on relationship building and acceptance of EC
   - Ways to build consumer trust in online purchasing
   - Role of certifications to ensure the trust
   - Factors that facilitate online loyalty

4. **Factors Used to Measure Online Customer Satisfaction with Metrics**
   - Technology acceptance behavior
   - Transaction cost
   - Service quality
   - Perceived importance of online support services
   - Expectations toward online services including both the desire for and the lack of confidence in the ability of those services

5. **Customer Relationship Management for EC Using Personalized Services**
   - Factors that determine customer retention in EC
   - Design of EC to enhance the stickiness for customer retention
   - Design of personalized services based on CRM
   - Impact of customer participation on brand loyalty
   - Information integration for relationship management
   - Consumer and product characteristics

6. **Internet Market Research**
   - Techniques and methods of online market research
   - Existing practices of Internet research
   - Consumer opportunity, ability, and motivation to participate in market research online
   - Cost and benefit of Internet market research methods in comparison with traditional research methods

7. **Impact of Internet Advertising**
   - Customer attitudes about online advertisement in comparison with other advertising channels
   - Design of Internet advertising methods
   - Negative impacts
   - Impact of Internet advertising on firm value
   - How to attract customers to Internet advertising
   - Selection of Web sites for online advertisement
   - Comparison challenge as an advertising model
   - How to design and use avatars

8. **Evaluating Internet Advertising Methods**
   - Algorithms for customized advertisement method
   - Business models for effective e-mail advertising
   - Effectiveness of banner advertising
   - Optimal ad placement method
   - The effectiveness of advergames
   - Does the use of color in e-mail matter?
   - Google's method versus its competitor's methods

9. **Effectiveness and Management Issues of Advertising**
   - Virtual advertising agencies
   - Web traffic aggregation

SUMMARY

In this chapter, you learned about the following EC issues as they relate to the learning objectives.

1. **Essentials of online consumer behavior.** Consumer behavior in EC is similar to that of any consumer behavior, but it has some unique features. It is described in a stimuli-based decision model that is influenced by independent variables (personal characteristics and environmental characteristics). The model also contains a significant vendor-controlled component that includes both market stimuli and EC systems (logistics, technology, and customer service). All of these characteristics and systems interact to influence the decision-making process and produce an eventual buyer decision.

2. **The online consumer decision-making process.** The goal of marketing research efforts is to *understand* the consumers' online decision-making process and formulate an appropriate strategy to *influence* their behavior. For each step in the process, sellers can develop appropriate strategies.

3. **Building one-to-one relationships with customers.** EC offers companies the opportunity to build one-to-one relationships with customers that are not possible in other marketing systems. Product customization, personalized service, and getting the customer involved interactively (e.g., in feedback, order tracking, and so on) are all practical in cyberspace. In addition, advertising can be matched with customer profiles so that ads can be presented on a one-to-one basis.

4. **Online personalization.** Using personal Web pages, customers can interact with a company, learn about products or services in real time, or get customized products or services. Companies can allow customers to self-configure the products or services they want. Customization also can be done by matching products with customers' profiles.

5. **Increasing loyalty and trust.** Customers can switch loyalty online easily and quickly. Therefore, enhancing e-loyalty (e.g., through e-loyalty programs) is a must. Similarly, trust is a critical success factor that must be nourished.

6. **EC customer market research.** Several fast and economical methods of online market research are available. The two major approaches to data collection are: (1) soliciting voluntary information from the customers and (2) using cookies, transaction logs, or clickstream data to track customers' movements on the Internet and find what their interests are. Understanding market segmentation by grouping consumers into categories is also an effective EC market research method. However, online market research has several limitations, including data accuracy and representation of the statistical population by a sample.

7. **B2B Internet marketing methods and organizational buyers.** Marketing methods and marketing research in B2B differ from those of B2C. A major reason for this is that the buyers must observe organizational buying policies and frequently conduct buying activities as a committee. Organizations use modified B2C methods such as affiliate marketing.

8. **Objectives and characteristics of Web advertising.** Web advertising attempts to attract surfers to an advertiser's site. Once at the advertiser's site, consumers can receive information, interact with the seller, and in many cases, immediately place an order. With Web advertising, ads can be customized to fit groups of people with similar interests or even individuals. In addition, Web advertising can be interactive, is easily updated, can reach millions at a reasonable cost, and offers dynamic presentation by rich multimedia.

9. **Major online advertising methods.** Banners are the most popular online advertising method. Other frequently used methods are pop-ups and similar ads (including interstitials), e-mail (including e-mail to mobile devices), classified ads, registration of URLs with search engines, and advertising in chat rooms. Some of these are related to search results obtained through search engines (especially Google).

10. **Various advertising strategies and types of promotions.** The major advertising strategies are ads associated with search results (text links), affiliate marketing, pay incentives for customers to view ads, viral marketing, ads customized on a one-to-one basis, and online events and promotions. Web promotions are similar to offline promotions. They include giveaways, contests, quizzes, entertainment, coupons, and so on. Customization and interactivity distinguish Internet promotions from conventional ones.

11. **Permission marketing, ad management, and localization.** In permission marketing, customers are willing to accept ads in exchange for special (personalized) information or monetary incentives. Ad management deals with planning, organizing, and controlling ad campaigns and ad use. Finally, in localization, attempts are made to fit ads to local environments.

12. **Intelligent agents.** Intelligent agents can gather and interpret data about consumer-purchasing behavior. Advanced agents can even learn about customer behavior and needs by observing their Web movements. Agents can facilitate or support all aspects of the purchasing process, including product brokering, merchant brokering, product comparison, buyer–seller negotiation, purchase and delivery, and after-sale customer service. Character-based interactive agents such as avatars and chatterbots "put a face" on the computing experience, making it more natural.

KEY TERMS

QUESTIONS FOR DISCUSSION

1. What would you tell an executive officer of a bank about the critical success factors for increasing the loyalty of banking customers by using the Internet?

2. Why is data mining becoming an important element in EC? How is it used to learn about consumer behavior? How can it be used to facilitate customer service?

3. Explain why online trust is more difficult to achieve than offline trust.

4. Discuss the similarities and differences between data mining and Web mining. (*Hint:* To answer this question, you will need to read Online Appendix W4A.)

5. How can research on satisfaction and dissatisfaction help online sellers?

6. Discuss why B2C marketing and advertising methods may not fit B2B.

7. Relate banner swapping to a banner exchange.

8. Discuss why banners are popular in Internet advertising.

9. Explain how Google generates ads for its customers.

10. Discuss the relationship between market research and advertisement (see Atlas DMT at atlasdmt.com for a start).

11. Discuss the advantages and limitations of listing a company's URL with various search engines.

12. How might a chat room be used for advertising?

13. Is it ethical for a vendor to enter a chat room operated by a competitor and pose queries?

14. Explain why online ad management is critical.

15. Examine some Web avatars and try to interact with them. Discuss the potential benefits and drawbacks of using avatars as an advertising medium.

16. Explain the advantages of using chatterbots. Are there any disadvantages?

17. Discuss the benefits of using software agents in marketing and advertising.

18. How can avatars increase trust?

19. Enter sric-bi.com/VALS. View their activities and discuss how they can facilitate online market segmentation.

20. When you buy a banner ad, you actually lease space for a specific time period. In milliondollarhomepage.com you buy space forever. Compare and discuss.

INTERNET EXERCISES

1. Enter **netflix.com/Affiliates?hnjr=3**. Describe the value of the program as a marketing channel.

2. Surf the Home Depot Web site (**homedepot.com**) and check whether (and how) the company provides service to customers with different skill levels. Particularly, check the "kitchen and bath design center" and other self-configuration assistance. Relate this to market research.

3. Examine a market research Web site (e.g., **acnielsen.com** or **claritas.com**). Discuss what might motivate a consumer to provide answers to market research questions.

4. Enter **mysimon.com** and share your experiences about how the information you provide might be used by the company for marketing in a specific industry (e.g., the clothing market).

5. Enter **marketingterms.com** and conduct a search by keywords as well as by category. Check the definitions of 10 key terms in this chapter.

6. Enter **2020research.com**, **infosurv.com**, and **marketingsherpa.com** and identify areas for market research about consumers.

7. Enter **nielsenmedia.com** and view the demos on e-market research. Then go to **clickz.com** and find its offerings. Summarize your findings.

8. Enter **selfpromotion.com** and find some interesting promotion ideas for the Web.

9. Enter the Web sites of **ipro.com** and **selfpromotion.com**. What Internet traffic management, Web results, and auditing services are provided? What are the benefits of each service? Find at least one competitor in each category (e.g., **netratings.com**). Compare the services provided and the prices.

10. Enter **hotwired.com** and **espn.com**. Identify all of the advertising methods used on each site. Can you find those that are targeted advertisements? What revenue sources can you find on the ESPN site? (Try to find at least seven.)

11. Compare the advertisements and promotions at **thestreet.com** and **marketwatch.com**. Write a report.

12. Enter **adweek.com**, **newroads.com**, **wdfm.com**, **ad-tech.com**, **iab.com**, and **adage.com** and find new developments in Internet advertisement. Write a report based on your findings.

13. Enter **clairol.com** to determine your best hair color. You can upload your own photo to the studio and see how different shades look on you. You can also try different hairstyles. It also is for men. How can these activities increase branding? How can they increase sales?

14. Enter **paf.bcentral.com** (part of Microsoft's "bCentral") and ask the Position Agent to rank your Web site or a site with which you are familiar. Assess the benefits of using the program versus the costs.

15. What resources do you find to be most useful at **targetonline.com**, **clickz.com**, **admedia.org**, **marketresearch.com**, and **wdfm.com**?

16. Enter **doubleclick.com** and examine all of the company's products. Prepare a report.

17. Enter **sitepal.com** and check out each of the chatterbots listed under "reasons for using SitePal." In your opinion, which of these bots best accomplished the goal of the site? Why?

18. Enter **zoomerang.com** and learn how it facilitates online surveys. Examine the various products, including those that supplement the surveys. Write a report.

19. Enter **pewinternet.org** and **pewresearch.org**. What research do they conduct that is relevant to B2C? To B2B? Write a report.

20. Enter **loomia.com**. Describe their recommendation engines.

TEAM ASSIGNMENTS AND ROLE PLAYING

1. Enter **harrisinteractive.com**, **infosurv.com**, and similar sites. Have each team member examine the free marketing tools and related tutorials and demos. Each team will try to find a similar site and compare the two. Write a report discussing the team's findings.

2. Each team will choose one advertising method and conduct an in-depth investigation of the major players in that part of the ad industry. For example, direct e-mail is relatively inexpensive. Visit **the-dma.org** to learn about direct mail. Then visit **ezinedirector.com** and **venturedirect.com** and similar sites. Each team will prepare and present an argument as to why its method is superior.

3. In this exercise, each team member will enter **uproar.com** or similar sites to play games and win prizes. What could be better? This site is the destination of choice for game and sweepstakes junkies and for those who wish to reach a mass audience of fun-loving people. Relate the games to advertising and marketing.

4. Let the team try the services of **constantcontact.com**. Constant Contact offers a turnkey e-mail marketing package solution. In less than five minutes, you can set up an e-mail sign-up box on your Web site. As visitors fill in their names and e-mail addresses, they can be asked to check off topics of interest (as defined by you) to create targeted groups.

   Constant Contact provides a system for creating custom e-mail newsletters that can be sent to your target users on a predetermined schedule. The site manages your mailings and provides reports that help you assess the success of your efforts. Pricing is based on the number of subscribers; less than 50 and the service is free. Write a report summarizing your experiences.

5. Netflix, Amazon.com, and others view historical purchases as input available for use in their recommendation systems. Some believe that this is an invasion of privacy. Debate this issue.

6. Enter **autonlab.org** and download tools for conducting data mining analysis (these downloads are free). Get data on customer shopping and analyze it.

Real-World Case

1-800-FLOWERS.COM USES DATA MINING TO FOSTER CUSTOMER RELATIONSHIP MANAGEMENT

1-800-FLOWERS.COM (*1-800-flowers.com*) is a true Internet pioneer. It had an Internet presence in 1992 and full-fledged e-store capabilities in 1995. Online sales are a major marketing channel (in addition to telephone and fax orders). Competition is very strong in this industry. The company's success was based on operational efficiency, convenience (24/7 accessibility), and reliability. However, all major competitors provide the same features today. To maintain its competitive advantage, the company transformed itself into a customer-intimate organization, caring for more than 15 million customers. The challenge was to make 1-800-FLOWERS.COM the only retailer that customers really trust when shopping for gifts online or by phone.

The company decided to cultivate brand loyalty through customer relationships, which is based on intimate knowledge of customers. How is this accomplished? SAS software spans the entire decision-support process for managing customer relationships. Collecting data at all customer contact points, the company turns that data into knowledge for understanding and anticipating customer behavior, meeting customer needs, building more profitable customer relationships, and gaining a holistic view of a customer's lifetime value. Using SAS Enterprise Miner, 1-800-Flowers.com sifts through data to discover trends, explain outcomes, and predict results so that the company can increase response rates and identify profitable customers. The rationale for the customer-intimate effort is to build loyalty. In addition to selling and campaign management, the ultimate goal is to make sure that when a customer wants to buy, he or she continues to buy from 1-800-Flowers.com and cannot be captured by a competitor's marketing. To build that kind of loyalty, it is necessary to know your customers and build a solid relationship with each one of them.

Identifying Each Customer

At 1-800-Flowers.com, the objective is not just about getting customers to buy more. It is about making sure that when they decide to purchase a gift online or by phone they do not think of going to the competition. Loyalty is earned through the quality of the relationship offered. The difficulty is that not every customer wants the same relationship. Some want you to be more involved with them than others; some will give you different levels of permission on how to contact them. At the end of the day, the data mining software helps the company identify the many different types of customers and how each would like to be treated.

The company plans its ad campaigns based on the results of the data mining done on a one-to-one basis. For example, some customers like to be notified about sales, others do not. Some prefer notification via e-mail. The data for the analysis is derived from the data center, which is backed-up by AT&T technology.

Many factors have contributed to the company's recent revenue growth—customer relationship management among them. The data mining analysis provides rapid access to better customer information and reduces the amount of time the company needs to spend on the phone with customers, which makes better use of everybody's time. The net result is that customer retention has increased 15 percent over 2 years.

Sources: Compiled from Anonymous (2006), Reda (2006), and *1-800-flowers.com* (accessed November 2006).

Questions

1. Why is being number one in operation efficiency not enough to keep 1–800-Flowers.com at the top of its industry?
2. How was the transformation to a customer-intimate business accomplished?
3. What is the role of data mining?
4. Why must the online presence and the telephone system be integrated?
5. How is the one-to-one relationship achieved?

REFERENCES

Agent Interactive. "Interactive Agents, 2006." **agentinteractive.se/en/interactive_agents.php** (accessed October 2006).

Akamai Technologies, Inc. "Best Practices for Successful Live Web Event." Akamai Technologies, Inc., report, 2000a.

Akamai Technologies, Inc. "Delivering the Profits: How the Right Content Delivery Provider Can Drive Traffic, Sales, and Profits Through Your Web Site." Akamai Technologies, Inc., white paper, 2000b.

Amato-McCoy, D. M. "The Power of Knowledge." *Chain Store Age*, June 2006.

Amiri, A., and S. Menon. "Effectiveness Scheduling of Internet Banner Advertisements." *ACM Transactions on Internet Technology*, November 2003.

Angel, G. "The Art and Science of Choosing Net Marketing Channels." *E-Commerce Times*, September 21, 2006. **ecommercetimes.com/story/53141.html** (accessed November 2006).

Anke, J., and D. Sundaram. "Personalization Techniques and Their Application," in Khosrow-Pour (2006).

Anonymous. "Ultimate Relationship in Bloom." Customer Success: 1-800-Flowers Sas.com, 2006. sas.com/success/1800flowers.html (accessed November 2006).

Anywhere You Go. "2006 Will Be Year of Mobile Advertising Experimentation." March 20, 2006. **anywhereyougo.com** (accessed March 2007).

Armstrong, G., and P. Kotler. *Marketing: An Introduction*, 7th ed. Upper Saddle River, NJ: Prentice Hall, 2007.

Atlantic Media Company. "American Advertising Federation's Survey on Digital Media Trends." 2006. **aaf.org/news/pdf/execsummarysurvey0606.doc** (accessed September 2006).

Baker, S. "The Online Ad Surge." BusinessWeek Online, November 22, 2004. businessweek.com/magazine/content/04_47/b3909401.htm (accessed March 2007).

Balabanis, G., N. Reynolds, and A. Simintiras. "Bases of E-Store Loyalty: Perceived Switching Barriers and Satisfaction." *Journal of Business Research* 59 (2006).

Birnbaum, M. H. "Human Research and Data Collection via the Internet." *Annual Review of Psychology* 55 (2004).

Blacharski, D. "Advertising as Lifeblood of the Internet." *ITWorld.com* (IT Insights), February 23, 2005. **itworld.com/Tech/2421/nls_itinsights050223/** (accessed February 2005).

Blanford, R. "Measuring Online Advertising's Effectiveness." *eMarketer Special Report*, July 2004.

Boswell, K. "Digital Marketing vs. Online Advertising Breaking Waves for Marketers to Catch." *The Marketleap Report* 2, no. 5 (2002). **marketleap.com/report/ml_report_24.htm** (accessed April 2003).

Boudriga, N., and M. S. Obaidat. "Intelligent Agents on the Web: A Review." *Computing Science and Engineering* 6, no. 4 (2004).

Brengman, M., M. Geuens, S. M. Smith, W. R. Swinyard, and B. Weijters. "Segmenting Internet Shoppers Based on Their Web-Usage-Related Lifestyle: A Cross-Cultural Validation." *Journal of Business Research* 58 (2005).

Bridges, E., R. E. Goldsmith, and C. F. Hofacker. "Businesses and Consumers as Online Customers," in Khosrow-Pour (2006).

Buckley, N. "E-Route to Whiter Smile." *Financial Times*, August 26, 2002.

Burns, E. "Shoppers Seek Web 2.0 E-Commerce." *Clickz.com*, October 2, 2006. **clickz.com/showPage. html?page=3623579** (accessed November 2006).

Castronova, E. "The Price of Bodies: A Hedonic Pricing Model of Avatar Attributes in a Synthetic World." *Kyklos* 57, no. 2 (2004).

Chan, S. *Strategic Management of e-Business*, 2d ed. Chichester, UK: John Wiley & Sons, 2005.

Chang, Y., and E. Thorson. "Television and Web Advertising Synergies." *Journal of Advertising* 33, no. 2 (2004).

Chase, L. "Advertisement Methods." *Web Digest for Marketing*, October 2, 2006.

Chase, L. "Top Ten Success Secrets of E-mail Marketing." 2004. **rightnow.com/resource/marketing-automa-tion-whitepapers.html** (accessed October 2006).

Chaudhury, A., D. Mallick, and H. R. Rao. "Web Channels in E-Commerce." *Communications of the ACM*, January 2001.

Chellappa, R., and R. G. Sin. "Personalization versus Privacy: An Empirical Examination of the Online Consumer's Dilemma." *Information Technology and Management* 4 (2005).

Chen, A. "Surveys Boost Satisfaction." *eWeek*, October 4, 2004.

Chen, A. Y. A., and D. McLeod. "Collaborative Filtering for Information Recommendation Systems," in Khosrow-Pour (2006).

Cheung, C. M. K., and M. K. O. Lee. "The Asymmetric Impact of Website Attribute Performance on User Satisfaction: An Empirical Study." *Proceedings of Hawaii International Conference on System Sciences*, Big Island, Hawaii, January 2005a.

Cheung, C. M. K., and M. K. O. Lee. "The Asymmetric Impact of Website Attribute Performance on User Satisfaction: An Empirical Study." *e-Service Journal* 3, no. 3 (2005b).

Cheung, C. M. K., and M. K. O. Lee. "Understanding Consumer Trust in Internet Shopping: A Multidisciplinary Approach." *Journal of the American Society for Information Science and Technology* 57, no. 4 (2006).

Cheung, C. M. K., L. Zhu, T. C. H. Kwong, G. W. W. Chan, and M. Limayem. "Online Consumer Behavior: A Review and Agenda for Future Research." *Proceedings of Bled eCommerce Conference*, Bled, Slovenia, June 2003.

Clow, K., and D. Baack. *Integrated Advertising, Promotion, and Marketing Communication*. Upper Saddle River, NJ: Prentice Hall, 2004.

Cognos.com. "High-Stakes Analytics." February 2006. **Cognos.Com/Pdfs/Success_Stories/Ss_Harrahs.Pdf** (accessed October 2006).

Collier, J. E., and C. C. Bienstock. "How Do Customers Judge Quality in an E-Tailer?" *MIT Sloan Management Review* 48, no. 1 (2006).

Computer Industry Almanac. "Worldwide Internet Users Top 1 Billion in 2005. USA Reach Nearly 200M Internet Users." January 4, 2006. **c-i-a.com/ pr0106.htm** (accessed September 2006).

Cone, E. "The Persona Next Door." *CIO Insights*, August 2005.

Cox, B., and W. Koelzer. *Internet Marketing*. Upper Saddle River, NJ: Prentice Hall, 2004.

Crampton, T. "10% of Population Has Shopped on Web, Study Shows." *International Herald Tribune*, October 2005. **iht.com/articles/2005/10/18/business/eshop.php** (accessed November 2006).

Cyr, D., C. Bonanni, J. Bowes, and J. Ilsever. "Beyond Trust: Website Design Preference Across Culture." *Journal of Global Information Management* 13, no. 4 (2005).

Delaney, K. J. "Once-Wary Industry Giants Embrace Internet Advertising," *The Wall Street Journal*, April 17, 2006.

DoubleClick. "Fifth Annual Consumer E-Mail Study." *DoubleClick.com*, 2004. **www3.doubleclick.com/ market/2004/10/dc/email.htm?c=0410_smrid_lead=n ewsletterid_source=newsletter_0410** (accessed December 2004).

Doyle, K., A. Minor, and C. Weyrich. "Banner Ad Location Effectiveness Study." University of Michigan, 1997. **webreference.com/dev/banners** (accessed November 2006).

Efendioglu, A. M. "E-Commerce Use by Chinese Consumers," in Khosrow-Pour, 2006.

eMarketer.com. "Measuring Online Advertising's Effectiveness." *eMarketer Daily Special Research Report*, July 28, 2004. **emarketer.com/ Report.aspx?on_ad_eff_jul04** (accessed March 2005).

eMarketer.com. "Social Network Ad Space: Sorry, Sold Out!" November 3, 2006. **emarketer.com/ Article.aspx?1004244** (accessed October 2006).

Evans, G. "The Big Payoff." *Teradata Magazine*, June 2006.

Extempo Systems, Inc. "Smart Interactive Characters: Automating One-to-One Customer Service." 1999. **extempo.com/company_info/press/webtechniques.sh tml** (accessed September 2002). Note: no longer available online.

Faught, K. S., K. W. Green Jr., and D. Whitten. "Doing Survey Research on the Internet." *Journal of Computer Information Systems* 44, no. 3 (2004).

Firstfold.com. "The Big E-Mail Opportunity Lies Ahead." September 29, 2006. **firstfold.com/category/survey-and-trends/page/2/** (accessed November 2006).

Fleita, A. "The Top Nine E-Mail Hoaxes." *MSN Money*, news item, November 15, 2003. **moneycentral.msn.com**.

Floh, A., and H. Treiblmaier. "What Keeps the E-Banking Customer Loyal? A Multigroup Analysis of the Moderating Role of Consumer Characteristics on E-Loyalty in the Financial Service Industry." *Journal of Electronic Commerce Research* 7, no. 2 (2006).

Flynn, L. J., "Like This? You'll Hate That. (Not All Web Recommendations Are Welcome)," *The New York Times*, January 23, 2006Fujitsu. **fujitsu.com** (accessed November 2006).

Gao, Y., M. Koufaris, and R. H. Ducoffe. "Negative Effects of Advertising Techniques in Electronic Commerce," in Khosrow-Pour, 2006.

Gelb, B. D., and S. Sundaram. "Adapting to 'Word of Mouse.'" *Business Horizons*, July–August 2002.

Georgia Institute of Technology, Graphics, Visualization, and Usability (GVU) Center. *Tenth WWW User Survey*. Georgia Institute of Technology, 1998. **cc.gatech.edu/gvu/user_surveys/survey-1998–10** (accessed February 2005).

Gold, R. Y. "Segmenting Strategically: Building Customer Piece of Mind." *RBC Royal Bank*, March 5, 2001. **royalbank.com/sme/articles/segmenting.html** (accessed April 2003).

Goldsmith, R. E. "Electronic Word-of-Mouth," in Khosrow-Pour (2006).

Goodman, A. E. *Winning Results with Google AdWords*. New York: McGraw Hill, 2005.

Gopal, R. D., A. K. Tripathi, and Z. D. Walter. "Economic Issues in Advertising via Email: A Role for A Trusted Third Party?" in *Contemporary Research in E-Marketing*, Volume 1, S. Krishnamurthy (ed.), Hershey, PA: The Idea Group Inc., 2005.

Graham, R. "Advergaming Goes Mainstream." *iMediaConnections*, December 5, 2005. **imediaconnection.com/content/7362.asp** (accessed March 2007).

Grainger, Inc. "E-Commerce Gaining Loyalty among Businesses Buying Operating Supplies Online." *PRNewswire*, December 10, 1998. **prnewswire.com/cgi-bin/stories.pl?ACCT=105&STORY=/www/story/12–10–1998/0000822471** (accessed March 2005).

Gregg, D. G., and S. Walczak. "Adaptive Web Information Extraction." *Communications of the ACM* (2006).

Greenwald, A., N. R. Jennings, and P. Stone. "Agents and Markets." *IEEE Intelligent Systems* 18, no. 6 (2003).

Guan, S.-U. "Intelligent Product Brokering and Preference Tracking Services," in Khosrow-Pour (2006).

Gurau, C. "Managing Advergames," in Khosrow-Pour (2006).

Guttman, R., A. G. Moukas, and P. Maes. "Agent-Mediated Electronic Commerce: A Survey." *Knowledge Engineering Review* 13, no. 3 (1998).

Hallerman, D. "The Death of Mass Marketing, *iMediaConnection*, June 16, 2006. **imediaconnection.com/index.asp** (accessed March 2007).

Harris, L. C., and M. M. H. Goode. "The Four Levels of Loyalty and the Pivotal Role of Trust: A Study of Online Service Dynamics." *Journal of Retailing* 80, no. 2 (2004).

Harrison-Walker, L. S., and S. E. Neeley. "Customer Relationship Building on the Internet in B2B Marketing: A Proposed Typology." *Journal of Marketing Theory and Practice* 12, no. 1 (2004).

He, M. H., and H. F. Leung. "Agents in E-Commerce: State of the Art." *Knowledge and Information Systems* 4, no. 3 (2002).

Hewson, C., et al. *Internet Research Methods*. London: Sage, 2003.

Hoffman, D. L., and T. P. Novak. "How to Acquire Customers on the Web." *Harvard Business Review*, May–June 2000.

Hoffman, L. J., K. Lawson-Jenkins, and J. Blum. "An Expanded Trust Model." *Communications of the ACM*, July 2006.

Inmon, B. "Why Clickstream Data Counts." *e-Business Advisor*, April 2001.

Interactive Prospect Targeting (IPT). "Consumers Respond Favorably to E-mail Marketing." *eMarketer*, 2004. **emarketer.com/Article.aspx?1003093** (accessed October 2004).

Iyer, G., and A. Pazgal. "Erratum: Internet Shopping Agents: Virtual Co-Location and Competition." *Marketing Science* 22, no. 2 (2003).

Jansen, B. J., and A. Spink. "How Are We Searching the World Wide Web? A Comparison of Nine Search Engine Transaction Logs." *Information Processing and Management* 42, no. 1 (2006).

Jeanson, B., and J. Ingham. "Consumer Trust in E-Commerce," in Khosrow-Pour (2006).

Jiang, Z., W. Wang, and I. Benbast, "Online Customer Decision Support," *Communications of the ACM* (2005).

Kalyanam, K., and M. Zweben. "The Perfect Message at the Perfect Moment." *Harvard Business Review* 83, no. 11 (2005).

Kent, P. *Search Engine Optimization for Dummies*. New York: Hungry Minds Inc., 2006.

Khosrow-Pour, M. (ed.). *Encyclopedia of E-Commerce, E-Government, and Mobile Commerce*. Hershey, PA: Idea Group Reference, 2006.

Kotler, P. *Marketing Management*, 11th ed. Upper Saddle River, NJ: Prentice Hall, 2005.

Kotler, P., and G. Armstrong. *Principles of Marketing*, 11th ed., Upper Saddle River, NJ: Prentice Hall, 2006.

Lee, M. K. O., C. M. K. Cheung, C. L. Sia, and K. H. Lim. "How Positive Informational Social Influence Affects Consumers' Decision of Internet Shopping." *Proceeding of the 39th Hawaii International Conference on System Sciences*, Kauai, Hawaii, January 4–7, 2006.

Lee, M., and E. Turban. "Trust in B2C Electronic Commerce: A Proposed Research Model and Its Application." *International Journal of Electronic Commerce* 6, no. 1 (2001).

Lewin, J. "Advertisers Confident in Online Ads." *ITWorld.com*, November 10, 2004. **itworld.com/Man/3827/nls_ecommercead041110** (accessed December 2004).

Lim, K. H., C. L. Sia, M. K. O. Lee, and I. Benbasat. "Do I Trust You Online, and If So, Will I Buy? An Empirical Study of Two Trust-Building Strategies." *Journal of Management Information Systems* 23, no. 2 (Fall 2006).

Limayem, M., C. Cheung, and G. Chan. "Online Consumer Behavior: What We Know and What We Need to Know." *Proceedings of the European and Mediterranean Conference on Information Systems*, Tunis, Tunisia, July 2004.

Marcus, C. "Loyal Customers Can't Be Strangers." *Microsoft Executive Circle* 1, no. 2 (May 2001).

Markellou, P., M. Rigou, and S. Sirmakessis. "A Closer Look to the Online Consumer Behavior," in Khosrow-Pour (2006).

Marketingsherpa.com. "How Southwest Airlines Sold $1.5 Million in Tickets by Posting Four Press Releases." *Marketingsherpa.com*, October 27, 2004. **library.marketingsherpa.com/barrier.cfm?ContentID=2845** (accessed February 2005).

Martin, T. N., and J. C. Hafer. "Internet Procurement by Corporate Purchasing Agents: Is It All Hype?" *SAM Advanced Management Journal* (Winter 2002).

Massad, N., R. Heckman, and K. Crowston. "Customer Satisfaction with Electronic Service Encounters." *International Journal of Electronic Commerce* 10, no. 4 (2006).

McDougall, P., and E. Malykhina. "Get E-Mail under Control." *InformationWeek*, August 21, 2006.

Meeker, N. *The Internet Advertising Report*. New York: Morgan Stanley Corporation, 1997.

Meskauskas, J. "Are Click-Through Rates Really Declining?" *Clickz.com*, January 16, 2001. **clickz.com/media/plan_buy/article.php/835391** (accessed April 2003).

Miles, G. E., A. Davies, and A. Howes. "A Framework for Understanding Human Factors in Web-Based E-Commerce." *International Journal of Human Computer Studies* 52, no. 1 (2000).

Mills, E. "How Deep Is the Online-Ad Well?" *ZDNet News*, May 9, 2006. **zdnet.com/ 2100-9595_22–6069983.html** (accessed September 2006).

Mirror99.com. "Lead Generation: Internet Marketing vs. Traditional Advertising as Seen By the "Net Generation." September 8, 2006. **Mirror99.Com/20060908/Lead_Generation_Internet_Marketing_Vs_Traditional_Advertising_As_Seen_By_The_Quot_Net_Fajg.Jspx** (accessed September 2006).

Moisander, J., and A. Valtonen. *Qualitative Marketing Research: A Cultural Approach*. Thousand Oaks, CA: Sage, 2006.

MoreBusiness.com. "Viral Marketing and Brand Awareness." March 29, 2006. **morebusiness.com/running_your_business/marketing/viral-marketing.brc** (accessed March 2007).

Mordkovich, B., and E. Mordkovich. *Pay-Per-Click Search Engine Marketing Handbook*. Morrisville, NC: Lulu.com, 2005.

NeoWiz.com. **neowiz.com** (accessed November 2006).

Netflix.com. "Netflix and *USA Weekend* Partner on 'Netflix Movie Picks' Promotion." September 13, 2006. **netflix.com/MediaCenter?id=5363** (accessed October 2006).

New Media Age. "Opinion: Providing Satisfaction Is the Key to Consumer Loyalty Today." *New Media Age*, March 2, 2006.

New Media Age. "Research Reveals Positive Effect of Web Advertising." *New Media Age*, March 2003.

New Media Age. "How to Get Users to Like Online Ads." *New Media Age*, April 2004.

Null, C. *How Netflix Is Fixing Hollywood by Finding a Market for Niche Titles*, July 1, 2003, **money.cnn.com/magazines/business2/business2_archive/2003/07/01/345263/index.htm** (accessed April 2006).

Nucifera, A. "Online Fantasy Sports Attract Real Fans." *The Alf Report*, July–August 2004. **nucifora.com/newsletter/0704–0804/estats.html** (accessed November 2006).

O'Keefe, R. M., and T. McEachern. "Web-Based Customer Decision Support System." *Communications of the ACM* (March 1998).

Oermann, A., and J. Dittmann. "Trust in E-Technologies," in Khosrow-Pour (2006).

Oh, M. S., J. W. Choi, and D.-G. Kim. "Bayesian Inference and Model Selection in Latent Class Logit Models with Parameter Constraints: An Application to Market Segmentation." *Journal of Applied Statistics* 30, no. 2 (2003).

Oliva, R. A. "Playing the Search." *Marketing Management* 13, no. 2 (2004).

Oliver, R. L. "Whence Consumer Loyalty." *Journal of Marketing* 63 (1999).

Paravastu, N., and D. Gefen. "Trust as an Enabler of E-Commerce," in Khosrow-Pour (2006).

Park, Y. H., and P. S. Fader. "Modeling Browsing Behavior at Multiple Websites." *Marketing Science* 23, no. 3 (2004).

Patrick, A. O. "Commercials by Cellphone," *The Wall Street Journal*, August 22, 2005.

PCMag.com. "Internet Radio: Definition," 2006. **pcmag.com/encyclopedia_term/0,2542,t=Internet+radio&i=45248,00.asp** (accessed October 2006).

Peppers and Rogers Group. "E-mail Marketing as a Relationship Strategy: The Four Steps to High Impact E-mail Marketing." Peppers and Rogers, white paper, 2004.

Petrecca, L. "In Limbo, Bidders Asked 'How Low Can You Go?'" *USA Today*, October 25, 2006.

Pons, A. P. "Biometric Marketing: Targeting the Online Consumer." *Communications of the ACM* (August 2006).

Ratnasingam, P. "Trust in Inter-Organizational Exchanges: A Case Study in Business to Business Electronic Commerce." *Decision Support Systems*, Vol. 39 no. 3, 2005.

Reda, S. "1-800-Flowers.Com and AT&T Cultivate Relationship Rooted in Common Business Objectives." *Stores*, October 2006.

Rehm, M., and E. André. "From Chatterbots to Natural Interaction—Face-to-Face Communication with Embodied Conversational Agents." *IEICE Transactions on Information and Systems* E88D, no. 11 (2005).

Sackmann S., J. Struker, and R. Accorsi. "Personalization in Privacy-Aware Highly Dynamic Systems." *Communications of the ACM* 49, no. 9 (2006).

Sanders, T. "Extortionists behind Million Dollar DoS Attack." *Computing*, January 19, 2006. **computing.co.uk/vnunet/news/2148849/cyber-criminals-target-pixel** (accessed March 2007).

SAS.com. "Harrah's Hits Customer Loyalty Jackpot." 2006. **sas.com/success/harrahs.html** (accessed October 2006).

Sayclub.com. **sayclub.com** (accessed November 2006).

Schonfeld, E., and J. Borzo. "The Next Disruptors." *Business 2.0*, October 2006.

Sen, A., P. A. Dacin, and C. Pattichis. "Current Trends in Web Data Analysis." *Communications of the ACM* 49, no. 11 (2006).

Shih, Y. Y., and K. Fang. "Overall Satisfaction Prediction," in Khosrow-Pour (2006).

Silverman, B. G., M. Bachann, and K. Al-Akharas. "Implications of Buyer Decision Theory for Design of E-Commerce Web Sites." *International Journal of Human Computer Studies* 55, no. 5 (2001).

Sim, K. M. (eds.). "Learning Approaches for Negotiation Agents and Automated Negotiation." *International Journal of Intelligent Systems* (January 2006).

Sloan, P. "Masters of Their Domains." *Business 2.0*, December 2005.

Sloan, P., and P. Kaihla. "Blogging for Dollars." *Business 2.0*, September 2006.

Sonal, K., and V. Preeta. "Practices, Perception and Avenues of Net-based Promotions." *Electronic Commerce Research* (October 2005).

Stafford, T. F., and A. Urbaczewski. "Spyware: The Ghost in the Machine." *Communications of the Association for Information Systems* 14, no. 15 (2004).

Sweiger, M., J. Langston, H. Lombard, and M. Madsen. *Clickstream Data Warehousing*. New York: Wiley, 2002.

Taylor, C. P. "Is One-to-One the Way to Market?" *Interactive Week*, May 12, 1997.

Tedeschi, B. "E-Commerce Report: New Alternatives to Banner Ads." *New York Times*, February 20, 2001.

Temkin, B. C. "Focus on Customer Experience, Not CRM." *Forrester Research*, September 2002.

TMCnet. "Procter & Gamble Applies RightNow to Deliver Superior Consumer Experience." August 30, 2006. **tmcnet.com/usubmit/2006/08/30/1846211.htm** (accessed October 2006).

Tode, C. "Survey: E-Commerce Leads in Customer Satisfaction." *DMNews*, February 21, 2006.

Turban, E., et al. *Information Technology for Management*, 6th edition. New York: John Wiley and Sons, 2007.

UCLA Center for Communication Policy. "UCLA Internet Report 2004: Surveying the Digital Future, Year 4." UCLA Center for Communication Policy, 2004. **ccp.ucla.edu/pages/NewsTopics.asp?Id=45** (accessed December 2004).

Urban, G. L., F. Sultan, and W. J. Qualls. "Placing Trust at the Center of Your Internet Strategy." *MIT Sloan Management Review* 42, no. 1 (2000).

Vert.net. "Patented Geo-Targeting Technology." 2006. **vert.net/geotargeting.html** (accessed October 2006).

Wang, N. "Marketers Connect with Online Video." *B2B Online*, August 9, 2004. **btobonline.com/article.cms?articleId=13042** (accessed February 2005).

Wang Y., K. L. Tan, and J. Ren. "Towards Autonomous and Automatic Evaluation and Negotiation in Agent-Mediated Internet Marketplaces." *Electronic Commerce Research* (October 2005).

Wang, E. T. G., H. Y. Yeh, and J. J. Jiang. "The Relative Weights of Internet Shopping Fundamental Objectives: Effect of Lifestyle Differences." *Psychology and Marketing* 23, no. 5 (2006).

Westcott, R. "Your Customers Are Talking, but Are You Listening?" *Quality Progress* 39, no. 2 (2006).

Witkowski, T. H. "Cross-Cultural Consumer and Business Research: An Introduction to the Special Section." *Journal of Business Research* 58, no. 1 (2005).

Yeo, A. Y. C., and K. M. Chiam. "E-Customer Loyalty," in Khosrow-Pour (2006).

Yoon, S. "Brand Names Are at the Virtual Mall." *Wall Street Journal Europe*, June 13, 2002.

Yoon, S. J., and J. H. Kim. "Is the Internet More Effective Than Traditional Media? Factors Affecting the Choice of Media." *Journal of Advertising Research* (November–December 2001).

B2B E-COMMERCE: SELLING AND BUYING IN PRIVATE E-MARKETS

Content

General Motors' B2B Initiatives

Managerial Issues

Real-World Case: Eastman Chemical Makes Procurement a Strategic Advantage

Learning Objectives

Upon completion of this chapter, you will be able to:

1. Describe the B2B field.
2. Describe the major types of B2B models.
3. Discuss the characteristics of the sell-side marketplace, including auctions.
4. Describe the sell-side intermediary models.
5. Describe the characteristics of the buy-side marketplace and e-procurement.
6. Explain how reverse auctions work in B2B.
7. Describe B2B aggregation and group-purchasing models.
8. Describe other procurement methods.
9. Explain how B2B administrative tasks can be automated.
10. Describe infrastructure and standards requirements for B2B.
11. Describe Web EDI, XML, and Web Services.

GENERAL MOTORS' B2B INITIATIVES

The Problem

General Motors (GM) is the world's second largest vehicle manufacturer. The company sells autos in 190 countries and has manufacturing plants in about 50. Because the automotive industry is very competitive, GM is always looking for ways to improve its effectiveness. Its most publicized new initiative is a futuristic project with which GM expects to custom build the majority of its cars in a few years. The company hopes to use the system to save billions of dollars by reducing its inventory of finished cars.

In the meantime, GM sells custom-designed cars online through its dealers' sites. Because such online sales are not considered direct marketing to the final consumers, GM is able to avoid *channel conflict* with the non–company-owned dealers. This collaboration requires sharing information with dealers for online marketing and service on cars and on warranties. Both GM and its many dealers also need to collaborate with GM's suppliers. These suppliers work with other automakers as well. Therefore, a good communications system is needed.

Besides the need for effective communication, GM faces many operational problems that are typical of large companies. One of these is an ongoing financial challenge of what to do with manufacturing machines that are no longer sufficiently productive. These capital assets depreciate (lose value) over time and eventually must be replaced. GM traditionally has sold these assets through intermediaries at physical auctions. The problem was that these auctions took weeks, even months, to conclude. Furthermore, the prices obtained at the auctions seemed too low, and a 20 percent commission had to be paid to the third-party auctioneers.

Another operational problem for GM relates to procurement of commodity products, which can be either *direct* materials that go into the vehicles or *indirect* materials, such as light bulbs or office supplies. GM buys about 200,000 different products from 20,000 suppliers, spending over $100 billion annually. The company was using a manual bidding process to negotiate contracts with potential suppliers. Specifications of the needed materials were sent by mail to the potential suppliers, the suppliers would then submit a bid, and GM would select a winner if a supplier offered a low enough price. If all the bids were too high, second and third rounds of bidding were conducted. In some cases, the process took weeks, even months, before GM was confident that the best deal, from both price and quality standpoints, had been achieved. The submission preparation costs involved in this process kept some bidders from submitting bids, so a less than optimal number of suppliers participated, resulting in higher prices paid by GM.

The Solution

To solve the problem of *connecting dealers and suppliers*, GM established an extranet infrastructure called *ANX* (Automotive Network eXchange). ANX, which was supported by other automakers, has evolved into a B2B exchange, Covisint (*covisint.com*), which is described in more detail in Online File W6.2. To address the *capital assets problem*, in early 2000 GM implemented its own electronic market on *covisint.com* from which *forward auctions* are conducted. The first items put up for bid were eight 75-ton stamping presses. GM invited 140 certified bidders to view the pictures and service records of the presses online. After only 1 week of preparation, the auction went live online, and the presses were sold in less than 2 hours.

For the *resource procurement problem*, GM automated the bidding process using *reverse auctions* on its e-procurement site. Qualified suppliers use the Internet to bid on each item GM needs to purchase. Bids are "open," meaning that all bidders can see the bids of their competitors. GM is able to accept bids from many suppliers concurrently and, using predetermined criteria, such as price, delivery date, and payment terms, can award jobs quickly to the most suitable bidder.

The Results

Within just 89 minutes of the opening of the first *forward auction*, eight stamping presses were sold for $1.8 million. With the old offline method, a similar item would have sold for less than half of its online price, and the process would have taken 4 to 6 weeks. Since 2001, GM has conducted hundreds of other electronic auctions. Other sellers were encouraged to put their items up for sale at the site as well, paying GM a commission on the final sales price.

In the first online *reverse auction*, GM purchased a large volume of rubber sealing packages for vehicle production. The price GM paid was significantly lower than the price the company had been paying for the same items previously negotiated by manual tendering. Now, many similar bids are conducted on the site every week. The administrative costs per order have been reduced by 40 percent or more.

Sources: Compiled from Ward's Auto World (2000) and miscellaneous press releases at *gm.com* (accessed August 2002).

WHAT WE CAN LEARN . . .

The GM case demonstrates the involvement of a large company in two EC activities: (1) electronically auctioning used equipment to buyers and (2) conducting purchasing via electronic bidding. The auctioning (selling) and purchasing activities were conducted from GM's *private e-marketplace*, and the transactions were B2B. In B2B transactions, the company may be a seller, offering goods or services to many corporate buyers, or it may be a buyer, seeking goods or services from many corporate sellers (suppliers). When conducting such trades, a company can employ auctions, as GM did, or it can use electronic catalogs or other market mechanisms. These mechanisms and methods are the subject of this chapter.

5.1 CONCEPTS, CHARACTERISTICS, AND MODELS OF B2B EC

B2B EC has some special characteristics as well as specific models and concepts. The major ones are described next.

BASIC B2B CONCEPTS

Business-to-business e-commerce (B2B EC), also known as *eB2B* (*electronic B2B*), or just *B2B*, refers to transactions between businesses conducted electronically over the Internet, extranets, intranets, or private networks (see Mockler et al. 2006; Sadeh 2003; Papazoglou and Ribbers 2006; and Haig 2003). Such transactions may take place between a business and its supply chain members, as well as between a business, its customers, and any other business. In this context, a business refers to any organization, private or public, for profit or nonprofit. The major characteristic of B2B is that companies attempt to electronically automate trading or communication and collaboration processes in order to improve them. Note that B2B commerce can also be done without the Internet.

Key business drivers for B2B are the availability of a secure broadband Internet platform and private and public B2B e-marketplaces; the need for collaborations between suppliers and buyers; the ability to save money, reduce delays, and improve collaboration; and the emergence of effective technologies for intra- and interorganizational integration. (See en.wikipedia.org/Wiki/B2B_ecommerce.)

business-to-business e-commerce (B2B EC) Transactions between businesses conducted electronically over the Internet, extranets, intranets, or private networks; also known as *eB2B* (*electronic B2B*) or just *B2B*.

MARKET SIZE AND CONTENT OF B2B

First let's look at the total B2B market. Gartner (*ePaynews* 2004, 2005) estimated that the worldwide B2B transaction volume in 2005 was $8.5 trillion. Market forecasters estimate that by 2008 the global B2B market (online and offline) may reach $10 trillion. Harris (2006) reports an Interactive Data Corporation (IDC) estimate of $1 trillion B2B online sales, approaching 10 percent of the total B2B market. Chemicals, computer electronics, utilities, agriculture, shipping and warehousing, motor vehicles, petrochemicals, paper and office products, and food are the leading items in B2B. According to *eMarketer* (2003), the dollar value of B2B comprises at least 85 percent of the total transaction value of e-commerce.

The B2B market, which went through major consolidation in 2000–2001, is growing rapidly. Different B2B market forecasters use different definitions and methodologies. Because of this, predictions frequently change and statistical data often differ. Therefore, we will not provide any more estimates here. Data sources that can be checked for the latest information on the B2B market are provided in Chapter 3 (Exhibit 3.1).

B2B EC is now in its fifth generation, as shown in Exhibit 5.1. This generation includes collaboration with suppliers, buyers, and other business partners (see Chapter 7), internal and external supply chain improvements (Chapter 7), and expert (intelligent) sales systems. Note that older generations coexist with new ones. Also, some companies are still using only EC from early generations. In this chapter, we mainly describe topics from the second and third generations. Topics from the fourth and fifth generations are covered in Chapters 6 through 13.

THE BASIC TYPES OF B2B TRANSACTIONS AND ACTIVITIES

The number of sellers and buyers and the form of participation used in B2B determine the basic B2B transaction types:

- ❱ **Sell-side.** One seller to many buyers (covered in Chapter 5)
- ❱ **Buy-side.** One buyer from many sellers (covered in Chapter 5)
- ❱ **Exchanges.** Many sellers to many buyers (covered in Chapter 6)
- ❱ **Supply chain improvements and collaborative commerce.** Activities other than buying or selling among business partners, for example, supply chain improvements, communicating, collaborating, and sharing of information for joint design, planning, and so on (covered in Chapter 7)

Exhibit 5.2 illustrates these four B2B types.

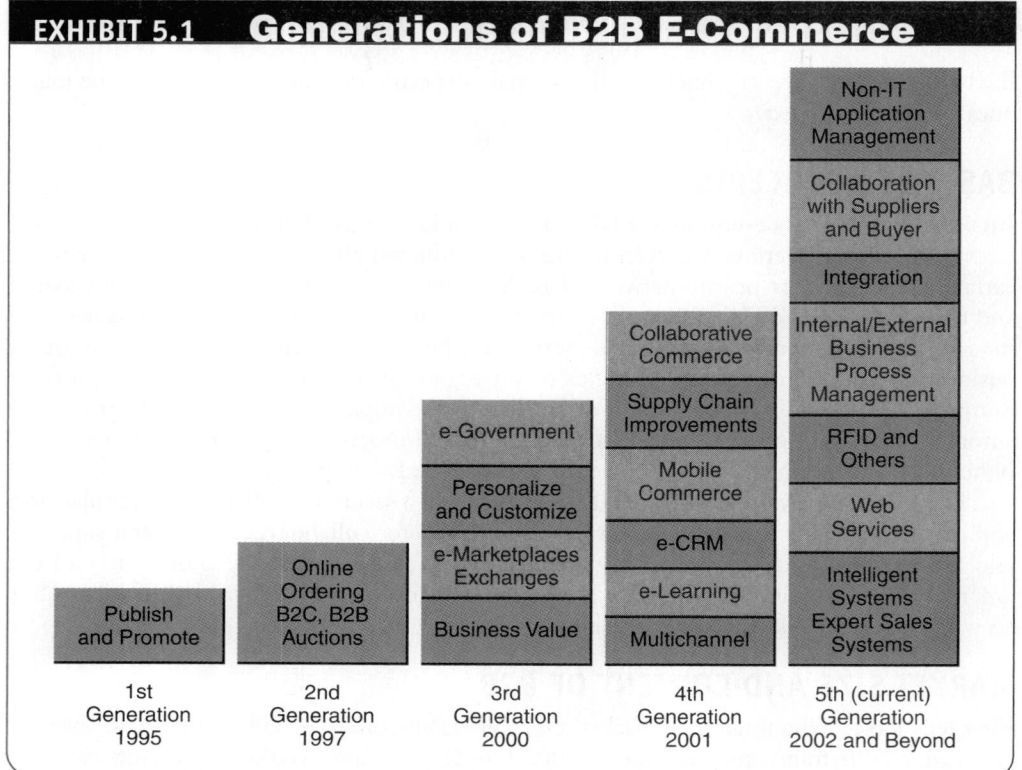

EXHIBIT 5.1   Generations of B2B E-Commerce

1st Generation 1995	2nd Generation 1997	3rd Generation 2000	4th Generation 2001	5th (current) Generation 2002 and Beyond
Publish and Promote	Online Ordering B2C, B2B Auctions	Business Value; e-Marketplaces Exchanges; Personalize and Customize; e-Government	Multichannel; e-Learning; e-CRM; Mobile Commerce; Supply Chain Improvements; Collaborative Commerce	Intelligent Systems Expert Sales Systems; Web Services; RFID and Others; Internal/External Business Process Management; Integration; Collaboration with Suppliers and Buyer; Non-IT Application Management

Source: Based on Gartner Inc. (2000).

EXHIBIT 5.2   Types of B2B E-Commerce

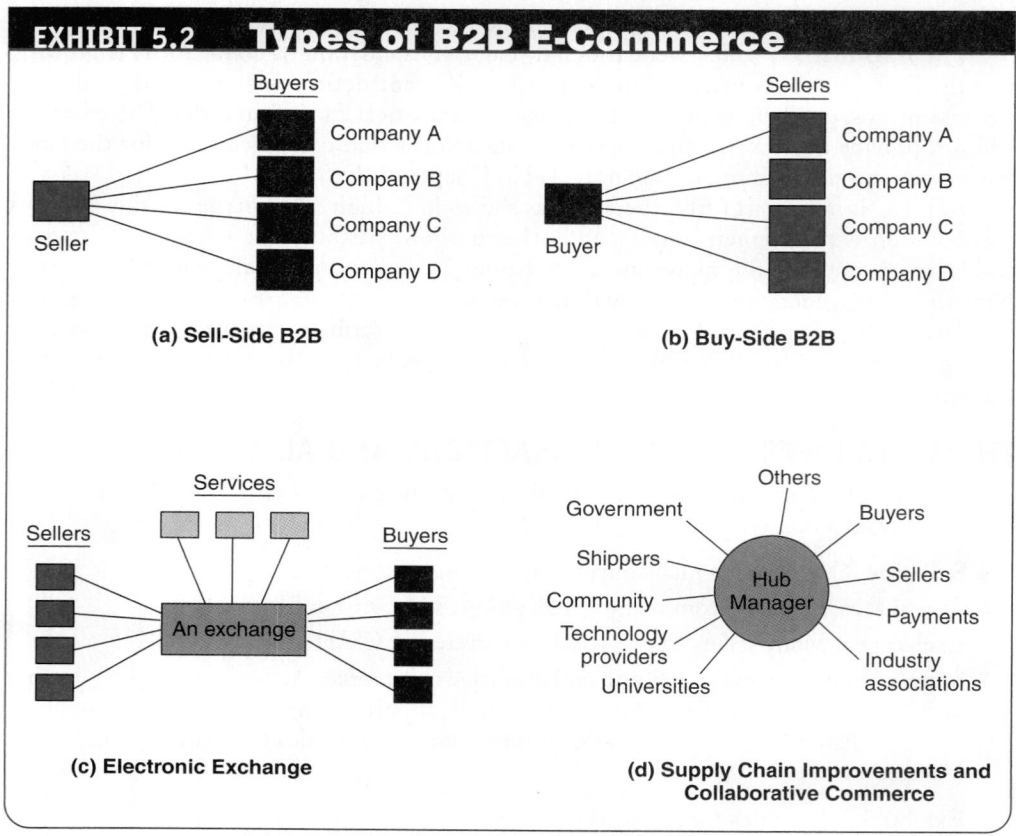

(a) Sell-Side B2B

(b) Buy-Side B2B

(c) Electronic Exchange

(d) Supply Chain Improvements and Collaborative Commerce

THE BASIC TYPES OF B2B E-MARKETPLACES AND SERVICES

The following are the basic types of B2B e-marketplaces.

One-to-Many and Many-to-One: Private E-Marketplaces

In one-to-many and many-to-one markets, one company does either all of the selling (*sell-side market*) or all of the buying (*buy-side market*). Because EC is focused on a single company's buying or selling needs in these transactions, this type of EC is referred to as **company-centric EC**. Company-centric marketplaces—both sell-side and buy-side—are the topic of this chapter.

In company-centric marketplaces, the individual sell-side or buy-side company has complete control over who participates in the selling or buying transaction and the supporting information systems. Thus, these transactions are essentially private. Therefore, sell-side and buy-side markets are considered **private e-marketplaces**. They may be at the sellers' Web sites or hosted by a third party.

company-centric EC
E-commerce that focuses on a single company's buying needs (many-to-one, or buy-side) or selling needs (one-to-many, or sell-side).

private e-marketplaces
Markets in which the individual sell-side or buy-side company has complete control over participation in the selling or buying transaction.

Intermediaries

Many one-to-many or many-to-one EC activities are conducted without the help of intermediaries. However, when it comes to auctions, aggregating buyers, or complex transactions, an intermediary frequently is used. (Even when an intermediary is used, the market is still considered private, because the single buyer or seller that hires the intermediary may maintain control of who is invited to participate in the market.)

Many-to-Many: Exchanges

In many-to-many e-marketplaces, many buyers and many sellers meet electronically for the purpose of trading with one another. There are different types of such e-marketplaces, which are also known as **exchanges, trading communities,** or **trading exchanges**. We will use the term *exchanges* in this book. Exchanges are usually owned and run by a third party or by a consortium. They are described in more detail in Chapter 6. Exchanges are open to all interested parties (sellers and buyers), and thus are considered **public e-marketplaces**.

exchanges (trading communities or trading exchanges)
Many-to-many e-marketplaces, usually owned and run by a third party or a consortium, in which many buyers and many sellers meet electronically to trade with each other.

public e-marketplaces
Third-party exchanges that are open to all interested parties (sellers and buyers).

Supply Chain Activities and Collaborative Commerce

B2B transactions are segments in the supply chain. Therefore, B2B initiatives need to be examined in light of other supply chain activities such as manufacturing, procurement of raw materials and shipments, and logistics (Chapter 13). Supply chain activities usually involve communication and collaboration.

Businesses deal with other businesses for purposes beyond just selling or buying. One example is that of *collaborative commerce*, which is communication, design, planning, and information sharing among business partners. To qualify as collaborative commerce, the activities that are shared must represent far more than just financial transactions. For example, they may include activities related to design, manufacture, or management. Supply chain issues and collaborative commerce are described in Chapter 7.

B2B2C

A special case of B2B is B2B2C (see the Godiva case in Chapter 1). With B2B2C, a business sells to a business but delivers small quantities to customers (individuals or business) of the buying business.

B2B CHARACTERISTICS

Similar to the classic story of the blind men trying to describe an elephant, B2B can be described in a variety of ways, depending on which characteristic is the focus. Here we examine various qualities by which B2B transactions can be characterized.

Parties to the Transaction: Sellers, Buyers, and Intermediaries

B2B commerce can be conducted *directly* between a *customer* and a *manufacturer* or it can be conducted via an **online intermediary**. The intermediary is an online third party that brokers the transaction between the buyer and seller; it may be a virtual intermediary or a click-and-mortar

online intermediary
An online third party that brokers a transaction online between a buyer and a seller; may be virtual or click-and-mortar.

intermediary. See Papazoglou and Ribbers (2006) for details. Some of the electronic intermediaries for consumers mentioned in Chapter 3 also can be referenced for B2B by replacing the individual consumers with business customers. Consolidators of buyers or sellers are typical B2B intermediaries (Section 5.3). Intermediaries can be distributors.

Types of Transactions

B2B transactions are of two basic types: spot buying and strategic sourcing. **Spot buying** refers to the purchasing of goods and services as they are needed, usually at prevailing market prices, which are determined dynamically by supply and demand. The buyers and the sellers may not even know each other. Stock exchanges and commodity exchanges (oil, sugar, corn, etc.) are examples of spot buying. In contrast, **strategic (systematic) sourcing** involves purchases based on *long-term contracts*.

Spot buying may be conducted most economically on the public exchanges. Strategic purchases can be supported more effectively and efficiently through direct buyer–seller offline or online negotiations, which can be done in private exchanges or private trading rooms in public exchanges.

Types of Materials Traded

Two types of materials and supplies are traded in B2B: direct and indirect. **Direct materials** are materials used in making the products, such as steel in a car or paper in a book. The characteristics of direct materials are that their use is usually scheduled and planned for. They are usually not shelf items, and they are frequently purchased in large quantities after extensive negotiation and contracting.

Indirect materials are items, such as office supplies or light bulbs, that support production. They are usually used in **maintenance, repair, and operation (MRO)** activities. Collectively, they are known as nonproduction materials.

Direction of Trade

B2B marketplaces may be classified as vertical or horizontal. **Vertical marketplaces** are those that deal with one industry or industry segment. Examples include marketplaces specializing in electronics, cars, hospital supplies, steel, or chemicals. **Horizontal marketplaces** are those that concentrate on a service or a product that is used in all types of industries. Examples are office supplies, PCs, or travel services.

The various characteristics of B2B transactions are presented in summary form in Insights and Additions 5.1.

SUPPLY CHAIN RELATIONSHIPS IN B2B

In the various B2B transaction types, business activities are usually conducted along the supply chain of a company. The supply chain process consists of a number of interrelated subprocesses and roles. These extend from the acquisition of materials from suppliers, to the processing of a product or service, to packaging it and moving it to distributors and retailers. The process ends with the eventual purchase of a product by the end consumer. B2B can make supply chains more efficient and effective or it can change the supply chain completely, eliminating one or more intermediaries (see Sadeh 2003).

Historically, many of the segments and processes in the supply chain have been managed through paper transactions (e.g., purchase orders, invoices, and so forth). B2B applications are offered online so they can serve as supply chain enablers that offer distinct competitive advantages. Supply chain management also encompasses the coordination of order generation, order taking, and order fulfillment and distribution (see Chapters 7, 13, and Online Tutorial T2 for more discussion of supply chain management).

Hoffman et al. (2002) looked at the effect of various B2B types on supply chain relationships. They found, for example, that a B2B private e-marketplace provides a company with high supply chain power and high capabilities for online interactions. This is basically how much bargaining and control power a company has. Joining a public e-marketplace, however, provides a business with high buying and selling capabilities but will result in low supply chain power. Companies that choose an intermediary to do their buying and selling will be low on

spot buying
The purchase of goods and services as they are needed, usually at prevailing market prices.

strategic (systematic) sourcing
Purchases involving long-term contracts that usually are based on private negotiations between sellers and buyers.

direct materials
Materials used in the production of a product (e.g., steel in a car or paper in a book).

indirect materials
Materials used to support production (e.g., office supplies or light bulbs).

MRO (maintenance, repair, and operation)
Indirect materials used in activities that support production.

vertical marketplaces
Markets that deal with one industry or industry segment (e.g., steel, chemicals).

horizontal marketplaces
Markets that concentrate on a service, materials, or a product that is used in all types of industries (e.g., office supplies, PCs).

Insights and Additions 5.1 Summary of B2B Characteristics

Parties to Transactions	Types of Transactions
Direct, seller to buyer or buyer to seller	Spot buying
Via intermediaries	Strategic sourcing
B2B2C: A business sells to a business but delivers to individual consumers	Spot buying
Types of Materials Sold	**Direction of Trade**
Direct	Vertical
Indirect (MROs)	Horizontal
Number and Form of Participation	**Degree of Openness**
One-to-many: Sell-side (e-storefront)	Private exchanges, restricted
Many-to-one: Buy-side	Private exchanges, restricted
Many-to-many: Exchanges	Public exchanges, open to all
Many, connected: Collaborative, supply chain	Private (usually), can be public

both supply chain power and buying/selling capabilities. Hoffman et al. (2002) recommend private e-marketplaces as most likely to result in effective supply chain relationships.

A major reason for companies to collaborate is to improve their joint supply chain. In Chapter 7, we illustrate how Cisco lost a large amount of money due to lack of collaboration along the supply chain.

VIRTUAL SERVICE INDUSTRIES IN B2B

In addition to trading products between businesses, services also can be provided electronically in B2B. Just as service industries such as banking, insurance, real estate, and stock trading can be conducted electronically for individuals, as described in Chapter 3, so they can be conducted electronically for businesses. The major B2B services are:

▶ **Travel and hospitality services.** Many large corporations arrange their travel electronically through corporate travel agents. To further reduce costs, companies can make special arrangements that enable employees to plan and book their own trips online. For instance, American Express Business Travel (formerly Rosenbluth International, see Online File W2.10) offers several tools to help corporate travel managers plan and control employee travel. In addition to traditional scheduling and control tools, in 2006 it started offering the following EC-based tools:

  ▶ *TrackPoint* enables travel managers, as well as security and risk professionals, to pinpoint a traveler's whereabouts at any time.

  ▶ *Travel Alert* and *Info Point* are information services that provide details about specific travel destinations. They are available free of charge to American Express Business Travel Clients.

  ▶ *Travel Insight Plus* consulting service identifies specific opportunities for savings in air travel expenditure for a given organization. The consulting study compares the client company's air travel expenditure against that of its true peers—other organizations that travel similar routes, over similar periods, with comparable volumes. Savings are identified through two key comparisons: the difference between the client and peer group's average spending on a route as well as highlighting the number of peers that are paying a lower average fare than the client's.

    Expedia, Travelocity, Orbitz, and other online travel services provide B2B services as well.

▶ **Real estate.** Commercial real estate transactions can be large and complex. Therefore, the Web may not be able to completely replace existing human agents. Instead, the Web can help businesses find the right properties, compare properties, and assist in negotiations. Some government-run foreclosed real estate auctions are open only to corporate real estate dealers and are conducted online.

▶ **Financial services.** Internet banking is an economical way of making business payments, transferring funds, or performing other financial transactions. For example, electronic funds transfer (EFT) is popular with businesses. Transaction fees over the Internet are less costly than any other alternative method. To see how payments work in B2B, see Chapter 12. Businesses can also purchase insurance online, both from pure online insurance companies and from click-and-mortar ones.

▶ **Online stock trading.** Some corporations are large stock investors. Online trading services are very attractive to institutional investors because fees for online trading are very low and flat, regardless of the trading amount. Most institutional investment is facilitated by electronic trading.

▶ **Online financing.** Business loans can be solicited online from lenders. Bank of America, for example, offers its commercial customers a matching service on IntraLoan (the bank's global loan syndication service), which uses an extranet to match business loan applicants with potential lending corporations. Several sites, such as garage.com, provide information about venture capital.

▶ **Other online services.** Consulting services, law firms, health organizations, and others sell knowledge and special services online. Many other online services, such as the purchase of electronic stamps (similar to metered postage, but generated on a computer), are available online (see stamps.com). Also, recruiting and staffing services are done online.

THE BENEFITS AND LIMITATIONS OF B2B

The benefits of B2B depend on which model is used. In general, though, the major benefits of B2B are that it:

▶ Creates new sales (purchase) opportunities
▶ Eliminates paper and reduces administrative costs
▶ Expedites processing and reduces cycle time
▶ Lowers search costs and time for buyers to find products and vendors
▶ Increases productivity of employees dealing with buying and/or selling
▶ Reduces errors and improves quality of services
▶ Makes product configuration easier
▶ Reduces marketing and sales costs (for sellers)
▶ Reduces inventory levels and costs
▶ Enables customized online catalogs with different prices for different customers
▶ Increases production flexibility, permitting just-in-time delivery
▶ Reduces procurement costs (for buyers)
▶ Facilitates customization via configuration (e.g., at Cisco)
▶ Provides for efficient customer service
▶ Increases opportunities for collaboration

B2B EC has limitations as well, especially regarding channel conflict and the operation of public exchanges. These will be discussed later in this chapter and in Chapter 6.

The introduction of B2B may eliminate the distributor or the retailer, which could be a benefit to the seller and the buyer (though not a benefit to the distributor or retailer). In previous chapters, such a phenomenon is referred to as *disintermediation* (Chapters 2 and 3).

In the remainder of the chapter, we will look at the company-centric B2B models and topics introduced in this opening section in more depth.

Section 5.1 ▶ REVIEW QUESTIONS

1. Define B2B.
2. Discuss the following: spot buying versus strategic sourcing, direct materials versus indirect materials, and vertical markets versus horizontal markets.
3. What are company-centric marketplaces? Are they public or private?
4. Define B2B exchanges.
5. Relate the supply chain to B2B transactions.
6. List the B2B online services.
7. Summarize the benefits and limitations of B2B.

5.2 ONE-TO-MANY: SELL-SIDE E-MARKETPLACES

Many B2B activities involve direct selling.

SELL-SIDE MODELS AND ACTIVITIES

In Chapter 3, we introduced the direct-selling B2C model in which a manufacturer or a retailer sells electronically directly to consumers from a *storefront*. In a **sell-side e-marketplace** a business sells products and services to business customers, frequently over an extranet. The seller can be a manufacturer selling to a wholesaler, to a retailer, or to an individual business. Intel, Cisco, and Dell are examples of such sellers. Or the seller can be a distributor selling to wholesalers, to retailers, or to businesses (e.g., W. W. Grainger). In either case, sell-side e-marketplaces involve one seller and many potential buyers. In this model, both individual consumers and business buyers may use the same sell-side marketplace (e.g., dell.com), or they may use different marketplaces. Exhibit 5.3 shows the architecture of sell-side B2B marketplaces, as compared to that of B2C (left side of figure).

The architecture of this B2B model is similar to that of B2C EC. The major differences are in the process (see Jakovljevic 2004). For example, in B2B, large customers may be provided with customized catalogs and prices. Usually, companies will separate B2C orders from B2B orders. One reason for this is that B2C and B2B orders have different *order-fulfillment processes* (see Chapter 13) and different pricing models, i.e., wholesale v. retail pricing. Technology

sell-side e-marketplace
A Web-based marketplace in which one company sells to many business buyers from e-catalogs or auctions, frequently over an extranet.

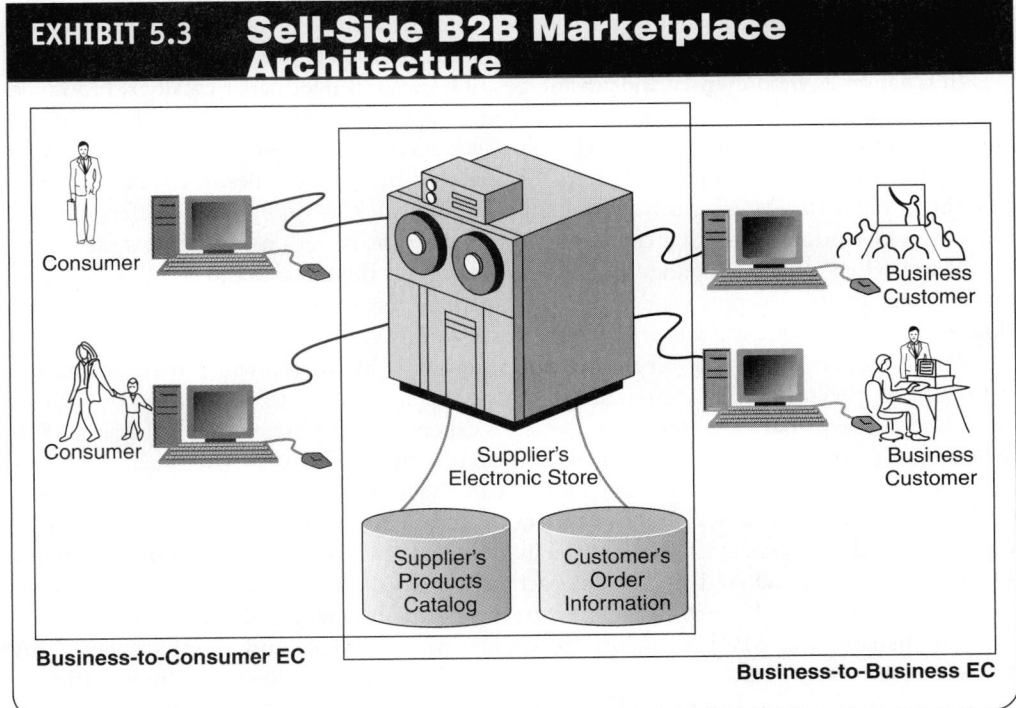

EXHIBIT 5.3   Sell-Side B2B Marketplace Architecture

Consumer

Consumer

Supplier's Electronic Store

Supplier's Products Catalog

Customer's Order Information

Business Customer

Business Customer

Business-to-Consumer EC

Business-to-Business EC

supports the ability to identify the customer and determine whether its a b or c customer and transact the order appropriately.

The one-to-many model has three major marketing methods: (1) selling from *electronic catalogs*; (2) selling via *forward auctions* (as GM does with its old equipment); and (3) *one-to-one* selling, usually under a *negotiated* long-term contract. Such one-to-one negotiating is familiar: The buying company negotiates price, quantity, payments, delivery, and quality terms with the selling company (see Section 5.8). We describe the first method in this section and the second in Section 5.3. For methods of improving B2B selling, see Hancock et al. (2005).

B2B Sellers

Sellers in the sell-side marketplace may be click-and-mortar manufacturers or intermediaries (e.g., distributors or wholesalers). The intermediaries may even be online pure companies (virtual), as in the case of Bigboxx.com, described in Online File W5.1.

Customer Service

Online sellers can provide sophisticated customer services. For example, General Electric receives 20 million calls a year regarding appliances. Although most of these calls come from individuals, many come from businesses. By using the Internet and automatic-response software agents (autoresponders), GE has reduced the cost of handling calls from $5 per call when done by phone to $0.20 per electronically answered call. Patton (2006) estimated that a call handled by a human agent costs $2 to $10. If answered automatically (e.g., autoresponder, interactive voice response [IVR]), the cost is between $.02 and $.20.

Another example of B2B customer service is that of Milacron, Inc., which produces consumable industrial products for metalworking. The company launched an award-winning EC site aimed at its more than 100,000 SME customers. The site provides an easy-to-use and secure way of selecting, purchasing, and arranging delivery (if needed) of Milacron's 55,000 products. From this site, the SMEs also can access a level of technical service beyond that provided previously to even Milacron's largest customers (see milacron.com).

We now turn our attention to the first of the sell-side methods—selling from electronic catalogs.

DIRECT SALES FROM CATALOGS

Companies can use the Internet to sell directly from their online catalogs. A company may offer one catalog for all customers or a *customized catalog* for each large customer (usually both).

In Chapter 2, we presented the advantages of e-catalogs over paper catalogs. However, this model may not be convenient for large and repetitive business buyers because the buyer's order information is stored in the supplier's server and is not easily integrated with the buyer's corporate information system. To facilitate B2B direct sales, the seller can provide the buyer with a buyer-customized shopping cart (such as Bigboxx.com offers), which can store order information that can be integrated with the buyer's information system.

Many sellers provide separate pages and catalogs to their major buyers. For example, Staples.com, an office-supply vendor, offers its business customers personalized software catalogs of about 100,000 products and pricing at stapleslink.com.

Another example of B2B direct sales from catalogs is Microsoft, which uses an extranet instead of an Electronic Data Interchange that is the application to application transfer of business documents between computers, which is expensive (see Chapter 6), to sell about $10 billion of software annually to its channel partners (distributors). Using Microsoft's extranet-based order-entry tool (MOET), distributors can check inventory, make transactions, and look up the status of orders. The online orders are automatically fed into the customer's SAP applications. MOET was started in Europe in 1997 and has since been rolled out worldwide. The extranet handles about 1 million transactions per year. The system significantly reduces the number of phone calls, e-mails, and incorrect product shipments (Microsoft 2006).

For distributors, MOET makes the order process faster and more efficient; for Microsoft, it ensures vendor compliance with business rules and allows for a more efficient use of internal resources. The bottom line is improved productivity and profitability for all.

CASE 5.1

EC Application

GREGG'S CYCLES GOES ONLINE

Reputable bicycle manufacturers such as Gregg's Cycles do not sell their products online, nor do they allow their bicycles to be sold online by others. These manufacturers also try to avoid conflicts with their dealers and the independent bike shops that sell their bikes. Gregg's Cycles believes that selling bikes is as much as about customer service as it is about the product.

Each bike sold in one of Gregg's stores is fitted to the customer and often customized for the rider in one way or another. This type of customer service cannot be done online. Therefore, when Gregg's Cycles decided to build a Web site, it decided to display all its bikes online so that customers could see the huge selection as well as use the site as a resource to learn about the bikes. As a bonus, the software Gregg's chose, CartGenie from J Street Technology, made it easy to sell online peripheral products, such as parts, clothing, accessories, and complementary products, such as snowboards and inline skates.

With the CartGenie software the company is able to show the specs of each bike so that viewers can compare up to three bikes on one screen. Oftentimes, customers come into the company's physical stores armed with printouts from the Web site, knowing exactly what they want. In addition, the site displays inventory availability. If a store has the bike that the customers are looking for, they will quickly come to the store to get their bike.

The online store now carries over 7,000 SKUs and caters to customers across the United States. Gregg's makes sure to mention its Web site address in all of its print ads and promotions. It also publishes an online newsletter to keep in touch with customers.

CartGenie enables bulk import of products to the corporate catalog, a most useful feature. Another useful feature is CartGenie Connect, which automatically updates pricing and availability. CartGenie Connect also takes

information directly from the point-of-sale database and syncs it with the online database. With over 7,000 SKUs, it would be close to impossible for a person to keep the site up-to-date.

CartGenie is available in the Standard, Pro, and Enterprise Editions. Key features include:

- Full support for B2B and B2C selling
- Multiple retail and wholesale price levels
- A built-in comparison engine for doing side-by-side product comparisons
- A complete inventory control module
- Integrated UPS shipping calculator
- Volume discount pricing
- Search engine friendly product catalog system
- Integration with PayPal
- Built-in product import utilities
- Full support for real-time credit card processing

The Web site also offers information on customizing bikes, bicycle repair, bike rental, blogging, store locations, job opportunities, coupons, bike events, and more. Customers love the Web site; the company gets favorable responses from most who send comments.

Sources: Compiled from Rincon (2006), from *greggcycles.com* (accessed October 2006), and from *jstreettech.com* (accessed October 2006).

Questions

1. Why is this a B2B sell-side case?
2. What are the benefits of this type of Web site for the company?
3. Relate the case to social networks.
4. How does CartGenie support the site?

In selling directly, manufacturers may encounter a similar problem to that of B2C, namely conflict with the regular distributors, including corporate dealers (channel conflict). An interesting solution is illustrated in Case 5.1, where Gregg's Cycles sells online (both B2B and B2C) but not its major product (bicycles), instead selling peripheral products, such as parts and accessories.

Configuration and Customization

As with B2C EC, B2B direct sales offer an opportunity for efficient customization (e.g., see Dell case in Chapter 1 and the Cisco case later in this chapter). As we will see in the case of Cisco, manufacturers can provide online tools for self-configuration, pricing, ordering, and so on. Business customers can customize products, get price quotes, and submit orders, all online.

Many click-and-mortar companies use a *multichannel distribution system*, in which the Internet is a new, but supplemental, channel that enables greater efficiency in the ordering process, as shown in the case of Whirlpool in Case 5.2.

CASE 5.2

EC Application

WHIRLPOOL B2B TRADING PORTAL

Whirlpool (*whirlpool.com*) is a $13-billion global corporation based in Benton Harbor, Michigan. It is in the company's best interest to operate efficiently and to offer as much customer service for the members (partners) of its selling chain as possible. It is a complex job, because the partners are located in 170 countries. Middle-tier partners, who comprise 25 percent of the total partner base and 10 percent of Whirlpool's annual revenue, were submitting their orders by phone or fax because they were not large enough to have system-to-system computer connections direct to Whirlpool.

To improve customer service for these dealers, Whirlpool developed a B2B trading partner portal (Whirlpool Web World), using IBM e-business solutions. The technologies enable fast, easy Web self-service ordering processes. Using these self-service processes, Whirlpool was able to cut the cost per order to under $5—a savings of 80 percent.

The company tested ordering via the Web by developing a portal for low-level products. It was so successful (resulting in a 100 percent ROI during the first 8 months of use) that Whirlpool went to a second-generation portal, which services the middle-tier partners. The Whirlpool Web World allows middle-tier trade partners to place orders and track their status through a password-protected site.

Simultaneously, the company implemented SAP R/3 for order entry, which is utilized by the middle-tier partners on the second-generation portal. The company also is using IBM's Application Framework for e-business, taking advantage of its rapid development cycles and associated cost reductions.

Whirlpool's global platform provides its operations with resources and capabilities few other manufacturers can match. Whirlpool's global procurement, product development, and information technology organizations help the company's operations reduce costs, improve efficiencies, and introduce a continuous stream of relevant innovation to consumers.

Using the same IBM platform, Whirlpool launched a B2C site for U.S. customers for ordering small appliances and accessories. The site was so successful that the company realized a 100 percent ROI in just 5 months.

Sources: Compiled from IBM (2000) and *whirlpoolcorp.com* (accessed September 2006).

Questions

1. How do Whirlpool's customers benefit from the portal?
2. What are the benefits of the trading portal for Whirlpool?
3. Relate the B2B sell-side to a B2C storefront.

Benefits and Limitations of Direct Sales from Catalogs

Successful examples of the B2B direct sales model include manufacturers, such as Dell, Intel, IBM, and Cisco, and distributors, such as Ingram Micro (which sells to value-added retailers; the retailer adds some service along with the product). Sellers that use this model may be successful as long as they have a superb reputation in the market and a large enough group of loyal customers.

Although the benefits of direct sales are similar to that of B2C, there also are limitations. One of the major issues facing direct sellers is how to find buyers. Many companies know how to advertise in traditional channels but are still learning how to contact would-be buyers online. Also, B2B sellers may experience channel conflicts with their existing distribution systems. Another limitation is that if traditional EDI (the computer-to-computer direct transfer of business documents) is used, the cost to the customers can be high, and they will be reluctant to go online. The solution to this problem is the transfer of documents over the extranets (see Appendix 6A). Finally, the number of business partners online must be large enough to justify the system infrastructure and operation and maintenance expenses.

DIRECT SALES: THE EXAMPLE OF CISCO SYSTEMS

Cisco Systems (cisco.com) is the world's leading producer of routers, switches, and network interconnection services. Cisco's portal has evolved over several years, beginning with technical support for customers and developing into one of the world's largest direct sales EC sites. Today, Cisco offers about a dozen Internet-based applications to both end-user businesses and reseller partners (see Slater 2003).

Customer Service

Cisco began providing electronic support in 1991 using value-added networks (VANs). The first applications offered were software downloads, defects diagnosis, and technical advice. In spring 1994, Cisco moved its system to the Web and named it Cisco Connection Online (CCO). By 2004, Cisco's customers and reseller partners were logging onto Cisco's Web site over 2 million times a month to receive technical assistance, place and check orders, or download software. The online service has been so well received that nearly 85 percent of all customer service inquiries and 95 percent of software updates are delivered online. The service is delivered globally in 16 languages. The CCO is considered a model for B2B success, and several books have been written about it (e.g., Slater 2003).

Online Ordering by Customers

Virtually all of Cisco's products are made-to-order. Before CCO, ordering a product was a lengthy, complicated, and error-prone process because it was done by fax or by "snail mail." Cisco began deploying Web-based commerce tools in July 1995, and within a year its Internet Product Center allowed users to configure and purchase any Cisco product over the Web. Today, a business customer's engineer can sit down at a PC, configure a product, and find out immediately if there are any errors in the configuration (some feedback is given by intelligent agents).

By providing online pricing and configuration tools to customers, 99 percent of orders are now placed through CCO, saving time for both Cisco and its customers. In the first 5 months of online ordering operations in 1996, Cisco booked over $100 million in online sales. This figure grew to $4 billion in 1998, to over $8 billion in 2002, and to about $12 billion in 2005 (Cisco Annual Report 2005).

TRACKING ORDER STATUS

Each month Cisco used to receive over 150,000 order-status inquiries such as, "When will my order be ready?" "How should the order be classified for customs?" "Is the product eligible for NAFTA agreement?" "What export control issues apply?" Cisco provides self-tracking and FAQ tools so that customers can find the answers to many of their questions by themselves. In addition, the company's primary domestic and international freight forwarders update Cisco's database electronically about the status of each shipment. CCO can record the shipping date, the method of shipment, and the current location of each product. All new information is made available to customers immediately. As soon as an order ships, Cisco notifies the customer via e-mail.

Benefits

Cisco reaps many benefits from the CCO system. The most important benefits include the following, per Interwoven (2001):

- **Reduced operating costs for order taking.** By taking its order process online in 1998, Cisco has saved $363 million per year, or approximately 17.5 percent of its total operating costs. This is due primarily to increased productivity of the employees who take and process orders.
- **Improved quality.** The system facilitates the Six Sigma mission of Cisco.
- **Enhanced technical support and customer service.** With more than 85 percent of its technical support and customer service calls handled online, Cisco's technical support productivity has increased by 250 percent per year.
- **Reduced technical support staff cost.** Online technical support has reduced technical support staff costs by roughly $125 million each year.
- **Reduced software distribution costs.** Customers download new software releases directly from Cisco's site, saving the company $180 million in distribution, packaging, and duplicating costs each year. Having product and pricing information on the Web and Web-based CD-ROMs saves Cisco an additional $50 million annually in printing and distributing catalogs and marketing materials to customers.
- **Faster service.** Lead times were reduced from 4–10 days to 2–3 days.

The CCO system also benefits customers. Cisco customers can configure orders more quickly, immediately determine costs, and collaborate much more rapidly and effectively with Cisco's staff. Also, customer service and technical support are faster.

In 2006, Cisco moved to selling its hardware (routers and switches and VoIP) and the software that powers them separately. This unbundling gives customers more flexibility (see Hoover 2006).

Section 5.2 ▶ REVIEW QUESTIONS

1. List the types of sell-side B2B transaction models.
2. Distinguish between the use and nonuse of intermediaries in B2B sell-side transactions.
3. What are buy-side and sell-side transactions? How do they differ?
4. Describe customer service in B2B systems.
5. Describe direct B2B sales from catalogs.
6. Discuss the benefits and limitations of direct B2B sales from catalogs.
7. Describe Cisco's B2B activities and list their benefits to Cisco and to its customers.

5.3 SELLING VIA INTERMEDIARIES AND DISTRIBUTORS

Manufacturers frequently use intermediaries to distribute their products to a large number of buyers, many of which are known as *distributors*. The intermediaries usually buy products from many vendors and aggregate them into one catalog from which they sell. Now, many of these distributors also are selling online.

As in B2C, many distributors (including retailers) also offer their products online via store-fronts. Some well-known online distributors for businesses are SAM's Club (of Wal-Mart), Avnet, and W. W. Grainger. Most e-distributors sell in horizontal markets, meaning that they sell to businesses in a variety of industries. However, some specialize in one industry (vertical market), such as Boeing PART (see Online File W5.2). A well-known intermediary of electrical parts is Marshall Industries. Its story is provided in Online File W5.3. Most intermediaries sell at fixed prices; however, some offer quantity discounts.

The case of W. W. Grainger is provided in Case 5.3.

Section 5.3 ▶ REVIEW QUESTIONS

1. What are the advantages of using intermediaries in B2B sales?
2. What special services are provided to buyers by Boeing Parts? (Online File W5.2)
3. Compare Grainger's case with Marshall's (Online File W5.3). What are the common elements? What are the differences?
4. Compare an e-distributor in B2B to Amazon.com. What are the similarities? What are the differences?

5.4 SELLING VIA AUCTIONS

Auctions are gaining popularity as a B2B sales channel (see Dasgupta et al. 2006). Some major B2B auction issues are discussed in this section.

USING AUCTIONS ON THE SELL SIDE

As you read in the opening case study, GM uses *forward auctions* to sell its unneeded capital assets. In such a situation, items are displayed on an auction site (private or public) for quick disposal. Forward auctions offer a number of benefits to B2B sellers:

▶ **Revenue generation.** Forward auctions support and expand online and overall sales. For example, Weirton Steel Corp. doubled its customer base when it started forward auctions (Fickel 1999). Forward auctions also offer businesses a new venue for quickly and easily disposing of excess, obsolete, and returned products (e.g., liquidation.com).

CASE 5.3
EC Application
W. W. GRAINGER AND GOODRICH CORPORATION

W. W. Grainger has a number of Web sites, but its flagship is *grainger.com*. In 2005, of Grainger's $6 billion in annual sales, more than $600 million was done over the Web, with the majority of those sales placed through *grainger.com*.

More than 800,000 brand-name MRO supplies from more than 1,000 suppliers are offered at *grainger.com*, and a growing number of Grainger's 2.2 million customers are ordering online. The Web site continues the same kind of customer service and wide range of industrial products provided by Grainger's traditional offline business with the additional convenience of 24/7 ordering, use of search engines, and additional services.

This convenience is what first attracted BFGoodrich Aerospace (now called Goodrich Corporation) in Pueblo, Colorado. It found *grainger.com* to be one of the most convenient and easy purchasing sites to use. The purchasing agent of this small Goodrich plant of approximately 250 employees used to call in an order to a supplier, give the salesperson a part number, and wait until the price could be pulled up. Goodrich's purchaser now can place orders online in a matter of minutes, and the purchaser's display has Goodrich's negotiated pricing built in.

Goodrich can get just about anything it needs from *grainger.com*. Grainger interfaces with other suppliers, so if Goodrich needs something specific that Grainger does not normally carry, Grainger will research and find the items through its *findmro.com* site. With Grainger's buying power, Goodrich can get better prices.

Goodrich has achieved additional savings from the tremendous decrease in paperwork that has resulted from buying through *grainger.com*. Individuals in each department now have access to purchasing cards, which allow them to do some of their own ordering. Before, the central purchasing department had to issue purchase orders for every single item. Now, employees with P-cards and passwords can place orders according to the spending limits that have been set up based on their positions.

In 2002, the Goodrich Pueblo operation spent $200,000 for purchases from *grainger.com*, which reflected a 10 to 15 percent savings on its purchases. Goodrich has now signed a company-wide enterprise agreement that allows every Goodrich facility in the country to order through *grainger.com*, with an expected savings of at least 10 percent.

Sources: Compiled from Fortune (2000), *grainger.com* (2006), and Lucas (2005).

Questions

1. Enter *grainger.com* and review all of the services offered to buyers. Prepare a list of these services.
2. Explain how Goodrich's buyers save time and money.
3. What other benefits does Goodrich enjoy by using *grainger.com*?
4. How was desktop purchasing implemented at Goodrich Corporation?

◗ **Cost savings.** In addition to generating new revenue, conducting auctions electronically reduces the costs of selling the auctioned items. These savings also help increase the seller's profits.

◗ **Increased stickiness.** Forward auctions give Web sites increased "stickiness." As discussed in Chapter 4, *stickiness* is a characteristic that describes customer loyalty to a site, demonstrated by the number and length of visits to a site. Stickiness at an auction site, for example, means that auction users spend more time on a site, generate more page views than other users, and trade more.

◗ **Member acquisition and retention.** All bidding transactions result in additional registered members, who are future business contacts. In addition, auction software aids enable sellers to search and report on virtually every relevant auction activity for future analysis and use.

Forward auctions can be conducted in two ways. A company may conduct its forward auctions from its own Web site or it can sell from an intermediary auction site, such as ebay.com or asset-auctions.com. Let's examine these options.

AUCTIONING FROM THE COMPANY'S OWN SITE

For large and well-known companies that frequently conduct auctions, such as GM, it makes sense to build an auction mechanism on the company's own site. Why should a company pay a commission to an intermediary if the intermediary cannot provide the company with added value? Of course, if a company decides to auction from its own site, it will have to pay for infrastructure and operate and maintain the auction site. However, if the company already has an electronic marketplace for selling from e-catalogs, the additional cost for conducting auctions may not be too high. On the other hand, a significant added value that could be provided by intermediaries is the attraction of many potential buyers to the auction site.

USING INTERMEDIARIES IN AUCTIONS

Several intermediaries offer B2B auction sites (e.g., see asset-auctions.com; others are discussed in Chapter 10). An intermediary may conduct private auctions for a seller, either from the intermediary's or the seller's site. Or a company may choose to conduct auctions in a public marketplace, using a third-party hosting company (e.g., eBay, which has a special "business exchange" for small companies).

Using a third-party hosting company for conducting auctions has many benefits. The first is that no additional resources (e.g., hardware, bandwidth, engineering resources, or IT personnel) are required. Nor are there any hiring costs or opportunity costs associated with the redeployment of corporate resources. B2B auctions also offer fast time-to-market: They enable a company to have a robust, customized auction up and running immediately. Without the intermediary, it may take a company weeks to prepare an auction site in-house.

Another benefit of using an intermediary relates to who owns and controls the auction information. In the case of an intermediary-conducted private auction, the intermediary sets up the auction to show the branding (company name) of the merchant rather than the intermediary's name. (For example, if an intermediary prepares a private auction for Blue Devils Company, customers see the Blue Devils name and logo.) Yet, the intermediary does the work of collecting data on Web traffic, page views, and member registration; setting all the auction parameters (transaction fee structure, user interface, and reports); and integrating the information flow and logistics. Of course, if a company wants to dispose of unwanted assets without advertising to the public that it is doing so, an inter-mediary-conducted public auction would be the logical choice. If a manufacturer is selling off products, buyers may become suspicious of the quality of the items. If an intermediary does the auction, it does not have to provide answers regarding the quality of the product.

Another benefit of using intermediaries relates to billing and collection efforts, which are handled by the intermediary rather than the company. For example, intermediaries calculate merchant-specific shipping weights and charge customers for shipping of auctioned items. All credit card data are encrypted for secure transmission and storage, and all billing information can be downloaded by the merchant company for integration with existing systems. These services are not free, of course. They are provided as part of the merchant's commission to the intermediary; a cost often deemed worth paying in exchange for the ease of the service.

For an example of using an intermediary to liquidate old equipment, see Case 5.4.

EXAMPLES OF B2B FORWARD AUCTION

The GM opening case provides an example of a company using a forward auction to sell surplus materials, which is a major objective of B2B EC auctions. Surpluses are sold online by intermediaries (e.g., asset-auctions.com) or by large manufacturers (e.g., Dell). The following are examples of B2B auctions:

- Whirlpool Corp. sold $20 million in scrap metal in 2003, increasing the price received by 15 percent (*Asset-auctions.com* 2006).
- SAM's Club (samsclub.com) auctions thousands of items (especially electronics) at auctions.samsclub.com. Featured auctions include the current bid, the number of bids, and the end date.
- ResortQuest, a large vacation rental company, uses auctionanything.com to auction rental space.
- At GovernmentAuctions.org (governmentauctions.org), businesses can bid on foreclosures, seized items, abandoned property, and more.
- Yahoo! conducts both B2C and B2B auctions of many items.

CASE 5.4
EC Application
HOW THE STATE OF PENNSYLVANIA SELLS SURPLUS EQUIPMENT

For many years, the Pennsylvania Department of Transportation (DOT) used a traditional offline auction process. In a radio address on December 6, 2003, Governor Ed Rendell announced that the state would begin holding online auctions to sell its surplus heavy equipment. The old, live in-person auction system generated about $5 million a year. Using the Internet, the DOT expected at least a 20 percent increase in revenue.

The Commonwealth of Pennsylvania conducted its initial online sale of surplus DOT items in October 2003. The sale consisted of 77 items (including 37 dump trucks). Onsite inspection was available twice during the 2-week bidding period. The online sale allowed the Commonwealth of Pennsylvania to obtain an average price increase of 20 percent, while reducing labor costs related to holding a traditional on-site sale. On high-value specialty items (i.e., a bridge inspection crane and a satellite van), results exceeded the estimated sale prices by over 200 percent.

The auction was conducted by Asset-auctions.com. The results of the auction are shown below:

- Total sales: $635,416.03.
- Half of the bidding activity occurred in the final 2 days.
- Every lot received multiple bids.

- Overtime bidding occurred in 39 lots.
- Over 200 bidders registered for the sale.
- 174 bidders from 19 states and Mexico made about 1,500 bids in 5 days.
- 47 different buyers participated.

The Commonwealth of Pennsylvania now sells surplus equipment and properties using both Asset-auctions.com and eBay.

Sources: Material compiled from *asset-auctions.com* (accessed November 2006) and the Commonwealth of Pennsylvania (2006).

Questions

1. Why is heavy equipment amenable to such auctions?
2. Why did the state generate 20 percent more in revenues with the online auction?
3. Why do you need an intermediary to conduct such an auction?
4. Comment on the number of bidders and bids as compared with offline auctions.

Section 5.4 ▶ REVIEW QUESTIONS

1. List the benefits of using B2B auctions for selling.
2. List the benefits of using auction intermediaries.

5.5 ONE-FROM-MANY: BUY-SIDE E-MARKETPLACES AND E-PROCUREMENT

When a buyer goes to a sell-side marketplace, such as Cisco's, the buyer's purchasing department sometimes has to manually enter the order information into its own corporate information system. Furthermore, manually searching e-stores and e-malls to find and compare suppliers and products can be slow and costly. As a solution, large buyers can open their own marketplaces, as GM did, called **buy-side e-marketplaces**, and invite sellers to browse and fulfill orders. The term *procurement* is used to refer to the purchase of goods and services for organizations. It is usually done by *purchasing agents*, also known as *corporate buyers*.

buy-side e-marketplace
A corporate-based acquisition site that uses reverse auctions, negotiations, group purchasing, or any other e-procurement method.

PROCUREMENT METHODS

Companies use different methods to procure goods and services depending on what and where they buy, the quantities needed, how much money is involved, and more. The major procurement methods include the following:

- Conduct bidding or tendering (a reverse auction) in a system in which suppliers compete against each other. This method is used for large-ticket items or large quantities (Section 5.6).
- Buy directly from manufacturers, wholesalers, or retailers from their catalogs, and possibly by negotiation. Frequently, a contract implements such a purchase (Section 5.8).

▶ Buy from the catalog of an intermediary (e-distributor) that aggregates sellers' catalogs, (Section 5.7).

▶ Buy from an internal buyer's catalog, in which company-approved vendors' catalogs, including agreed-upon prices, are aggregated. This approach is used for the implementation of *desktop purchasing,* which allows the requisitioners to order directly from vendors, bypassing the procurement department (Section 5.7).

▶ Buy at private or public auction sites in which the organization participates as one of the buyers (Section 5.6).

▶ Join a group-purchasing system that aggregates participants' demand, creating a large volume. Then the group may negotiate prices or initiate a tendering process (Section 5.7).

▶ Buy at an exchange or industrial mall (Chapter 6).

▶ Collaborate with suppliers to share information about sales and inventory, so as to reduce inventory and stock-outs and enhance just-in-time delivery. (See Chapter 7 on collaborative commerce.)

Some of these activities are done in private marketplaces, others in public exchanges. According to Wikipedia (2006), the six main types of e-procurement are as follow:

▶ **e-sourcing.** Identifying new suppliers for a specific category of purchasing requirements using Internet technology (discussed later in this chapter).

▶ **e-tendering.** Sending requests for information and prices to suppliers and receiving the suppliers' responses using Internet technology (discussed later in this chapter).

▶ **e-reverse auctioning.** Using Internet technology to buy goods and services from a number of known or unknown suppliers (discussed later in this chapter).

▶ **e-informing.** Gathering and distributing purchasing information both from and to internal and external parties using Internet technology (see Chapter 6).

▶ **Web-based ERP (electronic resource planning).** Creating and approving purchasing requisitions, placing purchase orders, and receiving goods and services by using a software system based on Internet technology (see Chapter 7).

▶ **e-MRO (maintenance, repair and operating).** The same as Web-based ERP except that the goods and services ordered are non–product-related MRO supplies (see Chapter 7).

INEFFICIENCIES IN TRADITIONAL PROCUREMENT MANAGEMENT

procurement management
The planning, organizing, and coordination of all the activities relating to purchasing goods and services needed to accomplish the mission of an organization.

Procurement management refers to the planning, organizing, and coordination of all the activities pertaining to the purchasing of the goods and services necessary to accomplish the mission of an enterprise. It involves the B2B purchase and sale of supplies and services, as well as the flow of required information and networking systems. Approximately 80 percent of an organization's purchased items, mostly MROs, constitute 20 to 25 percent of the total purchase value. Furthermore, a large portion of corporate buyers' time is spent on non–value-added activities such as data entry, correcting errors in paperwork, expediting delivery, or solving quality problems.

For high-value items, purchasing personnel spend a great deal of time and effort on procurement activities. These activities include qualifying suppliers, negotiating prices and terms, building rapport with strategic suppliers, and carrying out supplier evaluation and certification. If buyers are busy with the details of the smaller items (usually the MROs), they do not have enough time to properly deal with the purchase of the high-value items.

maverick buying
Unplanned purchases of items needed quickly, often at non-prenegotiated higher prices.

Other inefficiencies also may occur in conventional procurement. These range from delays to paying too much for rush orders. One procurement inefficiency is **maverick buying**. This is when a buyer makes unplanned purchases of items needed quickly, which results in buying at non-prenegotiated, usually higher, prices. The traditional procurement process, shown in Exhibit 5.4, often is inefficient. To correct the situation, companies reengineer their procurement systems, implement new purchasing models, and in particular, introduce e-procurement.

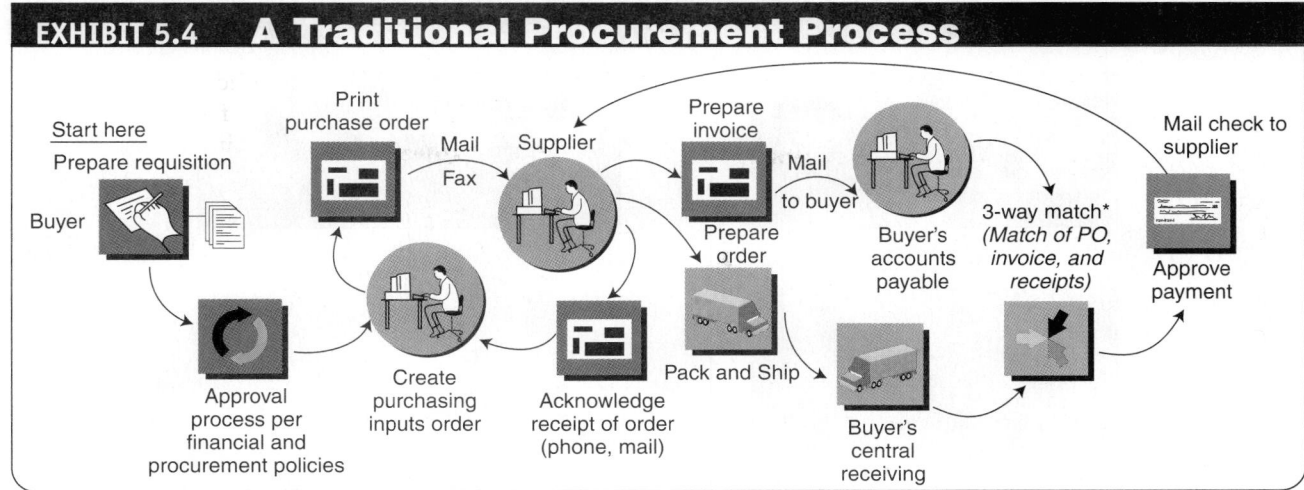

EXHIBIT 5.4   A Traditional Procurement Process

Source: *Ariba.com*, February 2001. Courtesy of Ariba Inc.

THE GOALS AND BENEFITS OF E-PROCUREMENT

Improvements to procurement have been attempted for decades, usually by using information technologies. The real opportunity for improvement lies in the use of **e-procurement**, the electronic acquisition of goods and services for organizations. For comprehensive coverage and case studies, see Saryeddine (2004). The general e-procurement process (with the exception of tendering) is shown in Exhibit 5.5.

By automating and streamlining the laborious routines of the purchasing function, purchasing professionals can focus on more strategic purchases, achieving the following goals and benefits:

e-procurement
The electronic acquisition of goods and services for organizations.

▶ Increasing the productivity of purchasing agents (providing them with more time and reducing job pressure)

▶ Lowering purchase prices through product standardization, reverse auctions, volume discounts, and consolidation of purchases

▶ Improving information flow and management (e.g., supplier's information and pricing information)

▶ Minimizing the purchases made from noncontract vendors (minimizing maverick buying)

▶ Improving the payment process and savings due to expedited payments (for sellers)

▶ Establishing efficient, collaborative supplier relations

▶ Ensuring delivery on time, every time

▶ Slashing order-fulfillment and processing times by leveraging automation

▶ Reducing the skill requirements and training needs of purchasing agents

▶ Reducing the number of suppliers

▶ Streamlining the purchasing process, making it simple and fast (may involve authorizing requisitioners to perform purchases from their desktops, bypassing the procurement department)

▶ Streamlining invoice reconciliation and dispute resolution

▶ Reducing the administrative processing cost per order by as much as 90 percent (e.g., GM achieved a reduction from $100 to $10)

▶ Finding new suppliers and vendors that can provide goods and services faster and/or cheaper (improved sourcing)

▶ Integrating budgetary controls into the procurement process

▶ Minimizing human errors in the buying or shipping processes

▶ Monitoring and regulating buying behavior.

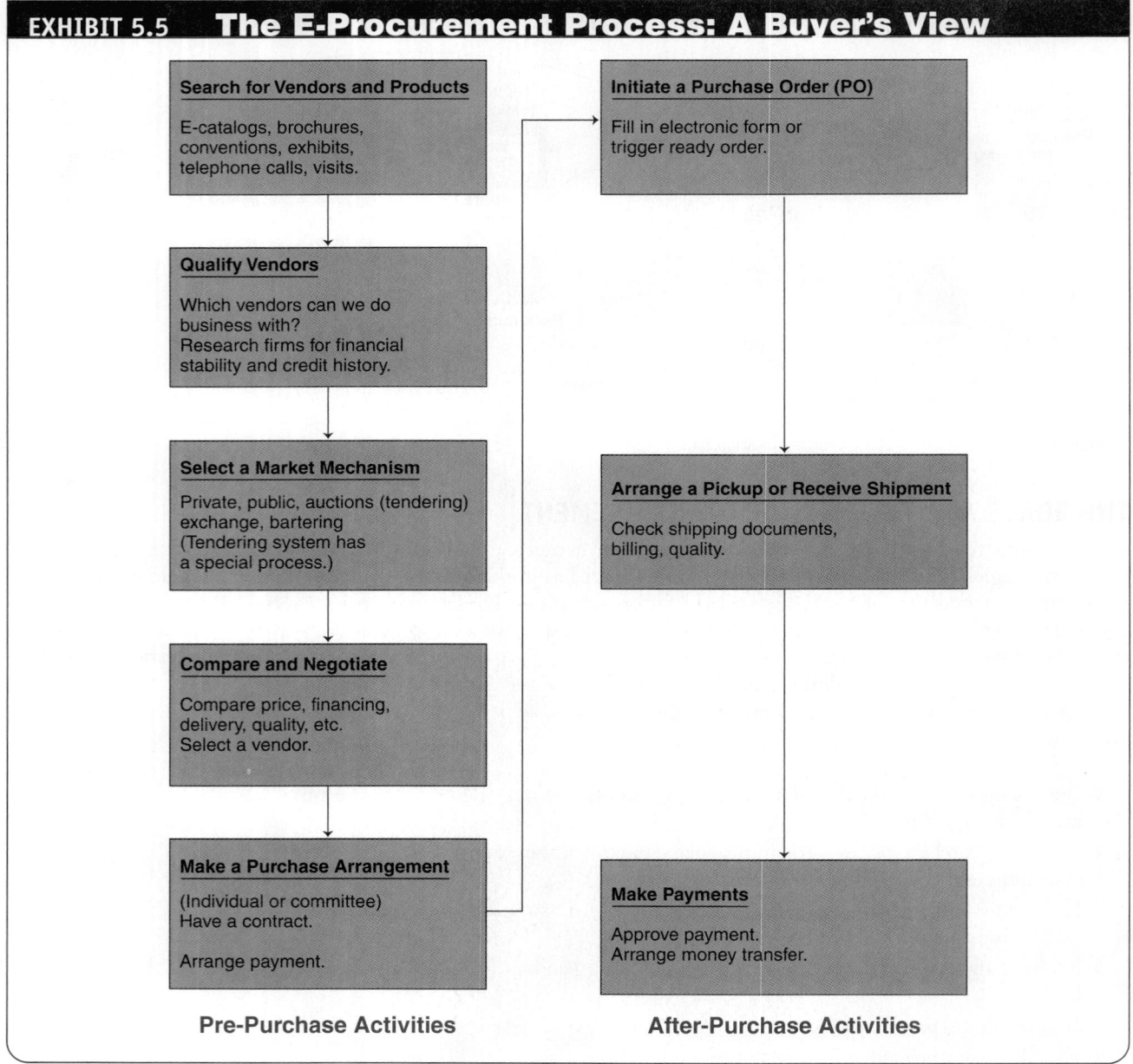

EXHIBIT 5.5   **The E-Procurement Process: A Buyer's View**

Search for Vendors and Products

E-catalogs, brochures, conventions, exhibits, telephone calls, visits.

Qualify Vendors

Which vendors can we do business with?
Research firms for financial stability and credit history.

Select a Market Mechanism

Private, public, auctions (tendering) exchange, bartering (Tendering system has a special process.)

Compare and Negotiate

Compare price, financing, delivery, quality, etc.
Select a vendor.

Make a Purchase Arrangement

(Individual or committee)
Have a contract.

Arrange payment.

Initiate a Purchase Order (PO)

Fill in electronic form or trigger ready order.

Arrange a Pickup or Receive Shipment

Check shipping documents, billing, quality.

Make Payments

Approve payment.
Arrange money transfer.

Pre-Purchase Activities   **After-Purchase Activities**

For additional benefits, see Saryeddine (2004).

E-procurement is relatively easy to implement (see Zhao 2006). Channel conflict usually does not occur, and resistance to change is minimal. Also, a wide selection of e-procurement software packages and other infrastructure is available at a reasonable cost. For details, see Wikipedia (2006).

MROs often are the initial target for e-procurement. However, improvements can be made in the purchasing of direct materials as well. All existing manual processes of requisition creation, requests for quotation, invitation to tender, purchase order issuance, receiving goods, and making payments can be streamlined and automated. However, to most effectively implement such automated support, the people involved in procurement must collaborate with the suppliers along the supply chain, as described in Chapter 7.

IMPLEMENTING E-PROCUREMENT

Putting the buying department on the Internet is the easy part of e-procurement. The more difficult part is implementing it. The components of e-procurement systems are shown in

Online File W5.4. For a model that simplifies the procurement process by performing tasks electronically, see Podlogar (2006).

The following are some of the major implementation issues that companies must consider when planning e-procurement initiatives:

▶ **Fitting e-procurement into the company's EC strategy.** For example, suppose the strategy is outsourcing. In this case, e-procurement can be done in an exchange, or the customer can buy at the sellers' Web sites.

▶ **Reviewing and changing the procurement process itself.** E-procurement may affect the number of purchasing agents, where they are located, and how purchases are approved. The degree of purchasing centralization also may be affected.

▶ **Providing interfaces between e-procurement and integrated enterprisewide information systems, such as ERP or supply chain management.** If the company does not have such systems, it may be necessary to do some restructuring before moving to e-procurement.

▶ **Coordinating the buyer's information system with that of the sellers.** Sellers have many potential buyers. For this reason, some major suppliers, such as SKF (a Swedish automotive parts maker; see skf.com), developed an integration-oriented procurement system for its buyers. The SKF information system is designed to make it easier for the procurement systems of others (notably the distributors in other countries) that buy the company's bearings and seals to interface with the SKF system. The SKF system allows distributors and large buyers to gain real-time technical information on the products, as well as details on product availability, delivery times, and commercial terms and conditions.

▶ **Consolidating the number of regular suppliers and integrating with their information systems and, if possible, with their business processes.** Having fewer suppliers minimizes the number of connectivity issues that need to be resolved and will lower expenses. Also, with fewer suppliers, the company will buy more from each supplier, allowing the company to get a quantity discount. Collaboration with each supplier also will be enhanced.

Many companies that have implemented e-procurement have been extremely satisfied with the payoffs. One such example is described in Case 5.5. Another case (Schlumberger) is available as Online File W5.5.

E-Sourcing

When implementing e-procurement, companies also should evaluate **e-sourcing**, the processes and tools that electronically enable any activity in the procurement process, such as quotation/tender requests and responses, e-auctions, online negotiations, and spending analyses (see ariba.com/solutions/sourcing_enterprise.cfm and Johnson and Klassen 2005). E-Sourcing is the automation of strategic sourcing.

Strategic sourcing is the process of identifying opportunities, evaluating potential sources, negotiating contracts, and managing supplier relationships to achieve corporate goals, such as cost reductions and increased quality and service. In an e-sourcing study by AMR (Murphree 2003), the companies surveyed reported savings of 10 to 15 percent in the cost of direct goods and 20 to 25 percent in the cost of indirect goods and services. Companies also reported reductions in sourcing cycle times.

Strategic sourcing requires a holistic process that automates the entire sourcing process, including order planning, RFQ creation, bid evaluation, negotiation, settlement, and order execution. The promise of strategic sourcing is in reducing total acquisition costs while increasing value. A fundamental shortcoming of sourcing tools today is their inability to allow the creation of complex RFQs that allow for a variety of bid structures that exploit complementarities and economies of scale in suppliers' cost structures.

E-sourcing attempts to improve strategic sourcing by making it more effective and efficient. For example, Moai Technologies (moai.com) provides the following e-sourcing solutions:

▶ **Just-in-Time Sourcing (JITS).** Moai's JITS integrates strategic consulting services with licensed software products. The software directs customers through the e-sourcing process, including negotiating with vendors and securing reliable suppliers, thereby lowering sourcing costs. According to Moai (2006), CompleteSource provides customized

e-sourcing
The process and tools that electronically enable any activity in the sourcing process, such as quotation/tender submittance and response, e-auctions, online negotiations, and spending analyses.

CASE 5.5
EC Application
REGENT INNS: SUCCESSFUL IMPLEMENTATION OF E-PROCUREMENT

Regent Inns PLC (*regentinns.co.uk*) operates 79 entertainment establishments in the United Kingdom. Regent Inns has two of the largest UK leisure brands in terms of average sales—Walkabout and Jongleurs Comedy Club.

When Regent Inns set out to implement a corporate-wide purchasing solution, the business set an audacious goal: "To implement a best practice procurement model across the Regent Inns brands that manages the process from cradle to grave" for all items and services. The company was not prepared to settle for less than 100 percent fit that included all services and products.

Two core elements of the project goal was the approach of "business process first—then technology." The other vital element of Regent Inns' style is the belief that "people and process excellence underpin business excellence."

The solution includes three components:

- **Back-office solution**—SunSystems from Systems Union PLC (*sunsystems.com*)
- **Procurement software solution**—iPOS from Professional Advantage (*suncompanion.com*)
- **Procurement consultancy service**—Foundation Services (*foundationsystems.co.uk*)

Results
The results were as follows:

- The purchasing cycle was reduced from months to weeks and from days to hours.
- Stock-holding costs were reduced dramatically.
- The number of food suppliers fell from 51 to fewer than 10.

- A single food supplier products reduced to 201 from 1,278
- The number of invoices with PO numbers increased from 20 to 97 percent (target was 95 percent).
- Automated invoice upload increased from 4 percent to 68 percent (target 90 percent)
- Incorrect delivery charges decreased by £50k/year
- Bottle deposit price errors 0.003p per bottle decreased by £80k/year
- Fewer deliveries
- Managers spend less time on administration and more time on the business.

The company attributed its success to management support; involvement of all types of users; high commitment from team members; in-depth study of all the processes; superb communication and collaboration; accurate definitions of all stakeholder requirements; a back-to-basics culture; and working closely with suppliers.

Sources: Compiled from Professional Advantage (2006) and from Sunsystems (2006).

Questions

1. What are the drivers of e-procurement?
2. How is e-procurement related to other information systems?
3. List the major benefits of the new e-procurement system to the company.

---

low-cost solutions at a flat fee. Those who are ready to take complete control of their sourcing process will benefit most from:

- **High ROI**—fixed subscription cost with huge savings
- **Maximum customization**—can be installed into unique workflows, applications, and processes
- **Maximum control**—"Behind the firewall" solution provides flexibility and control in administering, scheduling, branding ,and process integration
- **Strategic Consulting Services.** *RapidSource*, Moai's strategic consulting program, promotes testing and validation of e-sourcing to those new to the concept. With this guidance, users are guaranteed a return on investment in the program.
- **Hosted Sourcing Software.** Delays, IT complexities, and costs associated with in-house deployments are eliminated with Moai's hosted services.

Section 5.5 ▶ REVIEW QUESTIONS

1. Define procurement and list the major procurement methods.
2. Describe the inefficiencies of traditional procurement.
3. Define e-procurement and its goals.

4. How do direct materials and MROs differ? Why are MROs good candidates for e-procurement?

5. Describe the implementation of e-procurement.

6. Describe e-sourcing and its benefits.

5.6 BUY-SIDE E-MARKETPLACES: REVERSE AUCTIONS

One of the major methods of e-procurement is through reverse auctions. Recall from our discussions in Chapters 1 and 2 that a *reverse auction* is a tendering system in which suppliers are invited to bid on the fulfillment of an order and the lowest bid wins. In B2B usage of a reverse auction, a buyer may open an electronic market on its own server and invite potential suppliers to bid on the items the buyer needs. The "invitation" to such reverse auctions is a form or document called a **request for quote (RFQ)**. The reverse auction is referred to as the *tendering* or *bidding model*. Traditional tendering usually implied one-time sealed bidding (see Chapter 10), whereas the reverse auction opens the auction to competing sequential bidding. See Smeltzer and Carr (2002) for a comprehensive overview of reverse auctions.

Governments and large corporations frequently mandate reverse auctions, which may provide considerable savings. To understand why this is so, see Insights and Additions 5.2, which compares the pre-Internet tendering process with the Web-based reverse auction process. The electronic process is faster and administratively much less expensive. It also can result in locating the cheapest possible products or services.

request for quote (RFQ)
The "invitation" to participate in a tendering (bidding) system.

Insights and Additions 5.2 Comparison of Pre-Internet and Web-Based Reverse Auction Processes

The Pre-Internet Tendering System Process	The Web-Based Reverse Auction Process
The buyer prepares a paper-based description of the product (project) that needs to be acquired. The description includes specifications, blueprints, quality standards, delivery date, and required payment method.	The buyer gathers product information automatically from online sources and posts it on its secured corporate portal.
The buyer announces the RFQ via newspaper ads, direct mail, fax, or telephone.	The buyer sends e-mail alerts to selected vendors, inviting them to view the projects available for bid. Many suppliers constantly monitor buyers' sites or aggregator's sites.
Bidders (suppliers) that express interest receive detailed information (sometimes for a fee), usually by postal mail or a courier.	The buyer identifies potential suppliers from among those who responded to the online RFQ and invites suppliers to bid on the project. Bidders download the project information from the Web.
Bidders prepare proposals. They may call the company for additional information. Sometimes changes in the specs (specifications) are made, which must be disseminated to all interested bidders.	Bidders conduct real-time or delayed reverse auctions. Requests for more information can be made online. Changes in specs can be disseminated electronically.
Bidders submit paper proposals, usually several copies of the same documents, by a preestablished deadline.	Bidders submit proposals in electronic format.
Proposals are evaluated, usually by several departments, sequentially, at the buyer's organization. Communication and clarification may take place via letters or phone/fax.	The buyer evaluates the suppliers' bids (by several departments, simultaneously). Communications, clarifications, and negotiations to achieve the "best deal" take place electronically.
Buyer awards a contract to the bidder(s) that best meets its requirements. Notification is usually done via postal mail.	Buyer awards a contract to the bidder(s) that best meets its requirements. Notification is done online.

CONDUCTING REVERSE AUCTIONS

As the number of reverse auction sites increases, suppliers will not be able to manually monitor all relevant tendering sites. This problem has been addressed with the introduction of *online directories* that list open RFQs. Another way to solve this problem is through the use of monitoring software agents (see Chapter 10). Software agents also can aid in the bidding process itself. Examples of agents that support the bidding process are auctionsniper.com and auctionflex.com.

Alternatively, a third-party intermediaries may run the electronic bidding, as they do for forward auctions. General Electric's GXS (now an independent company, described in detail in Online File W5.6) is open to any buyer. Auction sites such as a-zuc.com, ariba.com, liquidation.com, and asset-auctions.com also belong to this category. Conducting reverse auctions in B2B can be a fairly complex process (see the United Technologies case in Online File W5.7). This is why an intermediary may be essential. (Examples of bidding managed by an intermediary are shown in Chapter 10.)

The reverse auction process is demonstrated in Exhibit 5.6. As shown in the exhibit, the first step is for the would-be buyer to post bid invitations. When bids arrive, contract and purchasing personnel for the buyer evaluate the bids and decide which one(s) to accept. The details of this process are explained in the General Electric case in Online File W5.6. For further discussion, see Bush (2006).

Some Implementation Issues

A special case of auctions is the bundling of multiple items and then auctioning them together. For actual practices and guidelines, see Schoenherr and Mabert (2006).

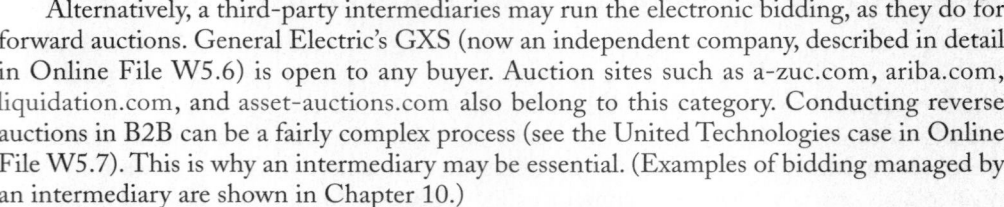

EXHIBIT 5.6   The Reverse Auction Process

Step I   Posting Bid Invitations

Buyers — Bidders

Contract & Purchasing Department → Requirement → Send Bid Invitation → Posted on Enterprise Web → E-mail → Bid

E-mail → Bid

Restricted Invitations   E-mail → Bid

Step II   Evaluation of Bids

Bidders — Evaluators

Bid 1 / e-mail, Bid 2 / e-mail, Bid 3 / e-mail → Contract & Purchasing Department → Rejection → Supplier 1

Evaluation → Rejection → Supplier 2

Acceptance → Supplier 3

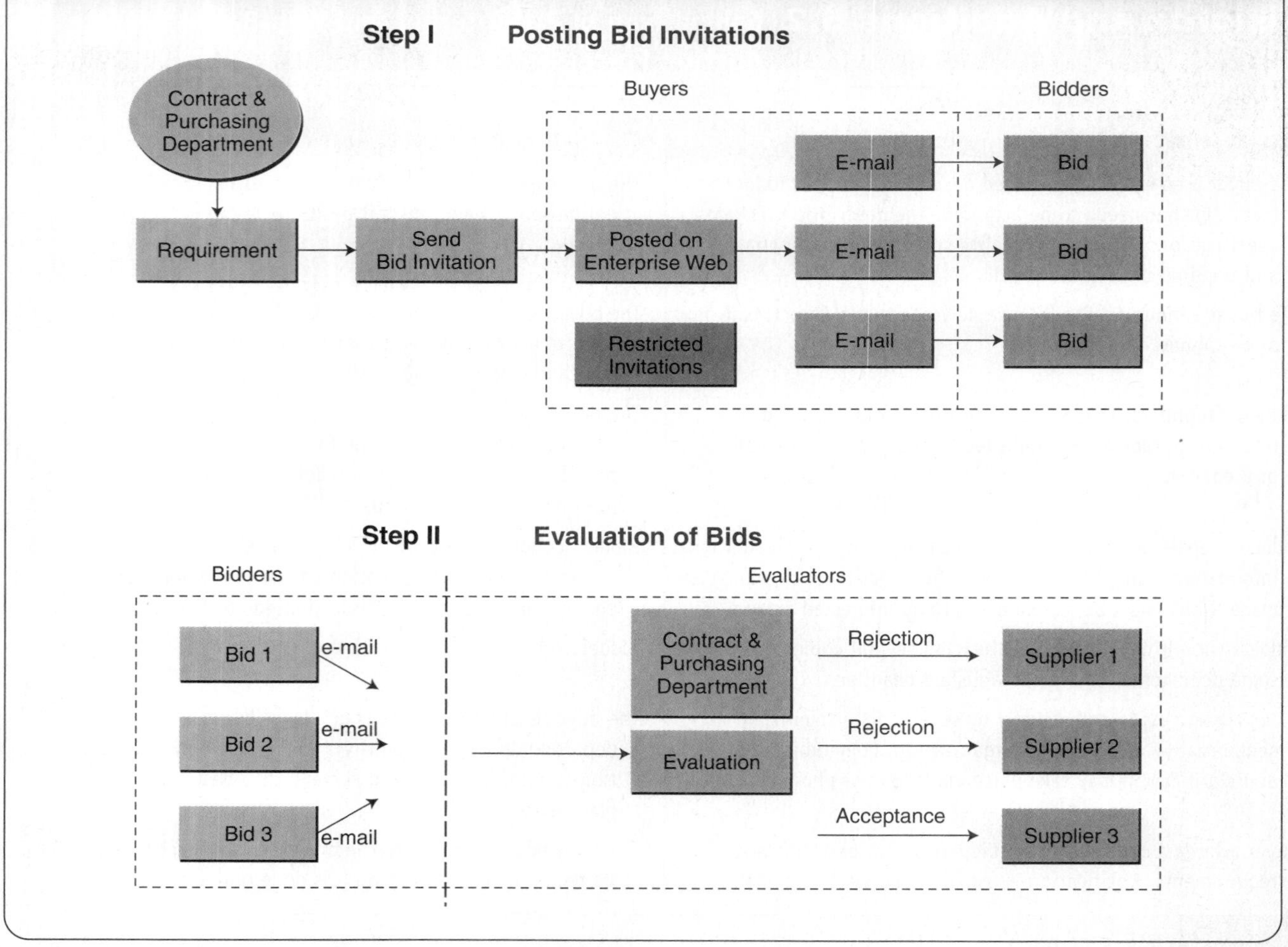

It is important to correctly calculate the *cost-benefit* of reverse auctions. Examining several case studies, Smith (2006) found that significant hidden costs may be associated with reverse auctions. These must be considered before a "go" decision is made.

E-Tendering by Governments

Most governments must conduct tendering when they buy or sell goods and services. Doing this manually is slow and expensive. Therefore, many are moving to e-reverse auctions, as illustrated in Case 5.6.

GROUP REVERSE AUCTIONS

B2B reverse auctions are done in a private exchange or at an aggregator's site for a group of buying companies. Such *group reverse auctions* are popular in South Korea and usually involve large conglomerates. For example, the LG Group operates the LG MRO auction for its members, and the Samsung Group operates iMarketKorea, as described in Chapter 6.

Section 5.6 ▶ REVIEW QUESTIONS

1. Describe the manual tendering system.
2. How do online reverse auctions work?
3. List the benefits of Web-based reverse auctions.
4. Describe the business drivers of GE's TPN now (GXS) and its evolution over time. (See Online File W5.6.)
5. What was a primary challenge to GE in implementing its e-procurement system? (See Online File W5.6.)

CASE 5.6

EC Application

REVERSE AUCTIONS BECOME A DIPLOMATIC TOOL

The U.S. State Department found a diplomatic solution to purchasing commercial products and technology without alienating vendors or paying top dollar. Foggy Bottom procurement officials now use FedBid's reverse auction technology to negotiate the lowest price for everything from light bulbs to laser printers.

In a reverse auction, sellers try to meet the specific needs of a purchaser by underbidding their competitors within an allotted time period. Registered agency procurement officials list their needs on FedBid's Web site, and vendors bid down the price. In the end, the lowest bidder gets the sale.

Starting in 2002, the State Department conducted more than 1,100 reverse auctions in a trial program worth about $39 million, for a net savings of $4.1 million. Initially, it purchased computer products, monitors, and commodity products from the major manufactures.

Since then, State has completed 4,700 reverse auctions worth $169 million, for a savings of $17.6 million from its original expected expenditure of $186.7 million. That doesn't even touch the fact that State hasn't had to increase procurement staffing in a long time.

The average savings between 2002 and 2005 have been 6 to 10 percent of estimated costs.

In one overseas' procurement, State used the reverse auction to solicit bids for Cisco Systems and Hewlett-Packard computers from resellers registered with the General Services Administration, according to Geoffrey Miller, FedBid's chief operating officer. State allocated $50,250 for the purchase. Six resellers bid to make the sale, which ended up costing State $45,375—a savings of $4,875.

Reverse auctions streamline the administrative burden and costs of collecting competing quotes in addition to the bottom-line savings. It's all about time—saving vendors' time to sell and purchasers' time to buy.

The U.S. government is not the only one conducting reverse auctions online. Dozens of governments around the globe are doing the same. Alexandersson and Hulten (2006) describe such a case in Sweden and raise the issue of multinational enterprises participating in local tenders submitting bids that are too low and subsidized by the government.

Sources: Compiled from Hubler (2006), Alexandersson and Hulten (2006), and *fedbid.com* (accessed October 2006).

Questions

1. List the drivers of the application.
2. What is the role of the intermediary? (See *fedbid.com*.)
3. What are the success factors in this case?

5.7   OTHER E-PROCUREMENT METHODS

Companies also have implemented other innovative e-procurement methods. Some common ones are described in this section.

AN INTERNAL PURCHASING MARKETPLACE: AGGREGATING SUPPLIERS' CATALOGS

Large organizations have many corporate buyers or purchasing agents that are usually located in different places. For example, Bristol-Myers Squibb Corporation has more than 3,000 corporate buyers located all over the world. These agents buy from a large number of suppliers. The problem is that even if all purchases are made from approved suppliers, it is difficult to plan and control procurement. In many cases, to save time, buyers engage in *maverick buying*. In addition, an organization needs to control the purchasing budget. This situation is especially serious in government agencies and multinational entities where many buyers and large numbers of purchases are involved.

One effective solution to the procurement problem in large organizations is to aggregate the catalogs of all approved suppliers, combining them into a single *internal* electronic catalog. Prices can be negotiated in advance or determined by a tendering, so that the buyers do not have to negotiate each time they place an order. By aggregating the suppliers' catalogs on the buyer's server, it also is easier to centralize and control all procurement. Such an aggregation of catalogs is called an **internal procurement marketplace**.

internal procurement marketplace
The aggregated catalogs of all approved suppliers combined into a single *internal* electronic catalog.

Benefits of Internal Marketplaces

Corporate buyers can use search engines to look through internal aggregated catalogs to quickly find what they want, check availability and delivery times, and complete electronic requisition forms. Another advantage of such aggregation is that a company can reduce the number of suppliers it uses. For example, Caltex, a multinational oil company, reduced the number of its suppliers from over 3,000 to 800. Such reduction is possible because the central catalog enables buyers at multiple corporate locations to buy from remote but fewer sellers. Buying from fewer sellers typically increases the quantities bought from each, lowering the per unit price.

Another example of a successful aggregation of suppliers' catalogs is that of MasterCard International, which aggregates more than 10,000 items from the catalogs of approved suppliers into an internal electronic catalog. The goal of this project is to consolidate buying activities from multiple corporate sites, improve processing costs, and reduce the supplier base. Payments are made with MasterCard's corporate procurement card. By 2006, the system was used by more than 2,500 buyers. MasterCard is continually adding suppliers and catalog content to the system (see Mastercard 2006).

Finally, internal marketplaces allow for easy financial controls. As buyers make purchases, their account balances are displayed. Once the budget is depleted, the system will not allow new purchase orders to go through. Therefore, this model is especially popular in public institutions and government entities. The implementation of internal purchasing marketplaces is frequently done via desktop purchasing.

Desktop Purchasing

desktop purchasing
Direct purchasing from internal marketplaces without the approval of supervisors and without the intervention of a procurement department.

Desktop purchasing implies purchasing directly from internal marketplaces without the approval of supervisors and without the intervention of a procurement department. This is usually done by using a *purchasing card* (*P-card*) (see Chapter 12). Desktop purchasing reduces the administrative cost and cycle time involved in purchasing urgently needed or frequently purchased items of small dollar value. This approach is especially effective for MRO purchases.

Microsoft built its internal marketplace, named MS Market, for the procurement of small items. The aggregated catalog that is part of MS Market is used by Microsoft employees worldwide, whose purchasing totals over $3.5 billion annually. The system has drastically reduced the role and size of the procurement department. For more on desktop purchasing (and other e-procurement activities) in the UK government, see Case 5.7.

The desktop-purchasing approach also can be implemented by partnering with external private exchanges. For instance, Samsung Electronics of South Korea, a huge global

CASE 5.7
EC Application
E-PROCUREMENT AT DEFRA

The UK Government Department for Environment, Food, and Rural Affairs (Defra) spends about £.5 billion (approximately US $2.5 billion) each year on prepurchasing from a pool of thousands of suppliers. The agency processes over 16,500 purchasing orders, 120,000 supplier invoices, and over 100,000 other payments.

The Problem

Defra set challenging e-procurement goals to provide systems and processes that would offer electronic solutions for all procurement processes, which included:

▶ Reduction of maverick spending
▶ Capture of all expenditures
▶ Full automation of month-end accrual processes
▶ Elimination of unmatched invoices and immediate invoice registration
▶ Reduction in the number of vendors supplying Defra
▶ Provide for better value for the money
▶ Alignment of corporate services and systems to business needs

The Process

The following e-procurement applications were implemented in Defra:

▶ Buy4defra (a desktop-purchasing method for initiating all maverick buying; many standard products and services are included in the online catalog)
▶ An e-contract management system
▶ An e-tendering system (reverse auction)
▶ e-auction4defra (regular auctions)
▶ e-billing4defra (electronic billing)

Implementation

The system was implemented with Oracle e-Business Suite 11i. Defra remodeled its processes to match the software using useful suggestions from Oracle User Group members. By the end of 2004, 1,000 users had registered, processing well over 2,500 requisitions per month; 20 supplier catalogs were online; and electronic transmission of purchase orders went live.

The major benefits of the new system are as follows:

▶ Savings of £600,000 each year.
▶ Removal of many unnecessary paper and manual processes in all areas of transactional activity.
▶ Reduction in maverick buying.
▶ 90 percent of supplier invoicing matched by mid-2005.
▶ By March 2006, over 60 percent of Defra's £1.4 billion expenditures had been processed through the e-procurement solution.

Sources: Compiled from *defra.gov.uk* (accessed June 2006) and from Office of Government Commerce (2005).

Questions

1. List three goals of the e-procurement systems. Explain.
2. Draw a flow chart of the new procurement process and explain it.
3. List three major benefits of the system.
4. List the critical success factors for this system.

---

manufacturer and its subsidiaries, has integrated its iMarketKorea exchange (see Chapter 6) with the e-procurement systems of its buying agents. This platform can be easily linked with *group purchasing*, which is described later in this section.

Desktop purchasing automates and supports purchasing operations such as product and supplier selection, requisitions, catalog searches, approval processes, purchase order processing, catalog updates and content management, and report generation. These systems are designed to support the nonpurchasing professional (employees whose job is other than purchasing agent) and casual end users. For details, see Segev and Gebauer (2001). A major vendor of such systems is Oracle.

BUYING AT E-AUCTIONS

Another popular approach to procurement is e-auctions. As described in Section 5.4, sellers are increasingly motivated to sell surpluses and even regular products via auctions. In some cases, e-auctions provide an opportunity for buyers to find inexpensive or unique items fairly quickly. A prudent corporate buyer should certainly look at both those manufacturers and distributors that conduct auctions periodically (e.g., GM or Dell) and at third-party auctioneers (e.g., eBay or auctions.yahoo.com). As will be shown in Chapter 10, auction aggregators can help purchasers find where and when auctions of needed items are being conducted.

GROUP PURCHASING

Many companies, especially small ones, are moving to group purchasing. With **group purchasing**, orders from several buyers are aggregated into volume purchases so that better prices can be negotiated. Two models are in use: *internal aggregation* and *external* (third-party) *aggregation*.

Internal Aggregation

Large companies, such as GE, buy billions of dollars of MROs every year. Company-wide orders, from GE companies and subsidiaries, for identical items are aggregated using the Web and are replenished automatically. Besides economies of scale (lower prices for large purchases) on many items, GE saves on the administrative cost of the transactions, reducing transaction costs from $50 to $100 per transaction to $5 to $10 (Rudnitsky 2000). With 5 million transactions annually at GE, this is a substantial savings.

External Aggregation

Many SMEs would like to enjoy quantity discounts but have difficulty finding others to join group purchasing to increase the procurement volume. Finding partners can be accomplished by an external third party such as BuyerZone.com (buyerzone.com), HIGPA (higpa.org), or United Sourcing Alliance (usa-llc.com). The idea is to provide SMEs with better prices, selection, and services by aggregating demand online and then either negotiating with suppliers or conducting reverse auctions (see Mudambi et al. 2004). The external aggregation group purchasing process is shown in Exhibit 5.7.

One can appreciate the importance of this market by taking into consideration some data about small businesses: In the United States, according to the U.S. Department of Commerce, 90 percent of all businesses have fewer than 100 employees, yet they account for over 35 percent of all MRO business volume (Small Business Administration 2002). Therefore, the potential for external aggregators is huge.

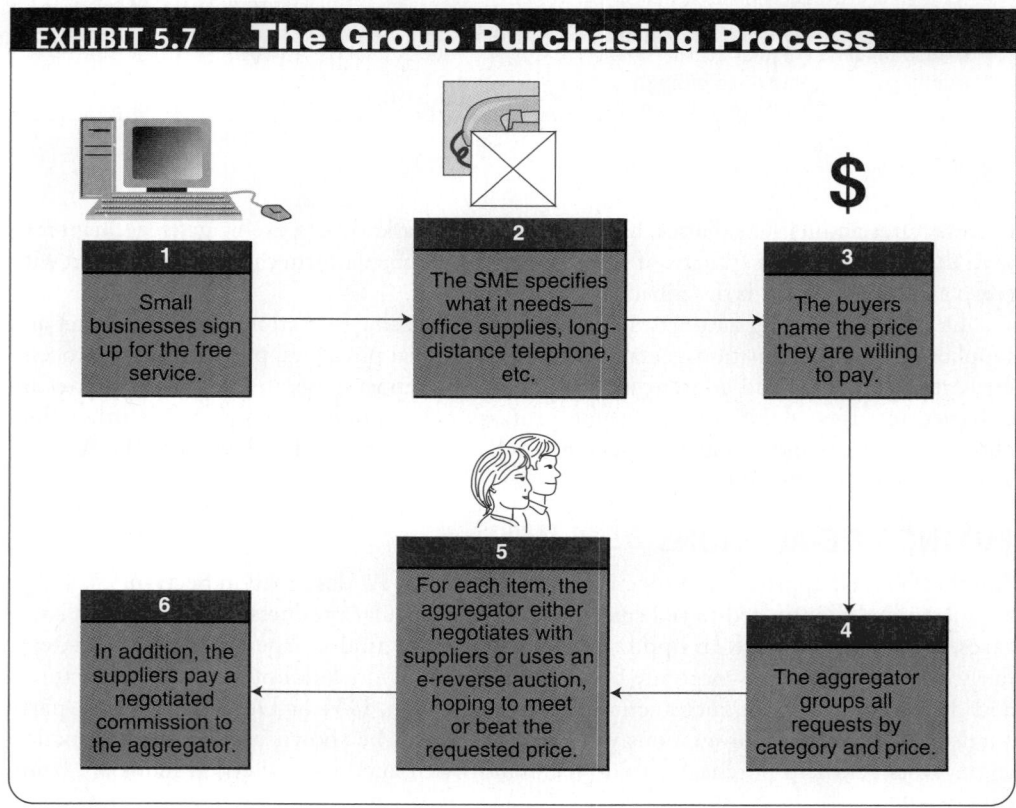

EXHIBIT 5.7   The Group Purchasing Process

1. Small businesses sign up for the free service.
2. The SME specifies what it needs—office supplies, long-distance telephone, etc.
3. The buyers name the price they are willing to pay.
4. The aggregator groups all requests by category and price.
5. For each item, the aggregator either negotiates with suppliers or uses an e-reverse auction, hoping to meet or beat the requested price.
6. In addition, the suppliers pay a negotiated commission to the aggregator.

Several large companies, including large CPA firms, EDS, and Ariba, are providing similar aggregation services, mainly to their regular customers. Yahoo! and AOL offer such services, too. A key to the success of these companies is a critical mass of buyers. An interesting strategy is for a company to outsource aggregation to a third party. For example, energy-solutions.com provides group buying for community site partners in the energy industry.

Group purchasing, which started with commodity items such as MROs and consumer electronic devices, has now moved to services ranging from travel to payroll processing and Web hosting. Some aggregators use Priceline's "name-your-own-price" approach. Others try to find the lowest possible price (see njnonprofits.org/groupbuy.html). Similar approaches are used in B2C, and several vendors serve both markets.

BUYING FROM E-DISTRIBUTORS

Section 5.3 described how companies use e-distributors as a sales channel (recall the case of W. W. Grainger). When buying small quantities, purchasers often buy from an e-distributor. If they buy online, it is considered e-procurement.

PURCHASING DIRECT GOODS

Until 2001, most B2B e-procurement implementations took place in the sell-side of large vendors (Cisco, Intel, IBM) and in the procurement of MROs. In general, MROs comprise 20 to 50 percent of a company's purchasing budget. The remaining 50 to 80 percent of corporate purchases are for *direct materials* and *services*. Therefore, most companies would reap great benefits in using e-purchasing to acquire direct goods: Buyers would be able to purchase direct goods more quickly, reduce unit costs, reduce inventories, avoid shortages, and expedite their own production processes. Sourcing direct materials typically involves more complex transactions requiring negotiation (Section 5.8) and *collaboration* between the seller and buyer and greater information exchange. This leads us to collaborative commerce, which will be discussed in Chapter 7.

ELECTRONIC BARTERING

Bartering is the exchange of goods or services without the use of money. As described Chapters 2 and 10, the basic idea is for a company to exchange its surplus for something that it needs. Companies can advertise their surpluses in classified ads and may find a partner to make an exchange, but in most cases a company will have little success in finding an exact match. Therefore, companies usually ask an intermediary to help.

A bartering intermediary can use a manual search-and-match approach or it can create an electronic bartering exchange. With a **bartering exchange**, a company submits its surplus to the exchange and receives points of credit, which the company can then use to buy items that it needs. Popular bartering items are office space, idle facilities and labor, products, and even banner ads. Examples of bartering companies are barteronline.com, itex.com, and tradeway.com (see Chapter 10).

BUYING IN EXCHANGES AND INDUSTRIAL MALLS

Another option for the e-procurer is to buy at a B2B exchange or shop at an industrial e-mall. These options are described in Chapter 6.

bartering exchange
An intermediary that links parties in a barter; a company submits its surplus to the exchange and receives points of credit, which can be used to buy the items that the company needs from other exchange participants.

Section 5.7 ❱ REVIEW QUESTIONS

1. Describe an internal procurement marketplace and list its benefits.
2. Describe the benefits of desktop purchasing.
3. Discuss the relationship of desktop purchasing with internal procurement marketplaces and with group purchasing.
4. Explain the logic of group purchasing and how it is organized.
5. Describe how e-distributors operate and discuss their appeal to buyers.
6. How does B2B bartering work?

5.8 AUTOMATING B2B TASKS

The previous section described how businesses sell and buy electronically. These activities involve many managerial and administrative tasks. Some of these tasks can be fully automated; others are done manually but can be supported by software. Most are provided through exchanges (Chapter 6) as well. Let's look at some representative tasks.

CONTRACT MANAGEMENT

To simplify, standardize, and better manage contracts, one can use software such as CompleteSource Contract Management from Moai Technologies (moai.com). This software provides advanced contract management capabilities and is integrated with the CompleteSource Sourcing Management and Spend Analysis solutions from Moai. The software provides companies with the ability to manage supplier relationships and the resultant contracts, terms, conditions, nested obligations, and complex pricing that are unique to a particular organization, business practice, or industry. For more about managed services solutions, see ariba.com.

In general, contract-management software can:

▶ Reduce contract negotiation time and efforts.
▶ Facilitate inter- and intracompany contract analysis and development.
▶ Provide for proactive contract compliance management.
▶ Enable enterprisewide standardization of contracts.
▶ Improve understanding of contract-related risks.
▶ Provide a more efficient approval process.

SPEND MANAGEMENT

Companies spend a considerable amount of money on goods and services. Companies can use spend-management software (e.g., from Ariba or Moai) to view their purchasing behavior in real time. Such software is designed to meet the needs of companies that require advanced spend-analysis capabilities. Spend-analysis software provides companies with the ability to view and analyze purchasing spend data across complex, multilocation, and multipurchasing organizations.

The following tools and features may be found in spend-management software:

▶ A data warehouse repository designed to manage data from multiple data sources
▶ Data management of contracts, supplier catalogs, and product content
▶ Data management of pricing
▶ Detailed standard and ad-hoc purchasing activity analysis and report tools
▶ Updates, notifications, and alerts regarding purchasing

SOURCING MANAGEMENT AND NEGOTIATION

Companies that want to implement an e-sourcing solution in house can use sourcing management software. Designed to meet the needs of customers that require advanced e-sourcing capabilities and integrated with spend-analysis and contract-management solutions, the software provides companies with the flexibility to create online negotiation scenarios that are unique to a particular organization, business practice, or industry.

Sourcing management software includes tools and features such as:

▶ Bid comparison, including exports of detailed bid data
▶ User management functions that eliminate data redundancy, simplify data management, and reduce risk to data integrity
▶ Weighted scoring of parameters to calculate the total value offered by suppliers
▶ Total merchandise purchased cost model with bids winners selection and ranking
▶ Reverse auctions and sealed bids, with a full set of features such as proxy bids and bid-time extensions (see Chapter 10)
▶ Negotiation support tools

Negotiation Support Tools

Companies are spending considerable amounts of time on price negotiations, payment schedules, delivery options, quality assurance, insurance, and more.

Ideally, the negotiation process would be automated. Indeed, studies of e-negotiation, both in B2C and B2B, are fairly popular in the academic environment, with a special journal dedicated to the topic (*Group Decision and Negotiation*). Representative efforts in e-negotiation are provided in Online File W5.8 and in Veit (2004).

In the real world, negotiations primarily are done manually. However, vendors do provide software tools to streamline the manual negotiation process. One such tool is Ozro Negotiate, which is described in Insights and Additions 5.3.

Insights and Additions 5.3 Ozro Negotiate

Ozro Negotiate is a patented negotiation engine at the center of the Ozro Agreements application suite from Eyedeas (*eyedeas.net*). The Ozro Agreement application offers an iterative multivariate negotiation solution and is designed to provide easy connectivity to enterprise data and third-party applications. The technology facilitates people-centric, iterative, and multiattribute negotiations by providing competitive advantage by prompting, capturing, and synchronizing communications and data and producing supporting documentation. Basically, it fosters comprehensive agreements in any context.

Ozro Negotiate approaches comprehensive agreement management in the following areas:

▶ **RFx management.** Buyers can create and manage their requests for information, such as proposals and quotes, which are known as RFx, online. Previous requests can be used as templates, or new information about products, delivery schedules, payment terms, etc., can be entered or imported.

▶ **Offer management.** Sellers can also create and manage their offers, such as proposals and quotes, online. Starting with a buyer's request, information about price lists, products, availability, terms and conditions, and so on is entered or imported into Ozro's system.

▶ **Negotiation.** Requests are exchanged between buyers and sellers in a structured manner. Well-established negotiation techniques are used to iteratively bring their exchanges to a conclusion and create detailed commercial agreement.

▶ **Contract management.** Ozro Negotiate is the foundation for Ozro's integrated contract management solutions—the Ozro Agreements application suite. Through its enterprise software applications, Ozro is dedicated to driving cost and time savings to both internal and business partner operations throughout the lifecycle of an agreement.

▶ **Workflow.** In order to streamline the highly collaborative process of creating a request or an offer in an organization, the software tracks current status and ownership in real time as users contribute and approve content.

▶ **Security.** Ozro utilizes leading-edge security mechanisms to safeguard the highly confidential and critical information contained in requests, offers, and agreements during exchanges between involved parties.

▶ **Notifications/alerts.** Ozro Negotiate notifies negotiation teams about changes by tracking the status of all requests, offers and agreements. Alerts are sent to end-users and other systems regarding any status changes to accelerate the development and advancement of commercial agreements.

▶ **Change and update management.** Commercial agreements are rarely constant, and relationships evolve to continue to meet the needs of the marketplace. Ozro Negotiate technology supplies end-users with the ability to reopen and reestablish agreements to ensure they consistently reflect the ever-shifting aspects of the relationship.

▶ **Audit trail.** Nonrepudiation (Chapter 11) is fundamental to the development and application of commercial agreements by preventing future disputes over the commitments that were made in support of each party's intent. Ozro Negotiate technology tracks all changes, including the identity of the user that makes the changes, which allows for complete nonrepudiation and ensures the validity of agreements reached through the Ozro solution.

▶ **Archives.** Creating and managing the volumes of approved terms and conditions for an enterprise is a complex procedure. Ozro Negotiate technology provides a "clause library" to store approved boilerplate text for standard terms that a company typically uses. The clauses are easily stored, updated, and retrieved for use across agreements.

Sources: Compiled from *eyedeas.net* (accessed 2006) and Zoominfo (2006).

Questions

1. Identify the direct support that Ozro Negotiate provides to negotiators.

2. Visit *eyedeas.net* and find the Ozro demo. View the demo. Which features are most important? Why?

3. Which companies, in your opinion, would benefit the most from the product? Why?

E-PROCUREMENT MANAGEMENT

If properly implemented, not only can an e-procurement system be used for making online purchases, but it can also be used to connect companies and their business processes directly with suppliers, all the while managing the interactions between them. This includes management of correspondence, bids, questions and answers, previous pricing, and e-mails sent to multiple participants.

A good e-procurement system helps a firm organize its interactions with its most important suppliers. It provides users a set of built-in monitoring tools to help control costs and ensure maximum supplier performance. In addition, it provides an organized system to help keep lines of communication open with potential suppliers during the business process. The system also allows managers to confirm previous pricing and to leverage agreements to make certain that each new price quote is more competitive than the previous one.

The decision-making process is enhanced by e-procurement, because relevant information is neatly organized and time-stamped. Template-driven e-procurement solutions guarantee that all transactions are standardized and traceable. This improves a company's ability to keep track of all bids, thereby allowing it to leverage its knowledge to obtain better pricing and to focus on its most lucrative trading partners and contracts. E-procurement systems that allow multiple access levels and permissions help managers organize administrative users by roles, groups, or tasks. Thus, procurement managers do not need extensive training or increased wages because software systems are standardized and easy to learn. For details on e-procurement, see epiqtech.com/e-procurement.htm and en.wikipedia.org/wiki/E-Procurement.

Selecting Methods and Infrastructure

Two interrelated issues in e-procurement adoption are deciding which method(s) to adopt and which infrastructure to use. Dai and Kauffman (2006) explore two alternatives for infrastructure—extranets and exchanges (Chapter 6)—and relate them to the first issue by providing guidelines for selecting e-procurement channels to fit different procurement needs.

Section 5.8 ▶ REVIEW QUESTIONS

1. How is contract management being automated?
2. Describe spend-management programs.
3. How is negotiation supported electronically?
4. Describe e-procurement management tools.

5.9 INFRASTRUCTURE, INTEGRATION, AND SOFTWARE AGENTS IN B2B EC

In implementing B2B EC, the following issues need to be examined: what infrastructure to use, how to integrate the applications, and which software agents should be employed. For these and other issues, see Papazoglou and Ribbers (2006) and Teo et al. (2006).

INFRASTRUCTURE FOR B2B

Large numbers of vendors, including Oracle, Microsoft, HP, and IBM (see Online Chapter 19 for a description of vendors' offerings), offer all of the necessary B2B tools. The major infrastructures needed for B2B marketplaces include the following:

- ▶ Software to support various B2B activities, for example, software for electronic catalogs, direct sales and auctions, e-procurement, reverse auctions, call centers, and Web storefronts.
- ▶ Telecommunications networks and protocols (including EDI, extranets, and XML)
- ▶ Server(s) for hosting databases and the applications
- ▶ Security for hardware and software

B2B software products are sold independently as components or integrated as suites. Most companies use vendors to build their B2B applications, as shown in the Real-World

Case at the end of this chapter. The vendor sells or leases the company all of the necessary software to create the e-marketplace.

The major tools are presented in the following sections. Further discussion is available in Online Chapter 19 and in Ratnasingam (2006).

Extranets and EDI

For business partners to effectively communicate online, companies must implement some type of secure interorganizational network, such as a VAN or an extranet, and a common protocol, such as EDI or XML. Briefly, *extranets* ("extended intranets") are secured networks, usually Internet based, that allow business partners to access portions of each other's intranets. Extranets and their core technology are explained more fully in Appendix 6A.

Electronic data interchange (EDI) is the electronic transfer of specially formatted standard business documents, such as bills, orders, and confirmations, sent between business partners. Traditional EDI systems, which have been around for about 30 years, were implemented in **value-added networks (VANs),** which are private, third-party-managed common carriers that also provide communications services and security. However, VANs are relatively expensive and inflexible, and so many SMEs found EDI over VANs to be unaffordable.

However, many companies have found **Internet-based (Web) EDI** to be more affordable. It can be used to replace or supplement traditional EDI. Downing (2002) discovered that companies using Web-based EDI experience superior performance, both internally and externally. Web-based EDI can be implemented easily on the Internet see (Whiteley 2006). See Online File W5.9 for more on the evolution of traditional EDI to Internet-based EDI.

According to Boucher-Ferguson (2002), all major retailers, from Home Depot to Wal-Mart, and many manufacturers, such as Sara Lee Corp., are *requiring* their suppliers to conduct business via regular or Web-based EDI. EDI services are provided by companies such as GXS (gxs.com) and Sterling Commerce (sterlingcommerce.com) (see Chapter 6).

According to Bury (2005), although the possibilities inherent to the Internet may not be influencing companies that have already made investments in traditional EDI to change, the cost of entry for EDI—traditional or not—has definitely come down. For example, AS2 applications that allow customers to replace VAN with EDI/Internet can cost as little as $40 per month for limited EDI with no upfront cost. As a result, smaller companies are getting involved as EDI penetrates further down the supply chain. According to *Network World*, Internet-based EDI transactions are growing 50 to 60 percent annually; other studies point to a 5 to 8 percent growth rate for traditional services (reported by Bury 2005).

electronic data interchange (EDI)
The electronic transfer of specially formatted standard business documents, such as bills, orders, and confirmations, sent between business partners.

value-added networks (VANs)
Private, third-party-managed networks that add communications services and security to existing common carriers; used to implement traditional EDI systems.

Internet-based (Web) EDI
EDI that runs on the Internet and is widely accessible to most companies, including SMEs.

INTEGRATION

A critical success factor for many B2B initiatives is the proper integration of the systems involved. Two major cases are distinguished: (1) integration with the existing internal infrastructure and applications and (2) integration with business partners' systems.

Integration with the Existing Internal Infrastructure and Applications

EC applications of any kind need to be connected with the company's existing internal information systems. For example, an ordering system in sell-side B2B is usually connected with a payment verification system and an inventory management application. Representative systems that must be integrated with EC applications include marketing databases and databases from other departments; legacy systems and their applications; ERP software, which may include procurement functions; catalog (product) information; the payment system; CRM software; logistics and inventory systems; workflow systems; sales statistics; SCM systems; and business intelligence applications. All major EC software vendors, including IBM, Microsoft, Oracle, and SAP, provide for such integration.

Integration with Business Partners

EC can be integrated more easily with internal systems than with external ones. For instance, in the sell-side e-marketplace, it is not easy for the many buying companies to connect with each seller. Similarly, a buy-side e-marketplace needs to be connected with hundreds or even thousands of suppliers for each buyer. One solution is to go to exchanges, where each buyer or seller is connected only once. The interface with back-end information systems allows the customer to put items from different sellers in a single cart. This makes shopping much more convenient, because the customer pays only one time even though purchases are made from multiple sites.

Systems integrators and middleware vendors (such as IBM and TIBCO Software) provide many solutions for both internal integration (called Enterprise Application Integration, EAI) and external integration (called B2Bi, the *i* standing for integration). Details on systems integration are provided in Online Chapter 19 and in Polgar et al. (2006). Examples of system integration are provided by Amato-McCay (2004), Ho et al. (2006), and ITWorld at itworld.com.

Two competing approaches are used to integrate B2B with exchanges. The first is ERP II (or Extended ERP) solutions. ERP II is provided by traditional ERP solution providers by adding B2B functions, such as supply chain management (SCM), supplier relationship management (SRM), and customer relationship management (CRM) to ERP. The other is the ECM (Electronic Commerce Management) approach, which provides a multivendor open architecture for the integration of B2B and ERP. ERP integrates all the back-office operations (accounting, inventory, finance, etc.). Back-office operations must be integrated with EC because when an order is received in the front office, fulfillment starts by checking payment credibility, inventory, and so on. Later in the purchase process, billing and insurance need to be arranged. Finally, both Web Services (Online Chapter 19) and XML (Online Technical Appendix B) are playing an increasing role in integration support.

THE ROLE OF STANDARDS, ESPECIALLY XML, IN B2B INTEGRATION

For B2B companies to interact with each other easily and effectively, they must be able to connect their servers, applications, and databases. For this to happen, standard protocols and data representation schemes are needed. EDI is one such standard, but it has several limitations and is not structured for the Internet (see Online Appendix W5A).

The Web is based on the standard communication protocols of *TCP/IP* (Transmission Control Protocol/Internet Protocol) and *HTTP* (Hypertext Transfer Protocol). Further, Web pages are written in the universally recognized standard notation of *HTML* (Hypertext Markup Language and its variants). However, this standard environment is useful only for displaying static, visual Web pages. To further extend the functionality of EC sites, one can use JavaScript and other Java and ActiveX programs. These tools allow for human interaction, but they still do not address the need of interconnecting back-end database systems and applications. For that purpose, the industry is pursuing several alternatives for standardized data representation, such as XML.

XML

XML (eXtensible Markup Language)
Standard (and its variants) used to improve compatibility between the disparate systems of business partners by defining the meaning of data in business documents.

One of the most promising standards is **XML (eXtensible Markup Language)** and its variants (see Raisinghani 2001; Linthicum 2000). XML is a simplified version of a general data description language known as SGML (Standard Generalized Markup Language). XML is promoted as a new platform for B2B and sometimes as a replacement for EDI systems. It is used to improve compatibility between the disparate systems of business partners by defining the meaning of data in business documents.

XML was created in an attempt at overcoming barriers to EDI implementation, which are discussed in Online File W5.9. XML can overcome EDI barriers for three reasons:

1. XML is a flexible language, therefore new requirements and changes can be incorporated into messages. This expands the rigid ranges of EDI.

2. Message content can be easily read and understood by people using standard browsers. Thus, receivers do not need EDI translators. This enables SMEs to receive, understand, and act on XML-based messages.

3. EDI implementation requires highly specialized knowledge of EDI methodology. Implementation of XML-based technologies requires less-specialized skills.

XML and other related standards require national and international agreements and cooperation. Several organizations are devoted to these topics. For example, ebXML, developed by UN/EDIFACT (EDI for Administration Commerce and Transport), is a popular standard, and most B2B XML protocols support it. See Online Technical Appendix B for the basics of XML and a list of some important standards organizations and links to their Web sites. XML is combined frequently with Web Services in a service-oriented architecture (Erl 2004). One XML variant is voice XML, which is used to increase interactivity and accessibility with speech-recognition systems.

For an example of how XML works, see Online File W5.10. See Online Chapter 19, Online Technical Appendix B, voiceingov.org/blog, and xml.org for more details on XML.

XBRL

XBRL (eXtensible Business Reporting Language) is a version of XML for capturing financial information throughout a business' information processes. XBRL makes it possible to format reports that need to be distributed to shareholders, Sarbanes-Oxley regulators, banks, and other parties. The goal of XBRL is to make the analysis and exchange of corporate information more reliable (trustworthy) and easier to facilitate. For details, see Online File W5.11.

Web Services

Web Services is a general-purpose architecture that enables distributed applications to be assembled from a Web of software services in the same way that Web sites are assembled from a web of HTML pages. It is a growing topic in e-commerce and IT (see Erl 2004). The major technologies behind Web Services include XML, SOAP, UDDI, and WDSL (see Online Chapter 19). Using these standards, Web Services allows different applications from different organizations to communicate data without custom coding. Because all communication is in XML, Web Services is not tied to any one operating system or programming language.

Web services' distributed computing model allows application-to-application communication. For example, one purchase-and-ordering application could communicate to an inventory application that specific items need to be reordered. Web Services are viewed as building blocks for distributed systems. Many believe that Web Services will trigger a fundamental shift in the way that most distributed systems are created. Thus, Web Services will play a major role in facilitating B2B because it makes it easier to meet the demands of business customers and channel partners.

THE ROLE OF SOFTWARE AGENTS IN B2B EC

Software (intelligent) agents play multiple roles in B2B (see Chapter 6, Section 6.8). Chapter 3 discussed how software agents are used to aid customers in the comparison-shopping process in B2C. The major role of software agents in B2C is collecting data from multiple sellers' sites. Similarly, in B2B, software agents collect information from business sellers' sites for the benefit of business buyers. For information about B2B collaborative agents, see Lakshmi et al. (2004) and Wang (2006).

Software agents play a similar role in the B2B buy-side marketplace. Suppose that a large number of buyers need to request quotes from multiple potential suppliers. Doing so manually would be slow, physically difficult, and uneconomical. Therefore, software agents are needed to assist both buyers and sellers. See Cheung et al. (2004). Also, agents are very useful in reverse auctions (see Chapter 10).

Section 5.9 ▶ REVIEW QUESTIONS

1. List the major infrastructures required for B2B EC.
2. Describe the difficulties of integration with business partners.
3. Describe the roles of extranets and EDI in interorganizational networks.
4. Distinguish traditional EDI from Web-based EDI.
5. Describe the purpose of XML.
6. Describe Web Services and its role in integration.
7. What role do software agents play in B2B?

XBRL (eXtensible Business Reporting Language)
A version of XML for capturing financial information throughout a business's information processes. XBRL makes it possible to format reports that need to be distributed to shareholders, SOX regulators, banks, and other parties. The goal of XBRL is to make the analysis and exchange of corporate information more reliable (trustworthy) and easier to facilitate.

Web Services
An architecture enabling assembly of distributed applications from software services and tying them together.

MANAGERIAL ISSUES

Some managerial issues related to this chapter are as follows.

1. **Can we justify the cost of B2B applications?** Because there are several B2B models and architectures (see Al Mosawi et al. 2006 and Papazoglou and Ribbers 2006), each of which can be implemented in different ways, it is critical to conduct a cost-benefit analysis of the proposed applications (projects). Such an analysis should include organizational impacts, such as possible channel conflicts, and how to deal with resistance to change within the organization. Also, implementation difficulties may increase costs (see Langelier and Lapierre 2003). One way to justify B2B is to look at the experiences of successful companies, best practices, and guidelines for success. For justification of reverse auctions see Emiliani (2006).

2. **Which vendor(s) should we select?** Vendors normally develop the B2B applications, even for large organizations. Two basic approaches to vendor selection exist: (1) Select a primary vendor such as IBM, Microsoft, or Oracle. This vendor will use its software and procedures and add partners as needed. (2) Use an integrator that will mix and match existing products and vendors to create "the best of breed" for your needs. See Online Chapter 19 for details.

3. **Which B2B model(s) should we use?** The availability of so many B2B models, especially in e-procurement, means that companies need to develop selection strategies based on preferred criteria. In addition to the company-centric models, several types of exchanges should be considered.

4. **Should we restructure our procurement system?** If volume is heavy enough to attract the attention of major vendors, the company that is doing the purchasing might decide to restructure the procurement process by establishing a buy-side marketplace on its server. For example, IBM completely restructured its procurement processes prior to moving them online. Many organizations fail to understand that a fundamental change in their internal processes must be implemented to realize the full benefits of e-procurement. The two critical success factors that many organizations overlook are the need to cut down the number of routine tasks and the reduction of the overall procurement cycle through the use of appropriate information technologies such as workflow, groupware, and ERP software.

5. **What are the ethical issues in B2B?** Because B2B EC requires the sharing of proprietary information, business ethics are a must. Employees should not be able to access unauthorized areas in the trading system, and the privacy of trading partners should be protected both technically and legally.

6. **Will there be *massive* disintermediation?** With the increased use of private e-marketplaces, disintermediation and channel conflicts are bound to occur. However, reintermediation may occur with those vendors that can adapt to EC (see Malhotra and Malhotra 2006 and Zeng et al. 2003).

7. **How can trust and loyalty be cultivated in B2B?** As discussed in Chapter 4, trust and loyalty are important in any type of EC in which the partners do not know each other. For a discussion and a case study, see Ratnasingam and Phan (2003).

8. **How is mobile B2B done?** Mobile B2B is used to facilitate order taking, provide order tracking (status reports), facilitate communication for salespeople in the field, facilitate desktop procurement, and more (see Chapter 9). The issue here is the cost-benefit of the mobile application.

RESEARCH TOPICS

Some research issues related to this chapter are provided next. For details, references, and additional topics, refer to the Online Appendix A "Current EC Research."

1. **Issues in Adopting B2B**
   - Surveys on factors that facilitate or hinder the adoption of B2B
   - Identification of CSFs
   - Who makes adoption decisions and how
   - Surveys can be done by industry, B2B business model, country, etc.

2. **B2B Relationship Management**
   - How important relationships are and how to find the optimal level of investment in such relationships

- ▶ Interactive buyer–seller relationships
- ▶ How to justify and budget such relationships

3. **Issues in E-Procurement**
   - ▶ Investigation of the selection model (methods) and the implementation processes of e-procurement
   - ▶ Investigation of the cost-benefit and impacts of e-procurement
   - ▶ The need for restructuring the procurement processes
   - ▶ Issues that determine either the diffusion or adoption of e-procurement throughout an organization
   - ▶ Issues relating to implementing reverse auctions (e.g., design, communication, process, security)
   - ▶ Optimization models

4. **Intelligent Agents in B2B**
   - ▶ Agents used for research, comparisons, evaluation, and control (e.g., in auctions)
   - ▶ The role of multiagent systems in B2B processes
   - ▶ B2B buyer–seller online negotiations

5. **Issues in B2B Integration.** This is one of the most difficult issues in B2B. In addition to the various options available (all with some advantages and limitations) one needs to investigate:
   - ▶ Issues such as information sharing, security, and cost-benefit analysis
   - ▶ When integrating systems with those of business partners, a slew of additional issues surfaces. What are they and how can they be handled?
   - ▶ Surveys of best practices and role of intermediaries can be useful.
   - ▶ Usability of Web Services

6. **Electronic Data Interchange**
   - ▶ The direction of EDI and the role of Internet-based and XML-based EDI
   - ▶ In addition to adoption, barriers and cost-benefit of various EDI configurations need to be analyzed.

7. **B2B Mechanisms and Models**
   - ▶ Investigation of the various B2B models
   - ▶ Examination of the B2B mechanisms such as customized catalogs, auctions, and negotiations
   - ▶ Identification of B2B international Internet marketing

8. **Conflict Resolution in B2B**
   - ▶ How changing selling channels creates conflicts with existing distribution channels
   - ▶ A close examination of how to handle such conflicts

9. **B2B Intermediation.** A large number of intermediaries may be needed for proper B2B EC.
   - ▶ What roles intermediaries play, how best to select an intermediary, and how to assess their contribution
   - ▶ Which services will suffer from disintermediation and what types of intermediation would be most useful

10. **B2B Auctions**
    - ▶ Barriers to adoption
    - ▶ Types of B2B auctions, characteristics, usability
    - ▶ Alternative Dutch auctions

SUMMARY

In this chapter, you learned about the following EC issues as they relate to the learning objectives.

1. **The B2B field.** The B2B field comprises e-commerce activities between businesses. B2B activities account for 77 to 85 percent of all EC. B2B e-commerce can be done using different models.

2. **The major B2B models.** The B2B field is very diversified. It can be divided into the following segments: sell-side marketplaces (one seller to many buyers), buy-side marketplaces (one buyer from many sellers), and trading exchanges (many sellers to many buyers). Intermediaries play an important role in some B2B models.

3. **The characteristics of sell-side marketplaces.** Sell-side B2B EC is the online direct sale by one seller (a manufacturer or an intermediary) to many buyers. The major

technology used is electronic catalogs, which also allow for efficient customization, configuration, and purchase by customers. In addition, forward auctions are becoming popular, especially for liquidating surplus inventory. Sell-side auctions can be conducted from the seller's own site or from an intermediary's auction site. Sell-side activities can be accompanied by extensive customer service.

4. **Sell-side intermediaries.** The role of intermediaries in B2B primarily is to provide value-added services to manufacturers and business customers. They also can aggregate buyers and conduct auctions.

5. **The characteristics of buy-side marketplaces and e-procurement.** Today, companies are moving to e-procurement to expedite purchasing, save on

item and administrative costs, and gain better control over the purchasing process. Major procurement methods are reverse auctions (bidding system); buying from storefronts and catalogs; negotiation; buying from an intermediary that aggregates sellers' catalogs; internal marketplaces and group purchasing; desktop purchasing; buying in exchanges or industrial malls; and e-bartering. E-procurement offers the opportunity to achieve significant cost and time savings.

6. **B2B reverse auctions.** A reverse auction is a tendering system used by buyers to get better prices from suppliers competing to fulfill the buyers' needs. Auctions can be done on a company's Web site or on a third-party auction site. Reverse auctions can dramatically lower buyer's costs, both product costs and the time and cost of the tendering process.

7. **B2B aggregation and group purchasing.** Increasing the exposure and the bargaining power of companies can be done by aggregating either the buyers or the sellers. Aggregating suppliers' catalogs into an internal marketplace gives buying companies better control of purchasing costs. In desktop purchasing, buyers are empowered to buy from their desktops up to a set limit without the need for additional approval. They accomplish this by viewing internal catalogs with pre–agreed-upon prices with the suppliers. Industrial malls specialize in one

industry (e.g., computers) or in industrial MROs. They aggregate the catalogs of thousands of suppliers. A purchasing agent can place an order at an industrial mall, and shipping is arranged by the supplier or the mall owner. Buyer aggregation through group purchasing is very popular because it allows SMEs to get better prices on their purchases. In addition to direct purchasing, items can be acquired via bartering.

8. **Administrative tasks.** The major administrative tasks that can be automated are contract management, spend management, e-sourcing management, and negotiation.

9. **Infrastructure and standards in B2B.** To implement B2B, an organization will need a comprehensive set of hardware and software that includes networks and protocols, multiple servers, application software, and security. Of special utility are extranets and EDI (both traditional and Web based).

10. **Web-based EDI, XML, and Web Services.** Traditional EDI systems were implemented over VANs, making EDI inaccessible to most small companies. Web-based EDI can replace traditional EDI or supplement it. To improve connectivity between business partners' systems, standards organizations are pursuing XML, a standard for defining data elements. The connectivity of B2B can be facilitated by XML-related Web Services.

KEY TERMS

QUESTIONS FOR DISCUSSION

1. Explain how a catalog-based sell-side e-marketplace works and describe its benefits.

2. Discuss the advantages of selling through online auctions over selling from catalogs. What are the disadvantages?

3. Discuss the role of intermediaries in B2B. Distinguish between buy-side and sell-side intermediaries.

4. Discuss and compare all of the mechanisms that group-purchasing aggregators can use.

5. Should desktop purchasing only be implemented through an internal marketplace?

6. How do companies eliminate the potential limitations and risks associated with Web-based EDI? (See Online File W5.9.)

7. How can software agents work for multiple sellers and buyers?

8. Discuss the role of XML in B2B. Why is it so important?

9. Discuss the importance of Web Services to B2B integration.

10. Relate e-procurement to sourcing.

11. Discuss the role of XBRL in financial management.

INTERNET EXERCISES

1. Enter gxs.com and review GXS Express's bidding process. Describe the preparations your company would make in order to bid on a job. Also, check how some of the customers are using the company (e.g., Rohm and Haas 2005 case study).

2. Enter inovis.com and view the capabilities of BizManager and BizConnect. Write a report.

3. Visit allsystem.com to learn about All-System Aerospace International, Inc., a company that handles aircraft parts from several vendors. From an aircraft repair technician's point of view, evaluate whether this site can compete with Boeing's PART system (see Online File W5.2).

4. Examine the following sites: ariba.com, trilogy.com, and icc.net. Match a B2B business model with each site.

5. Visit supplyworks.com and procuri.com. Examine how each company streamlines the purchase process. How do these companies differ from ariba.com?

6. Enter soho.org and locate EC applications for SOHOs. Also, check the business services for small businesses provided by officedepot.com.

7. Visit ebay.com and identify all of the activities related to its small business auctions. What services are provided by eBay?

8. Review the Cisco Connection Online (CCO) case.

   a. What is the CCO business model?

   b. What are the success factors of CCO?

   c. What kinds of inquiries are supported when customers check their order status?

   d. What are the major benefits of CCO to Cisco and its customers?

9. Enter ondemandsourcing.com and view the demo. Prepare a list of benefits to small and mid-tier organizations.

10. Enter bitpipe.com and find recent B2B vendor reports related to e-procurement. Identify topics not covered in this chapter.

11. Visit iasta.com, purchasing.com, and cognizant.com examine the tools they sell for conducting various types of e-procurement. List and analyze each tool.

12. Enter bambooweb.com and find information about EDI. Prepare a report.

13. Enter terrecom.com. Summarize the B2B technology it provides. Relate the sell side, buy side, and auctions.

14. Enter the-buying-group.com, omca.com/group_buying.htm, and other group purchasing sites. Report on B2B group buying activities.

15. Go to procurenet.biz. Prepare a list of resources related to e-procurement.

TEAM ASSIGNMENTS AND ROLE PLAYING

1. Predictions about the future magnitude of B2B and statistics on its actual volume in various countries keep changing. In this activity, each team will locate current B2B predictions and statistics for different world regions (e.g., Asia, Europe, North America). Using at least five sources, each team will find the predicted B2B volume (in dollars) for the next 5 years in their assigned region. Sources statistics are listed in Exhibit 3.1 (p. 94).

2. Your goal in this assignment is to investigate the major B2B vendors. Each team should investigate a major

vendor (e.g., Ariba, Microsoft, HP, mySAP SRM, Oracle, or IBM) or an application type (buy-side, sell-side, or auction). Find the major products and services offered. Examine customer success stories. Write a report based on your findings. Convince the class that your vendor is the best.

3. Each team should explore a different e-procurement method and prepare a paper for a class presentation. The paper should include the following about the e-procurement method:

   a. The mechanisms and technologies used

   b. The benefits to buyers, suppliers, and others (if appropriate)

   c. The limitations

   d. The situations for which each method is recommended

4. Each team will research vendors that produce software for reverse auctions and vendors that conduct reverse auctions for businesses. Some companies to consider are **hedgehog.com**, **purchasing.com**, **oltiby.com**, **sorcity.com**, **epiqtech.com**, and **bizauctions.com**. Each team will compile information about the reverse auction process, security, and so on. Prepare and make a presentation of your findings.

Real-World Case

EASTMAN CHEMICAL MAKES PROCUREMENT A STRATEGIC ADVANTAGE

Eastman Chemical (ECM) is a multinational corporation with 2005 sales of $7 billion with approximately 12,000 employees. The company operates in an extremely competitive environment (*eastman.com*). In response to competitive pressures, management decided to improve on the procurement of MRO items. In its effort to do so, the company embarked on two interrelated activities: integrating the supply chain and introducing e-procurement. The objectives of the project, which was implemented in 2001, were:

▶ To increase compliance with purchasing policies (reduce maverick buying)

▶ To support frontline employees while maintaining existing rules

▶ To reduce procurement transaction costs via elimination of non–value-added and redundant processes

▶ To leverage corporate spending to negotiate favorable trading terms with channel supply partners

Before the system was installed, the company purchased over $900 million in MROs from over 3,500 suppliers. The company used a SAP R/3 ERP system, part of the legacy system that interfaced with the e-procurement application. The system provided good control but at a cost of $115 per order when a purchasing card (see Chapter 12) was used. The ERP system helped to reduce the workload on accounts payable and procurement personnel; however, purchasing from noncontracted suppliers increased (the card made such purchasing easy). This maverick buying reduced purchase volumes with primary suppliers, thus reducing the company's negotiating power and increasing costs.

As part of its initiative to improve the MRO procurement process, Eastman Chemical established channel partnership relationships with its largest MRO suppliers. This increased the company's buying leverage and reduced costs and delays. Inventories and service levels were improved. In addition, the company introduced two new EC applications from CommerceOne (now Perfect at *perfect.com*) to its procurement system: Commerce One Buy e-procurement software (now PerfectProcure) for dealing with the suppliers and Commerce One Conductor (now PerfectManage) for transaction management, partner relationship management (PRM), and value-added services.

Using the Buy software, Eastman Chemical has created an *internal catalog* of all MRO products located in Eastman's storerooms. The software checks availability and prevents redundant purchases. The software also supplies catalog-management features that ensure that all vendors' changes and updates are entered into the internal catalog.

The Conductor application supported the creation of a portal that enables the following:

▶ Use of a common Web browser by all of Eastman Chemical's 16,000 employees

▶ Different types of employees can use the system without the need for additional training

▶ The ability to integrate the SAP R/3 with EC and the procurement card

▶ An effective and efficient catalog management strategy

▶ Maintenance of the existing systems infrastructure

▶ Simplification of business processes

▶ Flexibility and empowerment of frontline employees

The overall effect of the new portal has been reduced costs and increased profitability and competitiveness.

By 2004, the system was used by over 6,000 users in 83 countries in procuring over $2 billion worth of goods. The system delivers significant cost savings, improved productivity, and error reduction. A 2004–2005 initiative is automating the RFQ process and special request purchases, using the Commerce One Conductor platform that was designed to connect and compose business processes between systems and partners.

Eastman Chemical has a large sell-side marketplace as well. Customers order plastics, resins, and fibers online and track their purchases and transaction history, even down to the level of a part of a shipment. Eastman Chemical also auctions its surplus materials in the marketplace.

Overall, Eastman Chemical's e-business logged 11 percent of the company's revenue in 2001.

Sources: Compiled from *eastman.com* (accessed November 2006), Aberdeen Group (2006), King (2001), Business Wire (2003), and Microsoft (2000).

Questions

1. Enter *perfect.com* and find information about the capabilities of PerfectProcure. Write a report.

2. Why did Eastman Chemical start first with e-procurement rather than with the sell side? You may want to visit *eastman.com* to learn more about the company.

3. In July 2000, Eastman Chemical introduced an EC project that enables buyers to participate in its private online price negotiations using LiveExchange from Moai (*moai.com*). Explain how the software works and why it is referred to as "dynamic commerce."

4. Which of the problems cited in this case can be solved by other EC applications? Relate your answer to Ariba products (*ariba.com*).

REFERENCES

Aberdeen Group. **aberdeen.com** (accessed November 2006).

Alexandersson, G., and S. Hulten. "Predatory Bidding in Competitive Tenders: A Swedish Case Study." *European Journal of Law and Economics*, July 2006.

Al Mosawi, A., L. Zhao, and L. Macaulay, "A Model Driven Architecture for Enterprise Application Integration," *Proceedings of the 39th Annual Hawaii International Conference on Systems Sciences*, January 4–7, 2006, Kauai, HI.

Amato-McCay, D. "Michael Foods Dishes Out Superior Service with Business Integration Solution." *Stores*, February 2004.

Ariba.com. **ariba.com** (accessed March 2007).

Asset-Auctions.com. "CNC Machine Tools Case Study." **asset-auctions.com/casestudy_cnc.html** (accessed November 2006).

Boucher-Ferguson, R. "Writing the Playbook for B2B." *Wilson Internet*, January 29, 2002.

Bury, S. "Piggly Wiggly's Doing IT." *Manufacturing Business Technology*, February 2005. **mbtmag.com/current_issues/2005/feb/integInfra1.asp** (accessed September 2006).

Bush, D. "e-Sourcing Does Not Equal Reverse Auction." *E-Sourcing Forum*, March 24, 2006. **esourcingforum.com/?cat=8** (accessed September 2006).

Business Wire. "Commerce One's New Composite Application Platform Delivers Unprecedented Value to Customers." March 24, 2003.

Cheung, C. F., W. M. Wang, V. Lo, and W. B. Lee. "An Agent-Oriented and Knowledge-Based System for Strategic E-Procurement." *Expert Systems*, February 2004.

Cisco Annual Report. Cisco Systems, 2005. **cisco.com/web/about/ac49/ac20/ac19/ar2005/index.html** (accessed March 2007).

Commonwealth of Pennsylvania. "Pennsylvania's Surplus Property Programs." 2006. **dgs.state.pa.us/surp_prop/cwp/view.asp?a=3&q=120977** (accessed September 2006).

Dai, Q., and R. J. Kauffman. "To Be or Not to B2B: Evaluating Managerial Choices for E-Procurement Channel Adoption." *Information Technology and Management*, April 2006.

Dasgupta, P., L. E. Moser, and P. M. Melliar-Smith. "Dynamic Pricing for E-Commerce," in Khosrow-Pour (2006).

Downing, C. E. "Performance of Traditional and Web-Based EDI." *Information Systems Management* 19, no. 1 (2002).

Eastman. **eastman.com** (accessed November 2006).

eMarketer. "Has B2B E-Commerce Stagnated?" *Emarketer.com*, February 3, 2003. **emarketer.com/**

products/database.php?f_arg_0=B2B+85+percent+of+
e-commerce+2002&f_arg_0_b=B2B+85+percent+of+
e-commerce+2002&f_num_args_changed=1&f_num_
articles_found=2&f_num_charts_found=2&f_num_
reports_found=0&f_reports_found=&f_request=
&f_search_type=Basic&Image81.x=0&Image81.y=0
(no longer available online).

Emiliani, M. L. "Executive Decision-Making Traps and B2B
Online Reverse Auctions." *Supply Chain Management:
An International Journal* 11, no. 1 (2006).

ePaynews. "Statistics for Banking and Treasury
Management." *ePaynews.com*, 2005. **epaynews.com/
statistics/bankstats.html** (accessed September 2006).

ePaynews. "US Firms Favor E-Invoicing and Payment
Systems." *ePaynews.com*, August 12, 2004. **epaynews.com/
index.cgi?survey=&ref=browse&f=view&id=
1092329119622215212&block=** (accessed September
2006).

Erl, T. *Service-Oriented Architecture.* Upper Saddle River,
NJ: Prentice Hall, 2004.

Eyedeas.net. "Ozro Negotiate." **eyedeas.net/clients/ozro/
oursolutions/index.cfm** (accessed November 2006).

Fickel, L. "Online Auctions: Bid Business." *CIO Web Business
Magazine*, June 1, 1999.

Fortune. "E-Procurement: Unleashing Corporate Purchasing
Power." *Fortune*, 2000. available for download at
jobfunctions.bnet.com/whitepaper.aspx?docid=70133
(accessed March 2007).

General Motors. **gm.com** (accessed August 2002).

Grainger.com. "Grainger at a Glance." 2006.
**pressroom.grainger.com/phoenix.zhtml?c=194987&
p=irol-factsheet** (accessed September 2006).

Haig, M. *The B2B E-Commerce Handbook.* United
Kingdom: Kogan Page Ltd., 2003.

Hancock, M. Q., R. H. John, and P. J. Wojcik. "Better B2B
Selling." *The McKinsey Quarterly*, June 16, 2005.

Harris, L. "B2B E-Commerce Sites Increase Profitability
through Intelligent Search." **b2bmarketingtrends.com/
abstract.asp?id=198&groupid=9** (accessed August 2006).

Ho, G. T. S., C. K. M. Lee, H. C. W. Lau, A. W. H. Ip.
"A Hybrid Intelligent System to Enhance Logistics
Workflow: An OLAP-Based GA Approach." *International
Journal of Computer Integrated Manufacturing* 18, no. 1
(2006).

Hoffman, W., J. Keedy, and K. Roberts. "The Unexpected
Return of B2B." *The McKinsey Quarterly* no. 3 (2002).

Hoover, J. N. "The Cisco Premium." *InformationWeek*, July
31–August 7, 2006.

Hubler, D. "Reverse Auctions Become a Diplomatic
Tool." *FCW.com*, August 14, 2006. **fcw.com/
article95594-08-14-06-Print** (accessed March 2007).

IBM. *Whirlpool's B2B Trading Portal Cuts per Order Cost
Significantly.* White Plains, NY: IBM Corporation
Software Group, Pub. G325-6693-00, 2000.

Interwoven, Inc. "Interwoven Solutions Power Cisco
Connection Online." Interwoven case study, 2001.
**writeit4u.net/documents/interwoven/casestudy_cisc
o.pdf** (accessed March 2007).

Jakovljevic, P. J. "Differences in Complexity between B2C
and B2B E-Commerce." *TechnologyEvaluation.Com*,
March 4, 2004. **facweb.cs.depaul.edu/econfer/ect455/
Class%20Material/B2B%20B2C%20Distinctions.pdf**
(accessed March 2007).

Johnson, P. F., and R. D. Klassen. "E-Procurement." *MIT
Sloan Management Review*, Winter 2005.

King, J. "Chemical Weapon." *ComputerWorld*, July 16, 2001.
**computerworld.com/industrytopics/manufacturing/
story/0,10801,61471,00.html** (accessed March 2007).

Khosrow-Pour, M. (ed.). *Encyclopedia of E-Commerce,
E-Government, and Mobile Commerce.* Hershey, PA:
Idea Group Reference, 2006.

Lakshmi, I., R. Singh, and A. F. Salam. "Intelligent Agents to
Support Information Sharing in B2B E-Marketplaces."
Information and Management, Summer 2004.

Langelier, P., and V. Lapierre. *Winning Strategies for B2B
E-Commerce.* Montreal, Canada: IQ Collectif, 2003.

Linthicum, D. S. "Applications with XML." *e-Business
Advisor*, May 2000.

Lucas, H. C. *Information Technology: Strategic Decision
Making for Managers.* Hoboken, NJ: John Wiley and
Sons, 2005.

Malhotra, R., and D. K. Malhotra. "The Impact of Internet
and E-Commerce on the Evolving Business Models in
the Financial Services Industry." *International Journal of
Electronic Business* 4, no. 1 (2006).

Mastercard. "MasterCard Purchasing Card Program."
Mastercard.com, 2006. **mastercard.com/us/business/
en/pdf/MC%20Sell%20Sheet%20Purchasing%2005
3006.pdf** (accessed September 2006).

Microsoft. "Business Review: Eastman Chemical."
2000. **download.microsoft.com/documents/customer
evidence/5484_eastman_commerceone.doc** (accessed
November 2006).

Moai. "Solutions Overview." **moai.com/solutions/
solutions_overview.asp** (accessed September 2006).

Mockler, R. J., D. G. Dologite, and M. E. Gartenfeld.
"B2B E-Business," in Khosrow-Pour (2006).

Mudambi, R., C. P. Schunder, and A. Monger. "How
Co-Operative is Co-Operative Purchasing in Smaller
Firms." *Long-Range Planning*, February 2004.

Murphree, J. "Global Enabled Supply and Demand Chain
Series: Sourcing." *Source*, February–March 2003.
**sdcexec.com/publication/article.jsp?pubId=1&id=
4410** (accessed March 2007).

Office of Government Commerce. "E-Procurement in
Action." Spring 2005. **ogc.gov.uk/documents/cp0025.
pdf** (accessed March 2007).

Papazoglou, M., and P. Ribbers. *Building B2B Relationships—
Technical and Tactical and Implementations of E-Business
Strategy.* Hoboken, NJ: Wiley & Sons, 2006.

Patton, S. "Answering the Call." *CIO.com*, June 1, 2006.
**cio.com/archive/060106/call_center.html?action=
print** (accessed September 2006).

Podlogar, M. "Simplifying the Procurement Process by
Using E-Commerce." *International Journal of Internet
and Enterprise Management* 4, no. 2 (2006).

Polgar, J., R. M. Bram, and A. Polgar. *Building and Managing Enterprise-Wide Portals.* Hershey, PA: Idea Group Inc., 2006.

Professional Advantage. "Regent Inns PLC: eProcurement Case Study." **pa.com.au/sunsystems**(accessed October 16, 2006).

Raisinghani, M. S. "Extensible Markup Language: Synthesis of Key Ideas and Perspectives for Management." *Information Management* 14, no. 3, 4 (2001).

Ratnasingam, P. "The Evolution of Trust in Business-to-Business E-Commerce," in Khosrow-Pour (2006).

Ratnasingam, P., and D. D. Phan. "Trading Partner Trust in B2B E-Commerce: A Case Study." *Information Systems Management* (Summer 2003).

Rincon, A. "Gregg's Cycles Succeeds in E-Commerce by Not Selling Bikes Online." **onlinebusiness.about.com/od/ casestudies/a/greggscycles.htm** (accessed November 2006).

Rudnitsky, H. "Changing the Corporate DNA." *Forbes,* July 24, 2000.

Sadeh, N. M. "Advances in B2B E-Commerce and E-Supply Management." *Journal of Organizational Computing and E-Commerce* 13, no. 3 & 4 (2003).

Saryeddine, R. *E-Procurement: Another Tool in the Tool Box.* Ottowa Ontario, Canada: The Conference Board of Canada, 2004.

Schoenherr, T., and V. A. Mabert. "Bundling for B2B Procurement Auctions." *International Journal of Integrated Supply Management* 2, no. 3 (2006).

Segev, A., and J. Gebauer. "B2B Procurement and Marketplace Transformation." *Information Technology and Management* (July 2001).

Slater, R. *The Eye of the Storm: How John Chambers Steered Cisco through the Technology Collapse.* New York: Harper-Collins, 2003.

Small Business Administration. **sba.gov/advo/stats** (no longer available online).

Smeltzer, L. R., and A. Carr. "Reverse Auctions in Industrial Marketing and Buying." *Business Horizons,* March–April 2002.

Smith, A. D. "Supply Chain Management Using Reverse Auctions." *International Journal of Services and Standards* 2, no. 2 (2006).

Teo, T. S. H., C. Ranganathan, and J. Dhaliwal. "Key Dimensions of Inhibitors for the Deployment of Web-Based B2B E-Commerce." *IEEE Transactions on Engineering Management,* August 2006.

Veit, D. J. *Matchmaking in Electronic Markets.* New York: Springer-Verlag, 2004.

Wang, M. "Comparative Shopping on Agent Web Sites," in Khosrow-Pour (2006).

Ward's Auto World. "Auto Talk: GM Rings in Era of e-Commerce." March 2000. **findarticles.com/p/articles/ mi_m3165/is_2000_March/ai_62959140** (accessed November 2006).

Whirlpool. **whirlpoolcorp.com** (accessed November 2006).

Whiteley, D. "Electronic Data Interchange," in Khosrow-Pour (2006).

Wikipedia. "E-Procurement." 2006. **en.wikipedia.org/ wiki/E-procurement** (accessed March 2007).

Zeng, Y. E., H. J. Wen, and D. C. Yen. "Customer Relationship Management (CRM) in Business-to-Business (B2B) E-Commerce." *Information Management and Computer Security* 11 (2003).

Zhao, F. *Maximize Business Profits through E-Partnership.* Hershey, PA: Idea Group Inc., 2006.

Zoominfo. "Ozro Inc." 2006. **zoominfo.com/Search/ CompanyDetail.aspx?CompanyID=53035849&cs= QFDKUNJh0** (accessed December 2006).

B2B EXCHANGES, DIRECTORIES, AND OTHER SUPPORT SERVICES

Learning Objectives

Upon completion of this chapter, you will be able to:

1. Define exchanges and describe their major types.
2. Describe the various ownership and revenue models of exchanges.
3. Describe B2B portals.
4. Describe third-party exchanges.
5. Distinguish between purchasing (procurement) and selling consortia.
6. Define dynamic trading and describe B2B auctions.
7. Describe partner relationship management (PRM).
8. Discuss integration issues of e-marketplaces and exchanges.
9. Discuss B2B networks.
10. Discuss issues in managing exchanges, including the critical success factors of exchanges.

Content

CHEMCONNECT: THE WORLD COMMODITY CHEMICAL EXCHANGE

The Problem

The trading of raw and partially processed chemicals, plastics, fuel oil, and related materials is performed daily by thousands of companies in almost every country in the world. Before the Internet, the trading process was slow, fragmented, ineffective, and costly. As a result, buyers paid too much, sellers had high expenses, and intermediaries were needed to smooth the trading process.

The Solution

Today, buyers and sellers of chemicals and plastics can meet electronically in a large Internet public marketplace (founded in 1995) called ChemConnect (*chemconnect.com*). Global chemical industry leaders, such as BP, Dow Chemical, BASF, Hyundai, Sumitomo, and many more, make transactions over ChemConnect every day in real time. They save on transaction costs, reduce cycle time, and find new markets and trading partners around the globe. It was the first mover B2B e-market in the chemical industry.

ChemConnect provides a trading marketplace and an information portal to over 9,000 members worldwide in 150 countries. Members are producers, consumers, distributors, traders, and intermediaries involved in the chemical industry.

ChemConnect offers its members a Trading Center with three trading places:

1. **Marketplace for buyers.** In this marketplace, buyers can find suppliers all over the world. They can post RFQs with reverse auctions, negotiate, and more.

2. **Marketplace for sellers.** This marketplace provides sellers with exposure to many potential new customers. It provides automated tools for quick liquidation. More than 1,000 products are negotiated in auctions.

3. **Commodity markets platform.** This platform provides a powerful connection to the global spot marketplaces for chemicals, plastics, and other materials. Members can trade at market prices, access real-time market intelligence, and effectively manage risk. Traders can exchange bids and offers quickly, confidently, and anonymously, until the deal is complete.

ChemConnect members can use the Trading Center to streamline sales and sourcing processes by automating requests for quotes, proposals, and new suppliers. The center enables a member to negotiate more efficiently with existing business partners as well as with new companies the member may invite to the table—all in complete privacy. With over 9,000 companies, the Trading Center is a highly effective way to get the best prices and terms available on the worldwide market. In addition, members can access a database containing more than 63,000 chemicals and plastics—virtually any product members are ever likely to look for. In addition to trading, the exchange provides back-end fulfillment services (e.g., payments, delivery).

ChemConnect is an independent, third-party intermediary; thus, it works within certain rules and guidelines that ensure an unbiased approach to trades. All legal requirements, payments, trading rules, and other guidelines are fully disclosed. (Click "Policies, Fees, and Legal Information" on the site for more information on ChemConnect's disclosure policies.) The revenue model includes members' annual transaction fees, subscription fees (for trading and for auctions), and fulfillment transaction fees. Members pay transaction fees only for successfully completed transactions.

All three trading locations provide up-to-the-minute market information (via *bloomberg.com*) that can be translated into 30 different languages. Business partners provide several support services. For example, Citigroup and ChemConnect jointly offer several financial services for exchange members. ChemConnect also offers systems for connecting companies' back-end systems with their business partners and with ChemConnect itself.

ChemConnect is linked to GXS (see Insights and Additions 6.1), which manages a network of tens of thousands companies.

The Results

The overall benefits of ChemConnect to its members are more efficient business processes, lower overall transaction costs, and time saved during negotiation and bidding. For example, conducting a reverse auction in a trading room enables buyers to save up to 15 percent of a product's cost in just 30 minutes. The same process using manual bidding methods would take several weeks or months. One company that placed an RFQ for 100 metric tons of a certain acid to be delivered in Uruguay with a starting price of $1.10 per kilogram reduced the price to $0.95 in only six consecutive bids offered in 30 minutes.

In addition, sellers can reach more buyers and liquidate surpluses rapidly.

ChemConnect continues to grow, adding members and increasing its trading volume each year. (Transaction volume in 2004 was over $10 billion.) The company hopes to become profitable in 2004. One of the company's success factors is that 40 large chemical companies hold about one-third of the company's stock. Another factor is the fact that about 44 percent of the industry uses the exchange on a regular basis. ChemConnect market data are distributed by Bloomberg (*bloomberg.com*), a major financial information services company.

ChemConnect has expanded its coverage to become a more diversified company, offering midstream energy, such as ethanol, natural gas, and other commodities. It has also added negotiation solutions, collaboration hubs, data integration services, price discovery features, and more. Also, its community has been expanded. Participant companies include most producers,

consumers, distributors, traders, and transportation and logistics companies within each product class in addition to banks, hedge funds, and other interested financial institutions.

Sources: Based on information from *chemconnect.com* (accessed September 2006), Angwin (2004), and Rappa (2006).

WHAT WE CAN LEARN . . .

The ChemConnect story demonstrates an e-marketplace with many buyers and many sellers. Initially, all of its members were in the chemical industry (a vertical e-marketplace), but it has expanded to include other commodities. ChemConnect's buyers and sellers, as well as other business partners, congregate electronically to conduct business. This type of a marketplace is an *electronic exchange* that is owned and operated by a third-party intermediary. As will be seen later in the chapter, ownership of an exchange has some major implications for B2B marketplaces. The functions of the exchange expanded from transaction provider to transaction and value-added services provider.

In contrast to the company-centric models that were the focus of Chapter 5, the models in this chapter include *many buyers* and *many sellers*. They usually are *public* e-marketplaces, which are known by a variety of names and have a variety of functions. For now, we will simply call them *exchanges*.

6.1 B2B ELECTRONIC EXCHANGES—AN OVERVIEW

public e-marketplace (public exchange)
A many-to-many e-marketplace. Trading venues open to all interested parties (sellers and buyers); usually run by third parties. Some are also known as *trading exchanges*.

exchange
See public e-marketplace.

market maker
The third party that operates an exchange (and in many cases, also owns the exchange).

As defined in Chapter 2, **public e-marketplaces**, or **public exchanges** (in short *exchanges*), are trading venues open to all interested parties (many sellers and many buyers) that use a common technology platform and that are usually run by third parties or industry consortia (see Umar 2005). The term *exchange* implies many-to-many e-marketplaces. In the context of EC, exchanges are online trading venues. Many exchanges support community activities, such as distributing industry news, sponsoring online discussion groups, blogging, and providing research. Some also provide support services such as payments and logistics (see Iyer 2004 and Papazoglou and Ribbers 2006).

Exchanges are known by a variety of names: *e-marketplaces, e-markets,* and *trading exchanges.* Other terms include *trading communities, exchange hubs, Internet exchanges, Net marketplaces,* and *B2B portals.* We will use the term **exchange** in this book to describe the general many-to-many e-marketplaces, but we will use some of the other terms in more specific contexts (e.g., see epiqtech.com/others-B2B-Exchanges.htm).

Despite their variety, all exchanges share one major characteristic: Exchanges are electronic trading-community meeting places for many sellers and many buyers, and possibly for other business partners, as shown in Exhibit 6.1 At the center of every exchange is a **market maker**, the third party that operates the exchange and, in many cases, may also own it.

In an exchange, just as in a traditional open-air marketplace, buyers and sellers can interact and negotiate prices and quantities. Generally, free-market economics rule the exchange trade community, as demonstrated by ChemConnect.

According to Forrester Research (as reported by Shetty 2001), 2,500 exchanges worldwide, at several stages of operation, were in existence in the spring of 2001. Since then, more than 70 percent have folded due to a lack of customers, cash, or both (e.g., Chemdex and MetalSite). However, the companies that use exchanges, both as sellers and buyers, are generally pleased with them and plan to increase the number of exchanges they are participating in (from 1.7 to 4.1, on average), within 2 years (Dolinoy et al. 2001). Traders usually more than double the value of transactions that they do through an exchange after the first two years of participation.

EXHIBIT 6.1 The Community of an Exchange: Flow and Access to Information

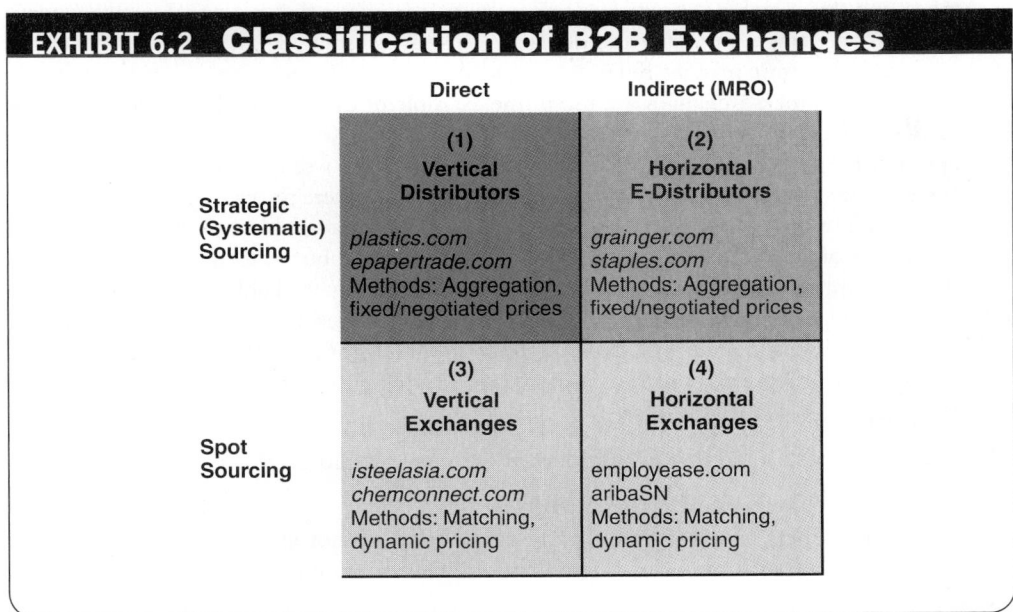

EXHIBIT 6.2 Classification of B2B Exchanges

CLASSIFICATION OF EXCHANGES

Exchanges can be classified in several ways. We will use the approach suggested by Kaplan and Sawhney (2000). According to this classification, an exchange can be classified into one of four cells of a matrix, as shown in Exhibit 6.2. The matrix has two dimensions. Across the top, two types of materials are traded, either *direct* or *indirect* (MRO), as defined in Section 5.1. Down the left side are two possible sourcing strategies: *strategic* and *spot* (see Section 5.1). The intersection of these characteristics results in four exchange classifications (the four cells of Exhibit 6.2).

If strategic sourcing is used for direct materials, the market maker aggregates the buyers, the sellers, or both, and provides the platform for *negotiated* prices and contracted terms (cell #1).

Strategic sourcing of direct materials, which are usually traded in large quantities, is frequently done with the aid of intermediaries. An example of this type of exchange can be found at plastics.com, an exchange for the plastics industry. Using the speed, access, and ease of the Internet, the exchange simplifies and streamlines the process of buying and selling at substantially reduced administrative costs, and sometimes reduced product costs as well.

In strategic sourcing of indirect materials (MROs) (cell #2), the market maker basically aggregates sellers' catalogs, as MRO.com (mro.com) does. MRO.com provides tools and technology in a hosted environment that enables manufacturers and distributors of industrial parts—the "supply" of the industrial supply chain—to participate in EC quickly and affordably. MRO.com creates one catalog containing products from multiple suppliers, connects the catalog to an order-processing system, and offers different types of industrial buyers a single source from which to buy their MROs.

Spot sourcing of *direct materials* (cell #3) takes place in **vertical exchanges**, which are considered vertical because sales take place in one industry or industry segment. Examples of vertical exchanges are ChemConnect and an exchange called ISteelAsia (isteelasia.com), which conducts online auctions and bids for steel.

Spot sourcing of indirect materials (cell #4) takes places in **horizontal exchanges**. These exchanges are considered horizontal because they handle materials traded for use by companies from different industries. For example, light bulbs and office supplies might be purchased in a horizontal exchange by both an automaker and a steelmaker. (In these horizontal exchanges, MROs can include both products, such as office supplies, as well as services, such as temporary labor.) Horizontal exchanges offer a variety of mechanisms, as shown in Online File W6.1.

DYNAMIC PRICING

The market makers in both vertical and horizontal exchanges match supply and demand in their exchanges, and this matching determines prices. In spot sourcing, the prices are usually *dynamic* and are based on changes in supply and demand. (In strategic sourcing, they are usually negotiated or fixed.) **Dynamic pricing** refers to a rapid movement of prices over time and possibly across customers. Stock exchanges are the prime example of dynamic pricing. Prices on stock exchanges sometimes change by the second, depending at any moment on how much buyers are willing to pay for a stock and how many sellers of that stock are willing to sell at various prices. Another good example of dynamic pricing occurs in *auctions*, where prices vary all the time.

Dynamic pricing is based on market information being available to buyers and sellers. One of the reasons the stock and some other exchanges are thought to work as well as they do is the amount of financial and other information generally available to the traders. The Internet provides a large amount of product information, sometimes in real time. Therefore, the Internet facilitates many of the dynamic pricing models for both B2B and B2C.

The typical process that results in dynamic pricing in most exchanges includes the following steps:

1. A company posts a bid to buy a product or an offer to sell one.
2. An auction (forward or reverse) is activated.
3. Buyers and sellers can see the bids and offers but may not always see who is making them. Anonymity is often a key ingredient of dynamic pricing.
4. Buyers and sellers interact with bids and offers in real time. Sometimes buyers join together to obtain a volume discount price (group purchasing).
5. A deal is struck when there is an exact match between a buyer and a seller on price, volume, and other variables, such as location or quality.
6. The deal is consummated, and payment and delivery are arranged.

Third-party companies usually provide supporting services such as credit verification, quality assurance, escrow service, insurance, and order fulfillment (see Exhibit 6.1). They ensure that the buyer has the money and that the product is in good condition. They also may coordinate product delivery (see Chapter 13).

In Chapter 5, we described group purchasing, negotiating, and forward auctions, which also employ dynamic pricing. When dynamic pricing is used with methods such as auctions, the process is referred to as *dynamic trading*. For example, IBM's WebSphere Commerce suite (see Online Chapter 19) includes a dynamic trading module that enables reverse auctions, exchanges, and contract negotiations.

FUNCTIONS OF EXCHANGES

According to Tumolo (2001), exchanges have three major functions:

1. **Matching buyers and sellers.** The matching of buyers and sellers includes such activities as:
   - ◗ establishing product offerings;
   - ◗ aggregating and posting different products for sale;
   - ◗ providing price and product information;
   - ◗ organizing bids, bartering, and auctions;
   - ◗ matching supplier offerings with buyer preferences;
   - ◗ enabling price and product comparisons;
   - ◗ supporting negotiations and agreements between buyers and suppliers; and
   - ◗ providing directories of buyers and sellers.

2. **Facilitating transactions.** Facilitating transactions includes the following activities:
   - ◗ providing the trading platform and mechanisms such as arranging logistics of delivering information, goods, or services to buyers;
   - ◗ providing billing and payment information, including addresses;
   - ◗ defining terms and other transaction values;
   - ◗ inputting searchable information;
   - ◗ granting exchange access to users and identifying company users eligible to use the exchange;
   - ◗ settling transaction payments to suppliers, collecting transaction fees and providing other escrow services;
   - ◗ registering and qualifying buyers and suppliers;
   - ◗ maintaining appropriate security over information and transactions; and
   - ◗ arranging for group (volume) purchasing.

3. **Maintaining exchange policies and infrastructure.** Maintaining institutional infrastructure involves the following activities:
   - ◗ ascertaining compliance with commercial code, contract law, export and import laws, and intellectual property law for transactions made within the exchange;
   - ◗ maintaining technological infrastructure to support volume and complexity of transactions;
   - ◗ providing interface capability to standard systems of buyers and suppliers; and
   - ◗ obtaining appropriate site advertisers and collecting advertising and other fees.

OWNERSHIP, GOVERNANCE, AND ORGANIZATION OF EXCHANGES

Let's look at several issues related to the ownership and operation of exchanges.

Ownership of Exchanges

Ownership models for Internet exchanges are of three basic types: industry giant, neutral entrepreneur, and a consortium.

◗ **One company, usually an industry giant.** In this model, one manufacturer, distributor, or broker sets up the exchange and runs it. An example is IBM, which established an exchange for the purpose of selling patents (delphion.com). In 1999, IBM placed 25,000 of its own patents up for sale and invited others to sell their patents as well. (Delphion is part of Thomson Corp. and has expanded to a portal for intellectual property.) This model is an extension of the sell-side model described in Chapter 5. General Electric's TPN (see Online File W5.9) is another classic example of a buy-side exchange that was initially controlled by an industry giant. It led to the creation of the GXS exchange, which is now owned by a group of investors. In the past, Samsung of South Korea manually brokered various commodities; as of 2002 it had several online exchanges, including one for fish. Note that one owner can set the policies, rules, and access to the market; hence, it is considered a *private exchange*, which is a many-to-many marketplace owned by one company. In contrast, a *private marketplace* has one seller and many buyers or one buyer and many sellers. The major issue for this type of exchange is whether the giant's large competitors will be willing to use it.

▶ **A neutral entrepreneur.** Under this model, a *third-party* intermediary sets up an exchange and promises to run an efficient and unbiased exchange. ChemConnect, for example, is a neutral exchange. (This type of exchange is discussed in Section 6.3.) The potential problem for such exchanges is whether buyers and sellers will use the exchange.

▶ **The consortium (or co-op).** With this type of exchange, several industry players get together and decide to set up an exchange so that all can benefit. (Consortia are discussed in Section 6.4.) A major potential problem with this model is determining who is in charge of the exchange.

Governance and Organization

Exchanges have their own board of directors and are governed by guidelines and rules, some of which are required by law. These rules and guidelines must be very specific regarding how the exchange operates, what the requirements are to join, what fees are involved, and what rules need to be followed. Furthermore, the governance document needs to specify security and privacy arrangements, what will happen in case of disputes, and so forth. The contract terms between an exchange and buyers and sellers also are critical, as are assurances that the exchange is fair.

Regardless of their ownership, revenue model, and governance structure, exchanges may include the following organizational elements.

Membership. Membership refers to the community's relationship to the exchange, to the fees charged, and to the class type of the member. Members can have full privileges or partial privileges (associate members). Also, there are different types of fees. For example, exchanges that do not charge members a fee to join (e.g., alibaba.com) may collect transaction or service fees. For exchanges that charge registration fees and annual membership fees (e.g., chemconnect.com), varying levels of membership may be offered. For example, members may be either *observing members*, who can only view what is going on but cannot trade, or *trading members*, who can make offers and bid, pay, and arrange deliveries. Trading members usually need to go through a qualification process with the market maker. In some cases, a cash deposit is required. There may be other categories of members. Some exchanges set limits on how much each member can trade.

Site Access and Security. Exchanges must be secure. Because members' activities may be strategic and competitors frequently congregate in the same exchange, information must be carefully protected. In addition to regular EC security measures, special attention should be made to prevent illegal offers and bids. Several exchanges have a list of individuals who are authorized to represent the participating companies.

Services Provided by Exchanges. Exchanges provide many services to buyers and sellers. The types of services offered depend on the nature of the exchange. For example, the services provided by a stock exchange are completely different from those provided by a steel or food exchange or by an intellectual property or patent exchange. However, most exchanges provide the services shown in Exhibit 6.3.

ADVANTAGES, LIMITATIONS, AND THE REVENUE MODEL OF EXCHANGES

Exchanges have several benefits, including making markets more efficient, providing opportunities for sellers and buyers to find new business partners, cutting the administrative costs of ordering MROs, and expediting trading processes. They also facilitate global trade and create communities of informed buyers and sellers.

Despite these benefits, beginning in 2001, exchanges started to collapse, and both buyers and sellers realized that they faced the risk of exchange failure or deterioration. In the case of exchange failure, the risk is primarily a financial one—of suddenly losing the market in which one has been buying and selling and, therefore, having to scramble to find a new exchange or to find buyers and sellers on one's own. In addition, finding a new place to trade is an operational risk. Buyers also risk potentially poor product performance and receipt of incomplete information from degraded exchanges, which is a risk the sellers may face, too. For more on competition among buyers in online exchanges, see Bandyopadhyay et al. (2005).

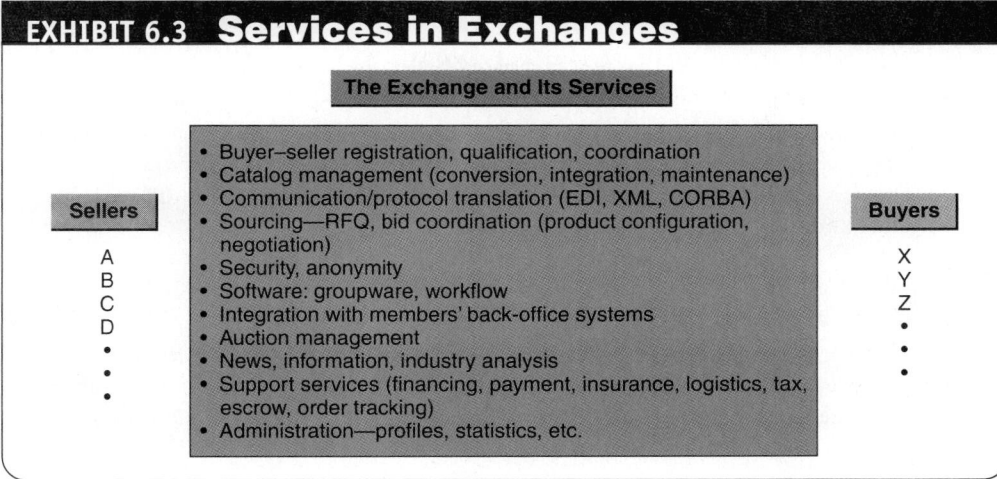

EXHIBIT 6.3 **Services in Exchanges**

The Exchange and Its Services

Sellers

A
B
C
D
•
•

- Buyer–seller registration, qualification, coordination
- Catalog management (conversion, integration, maintenance)
- Communication/protocol translation (EDI, XML, CORBA)
- Sourcing—RFQ, bid coordination (product configuration, negotiation)
- Security, anonymity
- Software: groupware, workflow
- Integration with members' back-office systems
- Auction management
- News, information, industry analysis
- Support services (financing, payment, insurance, logistics, tax, escrow, order tracking)
- Administration—profiles, statistics, etc.

Buyers

X
Y
Z
•
•

The potential gains and risks of B2B exchanges for buyers and for sellers are summarized in Exhibit 6.4. As the exhibit shows, the gains outnumber the risks.

Revenue Models

Exchanges, like all organizations, require revenue to survive. Therefore, an exchange's owners, whoever they are, must decide how they will earn revenue. The following are potential sources of revenue for exchanges.

▶ **Transaction fees.** Transaction fees are basically a commission paid *by sellers* for each transaction they make (see Chapter 1). However, sellers may object to transaction fees, especially when regular customers are involved. Exchanges charge relatively low transaction fees per order in order to attract sellers. Therefore, to cover its expenses the exchange must generate sufficient volume, find other revenue sources, or raise its transaction fees.

EXHIBIT 6.4 **Potential Gains and Risks in B2B Exchanges**

	for Buyers	for Sellers
Potential gains	• One-stop shopping, huge variety • Search and comparison shopping • Volume discounts • 24/7 ordering from any location • Make one order from several suppliers • Huge, detailed information • Access to new suppliers • Status review and easy reordering • Community participation • Fast delivery • Less maverick buying • Better partner relationship management	• New sales channel • No physical store is needed • Reduced ordering errors • Sell 24/7 • Community participation • Reach new customers at little extra cost • Promote the business via the exchange • An outlet for surplus inventory • Can go global more easily • Efficient inventory management • Better partner relationship management
Potential risks	• Unknown vendors; may not be reliable • Loss of customer service quality (inability to compare all services)	• Loss of direct CRM and PRM • More price wars • Competition for value-added services • Must pay transaction fees (including on seller's existing customers) • Possible loss of customers to competitors

▶ **Fee for service.** Some exchanges have successfully changed their revenue model from commission (transaction fee) to "fee for service." Sellers are more willing to pay for value-added services than for commissions. Sometimes buyers also pay service charges.

▶ **Membership fees.** A membership fee is a fixed annual or monthly fee. It usually entitles the exchange member to get some services free or at a discount. In some countries, such as China, the government may ask members to pay annual membership fees and then provide the participating sellers with free services and no transaction fees. This encourages members to use the exchange. The problem is that low membership fees may result in insufficient revenue to the exchange. However, high membership fees discourage participants from joining.

▶ **Advertising fees.** Exchanges also can derive income from fees for advertising on the information-portal part of the exchange. For example, some sellers may want to increase their exposure and will pay for special advertisements on the portal (like boxed ads in the yellow pages of telephone books).

▶ **Other revenue sources.** If an exchange is doing auctions, it can charge auction fees. License fees can be collected on patented information or software. Finally, market makers can collect fees for their services.

Section 6.1 ▶ REVIEW QUESTIONS

1. Define B2B exchanges and list the various types of public exchanges.
2. Describe strategic sourcing and spot sourcing.
3. Differentiate between a vertical exchange and a horizontal exchange.
4. What is dynamic pricing? How does it work?
5. Describe the types of ownership and the possible revenue models of exchanges.
6. List the potential advantages, gains, limitations, and risks of exchanges.

6.2   B2B PORTALS AND DIRECTORIES

B2C sometimes can be conducted in *information portals* (often called just *portals*), such as MSN or Yahoo!, where information (such as Yahoo!'s shopping directory) is targeted at individual customers or businesses. Buyers can place orders on some portals, but in many cases buyers are transferred to sellers' storefronts to complete their transactions, or they are just passive directories.

B2B portals
Information portals for businesses.

Similar situations exist in B2B. **B2B portals** are information portals for businesses. Some e-marketplaces act as pure information portals. They usually include *directories* of products offered by each seller, lists of buyers and what they want, and other industry or general information. Buyers then visit sellers' sites to conduct their transactions. The portal may get commissions for referrals or only derive revenue from advertisements. Thus, information portals may have a difficult time generating sufficient revenues. Because of this, many information portals are beginning to offer, for a fee, additional services that support trading, such as escrow and shipments. An example of a B2B portal is MyBoeingFleet.com (myboeingfleet.com), which is a Web portal for airplane owners, operators, and MRO operators. Developed by Boeing Commercial Aviation Services, MyBoeingFleet.com provides customers (primarily businesses) direct and personalized access to information essential to the operation of Boeing aircraft.

Like exchanges, information portals may be horizontal (e.g., Alibaba.com, described later), offering a wide range of products to different industries. Or they may be vertical, focusing on a single industry or industry segment. Vertical portals are often referred to as **vortals**.

vortals
B2B portals that focus on a single industry or industry segment; "vertical portals."

Some use the word *portal* when referring to an exchange. The reason for this is that many B2B portals are adding capabilities that make them look like exchanges. Also, many exchanges include information portals.

The two examples that follow illustrate some of the differences between *portals* and *exchanges*.

THOMAS GLOBAL

Thomas Global (thomasglobal.com) is a directory of over 700,000 manufacturers and distributors from 28 countries, encompassing over 11,000 products and service categories in 9 languages. It covers regional guides, such as Thomas Register of America (thomasnet.com), an information portal, which publishes a directory of millions of manufacturing companies. Thomas Register is basically an information portal for buyers using search engines because it does not offer any opportunity for transactions on its site. For example, it does not offer a list of products with quantities needed (requests to buy) or offer what is available from sellers. A similar information-only service is provided by Manufacturing.Net (manufacturing.net).

ALIBABA.COM CORPORATION

Another intermediary that started as a pure information portal but that is moving toward becoming a trading exchange is Alibaba.com (alibaba.com). Launched in 1999, Alibaba.com initially concentrated on China. It includes a large, robust community of international buyers and sellers who are interested in direct trade without an intermediary. Initially, the site was a huge posting place for classified ads. Alibaba.com is a portal in transition, showing some characteristics of an information portal plus some services of an exchange. Alibaba has today two complementary markets:

Alibaba International (alibaba.com) is an English-language Web site primarily serving small and medium-sized enterprises (SMEs) in the international trade community. It has more than 2 million registered users from over 200 countries and territories. More than 500,000 people visit the site every day, most of them global buyers and importers looking to find and trade with sellers in China and other major manufacturing countries.

Alibaba China (china.alibaba.com) is China's largest online marketplace for domestic trade among businesspeople. With more than 10 million registered users, Alibaba China is a trusted community of members who regularly meet, chat, search for products, and do business online. Customers pay an annual subscription fee for membership, which entitles them to post trade offers and products online. The subscription fee also includes authentication and verification of the member's identity, which is performed by a third-party credit reporting agency.

In addition, Alibaba owns yahoo.china.cn, a leading Internet search engine for businesses and japan.alibaba.com. It also had a major stake in taobao.com, a Chinese C2C auction site (see Heilemann 2006).

To understand the capabilities of Alibaba.com, we need to explore its marketplace (take the multimedia tour!).

The Database

The center of Alibaba.com is its huge database, which is basically a horizontal information portal with offerings in a wide variety of product categories. The portal is organized into 27 major product categories (as of 2006), including agriculture, apparel and fashion, automobiles, and toys. Each product category is further divided into subcategories (over 700 in total). For example, the toy category includes items such as dolls, electrical pets, and wooden toys. Each subcategory includes classified ads organized into four groups: sellers, buyers, agents, and cooperation. Each group may include many companies. The ads are fairly short. Note that in all cases a user can click an ad for details. In 2006, all postings were still free. Some categories have thousands of postings; therefore, a search engine is provided. The search engine works by country, type of advertiser, and age of the postings.

Reverse Auctions

Alibaba.com also allows buyers to post RFQs. Would-be sellers can then send bids to the buyer, conduct negotiations, and accept a purchase order when one is agreed upon (all via the exchange). As of March 2007, the process was not fully automated. (To see how the process works, go to "My trade activity" and take the tour, initiate a negotiation, and issue a purchase order.)

Features and Services

Alibaba.com provides the following features: free e-mail, Trust Service, FAQs, tutorials for traders, free e-mail alerts, a China club membership, news (basically related to importing and exporting), trade show information, legal information, arbitration, and forums and discussion groups. In addition, a member can create a personalized company Web page as well as a "sample house" (for showing their products); members also can post their own marketing leads (where to buy and sell). As of 2006, the site offers its services in English, Chinese, and Korean. Also, the site is doing e-tailing.

For-fee services include business credit reports, payment service (AliPay), export/import reports, and a quote center for shipping services. In the future, additional services will be added to increase the company's revenue stream.

Revenue Model

The site's revenue stream has been expanded from advertisements only to include fees for special services. For example, income is generated through paid memberships, online booths, priority listings, and so on. Alibaba.com competes with several global exchanges that provide similar services (e.g., see asia-links.com and globalsources.com). The advantage of Alibaba.com is its low operational costs. Therefore, it probably will be able to sustain losses much longer than its competitors. Someday in the future, Alibaba.com may be in a position that will enable it to make a great deal of money. Alibaba.com was strong enough to sustain losses until 2003, when it made $12 million profit.

DIRECTORY SERVICES AND SEARCH ENGINES

The B2B landscape is huge, with hundreds of thousands of companies online. Directory services can help buyers and sellers manage the task of finding specialized products, services, and potential partners. Some popular directories are listed and described in Exhibit 6.5. Note that the last three entries in the exhibit are specialized search engines, which can be used to find information about B2B. Some of these are embedded in the directories.

According to Killeen (2006), specialized search engines are becoming a necessity in many industries due to the information glut. The most useful search engines are those concentrating on vertical searches. Examples of vertical search engines and their services can be found at globalspec.com. In contrast to vertical searches, products such as Google Search provide search capabilities on many topics within one enterprise or on the Web in general.

Section 6.2 ▶ REVIEW QUESTIONS

1. Define B2B portals.
2. Distinguish a vortal from a horizontal portal.
3. List the major services provided by Alibaba.com.
4. Compare Alibaba.com with its competitors, such as asia-links.com and globalsources.com.
5. Describe some directory services in B2B.
6. Describe the role of search engines for B2B markets.

6.3 THIRD-PARTY AND DIRECTORIES EXCHANGES

The opening vignette introduced ChemConnect, a neutral, public, third-party-owned vertical market maker. ChemConnect's initial success was well publicized, and dozens of similar third-party exchanges, mostly in specific industries, have been developed since. A thriving example of a third-party exchange is Agentrics.com, which is described in Case 6.1 (p. 272).

Third-party exchanges are electronic intermediaries. In contrast with a portal, such as Alibaba.com, the intermediary not only presents catalogs (which the portal does) but also tries to *match* buyers and sellers and encourages them to make transactions by providing electronic trading floors and rooms (which portals, in general, do not).

EXHIBIT 6.5 B2B Directory Services

Directory	Description
b2business.net	A major resource for B2B professionals that provides listings of business resources in about 30 functional areas, company research resources (e.g., credit checks, customs research, financial reviews), and information on start-ups.
b2btoday.com	Contains listings of B2B services organized by type of service (e.g., Web site creation, B2B marketing, and B2B software) and product category (e.g., automotive, books).
communityb2b.com	Offers many B2B community services, such as news, a library, events calendar, job market, and resource directory.
a2zofb2b.com	Company directory organized in alphabetical order or industry order. Specifies the type and nature of the company, the venture capital (VC) sponsor, and the stock market ticker (if it is an IPO).
i-stores.co.uk	A UK-based directory of online stores; provides validation of secure Web sites.
dmoz.org/business	A large business directory organized by location and by product or service. Also provides listings by industry and subindustry (according to SIC code).
thomasnet.com	Directory of more than 150,000 manufacturers of industrial products and services.
dir.yahoo.com	Provides business directories that cover over 300,000 companies; see dir.yahoo.com/Business_and_Economy/Business_to_Business.
bocat.com	Bocat provides a B2B portal for marketplaces, directories, news, and resources supported by powerful search engines.
business.com	A comprehensive directory of B2B markets and services.
creditnet.com	A directory of 14 million companies. You can get credit reports on each for a monthly fee.
alibaba.com	Directory of suppliers for international customers.
sw365.com	Repository of B2B marketplaces.
Search Engines	
moreover.com	In addition to locating information, also aggregates B2B (and other business) news.
google.com	In addition to its search tools, offers a directory of components for B2B and B2C Web sites (e.g., currency exchange calculators, server performance monitors, etc.).
ientry.com	Provides B2B search engines, targeted "niche engines," and several industry-focused newsletters. Operates a network of Web sites and e-mail newsletters that reaches over 2,000,000 unique opt-in subscribers.
openbc.com	Finding partner's networks, job market.
hoovers.com	Financial information on 16 million companies. See company-information.

The following are some examples of other successful exchanges:

- Agentrics (agentrics.com), which serves the global retail industry
- Global Healthcare Exchange (ghx.com), which specializes in hospital and medical supplies
- i-MARK (imark.com), which sells surpluses
- Winery Exchange (wineryexchange.com), which specializes in wines
- ChemConnect (chemconnect.com), which offers chemicals and plastics
- Farms.com (farms.com), which specializes in agriculture-related products.

Third-party exchanges are characterized by two contradicting properties. On the one hand, they are *neutral* because they do not favor either sellers or buyers. On the other hand, because they do not have a built-in constituency of sellers or buyers, they sometimes have a problem attracting enough buyers and sellers to attain financial viability. Therefore, to increase their financial viability, these exchanges try to team up with partners, such as large sellers or buyers, financial institutions that provide payment schemes (as ChemConnect did with Citigroup), and logistics companies that fulfill orders. The goal of such partnerships and alliances is to cut costs, save cash, and possibly increase liquidity. **Market liquidity** is the

market liquidity
The degree to which something can be bought or sold in a marketplace without significantly affecting its price. It is determined by the number of buyers and sellers in the market and the transaction volume.

CASE 6.1
EC Application
AGENTRICS: A GIANT RETAIL EXCHANGE

Agentrics is the world's largest exchange for retail and packaged consumer goods. It was formed from the mergers of several exchanges, including the World Wide Retail Exchange (WWRE) and GNX. As of November 2006, it has 250 members, including 17 of the world's 25 top retailers (e.g., Best Buy, Sears, Safeway, Tesco). Its primary objective is to enable participating retailers and manufacturers to simplify, rationalize, and automate supply chain processes, thereby eliminating inefficiencies in the supply chain. Today, Agentrics is the premier Internet-based business-to-business (B2B) exchange in the retail e-marketplace. Utilizing the most sophisticated Internet technology available, the exchange enables retailers and manufacturers in the food, general merchandise, textile/home, and drugstore sectors to substantially reduce costs across product development, e-procurement, and supply chain processes. The exchange is used by more than 100,000 suppliers, partners, and distributors worldwide.

The exchange operates as an open, *independently* managed company that generates benefits for its members and ultimately the consumer. Agentrics is run as a private company with no plans of going public. Rather, it concentrates on bringing value to its members and customers.

Founding Principles
The following six principles guide the exchange's development and growth:

1. Openness
2. Commitment to utilizing the best available technology
3. Focus on improving efficiency and lowering costs for the retail industry
4. Operation as a neutral company
5. Equivalent fee structures for all participants
6. Confidentiality of transaction information

Value Proposition
Members realize value in seven key ways:

1. Low-cost product offerings that are robust, scalable, integrated, and fully supported
2. Shared technology investments and outsourced assets
3. Ability to access a global membership community and network with other retailers/manufacturers
4. Value-added services from a trusted source, at competitive costs
5. Participation in collaborative activities
6. Complex transactions and interactions made easy through automation
7. Standard-setting benefits for all B2B activities

The exchange offers about 20 different products and services. They are classified as those related to WWRE (e.g., global data synchronization, trading, sourcing, supply chain solutions) and those related to GNX (e.g., collaboration, performance and life cycle management, CPFR [see Chapter 7], and negotiation).

An example of one of the exchange's current projects is its Global Data Synchronization. Inaccurate product and item information costs the consumer goods industry more than $40 billion each year. Agentrics has developed a solution that enables retailers and suppliers to accurately maintain item information using industry standards and achieve a single point of entry into the Global Data Synchronization Network. The project is supported by webMethods Corporation, which provides the necessary integration.

Sources: Compiled from *agentrics.com* (accessed November 2006) and *webmethods.com* (accessed December 2005).

Questions

1. Enter *agentrics.com* and find information about services offered, including auctions and negotiations. Write a report.

2. Enter *agentrics.com* and identify the services offered and the benefits to retailers and to suppliers. Write a summary.

3. Enter *webmethods.com* and find information about the item synchronization project (for WWRE). Summarize the benefits to retailers and to suppliers.

degree to which something can be bought or sold in a marketplace without significantly affecting its price (e.g., without having to discount the price). To achieve market liquidity, there must be a sufficient number of participants in a marketplace, as well as a sufficient volume of transactions (see Section 6.7).

However, not all partnerships bring the desired results. In a partnership that did not work, Chemdex, a pioneering exchange that closed in late 2000, allied itself with VWR Scientific Products, a large brick-and-mortar intermediary. In the case of Chemdex, its liquidity was not large enough, despite the alliance.

Two major models of third-party exchanges exist: supplier aggregation and buyer aggregation.

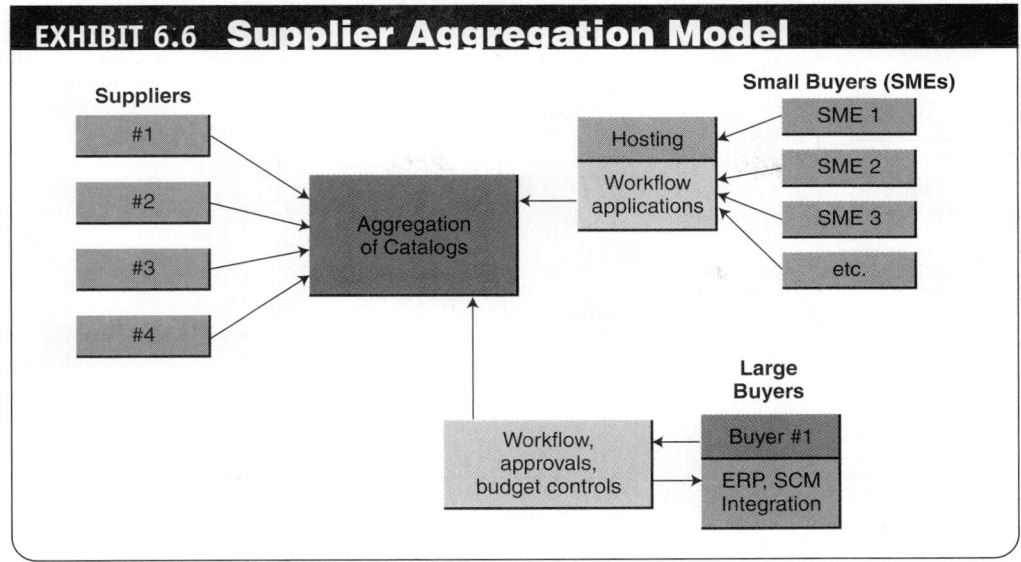

EXHIBIT 6.6 **Supplier Aggregation Model**

THE SUPPLIER AGGREGATION MODEL

In the *supplier aggregation model*, distributors standardize, index, and aggregate suppliers' catalogs or content and make this content available to buyers in a centralized location.

An example is the catalog of MRO suppliers at perfect.com. As shown in Exhibit 6.6, a market aggregator aggregates suppliers' catalogs and presents them to potential buyers. (This model is similar to the sell-side e-marketplace described in Chapter 5, but with *many* sellers, and it is more difficult to manage than B2C.)

Notice that Exhibit 6.6 shows two types of buyers: large and small (SMEs). Large buyers need software to support the purchase-approval process (e.g., workflow software; see Chapter 7), budgeting, and the tracking of purchases across the buying organization. This requires system integration with existing company regulations, contracts, pricing, and so forth. Such integration may be provided by an ERP architecture. As you may recall from Chapter 5, Bigboxx.com (Online File W5.2) provided such a service to its large buyers using SAP software. (For more on ERP integration, see Online Tutorial T1.) For smaller buyers, hosted workflow software and other applications are available from ASPs.

The major problems encountered in the supplier aggregation model are in recruiting suppliers and introducing the system to buyers. Solving these problems requires a strategic plan (see Epstein 2005).

THE BUYER AGGREGATION MODEL

In the *buyer aggregation model*, buyers' RFQs are aggregated (usually by a third party) and then linked to a pool of suppliers that are automatically notified of buyers' RFQs. The suppliers can then make bids. (This is similar to the buy-side e-marketplace described in Chapter 5, but with several buyers.) The buyers (usually small businesses) can benefit from volume discounts, especially if they use a group-purchasing approach. The sellers benefit from the new source of pooled buyers. Exhibit 6.7 shows the buyer aggregation model.

SUITABILITY OF THIRD-PARTY EXCHANGES

The aggregation models work best with MROs and services that are well defined, that have stable prices, and where the supplier or buyer base is fragmented. Buyers save on search and transaction costs and are exposed to more sellers. Sellers benefit from lower transaction costs as well as from an increase in their customer base.

As in other types of e-marketplaces, the most important key to the success of any third-party exchange is the critical mass of buyers and sellers. Fram (2002) believes that third-party

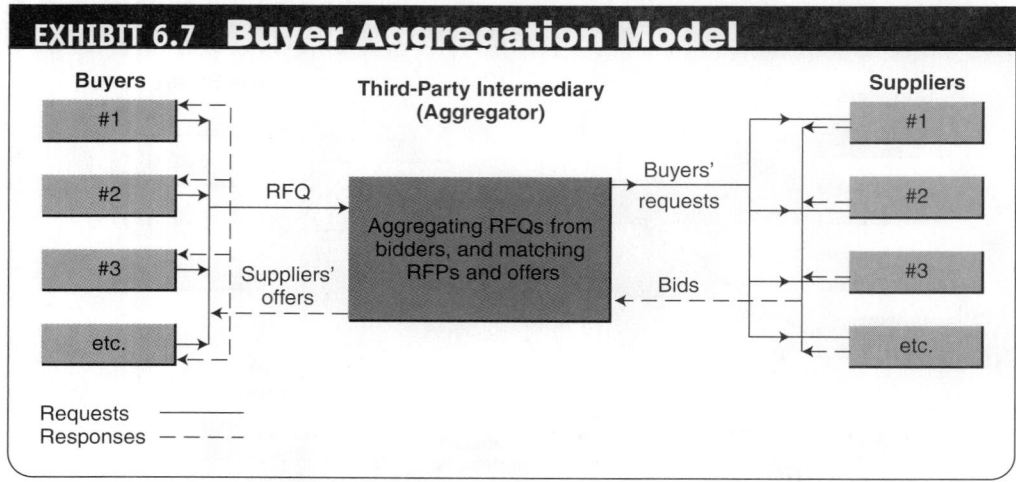

EXHIBIT 6.7 Buyer Aggregation Model

exchanges, if properly planned and built, will be one of the prominent EC pillars of the future. In 2006, many third-party exchanges were still struggling but on the whole performing better.

Section 6.3 ▶ REVIEW QUESTIONS

1. What is a third-party owned exchange?
2. Define liquidity.
3. Describe the supplier aggregation model.
4. Describe the buyer aggregation model.
5. List the market characteristics that are most suitable for third-party exchanges.

6.4 CONSORTIUM TRADING EXCHANGES

consortium trading exchange (CTE)
An exchange formed and operated by a group of major companies in an industry to provide industrywide transaction services.

A subset of third-party exchanges is a **consortium trading exchange (CTE)**, an exchange formed and operated by a group of major companies in one industry. The major declared goal of CTEs (also called *consortia*) is to provide industry-wide transaction services that support buying and selling. These services include links to the participants' back-end processing systems as well as collaborative planning and design services.

Markets operate in three basic types of environments, shown in the following list. The type of environment indicates which type of exchange is most appropriate.

1. **Fragmented markets.** These markets have large numbers of both buyers and sellers. Examples include the life sciences and food industries. When a large percentage of the market is fragmented, third-party managed exchanges are most appropriate.
2. **Seller-concentrated markets.** In this type of market, several large companies sell to a very large number of buyers. Examples are the plastics and transportation industries. In this type of market, consortia may be most appropriate.
3. **Buyer-concentrated markets.** In this type of market, several large companies do most of the buying from a large number of suppliers. Examples are the automotive, airline, and electronics industries. Here, again, consortia may be most appropriate.

According to Richard and Devinney (2005), CTEs fared much better than independent third-party exchanges during the dot-com shakeout that took place in 2000–2002. Yet, of the hundreds of CTEs that existed all over the world in 2000, by 2002 many had folded or were inactive, including giants such as Covisint (see Online File W6.2). By 2006, CTEs had achieved stability, and some new exchanges arrived on the business scene.

The four types of CTEs are classified by two main criteria: (1) whether they focus on buying or selling and (2) whether they are vertical or horizontal. The four types of consortia are:

1. Purchasing oriented, vertical
2. Purchasing oriented, horizontal
3. Selling oriented, vertical
4. Selling oriented, horizontal

In addition to these categories, some CTEs, such as GTN's Ocean Portal, described in the Case 6.2 at the end of the chapter, focus on providing services. The following sections describe the characteristics of each type of CTE, offer examples of each of type, and examine several issues related to consortia.

CASE 6.2
EC Application
GLOBAL TRANSPORTATION NETWORK OCEAN PORTAL

Although much publicity is given to public exchanges that deal with materials and products, such as ChemConnect, several service-oriented exchanges have been created, and some of them are growing rapidly. One such exchange is a global transportation exchange for ocean transportation named Global Transportation Network (GTN).

GTN was formed in 2001 by a consortium of 13 ocean carriers (lines) that collectively represent more than 40 percent of worldwide capacity, and a software company, GT Nexus (*gtnexus.com*) that specializes in global logistics and supply chain products.

The objective of the exchange, which is primarily a *portal* type, is to serve the ocean-shipping industry. The industry is composed of carriers, shippers (such as Wal-Mart and others who import many goods from abroad), and service providers (such as banks, insurance brokers, freight forwarders, and logistics providers). The mission of the exchange is to fundamentally change the process of getting goods around the world by using the Internet to provide superior service that maintains complete security for customers and the carriers. GT Nexus and its CEO are the exchange managers.

To develop the portal, the management team worked with many customers to identify customer needs and determine how the portal could help meet them. Customers wanted a multi-EC model that could meet their diversified needs in a unified way. Existing B2B software products were too narrow; a custom portal had to be built.

The GTN e-commerce platform is much more than a portal. It supports core transactional capabilities such as booking, invoicing, payment, tracking and tracing, rate negotiation, container management, and scheduling. GTN offers standardized booking, documentation, and tracking systems and provides better and more efficient customer support. In addition, it provides customized capabilities tailored for specific customers and carriers, including rate and contract management, cargo

forecasting, and resource allocation. The benefits of the system to the ocean-shipping industry include:

- **Significant efficiencies and cost savings.** A 2002 study conducted by Accenture estimated that cost savings from these process improvements and efficiencies alone resulted in savings of 5 to 10 percent for carriers and customers across a range of industries (Coia 2002a). GTN frees individual carriers from the huge capital costs associated with the advanced technologies and resources required to create proprietary technology methods.
- **Standardization and ease of use.** GTN automates core transactions and makes it easier for customers to conduct business with multiple providers using common standards.
- **Secure and confidential access.** GTN provides a secure and confidential environment for customers and carriers to conduct business over the Internet.

Industry experts have observed various improvements for the participants of the exchange (Goodman 2002). A single carrier cannot afford to offer as many EC applications as the exchange offers; therefore, the exchange has greatly expanded the number of applications available to carriers. The system also has enabled customers to do business electronically throughout every process in the shipment cycle. For example, contract negotiation, a very time-consuming process, has been speeded up by the exchange. In addition, because carriers now have access to many more shippers than they could have found on their own, the number of electronic transactions for carriers has doubled, even in the first year of operation in the exchange. Carriers have also been able to improve customer service, one of the major motivators for using the exchange.

The shipping industry is deregulated and very competitive. However, lots of cooperation, such as vessel sharing, still goes on. The GTN system helps to facilitate such collaboration.

(continued)

CASE 6.2   *(continued)*

Several alliances among carriers also exist, and they are supported by the system. Information sharing via open standards and Web-enabled systems is a primary objective of the portal.

The technology of the exchange has contributed to its effectiveness. Data fit the internal IT systems of all users. Standardized processes allow carriers to present their services to shippers in the same way. Clients are able to use one interface to retrieve any information, regardless of the carrier with which the booking was made. The system uses a secured Internet connection (with a VPN) and has an optional EDI for some transactions. It also allows for competitive tendering through *reverse auctions*. The exchange was recognized by *InfoWorld Magazine* (Sanborn 2002) as one of top three technology projects.

For the 2006 bid season, GT Nexus tallied the following results:

▶ Over 2.6 million TEUs procured and managed over the portal (one TEU is a 20-foot cargo container or its equivalent)
▶ More than $3.5 billion in transportation services contracted with carriers
▶ Participation of ocean carriers who together control more than 90 percent of global TEU capacity

These numbers are up 150 percent from 2005 and represent over 20 percent of all container volume moving in and out of North America. This demonstrates two things. First,

the concept of going online to handle a multimillion-dollar, strategic-transportation activity has become common for big shippers. And second, GT Nexus has become the industry standard and market leader for global transportation management.

Sources: Compiled from Goodman (2002), *gtnexus.com/gtn/en/company* (accessed 2004), Angwin (2004), Coia (2002b), GT Nexus (2002), and Sanborn (2002).

Questions

1. Identify the critical success factors of this exchange.
2. Is a consortium the best type of ownership for this kind of exchange?
3. Although there are thousands of shippers, some of them are very large (e.g., Wal-Mart), does it make sense to have them create a shippers' exchange? Why or why not?
4. What motivates a carrier to participate in the exchange?
5. What motivates a shipper to participate in the exchange?
6. How was customer service improved by the exchange?
7. Research GT Nexus' on-demand model and list its capabilities.

PURCHASING-ORIENTED CONSORTIA

Purchasing-oriented (procurement) consortia are by far the most popular B2B consortium model. The basic idea is that a group of companies join together to streamline purchasing processes. Some claim that another goal of procurement consortia is to pressure suppliers to cut prices. This model may be vertical or horizontal.

Vertical Purchasing-Oriented CTEs

Most CTEs are *vertical*, meaning that all the players are in the same industry. One example is Covisint, discussed in Online File W6.2.

Although the declared objective of vertical procurement CTEs is to support buying *and* selling, it is obvious that in a market owned and operated by large buyers the orientation is toward purchasing. Many of the consortia listed in Exhibit 6.8 are vertical exchanges (e.g., aerospace, airlines, hospitality, mining, retailers). Each exchange may have thousands of participating suppliers.

Horizontal Purchasing-Oriented CTEs

In a *horizontal* purchasing-oriented CTE, the owner–operators are large companies from different industries that unite for the purpose of improving the supply chain of MROs used by most industries. iMarketKorea (Real-World Case) started as a purchasing market for Samsung companies but later served other companies as well.

SELLING-ORIENTED CONSORTIA

Selling-oriented consortia are less common than buying-oriented ones. Most selling-oriented consortia are vertical. Participating sellers have thousands of potential buyers within a particular industry. The following are some examples of selling-oriented consortia:

▶ Cargill Foods (cargillfoods.com), a producer and marketer of basic food ingredients, has a wide range of buyers and has major ownership in a food exchange.

EXHIBIT 6.8 Representative Vertical Consortia

Consortium (CTE)	Industry Participants
Exostar (*exostar.com*)	Aerospace industry (Boeing, Lockheed Martin)
E-Markets (*e-markets.com*)	Agricultural commodities (Dow AgriSciences, Croplan Genetics)
Star Alliance (*staralliance.com*)	Airlines industry (Air Canada, Lufthansa)
Agentrics (*agentrics.com*)	Packaged consumer products (Sears, Best Buy, Safeway, Tesco)
Trade-Ranger (*trade-ranger.com*)	Energy industry (Royal/Dutch Shell, BP Amoco, Conoco)
Forest Express (*forestexpress.com*)	Paper and forest products (International Paper, Georgia-Pacific)
E2Open (*e2open.com*)	Personal computer manufacturers (Ariba, Hitachi, IBM, Netegrity, Oracle)
Amtrex Global Logistics (*amtrex.com*)	Global transport exchange (Bayer AG, Toshiba America, Newport Corp.)
Global Healthcare Exchange (*ghx.com*)	Medical services and supplies (AmeriNet, Neoforma)
Avendra (*avendra.com*)	Hospitality industry (Hyatt, Fairmont Hotels & Resorts, others)
Ocean Connect (*oceanconnect.com*)	Fuel trading for ocean shippers
Intercontinental Exchange (*theice.com*)	Petroleum industry (British Petroleum, PG&E Energy Trading, Royal Bank of Canada)
PlasticsNet (*plasticsnet.com*)	Plastics industry (Grand Effect Plastics, Strategic Systems International)
Constellation Real Technologies (*constellationllc.com*)	Real estate industry (Equity Office Properties Trust, Simon Property Group)
Rubber Network (*rubbernetwork.com*)	Rubber industry (Goodyear Tire & Rubber, Continental AG, Yokohama)
Transplace (*transplace.com*)	Transportation (air and land) industry (J.B. Hunt, U.S. Xpress, Werner)

- The major retailers are served by agentrix.com, which helps retailers in both selling and buying.
- Several international airline consortia act like large travel agencies, selling tickets or travel packages to business buyers (e.g., staralliance.com) and both to businesses and individuals (orbitz.com).
- Several consortia act as suppliers and distributors of health-care products (e.g., ghx.com).
- TRPlastics.com (trplastics.com) is a consortium that serves the plastics industry.

An example of a successful service-oriented exchange (vertical) is provided in Case 6.2. Note that the trend today is to get not only the first-tier suppliers, but also the second and even the third tier suppliers (Markus 2006). Large exchanges initially included only the first-tier suppliers. One exception was Covisint, which included additional tiers (see Online File W6.2).

LEGAL ISSUES FOR CONSORTIA

Consortia face a variety of issues, including legal challenges. This section presents the legal challenges (other issues that are common to all exchanges are discussed in Sections 6.9 and 6.10) and also looks at the critical success factors for consortia-based exchanges and the issue of combining consortia and third-party exchanges.

Legal Challenges for B2B Consortia

B2B exchanges and other e-marketplaces typically introduce some level of collaboration among both competitors and business partners. In both cases, antitrust and other competition laws must be considered. The concept of consortia itself may lead to antitrust scrutiny by governments, especially for industries in which either a few firms produce most or all of the output (oligopolies or duopolies) or in which there are only a few buyers. This could happen in many countries, especially in European countries, the United States, Australia, Japan, South Korea, Hong Kong, and Canada.

Momentive (gesilicones.com) is an exchange for industrial sealants (sold in 2006 to Appolo Management). GE Toshiba Silicone initiated this exchange and started discussions with other leading industrial sealant makers, such as Dow Corning, Wacker

Chemical, and Shin-Etsu Chemical, about joining the marketplace. The initial group of participants controls over 80 percent of the world market of industrial sealants. The potential exists for the participants to deal with some sensitive business issues, such as industry pricing policies, price levels, price changes, and price differentiations, in ways that may violate antitrust laws. Similarly, many fear that buyers' consortia will "squeeze" the small suppliers in an unfair manner. Antitrust issues and investigations may slow the creation of CTEs, especially global ones. For example, the Covisint venture (Online File W6.2) required government approval in the United Kingdom, the United States, and Germany. The German antitrust investigation was very slow and delayed the project by several months.

Critical Success Factors for Consortia

The critical success factors for consortia, according to Goldman Sachs (2000), include the following.

Appropriate Business and Revenue Models. B2B exchanges exhibit a variety of business and revenue models. The strategy of which revenue model to use and how much to charge can make or break the exchange.

Size of the Industry. The larger the industry, the larger the addressable market, which in turn means a greater volume of transactions on the site. This leads to greater potential cost savings to the exchange participants and ultimately more profitability for the exchange itself. The danger is that industry size may spawn several competing consortia, which has happened in the banking, mining, and airline industries.

Ability to Drive User Adoption. Consortia must have the ability to provide quick liquidity to an exchange. The more oligopolistic the consortium is (the more it is controlled by a few players), the more accelerated the adoption can be.

Elasticity. A critical factor for any exchange is the degree of elasticity the exchange fosters. **Elasticity** is a measure of the incremental spending by buyers as a result of price changes. The consortium has the potential to reduce prices of individual products, thus enabling and encouraging consortium members to buy more.

Standardization of Commodity-Like Products. The breadth of the suppliers brought in to transact with the buyers will help standardize near-commodity products due to content management and product-attribute description needs of online marketplaces. The more commodity-like the products are, the greater the market competition and the lower the prices.

Management of Intensive Information Flow. A consortium has the ability to be a repository for the huge amounts of data that flow through supply chains in a given industry. It can also enable information-intensive collaboration between participants, including product collaboration, planning, scheduling, and forecasting. The more information the exchange has, the more added value the exchange provides the participants, and the more buyers will come to the exchange.

Smoothing of Supply Chain Inefficiencies. It is important for the consortium-led exchange to help smooth inefficiencies in the supply chain, such as those in order fulfillment, logistics, and credit-related services.

Harmonized Shared Objectives. If the consortium cannot agree on shared objectives, the individual interests will be greater than the collective interests, and the exchange may fold.

Section 6.10 discusses critical success factors for exchanges in general, many of which also apply to consortia.

Combining Consortia and Third-Party Exchanges

Goldman Sachs (2000) suggested merging large consortia with a third-party owner (usually a dot-com) into what they call *dot-consortia*. Such a combination may bring about the advantages of ownership and minimize third-party limitations, such as low liquidity. Indeed, in a number of exchanges, several industry leaders are shareholders, but the exchange is managed by a third party.

According to Coia (2002b), consortia arrangements are common in the transportation industry. There, groups of shippers within an industry use a public exchange as a "semiprivate

elasticity
The measure of the incremental spending (demand) by buyers as a result of price changing.

exchange" to leverage the amount of freight that they ship, allowing greater opportunities for competitive rates.

Section 6.4 ▶ REVIEW QUESTIONS

1. Define CTEs.
2. Describe purchasing-oriented consortia and selling-oriented consortia.
3. Describe potential legal issues for consortia.
4. List the major critical success factors of consortia.

6.5   DYNAMIC TRADING: MATCHING AND AUCTIONS

One of the major features of exchanges is dynamic trading. **Dynamic trading** is trading that occurs in situations in which prices are determined by supply and demand, therefore changing continuously. Two major mechanisms are used in dynamic trading in exchanges: matching and auctions.

dynamic trading
Trading that occurs in situations when prices are changing continuously, being determined by supply and demand (e.g., in auctions).

MATCHING

An example of *matching* supply and demand is the stock market. When buyers place their bids and sellers list their asking prices, the market makers conduct the matching, sometimes by buying or selling stocks from their own accounts. The matching process may be more complex than buying and selling in regular auctions due to the need to match both prices and quantities. In other cases, quality, delivery times, and locations also need to be matched. Today, matching in stock exchanges is fully computerized. Most commodity exchanges (e.g., wheat, oil, silver) are B2B, as are some financial markets, and they are fully computerized.

AUCTIONS

As seen in the ChemConnect case, exchanges offer members the ability to conduct auctions or reverse auctions in *private trading rooms*. When this takes place, the one-to-many model is activated, as described in Chapter 5, with the hosting done by the exchange. The advantage of running an auction in an exchange is the ability to attract many buyers to a forward auction and many suppliers to a reverse auction. For SMEs that wish to buy or sell via auctions, finding auction participants can be a major problem. By going to an exchange, this problem may be solved.

Auctions can be arranged in several ways. Two options are as follows:

▶ An exchange offers auction services as one of its many activities, as ChemConnect does. Many vertical exchanges offer this option.

▶ An exchange is fully dedicated to auctions. Examples of this auctions-only arrangement are eBay for Businesses, Ariba's Dynamic Trading, FirstAuction.com, and QXL.com.

An exchange also can conduct many-to-many public auctions. These auctions may be vertical or horizontal and can run on the Internet or over private lines. Examples of auctions conducted over private lines are Aucnet in Japan, through which used cars are sold to dealers, and TFA, the Dutch flower market auction, described in Online File W6.3.

Exhibit 6.9 summarizes the major B2B, many-to-many mechanisms discussed thus far in the chapter. The remainder of the chapter deals with B2B implementation issues.

Section 6.5 ▶ REVIEW QUESTIONS

1. Explain how matches are made in exchanges.
2. Explain how private and public auctions are conducted in public exchanges.
3. Compare fully dedicated and partially dedicated auction exchanges.

EXHIBIT 6.9   Comparing the Major B2B Many-to-Many Models

Name	Major Characteristics	Types
B2B catalog-based exchanges	• A place for selling and buying • Fixed prices (updated as needed) • Search tools • Trading information	• Vertical, horizontal • Shopping directory, usually with hyperlinks (only) • Shopping carts with services (payment, etc.)
B2B portals and directories	• Community services, news, information • Communication tools • Classified ads • Employment markets • May support selling (buying) • Fixed prices • May do auctions	• Vertical (vortals), horizontal • Shopping directory, usually with hyperlinks
B2B dynamic exchanges	• Matches buyer/seller orders at dynamic prices, auctions • Provides trading-related information and services (payment, logistics) • Highly regulated • May provide general information, news, etc. • May provide for negotiations	• Vertical, horizontal • Forward auctions • Reverse auctions • Bid/ask exchanges

6.6 PARTNER AND SUPPLIER RELATIONSHIP MANAGEMENT

In order to succeed in B2B, and particularly in exchanges, it is necessary to have several support services.

PARTNER AND SUPPLIER RELATIONSHIP MANAGEMENT

Successful e-businesses carefully manage partners, prospects, and customers across the entire value chain, most often in a 24/7 environment. For benefits and methods, see Markus (2006). Therefore, one should examine the role of solution technologies, such as call centers and collaboration tools, in creating an integrated online environment for engaging e-business customers and partners. The use of such solutions and technology appears under two names: customer relationship management (CRM) and partner relationship management (PRM).

In Chapter 13, we will introduce the concept of CRM in the B2C environment. Here our interest is with the situation in which the customer is a business, shifting attention to business partners, such as suppliers. Many of the customer service features of B2C also are used in B2B. For example, it may be beneficial to provide corporate customers with a chat room and a discussion board. A Web-based call center also may be useful for companies with many partners.

Corporate customers may require additional services. For example, customers need to have access to the supplier's inventory status report so they know what items a supplier can deliver quickly. Customers also may want to see their historical purchasing records, and they may need private showrooms and trade rooms. Large numbers of vendors are available for designing and building appropriate B2B CRM solutions. The strategy of providing such comprehensive, quality e-service for business partners is sometimes called **partner relationship management (PRM)**.

In the context of PRM, business customers are only one category of business partners. Suppliers, partners in joint ventures, service providers, and others also are part of the B2B community in an exchange or company-centric B2B initiative, as illustrated in Exhibit 6.1.

partner relationship management (PRM)
Business strategy that focuses on providing comprehensive quality service to business partners.

PRM is particularly important to companies that conduct outsourcing (Hagel 2004). Companies with many suppliers, such as the automobile companies, may create special programs for them. Such programs are called *supplier relationship management (SRM)*.

Supplier Relationship Management

One of the major categories of PRM is **supplier relationship management (SRM)**, in which the partners are the suppliers. For many companies (e.g., retailers and manufacturers), the ability to work properly with suppliers is a major critical success factor. PeopleSoft, Inc. (an Oracle company), developed a model for managing relationships with suppliers in real time.

PeopleSoft's SRM Model. PeopleSoft's cyclical SRM model (see Schecterle 2003) is generic and could be considered by any large company. It includes 12 steps, illustrated in Exhibit 6.10. The details of the steps are shown in Online File W6.4. The core idea of this model is that an e-supply chain is based on integration and collaboration. The supply chain processes are connected, decisions are made collectively, performance metrics are based on common understanding, information flows in real time (whenever possible), and the only thing a new partner needs in order to join the SRM system is a Web browser.

Implementing PRM and SRM is different from implementing CRM with individual customers. For example, behavioral and psychological aspects of the relationships are less important in PRM than in CRM. However, trust, commitment, quality of services, and continuity are more important in PRM. For details, see McNichols and Brennan (2006) and Markus (2006).

E-COMMUNITIES AND PRM

B2B applications involve many participants: buyers and sellers, service providers, industry associations, and others. Thus, in many cases the B2B implementation creates a *community*. In such cases, the B2B market maker needs to provide community services such as chat rooms, bulletin boards, and possibly personalized Web pages. A detailed list of such services is provided in Online Chapter 19.

supplier relationship management (SRM)
A comprehensive approach to managing an enterprise's interactions with the organizations that supply the goods and services it uses.

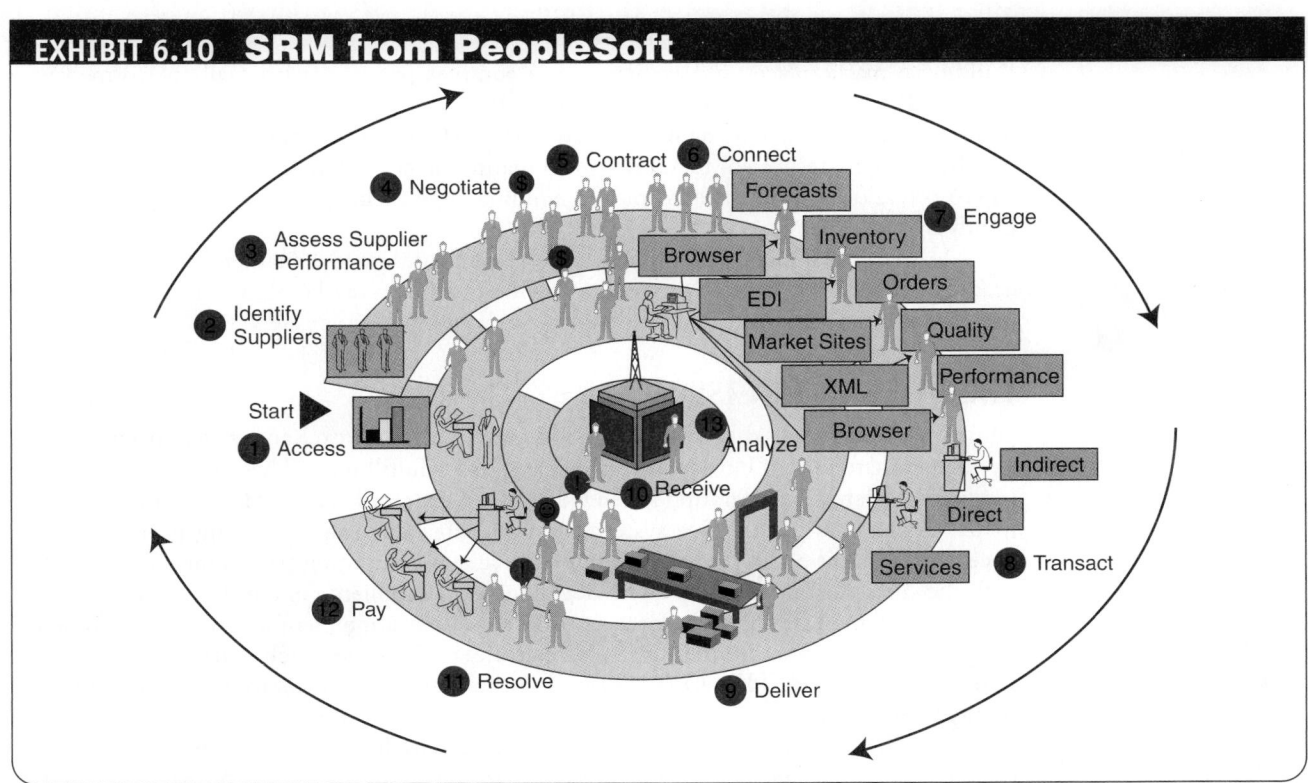

EXHIBIT 6.10 SRM from PeopleSoft

Source: Based on Schecterle, B., "Management and Extending Supplier Relationships," *People Talk,* April–June 2003.

E-communities are connecting personnel, partners, customers, and any combination of the three. E-communities offer a powerful resource for e-businesses to leverage online discussions and interaction in order to maximize innovation and responsiveness (e.g., see the Real-World Case at the end of this chapter). It is therefore beneficial to study the tools, methods, and best practices of building and managing e-communities. Although the technological support of B2B e-communities is basically the same as for any other online community (see Chapter 17), the nature of the community itself and the information provided by the community are different.

B2B e-communities are mostly communities of transactions, and as such, the major interest of the members is trading. Most of the communities are associated with vertical exchanges; therefore, their needs may be fairly specific. However, it is common to find generic services such as classified ads, job vacancies, announcements, industry news, and so on. Communities promote partnering. For further information, see *About.com* (2006).

Section 6.6 ▶ REVIEW QUESTIONS

1. What type of information is provided by B2B directory services and search engines?
2. How does PRM differ from SRM?
3. List five B2B services.
4. Describe e-communities in B2B.

6.7 BUILDING AND INTEGRATING E-MARKETPLACES AND EXCHANGES

Building large marketplaces, especially those that accommodate many sellers, buyers, and services, can be very complex. Also, consideration of how companies will be connected to the exchanges, as well as how the exchanges will be linked, is necessary. For a comprehensive discussion, see Papzoglou and Ribbers (2006).

BUILDING E-MARKETPLACES

Building e-marketplaces and exchanges is a complex process. It is usually performed by a major B2B software company, such as Ariba, Oracle, or IBM. In large exchanges, a management consulting company, such as PricewaterhouseCoopers, Gartner Group, or McKinsey, usually participates. Also, technology companies, such as IBM, Oracle, EDS, i2, Intel, Microsoft, and SAP, have major roles in building large exchanges. Most exchanges are built jointly by several vendors.

Most large B2B software vendors have specially designed e-marketplace packages. For example, IBM, Oracle, and Microsoft each has a set of e-marketplace solutions. A typical process for building a vertical e-marketplace is shown in Online File W6.5.

THE INTEGRATION ISSUE

Thus far, we have cited several value-added services that exchanges may offer, such as payments, matching of buyers and sellers, and order fulfillment. These services need to be integrated. Seamless integration is needed between the third-party exchange and the participants' front- and back-office systems. Communication among trading partners also is necessary. In addition, in private exchanges the seller's computing system must be integrated with the customers' systems (in a sell-side case) or its suppliers' systems (in a buy-side case). A number of applications and protocols make this integration possible. In addition, integration across multiple, frequently incompatible exchanges—each with its own XML scheme—is required. TIBCO (tibco.com) is the major infrastructure service provider for vertical exchanges. Some exchanges take care of the connectivity; others do not. For example, ChemConnect provides a central connectivity hub where members' communications needs are met no matter what message format they use. This eliminates the need to maintain multiple connections with supply chain partners.

The most common elements of B2B integration solutions are external communications, process and information coordination, Web Services, XBRL, and system and information management.

External Communications

External communications require the following:

▶ **Web/client access.** Businesses can use a Web browser, such as Internet Explorer, to interact with Web server applications hosted by other businesses.

▶ **Data exchange.** Information is extracted from an application, converted into a neutral data format, and sent to other businesses. Examples of data exchange include EDI over VANs, Internet-based EDI, and XML.

▶ **Direct application integration.** Application integration often requires middleware technologies, such as distributed object technologies, message queuing, and publish/subscribe brokers, to coordinate information exchange between applications (see ibm.com, oracle.com, and peregrine.com).

▶ **Shared procedures.** Businesses can agree to use the same procedures for certain processes. For example, a supplier and a buyer may agree to use the same order-management process.

Process and Information Coordination in Integration

Process and information coordination involves the coordination of *external communications* and *internal information systems*. This coordination includes external processes, internal processes, data transformation, and exception handling. For example, an online sales transaction must be processed directly to an internal accounting system.

Use of Web Services in Integration

Web Services essentially enable different Web-based systems to communicate with each other using Internet-based protocols such as XML (see Online Chapter 19 and Online Appendix B), SOAP (Simple Object Access Protocol), and UDDI (Universal Description Discovery and Integration). WSDL (Web Services Description Language) makes it expedient to use Web Services to connect different systems.

By using Web Services, the time it takes to connect complex systems can be reduced by about 75 percent. Also, development costs can be reduced by 10 percent (Ferris and Farrel 2003).

System and Information Management in Integration

System and information management involves the management of software, hardware, and several information components, including partner-profile information, data and process definitions, communications and security settings, and users' information. Furthermore, because hardware and software change rapidly (i.e., upgrades or releases of new versions), the management of these changes is an essential element of B2B integration. For more on B2B integration, see Executive Guide at searchcio.com.

Section 6.7 ▶ REVIEW QUESTIONS

1. List the steps in building a vertical exchange.

2. Describe the integration issues for third-party exchanges.

3. List some integration solutions.

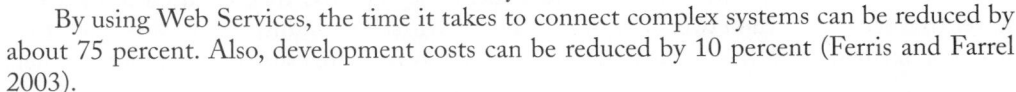

6.8 B2B NETWORKS

To implement any B2B system, it is necessary to consider the appropriate networks and their infrastructure. In Chapter 5, we mentioned the potential for the use of EDI between a company and its suppliers (Online File W5.9); in this chapter, we describe the use of extranets (Appendix 6A); private industry-wide networks, or *vertical networks* (*industrial networks*); company-centered networks; and global networks. Some of these are described next.

COMPANY-CENTERED (PRIVATE) NETWORKS

Also known as *private industrial networks*, company-centered networks are Web-based networks owned by one large seller (or one buyer) for the execution of interorganizational communications in buy-side and sell-side e-marketplaces. In contrast to EDI, such a network extends its activities to all business partners. An example of such a network is Boeing's PART (Online File W5.2), which connects Boeing's customers to Boeing and Boeing to its parts suppliers. Procter and Gamble, Coca-Cola, Dell, IBM, Cisco, Microsoft, Wal-Mart, and Nokia also operate company-centered networks. Most of these networks are direct descendents of the traditional company-owned (or leased) EDI. These networks encompass the companies' extended supply chain (see Online Tutorial T1).

The following are the major characteristics of such networks:

▶ Provide the infrastructure for e-marketplaces, enabling efficient and effective buying and selling along the extended supply chain.

▶ Allow suppliers to communicate effectively and efficiently with subsuppliers along several tiers.

▶ Increase the visibility of buyers, sellers, and other partners along the supply chain and around the globe (see Dubie 2003).

▶ Operate on a large scale, from one company with its thousands of suppliers to tens of thousands of firms globally.

▶ Foster collaboration and closer relationships among business partners.

▶ Enable industry-wide resource planning (Chapter 7).

▶ Provide support services, especially financial ones (e.g., settlements), for the benefit of trading partners.

▶ Provide insurance, financial derivatives, and so on to reduce risks in certain markets.

PUBLIC INDUSTRYWIDE (VERTICAL) NETWORKS

Company-centered networks may be a waste of money because they are used by only one buyer (buyer's industrial network) or by only one seller (seller's industrial network), and they may not be open to all. In contrast, public industry networks are usually open to many sellers and buyers in the industry. As such, they support exchanges, especially CTEs.

TRANSINDUSTRY AND GLOBAL NETWORKS

Companies sometimes need to collaborate with companies in other industries or with companies in other countries. In such situations, they can use horizontal exchanges or networks from several industries. An example is Nistevo Network (nistevo.com), which is a collaborative logistics network. It manages the entire shipment life cycle, from load planning to invoice auditing to performance management (see the demo on the Web site). Over 4,000 participants, including major companies such as International Paper, General Mills, Land O' Lakes, and Coca-Cola, participate. Nistevo coordinates, for example, members' excess shipping capacity in order to improve utilization. The participants manage over 4 million shipments a year (in 2006), saving 5 to 25 percent of their logistics expenses (*Nivesto.com* 2006).

A special network model that enables transindustry collaboration was proposed by the Keenan Report (2002). According to this model, business-to-exchange (B2X) hubs connect all Internet business services, e-merchant services, exchange infrastructures, buying and selling, member enterprises, and other B2X exchanges.

Networks of Exchanges (E2E)

With the increasing number of vertical and horizontal exchanges, some in different countries, it is logical to think about connecting them. Large corporations may work with several exchanges, and they would like these exchanges to be connected in a seamless fashion. Today,

EXHIBIT 6.11 How Several Exchanges Work in One Supply Chain

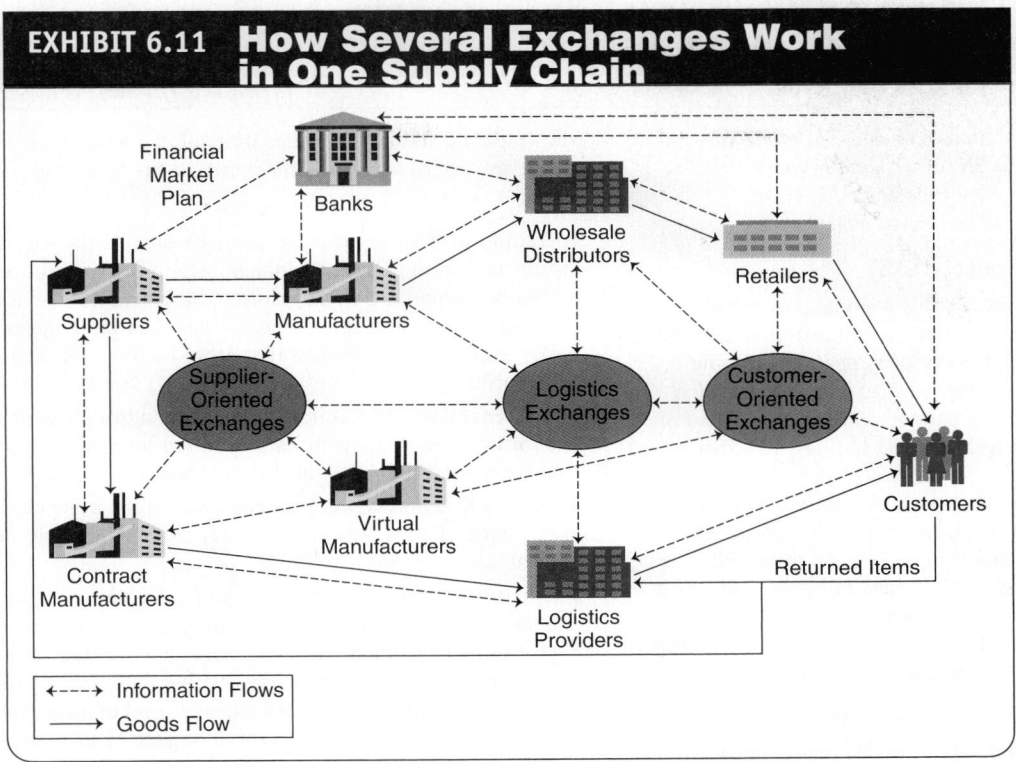

most exchanges have different log-on procedures, separate sets of rules for fulfilling orders, and different business models for charging for their services. Exchanges also can be connected in an industry's supply chain, as shown in Exhibit 6.11. Each exchange (oval) serves different participants, but some are members of two or more exchanges. Exchanges also may be connected via global networks.

Global Networks

Global networks serve multiple industries and countries. They provide international trade gateways. Notable vendors of such networks are GXS and Ariba (see Insights and Additions 6.1). Other vendors are Perfect Commerce (perfect.com) for suppliers and Sterling Commerce, which runs EDI networks for businesses.

Section 6.8 ▶ REVIEW QUESTIONS

1. Describe private B2B networks and list their characteristics.

2. Compare vertical and horizontal networks.

3. Describe the GXS network and its Trading Grid.

4. Describe Ariba's SN network.

6.9 OTHER B2B IMPLEMENTATION ISSUES

Large exchanges are supposed to bring together entire industry sectors, creating supply chain efficiencies and reduced costs for buyers and sellers alike. However, despite the fact that thousands of exchanges were created between January 1995 and December 2000, only a few hundred were active by the end of 2001, and less than half of these were conducting a high volume of transactions (AMR Research Staff 2001). By 2003, signs of improvement appeared. Existing exchanges solidified, and a few new exchanges appeared. However, due to the worldwide economic slowdown these exchanges were not doing so well. Let's look at some of the implementation issues that might explain why.

Insights and Additions 6.1 B2B Public Networks

The following are two examples of well-known networks: GXS and Ariba SN. Other large networks are offered by Sterling Commerce and by Covisint, (see Online File W6.2 and Team Assignment #4.)

Global eXchange Services (GXS)

Global eXchange Services (GXS) is a global provider of business-to-business integration, synchronization, and collaboration solutions. The company operates a highly reliable, secure *global network services platform*, enabling more than 100,000 trading partners, including over half of the *Fortune* 500, to actively conduct business together in real time.

GXS offers an extensive range of solutions to help companies, both large and small, connect worldwide with their business partners, synchronize product and price information, optimize inventory levels and demand forecasts, and speed the overall execution of their global supply chains.

GXS is providing traditional EDI services as well as other e-business services, which enable customers to:

▶ Accelerate the reliable exchange of information
▶ Provide all of the information needed along supply chains
▶ Serve large and small customers jointly and distinctly
▶ Streamline cross-enterprise business processes

To achieve this, GXS created the Extended Value Chain, shown below.

GXS provides its services via its Trading Grid, a global integration platform that enables and streamlines enterprise business processes.

As of late 2006, Microsoft's Biz Talk Server 2006 is embedded into the Trading Grid. This will help connect small suppliers with their global supply chain partners.

The Trading Grid has five major integrated components, which are described below and shown in the following figure:

▶ **Trading Grid Infrastructure Services** provide the foundation to Trading Grid and include an online, centralized, Web-based portal that allows users to register for services, self-provision, and self-service. A powerful data aggregation store also locates data that other Trading Grid services can utilize.

▶ **SMB Enablers and Enterprise Adapters** allow all users to effortlessly integrate with Trading Grid to conduct electronic commerce without changing existing business processes.

▶ **Trading Grid Messaging Services** assist in the event-driven exchange of data between business partners securely and reliably.

▶ A suite of **Trading Grid Intelligence Services** provides data and event processing according to each company's profile and business rules. Because moving data is not enough to give customers a competitive edge, Trading Grid Intelligence Services provide a superior level of responsiveness, which reduces the potential impact of unexpected changes in supply or demand. Analytics also provides real business insight.

▶ **Trading Grid Application Services** power the other services to automate industry-specific business processes. Customers' internal systems are complemented and additional software purchases are not required. Unlike with large software installations, businesses easily obtain a level of visibility, collaboration, and analytics. Small and medium-sized businesses can utilize these services to be more competitive with much larger businesses.

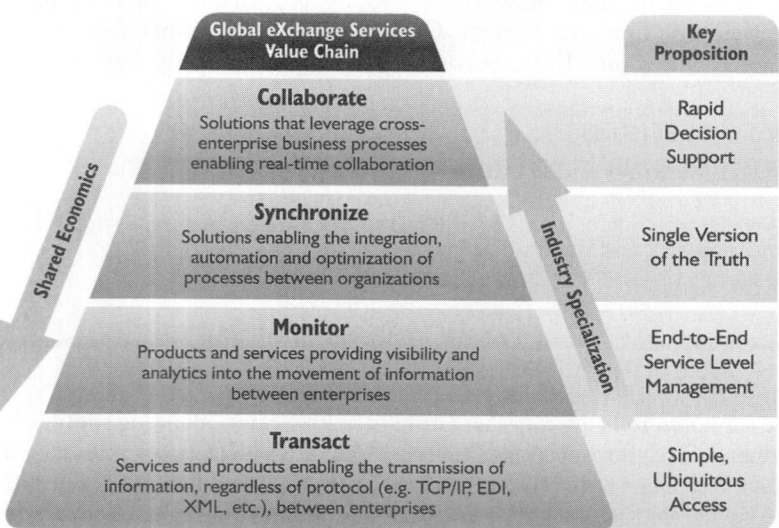

Source: Global eXchange Services Inc. "Global eXchange Service Mission." 2005. *gxs.com/pdfs/Data_Sheets/ DS_Mission_GXS.pdf* (accessed July 2007).

(continued)

Insights and Additions 6.1 *(continued)*

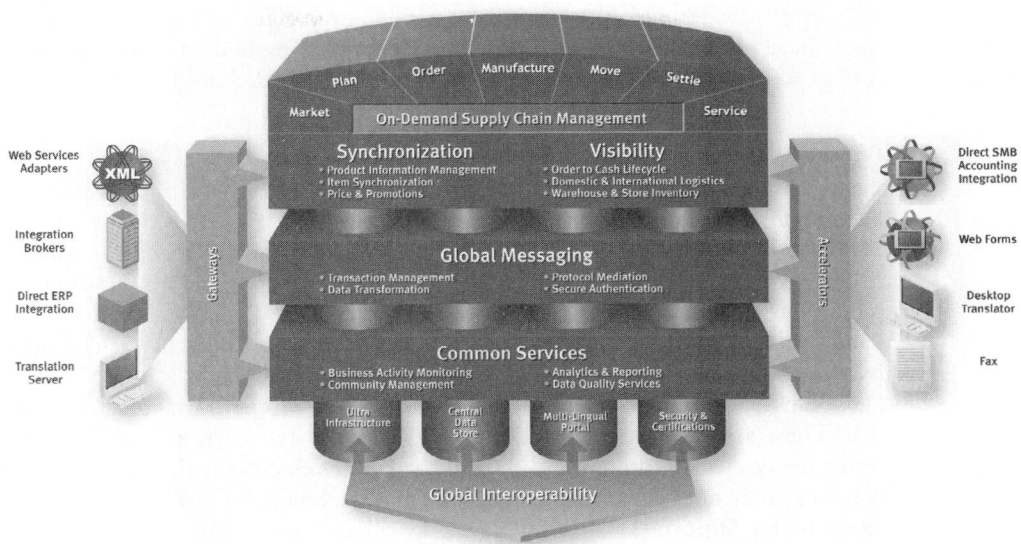

Source: Global eXchange Services, Inc. "Integrated Solutions That Streamline Cross-Enterprise Business Processes." 2006. *gxs.com/pdfs/Data_Sheets/DS_TG_GXS.pdf* (accessed April 2007).

Ariba Supplier Network (SN)

Ariba Supplier Network (Ariba SN) connects and transacts with a broad range of suppliers, partners, and distribution channels using Ariba's global eCommerce network. Ariba SN provides access to a global supplier community through a single connection. Buyers can leverage Ariba SN to access global public supplier directories of thousands of enabled suppliers while benefiting from negotiated visibility, security, and privacy. SN provides support for multiple content models, from static catalogs to robust, dynamic content, and reliable exchange of business documents, including invoice management.

Ariba Supplier Network is one of the world's largest open business-transacting systems, providing a single point of integration in which organizations can trade globally in real time. The network encompasses hundreds of buying organizations transacting with more than 140,000 e-enabled suppliers. The network delivers remarkable value for suppliers, grossing $90 billion in annual spending and driving 16 million purchase orders each year. Shared by suppliers in 115 countries worldwide, Ariba's Network provides a powerful solution to efficiently manage the entire prospecting-to-payment lifecycle.

Bringing suppliers online enables organizations to collaborate with each other as well as to better manage their expenditures by transacting business and exchanging documents electronically through a single, integrated supplier network. Because supplier participation is important for a business's success, SN provides software solutions—from zero-cost online tools to complete system-to-system XML integration—that help bring suppliers of all sizes in all industries online. In addition, Ariba SN enables suppliers to register and transact business free of charge.

The extensive resources and functionality of SN meet the needs of suppliers as well as buyers, giving companies the following advantages:

◗ Immediate network participation and robust connectivity to tens of thousands of trading partners worldwide

◗ Support for secure electronic transactions and routing of information and documents to achieve full-cycle process integration quickly and efficiently

◗ Lower operation costs using a single, consistent infrastructure

◗ Reduced process and content management costs through flexible, easy-to-use supplier enablement capabilities and efficient content management tools

◗ Instant access to robust, up-to-date business, product, and category information on suppliers

◗ Faster implementation and more rapid supplier adoption through seamless integration of all business processes and support for various messaging types

◗ Systematic deployment of best practices helps ensure highly profitable, long-term relationships with important suppliers

Sources: Compiled from *gxs.com* (accessed November 2006), *gxs.com/tradinggrid* (accessed November 2004), *ariba.com/suppliers/supplier_network.cfm* (accessed November 2006), and Boucher Ferguson (2006).

PRIVATE MARKETPLACES VERSUS PUBLIC EXCHANGES

private marketplaces
E-marketplaces that are owned and operated by one company. Also known as *company-centric marketplaces*.

As described earlier, exchanges owned by a third party are referred to as *public* or *independent exchanges*. In contrast, **private marketplaces** are owned and operated by one company. In October 2001, the Gartner Group (as reported by Konicki 2000) estimated that there were 30,000 active private marketplaces and 600 public exchanges in the United States, and the numbers have not changed much since then. Both have implementation and viability problems (e.g., see Saarinen, et al. 2006). For a comparison, see Richard and Devinney (2005).

Problems with Public Exchanges

Exchanges need to attract sellers and buyers. Attracting sellers, especially large businesses, to public exchanges is difficult for the following reasons.

Transaction Fees. One of the major reasons that large and successful suppliers refuse to join third-party exchanges is that they are required to pay transaction fees even when they engage in transactions with their existing customers.

Sharing Information. Many companies do not join public exchanges because they do not want to share key business data with their competitors.

Cost Savings. Many of the first-generation exchanges were horizontal, concentrating on MROs. These are low-value items. Although administrative costs can be reduced by online ordering, the cost of the products to the buyers remains essentially the same. Thus, the monetary savings may not be attractive enough for buyers, especially SMEs.

Recruiting Suppliers. One of the major difficulties facing public exchanges is the recruitment of large suppliers. For example, GE Plastics, a major vendor of plastic materials, said that it had been asked to join a public exchange, PlasticsNet (plasticsnet.com), but it did not see any benefit in doing so. There was simply no business case for it. Instead, GE Plastics decided to develop e-purchasing capabilities for its customers. The company likes the *direct contact* with its customers, which it would lose if it were part of a public exchange. Also, some suppliers just want to wait and see how exchanges will fare before they make a commitment to join.

Too Many Exchanges. When an exchange receives the publicity of being the *first mover*, as Chemdex did, or when it becomes a success, it is sure to attract some competition. Competitors believe that they can do a better job than the first mover or that they have "deeper pockets" to sustain losses and survive. Two chemical exchanges started a year after Chemdex. Because of the competition, Chemdex was forced to close in 2000.

Supply Chain Improvers

Public exchanges prepare the necessary infrastructure and ask suppliers to just "plug in" and start selling. However, companies also are interested in streamlining their internal supply chains, which requires integration with internal operations, not just plugging in. This is why companies such as i2 and Aspect, leaders in SCM, are partnering with some exchanges. According to *Business Review Weekly of Australia* (*BRW* Staff 2000), focusing on supply chain savings rather than on buy/sell savings can be very beneficial to exchanges. An example of an exchange that emphasizes supply chain improvement is Asite, as described in Case 6.3.

Problems with Private Exchanges

Some (e.g., Young 2002) believe that public exchanges will not do as well as private exchanges. However, private exchanges have their problems, too. The primary problem is that they may not be trusted because they are run by one company, usually a large one. Such distrust can lead to liquidity issues.

SOFTWARE AGENTS IN B2B EXCHANGES

The use of B2B exchanges has fostered a need within the B2B community for an efficient infrastructure to provide real-time, tighter integration between buyers and sellers and to facilitate management of multiple trading partners and their transactions across multiple virtual industry exchanges. Such capabilities can be provided by software agents.

CASE 6.3
EC Application

ASITE'S B2B E-MARKETPLACE FOR THE CONSTRUCTION INDUSTRY

Asite (*asite.com*) is a B2B e-marketplace for the construction industry in the United Kingdom that focuses on procurement and project management. The construction industry is typified by a high degree of physical separation and fragmentation, and communication among the members of the supply chain (e.g., contractors, subcontractors, architects, supply stores, building inspectors) has long been a primary problem. Founded in February 2000 by leading players in the construction industry, the company understands two of the major advantages of the Internet: the ability it provides to communicate more effectively and the increase in processing power that Internet technologies make possible. Taking advantage of the functions of an online portal as information broker and gateway to the services of technology partners, Asite developed a comprehensive portal for the construction industry.

Asite drew on employees from partner organizations with profound industry knowledge and expertise and has benefited from having an anchor group of buyers participating at an early stage of its development. This combination has enabled Asite to rapidly build up the liquidity that online portals require. The company's goal is to be the leading information and transaction hub in the European construction industry.

Asite made the decision not to build its own technology, but to establish partnerships with technology vendors that have highly specialized products. It formed core partnerships with Commerce One (which provides the business solution for the portal), Microsoft (which provides the technology platform and core applications), and Attenda (the designer and manager of the Internet infrastructure).

Asite set up seven interconnected marketplaces within its portal to serve all the needs of the participants in the construction industry—building owners, developers, trade contractors, general contractors, engineers, architects, and materials suppliers—from design through procurement to materials delivery (see exhibit). It began by addressing business problems, such as ineffective procurement processes and hit-or-miss information flows.

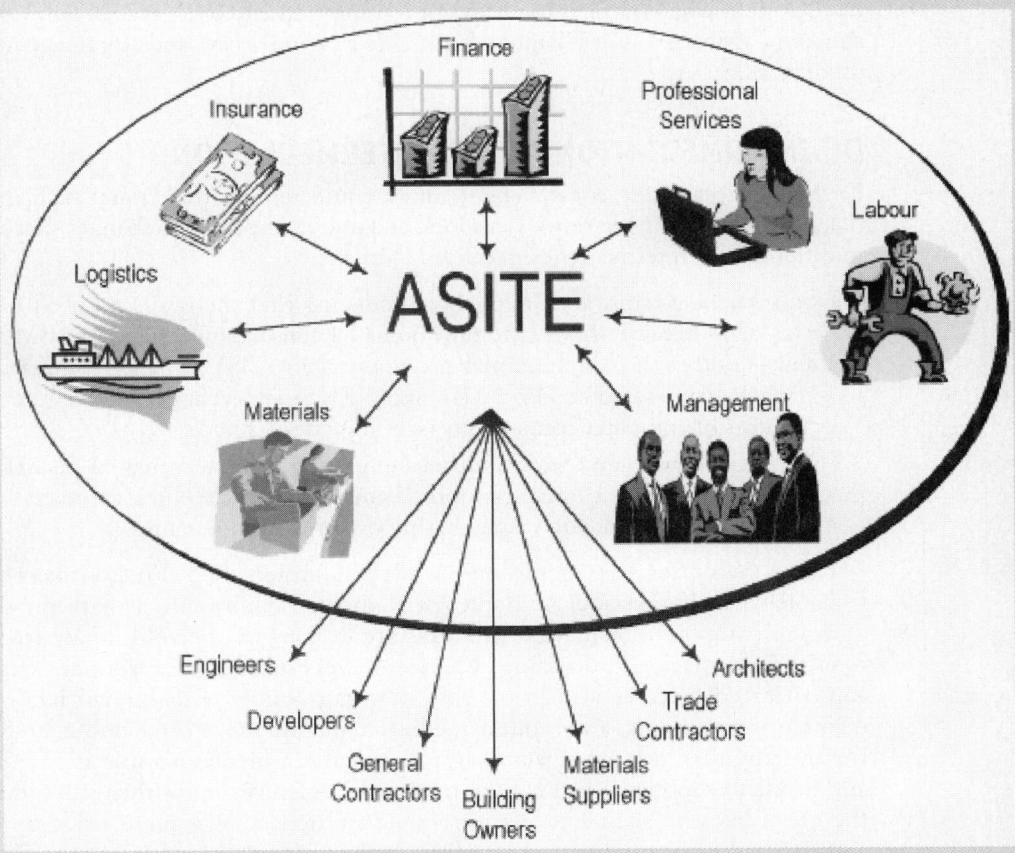

Source: Used by permission of Aberdeen Group.

(*continued*)

CASE 6.3   (continued)

Asite is committed to strong partnerships that enable it to seamlessly interact with other e-marketplaces. The open standards espoused by these vendors also mean that the technology can be incorporated easily with participating firms' back-end technologies, allowing full visibility of the supply and demand chains. Participating firms need nothing more sophisticated than a browser to connect to Asite's portal. This ease of access makes it particularly well suited to an industry such as construction, which is distinguished by a high proportion of small, and even single-person, firms.

The combination of strong backing from industry participants, experienced management from the construction industry, and the commitment to working with best-of-breed technology infrastructure providers is helping construction firms streamline their supply chains.

Sources: Compiled from Aberdeen Group (2001) and *asite.com* (accessed September 2006).

Questions

1. Identify the success factors of this company (see the list of success factors in Section 6.10).

2. How would you classify the ownership of this e-marketplace?

3. Examine the Webcor Case in Online File W7.3. How does Webcor differ from Asite? How is it similar?

4. Enter *asite.com* and read about any new developments (those within the last 6 months).

5. What is the exchange's revenue model?

6. Using the classification scheme presented in this chapter, is *asite.com* a portal or an exchange?

7. Examine the site's tendering, procurement, and project management tools.

One software agent, Dotcom-Monitor (dotcom-monitor.com), monitors traffic on a B2B exchange and takes appropriate actions when needed, such as sending an alert to management when traffic is too heavy or routing traffic to other places. Some of the types of shopping agents cited in Chapters 3 and 4 (e.g., comparison and search agents) also can be used for B2B purposes.

DISINTERMEDIATION AND REINTERMEDIATION

Exchanges, especially consortia-like ones, could replace traditional B2B intermediaries (i.e., cause disintermediation). Let's look at some examples of exchanges that might replace traditional B2B intermediaries in certain industries.

▶ Sun Microsystems, after publicly announcing that there was no need for third-party exchanges because they waste time, joined a consortium headed by IBM that develops and smoothes the computer maker's supply chain. This exchange competes with a similar exchange created by HP, AMD, and NEC. Such exchanges may eliminate some distributors of computer components (see Thibodeau 2005).

▶ Marriott, Hyatt, and several other competing hoteliers created an MRO exchange (avendra.com) concentrating on procurement that could eliminate many wholesalers in the hotel industry due to its purchasing power ($2 billion annually).

The Web offers new opportunities for reintermediation. First, brokers are especially valuable when the number of market participants is enormous, as with the stock market, or when complex information products are exchanged. Second, many trading services require information processing. Electronic versions of these services can offer more sophisticated features at a lower cost than is possible with human labor. Finally, for delicate negotiations, a computer mediator may be more predictable, and hence more trustworthy than a human. For example, suppose a mediator's role is to inform a buyer and a seller whether a deal can be made without revealing either side's initial price to the other because such a revelation would influence subsequent price negotiations. A software-based mediator will reveal only the information it is supposed to; a human mediator's fairness is less easily ensured.

An analysis of reintermediation strategies in B2B, including exchanges, is provided by Malhotra and Malhotra (2006).

Section 6.9 ▶ REVIEW QUESTIONS

1. List the major problems of public exchanges.

2. How can exchanges cause disintermediation?

3. What role do software agents play in B2B?

6.10 MANAGING AND THE FUTURE OF EXCHANGES

The topic of managing exchanges is very broad. This section will describe several major management-oriented issues. It concludes with an examination of the critical success factors for exchanges.

EVALUATING EXCHANGES

With the increasing number of competing exchanges, companies need to evaluate carefully which ones will work best for them. Online File W6.6 offers some useful questions that buyers and sellers should ask when evaluating exchanges and deciding whether to join (also see Ranganatan 2003).

CENTRALIZED MANAGEMENT

Managing exchanges and providing services to participants on an individual basis can be expensive. Therefore, it makes sense to have "families" of jointly managed exchanges. This way, one market maker can build and operate several exchanges from a unified, centralized location. The market maker manages all of the exchanges' catalogs, auction places, discussion forums, and so on, thus centralizing accounting, finance, human resources, and IT services. Furthermore, dealings with third-party vendors that provide logistic services and payment systems may be more efficient if a vendor is supplying services for many exchanges instead of just one.

Two such "families" of exchanges were those of VerticalNet and Ventro. They managed the administrative aspects involved for a large number of exchanges. However, due to the large number of exchange failures in 2001, Ventro (now nexprise.com) changed its business model and became a software provider. VerticalNet (verticalnet.com) is now a supply chain management software provider and consultant. In general, this model is very difficult to implement; thus, it has not yet been successful.

CRITICAL SUCCESS FACTORS FOR EXCHANGES

By early 2001, thousands of B2B exchanges were in existence. Since that time, as in the B2C area, many exchanges (perhaps 90 percent) have folded or are failing, including Chemdex. In certain areas or countries, there are too many competing exchanges. For example, Hong Kong probably did not have enough room for three toy exchanges (two failed by summer 2002). Therefore, B2B exchanges will continue to fail and consolidate. The question is what determines whether an exchange will survive.

According to Ramsdell (2000), of McKinsey & Company, a major management consulting firm, and Ulfelder (2004), the following five factors are influencing the outcome of the B2B exchange shakeout.

1. **Early liquidity.** Recall that liquidity requires having a sufficient number of participants and amount of transaction volume. The *earlier* a business achieves the necessary liquidity level, the better its chances for survival. The more buyers that trade on an exchange, the more suppliers will come, which will lead to lower transaction fees, which in turn will increase volume and liquidity even more.

2. **The right owners.** One way to increase liquidity is to partner with companies that can bring transactions to the exchange. For example, consortia members are committed to buying via the exchange. The desire to have committed partners is why many vertical exchanges are of the consortia type. In a situation where both the sellers and buyers are fragmented, such as in the bioscience industry, the best exchange owner may be an intermediary that can increase liquidity by pushing both the sellers and the buyers to use the exchange.

3. **The right governance.** Good management and effective operations and rules are critical to success. The governance provides the rules for the exchange, minimizes conflicts, and supports decision making. Furthermore, good management will try to induce the necessary liquidity. Also, good governance will minimize conflicts among the owners and the participants. Owners may try to favor some of their trading partners, a situation that may hurt the exchange if not checked by effective management. To succeed, good exchanges must be unbiased. In addition, good management of operations, resources, and people is mandatory for success. Finally, privacy must be protected.

4. **Openness.** Exchanges must be open to all, from both organizational and technological perspectives. Commitment to open standards is required, but there should be universal agreement on these standards. Using the wrong standards may hurt the exchange.

5. **A full range of services.** Although prices are important, buyers and sellers are interested in cutting their total costs. Therefore, exchanges that help cut inventory costs, spoilage, maverick buying, and so on, will attract participants. Many exchanges team up with banks, logistics services, and IT companies to provide support services. Furthermore, exchanges must be integrated with the information systems of their members—not a simple task (see the Real-World Case at the end of this chapter).

In addition to Ramsdell's five factors, a number of other factors are critical to the success of an exchange. These are presented and discussed in Insights and Additions 6.2 and in Diorio (2002), Woods (2003), and Online File W6.6. In order to achieve these critical success factors, market makers must carefully select the vendors that design and build the exchanges. For further discussion of critical success factors for exchanges, see Ordanini (2006) and Li and Li (2005).

NEW DIRECTIONS FOR B2B MARKETPLACES

The difficulties encountered by both third-party marketplaces and consortia have resulted in a search for new directions (such as the merger of the two). Berryman and Heck (2001) edited a special section of *The McKinsey Quarterly* in which they, with others, presented the *third wave of B2B exchanges.* (The first wave is dot-com-owned B2B exchanges; the second wave is consortia-owned exchanges.) After analyzing the problems of the first and second waves, they concurred with the view of Agrawal and Pak (2001) that many of the failures in the former waves mainly were due to the failure of these marketplaces to foster a broad-based sharing of information. The third wave contains both proven and potential success factors.

In the past, information flowed only between pairs of parties in a supply chain. The result was a multibillion-dollar version of the game of "telephone," in which small errors, magnified up and down the chain, led to incorrect forecasts and to either excessive or insufficient inventories. In contrast, marketplaces that became *information hubs* for distinct segments of the supply chain could instantaneously share data and insights gathered from each corporate participant. Such a hub-and-spoke model may be the way not only to save these B2Bs, but also to realize their value-creating potential.

Devine et al. (2001) explained why many consortia did not fare much better than third-party exchanges. In many cases, members of the consortium did not shift as much of their trading volume to the exchange as had been expected (*The Economist* 2004); thus, the liquidity that their participation was supposed to guarantee did not materialize. Such consortia must recognize the more fundamental asset provided by their member base—its unique knowledge of the industry. Such recognition should enable consortia to become arenas for *sharing this knowledge* and thereby make it possible to standardize products and processes, to spread risk, to uncover new opportunities, to do joint forecasting and demand planning, as well as to participate in the order–ship–settle process electronically (Brooks 2004). Marketplaces that offer their members such benefits will have no shortage of liquidity.

Hansen et al. (2001) and Richard and Devinney (2005) believe that one hallmark of third-wave B2B approaches is the idea of choosing a different model for each kind of transaction. Companies purchasing a commodity, for example, might value the liquidity, the transparency, and the price orientation of an online exchange (much like the benefits offered by commodity contracts already traded at the Chicago Mercantile Exchange and elsewhere).

Insights and Additions 6.2 Some Critical Success Factors for Exchanges

▶ **Importance of domain expertise.** To meaningfully aggregate buyers and sellers in a community and subsequently enable transactions among them, operators should have knowledge of a given industry's structure and business processes, the nature of buyer and seller behavior in the industry and government, and policy stipulations that impact the sector.

▶ **Targeting inefficient industry processes.** The traditional business processes in most industries have many inefficiencies. These contribute to increased costs and delays for businesses transacting with one another. Addressing these inefficiencies may create significant opportunities, especially for vertical exchanges to add value.

▶ **Targeting the right industries.** The most attractive characteristics suitable for vertical exchanges are: (1) a large base of transactions; (2) many fragmented buyers and sellers; (3) difficulties in bringing buyers and sellers together; (4) high vendor and product search/comparison costs, which may be caused by information-intensive products with complex configurations and nonstandard specifications; (5) high process costs associated with manual processes based on paper catalogs, manual requisitioning, telephone- or fax-based ordering, credit verification, and order tracking; (6) strong pressure to cut expenses; (7) a complex value chain, such as in the automotive industry; and (8) a climate of technological innovation. Targeting industries with some of these characteristics is desirable.

▶ **Brand building.** The low switching costs inherent in exchanges will make branding of exchanges of paramount importance to their long-term viability. Exchange operators must first invest in gaining brand awareness and getting businesses to use their exchange. For example, in Hong Kong, Bigboxx.com even advertises on buses. Exchange operators must then focus on customer retention. Adding valuable features and functionality is one way to increase switching costs (in this case, the services the customer would lose by switching).

▶ **Exploiting economies of scope.** Once a critical mass is reached, exchange operators must expand the services they provide to users. Value-added services, such as industry news, expert advice, or detailed product specification sheets, can make an exchange even more compelling. Expanding the range of services may also increase switching costs. Better-developed exchanges are now offering services such as systems integration, hosting, financial services (e.g., payment processing, receivables management, credit analysis), and logistics services (e.g., shipping, warehousing, and inspection), as well as risk-mitigation services.

▶ **Choice of business/revenue models.** To optimize the chances for success, exchange operators should generate multiple revenue streams, including software licensing, advertising, and sponsorship, and recurring revenues from transaction fees, subscription fees, and software subscription revenues. Other value-added services and applications, such as auctions, financial services, business reporting, and data mining services, may provide other sources of revenue.

▶ **Blending content, community, and commerce.** Exchanges differ in their approaches; some originate from a content/community perspective, whereas others have a focus on conducting EC transactions. Though content and community features have the advantage of stimulating traffic, the ability to conduct EC transactions is thought to create a higher level of customer "stickiness" and greater value for the exchanges. A successful exchange should combine rich content and community with the ability to conduct EC transactions.

▶ **Managing channel conflict.** The movement of buyers to interact directly with sellers and the consequent disintermediation of some portion of the supply chain intermediaries may be viewed as a hostile activity by existing fulfillment channels. The result sometimes is price erosion, which may affect a company's medium-term profitability. Exchanges are trying to minimize the conflict by using existing services of the major buyers and sellers.

▶ **Maximize the benefits for all participants.** Unless all parties are happy, the exchange will not have sufficient liquidity (see Markus 2006).

▶ **Other factors.** Diorio (2002) added the following critical success factors for exchanges: value-added content, expertise, trust relationships, appropriate financing, first-mover advantage, and availability of resources.

In contrast, companies making highly specialized purchases might value the possibilities for customization offered by the traditional bilateral relationship between buyers and sellers.

According to Baumgartner et al. (2001), sellers' reaction to B2B has ranged from skepticism to horror. Such negative reaction is based on the idea that these marketplaces serve a single overriding purpose—the promotion of price transparency—that entails a race to the profitless bottom. Of course, the authors note, certain buyers really are extremely price sensitive when they make certain purchases, and those buyers will naturally migrate to low-cost producers. However, many other purchases will continue to involve information-rich bilateral relationships. In fact, Ordanini et al. (2004) found in their survey that large private exchanges have a superior capability to generate turnover compared with vertical niche operators due to specific choices of content, structure, and governance.

A third model (Berryman and Heck 2001), is the *e-distributor* (see Chapter 5), which lies between the two extremes of the stand-alone third-party exchange and the consortium. In this model, e-distributors, like distributors in the offline world, take title to the goods they sell, aggregate those goods for the convenience of buyers and, because they only carry certain products, in effect advise buyers as to which products to purchase. In addition, e-distributors perform a critical service for sellers by reaching hard-to-find buyers, such as small ones. The result, in many cases, is significant *extra value* for buyers and decent profits for sellers. For an evaluation of the model, see Ranganatan (2003).

According to Bowness (2005), Forrester and Gartner both released predictions for several content fields. Among Forrester's Trend 2005 reports are predictions that continued consolidation will shrink the number of exchanges, that the focus on information quality will be significant, and that Web content management, e-learning, IP address management systems, and IP telephony will become even more important. Gartner suggests that the wireless will impact e-marketplaces via a diversity of devices, mobile infrastructure investments, and more business use of wireless technologies. Raisinghani and Hanabeck (2002) also believe that the use of wireless technology to facilitate collaboration among trading partners will help the expansion of the exchanges. Gartner also suggested that the continued worry over high human capital costs will encourage more offshore outsourcing, and business process outsourcing will be introduced into marketplaces.

Another set of interesting directions is presented by Dai and Kauffman (2002) in a special section of the journal *Electronic Markets* in which six research papers were presented. Of special interest are interviews with leading scholars in the field. This special presentation deals with many of the topics presented in Chapters 5 through 7. Finally, Murtaza et al. (2004) review the opportunities and challenges in different types of e-marketplaces. Ordanini (2006) developed a success model for exchanges that exploits content, governance, and structure to help generate revenues.

Section 6.10 ▶ REVIEW QUESTIONS

1. What are some of the questions one should ask when evaluating exchanges? (Hint: see Online File W6.4.)
2. Describe the concept of centrally managed exchanges.
3. List the five critical success factors for exchanges cited by Ramsdell.
4. Discuss other critical success factors for exchanges.
5. Describe the new directions of B2B exchanges.
6. Describe successful B2B exchange models.

MANAGERIAL ISSUES

Some managerial issues related to this chapter are as follows.

1. **Have we done our homework?** Study the options and select the most secure and economical choice for exchange implementation. Consult the technical staff inside and outside of each partnering company. Planning is essential. This is true for exchange creators, operators, and users.

2. **Can we use the Internet?** Review the current proprietary or leased networks and determine if they can be replaced by intranets and extranets (see Appendix 6A). Replacing them may reduce costs and widen connectivity for customers and suppliers. In making this decision, also consider whether it is safe enough to switch to the extranet.

3. **Which exchange to join?** One of the major concerns of management is selecting exchanges in which to participate. At the moment, exchanges usually are not tightly connected, so there may be a substantial start-up effort and cost for joining another exchange. This is a multicriteria decision that should be analyzed carefully. A related issue is whether to join a third-party public exchange or a consortium or to create a private exchange.

4. **Will joining an exchange force restructuring?** Joining an exchange may require a restructuring of the internal supply chain, which may be expensive and time consuming. Therefore, this possibility must be taken into consideration when deciding whether to join an exchange.

5. **Will we face channel conflicts?** Channel conflicts may arise when a company joins an exchange. You may anger your existing suppliers if you buy via an exchange. This issue must be considered, and an examination of its impact must be carried out.

6. **What are the benefits and risks of joining an exchange?** Companies must take very seriously the issues listed in Exhibit 6.4. The risks of joining an exchange must be carefully weighed against the expected benefits.

7. **Can we trust new trading partners?** Typical to the Internet, new partners are easy to find. But can they be trusted? As in B2C, intermediaries may provide services to increase trust. Also, trust involves a learning process (see Ratnasingam and Phan 2003).

RESEARCH TOPICS

Here are some suggested topics related to this chapter. For details, references, and additional topics, refer to the Online Appendix A "Current EC Research."

1. **Ownership Composition of B2B Marketplaces**
   - Evolution of B2B ownership alternatives and structures
   - Effect of existing corporate power in the market ownership structure
   - Why the buyer-centric marketplace is used most frequently
   - Why third-party exchanges have difficulties obtaining transactions
   - Competitive roles of public marketplaces in comparison with private marketplaces
   - Pros and cons of consortia for B2B marketplaces in different situations

2. **CSF of B2B Marketplaces**
   - Revenue models of successful B2B marketplaces
   - Metrics of CSFs of B2B marketplaces
   - Evolution of CSFs
   - Survival strategies of B2B marketplaces

3. **Matching Buyers and Sellers**
   - Representation of buyer's needs
   - Representation of seller's specifications for e-catalogs
   - Matching mechanisms of buyer's needs and seller's specifications
   - Products' configuration in a matching process
   - Standardizations for products and sellers' representation
   - Role of agents to discover the matched counterpart
   - Protocol of discovering matched counterparts
   - Web Services as a platform of matching services

4. **Case Studies of B2B Marketplaces: Successes and Failures**
   - Case studies of buyer-centric marketplaces
   - Case studies of seller-centric marketplaces
   - Case studies of the evolution of third party marketplaces such as GXS
   - Analysis of failures (e.g., Comdex, Covisint)
   - Comparative study between industries
   - Comparative study between countries

5. **Integration of Exchanges with External Components**
   - Architectures of business-to-exchange integration
   - Business models of exchange-to-exchange integration
   - Integrated services of marketplaces with ASP and collaboration hubs
   - International integration and interconnection of exchanges
   - Architectures of successful extranets

6. **Competition and Participation**
   - Competition among sellers in online exchanges
   - Competition among buyers in exchanges
   - Motivation of sellers and buyers to participate

SUMMARY

In this chapter, you learned about the following EC issues as they relate to the learning objectives.

1. **E-marketplaces and exchanges defined and the major types of exchanges.** Exchanges are e-marketplaces that provide a trading platform for conducting business among many buyers, many sellers, and other business partners. Other names used are *trading portals* or *Net marketplaces*. Types of public e-marketplaces include B2B portals, third-party trading exchanges, consortium trading exchanges, and dynamic trading floors for matching supply and demand and for auctions. Exchanges may be vertical (industry oriented) or horizontal. They may target systematic buying (long-term relationships) or spot buying (for fulfilling an immediate need).

2. **Ownership and revenue models.** Exchanges may be owned by one large buyer or seller, an intermediary (a neutral third party), or a large group of buyers or sellers (a consortium). The major revenue models are transaction fees (flat or percentage), fees for value-added services, annual membership fees, and advertisement income.

3. **B2B portals.** These portals are similar to B2C portals such as MSN or Yahoo! B2B portals are gateways to B2B community-related information. They are usually of a vertical structure, in which case they are referred to as *vortals*. Some B2B portals offer product and vendor information and even tools for conducting trades, sometimes making it difficult to distinguish between B2B portals and trading exchanges.

4. **Third-party exchanges.** Third-party exchanges are owned by an independent company and usually operate in highly fragmented markets. They are open to anyone and, therefore, are considered public exchanges. They try to maintain neutral relations with both buyers and sellers. Their major problem is acquiring enough participants to ensure liquidity. Two models of third-party exchanges are those that aggregate suppliers' catalogs and those that aggregate buyers' RFQs.

5. **Consortia and e-procurement.** A consortium trading exchange (CTE) is an exchange formed and operated by a group of major involved companies. Buying-oriented consortia are established by several large buyers (e.g., automakers). Their major objective is to smooth the procurement (purchasing) process.

Selling-oriented consortia are owned and operated by several large sellers, usually in the same industry (e.g., plastics, airlines). Their major objective is to increase sales and smooth the supply chain to their customers. CTEs sometimes face antitrust scrutiny by governments.

6. **Dynamic pricing and trading.** Dynamic pricing occurs when prices are determined by supply and demand at any given moment. Dynamic trading refers to trading in which prices are continuously changing. The two major dynamic pricing mechanisms are matching of supply and demand (such as in stock markets) and auctions (forward and reverse).

7. **Good relationship with business partners is critical to the success of B2B.** Similar to CRM in B2C, companies develop an electronic support of such relationships.

8. **Integrating marketplaces and exchanges.** One of the major problems in building e-marketplaces is systems integration, especially between business partners. In addition to application integration, there may also be problems of data and database integration as well as process integration. In the future, Web Services will provide a universal open environment that will ease the integration problem.

9. **B2B networks.** B2B requires networks that enable efficient and effective trade and communication. They may be company centered, for one industry, or global. Well-known examples are GXS and Ariba's Supplier Network.

10. **Management of exchanges and critical success factors for exchanges.** Customers will benefit if exchanges are connected to one another. Such integration is complex and may take years to complete. Managing individual exchanges can be expensive; therefore, "families" of exchanges may be managed centrally. The major implementation issues for exchanges are choosing between private and public exchanges (or their combination), evaluating exchanges, identifying problem areas, and using software agents as a support mechanism. Some of the major critical success factors for exchanges are early liquidity, proper ownership, proper governance and management, openness (technological and organizational), and a full range of services.

KEY TERMS

QUESTIONS FOR DISCUSSION

1. Discuss the advantages of a systematic SRM and PRM process.

2. Suppose a manufacturer uses an outside shipping company. How can the manufacturer use an exchange to arrange for the best possible shipping? How can a shipment's status be tracked?

3. Discuss the legal concerns regarding consortia.

4. Which types of exchanges are most suitable for third-party ownership and why?

5. Compare and contrast the supplier aggregation model with the buyer aggregation model in an industry of your choice.

6. Describe the various issues of integration related to B2B exchanges.

7. Explain the logic for networks of exchanges.

8. Discuss the need for auctions in exchanges and the types of auctions used.

9. Explain the importance of early liquidity and describe methods used to achieve it.

10. How do exchanges affect disintermediation? Reintermediation?

11. What questions should buyers and sellers ask when evaluating exchanges?

12. Compare and contrast a privately owned exchange with a private e-marketplace.

13. How does ChemConnect change the market for commodity chemicals?

INTERNET EXERCISES

1. Visit oracle.com and microsoft.com. Find software tools for building e-markets. Check the capabilities provided by each and comment on their differences.

2. Go to alibaba.com and sign up as a member (membership is free). Create a product and post it. Tell your instructor how to view this product.

3. Compare the services offered by globalsources.com with those offered by alibaba.com, and tradekey.com. Assuming you are a toy seller, with which one would you register? Why? If you are a buyer of auto parts, which one would you join and why?

4. Enter chemconnect.com and view the demos for different trading alternatives. Examine the revenue model. Evaluate the services from both the buyer's and seller's points of view. Also, examine the site policies and legal guidelines. Are they fair? Compare chemconnect.com with chemicalonline.com and trade-ranger.com. Which of these do you think will survive? Explain your reasoning.

5. Most of the major exchanges use an ERP/SCM partner. Enter i2.com and view its solutions. What are the benefits of these solutions?

6. Enter eBay's Business Industrial area (business.ebay.com or ebay.com and select "wholesale"). What kind of e-marketplace is this? What are its major capabilities?

7. Visit converge.com. What kind of exchange is this? What services does it provide? How do its auctions work?

8. Enter arbinet.com and explore its offerings. What kind of B2B is it? What services does it provide? What are its CSFs?

9. Enter mySAP, SRM at sap.com and identify what the software can do to improve SRM. List the benefits to both suppliers and buyers.

10. Enter globalspec.com. Find information about vertical search engines. Summarize in a report.

11. Enter marketsandexchanges.com. Prepare a list of resources about exchanges and B2B directories.

12. Enter google.com and find out how you can sell globally through a B2B exchange. Prepare a summary.

TEAM ASSIGNMENTS AND ROLE PLAYING

1. Form two teams (A and B) of five or more members. On each team, person 1 plays the role of an assembly company that produces television monitors. Persons 2 and 3 are domestic parts suppliers to the assembling company, and persons 4 and 5 play foreign parts suppliers. Assume that the TV monitor company wants to sell televisions directly to business customers. Each team is to design an environment composed of membership in exchanges they can use and present its results. A graphical display is recommended.

2. Enter **isteelasia.com**, **metalworld.com**, and **lme.co.uk**. Compare their operations and services. These exchanges compete in global markets. Examine the trading platforms, portal capabilities, and support services (e.g., logistics, payments, etc.) offered by each. In what areas do these companies compete? In what areas do they not compete? What are the advantages of **isteelasia.com** in dealing with Asian companies? Are regional exchanges needed? If it is good for Asia to have a regional exchange, why not have a Western European exchange, an Eastern European exchange, a Central American exchange, and so on? If regional exchanges are needed, can they work together? How? If there are too many exchanges, which are likely to survive? Research this topic and prepare a report.

3. Each team examines a public network: GXS, Sterling Commerce, Covisint, and Ariba SN. The mission is to convince your company to join the network. Specifically, look at what services they provide for B2B traders and how they support integration of their trading hub users' systems.

4. Enter **gtnexus.com** and look at their Private Logistics Networks model and offerings. Prepare a report on how exchanges can benefit from their services. How do they facilitate supply chains? Can they help e-marketplaces?

Real-World Case
IMARKETKOREA

iMarketKorea (iMK) is Korea's largest e-marketplace specializing in MRO items for the construction industry. Since its inception in 2000, the company has grown rapidly. From a market for Samsung's 45 affiliated companies, iMK grew to serve about 500 companies in 2007. Of these new companies, some are outside Korea and most are not Samsung affiliates. The exchange e-catalog includes over 400,000 MRO items.

Initially, IMK concentrated on acting as a procurement agent to the Samsung companies. By 2007, however, the company shifted its vision to become a B2B *procurement service provider*, providing end-to-end procurement services.

Among its most popular services are payments, deliveries, purchasing and budget management, internal approval process and inventory management, storage, and more (all for buyers). In addition, it helps to smooth its customers' supply chains (e.g., process improvement and workflow management). iMK also supports connectivity to enterprise systems (e.g., ERP, legacy systems).

The system architecture and the major participants are shown in Exhibit 6.12

One of the major services provided by iMK is the SRM orientation. This includes features such as:

▶ The ability to calculate "total cost of ownership" (for purchasing).

▶ Strategic sourcing processes.

▶ Formal evaluation of suppliers (assessment, selection, monitoring) through a formal scorecard grading system.

▶ Knowledge sharing about best practices of procurement.

▶ B2B auctions (forward and reverse, either as supporting the entire process or in helping customers take charge of the major activities, helping only with procedural matters during the auction).

▶ Spend management analysis and control.

▶ Provision of collaborative e-sourcing tools.

▶ Decision support and optimization models for buyers.

▶ Contract management.

EXHIBIT 6.12 iMK System Architecture

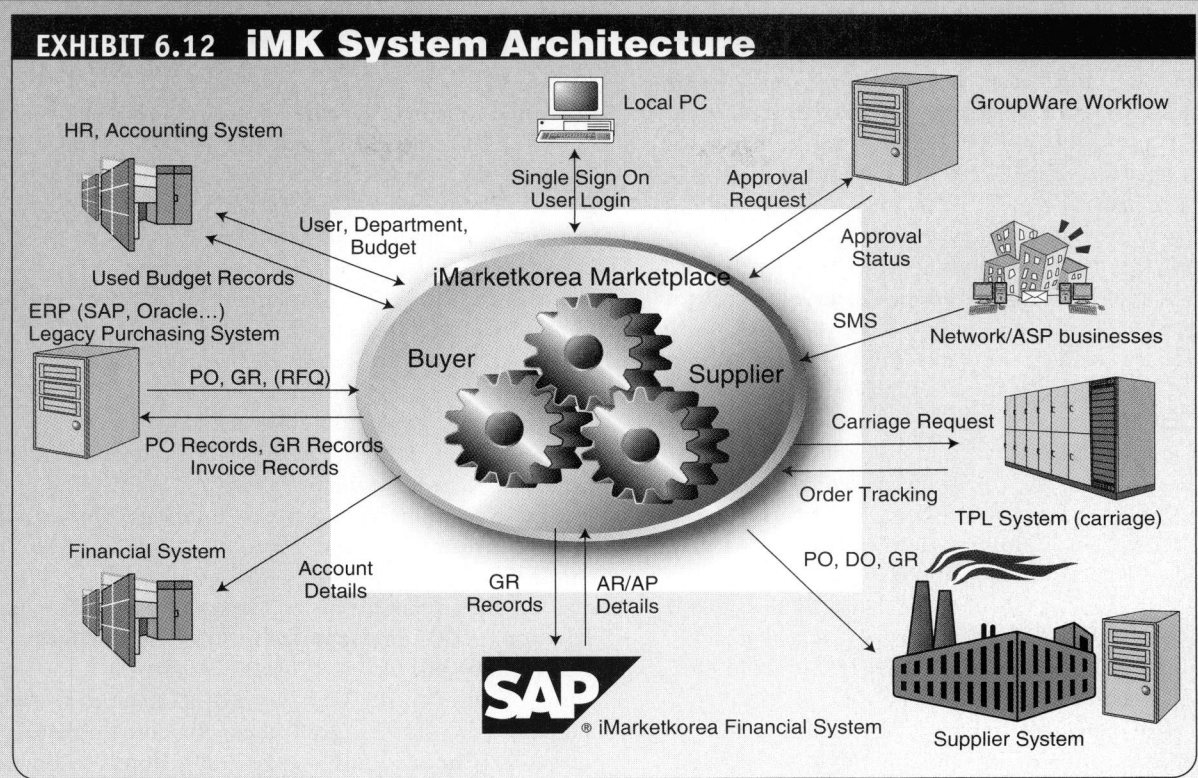

Source: iMarketKorea, "Purchasing Innovation: Value Proposition." 2006.
imarketkorea.co.kr/en_HD/DC9553ED_IMK_homepage_en_200408.pdf (accessed December 2006).

▶ Integrating suppliers by selecting those who are reliable and sound and who are able to provide value (price matters, too, of course), leading to long-term strategic relationships (win-win situation).

▶ Risk assessment and management.

▶ Item standardization for inventory and cost reduction at the suppliers' level. This enables better cataloging and faster and easier search (e.g., simultaneous search of many items).

▶ Analyzing replies to RFQs quickly, considering large amount of computerized information and knowledge.

▶ Joint process improvement, attempting to reduce supplier's TCO (providing suppliers with a comprehensive program of how to do it).

The following are some recent iMK initiatives:

▶ Alliance with the Japanese Samitomo Corp. (a top online trading company), kicking off global business expansion. iMK is already exporting MROs to 12 countries.

▶ iMK exported over $1 billion of MROs in 2005, plus $1.2 in raw materials (an over 30 percent increase over 2004).

▶ Collaborating with Woori Bank, iMK opened a B2C and B2B2C channel for selling gifts over the Internet to the bank's employees.

The results speak for themselves: on-time delivery increased from 72 percent to 93.7 percent; average lead-time was reduced from 5.3 days to 2.8 days; catalog search speed has increased 40 percent; 12 to 18 percent savings in purchase prices; 30 to 50 percent savings in

process costs; 5 to 15 percent savings in inventory management costs; and 40 to 60 percent savings in reduced inventory. All these savings have contributed to the success and growth of iMK. The site offers Korean, English and Japanese options to registered users.

Sources: Compiled from company brochure: Product Innovation-Value Proposition, accessed at *imarketkorea.com* (November 2006), Lee and Lee (2007), iMarketKorea.com (2005), and *iMarketKorea.com* (2006).

Questions

1. How do the support services benefit the exchange?

2. Relate this case to desktop purchasing (Chapter 5).

3. Write a summary of the benefits of the exchange to buyers.

4. Write a summary of the benefits of the exchange to sellers.

5. Compare iMK to Alibaba.com. What are the similarities and the differences?

6. Much of iMK's success is attributed to the understanding of the Korean culture and business environment. Given that iMK wants to expand internationally, what could be some of its stumbling blocks?

7. Check the recent news and press releases (last 6 months) at *imarketkorea.com*. Identify expansion patterns.

REFERENCES

Aberdeen Group, Inc. "Asite Builds E-Marketplace Using Combined Strength of Commerce One, Microsoft, and Attenda." *Aberdeen Group Profile*, May 2001, p. 5. **aberdeen.com/abpercent5Fabstracts/2001/05/05012573.htm** (accessed September 2002). Note: No longer available online.

About.com. "B2B Trading Communities Evolution." 2006. **logistics.about.com/library/weekly/aa060600a.htm** (accessed October 2006).

Agrawal, M. K., and M. H. Pak. "Getting Smart about Supply Chain Management." *The McKinsey Quarterly* no. 2 (2001).

Alibaba.com. **alibaba.com** (accessed November 2006).

AMR Research Staff. "B2B Marketplaces Report, 2000–2005." AMR Research, August 1, 2001. **amrresearch.com/Content/view.asp?pmillid=14510&docid=600** (accessed January 2003).

Angwin, J. "Top Online Chemical Exchange Is an Unlikely Success Story." *The Wall Street Journal Online*, January 8, 2004. **webreprints.djreprints.com/90766007 2246.html** (accessed March 2005).

Asite.com. **asite.com** (accessed September 2004).

Bandyopadhyay, S, J. M. Barron, and A. R. Chaturved. "Competition Among Sellers in Online Exchanges." *Information Systems Research*, March 2005.

Baumgartner, T., et al. "A Seller's Guide to B2B Markets." *The McKinsey Quarterly* no. 2 (2001).

Berryman, K., and S. Heck. "Is the Third Time the Charm for B2B?" *The McKinsey Quarterly* no. 2 (2001).

Boucher-Ferguson, R. "Microsoft, GXS Announce Partnership." *eWeek*, May 8, 2006.

Bowness, S. "No Matter What Your Expression, 2005 Will Be Interesting," E-Content Institute, February 2005. **econtentinstitute.org/issues/ISarticle.asp?id=159990&story_id=54579170437&issue=01012005&PC=** (accessed October 2006).

Brooks, A. "Exchange Values." *Purchasing B2B* 46, no. 3 (2004).

BRW Staff. "B2B: The Rocky Road to Profits for Exchanges." *Business Review Weekly of Australia*, November 10, 2000.

ChemConnect.com. **chemconnect.com** (accessed September 2006).

Coia, A. "Evolving Transportation Exchanges." *World Trade*, July 2002a.

Coia, A. "Going Online Brought Smooth Sailing to World of Ocean Shipping." **supplychainbrain.com** (accessed June 2002b).

Dai, Q., and R. J. Kauffman. "B2B E-Commerce Revisited: Revolution or Evolution." *Electronic Markets* 12, no. 2 (2002).

Devine, D. A., et al. "Building Enduring Consortia." *The McKinsey Quarterly* no. 1 (2001).

Diorio, S. *Beyond "e": 12 Ways Technology Is Transforming Sales and Marketing Strategy*. New York: McGraw-Hill, 2002.

Dolinoy, M., et al. "Customer Defined Networks." **forrester.com/ER/Research/Report/Summary/0,133 8,11071,FF.html** (accessed April 2001). Note: No longer available online.

Dubie, D. "Going Global." *Ebusinessiq.com*, March 13, 2003. **publish.com/article2/0,,1762086,00.asp** (accessed March 2005).

The Economist. "Survey: A Market Too Far." *The Economist* 371, no. 8375 (2004).

Epstein, M. J., *Implementing E-Commerce Strategies: A Guide to Corporate Success After the Dot.Com Bust*. Westport, CT: Praeger Publishers 2005.

Ferris, C., and J. Farrell. "E-Services: What Are Web Services?" *Communications of the ACM*, June 2003.

Fram, E. "E-Commerce Survivors: Finding Value Amid Broken Dreams." *Business Horizons*, July–August 2002, pp. 15–20.

Global eXchange Services, Inc. "Global eXchange Service Mission." 2004. **gxs.com/pdfs/DS_GXS_Mission_GXS_71604.pdf** (accessed December 2004).

Goldman Sachs. "B2B: 2B or Not 2B." *Goldmansachs.com*, January 5, 2000. **goldmansachs.com/hightech/research/b2b/** (accessed May 8, 2000). Note: No longer available online.

Goodman, R. "Going Online Brought Smooth Sailing to World of Ocean Shipping." *Supplychainbrain.com*, June 2002. **supplychainbrain.com/archives/6.02.ocean.htm?adcode=90** (accessed January 2003).

GT Nexus. "GT Nexus Names Jeff Lynch Vice President of Sales." GT Nexus press release, October 2002. **gtnexus.com/cgi-perl/press_releases.cgi? releaseID=45&lang=en** (accessed April 2004). Note: No longer available online.

Hagel, J. "Offshoring Goes on the Offensive." *The McKinsey Quarterly* no. 2 (2004).

Hansen, M. A., et al. "A Buyer's Guide to B2B Markets." *The McKinsey Quarterly* no. 2 (2001).

Heilemann, J. "Jack Ma Aims to Unlock the Middle Kingdom." *Business 2.0*, July 31, 2006.

iMarketKorea. "iMarketKorea Enters into Strategic Business Cooperation Agreement with Sumitomo Corporation Japan." January 25, 2006. **imarketkorea.com/en_HD/menu_05001–19view.jsp** (accessed November 2006).

iMarketKorea. "iMarketKorea Opens Woori Bank e-Shop." December 19, 2005. **imarketkorea.com/en_HD/menu_05001–17view.jsp** (accessed November 2006).

Iyer, G. R. *Customer Relationship Management in Electronic Markets*. Binghamton, NY: Haworth Press, 2004.

Kaplan, S., and M. Sawhney. "E-Hubs: The New B2B Market Places." *Harvard Business Review*, May–June 2000.

Keenan Report. "Internet Exchange 2000." **eyefortransport.com/archive/keenanvision17.pdf#search='Keenan%20Report.%20Internet%20Exchange%202000'** (accessed March 2005).

Killeen, J. F. "The Value of Vertical Search for B2B Markets." *Ecommercetimes.com*, October 27, 2006. **ecommercetimes.com/story/53931.html** (accessed March 2007).

Konicki, S. "Exchanges Go Private." *InformationWeek*, June 12, 2000. **informationweek.com/790/private.htm** (accessed September 2001).

Lee, Z., and D. S. Lee. "Transition from a Buyer's Agent to a Procurement Service Provider in B2B iMarketKorea." In Lee, J. K., et al., *Premier e-Business Cases from Asia*, Singapore: Prentice Hall and Pearson Education South Asia, 2007.

Li, J., and L. Li, "On the Critical Success Factors for B2B E-Marketplace," *Proceedings of the 7th international Conference on Electronic Commerce*, Xi'an, China, August 15–17, 2005.

Malhotra, R., and D. K. Malhotra, "The Impact of Internet and E-Commerce on the Evolving Business Models in the Financial Services Industry." *International Journal of Electronic Business* 4, no. 1 (2006).

Markus, L. "The Golden Rule." *CIO Insight*, July 2006.

McNichols, T., and L. Brennan. "Evaluating Partner Suitability for Collaborative Supply Networks." *International Journal of Networking and Virtual Organisations* 3, no. 2 (2006).

Murtaza, M. B., V. Gupta, and R. C. Carroll. "E-Marketplaces and the Future of Supply Chain Management: Opportunities and Challenges." *Business Process Management Journal* 10, no. 3 (2004).

Nivesto.com. "Cross-Road Transportation Management." 2006. Available for download at **nistevo.com/v1/downloads/index.html** (accessed March 2007).

Ordanini, A. "What Drives Market Transaction in B2B Exchanges?" *Communication of the ACM*, April 2006.

Ordanini, A. S., S. Micelli, and E. Di Maria. "Failure and Success of B-to-B Exchange Business Models: A Contingent Analysis of Their Performance." *European Management Journal* 22, no. 3 (2004).

Papazoglou, M., and P. Ribbers. *Building B2B Relationships—Technical and Tactical Implementation of an E-Business Strategy*. Hoboken, NJ: Wiley & Sons, 2006.

Raisinghani, M. S., and H. L. Hanabeck. "Rethinking B2B E-Marketplaces and Mobile Commerce: From Information to Execution." *Journal of Electronic Commerce Research* 3, no. 2 (2002).

Ramsdell, G. "The Real Business of B2B: Five Factors for Success." White paper, *McKinsey & Company*, October 2, 2000. **techupdate.zdnet.com/techupdate/stories/ main/0,14179,2635155–1,00.html** (accessed March 2005).

Ranganatan, C. "Evaluating the Options for B2B E-Exchanges." *Information Systems Management*, Summer 2003.

Rappa, M. "Case Study: ChemConnect—Managing the Digital Enterprise." 2006. **digitalenterprise.org/cases/chemconnect_text.html** (accessed November 2006).

Ratnasingam, P., and D. D. Phan. "Trading Partner Trust in B2B E-Commerce: A Case Study." *Information Systems Management*, Summer 2003.

Richard, P. J., and T. M. Devinney. "Modular Strategies: B2B Technology and Architecture Knowledge." *California Management Review*, Summer 2005.

Saarinen, T., M. Tinnild, and A. Tseng (eds.). *Managing Business in a Multi-Channel World: Success Factors for E-Business.* Hershey, PA: Idea Group, Inc., 2006.

Sanborn, S. "Sailing Online." *Infoworld Magazine*, October 18, 2002. **archive.infoworld.com/articles/fe/xml/02/11/04/021104fegtn.xml** (accessed December 2002). Note: No longer available online.

Schecterle, B. "Managing and Extending Supplier Relationships." *People Talk*, April–June 2003.

Shetty, B. "Forecast Online Sales by Exchange Type." *Forrester Research*, August 2001. **forrester.com/search/1,6260,,00.html?squery=2percent2C500+exchanges+worldwide** (accessed September 2002). Note: No longer available online.

Thibodeau, P. "IBM, Sun, HP and Intel Join on Grid Development." *Computerworld*, January 24, 2005.

Tumolo, M. "Business to Business Exchanges." *Brint.com*, February 2001. **brint.com/members/01040530/b2b exchanges** (accessed February 2005).

Ulfelder, S. "B2B Exchange Survivors." *Computerworld*, February 2, 2004.

Umar, A. *Third Generation Distributed Computing Environments*. New York: NGE Solutions, 2005.

webMethods. "Powering WWRE's Global Item Synchronization Solution." WWRE Success Story, 2005. **webmethods.com/meta/default/folder/0000006269? success storiesdetails_param0=3352** (accessed May 2005).

Woods, W. A. *B2B Exchange 2.0: Not All Are Dot-Bomb*. New York: ISI Publications, 2003.

WWRE. "WWRE Overview." 2005. **worldwideretail exchange.org/cs/en_US/about/wr0100.html** (accessed May 2005).

Young, E. "Web Marketplaces that Really Work." *Fortune/CNET Tech Review*, Winter 2002.

COMMUNICATION NETWORKS AND EXTRANETS FOR B2B

Chapter 5 pointed to the need for networks to support communication and collaboration among B2B business partners. It also described EDI and its supporting role in facilitating B2B communication and collaboration. This appendix looks at the networks needed for private e-marketplaces and public exchanges.

The major network structure used in e-marketplaces and exchanges is an *extranet*, or "extended intranet." An extranet uses the Internet to connect individual companies' intranets. Because the Internet is free, extranets are much less expensive than VANs. An extranet adds value to the Internet by increasing its security and expanding the available bandwidth. To better understand how an extranet interfaces with the Internet and intranets, we will first consider the basic concepts of the Internet and intranets and then turn our attention back to extranets.

THE INTERNET

Internet

A public, global communications network that provides direct connectivity to anyone over a LAN via an ISP.

The **Internet** is a public, global communications network that provides direct connectivity to anyone over a local area network (LAN), usually via an Internet service provider (ISP). Because access to the Internet is open to all, control and security are at a minimum.

INTRANETS

intranet

A private corporate LAN or WAN that uses Internet technology and is secured behind a company's firewalls.

An **intranet** is a private corporate LAN or wide area network (WAN) that uses Internet technology and is secured behind a company's firewalls. (Firewalls are discussed in Chapter 11.) An intranet links various servers, clients, databases, and application programs, such as ERP, within a company. Although intranets are based on the same TCP/IP protocol as the Internet, they operate as a private network with limited access. Only authorized employees are able to use them.

Intranets are limited to information pertinent to the company, and they contain exclusive, often proprietary, sensitive information. The intranet can be used to enhance communication and collaboration among authorized employees, customers, suppliers, and other business partners. Because an intranet allows access through the Internet, it does not require any additional implementation of leased networks. This open and flexible connectivity is a major capability and advantage of intranets. More on intranets can be found in Online Appendix W7A.

EXTRANETS

extranet

A network that uses a virtual private network to link intranets in different locations over the Internet; an "extended intranet."

An **extranet** uses the TCP/IP protocol to link intranets in different locations (as shown in Exhibit 6A.1). Extranet transmissions are usually conducted over the Internet, which offers little privacy or transmission security. Therefore, it is necessary to add security features. This is done by creating tunnels of secured data flows, using cryptography and authorization algorithms, to provide secure transport of private communications. An Internet with tunneling technology is known as a **virtual private network (VPN)** (see Chapter 11 for details).

Extranets provide secured connectivity between a corporation's intranets and the intranets of its business partners, materials suppliers, financial services, government, and customers. Access to an extranet is usually limited by agreements of the collaborating parties, is strictly controlled, and is available only to authorized personnel using a secure password and login. The protected environment of an extranet allows partners to collaborate and share information and to perform these activities securely.

virtual private network (VPN)

A network that creates tunnels of secured data flows, using cryptography and authorization algorithms, to provide secure transport of private communications over the public Internet.

Because an extranet allows connectivity between businesses through the Internet, it is an open and flexible platform suitable for B2B. To increase security, many companies replicate the portions of their databases that they are willing to share with their business partners and separate them physically from their regular intranets. However, even separated data need to be secured. (See Chapter 11 for more on EC network security.)

According to Szuprowicz (1998), extranet benefits fall into five categories:

1. **Enhanced communications.** The extranet enables improved internal communications; improved business partnership channels; effective marketing, sales, and customer support; and facilitated collaborative activities support.

2. **Productivity enhancements.** The extranet enables just-in-time information delivery, reduction of information overload, productive collaboration between workgroups, and training on demand.

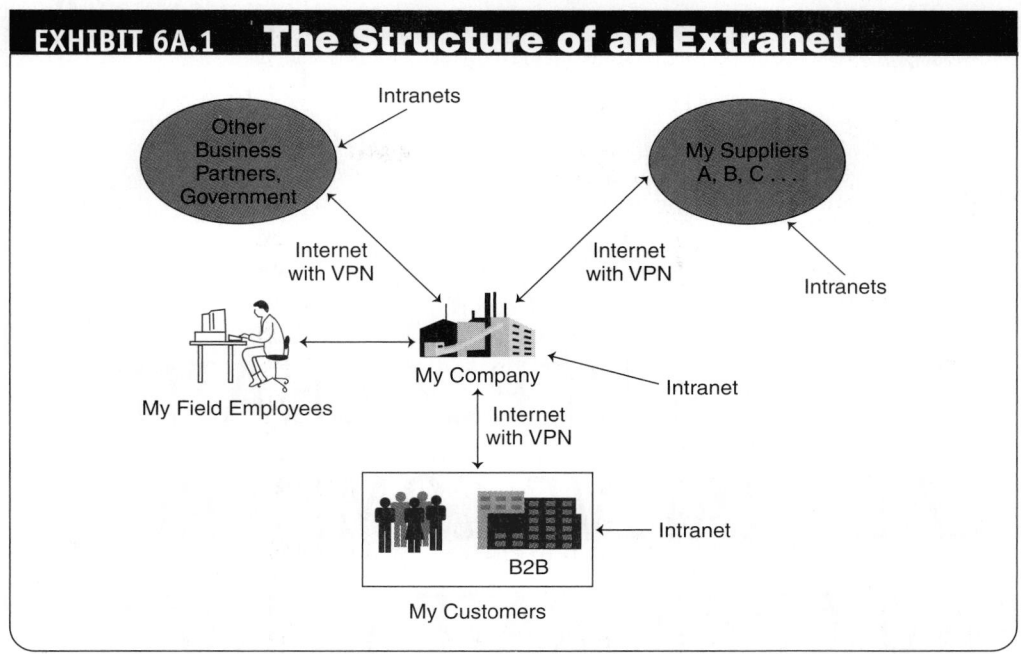

EXHIBIT 6A.1   The Structure of an Extranet

3. **Business enhancements.** The extranet enables faster time-to-market, potential for simultaneous engineering and collaboration, lower design and production costs, improved client relationships, and creation of new business opportunities.

4. **Cost reduction.** The extranet results in fewer errors, improved comparison shopping, reduced travel and meeting time and cost, reduced administrative and operational costs, and elimination of paper-publishing costs.

5. **Information delivery.** The extranet enables low-cost publishing, leveraging of legacy systems, standard delivery systems, ease of maintenance and implementation, and elimination of paper-based publishing and mailing costs.

Rihao-Ling and Yen (2001) reported additional advantages of extranets, such as ready access to information, ease of use, freedom of choice, moderate setup cost, simplified workflow, lower training cost, and better group dynamics. They also listed disadvantages, such as difficulty in justifying the investment (measuring benefits and costs), high user expectations, and drain on resources. Finally, Chow (2004) describes success factors of using extranets in e-supply chains.

KEY TERMS

Extranet 302	Intranet 302	Virtual private network (VPN) 302
Internet 302		

REFERENCES

Chow, W. S. "An Exploratory Study of the Success Factors for Extranet Adoption in E-Supply Chain." *Journal of Global Information Management*, January–March 2004.

Rihao-Ling, R., and D. C. Yen. "Extranet: A New Wave of Internet." *SAM Advanced Management Journal*, Spring 2001.

Szuprowicz, B. *Extranet and Intranet: E-Commerce Business Strategies for the Future.* Charleston, SC: Computer Technology Research Corp., 1998.

E-SUPPLY CHAINS, COLLABORATIVE COMMERCE, AND CORPORATE PORTALS

Learning Objectives

Upon completion of this chapter, you will be able to:

1. Define the e-supply chain and describe its characteristics and components.

2. List supply chain problems and their causes.

3. List solutions to supply chain problems provided by EC.

4. Describe RFID supply chain applications.

5. Define c-commerce and list the major types.

6. Describe collaborative planning and Collaboration, Planning, Forecasting, and Replenishing (CPFR) and list the benefits of each.

7. Discuss integration along the supply chain.

8. Understand corporate portals and their types and roles.

9. Describe e-collaboration tools such as workflow software and groupware.

Content

Boeing's Global Supply Chain for the Dreamliner 787

Managerial Issues

Real-World Case: Sysco—Excellence in Supply Chain Management through Business Process Innovation and IT

BOEING'S GLOBAL SUPPLY CHAIN FOR THE DREAMLINER 787

The Problem

Your company is losing market share to its major competitor. Your industry is in a bit of a slump, thanks in part to rising oil prices and global terrorism concerns. The next product, which may well be critical to the company's future success, will cost millions and take years to develop and produce. You can't afford to fail. This sounds like a high-pressure, risky undertaking. Essentially, this was the situation facing Boeing, a company with a proud tradition as leader of the civilian aircraft industry, when it announced the development of a super-efficient, midsized aircraft—the 787 Dreamliner.

Designing and manufacturing an aircraft is an immensely complex undertaking; the current Dreamliner project is said to be one the largest, most complex, and challenging engineering projects currently being undertaken in the world. The supply chain involved in the design and production of this aircraft involves millions of different parts and component materials and thousands of different suppliers, partners, contractors, and outsourcing vendors scattered across 24 countries working from 135 different sites. Absolute precision and meticulous attention to detail is required, and safety and quality are paramount. In addition to designing and producing a new aircraft, the new production processes had to be designed, tested, and implemented. Close collaboration and communication among thousands of employees, information and knowledge management, and sound management of this complex global supply chain were essential to the project's success.

The Solution

Boeing had been increasingly relying on sophisticated information technology (IT) to support its operations for some time and had been a user of CAD/CAM technologies since the early 1980s. The Dreamliner, however, was to be a "paperless airliner," with IT being employed to support many critical activities. Boeing teamed with Dassault Systemes to create a Global Collaboration Environment (GCE), a product management lifecycle solution, to support the virtual rollout of the new aircraft. The GCE enabled Boeing to digitally monitor the design, production, and testing of every aspect of the aircraft and its production processes before the actual production started.

The GCE included the following components:

- **CATIA.** A collaborative 3D-design platform that enabled engineers worldwide to collaborate on the design of each and every part of the 787.

- **ENOVIA.** A system that supported the accessing, sharing, and managing of all information related to the 787 design in a secure environment.

- **DELMIA.** An environment for defining, simulating, and validating manufacturing and maintenance processes and establishing and managing workflows before actually building tools and production facilities.

- **SMARTEAM.** A Web-based system to facilitate collaboration, which included predefined and auditable processes and procedures, project templates, and best-practice methodologies all geared toward ensuring compliance with corporate and industry standards.

In addition, Boeing also decided to integrate all databases associated with the Dreamliner, teaming up with IBM to employ a DB2 Universal Database for this purpose and ensuring partners access to the Dassault's suite of systems.

As the Dreamliner moved toward physical production using the new manufacturing processes (Boeing was to become the final assembler and integrator, rather than building much of the aircraft from scratch), excellent supply chain management was required to carefully coordinate the movement of components and systems across multiple tier partners around the world. Boeing teamed with Exostar to provide software to support its supply chain coordination challenges. The Exostar supply chain management solution enables all suppliers access to real-time demand, supply, and logistics information so that crucial components and systems arrive at Boeing's production facilities just in time for assembly over a 3-day period. The Exostar solution includes the following functionalities: planning and scheduling; order placement and tracking purchase order changes; exchanging shipping information; managing inventory consumption across suppliers; managing returns; and providing a consolidated view of all activities in the manufacturing process. Business process exceptions can also be monitored across partners, allowing for informed evaluation of the impacts of these exceptions to take place across affected parties.

RFID technologies will be deployed in the aircraft to support maintenance activities. By tagging component parts, Boeing expects to reduce maintenance and inventory costs.

The Results

The goal of the Dreamliner project was to produce a fuel-efficient (and less polluting, hence environmentally responsible), cost-effective, quiet, and comfortable mid-size aircraft that could travel long distances without stopping. It is a critical innovation for Boeing, which has in recent years struggled in the face of rising competition from Airbus. With the plane still some months out from its first flight, IT has played a critical role in supporting collaboration throughout this massive project, reducing the need for physical prototyping and testing, and making substantial impacts on the supply chain. IT has enabled faster decision making, better management of critical information and knowledge assets, increased sharing and exchange of product-related information and processes, reduced time-to-market, less rework, and reduced costs of manufacturing by reducing the assembly time for the aircraft from 13 to 17 days to just 3 days.

Boeing has received in excess of 300 orders for the plane to date and commitments in excess of $55 billion. Dreamliner may just be the most successful commercial airplane launch in history.

Sources: Kumar and Gupta (2006), Kidman (2006), *Supply and Demand Chain Executive* (2006), *RFID Gazette* (2006), and *TenLinks.com* (2006).

WHAT WE CAN LEARN . . .

In increasingly global industries, effective communication and collaboration are essential to an organization's success. Modern IT and Web-based systems have made collaboration, both internally and externally with key players along an industry supply chain, simpler and cheaper than ever before. Boeing recognized this, and implemented a range of technologies to facilitate the access, sharing, and storage of critical information related to the Dreamliner project. Vital, too, was its use of 3D virtual workspaces, removing the need for time-consuming and expensive physical prototyping of both aircraft components and the manufacturing process. The company also introduced IT to expedite design, reduce problems along the supply and value chains of the design process, reducing cost, cycle time, and assembly time dramatically. This case demonstrates several applications of EC, IT, and a range of Web-enabled technologies: collaborative commerce and streamlining complex supply chains. These and related issues are the topics of Chapter 7.

7.1 E-SUPPLY CHAINS

Many people equate e-commerce with selling and buying on the Internet. However, although a company's success is clearly dependent on finding and retaining customers, its success may be far more dependent on what is *behind* the Web page than on what is *on* the Web page. In other words, the company's internal operations (the back end) and its relationships with suppliers and other business partners are as critical, and frequently much more complex, than customer-facing applications such as taking an order online. This is of course true in the offline business world as well. In many cases, these non-customer-facing applications are related to the company's supply chain.

It has been well known for generations that the success of many organizations—private, public, and military—depends on their ability to manage the flow of materials, information, and money into, within, and out of the organization. Such a flow is referred to as a *supply chain*. Because supply chains may be long and complex and may involve many different business partners, we frequently see problems in the operation of the supply chains. These problems may result in delays, in products not being where they are required at the right time, in customer dissatisfaction, in lost sales, and in high expenses that result from fixing the problems once they occur. World-class companies, such as Dell, attribute much of their success to effective supply chain management (SCM), which is largely supported by IT and e-commerce technologies.

This chapter focuses on supply chain issues related to e-commerce. In addition, it covers several related topics such as collaboration and integration along the supply chain. The topic of financial supply chains (payment systems) is discussed in Chapter 12, and order fulfillment is presented in Chapter 13. The essentials of supply chains and their management are described in Online Tutorial T2.

DEFINITIONS AND CONCEPTS

To understand e-supply chains, one must first understand nonelectronic supply chains. A **supply chain** is the flow of materials, information, money, and services from raw material suppliers through factories and warehouses to the end customers. A supply chain also includes the *organizations* and *processes* that create and deliver products, information, and services to the end customers. The term *supply chain* comes from the concept of how the partnering organizations are *linked* together.

As shown in Exhibit 7.1, a simple linear supply chain links a company that manufactures or assembles a product (middle of the chain) with its suppliers (on the left) and distributors and customers (on the right). The upper part of the figure shows a generic supply chain. The bottom part shows a specific example of the toy-making process. The solid links in the figure show the flow of materials among the various partners. Not shown is the flow of returned goods (e.g., defective products) and money, which are flowing in the reverse direction. The broken links, which are shown only in the upper part of Exhibit 7.1, indicate the bidirectional flow of information.

A supply chain involves activities that take place during the entire product *life cycle*, "from dirt to dust," as some describe it. However, a supply chain is more than that, because it also includes the movement of information and money and the procedures that support the movement of a product or a service. Finally, the organizations and individuals involved are considered part of the supply chain as well. When looked at very broadly, the supply chain actually ends when the product reaches its after-use disposal—presumably back to Mother Earth somewhere.

The supply chain shown in Exhibit 7.1 is fairly simple. As will be shown in Online Tutorial T2, supply chains can be much more complex, and they are of different types.

supply chain
The flow of materials, information, money, and services from raw material suppliers through factories and warehouses to the end customers.

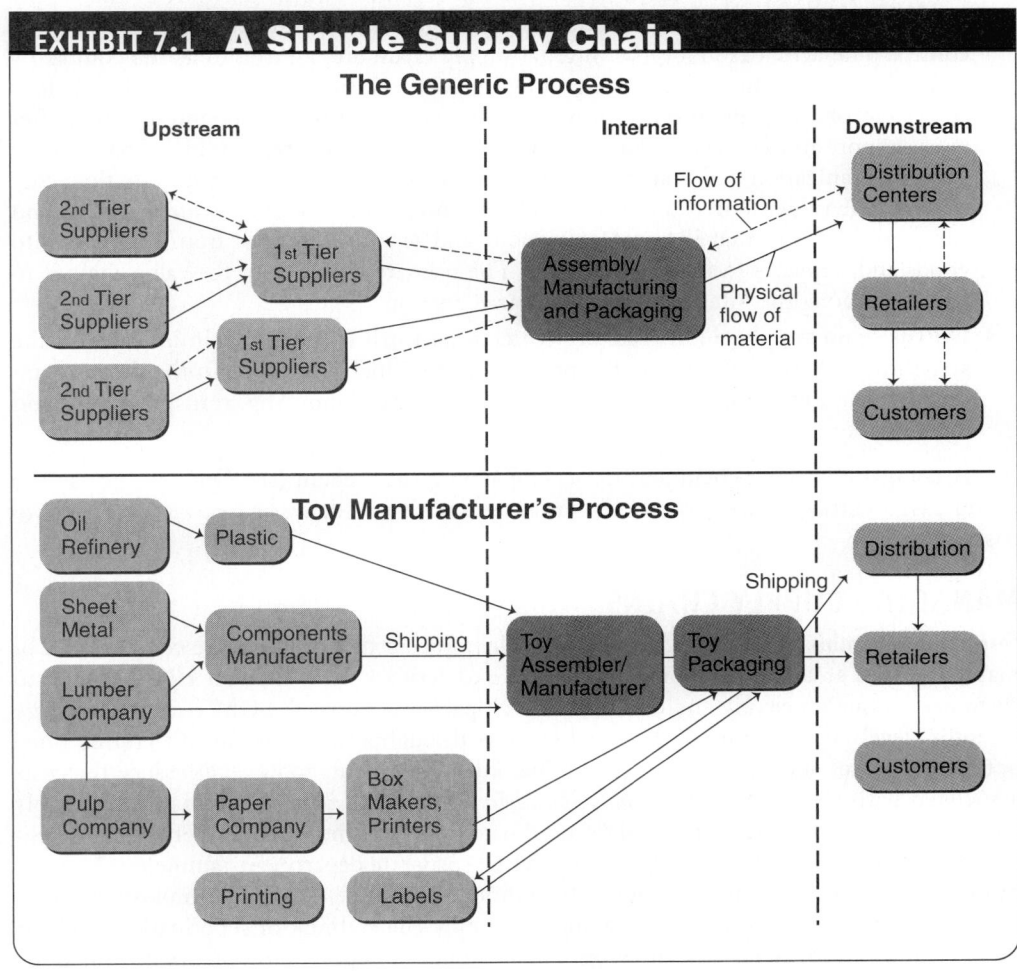

EXHIBIT 7.1 A Simple Supply Chain

e-supply chain

A supply chain that is managed electronically, usually with Web technologies.

When a supply chain is managed electronically, usually with Web technologies, it is referred to as an **e-supply chain**. As will be shown throughout this chapter, improvements in e-supply chains are a major target for EC applications. However, before examining how e-supply chains are managed, it is necessary to better understand the composition of supply chains.

SUPPLY CHAIN PARTS

A supply chain can be broken into three major parts: upstream, internal, and downstream, as was shown in Exhibit 7.1:

▶ **Upstream supply chain.** The upstream part of the supply chain includes the activities of a company with its suppliers (which can be manufacturers, assemblers, or both, or service providers) and their connections with their suppliers (second-tier suppliers). The supplier relationship can be extended to the left in several tiers, all the way to the origin of the material (e.g., mining ores, growing crops). In the upstream supply chain, the major activity is *procurement*. **Procurement** is the process made up of a range of activities by which an organization obtains or gains access to the resources (materials, skills, capabilities, facilities) they require to undertake their core business activities. Procurement and the technologies now used to support these activities are concerned with the consideration of what is required, where it should be obtained in a timely and cost effective manner, and issues such as spend analysis, sourcing strategies, supplier relationship management, reverse auctions, and the like, all informed by the organization's supply chain strategy (*Line56.com* 2006).

procurement

The process made up of a range of activities by which an organization obtains or gains access to the resources (materials, skills, capabilities, facilities) they require to undertake their core business activities.

▶ **Internal supply chain.** The internal part of the supply chain includes all of the in-house processes used in transforming the inputs received from the suppliers into the organization's outputs. It extends from the time the inputs enter an organization to the time that the products go to distribution outside of the organization. In this part of the supply chain, the major concerns are production management, manufacturing, and inventory control. The activities along the internal supply chain are referred to as the company's *value chain* (see Online Tutorial T2 and Davenport and Brooks 2004). The value chain is composed of a sequential set of primary activities (operations, outbound logistics, after sales support and service, etc.) and support activities (administration, HR, finance, etc.) that an organization undertakes in order to deliver a good or service of value to their customers. The value chain can thus be seen as an integrator between customers (B2C) and suppliers (B2B) in that it transforms goods and services obtained from suppliers into goods and services of value to customers. The primary objective of the value chain is to add value along the internal supply chain (see Section 7.5).

▶ **Downstream supply chain.** The downstream part of the supply chain includes all the activities involved in delivering the products to the final customers. In the downstream supply chain, attention is directed at distribution, warehousing, transportation, and after-sale service.

supply chain management (SCM)

A complex process that requires the coordination of many activities so that the shipment of goods and services from supplier right through to customer is done efficiently and effectively for all parties concerned. SCM aims to minimize inventory levels, optimize production and increase throughput, decrease manufacturing time, optimize logistics and distribution, streamline order fulfillment, and overall reduce the costs associated with these activities.

A company's supply chain and its accompanying value chain (see Online Tutorial T2) encompass an array of business processes that create value by delivering goods or services to customers.

MANAGING SUPPLY CHAINS

Supply chain management (SCM) is a complex process that requires the coordination of many activities so that the shipment of goods and services from supplier right through to customer is done efficiently and effectively for all parties concerned. SCM aims to minimize inventory levels, optimize production and increase throughput, decrease manufacturing time, optimize logistics and distribution, streamline order fulfillment, and overall reduce the costs associated with these activities (*SupplyChainManagement101.com* 2006). Managing supply chains can be difficult due to the need to coordinate several business partners, often in different countries and different time zones; several internal corporate departments; numerous business processes; and possibly many customers. In addition, complexity is added in industries where huge numbers of goods flow rapidly along the supply chain (think of supermarkets and the number and rate of items that flow on and off modern supermarket shelves). Managing medium to large supply chains manually is almost impossible. Information technology provides two types of software solutions: (1) SCM (including e-procurement) and (2) enterprise resource planning systems (ERP) (including e-business infrastructure, data warehouses, and the like) and its predecessors material requirements planning (MRP) and manufacturing resource planning (MRP II). (These types of software are defined and described in Online Tutorial T2.) A major requirement for any medium- to large-scale company that is moving to EC implies an integration between all the activities conducted on the Web and the ERP/MRP/SCM solutions—in other words, creating an e-supply chain and managing it. As these software packages evolve and become increasingly integrated, we see a new umbrella term, *enterprise systems*, being used to embrace all the functionality of ERP, SCM, CRM, and e-business solutions.

E-Supply Chains and Their Management

The capabilities of the Internet are having a profound impact on organizations' supply chains. Increasingly companies are recognizing that the efficient and effective flow of information and materials along their supply chains is a source of competitive advantage and differentiation. According to Norris et al. (2000), **e-supply chain management (e-SCM)** is the collaborative use of technology to enhance B2B processes and improve speed, agility, real-time control, and customer satisfaction. It involves the use of information technologies to improve the operations of supply chain activities (e.g., procurement), as well as the management of the supply chains (e.g., planning, coordination, and control). E-SCM is not about technology change alone; it also involves changes in management policies, organizational culture, performance metrics, business processes, and organizational structure across the supply chain. Interorganizational communication and cooperation (developing a win–win mentality, not a "them" and "us" approach) also are keys to success with e-SCM.

e-supply chain management (e-SCM) The collaborative use of technology to improve the operations of supply chain activities as well as the management of supply chains.

The success of an e-supply chain depends on the following:

- ⟩ **The ability of all supply chain partners to view partner collaboration as a strategic asset.** It is the tight integration and trust among the trading partners that generates speed, agility, and lower cost.
- ⟩ **A well-defined supply chain strategy.** This includes a clear understanding of existing strengths and weaknesses, articulating well-defined plans for improvement, and establishing cross-organizational objectives for supply chain performance. Senior executive commitment is essential and must be reflected through appropriate allocation of resources and priority-setting.
- ⟩ **Information visibility along the entire supply chain.** Information about inventories at various segments of the chain, demand for products, capacity planning and activation, synchronization of material flows, delivery times, and any other relevant information must be visible to all members of the supply chain at any given time. Therefore, information must be managed properly—with strict policies, discipline, and daily monitoring.
- ⟩ **Speed, cost, quality, and customer service.** These are the metrics by which supply chains are measured. Consequently, companies must clearly define the measurements for each of these four metrics, together with the target levels to be achieved. The target levels should be attractive to the business partners.
- ⟩ **Integrating the supply chain more tightly.** An e-supply chain will benefit from tighter integration, both within a company and across an extended enterprise made up of suppliers, trading partners, logistics providers, and the distribution channel.

Activities and Infrastructure of E-SCM

E-supply chain processes and activities include the following.

Supply Chain Replenishment. Supply chain replenishment encompasses the integrated production and distribution processes. Companies can use replenishment information to reduce inventories, eliminate stocking points, and increase the velocity of replenishment by synchronizing supply and demand information across the extended enterprise. Real-time supply and demand information facilitates make-to-order and assemble-to-order manufacturing strategies across the extended enterprise. Supply-chain replenishment is a natural companion to Web-enabled customer orders. (For more on this topic, see Stevenson 2004.)

E-Procurement. E-procurement serves to streamline a firm's purchasing processes and aims to eliminate paper-based documents, such as purchase orders and the like. As described in Chapter 5, **e-procurement** is the use of Web-based technology to support the key procurement processes, including requisitioning, sourcing, contracting, ordering, and payment. E-procurement supports the purchase of both direct and indirect materials and employs several Web-based functions, such as online catalogs, contracts, purchase orders, and shipping notices. E-procurement can improve the operation of the supply chain in various ways:

▶ Online catalogs can be used to eliminate redesign of components in product development.
▶ Visibility of available parts and their attributes enables quick decision making.
▶ Online purchase orders expedite the ordering process.
▶ Advanced-shipping notifications and acknowledgments streamline delivery.

e-procurement
The use of Web-based technology to support the key procurement processes, including requisitioning, sourcing, contracting, ordering, and payment. E-procurement supports the purchase of both direct and indirect materials and employs several Web-based functions such as online catalogs, contracts, purchase orders, and shipping notices.

From the purchaser's perspective, e-procurement can help better manage supplier relationships and accounts and allows for more effective tracking of orders. From the supplier's perspective, e-procurement enables them to respond more rapidly and effectively to the requirements of purchasers. Both purchasers and suppliers report that e-procurement can assist them in better managing their cash flows.

Supply Chain Monitoring and Control Using RFID. This is one of the most promising applications of RFID. We will return to this topic later in this chapter.

Inventory Management Using Wireless Devices. Many organizations are now achieving improvements in inventory management by using combinations of bar-coding technologies and wireless devices. For example, the auto industry is dependent on the supply of spare parts; in 2005, dealerships sold about $48.9 billion worth of spare parts. By combining bar coding and wireless technologies, dealers are now able to scan in goods as they arrive electronically and place them in inventory up to 50 percent faster than previously. This also means they are available for technicians to install in cars or for purchase by customers much faster than in the past. Dealers have a much more accurate picture of their inventory levels and are now able to avoid running out of stock (ThomasNet Industrial Newsroom 2006).

In some industries, such as supermarkets and hospitals, reorder points have been automated so that when inventory gets down to a certain point the system will automatically generate an order for new stock without human intervention. MemorialCare in Southern California is just one of many hospitals that are using PDAs to enter inventory item counts and then loading the data directly into the mainframe procurement system. This process is not only faster and less prone to error, but the data are processed in real time and orders (if needed) are generated automatically. The system is based on XML architecture. If orders are needed (based on the inventory count), the mainframe automatically transfers the order to an ERP system. This system creates purchase orders, e-mails them to the appropriate suppliers, generates invoices, and processes payments, all without any additional information.

collaborative planning
A business practice that combines the business knowledge and forecasts of multiple players along a supply chain to improve the planning and fulfillment of customer demand.

Collaborative Planning. **Collaborative planning** is a business practice that combines the business knowledge and forecasts of multiple players along a supply chain to improve the planning and fulfillment of customer demand (*Vics.org* 2006) Collaborative planning requires buyers and sellers to develop shared demand forecasts and supply plans for how to support demand. These forecasts and supply plans should be updated regularly, based on information shared over the Internet. Such collaborative planning requires B2B workflow across multiple enterprises over the Internet, with data exchanged among partners dynamically (see Brenchley 2004). This topic is discussed further in Section 7.4.

Collaborative Design and Product Development. Collaborative product development involves the use of product design and development techniques across multiple companies to improve product launch success and reduce time-to-market (as demonstrated in the Boeing opening case). During product development, engineering and design drawings can be shared over a secure network among the contract firm, testing facility, marketing firm, and downstream manufacturing and service companies. Other techniques include sharing specifications, test results, and design changes and using online prototyping to obtain customer feedback. Development costs can be reduced by tightly integrating and streamlining communication channels.

E-Logistics. E-logistics is the use of Web-based technologies to support the material acquisition, warehousing, and transportation processes. E-logistics enables distribution to couple routing optimization with inventory-tracking information. For example, Internet-based freight auctions enable spot buying of trucking capacity. Third-party logistics providers offer virtual logistics services by integrating and optimizing distribution resources. A company may consider collaboration with its competitors to improve its supply chain. For an example of how Land O'Lakes collaborates with its competitors via an electronic market, see Online File W7.1. This topic will be discussed more fully in Chapter 13.

Use of B2B Exchanges and Supply Webs. The B2B exchanges introduced in Chapter 6 could play a critical role in e-supply chain management. Supply webs, also known as *value nets* and *value webs,* emerge as alternative configurations to traditional supply chains. In a supply web, information, transactions, products, and funds all flow to and from *multiple* nodes. Premkumar et al. (2004) write that a supply web emerges when multiple organizations in customer and supplier partnerships can work together seamlessly, exchanging information, goods, and services dynamically so that value is created for all. Supply webs (or vortals) serve industry sectors by integrating the supply chain systems of various buyers and sellers, creating *virtual trading communities.*

Infrastructure for e-SCM

The key activities just described use a variety of infrastructure and tools. The following are the major infrastructure elements and tools of e-supply chains:

- **Electronic Data Interchange.** EDI (see Appendix 6A) is the major tool used by large corporations to facilitate supply chain relationships. Many companies are shifting from internal EDI to Internet-based EDI.
- **Extranets.** These are described in Appendix 6A. Their major purpose is to support interorganizational communication and collaboration. For details on success factors for using extranets in e-SCM, see Chow (2004).
- **Intranets.** These are the corporate internal networks for communication and collaboration.
- **Corporate portals.** These provide a gateway for external and internal collaboration, communication, and information search. They are described in Section 7.7.
- **Workflow systems and tools.** These are systems that *manage* the flow of information in organizations. They are described in Section 7.8. Also see van der Aalst and van Hee (2004).
- **Groupware and other collaborative tools.** A large number of tools facilitate collaboration and communication between two parties and among members of small as well as large groups. Various tools, some of which are collectively known as *groupware,* enable such collaboration, as described in Section 7.8.

Determining the Right Supply Chain Strategy

In a now classic *Harvard Business Review* article, Fisher (1997) indicated two fundamental approaches for devising an effective supply chain strategy. Fisher argued that there are critical differences between effective supply chains that deal with functional products and those that deal with innovative products. The differences in demand pattern, and hence the differences in the design and planning of the requisite or ideal supply chain, can be quite marked and fundamental for these two product types.

Functional products are staple products, such as groceries or gasoline, that have stable and predictable demand. For these products, an effective supply chain is an efficient, low-cost supply chain. Statistical analysis and forecasting tend to be effective for these supply chains, as does efficient logistics enabled by information technology in general and the Internet in particular.

Innovative products, such as fashion or high-technology products, tend to have higher profit margins, volatile demand, and short product life cycles. For example, products that might be fashionable or highly desirable today will be found discounted (or marked down) on sales racks tomorrow. Thus, such products require an approach to supply chain design and planning that emphasizes speed, responsiveness, and flexibility rather than low costs.

Thus, in summary, functional products require an efficient supply chain, whereas innovative products require a market-responsive supply chain. The design and implementation of these types of supply chains differ on major design parameters, including their primary purpose, inventory strategy, lead-time focus, supplier selection, and product design strategy.

The primary purpose of an efficient supply chain is that predictable demand should be met at the lowest possible cost. The market-responsive supply chain, in contrast, is designed to respond quickly to unpredictable demand in order to minimize stock outs, forced markdowns, and obsolete inventory.

When it comes to inventory strategy, the efficient supply chain is designed to minimize inventories, whereas the market-responsive supply chain's design is focused on deploying significant buffer stocks of parts or finished goods at strategic locations to enable quick and reliable supply. In an efficient supply chain, lead times are shortened as much as possible, as long as this does not increase costs significantly, whereas in the market-responsive supply chain there is aggressive investment in reducing lead times without the same concerns for cost factors.

For the efficient supply chain, suppliers are chosen primarily on their performance regarding cost and quality. With the market-responsive supply chain, although quality is a vitally important factor, so are speed, responsiveness, and flexibility.

The two different supply chain designs also imply different product design strategies. For the efficient supply chain, product design is focused on maximizing the product performance while simultaneously minimizing costs. In the market-responsive supply chain, product design tends to be focused on modular designs so that product differentiation can be postponed as long as possible, thus lessening the need for highly accurate finished product forecasts.

Section 7.1 ▶ REVIEW QUESTIONS

1. Define the e-supply chain and list its three major parts.
2. Describe success factors of e-supply chain management.
3. List the eight processes or activities of e-supply chains.
4. List the major e-supply chain management infrastructures and enabling tools.
5. Discuss the differences between efficient and market-responsive supply chains. Offer specific examples where each would be most applicable.

7.2   SUPPLY CHAIN PROBLEMS AND SOLUTIONS

Supply chains have been plagued with problems, both in military and business operations, for generations. These problems have sometimes caused armies to lose wars and companies to go out of business. The problems are most apparent in complex or long supply chains and in cases where many business partners are involved. Complex and long supply chains involving multiple business partners are becoming more common in the contemporary business world as globalization and offshoring of manufacturing operations continue to intensify. Thus, the problems faced by those managing supply chains are becoming both more complex and more critical to company competitiveness and survival (Kotabe and Mol 2006). As this section will show, some remedies are available through the use of IT and EC.

TYPICAL PROBLEMS ALONG THE SUPPLY CHAIN

With increasing globalization and offshoring, supply chains can be very long and involve many internal and external partners located in different places. Both materials and information must flow among several entities, and these transfers, especially when manually handled, can be slow and error prone (Christopher 2005).

In the offline world, there are many examples of companies that were unable to meet demand for certain products while having oversized and expensive inventories of other products. Similar situations exist online (see Chapter 13). Typical of the sorts of problems in EC that gain adverse publicity are when there is a supply–demand mismatch of goods or services during a period of particularly high demand, such as the holiday period. For example, a shortage of toys due to incorrect demand forecasting might attract negative attention. A demand forecast is influenced by a number of factors, including consumer behavior, economic conditions, competition, prices, weather conditions, technological developments, and so on. Companies can improve their demand forecasting by using IT-supported forecasts, which are done in collaboration with business partners.

Another problem is often related to shipping. A lack of logistics infrastructure might prevent the right goods (say toys) from reaching their destinations on time. Various uncertainties exist in delivery times, which depend on many factors ranging from vehicle failures to road conditions.

Quality problems with materials and parts also can contribute to deficiencies in the supply chain. The worst case is when quality problems create production delays, causing factories and workers to lie idle and disrupting inventories. Some companies grapple with quality problems due to general misunderstandings or to shipments of wrong materials and parts. Sometimes, the high cost of expediting operations or shipments is the unfortunate result.

Pure EC companies may be likely to have more supply chain problems because they may not have a logistics infrastructure and may be forced to use external logistics services. This can be expensive, plus it requires more coordination and dependence on outsiders. For this reason, some large virtual retailers, such as Amazon.com, have developed physical warehouses and logistics systems. Other virtual retailers are creating strategic alliances with logistics companies or with brick-and-mortar companies that have their own logistics systems. Other problems along the EC supply chain mainly stem from the need to coordinate several activities and internal units and business partners.

For further information on the problems, issues, and challenges of contemporary supply chain management, see Blanchard (2006) and Chopra and Meindl (2006).

The Bullwhip Effect

One additional supply chain problem, the **bullwhip effect**, is worth noting. The *bullwhip effect* refers to erratic shifts in orders up and down supply chains (see Davies 2004). This effect was initially observed by P&G with their disposable diapers in offline retail stores. Although actual sales in stores were fairly stable and predictable, orders from distributors had wild swings, creating production and inventory problems for P&G. An investigation revealed that distributors' orders were fluctuating because of poor demand forecasts, price fluctuations, order batching, and rationing within the supply chain. All of this resulted in unnecessary inventories in various places along the supply chain, fluctuations in P&G orders to its suppliers, and the flow of inaccurate information. Distorted or late information can lead to tremendous inefficiencies, excessive inventories, poor customer service, lost revenues, ineffective shipments, and missed production schedules.

bullwhip effect
Erratic shifts in orders up and down supply chains.

The bullwhip effect is not unique to P&G. Firms from HP in the computer industry to Bristol-Myers Squibb in the pharmaceutical field have experienced a similar phenomenon (Davies 2004). Basically, even slight demand uncertainties and variabilities become magnified when viewed through the eyes of managers at each link in the supply chain. If each distinct entity makes ordering and inventory decisions with an eye to its own interest above those of the chain, stockpiling may be occurring simultaneously at as many as seven or eight different places. Such stockpiling can lead to as many as 100 days of inventory waiting "just in case." Repeated studies in a number of different industries reveal a similar outcome: substantial benefits accrue in terms of profitability, inventory holding costs, reduced cash-to-cash cycle times, and better order fulfillment from improvements in demand driven forecasting and information sharing along the supply chain (Taylor and Fearne 2006). Thus, companies may avoid the "sting of the bullwhip" if they take steps to share information along the supply chain. For further information and explanation regarding information sharing in supply chains and the consequent impact on the bullwhip effect, see Fiala (2005). Such information sharing is, of course, implemented and facilitated by EDI, extranets, and groupware technologies and is delivered as part of interorganizational EC and *collaborative commerce*, topics discussed elsewhere in this chapter.

THE NEED FOR INFORMATION SHARING ALONG THE SUPPLY CHAIN

By definition, a supply chain includes the flow of information to and from all participating entities. The information can be supportive of physical shipments or of shipments of digitized products (or services). It includes product pricing, inventory, shipping status, credit and financial information, and technology news. Many, if not most, of the supply chain problems that occur are the result of poor flow of information, inaccurate information, untimely information, and so on. Information must be managed properly in each supply chain segment. Indeed, Finley and Srikanth (2005) emphasize communication and information sharing as critical imperatives in avoiding the bullwhip effect and achieving successful supply chain management.

Information systems are the links that enable communication and collaboration along the supply chain. According to Handfield and Nichols (2002), they represent one of the fundamental elements that link the organizations of the supply chain into a unified and coordinated system. In today's competitive business climate, information and information technology are one of the keys to the success, and perhaps even the survival, of any SCM initiative.

Case studies of some world-class companies, such as Wal-Mart, Dell, and FedEx, indicate that these companies have created very sophisticated information systems, exploiting the latest technological developments and creating innovative solutions. However, even world-class companies, such as Nike, may suffer from inappropriate information sharing resulting in poor forecasting and then severely underestimating the complexity of automating aspects of the supply chain (see Case 7.1).

EC SOLUTIONS ALONG THE SUPPLY CHAIN

Information technology, including Web-based EC technologies, provides solutions along the supply chain, as has been shown throughout this book. Such solutions are beneficial both to brick-and-mortar operations and to online companies (Craighead and Shaw 2003; Moody 2006). The following is a representative list of the major solutions provided by an EC approach and technologies:

- *Order taking* can be done over the Internet, EDI, EDI/Internet, or an extranet, and it may be fully automated. For example, in B2B, orders are generated and transmitted automatically to suppliers when inventory levels fall below certain levels. The result is a fast, inexpensive, and more accurate (no need to rekey data) order-taking process. In B2C, Web-based ordering using electronic forms expedites the process, makes it more accurate (intelligent agents can check the input data and provide instant feedback), and reduces processing costs (Leonard and Davis 2006).

- *Order fulfillment* can become instant if the products can be digitized (e.g., software). In other cases, EC order taking interfaces with the company's back-office systems, including logistics. Such an interface, or even integration, shortens cycle time and eliminates errors. (See Chapter 13 for more on order fulfillment.)

- *Electronic payments* can expedite both the order fulfillment cycle and the payment delivery period. Payment processing can be significantly less expensive, and fraud can be better controlled. (See Chapter 12 for more on electronic payments.)

- *Managing risk* to avoid supply-chain breakdown (Hillman 2006) can be done in several ways. Carrying additional inventories is effective against the risk of stockouts, and hence poor customer service, but can be expensive. Also, in certain cases the risk increases because products may become obsolete.

- *Inventories can be minimized* by introducing a build-to-order (on demand) manufacturing process as well as by providing fast and accurate information to suppliers. By allowing business partners to electronically track and monitor orders and production activities, inventory management can be improved and inventory levels and the expense of inventory management can be minimized.

- *Collaborative commerce* among members of the supply chain can be done in many areas ranging from product design to demand forecasting. The results are shorter cycle times, minimal delays and work interruptions, lower inventories, and lower administrative costs (Cassivi 2006; Finley and Srikanth 2005).

CASE 7.1
EC Application
NIKE'S SUPPLY CHAIN: FAILURE AND EVENTUAL SUCCESS

Increasingly demanding customers and the consequent increases in product sophistication lead to complex supply chains that are challenging to manage. Add increasing globalization to this mix, and supply chain management becomes an even more critical issue. Nike, along with other leading global companies, faced the challenge of a more complex and problematic supply chain in the late 1990s.

Back in the 1970s, retailers placed orders with Nike 6 months before the required delivery date. These orders were then forwarded to Nike's manufacturing units around the world. Nike guaranteed that 90 percent of their orders would be delivered within a set time period at an agreed-upon fixed price. This system initially worked well.

However, during the 1980s and 1990s, Nike's business expanded and became more and more global. Also during those years, customers became more demanding regarding quality, style, and comfort, and as a result, product sophistication and variety exploded, causing demand forecasting, manufacturing, and distribution to become increasingly complex. Nike's supply chain managers were soon dealing with thousands of styles of shoes, each offered in both a large number of different color combinations and sizes. Thus, even without considering the apparel and equipment sides of the business, Nike had an enormously complex global supply chain.

In 1999, supply chain problems, particularly demand and inventory forecasting, manifested themselves in the bottom line: profits dropped by 50 percent. Nike management's analysis and assessment of the situation led to the launch of NSC, the Nike Supply Chain project. This initiative was aimed at bringing about excellence in supply chain processes. The first element of the initiative was an attempt to improve the somewhat fragmented and failing demand forecasting and order management activities in Nike. In 1998, 27 order management systems led to poor demand forecasting and, hence, ineffective supply chain management overall. To overcome a number of the supply chain management problems, Nike decided to acquire and implement i2 Technologies' demand forecasting system.

The i2 Technologies implementation was begun in 1999 with a projected cost of $40 million. The objectives of the project were ambitious and included detailed forecasting of over one million stock keeping units (SKUs). Where the i2 Technologies' software did not exactly meet Nike's requirements, extensive customization was undertaken. Further, large amounts of data were fed into the i2 Technologies' system from legacy systems within Nike. From this data, sophisticated and complex algorithms automatically generated thousands of forecasts that were used to drive Nike manufacturing. Due to the ambitious nature of the project and the complexity of the undertaking, problems began to surface by June 2000.

In the latter half of 2000, Nike was overmanufacturing some products, while struggling to meet demand in others.

For example, Nike overproduced poor-selling shoe lines such as Air Garnett II by $90 million worth of product, while underproducing popular lines such as Air Force One by $80 million to $100 million worth of product. It took about 6 to 9 months for Nike to overcome its inventory imbalance and more than 2 years to make up the financial loss. In setting things right, many shoes were sold at heavily discounted prices.

Nike analyzed its i2 Technologies' demand forecasting application in an effort to correct the problems and move forward. Immediate lessons learned involved the need for more adequate training of users, more comprehensive testing of the application as the implementation presented, better data cleansing, and more careful integration of the application with other extant systems. The extensive customization of the i2 Technologies' software, which among other things, broke forecasts down to individual styles, added undue complexity to an already complex project. The customization increased the taxing amounts of data required by the system. Furthermore, the data requirements were made even more onerous by the decisions of the Nike planners and forecasters to require extensive historical data and to forecast too far ahead. Generally, the review of the project found that there was altogether too much reliance on automatically generated forecasts rather than a judicious blend of human judgment and intuition together with the statistical analysis.

Looking back over the problematic project, Nike management felt that the initial attempt to bring about supply chain improvements had been too ambitious. Deadlines had been too tight, and the implementation had been rushed. The complexity of the undertaking had been increased and focus had been lost because Nike had, in addition to the i2 Technologies' project, attempted to implement the SAP ERP system and Siebel's CRM system at the same time.

Nike moved to take control of its supply chain project, eventually moving its shoe product lines forecasting application onto SAP, where the forecasting was based more heavily on forward orders and planners' judgment rather than relying on statistical algorithms. After considerable improvements, i2 Technologies' system continued to be used for Nike apparel lines. By 2004, its implementation of i2 Technologies' forecasting system, SAP's ERP system, and Siebel's CRM system was complete, giving Nike an integrated and efficient supply chain.

Nike had spent 6 years and $800 million on the project. Generally speaking, despite the early problems, Nike management was well satisfied with the project. The project had enabled Nike to shorten its lead time for building footwear from 9 to 6 months, and its enhanced capabilities in planning and tracking inventory resulted in a return on investment of 20 percent in 2004.

Sources: Compiled from Koch (2004), Chaturvedi and Gupta (2005), and Datta (2005).

(continued)

CASE 7.1 *(continued)*

Questions	**3.** What was wrong with Nike relying heavily on automatic statistical forecasts generated by the i2 Technologies' software?
1. What developments led to Nike's supply chain being such a challenge to manage?	
2. What factors led to the i2 Technologies implementation being a highly complex project? Were the increased complexities really necessary?	

For implementation issues related to these technologies, see Singh et al. (2007).

Supply chain problems may become more serious when the supply chain involves global segments. Case 7.2 about Netafim reviews some of these problems and describes how they were successfully addressed.

The following section examines key enabling supply chain technologies that may be used to provide supply chain solutions. For implementation issues, see Sing et al. (2007).

Section 7.2 ▶ REVIEW QUESTIONS

1. Describe some typical problems along the supply chain.
2. Describe the reasons for supply-chain-related problems.
3. Describe the bullwhip effect.
4. Describe the benefits of information sharing along the supply chain.
5. List some EC solutions to supply chain problems.

CASE 7.2
EC Application

NETAFIM: PROBLEMS AND SOLUTIONS ON THE WAY TO AN AGILE GLOBAL SUPPLY CHAIN

Introduction

Netafim is an Israeli company that markets and sells irrigation solutions based on its irrigation system products. The company's vision is to "expand its presence as the global leader in the field of innovative irrigation-based solutions and water technologies" (*Netafim.com* 2007). The company Web site describes the Netafim mission as meeting the irrigation needs of customers wherever they are located, through innovative irrigation solutions.

Netafim was the first company to develop drip irrigation technology. Other firms quickly established themselves in this now highly competitive marketplace. The company had a decentralized operational and management structure through its early years and onward through its main period of growth.

Netafim had a significant advantage in the early days in that its early employees were farmers who had an intimate knowledge of farming in the arid and salty soils of Southern

Israel. Thus, with the knowledge possessed by such employees, Netafim was able to deliver complete and practical water management solutions to farmers. This led to the firm having remarkable success and growth through the next few decades, expanding its product range to a number of innovative irrigation solutions. By the early 2000s, Netafim was selling its products in 130 countries and had 30 subsidiary companies in different locations around the world, enabling Netafim to offer relevant and practical irrigation solutions tailored to local needs by drawing on local knowledge.

In the 1990s, to deal with the demands of the increasingly large and complex global supply chain, Netafim decided to build extrusion plants in some of its key markets, while keeping the production and assembly of the drippers themselves in Israel, so as to protect key company knowledge. Extrusion plants were built in Australia in 1996 and in Brazil and South Africa in 1998. Further, Netafim began to

(continued)

augment its irrigation pipe and dripper products with irrigation and related crop management products from other vendors in hopes of providing farmers with near-total solutions to water and crop management problems. By 2000, approximately 60 percent of Netafim's 50,000 SKUs were supplied by external vendors.

Supply Chain Problems

Initially, Netafim's decentralized structure allowed it to respond quickly to particular local needs in terms of designing solutions. However, an agile global supply chain was needed to deliver these solutions worldwide. Netafim had focused on developing its markets and its technologies, not on establishing an efficient and effective global supply chain, which was handled by manual and out-of-date methods. By the early 2000s, this was beginning to affect both Netafim's bottom line and competitiveness.

The company information systems were outdated, local, and fragmentary. Thus the company lacked any visibility of its total supply chain material flows. Furthermore, planning, forecasting, procurement, and distribution processes were inefficient, and hence, lead times were lengthy and variable. Adding to the lack of inventory visibility and the general lack of coordination was the fact that each subsidiary placed orders separately with the outside vendors of irrigation system and related products. In this environment of uncertainty, subsidiary companies, manufacturing plants, and the head office were forced to anticipate future needs without good information about production, orders and inventories. Unsure of production and inventory status up the line, subsidiaries, when they noticed a slight increase in demand, would order a little extra just in case they had noticed an upward trend. However, once they had received one or two overly large orders they would minimize or cancel the next order. When the manufacturing facilities received such orders they tended to follow similar practices. Given that orders tended to be large and infrequent, the upshot was the bullwhip effect, whereby the supply chain is characterized by infrequent, inappropriate, and fluctuating orders, as described in Section 7.2 above. Further, in an environment where demanding local customers wanted prompt order fulfillment, subsidiaries tended to cushion themselves against the poorly performing supply chain system by keeping high "safety" stocks. Despite the "safety stocks," out-of-stock instances at the subsidiaries continued to grow. In general the poorly performing supply chain was threatening the future performance and competitiveness of the company.

The Supply Chain Management Solution

In 2002, a new CEO quickly saw that one of his first priorities was a complete reorganization of the supply chain. He created a supply chain manager position as part of his executive team with two initial objectives. One was to create a uniform set of product codes across the organization. The other was to create information visibility and information sharing across the entire supply chain and to use this to increase efficiency and effectiveness. Eventually, a coherent set of

products emerged with multiple versions of the same or very similar products reduced to a minimum, while at the same time attention was paid to real customer needs.

To increase information visibility and information sharing in the supply chain, Netafim decided to implement SAP's ERP system. The idea was to use SAP to move the company to dynamic real-time production management and inventory control based, as much as was possible, on actual forward demand rather than forecasting. Staff in subsidiaries and headquarters redesigned and modernized the supply chain business processes of order management, procurement, and production and inventory management. Soon inventory levels across the entire supply chain were visible, and efforts could be focused on inventory reduction. Further, order placement and confirmation activities improved dramatically, with the average time for order placement and confirmation decreasing from 10 days to 1 day.

Some strategic structural decisions were also necessary. Regional Logistic Hubs (RLHs) were created in order to maintain customer service while minimizing total inventory in the supply chain. The RLHs would be located at strategic positions in the supply chain in order to be in locations that were in close proximity to the major points of demand. The plan was to get lead times regarding deliveries to subsidiaries and dealers down to under 20 days instead of 2 to 3 months. Further, it was hoped that through a combination of utilizing RLHs effectively and good planning and inventory control local inventories could be reduced by 50 percent or more. To ensure that inventories of external vendor's products were reduced, VMI (vendor managed inventory) was introduced, under which the vendor's owned and managed their stock items in the RLHs, the stock becoming Netafim's only when the subsidiary ordered the product. The SAP ERP system assisted in the implementation of VMI because it enabled an authorized individual at Netafim or one of its vendors to see both the Netafim and the vendor inventory at the RLHs.

To further improve supply chain management, a new procurement department was created and authorized to carry out central and strategic purchasing for all of Netafim, including the subsidiaries. The increased professionalism of this department, together with the ability to drive procurement discounts from the consolidated and increased purchasing power of the central department, led to decreases in procurement costs.

A new planning department also was created that engaged in forecasting and production planning and inventory control in the manufacturing units and the RLHs. Enabling this activity was a new software system called Viva Cadena. This system allowed a blend of statistical forecasting and inventory control, together with both planner's intuitive judgments and real-time information on current inventory status and forward order books. The system essentially made suggestions to planners rather than automatically determining orders and the like.

(continued)

CASE 7.2   (continued)

By 2005, the strategic decisions and information visibility across the entire supply chain began to bring results. Stock levels throughout the Netafim group had reduced significantly; customer service had improved dramatically; and general business competitiveness had been enhanced. The company's future seemed positive because with less energy being expended on managing problems in operations, a greater focus on technological innovation was now becoming possible.

Sources: Compiled from Lee and Michlin (2006) and *netafim.com* (accessed January 2007).

Questions

1. Describe the supply chain challenges the new CEO faced when he took over Netafim in 2002.

2. Describe the strategic and structural changes made to improve supply chain management at Netafim.

3. Discuss the role of SAP's ERP system in the improvements in Netafim's supply chain management.

7.3 KEY ENABLING SUPPLY CHAIN TECHNOLOGIES: RFID AND RUBEE

Two major technologies have the potential to revolutionize supply chain management: RFID and RuBee.

THE RFID REVOLUTION

radio frequency identification (RFID)
Tags that can be attached to or embedded in objects, animals, or humans and use radio waves to communicate with a reader for the purpose of uniquely identifying the object or transmitting data and/or storing information about the object.

One of the newest and most revolutionary solutions to supply chain problems is RFID. We introduced the concept of RFID in Chapter 2 by describing how Wal-Mart is mandating that its largest suppliers attach RFID tags to every pallet or box they ship to Wal-Mart. **Radio frequency identification (RFID)** tags can be attached to or embedded in objects, animals, or humans and use radio waves to communicate with a reader for the purpose of uniquely identifying the object or transmitting data and/or storing information about the object. Eventually, RFID tags will be attached to every item. This can be done due to the tag's relatively small size (although they are mostly still too large for some small items) and relatively low cost. Cost has been a real issue, and some would say an inhibitor of the uptake of RFID technology. In 2006, a major landmark was reached when Israeli RFID manufacturer SmartCode offered RFID tags for 5 cents per tag, providing orders were placed for 100 million tags at a time! This compares to Avery Dennison in the United States, which is offering tags at 7.9 cents for volumes of 1 million or more tags. Although few would be in a position to take up the SmartCode offer, it is an important signal that the cost of RFID technology is coming close to reaching a point where companies will be willing to invest in RFID because they can be more certain of achieving an ROI on their RFID investments (Roberti 2006). However, cost is just one issue. Organizations still need to learn exactly how to effectively use the capabilities of RFID technology in their supply chains with the back-office systems and how business processes may need to be redesigned and retooled so that solid business benefits accrue form the use of this technology (for benefits, see Loebbecke 2006).

Given these developments, what effect will RFID have on supply chains? Let's look at Exhibit 7.2, which shows the relationship between a retailer (Shopwell), a manufacturer (such as Heinz), and its suppliers. All of the companies in the figure use RFID tags. It is no longer necessary to count inventories, and all business partners are able to view inventory information. This transparency can go several tiers down the supply chain. Additional applications, such as rapid checkout, which eliminates the need to scan each item, will be provided by RFID in the future.

Other applications of RFID are shown in Exhibit 7.3 (page 320). The upper part of the figure shows how the tags are used as merchandise travels from the supplier to the retailer. Note that the RFID transmits real-time information on the location of the merchandise. The lower part shows the use of the RFID at the retailer, mainly to locate merchandise, control inventory, prevent theft, and expedite processing of relevant information. The RFID technology is presented in detail in Chapter 9 and Online File W7.2.

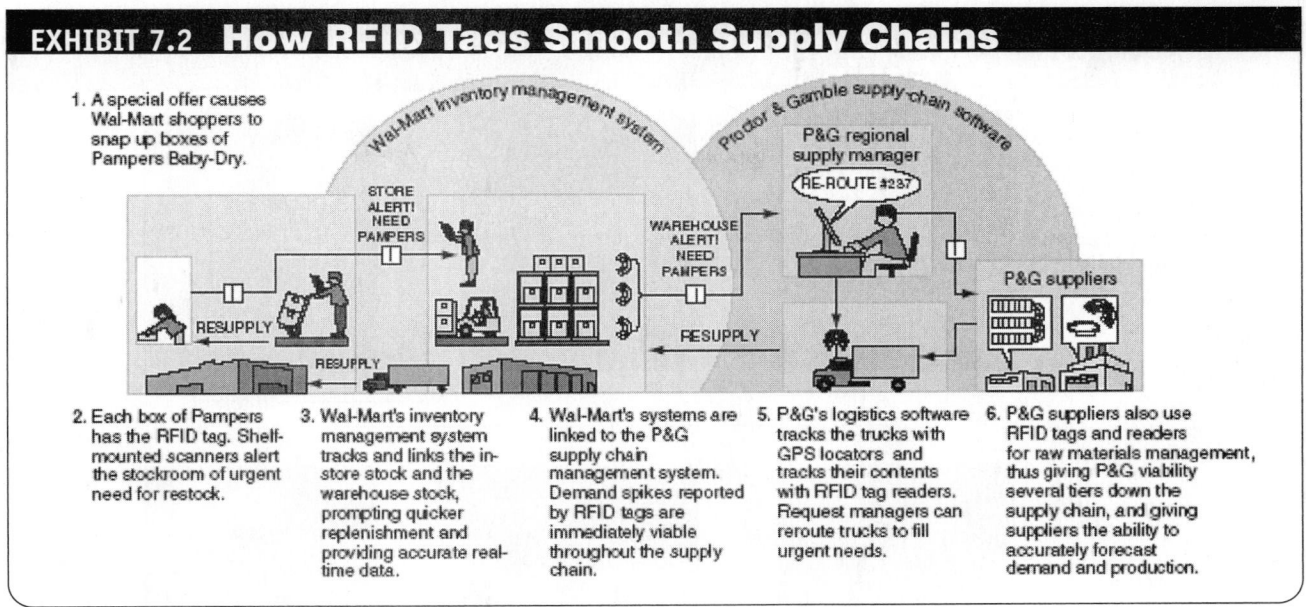

EXHIBIT 7.2 How RFID Tags Smooth Supply Chains

1. A special offer causes Wal-Mart shoppers to snap up boxes of Pampers Baby-Dry.

2. Each box of Pampers has the RFID tag. Shelf-mounted scanners alert the stockroom of urgent need for restock.

3. Wal-Mart's inventory management system tracks and links the in-store stock and the warehouse stock, prompting quicker replenishment and providing accurate real-time data.

4. Wal-Mart's systems are linked to the P&G supply chain management system. Demand spikes reported by RFID tags are immediately viable throughout the supply chain.

5. P&G's logistics software tracks the trucks with GPS locators and tracks their contents with RFID tag readers. Request managers can reroute trucks to fill urgent needs.

6. P&G suppliers also use RFID tags and readers for raw materials management, thus giving P&G viability several tiers down the supply chain, and giving suppliers the ability to accurately forecast demand and production.

RFID Applications in the Supply Chain

The following are examples of how RFID can be used in the supply chain.

RFID at Metro. Metro, a huge retailer from Germany, is using RFID tags in an attempt to speed the flow of goods from manufacturers in China to their arrival in Europe at the port of Rotterdam to distribution centers in Germany. Passive tags (see Online File W7.2) are being applied to cartons and cases of goods; active tags are being applied to the containers in which those goods are packed for shipping. At various points en route to Germany, the active tags are read and record the arrival of the cargo, enabling a record to be kept of where goods are located at any point in time. This gives Metro greater insights into the flow of goods along their supply chain, with bottlenecks or points that slow the delivery of goods becoming quickly evident. This allows for a review of business processes and work practices to ensure speedier handling and delivery. In addition, these RFID tags are equipped with intrusion sensors, which give an indication of whether any attempt has been made to open the sealed containers during the journey. If the container is tampered with, the tags can trigger flashing lights or a siren to alert staff. Thus, Metro will be able to detect any attempts to tamper with or pilfer stock (see Heinrich 2005).

The benefits of the RFID system to Metro are substantial. It is calculated that eliminating a single day from the supply chain will save Metro hundreds of thousands of dollars annually by reducing the amount of stock held in inventory, freeing this capital for other purposes. Estimates are that for large retailers (in excess of $1 billion in sales annually) a 1-day reduction in inventory can free up to $1 million in working capital (Sullivan 2006).

RFID at Starbucks. As Starbucks expands its range of fresh foods (such as salads, sandwiches, and the like) available at its outlets, the complexity and demands of managing this supply chain increases. Keeping the food fresh depends on keeping it at a steady cool state and in ensuring timely delivery. Starbucks is requiring its distributors to employ RFID tags to measure the temperature of the trucks. These tags are programmed to record the temperature inside the truck every few minutes, and on return to the depot this temperature data can be downloaded and analyzed carefully. If there are unacceptable readings (i.e. the temperature is deemed to have risen too high), efforts are made to determine the cause and remedy the problem. Often the cause is found to be process-related in that truck doors were left open during a delivery or a truck was left parked in a depot for too long. This can then cause a redesign of critical business processes with regard to the transportation and handling of food (*RFID Journal* 2006). As RFID technology matures, it is conceivable, that in the future, the tags themselves will be able to detect variation in temperature and send a signal to a thermostat to activate refrigeration fans within the truck.

EXHIBIT 7.3 How RFID Works in a Manufacturer–Retailer Supply Chain

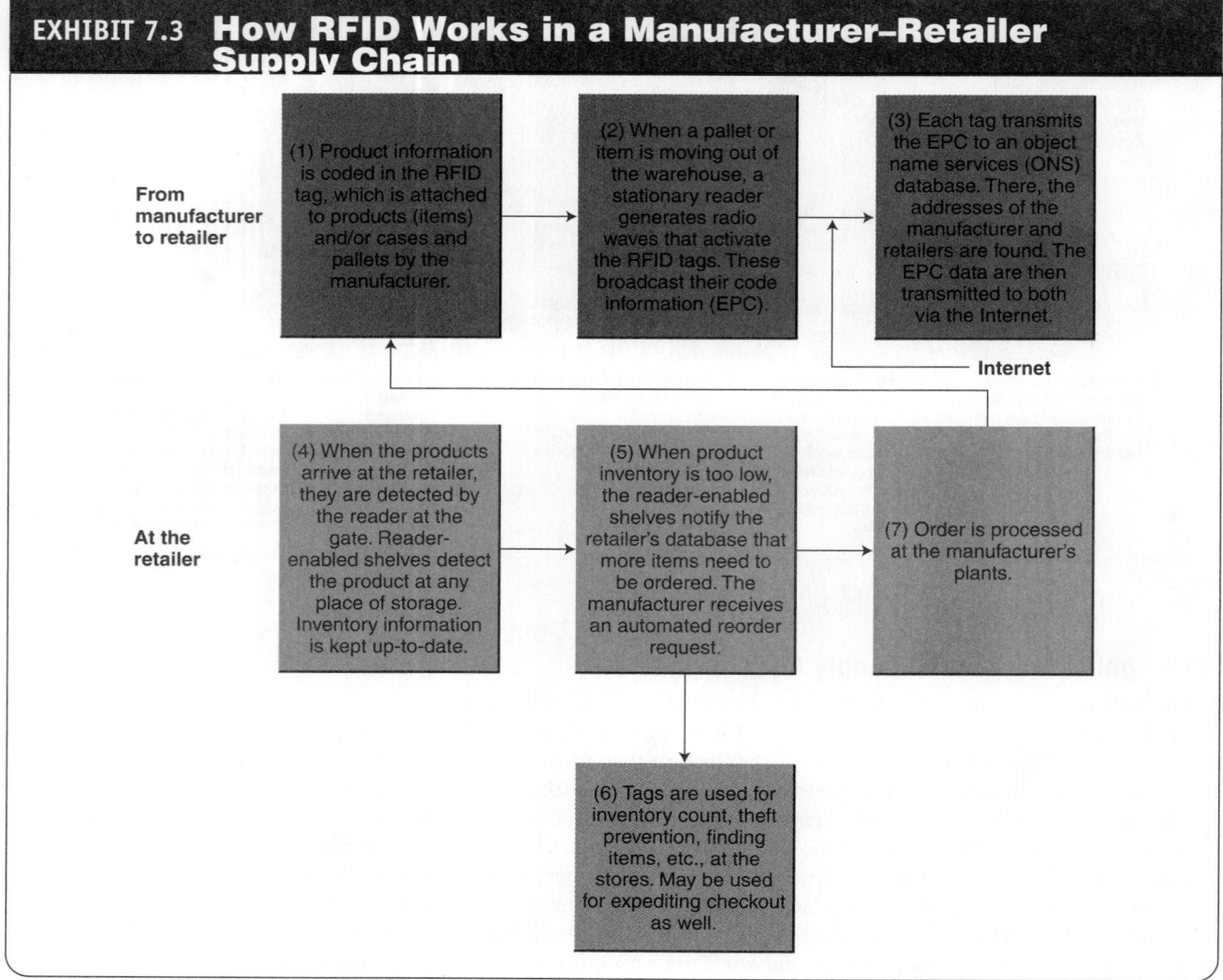

RFID at Harmon Hospital. Keeping track of relatively small, moveable assets (such as wheelchairs, pulse oximeters, and other medical devices) in hospitals can be time consuming and difficult. Equipment may be stored in cupboards, moved to other wards and not returned, and sometimes sent home with patients and not returned. Studies also suggest that when hospital staff are unable to find the equipment they need, rather than instigating a full-scale search, they tend to place an order for more equipment. Thus, hospitals incur significant costs in both searching for equipment and in ordering equipment that is not actually necessary. Harmon Hospital in Las Vegas is addressing these concerns by attaching active RFID tags on various medical devices and installing RFID readers at various points throughout the hospital. This enables staff to locate any required item of equipment, with the system providing a text-based report or a map of the hospital indicating the location of the desired piece of equipment (Bacheldor 2006a). Many other organizations in a variety of industries would clearly experience similar problems as those at Harmon Hospital; thus, the application of RFID tags to moveable assets is clearly an application with widespread potential.

RFID at Medway Maternity Unit. Security and safety in maternity wards is a priority, especially because of occasional cases of babies being snatched from hospital wards by unauthorized persons. Using the ideas gained from the application of RFID tags to released prisoners and asylum seekers at risk of absconding, Medway NHS in the United Kingdom became one of the first to attach RFID tags to newborns to track the movement of the infants, tightening security in their maternity wards. Immediately after birth, an RFID tag is attached to the baby's ankle (see Exhibit 7.4). The tag enables staff to monitor the baby's location on the ward. Any attempt by unauthorized personnel to move the baby out of the ward will trigger alarms and cause the doors to lock, thus ensuring that the babies are kept secure at all times. By providing each mother with a matching wrist tag, it is easy to ensure that babies are not inadvertently swapped when they are handed to their mother for feeding. The mother's tag can be activated to test match against the baby's. This is particularly important in preventing the accidental transfer of HIV or other infectious diseases through mistaken feeding of another mother's baby (Carvel 2006).

RFID in Philadelphia Cabs. As a result of collaboration between a number of companies, cabs in Philadelphia, Pennsylvania, are equipped to accept payments using RFID technologies. Passengers can use RFID-enabled credit cards, such as PayPass from MasterCard or similar cards from Visa or American Express, to pay their cab fares. A terminal is located behind the front seat, facing the passenger. To activate the system, passengers wave their RFID-enabled cards near the reader. The driver can then complete the transaction using either credit or debit facilities. Payments are processed by sending payment information over wireless networks. Such technologies are reducing the time taken to complete a transaction. This system also can be used by the cab driver for routing and navigational information, for work scheduling (signing on and off a shift), for keeping logs of trips, and for tracking items left by mistake by passengers in the cab (O'Connor 2006c).

RFID Use by CHEP. The Asia Pacific Division of CHEP (famous for its pallets and reusable containers, based in Florida) has developed an innovative use of RFID for the automotive industry in Australia. CHEP manufactures and then rents reusable, custom-made, plastic stacking crates for transporting parts and components along the automotive supply chain. In addition to the traditional text tags and bar-coded labels, CHEP has now added RFID tags to the outside of these crates. CHEP is thus able to easily determine which customer has which crate, while it gives the automotive companies much more precise insights into the location of parts both within their manufacturing environment and along their extended supply chains (Bacheldor 2006b).

RFID at Nokia. Not surprisingly, Nokia is combining RFID technology with mobile technology and coming up with some interesting applications. Security guards employed at Nokia facilities now carry a mobile phone handset with an RFID tag added and an RFID reader in the outer casing. At the start of a shift, guards use the phone to read their RFID enabled name badges. RFID tags are installed at various points around the facility. As security guards do their rounds, they open the handsets to read the tags as they pass. Details of the phone number and the RFID tag just read are transmitted over cellular phone networks. Supervisors are thus given accurate information as to when a particular guard started and finished a shift, whether the guard patrolled all the required locations, and where the guard was

EXHIBIT 7.4 RFID Ensures Security of Newborn Babies

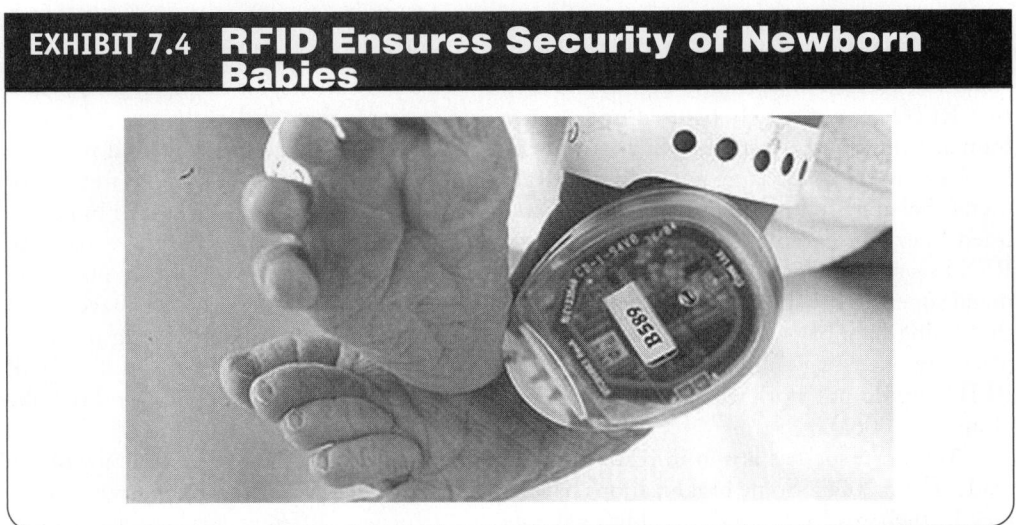

Carvel, J. "Babies Given Electronic Tags to Beat Abductors," *The Guardian* June 16, 2005. *guardian.co.uk/medicine/story/0,,1507510,00.html* (accessed January 2007).

at a particular point in time. In addition, supervisors can use the text and phone function to ask guards to recheck an area, vary their route, and the like.

The ability to link mobile phone technologies and RFID opens many more possibilities. For example, JCDecaux is considering using this Nokia application to track the installation and removal of billboard, posters, and rolling paid advertising displays at bus stops, train stations, movie theaters, roadsides, and other public locations (Bacheldor 2006d). Another company, Gentag, is developing technologies that will utilize mobile phones as RFID readers in healthcare applications. RFID-enabled skin patches will allow the remote monitoring of pulse rates, temperatures, glucose levels, and the like (Bacheldor 2006c).

RFID at Deutsche Post. Deutsche Post owns 6 million shipping containers that it uses to hold and transport about 70 million letters and other items that pass through its distribution centers daily. In order to process these crates, Deutsche Post prints in excess of 500 million thick paper labels, all of which are thrown away after a single use. It was environmental concerns, rather than purely economic ones, that have driven Deutsche Post's RFID initiative.

Deutsche Post is testing the use of passive RFID tags with a bistable display, meaning that the text displayed remains on-screen after power is removed and does not change until power is restored and the text is rewritten by an RFID interrogator. Tags on the crates must be readable from all angles and in all types of weather, requiring a robust tag. Furthermore, the tags will need to last about 5 years in order for the application to be financially viable. Deutsche Post is teaming with a number of partners to develop the tag, a custom RFID reader, and required specialized software in this innovative application of RFID that has produced fully functioning prototype tags but has not yet gone into full production (Wessel 2006).

For other applications and more details, refer to Loebbecke (2006) and Heinrich (2005).

LIMITATIONS OF RFID

RFID does have a number of limitations. For small companies, the cost of the system may be too high (at least for the near future). The lower-frequency systems (300 to 500Khz) required for passive tags are much cheaper but offer a decreased range. Radio frequency interference and the limited range of passive RFID tags also may be problematic, especially because passive tags are the most economically viable option for some businesses. These limitations should be minimized in the future as the cost of both passive and active RFID decreases and functionality increases. However, to date, many organizations have struggled to demonstrate the ROI of their RFID initiatives, raising the question of how long organizations will continue to invest in such technologies without gaining adequate returns (Schurman 2006).

Another major limitation of RFID currently is the restriction of the environments in which RFID tags are easily read. RFID tags do not work well in "harsh" environments, where reads are required in or around liquids and metals or around corners, for example. This means that RFID cannot readily be used underwater or near items that are largely liquid (such as human beings and livestock, which are mostly water!), nor do they function well in warehouses or areas where large amounts of metals are present (e.g., metal-lined deep freezers or metal shelving). Thus, in environments where foodstuffs must be kept deep frozen in metal-lined freezers (e.g., Sara Lee cakes, pastries, and ice-creams), getting accurate reads from RFID tags can be problematic. So, too, can getting reads of tagged items already placed on metal supermarket shelves or in metal supermarket trolleys. Ingenious shoplifters have found that lining handbags with aluminum foil will often render the security RFID tag on items placed in their bags unreadable, and hence they are able to pass out of stores undetected! RFID tags do not work well underground, around corners, through brick, rock, and the like (Johnson 2006a).

Another issue has arisen in real-world implementations of RFID—the accuracy of the reads (Finin 2006). Some organizations have reported achieving about 70 to 80 percent accuracy in their read rates and, of additional concern, achieving different levels of accuracy at different points along the supply chain (Schuman 2006a). Using active tags with a relatively large read range on individual items can prove problematic when passing through checkouts where there are many other items stocked proximate to the reader but not part of the shopping cart (O'Connor 2006a).

Concerns over customer privacy (see Chapter 9) are another issue and remain a significant point of contention in arguments about the appropriateness of wide-scale implementation of RFID. First and foremost are security concerns related to the potential of RFID tags to be tracked long after their SCM purpose has been served. The following are some concerns regarding customer privacy and RFID tags:

▶ The customer buying an item with an RFID tag may not be able to remove the tag or may be unaware that an RFID tag is attached to the item.

▶ The presence of a tag might mean that it would still be capable of being read from some distance away without the knowledge of the purchaser or user of that item. These two concerns have lead to comments such as a California state senator's remarking that "one day you realized your underwear was reporting your whereabouts!" (reported in en.wikipedia.org/wiki/RFID).

▶ If a purchase is made using a credit card, then the potential exists for the tag details to be linked directly to the personal details of the credit card holder (en.wikipedia.org/wiki/RFID).

Public confidence has not been allayed in this regard, with various incidents reported in the media involving linking RFID on products with smart shelves equipped with cameras, thus directly identifying the person buying an item with a photographic record (en.wikipedia.org/wiki/RFID).

As with most immature technologies, agreeing on universal standards, as well as connecting the RFIDs with existing IT systems is yet another issue. In 2006, however, the Gen 2 standard (a protocol for the exchange of information between the RFID tag and the reader) was announced, and it appears to be the major standard moving forward. However, some writers already suggest that Gen 2 will prove inadequate technically with the mass adoption of RFID technologies in the next 2 to 4 years, and they thus argue that Gen 3 will require a huge volume of item-level tagging and the alleviation of consumers' security concerns (Schuman 2006c). Moreover, the Gen 2 announcement certainly did not solve all problems relating to standards. Under the Gen 2 umbrella, in fact, two standards were announced: a high frequency (HF) air interface group and an ultrahigh frequency (UHF) air interface group. HF RFID tags work best on pallets, crates and cartons, for example, but may prove problematic for item-level tagging. UHF RFID tags work better for item-level tagging, particularly where security and data protection are important (*RFID Update* 2006).

In addition to technical standards, the players along the supply chain need to agree how particular items are to be labeled and categorized. Take, for example, a common product such as aspirin. Aspirin is manufactured by a pharmaceutical company but distributed to major supermarkets and retailers, such as Wal-Mart, pharmacies, and other convenience stores. The supermarket may categorize aspirin as a fast-moving consumer good (FMCG), and the pharmacist would consider it a pharmacy item, thus posing problems for the manufacturer as to how to categorize and hence identify the item. The manufacturer may prefer to use HF RFID tags, the supermarket UHF RFID tags. Unless agreement on these sorts of issues can be reached by all key players along a supply chain, significant problems may occur (O'Connor 2006a).

RUBEE: AN ALTERNATIVE TO RFID?

In 2006, a technology emerged that may act as an important complement to RFID in that it excels in situations where RFID has limitations. Known as RuBee, it relies on low-frequency magnetic waves to track products and transfer information. **RuBee** is defined as a bidirectional, on-demand, peer-to-peer radiating transceiver protocol (en.wikipedia.org/wiki/RuBee). It is currently being developed by the Institute of Electrical and Electronics Engineers. Exhibit 7.5 compares RuBee and RFID. Note that RuBee is not intended as a replacement for RFID but rather as a complement. As suggested in Exhibit 7.5, RFID is excellent for many applications, and indeed better than RuBee for some. However, RuBee tends to excel in areas where RFID has proven problematic; hence, it may prove vital in overcoming some of RFID's limitations. RuBee and RFID together may become partners in helping organizations better manage their global supply chains.

RuBee
Bidirectional, on-demand, peer-to-peer radiating transceiver protocol under development by the Institute of Electrical and Electronics Engineers.

EXHIBIT 7.5 Comparison of RuBee and RFID

	RuBee	RFID
Signal type	Magnetic waves (99.9% magnetic, 0.1% radio)	Radio waves (99.9% radio, 0.1% magnetic)
Frequency	Low frequency (below 450Khz, often 132KHz)	High and ultrahigh frequency (HF = 13.56Mhz and UHF = 916MHz)
Read speed	Slower 6–10 reads per second	Faster HF = 100 reads/second UHF = 150–200 reads/second
Battery life of active tags	Long (10–15 years)	Short (1–4 years)
Suitable for visibility	Locating items in warehouse, medical and health-care applications, livestock applications, obtaining real-time information on full history of item via the Internet, error detection, creation of smart store by reducing likelihood of stock-outs, theft prevention	Tracking, high-volume scanning Counting inventory moving on conveyor belts, ensuring inventory is moving along supply chain as planned
Tagging	Item-level tagging	Pallet, crate, carton tagging
Ability to handle harsh environments	Works under water, around metal, around corners	Does not always work effectively in harsh environments
Safety issues	Very safe, not absorbed through human tissue, lower field strengths than in airport metal detectors	Relatively safe
Cost	Infrastructure costs less than RFID; tag costs may be higher, depending on amount of intelligence built into tag	Infrastructure costs higher, tag costs depend on whether active or passive

Sources: Compiled from RFID Solutions Online (2006), Johnson (2006b), Schuman (2006b), Wikipedia (2007e), Schurman (2006), and O'Connor (2006b).

Section 7.3 ▶ REVIEW QUESTIONS

1. Describe how RFID can be used to improve supply chains.
2. Explain how RFID works in a supplier–retailer system.
3. Briefly explain the differences between active and passive RFID tags. (Note: see Online File W7.2.)
4. In what circumstances would it be better to use passive RFID tags? And in what circumstances might it be better to use active RFID tags? (Note: see Online File W7.2.)
5. What are some of the major limitations of RFID technology?
6. What is RuBee?
7. How does RuBee overcome some of the limitations of RFID?
8. Briefly describe the types of applications for which RuBee might be ideally suited.

7.4 COLLABORATIVE COMMERCE

collaborative commerce (c-commerce)
The use of digital technologies that enable companies to collaboratively plan, design, develop, manage, and research products, services, and innovative EC applications.

Previous chapters introduced B2B activities related mainly to selling and buying. E-commerce also can be used to improve collaboration within and among organizations along the supply chain.

ESSENTIALS OF COLLABORATIVE COMMERCE

Collaborative commerce (c-commerce) refers to the use of digital technologies that enable companies to collaboratively plan, design, develop, manage, and research products, services, and innovative EC applications. An example would be a company that is collaborating electronically with a vendor that designs a product or a part for the company, as was shown in the Boeing opening case. C-commerce implies communication, information sharing, and collaborative planning done electronically through tools such as groupware and specially designed EC collaboration tools.

Numerous studies (e.g., Microsoft.com 2006b) suggest that collaborative relationships result in significant impacts on organizations' performance. Major benefits cited are cost reduction, increased revenue, and better customer retention. These benefits are the results of fewer stock outs, less exception processing, reduced inventory throughout the supply chain, lower materials costs, increased sales volume, and increased competitive advantage.

COLLABORATION HUBS

One of the most popular forms of c-commerce is the **collaboration hub**, which is used by the members of a supply chain.

C-commerce activities usually are conducted between and among supply chain partners. Leightons Opticians, as shown in Case 7.3 uses a hub to communicate among all its business partners and is thus able to improve customer service. Finally, in Online File W7.3, the case of Webcor is described, a company using ProjectNet to better collaborate with its partners electronically.

There are several varieties of c-commerce, ranging from joint design efforts to forecasting. Collaboration can be done both between and within organizations. For example, a collaborative platform can help in communication and collaboration between headquarters and subsidiaries or between franchisers and franchisees. The platform provides, for example, e-mail, message

collaboration hub
The central point of control for an e-market. A single c-hub, representing one e-market owner, can host multiple collaboration spaces (c-spaces) in which trading partners use c-enablers to exchange data with the c-hub.

CASE 7.3
EC Application

LEIGHTONS OPTICIANS SEES THE VALUE OF COLLABORATIVE HUBS

Leightons Opticians was founded in 1928 in Southampton, United Kingdom. The business progressed throughout the decades, and a number of branches were opened. In 1996, Leightons launched a franchise business aimed at attracting high-quality and business-focused opticians and optometrists. Leightons now owns 25 branch stores and has 15 franchisees. Leightons still maintains its traditional family values of outstanding personal customer service delivered by highly professional staff offering excellent treatment and advice and the best quality lens and frame technologies. As the business expanded, however, the challenge was to ensure that staff spent time serving customers and not on administrative issues, such as order tracking, filing, and the like.

Leightons decided to implement a collaborative hub from Supply Chain Connect (*supplychainconnect.com*). All of the branches, franchises, and suppliers are able to connect to a single hub and seamlessly exchange information, irrespective of the internal systems operated at the respective sites. Leightons pays a monthly subscription fee for Supply Chain Connect's services, which meant that it was able to avoid making a substantial upfront investment in the technology.

Staff members at any of Leightons' branches are able to send orders electronically to a number of different suppliers. Because orders are sent through the hub, they can now be tracked, so Leightons' staff members are able to check the real-time status of any order at any time. Leightons has been very happy with the direct cost savings generated and also

believes that its staff is now able to spend more time delivering excellent personal customer service.

Leightons' two major suppliers are Luxottica and Marchon; both are enthusiastic users of Supply Chain Connect. They receive hundreds of orders daily from a variety of branches and franchisees, and the collaboration hub enables them to view all orders from a particular buyer very easily. The system is integrated with their back-office systems, eliminating any need for rekeying data, thus saving time and reducing errors. They are also better able to track the status of any particular order, meaning that they are better able to monitor the performance of their critical suppliers. Future expansion is planned to allow for automated matching of orders against invoices payment approvals.

Sources: Compiled from *SupplyChainConnect.com* (2005) and *LeightonsOpticians.com* (2006).

Questions

1. Why is this considered to be a collaboration hub?

2. What are the potential risks associated with participation in this collaboration hub?

3. In what other ways could these players utilize the collaboration hub?

4. Think of the various parties involved in this collaboration and identify the benefits that each derives from it.

boards and chat rooms, and online corporate data access around the globe, no matter what the time zone. The following sections demonstrate some types and examples of c-commerce.

COLLABORATIVE NETWORKS

Traditionally, collaboration took place among supply chain members, frequently those that were close to each other (e.g., a manufacturer and its distributor or a distributor and a retailer). Even if more partners were involved, the focus was on the optimization of information and product flow between existing nodes in the traditional supply chain. Advanced approaches such as Collaboration, Planning, Forecasting and Replenishing (CPFR), which is described in the next section, do not change the basic structure.

Traditional collaboration results in a vertically integrated supply chain. However, as stated in Chapters 1 and 2, EC and Web technologies can *fundamentally change* the shape of the supply chain, the number of players within it, and their individual roles. The new supply chain can be a hub or even a network. A comparison between the traditional supply chain and the new one, which is made possible by Web technologies, is shown in Exhibit 7.6. Notice that the traditional chain in Exhibit 7.6A is basically linear. The *collaborative network* in Exhibit 7.6B shows that partners at any point in the network can interact with each other, bypassing traditional partners. Interaction may occur among several manufacturers or distributors, as well as with new players, such as software agents that act as aggregators, B2B exchanges, hubs, or logistics providers.

The collaborative network can take different shapes depending on the industry, the product (or service), the volume of information flow, and more. For example, in the health-care sector the concept of regional health information organizations (RHIOs) is being discussed. RHIOs are electronic networks connecting communities of health-care providers that enable the exchange of relevant information among collaborating parties (including patients and consumers, medical staff of all sorts, hospitals, insurers, researchers, and educations) with the aim of improving the provision of health care. The goal is collaboration across the RHIO in order to promote the development, exchange and effective utilization of clinical care information and to service the constituents of the hub more efficiently in a variety of ways (Bazzoli 2006).

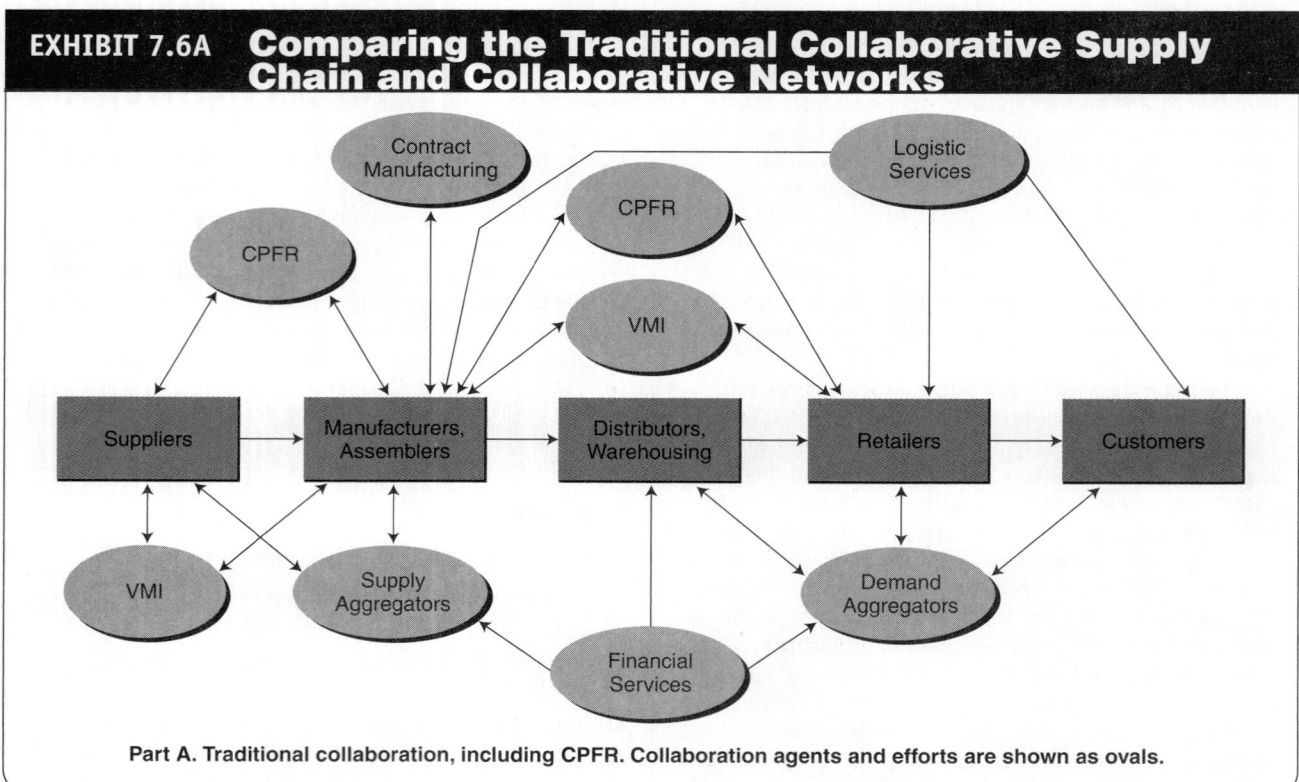

EXHIBIT 7.6A Comparing the Traditional Collaborative Supply Chain and Collaborative Networks

Part A. Traditional collaboration, including CPFR. Collaboration agents and efforts are shown as ovals.

EXHIBIT 7.6B

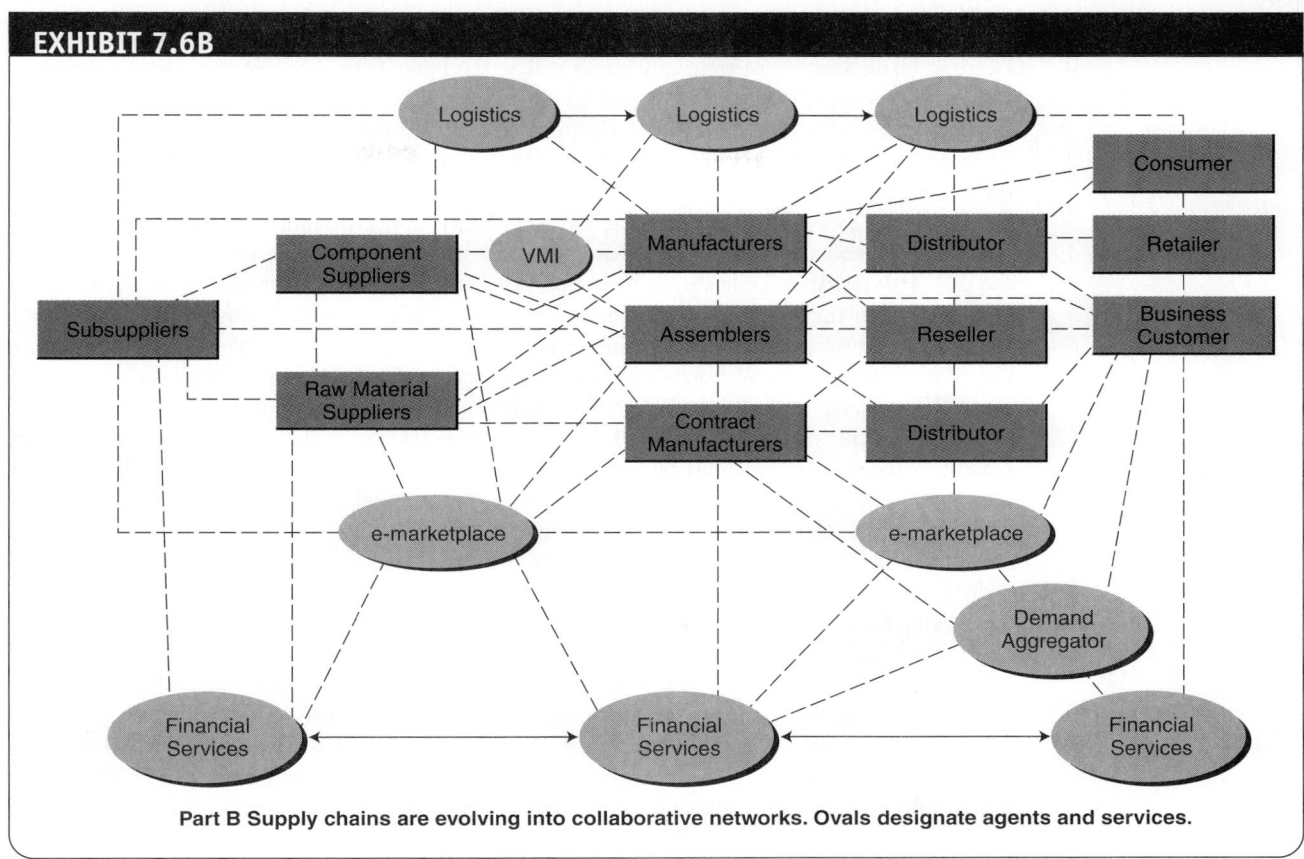

Part B Supply chains are evolving into collaborative networks. Ovals designate agents and services.

Source: Poirier, C., "Collaborative Commerce: Wave Two of the Cyber Revolution." *Computer Sciences Corporation Perspectives* (221): 8, pp. 9–8, fig. 1. Used with permission of Computer Sciences Corporation. All rights reserved.

Mobile Collaborative Networks, Grid Computing, and Service-Oriented Architectures

As mobile technologies become more and more mature, mobile collaborative networks are gradually coming into being. These networks have the ability to share valuable business information in mobile scenarios with those who are co-located or remote and who are not necessarily from the same enterprise. Mobile workers are able to communicate and share information anytime, anywhere (Divitini et al. 2004).

The latest and most ambitious type of collaborative network is grid computing. **Grid computing** is a form of distributed computing that involves coordinating and sharing computing, application, data, storage, or network resources across dynamic and geographically dispersed organizations. Grid technologies promise to change the way organizations tackle complex computational problems. However, the vision of large-scale resource sharing is not yet a reality in many areas. Grid computing is an evolving area of computing; standards and technology are still being developed to enable this new paradigm. Perhaps dynamic virtual corporations based on mobile technologies and grid computing will be the most common business model in the future. For further information about grid computing, see grid.org, www-1.ibm.com/grid, and oracle.com/grid.

The emerging area of **service-oriented architecture (SOA)** offers insights into the world of grid computing. It offers a model in which relatively loosely coupled collections of *Web Services* provide the functionality required by applications, management functions, and infrastructure. SOA facilitates integration by modularizing applications and viewing business processes as a set of coordinated services and activities. In this way, supply chain partners and value nets can more easily integrate business processes and applications across organizational boundaries and achieve better integration, greater flexibility, and improved ease of cooperation and collaboration (Kourpas 2006).

grid computing
A form of distributed computing that involves coordinating and sharing computing, application, data, storage, or network resources across dynamic and geographically dispersed organizations.

service-oriented architecture (SOA)
An architectural concept that defines the use of services to support a variety of business needs. In SOA, existing IT assets (called services) are *reused* and *reconnected* rather than the more time consuming and costly reinvention of new systems.

REPRESENTATIVE EXAMPLES OF E-COLLABORATION

Leading businesses are moving quickly to realize the benefits of c-commerce. Large companies such as Wal-Mart and Toyota have been leaders in the field in this regard for some time. However, smaller companies are now benefiting from the opportunities afforded by e-collaboration. ToySolution (toysolution.com) was established in Hong Kong to support collaboration between the many players in the toy industry. Within 6 months of launching, ToySolution had more than 700 active members in the system. ToySolution enables suppliers, manufacturers, designers, and toy retailers to collaborate online and improve process efficiency along the entire supply chain through the use of a variety of applications, including those involving document management, workflow processes, order tracking, online payments, arrangement of cargo inspections, insurance, logistics, and the like. It has successfully met the challenge of allowing small family owned and operated, low-tech companies to collaborate online with the large, sophisticated operators with large corporate ERP applications (*IBM.com* 2006a, *Toysolution.com* 2006).

Leading companies such as Dell, Cisco, and HP also use collaborative commerce strategically, enabling sophisticated business models while transforming their value chains. They also have implemented e-procurement and other mature collaboration techniques to streamline operations, reduce overhead, and maintain or enhance margins in the face of intense competition. For example, Dell implemented end-to-end integrated configuration and ordering, a single enterprise middleware backbone, and multitier collaborative planning. This has enabled Dell to support a make-to-order business model with best-in-class speed and efficiency. Cisco chose to support a virtual business model focusing on time-to-market and customer satisfaction. Cisco has integrated its order process with back-end processes, implemented purchase order automation, and enabled collaborative product development.

In addition, as described in Online File W7.4, Nygard of Canada has developed a collaborative system along its entire supply chain. There are many examples of e-collaboration. Some representative examples follow. For more, see Schram (2004) and Frank (2004).

Vendor-Managed Inventory

vendor-managed
inventory (VMI)
The practice of retailers'
making suppliers respon-
sible for determining
when to order and how
much to order.

With **vendor-managed inventory (VMI)**, retailers make their suppliers responsible for determining when to order and how much to order. The retailer provides the supplier with real-time information (e.g., point-of-sale data), inventory levels, and a threshold below which orders are replenished. The reorder quantities also are predetermined and usually recommended by the supplier. With this approach, the retailer is no longer burdened with inventory management, demand forecasting becomes easier, the supplier can see the potential need for an item before the item is ordered, there are no purchase orders, inventories are kept low, and out-of-stocks become infrequent. This method was initiated by Wal-Mart in the 1980s and was supported by EDI. Today, it can be supported by CFPR and special software. VMI software solutions are provided by Sockeye Solutions (sockeyesolutions.com) and JDA Software (jda.com). For details, see Richardson (2004).

Information Sharing Between Retailers and Suppliers: P&G and Wal-Mart

Information sharing among business partners, as well as among the various units inside each organization, is necessary for the success of SCM. Information systems must be designed so that sharing becomes easy. One of the most notable examples of information sharing is between P&G and Wal-Mart. Wal-Mart provides P&G access to sales information on every item P&G makes for Wal-Mart. The information is collected by P&G on a daily basis from every Wal-Mart store, and P&G uses the information to manage inventory replenishment for Wal-Mart. By monitoring the inventory level of each P&G item in every Wal-Mart store, P&G knows when the inventories fall below the threshold that triggers a shipment. All this is done electronically. The benefit for P&G is accurate demand information; the benefit for Wal-Mart is adequate inventory. P&G has similar agreements with other major retailers. For more on Wal-Mart, see Staff (2004a).

Retailer–Supplier Collaboration: Target Corporation

Target Corporation (targetcorp.com) is a large retail conglomerate. It conducts EC activities with about 20,000 trading partners. In 1998, then operating under the name Dayton-Hudson

Corporation, the company established an extranet-based system for those partners that were not connected to its VAN-based EDI. The extranet enabled the company not only to reach many more partners but also to use many applications not available on the traditional EDI. The system (based on GE's InterBusiness Partner Extranet platform, geis.com) enabled the company to streamline its communications and collaboration with suppliers. It also allowed the company's business customers to create personalized Web pages that were accessible via either the Internet or GE's private VAN, as shown in Exhibit 7.7. Target now has a Web site called Partners Online (partnersonline.com) which it uses to communicate with and provide an enormous amount of information to its partners.

Lower Transportation and Inventory Costs and Reduced Stockouts: Unilever

Unilever's 30 contract carriers deliver 250,000 truckloads of shipments annually. Unilever's Web-based database, the Transportation Business Center (TBC), provides the carriers with site-specification requirements when they pick up a shipment at a manufacturing or distribution center or when they deliver goods to retailers. TBC gives carriers all the vital information they need: contact names and phone numbers, operating hours, the number of dock doors at a location, the height of the dock doors, how to make an appointment to deliver or pick up shipments, pallet configuration, and other special requirements. All mission-critical information that Unilever's carriers need to make pickups, shipments, and deliveries is now available electronically 24/7. TBC also helps Unilever organize and automate its carrier selection processes based on contract provisions and commitments. When a primary carrier is unable to accept a shipment, TBC automatically recommends alternative carriers.

Reduction of Design Cycle Time: Clarion Malaysia

Clarion Malaysia, part of the global company the Clarion Group, employs approximately 700 people in Malaysia. It manufactures car audio electronic systems for cars. Over the years,

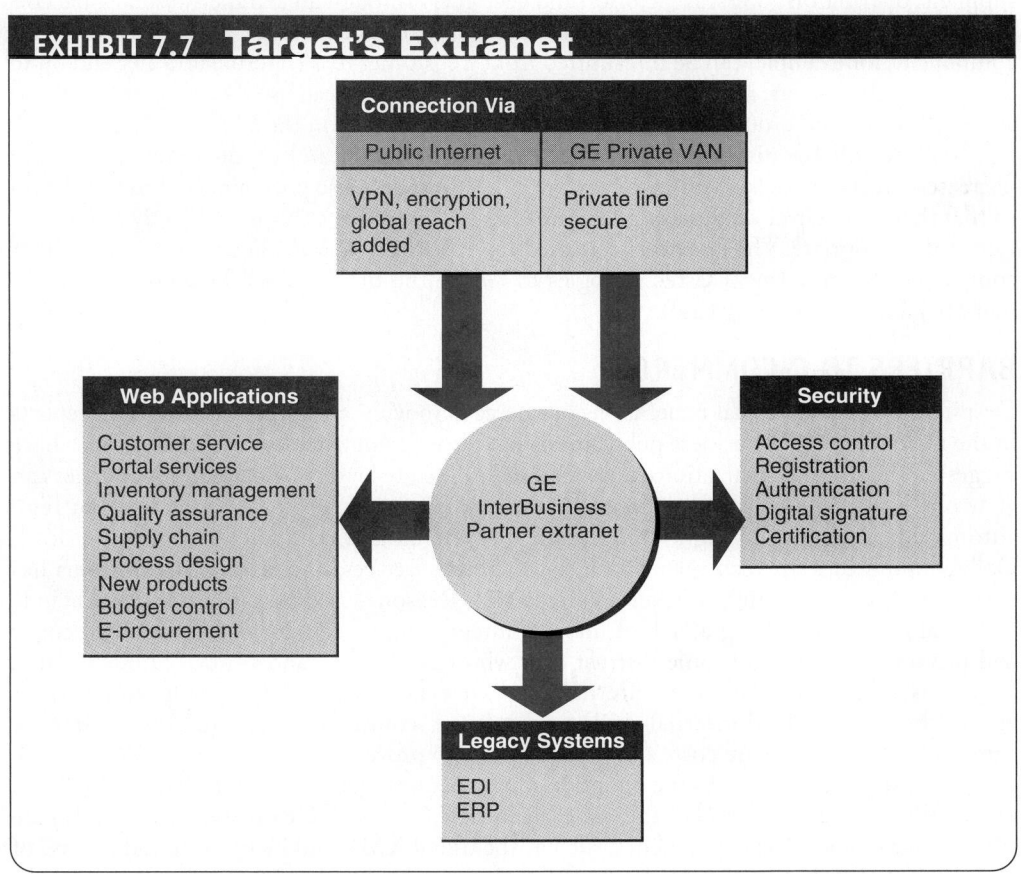

EXHIBIT 7.7 Target's Extranet

Connection Via

Public Internet	GE Private VAN
VPN, encryption, global reach added	Private line secure

Web Applications
Customer service
Portal services
Inventory management
Quality assurance
Supply chain
Process design
New products
Budget control
E-procurement

GE InterBusiness Partner extranet

Security
Access control
Registration
Authentication
Digital signature
Certification

Legacy Systems
EDI
ERP

the Clarion Group has developed an excellent reputation first for car radios (it produced Japan's first car radio in 1951) and more recently for offering a range of audiovisual, multimedia, car navigation, telematics, and automotive electronic components. Approximately 60 percent of its sales come from installing Clarion OEM systems in a range of cars, including Ford, GM, Honda, Mazda, Nissan, BMW, and most of the European manufacturers.

In an increasingly global and competitive market, Clarion recognized a need to improve product innovation, time-to-market, customer loyalty, and profitability. It aimed to align itself more closely with its customers' R&D processes and to dramatically cut lead times through more efficient and effective supply chains, thus forming the basis of strong partnerships with car manufacturers worldwide through outstanding business performance. It also recognized a need to understand collaborative projects with the auto manufacturers in terms of product development and delivery, quality control, and cost management. It also sought to protect its traditional markets in North America, Europe, and Japan while acquiring new customers in the burgeoning markets in China and other ASEAN countries.

Working with IBM through the implementation of CAD systems and collaborative product lifecycle management technologies, Clarion has slashed its time-to-market from 14 months to about 9 months, while at the same time improving the quality of the products because more time can be spent in yielding superior designs. The application of the latest information technology has also supported much closer cooperation with and responsiveness to customers throughout the design process, better use of materials through the deployment of 3D modeling, and a 60 percent reduction in tooling preparation time (Clarion Group 2006 and *IBM.com* 2006b).

Reduction of Product Development Time: Caterpillar, Inc.

Caterpillar, Inc. (caterpillar.com) is a multinational heavy-machinery manufacturer. In the traditional mode of operation, cycle time along the supply chain was long because the process involved the transfer of paper documents among managers, salespeople, and technical staff. To solve the problem, Caterpillar connected its engineering and manufacturing divisions with its suppliers, distributors, overseas factories, and customers through an extranet-based global collaboration system. By means of the collaboration system, a request for a customized tractor component, for example, can be transmitted from a customer to a Caterpillar dealer and on to designers and suppliers, all in a very short time. Customers also can use the extranet to retrieve and modify detailed order information while the vehicle is still on the assembly line.

Remote collaboration capabilities between the customer and product developers have decreased cycle time delays caused by rework time. Suppliers also are connected to the system so that they can deliver materials or parts directly to Caterpillar's shops or directly to the customer, if appropriate. The system also is used for expediting maintenance and repairs. Other companies also are using EC technologies to reduce the time needed for product development (e.g., see the opening case).

BARRIERS TO C-COMMERCE

Despite the many potential benefits, c-commerce is moving ahead fairly slowly, and reports in the media and other business publications have been somewhat hyped. Some studies have suggested that most organizations have achieved moderate levels of collaboration (parties can view one another's databases and engage in electronic exchanges of information, but high automated exchanges or tight integration of systems and databases is not the norm). Collaboration in high-tech manufacturing, financial services, and telecommunications has been found to be the highest (NerveWire 2002). Reasons cited in various studies include technical reasons involving a lack of internal integration, standards, and networks; security and privacy concerns, and some distrust over who has access to and control of information stored in a partner's database; internal resistance to information sharing and to new approaches; and lack of internal skills to conduct c-commerce (Schram 2004). Gaining agreement on how to share costs and benefits can also prove problematic (NerveWire 2002).

A big stumbling block to the adoption of c-commerce has been the lack of defined and universally agreed upon standards. Even early initiatives such as CPFR (see next section) are still in their infancy. New approaches, such as the use of XML and its variants and the use of Web Services, could significantly lessen the problem of standards.

Sometimes collaboration is an organizational culture shock—people simply resist sharing. One reason for this is lack of trust. According to Gibson-Paul (2003), companies such as Boeing are grappling with the trust factor. Some techniques Gibson-Paul suggests to increase trust include starting small (e.g., synchronizing one type of sales data), picking projects that are likely to provide a quick return on investment for both sides, meeting face-to-face in the beginning of a collaboration, and showing the benefits of collaboration to all parties. Despite an initial lack of trust, if potential collaborators judge the benefits of collaboration to be sufficient and distributed fairly among collaborators, they will be more eager to join in.

Finally, global collaboration involves all of the above potential barriers and more. Some of these additional barriers are described in Chapter 13. For more on c-commerce barriers, see Schrage (2004).

Specialized c-commerce software tools will break down some of the barriers to c-commerce (see Section 7.8). In addition, as companies learn more about the major benefits of c-commerce—such as smoothing the supply chain, reducing inventories and operating costs, and increasing customer satisfaction and the competitive edge—it is expected that more will rush to jump on the c-commerce bandwagon.

C-commerce is a response to business pressure (Chapter 1). Let's examine the case of a global supply chain in the fashion retailing industry (Insights and Additions 7.1).

Insights and Additions 7.1 Using EC in the Retail Industry to Reduce Time and Cost

Retailers, especially those dealing with fashion clothing (apparel), must deal with difficult environmental pressures (Chapter 1). Specifically, they must deliver products very quickly to their stores while cutting costs at the same time. In many cases, cost-cutting is done by moving production to Asia. This means creating a global supply chain because the major retailers are located mostly in Europe and the United States.

The fashion retail supply chain can be complex and long because it includes numerous functions—product design, merchandiser input, procurement of raw materials, manufacturing, and distribution. Therefore, communication and collaboration are critical. If lead time is not compressed, the risk of the product being too late on the shelf or obsolete is increased. All of this is done in an environment in which customer demand changes rapidly. If a retailer is too slow to react, store shelves will be stocked with uninspired fashions—resulting in substantial markdowns and anemic sales growth. As mentioned earlier in this chapter, demand forecasting can be very difficult.

Many retailers have implemented sourcing initiatives such as just-in-time (JIT) manufacturing, quick response (QR), efficient consumer response (ECR), and fast-moving consumer goods (FMCG). However, many retailers are still in trouble. Unfortunately, most solutions involve two contradicting factors: increasing speed and reducing or holding costs. If a company can do both simultaneously, it will be a winner. To do both, a company must change business processes and possibly look to adopt a range of EC tools and information systems. Changes in business processes may include component-based product design, e-sourcing, and supply chain improvements, all of which are supported electronically.

For example, Web-enabled planning, execution, and optimization tools improve data availability and boost collaborative efforts between retail and brand managers and their suppliers. Product development management (PDM) software allows brand managers to conduct online "what-if" scenarios relating to product design. To expedite cycle time, tools from companies such as Freeborders (*freeborders.com*), Logility (*logility.com*), SupplyChainge (*supplychainge.com*), and New Generation Computing (*ngcsoftware.com*), can be utilized. Lead time optimization (LTO) tools (e.g., from SupplyChainge) also are useful. These tools relate demand forecast to supply forecast and support planning in an uncertain environment from an enterprisewide perspective. For example, using optimization techniques, the tools enable performance of supply chain activities in parallel.

These solutions usually are limited to one segment of the internal supply chain. Unfortunately, this may not be sufficient because the supply chain crosses numerous functions, including product design, merchandiser's input, raw material procurement, manufacturing, and distribution. Therefore, collaboration and communication are needed to supplement these tools.

To enhance collaboration and communication, retailers can implement Web-based collaborative product design (CPD) solutions. With CPD tools, different people can work on the same design at the same or different times, from different locations. Yet another set of tools enables brand managers to build an item's design into a system and generate all of the cutting patterns and distribute them to manufacturers in seconds. A major factor in the success of all of these tools is partnership and collaboration. For details, see Reda (2003).

The fashion retail supply chain poses some unique and very challenging decisions for managers, and the adoption of appropriate technologies to support such supply chains is obviously critical. However, some fashion retailers are achieving extraordinary levels of success and are the envy of nearly all other players in this industry, yet have not adopted all the prescriptions we have detailed here. Zara (zara.com) is one such example. An examination of Zara and a consideration of how it has achieved success is detailed in Case 7.4.

CASE 7.4
EC Application
ZARA: FAST FASHION SUPPLY CHAIN INNOVATOR

The fashion industry is notoriously challenging: fashions and people's tastes are fickle, fast to change, and decidedly difficult to predict accurately. Achieving sustainability in this competitive industry is hard, market leadership almost impossible. Did a canny CEO and talented executive team with a deep understanding of their industry and market develop what at first sight can appear to be counterintuitive supply chain practices and win? Or does Zara display practices from which we all can learn?

Zara traces its origins to La Coruna, Spain, in the mid-1970s; since then it has grown into the flagship brand of its parent company, Inditex. Until 1987, Zara's operations were confined to Spain. In 1988, it opened in neighboring Portugal and then went international, opening in New York and Paris. By the end of the twentieth century, Zara was operating across Europe and Scandinavia, the United States, Japan, and South America. It now has expanded into a number of Southeast Asian countries, Russia, the Middle East, China, and Northern Africa. At the beginning of 2007, Zara operated from 991 stores in 65 countries, 24 of which are located in the United States. In this highly competitive market, Zara is now the third-largest apparel retailer in the world in terms of revenues and has approached 20 percent annual growth rates in sales and net income since the early 2000s.

To understand some of Zara's success, it is important to remember a key mantra for Zara: Success relied on having "five fingers touching the factory and five touching the customer" (Ortega, cited by Ferdows et al. 2004, p. 106). In other words, the decisions taken by Zara's executives are driven by a belief in being responsive to consumer demand and changing preferences and in meeting those needs by maintaining control of nearly all aspects of the supply chain. Zara has become famous for being able to go from the design phase to delivering the finished good to its warehouses in a 2- to 3-week time frame, compared with its competitors who might take 9 to 12 months. Zara's stores around the world receive these new designs 1 to 2 days after they reach the distribution center. Zara rolls out some 12,000 new items per year, compared to its competitors who average 2,000 to 4,000. Zara's customers visit their stores about 17 times per year compared, with about 4 visits per year to its competitors. It discounts only 18 percent of its clothes, compared to the industry average of about 35 to 40 percent. Zara spends a miserly 0.3 percent of sales on advertising, compared to an industry average of 3.5 percent. And, of interest here, it spends 5 to 10 times less on IT than its major rivals do.

It is generally acknowledged that Zara has a super-responsive supply chain. Rather than relying on sophisticated demand forecasting, Zara's strength lies in its ability to respond rapidly to changing trends (see Exhibit 7.8 illustrating Zara's core business activities). Zara has identified a few, critical processes (ordering, design and manufacturing, fulfillment) and gears those processes to meeting three discrete customer groups (men, women, children). Customer needs, preferences, and behaviors are the starting point of the Zara supply chain. Customer demand patterns and qualitative feedback from its stores drive much of the design and manufacturing activity. So, too, does market research into key fashion trends.

At a time when many other competitors are outsourcing much of the manufacturing, Zara outsources comparatively little other than the actual machining of garments. And unlike competitors who rely on low-cost producers in China and India, Zara elects to have garments sewn locally in Spain and northern Portugal. Zara also controls its distribution network, at times engaging in relatively high-cost practices that actually drive efficiencies elsewhere. Zara makes deliveries to its retail outlets twice weekly and in relatively small quantities, thus encouraging customers to buy now or miss out later. It also means that Zara carries much less in inventory. All clothes are tagged and priced in Spain, and many clothes are delivered on hangers and can be placed directly in the store without ironing. However, this practice costs more because it increases the volume of goods to be transported. Trucks and planes are used for delivery—a higher-cost option than trains and ships—allowing for rapid fulfillment.

Zara's supply chain is geared more toward maximizing revenues than toward reducing costs, and the organization appears to have uncanny insights into some of the more hidden costs associated with some very low-cost supply chain practices and activities.

Although Zara may spend less on IT than others in the fashion industry, it would be a mistake to think that IT is not regarded as critical to business success. Rather, Zara appears to adopt a philosophy that says (1) invest in mission-critical IT as a priority; (2) do not try to automate all functions, but allow IT to support information

CASE 7.4 (continued)

EXHIBIT 7.8   Zara's Core Business Activities

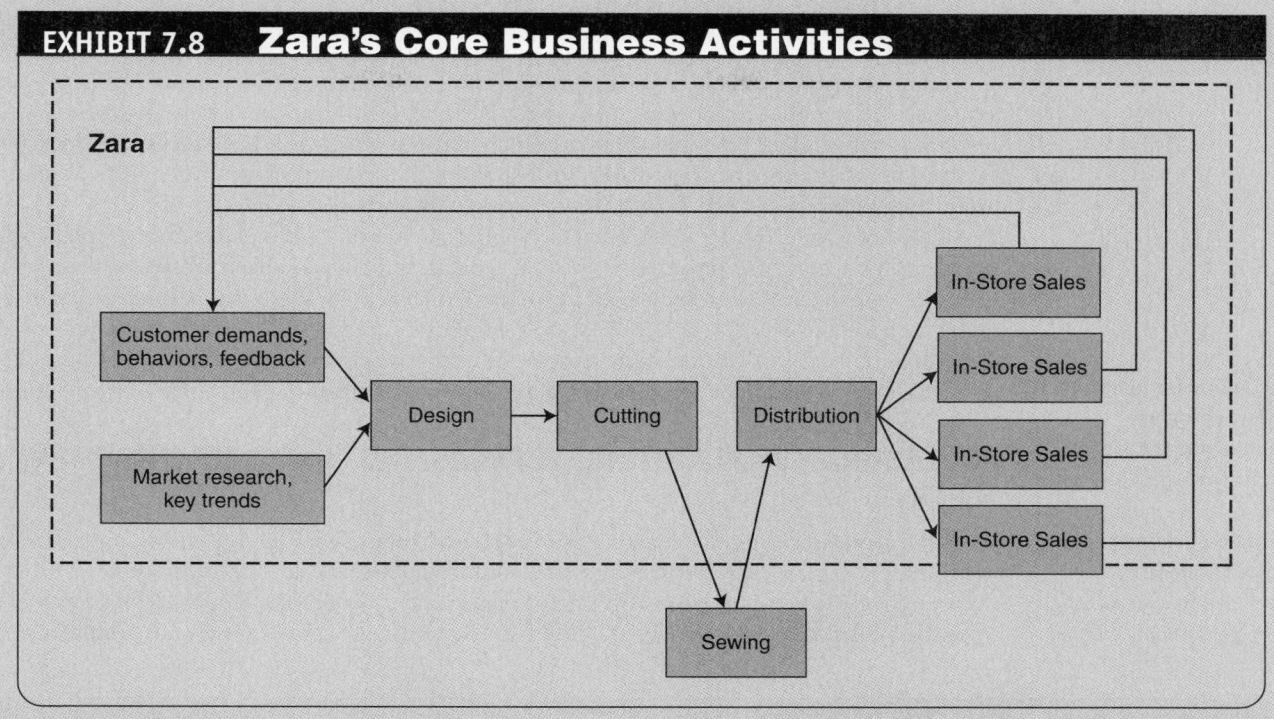

and knowledge sharing, collaboration, and inform the decision making; (3) simpler IT solutions that meet business needs are generally preferable to the more complex ones; and (4) ensure all investments in IT (many are in-house custom-built systems) are a very close match to required business functionality. Zara has made little investment in the Internet for B2C EC for two good reasons: (1) its distribution centers are not configured to support the picking and shipping of direct to consumer orders and (2) its research suggests that most mail-order businesses needed to deal with substantial returns, further complicating the management of their merchandise. The key to Zara's success is appropriate, business-driven IT investments, geared at supporting and automating parts of the critical core business processes.

Zara would appear to be a testimony to the successful design and implementation of a market-responsive supply chain strategy.

Sources: Compiled from *inditex.com* (2006), *zara.com* (accessed January 2007), Indu and Gupta (2006), Ferdows et al. (2004), and Ferdows et al. (2005).

Questions

1. Why is the fashion industry so competitive?
2. Why do you think excellence in supply chain management may be an important ingredient in success in the fashion industry?
3. What were the underlying reasons for Zara's success?
4. What is the meaning of the expression "five fingers touching the customer and five fingers touching the factory"? Would this be an appropriate mantra for a supermarket chain to adopt?
5. Discuss some of the risks you feel are evident in Zara's approach to supply chain management.

Section 7.4 ▶ REVIEW QUESTIONS

1. Define c-commerce.
2. List the major types of c-commerce.
3. Describe some examples of c-commerce.
4. Define collaborative networks and distinguish them from traditional supply chain collaboration.
5. Describe KM–collaboration relationships.
6. List some major barriers to c-commerce. How might these limitations be overcome?
7. How might collaboration support and improve industry supply chains?

7.5 COLLABORATIVE PLANNING, CPFR, AND COLLABORATIVE DESIGN

In *collaborative planning*, business partners—manufacturers, suppliers, distribution partners, and other partners—create initial demand (or sales) forecasts, provide changes as necessary, and share information, such as actual sales, and their own forecasts. Thus, all parties work according to a unified schedule aligned to a common view, and all have access to order and forecast performance that is globally visible through electronic links. Schedule, order, or product changes trigger immediate adjustments to all parties' schedules.

Collaborative planning is designed to synchronize production and distribution plans and product flows, optimize resource utilization over an expanded capacity base, increase customer responsiveness, and reduce inventories. Collaborative planning is a necessity in e-SCM (see Ireland and Crum 2005 and vics.org/committees/cpfr). The planning process is difficult because it involves multiple parties and activities, as shown in Exhibit 7.9.

This section examines several aspects of collaborative planning and collaborative design.

COLLABORATIVE PLANNING, FORECASTING, AND REPLENISHMENT (CPFR)

collaborative planning, forecasting, and replenishment (CPFR)
Project in which suppliers and retailers collaborate in their planning and demand forecasting to optimize flow of materials along the supply chain.

Collaborative planning, forecasting, and replenishment (CPFR) is a business practice in which suppliers and retailers collaborate in planning and demand forecasting in order to ensure that members of the supply chain will have the right amount of raw materials and finished goods when they need them. The goal of CPFR is to streamline product flow from manufacturing

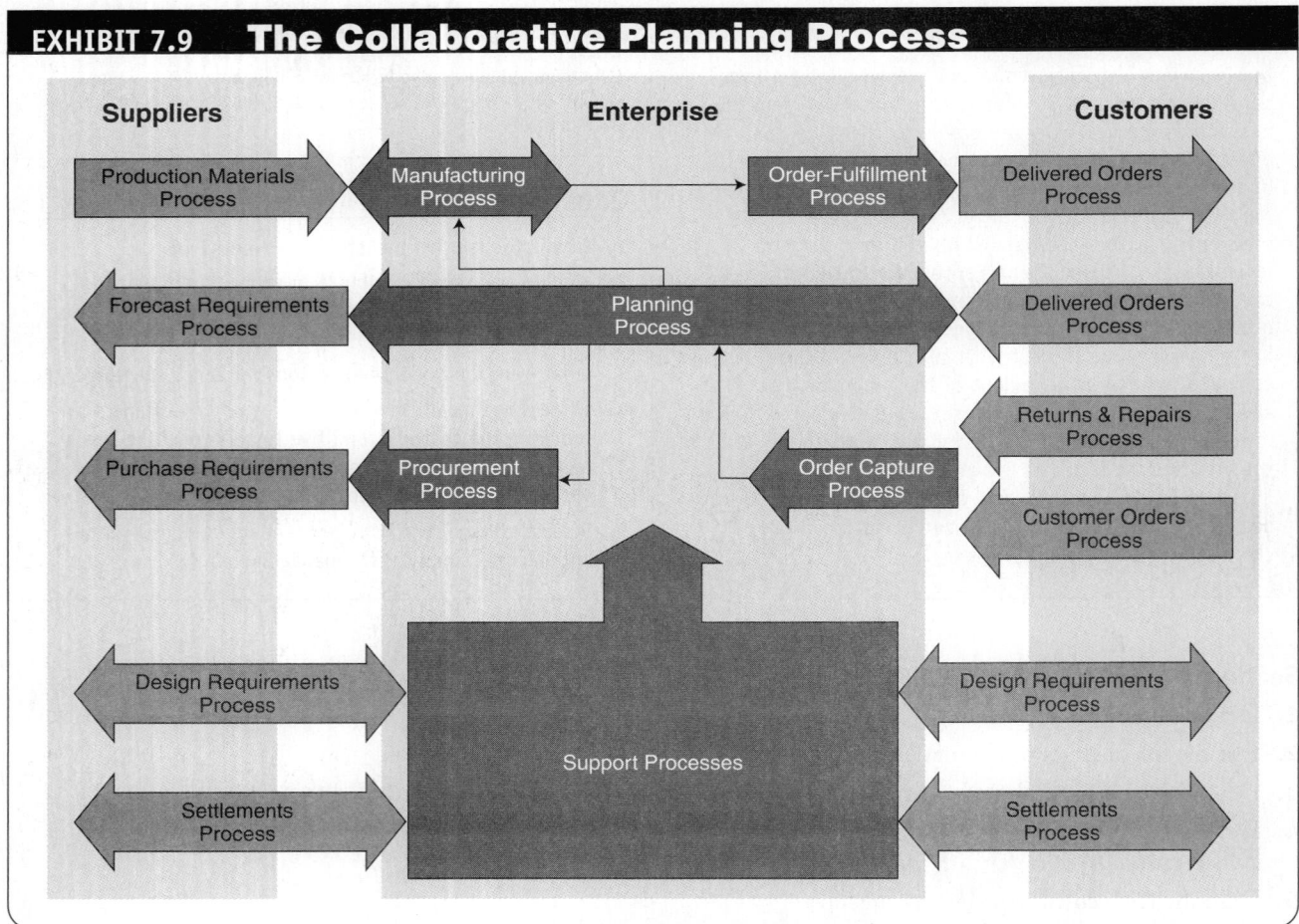

EXHIBIT 7.9   The Collaborative Planning Process

Source: Norris, G., et al. *E-Business and ERP: Transforming the Enterprise.* John Wiley & Sons, 2000. Reprinted by permission of John Wiley & Sons, Inc.

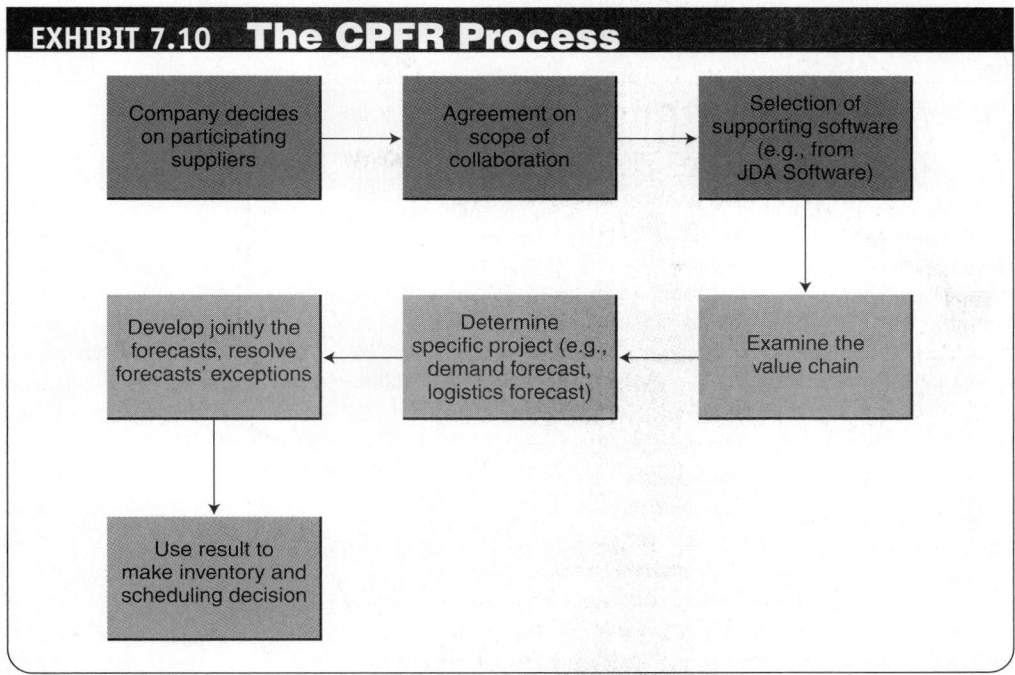

EXHIBIT 7.10 The CPFR Process

plants all the way to customers' homes. Large manufacturers of consumer goods, such as Warner-Lambert (WL), have superb supply chains resulting from their use of CPFR.

As part of a pilot project, WL shared strategic plans, performance data, and market insight with Wal-Mart. The company realized that it could benefit from Wal-Mart's market knowledge, just as Wal-Mart could benefit from WL's product knowledge. In CPFR, trading partners collaborate on making *demand forecasts*. Using CPFR, WL increased its products' shelf-fill rate (the extent to which a store's shelves are fully stocked) from 87 percent to 98 percent, earning the company about $8 million a year in additional sales.

When implementing a CPFR process, the collaborators agree on a standard process, shown in Exhibit 7.10. The process ends with an order forecast. CPFR provides a *standard framework* for collaborative planning. Retailers and vendors determine the "rules of engagement," such as how often and at what level information will be provided. Typically, they share greater amounts of more detailed information, such as promotion schedules and item point-of-sale history, and use store-level expectations as the basis for all forecasts.

The idea is to improve demand forecasting for all of the partners in the supply chain and then communicate forecasts using information-sharing applications (already developed by technology companies such as Oracle and i2). For the retailer, collaborative forecasting means fewer out-of-stocks and resultant lost sales and less stored inventory. For the manufacturer, collaborative forecasting means fewer expedited shipments, optimal inventory level, and optimally sized production runs.

Besides working together to develop production plans and forecasts for stock replenishment, suppliers and retailers also coordinate the related logistics activities (such as shipment or warehousing) using a common *language standard* and new information methodologies (Ireland and Bruce 2000).

A 2002 survey (Bradley 2002) found that 67 percent of 43 large food, beverage, and consumer products companies were researching, piloting, or implementing CPFR. About half of the respondents who were looking at CPFR said they planned to go ahead with their initiatives. However, CPFR is not the answer for all trading partners or all types of stock-keeping units (SKUs). According to Tim Paydos, a vice president of marketing at Syncra Systems, CPFR has generated the highest payback with either highly promoted or seasonal goods, whose inventories historically have often been misaligned with demand. "If I'm going to

CASE 7.5
EC Application
WEST MARINE: A CPFR SUCCESS STORY

West Marine is the largest boating-supply company in the United States. It has 400 stores and annual sales of $690 million. The company sells more than 50,000 different products, ranging from stainless-steel propellers and anchors to lifejackets and wetsuits, through its stores, Web site, catalog, and commercial sales arm.

West Marine has a dramatic story when it comes to its effective supply chain, which was guided and directed through its deep, intensive, and effective implementation of CPFR. West Marine is now regarded as having a showcase CPFR implementation; however, it wasn't always that way.

In 1997, West Marine acquired its East Coast competitor E&B Marine. As a result of the challenges of integrating the two companies, sales fell by almost 8 percent, and during the peak season out-of-stock situations rose by more than 12 percent over the previous year. Income dropped from $15 million in 1997 to little more than $1 million in 1998.

The situation was quite different when in 2003 West Marine purchased its largest competitor, BoatUS. West Marine successfully integrated BoatUS's distribution center in just 30 days. BoatUS's in-store systems were integrated into West Marine in just under 60 days. Further, supply chain performance and the bottom-line were not affected.

So why was this second acquisition so much smoother? The difference was that by 2003 the company had an effective IT-enabled supply chain management system driven by CPFR.

In reviewing the CPFR implementation in West Marine, it is clear that a key success factor was West Marine's commitment to technology enablement. Through the CPFR information systems, data such as seasonal forecasts, promotional stock levels, and future assortment changes are calculated automatically. Joint forecasting and order fulfillment are enabled by information systems that are suitably integrated between supply chain partners. As many similar case studies attest, such information sharing through integrated supply chain systems is one factor in successful supply chain management.

However, West Marine's successful CPFR implementation was not simply about the technology. Significant energy and resources were devoted to collaboration among the key supply chain personnel in West Marine and its supply chain partners. Joint skills and knowledge were developed along with the key elements of trust and joint understanding. These elements were built through joint education and training sessions as well as through the standard CPFR joint planning and forecasting sessions.

West Marine's CPFR program now involves 200 suppliers and more than 20,000 stock items, representing more than 90 percent of West Marine's procurement spending. Further, more than 70 of West Marine's top suppliers load West Marine's order forecasts directly into their production planning systems. In-stock rates at West Marine stores are well over 90 percent, forecast accuracy stands at 85 percent, and on-time shipments are now consistently better than 80 percent. Summing up West Marine's collaborative supply chain journey using CPFR, Larry Smith, Senior Vice President of Planning and Replenishment states, "The results, we believe, speak for themselves."

Sources: Compiled from Lee and Denend (2005) and Smith (2006).

Questions

1. What were the major elements of West Marine's CPFR success?
2. What were the benefits of the CPFR implementation for West Marine?

---

make the investment in CPFR," notes Paydos, "I want to do it with the products with the greatest return" (Bradley 2002).

The CPFR strategy has been driven by Wal-Mart and various benchmarking partners. After a successful pilot between Wal-Mart and Warner-Lambert involving Listerine products, a VICS (Voluntary Interindustry Commerce Standards) subcommittee was established to develop the proposed CPFR standard for the participating retailing industries (Wal-Mart's suppliers).

An interesting application of CPFR is that of West Marine presented in Case 7.5.

CPFR can be used with a company-centric B2B and with sell-side or buy-side marketplaces. For more on the benefits of CPFR, see cpfr.org/cpfr_pdf/index.html. Also, for comprehensive coverage, see Industry Directions (2000).

ADVANCED PLANNING AND SCHEDULING

advanced planning and scheduling (APS) systems
Programs that use algorithms to identify optimal solutions to complex planning problems that are bound by constraints.

Advanced planning and scheduling (APS) systems are math-based programs that identify optimal solutions to complex planning problems that are bound by constraints, such as limited machine capacity or labor. Using algorithms (such as linear programming), these systems

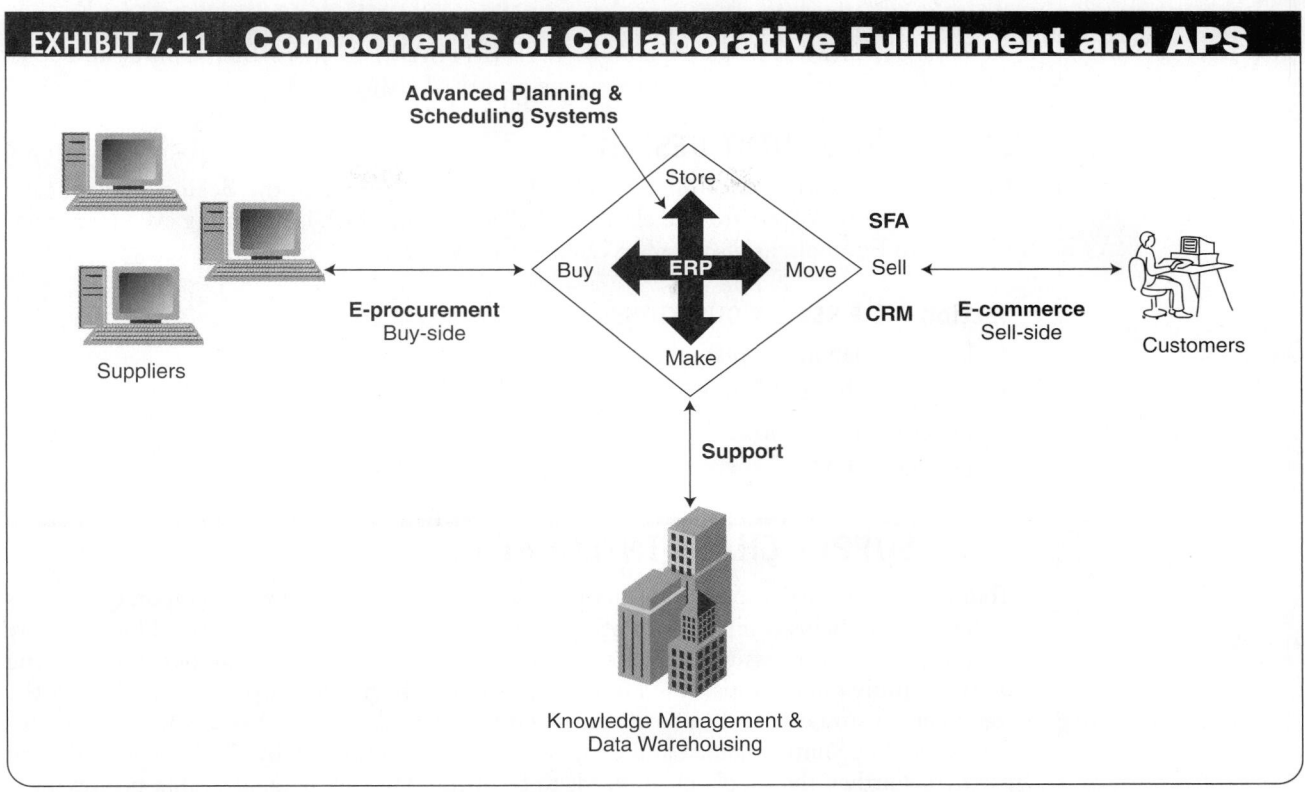

EXHIBIT 7.11 Components of Collaborative Fulfillment and APS

Advanced Planning &
Scheduling Systems

Store

SFA

Buy — ERP — Move — Sell

CRM

Make

E-procurement
Buy-side

Suppliers

E-commerce
Sell-side

Customers

Support

Knowledge Management &
Data Warehousing

Source: Modified from *E-Procurement: From Strategy to Implementation*, by Dale Neef, ©2001. Used by permission of Pearson Education, Inc., Upper Saddle River, NJ.

are able to solve a wide range of problems, from operational (e.g., daily schedule) to strategic (e.g., network optimization). For examples, see Gregory (2004).

The role of APS in EC is depicted in Exhibit 7.11. Basically, APS supplements ERP in revolutionizing a manufacturing or distribution firm's supply chain, providing a seamless flow of order fulfillment information from consumers to suppliers. It helps integrate ERP, CRM, SFA, KM, and more, enabling collaborative fulfillment and an integrated EC strategy. For additional details and discussion of ERP, SCM, and APS, see Online Tutorial T2.

PRODUCT LIFECYCLE MANAGEMENT

Product lifecycle management (PLM) is a business strategy that enables manufacturers to control and share product-related data as part of product design and development efforts and in support of supply chain operations (en.wikipedia.org/wiki/Product_Lifecycle_Management, IBM.com 2007). Internet and other new technologies can automate the *collaborative aspects* of product development that even within one company can prove tedious and time consuming if not automated. For example, by means of concurrent engineering and Web-based tools, companies simultaneously and interactively can design a product, its manufacturing process, and the supply chain that supports it. By overlapping these formerly disparate functions, a dynamic collaboration takes place among them, essentially forming a single, large product team.

PLM can have a significant beneficial impact in engineering change, cycle time, design reuse, and engineering productivity. Studies have shown that electronic-based collaboration can reduce product costs by 20 percent and travel expenses by 80 percent, as well as significantly reduce costs associated with product-change management. Moreover, an explosion of new products that have minimal life cycles, as well as increasing complexity in supply chain management, are driving the need for PLM.

PLM is a big step for an organization, requiring it to integrate a number of different processes and systems. Ultimately, information must be moved through an organization as quickly as possible to reduce cycle time and increase profitability. The faster different groups know that a new component or design change is on its way, the faster they can react and get

product lifecycle management (PLM)
Business strategy that enables manufacturers to control and share product-related data as part of product design and development efforts.

it manufactured or reengineered and out the door, and the sooner the organization can real-ize revenue. PLM tools are offered by SAP (MYSAP PLM, see Buxmann et al. 2004), Matrix One, EDS, PTC, Dassault Systems, and IBM (IBM PLM).

SUPPORTING JOINT DESIGN

Collaborative efforts are common in joint design, as illustrated in the Boeing opening case. This is one of the oldest areas of electronic collaboration, which is becoming even more pop-ular due to EC tools, as discussed in Online File W7.5.

Section 7.5 ▶ REVIEW QUESTIONS

1. Define collaborative planning.
2. Define CPFR and describe its advantages.
3. Describe APS efforts.
4. Describe PLM.

7.6 SUPPLY CHAIN INTEGRATION

Today, many business experts consider that the effective way to view contemporary business is that supply chains compete with other supply chains (Bendoly et al. 2004) This is a more insightful way of assessing business competitiveness than viewing competition as being between individual companies. Thus, supply chains from the suppliers' suppliers to the customers' customers need to be effective and efficient when viewed as a whole and, there-fore, should be jointly planned and designed for overall optimality by all of the supply chain partners. Further, the supply chain needs to be operationally integrated so that procurement activities link seamlessly to order management activities, inventory activities link seamlessly to manufacturing activities, and so on. This implies attention to business process design and management that includes not only organizational business process redesign but also *interorganizational* business process redesign (Jeston and Nelis 2006). Thus, supply chains require smooth and efficient flows of material and information between the operations of the supply chain, including, of course, interorganizational flows between each organization and its suppliers, business partners, and customers.

Within each organization in the supply chain, the primary value chain activities of inbound logistics, production, and outbound logistics must be integrated with supporting value chain activities such as marketing, customer service, after sales service, procurement, and product design. Further, outsourced elements of the primary value chain need to be inte-grated efficiently and effectively with the organization's primary value chain activities. When planning, designing and implementing such integrated operations, management requires a holistic focus that takes account of the factors of strategy, structure, people, and culture (including performance measurement, monitoring, and incentives), business processes, and IT. Further, these organizational dimensions need to be balanced along the entire supply chain. A myopic focus on, say, process logic or technology, will give suboptimal results.

HOW INFORMATION SYSTEMS ARE INTEGRATED

The integration issue can be divided into two parts: internal integration and integration with business partners. Internal integration includes connecting applications with databases and with each other and connecting customer-facing applications (front end) with order fulfillment and the functional information systems (back end). Internal integration is now commonly achieved through the implementation of an ERP system. Integration with business partners connects an organization's systems with those of its external business partners; for example, a company's ordering system to its suppliers' fulfillment systems. Another example of integration with business partners would be connecting an organization's e-procurement system to the engineering departments of bidding companies.

Where a company has implemented an ERP system, it is necessary to connect the EC applications to the ERP system (see Siau and Tian 2004). An ERP system automates the flow of routine and repetitive information, such as submission of purchasing orders, billing, and inventory management. An example of the integration of EC applications with an ERP system is provided in Online File W7.6. Increasingly, EC applications are incorporated into an ERP system's basic functionality.

ENABLING INTEGRATION AND THE ROLE OF STANDARDS AND WEB SERVICES

Web Services is an architecture that enables the assembly of distributed applications from software services and ties them together. Integrating EC systems can be a complex task. As described in Online Chapter 19, integration involves connectivity, compatibility, security, and scalability. In addition, applications, data, processes, and interfaces must be integrated. Finally, a major difficulty is the connection of Web-based systems with legacy systems.

Web Services
An architecture enabling assembly of distributed applications from software services and tying them together.

To ease the task of integration, vendors have developed integration methodologies and special software called *middleware* (see Online Chapter 19). In addition, major efforts are being undertaken to develop standards and protocols that will facilitate integration, such as XML. The topic of Web Services, one of the major goals of which is to facilitate seamless integration, is discussed in detail in Online Chapter 19.

INTEGRATION ALONG THE EXTENDED SUPPLY CHAIN

The discussion in Insights and Additions 7.2 provides an illustration of information integration along the extended supply chain—all the way from raw material to the customer's door. Such integration is possible with second-generation ERP systems (see Online Tutorial T2).

Insights and Additions 7.2   Seamless Integration of Business Partners' Systems

In Chapter 6, we raised the issue of B2B integration and some of the methods and standards used. One also can use these standards and methods, as well as some special tools that we describe here, to facilitate integration.

Retailers, such as Costco, Wal-Mart, QVC, Sears, Target, and Staples need to talk to their business partners in the "same language." They want to do so without learning "foreign" languages that may be used by their partners' systems. Those different languages are "translated" using special integration software and order management services from CommerceHub (*commercehub.com*). The company's translation platform enables retailers to electronically integrate with all of their suppliers, regardless of differing systems and incompatibilities. In addition to connectivity, the software provides real-time visibility and control over transactions. This enables better performance at a reduced cost.

According to Seideman (2004), QVC and its 200 suppliers tap into CommerceHub's universal translator instead of making separate links. The suppliers can be connected to QVC and to other retailers.

Companies that use traditional EDI have problems if their partners use different EDI standards or messages. Also, EDI runs on expensive VANs and is focused strictly on transactions. CommerceHub's service overcomes traditional EDI deficiencies. CommerceHub's software runs on Web EDI (see Online File W5.9), which is much cheaper, more flexible, and more capable than traditional EDI. The software also enables performance and expense monitoring, finds abnormalities, and solves order fulfillment problems.

A food distributor, Michael Foods, is using Sterling Commerce's (*sterlingcommerce.com*) Gentran Integration Suite to provide communication and collaboration when it deals with retailers such as Wal-Mart. Michael Foods uses collaboration tools and data synchronization to provide retail partners with assurance that products flow through the supply chain efficiently. The Gentran suite works with the EDI that is used by Michael Food and large retailers, but it also can accommodate new integration standards (e.g., ebXML, Web Services). The business partners can maintain their existing business processes and communication languages.

For example, in 2003 Michael Foods had to comply with Wal-Mart's requirement of moving to *AS2 Communication* (a new B2B protocol). Gentran Integration Suite made the transfer easy and inexpensive. Here is how it works: When a retail customer sends a purchase order EDI data file to Michael Foods, Gentran pulls the order and "wraps" it with the proper Internet elements to ensure security. It then translates the data file into the AS2 protocol and routes the order as a B2B file to the appropriate place at Michael Foods. There, the order is processed and fulfilled quickly and with fewer data errors. For details, see Amato-McCoy (2004).

Sources: Amato-McCoy (2004), Seideman (2004), *commercehub.com* (accessed January 2007), and *sterlingcommerce.com* (accessed January 2007).

Second-generation ERP systems include increasing amounts of SCM and CRM functionality, along with the internal ERP functionality.

A particular technology used in external supply chain integration is EDI. Large corporations have for some years used EDI to support their collaboration with partners. Increasingly, this EDI usage is becoming Internet based.

As an example of a corporation making extensive use of EDI, one can look at Boeing, which relies on hundreds of internal and external suppliers in dozens of different countries for the several million components needed to build a large airplane. Boeing is using EDI and other systems (e.g., PART, see Online File W5.2) to facilitate collaboration with its partners. For more information and examples, see Davenport and Brooks (2004).

Section 7.6 ▶ REVIEW QUESTIONS

1. Describe internal and external integration.

2. Explain the need to connect to an ERP system.

3. Describe the need for integrating standards and methodologies.

7.7 CORPORATE (ENTERPRISE) PORTALS

Portals and corporate portals were defined in Chapter 2. Corporate portals facilitate collaboration with suppliers, customers, employees, and others. This section provides in-depth coverage of corporate portals, including their support of collaboration and business process management.

CORPORATE PORTALS: AN OVERVIEW

corporate (enterprise) portal

A gateway for entering a corporate Web site, enabling communication, collaboration, and access to company information.

A **corporate (enterprise) portal** is a gateway to a corporate Web site that enables communication, collaboration, and access to company information. Kounadis (2000) more formally defines a corporate portal as a personalized, single point of access through a Web browser to critical business information located inside and outside of an organization. In contrast with commercial portals such as Yahoo! and MSN, which are gateways to general information on the Internet, corporate portals provide a single point of access to information and applications available on the intranets and extranets of a specific organization. Companies may have separate portals for outsiders and for insiders. One of the most pressing reasons for adopting modern portal technologies is to build a framework to host a variety of Web applications, each of which may serve different and distinct audiences and support differing requirements and preferences (BEA Systems 2006).

Corporate portals offer employees, business partners, and customers an organized focal point for their interactions with the firm. Through the portal, these people can have structured and personalized access to information across large, multiple, and disparate enterprise information systems, as well as the Internet. A schematic view of a corporate portal is provided in Exhibit 7.12. Increasingly the trend of seeing portals coalesce with other related technologies is being predicted. Some suggest that over time the achievement of business objectives through a closer integration of humans, business processes, and information systems will be achieved as portal and related technologies, such as collaboration tools, document and content management systems, e-mail, messaging of various types, and business processes converge to create a modern, flexible work environment (BEA Systems 2006).

Many large organizations are already implementing corporate portals. The reasons for doing so are to cut costs, to free up time for busy executives and managers, and to add to the bottom line. Corporate portals are especially popular in large corporations, as shown in Insights and Additions 7.3 (p. 342).

TYPES OF CORPORATE PORTALS

Corporate portals are either generic or functional. Generic portals are defined by their audience (e.g., suppliers, employees). Functional portals are defined by the functionalities they offer. Portals are popular both in the private and the public sectors. See BEA Systems (2006) for an interesting array of both generic and functional portal applications in both the public and private sectors.

EXHIBIT 7.12   Corporate Portal as a Gateway to Information

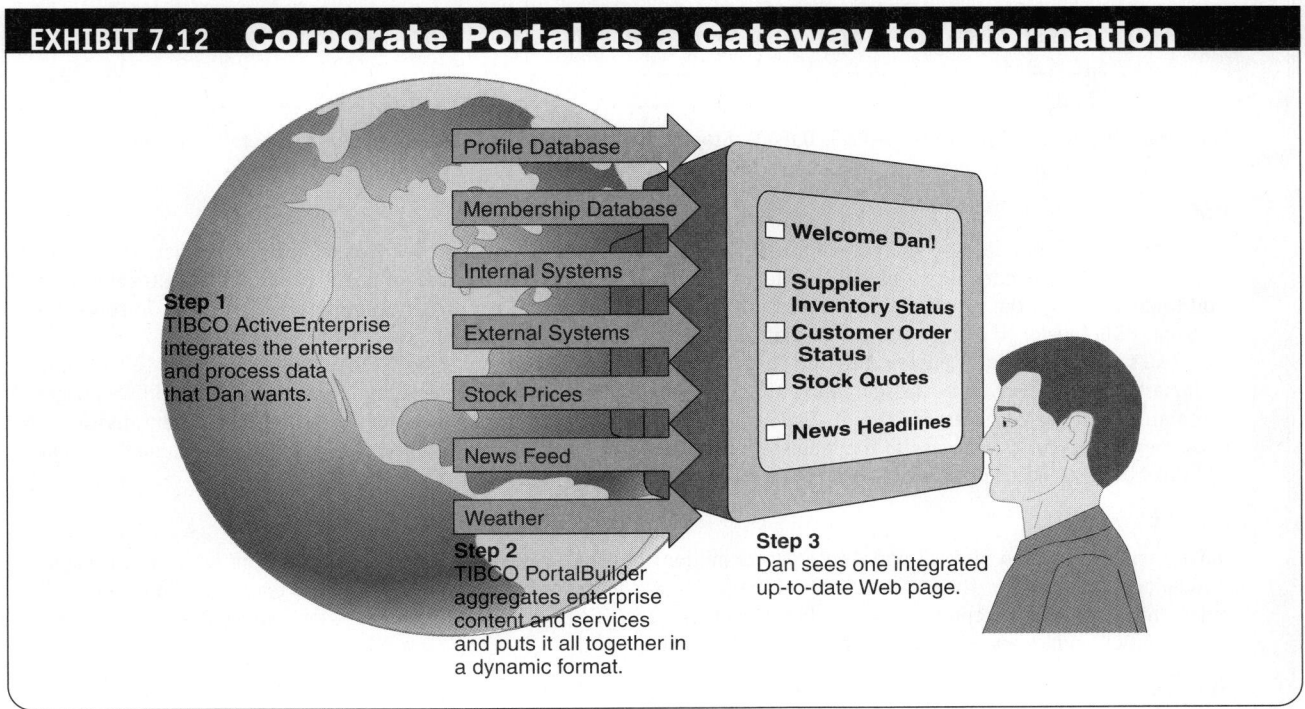

Step 1
TIBCO ActiveEnterprise integrates the enterprise and process data that Dan wants.

Profile Database

Membership Database

Internal Systems

External Systems

Stock Prices

News Feed

Weather

Step 2
TIBCO PortalBuilder aggregates enterprise content and services and puts it all together in a dynamic format.

☐ **Welcome Dan!**

☐ **Supplier Inventory Status**

☐ **Customer Order Status**

☐ **Stock Quotes**

☐ **News Headlines**

Step 3
Dan sees one integrated up-to-date Web page.

Source: Courtesy of TIBCO Software, Inc., *www.tibco.com.*

Types of Generic Portals

The following generic types of portals can be found in organizations.

Portals for Suppliers and Other Partners. Using such portals, suppliers can manage their own inventories online. They can view what they sold to the portal owner and for how much. They can see the inventory levels of the portal owner and send material and supplies when they see that a reorder level is reached, and they can collaborate with corporate buyers and other staff.

An example of a partners' portal is that of Samsung Electronic America's Digital IT. The company must keep in touch with 110,000 resellers and distributors. As part of its PRM, Samsung developed a portal that enables it to personalize relationships with each partner (e.g., conduct promotions, provide special pricing, etc.). The portal helped to increase sales by 30 percent; related expenses dropped by 25 percent. For details, see Schneider (2004).

Customer Portals. Portals for customers can serve both businesses and individual customers. Customers can use these *customer-facing portals* to view products and services and to place orders, which they can later track. They can view their own accounts and see what is going on with their accounts in almost real time. They can pay for products and services and arrange for warranties and deliveries.

At some portals, a repository of trending data enables a marketing manager to forecast whether a particular customer program would be useful based on usage patterns, transactional history, and data from similar customers. This enables marketing managers to push specific value-added programs to targeted customer segments at the customer portal.

In some applications, the relationship between the portal and its customers is completely transparent. A business customer, rather than calling, faxing, e-mailing, or using a catalog and creating a purchase order (PO), can go into its own system and create a PO. Then, the customer's system takes that PO and sends an XML message to the vendor's SCM system, which accepts the message. In this case, the communication back and forth between a customer and the company using the seller's portal is done largely at a system level. This creates a tighter integration between the seller and the customer. It gives both customers and suppliers more efficiency, and it facilitates more of a partnership than a typical customer–vendor relationship.

Insights and Additions 7.3 Some Large-Company Corporate Portals

Four examples of corporate portals—P&G, DuPont, Staples, and Redback Networks—are presented here to demonstrate how companies use corporate portals.

P&G

The IT division of P&G developed a system for sharing documents and information over the company's intranet. The scope of this system later expanded into a global knowledge catalog to support the information needs of all 98,000 P&G employees worldwide. Although the system helped in providing required information, it also led to information overload. To solve this problem, P&G developed a corporate portal that provides personalized information to each employee.

P&G's corporate portal, implemented by Plumtree (*plumtree.com*, now owned by BEA Systems), provides P&G's employees with marketing, product, and strategic information and with industry news documents numbering over 1 million Web pages. The corporate portal can be accessed through a Web browser without having to navigate through all of the different divisions' Web sites. Employees can gain access to the required information through customized preset views of various information sources and links to other up-to-date information.

DuPont

DuPont implemented an internal portal to organize millions of pages of scientific information stored in information systems throughout the company. The initial version of the portal was intended for daily use by over 550 employees to record product orders, retrieve progress reports for research products, and access customer-tracking information. Today, DuPont uses the portal for its 55,000 employees in 30 business units in 70 countries.

Staples

The corporate portal for Staples, an office supply company, was launched in February 2000. It was immediately used by the company's 3,000 executives, knowledge workers, and store managers; by 2003, over 10,000 users were registered, with the objective to reach 46,000 employees by 2004. The portal serves as the interface to Staples' business processes and applications. It offers e-mail, scheduling, headlines on articles about the competition, new product information, internal news, job postings, and newsletters. The portal is used by top management as well as by managers of contracts, procurement, sales and marketing, human resources, and retail stores and by the company's three B2B Web sites.

Redback Networks

A corporate enterprise portal implementation that is vital to the company's business performance is that of Redback Networks. Redback is meeting the growing demand for its computer networking products via a virtual manufacturing approach that leverages outsourcing to trusted partners and frees the company to focus on sales and product design. Redback's successful manufacturing strategy is based on its very creative and robust partnering strategy and the ICT infrastructure that connects Redback with its partners. Redback's connectivity includes three key portals: the Customer Portal, which connects the company with its customers; the Supplier Portal, which connects it with partners and suppliers; and the Employee Portal for its 600-plus employees.

Sources: Compiled from Konicki (2001), Regan (2006), and from press releases from the companies described (2002–2006).

Employee Portals. Such portals are used for training, dissemination of company news and information, discussion groups, and more. Employee portals also are used for self-service activities, mainly in the human resources area (e.g., change of address forms, tax withholding forms, expense reports, class registration, and tuition reimbursement forms). Employees' portals are sometimes bundled with supervisors' portals in what are known as *workforce portals* (e.g., Workbrain Enterprise Workforce Management, workbrain.com).

Executive and Supervisor Portals. These portals enable managers and supervisors to control the entire workforce management process—from budgeting to workforce scheduling. For example, Pharmacia (a Pfizer company) built a portal for its executives and managers worldwide, the Global Field Force Action Planner, which provides a single, worldwide view of the company's finances and performance. Business goals and sales figures are readily available on a consistent and transparent basis, allowing corporate management to evaluate and support field offices more effectively. Country managers also can share best practices with their peers and learn from other action plans, helping them to make better decisions.

Mobile Portals. Mobile portals are portals accessible via mobile devices, especially cell phones and PDAs. Most mobile portals are noncorporate information portals (i.e., they are commercial portals), such as DoCoMo's i-mode. (See the description of i-mode in Chapter 9.) Eventually, large corporations will introduce mobile corporate portals. Alternatively, they will offer access to their regular portals from wireless devices, which many already do (e.g., major airlines, banks, and retailers).

mobile portals
Portals accessible via mobile devices, especially cell phones and PDAs.

The Functionalities of Portals

Whoever their audience, the functionalities of portals range from simple **information portals** that store data and enable users to navigate and query those data to sophisticated **collaborative portals** that enable collaboration.

Several types of functional portals exist: *Business intelligence portals* are used mostly by middle- and top-level executives and analysts to conduct business analyses and decision-support activities (Ferguson 2001). For example, a business intelligence portal might be used to generate ad hoc reports or to conduct a risk analysis. *Intranet portals* are used mostly by employees for managing fringe benefits and for self-training (Ferguson 2001). *Knowledge portals* are used for collecting knowledge from employees and for disseminating collected knowledge. (For an example of a business intelligence and knowledge management portal, see Kesner 2003.)

information portals
Portals that store data and enable users to navigate and query these data.

collaborative portals
Portals that allow collaboration.

CORPORATE PORTAL APPLICATIONS

According to a 2002 Delphi Group survey (*DM Review* 2003), the top portal applications, in decreasing order of importance, are as follows: knowledge bases and learning tools; business process support; customer-facing (frontline) sales, marketing, and services; collaboration and project support; access to data from disparate corporate systems; personalized pages for various users; effective search and indexing tools; security applications; best practices and lessons learned; directories and bulletin boards; identification of experts; news; and Internet access.

Exhibit 7.13 depicts a corporate portal framework. This framework illustrates the features and capabilities required to support various organizational applications.

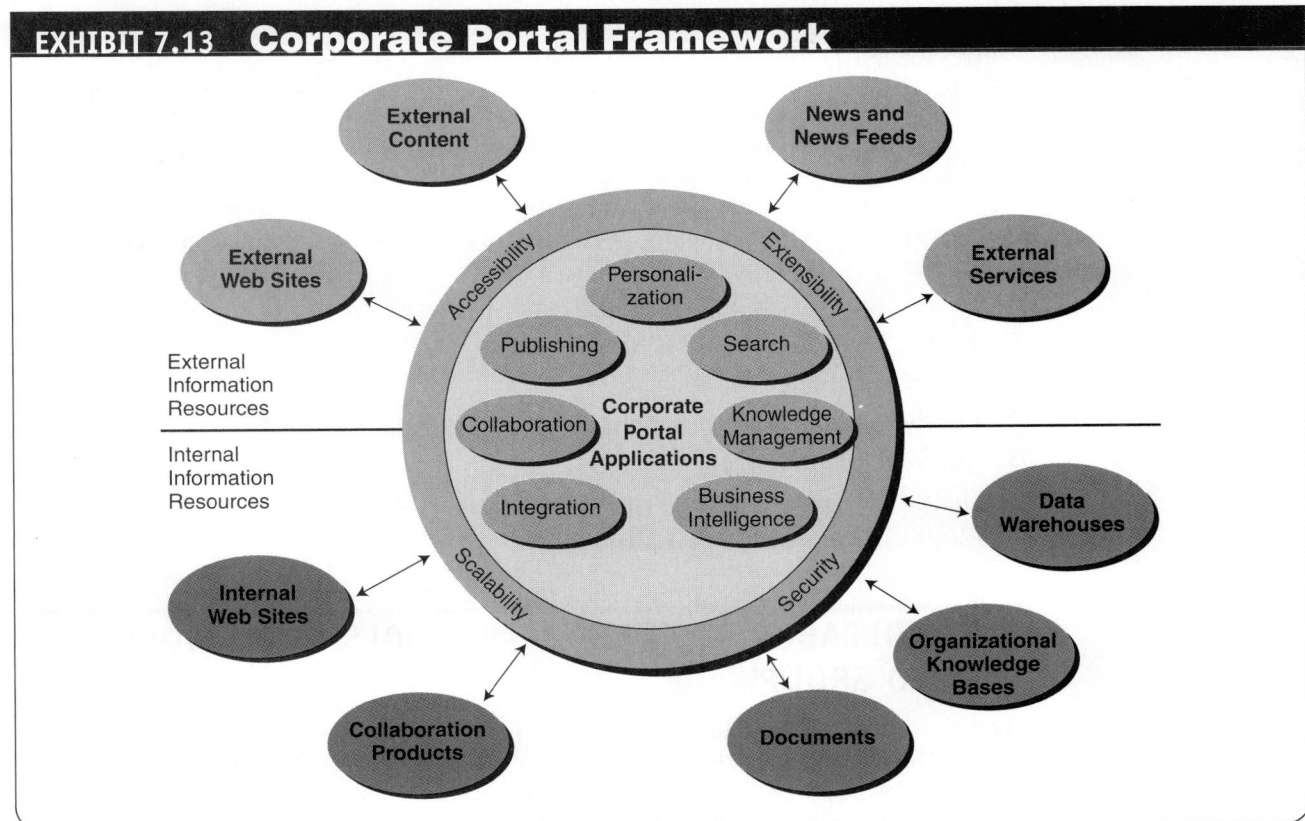

EXHIBIT 7.13 Corporate Portal Framework

Source: Compiled by N. Bolloju, City University of Hong Kong, from Aneja et al. (2000) and Kounadis (2000).

JUSTIFYING PORTALS

As with any IT project, management needs to be able to justify the development and use of a corporate portal by comparing its cost with its benefits. Some of the tangible benefits from investment in portal technology include revenue growth, call center productivity increases, and increased customer loyalty and retention. Adopters also report much improved trading relationships with suppliers and business partners (BEA Systems 2006). However, most of the benefits of portals are *intangible*. For example, Reda (2002) claims that employee portals have the potential to fundamentally change and improve employer–employee relationships—a desirable benefit, although somewhat difficult to measure. According to Ferguson (2001), portals offer the following benefits that are difficult to quantify:

▶ They offer a simple user interface for finding and navigating content via a browser.

▶ They improve access to business content and increase the number of business users who can access information, applications, and people.

▶ They offer access to common business applications from anywhere in a geographically distributed enterprise and beyond. Using Web-enabled mobile or wireless devices, content can be accessed from anywhere.

▶ They offer the opportunity to use platform-independent software (Java) and data (XML).

However, given that portals are relatively low-cost, low-risk devices (Cunningham 2002), it is not surprising that they are being adopted by thousands of organizations worldwide. A formal approach to justifying portals is offered by Plumtree (2002), which devised a framework for assessing the ROI of portals. BEA Systems offers several white papers and examples on this topic at its Web site (bea.com). For methods of justifying portals and intangible benefits, see Chapter 15.

DEVELOPING PORTALS

Before a company can develop a corporate portal, it must decide what the purpose and content of the portal will be. For some practical guidelines for determining a corporate portal strategy, see Smith (2004) and Online File W7.7. Others may be driven by more technical reasons, with the adoption of service-oriented architectures seen as a driver and/or complement to further development of portals (BEA Systems 2006).

Many vendors offer tools for building corporate portals as well as hosting services. Representative vendors are IBM, Microsoft, SAP, Oracle, BEA Systems, TIBCO (Portal Builder at tibco.com), Computer Associates (Jasmine II Portal at ca.com), Fujitsu, and Vignette.

Section 7.7 ▶ REVIEW QUESTIONS

1. What is a corporate portal?
2. List the types of corporate portals.
3. List five applications of portals.
4. Discuss the issue of justifying enterprise portals.
5. List the major benefits of corporate portals.

7.8 COLLABORATION-ENABLING TOOLS: FROM WORKFLOW TO GROUPWARE

As mentioned earlier, collaboration, knowledge management, and e-commerce are all vital ingredients in improving the performance of supply chains. A large number of tools and methodologies also are available that facilitate e-collaboration. This section presents workflow technologies, groupware, and other collaboration-enabling tools.

WORKFLOW TECHNOLOGIES AND APPLICATIONS

Workflow is the movement of documents and tasks (and hence information) as they flow through the sequence of steps that make up an organization's work processes and procedures. Workflow embraces how tasks are to be structured and performed, who should perform them, how they should be logically ordered and sequenced, how tasks are to be tracked and monitored, and most important, what information is required and generated from all these tasks and how and where it needs to be recorded (en.wikipedia.org/wiki/Workflow).

Workflow systems essentially help organizations analyze, model, automate, and electronically enact aspects of workflow and task performance among workers both within and across multiple organizations in a supply chain. These types of systems may include features that enable task scheduling and prioritization, job routing, tracking and control, document imaging, document management, management reporting, and the like.

Workflow management involves the management of workflows so that documents, information, or tasks are passed from one participant to another in a way that is governed by the organization's rules or procedures to achieve required deadlines. Workflow management also involves tracking of these tasks and documents, prioritizing tasks, and ensuring the allocation of adequate resources for the performance of these tasks. Workflow management involves all of the steps in a business process from start to finish, including all exception conditions. The key to workflow management is the tracking of process-related information and the status of each activity of the business process (see van der Aalst and van Hee 2004).

Types of Workflow Applications

Workflow applications fall into three major categories: collaborative, production, and administrative workflow.

▶ **Collaborative workflow.** Collaborative workflow refers to those software products that address project-oriented and collaborative types of processes. They are administered centrally yet are capable of being accessed and used by workers from different departments and in collaborative partner organizations and even from different physical locations. The goal of collaborative workflow tools is to empower knowledge workers. The focus of an enterprise solution for collaborative workflow is on allowing workers to communicate, negotiate, and collaborate within a unified environment. Collaborative workflow applications are generally a little less structured than some other application types. Some leading vendors of collaborative workflow applications are Lotus, JetForm, FileNet (an IBM company), Microsoft, and Action Technologies.

▶ **Production workflow.** Production workflow tools address mission-critical, transaction-oriented, high-volume processes. They are generally highly structured applications and clerical in nature. They usually are deployed in a single department or to a certain set of users within a department. These applications often include document imaging and storage and retrieval capabilities. They also may include the use of intelligent forms, database access, and ad hoc capabilities. The goal is to improve productivity and the quality of business processes. The leading vendors of workflow applications are FileNet, TIBCO, IBM, and Global 360. An example of production workflow that is mixed with collaborative workflow is presented in Case 7.6. For other applications, see SoftNet (2007), Torode (2004), and Staff (2004b).

▶ **Administrative workflow.** Administrative workflow deals with administrative tasks such as routing and approval functions for such things as travel requests, purchase orders, and leave requests. Some of these applications extend enterprise wide, such as recruitment, procurement, and expense reporting. Administrative workflow systems are usually based around electronic forms and documents and serve to automate parts of these previously paper-intensive processes. The major vendors are Lotus, TIBCO, and InTempo.

In conclusion, the benefits of workflow management systems include the following:

▶ Cycle time reduction achieved through improved control of business processes, with far less management intervention and fewer chances for delays or misplaced work than in

---

workflow
The movement of information as it flows through the sequence of steps that make up an organization's work procedures.

workflow systems
Business process automation tools that place system controls in the hands of user departments to automate information-processing tasks.

workflow management
The automation of workflows, so that documents, information, and tasks are passed from one participant to the next in the steps of an organization's business process.

POSTE ITALIANE GAINS EFFICIENCY AND COMPLIANCE THROUGH IMPLEMENTING WORKFLOW SYSTEMS

Poste Italiane (Italian Post) is a large, distributed organization with 146 branch offices, 14,000 postal offices, and about 158,000 employees, largely in Italy but also throughout Europe. In addition to the traditional postal services, it offers communications services, logistics, and financial services, including consumer banking services.

Banking is subject to substantial regulation, and Italian Post lacked the necessary infrastructure to ensure that important documents associated with banking rules and regulations, policies, reporting requirements, and the like were appropriately created, distributed, stored, and retrieved by authorized personnel. Most of these documents were created centrally and needed approval from different divisions before distribution across the network of postal offices, all within a strict timeframe. The original distribution method had been to manually fax documents to each of the post offices, an extremely inefficient, time-consuming, and labor-intensive activity. Furthermore, it was not possible to guarantee that the documents had been received, verify the delivery date, confirm that the documents had been read and enacted as required, or ensure that the documents were stored with appropriate levels of privacy and security.

A solution was found in a document management and workflow management system that is able to automate and simplify the creation, review, and distribution of these sensitive corporate documents. The system is also able to track a document's history; restrict access to particular documents; assign expiration dates, where appropriate; and archive documents.

Using components of Microsoft Office 2007 and Microsoft Windows Workflow Foundation, Italian Post employees now have access to a centralized portal where they can navigate through and review a large number of documents.

In addition, collaborative functions enable staff at the widely distributed offices to share, approve, and store these documents, using a procedure embedded in the software that ensures compliance with banking regulations and business rules. By restricting access to certain sensitive documents, document security is assured.

Italian Post benefits through a reduction in time spent on administrative tasks due to the automation of the workflows associated with the management of sensitive policy documents. In addition, collaboration and the management of corporate knowledge is improved through this system; documents are more accurate; and the process of creating, disseminating, storing, and securing these documents can be completed in a more timely manner.

Source: Compiled from *Microsoft.com* (2006a).

Questions

1. Briefly describe the major problems faced by Italian Post.

2. What was nature of the solution provided by document management and workflow management systems?

3. Draw the Italian Post process of document creation, dissemination, and storage outlined at the start of this case. Draw the same process following the introduction of the new technologies. Where are efficiencies being achieved?

4. Explain how the system has improved workflow.

5. In what ways do the new systems improve collaboration among the distributed postal offices?

other systems. Reductions in cycle times can also be achieved through minimizing reworks, using business rules to catch problem at their course, and so on.

▶ Productivity gains by helping individuals prioritize their activities, providing them with the necessary information to complete tasks, and balancing workloads across the entire workgroup.

▶ Improved process control, enabling the organization to improve quality and consistency.

▶ Improved quality of services through quicker response times with the best person available.

▶ Lower staff training costs because the work can be guided through complex procedures.

▶ Lower management costs, enabling managers to concentrate on nurturing employees and handling special cases rather than on routine reporting and distribution issues.

▶ Improved user satisfaction. Users typically have greater confidence that they are doing the best they can, and they enjoy greater satisfaction when completing their work with fewer conflicting requirements.

▶ More effective collaboration and knowledge sharing, especially the sharing of best practices.

A major area for EC workflow applications is the aggregation of sellers or buyers, which was described in Chapters 5 and 6. When large suppliers or buyers are involved, a workflow system is needed for both the collaborative efforts and for supply chain and production improvements.

For information on workflow management, see Fischer (2002). Additional information can be found at wfmc.org, aiim.org, BPM Focus (waria.com), and omg.org. For a discussion of the functionalities of workflow management systems, see Online File W7.8.

Because workflow management systems support more than one individual, they are considered by some to be a subset of groupware, our next topic.

GROUPWARE: COLLABORATION TOOLS

Groupware refers to software products that support groups of people who share a common task or goal and collaborate on its accomplishment. These products provide a way for groups to share resources and opinions. Groupware implies the use of networks to connect people, even if they are in the same room. Many groupware products are available on the Internet or an intranet, enhancing the collaboration of a large number of people worldwide (e.g., see Henrie 2004).

A number of different approaches and technologies are available for the support of groups on the Internet. Groupware tools and applications that support collaboration and conferencing are listed in Exhibit 7.14.

groupware
Software products that use networks to support collaboration among groups of people who share a common task or goal.

EXHIBIT 7.14 Major Features in Collaboration and Conferencing Tools

General

- Built-in e-mail, messaging system, instant messaging
- Browser interface
- Joint Web-page creation
- Sharing of active hyperlinks
- File sharing (graphics, video, audio, or other)
- Built-in search functions (by topic or keyword)
- Workflow tools
- Use of corporate portals for communication, collaboration
- Shared screens
- Electronic decision rooms
- Peer-to-peer networks

Synchronous (same time)

- Webinar
- Webcast
- Videoconferencing, multimedia conferencing
- Audioconferencing
- Shared whiteboard, smart whiteboard
- Text chart
- Brainstorming, polling (voting), and other decision support (consensus builder, scheduler)

Asynchronous (different times)

- Threaded discussions
- Voice mail
- Users can receive/send e-mail, SMS
- Users can receive activity notification via e-mail
- Users can collapse/expand threads
- Users can sort messages (by date, author, or read/unread)
- Chat session logs
- Bulletin boards, discussion groups
- Use of blogs, wikis
- Web publishing
- Collaborative planning and/or design tools

Synchronous Versus Asynchronous Products

Notice that the features in Exhibit 7.14 may be *synchronous*, meaning that communication and collaboration are done in real time, or *asynchronous*, meaning that communication and collaboration are done by the participants at different times (e.g., by leaving a message on a bulletin board to be read and answered later), potentially from disparate locations. Web conferencing and instant messaging as well as Voice-over-Internet Protocol (VoIP) are associated with synchronous mode. Associated with asynchronous mode are *online workspaces* where participants can collaborate on joint designs or projects but work at different times. Vignette (vignette.com), Google (google.com), and Groove Networks (groove.net) allow users to set up online workspaces for sharing and storing documents. According to Henrie (2004), many of the tools offered by vendors are converging. This is done with the help of new technologies, such as VoIP.

Groupware products are either stand-alone products that support one task (such as e-mail) or integrated kits that include several tools (such as e-mail and screen sharing). In general, groupware technology products are fairly inexpensive and can be easily incorporated into existing information systems.

The Internet, intranets, extranets, and private communication lines provide the infrastructure needed for groupware. Most of the software products are Web based. The following describes some of the most common groupware collaboration tools.

Electronic Meeting Systems

An important area of virtual collaboration is electronic meetings. For decades, people have attempted to improve face-to-face meetings, which are known to have many potential dysfunctions. Initially, people attempted to better organize group meetings by using a facilitator and established procedures (known as *group dynamics*). Numerous attempts have been made to use information technologies to improve meetings conducted in one room (see Nunamaker et al. 1997 for examples). The advancement of Web-based systems opens the door for improved electronically supported **virtual meetings**, where members are in different locations and even in different countries. For example, online meetings and presentation tools are provided by webex.com and by gotomeetings.com.

virtual meetings
Online meetings whose members are in different locations, even in different countries.

One of the major benefits of electronic meeting systems are the dramatic reductions in costs associated with business travel (en.wikipedia.org/wiki/Conferencing). In addition, improvements in supporting technology, reductions in the price of the technology, and the acceptance of virtual meetings as a respected way of doing business are fueling their growth (see Austin et al. 2006).

Virtual meetings are supported by a variety of groupware tools, as will be shown in the remainder of this section. We begin our discussion with the support provided to decision making.

Group Decision Support Systems

group decision support system (GDSS)
An interactive computer-based system that facilitates the solution of semistructured and unstructured problems by a group of decision makers.

A **group decision support system (GDSS)** is an interactive computer-based system that facilitates the solution of semistructured and unstructured problems by a group of decision makers. The goal of GDSSs is to improve the productivity of decision-making meetings, either by speeding up the decision-making process or by improving the quality of the resulting decisions, or both.

The major characteristics of a GDSS are as follows:

▶ Its goal is to support the group decision-making process by using IT tools to automate support subprocesses.

▶ It is a specially designed information system, not merely a configuration of already-existing system components. It can be designed to address one type of problem or a variety of group-level organizational decisions.

▶ It encourages idea generation, conflict resolution, and freedom of expression. It contains built-in mechanisms that discourage development of negative group behaviors, such as destructive conflict miscommunication and "groupthink."

First-generation GDSSs were designed to support face-to-face meetings in what is called a *decision room*. Today, support is provided over the Web to virtual groups (group members may be in different locations). The group can meet at the same time or at different times by using e-mail, sending documents, and reading transaction logs face-to-face. GDSS is especially useful when controversial decisions have to be made (such as resource allocation or determining which individuals to lay off). GDSS applications require a facilitator when done in one room or a coordinator or leader when done with virtual meetings.

GDSSs can improve the decision-making process in various ways. For one, GDSSs generally provide structure to the planning process, which keeps the group on track, although some permit the group to use unstructured techniques and methods for idea generation. In addition, GDSSs offer rapid and easy access to external information needed for decision making. GDSSs also support parallel processing of information and idea generation by participants and allow asynchronous computer discussion. They make possible larger meetings that would otherwise be unmanageable; a larger group means that more complete information, knowledge, and skills will be represented in the same meeting. Finally, voting can be anonymous, with instant results, and all information that passes through the system can be recorded for future analysis (producing organizational memory).

The major benefit of GDSSs, however, is in conducting virtual meetings. Meetings can be called very quickly, and the company can save on travel expenses. The major benefit over most Web conferencing tools, which are essentially unidirectional in their one-to-many pattern of communication, GDSSs were designed on a many-to-many basis, with a one-to-many facilitator role incorporated into most designs. Thus, in a GDSS people do not sit passively listening while information is distributed. The aim is for people to actively engage by adding their ideas, commenting on other's ideas, and actively engaging in the process (Austin et al. 2006).

GDSS Products. More general GDSS products, such as Microsoft NetMeeting, WebEx, and Lotus Notes/Domino, provide for some of the functionalities just discussed. A more specialized GDSS product is GroupSystems, which is a complete suite of electronic meeting software (both for one-room and virtual meetings). (Visit groupsystems.com and view the demo there.) Another specialized product is eRoom (now owned by EMC Documentum at documentum.com). This is a comprehensive Web-based suite of tools that can support a variety of collaboration scenarios (see Online File W7.9). A third product is Team Expert Choice, which is an add-on product for Expert Choice (expertchoice.com). It has limited decision-support capabilities, mainly supporting one-room meetings. Facilitate (facilitate.com) and Meetingworks (entsol.com) are both Web-based GDSSs designed to improve meeting productivity and support collaboration. WebIQ (webiq.net) offers similar functionality but includes a Web-based JAD tool. Grouputer (grouputer.com) offers the traditional GDSS functionality of supporting meetings and collaborative decision making but also offers tools specifically geared to support business process improvement initiatives, including Six Sigma. A number of these products can be used on an ASP basis in addition to being purchased and installed on a company's network.

Real-Time Collaboration Tools

The Internet, intranets, and extranets offer tremendous potential for real-time and synchronous interaction for people working in groups. *Real-time collaboration (RTC) tools* help companies bridge time and space to make decisions and collaborate on projects. RTC tools support synchronous communication of graphical and text-based information. These tools are being used in distance training, product demonstrations, customer support, e-commerce, and sales applications. RTC tools can be purchased as stand-alone tools or used on a subscription basis (as offered by many vendors).

Electronic Teleconferencing

Teleconferencing is the use of electronic communication that enables two or more people at different locations to have a simultaneous conference. It is the simplest infrastructure for supporting a virtual meeting. Several types of teleconferencing are possible. The oldest and simplest is a telephone conference call, wherein several people talk to each other from three or more locations. The biggest disadvantage of this is that it does not

teleconferencing
The use of electronic communication that allows two or more people at different locations to have a simultaneous conference.

allow for face-to-face communication. Also, participants in one location cannot see graphs, charts, and pictures at other locations. Although the latter disadvantage can be overcome by using a fax, this is a time-consuming, expensive, and frequently poor-quality process. One solution is *video teleconferencing*, in which participants can see each other, as well as the documents.

video teleconference
Virtual meeting in which participants in one location can see participants at other locations on a large screen or a desktop computer.

Video Teleconferencing. In a **video teleconference**, participants in one location can see participants at other locations. Dynamic pictures of the participants can appear on a large screen or on a desktop computer. Originally, video teleconferencing was the transmission of live, compressed TV sessions between two or more points. Today, video teleconferencing (or *videoconferencing*) is a digital technology capable of linking various types of computers across networks. Once conferences are digitized and transmitted over networks, they become a computer application.

data conferencing
Virtual meeting in which geographically dispersed groups work on documents together and exchange computer files during videoconferences.

With videoconferencing, participants can share data, voice, pictures, graphics, and animation. Data can be sent along with voice and video. Such **data conferencing** makes it possible to work on documents and to exchange computer files during videoconferences. This enables several geographically dispersed groups to work on the same project and to communicate by video simultaneously. Vendors of data conferencing tools include Microsoft, IBM (Lotus), NetSpoke, and WebEx.

Video teleconferencing offers various benefits. Two of them—providing the opportunity for face-to-face communication for individuals in different locations and supporting several types of media during conferencing—have already been discussed. Video teleconferencing also improves employee productivity, cuts travel costs, conserves the time and energy of key employees, and increases the speed of businesses processes (such as product development, contract negotiation, and customer service). It improves the efficiency and frequency of communications and saves an electronic record of a meeting, enabling specific parts of a meeting to be reconstructed for future purposes. Video teleconferencing also makes it possible to hold classes at different locations. Finally, the tool can be used to conduct meetings with business partners as well as to interview candidates for employment.

Web Conferencing. *Web conferencing* is conducted on the Internet for as few as two and for as many as thousands of people. It allows users to simultaneously view something on their computer screens, such as a sales presentation in Microsoft PowerPoint or a product drawing; interaction takes place via messaging or a simultaneous phone teleconference. Web conferencing is much cheaper than videoconferencing because it runs over the Internet.

The latest technological innovations support both B2B and B2C Web conferencing applications. For example, banks in Alaska use *video kiosks* in sparsely populated areas instead of building branches that will be underutilized. The video kiosks operate on the banks' intranet and provide videoconferencing equipment for face-to-face interactions. A variety of other communication tools, such as online polls, whiteboards, and question-and-answer boards may also be used. Such innovations can be used to educate staff members about a new product line or technology, to amplify a meeting with investors, or to walk a prospective client though an introductory presentation. People can use Web conferencing to view presentations, seminars, and lectures, and to collaborate on documents.

Web conferencing is becoming very popular. Almost all Web conferencing products provide whiteboarding and polling features and allow users to give presentations and demos and share applications. Popular Web conferencing products are Centra EMeeting, Genesys Meeting Center, Microsoft Office Live Meeting, and WebEx Meeting Center.

Voice-over-IP (VoIP)
Communication systems that transmit voice calls over Internet Protocol–based networks.

Voice-over-IP

Voice-over-IP (VoIP) refers to communication systems that transmit voice calls over Internet-Protocol–based networks. Corporations are moving their phone systems to Internet standards to cut costs and boost efficiency. Strategies for how to do this are described in Sturdevant (2004) and by Blickstein (2004). VoIP also is known as *Internet telephony*. Most browsers provide for VoIP capabilities. Users use their browsers to receive telephone calls initiated on the Internet (with a microphone and special VoIP software, which may be provided with the sender's browser). The market leader in VoIP is Skype, the world's fastest-growing Internet communication offering. Skype offers unlimited free voice, video, and instant messaging communication between users provided they also use the Skype software, which is available for free download over the Web (*Skype.com* 2007).

According to a Siemens Communication (communications.USA.Siemens.com) special advertisement, the following are the benefits of VoIP communications.

For the business:

- Allows chief information officers to explore different deployment options for company's communications needs
- Lowers total cost of ownership through voice/data convergence
- Lowers operational costs through use of integrated applications
- Reduces hardware requirements on the server side for certain applications (e.g., VoIP)
- Provides a holistic approach to security, enhanced by encryption and identity management
- Helps streamline workflows by empowering companies to communications-enable different business processes
- Enables optimized conferencing tools to replace business travel

For the user:

- Eliminates unwanted interruptions and unproductive actions by intelligently filtering communications
- Provides access to real-time presence information, which helps decisions get made faster
- Initiates ad hoc conferencing/collaboration sessions without the need to prearrange separate audio or videoconferencing bridges
- Enables participation in conferencing sessions quickly and easily via a variety of mobile devices

Interactive Whiteboards

Whiteboards are another type of groupware. Computer-based whiteboards work like real-world whiteboards with markers and erasers, except for one big difference: Instead of one person standing in front of a meeting room drawing on the whiteboard, all participants can join in. Throughout a meeting, each user can view and draw on a single document "pasted" onto the electronic whiteboard on a computer screen. Users can save digital whiteboarding sessions for future use. Some whiteboarding products let users insert graphics files that can be annotated by the group. Interactive whiteboards also enable the display of video clips, which can be frozen, then annotated and "cut" into PowerPoint presentations and the like.

Take, for example, an advertisement that needs to be cleared by a senior manager. Once the proposed ad has been scanned into a PC, both parties can see it on their screens. If the senior manager does not like something, she highlights what needs to be changed using a stylus pen. This tool makes communication between the two parties easier and clearer. The two parties also can share applications. For example, if party A works with Excel, party B does not have to have Excel in order to work with it in the whiteboarding tool.

Besides being used to support people working on the same task, whiteboards also are used for training and learning. The following are two examples of whiteboarding products: Digital Wall Display and Intelligent Whiteboard:

- Digital Wall Display from 3M Corp. (3m.com) is a multifunction whiteboard. It shows whatever is written on it, as well as anything—text, charts, still and moving pictures—that is stored in a computer and loaded onto the whiteboard. With a remote mouse, presenters or teachers can edit and move the material around on the touch-screen board. All of this, including audio, can be transmitted instantaneously to any connected board, anywhere in the world, making it useful for virtual, long-distance teaching or training. The system also is used for sharing research among colleagues.
- Intelligent Whiteboard from Smart Technologies Inc. (smarttech.com) was designed to support teaching. It has a "write" feature in electronic ink, a "touch" feature for controlling applications, and a "save" feature to save work to computer files. A model named Camfire is equipped with digital cameras that photograph what is written on the whiteboard. The images are then transferred to a Web site or e-mailed to students. The system also can connect to devices, such as a microscope, for presentation of hard-to-see information.

Another innovation to support group work collaboration involves the combination of intelligent whiteboards with Bridgit conferencing software. Bridgit allows users to share real-time voice, video, and data. Users can take over applications on another participant's computer or write notes in digital ink for all conference participants to see (Smart Technologies 2006).

Screen Sharing

screen-sharing software
Software that enables group members, even in different locations, to work on the same document, which is shown on the PC screen of each participant.

In collaborative work, members frequently are in different locations. Using **screen-sharing software**, group members can work on the same document, which is shown on the PC screen of each participant. For example, two authors can work on a single manuscript. One may suggest a correction and execute it so that the other author can view the change. Collaborators can work together on the same spreadsheet or on the resultant graphics. Changes can be done by using the keyboard or by touching the screen. This capability can expedite the design of products, the preparation of reports and bids, and the resolution of conflicts.

A special screen-sharing capability is offered by Groove Networks (groove.net). Its product enables the joint creation and editing of documents on a PC (see Team Assignment #1).

Instant Video

The spread of instant messaging and Internet telephony has naturally led to the idea of linking people via both voice and audio. Called *instant video*, the idea is for a kind of video chat room. It allows users to chat in real time and see the person(s) they are communicating with. A simple way to do this is to add video cameras to the participants' computers. A more sophisticated and better-quality approach is to integrate an existing online videoconferencing service with instant messaging software, creating a service that offers the online equivalent of a videophone.

This idea is still in the early stages. One instant video pioneer is CUworld (cuworld.com). Users get free software (CUworld 6.0) that can compress and decompress video signals sent over an online connection. To start a conference, a user sends a request to an online buddy (via instant messenger). The CUworld software goes to the directory of the instant messaging service to determine the Internet addresses of the users' connections, and, using the Web addresses, the computers of the video participants are linked directly via the Internet. A video conference can then begin.

Integration and Groupware Suites

Because groupware technologies are computer based, with the same objectives of supporting group work, it makes sense to integrate them among themselves and/or with other computer-based technologies. A *software suite* is created when several products are integrated into one system. Integrating several technologies can save time and money for users. For example, Polycom (polycom.com) is a market leader in combining video, voice, data, and Web conferencing capabilities into a single solution. Polycom has formed an alliance with Microsoft to deliver collaborative solutions across a range of communication devices and applications to allow participants to connect and share information both inside and between organizations worldwide. The alliance offers seamless real-time communication across a range of media, including video, instant messaging, business applications, business processes, Web Services, and Web collaboration. Polycom and Microsoft have achieved this through utilizing Session Initiation Protocol (SIP), which is a communication protocol that has the ability to merge previously separate infrastructures, such as multimedia conferencing, telecommunications, Web Services, wireless, and collaboration technologies (Polycom 2004). The following are some other examples of popular groupware suites.

Lotus Notes/Domino. The Lotus Notes/Domino suite includes a document management system, a distributed client/server database, a basis for intranet and e-commerce systems, and a communication support tool. It enhances real-time communications with asynchronous electronic connections (e.g., e-mail and other forms of messaging).

Group members using Lotus Notes/Domino may store all of their official memos, formal reports, and informal conversations related to particular projects in a shared database.

Lotus Notes provides online collaboration capabilities, workgroup e-mail, distributed databases, bulletin whiteboards, text editing, (electronic) document management, workflow capabilities, instant virtual meetings, application sharing, instant messaging, consensus building, voting, ranking, and various application development tools. All of these capabilities are integrated into one environment with a graphic-menu-based user interface. At the beginning of 2007, there were over 125 million Notes users worldwide (en.wikipedia.org/wiki/Lotus_Notes).

Microsoft NetMeeting. Microsoft's groupware suite, NetMeeting, is a real-time collaboration package that supports whiteboarding, application sharing (of any Microsoft Windows application document), remote desktop sharing, file transfer, text chat, data conferencing, desktop audio, and videoconferencing. The NetMeeting suite is included in Windows 98 and more recent versions.

Novell GroupWise. Novell's GroupWise offers a wide range of communication and collaboration capabilities integrated with document management capabilities, including e-mail, calendaring, group scheduling, imaging, workflow, electronic discussions, and more.

OTHER COLLABORATIVE TOOLS AND WIKIS

Many different collaborative tools are available. A sampler of these tools is provided in Online File W7.10. Consult that resource for information about collaborative tools in addition to those already discussed. Before closing this discussion of collaborative tools, however, we need to mention another tool—wikis (or wikilogs). Wikis, which are described in Chapters 8 and 18 enable people to work on the same files and documents, making changes in a very rapid way.

IMPLEMENTATION ISSUES FOR ONLINE COLLABORATION

This chapter has presented numerous online collaboration issues of one sort or another. The following are a few implementation issues that must be addressed when planning online collaboration. First, to connect business partners, an organization needs an effective collaborative environment. Such an environment is provided by groupware suites such as Lotus Notes/Domino or Cybozu Share360 (share360.com). Another issue is the need to connect collaborative tools with file management products on an organization's intranet. Two products that offer such connection capabilities are e/pop Web conferencing and online meeting software (wiredred.com) and eRoom's server (documentum.com).

In addition, protocols are required to create a truly collaborative environment. Protocols are needed to integrate different applications and for standardizing communication. One such protocol is WebDAV (Web Distributed Authoring and Versioning protocol; see webdav.org).

Finally, note that online collaboration is not a panacea for all occasions or all situations. Oftentimes, a face-to-face meeting is a must. People sometimes require the facial cues and the physical closeness that no computer system can currently provide. (A technology called *pervasive computing* attempts to remove some of these limitations by interpreting facial cues. For more, see Chapter 9.) However, face-to-face meetings may sometimes be improved by collaborative technologies, such as GDSS, described earlier.

Section 7.8 ▶ REVIEW QUESTIONS

1. Define workflow systems and management.
2. Explain the types of workflow systems and the benefits of such systems.
3. List the major groupware tools.
4. Describe GDSSs and electronic meeting systems.
5. Describe the various types of electronic teleconferencing, including Web-based conferencing.
6. Describe whiteboards and screen sharing.
7. Describe integrated suites and their benefits.

MANAGERIAL ISSUES

Some managerial issues related to this chapter are as follows.

1. **How difficult is it to introduce e-collaboration?** Dealing with the technology may be the easy part. Tackling the behavioral changes needed within an organization and its trading partners may be the greater challenge. Change management requires an understanding of the new interdependencies being constructed and the new roles and responsibilities that must be adapted in order for the enterprise and its business partners to collaborate. Finally, e-collaboration costs money and needs to be justified. This may not be an easy task due to the intangible benefits involved.

2. **How much can be shared with business partners? Can they be trusted?** Many companies are sharing forecast data and actual sales data. But when it comes to allowing real-time access to product design, inventory, and ERP systems, there may be some hesitation. It is basically a question of trust. The more information that is shared, the better the collaboration. However, sharing information can lead to the giving away of trade secrets. In some cases, there is a cultural resistance against sharing (some employees do not like to share information even within their own organization). The value of sharing needs to be carefully assessed against its risks.

3. **Who is in charge of our portal and intranet content?** Because content is created by many individuals, two potential risks exist. First, proprietary corporate information may not be secure enough, so unauthorized people may have access to it. Second, appropriate intranet "netiquette" must be maintained; otherwise unethical or even illegal behavior may develop. Therefore, managing content, including frequent updates, is a must (see Chapter 13).

4. **Who will design the corporate portal?** Corporate portals are the gateways to corporate information and knowledge. Appropriate portal design is a must, not only for easy and efficient navigation but also because portals portray the corporate image to employees and to business partners who are allowed access to it. Design of the corporate portal must be carefully thought out and approved by management.

5. **Should we conduct virtual meetings?** Virtual meetings can save time and money and if properly planned can bring as good or even better results than face-to-face meetings. Although not all meetings can be conducted online, many can. The supporting technology is getting cheaper and better with time.

RESEARCH TOPICS

Here are some suggested topics related to this chapter. For details, references, and additional topics, refer to the Online Appendix A "Current EC Research."

1. **Development of New Methods for Supply Chain Management**
   - The evolution of methods used to supporting SCM
   - Modeling intra- and interorganizational coordination for SCM
   - Collaboration methods for planning, forecasting, PLM, and other SCM topics
   - Appropriate methods for the implementation and use of VMI
   - Design protocols for continuous replenishment
   - Modeling of interorganizational workflow
   - Managing flexibility and agility in interorganizational supply chains
   - Demand chain management for multiple large customers
   - Restructuring the supply chain and related procedures using RFID

2. **Appropriate Design of SCM Systems**
   - Comparative evaluation of SCM solutions
   - Selection of and building a portfolio of SCM solutions
   - Standards for the deployment of CPFR
   - Integration of supply chain components with ERP and other IT systems
   - Using groupware in supply chain coordination and collaboration

- Using workflow to automate intra- and interorganizational SCM operations
- Using multi-agent technology for SCM improvements
- Using Knowledge Management Systems for SCM improvements

3. **Cost-Benefit Analysis of Supply Chain Management**
- Strategic and tactical issues for analyzing the supply chain in e-business
- Costs and benefits of supply chain collaboration for both industries and individual companies
- Real and ideal incentives for firms to share information vertically
- Risk of information sharing and protective measures to take
- Empirical studies of the value of electronic replenishment in supply chain
- Issues and solutions concerning the role of intermediaries in collaborative commerce
- Empirical studies concerning performance assessment of collaborative planning and forecasting

- Use of balanced scorecard for performance evaluation of different supply chain types

4. **Managerial Issues Related to SCM**
- Factors that determine trust building in B2B partnering
- Managing trust and commitment in collaborative supply chain relationships
- Relationship attributes in supply chain partnerships
- How to contract information sharing in demand forecasts
- Factors that impact the evaluation of suppliers and data collection methods
- Studying the behavior of suppliers who have adopted SRM systems
- An analysis of barriers to adoption of SCM
- How to motivate small suppliers to participate in EC-based SCM systems

5. **Other B2B Service Issues**
- Quality metrics of intranet-based services
- Design of corporate portals

SUMMARY

In this chapter, you learned about the following EC issues as they relate to the learning objectives.

1. **The e-supply chain, its characteristics, and its components.** Digitizing and automating the flow of information throughout the supply chain and managing it via the Web results in an entity called the *e-supply chain*. The major parts of the e-supply chain are the upstream (to suppliers), internal (in-house processes), and downstream (to distributors and customers) components. E-supply chain activities include replenishment, procurement, collaborative planning, collaborative design/development, e-logistics, and use of exchanges or supply webs—all of which can be Internet based.

2. **Supply chain problems and their causes.** The major supply chain problems are too large or too small inventories, lack of supplies or products when needed, the need for rush orders, deliveries of wrong materials or to wrong locations, and poor customer service. These problems result from uncertainties in various segments of the chain (e.g., in transportation), from mistrust of partners and a lack of collaboration and information sharing, and from difficulties in forecasting demand (e.g., the bullwhip effect). Also, lack of appropriate logistics infrastructure can result in problems.

3. **Solutions to supply chains problems provided by EC.** EC technologies automate and expedite

order taking, speed order fulfillment, provide for e-payments, properly control inventories, provide for correct forecasting and thus better scheduling, and improve collaboration among supply chain partners. Of special interest is the emerging RFID and RuBee technologies that could revolutionize supply chain management.

4. **RFID Tags and Rubee.** Replacing barcodes with wireless technologies can greatly improve locating items along the supply chain quickly. These technologies have many benefits and few limitations. They will revolutionize supply chain management.

5. **C-commerce: Definitions and types.** Collaborative commerce (c-commerce) refers to a planned use of digital technology by business partners. It includes planning, designing, researching, managing, and servicing various partners and tasks, frequently along the supply chain. Collaborative commerce can be between different pairs of business partners or among many partners participating in a collaborative network.

6. **Collaborative planning and CPFR.** Collaborative planning concentrates on demand forecasting and on resource and activity planning along the supply chain.

Collaborative planning tries to synchronize partners' activities. CPFR is a business strategy that attempts to develop standard protocols and procedures for collaboration. Its goal is to improve demand forecasting by collaborative planning in order to ensure delivery of materials when needed. In addition to forecasting, collaboration in design is facilitated by IT, including groupware. Product lifecycle management (PLM) enables manufacturers to plan and control product-related information.

7. **Integration along the supply chain.** Integration of various applications within companies and between business partners is critical to the success of companies. To simplify integration, one can use special software as well as employ standards such as XML. Web Services is a promising new approach for facilitating integration.

8. **Types and roles of corporate portals.** The major types of corporate portals are those for suppliers, customers, employees, and supervisors. There also are mobile portals (accessed by wireless devices). Functional portals such as knowledge portals and business intelligence portals provide the gateway to specialized knowledge and decision making. Corporate portals provide for easy information access, communication, and collaboration.

9. **Collaborative tools.** Hundreds of different collaboration tools are available. The major groups of tools are workflow and groupware. In addition, specialized tools ranging from group decision support systems (GDSSs) to devices that facilitate product design also are available.

KEY TERMS

Advanced planning and scheduling (APS) systems	336	E-supply chain management (e-SCM)	309	Service-oriented architecture	327
Bullwhip effect	313	Grid computing	327	Supply chain	307
Collaboration hub	325	Group decision support system (GDSS)	348	Supply chain management (SCM)	308
Collaborative commerce (c-commerce)	324	Groupware	347	Teleconferencing	349
Collaborative planning	310	Information portals	343	Vendor-managed inventory (VMI)	328
Collaborative planning, forecasting, and replenishment (CPFR)	334	Mobile portals	343	Video teleconference	350
		Procurement	308	Virtual meetings	348
Collaborative portals	343	Product lifecycle management (PLM)	337	Voice-over-IP (VoIP)	350
Corporate (enterprise) portal	340	Radio frequency identification (RFID)	318	Web Services	339
Data conferencing	350			Workflow	345
E-procurement	310	RuBee	323	Workflow management	345
E-supply chain	308	Screen sharing software	352	Workflow systems	345

QUESTIONS FOR DISCUSSION

1. Define *e-supply chain.* In the light of your definition, discuss the difference between an IT-enabled supply chain and an e-supply chain.

2. Discuss the benefits of e-supply chains.

3. Does a company's supply chain include the activities involving the movement of materials and information within the company? Discuss the difference between a value chain, an extended value chain, and a supply chain.

4. Discuss the relationship between c-commerce and corporate portals.

5. Compare and contrast a commercial portal (such as Yahoo!) with a corporate portal.

6. Describe how the advent of the Internet in the late 1990s has affected supply chain management. Include in your answer the contribution of the Internet to the following aspects and challenges:
   ▶ Globalization
   ▶ Outsourcing, including business process outsourcing
   ▶ Increasingly demanding customers
   ▶ Diminishing product life cycles

7. Discuss the proposition that competition in contemporary business is best described and conceptualized as competition between industry supply chains rather than between individual corporations.

8. Discuss the contribution of Web-enabled ERP systems to effective supply chain management.

9. Discuss the importance of taking a holistic view of supply chain management rather than simply approaching supply chain management from a business-process and IT viewpoint.

10. Discuss the major considerations that must be taken into account when implementing VMI.

11. Discuss the difference between a portal, a marketplace, and an e-hub. Do you think that there are any significant differences?

12. Discuss the difference between a focused application system using the Internet and a portal. Does the word "portal" serve any purpose in describing and explaining the contemporary role of IT in business, given that most application systems do have a focused and coherent objective and do, in most cases, utilize the Internet?

13. Explain the need for groupware to facilitate collaboration.

14. Discuss the need for workflow systems as a companion to e-commerce.

15. Discuss the relationship between portals and intranets at the same organization.

16. It is said that c-commerce signifies a move from a transaction focus to a relationship focus among supply chain members. Discuss.

17. Discuss the need for virtual meetings.

18. Discuss how CPFR can lead to more accurate forecasting and how it can resolve the bullwhip effect.

19. Describe the advantages of RFID over a regular bar code in light of supply chain management.

20. Compare a collaborative hub and a collaborative network.

21. Discuss the reasons why GDSSs have only had moderately limited use in business when meetings are so common and ubiquitous. Further, discuss why, for interspersed or distributed meetings, the major technologies used are simple telephone audioconferencing and videoconferencing rather than the use of GDSS tools for idea generation and the like. Does the IT in GDSSs, in your opinion, get in the way of natural and creative meeting behaviors?

INTERNET EXERCISES

1. Enter **ca.com/products** and register. Take the Clever Path Portal Test Drive. (Flash Player from Macromedia is required.) Then enter **ibm.com** and **bea.com**. Prepare a list of the major products available for building corporate portals.

2. Enter **bea.com**. Find the white papers about corporate portals and their justification. Prepare a report based on your findings.

3. Enter **doublediamondsoftware.com/product_overview. htm**. Identify all potential B2B applications and prepare a report about them.

4. Investigate the status of CPFR. Start at **vics.org/ committees/cpfr**, **google.com**, and **yahoo.com**. Also enter **supply-chain.org** and find information about CPFR. Write a report on the status of CPFR.

5. Enter **mysap.com** and **bea.com** and find the key capabilities of their enterprise portals. List the benefits of using five of the capabilities of portals.

6. Enter **nokia.com**, **mdsi.com**, and **symbolic.com**. Identify the B2E products you find at these sites. Prepare a list of the different products.

7. Enter **i2.com** and review its products. Explain how some of the products facilitate collaboration.

8. Enter **collaborate.com** and read about recent issues related to collaboration. Prepare a report.

9. Enter **kolabora.com** or **mindjet.com**. Find out how collaboration is done. Summarize the benefits of this site to the participants.

10. Enter **vignette.com** or **cybozu.com** and read the company vision for collaborative commerce. Then view the demo. Explain in a report how the company facilitates c-commerce.

11. Enter **lotus.com** and find the collaboration-support products. How do these products support groups?

12. Enter **supplyworks.com** and **worldchain.com**. Examine the functionalities provided for supply chain improvements (the inventory management aspects).

13. Enter **3m.com** and **smarttech.com**. Find information about their whiteboards. Compare the products.

14. Enter **electronicssupplychain.org**, then click "Resources." Find new information on supply chain automation.

15. Enter **epiqtech.com** and find information about products related to this chapter.

TEAM ASSIGNMENTS AND ROLE PLAYING

1. Have each team download a free copy of Groove from **groove.net**. Install the software on the members' PCs and arrange collaborative sessions. What can the free software do for you? What are its limitations?

2. Each team is assigned to an organization. The team members will attempt to identify several supply chains, their components, and the partners involved. Draw the chains and show which parts can be treated as e-supply chain parts.

3. Each team is assigned to a major vendor of corporate portals, such as BEA, TIBCO, IBM, or Oracle. Each team will check the capabilities of the corporate portal tools and try to persuade the class that its product is superior.

4. Each team is assigned to one area of collaborative commerce. The mission is to find recent applications and case studies in that area. Present the findings to the class.

Real-World Case

SYSCO—EXCELLENCE IN SUPPLY CHAIN MANAGEMENT THROUGH BUSINESS PROCESS INNOVATION AND IT

SYSCO is one of North America's leading distribution or food supply companies. It distributes food and related products to restaurants, hospitals and nursing homes, schools and colleges, and hotels. Under "Who We Are," SYSCO's Web site states:

> From the farm to the fork, SYSCO can provide everything to prepare meals away from home. Supported by more than 40,400 employees across North America, SYSCO is helping its customers create healthy, appetite-pleasing menus that will keep their dining patrons returning again and again. (sysco.com/aboutus/aboutus_ whoweare.html accessed December 2006).

In 2005, SYSCO served 390,000 customers, generating revenues of $30 billion. The company works through 100 operating companies and operates in 170 locations in the United States and Canada.

SYSCO is a highly successful company, having been ranked by *Fortune* as the number one wholesaler in the food and grocery industry in the United States. SYSCO's success is partly attributable to its excellence in supply chain management. This, in turn, comes from innovative business process redesign and management and the effective utilization of IT and the Internet. However, in striving for excellence in business processes and IT systems, SYSCO does not marginalize the importance of the contribution of people. Again, quoting from its Web site:

> SYSCO's men and women are the key to our diverse and fast moving business. Their talent coupled with technology has generated a level of innovation that is unsurpassed in food service distribution. (www.sysco.com/aboutus/aboutus_ whoweare.html).

The story of SYSCO's innovative IT-enablement of its supply chain begins in the late 1990s with the advent of the Internet. In those early days of electronic commerce, SYSCO introduced a system that enabled customers to choose products and place orders online. This was followed in 2001 by a partnership with InfoSys Technologies Ltd. of India that focused on increasing the efficiency of SYSCO's distribution activities.

InfoSys recommended introducing regional distribution centers placed strategically between SYSCO's 100 operating companies across the United States and its customers to consolidate distribution activities and increase logistics efficiencies. Together with this new distribution configuration, InfoSys worked with SYSCO to produce highly efficient and effective business processes and new IT systems that led to significant improvements in demand planning and forecasting, order management, inventory management, transportation economics, and warehouse management. Overall, significant improvements in transportation and inventory costs appeared across the entire supply chain.

SYSCO's supply chain innovations continued in 2001 with an agreement with CriticalArc Technologies to link SYSCO's Internet-based order entry system—eSYSCO—to CriticalArc's Web-enabled supply chain system. This was followed in 2003 by work with EFS Networks to improve electronic links between SYSCO and its suppliers and with Liberty IMS to improve the document management aspects of SYSCO's supply chain, particularly the handling and filing of invoices. The Liberty IMS project was particularly important, given that a typical SYSCO distribution point generated between 4,000 and 15,000 invoices per day and 1 million pages of reports per month.

In 2005, SYSCO introduced ChefEx. This system enabled the ordering and distribution of high-quality gourmet products and ingredients to SYSCO's customers. The program was especially valuable to chefs, enabling restaurants to offer more high-quality menu items without stocking the specialist ingredients, and allowing chefs to choose from a large range of gourmet products without having to interact with a formidable number of suppliers.

Also in 2005, SYSCO supplemented its bar-code technology with RFID technology. The RFID technology system was designed to SYSCO's cold chain (i.e., that part of its supply chain that is used for foods and perishable products that are stored and distributed at a defined temperature range, usually from 2°C to 8°C). The system helped SYSCO ensure product quality and reduce losses from spoilage.

Looking to the future, SYSCO continues to look for innovation, particularly technology innovation in its supply chain. However, the company takes a holistic view of its performance, using a "scorecard" approach, with important metrics in the areas of customer care, operations, finance, and human resources.

Sources: Compiled from Lambert (2006) and Tejomoortula and Fernando (2006), *www.sysco.com* (accessed January 2007).

Questions

1. What was the purpose of SYSCO's ChefEx system? What were the benefits of this system?

2. What was the objective of SYSCO's RFID system? What were the benefits of this system?

REFERENCES

Amato-McCoy, D. "Michael Foods Dishes out Superior Service with Business Integration Solution." *Stores*, February 2004.

Austin, T., N. Drakos, and J. Mann. "Web Conferencing Amplifies Dysfunctional Meeting Practices." *Gartner Research*, ID Number: G00138101, March 13, 2006.

Bacheldor, B. "Harmon Hospital Implements RFID to Track Assets." *RFID Journal*, December 22, 2006a. **rfidjournal.com/article/articleprint/2933/-1/1/** (accessed December 2006).

Bacheldor, B. "CHEP RFID-Enables Reusable Containers for Auto Industry." *RFID Journal*, December 1, 2006b. **rfidjournal.com/article/articleprint/2859/-1/1/** (accessed December 2006).

Bacheldor, B. "Gentag Foresees Cell Phones as Thermometers, Glucose Readers." *RFID Journal*, December 19, 2006c. **rfidjournal.com/article/articleprint/ 2910/-1/1/** (accessed December 2006).

Bacheldor, B. "Nokia Uses RFID-Enabled Phones to Police Its Security Guards." *RFID Journal*, December 18, 2006d. **rfidjournal.com/article/articleprint/2904/-1/1/** (accessed December 2006).

Bazzoli, F. "Report: Few RHIOs Are Up, Despite All the Talk." *Health Care IT News*, April 2006. **healthcareitnews.com/printStory.cms?id=4776** (accessed October 2006).

BEA Systems. "State of the Portal Market 2006: Portals and the New Wisdom of the Enterprise." 2006. **contact2.bea.com/bea/www/pswp/alsom_wp.jsp?PC =40TU2GXXWPBEm** (accessed January 2007).

Bendoly, E., A. Soni, and M. A. Venkatraman. "Value Chain Resource Planning: Adding Value with Systems beyond the Enterprise." *Business Horizons* 49, no. 2 (2004), pp. 79–86.

Blanchard, D. *Supply Chain Management Best Practices*. New York: John Wiley and Sons, 2006.

Blickstein, J. "Internet Telephony: A Sound Move?" *CIO Insight*, July 2004.

Bradley, P. "CPFR Gaining Converts." *Logistics*, April 2002.

Brenchley, D. "Collaboration Made Easy." *Supply Management* 9, no. 14 (2004).

Buxmann, P., et al. *Interorganizational Cooperation with SAP Solutions*. Boston: Springer, 2004.

Carvel, J. "Babies Given Electronic Tags to Beat Abductors." *The Guardian*. **guardian.co.uk/uk_news/ story/0,,1507497,00.html** (accessed December 2006).

Cassivi, L. "Collaboration Planning in a Supply Chain." *Supply Chain Management* 11, no. 3 (2006).

Chaturvedi, R. N., and V. Gupta. "SCM and ERP Software Implementation at Nike—From Failure to Success." *ICFAI Center for Management Research*, Hyderabad, India, 2005, OPER/049.

Chopra, S., and P. Meindl. *Supply Chain Management*, 3rd ed. Upper Saddle River, NJ: Prentice Hall, 2006.

Chow, W. S. "An Exploratory Study of the Success Factors for Extranet Adoption in E-supply Chain." *Journal of Global Information Management*, January–March 2004.

Clarion Group. "Clarion Group: Company Information." 2006. **clarion.com/au/en/company/index.htm** (accessed October 2006).

Craighead, C. W., and N. G. Shaw. "E-Commerce Value Creation and Destruction: A Resource-Based, Supply Chain Perspective." *Data Base*, Spring 2003.

Christopher, M. *Logistics and Supply Chain Management: Creating Value Adding Networks*, 3rd ed. Harlow, Essex, England: Financial Times Prentice Hall, 2005.

Cunningham, M. J. "Getting the Portal Payback." *e-Business Advisor*, March 2002.

Cybex International. **cybexintl.com** (accessed January 2007).

Datta, M. "Nike—Failure in Demand Forecasting." *ICFAI Center for Management Research*, Hyderabad, India, 2005, CLSCM004.

Davenport, T. H., and J. D. Brooks. "Enterprise Systems and the Supply Chain." *Enterprise Information Management* 17, no. 1 (2004).

Davies, C. "Game Shows It's Professionals Who Cause the Bullwhip Effect." *Supply Chain Europe* 13, no. 4 (2004).

Divitini, M., B. A. Farshchian, and H. Samset. "Mobile Computing and Applications (MCA): Collaboration Support for Mobile Users." *Proceedings of the 2004 ACM Symposium on Applied Computing*, Nicosia, Cyprus, March 14–17, 2004.

DM Review. "Top Priorities in Deploying Portal Software: Delphi Group." *DM Direct Special Report*, July 8, 2003. **dmreview.com/article_sub.cfm?articleId=7068** (accessed January 2007).

Ferdows, K., M. A. Lewis, and J. A. D. Machuca. "Zara's Secret for Fast Fashion." *Harvard Business School Working Knowledge for Business Leaders*, February 21, 2005, **hbswk.hbs.edu/archive/4652.html** (accessed December 2006).

Ferguson, M. "Corporate and E-Business Portals." *myITadviser*, April 2001.

Fiala, P. "Information Sharing in Supply Chains." *Omega* 33, no. 5 (2005), pp. 419–423.

Finin, T. "RuBee as RFID 2.0?" December 29, 2006. **ebiquity.umbc.edu/blogger/2006/06/15/rubee-as-rfid-20/** (accessed December 2006).

Finley, F., and S. Srikanth. "Seven Imperatives for Successful Collaboration." *Supply Chain Management Review* 9, no. 1 (2005).

Fisher, M. "What Is the Right Supply Chain for Your Products?" *Harvard Business Review* 75, no. 2 (1997), pp. 105–116.

Fischer, L. *Workflow Handbook 2002*. Lighthouse Point, FL: Future Strategies, Inc., 2002.

Frank, M. "Industry Showcase: LANSA Delivers e-Collaboration on Demand." *LANSA*, February 2004. **lansa.com/casestudies/ecollaboration.htm** (accessed January 2007).

Gibson-Paul, L. "Suspicious Minds." *CIO Magazine*, January 15, 2003.

Gregory, A. "How Best to Deal with the Unexpected?" *Works Management* 57, no. 6 (2004).

Handfield, R. B., and E. L. Nichols, Jr. *Supply Chain Management Redesign*. Upper Saddle River, NJ: Prentice Hall, 2002.

Heinrich, C. *RFID and Beyond*. Indianapolis, IN: Wiley Publishing Inc., 2005.

Henrie, K. S. "All Together Now." *CIO Insight*, July 2004.

Hillman, M. "Strategies for Managing Supply Chain Risk." *Supply Chain Management Review* 10, no. 5 (2006).

HP. **hp.com/support/jornada** (accessed January 2007).

IBM. "Product Lifecycle Management." **ibm.com/solutions/plm/** (accessed January 2007).

IBM. "Toysolution.com Pioneers Collaborative Commerce on Lotus Domino Infrastructure." 2006a. **www-8.ibm.com/hk/software/case_studies/lotus/toysolution1.html** (accessed October 2006).

IBM. "Clarion Malaysia Reduces Design Time by 50 Percent with CATIA V5." 2006b. **www-306.ibm.com/software/success/cssdb.nsf/CS/SDUY-6FCDCX?OpenDocument&Site=default** (accessed October 2006).

Indu, P., and V. Gupta. "Zara's Supply Chain Management Practices." *ICFAI Center for Management Research*, Hyderabad, India, OPER/055, 2006.

Industry Directions. "The Next Wave of Supply Chain Advantage: CPFR." White paper, April 2000. **industrydirections.com/pdf/CPFRPublicReport.pdf** (accessed January 2007).

Ireland, R., and R. Bruce. "CPFR: Only the Beginning of Collaboration." *Supply Chain Management Review*, September–October 2000.

Ireland, R. K., and C. Crum. *Supply Chain Collaboration: How to Implement CPFR and Other Best Collaborative Processes*. Boca Raton, FL: J. Ross Publishing, 2005.

Jeston, J., and J. Nelis. *Business Process Management: Practical Guides to Successful Implementation*. Burlington, MA: Butterworth-Heinemann, 2006.

Johnson, J. R. "Coming to a Store Near You." *DC Velocity*, August 2006a.

Johnson, J. R. "The Death Knell for RFID?" *DC Velocity*, June 21, 2006b. **dcvelocity.com/articles/rfidww/rfidww20060621/rfid_rubee.cfm** (accessed December 2006b).

Kesner, R. M. "Building a Knowledge Portal: A Case Study in Web-Enabled Collaboration." *Information Strategy: The Executive Journal*, Winter 2003.

Khosrow-Pour, M. (ed.). *Encyclopedia of E-Commerce, E-Government, and Mobile Commerce*, Hershey, PA: Idea Group Reference, 2006.

Kidman, A. "Dreamliner Sets SOA in Flight for Boeing." *Zdnet News*, July 12, 2006. **zdnet.com.au/news/software/soa/Dreamliner_sets_SOA_in_flight_for_Boeing/0,130061733,139263107,00.htm** (accessed January 2007).

Koch, C. "Nike Rebounds: How (and Why) Nike Recovered from Its Supply Chain Disaster." *CIO Magazine*, June 15, 2004. **cio.com/archive/061504/nike.html** (accessed January 2007).

Konicki, S. "The New Desktop: Powerful Portals." *InformationWeek*, May 1, 2001. **informationweek.com/784/portal.htm** (accessed January 2007).

Kotabe, M., and M. J. Mol. *Global Supply Chain Management*. North Hampton, MA: Edward Elgar Publishing, 2006.

Kounadis, T. "How to Pick the Best Portal." *e-Business Advisor*, August 2000.

Kourpas, E. "Grid Computing: Past, Present, and Future. An Innovation Perspective." IBM, June 2006. **www-1.ibm. com/grid/pdf/innovperspective.pdf** (accessed October 2006).

Kumar, M. V., and V. Gupta. "The Making of Boeing's 787 'Dreamliner.'" *ICFAI Center for Management Research*, Hyderabad, India, 2006, OPER/053.

Lambert, E. "SYSCO." *Forbes*, January 9, 2006.

Lee, H., and L. Denend. "West Marine: Driving Growth through Shipshape Supply Chain Management." *Stanford Graduate School of Business*, Case GS-34 (2005).

Lee, H., and G. Michlin. "Netafim: Migrating From Products to Solutions." *Stanford Graduate School of Business*, Case GS-46, February 2006.

LeightonsOpticians.com. "Leightons History." **leightonsopticians. com/aboutleightons.htm** (accessed October 2006).

Leonard, L. N. K., and C. C. Davis. "Supply Chain Replenishment: Before and After EDI Implementation." *Supply Chain Management* 11, no. 3 (2006).

Line56.com. "Procurement and Buy-Side." **line56.com/ topics/whatis.asp?TopicID-1** (accessed October 2006).

Loebbecke, C. "RIFD in the Retail Supply Chain," in Khosrow-Pour (2006).

Microsoft.com. "Italian Postal Provider Modernizes Document Workflow and Improves Efficiency and Compliance Using the 2007 Microsoft Office System." 2006a **microsoft.com/casestudies/casestudy.aspx? casestudyid=1000003951** (accessed January 2007).

Microsoft.com. "New Research Reveals Collaboration is a Key Driver of Business Performance Around the World." 2006b. **microsoft.com/presspass/press/2006/ jun06/06-05VerizonBusinessCollaborationPR.mspx** (accessed January 2007).

Moody, P. "With Supply Chain Management, Technology Rules!" *Supply Chain Management Review* 10, no. 4 (2006).

NerveWire. "Collaborative Commerce: Compelling Benefits, Significant Obstacles." 2002. **xml.coverpages.org/ Nervewire200210.pdf** (accessed December 2006).

Norris, G., et al. *E-Business and ERP: Transforming the Enterprise*. New York: McGraw-Hill, 2000.

Nunamaker, Briggs, R., Mittleman, D., Vogel, D., and Balthazard, P. "Lessons from a Dozen Years of Group Support Systems Research: A Discussion of Lab and Field Findings." *Journal of Management Information Systems*, 13, no. 3, 163–207.

O'Connor, M. C. "Wal-Mart Seeks UHF for Item-Level." *RFID Journal*, March 30, 2006a. **rfidjournal.com/ article/articleprint/2228/-1/1/** (accessed December 2006).

O'Connor, M. C. "Visible Assets Promotes RuBee Tags for Tough-to-Track Goods." *RFID Journal*, June 19, 2006b. **rfidjournal.com/article/articleprint/2436/-1/1** (accessed December 2006).

O'Connor, M. C. "Philly Cabs Taking RFID Payments on the Road." *RFID Journal*, November 29, 2006c.

rfidjournal.com/article/articleprint/2852/-1/1 (accessed December 2006).

Plumtree. "A Framework for Assessing Return on Investment for a Corporate Portal Deployment: The Industry's First Comprehensive Overview of Corporate Portal ROI." *Plumtree.com*, April 2002. **plumtree.com/webforms/ MoreInfo_FormActionTemplate.asp** (no longer available online).

Polycom. "Microsoft and Polycom Form Strategic Alliance to Deliver Rich Collaboration Solutions." 2004. **polycom.com/investor_relations/1,,pw-180-7992,00.html** (accessed January 2007).

Premkumar, G., V. J. Richardson, and R. W. Zmud. "Sustaining Competitive Advantage Through a Value Net: The Case of Enterprise Rent-A-Car." *MIS Quarterly Executive* 3, no. 4 (2004).

Reda, S. "New Systems Foster Interaction with Store Employees." *Stores*, February 2002.

Reda, S. "The Path to RFID." *Stores*, June 2003.

Regan, K. "Manufacturing in Action: Redback Networks." *The Manufacturer US*, October 2006. **themanufacturer.com/ us/detail.html?contents_id=4600&PHPSESSID= fd527f2956c982d428b907f96674ddfe** (accessed January 2007).

RFID Gazette. "RFID Used on Boeing's 787 Dreamliner." April 4, 2006. **rfidgazette.org/2006/04/rfid_used_ on_bo.html** (accessed January 2007).

RFID Journal. "Starbucks Keep Fresh with RFID." *RFID Journal*, December 13 2006. **rfidjournal.com/ article/articleprint/2890/-1/1/** (accessed December 2006).

RFID Solutions Online. "Active RFID Tag: AeroScout Enhances Industry's Leading Wi-Fi Based Active RFID Tag." September 6, 2006. **rfidsolutionsonline.com/ copntent/news/article.asp?docid=0fe8355e-e145-4fec-89f7-4f20536e43c3&atc~c=771+s=773+r=001+1= a&VNETCOOKIE=NO** (accessed December 2006).

RFID Update. "New RFID Standard Groups at EPCglobal." May 9, 2006. **rfidupdate.com/articles/ index.php?id=1113** (accessed December 2006).

Richardson, H. L. "The Ins & Outs of VMI." *Logistics Today* 45, no. 3 (2004).

Roberti, M. "A 5-Cent Breakthrough." *RFID Journal*, May 1, 2006. **rfidjournal.com/article/articleprint/2295/-1/2** (accessed October 2006).

Schneider, M. "Samsung's Partner Portal Delivers a 30 percent Sales Increase." *CRM Magazine*, May 2004.

Schrage, M. "Now You See It, Now You Don't." *CIO*, March 15, 2004.

Schram, P. *Collaborative Commerce: Going Private to Get Results*. New York: Deloitte Consulting. **dc.com** (accessed June 2004).

Schuman, E. "RuBee Offers Alternative to RFID." *Eweek*, June 9, 2006a. **eweek.com/article2/0,1895,1974931,00. asp** (accessed December 2006).

Schuman, E. "RuBee May Be Savior for Frustrated RFID Proponents." *Eweek*, June 10, 2006b. **eweek.com/**

article2/0,1895,1975003,00.asp (accessed December 2006).

Schuman, E. "Ready for RFID Gen3?" *Storefront Backtalk*, June 28, 2006c. **storefrontbacktoalk.com/story/062806Gen3.php** (accessed December 2006).

Schurman, K. "White Paper: RuBee Adding Flexibility to the RFID Market." *Computer Power User* 6, no. 9 (2006). **computerpoweruser.com/editorial/article.asp?article=articles/archive/c0609/29c09/29c09.asp&guid=668DE17F72E44FC4A135532323F722A0** (accessed December 2006).

Seideman, T. "QVC.com and Costco.com Talk to Business Partners in the Same Language." *Stores*, February 2004.

Siau, K., and Y. Tian. "Supply Chains Integration: Architecture and Enabling Technologies." *Journal of Computer Information Systems*, Spring 2004.

Singh, N., K.-H. Lai, and T. C. E. Cheng. "Intra-Organization Perspectives of IT-Enabled Supply Chains." *Communications of the ACM*, January 2007. **skype.com** (accessed January 2007).

Smart Technologies. "SMART Launches Rear Projection SMART 4000i Interactive Whiteboard." December 6, 2006. **smarttech.com/st/en-US/About+Us/News+Room/Media+Releases/2006+Media+Releases.htm?guid={3B0B3A41-C752-4085-998E-3E9EFB3FAC43** (accessed January 2007).

Smith, L. "West Marine: A CPFR Success Story." *Supply Chain Management Review* 10, no. 2 (2006).

Smith, M. A. "Portals: Toward an Application Framework for Interoperability." *Communications of the ACM*, October 2004.

SoftNet. "Lotus Domino Workflow." **softnet.ro/product.domino_apps.Dom_Work.jsp** (accessed January 2007).

Staff. "AS2 Is A-OK at Wal-Mart." *Chain Store Age* 80, no. 2 (2004a).

Staff. "Canadian Firm to Debut New Workflow Management System." *Operations Management* (2004b).

Stevenson, W. *Operations Management*, 8th ed. New York: McGraw-Hill, 2004.

Sturdevant, C. "How to Make the Move to IP Telephony." *CIO Insight*, Special Report, July 2004.

Sullivan, L. "Metro Moves Tagging Up the Supply Chain." *RFID Journal*, December 6, 2006. **rfidjournal.com/**

article/articleprint/2873/-1/1/ (accessed December 2006).

Supply and Demand Chain Executive. "Exostar Marks One Year Enabling Boeing's 787 Supply Chain." December 19, 2006. **sdcexec.com/online/article.jsp?id=9020&siteSection=29** (accessed January 2007).

SupplyChainConnect.com. "Leightons Opticians Sees the Business Case for Electronic Ordering in the UK Optical Industry." February 10, 2005. **supplychainconnect.com/pdfs/Leightons.pdf** (accessed October 2006).

SupplyChainManagement101.com. Info Guide to Supply Chain Management Software. **supplychainmanagement101.com/?gg=us&kw=supply%20chain&gclid=CL6i5MqI3ocCFSMhYQodWX8Bog** (accessed January 2007).

Taylor, D. H., and A. Fearne. "Towards a Framework for Improvement in the Management of Demand in Agri-Food Supply Chains." *Supply Chain Management: An International Journal* 11, no. 5 (2006).

Tejomoortula, S., and R. Fernando. "SYSCO's Supply Chain Management Practices." *ICFAI Center for Management Research*, Hyderabad, India, 2006, OPER/060.

TenLinks.com. "Boeing 787 Dreamliner Uses DELMIA, CATIA and ENOVIA." December 12, 2006. **tenlinks.com/NEWS/PR/DASSAULT/121206_boeing.htm** (accessed January 2007).

ThomasNet Industrial Newsroom. "Reynolds and Reynolds Introduces New Parts Barcoding Inventory Management Solution." 2006. **news.thomsnet.com/priontready.html?prid800331** (accessed October 2006).

Torode, C. "Kronos Plans Web-based Workflow Management." *Mass High Tech* 22, no. 35 (2004).

ToySolution.com. **toysolution.com** (accessed December 2006).

van der Aalst, W., and van Hee, K. *Workflow Management: Models, Methods and Systems.* Boston: MIT Press, 2004.

Vics.org. "CPFR Committee." 2006. **vics.org/committees/cpfr/2006** (accessed September 2006).

Wessel, R. "Environmental Concerns Lead Deutsche Post to RFID." *RFID Journal*, December 20, 2006. **rfidjournal.com/article/articleprint/2912/-1/1/** (accessed December 2006).

CHAPTER 8

INNOVATIVE EC SYSTEMS: FROM E-GOVERNMENT AND E-LEARNING TO CONSUMER-TO-CONSUMER COMMERCE

Content

Dresdner Kleinwort Wasserstein Uses Wiki for Collaboration and Information Dissemination

8.1   E-Government: An Overview

8.2   Implementing E-Government

8.3   E-Learning

8.4   Online Publishing and E-Books

8.5   Blogs and Wikis

8.6   Knowledge Management and E-Commerce

8.7   Customer-to-Customer E-Commerce

8.8   Peer-to-Peer Networks and Applications

Managerial Issues

Real-World Case: A Decade of E-Government Development in Hong Kong (1998–2007)

Learning Objectives

Upon completion of this chapter, you will be able to:

1. Describe various e-government initiatives.
2. Describe e-learning, virtual universities, and e-training.
3. Describe online publishing and e-books.
4. Discuss wikis and blogging.
5. Describe knowledge management and dissemination as an e-business.
6. Describe C2C activities.
7. Describe peer-to-peer networks and applications.

DRESDNER KLEINWORT WASSERSTEIN USES WIKI FOR COLLABORATION AND INFORMATION DISSEMINATION

Dresdner Kleinwort Wasserstein (DrKW) is the global investment banking arm of Dresdner Bank. Based in Europe, DrKW provides a range of capital markets and advisory services and employs approximately 6,000 people worldwide.

The Problem

Because of the large number of employees, their geographic distribution, and the diversity of cultures, it became necessary to provide computerized tools to support communication and collaboration in the company. However, providing e-mail and telephones proved to be insufficient. People wanted a diversity of tools—from e-mail to instant messenger, chat, and audio/videoconferencing—so that they could move between them, depending on which was most appropriate for a given situation. However, these tools were insufficient, and newer tools, such as blogs and wikis, were tempting.

The Solution

A *wiki* is a collaborative Web site whose content can be edited by anyone who has access to it. DrKW installed a primitive wiki in 1997, but it was not good enough. This first wiki was static and used only by IT people. The company needed a wiki that would be available to the rest of the business people for better communication and collaboration. The company reviewed SocialText wikis in March 2004 and ran a small pilot on the hosted service in July 2004. Based on the pilot, DrKW decided to upgrade to SocialText Enterprise, a comprehensive wiki-based system that was installed in the third quarter of 2004.

DrKW chose SocialText because the company was willing to work with DrKW on improving authentication, permissions, and sharing of information and communication among silos and understood the necessity for information to flow across multiple forms of communications. Because DrKW is highly regulated, everything must be able to be recorded, archived, searched, and retrieved.

The Results

The Information Strategy team was the first group to use the wiki on a hosted basis. Because the team's work needed a structured environment and skills were geographically dispersed, the SocialText workspace featured many individual-level publication and collaboration capabilities. The team uses the wiki as a communications tool, as a collective discussion tool, and as a storehouse for documents and information.

The User-Centered Design (UCD) team incorporated usability into external-facing applications used across all business lines. The wiki enables team members to upload information more easily, which encourages collaboration and transparency, and makes it simple to share ideas through e-mail conversations. UCD also uses the wiki to help explain what "user-centered design" is and why it is important to the wider DrKW community as a tool for sharing presentations, documents, and reports.

One of the most important of the wiki's roles is to track project development so that the team and management know what progress is being made regardless of individual geographical locations. It also enables the team to track what each team member is doing, the status of each project, and what actions should be taken.

By 2004, the Equity Delta 1 equity financing team was one of the largest users of the wiki. This unit deals with loans, equity swaps, and so on. It uses the wiki workspace to reduce the amount of e-mail, to view the development of business plans, and to store commonly used information. The team also has created an open forum where anyone can post views, comments, and questions on given subjects; publish and share white papers and bulletins; coordinate sales and marketing activities; and organize important team tasks.

The E-Capital London Team develops back-end applications for the Digital Markets business line and supports a number of legacy systems. It uses SocialText to share and develop new system specifications, product overviews, and help with documentation. The wiki provides an instantly editable collaboration platform that simplifies the publication process. The version history function is useful for product specs where it is important to retain a complete audit trail.

SocialText also enables individuals to edit the intranet quickly and easily. It also has been used to help build an internal glossary that defines the company's "jargon." The Wikipedia-style usage cuts down the training time and costs of new hires because it helps them to understand internal and external jargon and terms with less difficulty. It also simplifies the roles of people writing in other locations and languages. Eventually, the wiki will be used for informal training, which will encourage its use.

Sources: Compiled from SocialText (2004), *BusinessWeek* Online (2005), and from *socialtext.com* (accessed February 2007).

WHAT WE CAN LEARN . . .

A wiki is a Web page that can be edited by anyone with a standard Web browser. As such, individuals use it to publish content and share it with others. The technology enabled DrKW to improve communication and collaboration. Online publishing is one of the innovative topics discussed in this chapter that is used in e-business. It is related to some of the other topics presented in this chapter, such as e-government, e-learning, online publishing, blogs and wikis, knowledge management, consumer-to-consumer transactions, and peer-to-peer interactions.

8.1 E-GOVERNMENT: AN OVERVIEW

Electronic government, or e-government, is a growing e-commerce application that encompasses many topics (see U.S. Government 2003; Lee et al. 2005). This section presents the major e-government topics.

DEFINITION AND SCOPE

As e-commerce matures and its tools and applications improve, greater attention is being given to its use to improve the business of public institutions and governments (country, state, county, city, etc.). **E-government** is the use of information technology in general, and e-commerce in particular, to provide citizens and organizations with more convenient access to government information and services and to provide delivery of public services to citizens, business partners, and those working in the public sector. It also is an efficient and effective way of conducting government business transactions with citizens and businesses and within governments themselves. See Scholl (2006) and Marchioni et al. (2003) for details.

In the United States, the use of e-government by the federal government was driven by the 1998 Government Paperwork Elimination Act and by former President Clinton's December 17, 1999, Memorandum on E-Government, which ordered the top 500 forms used by citizens (such as tax forms) to be placed online by December 2000. The memorandum also directed agencies to construct a secure e-government infrastructure. Other drivers of e-government, according to Miller (2000), are increased computing power, the reduced cost of computing, the increased number of businesses and individuals on the Internet, and the need to make governments more efficient.

In this book, the term *e-government* will be used in its broader context—the bringing together of governments, citizens, and businesses in a network of information, knowledge, and commerce. In this broader view, e-government is both the advent of a new form of government and the birth of a new marketplace. It offers an opportunity to improve the efficiency and effectiveness of the functions of government and to make governments more transparent to citizens and businesses by providing access to more of the information generated by government, as well as facilitating transactions with and within governments.

Several major categories fit within this broad definition of e-government: government-to-citizens (G2C), government-to-business (G2B), government-to-government (G2G), Internal Efficiency and Effectiveness (IEE), and government-to-employees (G2E). The performance objectives of the first four categories are provided in Exhibit 8.1. For a comprehensive listing of e-government resources, tutorials, and more, see egov.gov. For a description of the range of e-government activities in the United States, see Moon (2004), U.S. Government (2003), and whitehouse.gov/egov/index.html.

e-government
E-commerce model in which a government entity buys or provides goods, services, or information to businesses or individual citizens.

GOVERNMENT-TO-CITIZENS

The **government-to-citizens (G2C)** category includes all of the interactions between a government and its citizens that can take place electronically. See U.S. Government (2003), Abramson and Means (2001), or Siau and Long (2006) for an overview of G2C. As described in the Real-World Case about Hong Kong at the end of the chapter, G2C can involve dozens of different initiatives. The basic idea is to enable citizens to interact with the government from their homes. G2C applications enable citizens to ask questions of government agencies and receive answers, pay taxes, receive payments and documents, and so forth. For example, citizens can renew driver's licenses, pay traffic tickets, and make appointments for vehicle emission inspections and driving tests. Governments also can disseminate information on the Web, conduct training, help citizens find employment, and more. In California, for example, drivers' education classes are offered online and can be taken anytime, anywhere.

Government services to citizens are provided via citizen portals. The services will vary depending on the country, on the level (city, county, country), and on the level of users' skills in using computers. An example of representative services in municipalities in Denmark is provided in Exhibit 8.2 (p. 367).

According to *Emarketer* (2002), the major features of government Web sites are phone and address information (96 percent), links to other sites (71 percent), publications (93 percent),

government-to-citizens (G2C)
E-government category that includes all the interactions between a government and its citizens.

EXHIBIT 8.1 Categories of E-Government Performance Objectives

G2C	G2B
Create easy-to-find single points of access to government services for individuals	Increase the ability for citizens and businesses to find, view, and comment on rules and regulations
Reduce the average time for citizens to find benefits and determine eligibility	Reduce burden on business by enabling online tax filing
Reduce the number of clicks to access relevant loan information	Reduce the time to fill out export forms and locate information
Increase the number of citizens who use the Internet to find information on recreational opportunities	Reduce time for businesses to file and comply with regulations
Meet the high public demand for information	Make transactions with the government easier, cheaper, quicker, and more comprehensible
Improve the value of government to citizen	
Expand access to information for people with disabilities	
Make obtaining financial assistance from the government easier, cheaper, quicker, and more comprehensible	

G2G	IEE
Decrease response times for jurisdictions and disciplines to respond to emergency incidents	Increase availability of training programs for government employees
Reduce the time to verify birth and death entitlement information	Reduce the average time to process clearance forms
Increase the number of grant programs available for electronic application	Increase use of e-travel services within each agency
Share information more quickly and conveniently between the federal and state, local, and tribal governments	Reduce the time for citizens to search for federal jobs
Improve collaborations with foreign partners, including governments and institutions	Reduce time and overhead cost to purchase goods and services throughout the federal government
Automate internal processes to reduce costs within the federal government by disseminating best practices across agencies	
Plan IT investments more effectively	
Secure greater services at a lower cost	
Cut government operating costs	

Sources: U.S. Government (2003), Lee et al. (2005), and Hyperion (2007).

and databases (57 percent). The major areas of G2C activities are tourism and recreation (77 percent), research and education (70 percent), downloadable forms (63 percent), discovery of government services (63 percent), information about public policy (62 percent), and advice about health and safety issues (49 percent).

An interesting recent application is the use of the Internet by politicians, especially during election periods. For example, the French political parties pursued millions of voters in the blogosphere for the 2007 presidential election (see Section 8.5). In the United States, during the 2004 presidential election both major-party candidates sent e-mail messages to potential voters and had comprehensive information portals. In South Korea, politicians log onto the Internet to recruit voters because many people who surf the Internet rarely read newspapers or watch TV. The target audience of these politicians is 20- to 30-year-olds, the vast majority of whom surf the Internet. Pasdaq, the Seoul-based over-the-counter stock exchange, offers an Internet game that simulates the stock market and measures the popularity of some 300 politicians by allowing players to buy "stocks" in a politician. In one year, over 500,000 members signed up. It became a necessity in South Korea for politicians to have a Web site. Involved citizens even make donations over the Internet using credit cards. Some politicians make decisions based on citizens' opinions collected on the Internet.

EXHIBIT 8.2 Sample G2C Municipal Services in Denmark

Service	Description
Your real estate	What information about real estate is stored in your municipality
Government housing eligibility	Self calculate eligibility for government housing; also can apply online
Child care option	What options are available for child care in your municipality; also, child care guides
Facts and statistics	All data available in your municipality of choice
Change of address	Do it yourself and get a receipt online
Pay tax and for services	Pay municipalities tax and for services (e.g., child care)
Calculate social benefits	Calculate social benefits (e.g., for elderly, children, pensions, maternity/paternity leave, sickness benefits for employees
Budget preparation	Calculators for budget preparations for individuals and small businesses
Tax calculations and matters	Calculate tax, get all forms and guides
Real estate information	Statistics, facts, and availability of real estate in Denmark, by municipality
Building guides	How to build on your property in each municipality; how to get permission (forms, guides)
Utility guides	Reports on water and electricity consumption in different cities
Education	How to sign up for a list of children waiting admission to educational institutions
Scholarships for nursery school	Application for scholarship for nursery schools (not provided to everyone)
Real estate appraisers/valuation	The official valuation of any real estate in Denmark

Sources: Compiled from Henriksen (2006), from *dst.dk* (accessed January 2007).

Another area of G2C activity is in solving constituents' problems. The government (or a politician) can use CRM-type software to assign inquiries and problem cases to the appropriate staff member. Workflow CRM software can then be used to track the problem's progress.

Yet another common G2C use is the broadcasting of city council meetings, press conferences, and public addresses. In many municipalities, delivering training and educational courses both to citizens and to employees is a very popular Internet activity. For more on G2C, see Paskaleva-Shapira (2006) and nbc.gov/g2c.cfm.

Electronic Voting

Voting processes inherently are subject to error and also are historically subject to manipulation and fraud. In many countries, there are attempts to "rig" the votes; in others, the losers want to count and recount. Voting may result in major political crises, as happened in the Ukraine in November 2004. Problems with the U.S. 2000 and 2004 presidential elections have accelerated the trend toward electronic voting.

The voting process requires extraordinary integrity (particularly for any computerized systems involved), as well as honesty and experience among the people involved in administering elections. In many countries, elections are observed by experts from other countries. The election process may require considerable sophistication on the part of voters as well.

Voting encompasses a broad spectrum of technological and social problems that must be systematically addressed—from registration and voter authentication to the casting of ballots and subsequent tallying of results. Because of this, **electronic voting** means different things to different people.

Each of the current voting technologies has its own set of vulnerabilities; none are infallible. However, fully electronic voting systems have raised considerable controversy because of a variety of factors, such as the proprietary nature of the software, the weakness of the certification criteria, the inability of black-box testing to provide full assurances of correctness, the general secrecy of the evaluation process, vendor-commissioned evaluations, and the lack of any mechanism whereby independent recounting of the ballots and auditing of the vote totals can be performed. Several of these issues are the subject of a special issue of the *Communications of the ACM* (see Neumann 2004). Also see several papers in Khosrow-Pour (2006).

The first country to use fully computerized balloting was Brazil. In the United States, electronic systems have been in use since 1980 (mainly for counting the results); large-scale implementation of touch-screen systems will probably occur only in 2008. It is interesting to note that several states (e.g., California, Nevada) require that touch-screen machines be able

electronic voting
Voting process that involves many steps ranging from registering, preparing, voting, and counting (voting and counting are all done electronically).

to produce a printed record. A good voting machine should show the voter what he or she has entered and ask for confirmation, much like when purchasing a book online from Amazon.com, transferring funds, or selling stocks.

From a technology point of view, voting machines make electronic fraud simple. Election fraud could easily be carried out by changing a program to count votes for X twice or not to count votes for Y at all. (See DiFranco et al. 2004 and Gibson and Brown 2006.) Therefore, security and auditing measures are key to the success of e-voting (Coggins 2004; Jones 2004; and Jefferson et al. 2004). However, considering the amount of fraud that occurs with traditional, non-e-voting systems and the fact that e-security is improving, e-voting eventually could be the norm. For more information on e-voting, see fcw.com.

Many believe that with the ever-increasing percentage of Internet users who get information about governments and politics online, also known as **Netizens**, the manner in which elections are conducted will change drastically in the not-so-distant future. For further discussion of online voting, and why it may take years to *fully* implement it in the United States, see Neumann (2004) and Jefferson et al. (2004).

Netizen
A citizen surfing the Internet.

Electronic Benefits Transfer

One e-government application that is not new is *electronic benefits transfer* (EBT), which has been available since the early 1990s. The U.S. government, for example, transfers around $1,000 billion in benefits to its citizens annually. In 1993, the U.S. government launched an initiative to develop a nationwide EBT system to deliver government benefits electronically. Initially, the attempt was made to deliver benefits to recipients' bank accounts. However, more than 20 percent of these transfers go to citizens who do not have bank accounts. To solve this problem, the government is initiating the use of smart cards (see Chapter 9). Benefit recipients will be able to load electronic funds onto the cards and use the cards at automated teller machines (ATMs), point-of-sale locations, and grocery and other stores, just like other bank card users do. When the smart card systems are in place, recipients will either get electronic transfers to their bank accounts or be able to download money to their smart cards. The advantage is not only the reduction in processing costs (from about 50 cents per paper check to 2 cents for electronic payment) but also the reduction of fraud. With biometrics (see Chapter 12) coming to smart cards and PCs, officials expect fraud to be reduced substantially.

The smart card system is part of a nationwide EBT system for miscellaneous payments, such as those for Social Security and welfare. Agencies at the federal, state, and local levels are expanding EBT programs into new areas, including health, nutrition, employment, and education. Also, many states operate EBT systems for state-provided benefits. Governments also use smart cards as purchasing media for G2B procurement. For more information on EBT in government, see fns.usda.gov/fsp/ebt/faq.htm.

Politicians to Citizens. Aspiring politicians are using blogs to promote themselves, and many use blogs after getting elected. As of 2006, social networks, especially MySpace, Facebook, and YouTube (see Chapter 18) are being used to reach the voters directly, especially young voters. For example, Keen (2006) reported that facebook.com created 1,400 candidate profiles for the November 2006 U.S. elections. Politicians use social networks not only to promote themselves but also to trash their opponents.

GOVERNMENT-TO-BUSINESS

Governments seek to automate their interactions with businesses. Although we call this category **government-to-business (G2B)**, the relationship works two ways: government-to-business and business-to-government. Thus, G2B refers to e-commerce in which government sells products to businesses or provides them with services as well as to businesses selling products and services to government (see Lee 2005). Two key G2B areas are e-procurement and the auctioning of government surpluses. For other U.S. G2B initiatives, see nbc.gov/g2b.cfm.

government-to-business (G2B)
E-government category that includes interactions between governments and businesses (government selling to businesses and providing them with services and businesses selling products and services to government).

Government E-Procurement

Governments buy large amounts of MROs and other materials directly from suppliers. In many cases, RFQ (or tendering) systems are mandated by law. For years, these tenderings were done manually; the systems are now moving online. These systems employ *reverse auctions*

EC Application
CONTRACT MANAGEMENT IN AUSTRALIA

The focus of the Western Australian (WA) government agency Contract and Management Services (CAMS) is to develop online contract management solutions for the public sector. CAMS Online allows government agencies to search existing contracts to locate commonly used ones. It also assists suppliers that want to sell to the government. Suppliers can view the current tenders (bids) on the Western Australia Government Contracting Information Bulletin Board and download tender documents from the site.

CAMS Online also provides government departments and agencies with unbiased expert advice on e-commerce, Internet, and satellite services as well as on building bridges between the technological needs of the public sector and the expertise of the private sector. The center offers various types of support for government procurement activities.

Support of E-Commerce Activities
WA's e-commerce activities include electronic markets for government purchasing. Government clients can purchase goods and services on the *CAMS Internet Marketplace,* which provides services ranging from sending a purchase order to receiving an invoice and paying for an item. The *WA Government Electronic Market* provides online supplier catalogs, electronic purchase orders, electronic invoicing, EFT, and check and credit card payments. The Victoria government and the New South Wales government in WA are spending over $500 million on e-procurement systems under the Government Electronic Market system.

Other WA e-commerce functions are *ProcureLink*, a CAMS service that sends electronic purchase orders to suppliers via EDI, EDI Post (an online hybrid mail service), fax, and the Internet; *SalesNet*, by which the government secures credit

card payments for the sale of government goods and services across the Internet; and *DataLink,* which enables the transfer of data using a secure environment for message management. DataLink is an ideal solution for government agencies that need to exchange large volumes of operational information.

Online Training
In addition to G2B functions, the site also offers online training to citizens. A service called *Westlink* delivers adult training and educational programs to remote areas and schools, including rural and regional communities. A video-conferencing service offers two-way video and audio links, enabling government employees to meet together electronically from up to eight sites at any one time.

Access to the Online Services Centre is given to government employees and businesses that deal with the government via the CAMS Web site at *doir.wa.gov.au/businessand industry*.

Sources: Compiled from *e-start.sbdc.com.au* (accessed February 2007) and *sbdc.com.au/drilldown/drilldown.asp?refid=7* (accessed February 2007).

Questions
1. How is contract management in WA facilitated by e-commerce tools?
2. What other e-commerce activities does the government perform?
3. Describe the WA online training program.

(buy-side auction systems), such as those described in Chapter 5. An example of a reverse auction used for G2B procurement in Hong Kong is described in the Real-World Case at the end of the chapter and at info.gov.hk. For additional information about such reverse auctions, see gsa.gov. In the United States, for example, the local housing agencies of HUD (Housing and Urban Development), which provides housing to low-income residents, are moving to e-procurement (see Kumar and Peng 2006 and U.S. Department of Housing and Urban Development 2006). Governments provide all the support for such tendering systems, as shown in Case 8.1

Procurement Marketing and Access Network (Small Business Administration) This service (pro-net.sba.gov) presents PRO-Net, a searchable database that contracting officers in various U.S. government units can use to find products and services sold by small, disadvantaged, or women-owned businesses.

Group Purchasing
The U.S. government also uses online group purchasing, which was introduced in Chapters 1 and 5. For example, the eFAST service conducts reverse auctions for aggregated orders (see gsa.gov). Suppliers post group-purchasing offers, and the prices fall as more orders are placed. Alternatively, government buyers may post product requests that other buyers may

review and join in on. Pooled orders are then forwarded to suppliers for reverse auction bidding. Also, government hospitals and public schools actively purchase in groups online.

Forward E-Auctions

Many governments auction equipment surpluses or other goods, ranging from vehicles to foreclosed real estate. Such auctions used to be done manually and then were done electronically over private networks. These auctions are now moving to the Internet. Governments can auction from a government Web site, or they can use third-party auction sites such as ebay.com, bid4assets.com, or governmentauctions.org for this purpose. In January 2001, the U.S. General Services Administration (GSA) launched a property auction site online (auctionrp.com) where real-time auctions for surpluses and seized goods are conducted. Some of these auctions are restricted to dealers; others are open to the public (see governmentauctions.org).

Tax Collection and Management

Every year millions of individuals file tax reports. Similarly, hundreds of thousands of businesses do the same. Businesses in the United States and other countries must file quarterly reports. Electronic filing of taxes is now available in over 100 countries, from Thailand to Finland to the United States. In addition to personal and income taxes, it also is possible to pay online sales taxes and value-added taxes. For a case study of successful online tax implementation in Thailand, see Hopfner (2002).

GOVERNMENT-TO-GOVERNMENT

government-to-government (G2G)
E-government category that includes activities within government units and those between governments.

The **government-to-government (G2G)** category consists of EC activities between units of government, including those within one governmental body. Many of these are aimed at improving the effectiveness or the efficiency of the government. Here are a few examples from the United States:

- **Intelink.** Intelink is an intranet that contains classified information that is shared by the numerous U.S. intelligence agencies.
- **Procurement at GSA.** The GSA's Web site (gsa.gov) uses technologies such as demand aggregation and reverse auctions to buy for various units of the federal government. (See also governmentauctions.org and liquidation.com). The agency seeks to apply innovative Web-based procurement methods to government buying. The site offers many services (see lvanj.org/government/directory.php?offset=0&searchterm= Government%20 Sales%20and%20Auctions).
- **Federal Case Registry (Department of Health and Human Services).** This service helps state governments locate information about child support, including data on paternity and enforcement of child-support obligations. It is available at acf.dhhs.gov/ programs/cse/newhire/fcr/fcr.htm.

For more examples of G2G services, see the Real-World Case at the end of the chapter, govexec.com, and nbc.gov/g2g.cfm. For implementation of G2G, see Joia (2006).

GOVERNMENT-TO-EMPLOYEES AND INTERNAL EFFICIENCY AND EFFECTIVENESS

government-to-employees (G2E)
E-government category that includes activities and services between government units and their employees.

Governments employ large numbers of people. Therefore, governments are just as interested as private-sector organizations are in electronically providing services and information to their employees. Indeed, because employees of federal and state governments often work in a variety of geographic locations, **government-to-employee (G2E)** applications may be especially useful in enabling efficient communication. One example of G2E is the Lifelines service provided by the U.S. government to U.S. Navy employees and their families, described in Case 8.2

CASE 8.2
EC Application
G2E IN THE U.S. NAVY

The U.S. Navy uses G2E to improve the flow of information to sailors and their families. Because long shipboard deployments cause strains on navy families, in 1995 the navy began seeking ways to ensure that quality-of-life information reaches navy personnel and their loved ones all over the world. Examples of quality-of-life information include self-help, deployment support, stress management, parenting advice, and relocation assistance.

Lifelines (*lifelines.navy.mil*) uses the Internet, simulcasting, teleconferencing, cable television, and satellite broadcasting to reach overseas personnel. The navy has found that certain media channels are more appropriate for different types of information. Lifelines regularly features live broadcasts, giving forward-deployed sailors and their families welcome information and, in some cases, a taste of home. On the Web, an average of 5,500 people access the Lifelines portal each day. In 2007, the portal covered dozens of topics ranging from jobs to recreation.

The government provides several other e-services to navy personnel. Notable are online banking, personal finance services, and insurance. Education and training also are provided online. In 2001, the navy started issuing mobile computing devices to sailors while they are deployed at sea. The handheld devices offer both entertainment and information to navy personnel on active duty.

Sources: Compiled from *GovExec.com* (2000), Dean (2000), and *lifelines.navy.mil* (accessed January 2007).

Questions

1. Why is the U.S. Navy using multiple media channels?
2. Compare the G2E services provided by the navy with the employee portal services discussed in Section 7.7.

Internal Efficiency and Effectiveness

These internal initiatives provide tools for improving the effectiveness and efficiency of government operations, and the processes are basically intrabusiness applications implemented in government units. The U.S. Office of Management and Budget (2002) provides the following examples:

- *E-payroll.* Consolidate systems at more than 14 processing centers across government.
- *E-records management.* Establish uniform procedures and standards for agencies in converting paper-based records to electronic files.
- *E-training.* Provide a repository of government-owned courseware.
- *Enterprise case management.* Centralize justice litigation case information.
- *Integrated acquisition.* Agencies share common data elements to enable other agencies to make better informed procurement, logistical, payment, and performance-assessment decisions.
- *Integrated human resources.* Integrate personnel records across government.
- *One-stop recruitment.* Automate federal government information on career opportunities, resume submission and routing, and assessment. Streamline the federal hiring process and provide up-to-the-minute application status for job seekers.

For more on using EC to improve the efficiency and effectiveness of government, see nbc.gov/iee.cfm.

FACILITATING HOMELAND SECURITY

A major responsibility of the government is homeland security. We introduced this topic briefly in Chapter 1. The government is using different electronic and other information technology systems to improve security. For more information on security in e-government, see Wang and Wang (2004). A list of such systems is provided in Online File W8.1.

Section 8.1 ▶ REVIEW QUESTIONS

1. Define *e-government*.
2. What are the four major categories of e-government services?

3. Describe G2C.
4. Describe how EBT works.
5. Describe the two main areas of G2B activities.
6. Describe e-government activities.

8.2 IMPLEMENTING E-GOVERNMENT

Like most other organizations, government entities want to move into the digital era and become click-and-mortar organizations. Therefore, one can find a large number of EC applications in government organizations. For information on the difficulties of implementing e-government, see Chen et al. (2006) and Rowe and Bell (2005). This section examines some of the issues involved in *implementing* e-government. Huang et al. (2006) review many implementation issues and trends in e-government. These are summarized in Exhibit 8.3.

EXHIBIT 8.3	**Key Issues and Trends of E-Government Development and Implementation**	
No.	**Key Issues and Trends**	**References**
1	Although there is a growing body of e-government literature, relatively little of it is empirical. More empirical investigation on e-government development and implementation will be needed in the future.	Norris and Moon (2005)
2	More research on privacy issue in e-government. The Central Intelligence Agency came under public criticism when it was discovered that their Web site used persistent "cookies" to track Web visits, in violation of federal privacy policy.	Stratford (2004)
3	E-government adoption and diffusion in public sector, especially in local governments. Prior study in the U.S. shows that e-government has been penetrating state government much more rapidly than local government. Future research should study the effects of factors such as proper marketing, privacy issues, equity, and financing on full penetration of e-government in the public sector.	Edmiston (2003)
4	Information technology provides some powerful supporting tools for e-government, which may empower government to provide additional and/or new services to the public that otherwise may not be possible. Future studies can look into how to provide new and value-added services through integrated e-government.	Pfaff and Simon (2002)
5	Very little is known about e-government usability issues for older citizens who don't have skills in computer usage or computer access.	Becker (2005)
6	Future research should study the relationship between e-government and e-governance; specifically how one issue influences another in e-government development and implementation.	Marche and McNiven (2003)
7	E-government and accountability. Will e-government lead to a more transparent, interactive, open and hence accountable, government? If not, what should we do to make it happen as e-government strategies are developed?	Wong and Welch (2004)
8	Qualification and training issues in e-government. While e-government has a potential to substantially change the current way the public sector operates and functions, new qualification requirements arise for users, managers, and decision makers in public administration. As a result, effective training programs should be worked out to meet this potentially large demand from the public sector. However, little research has been done in this area.	Kaiser (2004)
9	Risk issues in e-government. While e-government transaction services may offer a potential of increased efficiency and quality with minimum cost in the way the public administration deals with its customers, recent reports show that this is far from reality as e-government projects seem to be failing to deliver. Future study should look into this important issue on identifying key risk factors and how those factors influence the success or failure of e-government projects.	Evangelidis et al. (2004)

THE TRANSFORMATION TO E-GOVERNMENT

The transformation from traditional delivery of government services to full implementation of online government services may be a lengthy process. The business consulting firm Deloitte and Touche conducted a study (see Wong 2000) that identified six stages in the transformation to e-government. These stages are shown in Exhibit 8.4 and described in the following list.

▶ **Stage 1: Information publishing/dissemination.** Individual government departments set up their own Web sites. These provide the public with information about the specific department, the range of services it offers, and contacts for further assistance. In stage 1, governments may establish an electronic brochure, the purpose of which is to reduce the number of phone calls customers need to make to reach the employee who can fulfill their service requests. These online resources also help reduce paperwork and the number of help-line employees needed.

▶ **Stage 2: "Official" two-way transactions with one department at a time.** With the help of legally valid digital signatures and secure Web sites, customers are able to submit personal information to and conduct monetary transactions with single government departments. For example, the local government of Lewisham in the United Kingdom lets citizens claim income support and housing benefits by filing an electronic form and then receiving benefits online. In Singapore, payments to citizens and from citizens to various government agencies can be performed online. In many countries (e.g., United States, United Kingdom, Hong Kong), tax returns are filed online with attached payments, if needed. At this stage, customers must be convinced of the department's ability to keep their information private and free from piracy.

▶ **Stage 3: Multipurpose portals.** At this stage, customer-centric governments make a big breakthrough in service delivery. Based on the fact that customer needs can cut across department boundaries, a portal enables customers to use a single point of entry to send and receive information and to process monetary transactions across multiple departments. For example, in addition to acting as a gateway to its agencies and related governments, the government of South Australia's portal (sa.gov.au) features a "business channel" and a link for citizens to pay bills (utilities, automotive), manage bank accounts, and conduct personal stock brokering. The portal described in the Real-World Case at

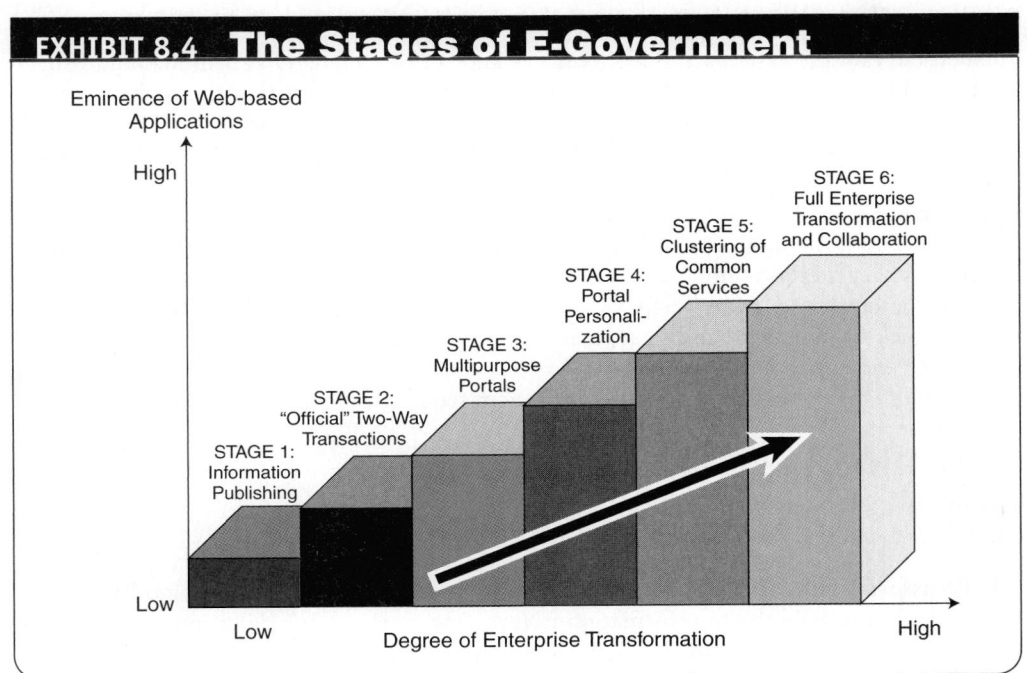

EXHIBIT 8.4 The Stages of E-Government

Eminence of Web-based Applications

STAGE 1: Information Publishing

STAGE 2: "Official" Two-Way Transactions

STAGE 3: Multipurpose Portals

STAGE 4: Portal Personalization

STAGE 5: Clustering of Common Services

STAGE 6: Full Enterprise Transformation and Collaboration

Degree of Enterprise Transformation

Source: Wong, W. Y. *At the Dawn of E-Government.* New York: Deloitte Research, Deloitte & Touche, 2000.

the end of this chapter is such a portal, as are Singapore's portals. See (ecitizen.gov.sg and gov.sg). The design of one-stop e-government sites is explored by Wimmer (2002), who developed a model for integrating multiple services in one location.

▶ **Stage 4: Portal personalization.** Through stage 3, customers can access a variety of services at a single Web site. In stage 4, government puts even more power into customers' hands by allowing them to customize portals with their desired features. To accomplish this, government sites require much more sophisticated Web programming that permits interfaces that can be manipulated by the users. The added benefit of portal personalization is that governments get a more accurate read on customer preferences for electronic versus nonelectronic service options. This allows for true CRM in government. Government use of such portals began in spring 2001. Many state and county governments in the United States (e.g., U.S. Department of Education at **ed.gov** and the Internal Revenue Service at **irs.gov**), Australia, Denmark, United Kingdom, and several other countries have now implemented such portals.

▶ **Stage 5: Clustering of common services.** Stage 5 is where real transformation of government structure takes shape. As customers now view once-disparate services as a unified package through the portal, their perception of departments as distinct entities will begin to blur. They will recognize groups of transactions rather than groups of agencies. To make this happen, governments will cluster services along common lines to accelerate the delivery of shared services. In other words, a business restructuring will take place. Initial stage 5 implementations were started in Australia, Canada, New Zealand, the United Kingdom, and the United States in late 2004.

▶ **Stage 6: Full integration and enterprise transformation.** Stage 6 offers a full-service center, personalized to each customer's needs and preferences. At this stage, old walls defining silos of government services have been torn down, and technology is integrated across the new structure to bridge the shortened gap between the front and back offices. In some countries, new departments will be formed from the remains of predecessors. Others will have the same names, but their interiors will look nothing like they did before the e-government implementation. Full electronic collaboration among government agencies and between governments, citizens, and other partners will occur during this phase, which is in its planning stage. Many countries, such as the United States, Norway, and Sweden, are planning for this stage or are in the early phases of implementation.

Example: Ilan County in Taiwan Promotes Tourism on a Portal

Situated on Taiwan's east coast, Ilan County is known for its quality agricultural and fishery products. The county government launched an online supermarket (agrishop.ilfa.org.tw) to showcase a wide array of products from its 10 township farmers' associations and 2 fishermen's association. Almost 2 million people visit the county's portal each year, mainly to buy agricultural products, generating about $60 million. The portal's objective is to promote the image of Ilan's agricultural produce, boosting the farmers and fishermen's business.

As of 2006, the site offered 150 fresh and processed products, as well as souvenirs. Buyers must register as members. The shoppers pay by credit card or at convenience stores. Most of the buyers are from Taipei (30 minutes driving time) and other large cities where they can pick up the merchandise at their nominated supermarkets. For further details, see Lin (2006) and agrishop.ilfa.org.tw.

For more on e-transformation in government, see Malkia et al. (2004).

IMPLEMENTATION ISSUES OF E-GOVERNMENT

The following implementation issues depend on which of the six stages of development a government is in and on its plan for moving to higher stages.

▶ **Transformation speed.** The speed at which a government moves from stage 1 to stage 6 varies, but usually the transformation is very slow. Some of the determining factors are the degree of resistance to change by government employees, the rate at which citizens adopt the new applications (see the following section), the available budget, and the legal environment.

▶ **G2B implementation.** G2B is easier to implement than G2C. In some countries, such as Hong Kong, G2B implementation is outsourced to a private company that pays all of the startup expenses in exchange for a share of future transaction fees. As G2B services have the potential for rapid cost savings, they can be a good way to begin an e-government initiative.

▶ **Security and privacy issues.** Governments are concerned about maintaining the security and privacy of citizens' data. According to Emarketer (2002), the number of U.S. government Web sites with *security policies* increased from 5 percent in 2000 to 63 percent in 2004. The percentage of those with *privacy policies* increased from 7 percent in 2000 to 43 percent in 2002 and 54 percent in 2003 (West 2004). An area of particular concern is health care. From a medical point of view, it is necessary to have quick access to people's data, and the Internet and smart cards provide such capabilities; however, the protection of such data is very expensive. Deciding on how much security to provide is an important managerial issue. In the United States, the 2002 E-Government Act requires all federal agencies to conduct privacy assessments of all government information systems.

▶ **Wireless applications.** Several wireless applications suitable for e-government will be presented in Chapter 9. Notable are B2E applications, especially for field employees, and B2C information discovery, such as the 511 system described in Online File W1.3 in Chapter 1. Another example is the city of Bergen, Norway, which provides wireless portable tourism services. An interesting wireless application in the city of Manchester (United Kingdom) is provided by Davies et al. (2002). Many more applications are expected in the future.

▶ **Business aspects.** Andersen (2006) points to the strategic management value of such initiatives. The author claims that the transformation of government to act "like business" requires internal analysis from a business point of view.

See Welch and Pandey (2006), Chao and Tong (2005), and Association for Federal Information Resources Management (2002), for additional implementation issues.

CITIZEN ADOPTION OF E-GOVERNMENT

One of the most important issues in implementing e-government is its adoption and usage by citizens. Warkentin et al. (2002) constructed a model that attempts to explore this issue. They believe that the adoption rate depends on many variables. One of the major variables is "trust in e-government," which is itself determined by several variables. Other variables, such as perceived ease of use and perceived usefulness, are generic to EC adoption. Moderating variables, such as culture, also are important.

NON–INTERNET E-GOVERNMENT

Today, e-government is associated with the Internet. However, governments have been using other networks, especially internal ones, to improve government operations for over 20 years. For example, on January 17, 1994, a major earthquake shook Southern California. About 114,000 buildings were damaged, and more than 500,000 victims turned to the Federal Emergency Management Agency (FEMA) for help. Initially, tired and dazed citizens stood hours in lines to register and have in-person interviews. To expedite the process, an e-government application was installed to expedite the issuance of checks to citizens. Citizens called an 800 number, and operators entered the information collected directly into online electronic forms. Then the data traveled electronically to the mobile disaster inspectors. Once checked, data went electronically to financial management and finally to check writing. The dataflow never touched paper, and the cycle time was reduced by more than 50 percent. Another example of non-Internet e-government is auctions conducted over private, secured telecommunication lines. Sooner or later, such non-Internet e-government initiatives will probably be converted to Internet-based ones.

Section 8.2 ▶ REVIEW QUESTIONS

1. List and briefly describe the six stages of e-government development.
2. Describe some e-government implementation issues.
3. Provide an example of a non-Internet e-government service.

8.3 E-LEARNING

The topic of e-learning is gaining much attention, especially because world-class universities such as MIT, Harvard, and Stanford in the United States and Oxford in the United Kingdom are implementing it. Exhibit 8.5 shows the forces that are driving the transition from traditional education to online learning in the academic setting. E-learning also is growing as a method for training and information delivery in the business world and is becoming a major e-business activity. In this section, we will discuss several topics related to e-learning.

THE BASICS OF E-LEARNING: DEFINITIONS AND CONCEPTS

e-learning

The online delivery of information for purposes of education, training, or knowledge management.

E-learning is the online delivery of information for purposes of education, training, or knowledge management. (See Aldrich 2006 and elearnmag.org.) It is a Web-enabled system that makes knowledge accessible to those who need it, when they need it, anytime, anywhere.

According to Wikipedia (2007), e-learning can refer to any method of computer-enhanced learning. This could be as simple a meaning as an extension of traditional mail-order distance learning where CD-ROMS are used for interactive and media-rich interaction with the student. Alternatively, the meaning can be extended all the way to fully interactive, institution-wide "managed learning environments" in which students communicate with professors and classmates, much like in a face-to-face delivered course. E-learning may include the use of Web-based teaching materials and hypermedia in general, multimedia CD-ROMs, Web sites, discussion boards, collaborative software, e-mail, blogs, wikis, chatrooms, computer-aided assessment, educational animation, simulations, games, learning management software, electronic voting systems, and more, with possibly a combination of different methods being used (see Ng 2006 for details).

EXHIBIT 8.5   The Effects of E-Commerce Forces in Education

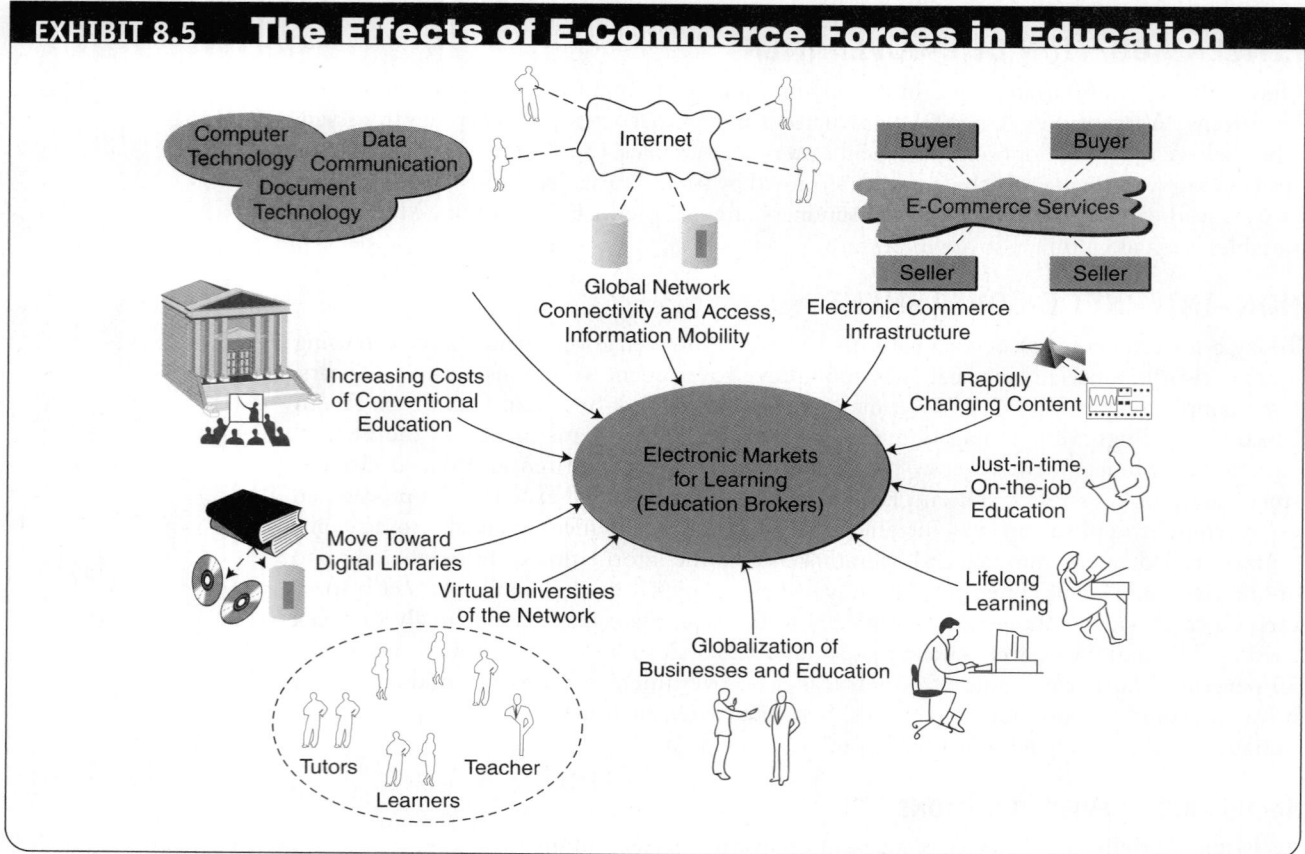

Source: Hamalainen, M. and A. Whinston. "Electronic Marketing for Learning: Education Brokerages on the Internet." *The Communications of the ACM*, ©1996, ACM, Inc.

E-learning is also broader than the term *online learning*, which generally refers to purely Web-based learning. The term *m-learning* has been proposed when the material is delivered wirelessly to cell phones or PDAs.

E-learning can be useful both as an environment for facilitating learning at schools and as an environment for efficient and effective corporate training, as shown in Case 8.3.

Aldrich (2006) surveyed the technological changes, such as simulations, open-source software, and content management, that have reshaped the e-learning landscape. Boehle (2005) described rapid development tools that enable organizations to create e-learning environments quickly and easily. For an overview and discussion of research issues related to e-learning, see Piccoli et al. (2001); this resource also compares e-learning with traditional classroom teaching. Comprehensive sites about e-learning, including videos and PowerPoint presentations, are available at e-learningcenter.com and e-learningcentre.co.uk.

CASE 8.3
EC Application
E-LEARNING AT CISCO SYSTEMS

The Problem

Cisco Systems (*cisco.com*) is one of the fastest growing high-tech companies in the world, selling devices that connect computers to the Internet and to other networks. Cisco's products continuously are being upgraded or replaced, so extensive training of employees and customers is needed. Cisco recognizes that its employees, business partners, and independent students seeking professional certification all require training on a continuous basis. Traditional classroom training was flawed by its inability to scale rapidly enough. Cisco offered in-house classes 6 to 10 times a year, at many locations, but the rapid growth in the number of students, coupled with the fast pace of technological change, made the training both expensive and ineffective.

The Solution

Cisco believes that *e-learning* is a revolutionary way to empower its workforce and its partners with the skills and knowledge needed to turn technological change to an advantage. Therefore, Cisco implemented e-learning programs that enable students to learn new software, hardware, and procedures. Cisco believes that once people experience e-learning, they will recognize that it is the fastest, easiest way to get the information they need to be successful.

To implement e-learning, Cisco created the Delta Force, which was made up of its CEO John Chambers, the IT unit, and the Internet Learning Solution Group. The group's first project was to build two learning portals, one for 40 partner companies that sell Cisco products and one for 4,000 systems engineers who deploy and service the products after the sale.

Cisco also wants to serve as a model of e-learning for its partners and customers, hoping to convince them to use its e-learning programs. To encourage its employees to use e-learning, Cisco:

- Makes e-learning a mandatory part of employees' jobs.
- Offers easy access to e-learning tools via the Web.

- Makes e-learning nonthreatening through the use of an anonymous testing and scoring process that focuses on helping people improve rather than on penalizing those who fail.
- Gives those who fail tests precision learning targets (remedial work, modules, exercises, or written materials) to help them pass and remove the fear associated with testing.
- Enables managers to track, manage, and ensure employee development, competency change, and ultimately, performance change.
- Offers additional incentives and rewards such as stock grants, promotions, and bonuses to employees who pursue specialization and certification through e-learning.
- Adds e-learning as a strategic top-down metric for Cisco executives, who are measured on their deployment of IT in their departments.

For its employees, partners, and customers, Cisco operates E-Learning Centers for Excellence. These centers offer training at Cisco's office sites as well as at customers' sites via intranets and the Internet. Some of the training requires the use of partnering vendors.

Cisco offers a variety of training programs supported by e-learning. For example, in 2001 Cisco converted a popular four-and-a-half-day, instructor-led training (ILT) course on Cisco's signature IOS (internetwork operating system) technologies into an e-learning program that blends both live and self-paced components. The goal was to teach seasoned systems engineers (SEs) how to sell, install, configure, and maintain those key IOS technologies and to do so in a way that would train more people than the 25 employees the on-site ILT course could hold.

The Results

With the IOS course alone, Cisco calculated its ROI as follows:

- It cost $12,400 to develop the blended course.
- The course saved each SE 1 productivity day and 20 percent of the travel and lodging cost of a 1-week training course in

(*continued*)

CASE 8.3   *(continued)*

San Jose. Estimating $750 for travel and lodging and $450 for the productivity day, the savings totaled $1,200 per SE.

▶ Seventeen SEs attended the course the first time it was offered, for a total savings of $20,400. Therefore, in the first offering of the course, Cisco recovered the development costs and saved $8,000 over and above those costs.

▶ Since March 2001, the IOS Learning Services team has presented two classes of 40 SEs per month. At that rate, Cisco saves $1,152,000 net for just this one course every 12 months.

In 2004, over 12,000 corporate salespeople, 150,000 employees of business partners, and 200,000 independent students were taking courses at Cisco learning centers, many using the e-learning courses. By 2004, Cisco had developed over 100 e-learning courses and was planning to develop

many more. According to Galagan (2002), e-learning is a major underpinning of Cisco's economic health.

Sources: Compiled from *cisco.com* (accessed January 2007), Galagan (2002), and Delahoussaye and Zemke (2001).

Questions

1. Use examples from the Cisco case to discuss the differences between e-learning and e-training.
2. What measures has Cisco adopted to encourage its employees to use e-learning?
3. Comment on the effectiveness of the e-learning programs of Cisco.

BENEFITS AND DRAWBACKS OF E-LEARNING

E-learning has many benefits. However, it also has several drawbacks, thus making it a controversial topic.

Benefits of E-Learning

E-learning can be a great equalizer: By eliminating barriers of time, distance, and socioeconomic status, it can enable individuals to take charge of their own lifelong learning. In the information age, skills and knowledge need to be *continually updated* and refreshed to keep up with today's fast-paced business environment. E-learning of new content will help organizations and countries adapt to the demands of the Internet economy by training their workers and educating their citizens. E-learning can save money, reduce travel time, increase access to experts, enable large numbers of students to take classes simultaneously, provide on-demand education, and enable self-paced learning. It also may make learning less frustrating by making it more interactive and engaging (e.g., see Kim and Ong 2005).

More specific benefits of e-learning are as follows:

▶ **Time reduction.** As shown in the Cisco case, e-learning can reduce training time by 50 percent.

▶ **Large volume and diversity.** E-learning can provide training to a large number of people from diverse cultural backgrounds and educational levels even though they are at different locations in different time zones.

▶ **Cost reduction.** One study reported that the cost of providing a learning experience can be reduced by 50 to 70 percent when classroom lectures are replaced by e-learning sessions (see Urdan and Weggen 2000).

▶ **Higher content retention.** E-learning students usually are self-initiated and self-paced. Their motive for acquiring more knowledge may be to widen their scope of view or to develop career skills. Urdan and Weggen (2000) contend that such self-motivation results in content retention that could be 25 to 60 percent higher than that of lecturer-led training.

▶ **Flexibility.** E-learners are able to adjust the time, location, content, and speed of learning according to their own personal schedules. For example, if necessary, they can refer back to previous lectures without affecting the learning pace of other students.

▶ **Updated and consistent material.** It is almost impossible to economically update the information in textbooks more frequently than every 2 or 3 years; e-learning can offer just-in-time access to timely information. In addition, as Urdan and Weggen (2000) reported, e-learning may be 50 to 60 percent more consistent than material presented than traditional classroom learning because variations between teachers are eliminated.

▶ **Fear-free environment.** E-learning can facilitate learning for students who may not wish to join a face-to-face group discussion or participate in class. This kind of behavior usually is attributed to their reluctance to expose their lack of knowledge in public. E-learning can provide a fear-free and privacy-protected environment in which students can put forth any idea without fear of looking stupid.

These benefits, according to Zhang et al. (2004), may enable remote learners to outperform traditional classroom students. Tutoring services that once required face time can also now be profitably handled online and offshored to low-cost countries such as India. For more discussion of the benefits of e-learning, see e-learningguru.com/articles/art1_3.htm and elearnmag.com.

E-learning provides a new set of tools that can add value to traditional learning modes. It may not replace the classroom, but it can enhance it, taking advantage of new content and delivery technologies. The better the match of the content and delivery vehicle to an individual's learning style, the greater the content retention and the better the learning results. Advanced e-learning support environments, such as Blackboard and WebCT, add value to traditional learning. See Insights and Additions 8.1 for descriptions of these e-learning tools.

As the Cisco case showed, e-learning also can be used in the business environment. Besides increasing access to learning and reducing costs, e-learning equips employees with the knowledge needed to help increase customer satisfaction, expand sales, and accelerate technology adoption. In short, e-learning enables companies to prepare their workforces for an increasingly competitive world marketplace.

For a classification of the dimensions of e-learning environments, see Piccoli et al. (2001) and Online File W8.2.

Insights and Additions 8.1 Blackboard and WebCT

Blackboard Inc. ("Blackboard"), the world's largest supplier of course management system software to educational institutions acquired rival WebCT Inc. ("WebCT") in early 2006 for $180 million. The merger has created an e-learning company with 3,700 customers, including colleges, universities, corporate and government users. There is a good chance that you will use the Blackboard or WebCT framework when using this text. These products provide the Internet software needed for e-learning and, thus, serve one of the fastest-growing industry segments in the world.

How do these products work? A publisher places a book's content, teaching notes, quizzes, and other materials on Blackboard or WebCT in a standardized format. Instructors can access modules and transfer them into their own specific Blackboard or WebCT sites, which can be accessed by their students.

Blackboard offers a complete suite of enterprise software products and services that power a total "e-education infrastructure" for schools, colleges, universities, and other education providers. Blackboard's two major lines of business are Course & Portal Solutions and Commerce & Access Solutions.

WebCT provides a similar set of tools but with a different vision and strategy. It uses advanced pedagogical tools to help institutions of higher education make distance-learning courses possible. Such courses enable schools to expand campus boundaries, attract and retain students and faculty, and continually improve course and degree program quality.

Textbook publishers are embracing these tools by making their major textbooks Blackboard and/or WebCT enabled. Thus, a professor can easily incorporate a book's content into the software that is used by thousands of universities worldwide. As of 2007, Blackboard/WebCT delivers corporate and government employee training programs that increase productivity and reduce costs in every major region of the world.

Sources: Compiled from *webct.com* (accessed January 2007) and *blackboard.com* (accessed January 2007).

Drawbacks and Challenges of E-Learning

Despite the numerous benefits, e-learning does have some drawbacks. The following issues have been cited as possible drawbacks of e-learning:

> ▶ **Need for instructor retraining.** Some instructors are not competent in teaching by electronic means and may require additional training. It costs money to provide such training.
>
> ▶ **Equipment needs and support services.** Additional funds are needed to purchase multimedia tools to provide support services for e-learning creation, use, and maintenance.
>
> ▶ **Lack of face-to-face interaction and campus life.** Many feel that the intellectual stimulation that takes places through instruction in a classroom with a "live" instructor cannot fully be replicated with e-learning.
>
> ▶ **Assessment.** In the environment of higher education, one criticism is that professors may not be able to adequately assess student work completed through e-learning. There is no guarantee, for example, of who actually completed the assignments or exams.
>
> ▶ **Maintenance and updating.** Although e-learning materials are easier to update than traditionally published materials, there are practical difficulties (e.g., cost, instructors' time) in keeping e-learning materials up-to-date. The content of e-learning material can be difficult to maintain due to the lack of ownership of and accountability for Web site material. In addition, no online course can deliver real-time information and knowledge in the way a "live" instructor can.
>
> ▶ **Protection of intellectual property.** It is difficult and expensive to control the transmission of copyrighted works downloaded from the e-learning platform.
>
> ▶ **Computer literacy.** E-learning cannot be extended to those students who are not computer literate or do not have access to the Internet.
>
> ▶ **Student retention.** Without some human feedback, it may be difficult to keep some students mentally engaged and enthusiastic about e-learning over a long period of time.

Some of these drawbacks can be reduced by advanced technologies. For example, some online products have features that help stimulate student thinking. Offsetting the assessment drawback, biometric controls can be used to verify the identity of students who are taking examinations from home. However, these features add to the costs of e-learning.

In addition to these drawbacks, e-learning faces challenges that threaten its acceptance (e.g., see Zhang et al. 2004). From the learner's perspective, the challenge is simply to change the mind-set of how learning typically takes place. Learners must be willing to give up the idea of traditional classroom training, and they must come to understand that continual, life-long learning will be as much a part of normal work life, past the college years, as voice mail and e-mail. From the teaching perspective, all learning objects must be converted ("tagged") to a digital format. This task can be challenging. Finally, another challenge for e-learning systems is the updating of the knowledge in them—who will do it and how often? Also, how will the cost of the updating be covered? For more on the strengths and weaknesses of e-learning, see Siemens (2004).

PREVENTING E-LEARNING FAILURES

Many of those who have tried e-learning have been pleased with it. In many cases, self-selection ensures that those who are likely to benefit from e-learning choose e-learning opportunities. For example, students who live at a great distance from school or who have family responsibilities during traditional school hours will be motivated to put in the time to make e-learning work. Similarly, employees for whom a training course at a distant site is a problem, either because of budget or personal constraints, are likely to be enthusiastic about e-learning programs.

E-learning does not work for everyone, though. It is believed that e-learning failures are due to the following issues (*Impact-information.com* 2006 and Weaver 2002):

▶ **Believing that e-learning is always a cheaper learning or training alternative.** E-learning can be less expensive than traditional instruction, depending on the number of students. However, if only a few students are to be served, e-learning can be very expensive because of the high fixed costs.

▶ **Overestimating what e-learning can accomplish.** People sometimes do not understand the limitations of e-learning and, therefore, may expect too much.

▶ **Overlooking the shortcomings of self-study.** Some people cannot do self-study or do not want to. Others may study incorrectly.

▶ **Failing to look beyond the course paradigms.** The instructor needs to look at the entire problem in the area of teaching and at material creation and delivery as well.

▶ **Viewing content as a commodity.** This results in a lack of attention to quality and delivery to individuals.

▶ **Ignoring technology tools for e-learning or fixating too much on technology as a solution.** A balanced approach is needed.

▶ **Assuming that learned knowledge will be applied.** This is difficult to accomplish successfully.

▶ **Believing that because e-learning has been implemented, employees and students will use it.** This is not always the case.

To prevent failure, companies and schools need to address these issues carefully and systematically. Balancing the benefits and the drawbacks of e-learning, many people remain enthusiastic about its potential.

DISTANCE LEARNING AND ONLINE UNIVERSITIES

The term **distance learning** refers to formal education that takes place off campus, often from home. The concept is not new. Educational institutions have been offering correspondence courses and degrees for decades. What *is* new, however, is the application of IT in general and the Web in particular to expand the opportunities for distance learning to the online environment (see Reisman 2006). Neal (2007) describes the role of the Web 2.0 tools (see Chapter 18) in distance learning in higher education, surveying implementation issues in terms of technology, course content, and pedagogy.

The concept of **virtual universities**, online universities from which students take classes from home or an off-site location via the Internet, is expanding rapidly. Hundreds of thousands of students in dozens of countries, from the United Kingdom to Israel to Thailand, are studying in such institutions. A large number of existing universities, including Stanford University and other top-tier institutions, offer online education of some form. Some universities, such as University of Phoenix (phoenix.edu), California Virtual Campus (cvc.edu), and the University of Maryland (umuc.edu/distance), offer hundreds of courses and dozens of degrees to students worldwide, all online See distancelearn.about.com for more resources of distance learning and online universities.

The virtual university concept allows universities to offer classes worldwide. Moreover, integrated degrees may soon appear by which students can customize a degree that will best fit their needs and take courses at different universities. Several other virtual schools include eschool-world.com, waldenu.edu, and trainingzone.co.uk.

ONLINE CORPORATE TRAINING

Like educational institutions, a large number of business organizations are using e-learning on a large scale (e.g., see Neal 2007). Many companies offer online training, as Cisco does. Some, such as Barclays Bank, COX Industries, and Qantas Airways, call such learning centers "universities." New employees at IBM Taiwan Corp. are given Web-based "electronic training," and KPMG Peat Marwick offers e-learning to its customers.

distance learning
Formal education that takes place off campus, usually, but not always, through online resources.

virtual university
An online university from which students take classes from home or other off-site locations, usually via the Internet.

Insights and Additions 8.2 Examples of Corporate Training

The following are a few examples of successful e-training:

▶ Sheetz operates approximately 300 convenience stores across 5 states. It uses e-training via a corporate portal to train and certify store associates in the proper procedures for alcohol sales. It uses a compliance-tracking tool from Compliance Solutions of Arlington, Virginia, to monitor employee participation in the classes. The employees must know both government and corporate policies and regulations. The program helped to train about 1,000 employees in 2003, saving the company a considerable amount of money. Compliance Solutions prepares teaching materials for the entire industry. For details, see Korolishin (2004a).

▶ Tweeter Home Entertainment Group must continuously train its 2,600 sales associates in the new technologies of electronic entertainment products, such as HDTV or surround sound. To help with its traditional classroom training, the company is using two e-learning products from OutStart (an e-learning software company). E-learning has been especially useful for people who are experts in the field. These people can log into the system from anywhere and do a quick brush-up. Two OutStart products are in use: Evolution (for content) and Evolution Learner Management (for course administration). The course content can be paced to fit the learners' time availability. For details, see Korolishin (2004b).

▶ Shoney's Restaurant chain (over 400 restaurants) needs to provide training continuously to its thousands of employees, from busboys to managers. A multicasting solution (RemoteWare from XcelleNet) is used to offer computer-based training. With multicasting, files are sent by telephone line or satellite from a server to many remote computers at the same time. The system helps both in communication and information dissemination as well as in training. These capabilities have allowed Shoney's to use PCs located at the chain's sites for computer-based training (CBT). Each restaurant has one computer (with speakers) used exclusively for staff training. Training files containing video clips, animation, and spot quizzes are easily transferred to the restaurants' computers. The solution also offers management and evaluation tools (e.g., which employees have completed which courses and how they scored on tests). Course evaluation also is done online. Test results provide indications that aid in improving content. The cost is much lower than training offered via videotape or CD-ROM. Training material is kept up-to-date and is consistent across the corporation. High-quality training has helped the company reduce employee attrition, which means people stay longer at their jobs and provide better customer service. For details, see McKinley (2003).

Corporate training often is done via intranets and corporate portals. However, in large corporations with multiple sites and for studies from home the Internet is used to access the online material. For discussion of strategies for implementing corporate e-learning, see Mahapatra and Lai (2005) and Sener (2006). Vendors of online training and educational materials can be found at digitalthink.com and deitel.com.

For examples of successful corporate training, see Insights and Additions 8.2.

The Drivers of E-Training

The business forces that are driving the transition from traditional education to online learning are described next. See elearnmag.org for more information on drivers and justification.

Technological Change. Technological changes and global network connectivity have increased the complexity and velocity of the work environment. Today's workforce has to process more and more information in a shorter amount of time. New products and services are emerging with accelerating speed. As product life cycles and life spans shorten, today's knowledge quickly will become obsolete. In the age of just-in-time (on demand) production, just-in-time training becomes a critical element to organizational success.

Competition and Cost Pressures. Fierce competition in most industries leads to increasing cost pressures. In today's competitive environment, organizations can no longer afford to inflate training budgets with expensive travel and lodging. Time spent away from the job, traveling or sitting in a classroom, tremendously reduces per-employee productivity and revenue.

Globalization. Globalization is resulting in many challenges. Today's businesses have more locations in different time zones and employ larger numbers of workers with diverse cultural backgrounds and educational levels than ever before. Corporations worldwide are seeking innovative and efficient ways to deliver training to their geographically dispersed workforces in other countries. E-learning is an effective way to achieve just this. Companies do not need to bring employees to a trainer or training facility (or even send a trainer to the employees); online classes can run anywhere in the world.

Continual Learning. In the new economy, corporations face major challenges in keeping their workforces current and competent. Learning has become a continual process rather than a distinct event. To retain their competitive edge, organizations have started to investigate which training techniques and delivery methods enhance motivation, performance, collaboration, innovation, and a commitment to lifelong learning.

Network Connectivity. The Internet provides an ideal delivery vehicle for education. The emergence of online education relates not only to economic and social change but also to access. Through its increasing penetration and simplicity of use, the Internet has opened the door to a global market where language and geographic barriers for many training products have been erased. Because of the popularity of the Internet, e-learning is perhaps the most effective way to deliver training electronically.

Fueling the boom in Internet-based management education are corporations hungry for better-trained executives. General Motors pays for its employees to earn an MBA through an Internet-based school launched in 2003 by the New York Institute of Technology and Cardean University. Ingersoll-Rand has a deal with the University of Indiana to customize an online MBA program for its employees. Capella offers tuition discounts to *Fortune* 500 companies such as Boeing, Johnson & Johnson, and Wells Fargo for putting the school on "preferred provider" lists. Online MBAs serve "a real market need," says Trace Urdan, an analyst with Robert W. Baird's equity research unit. "It's a win-win for companies and employees" (Crawford 2005).

Examples of top traditional MBA programs that are introducing e-learning are MIT, Kellogg (Northwestern), INSEAD, University of Chicago, Duke, Berkeley, Purdue, Wharton (University of Pennsylvania), and Cornell. Examples of joint ventures of MBA programs with industry can be seen at Duke, Darden (University of Virginia), UCLA, INSEAD (partners with Pensure), Columbia, Stanford, University of Chicago (partners with UNext), and Wharton (partners with FT Knowledge). Of special interest is the Harvard/Stanford Joint Venture in developing e-learning materials for executives. The materials are delivered in a combination of classroom teaching and e-learning known as Leading Change and Organizational Renewal. A similar venture is that of MIT (Sloan School) and IMD of Switzerland. As of 2007, more than 150 accredited business schools offer online versions of their curricula, according to *GetEducated.com*, which tracks online education trends.

IMPLEMENTING E-LEARNING AND E-TRAINING IN LEARNING CENTERS

Most schools and industries use e-learning as a *supplementary* channel to traditional classrooms. One facility that is used in the integration of the two approaches is the learning center. A *learning center* is a focal point for all corporate training and learning activities, including online ones. Some companies have a dedicated online learning center, a learning center dedicated only to online training. However, most companies combine online and offline activities, as done by W. R. Grace and described in Case 8.4

Learning center facilities may be run by a third party rather than connected to any particular corporation; these are referred to as *electronic education malls* (see Langenbach and Bodendorf 1999–2000). For example, Turbolinux (turbolinux.com), in collaboration with Hong Kong University, developed such a mall for primary and secondary schools in Hong Kong. For additional information about e-learning, see trainingmag.com, elearnmag.org, and learningcircuits.org.

EDUTAINMENT

Edutainment is a combination of education and entertainment, often through games. One of the main goals of edutainment is to encourage students to become active rather than passive learners. With active learning, a student is more involved in the learning process, which makes the learning experience richer and the knowledge gained more memorable. Edutainment embeds learning in an entertaining environment to help students learn almost without their being aware of it.

Edutainment covers various subjects, including mathematics, reading, writing, history, and geography. It is targeted at various age groups, ranging from preschoolers to adults, and it is also used in corporate training over intranets. Software Toolworks (toolworks.com, now a part of the Learning Company at broderbund.com) is a major vendor of edutainment products.

edutainment
The combination of education and entertainment, often through games.

CASE 8.4
EC Application
ONLINE GLOBAL LEARNING CENTER AT W. R. GRACE

The newest concept for training and development is the *online learning center*. Online learning centers combine the Internet, intranets, and e-delivered courses with conventional learning media, such as books, articles, instructor-led courses, and audio and videotapes.

W. R. Grace, a global specialty chemicals company (*grace.com*), initiated its online learning center in 2001. The company's human resources leaders were looking for a solution that would provide fast and easy access to a wide selection of tools for developing employee skills. Surveys indicated a need for self-paced professional and personal training support for employees. Strategic Partners' learning center concept provided the solution. A pilot program was initiated in March 2001. Within 6 months, the center was available 24/7 to 6,000 employees worldwide.

The learning center is organized around the core competencies that characterize the knowledge, skills, and abilities all W. R. Grace employees are expected to achieve. It offers internal classroom training; external courses; CD-ROM courses; self-paced learning tools; streaming video; Internet learning conferences; e-learning courses; coaching tips for managers and mentors; audio and videotapes; books and articles; information about the corporate mission, values, and strategy; strategy guides suggesting specific development actions, on-the-job and in the community; and corporate and industry news. Employees can access resources on a particular topic; they can search a range of appropriate tools and action alternatives specific to their needs, including training sessions, recommended readings, a rental library, and a strategy guide.

The center's Global Steering Committee, made up of representatives from all the functional areas of the business from around the world, keeps the center in tune with the development needs of employees and encourages the use of the center in all regions. The committee also provides human resources management with feedback on how the center is meeting identified needs.

Every 6 weeks, the center's electronic newsletter lands on each employee's desktop. The publication keeps employees up-to-date on the offerings of the center, reports on how employees are using the center, and encourages all employees to use the center as a source for learning and development. Corporate news also is included in the newsletter, keeping the company's initiatives and communications visible to all employees.

Based on its experience, W. R. Grace offers the following suggestions for the successful implementation of a learning center:

▶ Line up strong senior management support.
▶ Build gradually—start with a modest center, get it running smoothly, gather feedback from the users, make needed adjustments, and develop a more extensive center over time.
▶ Invite involvement—people support what they help to create.
▶ Provide a variety of learning tools, mixing in-house and external resources.
▶ Keep the learning center visible.
▶ Ensure the content is fresh and up-to-date.

W. R. Grace's Global Learning Center supports employee growth in a cost-effective manner while relating learning to performance and talent management, strategic communication, and individual development planning. It has proved to be a powerful learning and communications channel for the entire corporation.

Sources: Compiled from Boxer and Johnson (2002) and press releases at *grace.com* (accessed January 2007).

Questions

1. List the factors that drive e-learning at W. R. Grace.
2. How is e-learning integrated with other learning methods?
3. List the e-learning offerings of W. R. Grace's learning center.
4. Describe the critical success factors of e-learning offered by W. R. Grace.

For over a decade, educational games have been delivered mostly on CD-ROMs. However, since 1998, increasing numbers of companies now offer online edutainment in a distance-learning format (e.g., Knowledge Adventure products at sunburst.com and education.com).

E-LEARNING TOOLS

Many e-learning tools are available (e.g., see Zhang and Nunamaker 2003). WebCT and Blackboard, described earlier, are two such tools. One of the facilitators of e-learning is Web 2.0 technology such as wikipedia.org (see Chapter 18). The following are several other examples:

▶ IBM Workplace Collaborative Learning 2.6 software (ibm.com/software/workplace/collaborativelearning) is a Web-based tool that can be customized to fit a company's training needs. It uses customer-supplied job profile information to deliver role-based learning resources right to the users' desktops.

- ComputerPREP (computerprep.com) offers almost 400 e-learning products, including a comprehensive library of Web-based classroom, distance-learning, and self-study curricula. Students can even combine products from different categories to customize their learning environments.

- Macromedia offers tools for wireless devices at macromedia.com/software.

- eCollege (ecollege.com) offers an e-learning platform that includes free collaboration tools.

- Artificial Life, Inc., launched an e-learning portal based on intelligent agents for teaching English and basic sciences in China. This is done in collaboration with Extempo Systems, Inc., which offers an interactive character-based e-learning portal for teaching English as a second language.

For more e-learning tools, see Online File W8.3.

E-learning content can be facilitated with the aid of online publishing and e-books (Section 8.4), wikis and blogs (Section 8.5), and knowledge management (Section 8.6). The first two topics and their relationship to e-training are discussed by Weinstein (2006).

Section 8.3 ▶ REVIEW QUESTIONS

1. Define e-learning and describe its benefits.

2. List some of the major drawbacks of e-learning.

3. Describe virtual universities.

4. Define e-training and describe its drivers and how it is done.

5. List some e-learning tools and describe WebCT and Blackboard.

6. Describe learning centers in industry.

8.4 ONLINE PUBLISHING AND E-BOOKS

Moving paper information to electronic form has created a revolution that impacts both the dissemination of information and learning. **Online publishing** is the electronic delivery of newspapers, magazines, books, news, music, videos, and other digitizable information over the Internet (see Spanbauer 2006). Initiated in the late 1960s, online publishing was designed to provide online bibliographies and to sell knowledge that was stored in online commercial databases. Publicly funded online publishing was established for the purpose of disseminating medical, educational, and aerospace research information. It initially was conducted over private communication lines.

Today, online publishing has additional purposes. It facilitates e-learning, provides entertainment, disseminates knowledge, and supports advertising (because it is sometimes provided for free to attract people to sites where advertising is conducted). Publishers of traditional hard-copy media have expanded to add online operations. Magazine and newspaper publishers such as the *Time, PC Magazine*, the *Wall Street Journal*, and *Ad Week* all use online publishing to disseminate information online. Many magazines are offered only online; they are referred to as **e-zines** (e.g., technewsworld.com, pcai.com). Online publishing includes materials supplied for free or by subscription or per item fees; sometimes such material may be customized for the recipient. The potential of new interactive technologies and other Internet applications is expected to aid the growth of online publishing.

online publishing
The electronic delivery of newspapers, magazines, books, news, music, videos, and other digitizable information over the Internet.

e-zines
Electronic magazine or newsletter delivered over the Internet via e-mail.

APPROACHES AND METHODS TO ONLINE PUBLISHING

Several online publishing methods are in use. The following are common methods:

- **Online-archive approach.** The online-archive approach is a digital archive. Such an archive may be a library catalog or a bibliographic database. With this approach, paper publications are converted to a digitized format, without any changes, and are offered electronically.

- **New-medium approach.** The new-medium approach is used by publishers that seek to use the publication capabilities of the Web to create new material or add content and multimedia to paper publications. With this approach, publishers may provide extra analysis or additional information on any issue or topic online, offering more information than a traditional magazine or newspaper can offer. For example, chicagotribune.com (the online version of the *Chicago Tribune*) provides information from the paper's hard-copy issue plus additional news details, jobs and housing listings, and community service information. It also has an archive of past issues. One way of offering additional content is to offer integrated hypertext links to related stories, topics, and graphics. The Web medium also allows for easy customization or personalization, which old publishing media do not. Major journal publishers, such as Taylor and Francis Publishing Co., have placed many of their journals online. The publisher provides, at no charge, abstracts, search engines, and more. Users who want the full-version article are asked to pay. Subscribers are provided with research services, hypertext links, summaries, and more. The new-medium approach also offers up-to-date material, including breaking news. Examples of the new-medium approach include HotWired (wired.com), which complements a paper version of *Wired* magazine, and the *Wall Street Journal Online* (wsj.com). The student companion Web site (prenhall.com/turban) for this book is another example.

▶ **Publishing-intermediation approach.** The publishing-intermediation approach can be thought of as an online directory for news services. Publishing intermediation is an attempt to help people locate goods, services, and products online. Yahoo!, MSN Network, and other portals provide publishing-intermediation services.

▶ **Dynamic approach.** The dynamic approach personalizes content *in real time* and transmits it on the fly in the format best suited to the user's location, tastes, and preferences. This approach also is referred to as the *just-in-time* approach, *print-on-demand*, or *point casting*.

Content Providers and Distributors

Content providers and distributors are, as their name implies, those who provide and distribute content online (also see Chapter 16). These services are offered by several specialized companies (e.g., akamai.com and mirror-image.com), as well as by news services such as the Associated Press and ABC News. Due to the difficulty of presenting multimedia, especially in wireless systems, content providers face major challenges when operating in an environment of less-developed infrastructures. Also, the issue of intellectual property payments is critical to the success of content distribution. If authors do not receive payments for or recognition of their work, content providers may face legal problems. However, if payments *are* made, the providers' costs may be too high.

Many online content providers are starting to charge for content because advertising is proving insufficient to cover their expenses. In addition, more readers appear willing to pay for online publications. For example, the *New York Times* and *South China Morning Post* started to charge for articles in 2002.

Of special interest in this area is Digimarc (digimarc.com), which provides a tool for linking print publications to the Web.

Publishing of Music, Videos, Games, and Entertainment

The Internet is an ideal medium for publishing music, videos, electronic games, and related entertainment. As with content providers, a major issue here is the payment of intellectual property fees (see Chapter 17).

One of the most interesting new capabilities in this area is peer-to-peer networks over which people swap digital files, such as music or video files (Section 8.8). When such swapping is managed by a third-party exchange (e.g., Napster or Kazaa), the third party may be in violation of copyright law. (For more on the legal difficulties faced by Napster and its eventual collapse, see Chapter 3). For a discussion of the social and legal impacts of online music sharing activities, see Bhattacharjee et al. (2006). More and more people are willing to pay for digital music, as shown by the success of Apple's iTunes and others. For a survey, examples, and discussion, see Dahl (2003).

Webcasting

One way that new or obscure musicians promote their work on the Web is by using **Webcasting**, or "live Webcasting shows." For example, onlineevents.com.au broadcasts Webcasts to inform clients about Australian and international entertainment activities. Affiliate clubs and artists get royalty payments based on how many people purchase and download a performance. House of Blue's hob.com has been a pioneer, offering pay-per-view Webcasts.

Webcasting also can be used to broadcast public lectures. For example, *DM Review* (dmreview.com) offers Webcast Direct, a series of Webcast seminars, known as **Webinars**, or e-seminars, on topics related to business intelligence, data warehousing and mining, and data quality. Many other sites offer e-seminars.

Podcasting

A **podcast** is a media file that is distributed by subscription (paid or unpaid) over the Internet using syndication feeds for playback on mobile devices and personal computers. As with the term *radio*, a *podcast* refers to both the content and the method of syndication. The host or author of a podcast is often called a **podcaster**. The term *podcast* is derived from Apple's portable music player, the iPod. A *pod* refers to a container of some sort; thus, the idea of broadcasting to a container, or *pod*, correctly describes the process of podcasting.

Though podcasters' Web sites may also offer direct download or streaming content, a podcast is distinguished from other digital audio formats by its ability to be downloaded automatically, using software capable of reading feed formats such as RSS. (See Chapter 16 and en.wikipedia.org/wiki/Podcasts). For business applications of podcasts, see Gibson (2006).

ELECTRONIC BOOKS

An electronic book, or **e-book**, is a book in digital form that can be read on a computer screen, including handheld computers. A major event in electronic publishing occurred on March 24, 2000, when Stephen King's book *Riding the Bullet* was published exclusively online. For $2.50, readers could purchase the e-book at barnesandnoble.com/ebook and other e-book providers. Several hundred thousand copies were sold in a few days. However, the publishing event did not go off without some problems. Hackers breached the security system and distributed free copies of the book.

Publishers of e-books have since become more sophisticated, and the business of e-publishing has become more secure. E-books can be delivered and read in various ways:

- **Via Web access.** Readers can locate a book on the publisher's Web site and read it there. The book cannot be downloaded. It may be interactive, including links and rich multimedia.
- **Via Web download.** Readers can download the book to a PC.
- **Via a dedicated reader.** The book must be downloaded to a special device (an e-book reader).
- **Via a general-purpose reader.** The book can be downloaded to a general-purpose device, such as a Palm Pilot.
- **Via a Web server.** The contents of a book are stored on a Web server and downloaded for print-on-demand (see later discussion).

Most e-books require some type of payment. Readers either pay when they download a book from a Web site, or they pay when they order the special CD-ROM edition of the book.

Depending on the method by which the book is delivered, software and hardware may be needed to read the book. For example, e-book software such as Adobe Acrobat eBook Reader or Microsoft Reader may be required to read an e-book. These readers can be downloaded *for free* from Amazon.com or from other e-book sites. A portable hardware device such as Softbook or Rocket e-book also may be necessary. E-books can be downloaded in PDF, HTML, XML, JPEG, or MP3 formats (Miller 2005). After installing the software, the user downloads the e-book and within minutes can enjoy reading it. The books may be

Webcasting
A free Internet news service that broadcasts personalized news and information, including seminars, in categories selected by the user.

Webinars
Seminars on the Web (Web-based seminars).

podcast
A media file that is distributed over the Internet using syndication feeds for playback on mobile devices and personal computers. As with the term *radio*, it can mean both the content and the method of syndication.

podcaster
The host or author of a podcast.

e-book
A book in digital form that can be read on a computer screen or on a special device.

portable (e.g., see Pocket PC store at amazon.com) and convenient to carry. The Sony E-Book Reader (see Arar 2006) has a 64MB user-accessible memory and can hold approximately 80 (800KB or 500- to 800-page) books. More content can be loaded onto special memory cards that (in 2007) can store up to 100GB (see tigerdirect.com). Books also can be read online, in which case no special hardware is needed.

Several aids are available to help readers who want to read large amounts of material online. For example, ClearType from Microsoft and CoolType from Adobe can be used to improve screen display, colors, and font sizes.

Types of E-Books

Several types of e-books are available:

> **Traditional book format.** This type of e-book is a classic or new book that is presented in traditional linear format, usually without special features, such as hyperlinks or search mechanisms. With the right software (Adobe Portable Document Format), a reader can print the book.

> **Online bookshelf.** This is a *collection* of books (rather than just a single book) that can be read online or downloaded. They are simple in format and do not have hyperlinks.

> **The download.** This is an e-book in simple text files, HTML source documents, or Adobe Acrobat files that *can be downloaded* once the viewer has paid a fee.

> **The Rubics-cube hyperlink book.** This is a truly multimedia, online-only book. It has hyperlinks and provides three-dimensional text and display, employing graphics, audio, and video in a dramatically supportive manner. It supports nonlinear exploration of topics. It is especially useful in supporting learning.

> **The interactive, build-your-own (BYO) decision book.** This kind of book puts the reader "in the driver's seat." Combined with multimedia and VRML (a three-dimensional version of HTML), this e-book leads to dramatic engagement with content, plot, destiny, and responsibility. More information about BYO Decision books can be found at From Now On (fno.org).

> **The online reference book model.** The Safari, a joint venture of technical publishing giants O'Reilly and Pearson Technologies, provides online reference book services. Users search across the content of the Safari e-books, get relevancy ranked search results to answer their specific query, and then view the content immediately in a Web browser (see Miller 2005).

In addition to regular books, electronic *technical* documents and manuals are available from the eMatter division of Fatbrain (now a Barnesandnoble.com company). In addition to all the major publishers that sell e-books directly from their Web sites, readers also can buy e-books at electronic bookstores. All major textbook publishers (e.g., Pearson Education, the publisher of this text) are creating electronic companion textbooks that feature audio, video, and other interactive elements (see Spanbauer 2006).

Advantages and Limitations of E-Books

For e-books to make an impact, they must offer advantages to both readers and publishers. Otherwise, there would be little incentive to change from the traditional format. E-books, like any other books, can be used for pleasure reading and as textbooks to support learning (see Chu and Lam 2006).

The major advantage of e-books to readers is portability. As noted earlier, readers can carry as many as 80 books wherever they go (and more when portable memory drives are used). Other advantages are easy search capabilities and links; easy downloading; the ability to quickly and inexpensively copy material, including figures; easy integration of content with other text; no wear and tear on a physical book; ability to find out-of-print books; and books can be published and updated quickly, so they can be up-to-the-minute.

E-books also can reduce some of the physical burdens of traditional books. A number of studies have shown that 6 out of 10 students ages 9 to 20 report chronic back pain related to heavy backpacks filled with books. Some schools have eliminated lockers for safety reasons, causing students to carry heavy backpacks not only to and from school but all day long. A number of schools are experimenting with eliminating textbooks altogether and using an Internet-based curriculum or school materials on CD-ROMs (*Ergonomics Today* 2004).

The primary advantage that e-books offer publishers is lower production, marketing, and delivery costs, which have a significant impact on the price of books. Other advantages for publishers are lower updating and reproduction costs; the ability to reach many readers; the ease of combining several books, so professors can customize textbooks by using materials from different books by the same publisher; and lower advertising costs (see Chu and Lam 2006).

Of course, e-books have some limitations: They require hardware and software that may be too expensive for some readers; some people have difficulty reading large amounts of material on a screen; batteries may run down; there are multiple, competing standards; and finally, only a few books are available as e-books.

E-Book Issues

The functionality of e-books is increasing rapidly. Software providers are supplying tools that make e-books easier to use—tools that search like search engines and that enable easy annotation and bookmarks that enable readers to expedite research of large volumes of information. According to the Association of American Publishers (2006), e-book sales were up 26.2 percent for the year 2006. Despite persistent growth in the use of e-books and their advantages, e-books generally are not selling well in relation to the overall size of the book market. Although e-books are easy to read, are generally platform independent, have high-resolution displays, and can be read using long-lasting batteries, customers are still reluctant to change their habits. The following issues, when resolved, will contribute to the ease of use and popularity of e-books:

- How to protect the publisher's/author's copyright.
- How to secure content (e.g., use encryption, employ Digital Rights Management [DRM]; see Chapter 17).
- How to distribute and sell e-books.
- How much to charge for an e-book versus a hard copy, and how to collect payment for e-books.
- How to best support navigation in an e-book.
- Which standards to use (e.g., see the Online Information Exchange Standard [ONIX] developed by EDItEUR [editeur.org/onix.html]).
- How to increase reading speed. On the average screen, reading is 25 percent slower than hard-copy reading.
- How to transform readers from hard-copy books to e-books; how to deal with resistance to change.
- How to design an e-book (e.g., how to deal with fonts, typefaces, colors, etc., online).
- How publishers can justify e-books in terms of profit and market share.

Free e-books and white papers on e-publishing are available from a number of different sites (e.g., free-ebooks.net, fictionwise.com). For more information on e-books, see netlibrary.com.

Digital Libraries

Many organizations are building digital libraries of e-books, journals, periodicals, and other materials. In fact, most universities no longer subscribe to paper periodicals. Electronic library items (books, journals, and periodicals) are cheaper, easier to handle, do not require storage space, and are amenable to electronic searches.

The problem, according to Thong et al. (2004), is that millions of potential users are still ignoring these digital libraries. The search engine giant Google has been digitizing millions of print volumes to add to the Google Print database. Partnering with Google on this project are universities, including Harvard, Stanford, and Oxford, as well as the New York Public

Library (Price 2004). The British Library in London has partnered with Microsoft, digitizing around 25 million pages of its books (Schuman 2005).

PRINT-ON-DEMAND

A recent trend in publishing is *print-on-demand*, which refers to customized printing jobs, usually in small quantities, possibly only one document or book. The process is especially attractive for small print jobs because both the total fixed setup cost and the per unit setup cost can be very low.

The print-on-demand process has three steps:

1. A publisher creates a digital master, typically in Adobe Systems' Acrobat format, and sends it to a specialized print-on-demand company. The files are stored on the printing company's network.

2. When an order is placed, a print-on-demand machine prints out the text of the document or book and then covers, binds, and trims it. The entire process can take about a minute for a 300-page book.

3. The book is packaged and shipped to the publisher or the consumer.

Most textbook publishers now offer print-on-demand textbooks, including Pearson Education, the publisher of this book. Tarnoff (2007) suggests that print-on-demand technology has shifted students' financial responsibilities from traditional textbooks to other learning resources. For some issues related to the topic of print-on-demand, see Metz (2004).

Section 8.4 ❱ REVIEW QUESTIONS

1. Define online publishing and list some advantages it offers over traditional media.
2. List the major methods of online publishing.
3. What issues are involved in content creation and distribution?
4. Describe e-books and list their advantages and limitations.
5. List five e-books issues.
6. Describe print-on-demand.

8.5 BLOGS AND WIKIS

The Web enables easy and fast publishing by individuals and organizations via blogging and wikis.

BLOGGING (WEBLOGGING)

Weblogging (blogging)
Technology for personal publishing on the Internet.

blog
A personal Web site that is open to the public to read and to interact with; dedicated to specific topics or issues.

The Internet offers the opportunity for individuals to publish on the Web using a technology known as **Weblogging,** or **blogging**. A **blog** is a personal Web site, open to the public, in which the owner expresses his or her feelings or opinions. Blogs became very popular after the terrorist attacks of September 11, 2001. People were looking for as many sources of information as possible and for personal connections to the tragedy. Blogs comfort people in times of stress. They offer a place where people feel their ideas are noticed, and they can result in two-way communication and collaboration, group discussion, and so on.

Many types of blogs are available. According to Yap (2006), the most common types of blogs are professional blogs, which focus on professions, job aspects, and career building; personal blogs, which often take the form of an online diary, containing thoughts, poems, experiences, and other personal matters; topical blogs, which focus on a certain topic or niche, discussing specific aspects of the chosen subject; and business blogs, which are discussions about business and/or the stock market. Other types of blogs include, but are not limited to, science blogs, culture blogs, educational blogs, and photo blogs. Flynn (2006) estimates that one new blog is created every second. There were more than 1.6 million daily postings (or 66,600 hourly postings) on the blogosphere as of June 2006 (Sifry 2006). The

January 1, 2007, issue of *Time* was dedicated to blog communities. It described the story of 15 citizens—including a French rapper, a relentless reviewer, and a lonely girl—who are members of the new *digital democracy*.

Building Blogs

It is becoming easier and easier to build blogs. Programs from blogger.com, pitas.com, and others are very user-friendly. Blog space is free; the goal is to make it easy for users to create Web journals or blogs. Bloggers (the people who create and maintain blogs) are handed a fresh space on their Web site to write in each day. They can easily edit, add entries, and broadcast whatever they want by simply clicking the send key. Blogging software such as WordPress or Movable Type helps bloggers update their blogs easily. Free blog generators, such as Blogger, lets users host their content on Google servers without having to install any software or obtain a domain.

The crucial features that distinguish a blog from a regular Web page, according to Rapoza (2006) are trackbacks, blogrolls, pings, Feedblitz (an e-mail list management solution), and RSS feeds (see Chapter 16). Bloggers also use a special terminology. See samizdata.net for a dictionary of blog terms.

Datta (2006) suggests seven principles for building effective blogs:

1. Focus intently on a narrow niche, ideally one whose audience has a predilection for high-margin products.
2. Set up blogs so that each post gets its own permanent URL.
3. Think of a blog as a database, not a newspaper-like collection of dispatches.
4. Blog frequently and regularly, at least half a dozen posts every weekday.
5. Use striking images that liven up the pages and attract readers.
6. Enable comments and interact with readers.
7. Make friends with other bloggers, online and off.

Wikis

A wikilog, or wiki, is an extension of a blog. Whereas a blog usually is created by an individual (or maybe a small group) and may have an attached discussion board, a **wikilog**, or **wiki-blog** or **wiki**, is essentially a blog that enables everyone to participate as a peer. Anyone may add, delete, or change content. It is like a loose-leaf notebook with a pencil and eraser left in a public place. Anyone can read it, scrawl notes, tear out a page, and so on. Creating a wikilog is a *collaborative* process. For description and details, see usemod.com/cgi-bin/mb.pl? WikiLog. For further discussion, see Chapter 18 and en.wikipedia.org/wiki/wiki. A commercial use of a wiki was presented in the opening case.

wikilog (wikiblog or wiki)
A blog that allows everyone to participate as a peer; anyone may add, delete, or change content.

Commercial Uses of Blogs

The blog concept has transferred quickly to the corporate world. According to the 2006 Workplace E-mail, Instant Messaging & Blog Survey from the American Management Association (AMA) and the ePolicy Institute, 8 percent of U.S.–based organizations operate business blogs. Of that number, 55 percent operate external, or "facing out," blogs to communicate with customers and other third parties. Another 48 percent have established internal blogs to enhance employees' communication with one another (many operate both). Even CEOs are diving into the blogosphere, with 16 percent using blogs to build trust-based relationships, polish corporate reputations, promote social causes, and accomplish other professional goals. Blogging provides the ability to supplement corporate public relations, press releases, and brochures with more personal, "from the heart" talk and offer convenient links to related sources. A skillfully written, content-rich business blog can help organizations position executives as industry thought leaders, build brand awareness, facilitate two-way communication, and accomplish other important business goals. Blogs have gone from self-indulgent hobbies to flourishing businesses with the Web 2.0 wave (see Chapter 18). See Sloan and Kaihla (2006) for a survey of commercial uses of

CASE 8.5
EC Application
STONYFIELD FARM ADOPTS BLOGS FOR PUBLIC RELATIONS

Stonyfield Farm is the third largest organic company in the world, producing more than 18 million cups of yogurt each month and generating more than $50 million in annual sales in 50 states. The company's core values are promoting healthy food and protecting the environment. It guarantees the use of only natural ingredients in its products and donates 10 percent of its profit each year to efforts that protect the earth.

The company employs "word-of-mouth" marketing approaches that are compatible with its grassroots "people-friendly" image. Recently, Stonyfield has turned to blogs to further personalize its relationship with its customers and connect with even more people. The blogs provide the company with what the management calls a "handshake" with customers. Stonyfield publishes four different blogs on its Web site: (1) "Healthy Kids" encourages healthy food consumption in public schools; (2) "Strong Women Daily" features fitness, health tips, and stress-coping strategies; (3) "Baby Babble" provides a forum for child development and balancing work with family; and (4) "The Bovine Bugle" provides reports from organic dairy farms.

Stonyfield hires a journalist and almanac writer to post new content to each of the blogs daily, five days a week. When readers subscribe to the blogs, they will receive automatic updates, and they can also respond to the postings. The blogs have created a positive response for the Stonyfield brand by providing readers with topics that inspire them and piques their interests. They are also, of course, persuaded to try and buy Stonyfield products. The management believes that blogs are an excellent method of public relations.

Sources: Compiled from Needleman (2005), *BusinessWeek Online* (2006), and *stonyfield.com* (accessed January 2007).

Questions

1. How does Stonyfield Farms manage its business blogs?
2. How do the blogs help Stonyfield Farms build its corporate reputation?

blogs. Case 8.5 illustrates how one company uses blogs for building corporate reputations and providing CRM.

Potential Risks of Blogs

Some people see risks in corporate blogging (e.g., Lewin 2004). Two obvious examples are the risk of revealing trade secrets (in corporate-related blogs) and of making statements that are or could be construed as libel or defamation. Many companies have corporate policies on blogging. Groove Networks is one such example (see Ozzie 2002); the company even has corporate lawyers review the contents of its blogs.

According to Flynn (2006), blog-related risks can be minimized by establishing a strategic blog management program that incorporates the 3-Es of electronic risk management:

1. Establish comprehensive, written rules and policies. Make sure employees understand that all company policies apply to the blogosphere, regardless of whether employees are blogging at the office or from home.

2. Educate employees about blog-related risks, rules, and regulations. Be sure to address rights and privacy expectations, as well as the organization's blog-related risks and responsibilities.

3. Enforce blog policy with disciplinary action and technology. Take advantage of blog search engines to monitor the blogosphere and to keep track of what is being written about your company.

Bloggers and Politics

Bloggers are getting more and more active in politics. In France, politicians pursued millions of voters in the blogosphere during the 2007 presidential elections. In the United States, when Senator Tom Daschle (who lost the 2004 Senate election in South Dakota) went to court at the last minute to sue his opponent, several hundred bloggers in South Dakota and elsewhere attacked him, saying that the lawsuit was "pathetic" and showed desperation. One blogger even broadcasted the court hearing on its site.

Section 8.5 ▶ REVIEW QUESTIONS

1. Define *blogs* and *bloggers*.
2. Discuss the critical features that distinguish a blog from a regular Web page.
3. Describe the potential advantages and risks of blogs.
4. Define wikis.
5. Discuss the commercial uses of blogs.

8.6 KNOWLEDGE MANAGEMENT AND E-COMMERCE

The term *knowledge management* frequently is mentioned in discussions of e-learning. Why is this? To answer this question, one first needs to understand what knowledge management is.

Knowledge management and e-learning both use the same "coin of the realm"—knowledge. Whereas e-learning uses that "coin" for the sake of *individual* learning, knowledge management uses it to improve the functioning of an *organization*. Knowledge is one of the most important assets in any organization, and thus it is important to capture, store, and apply it. These are the major purposes of knowledge management. Thus, **knowledge management (KM)** refers to the process of capturing or creating knowledge, storing and protecting it, updating it constantly, and using it whenever necessary. For a comprehensive discussion of KM, see Naka (2007), Holsapple (2003), and kmworld.com. For KM resources, see en.wikipedia.org/wiki/knowledge_management.

Knowledge is collected from both external and internal sources. Then it is examined, interpreted, refined, and stored in what is called an **organizational knowledge base**, the repository for the enterprise's knowledge. A major purpose of an organizational knowledge base is to allow for *knowledge sharing*. Knowledge sharing among employees, with customers, and with business partners has a huge potential payoff in improved customer service, the ability to solve difficult organizational problems, shorter delivery cycle times, and increased collaboration within the company and with business partners. Furthermore, some knowledge can be sold to others or traded for other knowledge.

KM promotes an *integrated* approach to the process of handling an enterprise's information assets, both those that are documented and the tacit expertise stored in individuals' heads. The integration of information resources is at the heart of KM. EC implementation involves a considerable amount of knowledge—about customers, suppliers, logistics, procurement, markets, and technology. The integration of that knowledge is required for successful EC applications. These applications are aimed at increasing organizational competitiveness (see Putnik and Cunha 2007 and Holsapple 2003).

The KM/EC connection will be described in more detail later in this section. First, though, let's examine KM types and activities.

KM TYPES AND ACTIVITIES

According to Lai and Chu (2002), organizational knowledge is embedded in the following resources: (1) *human capital*, which includes employee knowledge, competencies, and creativity; (2) *structured capital (organizational capital)*, which includes organizational structure and culture, processes, patents, and the capability to leverage knowledge through sharing and transferring; and (3) *customer capital*, which includes the relationship between organizations and their customers and other partners.

This organizational knowledge must be properly managed, and this is the purpose of KM. According to Davenport and Prusak (2000), KM has four tasks: (1) creating knowledge repositories where knowledge can be stored and retrieved easily; (2) enhancing a knowledge environment in order to conduct more effective knowledge creation, transfer, and use; (3) managing knowledge as an asset so as to increase the effective use of knowledge assets over time; and (4) improving knowledge access to facilitate its transfer between individuals. The knowledge access and transfer between individuals is part of knowledge usage and sharing. For a comprehensive list of KM activities and tools, see Naka (2007) and kmworld.com.

knowledge management (KM)
The process of capturing or creating knowledge, storing it, updating it constantly, interpreting it, and using it whenever necessary.

organizational knowledge base
The repository for an enterprise's accumulated knowledge.

Knowledge Sharing

Knowledge is of limited value if it is not shared. The Web 2.0 boom discussed in Chapter 18 is based in part on online knowledge sharing (see Howe 2007). The ability to share knowledge decreases its cost and increases its effectiveness for greater competitive advantage. Thus, another major purpose of KM is to increase knowledge sharing. Song (2002) demonstrated that through effective knowledge sharing, organizations can reduce uncertainty and risk, improve efficiency, reduce training costs, and more. Roberts-Witt (2002) noted that KM used to be about sharing company databases but that increasingly it is also about sharing the information stored in people's heads.

Song (2002) proposed a framework for organizing and sharing knowledge gleaned from the Internet. According to this framework, organizations promote knowledge sharing via the use of rewards or incentives, through the use of different sharing mechanisms according to the type of knowledge, and by appropriately codifying knowledge. The proposed framework begins with the listing of strategic goals and objectives and the critical information needed for their attainment. Then, an analysis and storage mechanism is built as part of a business intelligence system (see Online File W4.3). The framework also deals with knowledge collection (from internal and external sources) and its dissemination in support of attaining the goals. An example knowledge sharing system at Xerox is provided in Case 8.6.

The KM discussion thus far has been fairly generic. For additional material regarding major KM activities, see the discussion of KM activities in Online File W8.4. Let's now consider how KM relates to EC.

HOW IS KNOWLEDGE MANAGEMENT RELATED TO E-COMMERCE?

As seen throughout this book, EC has many external as well as internal applications, including both CRM and PRM. To better perform their EC tasks, organizations need knowledge, which is provided by KM. For example, according to Sugumaran (2002), who

---

CASE 8.6
EC Application

ONLINE KNOWLEDGE SHARING AT XEROX

In the early 1990s, Xerox Corporation had a nationwide database that contained information that could be used to fix its copiers, fax machines, and high-speed printers. However, the information was not readily available to the 25,000 service and field employees and engineers whose job it is to repair the machines at customer sites. Satisfaction with customer service was low.

The engineers at Xerox's Palo Alto Research Center (PARC) spent 6 months observing repair personnel, watching how they worked, noting what their frustrations were, and identifying what kind of information they needed. They determined that the repair personnel needed to share their knowledge with their peers. PARC engineers developed Eureka, an online knowledge-sharing system created to assist the service people with time-consuming and complicated repair problems.

Ray Everett, program manager for Eureka, describes the powerful impact the program has had on service: "You went from not knowing how to fix something to being able to get the answer instantly. Even better, you could share any solutions you found with your peers around the globe within a day, as opposed to the several weeks it used to take."

Since its inception in 1996, Eureka has been implemented in 71 countries. It has helped solve 350,000 problems and has saved $3 to $4 million in parts and labor every year.

The system is available to all of Xerox's service engineers via notebook computers and is accessed through the Internet. Product fixes (50,000 of them), documentation updates, and product-update bulletins are delivered over the Web. Individual service employees and engineers can enter possible new solutions to problems into the system. The solution will appear in Eureka, giving credit to the author and noting the service employee's country of origin. An alert about a new solution is sent to validators who test the solution; if it works consistently, it is sent to all engineers via Eureka updates.

The 2006 version is designed to work over wireless Internet connections. Eureka is a constantly evolving and growing system that connects and shares the collective knowledge of Xerox's service force.

Sources: Compiled from Roberts-Witt (2002) and Xerox (2007).

Questions

1. What knowledge is shared via Eureka? How is it shared?
2. What EC technologies are described in this case? Classify the EC transactions.
3. What were the drivers of the program?
4. What advantages may be provided by the wireless system?

proposed a KM framework for EC organizations, strategic planning in traditional organizations needs considerable amounts of knowledge. To mitigate this problem, e-businesses can proactively incorporate KM processes to facilitate quick access to different types of knowledge.

In the EC marketspace, large amounts of data can be gathered easily, and by analyzing these data in a timely manner organizations can learn about their clients and generate useful knowledge for planning and decision making. For example, in the B2B market, organizations can scan the environment to monitor changes in a vertical industry and can form strategic alliances or partnerships in response to business pressures. For these activities to be successful in both B2B and B2C, appropriate knowledge is needed to interpret information and to execute activities.

Core knowledge management activities for companies doing EC should include the following electronically supported activities: identification, creation, capture and codification, classification, distribution, utilization, and evolution of the knowledge needed to develop products and partnerships. *Knowledge creation* involves using various computer-based tools and techniques to analyze transaction data and generate new ideas. *Knowledge capture and codification* includes gathering new knowledge and storing it in a machine-readable form. *Knowledge classification* organizes knowledge using appropriate dimensions relating it to its use. *Knowledge distribution* is sharing relevant information with suppliers, consumers, and other internal and external stakeholders through electronic networks—both public and private. *Knowledge utilization* involves appropriate application of knowledge to problem solving. *Knowledge evolution* entails updating knowledge as time progresses.

Jih et al. (2005) performed an empirical study of the casual relationship of knowledge management and e-commerce. Lin and Lee (2005) examined the impact of organizational learning factors and knowledge management processes on e-business systems adoption. Kumar and Thondikulam (2006) proposed a collaborative business framework for interorganizational knowledge sharing. Bose (2002) explored the relationship between KM and infrastructure for EC.

Fahey et al. (2001) believe that a major role of KM is linking e-business and operating processes. Specifically, knowledge generated in e-business contributes to the enhancement of three core operating processes: CRM, SCM, and product development management. For more on KM-enabling technologies and how they can be applied to business unit initiatives, see Online File W8.5, Rao (2004), and kmworld.com.

KNOWLEDGE PORTALS

Knowledge portals are single-point-of-access software systems intended to provide easy and timely access to knowledge and to support communities of knowledge workers who share common goals. Knowledge portals can be used for either external or internal use. A knowledge portal also can be defined as an information portal that will be used by knowledge workers.

Knowledge portals support various tasks performed by knowledge workers: gathering, organizing, searching for, and analyzing information; synthesizing solutions with respect to specific task goals; and then sharing and distributing what has been learned with other knowledge workers. These tasks are illustrated in Exhibit 8.6. In this example, Mack et al. (2001) illustrate how a knowledge portal was used to support the work of knowledge-work consultants at IBM and what technologies can be used to support each category of tasks. For further details on how knowledge portals are related to collaborative and intellectual capital management, see Jones et al. (2006) and Wimmer (2006).

Information Intelligence

Information intelligence refers to information, data, knowledge, and the semantic infrastructure that enables organizations to create more business applications. It creates a platform that leverages information analytics, patterns, and associations to extract business value from internal and external knowledge. For details, see Delphi Group (2004).

knowledge portal
A single-point-of-access software system intended to provide timely access to information and to support communities of knowledge workers.

information intelligence
Information, data, knowledge, and semantic infrastructure that enable organizations to create more business applications.

EXHIBIT 8.6 Knowledge Work Tasks with Examples of Supporting Technology

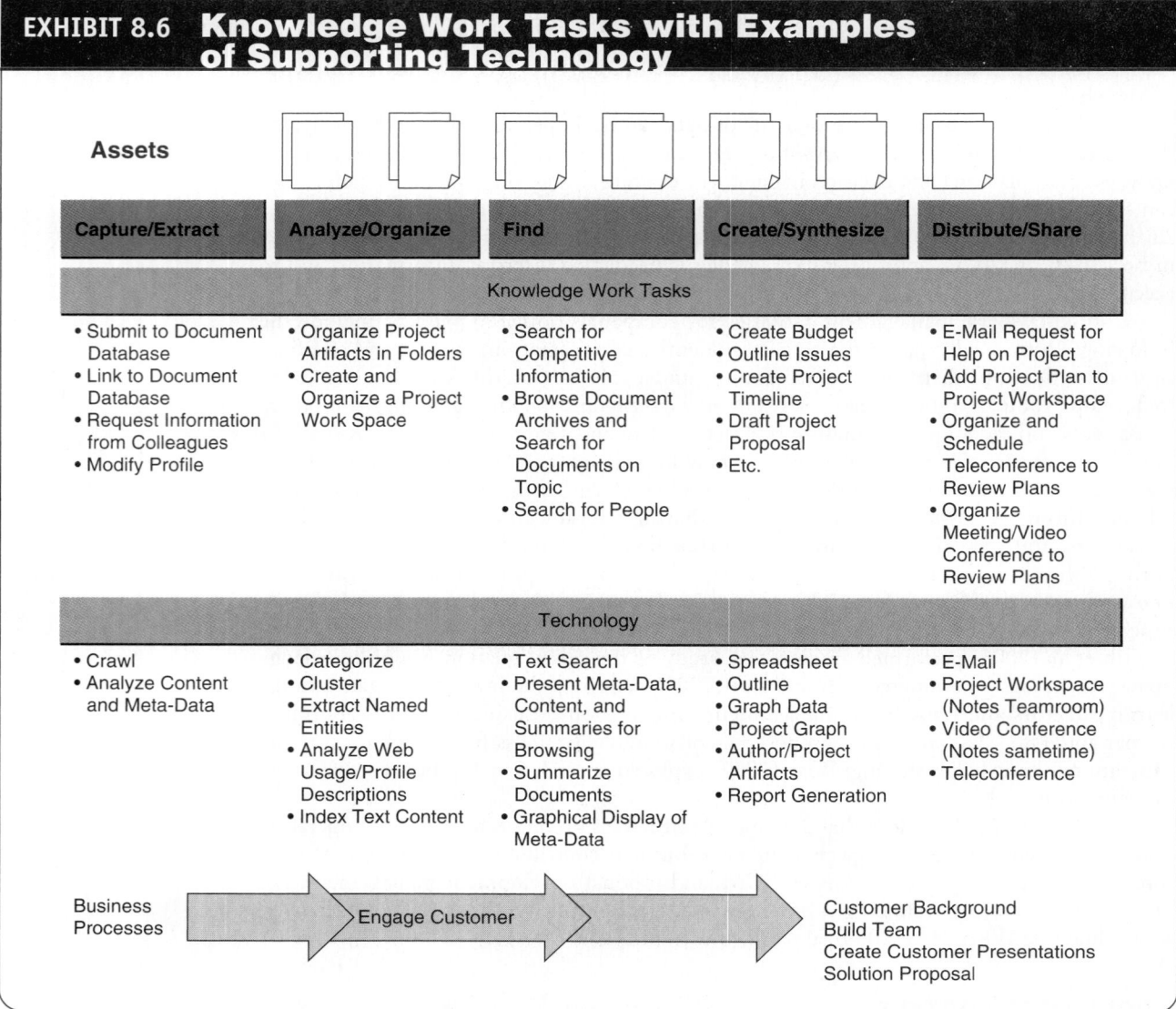

Assets

Capture/Extract	Analyze/Organize	Find	Create/Synthesize	Distribute/Share

Knowledge Work Tasks

Capture/Extract	Analyze/Organize	Find	Create/Synthesize	Distribute/Share
• Submit to Document Database • Link to Document Database • Request Information from Colleagues • Modify Profile	• Organize Project Artifacts in Folders • Create and Organize a Project Work Space	• Search for Competitive Information • Browse Document Archives and Search for Documents on Topic • Search for People	• Create Budget • Outline Issues • Create Project Timeline • Draft Project Proposal • Etc.	• E-Mail Request for Help on Project • Add Project Plan to Project Workspace • Organize and Schedule Teleconference to Review Plans • Organize Meeting/Video Conference to Review Plans

Technology

Capture/Extract	Analyze/Organize	Find	Create/Synthesize	Distribute/Share
• Crawl • Analyze Content and Meta-Data	• Categorize • Cluster • Extract Named Entities • Analyze Web Usage/Profile Descriptions • Index Text Content	• Text Search • Present Meta-Data, Content, and Summaries for Browsing • Summarize Documents • Graphical Display of Meta-Data	• Spreadsheet • Outline • Graph Data • Project Graph • Author/Project Artifacts • Report Generation	• E-Mail • Project Workspace (Notes Teamroom) • Video Conference (Notes sametime) • Teleconference

Business Processes → Engage Customer → Customer Background / Build Team / Create Customer Presentations / Solution Proposal

Source: Mack, R., et al. "Knowledge Portals and the Emerging Digital Knowledge Workplace." IBM Systems Journal 40, no. 4 (2001).

ONLINE ADVICE AND CONSULTING

Another use of knowledge online is offering advice and consulting services. The online advice and consulting field is growing rapidly as tens of thousands of experts of all kinds sell or provide for free their expertise over the Internet. The following are some examples:

▸ **Medical advice.** Companies such as WebMD (webmd.com) (see Chapter 2) and others (see kasamba.com) provide health-advice consultations with top medical experts. Consumers can ask specific questions and get an answer from a specialist in a few days. Health sites also offer specialized advice and tips for travelers.

▸ **Management consulting.** Many consultants are selling their accumulated expertise from organizational knowledge bases. A pioneer in this area was Andersen Consulting (now Accenture at accenture.com). Other management consultants that sell knowledge online are Aberdeen (aberdeen.com) and Forrester Research (forresterresearch.com). Because of their high consultation fees, such services mainly are used by corporations.

▸ **Legal advice.** Delivery of legal advice to individuals and businesses by consultation services has considerable prospects. For example, Atlanta-based law firm Alston & Bird coordinates legal counseling with 12 law firms for a large health-care company and for many other clients. The company created an organizational knowledge base that contains information from some of the best law firms in the country. This information is then made available to all 12 of the law firms in the consultation group. Also, many lawyers offer inexpensive consulting services online. Linklaters, a leading law firm in the United Kingdom, created a separate company (blueflag.com) to sell its legal services online. The company offers several products and also sells support technology to other law firms.

▶ **Gurus and answers to questions.** Several sites provide diversified expert services, some for free. One example is guru.com, which offers general advice and a job board for experts on legal, financial, tax, technical, lifestyle, and other issues. As of 2007, it has aggregated over 480,000 professional "gurus." Expertise is advertised at elance.com, where one can post a required service for experts to bid on. Of special interest is sciam.com, which offers advice from science experts at *Scientific American*.

Some of the most popular services that offer information from experts are answers.com (previously GuruNet), answers.yahoo.com, catholic.com, muslim-answers.com, healthanswers.com, wineanswers.com, and many, many more. These companies provide free answers and some charge fees for premium services. answers.com (with its teachers.answers.com) provides free access to over 4 million answers and generates income from advertisements.

▶ **Financial advice.** Many companies offer extensive financial advice. For example, Merrill Lynch Online (askmerrill.ml.com) provides free access to some of the firm's research reports and analyses.

▶ **Other advisory services.** Many other advisory services are available online—some for free and others for a fee. For example, guestfinder.com makes it easy for people who work in the media to find guests and interview sources.

One word of caution about advice: It is not wise to risk your health, your money, or your legal status on free or even for-fee online advice. Always seek more than one opinion, and carefully check the credentials of any advice provider.

EMPLOYEES' KNOWLEDGE NETWORKS AND EXPERT ADVICE WITHIN ORGANIZATIONS

Expert advice can be provided within an organization in a variety of ways. Human expertise is rare; therefore, companies attempt to preserve it electronically in corporate knowledge bases. Alternatively, electronic expert systems may be used. Although such systems are very useful and they can be used directly by nonexperts, they cannot solve all problems, especially new ones. For such cases, human experts are needed. In large organizations, it may be difficult to locate experts quickly.

Finding Experts Electronically

Companies know that information technology can be used to find experts. People who need help may post their problem on the corporate intranet and ask for help. Similarly, companies may ask for advice on how to exploit an opportunity. IBM frequently uses this method. Sometimes it obtains hundreds of useful ideas within a few days. It is a kind of brainstorming. The problem with this approach is that it may take days to get an answer if an answer is even provided, and the answer may not be from the top experts. Therefore, companies employ expert location systems.

Expert Location Systems

Expert location systems are interactive computerized systems that help employees find and connect with colleagues with expertise required for specific problems—whether they are across the country or across the room—in order to solve specific, critical business problems in seconds. Such software is made by companies such as AskMe, RightNow Technologies, and Tacit Knowledge Systems Inc. For example, AskMe Enterprise, a software solution for deploying employee knowledge networks, enables organizations to fully leverage employee knowledge and expertise to drive innovations and improve bottom-line performance. The solution is the result of AskMe's collaboration, experience and success with real-world

expert location systems
Interactive computerized systems that help employees find and connect with colleagues who have expertise required for specific problems—whether they are across the country or across the room—in order to solve specific, critical business problems in seconds.

EXHIBIT 8.7 How Expert Location Systems (Save) Work

Step 1:
An employee submits a question into the expertise location management system.

Step 2:
The software searches its database to see if an answer to the question already exists. If it does, the info (research reports, spreadsheets, etc.) is returned to the employee. If not, the software searches documents and archived communications for an "expert."

Step 3:
Once a qualified candidate is located, the system asks if he is able to answer a question from a colleague. If so, he submits a response. If the candidate is unable (perhaps he is in a meeting or otherwise indisposed), he can elect to pass on the question. The question is then routed to the next appropriate candidate until one responds.

Step 4:
After the response is sent, it is reviewed for accuracy and sent back to the querist. At the same time, it is added to the knowledge database. This way, if the question comes up again, it will not be necessary to seek real time assistance.

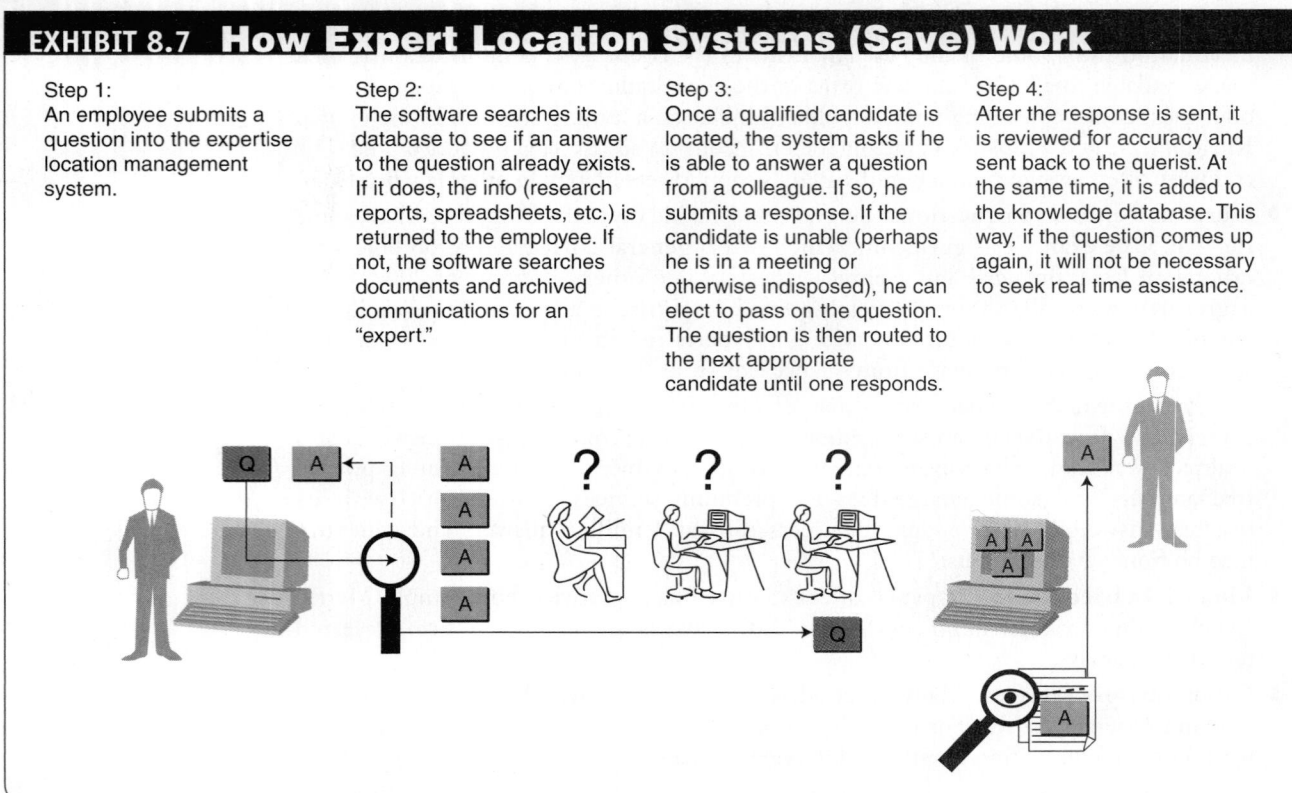

Source: D'Agostino D. "Expertise Management: Who Knows About This?" *CIO Insight,* July 1, 2004. Used with permission of artist, David Falherty.

customer deployments and many companies. For benefits, features, and demonstrations, see askmecorp.com. Most expert location systems work similarly, exploring knowledge bases for either an answer to the problem (if it exists there) or locating qualified experts. The generic process is shown in Exhibit 8.7. Case 8.7 demonstrates how such a system works for the U.S. government.

Desktop Search

With all of the challenges facing organizations, knowledge management is an essential function for capturing data that resides in a myriad of formats, systems, and locations. Although today's $12 billion knowledge management software market offers a variety of solutions for such obstacles, successful implementation of these solutions is highly dependent upon organizations' willingness and ability to pledge considerable resources as well as adaptation of employees. The inability to supply or control those factors often causes knowledge management efforts not to provide their desired effect.

desktop search
Search tools that search the contents of a user's or organization's computer files rather than searching the Internet. The emphasis is on finding all the information that is available on the user's PC, including Web browser histories, e-mail archives, and word-processor documents, as well as in all internal files and databases.

Desktop search is the name for the field of search tools that search the contents of a user's or organization's own computer files rather than searching the Internet. The emphasis is on finding all the information that is available on users' PCs, including Web browser histories, e-mail archives, and word-processor documents, as well as in all internal files and databases. For applications, see Chapter 18 and en.wikipedia.org/wiki/Desktop_search.

One of the main advantages of desktop search programs is that search results come up in a few seconds, much faster than was possible with previous tools such as Windows XP's search companions. A variety of desktop search programs are available. Examples are Google Desktop, Copernic Desktop Search, and X1 Enterprise (see Insights and Additions 8.3).

CASE 8.7
EC Application

HOW THE U.S. DEPARTMENT OF COMMERCE USES AN EXPERT LOCATION SYSTEM

The U.S. Commercial Service Division at the Department of Commerce (DOC) conducts approximately 200,000 counseling sessions a year involving close to $40 billion in trade. The division employs many specialists who frequently need to do research or call on experts to answer a question posed by a U.S. corporation.

For example, in May 2004 a U.S.–based software company called Brad Anderson, a DOC specialist, for advice. The software company wanted to close a deal with a customer in Poland, but the buyer wanted to charge the U.S. company a 20 percent withholding tax, a tax it attributed to Poland's recent admission into the European Union. Was the tax legitimate?

To find out, Anderson turned to the DOC Insider, an *expertise location system* (from AskMe). After typing in his question, Anderson first found some documents that were related to his query, but they did not explain the EU tax code completely. Anderson next asked the system to search the 1,700-strong Commercial Service for a real "live" expert, and within seconds, he was given a list of 80 people in the DOC who might be able to help him. Of those, he chose the six people he felt were most qualified and then forwarded his query.

Before the DOC Insider was in place, Anderson says, it would have taken him about 3 days to answer the same question. "You have to make many phone calls and deal with time zones," he says. Thanks to the expertise location system, however, he had three responses within minutes, a complete answer within an hour, and the sale went through the following morning. Anderson estimates that he now uses the system for roughly 40 percent of the work he does.

The DOC Insider is an invaluable tool. Anderson thinks the tool is vital enough to provide it to other units at the agency. In the first 9 months the system was in place, it saved more than 1,000 man hours.

Sources: Compiled from D'Agostino (2004) and *Askme.com* (2007).

Questions

1. What are the benefits of the expertise location system to the DOC? To U.S. companies?
2. Review Exhibit 8.7 and relate it to this case.
3. What in your opinion are the limitations of this system? Can they be overcome? How?

Insights and Additions 8.3 X1 Enterprise Software Searches for Knowledge

X1 Enterprise is a major desktop search tool from Yahoo! and X1 (*desktop.yahoo.com*). X1's knowledge management model is based on the intelligent indexing and searching of a company's data, no matter where it is stored or if it is organized. This solution acknowledges the fundamental truth that traditional knowledge management solutions do not: People have various organization skills and work in different ways. Many knowledge workers have too much information and not enough time to find it, so they generally seek some business rules or use intuition when needed.

X1 provides a state-of-the-art, customizable search interface that returns an entire data set of matching items, allows access to any element in the results, presents high-quality previews of each data item, allows real-time modification of multiple search parameters, and frees the IT department from management tasks required by other knowledge management systems.

One product is X1 Government Edition, which has been established for use and positioned at secure installations in both military and agency accounts. This is a certainly a positive step because a user-centric approach in knowledge management will support faster response times, especially in times of crisis. Because the actions of the government affect us all, we should be concerned about the knowledge management issues that government agencies face. Through user-centric technologies such as X1.com, the government will be better equipped to meet the needs of the people.

Sources: Compiled from Nenov (2005), *kmworld.com* (accessed January 2007), and *X1.com* (accessed January 2007).

Section 8.6 ▶ REVIEW QUESTIONS

1. Define *knowledge management*.
2. Discuss the relationship between KM and EC.
3. Describe knowledge portals.
4. Describe online advisory services.
5. Describe expert location systems and their benefits.
6. Describe software support to information discovery in organizations.

8.7 CUSTOMER-TO-CUSTOMER E-COMMERCE

customer-to-customer (C2C)
E-commerce model in which consumers sell directly to other consumers.

The section examines e-commerce transactions between individual consumers. **Customer-to-customer (C2C)** e-commerce refers to e-commerce in which both the buyer and the seller are individuals, not businesses. C2C is conducted in several ways on the Internet; the best-known C2C activities are auctions. Millions of individuals are buying and selling on eBay and hundreds of other auction sites worldwide. In addition to the major C2C activity of auctions, other C2C activities include classified ads, personal services, exchanges, selling virtual properties, and support services.

C2C AUCTIONS

In dozens of countries, selling and buying on auction sites is exploding. Most auctions are conducted by intermediaries (e.g., eBay). Consumers can select general sites such as ebay.com or auctionanything.com or they can use specialized sites such as ubid.com. In addition, many individuals are conducting their own auctions with the use of special software. For example, greatshop.com provides software to create C2C reverse auction communities online. See Chapter 10 for more on auctions.

CLASSIFIED ADS

People sell to other people every day through classified ads. Internet-based classified ads have several advantages over newspaper classified ads. They offer a national, rather than a local, audience. This greatly increases the supply of goods and services available and the number of potential buyers. One if the most successful sites of C2C classified ads is Craigslist (see Chapter 2). Other examples are classifieds2000.com, which contains a list of about 500,000 cars, compared with the much smaller number one might find locally. It also includes apartments for rent across the United States (powered by rent.com) and personal ads (powered by match.com). Another example is freeclassified.com. Both Google and Yahoo! are expanding their online classifieds. Many newspapers also offer their classified ads online. In many cases, placing an ad on one Web site brings it automatically into the classified sections of numerous partners. This increases ad exposure at no additional cost. To help narrow the search for a particular item, on some sites shoppers can use search engines. In addition, Internet-based classifieds often can be placed for free by private parties, can be edited or changed easily, and in many cases can display photos of the product offered for sale.

The major categories of classified ads are similar to those found in a newspaper: vehicles, real estate, employment, general merchandise, collectibles, computers, pets, tickets, and travel. Classified ads are available through most ISPs (AOL, MSN, etc.), in some portals (Yahoo!, etc.), and from Internet directories, online newspapers, and more. Once a person finds an ad and gets the details, he or she can e-mail or call the other party to find out additional information or to make a purchase. Most classified ads are provided for free. Some classified ad sites generate revenue from advertisers who pay for larger ads, especially when the sellers are businesses. Classified ad Web sites accept no responsibility for the content of any advertisement.

PERSONAL SERVICES

Numerous personal services are available on the Internet (lawyers, handy helpers, tax preparers, investment clubs, dating services). Some are in the classified ads, but others are listed in specialized Web sites and directories. Some are free, some charge a fee. Be very careful before purchasing any personal services. Fraud or crime could be involved (e.g., a lawyer online may not be an expert in the area professed or may not deliver the service at all). Online advising and consulting, described in Section 8.6, also are examples of personal services.

C2C EXCHANGES

C2C exchanges are of several types. They may be *consumer-to-consumer bartering exchanges* (e.g., targetbarter.com) in which goods and services are exchanged without monetary transactions. Or they may be *consumer exchanges* that help buyers and sellers find each other and negotiate deals. Another form of C2C exchange is one in which consumers exchange information about products (e.g., consumerdemocracy.com and epinions.com).

SELLING VIRTUAL PROPERTIES

Believe it or not, millions of online game players in Asia, and especially in China, are selling and buying online virtual properties. Here is how it works: With popular multiplayer online role playing games (MMORPG), such as Jianxia Qingyuan or Legend of MIR, players own virtual properties that are registered under their names. The players can buy or sell these virtual properties via auctions when playing the game. According to Ding (2004), who quoted an IDC report, 26.7 percent of the 13.8 million MMORPG players (or about 3.7 million) have bought or sold virtual a property, for about $120 million a year.

The trading platform is provided by companies such as Intelligence Dragon Software Technology. People win items in MMORPG games, such as rings or shields, and then they can sell them in e-auctions or classified ads. Of course, there are risks. Hackers may steal items, and even market organizers can sell them. Because the industry is not regulated, the player may have little chance of recovering the virtual property. In addition, there is the risk of the buyer's not paying for the item.

However, MMORPGs are very popular throughout the world, with combined global memberships in both subscription and nonsubscription games exceeding 15 million as of 2006 (see mmogchart.com). Revenues for MMORPGs exceeded half a billion dollars in 2005 (Parks Associates 2007) and are expected to reach over a billion dollars by 2009.

SUPPORT SERVICES FOR C2C

When individuals buy products or services from other individuals online, they usually buy from strangers. The issues of assuring quality, receiving payments, and preventing fraud are critical to the success of C2C. One service that helps C2C is payments by intermediary companies such as PayPal (paypal.com) (see Chapter 12). Other innovative services and technologies that support C2C are described in Chapter 18.

Section 8.7 ▶ REVIEW QUESTIONS

1. List the major C2C applications.
2. Describe how C2C works in classified online ads.
3. Describe C2C personal services, exchanges, and other support services.

8.8 PEER-TO-PEER NETWORKS AND APPLICATIONS

Several C2C applications are based on a computer architecture known as peer-to-peer. **Peer-to-peer (P2P)** computer architecture is a type of network in which each client computer can share files or computer resources (such as processing power) *directly* with others rather than through a central server. This is in contrast with a *client-server* architecture in which some computers serve other computers via a central server. (Note that the acronym P2P also can stand for *people-to-people, person-to-person,* or *point-to-point.* Our discussion here refers to *peer-to-peer networks* over which files and other computing resources are shared.)

P2P technology is really two different things—the direct sharing of digital files and the sharing of different computers' processing power. The main benefit of P2P is that it can expand enormously the universe of information accessible from a personal computer or a mobile device (users are not confined to just Web pages). Additionally, some proponents claim that a well-designed P2P system can offer better security, reliability, and availability of content than the client-server model on which the Web is usually based. Other advantages

peer-to-peer (P2P)
A network architecture in which workstations (or PCs) share data and processing with each other directly rather than through a central server; can be used in C2C, B2B, and B2C e-commerce.

over the client-server architecture include the following: no need for a network administrator, the network is fast and inexpensive to set up and maintain, and each PC can make a backup copy of its data to other PCs for security. P2P technology is more productive than client-server technology because it enables direct connections between computers. However, P2P has some drawbacks that limit its usability, including bandwidth limitations, privacy violations, and potential security problems.

CHARACTERISTICS OF P2P SYSTEMS

P2P systems have the following key characteristics: They provide for real-time access to other users through techniques such as instant messaging and multichannel collaboration applications. The users' computers can act as both clients and servers. The overall system is easy to use and is well integrated, and it includes tools for easy creation of content or for adding functionalities. P2P systems maximize the use of physical attributes such as processor cycles, storage space, bandwidth, and location on the network. They employ user interfaces that load outside of a Web browser. They address the need to reach content resources located on the Internet periphery. They support "cross-networking" protocols such as SOAP or XML-RPC (remote procedure call, a protocol that enables a program on one computer to execute a program on a server computer). Finally, they often do something new or exciting, which creates popular interest.

As these characteristics of P2P computing indicate, devices can join the P2P network from any location with little effort. Instead of dedicated LANs, the Internet itself becomes the network of choice. Easier configuration and control over applications enables non–network-savvy people to join the user community. In fact, P2P signifies a shift in peer-networking emphasis—from hardware to applications (e.g., see Lethin 2003).

P2P networking connects people directly to other people. It provides an easy system for sharing, publishing, and interacting that does not require knowledge of system administration. The system wraps everything up into a user-friendly interface and lets people share or communicate with each other (for details, see Kwok et al. 2002). P2P networks overcome existing client-server inefficiencies and limitations. They will not replace the client-server architecture, but they can be used to create hybrid P2P/client-server networks that are faster, cheaper, and more powerful. According to Kini (2002), P2P networking improves upon the existing client-server hierarchy to efficiently use the processing power, disk space, and data available in a significant number of information sharing and knowledge management applications.

An example of a P2P network is shown in Exhibit 8.8. The PCs shown in the drawing perform computer-to-computer communication directly through their own operating systems; individual resources such as printers, CD-ROM drives, or disk drives are transformed into shared, collective resources that are accessible from any PC on the P2P network.

Notice that these characteristics—such as self-expression, trading, selling—enable more Internet equality. Activities that previously required large amounts of money are now available at low costs, as suggested by Agre (2003).

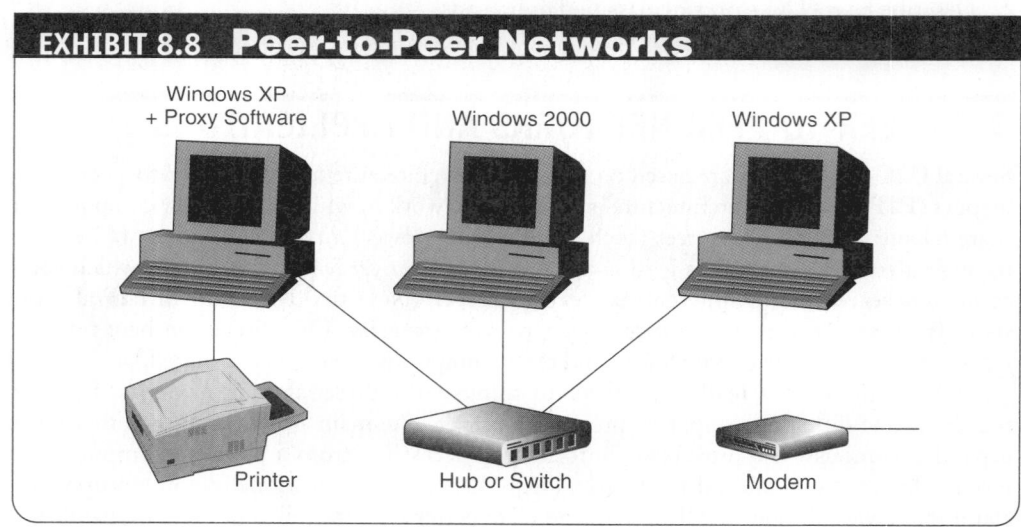

EXHIBIT 8.8 Peer-to-Peer Networks

Windows XP + Proxy Software

Windows 2000

Windows XP

Printer

Hub or Switch

Modem

MODELS OF P2P APPLICATIONS

Kwok et al. (2002) developed a framework of P2P business and service applications (see Online File W8.6). Four distinct models of P2P applications exist:

▶ **Collaboration.** This model allows real-time direct interactions between people, including instant messaging and videoconferencing applications.

▶ **Content distribution.** This model enables file sharing, made famous by Napster, Kazaa, and other music file-sharing services.

▶ **Business process automation.** This model is used to enhance existing business process applications. For example, users can control the type of data their e-mail client will accept.

▶ **Distributed search.** This model enables the sending of search requests in real time to multiple information repositories rather than searching a centralized index.

The characteristics and models just described allow for the various applications discussed next.

C2C P2P APPLICATIONS

The most publicized P2P applications are in the area of C2C. The most well known of these applications is the file sharing of music, software, movies, and other digital media.

Napster—The File-Sharing Utility

In Chapter 3, Napster was presented as an example of C2C EC. By logging onto services such as Napster, people could download files that other people were willing to share. The network enabled users to search other members' hard drives for a particular file, including data files created by users or copied from elsewhere. Digital music and games were the most popular files accessed. Napster had more than 60 million members in 2002 before it went out of business.

The Napster server functioned as a directory that listed the files being shared by other users. Once logged into the server, users could search the directory for specific songs and locate the file owner. They could then directly access the owner's computer and download the songs they had chosen. Napster also included chat rooms to connect its millions of users.

However, a U.S. federal court found Napster to be in violation of copyright laws because it enabled people to obtain music files without paying the creators of the music for access to their material. Following this ruling, in March 2002, Napster closed its free services. Napster continued to operate, with users paying a fee for file sharing and Napster passing along part of the fee to copyright owners.

In December 2002, Roxio, a software maker specializing in CD-burning software, bought Napster's intellectual property assets, including its patents and brand name. (Roxio did not assume any of Napster's legal or financial liabilities.) Napster's remaining hardware—servers, routers, and miscellaneous computers—became part of the company's bankruptcy proceedings and were auctioned off December 11, 2002. Roxio relaunched Napster in 2004 as a for-fee music service. (For more on Napster, see Chapter 17.)

Other File-Sharing Programs

A number of free file-sharing programs still exist. For example, an even purer version of P2P is Gnutella (gnutella.com), a P2P program that dispenses with the central database altogether in connecting the peer computers. Similarly, Kazaa (kazaa.com) offers music file sharing, and it is becoming very popular (see Reuters 2003). Attempts are being made to "kill" Kazaa (and others like it), but because Kazaa's servers are located in Denmark and it operates from Australia and users trade files using anonymous "supernodes," these attempts are facing legal difficulties (see Chapter 17). To access games over P2P networks, try fusiongames.com and battle.net. ICQ (the instant messenger-type chat room) can be considered a hybrid P2P technology because the chatters share the same screen.

A survey conducted by Ipsos-Reid in September 2002 reported that 49.7 percent of music files are downloaded by some P2P application without payment to their creators. The study found that 19.2 percent of people who use P2P file-sharing pay for downloading, and 24.8 percent buy music at e-tailers. By 2007, many people were downloading music legally for a fee (e.g., at iTunes).

Frost and Sullivan (an international strategic market consulting and training firm) performed an online survey that was taken by 150,000 people in 2004. The survey showed that the purchasing of music increases slightly for most people who used peer-to-peer file-sharing networks. It demonstrated that most people used P2P networks to find music that is actually worth buying (Mello 2004).

Despite the temptation to get "something for nothing," remember that downloading copyrighted materials for free is against the law; violators are subject to penalties if caught.

Other Commercial P2P Applications in C2C

With P2P, users can sell digital goods directly from their computers rather than going through centralized servers. If users want to sell on eBay, for example, they are required to go through eBay's server, putting an item on eBay's site and uploading a photo. However, if an auction site uses *file sharing*, it can direct customers to the seller's Web site, where buyers can find an extensive amount of information, photos, and even videos about the items being sold. In this case, an auction site serves as an intermediary making the P2P link between the sellers and buyers.

The following are some more C2C applications using P2P technologies:

▶ **Lending.** Individuals make loans to credit-worthy borrowers (e.g., zopa.com and prosper.com) See details in Chapter 18.

▶ **Bartering.** DVDs are offered for barter at peerflix.com. Also see bookins.com (trade books), lala.com (trade CDs), and swaptree.com (trade everything).

For several more P2P activities see Schonfeld (2006).

INTRABUSINESS P2P APPLICATIONS

Several companies are using P2P to facilitate internal collaboration. For example, in 1990 Intel wrote a file transfer program called NetBatch, which allows chip designers to use the additional processing power of colleagues' computers across sites in California, Arizona, and even foreign countries, such as Israel. Intel saved more than $500 million between 1992 and 2001 (Intel 2002). Under this arrangement, users were able to solve more complex problems that otherwise would have required the use of supercomputers.

After the Napster debacle, companies have been hesitant to use P2P collaboration tools. But tools such as those developed by Groove Networks (groove.net) are helping companies understand how the efficiency of P2P technologies can improve the fine art of collaboration and be incorporated into the work environment (Serva 2004).

B2B P2P APPLICATIONS

P2P could be a technology panacea for systems innovators building B2B exchanges. With P2P, people can share information, but they are not required to send it to an unknown server, as they do when using a regular exchange. Some companies fear that exchanges make it possible for unauthorized personnel to gain access to corporate data files. P2P applications enable such companies to store documents in-house instead of on an unknown, and possibly unsecured, server. According to McAffee (2000), P2P networks allow companies to avoid the fees charged by B2B exchanges and reduce the complexity and expense of the networking. Netrana Corporation's (netrana.com) software replaces the model of funneling all buyers and sellers into a central place with the ability of direct connection.

Several companies are using the P2P architecture as a basis for speeding up business transactions, as shown in the following examples:

▶ Groove Networks (now a Microsoft company) enables direct collaboration by small groups (see Kini 2002). Its products have many P2P-based capabilities.

▶ Hilgraeve of Monroe, Michigan, has a technology called DropChute hilgraeve.com/ dropchute that establishes a connection between two computers and allows users to transfer files. The company has won a U.S. patent for its P2P communication process, which touts four levels of encryption and virus-scanning protection. Fort Knox Escrow Service in Atlanta, Georgia, which transmits legal and financial documents that must be highly secure, has leveraged DropChute to enable clients to deliver material electronically. "Instead of having to wait for an overnight package, we can do it all over the Internet," said Jeanna Israel, Fort Knox's director of operations (Lason Company 2000).

▶ Biz2Peer Technologies offers a trading platform that allows P2P product searches, cataloging, and order entry.

▶ Blue Tiger Networks offers a platform for P2P trading between businesses.

▶ Consilient creates "sitelets," which are mobile XML documents designed to manage themselves through built-in workflow rules. (For further explanation of this complex technology, see openp2p.com; search for Consilient.)

Peer networks effectively address some of the Web's B2B deficiencies. The model is a natural fit for the needs of business because business relationships are intrinsically peer to peer. Peer networks enable businesses to communicate, interact, and transact with each other as never before by making business relationships interactive, dynamic, and balanced—both within and between enterprises.

However, the success of P2P in B2B is not guaranteed. It depends in part on the ability of the technology to address security and scalability issues. For additional information on P2P in B2B, see Gong (2002) and Internetnews.com (2001).

B2C P2P APPLICATIONS

P2P has potential applications to marketing, advertising, and B2C payments. For example, Certapay (certapay.com) is a P2P e-mail payment platform that enables e-banking customers to send and receive money using only an e-mail address. Another company, Fandango (fandango.com), combines P2P with collaborative filtering (Chapter 4) for online ticket-buying activities. Assuming a user is conducting a search for a ticket using Fandango's product, the user enters a search keyword, and the keyword is sent to 100 peers, which search local indexes of the Web pages they have visited. Those computers relay the query to 100 of their peers, and that group submits it to 100 of theirs, yielding, in theory, up to 1 million queries. The resulting URLs are returned to the user, weighted in favor of the most recently visited pages and peers with similar interests.

P2P is certain to enable new EC applications, but it has both technical and social limitations (see Lethin 2003). Although sensitive information may require special security arrangements and many users may encounter scalability issues, P2P is indeed a very promising technology.

Section 8.8 ▶ REVIEW QUESTIONS

1. Define P2P networks and list their major characteristics.
2. List the major P2P models.
3. Describe P2P applications in C2C.
4. Describe P2P applications in B2B.

MANAGERIAL ISSUES

Some managerial issues related to this chapter are as follows.

1. **Can we blog for business?** With one new blog created every second, the hype surrounding it is understandable. Everyone, it seems, is blogging. Is blogging just a hobby? Can we make real (big or small) money from our blogs? How can we turn our passion into an online business? Many companies are beginning to use blogging successfully.

2. **Are there e-learning and e-training opportunities?** Adding an e-learning component to a company's activities is useful when employees require retraining to keep up with new knowledge. Organizations can cut retraining costs and shorten the learning period. Also, companies can help customers train their employees in new products.

3. **Can we capitalize on C2C?** Businesses cannot capture much C2C activity unless they are providers of some innovative service, such as **paypal.com**. Businesses may consider using P2P to support C2C.

4. **How well are we managing our knowledge?** Connecting e-commerce initiatives with a KM program, if one exists, is a very viable strategy. The knowledge is needed for the operation and implementation of EC projects as well as for e-training.

5. **What are the e-government opportunities?** If an organization is doing business with the government, eventually some or all of it may be moved online. Organizations may find new online business opportunities with the government because governments are getting serious about going online. Some even mandate it as the only way to conduct B2G and G2B.

RESEARCH TOPICS

Here are some suggested topics related to this chapter. For details, references, and additional topics, refer to the Online Appendix A "Current EC Research."

1. **Multiple Technologies and Ranges of Expertise on Complex E-Government Issues**
   - Biodiversity
   - Data sharing and integration in e-government
   - Digital libraries and archives
   - Geographical information systems: applications in e-government sites
   - Security and privacy in e-government
   - Semantic Web applications
   - Wireless use in e-government

2. **E-Government Research Relevant to EC**
   - Communication model
   - Data privacy protection
   - Digital divide issues and solutions
   - E-government/service delivery
   - Intra/intergovernment relations
   - Political processes related to e-government

3. **Managerial and Political Issues Important to the Success of E-Government**
   - E-government architectures by applications
   - Metrics of e-government progress and evaluation (by countries)
   - Integration of governmental internal administrative systems with external e-marketplaces
   - Integration of departments on the Web Services platform
   - Secure Internet voting protocols
   - Citizen adoption of e-government services

4. **The Importance of E-Learning as a Medium for Public and Corporate Education**
   - Potential target market of e-learning
   - Impact and limitation of e-learning as a corporate training program
   - Propagation of e-learning by application and by country
   - Architecture of e-learning systems
   - Business models of e-learning systems
   - Hybrid design of online and offline learning services
   - The role of the virtual professor
   - Asynchronous collaboration in on-demand education
   - Transformation of knowledge process via Internet publishing
   - Comparative performance of blogs in building community

5. **Knowledge Management Used in the Context of EC**
   - When knowledge management succeeds and when it fails
   - Knowledge management for CRM
   - Knowledge management for SRM
   - Role of knowledge management in the online community
   - Using agents to collect knowledge about buyers and sellers
   - Architecture of knowledge management systems on Semantic Web Services
   - Framework of demand-driven knowledge management
   - Using knowledge management systems for decision support
   - Collaborative tools in building innovative virtual teams for interorganizational knowledge sharing
   - Ontologies in KM

SUMMARY

In this chapter, you learned about the following EC issues as they relate to the learning objectives.

1. **E-government activities.** Governments, like any other organization, can use EC applications for great savings. Notable applications are e-procurement using reverse auctions, e-payments to and from citizens and businesses, auctioning of surplus goods, and electronic travel and expense management systems. Governments also conduct electronic business with other governments. Finally, governments can facilitate homeland security with EC tools.

2. **E-government to citizens, businesses, and its own operations.** Governments worldwide are providing a variety of services to citizens over the Internet. Such initiatives increase citizens' satisfaction and decrease government expenses in providing customer service applications including electronic voting. Governments also are active in electronically trading with businesses. Finally, EC is done within and between governments.

3. **E-learning and virtual universities.** E-learning is the delivery of educational content via electronic media, including the Internet and intranets. Degree programs, lifelong learning topics, and corporate training are delivered by thousands of organizations worldwide. A growing area is distance learning via online university offerings. Some are virtual; others are delivered both online and offline. Online corporate training also is increasing and is sometimes conducted at formal corporate learning centers.

4. **Online publishing and e-books.** Online publishing of newspapers, magazines, and books is growing rapidly, as is the online publishing of other digitizable items, such as software, music, games, movies, and other entertainment. Of special interest are blogging, the publishing of newsletter-like commentaries by individuals on the Internet, and wikis, which enable people to collaborate in writing.

5. **Knowledge management and dissemination as an e-business.** Knowledge has been recognized as an important organizational asset. It needs to be properly captured, stored, managed, and shared. Knowledge is critical for many e-commerce tasks. Knowledge can be shared in different ways; expert knowledge can be provided to nonexperts (for fee or free) via a knowledge portal or as a personal service (e.g., via e-mail).

6. **C2C activities.** C2C consists of consumers conducting e-commerce with other consumers, mainly in auctions (such as at eBay). Buying and selling of goods and personal services can also take place through the use of online classified ads, exchanges, and special services.

KEY TERMS

Blog	390	**Expert location systems**	397	**Online publishing**	385
Customer-to-customer (C2C)	400	**Government-to-business (G2B)**	368	**Organizational knowledge base**	393
Desktop search	398	**Government-to-citizens (G2C)**	365	**Peer-to-peer (P2P)**	401
Distance learning	381	**Government-to-employees (G2E)**	370	**Podcast**	387
E-book	387	**Government-to-government (G2G)**	370	**Podcaster**	387
E-government	365	**Information intelligence**	395	**Virtual university**	381
E-learning	376	**Knowledge management (KM)**	393	**Webcasting**	387
E-zines	385	**Knowledge portal**	395	**Webinars**	387
Edutainment	383	**Netizen**	368	**Weblogging (blogging)**	390
Electronic voting	367			**WikiLog (wikiblog or wiki)**	391

QUESTIONS FOR DISCUSSION

1. Compare wikis to blogs.
2. Describe the social phenomenon of blogging and evaluate its commercial possibilities.
3. How can online publishing support paper-based publications?
4. Discuss the advantages and disadvantages of e-books.

5. Will paper-based books and magazines be eliminated in the long run? Why or why not?

6. Check an online version of a newspaper or magazine you are familiar with and discuss the differences between the print and online versions.

7. Discuss the advantages of e-learning for an undergraduate student.

8. Discuss the advantages of e-learning in the corporate training environment.

9. Discuss the relationship between KM and a portal.

10. In what ways does KM support e-commerce?

11. Why do you think people trade online virtual properties?

12. Discuss the advantages of expert location systems over corporate knowledge bases that contain experts' knowledge. What are the disadvantages? Can they be combined? How?

13. Some say that B2G is simply B2B. Explain.

14. Compare and contrast B2E with G2E.

15. Which e-government EC activities are intrabusiness activities? Explain why they are intrabusiness.

16. Identify the benefits of G2C to citizens and to governments.

17. How can e-government enhance homeland security?

18. Compare desktop searches to expert location systems.

INTERNET EXERCISES

1. Enter **blogger.com** and blog around. Create a blog based on your own personal interests. Try to apply the rules of blog building discussed in Section 8.5.

2. Enter **pcmag.com**, **fortune.com**, or other online versions of popular magazines. How would you compare reading the electronic magazine against the print version?

3. Enter **e-learningcentre.co.uk** and evaluate its resources and activities.

4. Enter **elearnmag.org** and **elearningpost.com**. Identify current issues and find articles related to the effectiveness of e-training. Write a report.

5. Identify a difficult business problem. Post the problem on **elance.com** and on **answers.com**. Summarize the offers to solve the problem.

6. Enter **kmworld.com** And find recent developments in KM. Prepare a report.

7. Enter **whitehouse.gov/government** and review the "Gateway to Government." Based on the stages presented in Exhibit 8.4, what stage does this site represent? Review the available site tours. Suggest ways the government could improve this portal.

8. Enter **oecd.org** and identify the studies conducted by the Organization for Economic Cooperation and Development (OECD) on the topic of e-government. What are the organization's major concerns?

9. Enter **fcw.com** and read the latest news on e-government. Identify initiatives not covered in this chapter. Check the B2G corner. Then enter **gcn.com**. Finally, enter **estrategy.gov**. Compare the information presented on the three Web sites.

10. Enter **procurement.com** and **govexec.com**. Identify recent e-procurement initiatives and summarize their unique aspects.

11. Enter **sbdc.com.au** and **fcw.com** and find the specific G2C information provided. Prepare a list.

TEAM ASSIGNMENTS AND ROLE PLAYING

1. Assign each team to a different country. Each team will explore the e-government offerings of that country. Have each team make a presentation to convince the class that its country's offerings are the most comprehensive. (Exclude Hong Kong.)

2. Create four teams, each representing one of the following: G2C, G2B, G2E, and G2G. Each team will prepare a plan of its major activities in a small country, such as Denmark, Finland, or Singapore. A fifth team will deal with the coordination and collaboration of all e-government activities in each country. Prepare a report based on the activity.

3. Have teams search for virtual universities (e.g., the University of Phoenix, **uophx.edu**), Liverpool University

in the UK, or **ecollage.com**). Write a summary of the schools' e-learning offerings.

4. Have each team represent one of the following sites: **netlibrary.com**, **ebooks.com**, and **zanderebooks.com**. Each team will examine the technology, legal issues, prices, and business alliances associated with its site.

Each team will then prepare a report answering the question, "Will e-books succeed?"

5. Have teams investigate various homeland security activities and how they are facilitated electronically. Write a report that expands on the material in Section 8.1. Investigate several countries.

Real-World Case

A DECADE OF E-GOVERNMENT DEVELOPMENT IN HONG KONG (1998 TO 2007)

Since 1998, the Hong Kong (HK) Special Administrative Region (SAR) government has implemented territory-wide e-government initiatives, which are pursuant to the Digital 21 Information Technology Strategy (*info.gov.hk/digital21*). Subsequently, the years 1998 to 2007 marked the initial stages of e-government development in HKSAR as information and services were made available online (refer to stages 1 to 4 of e-government in Exhibit 8.4). As a result, an infrastructure where citizens, business organizations, and the government can perform electronic transactions was established by February 2007. Moreover, the city of Hong Kong is now regarded as a "mature city" in terms of e-government development (Accenture 2003). The following are some of the key e-government projects in HKSAR that were developed from 1998 to 2007.

Electronic Service Delivery (ESD) Scheme

Since 2001, the Electronic Service Delivery Scheme, or ESD, has provided a central electronic platform through which the Hong Kong public can transact business with the government. ESDlife (*esdlife.com*), a Web portal launched under the ESD scheme, hosts over 200 e-government applications for more than 50 bureaus, departments, and agencies as of February 2007. Moreover, the average monthly number of visits to all government Web sites is 280 million, and over 90 percent of HKSAR government services are provided to the public with an e-option. Some examples of the ESD services include the following:

▶ Booking for leisure and sports facilities

▶ Performing civic duties, such as filing tax returns, paying tax bills, and purchasing tax reserve certificates

▶ Applying and subsequent registration for public examinations

▶ Searching for job vacancies

▶ Renewing driving and vehicle licenses

▶ Selling of statistical data and government publications

▶ Booking appointments for registration of identity card

▶ Booking appointments for giving marriage notice

▶ Registering to vote

▶ Applying for a senior citizen card

▶ Paying government bills

▶ Serving as a one-stop venue for changing one's address with multiple government departments

ESD employs a variety of CRM characteristics. For example, the 200 interactive and transactional services made available to the public are organized around their daily needs under the categories of "Health," "Personal Growth," "Leisure," "Household," and the like. A life event service index is also made available to facilitate the search for services under categories such as "Building a Career," "Establishing a Family," "Having a Baby," "Retiring," and so on. Some public services, such as the weather reports, air pollution index, and a government telephone directory, also are available through the mobile network.

The GovHK Web Portal

Between 2001 to late 2006, the HKSAR Government provided online government information and services through two Web portals—ESDlife (*esdlife.com*) and the Government Information Centre (GIC) (*info.gov.hk*). The former Web portal is controlled and operated by a private company and hosts all e-government applications. As a separate function, the GIC operated by the HKSAR Government provides easy access to some 200 departmental/thematic Web sites administered through different bureaus/departments (B/Ds). A new government Web portal GovHK (*gov.hk*) was launched in early 2007 to replace the government-centric GIC, and this new portal serves as the one-stop shop for online government information and services. For instance, related information and services provided by different B/Ds are brought together in service clusters on GovHK, the purpose of which is to serve one or more target customer groups with needs and interests within a particular subject (e.g., environment, employment, education, and transportation) or in a particular age range or role (e.g., business and trade, visitors, and residents). The goal is to migrate e-government applications hosted on

ESDlife to GovHK by January 2008. In its inception, the GovHK portal was developed to provide a citizen-centric way of e-government services delivery.

Smart Identity Card

The HKSAR government started issuing smart identity cards to its citizens in June 2003. By March 2007, Hong Kong's 7 million residents acquired the new generation of smart ID cards. This project has effectively made Hong Kong one of the largest populations in the world to use smart ID cards. The smart ID facilitated the formation of a community-wide information infrastructure for the government and the private sectors to introduce value-added e-applications.

The following are some applications provided on Smart ID cards:

▶ **E-certificates.** The embedding of a free e-Cert in the smart ID card presents Hong Kong citizens with an option to possess an "electronic-ID" that can be used for identity authentication and for ensuring confidentiality, integrity, and nonrepudiation of data transmitted in electronic transactions.

▶ **E-channels.** The Immigration Department of HKSAR introduced an automated passenger clearance system (e-channels) in December 2004. The e-channel system performs mutual authentication with the smart identity card key and then deploys fingerprint verification technology for the authentication of a person's identity. This way, HKSAR residents can use their smart identity cards to perform self-service immigration clearance.

▶ **E-library card.** Cardholders have the option to use their smart ID card as a library card.

▶ **E-driving licenses.** Smart ID card holders have the option not to carry their driving licenses when driving.

Hong Kong Education City

Set up in 2000, the Hong Kong Education City (HKedCity) provides an interactive electronic platform with rich e-learning resources for students, teachers, and parents. Users can exchange experiences and promote effective practices through the portal. As of February 2007, over 1.4 million registered users were on the platform.

Electronic Tendering System (ETS)

The Electronic Tendering System (ETS) enables international suppliers to do business with the HKSAR government online. Approximately 3,000 suppliers from over 30 countries were registered to use ETS in 2005.

Government Electronic Trading Service

The Government Electronic Trading Service (GETS) enables the trading community to submit official trade-related documents to the government through electronic means. Commercial service providers enable value-added services creating opportunities for the further enhancement of the local e-commerce service industry.

Between 1998 and 2007, HKSAR moved to the established stages of e-government, placing emphasis on the clustering of common services and full-enterprise reform and collaboration (refer to stages 5 and 6 of Exhibit 8.4). Refer to Online File W8.7 for the e-government activities of Hong Kong SAR, which are subject to implementation from 2007 to 2010.

Sources: Compiled from Accenture (2003); OGCIO (2005); and *govhk.com*, *esdlife.com*, and *smartid.com* (all accessed February 2007).

Questions

1. Identify each initiative as G2C, G2B, C2G, or G2E.
2. Visit *info.gov.hk/digital21* and identify the goals of the five e-government initiatives.
3. Section 8.1 and Exhibit 8.4 discuss the stages of e-government development. Specifically, the HKSAR government is at what stage of transformation?
4. How will the role of the HK government change when the initiatives mature and are fully utilized?
5. Compare the services offered by Hong Kong with those offered in other Asian cities, such as Taiwan (*gov.tw*) and Singapore (*ecitizen.gov.sg*). What are the major differences among these e-governments?

REFERENCES

Abramson, M. A., and G.E. Means (eds.). E-Government 2001. Lanham, MD: Rowman and Littlefield, 2001.

Accenture. *eGovernment Leadership: Engaging the Customer.* 2003. **accenture.com/xdoc/en/newsroom/epresskit/egovernment/egov_epress.pdf** (accessed February 2007).

Agre, P. E. "P2P and the Promise of Internet Equality." *Communications of the ACM*, February 2003.

Aldrich, C. "1996–2006 E-Learning in the Workplace." *TD*, September 2006.

Anderson, K. V. "e-Government: Five Key Challenges for Management." *Electronic Journal of E-Government* (**ejeg.com**), November 2006.

Arar, Y. "New E-Book Reader Is Worth Looking At." *PCWorld.com*, November 2006.

AskMe.com. "Demostrated ROI Prompts Department of Commerce to Expand Deployment Across Global Commercial Service Operations." **askme.com/press/docrelease.asp** (accessed February 2007).

Association for Federal Information Resources Management. "A Blueprint for Successful E-Government Implementation: Steps to Accelerate Cultural Change and Overcome Stakeholder Resistance." *Affirm.org,* June 2002. **affirm.org/Pubs/Affirm.pdf** (accessed January 2007).

Association of American Publishers. "Book Sales Continue To Climb In October." *AAP* press release, December 11, 2006. **publishers.org/press/releases.cfm?PressRelease ArticleID=360** (accessed January 2007).

Becker, S. A. "E-Government Usability for Older Adults." *Communications of the ACM* 48, no. 2 (2005).

Bhattacharjee, S., R. D. Gopal, K. Lertchwara, and J. Marsden. "Impact of Legal Threats on Online Music Sharing Activity: An Analysis of Music Industry Legal Actions." *The Journal of Law and Economics* 49 (2006).

Blackboard. **blackboard.com** (accessed January 2007).

Boehle, S. "Rapid e-Learning." *Training,* July 2005.

Bose, R. "Knowledge Management Capabilities and Infrastructure for E-Commerce." *Journal of Computer Information Systems* 42, no. 5 (2002).

Boxer, K. M., and B. Johnson. "How to Build an Online Center." *Training and Development,* August 2002. **findarticles.com/p/articles/mi_m0MNT/is_8_56/ai_90512522** (accessed February 2007).

BusinessWeek Online. "E-Mail Is So Five Minutes Ago." November, 28, 2005. **businessweek.com/magazine/content/05_48/b3961120.htm** (accessed February 2007).

BusinessWeek Online. "The Organic Myth." October 16, 2006. **businessweek.com/magazine/content/06_42/b4005001.htm** (accessed January 2007).

Chao, Y., and F. Tong. "The Problems in the Implementation of E-Government Administration, the Analysis and Strategies." *Proceedings of the 7th International Conference on Electronic Commerce,* Xi'an, China, August 15–17, 2005.

Chen, Y. N., H. M. Chen, W. Huang, and R. K. H. Ching. "E-Government Strategies in Developed and Developing Countries: An Implementation Framework and Case Study." *Journal of Global Information Management* 14, no. 1 (2006).

Chu, K. C., and Q. Lam. "Using an E-Book for Learning," in Khosrow-Pour (2006).

Ciment, M. "A Personal History of the NSF Digital Government Program." *Communications of the ACM,* January 2003.

Cisco. **cisco.com** (accessed January 2007).

Coggins, C. "Independent Testing of Voting Systems." *Communications of the ACM* 47, no. 10 (October 2004).

Crawford, K. "A Degree of Respect for Online MBAs." *Business 2.0,* December 2005.

D'Agostino, D. "Expertise Management: Who Knows about This?" *CIO Insight,* July 1, 2004.

Dahl, E. "Online Music: New Hits and Misses." *PCWorld,* September 2003.

Datta, S. "The 7 Habits of Highly Effective Bloggers." *Business 2.0,* September 2006.

Davenport, T. H., and L. Prusak. *Working Knowledge: How Organizations Manage What They Know.* Cambridge, MA: Harvard Business School Press, 2000.

Davies, N., K. Cheverst, A. Friday, and K. Mitchell. "Future Wireless Applications for a Networked City." *IEEE Wireless Communications,* February 2002.

Dean, J. "E-Gov in the Works." *GOVEXEC.com,* November 2000. **govexec.com/features/1100/egov/egovworks.htm** (accessed January 2007).

Delahoussaye, M., and R. Zemke. "About Learning Online." *Training,* September 2001.

Delphi Group. "Information Intelligence: Content Classification and the Enterprise Taxonomy Practice." *Delphi Group Report,* June 2004.

DiFranco, A., A. Petro, E. Shear, and V. Vladimirov. "Small Vote Manipulations Can Sway Elections." *Communications of the ACM* 4, no. 10 (October 2004).

"Digital 21 IT Strategies." **info.gov.hk/digital21,** student interview, February 2001 and 2002 (accessed January 2007).

Ding, E. "Virtual Property: Treasure or Trash?" *China International Business,* September 2004.

Edmiston, K. D. "State and Local E-Government—Prospects and Challenges." *American Review of Public Administration* 33, no. 1 (2003).

eLearn Magazine. **elearnmag.org** (accessed January 2007).

Emarketer. "U.S. Government Web Sites Concentrate on Security, Privacy." October 2, 2002.

Ergonomics Today. "Study Links Long-Term Back Pain to Backpacks." *Ergonomics Today,* September 8, 2004. **ergoweb.com/news/detail.cfm?id=985** (accessed January 2007).

Evangelidis, A., A. Macintosh, and E. Davenport. "Frames Towards Risk Modeling in E-Government Services: A UK Perspective." *Proceedings of the Third International Conference on Electronic Government,* Zaragoza, Spain, August 30–September 3, 2004.

Fahey, L., R. Srivastava, J. S. Sharon, D. E. Smith-Textkörper. "Linking E-Business and Operating Processes: The Role of KM." *IBM Systems Journal* 40, no. 4 (2001).

Flynn, N. *Blog Rules: A Business Guide to Managing Policy, Public Relations, and Legal Issues.* New York: AMACOM/American Management Association, 2006.

Galagan, P. A. "Delta Force at Cisco." *Training and Development,* July 2002.

Gibson, R., and C. Brown. "Electronic Voting as the Key to Ballot Reform," in Khosrow-Pour (2006).

Gibson, S. "Podcasting: An Enterprise Hit." *eWeek,* October 2, 2006.

Gong, L. (ed.). "Peer-to-Peer Networks in Action." *IEEE Internet Computing*, Special Issue (January–February 2002).

Grace.com. **grace.com** (accessed January 2007).

Henriksen, H. Z. "Fad or Investment in the Future: An Analysis of the Demand of E-Services in Danish Municipalities." *Electronic Journal of e-Government* 4, no. 1 (2006).

Holsapple, C. W. (ed.) *Handbook on Knowledge Management.* Heidelberg, Germany: Springer Computer Science, 2003.

Hopfner, J. "A Revolution in (Tax) Revenue." *MIS Asia*, May 2002.

Howe, J. "Your Web, Your Way." *Time,* December 17, 2006. **time.com/time/magazine/article/0,9171,1570815,00.html** (accessed January 2007).

Huang, W., et al. "E-Government Development and Implementation," in Khosrow-Pour (2006).

Hyperion. "Federal Government—Additional Details." 2007. **hyperion.com/solutions/federal_division/legislation_summaries.cfm** (accessed February 2007).

Impact-information.com. "Making e-Learning Work." July 18, 2006. **impact-information.com/impactinfo/newsletter/plwork26.htm** (accessed January 2007).

Intel. "Peer-to-Peer: Spreading the Computing Power." **intel.com/eBusiness/products/peertopeer/ar011102.htm** (accessed June 2002). Note: no longer available online.

Internetnews.com. "CommerceNet and Peer Intelligence Research P2P for Business." *SiliconValley.Internet.com*, August 17, 2001. **siliconvalley.internet.com/news/article.php/868511** (accessed July 2002).

Jefferson, D., A. D. Rubin, B. Simons, and D. A. Wagner. "Analyzing Internet Voting Security." *Communications of the ACM* 47, no. 10 (October 2004).

Jih, W. K., M. M. Helms, and D. T. Mayo. "Effects of Knowledge Management on Electronic Commerce: An Exploratory Study in Taiwan." *Journal of Global Information Management* 13, no. 4 (2005).

Joia, L. A. "Building Government-to-Government Enterprise," in Khosrow-Pour (2006).

Jones, D. W. "Auditing Elections." *Communications of the ACM* 47, no. 10 (October 2004).

Jones, N. B., D. Provost, and D. Pascale. "Developing a University Research Web-Based Knowledge Portal." *International Journal of Knowledge and Learning*, January–February 2006.

Kaiser, S. "Qualification Requirements in E-Government: The Need for Information Systems in Public Administration Education." *Proceedings of the Third International Conference on Electronic Government*, Zaragoza, Spain, August 30–September 3, 2004.

Keen, J. "Politicians' Campaigns Invade MySpace." *USA Today*, October 17, 2006.

Khosrow-Pour, M. (ed.). *Encyclopedia of E-Commerce, E-Government, and Mobile Commerce.* Hershey, PA: Idea Group Reference, 2006.

Kim, G., and S. M. Ong., "An Exploratory Study of Factors Influencing M-Learning Success." *Journal of Computer Information Systems*, Fall 2005.

Kini, R. B. "Peer-to-Peer Technology: A Technology Reborn." *Information Systems Management*, 2002.

KMworld.com. **kmworld.com** (accessed January 2007)

Korolishin, J. "Sheetz Keeps Tabs on Training Compliance via Web Portal." *Stores*, February 2004a.

Korolishin, J. "Tweeter Gives Training a Tweak." *Stores*, August 2004b.

Kumar, N., and Q. Peng. "Strategic Alliances in E-Government Procurement." *International Journal of Electronic Business* 4, no. 2 (2006).

Kumar, S., and G. Thondikulam. "Knowledge Management in a Collaborative Business Framework." *Information, Knowledge, Systems Management* 5, no. 3 (2006).

Kwok, S. H., K. R. Lang, and K. Y. Tam. "Peer-to-Peer Technology Business and Service Models: Risks and Opportunities." *Electronic Markets* 12, no. 3 (2002).

Lai, H., and T. H. Chu. "Knowledge Management: A Review of Industrial Cases." *Journal of Computer Information Systems*, special issue 42, no. 5 (2002).

Langenbach, C., and F. Bodendorf. "The Electronic Mall: A Service Center for Distance Learning." *International Journal of Electronic Commerce*, Winter 1999–2000.

Lason Company. "Fort Knox Escrow Services—A Lason Company—Unveils Escrow Direct." Lason Company press release, March 20, 2000. **lason.com** (accessed June 2003).

Lee, D. H. "Contextual IT Business Value and Barriers: An E-Government and E-Business Perspective." *Proceedings 38th HICSS*, Big Island, Hawaii, January 2005.

Lee, S. M., X. Tan, and S. Trimi. "Current Practices of Leading E-Government Countries." *Communications of the ACM* 48, no. 10 (October 2005).

Lethin, R. (ed.). "Technical and Social Components of Peer-to-Peer Computing." *Communications of the ACM*, February 2003.

Lewin, J. "Blog Risk." *E-Commerce in Action*, September 29, 2004. **66.51.97.137/2367202.txt** (no longer available online).

lifelines.navy.mil (accessed January 2007).

Lin, H., and G. Lee. "Impact of Organizational Learning and Knowledge Management Factors on E-Business Adoption." *Management Decision* 43, no. 2 (2005).

Lin, J. "Ilan County Seeks Online Buyers for Produce." *Taipei Times*, November 16, 2006.

Mack, R., Y. Ravin, and R. J. Byrd. "Knowledge Portals and the Emerging Digital Knowledge Workplace." *IBM Systems Journal* 40, no. 4 (2001).

Mahapatra, R., and V. S. Lai. "Evaluating End-User Training Programs." *Communications of the ACM*, January 2005.

Malkia, M., et al. *E-Transformation in Governance: New Directions in Government.* Hershey, PA: The Idea Group, 2004.

Marche, S., and J. D. McNiven. "E-Government and E-Governance: The Future Isn't What It Used to Be." *Canadian Journal of Administrative Sciences* 20, no. 1 (2003).

Marchioni, G., et al. (eds.). "Digital Government." *Communications of the ACM*, Special Issue (January 2003).

McAffee, A. "The Napsterization of B2B." *Harvard Business Review*, November–December 2000.

McKinley, E. "Multitasking Solution Ushers in New Era of Computer-Based Training at Shoney's." *Stores*, April 2003.

Mello, J. P. "Survey Finds File-Sharing Networks Boost CD Buys." *TechNewsWorld*, June 17, 2004. **technewsworld. com/story/34544.html** (accessed January 2005).

Metz, C. "Who Owns Print-on-Demand." *PCMagazine*, March 2004.

Miller, J. R. "Technology, Digital Citizen, and E-Government: The E-Invention Revolution." World Markets Research Center, 2000. **wmrc.com/business briefing/pdf/wued2000/Publication/miller.pdf** (no longer available online).

Miller, R. "Ebooks Worm Their Way into the Reference Market." *EcontentMag.com*, July–August 2005. **econtent mag.com/Archives/Issue.aspx?IssueID=219** (accessed January 2007).

Moon, J. M. *From E-Government to M-Government: Emerging Practices in the Use of Mobile Technology by State Governments*. Arlington, VA: IBM Center for the Business of Government, 2004.

Naka, I. *Knowledge Management and Risk Strategy*. Taipei, Taiwan: World Scientific Publishing Company, 2007.

Neal, L. "Predictions for 2007." *eLearn Magazine*, January 12, 2007. **elearnmag.org/subpage.cfm?section=articles& article=42–1** (accessed January 2007).

Needleman, S. "Blogging Becomes a Corporate Job: Digital 'Handshake'?" *Wall Street Journal*, May 2005.

Neumann, P. (ed.). "The Problems and Potentials of Electronic Voting Systems." *Communications of the ACM*, October 2004.

Ng, F. F. "E-Learning Concepts and Development," in Khosrow-Pour (2006).

Norris, D. F., and M. J. Moon. "Advancing E-Government at the Grassroots: Tortoise or Hare?" *Public Administration Review* 65, no. 1 (2005).

OGCIO. "Success Story of Project Completed for the Government." *Info.gov.hk*, December 12, 2005. **info. gov.hk/digital21/eng/scp/success_stories/ESDServics_ Success_Story_ESD.pdf** (accessed January 2007).

Ozzie, R. CEO of Groove Networks personal blog, August 24, 2002. **ozzie.net/blog/2002/08/24.html** (accessed January 2007).

Parks Associates. **parksassociates.com** (accessed January 2007).

Paskaleva-Shapira, K. "Transitioning from e-Government to e-Governance in the Knowledge Society: The Role of the Legal Framework for Enabling the Process in the European Union's Countries." *Proceedings of the 7th Annual International Conference on Digital Government*, San Diego, California, May 21–24, 2006.

Pfaff, D., and B. Simon. "New Services through Integrated E-Government." Proceedings of the First International Conference on *Electronic Government*, Aix-en-Provence, France, September 2–5, 2002.

Piccoli, G., R. Ahmad, and B. Ives. "Web-Based Virtual Learning Environments." *MIS Quarterly*, December 2001.

Price, G. "Google Partners with Oxford, Harvard, and Others to Digitize Libraries." *SearchEngineWatch*, December 14, 2004. **searchenginewatch.com/search day/article.php/3447411** (accessed January 2007).

Putnik, G., and M. M. Cunha (eds.). *Knowledge And Technology Management in Virtual Organizations*, Hershey, PA: Idea Group Publishing, 2007.

Rao, M. *Knowledge Management Tools and Techniques*. Burlington, MA: Elsevier, 2004.

Rapoza, J. "How to Spot Fake Blogs." *eWeek*, October 2006.

Reisman, S. "Evolution of Computer-Based Distance Learning," in Khosrow-Pour (2006).

Reuters (TechNews). "Kazaa Nears Download Record." *News.com*, May 22, 2003.

Roberts-Witt, S. "A 'Eureka!' Moment at Xerox." *PC Magazine*, March 26, 2002. **pcmag.com/ article2/0,4149,28792,00.asp** (accessed January 2007).

Rowe, D. and O. Bell. "Experiences in E-Government Best Practices and Solution Sharing." *Journal of E-Government* 1, no. 3 (2005).

Scholl, H. "What Can E-Commerce and E-Government Learn from Each Other?" *Proceedings of the 7th Annual International Conference on Digital Government*, San Diego, California, May 21–24, 2006.

Schonfeld, E. "P2P Gets Personal." *Business 2.0*, November 2006.

Schuman, E. "Microsoft, Amazon and Google Tackle E-Books Their Own Way." *e Week*, November 2005.

Sener, J. "Effectively Evaluating Online Learning Programs." *eLearn Magazine*, May 2006. **elearnmag.org/ subpage.cfm?section=tutorials&article=23–1** (accessed January 2007).

Serva, S. "P2P Collaboration Tools at Work." *Econtentmag.com*, June 1, 2004. **econtentmag.com/ Articles/ArticlePrint.aspx?ArticleID=6599IssueID= 208** (accessed January 2005).

Siau, K., and Y. Long "Using Social Development Lenses to Understand E-Government Development." *Journal of Global Information Management* 1, no. 1 (2006).

Siemens, G. "Categories of E-Learning." *Elearnspace. org*, October 18, 2004. **elearnspace.org/Articles/ elearningcategories.htm** (accessed February 2007).

Sifry, D. "State of the Blogosphere." *Sifry.com*, August 7, 2006. **sifry.com/alerts/archives/000436.html** (accessed February 2007).

Sloan, P., and P. Kaihla. "Blogging for Dollars." *Business 2.0*, September 2006.

SocialText. "Dresdner Kleinwort Wasserstein (DrKW)." *Customer Success Story at SocialText.com*, 2004. **socialtext. com/node/80** (accessed February 2007).

Song, S. "An Internet Knowledge Sharing System." *Journal of Computer Information Systems*, Spring 2002.

Spanbauer, S. "Internet Tips: Self-Publish Your Books, Songs, and Movies Online." *PCWorld.com*, September 22, 2006. **pcworld.com/article/id,127053c,webauthoringsoftware/article.html** (accessed January 2007).

Stonyfield. **stonyfield.com** (accessed January 2007).

Stratford, J. "Computerized and Networked Government Information Column—Developments in U.S. Federal E-Government Efforts." *Journal of Government Information* 30, nos. 5–6 (2004).

Sugumaran, V. *Intelligent Support Systems Technology: Knowledge Management.* Hershey, PA: Idea Publishing Group, 2002.

Tarnoff, D. L. "Shifting Students' Financial Responsibilities from Textbooks to Laboratory Resources." *Journal of Computing Sciences in Colleges* 22, no. 3 (January 2007).

Thong, J. Y., L. H. Weiyin, and Y. T. Kar. "What Leads to User Acceptance of Digital Libraries." *Communications of the ACM*, November 2004.

U.S. Department of Housing and Urban Development. *FY 2006 Performance and Accountability Report.* November 2006. **hud.gov/offices/cfo/reports/2006/2006par.pdf** (accessed January 2007).

U.S. Government. "E-Government Strategy." Office of the President of the United States, Special Report, 2003. **whitehouse.gov/omb/egov/2003egov_strat.pdf** (accessed January 2007).

U.S. Office of Management and Budget. "E-Government Strategy: Delivery of Services to Citizens." *OMB Internal Report*, February 27, 2002.

Urdan, T., and C. Weggen. "Corporate E-Learning: Exploring a New Frontier." W. R. Hambrecht & Co., March 2000. **spectrainteractive.com/pdfs/CorporateELearingHamrecht.pdf** (accessed January 2007).

Wang, H., and S. Wang. "Cyber Warfare: Steganography vs. Steganalysis." *Communications of the ACM*, October 2004.

Warkentin, M., D. Gefen, P. A. Pavlou, and G. M. Rose. "Encouraging Citizen Adoption of E-Government by Building Trust." *Electronic Markets* 12, no. 3 (2002).

Weaver, P. "Preventing E-Learning Failure." *Training and Development* 56, no. 8 (2002).

WebCT. **webct.com** (accessed January 2007).

Weinstein, M. "On Demand Is in Demand." *Training Magazine*, October 2006.

Welch, E. W., and S.K. Pandey "E-Government and Bureaucracy: Toward a Better Understanding of Intranet Implementation and Its Effect on Red Tape." *Journal of Public Administration Research and Theory*, October 2006. **doi:10.1093/jopart/mul013** (accessed January 2007).

West, D. "State and Federal E-Government in the United States, 2004." Center for Public Policy Report, September 2004. **insidepolitics.org/egovt04us.html** (accessed January 2007).

Wikipedia. "E-Learning." 2007. **en.Wikipedia.org/wiki/Elearning** (accessed January 2007),

Wimmer, M. A. "Integrated Service Modeling for Online One-Stop Government." *Electronic Markets 12*, no. 3 (2002).

Wimmer, M. A. "Implementing a Knowledge Portal for Egovernment Based on Semantic Modelling: The E-Government Intelligent Portal." *Proceedings 39th Hawaiian International Conference on Systems Sciences*, Kauai, Hawaii, January 4–7, 2006.

Wong, W. Y. *At the Dawn of E-Government.* Report, Deloitte & Touche, New York, 2000.

Wong, W., and E. Welch. "Does E-Government Promote Accountability? A Comparative Analysis of Web Site Openness and Government Accountability." *Governance—An International Journal of Policy and Administration* 17, no. 2 (2004).

Xerox. "Eureka." PARC Research. **parc.xerox.com/research/projects/commknowledge/eureka.html** (accessed January 2007).

Yap, A. "Secrets to Successful Blogging." *Searchwarp.com*, May 3, 2006. **searchwarp.com/swa60483.htm** (accessed January 2007)

Zhang, D., and J. F. Nunamaker. "Powering E-Learning in the New Millennium: An Overview of E-Learning Enabling Technology." *Information Systems Frontiers*, April 2003.

Zhang, D., J. L. Zhao, L. Zhou, and J. Nunamaker. "Can E-learning Replace Classroom Learning?" *Communications of the ACM*, May 2004.

CHAPTER 9

MOBILE COMPUTING AND COMMERCE AND PERVASIVE COMPUTING

Content

Learning Objectives

Upon completion of this chapter, you will be able to:

1. Describe the mobile computing environment that supports m-commerce (devices, software, services).

2. Describe the four major types of wireless telecommunications networks.

3. Define mobile commerce and understand its relationship to e-commerce.

4. Discuss the value-added attributes, benefits, and fundamental drivers of m-commerce.

5. Discuss m-commerce applications in finance, shopping, advertising, and provision of content.

6. Describe the application of m-commerce within organizations.

7. Understand B2B and supply chain management applications of m-commerce.

8. Describe consumer and personal applications of m-commerce.

9. Understand the technologies and potential application of location-based m-commerce.

10. Describe the major inhibitors and barriers of m-commerce.

11. Discuss the key characteristics and current uses of pervasive computing.

FOOD LION'S M-COMMERCE INNOVATIONS

The Problem

Food Lion is a supermarket chain (1,200 stores) that decided to distinguish itself from the competition, which is extremely strong (e.g., Wal-Mart is a major competitor). The company wanted to create *Bloom*, an upscale grocery store brand that would provide a sensible, uncomplicated, hassle-free shopping experience that would leave shoppers feeling smart, relaxed, and confident. The problem was finding the appropriate technology to do it.

The Solution

The company decided to use m-commerce technology. The following are some of the applications implemented by Food Lion:

- **Mobile checkstand.** This is a mobile checkout POS terminal equipped with wheels that can be moved to any location in the store as well as outside (e.g., storefront for special sales). This brings flexibility and ability to expedite checkout time. These devices can be added whenever checkout lines are getting long.

- **Personal scanner.** This handheld device is a POS terminal that emulates the system used at checkout. The device is given to the customers. When a customer picks up an item off the shelf, the customer scans the item with the device and then bags the item. The device shows the price of the item and the running total of all items bagged. Food Lion can also use the personal scanner (from Symbol Technology) to send messages, such as special marketing offers, to customers while they are shopping. The final bill is downloaded to the cash register.

- **Employee's handheld devices.** These devices enable employees to execute inventory counts, enter orders for depleted items, do shelf-tag printing, and conduct price management from anywhere in the store.

- **Cart-mounted table PC.** This device enables customers to check prices and get product location and information while pushing their carts. Currently, this is done on an experimental basis due to the high cost.

- **Tablet PCs for employees.** The device is docked in the office and carried around wherever the manager goes while maintaining a wireless connection to the store system. Employees prefer it over PDAs and smart cell phones due to the large screen (but they are heavy, so not all employees like them).

- **Mobile manager.** This is a cell-phone sized portable device used to improve in-store communication and supervision.

- **Wi-Fi access.** This is an in-store wireless network (WLAN) that supports the above devices.

To deter cheating in the self-scanning, a random audit is done, but this may alienate a customer, especially if the customer is in a hurry. In the future, the company will install an RFID system that will improve the existing system and reduce the potential for cheating.

Results

Speedier checkout is the main benefit, because all the customer has to do is to pay. Also, in the future, the purchase can be debited automatically directly from the customers' bank account to make checkout even faster. The customers also are happy because they can compare the running total while shopping against their budget. The use of the personal scanner enables the company to reduce prices and increase revenue. The other devices have helped increase employee productivity and satisfaction.

The *Bloom* concept is still under experimentation in several stores. If successful, it will be installed in many stores.

Food Lion is not the only retailer experimenting with wireless devices. Metro Group in Germany (2,400 stores) is experimenting with all the devices cited earlier plus more. For example, a Tablet PC helps shoppers navigate their way to any product, using the store map.

Sources: Compiled from Clark (2005), McGuire (2004), and Heinrich (2005).

WHAT WE CAN LEARN . . .

The opening case illustrates several applications of different wireless devices that have the potential to improve Food Lion's operations. Benefits were observed for the customers, employees, and management. Using wireless technologies, one can create EC applications that are not available with wireline systems; however, some may be expensive (e.g., the cart-mounted Tablet PCs). The case's applications are based on a local area infrastructure called Wi-Fi. All this is part of an emerging technology called *mobile computing,* which is the subject of this chapter.

9.1 MOBILE COMPUTING: CONTENT, INFRASTRUCTURE, AND SERVICES

In the traditional computing environment, users require a desktop computer, and computers are connected to each other, to networks, to servers, and to peripheral devices, such as printers, via wires and cables (Longino 2006). This situation has limited the use of computers to wired locations and has created difficulties for people who need to be mobile in their work. Specifically, salespeople, field service employees, law enforcement agents, inspectors, utility workers, and executives who travel frequently can be more effective if they can use information technology while at their jobs in the field or in transit. Additionally, most people want to be able to connect to the Internet or use mobile telephone services anyplace, anytime. A solution to this situation is mobile computing.

NEW COMPUTING ENVIRONMENT: MOBILE COMPUTING

Mobile computing refers to a computing paradigm designed for workers who travel outside the boundaries of their organizations or for anyone on the move. Salespeople are able to make proposals at customers' offices; a traveler could read and answer all of the day's e-mails while on the road. One could work with the mobile device as long as the battery is working. This paradigm is illustrated in Exhibit 9.1; it shows that small mobile computers can be wired or wireless.

Mobile Devices

Mobile and wireless computing required two solutions. The first solution was to make computers small enough so that they could be carried around easily—in other words, mobile (as shown on the vertical axis in Exhibit 9.1). The desktop computer was made smaller so that it was easier to carry and operated on batteries. First came the laptop computer, which was followed by the smaller but powerful, palmtop computer, recently exemplified by the OQO (pronounced OH-cue-oh). As of 2006, OQO devices have a 1-GHz processor, 30GB HD, 512MB RAM, Wi-Fi card, Bluetooth®, USB 2.0, FireWire, audio, thumb keyboard, and 800×480 indoor/outdoor readable LCD. It also includes a removable lithium battery, a docking cable, a desktop stand, a universal power supply, an air/auto cable, a carrying sleeve,

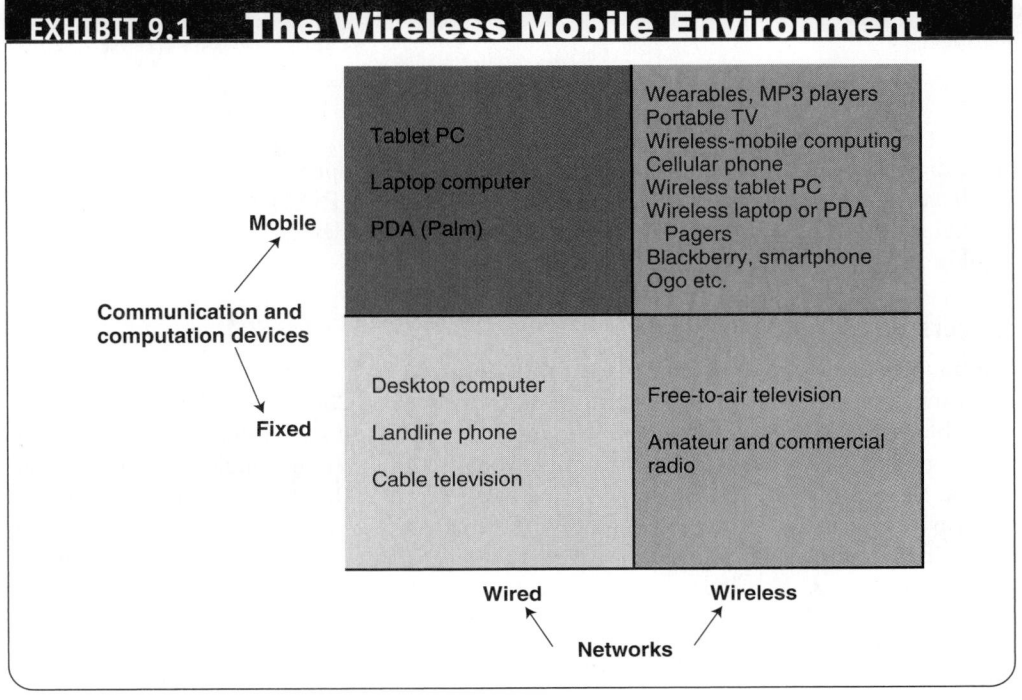

EXHIBIT 9.1 The Wireless Mobile Environment

EXHIBIT 9.2   Mobile Computing Devices

Device	Applications
Wireless portable computer: A laptop or notebook computer can become wireless with the addition of a wireless network card.	Full functionality of a desktop computer, including Microsoft Office, Internet connectivity, and a wide range of business applications.
Tablet PC: A favorite of salespersons and "meeting warriors"; a tablet PC typically includes a stylus, handwriting-recognition software, a virtual on-screen keyboard, and an attachable keyboard for data entry.	Full functionality of a desktop computer, including Microsoft Office, Internet connectivity, and a wide range of business applications. The Microsoft XP Tablet Edition is the most widely used tablet operating system.
Palmtop: Early palmtop computers had limited functionality and poor usability factors. The new OQO features a thumb keyboard, miniature joystick mouse, thumb-wheel scroll device, a stylus-sensitive touch screen, microphone, USB port, Wi-Fi antenna, Bluetooth transmitter, and a 20–40 Gb hard drive.	The OQO supports Microsoft Office, other Windows applications, and Internet connectivity. Memory-intensive programs such as desktop publishing, video editing, and 3D highly interactive games will not work well due to limited memory (256 Mb) and the smalll screen.
Personal digital assistant (PDA): The first handheld computing device has come a long way from its humble beginnings. Modern PDAs feature color screens, tiny keyboards, and many are mobile telephones, too. Indeed, PDAs are converging with smartphones.	Personal information management applications such as calendars, address books, and task lists. Windows Mobile offers Pocket Word and Excel and some PDAs have video and still cameras, audio notebooks, and USB, infrared, Bluetooth, and Wi-Fi connectivity.
Smartphone: All major cell phone manufacturers now make Internet-enabled cell phones. For a list of vendors, models, and capabilities see Malykhina (2006a).	Of course, a smartphone offers a telephone connection similar to a cell phone. Other applications include SMS (texting), Internet access, games, calendars, address books, alarm clocks, and calculators.
Blackberry: A handheld device for e-mail. A screen, tiny keyboard, and innovative interface keep office workers connected to e-mail while traveling or at leisure.	The primary application of Blackberry is e-mail. However, it also has personal information management applications (contacts, calendars, tasks) and a mobile phone. Blackberry offers an integrated user environment; no ISP is required.
Ogo: Similar to Blackberry, but targeted at the "thumb tribe" (younger users who use text and instant messaging); this inexpensive handheld device just sends and receives text. Slightly larger than a cell phone, the Ogo includes a thumb keyboard and special navigation keys for messaging. It is a Palm companion.	Supports instant messaging and e-mail to/from AOL, MSN, and Yahoo! Also supports Short Message Service (SMS) to/from any SMS-capable mobile phone.

personal digital assistant (PDA)
A handheld computer principally used for personal information management.

smartphone
Internet-enabled cell phone that can support mobile applications.

Blackberry
A handheld device principally used for e-mail.

and a digital pen. For details, see oqo.com (2006). Portable specialized computing devices also have emerged, such as the **personal digital assistant (PDA)**, the **smartphone**, the **Blackberry**, and now the Ogo (pronounced O-Go). These devices are explained in more detail in Exhibit 9.2.

Conversion of Devices

The number of new mobile devices continues to grow—for example, the Ogo was introduced into the market in late 2004 and came to the U.S. in 2007. These handheld devices blend blogging, Instant Messages, SMS, and other forms of social networking in which Web browsing is easy, especially with a full keyboard. Other features include a 2-megapixel camera, music streamer, and Bluetooth capability (White 2007). Other devices are declining in widespread use or are converging with other devices into what is called *all-in-one devices*. For example, cell phones have largely replaced interactive pagers except in small niche markets (e.g., hospitals, emergency services). The next casualty may be the stand-alone PDA; mobile users want portable devices that integrate cell phones, personal information management, wireless Web surfing, and streaming video and audio. Overall, PDA sales were down more than $23 billion for the 12 months ending March 30, 2004.

According to Ross Rubin from NPD TechWorld, "Over time, I think the PDA just failed to establish a killer application beyond personal information management" (Diaz 2004). In the future, smartphones and PDAs are likely to converge, offering users a range of voice and data connectivity options and with a variety of software for personal information management, office applications, and Internet access. For a discussion and list of all-in-one devices, see Malykhina (2006a).

The first solution used portable devices to store and process data. Whenever possible, the device was connected to a wired network via *synchronization*.

The second solution was to replace wires with wireless networks. Radios, televisions, and telephones have been wireless for a long time, so it was natural to adapt this technology to the computing environment (Longino 2006). The two solutions combined resulted in wireless mobile computing.

Wireless Mobile Computing

Combining the two solutions (mobile devices and wireless solutions) is shown in the upper-right quadrant in Exhibit 9.1. **Wireless mobile computing** (or just **mobile computing**) enables a real-time connection between a mobile device and computing networks or to another computing device, anytime, anywhere. Mobile computing offers a computing environment suitable for workers who travel outside the boundaries of their workplace or for anyone on the move. Salespeople are able to "close the deal" at a customer's office instead of having to say, "I'll have to check on that at the office," and perhaps lose the sale. A busy executive can receive and send e-mail during normally unproductive "dead" time in an airport lounge. A field service worker can conduct an inventory check for a faulty part, find the closest source, and arrange for delivery time of a replacement. The innovation of mobile computing is creating a revolution in the manner in which people use computers at work, home, and school and in health care, entertainment, security, and much more.

wireless mobile computing (mobile computing) Computing that connects a mobile device to a network or another computing device, anytime, anywhere.

ENABLING TECHNOLOGIES FOR MOBILE COMPUTING

Behind every m-commerce transaction or activity there are hardware and software infrastructures and their support. Some of these infrastructures (e.g., network access points, mobile communications server switches, cellular transmitters and receivers) support the wireless connection. Other parts of this infrastructure (e.g., WAP gateways, GPS locators, GPS satellites) support delivery of services over the wireless connection. Most of these components of the mobile computing infrastructure are discussed elsewhere in this chapter in the context in which they are used (see Hu et al. 2006 and Kou and Yesha 2006).

As one would expect, other infrastructure components support m-commerce activity in the same way as in typical e-commerce transactions. For example, a Web server, database server, and enterprise application server offer the same services to a wireless device as they do to a wired computer, with one significant exception. Certain characteristics of mobile devices—small screens, reduced memory, limited bandwidth, and restricted input capabilities—means that hardware and software designers need to anticipate special requirements and design the system accordingly. For example, a Web server may need two versions of the same Web page—a "normal" page with full graphics for desktop computers and a "mobile" page for PDAs and smartphones—as well as a way to distinguish between devices requesting the Web page.

The infrastructure to support mobile commerce is not cheap, and it is not simple to put in place. A more extensive discussion of mobile hardware infrastructure is available in Elliott and Phillips (2004), Hu et al. (2006), and mobile computing professional books. The major components of the infrastructure are devices, software, and services (to be discussed in this section) and networks (Section 9.2).

MOBILE COMPUTING SOFTWARE

Developing software for wireless devices is challenging for several reasons. First, there are a number of competing standards for application development on various devices. This means that software applications must be customized for each type of device with which the application may communicate. Second, software applications have to adapt to match the requirements of the device, not the other way around. Specifically, all software must deal with the technological challenges of small display screens, reduced bandwidth, limited input capabilities, and restricted memory that are common on most mobile devices. In the desktop computing world, the inability of a computer to properly load an application due to insufficient memory is solved by adding more memory. In the mobile computing world, the solution is to redesign the application.

The following are the major software components associated with mobile computing.

Mobile Operating System

Microsoft, Symbian, Linux, and other, more specialized, operating systems are available for most mobile devices. For example, PDA manufacturers have a choice of operating systems: Palm OS from Palm Computing, Windows CE (PocketPC) from Microsoft, and EPOC from the Symbian consortium.

Mobile Application User Interface

The interface is the application logic in a PDA, smartphone, Wintel notebook, or other device. Small handheld computing devices use a variety of interface approaches including a touch screen, mini-joystick, jog dial, and thumb wheel.

Microbrowsers

microbrowser
Wireless Web browser designed to operate with small screens and limited bandwidth and memory requirements.

Microbrowsers, as their name implies, resemble standard Internet browsers on desktop computers and are used to access the Web. However, they have been adapted to deal with the special requirements of mobile devices, especially small screens, limited bandwidth, and minimal memory.

Wireless Application Protocol

Wireless Application Protocol (WAP)
A suite of network protocols designed to enable different kinds of wireless devices to access WAP-readable files on an Internet-connected Web server.

The **Wireless Application Protocol (WAP)** is a suite of network protocols designed to enable different kinds of wireless devices (e.g., mobile phones, PDAs) to access WAP-readable files on an Internet-connected Web server. The central part of the WAP architecture (see Exhibit 9.3) is a WAP gateway server that sits between the mobile device and the Internet.

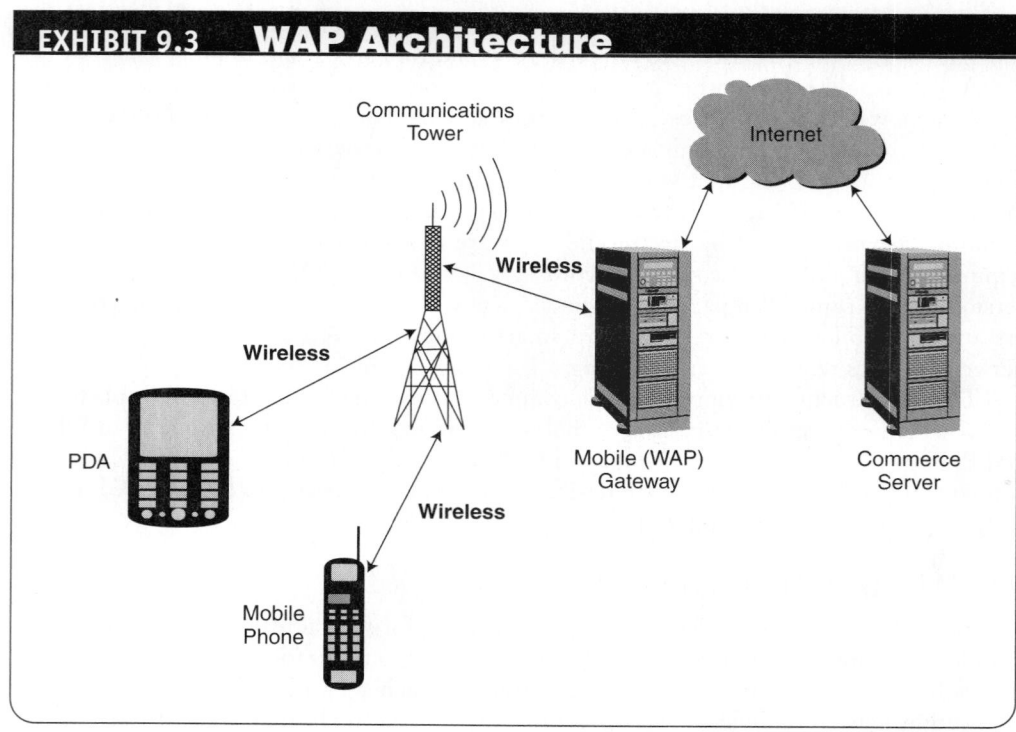

EXHIBIT 9.3   WAP Architecture

The gateway server is responsible for translating information requests from the device into an HTTP request that the Web server can understand. The server also checks ("parses") the WAP-compatible file from the Web server to ensure it is correct for the device and then forwards the file to the device. WAP was the first standard for accessing data from the Internet, but today WAP is being challenged by several other competing standards, including Java-based applications (the J2ME platform), which offer better graphics and security.

Markup Languages

An area of competing standards is the Internet software languages used to write applications for mobile devices. **Wireless Markup Language (WML)** is the scripting language used to create content in the WAP environment. WML is based on XML, and pages written in WML are usually abbreviated versions of their HTML counterparts, sometimes offering only the most relevant text-based content.

    Compact Hypertext Markup Language (cHTML) is the scripting language used in i-mode, an extremely popular mobile Internet service that originated in Japan (i-mode is described in more detail in Online File W9.7).

    Extensible Hypertext Markup Language (xHTML) is the most recent software language to be offered to application developers. xHTML has considerable potential, especially to replace WML, for several reasons. First, xHTML is a subset of XML, but it is compatible with HTML. This means that normal Web browsers can view pages developed in xHTML. Second, the xHTML standard has been set by the World Wide Web Consortium, the most widely recognized standards-setting organization for the Web. More than any other scripting language, xHTML represents increased compatibility between the "normal Web" and the "mobile Web." Finally, there is **voice XML (VXML)**, which is an extension of XML designed to accommodate voice.

Supporting Devices

The following are some supporting devices used in mobile computing.

    Synchronization. Synchronization, the exchange of updated information with other computing devices, is a requirement of any mobile computing device that stores data. Some mobile devices use wires (e.g., a USB cable, a docking station) to exchange information with other devices or the network. For example, Millstone Coffee, a U.S. distributor of roasted coffee beans, has equipped its 300 drivers with handheld devices to track inventory, generate invoices, and capture detailed sales and marketing data at each store. The devices are not wireless. Instead, drivers synchronize their handheld computers with the company's main systems at the end of the day, a process that takes only 2 minutes (Cohen 2002). Similarly, changes made to a PDA's calendar during the day need to be synchronized with the central-ized office calendar. Even if a mobile device is able to make a wireless connection, it may be inconvenient or temporarily impossible for real-time updates. For example, changes in the electronic product catalog made by the home office need to be exchanged with a salesperson's catalog on her (his) Tablet PC, but it is more convenient to do so when the salesperson is not actively using it, using a docking station.

    Docking Stations. At the end of the mobile computing day, most devices need to be plugged into a docking station or docking cradle to recharge their batteries, to connect to attachable keyboards or larger display screens, or to provide for faster *synchronization*, as illus-trated in Online File W9.1.

    Attachable Keyboards. Because of their small size, mobile devices generally use a minia-ture keyboard, a keypad, or a stylus-activated touch screen for data entry. These data input solutions are not satisfactory for significant data entry tasks; many tablet PCs, smartphones, PDAs, and other mobile devices come with small attachable keyboards that can be used at a table or desk. Attachable desktop display screens, memory sticks, and CD-ROM drives, also are available for some devices.

    Batteries. Rechargeable lithium batteries are most commonly used by handheld devices. The life of this kind of battery is short, generally only a few hours of operating time. Battery technology will not significantly improve unless and until manufacturers begin to switch to fuel cells, which is unlikely in the near future.

Wireless Markup Language (WML)
A scripting language used to create content in the WAP environment; based on XML, minus unneces-sary content to increase speed.

Compact Hypertext Markup Language (cHTML)
A scripting language used to create content in i-mode.

Extensible Hypertext Markup Language (xHTML)
A general scripting lan-guage; compatible with HTML; a standard set by W3 Consortium.

voice XML (VXML)
An extension of XML designed to accommodate voice.

synchronization
The exchange of updated information with other computing devices.

Media Players. Large numbers of devices are used as media players, mostly for MP3 listening and video viewing. Apple's iPod and Microsoft's Zune are major vendors. In fall 2006, many airlines allowed passengers to connect their iPods to in-flight entertainment systems, saving battery power for the devices. Motorola and Apple have developed a combination cell phone and portable music player called POKR.

MOBILE COMPUTING SERVICES

In a separate category all their own—software-enabled but not truly applications—are a range of mobile computing services mostly developed for mobile phones. These services fulfill the needs of mobile device users, but they also provide a foundation for supporting many applications described later in this chapter. For example, SMS is the underlying service that supports communication.

Short Message Service

Short Message Service (SMS)
A service that supports the sending and receiving of short text messages on mobile phones.

Short Message Service (SMS), frequently referred to as *text messaging*, or simply *texting*, is a service that supports the transmittal of short text messages (up to 160 characters) between mobile phones on a cellular telephone network. The limited message length means users often use acronyms to convey the message in shorthand text. Examples include "how are you" becomes "how r u," and "great" becomes "gr8." Texting has been wildly popular in Asia and Europe for some time, and now it is increasing in popularity in the United States. In China, 550 billion text messages were sent in 2004, a figure expected to rise to 1.4 trillion messages by 2006 (*Designerz.com* 2004).

Enhanced Messaging Service

Enhanced Messaging Service (EMS)
An extension of SMS that can send simple animation, tiny pictures, sounds, and formatted text.

Enhanced Messaging Service (EMS) is an extension of SMS that can send tiny pictures, simple animations, sounds, and formatted text. EMS is sometimes referred to as *picture texting* or *pictxt*. The Network for Online Commerce (2006) reported an increase in text messages of 30 to 40 percent in 2005 compared to 2004 in many European countries and in Asia, especially on New Year's Day.

Multimedia Messaging Service

Multimedia Messaging Service (MMS)
The emerging generation of wireless messaging; MMS is able to deliver rich media.

Multimedia Messaging Service (MMS) is the emerging generation of wireless messaging, delivering rich media, including video and audio, to mobile phones and other devices. MMS enables the convergence of mobile devices and personal computers because MMS messages can be sent between PCs, PDAs, and mobile phones that are MMS enabled (Elliott and Phillips 2004).

micropayments
Electronic payments for small-purchase amounts (generally less than $10).

Micropayments Micropayments, which are electronic payments for small-purchase amounts, generally less than $10, have not become widespread in EC, at least in part because of the relatively high cost of conducting such transactions (see Chapter 12). However, cellular telephone companies already have mechanisms for billing small amounts (e.g., send a text message for 10 cents) and charging them to the phone owner's account. Accordingly, many mobile commerce transactions may use micropayment services offered by mobile network providers. However, the provision of this service does incur an element of financial risk for the network provider. Unless a subscription revenue model is used, the cellular telephone company incurs the obligation to pay the debt without guarantee of payment from the customer. This means that the mobile telephone company acts as a bank, with much of the risk but few of the benefits or protections of a bank. Other examples of m-commerce applications that use micropayments are provided in the discussion of wireless electronic payment systems in Section 9.4.

Location-Based Services

global positioning system (GPS)
A worldwide satellite-based tracking system that enables users to determine their position anywhere on the earth.

Another support service that can be built into many m-commerce applications, location-based services use the **global positioning system (GPS)**, a worldwide satellite-based tracking system that enables advertisers and sellers to determine the position of potential customers anywhere on the earth. This supports localization of products and services (see Section 9.3) and location-based m-commerce (see Section 9.8).

Voice-Support Services

The most natural mode of human communication is voice. Voice recognition and voice synthesization in m-commerce applications offer advantages such as hands- and eyes-free operation, better operation in dirty or moving environments, faster input (people talk about two-and-a-half times faster than they type), and ease-of-use for disabled people. Most significantly, increased use of voice-support services exploits the built-in audio capabilities of many mobile devices and reduces their dependence on less-than-satisfactory input solutions, such as handwriting recognition, keypads, or virtual touch-screen keyboards.

Voice support applications such as **interactive voice response (IVR)** systems enable users to interact with a computerized system to request and receive information and to enter and change data using a telephone. These systems have been around since the 1980s but are becoming more functional and widespread as artificial intelligence and voice recognition capabilities continue to improve.

The highest level of voice support services is a **voice portal**, a Web site with an audio interface that can be accessed through a telephone call. A visitor requests information by speaking, and the voice portal finds the information on the Web, translates it into a computer-generated voice reply, and provides the answer by voice. For example, tellme.com and bevocal.com allow callers to request information about weather, local restaurants, current traffic, and other handy information. IVR and voice portals are likely to become important ways of delivering m-commerce services over audio-enabled computing devices.

Mobile services is a rapidly developing area in mobile computing, and additional services can be expected to be offered as mobile computing devices become more powerful, as increased bandwidth (e.g., 3G and WiMax) becomes widespread and as m-commerce becomes more commonplace. In other words, "watch this space."

interactive voice response (IVR)
A voice system that enables users to request and receive information and to enter and change data through a telephone to a computerized system.

voice portal
A Web site with an audio interface that can be accessed through a telephone call.

Section 9.1 ▶ REVIEW QUESTIONS

1. Define *mobile computing*.
2. What two needs of users have propelled the development of *wireless* mobile devices?
3. List and describe the major mobile devices used in m-commerce.
4. Define synchronization and give a business example of its use.
5. List the major software components of mobile computing.
6. Distinguish between WML, cHTML, xHTML, SMS, EMS, and MMS.
7. List and briefly describe the major mobile computing services.

9.2 WIRELESS TELECOMMUNICATIONS NETWORKS

All mobile devices need to connect with a telecommunications network or with another device. How they do this depends on the purpose of the connection, the capabilities and location of the device, and what connection options are available at the time. This section explores four levels of telecommunication networks: (1) personal area networks for device-to-device connections up to 30 feet; (2) wireless local area networks for medium-range connections, typically up to 300 feet; (3) wireless metropolitan area networks for connections up to 31 miles; and (4) wireless wide area networks for connecting to a network from anywhere with cellular phone coverage.

PERSONAL AREA NETWORKS

A good place to begin a discussion of mobile wireless networks is at the personal level. A **personal area network (PAN)** is suitable for mobile users who need to make very short-range device-to-device wireless connections within a small space, typically a single room. The most common way to establish a PAN is with Bluetooth.

Bluetooth is a set of telecommunications standards that enables wireless devices to communicate with each other over short distances of up to 20 meters (60 feet). Bluetooth uses low-power radio technology in the 2.4GHz radio spectrum, and up to seven simultaneous connections can be made to link individual devices. Bluetooth operates under the IEEE

personal area network (PAN)
A wireless telecommunications network for device-to-device connections within a very short range.

Bluetooth
A set of telecommunications standards that enables wireless devices to communicate with each other over short distances.

(Institute of Electrical and Electronic Engineers) 802.15 standard. (Bluetooth gets its curious name from the heroic tenth-century Viking king who united Denmark and conquered Norway.) More information about Bluetooth technology is available from bluetooth.com.

Why would someone want to create a PAN? Suppose a mobile worker with a cell phone and a wireless laptop needs to connect to the Internet from a rural area. The laptop has a Web browser, but it is unable to connect to the Internet without a wireless network signal, which is unavailable in this remote location. The cell phone can make a dial-up connection to the Internet, but it does not have a Web browser. If both devices are Bluetooth enabled, then the worker can *pair* the devices ("introduce" one device to another through a shared profile) to establish a communication link between them. Now the mobile user can dial up an ISP on the cell phone and wirelessly pass the information to the laptop, where it is displayed on the Web browser.

Another common PAN is Bluetooth-enabled headsets that some people use with their cell phones. Once the Bluetooth-enabled headset is paired with the mobile phone, the wearer can answer a call, speak, listen, and terminate a call through the headset; the wearer can do everything except place an outgoing call (at least not until speech recognition becomes commonplace in mobile phones). The mobile phone can be on the person, in a purse, in a briefcase, in a docking station, or some other location as long as it is within Bluetooth's radio range.

Bluetooth can be used to pair a number of different devices—wireless keyboards with tablet PCs, PDAs with computers for easy data synchronization, and digital cameras with printers. Bluetooth also can link more than two devices, as is done in connectBlue's (connectblue.se) operating-room control system. Equipment that monitors a patient's heartbeat, ECG, respiration, and other vital signs all can be linked via Bluetooth, eliminating obstructive and dangerous cables and increasing the portability of the equipment.

Bluetooth does have some limitations, however, other than the obvious one of its short range. First, the communication is very directional, and objects located between paired devices can interrupt the connection. Similarly, because 2.4GHz is a commonly used radio range, interferences can arise from microwave ovens, cordless phones, and similar sources. Security can be a problem, too, especially if the default low-level security setting is used. Finally, first-time and infrequent users sometimes have difficulty finding the right configurations and doing the necessary setup procedures to make the initial pairing.

For additional information, see Wikipedia (2006) and bluetooth.org.

WIRELESS LOCAL AREA NETWORKS AND WI-FI

wireless local area network (WLAN)
A telecommunications network that enables users to make short-range wireless connections to the Internet or another network.

In the past few years, the fastest-growing area of wireless connectivity has been in making short-range network connections inside a building or a house. As its name implies, a **wireless local area network**, or **WLAN**, is equivalent to a wired LAN, but without the cables.

Most WLANs run on a telecommunications standard known as IEEE 802.11 or, more commonly, as **Wi-Fi** (for **wireless fidelity**). IEEE 802.11 comes in four forms:

Wi-Fi (wireless fidelity)
The common name used to describe the IEEE 802.11 standard used on most WLANs.

- **802.11b** is the most widely used standard. WLANs employing this standard have communication speeds of 11 Mbps for ranges up to 100 meters (300 feet) for indoor use and up to 275 meters (900 feet) for open space or outdoor use. The 802.11b standard operates in the 2.4GHz range, and microwave ovens, cordless phones, and other devices using this same range can cause interference.

802.11b
The most popular Wi-Fi standard; it is inexpensive and offers sufficient speed for most devices; however, interference can be a problem.

- **802.11a**, which was issued at the same time as 802.11b, offers faster transfer rates (54 Mbps) but a weaker signal range (maximum of 30 meters or 100 feet) indoors.

- **802.11g** is a standard that attempts to combine the best of both of the other standards. 802.11g offers the high transfer rate (54 Mbps) of 802.11a, a strong signal range like 802.11b, and is backward compatible with 802.11b. However, few mobile devices can utilize the higher transfer rate, and 802.11g is more expensive.

802.11a
This Wi-Fi standard is faster than 802.11b but has a smaller range.

- A standard currently under development, 802.11n, promises bandwidth transfer rates of 200 to 540 Mbps. Although currently not very practical because it exceeds the limits of most broadband connections used by homes and businesses, as Internet connections move from cable or DSL to fiber-optic cables, the need for Wi-Fi connections at these high speeds will grow (Asaravala 2004).

802.11g
This fast but expensive Wi-Fi standard is mostly used in businesses.

Increasingly, 802.11g is being used in commercial environments where cost is not a major issue and where laptop computers can take advantage of the 54 Mbps transfer rate. 802.11b remains the Wi-Fi standard of choice for inexpensive installations in most public areas and homes. For details, see Wikipedia (2006); look for IEEE 802.11n.

Physically, the heart of a WLAN is a **wireless access point** that connects wireless devices to the desired network (see Exhibit 9.4). The access point is analogous to the network cable plugged into a desktop computer but without the wires. On the back end, the wireless access point makes a wired connection to the Internet, an intranet, or any other network in the same manner as a wired LAN cable. Mobile devices send and receive signals from the access point via a wireless network card, installed by the user or built into the device by the manufacturer.

WLANs provide fast and easy Internet or intranet broadband access from public **hotspots** located in airports, hotels, restaurants, and conference centers. A California vineyard is using Wi-Fi to monitor field conditions (see Case 9.2 later in this chapter).

Wi-Fi has residential applications, too. Many homeowners install a WLAN to enable Internet connectivity throughout their homes without the need to retrofit the house with cables. However, security is sometimes lacking in these residential installations. Unprotected WLANs in homes and small businesses can be discovered via *war driving*, with unanticipated consequences for the homeowner (see Online File W9.2).

wireless access point
An antenna that connects a mobile device to a wired LAN.

hotspot
An area or point where a wireless device can make a connection to a wireless local area network (using Wi-Fi).

EXHIBIT 9.4   How Wi-Fi Works

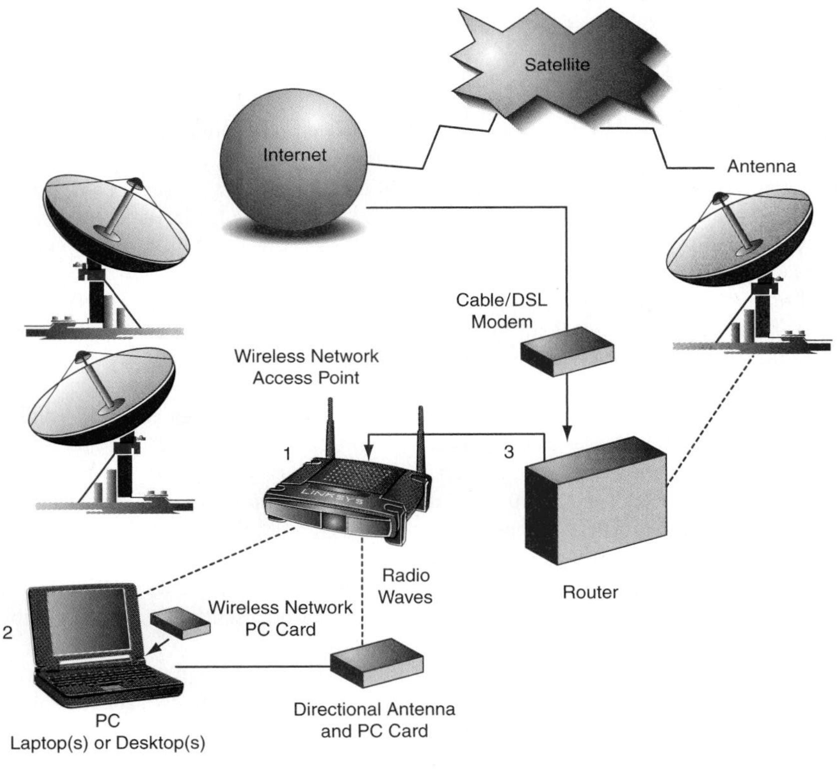

Satellite

Internet

Antenna

Cable/DSL Modem

Wireless Network Access Point

Router

1

3

Radio Waves

Wireless Network PC Card

2

Directional Antenna and PC Card

PC
Laptop(s) or Desktop(s)

1   Radio-equipped access point connected to the Internet (or via a router). It generates and receives radio waves (up to 400 feet).
2   Several client devices, equipped with PC cards, generate and receive radio waves.
3   Router is connected to the Internet via a cable or DSL modem or connected via a satellite.

One wireless access point or hotspot can provide service to between 4 and 16 users within a small geographical area. Several wireless access points can be used to support a larger number of users across a larger geographical area. Multiple hotspots can operate simultaneously in any given area, providing overlapping coverage. The hotspots do not interfere with each other as long as they are operating on different radio channels. A sample application of Wi-Fi is provided in Insights and Additions 9.1.

Insights and Additions 9.1 Wi-Fi Takes Off

Perhaps nowhere else in the world is there a more compelling case for Wi-Fi connectivity than in the travel industry. Airports, airplanes, and hotels are the places that travelers are most likely to have spare time on their hands. Business travelers are keen to make productive use of this "dead" time by answering e-mail or conducting business research on the Web. Recreational travelers frequently want to send e-mail to or read e-mail from friends and family, catch up with fellow travelers through instant messaging, or investigate activities at their next destination. Both types of travelers may need to book accommodations, alert contacts at their destination of expected arrival times, or reserve taxis or shuttles.

The air transport and travel industries know this, and Wi-Fi is taking off in airports and hotels around the world. According to a report by IT-industry research firm IDC, Wi-Fi hotspots doubled at U.S. airports in 2004 (compared to 2003) and will nearly triple again by 2008, exceeding the growth rate at hotels, cafes, and restaurants.

Not only is the number of airport-based hotspots increasing faster than in other locations, but the number of users using Wi-Fi is expected to grow faster because of the nature of the target audience—travelers need Internet connectivity more than restaurant patrons or even hotel visitors.

Airport hotspots are being installed in a number of ways. Terminal-wide access is available at all major U.S. airports. Access is restricted to certain terminals or gate areas at airports, such as Kennedy and La Guardia in New York City and Newark Liberty in Newark, New Jersey. In other airports, airport authorities have left it to restaurants (e.g., McDonald's, Starbucks) or airlines to offer Wi-Fi services to their customers.

Like a number of airports in the United States, the Minneapolis–St. Paul International airport is served by Wi-Fi. The fee is $7.95 for unlimited daily access. Northwest Airlines has 570 hotspots in the United States.

Wi-Fi access usually is free in the business-class lounges of all major airlines. However, most airport authorities, restaurants, and airlines view Wi-Fi access as something travelers are willing to pay for and charge for it. Rates usually are set by the Wi-Fi provider (e.g., T-Mobile, Wayport) and tend to be $7 to $10 per day or $20 to $40 per month. Business centers in some airports offer Wi-Fi connections as well.

Of course, another source of unproductive travel time is in the airplane itself, and Wi-Fi is taking off into the skies as well. Lufthansa offers in-flight Wi-Fi service on its long-haul fleet. The hotspots are connected to the Internet via satellites, and the user pays $25 or $35 to use the service. However, several airlines discontinued the service in 2006 due to low usage.

Since 2002, T-Mobile has installed Wi-Fi networks in several thousand Starbucks in the United States. T-Mobile is also installing Wi-Fi in hundreds of Borders locations. T-Mobile charges annually, monthly, daily, or pay as you go (see *hotspot.t-mobile.com/services_plans.htm*).

McDonald's now offers Wi-Fi "hotspots" in more than 7,000 restaurants around the world, and the number is increasing daily. Local service providers provide high-quality wireless service through online credit card payment, subscriptions, prepaid cards, and sometimes promotional coupons (see *mcdonalds.com/wireless.html*).

Using a wireless ticketing system, Universal Studios in Hollywood is shortening the waiting lines for tickets at its front gate. Ticket sellers, armed with Wi-Fi–enabled devices and belt-mounted printers, not only sell tickets, but also provide information. For details, see Scanlon (2003).

CVS Corp., the largest retail pharmacy in the United States, uses Wi-Fi–based devices throughout its 4,100 stores. The hand-held computers support a variety of in-store applications, including direct store delivery, price management, inventory control, and receiving. Benefits include faster transfer rates, increasing productivity and performance, reduced cost, and improved customer service.

Several mining companies in Europe installed several hundred Wi-Fi hot spots in their coal mines. Information from drills and trucks, such as their positions and the weight of their loads, is related wirelessly to the control center. It increases both productivity and safety.

Many hotels, from five-star to budget-oriented inns, offer free Internet connections in their lobby or guest rooms.

Sources: Compiled from Levere (2004), Fleishman (2003), Gleishman (2006), Scanlon (2003), and *jiwire.com* (2006).

MUNICIPAL WI-FI NETWORKS

By using a large number of connected hot spots, one can create a wireless city. This is known as a municipal Wi-Fi network. Wi-Fi signals are irregular and hard to predict, so coverage varies depending on the user's location, the proximity of a node, and what the user's house is made of. However, users experiencing weak signals can purchase cheap repeater devices to strengthen the reception in their homes.

For example, on August 16, 2006, Google created a network of 380 access points posted on light poles throughout the city of Mountain View, California. Residents of Mountain View just have to choose the "GoogleWiFi" signal and sign into their Google accounts with their user I.D. and password in order to access the Web through the free Wi-Fi service. These networks also are known as *mesh networks* (see Online File W9.3).

Wi-Fi networks are not cheap. For example, the city of Philadelphia debated whether to go forward with its plan to install a wireless network, which would cost the 135-square-mile city $10 million to install, or about $75,000 per square mile. The cost of running the network during the first 2 years would be $5 million. The city put the project into action in April 2006 with the hopes of closing the digital divide within the city and enhancing economic development (Lindstrom 2006). In February 2007, the city began testing "Proof of Concept" zone (most of northern Philadelphia). Once the testing was completed, the construction of the network continued in other areas of the city (WirelessPhiladelphia.org 2007).

Municipal Wi-Fi networks compete with a related technology called WiMax.

WIRELESS METROPOLITAN AREA NETWORKS AND WIMAX

One obvious limitation of wireless local area networks is the word *local*. A nomadic worker traveling around a city will always have to search for another hotspot to make an Internet connection. Municipal governments have recognized this limitation and, wanting to promote an image of being a "wired town" or "connected city," many have encouraged or sponsored widespread distribution of hotspots. For example, in Wellington, New Zealand, CityLink has installed over 90 hotspots in the city's central business district (see cafenet.co.nz). American cities with widespread Wi-Fi initiatives underway include New York City (where wireless access points would be placed on top of 18,000 lampposts), Philadelphia, San Francisco, Cleveland, and Corpus Christi (*SiliconValley.com* 2004). Chaska, Minnesota, too, has plans to provide inexpensive, widespread Wi-Fi service to its 18,000 residents. However, one industry expert has questioned the initiative. According to Derek Kerton, using a series of overlapping Wi-Fi hotspots for broad coverage is like "using a hammer to drive in a screw. You can do it, but wouldn't it be better if you found a better tool?" (Ojeda-Zapata 2004). That better tool is WiMax.

WiMax

WiMax (Worldwide Interoperability for Microwave Access) is a wireless standard (IEEE 802.16) for making broadband network access widely available for data and voice over a medium-sized area of up to 50 kilometers (31 miles). WiMax, which is a technology for **wireless metropolitan area networks (WMANs)**, was released in 2005. The WiMax Forum (wimaxforum.org) describes WiMax as "a standards-based technology enabling the delivery of last mile wireless broadband access as an alternative to cable and DSL." WiMax does not require a clear line of sight to function, as satellites do.

WiMax uses the same technology as Wi-Fi, but its potential is more like the fast data communications services being developed by cell phone companies. WiMax uses a radio-based, ultrawide bandwidth, offering normal data transfer speeds of 70 Mbps and peaks of up to 268 Mbps. The first step of WiMax is the installation and support of fixed rooftop antennas. The second phase is the rollout of indoor antennas, greatly reducing installation costs. The third step moves wireless connectivity down to mobile devices such as notebooks, PDAs, and 3G phones, allowing connectivity anywhere within range of an antenna. Intel integrated WiMax into its Centrino wireless chip beginning in late 2006.

The architecture of WiMax is illustrated in Exhibit 9.5.

Despite its designation for use in WMANs, WiMax's biggest impact may not be in cities. In large markets with crowded airwaves, a WiMax service would have to use a costly

WiMax
A wireless standard (IEEE 802.16) for making broadband network connections over a medium size area such as a city.

wireless metropolitan area network (WMAN)
A telecommunications network that enables users to make medium-range wireless connections to the Internet or another network.

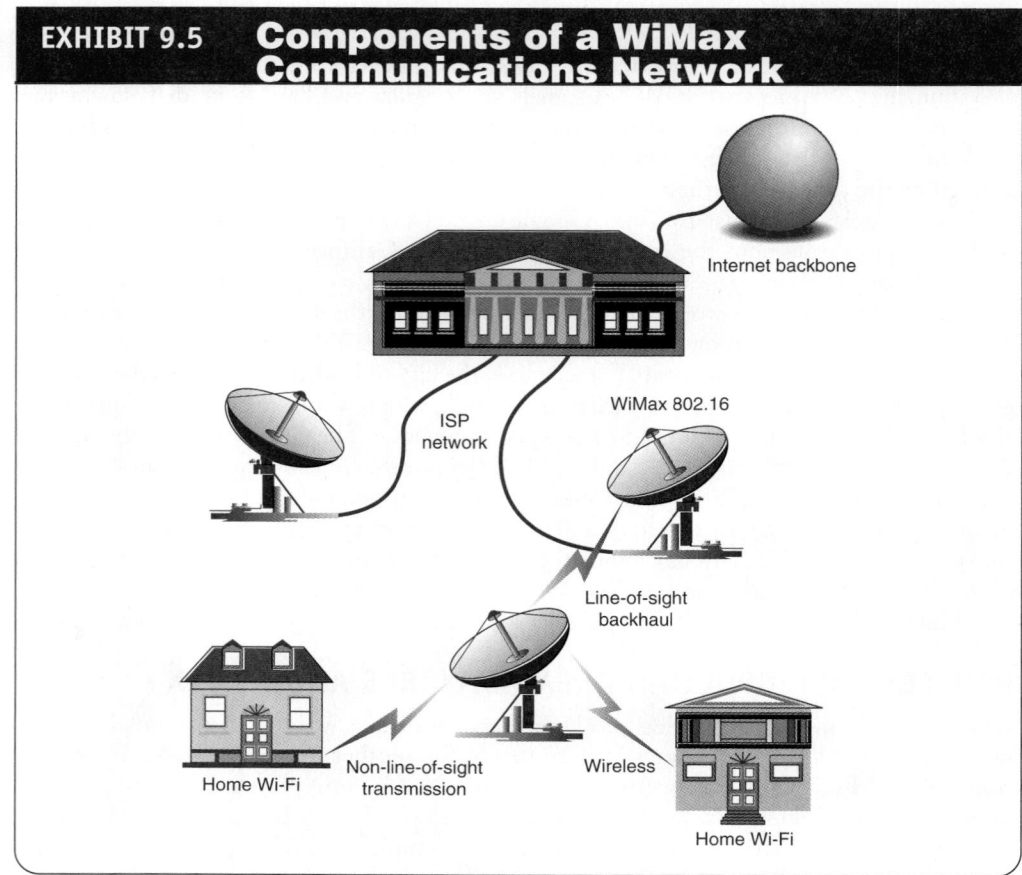

EXHIBIT 9.5   Components of a WiMax Communications Network

spectrum. Competition from mobile telephone carriers and Wi-Fi also may tend to blunt its impact. Instead, WiMax seems ideal for the delivery of high broadband speeds to rural areas of the developed countries and to cities and towns in developing countries that do not have a mature communications infrastructure (Davidson 2004).

WiMax is still an evolving telecommunications standard, and its eventual impact on m-commerce is speculative. As with other aspects of rapidly developing wireless technologies, the only sure thing that can be said is "watch this space."

WIRELESS WIDE AREA NETWORKS

The broadest wireless coverage is offered by the world's most well-established wireless communications network—cellular networks operated by telecommunications companies. A **wireless wide area network (WWAN)** offers widespread wireless coverage over a large geographical area. Most WWANs are cellular phone networks.

Physical Topology of a WWAN

A WWAN achieves its widespread coverage through a set of overlapping cells that collectively form a cell cluster. At the center of each cell is a base station transceiver or cell tower that is used to send and receive signals to and from mobile devices operating within the cell. These signals are, in turn, communicated to a base station controller (BSC) that is connected to a mobile switching center (MSC) that is connected to the land-based public switched telephone network.

A unique feature of a WWAN is how the mobile switching station tracks a cellular phone user as the user moves from cell to cell. When a device is turned on, a **subscriber identification module (SIM) card** inside the device identifies itself to the network. This SIM card is an extractable memory storage card that is used for identification, customer location information, transaction processing, secure communications, and the like. A SIM card also makes it possible for a handset owner to change phone numbers.

wireless wide area network (WWAN)
A telecommunications network that offers wireless coverage over a large geographical area, typically over a cellular phone network.

subscriber identification module (SIM) card
An extractable storage card used for identification, customer location information, transaction processing, secure communications, etc.

As the mobile phone user changes physical location, the "mobility management protocol" in the mobile switching station directs each base station controller to make the handoff from one transceiver to the next as the user moves from cell to cell and cell cluster to cell cluster.

The size of a cell is determined by the number of objects that may interfere with the signal and the traffic volume. For both of these reasons, a cell in a dense urban area is likely to be small, perhaps a few hundred feet wide, whereas a cell in a rural area may be over 6 miles (10 kilometers) in size.

WWAN Communication Bandwidths

All WWANs are not equal. Currently, four generations of communications technology can be distinguished:

▶ **1G**. This was the first generation of wireless technology. It was an analog-based technology in effect from 1979 to 1992 and was used exclusively for voice.

▶ **2G**. This second generation of digital wireless technology is in widespread existence today. 2G is based on digital radio technology and is able to accommodate text messages (SMS).

▶ **2.5G**. An interim technology based on new cell phone protocols such as GPRS (General Packet Radio Service) and CDMA2000 (Code Division Multiple Access). This generation can communicate limited graphics, such as in picture text messages.

▶ **3G**. The third generation of digital wireless technology will support rich media, such as video. 3G utilizes packet switching in the high 15 to 20 MHz range. 3G started in Japan in 2001, reached Europe in 2002, and the United States and much of Asia in 2003. As of 2004, the number of 3G-enabled devices was only a tiny fraction of the cell phone market. However, sales are projected to increase gradually as more 3G networks and applications become available. IT research firm IDC projects annual sales of 3G handsets will reach 100 million by 2007 (Sharma 2004).

▶ **3.5G**. This generation is expected to be about seven times better than 3G. It promises data download speeds of 14 Mbps and upload speeds of up to 1.8 Mbps. This means major improvement in mobile voice telephony, video telephony, mobile TV, and other media. For details see softpedia.com.

▶ **4G**. The expected next generation after 3.5G. The arrival of 4G, which will provide faster display of multimedia, is expected between 2008 and 2010.

Exhibit 9.6 compares 2G and 3G on a number of important variables. Of most interest for m-commerce are the faster download speeds and the extension of cellular connectivity to mobile devices other than phones.

1G
The first generation of wireless technology, which was analog based.

2G
The second generation of digital wireless technology; accommodates voice and text.

2.5G
An interim wireless technology that can accommodate voice, text, and limited graphics.

3G
The third generation of digital wireless technology; supports rich media such as video.

3.5G
This generation was inserted into the ranks of cellphone generations; it refers to the packet-switched technologies used to achieve higher transmission speeds.

4G
The expected next generation of wireless technology that will provide faster display of multimedia.

EXHIBIT 9.6	Comparison of 2G and 3G Communication Bandwidth	
	2G	**3G**
Bandwidth	30 to 200 KHz	15 to 20 MHz
Connectivity	Dial up	Always on
Hardware	Telephone handset	Mobile computing device
Speed	9.6 to 384 Kbps	144 Kbps to 2 Mbps
Download delivery times:		
E-mail file (10 Kb)	8 seconds	0.04 second
Web page (9 Kb)	9 seconds	0.04 second
Text file (40 Kb)	33 seconds	0.2 second
Large report (2 Mb)	28 minutes	7 seconds
Video clip (4 Mb)	48 minutes	14 seconds
TV quality movie (6 Gb)	1,100 hours	5 hours (approximately)

Sources: Hansmann et al. (2003), p. 278, and Burkhardt et al. (2002), p. 94.

In addition to the high data transmission rates illustrated in Exhibit 9.6, all 3G networks aim to offer efficient spectrum utilization (see communication protocols immediately below) and worldwide connectivity or global roaming (see network systems below). These benefits come at a cost, however. A fairly complete new infrastructure has to be built on top of the existing one, and telecommunications providers have already paid high prices for 3G frequencies in frenzied auctions at the height of the dot-com boom. The rollout of 3G has been slow, and large profits remain uncertain. However, the potential is there for 3G to change the way mobile devices are used and dramatically increase m-commerce applications and activities.

WWAN Communication Protocols

A second way WWANs differ is in the communication protocols they use. These multiplexing communication protocols are used to provide service to large numbers of users with limited communication bandwidth. In today's mobile world, there are three main multiplexing protocols:

- **Frequency Division Multiple Access (FDMA).** This protocol divides the available bandwidth into different frequency channels, and each device is given its own frequency on which to operate. Although easy to implement and necessary in the circuit-switched analog world of 1G, it is terribly wasteful of limited bandwidth.
- **Time Division Multiple Access (TDMA).** Widely used in 2G networks, TDMA assigns different users different time slots on a communications channel (e.g., every one-eighth time slot). TDMA is sometimes used in conjunction with FDMA; the available bandwidth is divided into frequencies, and each frequency is divided into time slots.
- **Code Division Multiple Access (CDMA).** Designed for 3G networks, this protocol divides data into small packets that are distributed across the frequency spectrum in a set pattern. CDMA is very reliable and efficient (Hansmann et al. 2003).

Even more advanced communications protocols, such as orthogonal frequency-division multiplexing (OFDM), are emerging.

WWAN Network Systems

A third way WWANs differ is in the network standards they use. These competing standards resulted from the simultaneous development of cellular networks in different countries (e.g., Global System for Mobile Communications [GSM] in Europe, Personal Digital Cellular [PDC] in Japan, both IS-95 and IS-136 in the United States). The differences among these systems have been the primary cause for incompatibility of handsets between different countries, and even within countries, in the first decade of cellular networks.

Global System for Mobile Communications (GSM)
An open, nonproprietary standard for mobile voice and data communications.

The **Global System for Mobile Communications (GSM)** has emerged as the most popular standard, currently in use in over 170 countries and with 72 percent of the world's mobile market (Yapp 2004). GSM's popularity is likely to increase; according to the GSM Association, 85 percent of the world's mobile network operators have chosen 3GSM for delivery of 3G services (*GSM World* 2004). To learn more about GSM, visit gsmworld.com.

This concludes our overview of the technological foundations upon which mobile commerce is based. Mobile computing—devices, infrastructure, software, and services—and wireless telecommunications networks—personal, local, metropolitan, and wide area—have been presented and discussed. These two sections explored the *mobile* part of mobile commerce. Next we turn our attention to an in-depth exploration of the *commerce* aspect.

Section 9.2 ❯ REVIEW QUESTIONS

1. Define *personal networks*.
2. Describe a scenario in which Bluetooth might be used.
3. Define Wi-Fi and list some of its applications.
4. List the distinguishing characteristics of each of the three Wi-Fi standards.

5. What is war driving? List at least two reasons why someone would war drive. (See Online File W9.2.)

6. What distinguishes WiMax from the other telecommunication networks discussed in this section?

7. Describe WWAN and list its communication bandwidth.

8. Define 3G and list some potential uses of 3G technology.

9.3 MOBILE COMMERCE: ATTRIBUTES, BENEFITS, AND DRIVERS

Mobile commerce is growing rapidly, especially due to smart phones. Let's examine its foundations.

OVERVIEW OF MOBILE COMMERCE

Mobile commerce (m-commerce), also known as **m-business**, includes any business activity conducted over a wireless telecommunications network. This includes B2C and B2B commercial transactions as well as the transfer of information and services via wireless mobile devices, especially in intrabusiness. Some authors (e.g., Paavilainen 2002) make a distinction between m-commerce and m-business, defining *m-business* broadly, as we do here, but restricting *m-commerce* activities to financial transactions. However, as used in this chapter, *m-commerce* and *m-business* are any e-commerce or e-business activity conducted in a wireless environment. Like regular EC applications, m-commerce can be done via the Internet, via private communication lines, or over other computing networks. For an overview, see Pierre (2006), Deans (2005), and Petrova (2006).

> **mobile commerce (m-commerce, m-business)** Any business activity conducted over a wireless telecommunications network or from mobile devices.

M-commerce is a natural extension of e-commerce. Mobile devices create an opportunity to deliver new services to existing customers and to attract new customers. However, the small screen size and limited bandwidth of most computing devices have limited consumer interest. So even though the mobile computing industry recognizes the potential for B2C m-commerce applications, the number of existing applications is quite small and uptake has been minimal. Instead, it is intrabusiness and B2B applications that are receiving most of the attention and that offer the best short-range benefits for businesses. Thirteen categories of m-commerce applications are provided in Online File W9.4 on the book's Web site. Academic journals specializing in mobile commerce include the *International Journal of Mobile Communications* and the *International Journal of Mobile Computing and Commerce*. Online resources for monitoring the development of m-commerce include wireless.ittoolbox.com, mobileinfo.com, mobiforum.org, and mobilemediajapan.com.

The technological foundations presented in Sections 9.1 and 9.2 create the commercial capabilities of m-commerce, as shown in Exhibit 9.7. In Section 9.3, the value-added attributes and various drivers of mobile commerce are discussed (the middle column in Exhibit 9.7). The various applications of m-commerce are examined in Sections 9.4 through 9.8, the third column in Exhibit 9.7. Because m-commerce is, after all, commerce, underpinning this whole discussion are management and financial considerations, such as planning, implementation, cost-benefit analysis, risk assessment, profits, and much more, which are represented by the horizontal bar in Exhibit 9.7.

ATTRIBUTES OF M-COMMERCE

Generally speaking, many of the EC applications described in this book also apply to m-commerce. For example, online shopping, Internet banking, e-stock trading, and online gambling are gaining popularity in wireless B2C. Auction sites are starting to use m-commerce (e.g., sending a text-message alert when an auction is about to close), and wireless collaborative commerce in B2B EC is emerging. The major attributes described next offer the opportunity for development of new applications that are possible only in the mobile environment.

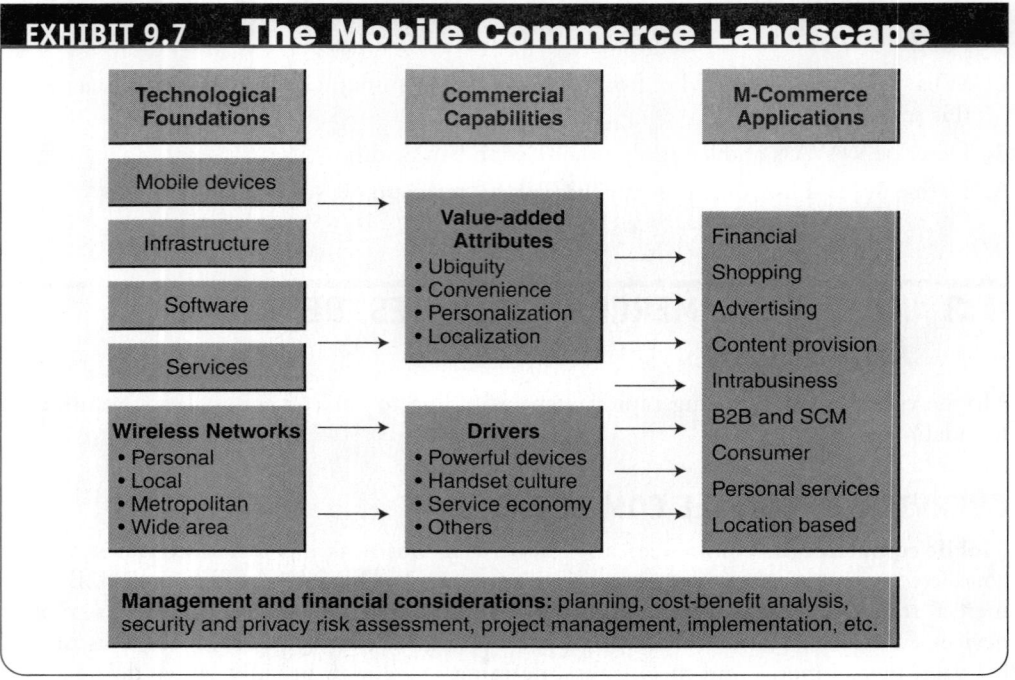

EXHIBIT 9.7   The Mobile Commerce Landscape

Ubiquity. *Ubiquity* means being available at any location at any time. A wireless mobile device such as a smartphone or tablet PC can deliver information when it is needed, regardless of the user's location. Ubiquity creates easier information access in a real-time environment, which is highly valued in today's business and consumer markets.

Convenience. It is very convenient for users to operate in the wireless computing environment. Mobile computing devices are increasing in functionality and usability while remaining the same size or becoming smaller. Unlike traditional computers, mobile devices are portable, can be set in a variety of monitoring modes, and most feature instant connectivity (i.e., no need to wait for the device to boot up). Mobile devices enable users to connect easily and quickly to the Internet, intranets, other mobile devices, and online databases. Thus, the new wireless devices could become the most convenient, preferred way to access many forms of information.

Interactivity. In comparison with the desktop computing environment, transactions, communications, and service provision are immediate and highly interactive in the mobile computing environment. Businesses in which customer support and delivery of services require a high level of interactivity with the customer are likely to find a high value-added component in mobile computing.

Personalization. Mobile devices are truly personal computing devices. Whereas a computer in a home, library, or Internet café may be used by a number of people, mobile devices are almost always owned and operated by a single individual. This enables consumer personalization—the delivery of information, products, and services designed to meet the needs of individual consumers. For example, users planning a trip can be sent travel-related information for retrieval when and where they want. Consumer personalization applications on mobile devices are still limited. However, the personal nature of the computing device, the increasing availability of personalized services, and transaction feasibility via mobile portals means that the mobile computing device could become the primary EC tool for delivering personalized information, products, and services.

Localization. Knowing where a user is physically located at any particular moment is key to offering relevant services. Such services are known as location-based m-commerce (see Section 9.8). Localization may be general; for example, targeting everyone in a certain location (e.g., all shoppers at a shopping mall). Or, even better, it may be targeted so that users get messages that depend both on where they are and what their preferences are, thus combining personalization and localization. For instance, if it is known that a person likes Italian food and that person is strolling in a mall that has an Italian restaurant, the device owner could receive a text message that displays the restaurant's menu offerings and offers a 10 percent discount.

Vendors and carriers can differentiate themselves in the competitive marketplace by offering new, exciting, and useful services based on these attributes. These value-adding attributes can be the basis for businesses to better deliver the value proposition they offer to customers. The services these attributes represent will help e-businesses attract and keep customers and grow their revenues.

DRIVERS OF M-COMMERCE

In addition to the value-added attributes just discussed, the development of m-commerce is being driven by the following technological, business, social, and economic factors:

- **Widespread Availability of More Powerful Devices.** As of the end of 2004, the number of cell phones throughout the world exceeded 1.5 billion (*CellularOnline* 2004). In 120 countries, the number of mobile phones exceeds the number of landline phones (Yapp 2004), and total worldwide mobile phone ownership was predicted to top 2 billion by 2006 (*The Age* 2004b). These devices are increasing in power, functionality, and features (e.g., color screens, GPS locators, Internet access) that support m-commerce. Thus, a potential mass market for conducting m-commerce is emerging.
- **The Handset Culture.** A closely related driver is the widespread use of cell phones among the 15- to 25-year-old age group. These users will constitute a major market of online buyers once they begin to make and spend reasonable amounts of money.
- **The Service Economy.** The transition from a manufacturing to a service-based economy is encouraging the development of mobile-based services, especially when customer service is a differentiator in highly competitive industries. Time-starved but resource-rich individuals will pay for mobile services that perform a range of tasks (e.g., locating a restaurant or dry cleaner in close proximity to the user's position and mobile banking allows users to pay bills online from their cell phones) at their convenience (McKay and Marshall 2004).
- **Vendor's Push.** Both mobile communication network operators and manufacturers of mobile devices are advertising the many potential applications of m-commerce so that they can push new technologies, products, and services to buyers. The advertising expenditure by these companies to encourage businesses to "go mobile" or "mobilize your business" is huge.
- **The Mobile Workforce.** Some workers, such as salespeople and field service employees, have always worked away from an office. Increasingly, other sectors of the workforce also are "going mobile." This is being driven by social work trends such as telecommuting, employers' concerns about security, employees' desires for improved work–life balance, and a general questioning of where knowledge workers need to be located to conduct their work.
- **Increased Mobility.** The most widely recognized benefit of increased mobility is the productive use of travel time. Workers who commute long distances, and especially executives who travel frequently, want to make more productive use of time they spend in public transportation vehicles or in airport lounges. However, there also are spatial, temporal, and contextual aspects of increased mobility that introduce business and personal benefits.

> ▶ **Improved Price/Performance.** The price of wireless devices and the per-minute pricing of mobile services continues to decline even as available services and functionality are increasing. This is leading to improvements in the price/performance ratio. This is enticing new owners into the market and encouraging existing owners to increase consumption of services and to upgrade their handsets.
>
> ▶ **Improvement of Bandwidth.** To properly conduct m-commerce, it is necessary to have sufficient bandwidth to transmit the desired information via text, picture, voice, video, or multimedia. The 3G communications technology is providing a data rate of up to 2 Mbps.

For more on m-commerce applications and adoption, see Petrova (2006) and Deans (2005). The drivers and attributes of m-commerce are the basis for the applications discussed next.

Section 9.3 ▶ REVIEW QUESTIONS

1. Briefly describe the value-added attributes of m-commerce.
2. List and briefly describe eight major drivers of m-commerce.

9.4 MOBILE FINANCIAL APPLICATIONS

Most mobile financial applications are simply a mobile version of their wireline counterparts, but they have the potential to turn a mobile device into a business tool, replacing bank branches, ATMs, and credit cards by letting a user conduct financial transactions with a mobile device, anytime, anywhere (see Gressgard and Stensaker 2004). In this section, we will look at some of the most popular mobile applications in financial services.

MOBILE BANKING AND FINANCIAL SERVICES

Throughout Europe, the United States, and Asia, an increasing percentage of banks are offering mobile access to financial and account information. For instance, Merita Bank in Sweden pioneered many services (Sadeh 2002), and Citibank in the United States has a diversified mobile banking service. Customers of such banks can use their mobile handsets to access account balances, pay bills, and transfer funds using SMS. The Royal Bank of Scotland, for example, uses a mobile payment service, and Banamex, one of Mexico's largest banks, is a strong provider of wireless services to customers. Many banks in Japan, Korea (Infobank), and Hong Kong allow for banking transactions to be done via cell phone. Banks in Germany, Switzerland, Sweden, Finland, and Austria offer several mobile financial services. Of special interest to banking customers are financial-alert applications (e.g., a loan payment is due, a scheduled rental payment has not been made, a bank balance has fallen below a specified amount).

To date, though, the uptake of mobile banking is still low. However, surveys indicate a strong latent demand for these offerings; customers may be waiting for the technology and transmission speeds to improve (e.g., mobile banking support is now offered in the United States by Cingular and other major carriers). The same can be said for other mobile financial applications, such as mobile *real estate*, *insurance*, and *stock market* trades.

WIRELESS ELECTRONIC PAYMENT SYSTEMS

Wireless payment systems transform mobile phones into secure, self-contained purchasing support tools capable of instantly authorizing payments over the cellular network. In the United States, for example, Cellbucks offers a mobile payment service that enables fans at participating sports stadiums to purchase food, beverages, and merchandise by cell phone and have it delivered to their seats. Any fan who is a member of the Cellbucks Network can dial a toll-free number, enter his or her pass code and seat location, and then select numbered items that correspond to desired menu selections. Once authorized, the purchase request is passed on to stadium personnel who prepare the food and deliver it to the fan's seat. An e-mail detailing the

EXHIBIT 9.8   Purchasing Movie Tickets with WAP Solo

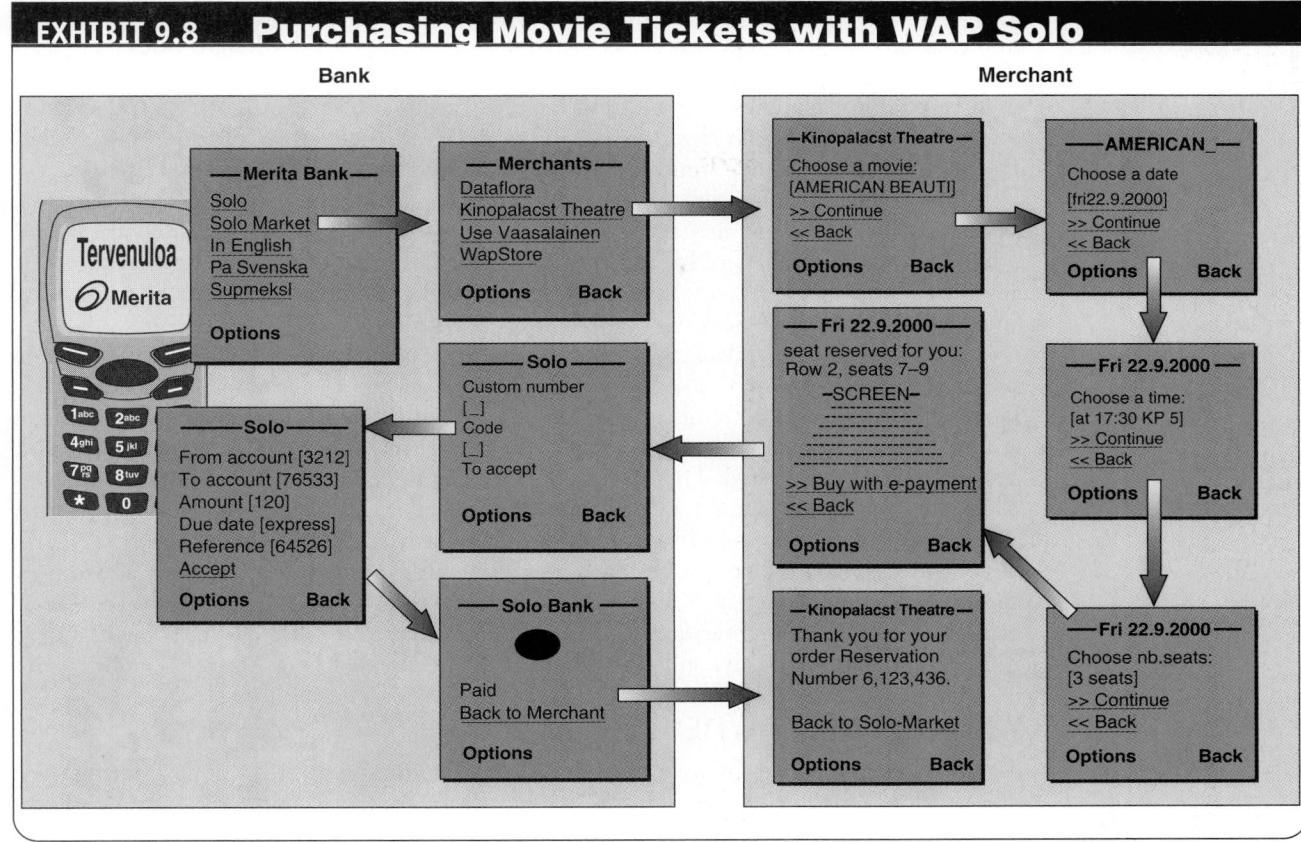

Source: Sadeh, N., *M-Commerce*. New York: Wiley, 2002, Figure 1.5. Reprinted by permission of John Wiley & Sons, Inc.

transaction is sent to the fan as further confirmation of the order. In Europe and Japan, using wireless technology to buy tickets to movies and other events is popular (see Exhibit 9.8).

In Frankfurt, Germany, people can use cell phones to pay for taxi rides. In Japan, Hong Kong, Korea, and Israel, people can purchase drinks from vending machines with their mobile phones. In Italy and New Zealand, cell phones can be used to pay for time on parking meters (Synergy 2004). As discussed earlier in this chapter, these micropayments are likely to become one of the most popular support services for m-commerce applications. An A. T. Kearney study (*ClickZ Stats* 2002) found that more than 40 percent of mobile phone users surveyed would like to use their mobile phone for small cash transactions, such as transit fares or vending machines. The desire for such services was highest in Japan (50 percent) and lowest in the United States (38 percent). The percentage of mobile phone users who had actually used their phones for such purposes was only 2 to 3 percent, reflecting the fact that very few vendors were offering micropayments in their applications as of 2006.

Micropayment technology has wide-ranging applications, such as making payments to parking garages, restaurants, grocery stores, and public transportation. The success of micropayment applications, however, ultimately depends on the cost of the transactions (transaction costs will be small only if there is a large volume of transactions) and the willingness of the mobile service provider to accept the risk of potential nonpayments by customers. For details, see Karnouskos and Vilmos (2006) and Chapter 12.

Wireless Wallets

An *e-wallet* (see Chapter 12) is a piece of software that stores an online shopper's credit card numbers and other personal information so that the shopper does not have to reenter that information for every online purchase. In the recent past, companies such as SNAZ offered **m-wallet (mobile wallet)** (also known as *wireless wallet*) technologies that enabled cardholders to make purchases with a single click from their mobile devices. Although most

m-wallet (mobile wallet)
Technologies that enable cardholders to make purchases with a single click from their wireless device.

of these companies are now defunct, some cell phone providers have incorporated m-wallets into their offerings. A good example is the Nokia wallet. This application provides users with a secure storage space in their phones for information (such as credit card numbers) to be used in mobile payments. The information also can be used to authenticate transactions through the use of *digital signatures* (see Chapter 12). Microsoft is offering its e-wallet, Passport, in a wireless environment. Another example is Google Toolbar AutoFil.

The mobile wallet is a versatile application that includes elements of mobile transactions, as well as other items one may find in a wallet, such as membership cards, loyalty cards, and other forms of identification. In-Stat (instat.com) believes that the market can grow only by adopting a technology that offers the most versatility by providing both transaction capability and content discovery (*Mobile Marketing Magazine* 2005).

According to *Mobile Marketing Magazine* (2005), as many as 25 million wireless phone subscribers in North America could be using their mobile phones as mobile wallets by 2011. However, market research indicates that the attitudes of U.S. users toward mobile wallets are at best lukewarm, with roughly one-third of respondents interested, one-third indifferent, and one-third uninterested. The most frequently mentioned barrier to the mobile wallet is added fees for its use (cited by 72 percent of respondents), followed by security concerns about loss of the phone and privacy. This problem may be alleviated by new security. NTT's DoCoMo has been selling phones with m-wallet chips in Japan that can be scanned by a short-range wireless reader at tens of thousands of stores since 2004. Similar capabilities using Near Field Communications (NFC) are forecasted for the United States beginning in 2007. More than half of all handsets sold by 2010 could be m-wallets (Smith 2006).

WIRELESS BILL PAYMENTS

A number of companies are now providing their customers with the option of paying their bills directly from a cell phone. HDFC Bank of India (hdfcbank.com), for example, allows customers to pay their utility bills using SMS. An example of how bill payments can be made using a mobile device is shown in Online File W9.5. This service is offered by Nordea, a pioneering provider of wireless banking services in Scandinavia. According to Poropudas (2003), more and more ATMs and vending machines can communicate with mobile phones, giving consumers the opportunity to access virtual cash, buy goods or services, or pay bills.

According to *Payment News* (2006), mobile payments are set to rise to $10 billion in total revenue by 2010, thanks to the entrance of new players offering m-payment schemes and subsequent consumer demand. The expansion of PayPal services into the micropayment and m-retail sector will serve to facilitate a fundamental shift in global consumer payment services now and into the future.

Closing the Digital Divide

Mobile devices, especially smartphones and even regular cell phones, are closing the digital divide in developing countries such as China, India, and the Philippines. These developing countries do not have the money to implement wireline phone systems, but they can afford WWANs. As a result, people can afford telephones, and with declining Internet access fees, they can do m-commerce. Even if they do not have Internet access, they can still pay bills, as is the case in China.

SmartPay Jieyin, working with banks and utility companies, provides a service for people in Shanghai and Beijing, China, to pay their utility bills by cell phone. Most people in China do not have checking accounts, and very few have credit cards, so bills must be paid by standing in a long line at a bank. The system sends an SMS message on a subscriber's cell phone when a payment is due. The user then types in a PIN number to authorize the money transfer from his or her bank account.

Section 9.4 ▶ REVIEW QUESTIONS

1. Describe some of the services provided by mobile banking.
2. Discuss mobile payments, especially the potential for wireless micropayments.
3. Describe the m-wallet and discuss wireless bill payments.

9.5 MOBILE SHOPPING, ADVERTISING, AND CONTENT PROVISION

As in e-commerce, m-commerce B2C applications are concentrated in three major areas: retail shopping for products and services, advertising, and providing content for a fee.

WIRELESS SHOPPING

An increasing number of online vendors allows customers to shop from wireless devices, especially cell phones and PDAs (see pilotzone.com for more information on how this is done). Customers can use their wireless devices to perform quick searches, compare prices, use a shopping cart, order, and view the status of their order. Wireless shoppers are supported by services similar to those available for wireline shoppers. For example, mobile shoppers have access to shopping carts, as well as product search and price comparison tools. Japan has the highest number of 3G service users of any country in the world. Eighty percent of e-commerce by teenagers between 15 and 19 was done on mobile phones in 2005 (Belew 2006).

An example of restaurant shopping from wireless devices is those restaurant chains that enable consumers to place an order for pickup or delivery virtually anytime, anywhere. Donatos Pizzeria was the first chain to implement the system in 2002.

Cell phone users also can participate in online auctions. For example, eBay offers "anywhere wireless" services. Account holders at eBay can access their accounts, browse, search, bid, and rebid on items from any Internet-enabled phone or PDA. The same is true for participants in Amazon.com Auctions.

MOBILE AND TARGETED ADVERTISING

Knowing the real-time location of mobile users and their preferences or surfing habits, marketers can send user-specific advertising messages to wireless devices. Location-sensitive advertising (using GPS) to find where a customer is can inform a potential buyer about shops, malls, and restaurants close to where the mobile device owner is. This topic is discussed in more detail in Section 9.8. Examples of companies capitalizing on targeted advertising, including paying users to listen to advertising, are included in Online File W9.6 at the book's Web site.

Currently SMS and e-mails are the principal technologies used to deliver advertisements to cell phones. However, as more wireless bandwidth becomes available, content-rich advertising involving audio, pictures, and video clips will be generated for individual users with specific needs, interests, and inclinations.

For example, Expedia (expedia.com, the largest online travel company, sends SMSs to targeted segments of frequent travelers offering incentives to enter the Expedia.com Web site, where the cell phone users can opt in for free services and for information to be delivered to their phones.

A mobile advertising campaign should be pursued with some caution. The number of ads pushed to an individual customer should be limited, to avoid overwhelming a user with too much information and also to avoid the possibility of congestion over the wireless networks. Wireless network managers may consider ad traffic to be of a lower priority compared with purchases or customer interaction. Finally, because advertisers need to know a user's current location, a third-party vendor may be used to provide location services. This will require the sharing of revenues with a location service provider. Mobile advertisements can also be unrelated to location. For details, see *3GNewsroom.com* (2006). For permission-based m-advertising and factors affecting mobile advertisements, see Salo and Tahtinen (2006). For other topics, see Pierre (2006).

mobile portal
A customer interaction channel that aggregates content and services for mobile users.

MOBILE PORTALS

A **mobile portal** is a customer access and interaction channel, optimized for mobility, that aggregates and provides content to and services for mobile users (see Chapters 6 and 7 for additional discussion of portals). Zed (zed.com) from Sonera in Finland is Europe's leading mobile portal. Nordea's Solo banking portal was illustrated in Online File W9.5. Vodafone offers its customers Vodafone Live! The world's best-known mobile portal, with over 40 million members, mostly in Japan, is i-mode, which is described in Online File W9.7.

Mobile portals offer news, sports, entertainment, and travel information; restaurants and event information; leisure-related services (e.g., games, videos, and movies); e-mail; community services; and stock trading. A sizeable percentage of the portals also provides downloads and messaging, music-related services, and health, dating, and job information. Mobile portals frequently charge a monthly fee to access basic information services and a per-service fee for premium content, such as location-based weather reports or downloads.

Specifically designed for m-commerce, mobile portals plan their pages with minimum information and very few graphics. Examples are MSN and Yahoo!'s mobile portals, which offer short menus of popular topics (e.g., news, sports, finance, e-mail, instant messenger, and search capabilities).

Section 9.5 ▶ REVIEW QUESTIONS

1. Describe how mobile devices can be used to shop.
2. Explain targeted advertising in the wireless environment.
3. Describe mobile portals and the types of information they provide.

9.6   MOBILE ENTERPRISE AND SUPPLY CHAIN

Although B2C m-commerce gets considerable publicity in the media and first mention in most discussions of m-commerce, for most organizations the greatest short-term benefit from mobile commerce is likely to come from intrabusiness applications, especially B2E (business-to-employee) ones. This section looks at how mobile devices and technologies can be used within organizations.

SUPPORT OF MOBILE EMPLOYEES

Mobile workers are employees who work outside the corporate premises. Examples of mobile workers are members of sales teams, traveling executives, telecommuters, people working in corporate yards or warehouses, and repair or installation employees who work at customers' sites or in the field. These mobile workers need the same corporate data available to employees working inside the company's offices. However, it may be inconvenient or impossible for these off-site employees to use wireline-based devices, even portable ones.

The solution is smaller, simpler wireless devices such as tablet PCs, PDAs, and smartphones. Increasingly, companies are realizing that equipping their mobile employees with mobile computing devices will increase employee productivity (Kakihara and Sorensen 2003), improve customer service, and increase employee morale and job satisfaction. According to Intel (2006), a new wireless notebook PC can provide nearly 100 hours of additional productivity per employee per year. That is what Intel's IT department found when it began migrating users from mobile Pentium III processor-based notebooks to Intel Centrino mobile technology-based notebooks in early 2003. In short, the company will receive considerable gains from the investment. Perhaps in no area is this truer than in the use of mobile devices in mobile offices and sales force mobilization and automation.

According to Malykhina (2006b), the major enterprise mobile applications are e-mail, cell phone contacts, calendaring, customer relations, sales force automation, field service, logistics and supply chain, HRM, and financial (in descending order of frequency). Let's look at some of these applications in more detail.

Mobile Office

The most obvious application of supporting employees is the ability to work from the car, at airports, hotels, and so on. The simplest form is that of communication (e.g., via SMS) or connection to the Web for downloading or uploading data. In the following applications, both technologies are used. For details, see Pierre (2006).

Sales Force Mobilization and Automation

Many employees who sell must travel. Whether making a sales pitch to a potential customer, demonstrating a new product to an existing customer, checking inventory in the customer's store, or maintaining a close working relationship with customers, salespeople spend a lot of time away from the office. Mobile computing devices can keep these employees better informed about new product launches, product information, pricing schedules, order status, manufacturing schedules, inventory levels, and delivery schedules. Popular devices used by salespeople are the Treo 700W and 700 WK and Blackberry 8700C. For details, see Chen (2006) and Malykhina (2006a).

The business case for **sales force mobilization**—equipping sales force employees with wireless Internet-enabled computing devices—is a compelling one. Sales staff can enter sales meetings with the most current and accurate information, perhaps even checking sales and product information during the meeting itself. When it is time to close the deal, the salesperson can wirelessly check production schedules and inventory levels to confirm product availability and even specify a delivery date. This available-to-promise/capacity-to-promise (ATP/CTP) capability means no more "I will have to check on that" promises that can sometimes delay or cancel a sale. It also can mean more competitive and realistic offers to customers.

If taking inventory of existing product on a client's shelf is part of the sales duties, the time devoted to this can be dramatically reduced through RFID tags (introduced in Chapter 7, described further in Section 9.10 and illustrated in the Real-World Case at the end of this chapter). Making this task easier and less time consuming can increase employee job satisfaction and make more time available for higher-revenue-generating activities.

Finally, by enabling sales force employees to record orders in real time, the organization benefits through improved manufacturing and delivery scheduling, fewer data entry errors, less clerical and administrative overhead, and better decision making. An example of improved sales productivity through wireless mobile computing is provided in Case 9.1.

sales force mobilization
The process of equipping sales force employees with wireless Internet-enabled computing devices.

CASE 9.1
EC Application
MARKETSOURCE MOBILIZES ITS WORKFORCE

As a provider of outsourced sales and marketing programs, MarketSource knows sales. With approximately 80 percent of its 2,000 employees working away from the office, either calling on customers or working on site, MarketSource also knows from firsthand experience the impact of mobile computing on sales force automation.

The majority of the company's employees work remotely from retailer sites or from home offices, so connectivity and communications are critical to using their time efficiently. MarketSource representatives need to capture sales information, competitive data, and point-of-sale activity in the field through the firm's Web-based applications and transmit that information back to the corporate office to produce vital sales reports.

One solution MarketSource uses to accomplish this is tablet PCs running the Windows XP Tablet PC Edition operating system. As of May 2003, approximately 5 percent of MarketSource's full-time staff were using tablet PCs, a percentage that is expected to grow.

"We're primarily deploying tablet PCs to people who go to a lot of meetings and travel a lot," says Jim Hibbard, MarketSource Manager of QA and Training. "This group takes advantage of the handwriting recognition and digital ink capabilities built into Windows XP Tablet PC Edition to take notes in meetings and store them electronically so that they can be quickly searched or sent in e-mail."

Using tablet PCs, MarketSource sales representatives do in-store surveys in real time and easily send and receive e-mail throughout the workday. This gives them more "face time" with the customer and helps them get reporting done faster, which reduces the amount of time spent working at home.

The wireless network support in Windows XP Professional also helps make meetings more productive. "People bring their notebook computers or tablet PCs to meetings because they can access things on the network from the conference room rather than run back to their office for something," Hibbard says. "When a question comes up in a meeting, they just connect where they are and immediately get answers. They can send files back and forth to other users in the meeting, which also saves time."

The deployment "has made a significant impact on the organization in terms of productivity and lowered TCO [total cost of ownership]," says Kristin McQuiddy, MarketSource Director of Business Development. "But the real value comes from our ability to deliver better results for our partners."

Source: Compiled from Microsoft (2003).

Questions

1. Which MarketSource employees use tablet PCs and for what purposes?
2. What benefits are MarketSource and its employees receiving from this deployment of intrabusiness m-commerce?

Worker Support in Retailing

Symbol Technology (symbol.com) provides rugged handheld, small computers that enable data capture applications, collaboration, and price markdowns. The Symbol MC series, for example, can facilitate inventory taking and management. Warehouse management systems are greatly improved with software that is combined with the device (e.g., from M-Netics). Wild Oats employees use handheld computers to reorder. When an employee scans a product's bar code, the handheld recommends how much to order. All the employee has to do is accept or modify the recommendation and press "execute."

Support in Hospitals

Many hospitals have introduced wireless applications ranging from wearable push-button communication devices (badge clips from Vocera Communications) to wireless laptops for bedside registration (Walsh and Yamarick 2005).

Support in Operations

Many devices are available to facilitate different tasks of mobile employees. For example, Driscoll Strawberry Associates uses wireless data collection devices, mobile printers, and handheld devices to accelerate transactions, increase accuracy, and enable real time receiving and inventory management. The company arranges the delivery of berries to market. The company achieved a 25 percent reduction in transaction processing time, 30 percent reduction in account reconciliation errors, and improved employee feedback on ease of use. For details see the Driscoll's Berries case study at symbol.com.

Home Depot equipped close to 12,000 service agents with the Wi-Fi–based Enfo Trust system. The system can take photos as well. See Nobel (2005) for details.

Tracking Employees

Using PDAs, Todd Pacific Shipyards knows that accurately locating employees, including the hours and projects they've worked, and assessing daily staffing needs is a key to profitability (see Schuman 2004).

Job Dispatch

Another group of inherently mobile employees are those involved in delivery and dispatch services, including transportation (e.g., delivery of food, oil, newspapers, and cargo; courier services; tow trucks; taxis), utilities (e.g., gas, electricity, phone, water), field services (e.g., computer, office equipment, home repair), health care (e.g., visiting nurses, doctors, social services), and security (e.g., patrols, alarm installation). Mobile devices are becoming an integral part of the groupware and workflow applications that support these employees. Mobile computing can assist in dispatch functions—assigning jobs to mobile employees—and provide workers with detailed information about the task.

A dispatching application for wireless devices enables improved response with reduced resources, real-time tracking of work orders, increased dispatcher efficiency, and a reduction in administrative work. For example, AirIQ's OnLine system (airiq.com) combines Internet, wireless, GPS, digital mapping, and intelligent information technologies. The system collects information about a vehicle's direction, speed, and location from a device housed in each vehicle. Managers can view and access information about the fleet on digital maps, monitor vehicles on the Internet, and monitor the operating condition of their fleet. AirIQ promises savings of about 30 percent in communication costs and increases in workforce efficiency of about 25 percent. Online File W9.8 at the book's Web site provides a detailed description of a job-dispatching system that a truck service company has used to provide benefits to both itself and its customers.

Maintenance and Repair at Remote Sites

Many companies have maintenance and repair people in their own field or at customers' sites. These employees need to be in constant contact with the office, warehouse, engineering, and so. Cell phones are useful but not sufficient in all cases. Tablet PCs, PDAs, smart phones, and cameras that can be connected to the corporate intranets are useful as well. One category of devices of particular interest for maintenance and repair at remotes sites is *wearable devices*.

Wearable Devices

Employees who work on buildings, electrical poles, or other "climbable workplaces" may be equipped with special mobile wireless computing devices called **wearable devices**. Workers wear these devices on their arms, clothes, helmets, or other parts of their bodies. The following are examples of wearable devices:

> ▶ **Screen.** A computer screen is mounted on a safety hat in front of the worker's eyes, displaying information to the worker.
> ▶ **Camera.** A camera is mounted on a safety hat. Workers can take digital photos and videos and transmit them instantly to a portable computer nearby. Photo transmission is usually made possible by Bluetooth.
> ▶ **Keyboard.** A wrist-mounted keyboard can be typed on by the other hand. Wearable keyboards are an alternative to voice recognition systems, which also are wireless.
> ▶ **Touch-panel display.** In addition to the wrist-mounted keyboard, mobile employees can use a flat-panel screen attached to a hand that responds to the tap of a finger or stylus.
> ▶ **Speech translator.** For those mobile employees who do not have their hands free to use a keyboard, a wearable speech translator is handy (see Smailagic et al. 2001).

wearable devices
Mobile wireless computing devices, attached to various parts of employees, for employees who work on buildings and other climbable workplaces.

For an example of wearable devices used to support mobile employees, see Online File W9.9 at the book's Web site. Other sources of information about wearable wireless devices are xybernaut.com, essworld.net, and media.mit.edu/wearables.

SUPPORTING OTHER TYPES OF WORK

There are many other examples of how wireless devices can support workers. The applications will surely grow as the technology matures and as workers discover new ways to apply the functions of wireless devices to their jobs. Consider the following examples:

> ▶ Wireless devices can be used to support traveling (or off-corporate-site) executives, managers, or other employees. The iPaq Travel Companion is not only a smartphone, but it even has a GPS receiver. With Windows Mobile, it offers business travelers effective navigation, connectivity, and entertainment options.
> ▶ Tractors equipped with sensors, onboard computers, and a GPS unit help farmers save time, effort, and money. GPS determines the precise location of the tractor and can direct its automatic steering. Because the rows of planting resulting from GPS-guiding are more exact, farmers save both on seeds and on fertilizers due to minimized overlapping and spillage. Farmers also can work longer hours (at dark) with the satellite-controlled steering to take advantage of good weather. Another savings is due to the instant notification to the service department of any machine that breaks down. For details, see Scanlon (2003).
> ▶ Taco Bell provides its mystery shoppers (shoppers who visit restaurants to conduct a survey unknown to the owners) with handheld computers so that they can communicate more quickly with the company's headquarters (Microsoft 2002). The mystery shoppers must answer 35 questions, ranging from the speed of service to food quality. Prior to the use of the devices, information was provided by filling out paper forms that were mailed overnight and scanned into computers for processing. The information flow using the handheld computers is both faster and more accurate.
> ▶ Like e-mail, SMS can be used to bolster collaboration. According to Kontzer (2003), the following are 10 applications of SMS for mobile workers: (1) alerting mobile technicians to system errors; (2) alerting mobile executives to urgent voice messages; (3) confirming

with mobile sales personnel that a faxed order was received; (4) informing travelers of delays and changes; (5) enabling contract workers to receive and accept project offers; (6) keeping stock traders up to date on urgent stock activity; (7) reminding data services subscribers about daily updates; (8) alerting doctors to urgent patient situations; (9) enabling mobile sales teams to input daily sales figures into corporate databases; and (10) sending mobile sales representatives reminders of appointments and other schedule details.

▶ To increase national security and safeguard national borders, countries are using facial-recognition and iris-scanning biometrics (see Chapter 11), both of which are supported by wireless systems.

▶ Companies are using mobile devices to locate items in warehouses.

▶ In some amusement parks (e.g., Lego/Denmark), children are tagged so they can be easily found.

CUSTOMER AND PARTNER SUPPORT

Mobile access extends the reach of customer relationship management (CRM) to both employees and business partners on a 24/7 basis to any place where recipients are located. In large software suites, such as Siebel's CRM (from Oracle), the two CRM functions that have attracted the most interest are sales force mobilization and field service, both discussed earlier. Two illustrations of the use of mobile technologies for sales support and customer service support are provided in Online File W9.10 at the book's Web site.

Voice portals also can be used to enhance customer service or to improve access to data for employees. For example, customers who are away from the office could use a vendor's voice portal to check on the status of deliveries to a job site. Salespeople could check on inventory status during a meeting to help close a sale. There are a wide variety of CRM applications for voice portal technology. The challenge is in learning how to create the navigation and other aspects of interaction that makes customers feel comfortable with voice-access technology.

NON–INTERNET ENTERPRISE APPLICATIONS

Wireless applications in the non–Internet environment have been around since the early 1990s. Examples include wireless networking, used to pick items out of storage in warehouses via laptops mounted on forklifts; delivery-status updates, entered on PCs inside distribution trucks; and collection of data, such as competitors' inventories in stores and customer orders, using a handheld (but not wireless) device, from which data are transferred to company information systems each evening. Also, using cell phones (but not Internet connected) is popular with many applications. The following are three recent examples of such intrabusiness applications.

▶ Employees at companies such as Telecom Italia Mobile (*Republica.IT* 2001) get their monthly pay slips as SMS messages sent to their mobile phones. The money itself is transferred electronically to a designated bank account. The method is much cheaper for the company and results in less paperwork than the old method of mailing monthly pay slips.

▶ Kemper Insurance Company has piloted an application that lets property adjusters report from the scene of an accident. Kemper attached a wireless digital imaging system to a camera that lets property adjusters take pictures in the field and transmit them to a processing center (Nelson 2000). The cameras are linked to Motorola's StarTac data-enabled cellular phone service, which sends the information to a database. These applications eliminate delays in obtaining information and in film processing that exist with conventional methods.

▶ A medical-supplies vendor developed a mobile enterprise application that allows sales representatives to check orders and inventories during their visits with physicians and instantly determine what they can deliver to the physician's office and when (Ellison 2004).

The use of RFID to improve productivity in intrabusiness applications will be discussed in Section 9.10. Now, however, our examination of m-commerce applications leaves the one company organizational boundaries to look at interbusiness applications in B2B m-commerce and supply chain management.

B2B M-COMMERCE AND SUPPLY CHAIN MANAGEMENT

Timely access to accurate information is critical for B2B EC success. Companies must be able to respond to business partner requirements in real time, and speedy response is especially important in managing the supply chain. Mobile computing solutions enable organizations to respond faster to supply chain disruptions by proactively adjusting plans or by shifting resources related to critical supply chain events as they occur (see details in Chapter 7).

The two greatest opportunities in B2B mobile commerce are to use wireless communication to share information along the supply chain and to collaborate with partners. By integrating the mobile computing device into supply chain communications, it is possible to make mobile reservations of goods, remotely check availability of a particular item in the warehouse, order a customized product from the manufacturing department, or provide secure access to confidential financial data from a management information system.

One way to share information with supply chain partners is wireless *telemetry*, which is the science of measuring physical phenomena such as temperature, volume, or an on/off condition at a remote point and transmitting the value to a distant recorder or observer. (Telemetry is described further in Section 9.8.) This technology enables automated data capture, improved timeliness and accuracy of billing, lower overheads, and increased customer satisfaction through faster and more complete service responsiveness. For example, vending machines can be kept replenished and in reliable operation if suppliers can wirelessly check inventory and service status. RFID tags (described in Section 9.10) can be used to monitor and control the flow of goods up and down the supply chain more efficiently.

Mobile devices also can facilitate collaboration among members of the supply chain. It is no longer necessary for a company to call a partner company to find its offsite employees. Instead, managers can contact these employees directly on their mobile devices.

Finally, many of the organizational benefits of sales force mobilization mentioned earlier flow up and down the supply chain, too. Direct, remote, real-time entry of sales into ERP systems can improve supply chain operations because today's ERP systems tie into broader supply chain management solutions that extend visibility across multiple tiers in the supply chain. Mobile supply chain management (mSCM) empowers the workforce to leverage these broader systems through improved inventory management and ATP/CTP functionality that extends across multiple supply chain partners and takes into account logistics considerations.

Section 9.6 ▶ REVIEW QUESTIONS

1. In what ways does an organization benefit from providing mobile wireless devices to its sales employees?
2. Describe wireless job dispatch.
3. List some of the non–Internet intrabusiness mobile applications.
4. Briefly describe two ways wireless communications can support B2B commerce and supply chain management.
5. What are the benefits of mSCM?

9.7 MOBILE CONSUMER AND PERSONAL SERVICE APPLICATIONS

A large number of wireless applications exist that support consumers and provide personal services (see Kou and Yesha 2006). As an example, consider the situation of a traveler taking an international flight. Before leaving home, the traveler uses his or her cell phone to query the airline's WAP-enabled Web site or SMS messaging system to see if there has been a flight delay. Upon arrival at the airport, entering the flight number into the device returns a message from the airline indicating the correct check-in desk and confirming the flight time. Singapore Airlines even allows passenger check-in via SMS at 12 international airports.

Upon arrival at the airport, Singapore passengers check in luggage and pick up boarding passes from a dedicated counter rather than wait in regular queues (*The Age* 2004a). After check-in, a GPS-enabled device could be used to determine the nearest washroom or restaurant and provide directions. Information about today's specials at a duty free store can be requested through an SMS number posted on advertising in the terminal's lobby. A text message from the airline alerts the traveler when boarding is about to commence. Finally, the traveler can make a taxi reservation at the destination while waiting in the airport lounge for boarding. All of these services are possible in some places and are expected to be widely available soon.

Similar scenarios can be created for hotels, a day at a theme park, conference attendance, entertainment facility, or a night out on the town. The purpose of this section is to introduce the reader to a few of the consumer and personal service areas in which wireless devices can be used.

MOBILE ENTERTAINMENT

Mobile entertainment is available on many mobile devices, ranging from smartphones to iPods. Notable applications are music, videos, games, adult entertainment, sports, gambling, and more. Several examples of mobile sports offerings are presented in Insights and Additions 9.2 For other examples of mobile entertainment applications, see Online File W9.11.

Mobile Games and Gambling

According to Telephia Research (2006), nearly 13.5 million mobile subscribers downloaded a game in the second quarter of 2006, representing average monthly revenues for the major U.S. vendors of $46.9 million for the quarter. Since the third quarter of 2005, the number of subscribers who have downloaded mobile games from game portals has increased by 15 percent. During the same time period, revenues for game providers jumped 63 percent. Sega Corp. has capitalized on the popularity of games such as Sonic the Hedgehog to garner 2.5 million Japanese subscribers for its mobile game and entertainment services (Becker 2002). In Japan, where millions of commuters spend time during long train rides, cell phone games have become a cultural phenomenon. For growth projections, see Kolenikov-Jessop (2005).

With more than 2 billion cell phones in use by the end of 2006 (Goodman 2006), the potential audience for mobile games is substantially larger than the market for other platforms, such as PlayStation and Gameboy. Because of the market potential, cell phone manufacturer Nokia has decided to enter the mobile-gaming world, producing not only the phone/console, but also the games, which are delivered on memory sticks. It is developing and marketing short-distance multiplayer gaming over Bluetooth and wide area gaming using cellular networks.

In July 2001, Ericsson, Motorola, Nokia, and Siemens established the Mobile Games Interoperability Forum to define a range of technical standards that will make it possible to deploy mobile games across multigame servers, wireless networks, and over different mobile devices. Microsoft is moving into this field as well. This organization is now called Open Mobile Alliance (see OMA 2006).

Mobile gambling, a related topic, is extremely popular in some countries (e.g., horse racing in Hong Kong and racing and other events in Australia). For more on mobile gambling, see sportbet.com.

Hands-Free Driving

Ford and Microsoft are bringing wireless Windows to cars in February 2007. The new technology, called Sync, uses Bluetooth to enable connections between the car and devices such as cell phones and iPods, allowing for hands-free driving (Hoffman 2006). According to Elliot (2007), soon it will be possible to connect to high-speed wireless from a car.

Insights and Additions 9.2 Sports-Related Mobile Applications

▶ In May 2006, Nike and Apple introduced an iPod shoe called the Nano that can provide real-time feedback on distance, time, and calories burned during a workout. A sensor and receiver embedded in the shoe provide a wireless connection to the iPod; workout information is stored in the device and displayed on the screen. Runners can get audible feedback through the headphones, and data stored on the Nano can be downloaded to a Mac or PC after a run. In addition to these functions, the system delivers music and commentary to help joggers make it through their workouts. Nike also is offering workout-related podcasts that include advice from marathon runner Alberto Salazar and inspiration from bicycling champion Lance Armstrong. In fall 2006, Nike delivered six additional footwear styles designed to hold the iPod sensor. The company also is planning to unveil a collection of jackets, tops, shorts, and armbands designed for the Nike+iPod Sport Kit. A similar service is offered by Bones in Motion (*bonesinmotion.com*) together with Sprint. It uses GPS to turn mobile phones into exercise-tracking devices.

▶ In winter 2006, Levi Strauss introduced a new line of jeans specifically geared toward iPod users. The $200 trousers come complete with headphones, a joystick, and even a docking cradle.

▶ Apparel maker Burton got a great deal of attention during the 2006 Winter Olympics with its Bluetooth-enabled snowboard jackets featuring padded casings for cell phones and MP3 players, removable speakers in the hood, and built-in control pads on the sleeves.

▶ ESPN's Sport Center with Sanyo offers a cell phone dedicated to sports. Users can get quick access to news about their favorite teams. Video clips of up to 30 seconds are available, and so is a built-in camera. Sports trivia also are offered. Alerts are sent by request. The service is relatively expensive.

▶ A grocery phone is used in Finland to calculate how much exercise a shopper will have to perform to burn off the calories of any food consumed. To access the information, users take a photo of the product bar code and enter their age, weight, and height.

WIRELESS TELEMEDICINE

Today, two different technologies are being used for telemedicine applications: (1) storage of data and transferring of digital images from one location to another and (2) videoconferencing used for real-time consultation between a patient in one location and a medical specialist in another. In most of the real-time consultations, the patient is in a rural area and the specialist is in an urban location.

Telemedicine faces a number of obstacles. Some states do not allow physicians to provide medical advice across state lines. The threat of malpractice suits is another issue because there is no hands-on interaction between the remote physician and the patient. In addition, from a technical standpoint, many telemedicine projects are hindered by poor telecommunications support. However, those who are looking ahead to the needs of an aging population are seeing opportunities to meet some of those needs in emerging technologies. The new wireless and mobile technologies such as 3G and WiMax not only offer the possibility of overcoming the hurdles imposed by remote locations but also open a number of new and novel application opportunities. Examples include the following:

▶ Typically, physicians write a prescription, and the patient takes it to the pharmacy where there is typically a 15- to 30-minute wait for it to be filled. Some new mobile systems allow physicians to enter patient prescriptions into a palm-sized device. The information is transmitted by cellular modem (or Wi-Fi) to Med-i-nets (med-i-nets.com) or a similar company. There, the information is checked for insurance eligibility and conformity to insurance company and government regulations. If everything checks out, the prescription is transferred electronically to the appropriate pharmacy for a no-wait pick-up by the patient. In addition, for patients who need refills, the system tracks and notifies physicians when it is time to reorder, and the doctor can reissue a prescription with a few clicks.

▶ Fast response is absolutely critical in the case of a heart-attack victim. Manufacturers are developing wearable heart monitors linked to a cell phone that can automatically contact doctors or family members at the first sign of trouble.

▶ The Swiss Federal Institute of Technology has designed portable devices that transmit the vital signs of avalanche victims up to 80 meters (262 feet) away (Baard 2002). Not only does the device provide location information, it also provides information about body orientation that helps reduce injuries as rescuers dig for the victims.

▶ In-flight medical emergencies occur much more frequently than one might think. Alaskan Airlines, for example, deals with about 10 medical emergencies per day (Conrad 2002). Mobile communications already are being used to attend to medical emergencies on planes. MedLink, a service of MedAire in Phoenix, provides around-the-clock access to board-certified emergency physicians. These mobile services also can remotely control medical equipment, such as defibrillators, located onboard the plane.

▶ The military is involved in developing mobile telesurgery applications that enable surgeons in one location to remotely control robotic arms for surgery in another location. The technology could be particularly useful in battlefield situations.

OTHER MOBILE COMPUTING SERVICES FOR CONSUMERS

Many other mobile computer services in a variety of service categories are available to consumers. Examples include services providing news, weather, and sports reports; language translators; information about tourist attractions (hours, prices); currency, time zone, and other converters for travelers; and emergency services. At CVS Pharmacy, customers can print photos directly from their mobile phones to store kiosks (*Pmai.org* 2005). For more examples, see the case studies at mobileinfo.com/case_study/index.htm.

NON–INTERNET MOBILE APPLICATIONS FOR CONSUMERS

Non–Internet mobile applications for consumers have mainly been in the transportation industry. Millions of "contactless" smart cards (also called *proximity cards*) are used to pay bus and subway fares and road tolls worldwide. Amplified remote-sensing cards that have an RF (radio frequency) of up to 30 meters (100 feet) are used in several countries for toll collection.

Section 9.7 ▶ REVIEW QUESTIONS

1. List a few ways wireless communications can assist a traveler who is about to take a trip.
2. Describe some potential uses of mobile and wireless technologies in providing medical care.
3. How are wireless smart cards used in the transport industry?

9.8 LOCATION-BASED MOBILE COMMERCE

location-based m-commerce

Delivery of m-commerce transactions to individuals in a specific location, at a specific time.

As discussed earlier in this chapter, the use of GPS enables localization of mobile services, a value-added attribute of mobile commerce (Section 9.3). Formally, **location-based m-commerce (l-commerce)** refers to the use of GPS-enabled devices or similar technologies (e.g., triangulation of radio- or cell-based stations) to find where a customer is and deliver products and services based on the customer's location. Location-based services are attractive to both consumers and businesses alike. From a consumer or business user's viewpoint, localization offers safety (emergency services can pinpoint the mobile device owner's exact location), convenience (a user can locate what is nearby without consulting a directory, pay phone, or map), and productivity (time can be optimized by determining points of interest within close proximity). From a business supplier's point of view, location-based m-commerce offers an opportunity to provide services that more precisely meet a customer's needs.

The services provided through location-based m-commerce focus on five key factors:

1. **Location.** Determining the basic position of a person or a thing (e.g., car or boat)
2. **Navigation.** Plotting a route from one location to another
3. **Tracking.** Monitoring the movement of a person or a thing (e.g., a package or vehicle)
4. **Mapping.** Creating maps of specific geographical locations
5. **Timing.** Determining the precise time at a specific location

THE TECHNOLOGY FOR L-COMMERCE

Technologically, the ability of a location-based service to identify where a mobile consumer is located depends on the global positioning system and geographical information system.

Global Positioning System

The global positioning system (GPS) is based on a worldwide satellite-based tracking system that enables users to determine exact positions anywhere on the earth. GPS was developed by the U.S. Defense Department for military use, but its high value for civilian use was immediately recognized, and the technology was released into the civilian domain, originally for use by commercial airlines and ships. In recent years, GPS locators have become a part of the consumer electronics market and are used widely for business and recreation (e.g., see geocaching.com).

GPS is supported by 24 U.S. government satellites. Each satellite orbits the earth once every 12 hours on a precise path at an altitude of 10,900 miles. At any point in time, the exact position of each satellite is known, because the satellite broadcasts its position and a time signal from its onboard atomic clock, which is accurate to one-billionth of a second. Receivers on the ground also have accurate clocks that are synchronized with those of the satellites.

GPS locators may be stand-alone units or embedded into a mobile device. Using the fast speed of the satellite signals (186,272 miles, or 299,775 kilometers, per second; the speed of light) the system can determine the location (latitude and longitude) of any GPS locator, to within 50 feet (15 meters) by triangulation, using the distance from the GPS locator to three satellites to make the computation. GPS software then computes the latitude and longitude of the receiver. More information on how the GPS system works is available in Online File W9.12 at the book's Web site. An online tutorial on GPS is available at trimble.com/gps.

Geographical Information System and GPS

The location provided by GPS is expressed in terms of latitude and longitude. To make that information useful to businesses and consumers, these measures need to be related to a specific place or address. This is done by inserting the latitude and longitude onto an electronic map, which is known as a *geographical information system (GIS)*. A **geographical information system (GIS)** is a computer system capable of integrating, storing, editing, analyzing, sharing, and displaying geographically-referenced (spatial) information. For details, see en.wikipedia.org/wiki/Geographic_information_system. The GIS data visualization technology integrates GPS data into digitized map displays (see idelix.com for an explanation of how this is done). Companies such as mapinfo.com and navteq.com provide the GIS core spatial technology, maps, and other data content needed in order to deliver location-based services such as emergency assistance, restaurant locators, buddy finders, and service-call routing.

geographical information system (GIS)
A computer system capable of integrating, storing, editing, analyzing, sharing, and displaying geographically-referenced (spatial) information.

An interesting application of GPS/GIS is now available from several car manufacturers (e.g., Toyota, Cadillac) and car rental companies (e.g., Hertz, Avis). Some cars have a navigation system that indicates how far away the driver is from gas stations, restaurants, and other locations of interest. The GPS knows where the car is at any time, so the application can map the route for the driver to a particular destination. Another example of a location-based application in the transportation industry is NextBus, as described in Online File W9.13 at the book's Web site. Any GPS application can be classified as *telemetry*, a topic discussed later in this section. Other examples are provided next.

GPS/GIS Applications

The following are illustrative examples of various GPS/GIS applications:

▶ UltraEx, a West Coast company that specializes in same-day deliveries of items such as emergency blood supplies and computer parts, equips all of its vehicles with @Road's GPS receivers and wireless modems. In addition to giving dispatchers a big-picture view of the entire fleet, @Road helps UltraEx keep clients happy by letting *them* track the location and speed of their shipments on the Web in real time. This service shows customers a map of the last place the satellite detected the delivery vehicle and how fast it was traveling. Drivers use AT&T's Mobile Data Service to communicate with dispatch, and drivers who own their vehicles are unable to falsify mileage sheets because @Road reports exact mileage for each vehicle.

▶ The Mexican company Cemex is the third largest cement producer in the world. Concrete is mixed en route to construction sites and must be delivered within a certain time period or it will be unusable. Rather than waiting for orders, preparing delivery schedules, and then sending out the deliveries as most companies do, Cemex has trucks fitted with GPSs patrolling the road at all times, waiting for orders; this allows the company to guarantee delivery within 20 minutes of the agreed time. Real-time data on each truck's position are available not only to company managers but also to clients and suppliers, enabling them to plan their schedules to fit in with the next available truck. Digital maps help locate the customers and the trucks, allowing the use of shortcut routes.

▶ CSX Transportation Inc. has equipped all its 3,700 locomotives with a GPS. The Union Pacific Railroad has installed satellite-based monitoring devices on thousands of its freight cars for car tracking. By combining GIS with a GPS, a freight company can identify the position of a railroad car or truck within 100 meters at any time. For example, it can identify locomotives that have left their route and the specific cars that have been left behind or sent with the wrong locomotive. Further benefits include the ability to minimize accidents.

▶ The city of Beijing, China, is preparing a network of intelligent transportation systems for the 2008 Summer Olympics. A major portion of the system is a real-time traffic control based on GPS/GIS technology. For details, see Wang et al. (2003).

LOCATION-BASED ADVERTISING

Imagine that you are walking near a Starbucks, but you do not even know that one is there. Suddenly your cell phone beeps with a message: "Come inside and get a 15 percent discount." Your wireless device was detected, and similar to the pop-up ads on your PC, advertising was directed your way (Pierre 2006). You could use permission marketing to shield yourself from location-based advertising; if the system knows that you do not drink coffee, for example, you would not be sent a message from Starbucks.

Another use of wireless devices for advertising is described by Raskin (2003). In this case, a dynamic billboard ad could be personalized specifically for you when your car approaches a certain billboard and the system knows your preferences. Your car will be tracked by a GPS every 20 seconds. A computer scans the areas in which billboards are visible, and by cross-referencing information about your location and your preferences, a personalized ad could be placed on the billboard so you would see it as you pass.

Yet another method of location-based advertising involves putting ads on the top of taxi-cabs. The ads change based on the taxi's location. For example, a taxi cruising in the theater district in New York City might show an ad for a play or a restaurant in that area; when the cab goes to another neighborhood, the ad might be for a restaurant or a business in that part of the city.

EMERGENCY RESPONSE CELL PHONE CALLS

If someone dials an emergency response number (e.g., 911 in the United States; 111, 110, or 999 in many other countries) from a regular wired phone, it is easy for the emergency response service to pinpoint the phone's location. But what happens if someone places an emergency call from a mobile phone? How can the emergency response dispatcher locate the caller? A few years ago, the U.S. Federal Communication Commission (FCC) issued a directive to wireless carriers, requiring that they establish services to handle **wireless 911 (e-911)** calls. To offer an idea of the magnitude of this requirement, more than 156,000 wireless 911 calls are made every day, representing more than half of the 911 calls made daily in the United States (Schwartz 2006).

wireless 911 (e-911)
In the United States, emergency response system that processes calls from cellular phones.

The e-911 directive is implemented in two phases, although the specifics of each phase vary from one wireless carrier (e.g., T-Mobile, Cingular, Sprint) to another. Phase I requires carriers, upon appropriate request by a local Public Safety Answering Point (PSAP), to report the telephone number of the wireless 911 caller and the location of the cellular antenna that received the call. Phase II requires wireless carriers to provide information that will enable the PSAP to locate a caller within 50 meters 67 percent of the time and within 150 meters 95 percent of the time. By the end of Phase II, it is expected that 95 percent of all new cell phones will have these location capabilities. It is expected that many other countries will follow the example of the United States in providing this type of emergency response service.

Some expect that in the future cars will have an **automatic crash notification (ACN)** device. These still-experimental devices will automatically notify the police of an accident involving an ACN-equipped car and its location. Also, following a school bus hijacking in Pennsylvania, the Pennsylvania legislature is considering a bill to mandate real-time satellite tracking of all school buses.

TELEMATICS AND TELEMETRY APPLICATIONS

Telematics refers to the integration of computers and wireless communications in order to improve information flow (see Chatterjee et al. 2002 and Cybit 2006). It uses the principles of *telemetry*, the science that measures physical phenomena at a remote point and transfers the value to a receiving station. Wireless Matrix (wirelessmatrix.com), for example, tracks and monitors trucks and containers for fleet management, driver communication, environmental changes, and intrusion detection, all while the vehicle or container is in motion.

Using *mobile telemetry*, technicians can diagnose maintenance problems in equipment from a remote distance. Car manufacturers use the technology for remote vehicle diagnosis and preventive maintenance. Finally, doctors can use mobile telemetry to monitor patients and control medical equipment from a distance.

Imagine the following scenario, an example of *mobile inventory* (Pierre 2006): As soon as a store (e.g., 7-Eleven) requires a certain item, the wireless system can automatically locate a truck that carries item, preferably one in the area, and obtain just-in-time (or on-demand) delivery. Similar applications can be used in hospitals. This reduces the storage space and the inventory holding costs as well.

One of the major problems in many cities is the lack of sufficient parking spaces. This is the situation in Paris, France, where as many as 20 to 25 percent of all vehicles may circulate the city looking for a parking space at certain times of the day. This causes more traffic jams and wastes gasoline.

As of December 2006, relief is in sight. Orange, a large mobile telecommunications company, and its partners organized a system that allows drivers to find the empty parking spaces quickly in one of the nearest parking garages. Here is how it works: The 120 participating garages collect information electronically about open parking spaces and send the information to a central server at Orange. The messages are transmitted over the Internet. As soon as an open space is occupied, the information is updated. Drivers call Orange for help in finding a parking space using their cell phones. Orange knows their location by the location of the antenna being used to make the cell phone call. As of 2007, the system will find the location of those with GPS embedded in their cell phones. The system matches drivers with available spaces. Those who have GPSs are guided to the available space. As a bonus, the system tells the drivers when they approach a speed camera (*Taipei Times* 2006; Mullen 2006).

General Motors popularized automotive telematics with its OnStar system (see Online File W9.14). Nokia has set up a business unit, Smart Traffic Products, that focuses solely on telematics. Nokia believes that every vehicle will be equipped with at least one Internet Protocol (IP) address by the year 2010. Smart cars are discussed in more detail in Section 9.10.

OTHER APPLICATIONS OF LOCATION-BASED SYSTEMS

New and innovative applications of location-based systems (LBS) appear almost daily. The following are some examples:

- In Las Vegas, the Luxor preregisters guests when their airplane lands and they turn on their cell phones. Also, the hotel can determine when guests leave the hotel, luring them back (to gamble) with mobile incentives and pitches.
- SearchQuest from Realtors by Realtors is an LBS application designed to help real estate agents showcase houses. The company hopes to release the service in August 2006 (see searchquest.com).

automatic crash notification (ACN)
Device that automatically sends the police the location of a vehicle that has been involved in a crash.

telematics
The integration of computers and wireless communications to improve information flow using the principles of telemetry.

▶ Jewel Chaser from TikGames (tikgames.com), due in the United States by early 2007, is a cops-and-robbers game that puts players in the role of detective, deciphering clues and navigating their way through the real world in order to capture runaway thieves. Loc-Aid (loc-aid.net) has unveiled a location-based treasure hunt game played on a mobile phone.

▶ GlobalPetFinder (globalpetfinder.com) is small device that pet owners can snap onto their pet's collar. If a pet wanders outside the "virtual fence," the pet's owner will receive a text alert of the pet's whereabouts.

▶ KnowledgeWhere's Mobile Pooch (knowledgewhere.ca), Kamida's Socialight (socialight.com) and Proxpro (proxpro.com) are applying LBS to social networking. Socialight, now in beta, lets users publish pictures, words, sound, and video tagged to specific locales.

BARRIERS TO LOCATION-BASED M-COMMERCE

What is holding back the widespread use of location-based m-commerce? Several factors come into play, including the following:

▶ **Accuracy of devices.** Some of the location technologies are not as accurate as people expect them to be. A good GPS provides a location that is accurate up to 15 meters (50 feet). Less expensive, but less accurate, locators can be used to find an approximate location within 500 meters (1,640 feet).

▶ **The cost-benefit justification.** For many potential users, the benefits of location-based services do not justify the cost of the devices or the inconvenience and time required to utilize the service (e.g., Bial and Mayhew 2005). After all, many seem to feel that they can just as easily obtain information the old-fashioned way.

▶ **Limited network bandwidth.** Wireless bandwidth is currently limited; it will be improved as 3G technology spreads. As bandwidth improves, applications will improve, which will attract more customers.

▶ **Invasion of privacy.** When "always-on" cell phones are a reality, many people will be hesitant to have their whereabouts and movements tracked throughout the day, even if they have nothing to hide. This issue will be heightened when our cars, homes, appliances, and all sorts of other consumer goods are connected to the Internet and have a GPS device embedded in them, as discussed in Section 9.10.

Section 9.8 ▶ REVIEW QUESTIONS

1. Describe some of the potential uses of location-based m-commerce.
2. Discuss the technologies used in providing location-based services.
3. Describe GPS and GIS.
4. Discuss telematics.
5. List some of the barriers to location-based m-commerce.

9.9 SECURITY AND OTHER IMPLEMENTATION ISSUES IN M-COMMERCE

Despite the vast potential for mobile commerce to change the way many companies do business, several barriers are either slowing down the spread of mobile commerce or leaving many m-commerce businesses and their customers disappointed or dissatisfied (e.g., see Islam and Fayad 2003). Security of mobile communications and mobile computing systems is a major concern, and this topic is addressed first.

M-COMMERCE SECURITY ISSUES

Many m-commerce security issues mirror those of e-commerce security (see Chapter 11).

Malicious Code. In 2001, a hacker sent an e-mail message to 13 million users of the i-mode wireless data service in Japan. The message had the potential to take over the recipient's phone, causing it to dial Japan's emergency hotline (1–1–0). DoCoMo rapidly fixed the problem, so no damage was done. At the beginning of 2002, researchers in the Netherlands discovered a bug in the operating system used by many Nokia phones that would enable a hacker to send a malformed SMS message capable of crashing the system. Again, no real damage was done. In 2004, Cabir became the first known virus capable of spreading through mobile phones. Fortunately, the virus was not launched, because it was developed by a global group that creates viruses to demonstrate that no technology is reliable and safe from viruses (see *Forbes* 2004).

These three cases are indicative of the malicious code threat that may someday plague mobile computing as much as it does desktop computing. Most Internet-enabled cell phones in operation today have their operating systems and other functional software "burned" into the hardware. This makes them incapable of storing applications and, in turn, incapable of propagating a virus, worm, or other rogue program from one phone to another. However, as the capabilities of cellular phones increase and the functionality of PDAs and cell phones converge, the threat of attack from malicious code will certainly increase.

Transaction Security. The basic security goals of confidentiality, authentication, authorization, and integrity are just as important for m-commerce as they are for e-commerce but are more difficult to ensure. Specifically, m-commerce transactions almost always pass through several networks, both wireless and wired. An appropriate level of security must be maintained on each network, and this interoperability is difficult. Similarly, posttransactional security issues of auditing and nonrepudiation are more difficult because cell phones do not yet have the capability to store the digital equivalent of a receipt.

Other m-commerce security challenges are unique because of the nature of the mobile computing environment. Some of the security issues include the following.

Wireless Communication. The open-air transmission of signals opens up new opportunities, but security may be compromised. Interception of a communication in a wired network requires physical access to the wires in which the signal is being carried. Interception of a communication in a wireless network can be done with a carefully aimed, even crude, antenna (e.g., a legendary war-driving tip is how to use a Pringles potato chip can to hone in on a rogue Wi-Fi signal).

Physical Security of Mobile Devices. Because of their small size, mobile devices are easily lost or stolen. Similarly, because they are mobile, cell phones, PDAs, Blackberries, and other devices are sometimes dropped, crushed, or damaged by water and extreme temperature. A stolen device can provide the thief with valuable data and digital credentials that can be used to compromise an m-commerce network. A lost or damaged device is a security threat because of the loss of any stored data or device settings.

Ease of Use and Poor Security. The very same ease-of-use factors that mobile computing users appreciate work against fulfillment of security goals. Couple this with the privacy and apparent anonymity that personal computing devices provide, and the opportunities for abuse rise dramatically (Elliott and Phillips 2004).

Many of the processes, procedures, and technologies used for e-commerce security and for general organizational computer security also apply to m-commerce security. Passwords, encryption, active tokens, and user education (all discussed in Chapter 11) also apply to m-commerce security.

Security Measures. Special security measures for m-commerce may be required. For example, to prevent the theft of a mobile device, a user might carry a "wireless tether" that sounds a warning if a device is left behind or carried away. Wi-Fi networks have their own built-in security system known as Wired Equivalent Privacy (WEP), which is, as the name suggests, similar to encryption protocols used on wired networks. Similarly, WAP networks depend on the Wireless Transport Layer Security (WTLS), and cell phones can be protected by SIM-based authentication. These three approaches to m-commerce security are discussed in more detail in the Online File W9.15 at the book's Web site. Additional information about mobile commerce security is available in Commonwealth Telecommunications Organisation (2006) and Elliott and Phillips (2004).

TECHNOLOGICAL BARRIERS TO M-COMMERCE

When mobile users want to access the Internet, the *usability* of the site is critical to achieve the purpose of the visit and increase user stickiness (the degree to which users stay at a site). However, many Web sites are not designed for viewing by mobile devices and, thus, are unviewable or unfriendly to mobile devices.

A related problem, referred to earlier, is the technological limitations of most mobile computing devices. Current devices have limited usability, particularly with respect to pocket-size screens or data input devices. In addition, because of the limited storage capacity and information access speed of most smartphones and PDAs, it is often difficult or impossible to download large files to these devices.

Mobile visitors to a Web site are typically paying premium rates for Internet connections and are focused on a specific goal (e.g., conducting a stock trade). For visitors to find exactly what they are looking for easily and quickly, the navigation systems have to be fast and designed for mobile devices. Similarly, the information content needs to meet the user's needs. For example, many WAP screens are text based and have only simple black-and-white graphics. This means that mobile users cannot browse an online picture-based catalog, which makes mobile shopping difficult. This situation is improving as devices become more powerful and as 3G bandwidth becomes more commonplace. Today, some users can watch videos and movies on their cell phones.

Other technical barriers related to mobile computing technology include limited battery life and transmission interference with home appliances. These barriers and others are listed in Exhibit 9.9.

EXHIBIT 9.9	Technical Limitations of Mobile Computing
Limitation	**Description**
Insufficient bandwidth	Sufficient bandwidth is necessary for widespread mobile computing, and it must be inexpensive. It will take a few years until 3G and WiMax are available in many places. Wi-Fi solves some of the problems for short-range connections.
Security standards	Universal standards are still under development. It may take 3 or more years for sufficient standards to be in place.
Power consumption	Batteries with long life are needed for mobile computing. Color screens and Wi-Fi consume more electricity, but new chips and emerging battery technologies are solving some of the power-consumption problems.
Transmission interferences	Weather and terrain, including tall buildings, can limit reception. Microwave ovens, cordless phones, and other devices on the free, but crowded, 2.4GHz range interfere with Bluetooth and Wi-Fi 802.11b transmissions.
GPS accuracy	GPS may be inaccurate in a city with tall buildings, limiting the use of location-based m-commerce.
WAP limitations	Many mobile phone users find that WAP is expensive and difficult to access.
Potential health hazards	Potential health damage from cellular radio frequency emission is not known yet. Known health hazards include cell phone addiction, thumb-overuse syndrome, and accidents caused by people using cell phones while driving.
Human–computer interface	Screens and keyboards are too small, making mobile devices uncomfortable and difficult for many people to use.
Complexity	Too many optional add-ons are available (e.g., battery chargers, external keyboards, headsets, microphones, cradles). Storing and using the optional add-ons can be a problem.

ETHICAL, LEGAL, AND HEALTH ISSUES IN M-COMMERCE

The increasing use of mobile devices in business and society raises new ethical, legal, and health issues that individuals, organizations, and society will have to resolve.

One workplace issue is the isolation that mobile devices can impose on a workforce. The introduction of desktop computing invoked a profound change on social interaction in the workplace, illustrated by the walled cubicles featured in Dilbert cartoons. Some workers had difficulty adjusting to this new environment and sought to replace face-to-face interactions with e-mail interactions, prompting organizational policies against the forwarding of non-business-related e-mail and IM messages.

Equipping the workforce with mobile devices may have similar impacts. Field service employees dispatched remotely and who acquire replacement parts from third-party sources will visit "the office" only briefly at the start and end of each day, if at all. The result could be a reduction in organizational transparency, making it difficult for employees to know what other employees do, how the organization is evolving, and how they fit into it. These changes have powerful implications for individuals and the organization for which they work. Whether the results are good or bad depends on how the change is managed (Elliott and Phillips 2004).

The truly personal nature of the mobile device also raises ethical and legal issues in the workplace. Most employees have desktop computers both at home and at work, and separate business and personal work accordingly. However, it is not so easy to separate work and personal life on a cell phone, unless one is willing to carry two phones or two PDAs. And if an organization has the right to monitor e-mail communications on its own network, does it also have the right to monitor voice communications on a company-owned cell phone?

The widespread appearance of mobile devices in society has led to the need for cell phone etiquette, the creation of "cell free" zones in hospitals and airport lounges, and National Cell Phone Courtesy Month. For an insightful essay into the impact of cell phones in work and social spaces, see Rosen (2004).

A widely publicized health issue is the potential, but not yet proven, health damage from cellular radio frequency emissions. Cell phone addiction also is a problem. A study by Seoul National University found that 30 percent of South Korean high school students reported addiction effects, such as feeling anxious when they did not have their phones with them. Many also displayed symptoms of repetitive stress injury from obsessive text messaging (Rosen 2004).

Other ethical, legal, and health issues include the ethics of monitoring staff movements based on a GPS-enabled devices or vehicles, maintaining an appropriate work–life balance when work can be conducted anywhere at anytime, and the preferred content of an organizational policy to govern use and control of personal mobile computing devices in and out of the workplace.

BARRIERS FOR ENTERPRISE MOBILE COMPUTING

According to Malykhina (2006b), the following are the major barriers to enterprise mobile computing (based on the percentage of companies experiencing them): high cost (59 percent), inadequate security (48 percent), lack of integration (46 percent), insufficient broadband (41 percent), inadequate mobile applications development (36 percent), not a high IT priority (34 percent), short battery life (32 percent), management requirements (32 percent), small screens (30 percent), lack of industry standards (21 percent), and inadequate device memory (18 percent).

PROJECT FAILURES IN M-COMMERCE

As with any other technology, especially a new one, applications, as well as entire companies, have failed in their attempts to implement an m-commerce strategy. It is important to anticipate and plan for possible failures as well as to learn from them.

The case of Northeast Utilities provides some important insights. According to Hamblen (2001), Northeast Utilities, which supplies energy products and services to 1.2 million customers from Maine to Maryland, embarked on a wireless project in 1995 in which its field inspectors used wireless devices to track spills of hazardous material and report them to headquarters in real time. After 18 months and spending $1 million, the project failed. The following are some of the lessons learned from this failure:

▶ Do not start a project without the appropriate infrastructure.
▶ Do not start a full-scale implementation; use a small pilot for experimentation.
▶ Pick an appropriate architecture (e.g., some users do not need to be persistently connected).
▶ Talk with a range of users, some experienced and some not, about usability issues.
▶ Users must be involved; hold biweekly meetings if possible.
▶ Employ wireless experts.
▶ Wireless is a different medium from other forms of communication. Remember that people are not used to the wireless paradigm.

Having learned from the failure, Northeast made its next wireless endeavor a success. Today, 15 field inspectors carry rugged wireless laptops that are connected to the enterprise intranet and databases. The wireless laptops are used to conduct measurements related to electricity transformers, for example. The laptops transmit the results, in real time, to chemists and those who prepare government reports about hazardous materials spills. In addition, time is saved because all the information is entered directly into proper fields of electronic forms without having to be transcribed. The new system is so successful that it has given IT workers the confidence to launch other applications, such as sending power-outage reports to executives via smartphones and wireless information to crews repairing street lights.

Section 9.9 ▶ REVIEW QUESTIONS

1. Discuss how m-commerce security is similar to e-commerce security.
2. Identify three unique security challenges for mobile devices.
3. Discuss the role that usability plays in the adoption of m-commerce.
4. List the technical limitations of m-commerce.
5. Discuss the potential impact of mobile devices on the workplace.
6. Describe the potential health hazards of mobile devices.
7. List the lessons learned in the implementation of m-commerce at Northeast Utilities.

9.10   PERVASIVE COMPUTING

Many experts believe that the next major step in the evolution of computing will be pervasive computing. In a *pervasive computing* environment, almost every object has processing power and a wired or wireless connection to a network. The use of RFID tags mentioned in several earlier chapters is an example of pervasive computing. Many other initiatives already underway—smart homes, smart appliances, and sensor networks—are described in the second part of this section. The section begins with an overview of pervasive computing.

OVERVIEW OF PERVASIVE COMPUTING

pervasive computing
Invisible, everywhere computing that is embedded in the objects around us.

Pervasive computing is invisible, everywhere computing; it is computing capabilities being embedded into the objects around us. In contrast, mobile computing is usually represented by devices—handheld computers, handset phones, headsets, and so on—that users hold, carry, or wear. Even as mobile computing devices continue to mature in functionality, power, and usefulness, pervasive computing technologies are emerging (see Streitz and Nixon 2005).

Pervasive computing also is called *embedded computing*, *augmented computing*, or *ubiquitous computing*. However, some in this still-emerging field make a distinction between pervasive and ubiquitous computing. According to Lyytinen and Yoo (2002), *pervasive computing* is embedded in the environment but typically not mobile. They define *ubiquitous computing* as computing that combines a high degree of mobility with a high degree of embeddedness. So, for example, most smart appliances in a smart home represent wired, pervasive computing, and mobile objects with embedded computing, such as in clothes, cars,

and personal communication systems, represent ubiquitous computing. This distinction is illustrated in Online File W9.16 at the book's Web site. In this chapter, however, we treat *pervasive* and *ubiquitous* as equivalent terms; pervasive computing devices are embedded in the environment around us, and they may be mobile or stationary.

The idea of pervasive computing has been around for years. Mark Weiser first articulated the current version in 1988 at Xerox's computer science laboratory, the Palo Alto Research Center (PARC). Weiser and his colleagues were attempting "to conceive a new way of thinking about computers, one that takes into account the human world and allows the computers themselves to vanish into the background" (Weiser 1991, p. 94). According to Weiser, pervasive computing is the opposite of virtual reality. In virtual reality, the user is immersed in a computer-generated environment. In pervasive computing, the user is immersed in an invisible "computing is everywhere" environment—in cars, clothes, homes, the workplace, and so on (Weiser 1991).

Invisible Computing

By invisible, Weiser did not mean to imply that pervasive computing devices would not be seen but, rather, that, unlike a desktop or handheld computer, these embedded computers would not intrude on our consciousness. Think of electric motors. They exist in the devices all around us, but they are invisible to us, and we do not think about using them. This is Weiser's vision for pervasive computing. The user will not think about how to use the processing power in the object; rather, the processing power automatically helps the user perform the task.

Principles of Pervasive Computing

Underlying the embeddedness of pervasive computing are four principles that will define its development (Hansmann et al. 2003):

- ▶ **Decentralization.** The decentralization of computing that began with the transition from the centralized mainframe computer to the personal computer will continue in pervasive computing. Indeed, computing devices in the future will not be computers but tags, sensors, badges, and commonplace objects all cooperating together in a service-oriented infrastructure.
- ▶ **Diversification.** Computing devices will evolve from a fully functional one-computer-does-all paradigm to one in which specialized, diversified devices will suit the requirements of an individual for a specific purpose. A person may own several devices that slightly overlap in functionality, but each will be the preferred tool for each specific purpose.
- ▶ **Connectivity.** The independent pervasive computing devices—tags, sensors, badges—will be seamlessly connected to the network or to each other. Open, common standards will be required to achieve this level of connectivity and interoperability.
- ▶ **Simplicity.** These devices must be designed for simplicity of use. Intuitive interfaces, speech recognition, one-handed operation, instant on, and always connected are a few of the requirements for high, but simple, usability.

In addition to the four principles outlined here, a list of the technical foundations for pervasive computing is provided in Online File W9.17 at the book's Web site.

Contextual Computing (Context Awareness)

As described earlier, location can be a significant differentiator when it comes to providing services. However, knowing that the user is at a particular street corner is not enough to fully anticipate and meet the user's needs. For this, we need to know information such as the weather, the time of day, what is on the user's calendar, and other relevant *contextual attributes*. *Context awareness* refers to capturing a broad range of contextual attributes to better understand the consumer's needs and to determine what products or services may be required to fulfill those needs. For an illustrative example, see the Carnegie Mellon University case in Online File W9.18.

Context awareness is part of **contextual computing**, which refers to the enhancement of a user's interactions by understanding the user, the context, and the applications and information required, typically across a wide set of user goals (see Pitkow et al. 2002 for details). Contextual computing is about actively adapting the computational environment for each user based on a variety of factors.

Many strategists working in this field view contextual computing and context awareness as the Holy Grails of m-commerce. Contextual computing offers the prospect of applications that could anticipate our every wish and provide us with the exact information and services we are looking for—and also help us filter all those annoying promotional messages that we really do not care for. Such applications are futuristic at the present time, but they become more possible in a world of pervasive computing.

contextual computing
The enhancement of a user's interactions by understanding the user, the context, and the applications and information required.

RADIO FREQUENCY IDENTIFICATION (RFID)

A number of pervasive computing initiatives are underway that hold substantial promise for the future of EC and m-commerce and that have the substantial financial backing that will be needed for commercial success. A major one is RFID.

The Basics of RFID

radio frequency identification (RFID)
Technology that uses radio waves to identify items.

Radio frequency identification (RFID) technology uses radio waves to identify items (see wikipedia.org). An RFID system consists of (1) an *RFID tag* that includes an antenna and a chip with information about the item and (2) an *RFID reader* that contains a radio transmitter and receiver. An RFID tag remains inactive until radio frequency energy from the radio transmitter (on the tag) hits its antenna, giving the chip enough power to emit a 96-bit string of information, which is read by the radio receiver. This is three times the amount of information a bar code can hold, and the tag can be read through cardboard, wood, and plastic at a range of up to 30 feet. The reader then passes the information, wirelessly or through a docking station, to a computer for processing (see Exhibit 9.10). For a comprehensive overview see Heinrich (2005).

RFID Applications

The number of applications for RFID is increasing. A 2006 study (Ferguson 2006) revealed that RFID is most often used for the tracking of items in factories and stores. This was

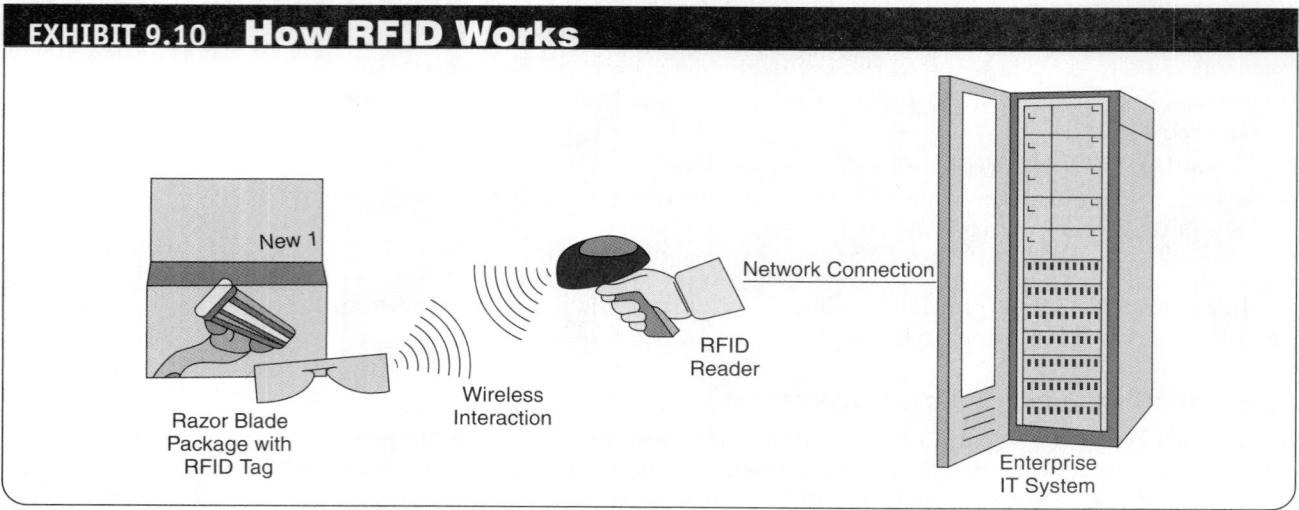

EXHIBIT 9.10 How RFID Works

New 1

Razor Blade Package with RFID Tag

Wireless Interaction

RFID Reader

Network Connection

Enterprise IT System

Source: Heinrich,C. *RFID and Beyond*, Indianapolis, Wiley Publishing, 2005, Figure 3.5, p. 65. Reprinted by permission of John Wiley & Sons, Inc.

demonstrated in the Wal-Mart case (Chapter 2). Fifty-five percent of all companies use RFID for this purpose or plan to in the near future. In addition, almost 50 percent of companies use RFID in real-time locating systems (Chapter 7).

RFID has been around for almost 60 years, but only now has it begun to receive widespread attention. Until recently, RFID was expensive, with tags costing 50 cents or more. However, as the cost of the tags continues to decline, the use of the technology is expected to expand. RFID technology is already being used for a variety of purposes:

> ▶ **Track moving vehicles.** The E-Z Pass (ezpass.com) prepay toll system uses RFID, as does Singapore's Electronic Road Pricing system, which charges different prices to drive on different roads at different times. Online File W9.19 at the book's Web site provides an example of the use of RFID technology for toll collection on a Los Angeles' highway.
>
> ▶ **Track people.** In some Japanese schools, tags in backpacks or clothes track students' entry and departure from school buildings. In Denmark, the Legoland amusement park offers parents a child-tracking system that combines RFID and Wi-Fi. As of 2006, all new U.S. passports contain an RFID tag that can be scanned upon entry and departure from the United States. About 47 percent of all companies used, or planned to use, RFID for such tracking purposes in 2005 (Teradata 2006).
>
> ▶ **Track individual items.** The Vatican Library is tagging over 2 million items in its collection. Retail giant Marks & Spencer is using antitheft tags on clothes and is tagging employee ID cards to control entrance into secure areas. The Jacksonville, Florida, airport has a pilot test for RFID tracking of luggage. The U.S. army is tracking inventory, including weapons, with RFID tags. The Star City Casino in Sydney, Australia, is using RFID to keep track of 80,000 costumes and uniforms.
>
> ▶ **Protect secure areas.** FedEx uses RFID-tagged wristbands to give drivers access to their vehicles, reducing theft and speeding delivery time. The New York Police Department uses RFID tags embedded in ID tags to track visitors (Ferguson 2006).
>
> ▶ **Record transactions.** Exxon Mobil Corp.'s Speedpass cards and key rings allow customers to speed through checkout lines. At the Baja Beach Club in Barcelona, Spain, an RFID chip embedded just under a guest's skin is used to pay for purchases, including drinks at the pool.

For a list of additional RFID applications, see Online File W9.20. As suggested in the Real-World Case at the end of this chapter and in Chapter 7, the greatest interest in this technology is to track individual items to improve inventory and supply chain management. An indication of the high interest in this was the purchase of 500 million RFID tags in early 2003 by Gillette (*RFID Journal* 2002). Gillette is using the tags in a number of trial programs, including the largest RFID trial in the world at Wal-Mart (see the Real-World Case in Chapter 2). Retail giants such as Albertson's, Target, and Best Buy also are supporting adoption of the technology by their suppliers (Feder 2004).

One initiative underway that could lead to widespread support for the introduction of RFID is the **Electronic Product Code (EPC)**. The EPC identifies the manufacturer, producer, version, and serial number of each item. The concept is similar to the Universal Product Code (UPC) that currently appears on almost every consumer product. The UPC is a 12-digit number that is represented by bars and spaces of varying widths, readable by a bar code scanner. The use of an EPC-enabled RFID tag instead of a UPC bar code offers several advantages. First, an RFID tag does not require line-of-sight contact to be read. Second, RFID tags are not printed on paper, so they are less likely to be ripped, soiled, or lost. Third, the RFID tag identifies the item, not just the manufacturer and product. EPC will provide the ability to track individual items as they move from factories to store shelves, considerably improving supply chain collaboration; eliminating human error from data collection; reducing inventories, loss, and waste; and improving safety and security.

Electronic Product Code (EPC) An RFID code that identifies the manufacturer, producer, version, and serial number of individual consumer products.

Several factors will determine the speed with which RFID will take off. The first of these is how many companies will mandate that business partners use RFID. So far, only major retailers, such as Wal-Mart, and the U.S. Department of Defense require its use. The second factor is concerns about privacy issues raised by the use of the tags (see Online File W9.21; *Wired* 2004). Finally, the cost of the tags and the needed information systems to support RFID use is still high and is likely to remain so (Spivey-Overby 2004). However, Ryan (2004) suggests that in order to be winners, manufacturers must embrace the technology. For an overview of RFID implementation issues and attempted solutions, see Kharif (2004).

SMART APPLICATIONS: HOMES, CARS, AND MORE

Pervasive computing, with its tiny devices and tags, including RFID tags, is the key to many applications.

Smart Homes

In a smart home, the home computer, television, lighting and temperature controls, home security system, and many appliances within the home can "talk" to each other via the Internet or a home intranet. These linked systems can be controlled through various devices (see Bertolucci 2006).

In the United States, tens of thousands of homes are already equipped with home-automation devices, and there are signs that Europe is also warming to the idea. For instance, a 2001 study by the United Kingdom's Consumers' Association found that almost half those surveyed were interested in having the functions a "smart home" could offer if they were affordable (Edgington 2001).

Currently, home automation systems support a number of different tasks:

- **Lighting.** Users can program their lights to go on and off or dim them to match their moods and needs for comfort and security.
- **Energy management.** A home's HVAC (heat, ventilation, and air conditioning) system can be programmed for maximum energy efficiency and controlled with a touch panel or a telephone.
- **Water control.** Watercop (watercop.com) is a device that relies on a series of strategically placed moisture-detection sensors. When the moisture level rises in one of these sensors, it assumes a water leak has occurred and sends a wireless signal to the Watercop control unit, which turns off the main water supply.
- **Home security and communications.** The window blinds, garage doors, front door, smoke detectors, and home security system all can be automated from a network control panel. These can all be programmed to respond to scheduled events (e.g., when the home owner goes on vacation).
- **Home entertainment.** Users can create a multisource audio and video center around their house that can be controlled with a touch pad or remote. For example, if a person has a DVD player in the master bedroom but wants to see a movie in a child's room, with the click of a remote the signal can be directed to the child's room.

Analysts generally agree that the market opportunities for smart homes will take shape over the next 3 to 5 years. These opportunities are being driven by the increasing adoption of broadband (cable and DSL) services and the proliferation of LANs and WLANs within the home. Online File W9.22 at the book's Web site shows how pervasive computing can be used to manage the care of the elderly at an assisted-living facility. Related to smart homes are smart appliances and clothes (see Online File W9.23).

Smart Cars

The average automobile on the road today contains at least 20 microprocessors that are truly invisible. They are under the hood, behind the dash, in the door panels, and on the under-carriage. Microprocessors control the entertainment system, decide when the automatic transmission should shift gears, remember seat positions for different drivers, and control the inside temperature. Car computers often operate independently, but some swap data among themselves—a growing trend. They require little maintenance and operate under extreme temperature, vibration, and humidity. In the shop, the onboard microprocessors are used to diagnose problems.

Following U.S. Department of Transportation (USDOT) guidelines (U.S. Department of Transportation 2002), the automotive industry is in the process of testing a variety of experimental systems to improve auto safety in areas such as collision avoidance, computer vision for cars, vehicle stability, and driver monitoring. For example, General Motors (GM), in partnership with Delphi Automotive Systems, has developed an Automotive Collision Avoidance System that employs radar, video cameras, special sensors, and GPS to monitor traffic and driver actions in an effort to reduce collisions with other vehicles and pedestrians (Sharke 2003).

There also is a growing trend to connect car microprocessors to mobile networks and to the Internet to provide emergency assistance, driving directions, e-mail, and other services. GM's OnStar system (onstar.com) introduced in Section 9.8, for example, uses cellular telephone and satellite technology to connect a vehicle with a 24-hour service center. Some of the services provided by OnStar include automatic air-bag deployment notification, route support to guide drivers to their destinations, stolen vehicle tracking, and remote unlocking of doors.

OnStar is the forerunner of smart cars of the future. The next generation of smart cars is likely to provide even more automated services, especially in collision prevention and emergency situations. For instance, although OnStar automatically notifies the service center when a vehicle's air bags have been deployed and immediately contacts emergency services if the driver and passengers are incapacitated, OnStar cannot provide detailed information about a crash. Newer systems are under development that will automatically determine the impact speed, whether the car has rolled over, and whether the driver and passengers were wearing seat belts. Information of this sort might be used by emergency personnel to determine the severity of the accident and what types of services will be needed. For further details, see Online File W9.14.

Ideally, smart cars eventually will be able to drive themselves. Known as *autonomous land vehicles* (ALVs), these cars follow GIS maps and use sensors in a wireless environment to identify obstacles. These vehicles are being tested on experimental roads in California, Pennsylvania, and Germany.

Sensor Networks

Sensor networks are an area of pervasive computing with applications in homes, workplaces, and agricultural areas. A **sensor network** consists of a series of interconnected sensors that monitor the environment in which they are placed and report collected information to a network. Typically, each sensor has (1) a device to measure temperature, humidity, vibration, sound, motion, or whatever is being measured and (2) a weak radio transmitter capable of transmitting its data to the nearest sensor in a line or grid pattern. Each sensor passes its information, bucket-brigade style, along the network to a gateway node, which transmits the information to a computer for processing or storage. Companies such as Millennial Net, Crossbow Technology, and Ember are developing sensor nets that are capable of the following (Ricadela 2005; Feder 2004):

sensor network
A series of interconnected sensors that monitor the environment in which they are placed.

◗ **Protect the environment.** Sensor nets are being used to warn when oil tanker equipment is in danger of failing, when nitrates in wastewater being used for irrigation begin to exceed toxic levels, and when a forest fire has been detected. At Great Duck Island off the coast of Maine, 190 sensors form a sensor net that monitors the daily life of the Leach's storm petrel.

◗ **Enhance homeland security.** Science Applications International Corporation (saic.com) is using sensors from Dust Networks (dust-inc.com) to help secure border crossings and other sensitive areas. This application combines networked motes (sensors), which can detect people, vehicles, voices, and motion, with a tiny camera for capturing images. SAIC is also working on applications to use motes on ships or in shipping containers to detect radiation emitted from a nuclear weapon during transit. See Ricadela (2005) for additional homeland security applications.

▶ **Public safety.** Sensor nets assist in air traffic control, monitor stresses on aging bridges, and look for seismic activity along earthquake faults.

▶ **Monitor business and agricultural areas.** Company warehouses, open storage areas, and offices can be monitored inexpensively for detrimental environmental changes and security. In North Dakota, a sensor net in a sugar beet warehouse looks for pockets of heat buildup that can start to break down the sugar in the beets. In Western Australia, a variation of a sensor net puts up a "virtual fence" to detect livestock that have wandered out of a designated area. In California, a Wi-Fi–enabled sensor net is being used to improve grape production for premium wines (see Case 9.2). For more on agricultural applications, see Crossbow Technology (2005).

CASE 9.2
EC Application
WI-FI SENSOR NET AIDS WINE MAKERS

Pickberry, a California vineyard, is using a sensor network to answer an age-old question: how to grow better grapes. Grapes that produce good wine sell at a premium, so getting the right conditions for good growth can mean the difference between profit and loss for small vineyards.

One problem Pickberry faces is that the Sonoma County vineyard is spread over a hill, and growing conditions vary over the different parts of the slope. In order to monitor key growing conditions, such as temperature, humidity, and soil moisture, measurements need to be taken at various points throughout the vineyard. Field monitor sensors have been available for some time, but it has been prohibitively expensive and impractical to run data cables through the vineyard.

Pickberry's viticulturists also want information that can help them work out what grape-growing conditions produce good quality grapes. In the past, they have had to retrospectively speculate why vines growing in one part of the vineyard in one year produced better grapes than vines in another part of the vineyard in another year.

The solution is a sensor net that uses Wi-Fi for data connectivity. Sensors that monitor the conditions known to be key influences on grape quality have been placed throughout the vineyard. A sensor communicates its data to a central server by hopping from one Wi-Fi access point to another. The analysis engine on the server has a series of alerts built in that tells the growers when particular levels of indicators, such as soil moisture or temperature, are reached. Then corrective action can be taken.

Wireless was a natural choice for the grape growers, according to Bill Westerman, an associate partner at Accenture who worked on the project. "We are able to get data from 30 acres back to home base without having to run cables and without having to have radio transmitters that are powerful enough to make the leap from one end of the field to the other," said Westerman.

The Remote Sensor Network provides Pickberry with the ability to:

▶ Make calculated decisions—almost vine-by-vine—thanks to the granular level of the data obtained in near real time.

For example, Pickberry can use the data to adjust watering schedules for a specific area.

▶ Combine vineyard data with other data sources. This enables Pickberry to manage operations and resources, such as water usage, more scientifically. Live data on soil moisture and air humidity can be correlated with weather forecast data to match estimated water demand with well supply.

▶ Detect potentially devastating events such as frost, disease, and pests early on.

What are the results? Obviously the data are helping the Pickberry grape growers know much more about the health of their vines in different parts of the vineyard. They better understand how water is being retained and how much water needs to be applied, promoting both healthy vines and water conservation. The analysis also has been used to reduce the application of fungicides to control mildew. Now fungicides are applied only when and where they are needed rather than blanket coverage on a regular schedule, as was done before the sensor net.

The data also are helping the viticulturists work out the conditions that produce the best grapes. According to Westerman, "They are using this data in part to verify what they did before and to get details they never had before."

Armed with insight provided from sensor applications, Pickberry can take immediate action. These capabilities lead to more effective crop management, lowering costs while raising product quality.

Sources: Compiled from Ward (2004) and Accenture (2006).

Questions

1. How is the Wi-Fi sensor net contributing to Pickberry's core competency of grape production?

2. Why is Wi-Fi such an important part of this solution?

3. What are the benefits for Pickberry, the environment, and for the wine industry?

Other, far more advanced sensor networks are on the drawing boards or in the imaginations of technologists and scientists. *Smart dust* particles are sensor circuits so small and inexpensive that they can be scattered anywhere a sensor net is needed. Potential smart dust applications include fighting forest fires (to closely monitor the spread of the fire) and the tracking of enemy troop movements in military operations (Webb 2003). Advanced machine-to-machine (M2M) integration is possible with sensor networks. An embedded sensor net with actuators and activators and a hierarchy of controlling computers can control the environment of a building without human intervention.

BARRIERS TO PERVASIVE COMPUTING

Considering that pervasive computing is a technological area still under development, it is not surprising to find that a number of technological, legal, and ethical issues still need to be fully explored and resolved if the promises of pervasive computing are to be realized.

Invisible, everywhere computing offers an opportunity to deliver new products and services to customers, but privacy is in great danger in a world of embedded internetworked devices (Cas 2005). For example, fashion retailer Benetton Group SpA was considering attaching RFID tags to its Sisley line of clothing to help track shipping, inventory, shoplifting, and sales in the company's 5,000 stores. The idea was to integrate the RFID tag into the clothing labels. However, privacy groups expressed concern that the tags could also be used to track buyers, and some groups even urged that the company's clothing be boycotted. As a result, Benetton backed away from the plan, at least until an impact study is completed (Rosencrance 2003). The ethics of using RFID tags to track customers in a children's clothing store is explored in a *Harvard Business Review* business case study (Fusaro 2004). Privacy also is difficult to control in context-aware systems.

For pervasive systems to be widely deployed, it is necessary to overcome many of the technical, ethical, and legal barriers associated with mobile computing (see Section 9.9) as well as a few barriers unique to ubiquitous computing. Streitz and Nixon (2005) provide a comprehensive list of technical challenges, social and legal issues, and economic concerns (including finding appropriate business models) in deploying pervasive computing systems. They also cite research challenges, such as component interaction, adaptation and contextual sensitivity, user interface interaction, and appropriate management mechanisms.

Section 9.10 ▶ REVIEW QUESTIONS

1. Define *pervasive computing*.
2. List four principles of pervasive computing.
3. Define *contextual computing*.
4. Describe how RFID works.
5. Discuss some of the ways that pervasive computing can be used in the home.
6. Describe a sensor net.

MANAGERIAL ISSUES

Some managerial issues related to this chapter are as follows.

1. **What's our timetable?** Although there has been a great deal of hype about m-commerce in the last few years, only a small number of large-scale m-commerce applications have been deployed to date. This means that companies still have time to carefully craft an m-commerce strategy. This will reduce the number of failed initiatives and bankrupt companies.

2. **Which applications first?** Finding and prioritizing applications is part of an organization's e-strategy. Although location-based advertising is logically attrac-

tive, its effectiveness may not be known for several years. Therefore, companies should be very careful in committing resources to m-commerce. For the near term, applications that enhance the efficiency and effectiveness of mobile workers are likely to have the highest payoff as well as advertisement-related applications. For adoption issues, see Petrova (2006).

3. **Is it real or just a buzzword?** In the short run, m-commerce and location-based m-commerce may be just buzzwords due to the many limitations they now

face. However, in the long run, both concepts will fly. Management should monitor technological developments and make plans accordingly.

4. **Which system to use?** The multiplicity of standards, devices, and supporting hardware and software can confuse a company planning to implement m-commerce. An unbiased consultant can be of great help. Researching the vendors and products carefully is important. Making sure an m-commerce strategy fits into the organization's overall business strategy is most critical of all.

5. **Is an all-in-one device a winner?** It looks like it. Almost all vendors are moving in this direction. PDAs now include cell phones, Internet access, GPS, and more, and cell phones often have PDA and GPS capabilities.

6. **Which will win the wireless race: WiMax, Wi-Fi, or 3G?** It is difficult to say at this time. WiMax is cost effective, but some issues regarding its use have not been resolved. Each technology will probably prosper in certain areas and applications.

RESEARCH TOPICS

Here are some suggested topics related to this chapter. For details, references, and additional topics, refer to the Online Appendix A "Current EC Research."

1. **Value Chain and Business Models of M-Commerce**
   - Identification of value chain of m-commerce in various industries
   - Framework of business models in m-commerce
   - Comparison of the attributes and value of different m-commerce business models
   - Analysis of potential and existing inhibitors of m-commerce
   - The value of all-in-one devices versus separate devices

2. **Impact of M-Commerce Applications and Devices**
   - Comparison of m-commerce platforms, such as mobile phones, PDAs, and pocket PCs
   - Comparison of mobile platforms with the wired PC applications
   - Information quality of m-commerce applications and customers' relative preference
   - Synergistic design of wired and wireless applications to maximize customer satisfaction
   - Potential of portable Internet using the notebook PC as a terminal
   - Pricing of portable Internet services
   - Security issues and protection schemes of m-commerce

3. **M-Payments and Mobile Banking**
   - Business models and protocols of mobile payment gateways
   - Effectiveness of mobile payment methods in comparison with other micropayment methods, such as e-cash and e-mail payment

   - Alliance and competition of mobile service providers with banks

4. **Development of Context-Aware Computing and Its Applications in M-Commerce**
   - Factors that dynamically determine mobile contexts (e.g., location and user information)
   - Applications and potentials of context-aware computing
   - Intelligence- and CRM-backed models for context-aware computing

5. **Intelligent M-Commerce Search Aids**
   - Search algorithms using collaborative filtering and contents-based search
   - Personalized search aids backed by CRM systems

6. **Applications of RFID for Pervasive Computing**
   - Design of RFID applications for supply chain management and logistics
   - Pilot and case studies of RFID applications
   - Determining the costs and benefits of RFID applications
   - Privacy and ethical issues of RFID

7. **Implementing M-Commerce**
   - Social issues and cross-cultural differences in mobile Internet usage
   - Mobility modeling
   - Application adoption

SUMMARY

In this chapter, you learned about the following EC issues as they relate to the learning objectives.

1. **What is mobile computing?** Mobile computing refers to computing done with mobile devices, usually in a wireless environment.

2. **Characteristics of mobile devices.** Mobile computing devices vary in size and functionality. One limitation of m-commerce is the poor usability of mobile devices with small screens, reduced memory, limited bandwidth, and restricted input capabilities.

3. **Mobile computing support services.** A range of support services, principally SMS, micropayments, voice, and location-based services, at present, support mobile computing and the implementation of m-commerce applications.

4. **Wireless telecommunications networks.** Mobile computing devices connect to networks or other devices at a personal, local, metropolitan, or wide-area level. Bluetooth (personal) and especially cellular phone networks (wide area) are known technologies and are well established in the marketplace. Wi-Fi (local) is new but increasingly popular. WiMax (metropolitan) is emerging as an important technology.

5. **What is m-commerce?** M-commerce is any business activity conducted over a wireless telecommunications network. M-commerce is a natural extension of e-commerce.

6. **Value-added attributes of m-commerce.** M-commerce can help a business improve its value proposition to customers by utilizing its unique attributes: ubiquity, convenience, interactivity, personalization, and localization.

7. **Drivers of m-commerce.** The following are the major drivers of m-commerce: large numbers of users of mobile devices; a developing "cell phone culture" among youth; demands from service-oriented customers; vendor marketing; declining prices; a mobile workforce; improved performance for the price; and increasing bandwidth.

8. **Finance, shopping, advertising, and content-providing applications.** Many EC applications in the service industries (e.g., banking, travel, and stocks) can be conducted with wireless devices. Also, shopping can be done from mobile devices. Location-based advertising and advertising via SMSs is expected to increase. Mobile portals aggregate and provide content and services for mobile users.

9. **Intrabusiness applications.** Intrabusiness applications such as sales force mobilization, inventory management, and wireless job dispatch offer the best opportunities for high return on investment for most organizations, at least in the short term.

10. **B2B and SCM applications.** Emerging B2B applications are being integrated with the supply chain and are facilitating cooperation between business partners.

11. **Consumer applications.** M-commerce is being used to provide applications in travel, gaming, information services, and health care.

12. **Location-based commerce.** The delivery of services based on the location of a device, as determined by GPS, is emerging in the advertising, emergency response, and transport industries. These applications utilize the localization attribute of m-commerce.

13. **Limitations of m-commerce.** The mobile computing environment offers special challenges for security, including the need to secure transmission over open air and through multiple connecting networks. The biggest technological changes relate to the usability of devices. Finally, ethical, legal, and health issues can arise from the use of m-commerce, especially in the workplace.

14. **Pervasive computing.** This is the world of invisible computing in which virtually every object has an embedded microprocessor that is connected in a wired or wireless fashion to the Internet. Smart homes, smart appliances, smart cars, and other applications of pervasive computing will provide a number of life-enhancing, consumer-centric, and B2B applications.

KEY TERMS

QUESTIONS FOR DISCUSSION

1. Discuss how m-commerce can solve some of the problems of the *digital divide* (the gap within a country or between countries with respect to people's ability to access the Internet).
2. Discuss how m-commerce can expand the reach of EC.
3. Explain the role of wireless telecommunications networks in m-commerce.
4. Discuss the impact of m-commerce on emergency medical services.
5. How are GIS and GPS related?
6. What sells best in m-commerce? Make a list of products and services that offer the best opportunity for the development of m-commerce.
7. List three to four major advantages of wireless commerce to consumers presented in this chapter and explain what benefits they provide to consumers.
8. Location-based services can help a driver find his or her car or the closest gas station. However, some people view location-based services as an invasion of privacy. Discuss the pros and cons of location-based services.
9. Discuss how wireless devices can help people with disabilities.
10. Discuss the benefits of IVR.
11. Based on what you know about Internet services and wireless technology in your own country, what success and risk factors should DoCoMo consider if it wanted to offer i-mode services in your country?
12. What is the relationship between sales force mobilization and mobile supply chain management?
13. Discuss the benefits of telemetry-based systems.
14. Discuss the ways in which Wi-Fi is being used to support m-commerce. Describe the ways in which Wi-Fi is affecting the use of cell phones for m-commerce.
15. Which of the m-commerce limitations listed in this chapter do you think will have the biggest negative impact on m-commerce? Which ones will be minimized within 5 years? Which ones will not?
16. Describe two scenarios, one personal and one professional, in which contextual computing could apply.
17. Which of the following applications of pervasive computing—smart homes, smart appliances, and smart cars—are likely to gain the greatest market acceptance over the next few years? Why?
18. If a company monitors desktop e-mails, should it monitor company owned cell phones? Debate this issue.

INTERNET EXERCISES

1. Learn about PDAs by visiting vendors' sites such as Palm, HP, Phillips, NEC, Hitachi, Compaq, Casio, Brother, Texas Instruments, and others. List the m-commerce devices manufactured by these companies.

2. Access **progressive.com**, an insurance company, from your cell phone (use the "Go to . . ." feature). If you have a Sprint PCS wireless phone, do it via the Finance menu. If you have a Palm i705, you can download the Web-clipping application from Progressive. Report on these capabilities.

3. Research the status of 3G and the future of 4G by visiting **3gnewsroom.com**. Prepare a report on the status of 3G and 4G based on your findings.

4. Explore **nokia.com**. Prepare a summary of the types of mobile services and applications Nokia currently supports and plans to support in the future.

5. Enter **kyocera-wireless.com** and view the demos. What is a smartphone? What are its capabilities? How does it differ from a regular cell phone?

6. Enter **ibm.com**. Search for *wireless e-business*. Research the resulting stories to determine the types of wireless capabilities and applications supported by IBM software and hardware. Describe some of the ways these applications have helped specific businesses and industries.

7. Go to **wi-fihotspotlist.com** and **hotspot-locations.com** to determine whether there are any Wi-Fi hotspots in your area. Enter **wardriving.com**. Based on information provided at this site, what sorts of equipment and procedures could you use to locate hotspots in your area?

8. Enter **mapinfo.com** and look for the location-based services demos. Try all the demos. Find all of the wireless services. Summarize your findings.

9. Enter **smarthome.com** and **homeauto.com**. Identify intelligent (smart) home appliances. Also visit **ieee.org**, **ieeecomputersociety.org**, and **resources.ecommercetimes.com** to find information on smart home appliances. Prepare a report.

10. Enter **packetvideo.com** and **microsoft.com/mobile/pocketpc**. Examine their demos and products and list their capabilities.

11. Enter **callmania.com** and **ranosofttechnologies.com** and similar sources and identify location-based m-commerce applications including personalization. Write a report.

12. Enter **onstar.com**. What *fleet* services does OnStar provide? Do they differ from the services OnStar provides to individual car owners?

13. Enter **hp.com** and find information about iPaq rx5–900. Why is it called the travel companion? Find a competing device and compare the two.

14. Find information about Google Maps for mobile devices. Also review the capabilities of Google SMS and other Google applications. Write a report on your findings.

TEAM ASSIGNMENTS AND ROLE PLAYING

1. Each team should examine a major vendor of mobile devices (Nokia, Kyocera, Motorola, Palm, Blackberry, etc.). Each team will research the capabilities and prices of the devices offered by each company and then make a class presentation, the objective of which is to convince the rest of the class why they should buy that company's products.

2. Each team should explore the commercial applications of m-commerce in one of the following areas: financial services, including banking, stocks, and insurance; marketing and advertising; manufacturing; travel and transportation; human resources management; public services; and health care. Each team will present a report to the class based on their findings. (Start at **mobiforum.org**.)

3. Each team will investigate a global organization involved in m-commerce, such as **gsmworld.com**, **wimaxforum.com**, and **openmobilealliance.com**. The teams will investigate the membership and the current projects each organization is working on and then present a report to the class based on their findings.

4. Each team will investigate a standards-setting organization and report on its procedures and progress in developing wireless standards. Start with the following: **atis.org**, **etsi.org**, and **tiaonline.org**.

5. Each team should take one of the following areas—homes, cars, appliances, or other consumer goods, such as clothing—and investigate how embedded microprocessors are currently being used and will be used in the future to support consumer-centric services. Each team will present a report to the class based on its findings.

Real-World Case

7-ELEVEN TRACKS INVENTORY WIRELESSLY

The Problem

Despite the origins of its name—"open from 7 a.m. until 11 p.m."—most of the 27,000 stores in the worldwide chain of 7-Eleven stores operate 24 hours per day in a unique market, one quite different from many other retailers.

One unique feature of this $36-billion retail convenience store giant is its large and varied product mix. A typical 7-Eleven carries about 2,500 different products, from gasoline and sandwiches to prepaid phone cards and money orders. A large portion of that inventory—sandwiches, fresh food, and dairy products—is perishable, requiring constant monitoring for freshness and strategies to reduce the amount of spoilage, or goods that have to be thrown away. The amount of inventory that goes out the back door, not the front door, can have an immediate and dramatic impact on profits.

Also consider the broad demographic mix of 7-Eleven's 6 million daily customers. The 7-Eleven customer base is one of the most diversified in the retail market, cutting across all ages and income categories. Because of its diverse customer base and neighborhood locations, 7-Eleven delegates an unusually high proportion of its purchasing decisions to the store-manager level. In some areas, customer demands vary from street to street, and management has to be responsive to this diversity.

Finally, consider the small size of each store. Despite a large and varied product mix, on-site inventory is minimal. At any point, a large proportion of 7-Eleven's inventory is on a truck somewhere on its way to a store.

The small store size also means that often there are only two or three checkout, or point-of-sale (POS), stations. Because the customer expects a quick trip in and out of the store, the POS hardware and software must be fast and responsive. An inconvenient convenience store is not long for this world.

The Solution

Sherry Neal is checking the refrigerated shelves of her 7-Eleven store in Rockwall, Texas. She touches the screen of a small handheld computer and gets an instant 4-week sales history on turkey sandwiches. With a couple of keystrokes on the wireless computer, this 7-Eleven store manager places an order for the next day's supply without ever leaving the aisle.

At the same time, a dairy truck driver pulls up to another 7-Eleven store and prepares to deliver crates of milk when the store manager stops him. "Hold on a moment," the manager says, as he looks at his RFID reader. "These crates over here are bad. Sure, they're registering a good temperature now, but it looks like they were warm for 9 hours yesterday. Sorry, I won't take these three, but the others are fine. Bring them in."

The milk-delivery scenario is hypothetical, but Sherry Neal's small handheld computer is real. The technology is not yet commonplace at 7-Eleven stores, but it is used in many stores where it is being tested for widespread roll out.

Both scenarios depend on RFID technology. A "passive" RFID tag on each sandwich contains information, such as the manufacture date, sell-by date, origin, and lot number, that was loaded onto a computer chip when the sandwich was packaged for sale. When activated by a radio wave from an RFID reader, the chip sends its information to the reader. The manager can then compare current inventory, and its freshness, with recent sales and place a new order with increased confidence. The milk-delivery scenario depends on a "smart" RFID tag that can record changing environmental conditions; however, this technology is still too expensive for widespread use.

Keith Morrow, 7-Eleven's CIO, says that his chain is very interested in RFID and that it is item-level tracking that interests him most. He says, "We want that information at a more granular level about products, especially at the food and drink level. In a perfect world, we'd be able to monitor [everything] through the life of fresh products."

But at what cost? Morrow adds that his chief worry is the pricing impact: "What would it do to the cost of a sandwich?" At today's cost per tag and reader, widespread use of RFID technology is not realistic. However, RFID costs are expected to decrease sharply between now and when per-item tracking is ready for wide-scale deployment, around 2010.

In the meantime, 7-Eleven recently signed a deal to combine its own proprietary POS software with hardware from HP, NCR, and NEC. This technology, in the process of being rolled out to its 5,300 U.S. locations, is the kind of technology that promises to change the way that convenience stores are run. It offers some of the fastest checkout speeds in the business, but it is just the beginning. The company is testing prepaid payment cards at stores in Texas and Florida. These cards—similar to Exxon Mobil Corp.'s Speedpass—mean even faster checkout for 7-Eleven customers.

The most visible part of 7-Eleven's *mobile commerce* future is the NEC handheld ordering device. 7-Eleven stores in Japan, licensed by 7-Eleven's parent company Ito-Yokado Co., have had a basic version of the small handheld computers for several years. However, the tool is not totally wireless—store employees still must transfer data into a networked computer in the back office before placing an order. For inventory and asset surveys, employees use Tablet PC.

The Results

7-Eleven officials say that the wireless version of the handheld computer being tested by Sherry Neal will help managers do a better job of balancing inventory with demand. The device is designed to help store managers handle one of their most challenging tasks: ordering just the right amount of each item. Empty shelves mean lost sales, and getting stuck with leftovers means costly

write-offs due to spoilage, as well as high inventory keeping costs.

The device also must meet the special needs of retailers, who often have high employee turnover. The device has a touch screen and pictures of items, not just bar code numbers. According to Morrow, "It's got to be simple to use, reliable and rugged or it won't work in a convenience store."

The NEC handheld was tested in 10 Dallas-area stores beginning in March 2004 and is now in use at the Rockwall and several other stores.

Sherry Neal gives the mobile technology the big tick. "It brings the computer out here on the floor, and it saves time," Neal said. "I'm not a backroom manager. I'd rather be out front helping the customers." A savings of $3 million to $5 million per year is estimated from using Tablet PCs for inventory counts.

Sources: Compiled from Koenig (2004), Schuman (2004), and Infologic (2006).

Questions

1. Relate this case to pervasive computing.
2. What m-commerce applications are evidenced in this case?
3. Describe the use of RFID. What could be the benefits of attaching a tag to each item in the store?
4. What is the handheld device? Is it a PDA? A Tablet PC? Or some other type of device?

REFERENCES

3GNewsroom.com. "2006 Will Be Year of Mobile Advertising Experimentation." March 19, 2006. 3gnewsroom.com/3g_news/mar_06/news_6820.shtml (accessed December 2006).

Accenture. "Pickberry Vineyard: Accenture Prototype Helps Improve Crop Management." 2006. accenture.com/xd/xd.asp?it=enweb&xd=services%5Ctechnology%5Ccase%5Cpickberry.xml (accessed October 2006).

The Age. "Singapore Airlines Introduces SMS Check-In." *The Age*, August 3, 2004a. theage.com.au/articles/2004/08/03/1091476476848.html (accessed April 2007).

The Age. "Landlines Yield to Mobiles in India." *The Age*, October 25, 2004b. theage.com.au/articles/2004/10/25/1098667675148.html (accessed April 2007).

Asaravala, A. "Four Wireless Technologies Move Toward Starting Gate." *USA Today*, March 28, 2004. usatoday.com/tech/wireless/data/2004-03-28-coming-tech_x.htm (accessed April 2007).

Baard, M. "After the Fall: Help for Climbers." *Wired*, December 24, 2002. wired.com/news/technology/0,1282,56146,00.html (accessed April 2007).

Becker, D. "Sega Forms Mobile Games Division." *CNET News*, April 2002. news.zdnet.co.uk/story/0,,t269-s2108679,00.html (accessed April 2007).

Belew, B. "M-Commerce is Future of Japan Retail." *Rising Sun of Nihon*, September 15, 2006.

Bertolucci, J. "Make Your Home a Smart Home." *Kiplinger's*, May 2006.

Bial, R. G., and D. J. Mayhew. *Cost-Justifying Usability: An Update for the Internet Age*, 2nd ed. San Francisco: Elsevier, 2005.

Cas, J. "Privacy in Pervasive Computing Environments. A Contradiction in Terms." *IEEE Technology and Society Magazine*, Spring 2005.

CellularOnline. "Latest Global, Handset, Base Station, & Regional Cellular Statistics." cellular.co.za/stats/stats-main.htm (accessed April 2007).

Chatterjee, A., H.-W. Kaas, T. V. Kumaresh, and P. J. Wojcik. "A Road Map for Telematics." *McKinsey Quarterly*, April–June 2002.

Chen, A. "Dot Net and J2EE for Web Services," in Khosrow-Pour (2006).

Clark, K. "Food Lion's High Wireless Act." *Retail Technology Quarterly*, July 2005.

ClickZ Stats. "Mobile Users Yearning for Micro-payments." *Clickz.com*, March 21, 2002. **clickz.com/stats/sectors/wireless/article.php/995801** (accessed April 2007).

Cohen, A. "Millstone Mobilizes to Deliver Coffee." *PC Magazine*, September 17, 2002. **pcmag.com/article2/0,1895,1160212,00.asp** (accessed April 2007).

Commonwealth Telecommunications Organization. "Barriers and Enablers to Sustainable Growth in Emerging Markets." CTO Forum 2006, London, England, September 4–6, 2006.

Conrad, D. "Medlink to the Rescue." *Alaskas World*, March 11, 2002. **alaskasworld.com/news/2002/03/11_MedLink.asp** (no longer available online).

Crossbow Technology. "Motes in 'Controlled Environment Agriculture.'" *Crossbow Solutions Newsletter* 8, Fourth Quarter (2005).

Cybit. "Cybit Announces Total Mobile Resource Management (MRM) Solution for Managing Mobile Workforce." August 30, 2006. **cybit.co.uk/RecentNews.aspx** (accessed October 2006).

Davidson, P. "Inventive Wireless Providers Go Rural." *USA Today*, July 14, 2004. **usatoday.com/tech/news/2004-07-14-wireless_x.htm** (accessed April 2007).

Deans, C. (ed.). *E-Commerce and M-Commerce Technologies.* Hershey, PA: The Idea Group, IRM Press, 2005.

Designerz.com. "Chinese People to Send 550 Billion Text Messages This Year." *Designerz.com News*, August 10, 2004. **3d2f.com/news/18-257-chinese-people-to-send-billion-text-messages-this-year-read.shtml** (accessed April 2007).

Diaz, S. "Sony Retreat on Handhelds Is a Blow to Palm OS." *SiliconValley.com.* **siliconvalley.com/mld/siliconvalley/8818846.htm** (no longer available online).

Edgington, C. "How Internet Gateways and Smart Appliances Will Transform Our Homes." *TNTY Futures*, 2001. **tnty.com/newsletter/futures/technology.html** (accessed November 2006).

Elliot, C., "Start-Up Expected to Announce Deal for Wi-Fi in Avis Cars." *International Herald Tribune*, January 2, 2007. **iht.com/bin/print/php?id=4073518** (accessed January 2007).

Elliott, G., and N. Phillips. *Mobile Commerce and Wireless Computing Systems.* Harlow, England: Pearson Education, 2004.

Ellison, C. "Palm Sees Uptick in Development of Mobile Enterprise Applications." *e-Week*, May 18, 2004. **eweek.com/article2/0,1759,1594712,00.asp** (accessed April 2007).

Feder, B. J. "Wireless Sensor Networks Spread to New Territory." *New York Times*, July 26, 2004. **onworld.com/html/newswsnnytimes7-04.htm** (accessed April 2007).

Ferguson, S. "HP Announces RFID Technology." *eWeek*, October 23, 2006.

Fleishman, G. "Lufthansa Says Achtzig, Bitte!" *Wi-Fi Net News*, May 28, 2003. **wifinetnews.com/archives/001686.html** (accessed April 2007).

Forbes. "Software Experts Find 'First' Mobile Virus: No Harmful Effects Yet." *Forbes.com*, June 15, 2004. **forbes.com/technology/feeds/wireless/2004/06/16/wireless01087398037128-20040615-152500.html** (accessed April 2007).

Fusaro, R. A. "None of Our Business?" *Harvard Business Review* (December 2004): 33–46.

Gleishman, G. "Comprehensive U.S. Airport Wi-Fi Guide." *Wifinetnews.com*, September 12, 2006. **wifinetnews.com/archives/cat_air_travel.html** (accessed October 2006).

Goodman, D. N. "Recycled Cell Phones Help Drive Third World Wireless Boom." *SanLuisObispo.com*, August 19, 2006. **sanluisobispo.com/mld/sanluisobispo/business/15313959.htm** (accessed October 2006).

Gressgård, L. J., and I. Stensaker. "Future Mobile Internet Services: Business Model Scenarios." *SNF Report*, June 2004.

GSM World. "Setting the Record Straight." 2004. **gsmworld.com/technology/3g/intro.shtml** (accessed April 2007).

Hamblen, M. "Get Payback on Wireless." *Computerworld*, January 1, 2001. **computerworld.com/mobiletopics/mobile/story/0,10801,54798,00.html** (accessed April 2007).

Hansmann, U., et al. *Pervasive Computing: The Mobile World,* 2nd ed. Berlin: Springer, 2003.

Heinrich, C. *RFID and Beyond.* Indianapolis, IN: Wiley, 2005.

Hoffman, B. G. "Ford, Microsoft Team Up on Tech Collaboration to Foster Wireless Links Between Autos and Devices Such as Cell Phones and iPods." *Detroit News*, December 30, 2006. **detnews.com/apps/pbcs.dll/article?AID=/20061230/AUTO01/612300351/1148** (accessed January 2007).

Hu, W.-C., J.-H. Yeh, H.-J. Yang, and C.-W. Lee. "Mobile Handheld Devices for Mobile Commerce," in Khosrow-Pour (2006).

Intel. "Building the Foundation for Anytime Anywhere Computing." White Paper 25 1290-002 Intel Corporation, June 13, 2002, **intel.com/pressroom/kits/events/idffall_2002/wireless_mobility_whitepaper.pdf** (accessed April 2007).

Islam, N., and M. Fayad. "Toward Ubiquitous Acceptance of Ubiquitous Computing." *Communications of the ACM* 46, no. 2 (2003).

Jiwire.com. **jiwire.com** (accessed May 2006).

Kakihara, M., and C. Sorensen. "Mobile Urban Professionals in Tokyo: Tales of Locational, Operational, and Interactional Mobility." Paper presented at the Stockholm Mobility Roundtable, Stockholm, Sweden, May 22–23, 2003.

Karnouskos, S., and A. Vilmos. "Universal Approach to Mobile Payments," in Khosrow-Pour (2006).

Kharif, O. "Like It or Not, RFID Is Coming." *Business Week Online*, March 18, 2004.

Khosrow-Pour, M. (ed.). *Encyclopedia of E-Commerce, E-Government, and Mobile Commerce.* Hershey, PA: Idea Group Reference, 2006.

Koenig, D. "7-Eleven Adopting Wireless Technology." *eWeek*, October 11, 2004.

Kolesnikov-Jessop, S. "Wireless: Bets Are Down on Mobile Gambling." *International Herald Tribune*, November 13, 2005. **iht.com/articles/2005/11/13/business/wireless14.php** (accessed October 2006).

Kontzer, T. "Top Ten Uses for SMS." *Information Week*, June 11, 2003. **informationweek.com/techcenters/networking/wireless** (no longer availabel online).

Kou, W., and Y. Yesha (eds.) *Enabling Technologies for Wireless E-Business*. Heidelberg, Germany: Springer, 2006.

Levere, J. "Wi-Fi Service Expands Its Reach." *New York Times*, July 27, 2004. **nytimes.com/2004/07/27/business/27wifi.html** (accessed April 2007).

Lindstrom, A. "Dianah Neff, CIO for the City of Philadelphia, Discusses Municipal Broadband in Urban Areas." Motorola Connections, February 3, 2006. **connectwithcanopy.com/index.cfm?canopy=stop.story&aid=367** (accessed April 2007).

Longino, C. "Your Wireless Future." *Business 2.0*, May 2006.

Lyytinen, K., and Y. Yoo. "Issues and Challenges in Ubiquitous Computing." *Communications of the ACM* 45, no. 12 (2002): 63–65.

Malykhina, E. "Get Smart." *InformationWeek*, October 30, 2006a.

Malykhina, E. "Leave the Laptop Home." *InformationWeek*, October 30, 2006b.

McGuire, C. "Food Lion Checking Out with Wi-Fi." *Wi-Fi Plant News*, May 27, 2004. **internetnews.com/wireless/article.php/3360601** (accessed April 2007).

McKay, J., and P. Marshall. *Strategic Management of eBusiness.* Milton, Australia: John Wiley and Sons, 2004.

Microsoft. "Taco Bell Builds a Microsoft Windows CE-Based Solution in Support of Their Mystery Shopper Program." Microsoft.com, August 27, 2002. **microsoft.com/casestudies/casestudy.aspx?casestudyid=51345** (accessed April 2007).

Microsoft. "Your Mobile Work Force Needs Mobile Solutions" *MSN Tech and Gadgets*, 2003. **tech.msn.com/guides/670780.armx** (accessed October 2006).

Mobile Marketing Magazine. "Is It a Phone? No It's a Wallet!" April 21, 2006. **mobilemarketingmagazine.co.uk/stats/index.html** (accessed October 2006).

Mullen, J. "For Those in Paris about to Park, a Service That Tells Them Where." *The New York Times*, November 21, 2006. **nytimes.com/2006/11/20/business/worldbusiness/20garage.html?ex=1321678800&en=9e1908a053b88365&ei=5088&partner=rssnyt&emc=rss** (accessed December 2006).

Nelson, M. "Kemper Insurance Uses Wireless Digital Imaging to Lower Costs, Streamline Process." *InformationWeek*, September 25, 2000. **informationweek.com/805/photo.htm** (no longer available online).

Network for Online Commerce. "2006 New Year SMS Records Rocket Around the World." January 27, 2006. **newsweaver.co.uk/noc/e_article000520133.cfm?x=b11,0,w** (accessed October 2006).

Nobel, C. "Home Depot Tackles Network Challenge." *eWeek*, November 21, 2005.

Ojeda-Zapata, J. "Chaska Goes Wi-Fi." *Twin Cities Pioneer Press*, May 26, 2004. **twincities.com/mld/twincities/business/technology/personal_technology/8759053.htm?1c** (no longer available online).

Open Mobile Alliance. "Mobile Games Interoperability Forum." 2006. **openmobilealliance.org/tech/affiliates/mgif/mgifindex.html** (accessed October 2006).

Paavilainen, J. *Mobile Business Strategies: Understanding the Technologies and Opportunities.* London: Pearson Education, 2002.

Payment News. "Mobile Banking Stages a Remarkable Comeback." *Paymentnews.com*, February 6, 2006. **paymentsnews.com/2006/02/mobile_banking_.html** (accessed April 2007).

Petrova, K. "Mobile Commerce Applications and Adoption," in Khosrow-Pour (2006).

Pierre, S., "Mobile Electronic Commerce," in Khosrow-Pour (2006).

Pitkow, J., H. Schutze, T. Cass, R. Cooley, D. Turnbull, A. Edmonds, et al. "Personalized Search: A Contextual Computing Approach May Prove a Breakthrough in Personalized Search Efficiency." *Communications of the ACM* 45, no. 9 (2002): 50–55.

Pmai.org. "'Sony Electronics' ImageStation.com Joins with CVS/Pharmacy on In-Store Photo Pick-up Service." *Pmai.org*, February 19, 2005. **news.sel.sony.com/en/press_room/consumer/digital_imaging/image_station/archive/8941.html?archive=1** (accessed April 2007).

Poropudas, T. "ATM Connection to Boost Mobile Payments." *Mobile CommerceNet*, February 15, 2003.

Raskin, A. "Your Ad Could Be Here! (And Now We Can Tell You Who Will See It)." *Business 2.0*, May 2003.

Republica.IT. "Busta Paga in Pensione Lo Stipendio Arriva via SMS." March 20, 2001. **repubblica.it/online/tecnologie_internet/tim/tim/tim.html** (no longer available online).

RFID Journal. "Gillette to Buy 500 Million EPC Tags." *RFID Journal*, November 15, 2002. **rfidjournal.com/article/articleview/115/1/1** (accessed April 2007).

Ricadela, A. "Sensors Everywhere." *Information Week*. January 24, 2005.

Rosen, C. "Our Cell Phones, Ourselves." *The New Atlantis*, Summer 2004. **thenewatlantis.com/archive/6/rosen.htm** (accessed April 2007).

Rosencrance, L. "Update: Benetton Backs Away from 'Smart Tags' in Clothing Line." *ComputerWorld*, April 4, 2003. **computerworld.com/industrytopics/retail/story/0,10801,80061,00.html** (accessed April 2007).

Ryan, T. "RFID in the Consumer Industries." Research Report, Aberdeen Group, March 2004.

Sadeh, N. *M-Commerce*. New York: Wiley, 2002.

Salo, J., and J. Tähtinen. "Special Features of Mobile Advertising and Their Utilization," in Khosrow-Pour (2006).

Scanlon, J. "The Way We Work." *Wired*, May 2003. **wired.com/wired/archive/11.05/unwired/work.html** (accessed April 2007).

Schuman, E. "RFID to Be Served 7-Eleven Style." *eWeek*, September 11, 2004. **eweek.com/article2/0%2C1895%2C1644885%2C00.asp** (accessed April 2007).

Schwartz, E. "FBI Phone Tapping And Locating Cell Phones Making 911 Calls: Is It Privacy or Paranoia?" *InfoWorld*, 2006. **infoworld.com/articles/op/xml/01/01/15/010115opwireless.html** (accessed October 2006).

Sharke, P. "Smart Cars." *Mechanical Engineering*, 2003. **memagazine.org/contents/current/features/smartcar/smartcar.html** (accessed April 2007).

Sharma, D. "Cell Phone Shipments on the Rise." *CNET News*, May 6, 2004. **news.zdnet.com/2100–9584_22–5207340.html** (accessed April 2007).

SiliconValley.com. "Philadelphia Joins List of Cities Mulling Wireless Internet for All." September 1, 2004. **siliconvalley.com/mid/siliconvalley/9553298.html** (no longer available online).

Smailagic, A., et al. "CMU Wearable Computers for Real-Time Speech Translation." *IEEE Personal Communications* 8, no. 2 (April 2001).

Smith, B. "Goodbye Wallet, Hello Phone." *Wireless Week*, April 1, 2006. **wirelessweek.com/article/CA6321122.html?spacedesc=Features** (accessed June 2006).

Spivey-Overby, C. "RFID at What Cost? What Wal-Mart Compliance Really Means." ForrTel (Webcast plus telephone), *Forrester Research*, May 25, 2004.

Streitz, N., and P. Nixon (eds.). "The Disappearing Computer," *Communications of the ACM*, March 2005.

Synergy. "TXT-a-Park." *Synergy.com*, March 2004. **synergy.co.nz/case-studies/archive/txt-a-park-case-study.htm** (no longer available online).

Taipei Times. "New GPS Parking Hits the Spot for Paris." November 21, 2006. **taipeitimes.com/News/world/archives/2006/11/21/2003337287** (accessed December 2006).

Telphia Research. "Telephia Research Shows Nearly 13.5 Million Wireless Subscribers Downloaded a Mobile Game, with Average Monthly Revenues Reaching $46.9 Million in Q2 2006." August 24, 2006, **telephia.com/html/insights_082406.html** (accessed October 2006).

Teradata. "Technology Investments Pushed by Business Users, Retail Survey Finds." *Tearadata.com*, January 31, 2006. **teradata.com/t/page/145593/index.html** (accessed April 2007).

U.S. Department of Transportation. "Intelligent Vehicle Initiative." May 13, 2002. **its.dot.gov/ivi/ivi.htm** (accessed April 2007).

Walsh, B., and W. K. Yamarick. "Beam Me Up, Scotty." *Health Management Technology*, July 2005.

Wang, F. Y., S. Tang, Y. Sui, X. Wang. "Toward Intelligent Transportation System for the 2008 Olympics." *IEEE Intelligent Systems*, November–December 2003.

Ward, M. "Wi-Fi Sensor Net Aids Wine Makers." BBC News, July 6, 2004. **news.bbc.co.uk/1/hi/technology/3860863.stm** (accessed July 2007).

Webb, W. "Smart-Dust Designers Deliver Dirt-Cheap Chips." *EDN Magazine*, November 27, 2003. **edn.com/article/CA336870.html** (accessed April 2007).

Weiser, M. "The Computer for the Twenty-First Century." *Scientific American* 265 (1991): 94–104.

White, D. "Ogo Handhelds Coming to U.S." Mobile Magazine, March 29, 2007. **mobilemag.com/content/100/333/C12202** (accessed April 2007).

Wikipedia. "IEEE 802.11," 2006. **en.wikipedia.org/wiki/IEEE_802.11** (accessed October 2006).

Wired. "American Passports to Get Chipped." *Wired*, October 21, 2004. **wired.com/politics/security/news/2004/10/65412** (accessed April 2007).

WirelessPhiladelphia.org. "Network Testing Has Begun." February 2007. **wirelessphiladelphia.org/newsletter_feb_07.htm** (accessed April 2007).

Yapp, E. "Connecting the Unconnected." *The Star Online*, October 21, 2004. **gsmworld.com/news/media_2004/asia04_connecting.shtml** (accessed April 2007).

CHAPTER 10

DYNAMIC TRADING: E-AUCTIONS, BARTERING, AND NEGOTIATIONS

Content

Learning Objectives

Upon completion of this chapter, you will be able to:

1. Define the various types of e-auctions and list their characteristics.

2. Describe forward and reverse auctions.

3. Describe the benefits and limitations of e-auctions.

4. Describe some unique e-auction models.

5. Describe the various services that support e-auctions.

6. Describe bartering and negotiating.

7. Describe the hazards of e-auction fraud and discuss possible countermeasures.

8. Describe e-auction deployment and implementation issues.

9. Analyze mobile and future directions of e-auctions.

EBAY—THE WORLD'S LARGEST AUCTION SITE

The Opportunity

eBay is one of the most profitable e-businesses. The successful online auction house has its roots in a 50-year-old novelty item—Pez candy dispensers. Pam Omidyar, an avid collector of Pez dispensers, came up with the idea of trading them over the Internet. When she expressed this idea to her boyfriend (now her husband), Pierre Omidyar, he was instantly struck with the soon-to-be-famous e-business auction concept.

The Solution

In 1995, the Omidyars created a company called AuctionWeb. The company was renamed eBay and has since become the premier online auction house in many countries, with millions of unique auctions in progress and over 500,000 new items added each day. Almost 194 million registered buyers and sellers use eBay. Today, eBay is much more than an auction house, but its initial success was in electronic auctions.

eBay's initial business model was to provide an electronic infrastructure for conducting mostly C2C auctions. eBay auctions do not require an auctioneer; technology manages the auction process.

On eBay, people can buy and sell just about anything. The company collects a submission fee upfront, plus a commission that is a percentage of the final sale amount. The submission fee is based on the amount of exposure the seller wants the item to receive, with a higher fee if the seller would like the item to be among the featured auctions in a specific product category, and an even higher fee if the seller wants the item to be listed on the eBay homepage under *Featured Items*. Another attention-grabbing option is to publish the product listing in a boldface font (for an additional charge).

The auction process begins when the seller fills in the appropriate registration information and posts a description of the item for sale. The seller must specify a minimum opening bid. If potential buyers feel this price is too high, the item may not receive any bids. Sellers may set the opening bid lower than the *reserve price,* a minimum acceptable bid price, to generate bidding activity.

If a successful bid is made, the seller and the buyer negotiate the payment method, shipping details, warranty, and other particulars. eBay serves as a liaison between the parties; it is the interface through which sellers and buyers can conduct business. eBay does not maintain a costly physical inventory or deal with shipping, handling, or other services that businesses such as Amazon.com and other retailers must provide. The eBay site basically serves individuals, but it also caters to small businesses.

In 2001, eBay started to auction fine art in collaboration with icollector.com (*icollector.com*) of the United Kingdom and with the art auction house Sotheby's (*sothebys.com*), whose auction page is on eBay's main menu. Due to lack of profit, as of May 2003, eBay and Sotheby's discontinued separate online auctions and began placing emphasis on promoting Sotheby's live auctions through eBay's Live Auctions technology while continuing to build eBay's highly successful arts and antiques categories. The Sotheby Web site still exists, but now is focused on supporting Sotheby's live auction business.

In addition, eBay operates globally, permitting international auctions to take place. Country-specific sites are located in over 31 countries, including the United States, Canada, France, Sweden, Brazil, the United Kingdom, Australia, Singapore, and Japan. eBay also has equity in or owns several country-specific sites, such as those in China, India, Korea, and Japan, that generate 46 percent of eBay's business. Buyers from more than 150 other countries participate. eBay also operates a business exchange in which SMEs can buy and sell new and used merchandise in B2B or B2C modes.

eBay has over 60 local sites in the United States that enable users to easily find items located near them, to browse through items of local interest, and to meet face-to-face to conclude transactions. In addition, some eBay sites, such as eBay Motors, concentrate on specialty items. Trading can be done anywhere, anytime. Wireless trading also is possible.

In 2002, eBay Seller Payment Protection was implemented to make it safer to sell on eBay. Now sellers are protected against bad checks and fraudulent credit card purchases. The service offers credit card chargeback protection, guaranteed electronic checks, secure processing, and privacy protection. After a few years of successful operation and tens of million of loyal members, eBay decided to leverage its large customer base and started to do e-tailing, mostly at fixed prices. This may have been in response to Amazon.com's decision to start auctions, or it may have been a logical idea for a diversification. By 2003, eBay operated several specialty sites.

In addition to eBay Motors cited earlier, *half.com*, the famous discount e-tailer, is now part of eBay, as is PayPal, the P2P payment company.

A special feature is eBay Stores. These stores are rented to individuals and companies. The renting companies can use these stores to sell from catalogs or conduct auctions. In 2002, eBay introduced the Business Marketplace, located at *ebay.com/businessmarketplace*. This site brings together all business-related listings on eBay to one destination, making it easier for small businesses to find the equipment and supplies they need. eBay also offers software for building customized storefronts that eBay hosts (Prostores products), and provides templates for building standard storefronts.

eBay is used by individuals, small businesses, large enterprises, and governments (See *auctionbiz.com*.).

Many individuals are using eBay Stores and Marketplace to make a living. Some of them are very successful. Holden (2006) describes how 10 different entrepreneurs have tapped into the power of eBay and are making millions.

In 2006, eBay launched "eBay Express," which enables instant-purchasing using a shopping cart to buy multiple items at the prices set by the sellers. eBay also allows Web site affiliates to run contextual ads for eBay auctions in exchange for a cut of resulting ad sales. (The program is called eBay AdContext.) As of June 2006, eBay offers eBay Community Wiki, where buyers and sellers can exchange best practices and tips. eBay owns Skype, a VoIP provider of Internet communication, to streamline complex auctions (e.g., if you want to buy a car on eBay you may want to ask the seller a number of questions). Also, some sellers need information from buyers so they can customize their products.

The Results

The impact of eBay on e-business has been profound. Its founders took a limited-access offline business model and, by using the Internet, were able to bring it to the desktops of consumers worldwide. This business model consistently generates a profit and promotes a sense of community—a near addiction that keeps traders coming back.

eBay is the world's largest auction site, with a community of close to 194 million registered users as of spring 2006, about half of them outside the United States. According to company financial statements, in 2004, eBay transacted over $40 billion in sales for net revenue close to $6 billion and net income of about $500 million (Schonfeld 2005 and *ebay.com*).

As a matter of fact, the only place where people are doing more business online than offline (and considerably more, at that) is auctions. For comparison, e-tailing is less than 5 percent of total retail sales.

Sources: Compiled from *eMarketer* (2004), eBay (2006a), Search Engine Roundtable (2006), Stroebel (2003), Coffin (2004), Prince (2004), Schonfeld (2005), Park (2006), and Holden (2006).

WHAT WE CAN LEARN . . .

The eBay case demonstrates the success of a company that implemented an EC business model that took off very rapidly. The case presents some of the ideas of auctioning. It also demonstrates that auctions can be an online-only e-commerce channel, or they can be a supplementary channel. The operations and issues of auctions, as well as their variations and economic impacts, are the subject of this chapter.

10.1 FUNDAMENTALS OF DYNAMIC PRICING AND E-AUCTIONS

As described in Chapter 2, an **auction** is a market mechanism by which sellers place items for buyers to make bids on (forward auction) or buyers place RFPs for specific items and sellers place bids to win the jobs (reverse auction). Auctions are characterized by the competitive and dynamic nature by which a final price is reached. Auctions, an established method of commerce for generations, deal with products and services for which conventional marketing channels are ineffective or inefficient.

The Internet provides an infrastructure for executing auctions at lower administrative costs and with many more participating sellers and buyers. **Electronic auctions (e-auctions)**, which are auctions conducted online, have been in existence for several years. Individual consumers and corporations alike can participate in this rapidly growing and very convenient form of e-commerce. For an elementary introduction to auctions, see Kobler et al. (2005). For more on how to conduct online auctions, see the tutorial at ebay.com as well as the glossary at dellauction.com.

Although many consumer goods are not suitable for auctions and are best sold through conventional sales techniques (i.e., posted-price retailing), the flexibility offered by online auction trading may offer innovative market processes. For example, instead of searching for products and vendors by visiting sellers' Web sites, a buyer may solicit offers from all potential sellers. Such a buying mechanism is so innovative that it has the potential to be used for almost all types of consumer goods (e.g., see bidville.com). By soliciting a wide range of bids from many suppliers or customers, auctions improve the chances of finding the optimal match, particularly in B2B. Charities have taken silent auctions online. For example, see GoBid (gobid.ca).

auction
Market mechanism by which buyers make bids and sellers place offers; characterized by the competitive and dynamic nature by which the final price is reached.

electronic auctions (e-auctions)
Auctions conducted online.

EXHIBIT 10.1   Types of Dynamic Pricing

	One	Negotiation, Bartering, Bargaining	Reverse auctions, RFQ, Tendering
Buyers	Many	Forward (regular) auctions	Dynamic exchanges
		One	Many
		Sellers	

dynamic pricing
Fluctuating prices that are determined based on supply and demand relationships at any given time.

Many major manufacturers and e-tailers are using auctions to sell products and services (e.g., Dell, Amazon.com, Sam's Club of Wal-Mart) or to buy products and services (e.g., GE, GM, Boeing). Also, hundreds of intermediaries, ranging from ebay.com to ubid.com, are active in this fast-growing, multibillion-dollar market.

As discussed in Chapter 2, the major characteristic of an auction is that it is based on dynamic pricing. **Dynamic pricing** refers to a transaction in which the price is not fixed but fluctuates based on supply-and-demand relationships (see Dasgupta et al. 2006).

There are several types of auctions, each with its own goals and procedures. It is customary to classify dynamic pricing into four major categories depending on how many buyers and sellers are involved, as shown in Exhibit 10.1 and described here. Each of the following auction types can be done online or offline.

ONE BUYER, ONE SELLER

In the first configuration (pictured in the upper-left-hand box in Exhibit 10.1), each party can use negotiation, bargaining, or bartering. The resulting price will be determined by bargaining power, supply and demand in the item's market, and possibly business-environment factors. This model is popular in B2B (see Chapter 5, Chapter 6, and the Real-World Case at the end of this chapter).

ONE SELLER, MANY POTENTIAL BUYERS

forward auction
An auction in which a seller offers a product to many potential buyers.

In the second configuration (in the bottom-left-hand box of Exhibit 10.1), one seller uses a **forward auction** to offer a product to many potential bidders. Forward auctions have two major purposes: liquidation and market efficiency (Exhibit 10.2). For additional details on forward auctions, see Kollmann and Häsel (2006), Cook (2006), and Kambil and van Heck (2002). An example of B2C forward auctions is provided in Insights and Additions 10.1. The following is an example of a company that started auctions for liquidation but then moved to auction regular products.

American Power Conversion Corp. (APC; apcc.com) needed a channel for end-of-life (old models) and refurbished power-protection products. These were difficult to sell in regular distribution channels. Before using auctions, the company used special liquidation sales that were not very successful. APC decided to use auctions to sell these items. APC turned to FreeMarkets to help it establish an online auction. (Note: This company was integrated into Ariba.com.) It also helped the company determine the best auction strategies (such as starting bid price and auction running length). The site became an immediate success. APC also started to auction some of its regular products (only merchandise for which there would be no conflict with the company's regular distributors).

sealed-bid auction
Auction in which each bidder bids only once; a silent auction, in which bidders do not know who is placing bids or what the bid prices are.

Sealed-bid auctions are another example of one seller, many potential buyers auctions. In a **sealed-bid auction**, a bidder bids only once. It is a *silent auction*, and the bidders do not know who is placing bids or what the bids are. In a *first-price* sealed-bid auction, the item is awarded to the highest bidder. (Sealed-bid auctions also can be conducted in reverse auctions.)

EXHIBIT 10.2   Two Types of Forward Auctions

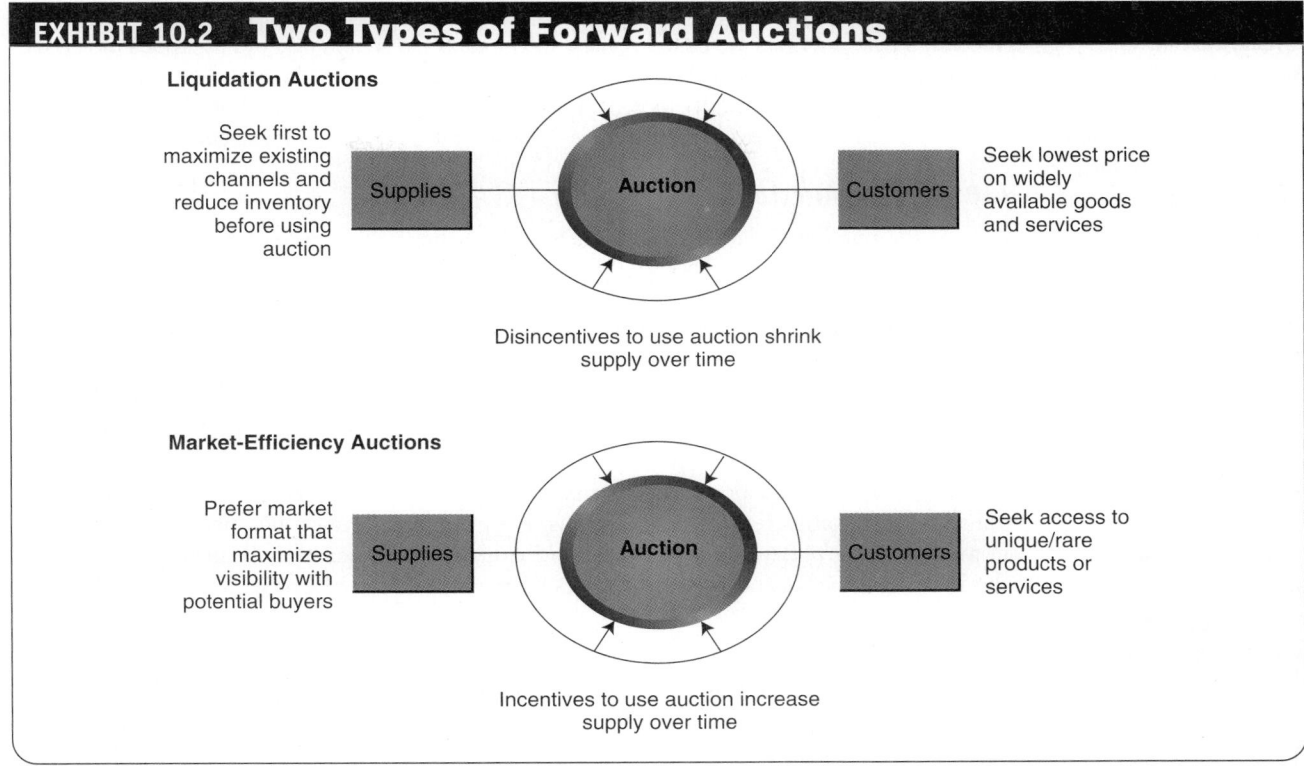

Liquidation Auctions

Seek first to maximize existing channels and reduce inventory before using auction

Supplies → Auction → Customers

Seek lowest price on widely available goods and services

Disincentives to use auction shrink supply over time

Market-Efficiency Auctions

Prefer market format that maximizes visibility with potential buyers

Supplies → Auction → Customers

Seek access to unique/rare products or services

Incentives to use auction increase supply over time

Source: Gallaugher, J. M. "E-Commerce and the Undulating Distribution Channel." *Communications of the ACM* (July 2002), Figure 3, p. 91.

In a *second-price* sealed-bid auction (also called a **Vickrey auction**), the item is awarded to the highest bidder, *but at the second-highest price that was bid.* This is done to alleviate bidders' fears of significantly exceeding the item's true market value.

Vickrey auction
Auction in which the highest bidder wins but pays only the second-highest bid.

ONE BUYER, MANY POTENTIAL SELLERS

In auctions in this category (pictured in the upper-right-hand corner of Exhibit 10.1) one buyer solicits bids from many sellers or suppliers (see examples of GE and GM in Chapter 5). An item the buyer needs is placed on an RFQ (request for quote), and potential sellers bid on

Insights and Additions 10.1   B2C Forward Auctions: Dell Auction

Consumers who want to buy or sell used or obsolete Dell products can go to *dellauction.com*. Buyers will find lots of information on the items they are interested in. For example, a buyer can find out if the seller is Dell (B2C) or an individual (C2C). The buyer also can check product details, such as the item's warranty and condition. The site also offers general services, such as escrow. Everything on the site is organized for both buyers and sellers, from shopping carts and account management features to payment and shipping services.

The site is clearly marked with icons that denote and allow for the following:

▶ Reserve price, which is the lowest price at which a seller is willing to sell an item

▶ English auction, in which items are sold to the highest bidder at the end of auction period

▶ Dutch auction, in which more than one item is up for bid at a time and all winning bidders pay the same price, which is the *lowest* winning bid on the items

▶ QuickWin auction, in which an item is sold to the first bidder who meets the threshold price (set by the seller)

▶ Classified listings, in which the buyer and seller communicate offline to decide on a price for the item

▶ AutoMarkdown listings, which are designed to sell large quantities of items and are posted with an initial price that declines over the course of the auction until the quantities run out

▶ Fixed-price listings that offer items for sale at the price listed

▶ "Hot" listings, indicating that an item has generated a high level of bidding interest

reverse auction

Auction in which the buyer places an item for bid (*tender*) on a request for quote (RFQ) system; potential suppliers bid on the job, with bid price reducing sequentially, and the lowest bid wins; used mainly in B2B and G2B e-commerce.

the item, *reducing the price sequentially*. (Refer to Exhibit 2.5, page 54, for an illustration of this process.) These auctions are called **reverse auctions** because *suppliers* bid on goods or services the buyer needs. In reverse auctions, the price is reduced sequentially, and the lowest bid wins. These auctions are used mainly in B2B (both large and small businesses) or G2B; they may be combined with negotiations (see the Real-World Case at the end of this chapter).

B2B Reverse Auctions

Most of the publicity related to auctions is around the C2C and B2C markets. However, as described in Chapters 5 through 7, B2B reverse auctions are gaining popularity as an online mechanism for buying goods and services. Hedgehog.com/onlinereverseauctions.htm presents the opportunities, advantages, and economic benefits of such B2B e-auctions. An example of a reverse auction using an intermediary is provided in Case 10.1. For more on reverse auctions, see Chapter 5, Carbone (2005), and hedgehog.com/onlinereverseauctions .htm (accessed April 2007).

C2C Reverse Auctions

Although most C2C auctions are of a forward nature (usually the English type), increasingly, individuals are conducting reverse auctions. For example, a person who wants to buy a used car may create a *request-for-bid* (RFB, for individuals) for the car of their dreams and let those who have such cars contact them. C2C auctions are provided by eBay.

"name-your-own-price" model

Auction model in which would-be buyers specify the price (and other terms) they are willing to pay to any willing seller; a C2B model pioneered by Priceline.com.

"Name-Your-Own-Price" Model

Another type of auction in the one buyer, many potential sellers category is the **"name-your-own-price" model** pioneered by Priceline.com (Section 10.3). In this model, a would-be buyer specifies the price (or other terms) that he or she is willing to pay to any willing and able seller. This is basically a C2B model, although it is also used by some businesses. Competitors to Priceline.com offer similar models.

CASE 10.1
EC Application
PROCUREMENT VIA AUCTIONS AT STE

Singapore Technologies Engineering (STE) (*stengg.com*), a large, integrated global engineering group specializing in the fields of aerospace, electronics, and land and marine systems, wanted to improve its e-procurement (sourcing) through the use of reverse auctions. Specifically, STE had the following goals:

▶ Minimize the cost of products it needed to buy, such as board parts.
▶ Identify a new global supply base for its multisourcing strategy.
▶ Maximize efficiency in the procurement process.
▶ Find new, quality suppliers for reliability and support.
▶ Consolidate existing suppliers.

Such goals are typical of business purchasers. STE decided to use an intermediary. The vendor started by training STE's corporate buyers and other staff on the new system. Then it designed an improved process that replicated the traditional negotiations with suppliers. Finally, it took a test item (printed circuit board assemblies) and prepared an RFQ, placing it for bid on the software vendor's global supply network, the database of suppliers that are exposed to the RFQs of buyers. The vendor used a five-step process that started with the RFQ and ended with supplier management

(which included supplier verification and training). At the end of the trial, STE saved 35 percent on the cost of printed circuit board assemblies.

It is interesting to note that one of STE's traditional suppliers threatened not to participate in the event. The supplier claimed that its prequoted price was so competitive that it would be impossible to beat the price through online bidding. In spite of these claims, STE followed through with the auction and subsequently awarded the business to another high-quality bidder with even better pricing.

Sources: Compiled from Kheng and Al-Hawamdeh (2002) and *Asia.Internet.com* (2006).

Questions

1. Why was it necessary to restructure the purchasing process?
2. Why, in your opinion, was it beneficial for STE to use an intermediary? (Hint: See Chapter 5.)
3. Explain how STE's five goals can be achieved by using a reverse-auction process.

MANY SELLERS, MANY BUYERS

In this final configuration (the bottom-right-hand box in Exhibit 10.1), buyers and their bidding prices are matched with sellers and their asking prices based on the quantities on both sides and the dynamic interaction between the buyers and sellers. Stocks and commodities markets are typical examples of this type of configuration (see also Chapter 6 and the Real-World Case at the end of this chapter). Buyers and sellers may be individuals or businesses. Such auctions, which are usually done in exchanges, are called *double auctions* (see Section 10.5).

Vertical auction. A **vertical auction** is one that takes place between sellers and buyers in one industry or for one commodity (e.g., flowers, cars, or cattle). It is considered vertical because activity goes up and down the supply chain in a single industry, rather than horizontally between members of supply chains in different industries. Specialized sites for such auctions (in one industry) are sometimes referred to as **auction vortals**. Vertical auctions are particularly useful in B2B. At eBay "anything goes" (i.e., almost anything can be sold), but many auction sites specialize in one area. For example, policeauctions.com specializes in selling unclaimed or seized properties.

vertical auction
Auction that takes place between sellers and buyers in one industry or for one commodity.

auction vortals
Another name for a vertical auction vertical portal.

Section 10.1 ▶ REVIEW QUESTIONS

1. List the four categories of auctions.
2. List the major auction models available to one seller.
3. List the auction models available to one buyer.

10.2 BENEFITS, LIMITATIONS, AND STRATEGIC USES OF E-AUCTIONS

Electronic auctions are becoming important selling and buying channels for companies and individuals. Almost perfect market information is available to both buyers and sellers about prices, products, current supply and demand, and so on. These features provide benefits to all.

BENEFITS OF E-AUCTIONS

Electronic auctions create some economic changes that benefit both sellers and buyers. The major economic impacts of auctions are summarized in Exhibit 10.3.

EXHIBIT 10.3 Economic Impacts of Auctions

Impact	Description
Market liquidity	Increases the number of buyers and sellers who can easily find each other and the auction place online and participate in the auction. This includes global participation.
Coordination mechanism for equilibrium in prices	Efficient mechanism for setting prices based on supply, demand, and participants' requirements.
Price discovery	Both buyers and sellers can easily find existing offers and bids, as well as historical price settlements. This is especially important for rare or valuable items.
Highly visible distribution mechanism	Via special offers, attention is given to certain groups of sellers (e.g., liquidators) and buyers (e.g., bargain hunters).
Price transparency	Prices are visible to all; this allows sellers to be more realistic, and buyers to be more careful in making offers.
Volume effect	The larger the auction site (e.g., eBay), the more the previous impacts are felt. Thus, transaction costs are lower, more people can find what they want, and more sellers can sell quickly at reasonable prices.

Benefits to Sellers

Electronic auctions provide the following benefits to sellers. (See hedgehog.com and purchasing.com.)

Larger Reach and Increased Revenues. By broadening the customer base and shortening the disposal cycle, sellers can reach the most interested buyers in the most efficient and fastest way possible and sell more at a price equal to buyer valuation of the product.

Optimal Price Setting. Sellers can make use of the information about price sensitivity collected in auctions to set prices in fixed-price markets. This eliminates the risk of pricing items too high or too low.

Removal of Expensive Intermediaries. Sellers can gain more customer dollars by offering items directly rather than going through an expensive intermediary or by using an expensive physical auction. Furthermore, using e-auctions via intermediaries can be more cost-effective than using a physical auction place.

Liquidation. Sellers can liquidate large quantities of obsolete or surplus items very quickly (see liquidation.com).

Lower Transaction Costs. Compared with manual auctions and liquidations, e-auctions offer lower transaction costs.

Lower Administrative Costs. The cost of selling via e-auctions can be much lower than the costs of selling via e-tailing or via non-Internet auctions.

Better Customer Relationships. Buyers and sellers have more chances and time to interact with each other, thus creating a sense of community and loyalty. Additionally, by making use of information gathered on customer interests, sellers can improve the overall e-commerce experiences of buyers and deliver more personalized content, thus enhancing customer relationships.

Benefits to Buyers

Electronic auctions provide the following benefits to buyers.

Opportunities to Find Unique Items and Collectibles. Items that are hard to find in certain areas or at certain times are auctioned regularly on the Internet. Stamps, coins, Barbie dolls, and the Pez dispensers that started the idea of eBay are examples of popular collectible items on the Internet.

Lower Prices. Instead of buying at a fixed price, buyers can use the bidding mechanism to reduce prices.

Anonymity. With the help of a third party, e-auction buyers can remain anonymous if they choose to.

Convenience. Buyers can trade from anywhere, even with a cell phone (m-commerce auctions).

Entertainment. Participating in e-auctions can be entertaining and exciting. The competitive environment, as well as the interaction between buyers and sellers, may create goodwill and positive feelings. Buyers can interact with sellers as much or as little as they like.

Benefits to E-Auctioneers

Electronic auctions provide the following benefits to e-auctioneers.

Higher Repeat Purchases. Jupiter Communications conducted a study in 1998 that showed comparative repeat-purchase rates across some of the top e-commerce sites (Subramaniam 2000). The findings indicated that auction sites, such as eBay and uBid, tend to garner higher repeat-purchase rates than the top e-commerce B2C sites, such as Amazon.com.

A Stickier Web Site. *Stickiness* refers to the tendency of customers to stay at Web sites longer and come back more often (Chapter 4). Auction sites often are stickier than fixed-priced sites. With sticky sites, more advertising revenue can be generated because of more impressions and longer viewing times.

Expansion of the Auction Business. Auctioneers easily can expand their markets (usually with the help of local partners). An example of how auctioneers can expand their business can be seen in the example of Manheim Auctions (*Business Journal of Phoenix* 2005 and Schermerhorn 2004).

Consider the following example. In response to the Japanese company Aucnet's efforts to penetrate the U.S. car auction business, Manheim Auctions, the world's largest conventional auction house, created Manheim Online (MOL) in 1999 to sell program cars (cars that have been previously leased or hired). This Internet-based system is changing the car auction business. The United States has over 80,000 used car dealers, and Manheim auctions some 6 million cars for them each year. Trying to leverage its knowledge of the automobile market to provide services to its customers, Manheim developed two other products, Manheim Market Report and AutoConnect. It also is expanding its auction business in Europe. Manheim wants to continue to add value to Manheim Online as a way of discouraging competition and of extending sales through the Internet without cannibalizing Manheim's core business. By 2003, hundreds of car auction sites had gone online. Portals such as eBay, Yahoo!, Amazon.com, and MSN offer thousands of cars each year.

LIMITATIONS OF E-AUCTIONS

As discussed in Chapter 2, e-auctions have several limitations, including the following.

Possibility of Fraud. The fraud rate in e-auctions is very high. Auction items are in many cases unique, used, or antique. Because buyers cannot see the item, they may get a defective product. Buyers also may commit fraud. (For specific fraud techniques and how to prevent them, see Section 10.7.)

Limited Participation. Some auctions are by invitation only; others are open only to dealers.

Security. Some of the C2C auctions conducted on the Internet are not secure, and some potential participants are scared away by the lack of security.

Auction Software. Unfortunately, auction software is limited. Only a few off-the-shelf software solutions that can support the dynamic commerce functionality required for optimizing pricing strategies and that can be easily customized to a company or industry are available. However, this situation is improving with time.

Long Cycle Time. Some auctions last for days, and in some cases sellers and buyers need to meet face-to-face or with an escrow agent to complete a deal. This may take time, and buyers and sellers may not want or be able to invest such time.

Monitoring Time. Although in some cases buyers can use intelligent agents to monitor an auction and place bids, in others they have to do this time-consuming job themselves.

Equipment for Buyers. Buyers need a PC to engage in electronic auctions, and they also need to pay for Internet access. These requirements have somewhat limited the number of potential auction participants. These requirements are changing as people are starting to use their smart cell phones for auctions; however, this requires a cell phone with Internet capabilities.

Order Fulfillment Costs. Buying at an auction site means that the buyer will pay shipment and handling costs plus any extra insurance cost.

STRATEGIC USES OF AUCTIONS AND PRICING MECHANISMS

Through dynamic pricing, buyers and sellers are able to adjust pricing strategies and optimize product inventory levels very quickly. For example, by using Web-based auctions and exchanges, suppliers can quickly flush excess inventory and liquidate idle assets. Buyers may end up with the power to procure goods and services at the prices they desire. The end game is to accurately assess and exploit market supply-and-demand requirements faster and more efficiently than the competition.

Aberdeen Group (2000) showed that e-marketplaces that are using auctions extensively are reaching liquidity ("critical mass") more rapidly than those utilizing only catalog-order-based trading environments. However, businesses are still struggling to understand how to truly implement dynamic pricing models to augment existing business practices.

One suggestion of how to do so was provided by Westland (2000), who observed that e-auctions place much more power in the hands of the consumer than does catalog-based e-tailing. He suggested that a number of lessons from stock exchange trading can be applied to e-tailing auctions; these lessons are listed in Online File W10.1.

For a summary of the impacts of electronic auctions on their subjects, see Online File W10.2.

AUCTIONS FOR PUBLICITY

Auctions can be used to attract attention. An interesting case is provided in the following example.

In forward auctions (Chapters 2 and 10), the winner is the highest bidder. But in doing promotions online, the opposite is true. Hard to believe? Go to Limbo 41414 (41414.com). Here is how it works: The site auctions several prizes on which people can bid online from cell phones (see Chapter 9). The winner is the person with the lowest bid that no one else duplicates. For example, if two or more people bid a penny, they all lose. Petrecca (2006) reports that a Ms. Winegarner won a 2007 Harley-Davidson motorcycle for $7.35. Each interactive auction lasts from a day to a month (as determined by the sponsor). Bidders get messages from Limbo about the status of each auction.

Section 10.2 ▶ REVIEW QUESTIONS

1. List the major benefits of auctions to buyers.
2. List the major benefits of auctions to sellers.
3. List the benefits of auctions to auctioneers.
4. List the limitations of auctions.

10.3 THE "NAME-YOUR-OWN-PRICE" C2B MODEL

One of the most interesting e-commerce models is the *"name-your-own-price"* model. This model, pioneered by Priceline.com (priceline.com), enables consumers to achieve significant savings by naming their own price for goods and services. Basically, the concept is that of a C2B reverse auction, in which vendors bid on a job by submitting offers and the lowest-priced vendor or the one that meets the buyer's requirements gets the job.

Priceline.com either presents consumer offers to sellers who can fill as much of that guaranteed demand as they wish at price points requested by buyers or, more likely, searches a Priceline.com database that contains vendors' minimum prices and tries to match supply against requests. Priceline.com asks customers to guarantee acceptance of the offer if it is at or below the requested price. Priceline.com guarantees this by having the buyer's credit card number. Priceline.com's "virtual" business model allows for rapid scaling; it uses the Internet to determine consumer demand and then tries to fill it. The approach is based on the fundamental concept of the downward-sloping demand curve in which prices vary based on demand.

However, Priceline.com and similar companies have one limitation: When a buyer names a price for an airline ticket, the buyer is *not* told the airline, how many stops are involved, or what time of the day the flight will depart until the buyer accepts the offer and pays. Then, the buyer must take the offer or lose that money that was guaranteed by a credit card. To overcome this problem, travelers can go to online travel sites such as expedia.com, orbitz.com, travelocity.com, aa.com, or others that provide price comparisons. By becoming familiar with the routes and flights, a buyer may be able to find what is available and then go to Priceline.com and bid for lower prices, knowing basically who is offering what. This way, buyers will get real bargains.

Priceline.com has offered multiple products and services: travel services, personal finance services, an automotive service that offers new cars for sale, and credit cards and long-distance calling. (In 2000, Priceline.com suspended the delivery of food, gasoline, and groceries due to accumulated losses.) Some of the services are offered via partners. Priceline.com receives either a commission for referrals or royalties for use of its technology. In 2000, the company teamed up with Hutchison Whampoa Limited, one of Asia's largest owners of telecommunications and Internet infrastructure, to offer a range of services in Asia. Priceline.com also has business offices in many other countries.

By 2002, the company offered products for sale in two categories: (1) a travel service that offers leisure airline tickets, hotel rooms, rental cars, vacation packages, and cruises, and (2) a personal finance service that offers home mortgages, refinancing, and home equity loans through an independent licensee. Also in 2002, Priceline.com purchased the Internet domain name and trademark of LowestFare.com, another Web-based travel site. With Priceline.com, you can now choose your exact flights and times for incredible travel savings or name your own price and save even more. All it takes is a little flexibility with your travel plans. In addition, Priceline.com now offers low-price, fixed-rate flights. Priceline.com also licenses its business model to independent licensees.

At one point, Priceline.com initiated a service to help people get rid of old things that they no longer wanted. It was similar to an auction site, with heavy emphasis on second-hand goods but with a different auction process. The site, named Perfect YardSale, was intended to let a user make an offer below the seller's asking price for an item, a system that is similar to the haggling that goes on at garage and yard sales. Perfect YardSale transactions were limited to local metropolitan areas, so that the buyer and seller could meet face-to-face. Buyers and sellers would be able to swap goods in person, eliminating the expense of shipping. This service was discontinued in 2001 due to incurred losses. A variation of this service is the sale of previously owned items at fixed prices by half.com (a subsidiary of eBay).

Section 10.3 ▶ REVIEW QUESTIONS

1. What is the logic behind the "name-your-own-price" model?
2. Describe Priceline.com's business model.
3. How does Priceline.com match supply and demand?
4. Enter priceline.com and try to book a flight but stop short of giving your credit card number. Comment on your experience.

10.4   THE FORWARD E-AUCTION PROCESS AND SOFTWARE SUPPORT

A number of software products and intelligent tools are available to help buyers and sellers find an auction site, identify what is going on there, or complete a transaction. In an auction, sellers and buyers usually complete a four-phase process: Searching and comparing, getting started at an auction, bidding, and conducting postauction activities (see Exhibit 10.4). The details of these steps for eBay users are available at Kobler et al. (2005). Each phase has several support tools (see allauctiontools.com). Many of these are intelligent agents (see Guan 2006). Let's explore them by the auction phase in which they are used.

PHASE 1: SEARCHING AND COMPARING

Auctions are conducted on hundreds of sites worldwide. Therefore, sellers and buyers need to execute extensive searches and comparisons to select desirable auction locations. Sellers can also search auction sites to get an idea of the minimum and reserve prices.

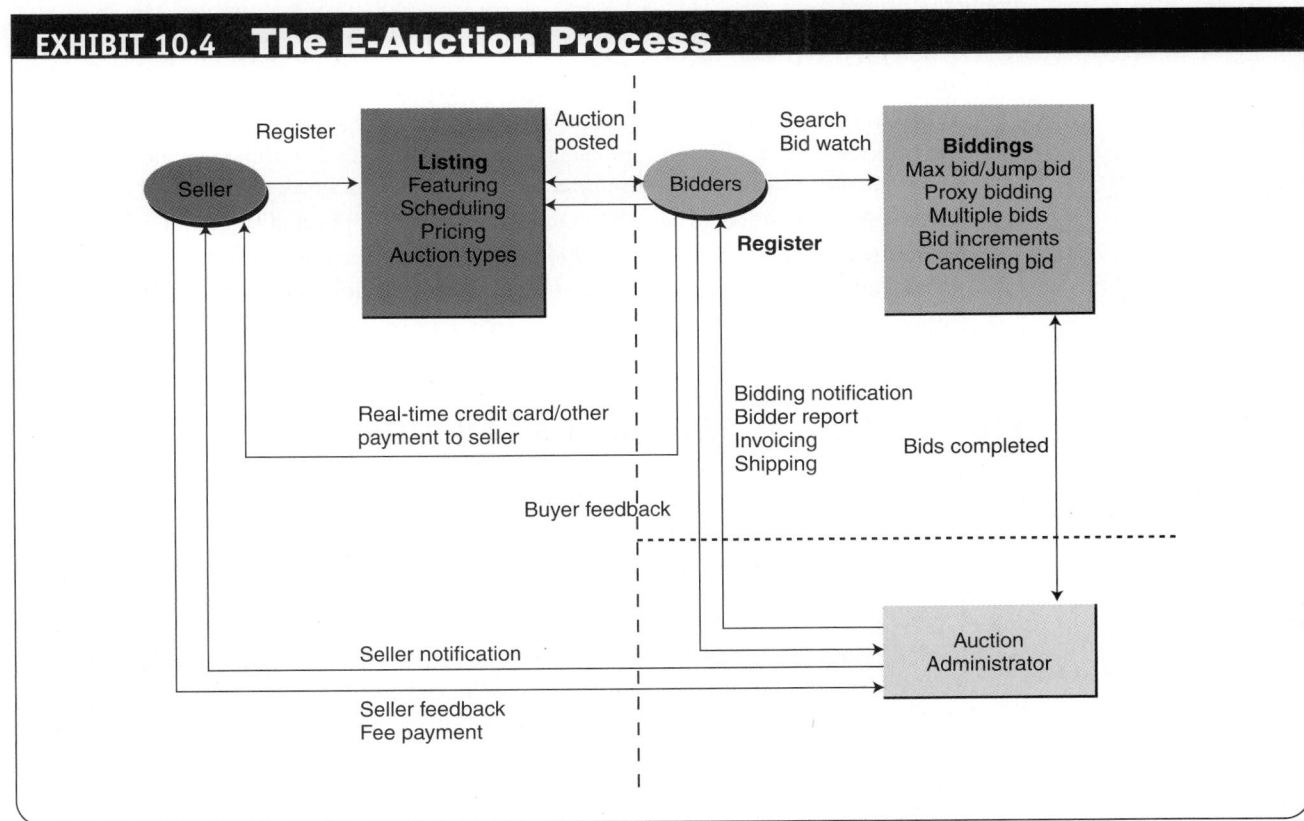

EXHIBIT 10.4   The E-Auction Process

Auction Aggregators and Notification. The search to find what is being auctioned and where can be difficult; there are thousands of auction sites, some of which are very specialized. **Auction aggregators** are companies that use software agents to visit Web auction sites, find information, summarize and organize it, and deliver it to users. Leading aggregators are vendio.com, bidfind.com, and bidxs.com.

auction aggregators
Companies that use software agents to visit Web auction sites, find information, summarize it, and deliver it to users.

At these aggregation sites, buyers (sellers, too) fill out electronic forms specifying the item they want. Then the aggregators keep tabs on various auction sites and notify buyers by e-mail when the items they wish to bid on appear. There are two types of notification services: those that supply notification only for their own sites (e.g., eBay or Ubid.com) and those that report what is going on at many sites (e.g., bidslammer.com).

Aggregation services such as auction-portal.com are beneficial to users but may not be appreciated by the auction sites, as discussed in Online File W10.3 at the book's Web site.

The task of auction aggregation can be complex when the aggregators have to monitor several items at several auction sites in several auction formats. The first international competition took place in 2000 called the Trading Agent Competition (TAC) to identify the best aggregators. See sics.se/tac/page.php?id=1 to read about recent TAC competitions, including TAC classic/travel and TAC SCM.

Browsing Site Categories. Almost all auction homepages contain a directory of categories. Buyers can browse a category and its subcategories to narrow a search. Some sites also enable users to sort items according to the time a specific auction is being conducted.

Basic and Advanced Searching. Buyers can use search engines to look for a single term, multiple terms, or keywords. To conduct an advanced search, buyers can fill in a search form to specify search titles, item descriptions, sellers' IDs, auction item numbers, price ranges, locations, closing dates, completed auctions, and so forth.

Both buyers and sellers want to find specific items and auctions relevant to these items so they can determine ask and bid prices more realistically. Many Web sites offer links to hundreds of auction sites or provide search tools (e.g., see bidfind.com) to locate specific sites. The searching utility not only helps sellers find suitable locations to list their items but also enables buyers to browse available auction sites efficiently. See Insights and Additions 10.2 for an example of how to find when and where an item is being auctioned.

The following support services may be helpful in conducting searches and comparisons:

- Online Auctions Network (online-auctions.net) contains a directory of auction sites organized by categories, as well as auction news.
- The Internet Auction List (internetauctionlist.com) is packed with news about e-auctions worldwide and features access to innumerable specialty auctions.
- Yahoo!'s auction list (auctions.yahoo.com) contains a list of over 400 auction-related links.
- Theinfo (theinfo.com) conducts searches across multiple auction houses for specific auction products and pricing information. It provides detailed historical information on previous sales.
- Turbobid (etusa.com) provides a megasearch service that helps local bidders look for items they want from a pool of e-auction sites.

PHASE 2: GETTING STARTED AT AN AUCTION

To participate in a third-party–managed auction, both the sellers and buyers need to register at the selected site. After registration, sellers can list, feature, schedule, and price their items on the site. Buyers can check sellers' profiles and other details, such as the auction rules and policy and the payment methods allowed, and then place their bids.

Registration and Participants' Profiles. Sellers and buyers must usually register their names, user IDs, and passwords before they can participate at a specific auction site. The user's page header (heading at the top of the screen) and the auction listing will display a basic description of sellers and their listings. Before submitting a bid, buyers can check a seller's profile, including the seller's membership ID and previous transactions. If the auction site provides voluntary verified-user programs, such as those at winecommune.com and eBay, buyers can check whether sellers are qualified auction community members, as verified by a third-party security source.

Listing and Promoting. Several software programs are available that can help sellers list and promote their items:

Insights and Additions 10.2 Finding a Pool Table and More

Assume a potential buyer is interested in purchasing a pool table. The following process is one example of how that buyer might use the Internet to locate the desired pool table. To find auctions that feature pool tables, the would-be buyer performs the following three steps:

1. Enter *bidfind.com*.
2. Choose "auctions."
3. Enter "pool table" as the keyword option.

The search engine claims that it searches more than 1,000 online dynamic pricing sites, including auctions, shopping sites, and classified ads. The buyer's keyword search found seven auctions, organized as shown here. BidFind links to the auction sites where the searched items are found.

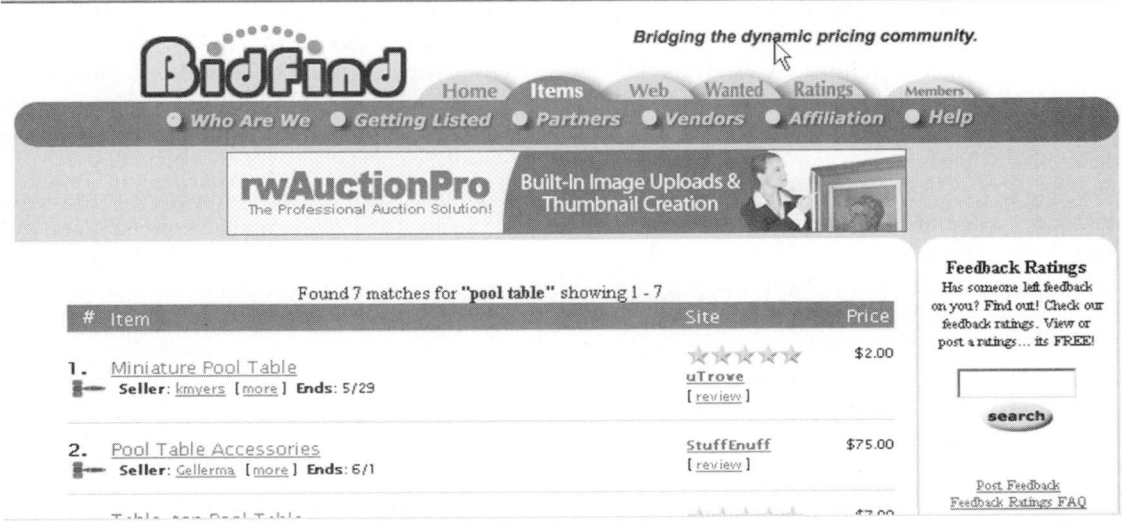

Source: Courtesy of VisionNetwork. Copyright ©1995–2005 VisionNetwork. All Rights Reserved. BidFind® is a registered trademark.

- ◗ AuctionSplash (see auctionsplash.com) helps users create attractive auction postings. With simple-to-use templates, users can create great-looking advertisements for e-auctions or for other purposes.
- ◗ Auction Assistant (see tucows.com) and Ad Studio (adstudio.net) can be combined to create auction listings. This combination enables users to manipulate fonts, backgrounds, and themes on their listings. It also enables users to include standard details, such as shipping policy and payment terms, and to track sales, payments, and shipping.
- ◗ Auctiva Mr. Poster (auctiva.com), a software program that interacts directly with eBay, makes it simple to add pictures to a listing. The program can create up to 100 ads at a time, and it supports bulk listings.
- ◗ Auction Wizard (auctionwizard2000.com) can upload up to 100 items simultaneously. It is an auction-posting tool that saves time spent cutting and pasting. Auction Wizard also enters user ID, password, auction title, location, opening bid, category, and auction duration.
- ◗ eBay Turbo Lister is a free listing tool to help you create professional-looking listings and upload thousands of items in bulk. The 2006 version of eBay Turbo Lister has improved speed and reliability, easier listing and editing capability, sleek new design, and same bulk listing benefits as the original Turbo (Mister) Lister. It's still free. (See pages.ebay.com/turbo_lister/index.html?ssPageName=STRK:SRVC:010). Similarly, using Bulk Loader (see Yahoo! Auctions at auctions.yahoo.com), sellers can load several auctions into a spreadsheet program, such as Microsoft Excel.

Pricing. To post an item for bid, sellers have to decide the minimum bid amount, the bid increment, and the reserve price. Sellers can search for guides for setting minimum bid amounts, the bid increments, and reserve prices for comparable auctions with Web search engines such as bidfind.com, freemerchant.com, pricescan.com, and vendio.com. If the auction site allows users to search the history of completed auctions, the transacted prices of similar items can provide a benchmark for a buyer's bidding strategy or a minimum acceptable price for a seller.

PHASE 3: BIDDING

In the bidding phase, buyers can submit bids themselves or can make use of software tools that place bids on their behalf. They also can use software tools to view the bidding status and to place bids across different sites in real time.

Bid Watching and Multiple Bids. Buyers can visit their personalized page at an e-auction Web site at any time and keep track of the status of active auctions. They can review bids and auctions they are currently winning or losing or have recently won. Tools provided in the United States by Bid Monitor (see bruceclay.com) enable bidders to view their bids across different auction sites in an organized way. Bidders also can use the tools to place bids at multiple auction sites using a single screen without switching from one window to another.

sniping

Entering a bid during the very last seconds of an auction and outbidding the highest bidder.

Sniping. The act of entering a bid during the very last seconds of an auction and outbidding the highest bidder is called **sniping**. Auto-sniping involves the use of electronic tools to perform the sniping automatically.

Occasionally, sellers use sniping in a fraudulent way: When the bidding price seems to be too low, they may enter the auction and bid for their own goods or services, pretending they are buyers. In this way, they hope to inspire other bidders to submit higher bids. (Being aware of this possible activity should help one avoid being caught up in last-minute bidding frenzy and overpaying in an online auction.)

proxy bidding

Use of a software system to place bids on behalf of buyers; when another bidder places a bid, the software (the proxy) will automatically raise the bid to the next level until it reaches the buyer's predetermined maximum price.

Proxy Bids. A software system can be used for **proxy bidding**, in which the system operates as a proxy (agent) to place bids on behalf of buyers. In proxy bidding, a buyer should determine the maximum bid he or she is willing to offer and then place the first (low) bid manually. The proxy will then execute the buyer's bids, trying to keep the bids as low as possible. When someone enters a new bid, the proxy will automatically raise the bid to the next level until it reaches the predetermined maximum price set by the bidder. This function is not applicable in a Dutch auction.

PHASE 4: POSTAUCTION FOLLOW-UP

Postauction activities take place once an auction is completed. These activities include e-mail notifications and arrangements for payment and shipping.

Postauction Activities. Typical postauction activities include the following:

- **Bidding notifications.** Buyers receive e-mail, SMS messages, or beeper messages notifying them each time they win an auction and sometimes when they are outbid.
- **End-of-auction notices.** When an auction closes, the seller receives an e-mail (or SMS) message naming the highest bidder. End-of-auction e-mails provide seller and buyer IDs; seller and winner e-mail addresses (or cell phone numbers); a link to the auction ad, auction title, or item name; the final price; the auction ending date and time; the total number of bids; and the starting and highest bid amounts.
- **Seller notices.** After an auction ends, the seller generally contacts the buyer. The seller's notice typically provides the auction number and item name, total purchase price (winning bid plus shipping), payment preferences, mailing address, and so on.
- **Postcards and thank-you notes.** Sites such as vendio.com help sellers create a customized close-of-auction or thank-you note for winning bidders.

User Communication. User-to-user online communication provides an avenue by which auction participants can share information about goods and services being offered and about the process of online auctions. User communication appears in a number of forms:

- **Chat groups.** Areas on e-auction sites and auction-related sites where people can post messages in real time to get quick feedback from others.

- ▶ **Mailing lists.** A group of people talking about a chosen topic via e-mail messages.
- ▶ **Message boards.** Areas on e-auction and auction-related sites where people can post messages that other users can read at their convenience. Other message board participants can post replies for all to read.

Feedback and Ratings. Most e-auction sites provide a feedback and rating feature that enables auction community members to monitor each other. This feature enables users to rank sellers or bidders and to add short comments about sellers, bidders, and transactions.

Invoicing and Billing. An invoicing tool (invoicing utility) can e-mail and print one or all invoices, search and arrange invoices in a number of ways, edit invoices, and delete incorrect invoices. This utility automatically calculates shipping charges and sales tax. It also can automatically calculate and charge the seller with the listing fees and/or a percentage of the sale as commission. An example of such a tool is Simplybill from (simplybill.com).

Payment Methods. Sellers and winning bidders can arrange payment to be made by P2P payment service (e.g., paypal.com), cashier's check, C.O.D. (cash on delivery), credit card, electronic transfer, or through an escrow service (see Chapter 12). A number of online services are available for electronic transfer of money, escrow services, and credit card payment, including the following:

- ▶ **P2P transfer service.** Buyers can pay electronically via services at sites such as paybyweb.com, paypal.com, and bidpay.com. (See Chapter 12 for further discussion.)
- ▶ **Escrow service.** An independent third party holds a bidder's payment in trust until the buyer receives and accepts the auction item from the seller. The third party charges a fee for the escrow service, and the service is usually reserved for high-end transactions. Examples of escrow service provider sites are moneybookers.com, i-escrow.com, fortis-escrow.com, and escrow.com.
- ▶ **Credit card payment.** PayPal (paypal.com) and CCNow (ccnow.com) facilitate person-to-person credit card transactions (see Chapter 12).

Shipping and Postage. Finally, to complete the auction process, the purchased goods must be shipped from the seller to the buyer. Shipping providers such as iship.com help sellers by providing a one-stop integrated service for processing, shipping, and packing e-commerce goods. UPS, FedEx, the U.S. Postal Service, and other shippers move most of the purchases to their destinations (see Chapter 13 for details).

ADDITIONAL TERMS AND RULES

Each auction house has its own rules and guides. The following are some examples:

- ▶ **Bid retraction.** This is the cancellation of a bid by a bidder. It is used only in special circumstances. Usually a bid is considered to be a binding contract.
- ▶ **Featured auctions.** These are auctions that get added exposure on the auction Web site. Sellers pay extra for this service.
- ▶ **Other Services.** eBay provides many other services. For example, equipment financing is available, as are buyer tools, warranty programs, seller tools, security tools (to be discussed in Section 10.7), buyer and seller education, software downloads, and much more (see pages.ebay.com/services).

Section 10.4 ▶ REVIEW QUESTIONS

1. List the activities of phase 1. What software tools or agents are available to support these activities?
2. List the activities of phase 2. What software tools or agents are available to support these activities?
3. List the activities of phase 3. What software tools or agents are available to support these activities?
4. List the activities of phase 4. What software tools or agents are available to support these activities?

10.5 DOUBLE AUCTIONS, BUNDLE TRADING, AND PRICING ISSUES

Other issues to be considered in a discussion of auctions are single versus double auctions, bundling of goods or services to attract buyers, and pricing.

DOUBLE AUCTIONS

single auction
Auction in which at least one side of the market consists of a single entity (a single buyer or a single seller).

double auction
Auction in which multiple buyers and sellers may be making bids and offers simultaneously; buyers and their bidding prices and sellers and their asking prices are matched, considering the quantities on both sides.

Auctions may be single or double. In a **single auction**, an item (or several identical items) is either offered for sale by one seller and the market consists of multiple buyers making bids to buy, or an item is wanted by one buyer and the market consists of multiple sellers making offers to sell. In either case, one side of the market consists of a single entity.

In a **double auction**, multiple buyers and sellers may be making bids and offers simultaneously. An example of a double auction is stock trading. In double auctions, multiple units of a product may be auctioned off at the same time. The situation becomes complicated when the quantity offered is more than one and buyers and sellers bid on varying quantities.

Although many online auctions are single, double auctions are the form used for transactions involving corporate stocks and commodities (grains, metals, livestock, etc.). In a given trading period, any seller may make an offer while any buyer makes a bid. Either a seller or a buyer may accept the offer or bid at any time. The difference between the cost and price paid is the seller's profit (loss); the difference between the price paid and valuation is the buyer's surplus. If quantities vary, as in a stock market, a *market maker* needs to *match* both prices and quantities. For details, see Choi and Whinston (2000).

Prices in Double Auctions

According to Rouchier and Robin (2006) and Trevathan and Ghodosi (2006), double-auction markets tend to generate competitive outcomes. Simply put, a double auction is an interactive market in which both buyers and sellers are competitive. In contrast, in a single auction, contract prices may be much higher or much lower than in a competitive format. This conclusion may have a significant effect on the future use of double auctions in the digital economy.

Ideally, any effort to promote competitiveness should include expanding online double auctions and similar market mechanisms because they offer an opportunity to raise economic efficiencies that is unsurpassed by any physical market organization. Note, however, that in many cases double auctions are not feasible due to lack of multiple sellers (e.g., in cases of collectible items). For auctioneers, however, single auctions generate substantially more revenue than double auctions.

BUNDLE TRADING

bundle trading
The selling of several related products and/or services together.

One of the major characteristics of the digital economy is the ability of businesses to personalize and customize products and services. Many e-businesses do this by offering their customers a customized collection of complementary goods and services. **Bundle trading** involves selling (auctioning) several related products or services together. For example, airline tickets, hotel rooms, rental cars, meals, and amusement park admission tickets can be *bundled* as a packaged leisure product. Some bundled products that are vertically related (e.g., a software product and a hardware product) may be provided by different vendors.

The management and operation of a bundle market is complex, and it differs considerably from those of single or double auction markets. For a discussion of the bundle market, see Wigand and Tan (2005) and Rezabakhsh et al. (2006).

PRICES IN AUCTIONS: HIGHER OR LOWER?

Compared with competitive (nonauction) markets, prices in forward auctions tend to be higher, reaching monopoly level when there is only one seller or one product, such as an old painting. In general, the auction seller is in a better position to maximize revenues than is the seller in a competitive market. When the auction seller is selling a product among multiple bidders, the expected price is often higher than in the competitive market.

However, in many instances, prices in auctions are lower. This may happen in cases of liquidation, in which the seller's objective is to sell as quickly as possible. For example, truckers or airlines selling unused capacity at the last minute usually do so at a lower price. Alternatively, buyers go to online global markets where they can get products more cheaply than those imported by intermediaries. In general, buyers expect online prices to be lower, and they compare prices at aggregating auction sites. Also, considering the fact that most C2C auctions are for used merchandise and many B2B auctions may include used or obsolete products, bargain prices are likely to prevail.

Finally, a more fundamental reason for lower online auction prices is that an online auction is usually an alternative selling channel rather than an exclusive selling arrangement. Therefore, buyers can always revert to physical markets if online bids exceed prices posted in physical markets. In short, few people in online auctions are willing to pay what they are expected to pay in physical markets or in online markets with fixed prices.

Pricing Strategies in Online Auctions

Both sellers and buyers may develop pricing strategies for online auctions. Sellers have the option to use different auction mechanisms, such as English, Dutch, sealed-bid first price, and sealed-bid second price. Buyers need to develop a strategy regarding how much to increase a bid and when to stop bidding. These topics are relevant to offline auctions as well and will not be dealt with here.

Section 10.5 ▶ REVIEW QUESTIONS

1. Describe double auction operations and pricing.
2. What is bundle trading?
3. Discuss the conditions under which prices in online auctions are higher or lower than prices in physical markets or in online with fixed prices.

10.6 BARTERING AND NEGOTIATING ONLINE

In addition to auctions, in which money is exchanged for goods, dynamic pricing can also take the form of online bartering. Also, prices in e-commerce can be arrived at through a process of negotiation.

BARTERING ONLINE

Bartering is an *exchange* of goods and services. The oldest method of trade, bartering today is usually conducted between organizations, but some individuals exchange goods and services as well. The problem with bartering is that it is often difficult to find partners. As discussed in Chapter 2, *bartering exchanges*, in which intermediaries arrange the matching and transactions, were created to address this problem.

Electronic bartering (e-bartering)—bartering conducted online, frequently in a bartering exchange—can improve the matching process by inducing more customers to take part in the exchange. Items that are frequently bartered electronically include office space, storage space, factory space, idle facilities and labor, surplus products, and banner ads. E-bartering may have tax implications that need to be considered.

Bartering Web sites include intagio.com, itex.com, u-exchange.com, and whosbartering.com. Bartering is popular today not only between organizations but also among individuals (e.g., see web-barter.com). A bartering matching service for professionals is available at barteryourservices.com.

Until recently, e-bartering matched only two individuals at a time who basically exchanged products or services (e.g., see PeerFlix, Bookins, and LaLa). However, Swaptree (swaptree.com) has developed a mechanism that enables up to four traders to exchange products or services in one transaction (initially CDs, videogames, books, and DVDs). The traders list what they have to give and what they need. Swaptree does the matching, assuming all

bartering
The *exchange* of goods and services.

electronic bartering (e-bartering)
Bartering conducted online, usually by a bartering exchange.

items have the same value. Swaptree.com provides the service for free and plans to make money from advertisements. For details, see Copeland (2006).

Consumer-to-Consumer Barter Exchanges

More and more individuals use the bartering method online. The following are some examples of bartering sites:

▶ **SwapVillage.** SwapVillage (swapvillage.com) offers a complete swapping service, from item listings to actual exchanges. Users can make a swap with their items, Village$ (SwapVillage's currency), or any combination of the two.

▶ **Nintari.** This site (nintari.net) is dedicated to bringing together millions of people on the Internet and facilitating the swap of durable entertainment goods such as video games and DVDs.

▶ **Trade Away.** Trade Away (tradeaway.com) offers consumers and businesses the opportunity to get value for their unused goods or services without the use of cash.

▶ **WebSwap.** WebSwap (webswap.com) matches swappers interested in exchanging goods, allowing use of money to equalize deals if necessary. In addition to swapping, users can buy and sell goods.

▶ **BarterBee.** (barterbee.com) users swap CDs, DVDs, and games.

▶ **Lala.com.** Lala.com helps people swap CDs. Sign-up is free. Just list the discs you're trying to peddle and draft a wish list of the discs you want. When another user requests one of your discs, Lala mails you a prepaid envelope to send it in. Once your disc is received, the first available disc on your wish list is sent to you. Lala charges $1 for every CD you receive and 49 cents for shipping; 20 percent of the trading revenue goes to the "Z" Foundation, a nonprofit founded by Lala.com to help working musicians obtain health care. Similar sites are Peerflix and Bookins.

▶ **Craigslist.org.** The barter option in craigslist.org enabled Kyle MacDonald to turn a paper clip into a house. See Case 10.2 for details. For additional sites, see Copeland (2006).

CASE 10.2
EC Application
TURNING A PAPER CLIP INTO A HOUSE

When Kyle McDonald told people about his idea, people thought that he had lost his mind. McDonald's idea was to trade a paper clip for something more valuable, and to do so many times until he traded for a house. His goal was to do it within one year. And indeed, he did it. Kyle was inspired by a childhood barter game called Bigger and Better, but this time he used e-commerce technology.

McDonald's first step was to post a message "for barter" on *craigslist.org* (Chapter 2). In 2 days, he bartered the paper clip for a fish-shaped pen, which he then swapped for a doorknob with a smiley face. The swapping continued, next to a Coleman camping stove.

To reach a larger audience, Kyle created a special Web site: *oneredpaperclip.com*, where he received more responses, as well as strange offers, ranging from body parts to souls. With some publicity in TV and newspapers, the offers kept coming. The camping stove was traded for a power generator, and with a few more trades he owned a snowmobile. By the time he had acquired a truck, he was getting closer to his goal. Soon, he received a half day with the rock legend Alice Cooper. Then his

trades concentrated in show-business ventures. Finally, after 14 trades, the town of Kipling, Saskatchewan, Canada, offered him a three-bedroom house for a speaking role in a new film.

Today, a swapping marketplace called SwapAce uses *oneredpaperclip.com.au* to advertise swapping, and Kyle McDonald uses *oneredpaperclip.com* as a blogging space.

Sources: Compiled from Anonymous (2006), *oneredpaperclip.com*, and CBC News (2006).

Questions

1. Is such a barter possible offline? Why or why not?
2. Why did Kyle use Craigslist.org to begin with, and why did he shift to a special Web site?
3. Speculate on why people are willing to swap and get items of lower monetary value?
4. Do you think that many people can conduct such a deal? Why or why not?

Many other variations of bartering exist both in B2B and C2C. Although many barters are done on a one-to-one basis, several bartering exchanges facilitate three-way (or four) trades. For example, see swaptree.com and Copland (2006).

NEGOTIATION AND BARGAINING

Dynamic prices also can be determined by **online negotiation**, a back-and-forth process of bargaining until a buyer and seller reach a mutually agreeable price. Negotiation is a well-known process in the offline world, especially for expensive or specialized products, such as real estate, automobiles, and jewelry. Negotiations also deal with nonpricing terms, such as shipment, warranties, payment methods, and credit. E-markets allow negotiations to be used for virtually all products and services. Three factors may facilitate negotiated prices (see Veit and Veit 2003): (1) intelligent agents that perform searches and comparisons; (2) computer technology that facilitates the negotiation process; and (3) bundling and customization of products.

Negotiation can take place in B2B, especially when large contracts are involved, and several companies have developed software support for such situations (see Chapters 5 and 6; e.g., ariba.com). Negotiation can take place in G2B (similar to B2B), and P2P transactions as well.

online negotiation
A back-and-forth electronic process of bargaining until the buyer and seller reach a mutually agreeable price; sometimes supported by software (intelligent) agents.

P2P Online Negotiations

A common phenomenon is negotiation between an individual buyer and seller. The seller can be a company or an individual. One such tool designed especially to support person-to-person negotiation is iOffer (ioffer.com). iOffer is a trading community based on negotiation; buyers can make offers on one or more items. Sellers can accept, change, or decline offers. Buyers get a good price. Sellers get the price they want. See Internet Exercise 16 to learn the details about this tool.

Technologies for Electronic Bargaining

According to Choi and Whinston (2000), negotiation and bargaining involve a bilateral interaction between a seller and a buyer who are engaged in the following five-step process that is necessary to complete a transaction:

1. **Search.** Bargaining starts with the collection of all relevant information about products and sellers or buyers. Computer-mediated markets excel in raising the search efficiency. (Search tools are described in Chapters 3 and 4.)

2. **Selection.** Selection filters retrieve screened information that helps the buyer and seller determine what to buy (sell) and from whom to buy (sell). This filtering process encompasses the purchasing evaluation of products and seller alternatives, based on consumer-provided criteria such as price, warranty, availability, delivery time, and reputation. The screening/selection process results in a set of names of products and partners to negotiate with in the next step. Software agents, such as Pricemix (bizrate.com), and other tools can facilitate the selection (see Chapter 4).

3. **Negotiation.** The negotiation stage focuses on establishing the terms of the transaction, such as price, product quality, delivery, and payment terms. Negotiation varies in duration and complexity depending on products, partners, economy, and the market. In online markets, all stages of negotiation can be carried out by automated programs or software agents (see Appendix C at the book's Web site).

Negotiation agents are software programs that make independent decisions to make bids within predetermined constraints or to accept or reject offers. The agents may be bound by negotiation rules or protocols that control how sellers and buyers interact. For example, price negotiation may start with a seller's list price as a starting point, or it may start with any bid or offer depending on the rule. For an overview of electronic negotiation and comparison, see Cellich and Jain (2003).

4. **Continuing Selection and Negotiation.** The previous steps are repeated sequentially, if necessary, until an agreement is reached and a contract is written.

5. **Transaction Completion.** After product, vendor, and price are determined, the final step is to complete the transaction. This involves online payment and product delivery in accordance with the terms determined in the negotiation phase. Other characteristics, such as customer service, warranty, and refunds, also may be implemented.

Negotiating tools can be used for a number of applications; for example, a factory-floor-scheduling domain, where different companies in a subcontracting web negotiate over a joint scheduling problem, and an airport resource management domain, where negotiations take place for the servicing of airplanes between flights. Another application is to optimize the negotiation considering constraints such as the company's employee turnover rate. In this approach, a sales schedule is developed dynamically by all of the concerned participants. The negotiation methodology enables agents to negotiate with other agents in a certain geographical area based on their sales capacity, commission percentage, and the area's sales turnover. For details, see Protogeros et al. (2006). For bargaining mechanisms, see Sim (2006).

The following are the major *benefits* of electronic negotiations:

▶ Buyers and sellers do not need to determine prices beforehand and, therefore, do not have to engage in the difficult process of collecting relevant information. Negotiating prices transfers the burden of determining prices (i.e., market valuation) to the market itself. Insofar as the market process is efficient, the resulting negotiated prices will be fair and effective.

▶ Intelligent agents can negotiate both price and nonprice attributes, such as delivery time, return policy, and other transactions that add value. In addition, intelligent agents can deal with multiple partners (see Appendix C at the book's Web site). An example of such an application is negotiation among several freight dispatch centers of different companies to solve their vehicle routing problems.

Section 10.6 ▶ REVIEW QUESTIONS

1. What are the major reasons for e-bartering?
2. List the factors that may facilitate price negotiation.
3. Discuss the benefits of electronic negotiation.
4. What are the five steps of online negotiation?
5. Describe the role of software agents in negotiation.

10.7 E-AUCTION FRAUD AND ITS PREVENTION

According to the National Consumers League (nclnet.org), McKay (2003), and NCL's National Fraud Information Center (2004), of all of the e-commerce activities conducted over the Internet, fraud was the most prevalent and serious in e-auctions until 2005. The U.S. Fraud Complaint Center says that the median dollar loss per auction fraud was $225 in the first half of 2001 but jumped to $489 in the second half of the year, as criminals evidently focused on high-tech, big-ticket items (Lee 2002) and to $803 in 2004 (National Fraud Information Center 2006). In 2003, auction fraud was 35 to 40 percent more prevalent than in 2002, judging from the reported 400 frauds at any given time, as compared with 250 in 2002 (Sullivan 2003). However, in 2005 identity theft became the major problem (37 percent of all complaints), and auctions moved to second place (12 percent). See *ftc.gov* (2006). According to Hearn (2005), almost 50 percent of all eBay users have had problems, and 39 percent of those affected complain that their problems have never been resolved.

TYPES OF E-AUCTION FRAUD

bid shielding

Having phantom bidders bid at a very high price when an auction begins; they pull out at the last minute, and the real bidder who bid a much lower price wins.

Fraud may be conducted by sellers, buyers, or others (for a list, see ftc.gov/bcp/pubsauctions.htm). The following are some examples of fraud; some are unique to e-auctions; others can be found in any type of EC.

Bid Shielding. The use of phantom bidders to bid at a very high price when an auction begins is called **bid shielding**. The phantom bidders pull out at the last minute, and the bidder (friend of the phantom bidder) who bids with a very low price wins. The bogus bidders were the shields, protecting the low bid of the real bidder in the stack by scaring off other real bidders.

Shilling. A similar type of fraud can be conducted by sellers. In this fraud, called **shilling**, sellers arrange to have fake bids placed on their items (either by associates or by using multiple user IDs) to artificially jack up bids. If they see that the legitimate high bid does not meet their expectations as the end of an auction draws near, they might pop in to sell the item to themselves. This way they can put the item up again for auction, attempting to get a higher price next time.

shilling
Placing fake bids on auction items to artificially jack up the bidding price.

Fake Photos and Misleading Descriptions. In reaching for bidders' attention, some sellers distort what they can truly sell or fail to disclose all relevant information about the item(s). Borrowed images, ambiguous descriptions, and falsified facts are some of the tactics that sellers might employ to convey a false impression of the item.

Improper Grading Techniques. The grading of items is one of the most hotly debated issues among buyers and sellers. A seller might describe an item as 90 percent new, whereas the bidder, after receiving the item and paying the full amount, feels that it is only 70 percent new. Condition is often in the eye of the beholder. Although many grading systems have been devised and put to use, condition is still subject to interpretation.

Bid Siphoning. Luring bidders to leave a legitimate auction by offering to sell the "same" item at a lower price. The buyer then loses protections offered by the auction site, such as insurance, guarantees, quality, and so on.

Selling Reproductions as Originals. A seller sells something that the seller claims is original, but it turns out to be a reproduction.

Failure to Pay. Buyers do not pay after a deal is agreed upon.

Failure to Pay the Auction House. Sometimes sellers fail to pay the auction's listing or transaction fees.

High Shipping Costs and Handling Fees. Some sellers just want to get a little more cash out of bidders. Postage and handling rates vary from seller to seller. Some charge excessive rates to cover the cost of packaging supplies, "handling" costs, or other overhead intangibles.

Failure to Ship Merchandise. This is the old collect-and-run routine. Money was paid out, but the merchandise never arrives. A lesser problem is failure to deliver on time.

Loss and Damage Claims. Buyers claim that they did not receive an item or that they received it in damaged condition and then ask for a refund. In some cases, they might be trying to get a freebie. The seller sometimes cannot prove whether the item ever arrived or whether it was in perfect condition when shipped.

Fake Escrow Services. Presenting itself as an independent trusted third party, a fake service will take the seller's items and the buyer's money and disappear.

Switch and Return. The seller has successfully auctioned an item, but when the buyer receives it, the buyer is not satisfied. The seller offers a cheerful refund. However, what the seller gets back is a mess that does not much resemble the item that was originally shipped. Some buyers may attempt to swap out their junk for someone else's jewels.

Other Frauds. Many other types of fraud also are possible, including the sale of stolen goods, the use of false identities, providing false contact information, and selling the same item to several buyers.

For more about auction frauds see Gavish and Tucci (2006), ftc.gov, and scambusters.org.

PROTECTING AGAINST E-AUCTION FRAUD

The largest Internet auctioneer, eBay, has introduced several measures in an effort to reduce fraud. Some are free; others are not. The company has succeeded in its goal: less than one-tenth of 1 percent of the transactions at eBay were fraudulent in 2001 (Konrad 2002). The following are some of eBay's antifraud measures.

User Identity Verification. eBay uses the services of Equifax to verify user identities for a $5 fee. Verified eBay User, a voluntary program, encourages users to supply eBay with information for online verification. By offering their Social Security number, driver's license number, and date of birth, users can qualify for the highest level of verification on eBay.

Authentication Service. Product authentication is a way of determining whether an item is genuine and described appropriately. Authentication is very difficult to perform because it relies on the expertise of the authenticators. Because of their training and experience, experts can (for a fee) often detect counterfeits based on subtle details. However, two expert authenticators may have different opinions about the authenticity of the same item. eBay has links to companies that provide this specialized service.

Grading Services. Grading is a way of determining the physical condition of an item, such as "poor quality" or "mint condition." The actual grading system depends on the type of item being graded. Different items have different grading systems—for example, trading cards are graded from A1 to F1, whereas coins are graded from poor to perfect uncirculated. For a tutorial on grading diamonds, see bluenile.com.

Feedback Forum. The eBay Feedback Forum allows registered buyers and sellers to build up their online trading reputations (see Insights and Additions 10.3). (Each eBay member has a feedback score.) It provides users with the ability to comment on their experiences with other individuals.

Insurance Policy. eBay offers insurance underwritten by Lloyd's of London. Users are covered up to $200, with a $25 deductible. The program is provided at no cost to eBay users. Supplementary insurance is available from companies such as AuctionInsurance.com. At other auction sites, such as amazon.com/auctions, some insurance is provided, but extra insurance may be needed.

Escrow Services. For items valued at more than $200 or when either the buyer or seller feels the need for additional security, eBay recommends escrow services (for a fee). With an easy-to-access link to a third-party escrow service, both partners in a deal are protected. The buyer mails the payment to the escrow service, which verifies the payment and alerts the seller when everything checks out. At that point, the seller ships the goods to the buyer. After an agreed-upon inspection period, the buyer notifies the service, which then sends a check to the seller. eBay, Yahoo!, and other large online auction sites provide their own escrow services. (Examples of a third-party provider of online escrow services can be found at i-escrow.com and fortis-escrow.com.) For details on how escrow services work for auctions, see auctions.yahoo.com and ftc.gov.

Nonpayment Punishment. eBay implemented a policy against those who do not honor their winning bids. To help protect sellers, a first-time nonpayment by a buyer results in a friendly warning. A sterner warning is issued for a second-time offense, a 30-day suspension for a third offense, and indefinite suspension for a fourth offense.

Appraisal Services. Appraisers use a variety of methods to appraise items, including expert assessment of authenticity and condition and reviewing what comparable items have sold for in the marketplace in recent months. An appraised value is usually accurate only at the time of appraisal. Eppraisals.com (eppraisals.com) offers users access to over 700 experts and a selection of online appraisal services that are located throughout eBay's categories of fine art, antiques, and collectibles, as well as on eBay Premier.

Physical Inspection. Providing for a physical inspection can eliminate many problems. This is especially true for collectors' items. When the seller and buyer are in the same vicinity, it is easy to arrange for such inspections. eBay offers inspection services on a regional basis, so buyers can arrange for nearby inspections.

Item Verification. One way of confirming the identity and evaluating the condition of an item is through verification. With verification, neutral third parties will evaluate and identify an item through a variety of means. For example, some collectors have their item "DNA tagged" for identification purposes. This provides a way of tracking an item if it changes ownership in the future. In addition to the antifraud measures discussed here, one can use the general EC fraud protection measures suggested in Chapters 11 and 17, at ftc.gov, and at infofaq.com (see online auctions).

Buyer Protections. The PayPal Protection Program shields buyers by covering up to $500 of their purchase at no additional cost. The eBay Standard Purchase Protection Program provides up to $200 coverage (minus a $25 processing cost) for items that are not received or items that are not as described in the listing.

Spoof (Fraudulent) Web Site Protection. The eBay Toolbar with Account Guard enables eBay members to protect their accounts by indicating when they are on an eBay or PayPal site.

eBay Security Center. The eBay Security Center provides guidance on buying safely, selling safely, and paying safely, as well as valuable third-party, government, and law-enforcement resources. The Security Center is a valuable resource for all users, from first-time buyers who want information on safeguarding online transactions to high-volume sellers who want to protect their copyrights. It also offers a dispute resolution service.

For more on eBay's antifraud and security efforts, see eBay (2006), Gavish and Tucci (2006), Hof (2005), and Kobler et al. 2005.

Insights and Additions 10.3 Analysis Predicts Auction Fraud

At online auction sites like eBay, buyers rate their transaction experiences with sellers, thereby recording fraudsters. This information is used to warn other buyers. However, savvy fraudsters get around it by conducting fake transactions with friends, friends of friends, or even themselves, using alternate user names. This way they can give themselves high satisfaction ratings, so unsuspecting buyers will buy from them.

To fight such fraud, researchers at Carnegie Mellon University (CMU) developed intelligent software called NetProbe that looks for patterns of users who have repeated dealings with one another. Based on the analysis, they can identify those who are likely to conduct fake transactions and alert honest buyers.

To develop the software, CMU researchers analyzed over 1 million transactions involving 66,000 eBay users.

The software is being improved and will be available for use in spring 2007. Finding those fraudsters who make positive recommendations for each other may not be 100 percent correct. The software points to those who are "likely" to commit fraud, but it may also point to innocent sellers who repeatedly buy from one another (e.g., baseball card collectors).

According to eBay, protecting more than 212 million users from fraud is top priority, and any innovation in this area is welcomed. For further details, see CMU (2006).

Source: Carnegie Mellon University, "Carnegie Mellon Researchers Uncover Online Auction Fraud: Data Mining Software Finger Both Perpetrators and Accomplices." December 5, 2006. *news.cs.cmu.edu/ Releases/demo/257.html* (accessed December 2006).

Section 10.7 ▶ REVIEW QUESTIONS

1. What types of fraud can be perpetuated by sellers?
2. What types of fraud can be perpetuated by buyers?
3. What kinds of protections exist for sellers?
4. What kinds of protections exist for buyers?

10.8 ISSUES IN E-AUCTION IMPLEMENTATION

Implementing auctions may not be a simple task, and for this reason many companies use intermediaries. This section presents some issues that are relevant to auction implementation and use.

USING INTERMEDIARIES

Any seller can auction from a Web site. The question is: Will the buyers come? A similar issue was raised in Chapter 3: Should sellers sell from their own storefront, join an online mall, or use another third-party arrangement?

Large companies often choose to auction from their own Web sites. If their name is well recognized, they can feel some assurance that buyers will come. Chapter 5 presented the example of GM's selling obsolete equipment from its site. Governments and large corporations also are using reverse auctions from their sites for procurement purposes. Some individuals even conduct auctions from their own Web sites.

However, most individuals, SMEs, and many large companies use third-party intermediaries whose charges are fairly low compared with the charges in physical auctions and who provide many services that are critical to the success of auctions.

The following are some of the popular third-party auction sites:

▶ **General sites.** Such sites include eBay, auctions.amazon.com, auctions.yahoo.com, bidz.com, auctions.overstock.com, and ubid.com.

▶ **Specialized sites.** Such sites are focused on a particular industry or product; examples include americanautobargains.com and autocastle.com (cars), baseball-cards.com, teletrad.com (coins), and oldandsold.com (antiques).

▶ **B2B-oriented sites.** Such sites are focused on B2B transactions; examples include asset-auctions.com and liquidation.com.

TRADING ASSISTANTS

To encourage people to auction online, eBay and some other auction sites provide trading assistants, as described in Insights and Additions 10.4.

AUCTION RULES

The success of auctions depends on complying with auction rules. These rules are intended to smooth the auction mechanism and to prevent fraud. Wurman (2001) divides the rules into three major categories: bidding rules, clearing rules, and information-revelation rules. These rules are provided by Wurman (2001) and by the U.S. Federal government at ftc.gov/bcp/online/pubs/online/auctions.htm. The rules provide definitions, restrictions, and timing constraints.

Auction rules may vary from country to country due to legal considerations. They may also vary within a country due to the nature of the items auctioned, the auctioneer's policies, and the nature of competition among the auction houses.

STRATEGIC ISSUES

When a company decides to use auctions as a sales channel, it must make several important strategic decisions, such as which items (services) to auction; what type of auction to use; whether to do the auction in-house or to use an auctioneer (and which one); how long to run each auction; how to set the initial prices; how to accept a bid; what increments to allow in the bidding; and what information to disclose to the participants (e.g., the names of bidders, the current prices, etc.). For help in making such decisions, see Becherer and Halstead (2004).

One of the strategic issues in B2B is the potential conflict with existing distributors and distribution channels. Therefore, some companies use auctions only to liquidate obsolete, used, refurbished, or damaged products.

Insights and Additions 10.4 Using Trading Assistants at eBay

What if a person wants to sell on eBay but is not familiar with computers? What if an escrow service is needed? What if items need to be picked up? eBay provides a complete solution called Trading Assistants that helps people sell their items on eBay. To execute this service, eBay has trading assistants (or advisors) in many cities (and even countries).

What do eBay's trading assistants do? A trading assistant will pick up the items to be sold. The total value of the items to be auctioned must be $200, and there is a minimum value of $50 per item. The trading assistant will store the items, and the items are insured. The trading assistant will prepare photos and offer the seller suggestions on how to advertise the items.

The assistant will list the items on eBay's auction site. Auctions last 7 to 10 days. If an item does not sell, it is relisted, and it is auctioned again (twice). If the item does not sell after the second auction listing, the seller can lower the minimum acceptable price or pick up the item. After successful completion of the auction, the trading assistant packs and ships the item and collects the money from buyers.

Trading Assistant provides the following benefits:

- **Saves time and effort.** The Trading Assistant handles every aspect of selling an item on eBay, from listing the item to shipping it to the buyer.
- **Takes advantage of selling expertise.** All Trading Assistants have experience selling on eBay and are in good standing in the eBay community. Many of them specialize in certain categories and know how to sell an item for maximum value.
- **Makes sellers money.** When an item sells, the Trading Assistant passes the profit on to the seller (after taking out fees).

The Trading Assistant will collect payment from the buyer, deduct any fees, and pass the money on to the seller. Trading Assistants receive a commission of the sale price. The commission normally is 25 percent, and the seller pays only after the item sells. eBay employs tens of thousands of trading assistants. Some of them earn $100,000 to $150,000 a year in commissions. By selling an item on eBay, a seller is able to reach about 120 million potential buyers. Of course, sellers can do everything themselves and pay little commission. For more information on eBay's Trading Assistant service, see *pages.ebay.com/tradingassistants*.

AUCTIONS IN EXCHANGES

Chapter 6 mentioned that exchanges are using auctions to supplement their regular buying/selling channels. An example of such an auction is provided in Case 10.3.

INFRASTRUCTURE FOR E-AUCTIONS

Auction sites can be built as special, independent buy-side systems, integrated with sell-side or buy-side systems, or run over the Internet or private lines.

Building Auction Sites

The process of building auction applications is complex for two reasons. First, as shown in Exhibit 10.5, the number of needed features can be very large. Second, in the case of B2B auctions, auctions must be integrated with the back-end offices and with the legacy systems of participating companies. Exhibit 10.6 shows a sample integrated auction process. Because of these two complexities, even large companies typically outsource the construction of auction sites.

AUCTIONS ON PRIVATE NETWORKS

Electronic auctions that run on private networks have been in use for about 20 years. Chapter 6 introduced the flower market in the Netherlands as a B2B example of an auction on a private network. The following are additional B2B examples of auctions on private networks.

Pigs in Singapore and Taiwan

The auctioning of pigs in Singapore and Taiwan has been conducted over private networks for over 15 years (see Neo 1992). Farmers bring the pigs to one area where they are

---

CASE 10.3
EC Application
ONLINE GRAPES AND WINE AUCTIONS

The wine industry is hundreds of years old, consisting of established associations between grape growers and wineries. Typically, vintners have multiyear buying contracts with growers. The adoption of the Internet to facilitate the trading of grapes was slow, but in March 2001, 2,000 tons of grapes were traded in the first of many online grape auctions.

The WineryExchange (*wineryexchange.com*), based in Novato, California, conducted the first online grape auction. "In the past, most of the deals have been cut on the tailgate of a truck," said Doug Wilson, director of grower relations at Fetzer Vineyards, producer of 4 million cases of wine each year. His company was among some 30 buyers who intended to make $10 to $50 bottles of wine from the "super premium" grapes to be offered by 36 California coastal growers.

Unfortunately, WineryExchange had to stop auctioning grapes because it became uneconomical to manage such auctions. It has changed into an information portal for the grape-grower community. It also is a storefront for wine sellers.

Selling wines, especially antique ones, online is very popular. Although regular wines are sold via catalogs, antique, expensive wines are selling at auction much of the time. WineBid conducts auctions regularly for wine collectors (see the Auction Index at *winebid.com*). Such auctions are usually of a C2B type. If a buyer finds what he or she wants and the price is right, the buyer can track the lot (12-bottle case) or an individual bottle and see current bids before placing a new one. For instructions, see "Buying" at *winebid.com*. Several other types of wine auctions exist, including forward B2C and C2C auctions at eBay.

Sources: Compiled from Reuters (2001), *wineryexchange.com* (accessed November 2006), and *winebid.com* (accessed November 2006).

Questions

1. What drives auctions in the winery exchange?
2. Enter *winebid.com* and find how auctions are conducted.
3. Why is the C2B model successful?
4. Find other sites that auction wines and compare them with *winebid.com*.

EXHIBIT 10.5 **Components of a Comprehensive Auction Site**

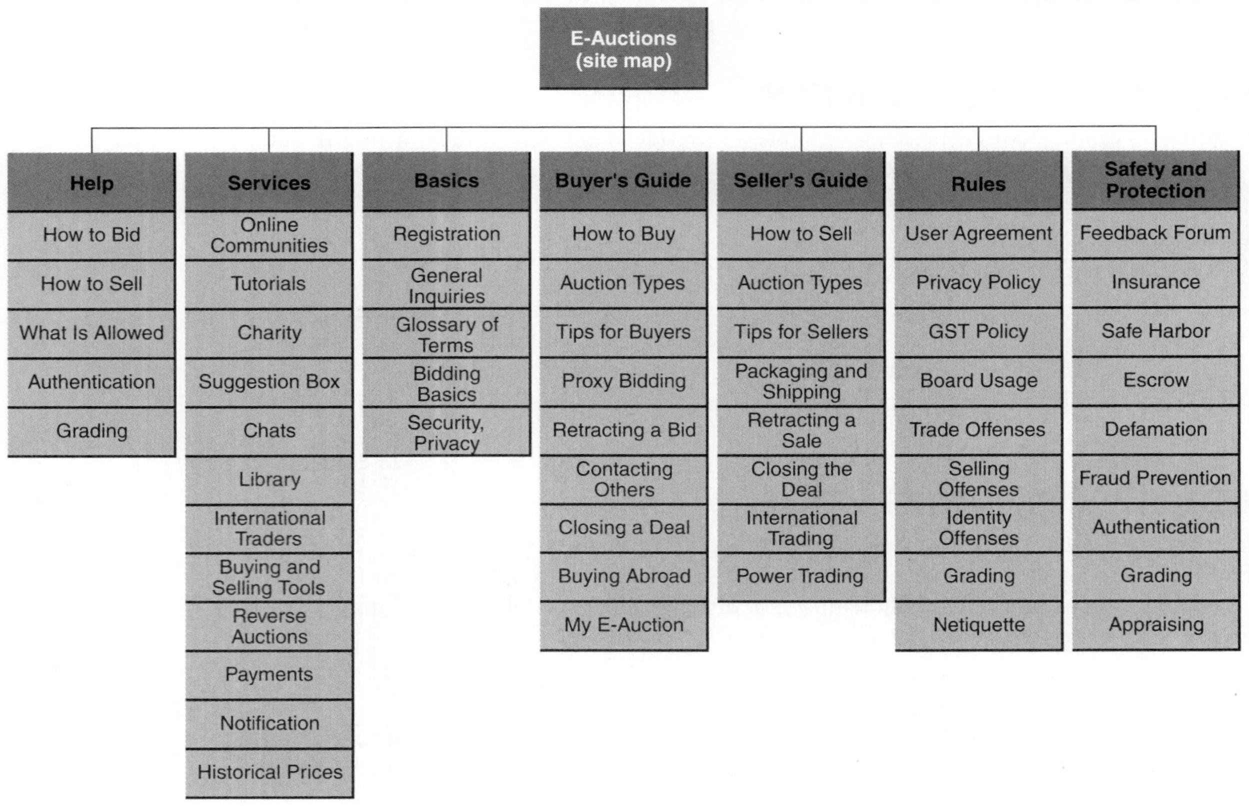

E-Auctions (site map)
Help
How to Bid
How to Sell
What Is Allowed
Authentication
Grading
Services
Online Communities
Tutorials
Charity
Suggestion Box
Chats
Library
International Traders
Buying and Selling Tools
Reverse Auctions
Payments
Notification
Historical Prices
Basics
Registration
General Inquiries
Glossary of Terms
Bidding Basics
Security, Privacy
Buyer's Guide
How to Buy
Auction Types
Tips for Buyers
Proxy Bidding
Retracting a Bid
Contacting Others
Closing a Deal
Buying Abroad
My E-Auction
Seller's Guide
How to Sell
Auction Types
Tips for Sellers
Packaging and Shipping
Retracting a Sale
Closing the Deal
International Trading
Power Trading
Rules
User Agreement
Privacy Policy
GST Policy
Board Usage
Trade Offenses
Selling Offenses
Identity Offenses
Grading
Netiquette
Safety and Protection
Feedback Forum
Insurance
Safe Harbor
Escrow
Defamation
Fraud Prevention
Authentication
Grading
Appraising

EXHIBIT 10.6 **Integrated Auction Business Process**

Business Rules
Customers
Inventory Management
Items–offline
Items
Prices
Buying Trends
E-Commerce
Online Auction
Items
Price
Bidding Habits
Bidding Trends
Customer Data
Purchases
Accounting System

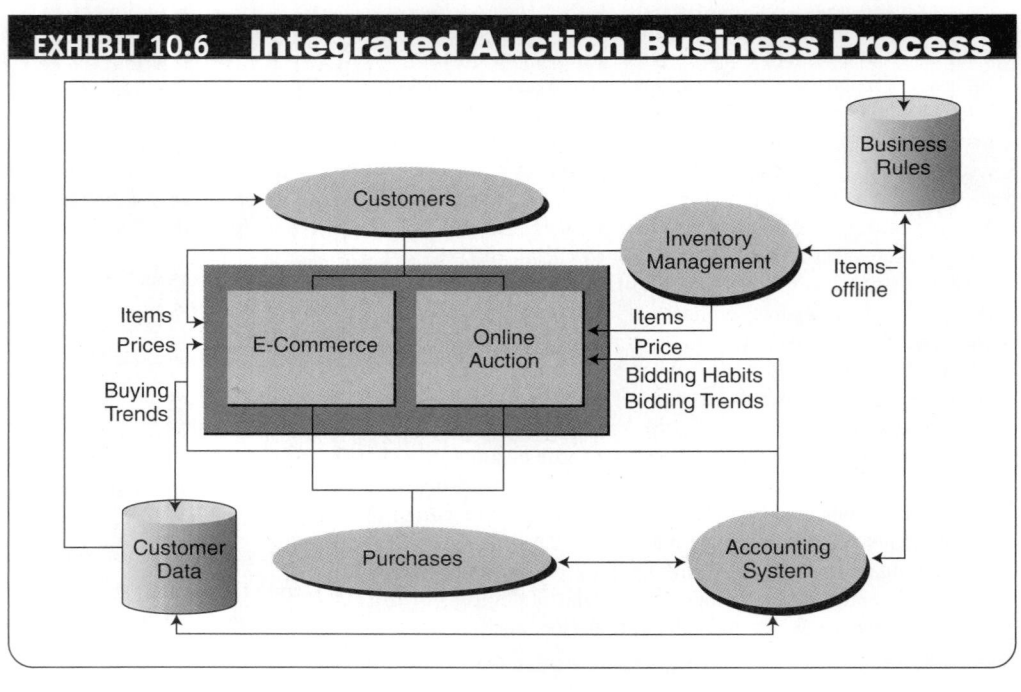

washed, weighed, and prepared for display. The pigs are auctioned (via a forward auction) one at a time while the data on each pig are displayed to approved bidders who bid by watching a displayed price. If bids are submitted, the price can be increased incrementally only by 20 cents per kilogram. The process continues until no further bids occur. The bidders' financial capability is monitored by a computer. (The computer verifies that the bidder has available funds in the prepaid account that was opened for the auction.) The process is illustrated in Exhibit 10.7.

EXHIBIT 10.7 Auctioning Pigs in Singapore

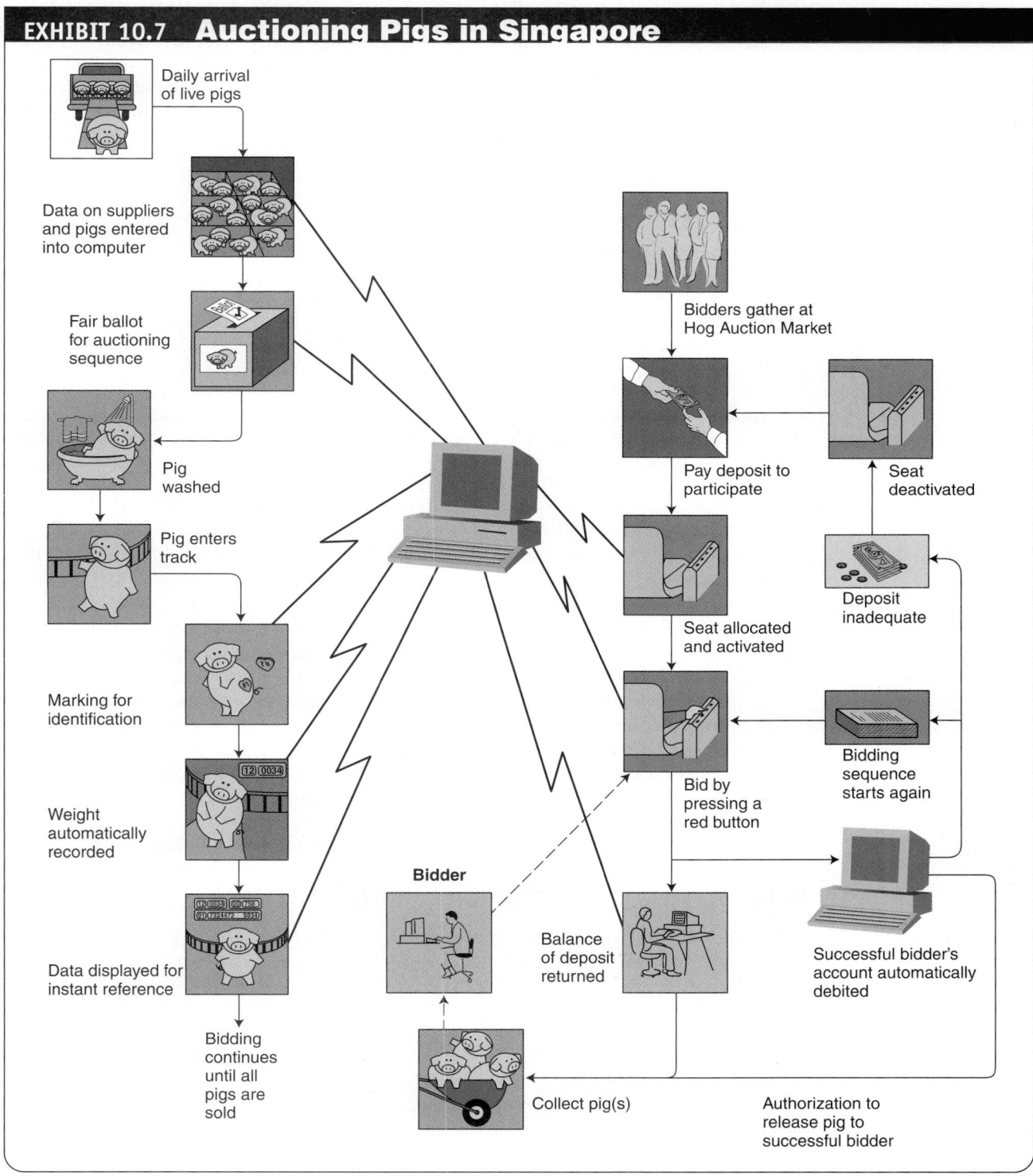

Livestock Auctions in Australia

Computer Aided Livestock Marketing (CALM) is an online system for trading cattle and sheep that has been in operation since 1986. In contrast with the pig-auctioning system in Singapore, livestock do not have to travel to CALM, a feature that lowers stress in the animals and reduces sellers' costs. The buyers use PCs or Vt100 terminals to connect to the auction. The system also handles payments to farmers.

The original system is now operating as Auctions Plus. A second system, the Saleyards livestock marketing system (saleyards.com.au), facilitates direct sales between independent agents and producers, which account for the majority of Australian livestock sales. Auctions Plus runs auctions that are listed on a regular basis and are viewable through a single activity screen; Saleyards operates an online advertising display system with the future ability for online trading. Its power lies in automated, active direct matching between buyers and sellers who list stock availability and requirements. Saleyards works directly with livestock producers (farmers) and agents, with the goal of saving all participants involved time and money; Auctions Plus operates mainly along the lines of the traditional agent-facilitated sales. For further details, see Answers.com (2007).

Section 10.8 ▶ REVIEW QUESTIONS

1. What are the reasons for using auction intermediaries?
2. What types of intermediaries exist?
3. List some of the necessary auction rules.
4. List major strategic issues in conducting B2B auctions.
5. Describe auctions that run on private networks.

10.9 MOBILE E-AUCTIONS AND THE FUTURE OF AUCTIONS

There were 420 million Internet users in 2000; the number topped 1 billion in mid-2005. The expected number for 2011 is 2 billion (per Computer Industry Almanac 2006 and eTForecasts 2006). Of those users, 44 percent in 12 key global markets browsed the Internet wirelessly in 2004 (European Travel Commission 2004). Forecasts by such agencies as Ipsos-Insights predict strong growth of wireless Web usage because for many new Internet users the cell phone may be their only Internet access device (reported by the European Travel Commission 2004).

Because mobile phones and other wireless devices could be the primary way that people access the Internet, large-volume m-commerce may result. In response, many auction sites are implementing m-commerce applications.

In the United States, eBay went wireless in October 1999 (eBay Anywhere), and uBid followed in 2000. Yahoo!, Amazon.com, and other auction sites provide wireless access to auctions. In the United Kingdom, BlueCycle (bluecycle.com), which conducts used car auctions for dealers, allows dealers to use their cell phones to bid from anywhere. Many auctions notify both buyers and sellers with SMS alerts at different stages of the bidding progress (e.g., eBay and Amazon.com).

The use of cell phones for online auctions presents a number of benefits and some limitations.

BENEFITS AND LIMITATIONS OF MOBILE AUCTIONS

The *benefits* of mobile auctions are as follows:

▶ **Convenience and ubiquity.** People can conduct auction business on the go and from any location via a mobile phone. One can auction anything from anywhere and search for information even in the middle of a discussion around a café table. Bids can be checked on the run.

▶ **Privacy.** The Internet cell phone is more private than a PC. Cell phone users can conduct business away from prying eyes; thus, participation in an auction can take place in a secure and private environment.

> ▶ **Simpler and faster.** Because online auctions require a limited amount of information, it is relatively easy to adapt Internet-enabled phones to display auction information, even if they can only handle limited bandwidth and data.

The *limitations* of mobile auctions are as follows:

> ▶ **Visual quality.** Portable devices are small and may have a problem showing pictures of auction items. One solution is provided by Sony. In 2004, the company started mass production of full-color OLED (organic light emitting diode) displays for use in a wide range of portable devices. The OLED technology provides a brighter and thinner screen that offers faster response time and better contrast. This improvement to smaller screens enhances wireless Internet use (Kallender 2004).
>
> ▶ **Memory capacity.** Internet-enabled phones have limited memory capacity. In the near future, the development of new WAP services will probably press hardware producers to come up with better memory systems for mobile terminals.
>
> ▶ **Security.** Wireless systems are not as safe as wireline ones. These security issues, such as protecting personal data transmitted via wireless communications and avoiding computer viruses, must be addressed. As of 2006, new security standards, such as SIM Toolkit and WTLS, were still evolving. For further details, see en.Wikipedia.org/wiki/IEEE_802.11.

See Chapter 9 for more on these and other benefits and limitations of m-commerce.

THE FUTURE OF E-AUCTIONS

The online auction industry is growing. The following are areas of potential growth.

Global Auctions

Many of the auction companies that sell products and services on the Web are extending their reach. One way to do so is by going global. However, companies that seek to serve the international market may face all the regular problems of selling online in foreign countries (see Chapter 14). Therefore, companies such as eBay are acquiring auction companies in other countries. In 2006, eBay, for example, transferred its auction business in China to tom.com.

Wireless Auctions

The use of mobile auctions is increasing rapidly due to support from eBay and other auction sites. For example, in 2006 eBay introduced eBay Alerts, an extension of eBay Wireless, which enables wireless device users to access eBay listings. eBay Alerts provides wireless device users with eBay listing updates through phone calls, text messages, and instant messages and enables users to bid on auction-style listings from their wireless devices. eBay Alerts helps mobile customers by driving more demand to the sellers and making it easier for buyers to stay involved in the auction process before an item listing closes.

eBay buyers can elect to receive a phone call alerting them that 3 minutes remain before a listing ends. The service gives buyers an easy and convenient way to check an item's status or place bids by phone. This feature was rolled out as a pilot program. The phone call alerts are powered by UnWired Buyer, which provides the event-triggered, voice-based e-commerce platform.

Similarly, buyers can now receive "outbid" and "item ending soon" alerts using AOL Instant Messenger, Yahoo! Messenger, or MSN Messenger for any of the items they are bidding on. This service also is available via Skype. As a part of this free notification service, eBay sends a link leading back to the item on eBay, where buyers can increase their bid if they wish.

Selling Art Online in Real-Time Auctions

As of January 2001, collectors in the United Kingdom were able to bid online for the first time in live showroom auctions using an application provided by eBay and Icollector.com (icollector.com). Icollector.com provides real-time access to 300 independent auction houses, such as the United Kingdom's Charter House Auctioneers and Valuers. Christie's has an online site, but as of winter 2002, it was not allowing online bidding for live showroom auctions. In the United States, Butterfields (butterfields.com) allows for real-time auction bidding and has a relationship with eBay. Butterfields.com has been purchased by Bonhams but will continue to sell through eBay's Live Auctions feature, allowing online bidders to participate in auctions at traditional auction houses in real time. See Mirapaul (2001) to find out how individual artists use Internet auctions.

Strategic Alliances

Auctions may have a major impact on competition and on industry structure because they put sellers and buyers together more directly, cutting out intermediaries. In addition, auctions may be used as a strategic tool by both online and offline companies. An example of such a strategy is provided in Online File W10.4, which describes an online auction site in Australia that enables SMEs to offer heavily discounted merchandise to consumers. It appears that this type of strategic alliance will be very popular in the future due to its win–win possibilities.

Section 10.9 ▶ REVIEW QUESTIONS

1. Describe the benefits of wireless auctions.
2. Describe the limitations of wireless auctions.
3. Describe the future of global auctions.
4. Describe auctioning of art on the Internet.
5. Why are strategic alliances used in auctions?

MANAGERIAL ISSUES

Some managerial issues related to this chapter are as follows:

1. **Should we have our own auction site or use a third-party site?** This is a strategic issue, and there are pluses and minuses to each alternative. If you decide to auction from your site, you will need to advertise and attract visitors, which may be expensive. Also, you will need to install fraud-prevention mechanisms and provide services. Either way, you may need to consider connectivity to your back-office and logistics system.

2. **What are the costs and benefits of auctions?** A major strategic issue is whether you need to do auctions. Auctions do have risks, and in forward auctions you may create conflicts with your other distribution channels. In addition, auctions may change the manner in which companies sell their products. They also may change the nature of competition in certain industries, as well as price and margin levels. Therefore, conducting a cost-benefit analysis is essential.

3. **What auction strategies would we use?** Selecting an auction mechanism, pricing, and bidding strategy can be very complex for sellers. These strategies determine the success of the auction and the ability to attract and retain visitors on the site. Management should understand and carefully assess the options.

4. **What about support services?** Auctions require support services, such as those for escrow service, payment, and delivery. Decisions about how to provide them and to what extent to use business partners are critical to the success of repeated high-volume auctions. An efficient payment mechanism is also essential for auctions, especially when the buyers or sellers are individuals. Some innovative methods can solve the payment problem.

5. **What would we auction?** Both individuals and companies would like to auction everything. However, is it ethical or even legal to do it? Ask eBay, which is trying, for example, to clean up pornographic auctions by

banning some items and directing some items into a "mature audiences" area. Another issue is pirated software, which is offered on about 2,000 auction sites worldwide. As a matter of fact, eBay was sued in 2000 by videogame manufacturers Nintendo, Sega, and Electronic Arts. eBay immediately began working with software companies and other owners of intellectual property to halt the sale of pirated items (Wolverton 2000).

6. **What is the best bartering strategy?** Bartering can be an interesting strategy, especially for companies that have limited cash and have some surpluses. However, the valuation of what is bought or sold may be difficult, and the tax implications in some countries are not clear. Nevertheless, e-bartering can be rewarding and should be considered as an alternative to regular auctions.

7. **How can we promote our auction?** By monitoring what is going on in auctions (e.g., what people like, how much bidders are willing to pay, etc.), both sellers and auctioneers can foster selling strategy. Sometimes auctions bring very high prices to sellers. Auction houses such as eBay do analyses to determine advertising strategy for their business.

8. **Should we combine auctions with other models?** Consider combining auctions with other EC models. For example, group purchasing is often combined with a reverse auction once orders are aggregated.

RESEARCH TOPICS

Here are some suggested topics related to this chapter. For details, references, and additional topics, refer to the Online Appendix A "Current EC Research."

1. **E-Auctions, Negotiation, and Dynamic Pricing**
   - Types of negotiation and the contract process
   - Using software agents and methods of automating negotiation
   - Concepts, architectures, and protocols of negotiation
   - Effect of the seller's size in Internet auctions
   - Effect of dynamic pricing on Internet trading

2. **Measurement of the Effect of E-Auctions and Applications**
   - Framework of estimating the benefits of using e-auctions
   - Social and entertainment effects of online auctions
   - Importance of reputation in closing prices of online auction sites
   - Relationship between products, auction rules, and trading types
   - Experimental investigation of online electric power auctions

3. **Measurement Performance of Complex Auctions**
   - Performance of multiattribute auctions
   - Performance of multi-item auctions
   - Performance of Vickrey second-price auctions
   - Winner determination methods for combinatorial auctions
   - Algorithms to reduce the computational complexity of winner determination

   - Combinatorial auction procedures with multiple winners
   - User understanding of the complex auction process and its adoption
   - Auction-based review management

4. **Bidding and Negotiation behavior**
   - Bidding behavior on B2C and C2C auction sites
   - Reasons why consumers use Internet auction sites
   - Gender salience in e-negotiation
   - Behavior pattern in electronic negotiation

5. **Design of E-Auction Systems and Software Agents**
   - Optimal design of online auction channels with analytical, empirical, and computational perspectives
   - Software agents to support real-time multiple auctions
   - Auction agents for transfer protocols
   - Importance of ordering in sequential auctions
   - Genetic algorithm to find optimal parameter values for trading agents
   - Multiagent framework for automated online negotiation
   - Time-bounded negotiation for EC agents
   - Strategies for agents' learning the principals' behavior patterns

6. Security and Ethics in E-Auctions

- Privacy preserved protocols for sealed-bid auctions
- Security design for sealed-bid auctions
- Cryptographic protocol with semitrusted auctioneers
- Types of fraud in online auctions and new preventive schemes
- Effect of feedback-posting mechanisms in preventing illegal behavior in auctions
- Risks from the employees of auctioneer site and assurance of their ethics
- Monitoring and enforcing online auction ethics

SUMMARY

In this chapter, you learned about the following EC issues as they relate to the learning objectives.

1. **The various types of auctions and their characteristics.** The classification and types of auctions are based on the numbers of buyers and sellers involved. One seller and many buyers characterize forward auctions. One buyer and many sellers typify reverse auctions. "Name-your-own-price" auctions are a form of reverse auctions. Many buyers and many sellers can participate simultaneously in auctions (called double auctions) in which prices are determined dynamically, based on supply and demand.

2. **The processes of forward and reverse auctions.** In a forward auction, the seller places the item to be sold on the auction site, specifying a starting price and closing time. Bids from buyers are placed sequentially, either increasing (English mode) or decreasing (Dutch mode). At the close, the highest bidder wins. In reverse auctions, buyers place an RFQ for a product or service, and suppliers (providers) submit offers in one or several rounds. The lowest-price bidder wins.

3. **Benefits and limitations of auctions.** The major benefits for sellers are the ability to reach many buyers and to sell quickly. Also, sellers save the high commissions they pay to off-line intermediaries. Buyers have a chance to obtain collectibles while shopping from their homes, and they can find bargains. The major limitation is the possibility of fraud.

4. **Unique auction models.** In the "name-your-own-price" reverse auction, buyers specify how much they are willing to pay for a product or service, and an intermediary tries to find a supplier to fulfill the request. Also, auctions can be conducted on private networks (e.g., pigs in Singapore), can be organized as double auctions (multiple buyers and sellers bidding simultaneously), or can offer bundle trading (related products or services auctioned together).

5. **Services that support auctions.** Auction-support services exist along the entire process and include tools for (1) searching and comparing auctions for specific items; (2) registering, promoting, pricing, and so on; (3) bid watching, making multiple bids, and proxy bidding; and (4) notification, payment, and shipping.

6. **Bartering and negotiating.** Electronic bartering can greatly facilitate the swapping of goods and services among organizations thanks to improved search and matching capabilities. Negotiations online can be facilitated with software agents.

7. **Hazards of e-auction fraud and countermeasures.** Fraud can be committed either by sellers or by buyers. Good auction sites provide protection that includes voluntary identity verification, monitoring of rule violations, escrow services, and insurance.

8. **Auction deployment and implementation.** Some implementation issues are whether to use an intermediary or to run the auction oneself, various strategic issues (e.g., what rules to use and competition with regular channels), and whether to outsource construction of the auction site.

9. **Future directions and the role of mobile auctions.** B2B, C2C, G2B, and B2C auctions are all expanding rapidly. Future directions include use of wireless devices to monitor and trade at auctions, an increase in global auctioning, and strategic alliances.

KEY TERMS

QUESTIONS FOR DISCUSSION

1. Discuss the advantages of dynamic pricing over fixed pricing. What are the potential disadvantages?

2. The "name-your-own-price" model is considered to be a reverse auction. However, there is no consecutive bidding, so why is it called an auction? Is it an auction at all?

3. Find some material on why individuals like C2C auctions so much. Write a report.

4. Compare the "name-your-own-price," i-offer, and tendering (RFQ) approaches. Under what circumstances is each advantageous?

5. Identify three fraud practices in which a seller might engage. How can buyers protect themselves? Be specific.

6. Identify three fraud practices in which a buyer might engage. How can sellers protect themselves?

7. It is said that Manheim Auction is trying to sell more online without cannibalizing its core business. Discuss this situation.

8. Discuss the need for software agents in auctions. Start by analyzing *proxy bidding* and *auction aggregators*.

9. Discuss the role of auction aggregators.

10. It is said that *individuals* prefer an English auction, whereas *corporations* prefer a Dutch one. Speculate on the reasons for this.

11. Discuss why eBay considers itself a community-driven company.

12. Relate consumer trust to auctions.

13. List three to five circumstances under which double auctions are *not* possible.

14. Swaptree's revenue model is based solely on selling ads. Do you think the company will succeed? Why or why not?

INTERNET EXERCISES

1. Enter eBay's online partner (**elance.com**). Post a project and see how professionals bid on this work. Summarize your experience.

2. Enter **dellauction.com** and click on "site terms" of use. Examine the policies, security and encryption statement, privacy protection statement, escrow services, payment options, and other features. Read the FAQs. Which of the following auction mechanisms are used on the Dell site: English, Dutch (declining), reverse, etc.

   Write a report describing all the features available at this site. (*Note:* If you are outside the United States, use an auction site accessible to you.)

3. Enter **auctions.yahoo.com**. Register (for free) and then bid on an item you need. Alternatively, try to sell an item you wish to sell. Write a report on your experiences.

4. Visit **ebay.com** and examine all of the quality assurance measures available either for a fee or for free. Prepare a list.

5. Visit **vendio.com** and **oltiby.com** and report on the various services offered at each site. What are the sites' revenue models?

6. Enter **bidfind.com** and report on the various services provided. Check its affiliate program. What is the site's revenue model?

7. Enter **ebay.com** and investigate the use of "anywhere wireless." Review the wireless devices and find out how they work.

8. Enter **asset-auctions.com** and **liquidations.com**. Compare the sites.

9. Enter **escrow.com**. Read the tutorial on how escrow services work for both buyers and sellers in electronic commerce. Write a summary.

10. Enter **priceline.com** and name a price to travel from where you live to a place you would like to visit. Go through the process without actually buying the ticket (stop short of giving your credit card number). Summarize your experience.

11. Enter **icollector.com** and review the process used to auction art. Find support services, such as currency conversion and shipping. Take the tour of the site. Prepare a report on buying collectibles online.

12. Enter **ubid.com** and examine the "auction exchange." What is unique about it? Compare this auction with those conducted on **ebay.com**. What are the major differences between the auctions on the two sites?

13. Enter **autoparts.com** and describe how auctions are being conducted there.

14. Enter **web-barter.com** and **bigvine.com** and examine their services. Summarize them in a report.

15. Enter **ioffer.com** and review the negotiation process. Write a report.

16. Enter **ioffer.com**. Read the Q&A at the help center. Write a report on the logistics, payments, and rules involved. How is fraud prevented?

TEAM ASSIGNMENTS AND ROLE PLAYING

1. Each team is assigned an auction method (English, Dutch, etc.). Each team should convince a (hypothetical) company that wants to liquidate items that its method is the best. Items to be liquidated include the following:

   a. Five IBM top-of-the-line mainframe systems valued at about $500,000 each

   b. 750 PCs valued at about $1,000 each

   c. A property valued at about $10 million

   Present arguments as to which auction method should be used with each item.

2. Assign teams to major third-party auction sites from your country and from two other countries. Each team should present the major functionalities of the sites and the fraud protection measures they use. Convince a user that your site is the best.

3. Each team investigates a B2B reverse auction site such as: **asset-auctions.com**, **liquidation.com**, **overstock.com**, and **bizauctions.com**. Compare features and report their strengths and limitations.

4. Each team examines two or three of the following sites: **prosper.com**, **swapthing.com**, **swaptree.com**, **peerflix.com**, **lala.com**, **ipswap.com**, **swapvillage.com**, **webswap.com**, **bigvine.com**, etc. Compare their business and revenue models.

5. Create an eBay group. Enter **ebay.com**, click the "Community" button, click "Groups," sign in to enter, click "Start Group," and follow the instructions to create a group of five members in your class and select common interest (e.g., collecting stamps or toy trains). You will moderate the group, invite the group to discussions, and create polls. Write a report on your experience.

Real-World Case

DYNAMIC TRADING AT OCEANCONNECT.COM

OceanConnect.com (*oceanconnect.com*) is an e-marketplace for selling and buying marine fuels. It is a consortium backed by the major global suppliers and some large buyers of such fuels. More than 700 registered users from about 50 countries deal in this market. Marine fuels vary in quality and type, and they represent 30 to 50 percent of total operating expenses of oceangoing vessels. Traditional trading is complex, inefficient, and expensive. Trading in marine fuels is done by auctions and negotiations. Thus, an electronic solution has the potential for substantial savings if the e-commerce platform can be cost-effective and scalable. Furthermore, it must allow for negotiations on attributes other than price, and it needs to have a robust architecture.

OceanConnect.com found the proper solution with LiveExchange Enterprise (from Moai Technologies). The solution supports complex marine fuel requirements, specifically addressing the issue of different prices of different products at different ports and offering the ability to compare prices in real time and to negotiate. To do all this, OceanConnect.com uses a variety of transaction models ranging from the more traditional sealed-bid process to reverse auctions to complex, multistage online negotiations on multiple parameters. These mechanisms allow marine fuel purchasers to invite selected participants, specify the time and place of an online transaction event, and customize product specifications and requirements. Having the ability to bid on several parameters in addition to price (such as fuel quality and delivery time and location) allows buyers and sellers to reach agreements that improve total cost of transactions, saving money for buyers and sellers alike.

OceanConnect.com supplements the auctions with features that better serve the market. For example, noticing that bidding activity peaked near the end of auction events, OceanConnect.com added an "Extension Window" feature that extends the bidding for 3 minutes if a lower bid comes in during the last 3 minutes. This feature continues as long as new bids are entered, allowing suppliers to have a "last look" at the lowest bid and affording them additional time to offer their best price.

A typical example of how OceanConnect.com brings greater efficiency to the marine fuels market is that of Neptune Orient Lines Ltd. (NOL), one of the world's largest container shipping lines, which created a transaction that generated 14 bids by 4 suppliers and closed online with one of them. NOL said that the auctions save time and money and are the best platform for bunker purchasing. Throughout the auction, NOL communicated with suppliers via OceanConnect.com's Instant Messaging feature, which allowed the buyer to request clarification on bids or answer supplier questions. The deal's closing price came in underneath the market's average low for that day.

Another feature is the "Bid Box," which enables a supplier to indicate whether there are additional charges associated with the offered price, such as barging or port charges. As a result, the total transaction cost is transparent and can be analyzed by prospective buyers when making their final purchasing decisions.

OceanConnect.com provides extra services, such as access to online credit insurance. In addition, the company offers users specially developed content, including daily bunker pricing, weekly bunker market reports, top expert commentary, forward price indications, and average price charts. OceanConnect.com has added functions to the platform that allow suppliers to signal whether they plan to participate in an auction and allow participants to communicate with each other throughout the auction.

The e-commerce tools gave OceanConnect's e-marketplace the flexibility and scalability necessary to meet the rapidly changing needs of its customers. It also allowed the company to expand both its product offerings and geographic reach.

Sources: Compiled from Moai Technologies (2006) and from *oceanconnect.com* (accessed December 2006).

Questions

1. Why is it important to consider more than the price in auctions?

2. Additional parameters, such a delivery time and location, are often part of the negotiation process. How do these parameters relate to the bidding price? Why is software support of negotiation so critical? Explain the value of the Instant Messaging to the negotiation process.

3. Comment on the complexity of a market such as this one.

4. Why does OceanConnect.com need several transaction modes?

5. OceanConnect.com is an exchange. Given what you have learned about the successes and failures of exchanges, identify the success factors of this exchange.

6. Do you think that the negotiated parameters can be incorporated into the electronic bidding process someday? Why or why not?

REFERENCES

Aberdeen Group. "The Moment: Providing Pricing Flexibility for eMarkets." Aberdeen Group, July 27, 2000. **aberdeen.com** (no longer available online).

Anonymous. "How to Turn a Paper Clip into a House." *ABC News*, July 14, 2006.

Answers.com. "Australian Online Rural Livestock Trading Systems." 2006. **answers.com/topic/australian-online-rural-livestock-trading-systems** (accessed April 2007).

Asia.Internet.com. "Auction Pioneer Signs Up First Asia Customer." September 1, 2000. **asia.internet.com/news/article.php/670841** (accessed October 2006).

Becherer, R. C., and D. Halstead. "Characteristics and Internet Marketing Strategies of Online Auction Sellers." *International Journal of Internet Marketing and Advertising* 1, no. 1 (2004).

Business Journal of Phoenix. "Online Auction Gives Businesses Marketing Tool." December 16, 2005. **bizjournals.com/phoenix/stories/2005/12/19/smallb 1.html** (accessed October 2006).

Carbone, J. "Reverse Auctions Become More Strategic for Buyers." *Purchasing Magazine Online,* December 8, 2005.

Carnegie Mellon University. "Carnegie Mellon Researchers Uncover Online Auction Fraud: Data Mining Software Finger Both Perpetrators and Accomplices." December 5, 2006. **news.cs.cmu.edu/Releases/demo/257.html** (accessed December 2006).

CBC News. "From Paper-Clip to House, in 14 Trades." July 7, 2006. **cbc.ca/canada/story/2006/07/07/paperclip-house.html** (accessed November 2006).

Cellich, C., and S. Jain. *Global Business Negotiations: A Practical Guide.* Cincinnati: Southwest Publishers, 2003.

Choi, S. Y., and A. B. Whinston. *The Internet Economy: Technology and Practice.* Austin, TX: SmartconPub, 2000.

Coffin, A. M. *eBay for Dummies,* 4th ed. Hoboken, NJ: John Wiley & Sons, 2004.

Computer Industry Almanac. "Worldwide Internet Users Top 1 Billion in 2005. USA Reach Nearly 200M Internet Users." January 4, 2006. **c-i-a.com/pr0106.htm** (accessed October 2006).

Cook, T. "Success with Internet Auctions: Tips and Techniques." *PowerHomeBiz.com,* 2006. **powerhomebiz.com/column/terri/tips.htm** (accessed October 2006).

Copeland, M. V. "Swaptree: The eBay of Swap." *CNNMoney.com,* May 11, 2006. **money.cnn.com/magazines/business2/business2_archive/2006/05/01/8375930/index.htm** (accessed November 2006).

Dasgupta, P., L. E. Moser, and P. M. Melliar-Smith. "Dynamic Pricing," in Khosrow-Pour (2006).

eBay. "eBay Express." 2006a. **pages.ebay.com/sell/announcement/overview/express.html** (accessed December 2006).

eBay. "Trust and Safety." 2006b. **pages.ebay.com/aboutebay/trustandsafety.html** (accessed December 2006).

eTForecasts. "Worldwide Internet Users Top 1 Billion in 2005." January 3, 2006. **etforecasts.com/pr/pr106.htm** (accessed October 2006).

European Travel Commission. "New Media Review." December 3, 2004. **etcnewmedia.com/review/default.asp?SectionID=10&OverviewID=6** (accessed January 2005).

ftc.gov. "FTC Releases Top 10 Consumer Fraud Complaint Categories." January 25, 2006. **ftc.gov/opa/2006/01/topten.htm** (accessed December 2006).

Gavish, B., and C. L. Tucci. "Fraudulent Auctions on the Internet." *Electronic Commerce Research,* April 2006.

Guan, S. U. "Mobile Agent-Based Auction Services," in Khosrow-Pour (2006).

Hearn, L. "Buyer Beware at Online Auctions." *The Age,* July 26, 2006. **theage.com.au/news/biztech/buyer-beware-at-online-auctions/2006/07/26/1153816238964.html** (accessed December 2006).

Hof, R. "Lessons from eBay Live!" *BusinessWeekOnline,* June 27, 2005. **businessweek.com/the_thread/techbeat/archives/2005/06/after_spending.html** (accessed October 2006).

Holden, G. "Fast Forward." *Entrepreneur,* May 2006.

Kallender, P. "Sony to Mass Produce OLEDs for Small Screens from 2005." *CIO.com,* September 17, 2004. **cio.co.nz/cio.nsf/0/977FB86373ADE4EECC256F110078E5FF?OpenDocument** (accessed January 2005).

Kambil, A., and E. van Heck. *Making Markets.* Boston: Harvard Business School Press, 2002.

Kheng, C. B., and S. Al-Hawamdeh. "The Adoption of Electronic Procurement in Singapore." *Electronic Commerce Research,* January 2002.

Khosrow-Pour, M. (ed.). *Encyclopedia of E-Commerce, E-Government, and Mobile Commerce.* Hershey, PA: Idea Group Reference, 2006.

Kobler, et al. (eds.). *The Complete Guide to Using eBay.* Special Publication, Lincoln, NE: Smart Computing, 2005.

Kollmann, T., and M. Häsel. *Cross-Channel Cooperation: The Bundling of Online and Offline Business Models.* Wiesbaden, Germany: Deutscher Universitäs-Verlag, 2006.

Konrad, R. "eBay Touts Anti-Fraud Software's Might." *News.com,* June 5, 2002. **marketwatch-cnet.com.com/2100–1017_3–932874.html** (accessed December 2006).

Lee, B. "Web's Bloom a Garden for Sophisticated Scammers." *Chicago Tribune,* March 11, 2002. **chicagotribune.com/technology/local/chi-020311crime,0,6398375.story** (no longer available online).

McKay, C. "Online Auctions Dominant Consumer Fraud." *National Consumers League,* March 25, 2003. **fugitive.com/c-online-auction-fraud.html** (accessed December 2006).

Mirapaul, M. "The New Canvas: Artists Use Online Auctions for Art Projects." *New York Times*, February 5, 2001.

Moai Technologies. "Fueling Efficient Gains." **moai.com** (accessed November 2006).

National Fraud Information Center. "Internet Scams Fraud Trends, January–December 2005." 2006. **fraud.org/2005_Internet_Fraud_Report.pdf** (accessed October 2006).

National Fraud Information Center. "Internet Fraud Statistics, January–June 2004." 2004. **fraud.org/janjune2004ifw.htm** (accessed November 2006).

Neo, B. S. "The Implementation of an Electronic Market for Pig Trading in Singapore." *Journal of Strategic Information Systems* 1, no. 5 (1992).

Park, S. "eBay's Dominance in Internet Auctions," in Khosrow-Pour (2006).

Petrecca, L. "In Limbo, Bidders Asked, 'How Low Can You Go?'" *USA Today*, October 25, 2006.

Prince, D. L. *How to Sell Anything on eBay . . . and Make a Fortune.* New York: McGraw-Hill, 2004.

Protogeros, N., J. Mylonakis, P. Tahinakis, and D. Ginoglou. "Sales Schedule Optimisation in an Agent-Based Technology." *International Journal of Technology Marketing* 1, no. 2 (2006).

Reuters. "Grape Auction Goes Online." *CNN.com*, March 20, 2001. **cnn.com/2001/BUSINESS/03/20/wine.online.reut/** (no longer available online).

Rezabakhsh, B., D. Bornemann, U. Hansen, and U. Schrader. "Consumer Power: A Comparison of the Old Economy and the Internet Economy." *Journal of Consumer Policy*, March 2006.

Rouchier, J., and S. Robin. "Information Perception and Price Dynamics in a Continuous Double Auction." *Simulation and Gaming*, June 2006.

Schermerhorn, J. R. *Management*, 8th ed. New York: John Wiley & Sons, 2004.

Schonfeld, E. "The World According to eBay." *CNNMoney.com.*, January 1, 2005. **money.cnn.com/magazines/business2/business2_archive/2005/01/01/8250238/index.htm** (accessed December 2006).

Search Engine Roundtable. "eBay AdContext—eBay's Contextual Ad System." June 12, 2006. **seroundtable.com/archives/003926.html** (accessed December 2006).

Sim, K. M. "A Survey of Bargaining Models for Grid Resource Allocation." *Communications of the ACM*, January 2006.

Stroebel, M. *Engineering Electronic Negotiations.* Boston: Klewer Academics, 2003.

Subramaniam, R. "Experience Pricing." *Business Line*, August 31, 2000. **blonnet.com/businessline/2000/08/31/stories/043101ra.htm** (no longer available online).

Sullivan, B. "Auction Fraud on the Rise Some Say." *MSNBC*, July 29, 2003. **msnbc.msn.com/id/3078737** (accessed December 2006).

Trevathan, J., H. Ghodosi, and W. Read. "An Anonymous and Secure Continuous Double Auction Scheme." *Proceedings of the 39th Annual Hawaii International Conference on System Sciences*, Kauai, Hawaii, January 4–7, 2006.

Veit, D., and D. J. Veit. *Matchmaking in Electronic Markets: An Agent-Based Approach Towards Matching in Electronic Negotiation.* Berlin/Heidelberg: Springer, 2003.

Westland, J. C. "Ten Lessons that Internet Auction Markets Can Learn from Securities Market Automation." *Journal of Global Management* 8, no. 1 (2000).

Wigand, R. T., and Y.-H. Tan. "Introduction to the Special Section: Identity Management, Value Webs, and Business Models in the Networked Economy." *International Journal of Electronic Commerce*, Spring 2005.

WineBid. **winebid.com** (accessed December 2006).

WineryExchange. **wineryexchange.com** (accessed December 2006).

Wolverton, T. "Survey Finds Pirates Rule Online Auctions." *CNET News*, April 11, 2000. **news.com.com/Survey+finds+pirates+rule+online+actions/2100–1017_3–239146.html** (accessed December 2006).

Wurman, P. "Dynamic Pricing in the Virtual Marketplace." *IEEE Internet Computing* (March–April 2001): 38–39.

E-COMMERCE SECURITY

Learning Objectives

Upon completion of this chapter, you will be able to:

1. Explain EC-related crimes and why they cannot be stopped.

2. Describe an EC security strategy and why a life cycle approach is needed.

3. Describe the information assurance security principles.

4. Describe EC security issues from the perspective of customers and e-businesses.

5. Identify the major EC security threats, vulnerabilities, and risk

6. Identify and describe common EC threats and attacks.

7. Identify and assess major technologies and methods for securing EC communications.

8. Identify and assess major technologies for information assurance and protection of EC networks.

Content

Cyber Cons Target Online Shoppers

Managerial Issues

Real-World Case: UBS PaineWebber's Business Operations Debilitated by Malicious Code

CYBER CONS TARGET ONLINE SHOPPERS

The Problem

"Cyber Monday" is the name retailers gave to the first Monday after the U.S.'s Thanksgiving holiday weekend because that day kicks off the busiest online shopping period of the year. EC sales hit a record high $608 million on Cyber Monday in November 2006—a 26 percent gain in sales over Cyber Monday in 2005. During the first three quarters prior to Cyber Monday, online shoppers had spent $79 billion, up 23 percent from the same period in 2005. This growth in EC sales and number of shoppers has attracted cyber cons aimed at identity theft and fraud. **Fraud** is any business activity that uses deceitful practices or devices to deprive another of property or other rights.

Online shoppers are attractive targets because they typically have higher incomes. Phishers, electronic shoplifters, con artists, and scammers stalk online shoppers because these cyber cons want *information*—today's most valuable form of international currency. What's alarming is that most new scammers are not computer geniuses. They are low-end criminals who have discovered effective phishing schemes to trick people into giving up account numbers or to intercept the transmission of information to access accounts. Scammers even outsource work to programmers to seize control of vulnerable computers or wireless networks.

Identity theft is the number one concern of all online shoppers, according to the U.S. Federal Trade Commission (FTC; *ftc.gov*). Selling information, like selling illegal drugs, is profitable and unstoppable. In a 2006 survey, 21 percent of potential customers listed "too much risk of fraud, I don't trust online merchants" as their primary reason for not shopping online. Of the total fraud complaints reported to the FTC, Internet-related fraud complaints jumped from 1 percent in 1996 to 46 percent in 2006. (See *ftc.gov/opa/2006/01/topten.htm*.) Not only do concerns about cyber cons stunt EC growth, defending against these cons and compensating for damages significantly increase the costs of EC. As companies try to expand their e-business in countries where consumers have limited purchasing power and legal systems are underdeveloped, opportunities for fraud expand with it.

fraud
Any business activity that uses deceitful practices or devices to deprive another of property or other rights.

The Solution

Con artists have gone high-tech, using the Internet to defraud consumers in many clever ways, such as through phishing sites. Scam artists use the excitement of Internet auctions to entice consumers. They e-mail frightening warnings to prey on the fears of online shoppers. And they exploit people's weaknesses by offering false promises of irresistible deals. Individuals need to fear the sender—and not let the message intimidate them. Users can no longer trust Web sites or e-mails without the extra effort of verifying their authenticity. Likewise, EC retailers cannot trust buyers without authentication processes.

The High-Tech Crime Network (HTCN, *htcn.org*), Anti-Phishing Working Group (APWG; *antiphishing.org*), and FTC are dedicated to eliminating fraud resulting from phishing and crimeware. The APWG publishes the *Phishing Trends Activity Report* (Anti-Phishing Working Group 2006). **Crimeware** is software designed to infect a computer and take personal information that can be used to steal from the computer user. **Phishing** is a crimeware technique used to steal the identity of a target company to get the identities of its customers. **Spy-phishing** is a blended threat that uses the phishing technique with spyware programs to target online banks and other password-driven sites. Computer security companies, such as VeriSign (*verisign.com*) and NameProtect (*nameprotect.com*), offer services that search the Web (domain name servers, pages, sites, news groups, chat rooms, etc.) for signs of phishing. While their services help companies whose brands are exploited, they do not help individuals who are scammed. From an EC perspective, individuals need to protect themselves by:

crimeware
Software designed to infect a computer and take personal information that can be used to steal from the computer user.

phishing
A crimeware technique to steal the identity of a target company to get the identities of its customers.

spy-phishing
A blended threat that uses the phishing technique with spyware programs to target online banks and other password-driven sites.

- Verifying the authenticity and security of Web sites, particularly EC sites.
- Not shopping online while using an unencrypted or open wireless network.
- Securing computers before shopping online by keeping antivirus, antispam, and firewall software up-to-date.
- Reviewing credit card and financial statements for unauthorized charges.
- Never replying to e-mail or pop-up messages from companies that ask for personal, financial, or password information.
- Never following directions asking you to reveal information or delete a file that is received in e-mail or pop-up messages from seemingly trusted companies. (These tactics work because people tend to give others the benefit of the doubt and naturally want to help, which is a vulnerability that is exploited.)

The Results

Profit-driven cybercrimes are increasing with EC. Crimeware consisting of blended threats or hybrid attacks—comprised of malware plus spam plus *pretexting*—evade IT security programs and make them harder to detect. **Pretexting** is impersonating someone else to gain access to information that is restricted. Under U.S. law, it is illegal to use pretexting to gain access to financial records. Cybercriminals continuously adopt new tactics to con even the most cautious users. In early 2007, RSA Security Inc. (*rsasecurity.com*) reported a powerful new phishing tool fraudsters are selling via online forums and using to dupe consumers. Phishers use the tool, called a **universal man-in-the-middle phishing kit,** to set up a URL that can interact in real-time with the content of a legitimate Web site, such as a bank or EC site. In this way, fraudsters can intercept data entered by customers at log-in or checkout pages. They then send out phishing e-mails containing links that send recipients to the fake URL, where the user can see an organization's legitimate Web site—and where the fraudsters will hijack inputted information being typed. Unfortunately, the trend is toward continuously harder-to-detect online fraud.

Sources: *Seventh Annual Online Fraud Report, 2006 Edition. Comscore.com*, FTC (2005), *Net-security.org, RSAsecurity.com*, and Van Riper (2006).

pretexting
Impersonating someone else to gain access to information that is restricted.

universal man-in-the-middle phishing kit
A tool used by phishers to set up a URL that can interact in real-time with the content of a legitimate Web site, such as a bank or EC site, to intercept data entered by customers at log-in or check out Web pages.

WHAT WE CAN LEARN . . .

Electronic transactions and Web sites create business risks. Criminals around the world are stealing credit card information, bank account passwords, and other personal information in greater numbers than ever before. Threats range from high-tech blended attacks to low-tech pretexting cons. As such, an **EC security strategy** consisting of multiple layers of defense is needed. This strategy views EC security as the *process of preventing and detecting* unauthorized use of the organization's brand, identity, Web site, e-mail, information, or other assets and attempts to defraud the organization, its customers, and employees. **Prevention measures** help stop unauthorized users (also known as "intruders") from accessing any part of the EC system. **Detection measures** help determine whether intruders attempted to break into the EC system; whether they were successful; and what they may have done.

Making sure that a shopping experience is a safe and secure one is a crucial part of improving the buyer experience. The ultimate goal of EC security is often referred to as **Information assurance (IA).** IA is the protection of information systems against unauthorized access to or modification of information whether in storage, processing, or in transit; protection against the denial of service to authorized users; and those measures necessary to detect, document, and counter threats.

In this chapter, you will learn about EC security strategies, prevention and detection measures, and the need for a defense-in-depth security approach. Firewalls protecting business networks, for example, cannot prevent an attack if the company lacks **human firewalls** that limit employees' access to critical business documents and enforce strict security policies. Like multiple layers of defense, companies also need multiple layers of recovery. You will also learn how EC companies should prepare for the attacks and compromises that will occur. Incident response and disaster recovery plans are crucial and may be required by law.

Because of the complexity of EC and network security, this topic cannot be covered in a single chapter. Those readers interested in a more comprehensive discussion should see the *Prentice Hall Security Series (prenhall.com).*

EC security strategy
A strategy that views EC security as the process of preventing and detecting unauthorized use of the organization's brand, identity, Web site, e-mail, information, or other asset and attempts to defraud the organization, its customers, and employees.

prevention measures
Ways to help stop unauthorized users (also known as "intruders") from accessing any part of the EC system.

detection measures
Ways to determine whether intruders attempted to break into the EC system; whether they were successful; and what they may have done.

11.1 STOPPING E-COMMERCE CRIMES

Why can't we stop these criminals? One reason is that strong EC security makes online shopping inconvenient and demanding on customers. The EC industry does not want to enforce safeguards that add friction to the profitable wheels of online commerce. It is possible, for example, to demand passwords or PINs for all credit card transactions, but that could discourage or prevent customers from completing their purchase. It is also possible to demand delivery only to the billing address for a credit card, but that would eliminate an important convenience for gift senders. In EC transactions, new and better ways of authenticating legitimate customers and identifying fraudsters could complement user names and passwords, but that increases transaction costs and time.

A second reason is the lack of cooperation from credit card issuers and foreign ISPs. There are insufficient incentives for credit card issuers to share leads on criminal activity with each other or law enforcement. It is much cheaper to block a stolen card and move on than to invest time and money in a prosecution with an uncertain outcome. While in the past, not disclosing breaches or attacks might have protected a company's reputation, today's laws requiring full disclosure when personal data has been compromised make it difficult to keep secret.

Most foreign ISPs have no incentive to cooperate. If the source ISP would cooperate and suspend the hacker's access, it would be very difficult for hackers to do what they do. The hacker would not be able to hack from the comfort of home because that street address would be blacklisted by the ISP.

Consider this scenario, which shows the importance of cooperation. A hacker compromises an EC Web site's database and extracts all the credit card numbers. The hacker uses those numbers to order services, such as Web hosting and domains via the Internet. In turn, those services are used for even more malicious activity, primarily for phishing or to host hacking exploit tools. Most U.S. Web hosting providers log all activity so, in most cases, they can identify the source IP address and source ISP with timestamps and other identifying information. In addition, most ISPs throughout the world log or have the capability to log which customer is or was using this IP address on this day and this time.

However, requiring stronger EC standards and information sharing by the credit card companies would not fix the problem. Many cybercriminals, especially ones that do not reside in a G8 nation, do not need to worry about prosecution from their government or even suspension from their ISP. (The Group of Eight [G8] is an international forum for the governments of Canada, France, Germany, Italy, Japan, Russia, the United Kingdom, and the United States). This situation helps explain why a huge majority of the hackers (some estimate about 95 percent) reside in Turkey, China, Romania, or Brazil.

The third reason pertains to customers. Online shoppers are to blame for not taking necessary precautions to avoid becoming a victim. Some shoppers rely too heavily on fraud protection provided by credit card issuers ignoring the bigger risk of identity theft. Phishing is rampant because some people respond to it—making it profitable. While phishing gets most of the media attention, there are equally dangerous risks that users expose themselves to by using debit cards on online gambling sites or revealing themselves in online communities like MySpace (myspace.com), Facebook (facebook.com), and France's Skyblog (skyblog.com). Personal information posted on these sites is used for identity theft or to infect users' PCs with malware converting them into zombie computers, or **zombies,** for launching attacks or sending e-mail spam. The vast majority of spam is relayed by zombies because it allows spammers to avoid detection and save bandwidth costs by using the PCs of others (Sophos 2006).

A fourth reason arises from IS design and security architecture issues. It is well known that preventing vulnerability during the EC design and preimplementation stage is far less expensive than mitigating problems later. The IS staff needs to plan security from the design stage because simple mistakes, such as not insuring that all traffic into and out of a network pass through a firewall, are often to blame for letting in hackers. If companies don't invest the resources needed to insure that their applications are secure, they may as well forget about security elsewhere on the Web site. Security needs to be built into an EC site from the very beginning and also into the application level. Protection can be added later, but if it has not been built into the server application level, it may be impossible to block some types of attack. Sophisticated hackers do not use browsers to crack into Web sites, but rather use toolkits to gain access to networks or applications and ultimately get into databases from them.

Previously, it was thought that if a front-end application, such as a Web site, was secured, then the data itself would be secured, but that's not true because sometimes applications

Information assurance (IA)
The protection of information systems against unauthorized access to or modification of information whether in storage, processing or transit, and against the denial of service to authorized users, including those measures necessary to detect, document, and counter such threats.

human firewalls
Methods that filter or limit people's access to critical business documents.

zombies
Computers infected with malware that are under the control of a spammer, hacker, or other criminal.

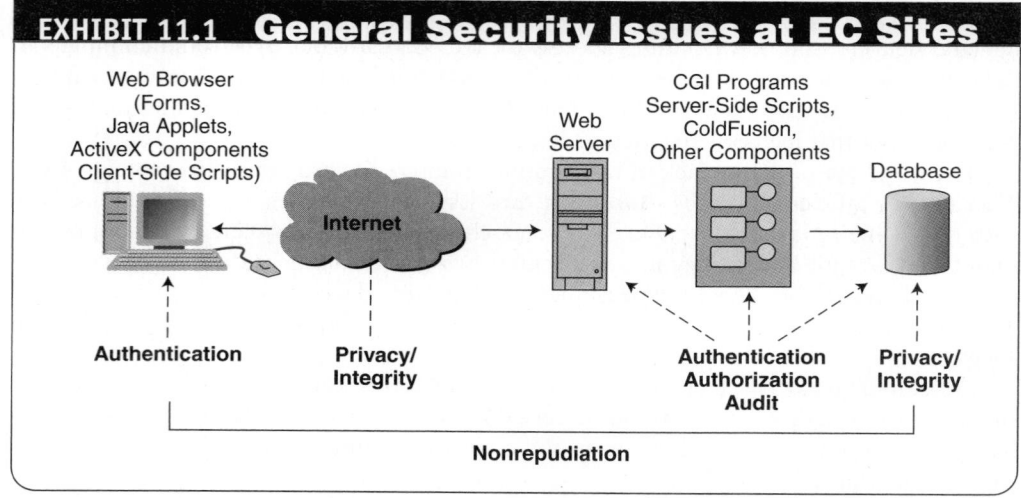

EXHIBIT 11.1   General Security Issues at EC Sites

Source: Scambray, J. et al. *Hacking Exposed*, 2d ed. New York: McGraw-Hill, 2000. Copyright ©The McGraw-Hill Companies.

application firewalls
Specialized tools designed to increase the security of Web applications.

common (security) vulnerabilities and exposures (CVE)
Publicly known computer security risks, which are collected, listed, and shared by a board of security-related organizations (cve.mitre.org).

vulnerability
Weakness in software or other mechanism that threatens the confidentiality, integrity, or availability of an asset (recall the CIA model). It can be directly used by a hacker to gain access to a system or network.

risk
The probability that a vulnerability will be known and used.

exposure
The estimated cost, loss, or damage that can result if a threat exploits a vulnerability.

standard of due care
Care that a company is reasonably expected to take based on the risks affecting its EC business and online transactions.

do not function as planned or expected. Web applications that provide access to back-end databases or banking applications can provide an attack vector. Since Web applications can expose critical systems to threats from internal and external sources, application firewalls are needed. **Application firewalls** are specialized tools designed to increase security in Web applications.

There's no doubt that Web applications are attackers' target of choice and that every component in an EC application is subject to some sort of security threat. Exhibit 11.1 depicts some of the major components involved in EC applications and indicates where security issues come into play. In 2006, Mitre Corporation, which publishes a list of vulnerabilities called **common vulnerabilities and exposures (CVE)**, (cve.mitre.org), reported that four of the top five reported vulnerabilities were within Web applications. **Vulnerabilities** are weaknesses in software or other mechanisms that a hacker can use directly to gain access to a system or network. Vulnerabilities create **risk**, which is the probability that this weakness will be known and used. **Exposure** is the estimated cost, loss, or damage that can result if a threat exploits a vulnerability. Exposure exists when a computing system:

◗ Allows an attacker to conduct information gathering activities,
◗ Allows an attacker to hide activities,
◗ Includes a capability that behaves as expected, but can be easily compromised,
◗ Is a primary point of entry that an attacker may attempt to use to gain access to the system or data, or
◗ Is considered a problem according to some reasonable security policy.

Software vulnerabilities (bugs) are a huge security problem. The well-documented vulnerabilities in the wireless 802.11 standard were built into the protocols (Berghel and Uecker 2005). Vulnerabilities cost money through increased maintenance, reduced sales, even a drop in the stock price. Keeping the bug-rate down can be expensive too. Understandably, many vulnerabilities in applications cannot be prevented at the design stage because they become known much later. Those vulnerabilities need to be managed with patches. Patch management issues will be discussed later in this chapter. The challenge is for EC systems designers and network administrators to integrate risk management into the system development life cycle (SDLC).

The final reason is the lack of due care in business or hiring practices, outsourcing, and business partnerships. The **standard of due care** comes from the law and is also known as the "duty to exercise reasonable care." Due care in EC is care that a company is reasonably expected to take based on the risks affecting its EC business and online transactions. If managers ignore the standard of due care in business practices, hires criminals, outsources to fraudulent vendors, or partners with unsecured companies, they put their EC business and confidential data at risk exposing themselves to legal problems. Those problems include violating laws like the Foreign Corrupt Practices Act (FCPA) and the Sarbanes-Oxley Act, facing lawsuits and fines from regulators, such as the FTC and Securities and Exchange Commission (SEC), and not following industry-specific standards, such as the Payment Card Industry (PCI) requirements of the Visa, MasterCard, American Express, and Discover Card standard. See Online File W11.1 for a discussion of the impacts on ChoicePoint for its negligence for not following *reasonable* information security and privacy practices. For a description of the PCI standard and requirements, see pcistandard.com.

No one really knows the true impact of online security breaches because only 20 percent of businesses report computer intrusions to legal authorities, according to the FBI (2005) and the Computer Security Institute (CSI, gocsi.com). See the Center for Public Policy and Private Enterprise (2005) for the 2005 **CSI/FBI Computer Crime and Security Survey** full report. It is the annual security survey of U.S. corporations, government agencies, financial and medical institutions, and universities conducted jointly by the FBI and the Computer Security Institute. Highlights from that *Tenth Annual CSI/FBI Computer Crime and Security Survey*, which was based on responses from 700 U.S. corporations, government agencies, financial and medical institutions, and universities, include the following:

CSI/FBI Computer Crime and Security Survey Annual security survey of U.S. corporations, government agencies, financial and medical institutions, and universities conducted jointly by the FBI and the Computer Security Institute.

1. **Total financial losses from attacks have declined dramatically.** They were down 61 percent on a per respondent basis from 2004 but were still a reported $130 million. Of the types of attacks:
    ▶ Virus attacks ranked first.
    ▶ Unauthorized access ranked second.
    ▶ Theft of proprietary information ranked third.
    ▶ Denial of service (DOS) attacks ranked a distant fourth.

2. **Attacks on computer systems or (detected) misuse of these systems have been slowly but steadily decreasing in all areas.** The one exception was a slight increase in the abuse of wireless networks.

3. **Defacements of Internet Web sites have increased dramatically.** Ninety-five percent of organizations experienced more than 10 Web site incidents in 2004.

4. **"Inside jobs" occur about as often as external attacks.** The lesson is to anticipate attacks from current and former employees as well as hackers.

5. **Organizations largely defend their systems through firewalls, antivirus software, intrusion detection systems, and server-based access control lists.** The use of smart cards and other one-time password tokens increased, while use of intrusion prevention systems decreased.

6. **More organizations are conducting security audits to serve as a baseline for a meaningful security program.** Eighty-seven percent had conducted security audits, possibly in response to regulatory or insurance mandates.

7. **Computer security investments per employee vary widely.** State governments had the highest investments at $497 per employee, which was followed in descending order by utilities, transportation, telecommunications, manufacturing, high-tech, and the federal government. For the federal government, the investment was $49 per employee.

Every EC business knows the threat of bogus credit card purchases, data breaches, phishing, malware, and pretexting never end—and that these threats must be addressed comprehensively and strategically. We cannot expect an end to a majority of cybercrime until there are international Internet laws that have teeth and an international task force to enforce them.

Section 11.1 ▶ REVIEW QUESTIONS

1. Why can't cybercrimes or cybercriminals be stopped?
2. What risks do people expose themselves to on social networks?
3. Why are zombie PCs used to send spam?

11.2 E-COMMERCE SECURITY STRATEGY AND LIFE CYCLE APPROACH

EC security is an evolving discipline. Threats change, e-business needs change, and Web-based technologies to provide greater service change—and so must the methods to defend against those threats. Information security departments with big workloads and small budgets are not able to optimize their EC security program for efficiency. Endless worms, spyware, data privacy vulnerabilities, and other crises keep them working reactively rather than strategically. And they address security concerns according to attackers' schedules instead of their own. As a result, their security costs and efforts from reacting to crises and paying for damages are greater than if they had an EC security strategy. The underlying reasons why a comprehensive EC security strategy is needed are discussed next.

THE INTERNET'S VULNERABLE DESIGN

It's important to recognize that the Internet, or more specifically the Internet and network protocols, was never intended for use by untrusted users or components. It was designed to accommodate computer-to-computer communications in a closed community. But it evolved into an any-to-any means of communication in an open community. As you know, that community is global in scope, totally unregulated, and out of control. Furthermore, the Internet was designed for maximum efficiency without regard for security or the integrity (or malicious intent) of a person sending a message or requesting access. Error checking to ensure that the message was sent and received correctly was important at that time but not user authentication or access control. The Internet is still a fundamentally insecure infrastructure. For more information on the history of the Internet, visit the Internet Society at isoc.org/internet/history.

domain name system (DNS)

Translates (converts) domain names to their numeric IP addresses.

IP address

An address that uniquely identifies each computer connected to a network or the Internet.

Because virtually every Internet application relies on the reliable operation of the *domain name system* services, the lack of source authentication and data integrity checking in DNS operations leave nearly all Internet services vulnerable to attacks. The **domain name system (DNS)** translates (converts) domain names (e.g., prenhall.com and fbi.gov) to their numeric IP addresses. An **IP address** is an address that identifies your computer on a network or Internet. When a computer is connected to a LAN or the Internet, it is assigned an IP address that is either static, meaning it never changes, or dynamic, meaning that it changes with each log-in. For more information on the deployment of DNS Security Extensions (DNSSEC), see UCLA's Internet Research Lab at irl.cs.ucla.edu.

There are still many Internet-design problems that become EC problems. Consider the following cases and reports.

- In 2006, the Web sites of three Florida banks, Premier Bank, Wakulla Bank, and Capital City Bank, were hacked in an attack that security experts described as the "first of its kind." Hackers broke into servers of the ISP hosting the three banks' sites and redirected their traffic to a bogus server to steal credit card numbers, PINs, and other personal information about the banks' customers. Though the scam affected fewer than 20 customers, the ability of fraudsters to link a bogus server to a legitimate Web site was an alarming development.

- In January 2007, a worm attack that started in Europe quickly spread across the globe. The *Small.Dam* worm was dubbed *Storm* because it referenced a major storm in Europe in its subject line. In addition to propagating spam, this malware installed Trojans that created back doors into systems that could be exploited by future attacks. Experts forecasted a huge increase in spam because the *Storm* worm sent out six separate waves containing hundreds of thousands of e-mails within days. *Storm* was distributed to set up a network of infected zombie computers to be used to launch massive spam campaigns (Prince 2007).

- E-mail security firm Commtouch Software (commtouch.com) named 2006 the *Year of the Zombies*. According to a 2006 report, their study found that remote-controlled zombies can number up to 8 million hosts globally on a given day. Zombies were responsible for increasing the volume of spam by 30 percent in 2006.

- On January 25, 2007, Internet security company Symantec elevated the *Trojan.Peacomm* from a category 2 out of 5 to a category 3 threat because of the speed and volume at which it was aggressively spammed across the Internet. *Trojan.Peacomm* was first detected on January 17, 2007. Its threat level was raised to a higher category after a sustained increase in new versions of the attack. The author of *Trojan.Peacomm* had responded to the defensive efforts by security companies by adjusting his tactics to overcome new defenses to stop the malware. *Trojan.Peacomm* was one of several spamming Trojan horse programs, which appeared to originate from Russia, that were clearly aimed at making money for the author by pumping up penny stocks. The victims were enticed through social engineering techniques to open an e-mail attachment, which appeared to be a video clip on a recent news story. The e-mail itself had no message body, but had one of several attention grabbing subject lines such as "A killer at 11, he's free at 21 and kills again!" "Fidel Castro Dead," or "Re: Your Text."

Safe, dependable Internet service does not exist. No matter how you view it, we are not winning the war on Internet and EC criminal activities.

THE SHIFT TO PROFIT-MOTIVATED CRIMES

In the early days of e-commerce, many hackers simply wanted to gain fame or notoriety by defacing Web sites or "gaining root," that is, root access to a network. As the *Trojan.Peacomm* and other malware attacks illustrate, criminals are now profit-oriented, and there are many more of them. And their tactics are not limited to the cyberworld. For example, in June 2006, international insurance company AIG, with operations in over 130 countries and $109 billion in revenues, admitted that the personal data of almost one million people had been stolen a month earlier. Firewalls and intrusion detection systems were irrelevant in this breach. Thieves physically broke into an AIG Midwestern regional office through the ceiling and carried off a server and laptop. That server contained detailed personal data from 930,000 prospective AIG customers, whose information had been forwarded to the insurance firm from 690 insurance brokers around the country. Ironically, AIG had recently begun offering identity theft insurance coverage.

Countless and continuing e-business security crises prove that a company needs to have in place a risk management process to methodically assess potential risks and vulnerabilities and incident response processes when compromises occur. Such processes are crucial, as the intrusion to access corporate data at discount retail conglomerate TJX illustrates. See Online File W11.2 to read about the network intrusion at TJX.

Experts believe that a stringent e-business risk management program rigorously managed could have prevented many former and recent data breaches. For a chronology of data breaches and how they occurred, see privacyrights.org/ar/ChronDataBreaches.htm. These security risks cannot be eliminated, but they can be mitigated to reduce them to a level of residual risk that is acceptable from an operational and legal standpoint and that still allows the e-business to function.

TREATING EC SECURITY AS A PROJECT

EC security programs have a life cycle, and throughout that life cycle the EC security requirements must be continuously evaluated and adjusted. An **EC security program** is the set of controls over security processes to protect organizational assets. There are four high-level stages in the life cycle of an EC security program, which are

EC security program
Set of controls over security processes to protect organizational assets.

1. Planning and organizing
2. Implementation
3. Operations and maintenance
4. Monitoring and evaluating

Organizations that do not follow such a life cycle approach in developing, implementing, and maintaining their security management program usually:

▶ Do not have policies and procedures that are linked to or supported by security activities
▶ Suffer disconnect, confusion, and gaps in responsibilities for protecting assets
▶ Lack methods to fully identify, understand, and improve deficiencies in the security program

> Lack methods to verify compliance to regulations, laws, or policies

> Have to rely on *patches, hotfixes,* and *service packs* because they lack a holistic EC security approach.

A **patch** is a program that makes needed changes to software that is already installed on a computer. Software companies issue patches to fix bugs in their programs, to address security problems, or to add functionality. A **hotfix** is Microsoft's name for a patch. Microsoft bundles hotfixes into service packs for easier installation. **Service packs** are the means by which product updates are distributed. Service packs may contain updates for system reliability, program compatibility, security, and more. For more information about what particular Microsoft service packs contain and how to obtain them, visit support.microsoft.com/sp. Other companies have adopted Microsoft's nomenclature of hotfixes and service packs for updates to their own software.

If a life cycle approach is not used to maintain an EC security program, an organization is doomed to treating security as a project. Projects have a starting date and ending date, at which time the resources and project team are reallocated to other projects. A project approach results in a lot of repetitive work that costs much more than a life cycle approach and with diminishing results.

IGNORING EC SECURITY BEST PRACTICES

Many companies of all sizes fail to implement basic IT security management best practices, business continuity plans, and disaster recovery plans. In its fourth annual study on information security and the workforce released in 2006, the **Computing Technology Industry Association (CompTIA),** a nonprofit trade group, said human error was responsible for nearly 60 percent of information security breaches in organizations in 2005—up from 47 percent the year before (CompTIA 2006). Yet despite the known role of human behavior in information security breaches, only 29 percent of the 574 government, IT, financial, and educational organizations surveyed worldwide had mandatory security training. Only 36 percent offered end-user security awareness training.

In the next section, you will learn the fundamentals of a reasonable EC security strategy, which is based on the IA model.

Section 11.2 ▶ REVIEW QUESTIONS

1. How have the motives of cybercriminals changed?

2. Why is a project management approach to EC security inadequate?

3. What did CompTIA's survey results reveal?

11.3 INFORMATION ASSURANCE

Recall that IA is the protection of information systems against unauthorized access to or modification of information that is stored, processed, or being sent over a network. The importance of the IA model to EC is that it represents the processes for protecting information by insuring its confidentiality, integrity, and availability. This model is referred to as the **CIA security triad,** or simply the **CIA triad,** and is typically diagrammed as shown in Exhibit 11.2.

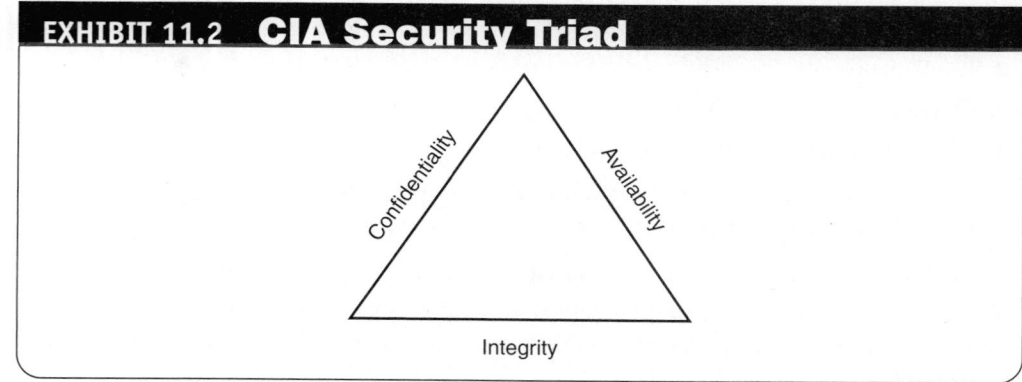

EXHIBIT 11.2 CIA Security Triad

EXHIBIT 11.3 Encryption Components

Component	Description	Example or Description
Plaintext	The original message or document is created by the user, which is in human-readable form.	Credit Card Number 5342 8765 3652 9982
Encryption algorithm	The set of procedures or mathematical functions to encrypt or decrypt a message. Typically, the algorithm is not the secret piece of the encryption process.	Add a number (the key) to each number in the card. If the resulting number is greater than 9, wrap around the number to the beginning (i.e., modulus arithmetic). For example, add 4 to each number so that 1 becomes 5, 9 becomes 3, etc.
Key or Key Value	The secret value used with the algorithm to transform the message.	The key dictates what parts (functions) of the algorithm will be used, in what order, and with what values.
Keyspace	The large number of possible key values (keys) created by the algorithm to use when transforming the message.	The larger the keyspace, the greater the number of possibilities for the key, which makes it harder for an attacker to discover the correct key.
Ciphertext	Message or document that has been encrypted into unreadable form.	The original 5342 8765 3652 9982 becomes 9786 2109 7096 3326.

CONFIDENTIALITY, INTEGRITY, AND AVAILABILITY

The success and security of EC depends on the confidentiality, integrity, and availability of information and the business Web site.

1. **Confidentiality** is the assurance of data privacy. The data or transmitted message is encrypted so that it is readable only by the person for whom it is intended, as shown in Exhibit 11.3. Depending on the strength of the encryption method, intruders or eavesdroppers might not be able to break the encryption to read the data or text. The confidentiality function prevents unauthorized disclosure of information.

2. **Integrity** is the assurance that data is accurate or that a message has not been altered. It means that stored data has not been modified without authorization; a message that was sent is the same message that was received. The integrity function detects and prevents the unauthorized creation, modification, or deletion of data or messages.

3. **Availability** is the assurance that access to data, the Web site, or other EC data service is timely, available, reliable, and restricted to authorized users.

Although the basic security concepts important to information on the Internet are confidentiality, integrity, and availability, concepts relating to the people (users) are authentication, authorization, and nonrepudiation. Confidentiality, integrity, availability, authentication, authorization, and nonrepudiation are all assurance processes.

AUTHENTICATION, AUTHORIZATION, AND NONREPUDIATION

All the CIA functions depend on authentication. **Authentication** is a process to verify (assure) the real identity of an entity, which could be an individual, computer, computer program, or EC Web site. For transmissions, authentication verifies that the sender of the message is who the person or organization claims to be.

Authorization is the process of determining what the authenticated entity is allowed to access and what operations it is allowed to perform. Authorization of an entity occurs after authentication.

Closely associated with authentication is **nonrepudiation,** which is assurance that online customers or trading partners cannot falsely deny (repudiate) their purchase, transaction, and so on. For EC and other electronic transactions, including cash machines or ATMs, all parties in a transaction must be confident that the transaction is secure; the parties are

confidentiality
Assurance of data privacy and accuracy. Keeping private or sensitive information from being disclosed to unauthorized individuals, entities, or processes.

integrity
Assurance that stored data has not been modified without authorization; and a message that was sent is the same message that was received.

availability
Assurance that access to data, the Web site, or other EC data service is timely, available, reliable, and restricted to authorized users.

authentication
Process to verify (assure) the real identity of an individual, computer, computer program, or EC Web site.

authorization
Process of determining what the authenticated entity is allowed to access and what operations it is allowed to perform.

nonrepudiation
Assurance that online customers or trading partners cannot falsely deny (repudiate) their purchase or transaction.

digital signature
or digital certificate
Validates the sender and time stamp of a transaction so it cannot be later claimed that the transaction was unauthorized or invalid.

who they say they are (authentication), and that the transaction is verified being completed or final. Nonrepudiation involves many assurances, including providing:

▶ The sender (customer) of data with proof of delivery

▶ The recipient (EC company) with proof of the sender's identity

▶ Authentication and nonrepudiation are potential defenses against phishing and identity theft. To protect and ensure trust in EC transactions, **digital signatures**, or **digital certificates**, are often used to validate the sender and time stamp of the transaction so it cannot be later claimed that the transaction was unauthorized or invalid. Exhibit 11.4 shows how digital signatures work. A technical overview of digital signatures and certificates and how they provide verification is presented in Section 11.7. Unfortunately, phishers and spammers have devised ways to compromise digital signatures (Jepson 2006).

New or improved methods to ensure the confidentiality of credit card numbers, integrity of entire messages, authentication of the buyer and seller, and nonrepudiation of transactions are being developed as older ones become ineffective. The trend toward more menacing cybercrimes and intrusions is evidence that EC security is still a huge problem that can cause significant financial losses for an organization. Organizations continue to take the problem seriously and exert considerable effort to prevent unauthorized and illegal activities.

EXHIBIT 11.4 Digital Signatures

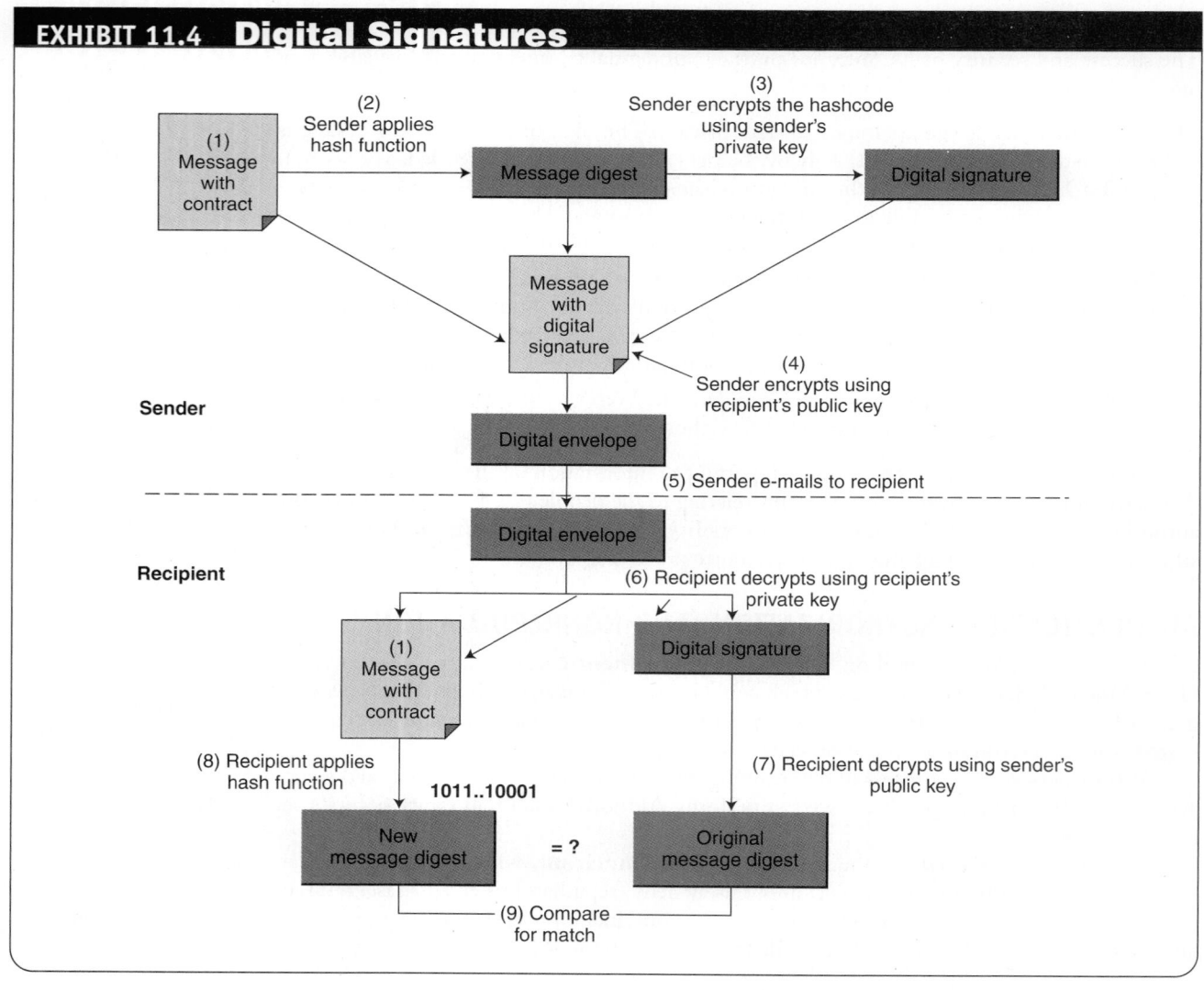

EXHIBIT 11.5   E-Commerce Security Taxonomy

E-Commerce Security Strategy

Regulatory (External)	**Financial** (Internal)	**Marketing & Operations** (Internal)
Control: Database and network security **Assurance metrics:** Confidentiality, integrity, authorization **Protect against:** Unauthorized access by hackers, former employees, malware, and crimeware Privacy violations	**Control:** Fraud; embezzlement, bad debt expense **Assurance metrics:** Authentication and integrity **Protect against:** Transactions using stolen identities, debit or credit cards, and checks. Unauthorized transactions and overrides Pretexting	**Control:** Web site functions, customer transactions, electronic documents, intellectual property **Assurance metrics:** Availability, nonrepudiation. **Protect against:** Phishing Spoofing Denial of service attacks Industrial espionage

E-COMMERCE SECURITY TAXONOMY

An EC security strategy needs to address the three information assurance metrics and three user assurance metrics. In Exhibit 11.5, an EC security taxonomy is presented that defines the high-level categories the six assurance metrics map to and their controls. The three major categories are regulatory, financial, and marketing and operations. Only the key metrics are listed in the taxonomy, but there is overlap in requirements in each category.

FTC and other regulatory agencies mandate that organizations protect against unauthorized access and privacy violations. Given the staggering number of data breaches, these external agencies are imposing increasingly harsh penalties for inadequate database and network security. The most critical assurance metrics are confidentiality, integrity, and authorization.

The financial health of an organization is at risk if fraud, embezzlement, and bad debt expense are not rigorously contained. Doing so requires protecting against the use of stolen identities, checks, debit cards, and credit cards and against unauthorized transactions and overrides of accounting controls.

EC marketing depends on the trust and confidence of customers. The ability to operate depends on the availability of the EC site and its ability to provide shopping features and process the transaction. Among the many ways of impairing marketing and operations are phishing, spoofing, denial of service attacks, and industrial espionage.

Being proactive by setting the assurance requirements correctly as a first step in the EC security life cycle and following a strategy to meet regulatory, financial, and marketing and operations is the most cost-effective approach. But that approach requires significant investments, inconvenience, and commitment, as you will learn in the next section.

Section 11.3 ▶ REVIEW QUESTIONS

1. What is information assurance?
2. What are the six assurances for information and people (that is, senders and receivers of information)?
3. Why is authentication so difficult in an EC transaction?

11.4   ENTERPRISEWIDE E-COMMERCE SECURITY AND PRIVACY MODEL

The success of an EC security strategy and program depends on the commitment and involvement of executive management. This is often called the "tone at the top." A genuine and well-communicated executive commitment about EC security and privacy measures is

EXHIBIT 11.6 Enterprisewide EC Security and Privacy Model

| Senior Management Commitment & Support | → | Security Policies & Training | → | Security Procedures & Enforcement | → | Security Tools: Hardware & Software |

needed to convince users that insecure practices, risky or unethical methods, and mistakes due to ignorance will not be tolerated. Most forms of security (e.g., airport and sports arena security) are unpopular because they are inconvenient, restrictive, time consuming, and expensive. Security practices tend not to be a priority unless they are mandatory and there are negative consequences for noncompliance.

Therefore, an EC security and privacy model for effective enterprise-wide security begins with senior management commitment and support, as shown in Exhibit 11.6 The model views EC security (as well as the broader IT security) as a combination of commitment, people, processes, and technology.

SENIOR MANAGEMENT COMMITMENT AND SUPPORT

The authority of senior managers is needed to establish and maintain EC security programs. EC security programs consist of all the policies, procedures, documents, standards, hardware, software, training, and personnel that work together to protect information, the ability to conduct business, and other assets. Regulators and government agencies, most often the FTC and SEC, are imposing harsh penalties to deter weak security programs that allow confidential data to be compromised. For further information about management accountability and standards of the attorneys general, see naag.org.

EC SECURITY POLICIES AND TRAINING

The next step is to develop a general EC security policy, as well as policies that specify acceptable use of computers and networks, access control, enforcement, roles, and responsibilities. The policies need to be disseminated throughout the organization and necessary training provided to ensure that everyone is aware of and understands them. These policies are important because access control rules, access control lists, monitoring, and rules for firewalls and routers are derived from them. For example, to avoid violating privacy legislation when collecting confidential data, policies need to specify that customers:

▶ Know they are being collected
▶ Give permission, or "opt in," for them to be collected
▶ Have some control over how the information is used
▶ Know they will be used in a reasonable and ethical manner

acceptable use policy (AUP)
Policy that informs users of their responsibilities when using company networks, wireless devices, customer data, and so forth.

The greater the understanding of how security issues directly impact production levels, customer and supplier relationships, revenue streams, and management's liability, the more security will be incorporated into business projects and proposals. It is essential to have a comprehensive and up-to-date **acceptable use policy (AUP)** that informs users of their responsibilities when using company networks, wireless devices, customer data, and so forth. To be effective, the AUP needs to define the responsibilities of every user by specifying both acceptable and unacceptable computer usage. Access to the company networks, databases, and e-mail should never be given to a user until after this process is completed. Recall that human error was responsible for nearly 60 percent of information security breaches in organizations in 2005, up from 47 percent in 2004 (CompTIA 2006).

EC SECURITY PROCEDURES AND ENFORCEMENT

EC security procedures require an evaluation of the digital and financial assets at risk—including cost and operational considerations. To calculate the proper level of protection,

EXHIBIT 11.7   Risk Exposure Model for Digital Assets

Factor	Cost and Operational Considerations
Asset's value to the company	What are the costs of replacement, recovery, or restoration? What is the recoverability time?
Attractiveness of the asset to a criminal	What is the asset's value (on a scale of low to high) to identity thieves, industrial spies, terrorists, or fraudsters?
Legal liability attached to the asset's loss or theft	What are the potential legal costs, fines, and restitution expenses?
Operational, marketing, and financial consequences	What are the costs of business disruption, delivery delays, lost customers, negative media attention, inability to process payments or payroll, or a drop in stock prices?
Likelihood of a successful attack against the asset	Given existing and emerging threats, what is the probability the asset will be stolen or compromised?

managers responsible for a digital asset need to assess its risk exposure. The risk exposure model for digital assets is comprised of the five factors, which are shown in Exhibit 11.7.

Another assessment is the business impact analysis. **Business impact analysis (BIA)** is an exercise that determines the impact of losing the support of an EC resource to an organization; estimates how that loss may escalate over time; identifies the minimum resources needed to recover from the loss; and prioritizes the steps in the recovery of the processes and supporting systems. A BIA needs to be done when conditions change, new threats emerge, or risks get worse. Consider changes in customers' attitudes, for example. According to a 2004 Harris Interactive study, more than 80 percent of consumers said they would stop doing business entirely with companies that misuse information (Ewing et al. 2006). Over 50 percent said they would buy more frequently and in higher volume from companies perceived to have sound privacy practices. These results clearly demonstrate both the financial risk that can accompany a privacy breach and the financial opportunity for organizations that can earn customer confidence with their privacy practices and commitments. See Online File W11.3 to learn about consumer privacy problems and brand image.

After estimating the risk exposure of digital assets, focus resources on the risks that are the greatest. This is an intelligent method for allocating resources because it ensures the protection of assets according to their risk exposure rather than for political or other reasons.

business impact analysis (BIA)
An exercise that determines the impact of losing the support of an EC resource to an organization and establishes the escalation of that loss over time, identifies the minimum resources needed to recover, and prioritizes the recovery of processes and supporting systems.

SECURITY TOOLS: HARDWARE AND SOFTWARE

After the EC security program and policies are defined and risk assessment completed, then the software and hardware needed to support and enforce them can be put in place. Decisions regarding data encryption are implemented at this stage. While encryption to protect moving or static data is not foolproof, it helps protect a company from customer outrage and public outcry if it suffers a data breach.

Keep in mind that security is an ongoing, multilayered (or *defense in depth*) process and not a problem that can be solved only with hardware or software tools. Nor can hardware and software security defenses protect against irresponsible business practices or corrupt management. Managers and employees are potential attack vectors just as hackers and criminal communities are. For more information on the reasons for a multilayered security approach, read Online File W11.4. There is no single hardware or software solution, and tools, such as firewalls and antivirus software, that have been implemented require constant monitoring and frequent upgrading to remain useful.

Section 11.5 discusses the technical defenses—hardware and software.

Section 11.4 ❿ REVIEW QUESTIONS

1. If senior management is not committed to EC security, how might that impact the e-business?
2. What is a benefit of using the risk exposure model for EC security planning?
3. Why should every company implement an acceptable use policy?

11.5 BASIC E-COMMERCE SECURITY ISSUES AND PERSPECTIVES

EC security involves more than just preventing and responding to cyberattacks and intrusion. Consider, for example, the situation in which a user connects to a Web server at a marketing site to obtain some product literature. In return, the users are asked to fill out a Web form providing information about themselves or their employers before receiving the literature. In this situation, what kinds of security questions arise?

From the user's perspective:

▶ How can the user know whether the Web server is owned and operated by a legitimate company?

▶ How does the user know that the Web page and form have not been compromised by spyware or other malicious code?

▶ How does the user know that an employee won't intercept and misuse the information?

From the company's perspective:

▶ How does the company know the user will not attempt to break into the Web server or alter the pages and content at the site?

▶ How does the company know that the user will not try to disrupt the server so that it is not available to others?

From both parties' perspectives:

▶ How do both parties know that the network connection is free from eavesdropping by a third party "listening" on the line?

▶ How do they know that the information sent back and forth between the server and the user's browser has not been altered?

These questions illustrate the types of security issues that arise in an EC transaction. For transactions involving e-payments, additional types of security issues must be confronted. The following list summarizes some of the major technology defenses to address these security issues that can occur in EC:

▶ **Authentication.** Authentication requires evidence in the form of credentials, which can take a variety of forms, including something known (e.g., a password), something possessed (e.g., a smart card), or something unique (e.g., a signature).

▶ **Authorization.** Authorization requires comparing information about the person or program with access control information associated with the resource being accessed.

▶ **Auditing.** When a person or program accesses a Web site or queries a database, various pieces of information are recorded or logged into a file. The process of recording information about what was accessed, when, and by whom is known as **auditing.** Audits provide the means to reconstruct what specific actions had occurred and may help IT personnel identify the person or program that performed the actions.

▶ **Confidentiality (privacy) and Integrity (trust).** The most common method is encryption.

▶ **Availability.** Technologies such as load-balancing hardware and software help ensure availability.

▶ **Nonrepudiation.** One nonrepudiation method is the use of a digital signature that makes it difficult for people to dispute that they were involved in an exchange.

auditing
Process of recording information about what Web site, data, file, or network was accessed, when, and by whom or what.

Section 11.5 ▶ REVIEW QUESTIONS

1. If a customer purchases an item from an online store, what are some of the security concerns that might arise?

2. What technical methods help the parties in a transaction trust each other?

11.6 THREATS AND ATTACKS

It's helpful to distinguish between two types of attacks—nontechnical and technical. **Nontechnical attacks** are those in which a perpetrator uses some form of deception or persuasion to trick people into revealing information or performing actions that can compromise the security of a network. Examples of nontechnical attacks are pretexting and *social engineering*. **Social engineering** is a type of nontechnical attack that uses some ruse to trick users into revealing information or performing an action that compromises a computer or network. Like hacking, the goals of social engineering are to gain unauthorized access to systems or information. Phishing attacks rely on social engineering.

In contrast, software and systems knowledge are used to perpetrate technical attacks. A computer worm is an example of a technical attack. Most attacks involve a combination of the two types. For instance, an intruder may use an automated tool to post a message to an instant messaging service offering the opportunity to download software of interest to the reader (e.g., software for downloading music or videos). When an unsuspecting reader downloads the malicious software, it automatically runs on his or her computer, enabling the intruder to turn the machine into a zombie to perpetrate a technical attack.

SOCIAL NETWORKING MAKES SOCIAL ENGINEERING EASY

Social engineering tactics have changed. In the past, social engineers used dumpster diving or cleverly worded conversations to get information to launch attacks. But now, social networking sites are goldmines of information that is readily available. Social engineering tactics or scams that depended on user interaction to execute an attack against them rose dramatically in 2006 (LeClaire 2007). At a high level, social engineering attacks are Web 2.0 attacks. As more users take advantage of Web 2.0 applications like social networking sites, blogs, wikis, and RSS feeds, malware authors, identity thieves, and other criminals are going to exploit them. With the rise of Web 2.0 and more social interaction on sites like MySpace (myspace.com), LinkedIn (linkedin.com), and YouTube (youtube.com), security experts warned of an increase in the incidence of hackers inserting malicious code into dynamically generated Web pages in 2007.

Despite all the social engineering incidents in 2006, it wasn't until the worm and phishing attack against MySpace in early December 2006 that the public realized what some security experts are calling the next big Internet threat. The attack forced MySpace to shut down hundreds of user profile pages after a worm converted legitimate links to those that sent users to a phishing site. The phishing site attempted to obtain personal information, including MySpace user names and passwords.

Because successful social engineering depends, in effect, on the cooperation of the victims, stopping social engineering attacks also depends on the victims. Certain positions within an organization are clearly vulnerable, such as those with access to private and confidential information or who interact with customers or vendors. In the AUP and employee training programs, all users should learn how to avoid becoming a victim of manipulation. Specific policies and procedures need to be developed for securing confidential information, guiding employee behavior with respect to confidential information, and taking the steps needed to respond to and report any social engineering breaches.

TECHNICAL ATTACKS

Software and systems knowledge are used to carry out **technical attacks**. Hackers often use several software tools readily and freely available over the Internet and study hacker and security Web sites to learn of vulnerabilities. Although many of these tools require expertise, novice hackers easily can use many of the existing tools.

The time-to-exploitation of today's most sophisticated spyware and worms has shrunk from months to days. **Time-to-exploitation** is the elapsed time between when a vulnerability is discovered and the time it is exploited. For more on spyware, see **SpywareGuide**, a public reference site, at spywareguide.com. As a result, companies have an ever shorter time frame to find and fix flaws before an attack compromises them. New vulnerabilities are continuously being found in operating systems, applications, and networks. Left undetected or

nontechnical attack
An attack that uses chicanery to trick people into revealing sensitive information or performing actions that compromise the security of a network.

social engineering
A type of nontechnical attack that uses some ruse to trick users into revealing information or performing an action that compromises a computer or network.

technical attack
An attack perpetrated using software and systems knowledge or expertise.

time-to-exploitation
The elapsed time between when a vulnerability is discovered and the time it is exploited.

SpywareGuide
A public reference site for spyware.

unprotected, these vulnerabilities provide an open door for attacks—and business interruptions and their financial consequences.

The SANS Institute publishes a document summarizing the "Top 20 Internet Security Vulnerabilities" (SANS 2007). The SANS Top-20 2006 is a consensus list of vulnerabilities that require immediate remediation. It is the result of a process that brought together dozens of leading security experts. Organizations use this to prioritize their security efforts, allowing them to address the most dangerous vulnerabilities first.

A 2006 security report from the SANS Institute noted that companies were seeing an increasing number of **zero-day incidents,** or attacks through previously unknown weaknesses in their computer networks. This suggests cybercrime has become so lucrative that hackers are now willing to invest more time and effort on researching new ways of getting in.

Next, we discuss the worst threats facing e-commerce.

Denial of Service, Zombies, and Phishing

A **denial of service (DOS)** is an attack in which so many requests (for service or access) bombard a system that it crashes or cannot respond. In a DOS attack, an attacker uses specialized software to send a flood of data packets to the target computer, with the aim of overloading its resources. Many attackers rely on software created by other hackers and made available over the Internet rather than developing it themselves.

In the beginning of 2004, the MyDoom.A e-mail viruses infected hundreds of thousands of PCs around the world (Fisher 2004). Like many other e-mail viruses, this virus propagated by sending an official-looking e-mail message with a zip file attached. When the victim opened the zip file, the virus automatically found other e-mail addresses on the victim's computer and forwarded itself to those addresses. However, there was more to MyDoom.A than simple propagation. When the victim opened the zip file, the virus code also installed a program on the victim's machine that enabled the intruders to automatically launch what is known as a DOS attack against a company called the SCO Group. The attack involved nothing more than having hundreds of thousands of infected machines send page requests to SCO's Web site. The site was brought to a standstill because it was overwhelmed by the large number of requests. It was first thought that SCO was a victim of irate Linux proponents who were angered by SCO's multimillion-dollar lawsuit against IBM for having allegedly included SCO's code in IBM's Linux software. Later, it was suggested that the attack was actually launched by spammers out of Russia.

Due to the widespread availability of free intrusion tools and scripts and the overall interconnectivity on the Internet, virtually anyone with minimal computer experience (often a teenager with time on his or her hands) can mount a DOS attack.

DOS attacks can be difficult to stop. Fortunately (or unfortunately), they are so commonplace that over the past few years the security community has developed a series of steps for combating these costly attacks. In the case of SCO, the attacks were scheduled to run from February 1, 2004, to February 12, 2004. During that time, SCO shut off its original Web site, sco.com, and set up a new home page at thescogroup.com. Microsoft, which was the target of MyDoom.B, redirected its Web to specialized security servers run by Akamai Technologies Inc. (akamai.com). Depending on the type of attack, a company can sometimes thwart a DOS attack by reconfiguring its network routers and firewalls (see Section 11.7).

Zombied PCs—and the spyware that controls them—can be used to launch DOS attacks or spread adware. Connecting wireless laptops and palmtops to insecure networks in airport WiFi facilities, hotels, and Internet cafés totally exposes data to threats.

Even though most people are aware of phishing scams, phishers still remain a serious threat because they change their tactics. According to David Sancho, an engineer with Trend Micro, German phishers sent out messages pretending to come from a utility that provides an electronic invoice as an Adobe PDF file. This social engineering trick worked. Many customers clicked the link to download an "important document," which contained a trojan, a program that gave the sender control of the infected machine. The trojan monitored every Internet connection and keystroke to capture and report passwords back to the Trojan's creator.

zero-day incidents
Attacks through previously unknown weaknesses in their computer networks.

denial of service (DOS) attack
An attack on a Web site in which an attacker uses specialized software to send a flood of data packets to the target computer with the aim of overloading its resources.

Web Server and Web Page Hijacking

Web servers and Web pages can be hijacked and configured to control or redirect unsuspecting users to scam or phishing sites. This technique uses 302 server redirects. This exploit allows *any* Web master (including criminals) to have his or her own "virtual pages" rank for pages belonging to another Web master (e.g., legitimate EC site). Successfully employed, this technique will allow the offending Web master ("the hijacker") to displace the pages of the "target" or victim Web site in the search engine results pages (SERPS). This causes search engine traffic to the target Web site to vanish or redirects traffic to any other page of choice.

Criminal organizations, crime networks, and terrorist groups have used Web server hijacking and exploited the global information, financial, and transportation networks (Hearing of the Senate Armed Services Committee 2006). Case 11.1 describes such attacks.

Botnets

A **botnet** is a huge number (e.g., hundreds of thousands) of hijacked Internet computers that have been set up to forward traffic, including spam and viruses, to other computers on the Internet. An infected computer is referred to as a computer robot, or bot. Botmasters, or bot herders, control botnets. The combined power of these coordinated networks of computers can scan for and compromise other computers and perpetrate DOS attacks. On May 4, 2006, Christopher Maxwell pleaded guilty in U.S. District Court in Seattle to computer fraud for operating a botnet that disrupted Northwest Hospital's critical care system. Maxwell's attack disrupted operating room doors, physicians' pagers, and computers in the intensive care unit.

Malicious Code: Viruses, Worms, and Trojan Horses

Sometimes referred to as **malware** (for malicious software), malicious code is classified by how it propagates (spreads). A **virus** is a piece of software code that inserts itself into a host, including the operating systems; running its host program activates the virus. A virus has two components. First, it has a propagation mechanism by which it spreads. Second, it has a payload that refers to what the virus does once it is executed. Sometimes a particular event triggers the virus's execution. For instance, Michelangelo's birth date triggered the Michelangelo virus. Some viruses simply infect and spread. Others do substantial damage (e.g., deleting files or corrupting the hard drive).

botnet
A huge number (e.g., hundreds of thousands) of hijacked Internet computers that have been set up to forward traffic, including spam and viruses, to other computers on the Internet.

malware
A generic term for malicious software.

virus
A piece of software code that inserts itself into a host, including the operating systems, in order to propagate; it requires that its host program be run to activate it.

CASE 11.1

EC Application

WHO IS USING YOUR PC?

International organized crime syndicates, al-Qaida groups, and other cybercriminals steal hundreds of billions of dollars every year. Cybercrime is safer and easier than selling drugs, dealing in black market diamonds or robbing banks. Online gambling offers easy fronts for international money laundering operations. And hack attacks are a key weapon of global jihad.

A customer, Stacey, placed an order online with an English motorcycle accessory company, Davida. After her purchase of a $255 Deluxe Jet helmet, she found herself in the shadowy world of global jihad. Stacey, a St. Petersburg lawyer, learned that she was among several Davida customers whose personal and credit information was placed on a public Web site *3asfh.net*. The site, hosted temporarily by a Tampa-based ISP, has been used to exchange information on hacking by people waging war in the name of Islam. Her loss was modest with no charges over $40, but other victims discovered attempts to charge more than $1,000. Investigators and Internet security experts knew more was at stake.

For example, credit card fraud financed the 2002 explosion that killed more than 200 people at a nightclub in Bali, Indonesia. Imam Samudra, the man behind the attack, wrote a book in jail in which he exhorts followers to "learn to hack." The book continues, "Not just because it makes more money in three to six hours than a policeman makes in six months, because it is how we can bring America and its cronies to its knees."

Sources: Compiled from Altman (2006) and Wolfe (2006).

Questions

1. What sorts of precautions do most online shoppers use to secure their computers?

2. What are some of the major vulnerabilities on home users' computers?

worm
A software program that runs independently, consuming the resources of its host in order to maintain itself, that is capable of propagating a complete working version of itself onto another machine.

macro virus (macro worm)
A virus or worm that executes when the application object that contains the macro is opened or a particular procedure is executed.

Trojan horse
A program that appears to have a useful function but that contains a hidden function that presents a security risk.

Trojan-Phisher-Rebery
A new variant of a Trojan program that stole tens of thousands of stolen identities from 125 countries that the victims believed were collected by a legitimate company.

banking Trojan
A trojan that comes to life when computer owners visit one of a number of online banking or e-commerce sites.

rootkit
A special Trojan horse program that modifies existing operating system software so that an intruder can hide the presence of the Trojan program.

Unlike a virus, a **worm** can spread itself without any human intervention. Worms use networks to propagate and infect a computer or handheld device (e.g., cell phone) and can even spread via instant messages. Also unlike viruses that generally are confined within a target computer, a worm's ability to self-propagate can degrade network performance. Worms consist of a set of common base elements: a warhead, a propagation engine, a payload, a target-selection algorithm, and a scanning engine. The warhead is the piece of code in a worm that exploits some known vulnerability. Once a worm exploits the vulnerability, its propagation engine moves the rest of the worm's code across the network. A file transfer program usually accomplishes the move. Once the entire worm moves across, it delivers its payload and then utilizes its target-selection algorithm to look for other potential victims to attack (e.g., e-mail addresses on the victimized machine). The scanning engine determines which of the other potential victims it can exploit. When it finds a suitable target, it repeats the entire process. The entire process takes seconds or less, which is why a worm can spread to thousands of machines.

A **macro virus** or **macro worm** is executed when the application object that contains the macro is opened or a particular procedure is executed.

Antivirus software can stop viruses and other forms of malware, including worms. Because worms spread much more rapidly than viruses, organizations need to proactively track new vulnerabilities and apply system patches as a defense against their spread.

A **Trojan horse** is a program that appears to have a useful function but contains a hidden function that presents a security risk. The name is derived from the Trojan horse in Greek mythology. Legend has it that during the Trojan War the city of Troy was presented with a large wooden horse as a gift to the goddess Athena. The Trojans hauled the horse into the city gates. During the night, Greek soldiers, who were hiding in the hollow horse, opened the gates of Troy and let in the Greek army. The army was able to take the city and win the war.

There are many types of Trojan horse programs. The programs of interest are those that make it possible for someone else to access and control a person's computer over the Internet. This type of Trojan horse has two parts: a server and a client. The *server* is the program that runs on the computer under attack. The *client* program is the program used by the person perpetrating the attack. For example, the Girlfriend Trojan is a server program that arrives in the form of a file that looks like an interesting game or program. When the unsuspecting user runs the program, the user unknowingly installs the Trojan program. The installed program executes every time the user turns on the attacked computer. The server simply waits for the associated client program to send a command. This particular Trojan horse enables the perpetrator to capture user IDs and passwords, to display messages on the affected computer, to delete and upload files, and so on.

Malware is used to commit new computer crimes. For example, spyware researchers at Webroot Software uncovered a stash of tens of thousands of stolen identities from 125 countries that they believe were collected by a new variant of a Trojan program the company named **Trojan-Phisher-Rebery** (Roberts 2006). The Rebery malicious software is an example of a **banking Trojan**, which is programmed to come to life when computer owners visit one of a number of online banking or e-commerce sites. Without strong defenses—including AUP and secure procedures—e-commerce can lose a lot of customers.

Bank of America has 19 million customers online and processes more transactions online than it does in all its physical banking centers. In February 2005, a customer, Ahlo, a Miami wholesaler of ink and toner cartridges, sued Bank of America (Gage 2006). Ahlo held the bank responsible for an unauthorized transfer of more than $90,000 from Ahlo's account to a bank in Latvia. A Coreflood Trojan infected the company's PC. The Trojan was spread by a phishing attack—fraudulent e-mails that tricked bank customers into giving up their account information and infecting their computers with malware that logged keystrokes. (The bank does not discuss individual phishing attempts but posted information on its Web site, bofa.com/privacy, to educate customers about online fraud.) Bank of America's battle against phishing shows how hard it is for businesses that have grown by acquiring companies with incompatible information systems to protect gullible and sometimes lazy or "can't happen to me" mentality customers from cybercrime.

One key malware trend is the rise of code that exploits and alters the user's operating system down to the kernel level. The *kernel* controls things such as a computer's memory, file system, hardware, and other critical components that are crucial to the operation of the machine. **Rootkits** fall into this category of code; they are special Trojan horse programs that modify the existing operating system software so that an intruder can hide the presence of the Trojan program. For example, in the UNIX operating system the "–ls" command is used to list the files on the machine. Using a rootkit, an intruder could substitute his or her own "-ls" command that would hide the Trojan program's presence by failing to list it when the "-ls" command is issued.

The best way to defend against Trojan horses is to implement strict AUPs and procedures for installing new software. In an organization, end users should be forbidden from installing unauthorized programs. Administrators need to check the integrity of programs and patches that are installed. In the same vein, new programs and tools should be installed in a test environment before putting them into a production environment.

Section 11.6 ▶ REVIEW QUESTIONS

1. Describe the difference between a nontechnical and a technical cyberattack.
2. How has the time-to-exploitation changed, and what is the impact of that change?
3. How are DOS attacks perpetrated?
4. What are the major forms of malicious code?
5. What factors account for the increase in malicious code?
6. What are some of the major trends in malicious code?

11.7 SECURING E-COMMERCE COMMUNICATIONS

Most organizations rely on multiple technologies to secure their networks. These technologies can be divided into two major groups: those designed to secure communications *across* the network and those designed to protect the servers and clients *on* the network. This section considers the first of these technologies.

ACCESS CONTROL

Network security depends on access control. **Access control** determines who (person, program, or machine) can legitimately use a network resource and which resources he, she, or it can use. A resource can be anything—Web pages, text files, databases, applications, servers, printers, or any other information source or network component. Typically, access control lists (ACLs) define which users have access to which resources and what rights they have with respect to those resources (i.e., read, view, write, print, copy, delete, execute, modify, or move). Each resource needs to be considered separately, and the rights of particular users or categories of users (e.g., system administrators, northwest sales reps, product marketing department, trading partners, etc.) need to be established. Creating various roles or groups assigning rights to those groups and then specifying the individuals within those groups simplifies the process and reduces errors. Users' network login IDs, which are checked when the user first accesses the system, identifies them.

After a user has been identified, the user must be authenticated. As noted earlier, authentication is the process of verifying that the user is who he or she claims to be. Verification usually is based on one or more characteristics that distinguish the individual from others. The distinguishing characteristics can be based on something one knows (e.g., passwords), something one has (e.g., a token), or something one possesses (e.g., fingerprint). Traditionally, authentication has been based on passwords. Passwords are notoriously insecure because people have a habit of writing them down in easy-to-find places, choosing values that are guessed easily, and willingly telling people their passwords when asked.

Combining something a user knows with something a user has, a technique known as *two-factor authentication*, achieves stronger security. Tokens qualify as something a user has. Tokens come in various shapes, forms, and sizes. **Passive tokens** are storage devices that contain a secret code. The most common passive tokens are plastic cards with magnetic strips containing a hidden code. With passive tokens, the user swipes the token through a reader attached to a personal computer or workstation and then enters his or her password to gain access to the network.

Active tokens usually are small stand-alone electronic devices (e.g., key chain tokens, smartcards, calculators, USB dongles) that generate one-time passwords. In this case, the

access control
Mechanism that determines who can legitimately use a network resource.

passive token
Storage device (e.g., magnetic strip) that contains a secret code used in a two-factor authentication system.

active token
Small, stand-alone electronic device that generates one-time passwords used in a two-factor authentication system.

user enters a PIN into the token, the token generates a password that is only good for a single log-on, and the user then logs on to the system using the one-time password. ActivIdentity (actividentity.com) and CRYPTOcard (cryptocard.com) are companies that provide active token authentication devices.

Biometric Systems

Two-factor authentication also can be based on a biological or physical trait. Fingerprint scanners, iris scanners, facial recognition systems, and voice recognition all are examples of **biometric systems** that recognize a person by some physical trait. Biometric systems can *identify* a person from a population of enrolled users by searching through a database for a match based on the person's biometric trait, or the system can *verify* a person's claimed identity by matching the individual's biometric trait against a previously stored version. Biometric verification is much simpler than biometric identification, and it is the process used in two-factor authentication. See Case 11.2.

Interest in biometric security is increasing, spurred by declining prices in biometric systems, the worldwide focus on terrorism, and soaring fraud and identity theft. Many financial institutions, for instance, are interested in using a combination of smartcards and biometrics to authenticate customers and ensure nonrepudiation for online banking, trading, and purchasing transactions. Retail point-of-sale system vendors are looking to biometrics to supplement signature verification for credit card purchases. Biometrics also are being tested in various national security and governmental applications, including airport security, passport verification, and social service fraud prevention. Fingerprint scanning is the most widely used biometric, with scans of irises, hands, and facial characteristics the next most popular.

To implement a biometric authentication system, the physiological or behavioral characteristics of a participant must be scanned repeatedly under different settings. The scans are then averaged to produce a biometric template, or identifier. The template is stored in a database as a series of numbers that can range from a few bytes for hand geometry to several thousand bytes for facial recognition. When a person uses a biometric system, a live scan is conducted, and the scan is converted to a series of numbers that is then compared against the template stored in the database.

PUBLIC KEY INFRASTRUCTURE

The "state of the art" in authentication rests on the **public key infrastructure (PKI).** In this case, the something a user has is not a token, but a certificate. PKI has become the cornerstone for secure e-payments. It refers to the technical components, infrastructure, and practices needed to enable the use of public key encryption, digital signatures, and digital certificates with a network application. PKI also is the foundation of a number of network applications, including SCM, VPNs, secure e-mail, and intranet applications.

Private and Public Key Encryption

PKI is based on *encryption*. **Encryption** is the process of transforming or scrambling (encrypting) data in such a way that it is difficult, expensive, or time-consuming for an unauthorized person to unscramble (decrypt) it. All encryption has five basic parts (refer again to Exhibit 11.3): *plaintext, ciphertext,* an *encryption algorithm,* the *key,* and *key space.* **Plaintext** is a human-readable text or message. **Ciphertext** is not human-readable because it has been encrypted. The **encryption algorithm** is the set of procedures or mathematical functions to encrypt or decrypt a message. Typically, the algorithm is not the secret piece of the encryption process. The **key** (or **key value**) is the secret value used with the algorithm to transform the message. The **key space** is the large number of possible key values (keys) created by the algorithm to use when transforming the message.

The two major classes of encryption systems are *symmetric systems,* with one secret key, and *asymmetric systems,* with two keys.

biometric systems
Authentication systems that identify a person by measurement of a biological characteristic, such as fingerprints, iris (eye) patterns, facial features, or voice.

public key infrastructure (PKI)
A scheme for securing e-payments using public key encryption and various technical components.

encryption
The process of scrambling (encrypting) a message in such a way that it is difficult, expensive, or time-consuming for an unauthorized person to unscramble (decrypt) it.

plaintext
An unencrypted message in human-readable form.

ciphertext
A plaintext message after it has been encrypted into a machine-readable form.

encryption algorithm
The mathematical formula used to encrypt the plaintext into the ciphertext, and vice versa.

Key (key value)
The secret code used to encrypt and decrypt a message.

key space
The large number of possible key values (keys) created by the algorithm to use when transforming the message.

CASE 11.2
EC Application
THE EYES HAVE IT

With increasing concerns over terrorism, air safety, and fraud, the United Kingdom has begun testing biometric identification and authentication for both security and commercial purposes. In one pilot project, British Airways and Virgin Atlantic tested an iris-scanning system from EyeTicket Corporation at Heathrow Airport in London, JFK Airport in New York City, and Dulles Airport outside Washington, D.C. The six-month pilot, which occurred in 2002, was arranged by the UK's Simplifying Passenger Travel Project (SPT) of the International Air Transport Association (IATA). The major goal of the project was to determine whether iris scanning could be used with passports to speed the authentication process for international travelers entering the United Kingdom.

The two airlines chose participants from among their frequent-flyer programs, focusing on passengers who made frequent trips between the United States and the United Kingdom. Potential participants registered for the program via e-mail. The UK Immigration Service interviewed them to ensure that there were no security issues. Approximately 900 people registered for the program.

The actual tests involved iris-scanning enrollment stations at Heathrow, JFK, and Dulles, as well as video cameras and a recognition station located at Heathrow. Passengers who participated in the program enrolled only once. This was done at the enrollment stations by taking a close-up digital image of the passenger's iris. The image was then stored as a template in a computer file. When a passenger landed at Heathrow, the passenger's iris was scanned at the recognition station and compared to the stored template. If a match occurred, the passenger passed through immigration. On average, the scan and match took about 12 seconds. If the match failed, the passenger had to move to the regular immigration line. The failure rate was only 7 percent. Watery eyes and long eyelashes were some of the major sources of failure.

According to the IATA's SPT regional group in charge of the project, the initial findings of the pilot project were encouraging. Not only did the biometric system simplify and speed the arrival process, but the system also successfully verified passengers, maintained border integrity, and was well received by the participants.

Despite the success of the pilot project, there are barriers to using the system for larger populations of passengers. One of the major barriers is the initial registration. According to the Immigration Service, the most difficult and time-consuming aspect of the pilot program was working through the processes and procedures for registration and risk assessment. As noted, the pilot only involved around 900 passengers. It would be much more difficult to register thousands or millions of passengers. Likewise, it would be a much slower process to compare a scanned iris against thousands or millions of iris templates.

Another barrier to wider deployment is the lack of technical and procedural standards. On the technical front, there are no standards for iris scanning. The EyeTicket system is based on an iris-scanning algorithm originally created by Jeffrey Daugman, a professor at Cambridge University. Other iris enrollment and scanning devices use other algorithms. This makes it difficult to share templates across systems and across borders. There is also a need for standard procedures. Without common enrollment, authentication, and identification procedures, there is little basis for trust among different government agencies or different governments.

Even with standards, the prospects for using iris scanning or any other biometric at airports for identification are poor. In 2003, face-recognition systems at Boston's Logan Airport failed to recognize volunteers posing as terrorists 96 times during a three-month period and incorrectly identified the innocent an equal number of times. Similar results were obtained in an earlier trial at Palm Beach International Airport, with more than 50 percent of those who should have been identified going undetected and two to three innocent passengers being flagged every hour. Such results in a larger population would bring airport security to its knees.

According to the TSSI Biometrics in Britain Study 2006, undertaken by TSSI Systems, Britain's document and identity security specialists, the UK public is now overwhelmingly in favor of wider biometrics use. Seventy-six percent are more in favor of biometrics than they were in 2005. The striking opinion change comes after a year in which the United Kingdom has thwarted an airline terrorist plot and 15 months after the London transport bombings of July 2005. Personal safety was identified as the biggest driver for the change: three-quarters of people believed it was important for combating terrorism. However, there is widespread public confusion about what biometrics mean in practice, with the majority of people confused about the terminology. In addition, concerns about civil liberties were highlighted by almost a third of respondents. The TSSI Biometrics in Britain Study 2006 management report with full details of the findings, issues raised, and recommendations can be requested from TSSI at tssi.co.uk/tssi/biometric-britain.html.

Sources: Emigh (2004), TSSI (2006), and Venes (2004).

Questions

1. What were the major components in the EyeTicket iris-scanning system?

2. What are some of the difficulties in using iris scanning to verify passengers for passport control?

3. Is it reasonable to use iris scanning or any other biometric to identify terrorists at airports?

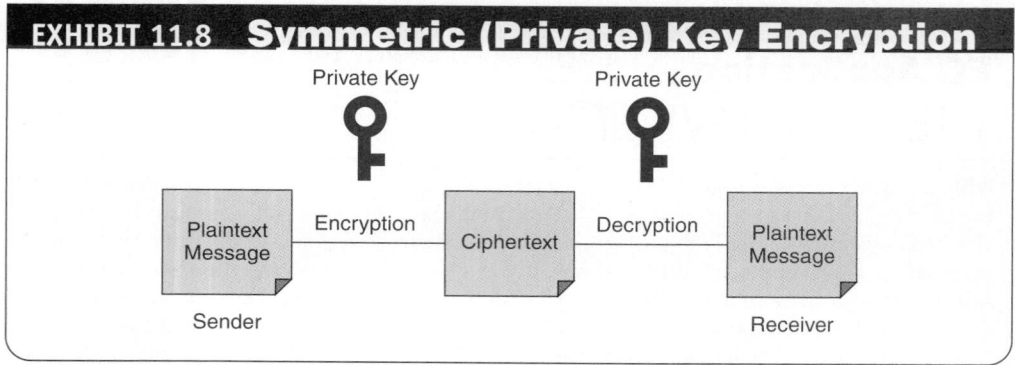

EXHIBIT 11.8 Symmetric (Private) Key Encryption

symmetric (private) key system
An encryption system that uses the same key to encrypt and decrypt the message.

Data Encryption Standard (DES)
The standard symmetric encryption algorithm supported by the NIST and used by U.S. government agencies until October 2000.

Rijndael
An advanced encryption standard (AES) used to secure U.S. government communications since October 2, 2000.

public (asymmetric) key encryption
Method of encryption that uses a pair of matched keys—a public key to encrypt a message and a private key to decrypt it, or vice versa.

public key
Encryption code that is publicly available to anyone.

private key
Encryption code that is known only to its owner.

RSA
The most common public key encryption algorithm; uses keys ranging in length from 512 bits to 1,024 bits.

Symmetric (Private) Key System

In a **symmetric (private) key system,** the same key is used to encrypt and decrypt the plaintext (see Exhibit 11.8). The sender and receiver of the text must share the same key without revealing it to anyone else—making it a so-called *private* system.

The **Data Encryption Standard (DES)** had been the standard symmetric encryption algorithm supported by U.S. government agencies. In 2000, the National Institute of Standards and Technology (NIST) replaced DES with **Rijndael**, the new advanced encryption standard for encrypting sensitive but unclassified government data. DES had become too susceptible to attacks.

Because the algorithms used to encrypt a message are well known, the confidentiality of a message depends on the key. It is possible to guess a key simply by having a computer try all the encryption combinations until the message is decrypted. High-speed and parallel-processing computers can try millions of guesses in a second. This is why the length of the key (in bits) is the main factor in securing a message. If a key were 4 bits long (e.g., 1011), there would be only 16 possible combinations (i.e., 2 raised to the fourth power). However, a 64-bit encryption key would take 58.5 years to be broken at 10 million keys per second.

Public (Asymmetric) Key Encryption

Imagine trying to use one-key encryption to buy something offered on a particular Web server. If the seller's key was distributed to thousands of buyers, then the key would not remain secret for long. This is where public key (asymmetric) encryption comes into play. **Public (asymmetric) key encryption** uses a pair of matched keys—a **public key** that is publicly available to anyone and a **private key** that is known only to its owner. If a message is encrypted with a public key, then the associated private key is required to decrypt the message. If, for example, a person wanted to send a purchase order to a company and have the contents remain private, he or she would encrypt the message with the company's public key. When the company received the order, it would decrypt it with the associated private key.

The most common public key encryption algorithm is **RSA** (rsa.com). RSA uses keys ranging in length from 512 bits to 1,024 bits. The main problem with public key encryption is speed. Symmetrical algorithms are significantly faster than asymmetric key algorithms. Therefore, public key encryption cannot be used effectively to encrypt and decrypt large amounts of data. In practice, a combination of symmetric and asymmetric encryption encrypts messages.

Digital Signatures and Certificate Authorities

In effect, a digital signature is the electronic equivalent of a personal signature that cannot be forged. Digital signatures are based on public keys for authenticating the identity of the sender of a message or document. They also can ensure that the original content of an electronic message or document is unchanged. Digital signatures have additional benefits in the online world. They are portable, cannot be easily repudiated or imitated, and can be time-stamped.

See Exhibit 11.4 to review how a digital signature works. Suppose a person wants to send the draft of a financial contract to a company with whom he or she plans to do business as an e-mail message. The sender wants to assure the company that the content of the draft has not been changed en route and that he or she really is the sender. To do so, the sender takes the following steps:

1. The sender creates the e-mail message with the contract in it.

2. Using special software, a mathematical computation called a **hash** function is applied to the message, which results in a special summary of the message, converted into a string of digits called a **message digest (MD)**.

3. The sender uses his or her private key to encrypt the hash. This is the sender's *digital signature*. No one else can replicate the sender's digital signature because it is based on the sender's private key.

4. The sender encrypts both the original message and the digital signature using the recipient's public key. This is the **digital envelope**.

5. The sender e-mails the digital envelope to the receiver.

6. Upon receipt, the receiver uses his or her private key to decrypt the contents of the digital envelope. This produces a copy of the message and the sender's digital signature.

7. The receiver uses the sender's public key to decrypt the digital signature, resulting in a copy of the original message digest.

8. Using the same hash function employed in step 2, the recipient then creates a message digest from the decrypted message.

9. The recipient compares this digest with the original message digest.

10. If the two digests match, then the recipient concludes that the message is authentic.

In this scenario, the company has evidence that the sender sent the e-mail because (theoretically) the sender is the only one with access to the private key. The recipient knows that the message has not been tampered with because if it had been, the two hashes would not have matched.

According to the U.S. Federal Electronic Signatures in Global and National Commerce Act that went into effect in October 2000, digital signatures in the United States have the same legal standing as a signature written in ink on paper. Although PKI is the foundation of digital signatures, two-factor authentication often is used to verify a person's legal identity. For example, PKI can be used with personal smart cards or biometric systems to corroborate an identity.

Third parties called **certificate authorities (CAs)** issue digital certificates. A certificate contains things such as the holder's name, validity period, public key information, and a signed hash of the certificate data (i.e., hashed contents of the certificate signed with the CA's private key). There are different types of certificates, namely those used to authenticate Web sites (*site certificates*), individuals (*personal certificates*), and software companies (*software publisher certificates*).

There are a large number of third-party CAs. VeriSign (verisign.com) is the best known of the CAs. VeriSign issues three classes of certificates: Class 1 verifies that an e-mail actually comes from the user's address. Class 2 checks the user's identity against a commercial credit database. Class 3 requires notarized documents. Companies such as Microsoft offer systems that enable companies to issue their own private, in-house certificates.

Secure Socket Layer (SSL)

If the average user had to figure out how to use encryption, digital certificates, digital signatures, and the like, there would be few secure transactions on the Web. Fortunately, Web browsers and Web servers handle many of these issues in a transparent fashion. Given that different companies, financial institutions, and governments in many countries are involved in e-commerce, it is necessary to have generally accepted protocols for securing e-commerce. One of the major protocols in use today is Secure Socket Layer (SSL), also known as Transport Layer Security (TLS).

The **Secure Socket Layer (SSL)** was invented by Netscape to use standard certificates for authentication and data encryption to ensure privacy or confidentiality. SSL became a de facto standard adopted by the browsers and servers provided by Microsoft and Netscape. In 1996, SSL was renamed **Transport Layer Security (TLS),** but many people still use the SSL name. It is the major standard used for online credit card payments.

SSL makes it possible to encrypt credit card numbers and other transmissions between a Web server and a Web browser. In the case of credit card transactions, there is more to

hash
A mathematical computation that is applied to a message, using a private key, to encrypt the message.

message digest (MD)
A summary of a message, converted into a string of digits after the hash has been applied.

digital envelope
The combination of the encrypted original message and the digital signature, using the recipient's public key.

certificate authorities (CAs)
Third parties that issue digital certificates.

Secure Socket Layer (SSL)
Protocol that utilizes standard certificates for authentication and data encryption to ensure privacy or confidentiality.

Transport Layer Security (TLS)
As of 1996, another name for the SSL protocol.

making a purchase on the Web than simply passing an encrypted credit card number to a merchant. The number must be checked for validity, the consumer's bank must authorize the card, and the purchase must be processed. SSL is not designed to handle any of the steps beyond the transmission of the card number.

Section 11.7 ▶ REVIEW QUESTIONS

1. What are the basic elements of an authentication system?
2. What is a passive token? An active token?
3. Describe the five basic components of encryption.
4. What are the key elements of PKI?
5. What are the basic differences between symmetric and asymmetric encryption?
6. What role does a certificate authority play?
7. What is the SSL protocol?

11.8 SECURING E-COMMERCE NETWORKS

Several technologies exist that ensure that an organization's network boundaries are secure from cyberattack or intrusion and that if the organization's boundaries are compromised the intrusion is detected. The selection and operation of these technologies should be based on certain design concepts:

▶ **Defense in depth.** Relying on a single technology to defend against attacks is doomed to failure. Layers of security technologies must be applied at key points in a network (see Exhibit 11.9). This is probably the most important concept in designing a secure system.

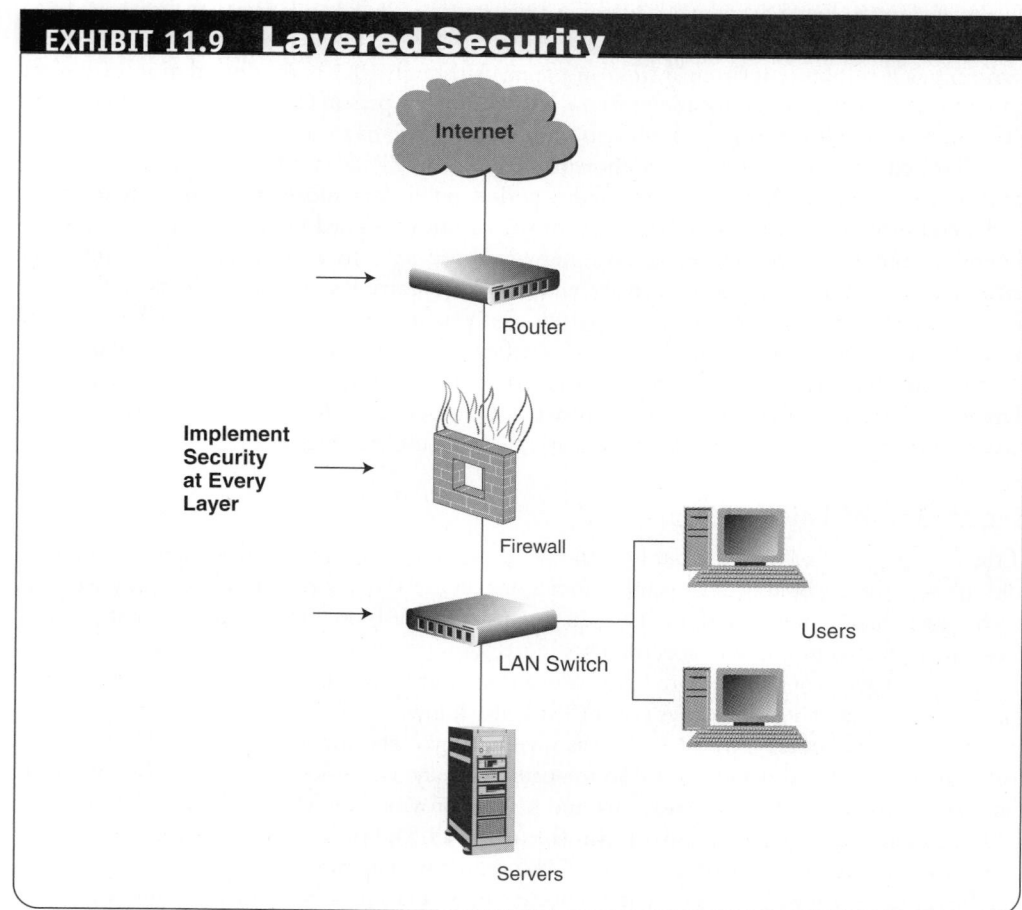

EXHIBIT 11.9 Layered Security

- **Need-to-access basis.** Access to a network ought to be based on the **policy of least privilege (POLP).** By default, access to network resources should be blocked and permitted only when needed to conduct business.
- **Role-specific security.** As noted in Section 11.7, access to particular network resources should be based on a user's role within an organization.
- **Monitoring.** Real-time monitoring has become essential because of zero-day exploits and emerging hacker threats.
- **Patch management.** Vendors (such as Microsoft) are continually patching or upgrading their software, applications, and systems to plug security holes. The only way to take advantage of these fixes is to install the patches or upgrades. Newer versions of software (e.g., operating systems such as Windows Vista) have automatic update functionality built in. This makes it easier for organizations and individuals to track fixes.
- **Incident response team (IRT).** Regardless of the organization's size, its networks will be attacked. For this reason, organizations need to have a team in place that can respond to these attacks. The team needs to have well-established plans, processes, and resources and should practice responding when the pressure is off rather than learning during a crisis.

> **policy of least privilege (POLP)**
> Policy of blocking access to network resources unless access is required to conduct business.

FIREWALLS

Firewalls are barriers between a trusted network or PC and the untrustworthy Internet. Technically, it is a network node consisting of both hardware and software that isolates a private network from a public network. On the Internet, the data and requests sent from one computer to another are broken into segments called **packets.** Each packet contains the Internet address of the computer sending the data, as well as the Internet address of the computer receiving the data. Packets also contain other identifying information that can distinguish one packet from another. A firewall examines all data packets that pass through it and then takes appropriate action—to allow or not to allow. Firewalls can be designed to protect against:

Remote login. When someone connects to your PC and gains control of it. Examples: being able to view or access your files; running programs on your PC.

Application backdoors. Some programs have special features that allow for remote access. Others contain bugs that provide a backdoor, or hidden access, that provides some level of control of the program.

SMTP session hijacking. SMTP is the most common method of sending e-mail over the Internet. By gaining access to a list of e-mail addresses, a person can send spam to thousands of users. This is done quite often by redirecting the e-mail through the SMTP server of an unsuspecting host, making the actual sender of the spam difficult to trace.

Macros. To simplify complicated procedures, many applications allow you to create a script of commands that the application can run. This script is known as a macro. Hackers create their own macros that, depending on the application, can destroy your data or crash your PC.

Viruses. Range from harmless messages to erasing all your data.

Spam. The electronic equivalent of junk mail. Spam can be dangerous. Often it contains links to dangerous Web sites.

Some firewalls filter data and requests from the Internet to a private network based on the network IP addresses of the computer sending or receiving the request. These firewalls are called **packet-filtering routers. Packet filters** are rules that can accept or reject incoming packets based on source and destination addresses and the other identifying information. Some simple examples of packet filters include the following:

- **Block all packets sent from a given Internet address.** Companies sometimes use this to block requests from computers owned by competitors.
- **Block any packet coming from the outside that has the address of a computer on the inside.** Companies use this type of rule to block requests where an intruder is using his or her computer to impersonate a computer that belongs to the company.

> **firewall**
> A single point between two or more networks where all traffic must pass (choke point); the device authenticates, controls, and logs all traffic.

> **packet**
> Segment of data sent from one computer to another on a network.

> **packet-filtering routers**
> Firewalls that filter data and requests moving from the public Internet to a private network based on the network addresses of the computer sending or receiving the request.

> **packet filters**
> Rules that can accept or reject incoming packets based on source and destination addresses and the other identifying information.

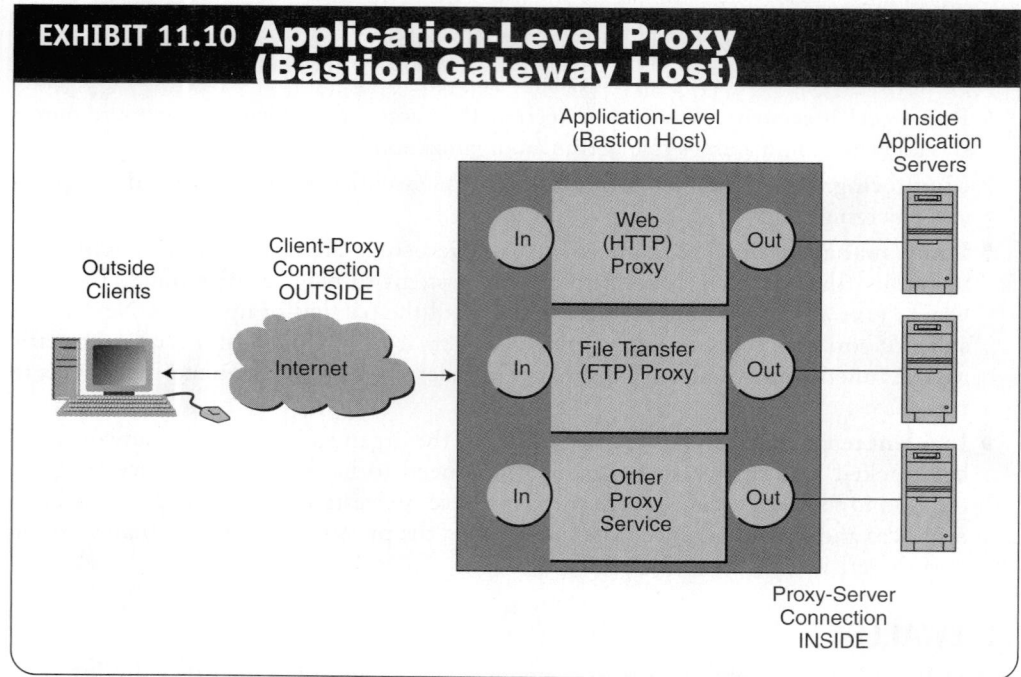

EXHIBIT 11.10 Application-Level Proxy (Bastion Gateway Host)

application-level proxy
A firewall that permits requests for Web pages to move from the public Internet to the private network.

bastion gateway
A special hardware server that utilizes application-level proxy software to limit the types of requests that can be passed to an organization's internal networks from the public Internet.

proxies
Special software programs that run on the gateway server and pass repackaged packets from one network to the other.

demilitarized zone (DMZ)
Network area that sits between an organization's internal network and an external network (Internet), providing physical isolation between the two networks that is controlled by rules enforced by a firewall.

However, packet filters have their disadvantages. In setting up the rules, an administrator might miss some important rules or incorrectly specify a rule, thus leaving a hole in the firewall. Additionally, because the content of a packet is irrelevant to a packet filter, once a packet is let through the firewall, the inside network is open to data-driven attacks. That is, the data may contain hidden instructions that cause the receiving computer to modify access control or security-related files.

Packet-filtering routers often are the first layer of network defense. Other firewalls form the second layer. These later firewalls block data and requests depending on the type of application being accessed. For instance, a firewall may permit requests for Web pages to move from the public Internet to the private network. This type of firewall is called an **application-level proxy.** In an application-level proxy, there is often a special server called a **bastion gateway.** The bastion gateway server has two network cards so that data packets reaching one card are not relayed to the other card (see Exhibit 11.10). Instead, special software programs called **proxies** run on the bastion gateway server and pass repackaged packets from one network to the other. Each Internet service that an organization wishes to support has a proxy. For instance, there is a Web (i.e., HTTP) proxy, a file transfer (FTP) proxy, and so on. Special proxies also can be established to allow business partners, for example, to access particular applications running inside the firewall. If a request is made for an unsupported proxy service, then it is blocked by the firewall.

In addition to controlling inbound traffic, the firewall and proxies control outbound traffic. All outbound traffic requests are first sent to the proxy server and then forwarded by the proxy on behalf of the computers behind the firewall. This makes all the requests look as if they were coming from a single computer rather than multiple computers. In this way, the Internet addresses of the internal computers are hidden to the outside.

One disadvantage of an application-level proxy firewall is performance degradation. It takes more processing time to tie particular packets to particular applications. Another disadvantage is that the users on the internal network must configure their machines or browsers to send their Internet requests via the proxy server.

DEMILITARIZED ZONE

A **demilitarized zone (DMZ)** is a network area that sits between an organization's internal network and an external network (Internet), providing physical isolation between the two networks that is controlled by rules enforced by a firewall. For example, suppose a company

EXHIBIT 11.11 Demilitarized Zone (DMZ)

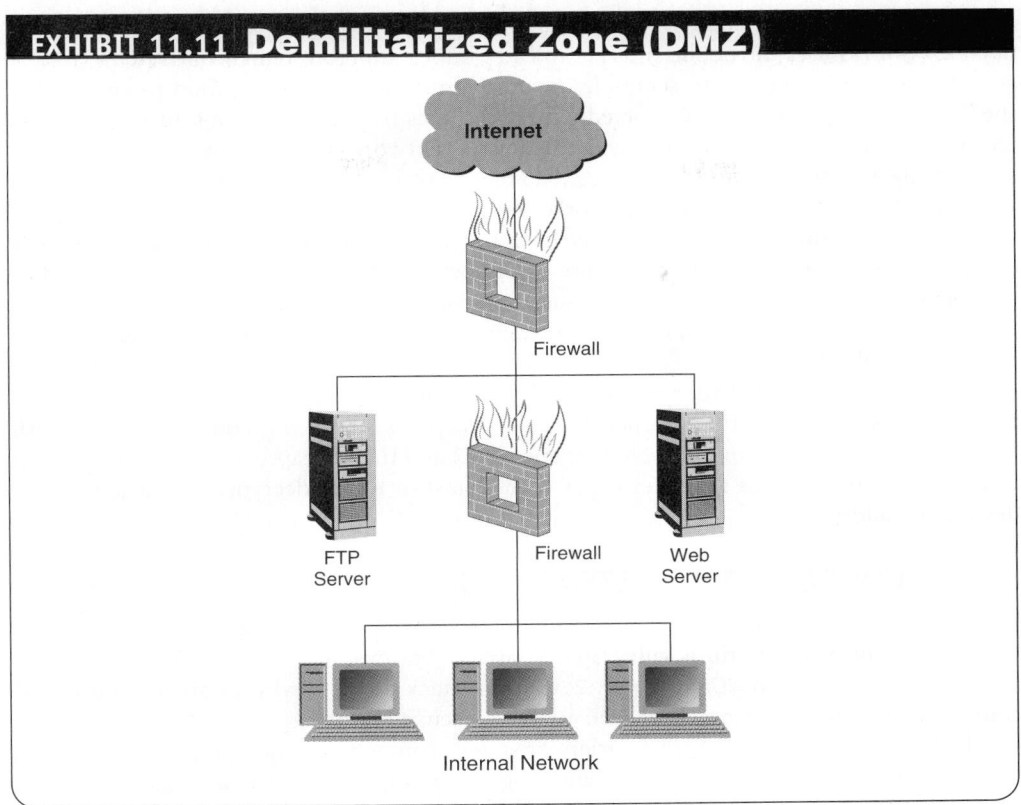

wants to run its own Web site. In a DMZ setup, the company would put the Web server on a publicly accessible network and the rest of its servers on a private internal network. A firewall would then be configured to direct requests coming from the outside to the appropriate network and servers. In most cases, a second firewall fronts the internal network to doubly ensure that intrusive requests do not get through to the private network (see Exhibit 11.11).

PERSONAL FIREWALLS

Users with high-speed broadband (cable modem or digital subscriber lines [DSL]) Internet connections to their homes or small businesses have increased. These "always-on" connections are much more vulnerable to attack than simple dial-up connections. With these connections, the homeowner or small business owner runs the risks of information being stolen or destroyed, of sensitive information (e.g., personal or business financial information) being accessed, and of the computer being used in a DOS attack on others.

Personal firewalls protect desktop systems by monitoring all the traffic that passes through the computer's network interface card. They operate in one of two ways. With the first method, the owner can create filtering rules (much like packet filtering) that the firewall uses to permit or delete packets. With the other method, the firewall can learn, by asking the user questions, how it should handle particular traffic. For a detailed comparison of a number of these products, see firewallguide.com/software.htm.

personal firewall
A network node designed to protect an individual user's desktop system from the public network by monitoring all the traffic that passes through the computer's network interface card.

VPNs

Suppose a company wants to establish a B2B application, providing suppliers, partners, and others access not only to data residing on its internal Web site, but also to data contained in other files (e.g., Word documents) or in legacy systems (e.g., large relational databases). Traditionally, communications with the company would have taken place over a private leased line or through a dial-up line to a bank of modems or a remote access server (RAS) that provided direct connections to the company's LAN. With a private line, the chances of a hacker eavesdropping on the communications between the companies would be nil, but it is an expensive way to do business.

virtual private network (VPN)

A network that uses the public Internet to carry information but remains private by using encryption to scramble the communications, authentication to ensure that information has not been tampered with, and access control to verify the identity of anyone using the network.

protocol tunneling

Method used to ensure confidentiality and integrity of data transmitted over the Internet, by encrypting data packets, sending them in packets across the Internet, and decrypting them at the destination address.

intrusion detection systems (IDSs)

A special category of software that can monitor activity across a network or on a host computer, watch for suspicious activity, and take automated action based on what it sees.

honeynet

A network of honeypots.

honeypot

Production system (e.g., firewalls, routers, Web servers, database servers) that looks like it does real work, but which acts as a decoy and is watched to study how network intrusions occur.

A less expensive alternative would be to use a *virtual private network*. A **virtual private network (VPN)** uses the public Internet to carry information but remains private by using a combination of encryption to scramble the communications, authentication to ensure that the information has not been tampered with and comes from a legitimate source, and access control to verify the identity of anyone using the network. In addition, a VPN can also support site-to-site communications between branch offices and corporate headquarters and the communications between mobile workers and their workplace.

VPNs can reduce communication costs dramatically. The costs are lower because VPN equipment is cheaper than other remote solutions; private leased lines are not needed to support remote access; remote users can use broadband connections rather than make long distance calls to access an organization's private network; and a single access line can be used to support multiple purposes.

The main technical challenge of a VPN is to ensure the confidentiality and integrity of the data transmitted over the Internet. This is where *protocol tunneling* comes into play. With **protocol tunneling**, data packets are first encrypted and then encapsulated into packets that can be transmitted across the Internet. A special host or router decrypts the packets at the destination address.

INTRUSION DETECTION SYSTEMS (IDSs)

Even if an organization has a well-formulated security policy and a number of security technologies in place, it still is vulnerable to attack. For example, most organizations have antivirus software, yet most are subjected to virus attacks. This is why an organization must continually watch for attempted, as well as actual, security breaches.

In the past, *audit logs*, which a variety of system components and applications produce, were reviewed manually for excessive failed log-on attempts, failed file and database access attempts, and other application and system violations. This manual procedure had its flaws. For example, if intrusion attempts were spread out over a long period of time, they could be easily missed. Today, a special category of software exists that can monitor activity across a network or on a host computer, watch for suspicious activity, and take automated action based on what it sees. This category of software is called **intrusion detection systems (IDSs).**

IDSs are either host based or network based. A *host-based IDS* resides on the server or other host system that is being monitored. Host-based systems are particularly good at detecting whether critical or security-related files have been tampered with or whether a user has attempted to access files that he or she is not authorized to use. The host-based system does this by computing a special signature or check-sum for each file. The IDS checks files on a regular basis to see if the current signatures match the previous signatures. If the signatures do not match, security personnel are notified immediately. Some examples of commercial host-based systems are Symantec's Intruder Alert (symantec.com), Tripwire Security's Tripwire (tripwiresecurity.com), and McAfee's Entercept Desktop and Server Agents (mcafee.com).

A *network-based IDS* uses rules to analyze suspicious activity at the perimeter of a network or at key locations in the network. It usually consists of a monitor—a software package that scans the network—and software agents that reside on various host computers and feed information back to the monitor. This type of IDS examines network traffic (i.e., packets) for known patterns of attack and automatically notifies security personnel when specific events or event thresholds occur. A network-based IDS also can perform certain actions when an attack occurs. For instance, it can terminate network connections or reconfigure network devices, such as firewalls and routers, based on security policies. Cisco Systems' NetRanger (cisco.com) and Computer Associates' eTrust Intrusion Detection (www3.ca.com/solutions/product.asp?id=163) are examples of commercially available network-based IDSs.

HONEYNETS AND HONEYPOTS

Honeynets are another technology that can detect and analyze intrusions. A **honeynet** is a network of honeypots designed to attract hackers like honey attracts bees. In this case, the **honeypots** are information system resources—firewalls, routers, Web servers, database servers, files, and the like—that look like production systems but do no real work. The main difference between a honeypot and the real thing is that the activities on a honeypot come from intruders attempting to compromise the system. In this way, researchers watching the honeynet can gather information about why hackers attack, when they attack, how they attack, what they do after the system is compromised, and how they communicate with one another during and after the attack.

Honeynets and honeypots originated in April 1999 with the Honeynet Project (Honeynet 2004; see honeynet.org/misc/project.html). The Honeynet Project is a worldwide, not-for-profit research group of security professionals. The group focuses on raising awareness of security risks that confront any system connected to the Internet and teaching and informing the security community about better ways to secure and defend network resources. The project runs its own honeynets but makes no attempt to attract hackers. They simply connect the honeypots to the Internet and wait for attacks to occur.

Before a company deploys a honeynet, it needs to think about what it will do when it becomes the scene of a cybercrime or contains evidence of a crime and about the legal restrictions and ramifications of monitoring legal and illegal activity. Case 11.3 discusses these issues.

CASE 11.3
EC Application

HONEYNETS AND THE LAW

Millions of networks and computers are on the Internet. Given this, what is the chance that an outside intruder will victimize a small collection of computers connected to the Internet? In the first phase of the Honeynet Project, which ran from 1999 to 2001, the honeynet consisted of eight honeypots that mimicked a typical home computer setup. Within 15 minutes of being connected to the Internet, one of the honeypots was hit. Over the course of the next few days, all the honeypots were compromised, and over the course of the next two years they were attacked repeatedly.

During the first phase, many of the attacks were crude and fairly innocuous. Today, the character of both the intrusions and the intruders has changed. The proportion of hackers involved in illegal activities of all sorts has risen dramatically. If a company deploys a honeynet, there is a good chance that it will be the scene of a cybercrime or contain evidence of a crime. Some intruders may be focused solely on attacking the honeynet itself. Others may want to use it as a zombie for launching attacks, as a place to store stolen credit cards, or as a server to distribute pirated software or child pornography. Regardless, companies need to understand the types of crimes that may occur and the legal issues that may ensue if they choose to either report or ignore these crimes. Just because the activities on a honeynet are perpetrated by intruders, it does not mean that the operator has unlimited rights to monitor the users of the network.

Although many crimes can be perpetrated against or with a honeynet, the most frequent and obvious crime is network intrusion. The Computer Fraud and Abuse Act (CFAA) is a federal law passed by the U.S. Congress in 1986 intended to reduce "hacking" of computer systems. It was amended in 1994, 1996, and 2001 by the USA PATRIOT Act. The CFAA makes it a crime to attack "protected computers," including computers "used in interstate or foreign commerce or communication." If a computer is on the Internet, it is used in interstate communication. The CFAA protects all government

computers and those used by banks and financial institutions. This means that the CFAA is going to protect most honeynets.

The Act also defines the types of attacks that constitute a crime. It is a felony if an attacker "knowingly causes the transmission of a program, information, code, or command, and as a result of such conduct, intentionally causes damage without authorization, to a protected computer." Damage occurs when there is "any impairment to the integrity or availability of data, a program, a system or information." The limitations are that in order for an attack to be a felony, one or more of the following must result: aggregate damage of at least $5,000; modification or impairment to the medical examination, diagnosis, treatment, or care of one or more individuals; physical injury to a person; a threat to public health or safety; or damage to a government computer used for the administration of justice, national defense, or national security. Under these provisions, the Act covers a wide range of activities, including:

▶ DOS attacks, viruses, and worms
▶ Simple intrusions in which the attacker causes damage
▶ Unauthorized information gathering, especially if the information is used for commercial advantage, financial gain, in furtherance of another crime, or the information is worth more than $5,000
▶ Unauthorized access to nonpublic U.S. government computers
▶ Using computers to obtain classified information without authorization
▶ Computer-related espionage, which may also constitute terrorism
▶ Trafficking in passwords
▶ Threatening to damage a computer
▶ Attempting to commit a network crime, even though the crime was never consummated

(continued)

CASE 11.3 (continued)

In running a honeynet, a company needs to be careful to ensure that it is not facilitating or helping further a crime. Precautions and actions must be taken to prevent potential or actual criminal activity from harming others; to inform authorities when criminal activities or evidence comes to light; and to ensure that the data, code, programs, and systems running on the honeynet are legal (e.g., do not store contraband on the system in an effort to trap an intruder).

The primary purpose of a commercial honeynet is to monitor and analyze intrusion and attacks. Under certain circumstances, the monitoring of these activities may constitute a criminal or civil action. In the United States, the federal Wiretap Act and the Pen Register, Trap, and Trace Devices statute place legal limits on monitoring activity. The Wiretap Act makes it illegal to intercept the contents of a communication. If intruders cannot store (either directly or indirectly) data or information on a honeynet, then the Act does not apply. If they can, then there are exceptions to the rule. For instance, if the monitoring is done to prevent abuse or damage to the system, then monitoring it is not illegal. The implication is that certain honeynet purposes and configurations are illegal and others are not.

In contrast to the Wiretap Act, the federal Pen Register, Trap, and Trace Devices statute applies to the "noncontent" aspects of a communication. For example, with telephones, telephone numbers are "noncontent." Similarly, in a network communication, network addresses are "noncontent." This statute makes it illegal to capture the noncontent information of a communication unless certain exceptions apply. The exceptions pertain primarily to actions that are taken by the communication provider (in this case the honeynet operator) to protect its rights or property. Again, certain honeynet purposes and configurations are legal and others are not.

When a company monitors the network activities of insiders and outsiders, a number of legal issues arise. Because monitoring is one of the primary activities of a honeynet, a company should consult legal counsel before deploying a honeynet and should become familiar with local law enforcement agencies that should be involved if illegal activities are observed.

Sources: Legal Information Institute of the Cornell Law School (2007), Honeynet.org, and Honeynet (2004).

Questions

1. What constitutes a crime under the CFAA?
2. What types of activities are prohibited by the CFAA?
3. What types of activities are illegal under the federal Wiretap Act? The Pen Register, Trap, and Trace Devices statute?

Section 11.8 ▶ REVIEW QUESTIONS

1. List the basic types of firewalls and briefly describe each.
2. What is a personal firewall?
3. How does a VPN work?
4. Briefly describe the major types of IDSs.
5. What is a honeynet? What is a honeypot?

MANAGERIAL ISSUES

Some managerial issues related to this chapter are as follows.

1. **Why should managers learn about EC security?** Because debilitating and devastating EC crimes cannot be stopped. Because the consequences of poor network security can be severe, it is imperative that senior management have a basic understanding of best practices in network risk management.

2. **Why is an EC security strategy and life cycle approach needed?** Without an EC security strategy to guide investments and defenses, security efforts tend to be reactive and more expensive to manage. Ineffective security opens the door to computer and network attacks that can result in damage to technical and information assets; theft of information and information services; temporary loss of a Web site and Internet access; loss of income; litigation brought on by dissatisfied organizational stakeholders; loss of customer confidence; and damaged reputation and credibility. In some cases, attacks literally can put a company out of business, especially if EC is its sole source of revenue.

3. **How should managers view EC security issues?** Suppose you decide to set up a B2B site in order to service your suppliers and partners. Because it is not a public site, the only ones who are likely to know of its existence are you, your suppliers, and your partners. You assume that there is no need to institute strong security measures. Wrong! Because of the prevalence of automated scanning tools, it will be only a matter of time before breached companies must thoroughly review their security requirements and institute stringent measures to guard against high-priority threats.

4. **What is the key to establishing strong e-commerce security?** Most discussions about security focus on technology, with statements like "firewalls are mandatory" or "all transmissions should be encrypted." Although firewalls and encryption can be important technologies, no security solution is useful unless it solves a business problem. Determining your business requirements is the most important step in creating a security solution. Business requirements, in turn, determine your information requirements. Once you know your information requirements, you can begin to understand the value of those assets and the steps that you should take to secure those that are most valuable and vulnerable.

5. **What steps should businesses follow in establishing a security plan? Security risk management** is an ongoing process involving three phases: asset identification, risk assessment, and implementation. By actively monitoring existing security policies and measures, companies can determine which are successful or unsuccessful and, in turn, which should be modified or eliminated. However, it also is important to monitor changes in business requirements, changes in technology and the way it is used, and changes in the way people can attack the systems and networks. In this way, an organization can evolve its security policies and measures, ensuring that they continue to support the critical needs of the business.

6. **Should organizations be concerned with internal security threats?** Except for malware, breaches perpetrated by insiders are much more frequent than those perpetrated by outsiders. This is true for both B2C and B2B sites. Security policies and measures for EC sites need to address these insider threats.

RESEARCH TOPICS

Here are some suggested topics related to this chapter. For details, references, and additional topics, refer to the Online Appendix A "Current EC Research."

1. **Certification Programs**
   - Limitations on the use of digital certificates
   - Certification programs that ensure trust, privacy, and safety
   - Effectiveness of certification programs in enhancing security
   - Evaluation factors for certification
   - International certification programs for secure international trades

2. **Risk Perception and the Adoption of Security Measures**
   - Customers' perceptions of risk in e-commerce and e-payment
   - Impact of consumers' perceptions of risk in conducting EC transactions
   - Inhibitors of security measure adoption
   - Relationship between a corporation's risk management system and their overall values
   - Reducing operational risk to cope with the BASEL II Accord

3. **EC Security Technologies**
   - The application of biometric technologies to authentication
   - Customer preferences for authentication schemes
   - Intelligent detection of criminal patterns on the Internet

4. **Secure Electronic Payment Protocols**
   - Protocols that avoid the disclosure of customers' bank and credit account information to merchants
   - Comparative evaluation of protocols
   - Problems with adopting the Secure Electronic Transaction (SET) protocol

5. **Design of Secure E-Commerce Sites**
   - Framework for designing secure e-commerce sites
   - Risk assessment of e-commerce sites
   - Cost and benefit of security systems for e-commerce

6. **Study Security Violation Cases and Lessons to Avoid Mistakes**
   - Cases concerning disasters caused by violated security
   - Measurements taken and studied after the violation
   - Protection schemes before the crucial violation
   - Security ethics
   - Effect of codes of conduct and certificates

SUMMARY

In this chapter, you learned about the following EC issues as they relate to the learning objectives.

1. **Stopping E-Commerce Crimes.** Responsibility or blame for cybercrimes can be placed on criminals and victimized industries, users, and organizations. The EC industry does not want to enforce safeguards that add friction to the profitable wheels of online commerce. Credit card issuers try to avoid sharing leads on criminal activity with each other or law enforcement. Online shoppers fail to take necessary precautions to avoid becoming a victim. IS designs and security architectures are still incredibly vulnerable. Organizations fail to exercise due care in business or hiring practices, outsourcing, and business partnerships. Every EC business knows that the threats of bogus credit card purchases, data breaches, phishing, malware, and pretexting never end—and that these threats must be addressed comprehensively and strategically.

2. **EC Security Strategy and Life Cycle Approach.** EC security will remain an evolving discipline because threats change, e-business needs change, and Web-based technologies to provide greater service change. An EC security strategy is needed to optimize EC security programs for efficiency and effectiveness. There are several reasons why. EC security costs and efforts from reacting to crises and paying for damages are greater than if organizations had an EC security strategy. The Internet is still a fundamentally insecure infrastructure. There are many criminals, and they are intent on stealing information for identity theft and fraud. Without a strategy, EC security is treated as a project instead of an ongoing, never-ending process.

3. **Information Assurance.** The importance of the Information Assurance model to EC is that it represents the processes for protecting information by ensuring its confidentiality, integrity, and availability. Confidentiality is the assurance of data privacy. Integrity is the assurance that data is accurate or that a message has not been altered. Availability is the assurance that access to data, the Web site, or other EC data service is timely, available, reliable, and restricted to authorized users.

4. **Enterprisewide EC Security and Privacy Model.** EC and network security are inconvenient, expensive, tedious, and never ending. A defense-in-depth model that views EC security as a combination of commitment, people, processes, and technology is essential. An effective program starts with senior management's commitment and budgeting support. This sets the tone that EC security is important to the organization. Other components are security policies and training. Security procedures must be defined with positive incentives for compliance and negative consequences for violations. The last stage is the deployment of hardware and software tools based on the policies and procedures defined by the management team.

5. **Basic EC Security Issues and Perspectives.** Owners of EC sites need to be concerned with multiple security issues: authentication, verifying the identity of the participants in a transaction; authorization, ensuring that a person or process has access rights to particular systems or data; auditing, being able to determine whether particular actions have been taken and by whom; confidentiality, ensuring that information is not disclosed to unauthorized individuals, systems, or processes; integrity, protecting data from being altered or destroyed; availability, ensuring that data and services are available when needed; and nonrepudiation, the ability to limit parties from refuting that a legitimate transaction took place.

6. **Threats and attacks.** EC sites are exposed to a wide range of attacks. Attacks may be nontechnical (social engineering), in which a perpetrator tricks people into revealing information or performing actions that compromise network security. Or they may be technical, whereby software and systems expertise are used to attack the network. DOS attacks bring operations to a halt by sending floods of data to target computers or to as many computers on the Internet as possible. Malicious code attacks include viruses, worms, Trojan horses, or some combination of these. Over the past couple of years, various trends in malicious code have emerged, including an increase in the speed and volume of attacks; reduced time between the discovery of a vulnerability and the release of an attack to exploit the vulnerability; the growing use of bots to launch attacks; an increase in attacks on Web applications; and a shift to profit-motivated attacks.

7. **Securing EC communications.** In EC, issues of trust are paramount. Trust starts with the authentication of the parties involved in a transaction; that is, identifying the parties in a transaction along with the actions they can perform. Authentication can be established with something one knows (e.g., a password), something one has (e.g., a token), or something one possesses (e.g., a fingerprint). Biometric systems can confirm a person's identity. Fingerprint scanners, iris scanners, facial recognition, and voice recognition are examples of biometric systems. Public key infrastructure (PKI), which is the cornerstone of secure e-payments, also can authenticate the parties in a transaction. PKI uses encryption (private and public) to ensure privacy and integrity and digital signatures to ensure authenticity and nonrepudiation. Digital signatures are themselves authenticated through a system of digital certificates issued by certificate authorities (CAs). For the average consumer and merchant, PKI is simplified because it is built into Web browsers and services. Such tools are secure because security is based on SSL (TSL) communications.

8. Technologies for securing networks. At EC sites, firewalls, VPNs, and IDSs have proven extremely useful. A firewall is a combination of hardware and software that isolates a private network from a public network. Firewalls are of two general types—packet-filtering routers or application-level proxies. A packet-filtering router uses a set of rules to determine which communication packets can move from the outside network to the inside network. An application-level proxy is a firewall that accepts requests from the outside and repackages a request before sending it to the inside network, thus, ensuring the security of the request.

Individuals with broadband access need personal firewalls. VPNs are used generally to support secure site-to-site transmissions across the Internet between B2B partners or communications between a mobile and remote worker and a LAN at a central office. IDSs monitor activity across a network or on a host. The systems watch for suspicious activity and take automated actions whenever a security breach or attack occurs. In the same vein, some companies are installing honeynets and honeypots in an effort to gather information on intrusions and to analyze the types and methods of attacks being perpetrated.

KEY TERMS

Acceptable use policy (AUP)	520	Domain name system (DNS)	514	Pretexting	510
Access control	527	EC security program	515	Prevention measure	510
Active tokens	527	EC security strategy	510	Private key	530
Application firewall	512	Encryption	528	Protocol tunneling	536
Application-level proxy	534	Encryption algorithm	528	Proxies	534
Auditing	522	Exposure	512	Public key	530
Authentication	517	Firewall	533	Public (asymmetric) key	
Authorization	517	Fraud	509	encryption	530
Availability	517	Hash	531	Public key infrastructure (PKI)	528
Banking Trojan	526	Honeynet	536	Rijndael	530
Bastion gateway	534	Honeypot	536	Risk	512
Biometric system	528	Hotfix	516	Rootkit	526
Botnet	525	Human firewall	511	RSA	530
Business impact analysis (BIA)	521	Information assurance (IA)	511	Secure Socket Layer (SSL)	531
Certificate authorities (CAs)	531	Integrity	517	Service pack	516
CIA security triad (CIA triad)	516	Intrusion detection system (IDS)	536	Social engineering	523
Ciphertext	528	IP address	514	SpywareGuide	523
Common (security) vulnerabilities		Key	528	Spy-phishing	509
and exposures (CVEs)	512	Key space	528	Standard of due care	512
Computing Technology Industry		Macro virus (macro worm)	526	Symmetric (private) key system	530
Association (CompTIA)	516	Malware	525	Technical attacks	523
Confidentiality	517	Message digest	531	Time-to-exploitation	523
Crimeware	509	Nonrepudiation	518	Transport Layer Security (TLS)	531
CSI/FBI Computer Crime		Nontechnical attack	523	Trojan horse	526
and Security Report	513	Packet	533	Trojan-Phisher-Rebery	526
Data Encryption Standard		Packet filter	533	Universal man-in-the-middle	
(DES)	530	Packet-filtering router	533	phishing kit	510
Demilitarized zone (DMZ)	534	Passive token	527	Virtual private network (VPN)	536
Denial of service (DOS) attack	524	Patch	516	Virus	525
Detection measures	510	Personal firewall	535	Vulnerability	512
Digital envelope	531	Phishing	509	Worm	526
Digital signature (digital		Plaintext	528	Zero-day incident	524
certificate)	518	Policy of least privilege (POLP)	533	Zombie	511

QUESTIONS FOR DISCUSSION

1. Survey results on the incidence of cyberattacks paint a mixed picture; some surveys show increases, others show decreases. What factors could account for the differences in the results?

2. Consider how a hacker would like to trick people into giving you their user IDs and passwords to their Amazon.com accounts. What are some of the ways that they might accomplish this?

3. B2C EC sites continue to experience DOS attacks. How are these attacks perpetrated? Why is it so difficult to safeguard against them? What are some of the things a site can do to mitigate such attacks?

4. All EC sites share common security threats and vulnerabilities. Discuss these threats and vulnerabilities and some of the security policies that can be implemented to mitigate them. Do you think that B2C Web sites face different threats and vulnerabilities than B2B sites? Explain.

5. How are botnet identity theft attacks and Web site hijacks perpetrated? Why are they so dangerous to e-commerce?

6. A business wants to share its customer account database with its trading partners and customers, while at the same time providing prospective buyers with access to marketing materials on its Web site. Assuming that the business is responsible for running all these network components, what types of security components (e.g., firewalls, VPNs, etc.) could be used to ensure that the partners and customers have access to the account information and others do not? What type of network configuration (e.g., bastion gateway server) will provide the appropriate security?

7. A company is having problems with its password security systems and decides to implement two-factor authentication. What biometric alternatives could the company employ? What are some of the factors it should consider when deciding among the alternatives?

INTERNET EXERCISES

1. Attrition organization provides an open source database of its data breach records, called the Data Loss Database–Open Source, or DLDOS. It is a flat comma-separated value (csv) file that can be imported into a database or spreadsheet program for data analysis. Visit **attrition.org/dataloss/dataloss.csv** to access the spreadsheet. Using cases that were reported in the prior year, create a table that summarizes the breach types. For each breach type, show the frequency for each of the following factors: whether the breach was outside or inside, the total affected, and whether there was an arrest or prosecution. Discuss your results.

2. The National Vulnerability Databases (NVD) are a comprehensive cybersecurity vulnerability database that integrates all publicly available U.S. government vulnerability resources and provides references to industry resources. Visit **nvd.nist.gov** and review 10 of the recent CVE vulnerabilities. For each vulnerability, list its publish date, CVSS severity, impact type, and the operating system or software with the vulnerability.

3. The Computer Vulnerabilities and Exposures Board (**cve.mitre.org**) maintains a list of common security vulnerabilities. Review the list. How many vulnerabilities are there? Based on the list, which system components appear to be most vulnerable to attack? What impact do these vulnerable components have on EC?

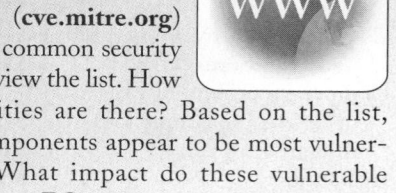

4. Your B2C site has been hacked. List two organizations where you would report this incident so that they can alert other sites. How do you do this, and what type of information do you have to provide?

5. The McAfee Avert Labs Threat Library has detailed information on viruses, Trojans, hoaxes, vulnerabilities and potentially unwanted programs (PUPs), where they come from, how they infect your system, and how to mitigate or remediate them (**vil.nai.com**). Select one *Newly Discovered Malware* and one *Newly Discovered PUP*. Using other online resources, describe these threats and the steps needed to combat it. Why is adware listed as a PUP?

6. Connect to the Internet. Determine the IP address of your computer by visiting at least two Web sites that provide that feature. You can use a search engine to locate Web sites or visit **ip-adress.com** or **whatismyipaddress.com**. What other information does the search reveal about your connection? Based on this information, how could a company or hacker use that information?

7. ICSA Labs (**icsalabs.com**) provides a detailed list of firewall products for corporate, small business, and residential use. Select three corporate firewall products from the list. Using online materials, research and compare the benefits of each product. Based on the comparison, which product would you choose and why?

8. Select a single type of physiological biometric system. Using the Internet, identify at least two commercial vendors offering these systems. Based on the information you found, what are the major features of the systems? Which of the systems would you select and why?

9. *The National Strategy to Secure Cyberspace* provides a series of actions and recommendations for each of its five national priorities. Search and download a copy of the strategy online. Selecting one of the priorities, discuss in detail the actions and recommendations for that priority.

10. The *Symantec Internet Security Threat Report* provides details about the trends in attacks and vulnerabilities in Internet security. Obtain a copy of the report and summarize the major findings of the report for both attacks and vulnerabilities.

TEAM ASSIGNMENTS AND ROLE PLAYING

1. The text identifies hackers' motives, which are money, entertainment, ego, cause, entrance to social groups, and status. Using the Web as your primary data source, have each team member explore one or more of these motives. Each member should describe the motive in detail, how widespread the motive is, the types of attacks that the motive encourages, and the types of actions that can combat the associated attacks.

2. Several personal firewall products are available. A list of these products can be found at **firewallguide.com/software.htm**. Assign each team three products from the list. Each team should prepare a detailed review and comparison of each of the products they have been assigned.

3. Assign each team member a different B2C or B2B Web site. Have each team prepare a report summarizing the site's security assets, threats, and vulnerabilities. Prepare a brief EC security strategy for the site.

Real-World Case
UBS PAINEWEBBER'S BUSINESS OPERATIONS DEBILITATED BY MALICIOUS CODE

Employee (Allegedly) Planned to Crash All Computer Networks

In June 2006, former systems administrator at UBS PaineWebber, Roger Duronio, 63, was charged with building, planting, and setting off a software logic bomb designed to crash the network. His alleged motive was to get revenge for not being paid what he thought he was worth. He designed the logic bomb to delete all the files in the host server in the central data center and in every server in every U.S. branch office. Duronio was looking to make up for some of the cash he felt he had been denied. He wanted to take home $175,000 a year. He had a base salary of $125,000 and a potential annual bonus of $50,000, but the actual bonus was $32,000.

Duronio quit his job, within hours went to a broker, and bought stock options that would only pay out if the company's stock plunged within 11 days. By setting a short expiration date of 11 days instead of a year, the gain from any payout would be much greater. He tried to ensure a stock price crash by crippling the company's network to rock their financial stability. His "put" options expired worthless because the bank's national network did go down, but not UBS stock.

Discovering the Attack

In a federal court, UBS PaineWebber's IT manager Elvira Maria Rodriguez testified that on March 4, 2002, at 9:30 a.m. when the stock market opened for the day, she saw the words "cannot find" on her screen at the company's Escalation Center in Weehawken, New Jersey. She hit the enter key to see the message again, but her screen was frozen. Rodriguez was in charge of maintaining the stability of the servers in the company's branch offices.

When the company's servers went down that day in March 2002, about 17,000 brokers across the country were unable to make trades; the incident affected nearly 400 branch offices. Files were deleted. Backups went down within minutes of being run. Rodriguez, who had to clean up after the logic bomb, said "How on earth were we going to bring them all back up? How was this going to affect the company? If I had a scale of one to 10, this would be a 10-plus."

The prosecutor, Assistant U.S. Attorney V. Grady O'Malley, told the jury: "It took hundreds of people, thousands of man hours and millions of dollars to correct." The system was offline for more than a day, and UBS PaineWebber (renamed UBS Wealth Management USA in 2003) spent about $3.1 million in assessing and restoring the network. The company did not report how much was lost in business downtime and disruption.

Tracking Down the Hacker

A computer forensics expert testified that Duronio's password and user account information were used to gain remote access to the areas where the malicious code was built inside the UBS network. The U.S. Secret Service agent who had investigated the case found a hardcopy of the logic bomb's source code on the defendant's bedroom dresser. A *computer forensics* investigator found electronic copies of the code on two of his four home computers.

Defense Blames USB Security Holes

Chris Adams, Duronio's defense attorney, offered another scenario. Adams claimed that the code was planted by someone else to be a nuisance or prank. Adam also said the UBS system had many security holes and *backdoors* that gave easy access to attackers. Adams told the jury:

> UBS computer security had considerable holes. There are flaws in the system that compromise the ability to determine what is and isn't true. Does the ability to walk around in the system undetected and masquerade as someone else affect your ability to say what has happened?

He also claimed that UBS and @Stake, the first computer forensic company to work on the incident, withheld some information from the government and even "destroyed" some of the evidence. As for the stock options, Adams explained that they were neither risky bets nor part of a scheme, but rather a common investment practice.

Disaster Recovery Efforts

While trying to run a backup to get a main server up and functional, Rodriguez discovered that a line of code (MRM-r) was hanging up the system every time it ran. She renamed the command to hide it from the system and rebooted the server. This action stopped the server from deleting anything else. After testing to confirm the fix, backup tapes brought up the remaining two thousand servers, and the line of code was deleted from each one. Restoring each server took from 30 minutes to two hours unless there was a complication. In those cases, restoration took up to six hours. UBS called in 200 IBM technicians to all the branch offices to expedite the recovery.

Many of the servers were down a day and a half, but some servers in remote locations were down for weeks. The incident impacted all the brokers who were denied access to critical applications because the servers were down.

Minimizing Residual Damages

UBS asked the judge to bar the public from Duronio's trial to avoid "serious embarrassment" and "serious injury" to the bank and its clients and possibly reveal sensitive information about the UBS network and operations. UBS argued that documents it had provided to the court could help a criminal hack into the bank's computer systems to destroy critical business information or to uncover confidential client information.

Duronio faced federal charges, including mail fraud, securities fraud, and computer sabotage, which carry sentences of up to 30 years in jail, $1 million in fines, and restitution for recovery costs. See *informationweek.com/ showArticle.jhtml?articleID=189500138* or *usdoj.gov/ usao/nj/press/files/pdffiles/duro1213rel.pdf*.

Sources: Compiled from DOJ (2002), Gaudin (2006), and Whitman (2006).

Questions

1. What might have been some "red flags" indicating that Duronio was a disgruntled employee? Would any of those red flags also indicate that he would sabotage the network for revenge?

2. How could this disaster have been prevented? What policies, procedures, or technology could have prevented such an attack by an employee with full network access?

3. Did USB have a disaster recovery plan in place for an enterprisewide network crash?

4. Do you agree with the defense lawyer's argument that anyone could have planted the logic bomb because USB's computer security had considerable holes?

5. Given the breadth of known vulnerabilities, what sort of impact will any set of security standards have on the rise in cyberattacks?

REFERENCES

Altman, H. "Jihad Web Snares Online Shops, Buyers." *Tampa Tribune*, February 20, 2006.

Anti-Phishing Working Group (APWG). "Phishing Trends Activity Report for November 2006." **antiphishing.org/ reports/apwg_report_november_2006.pdf** (accessed January 2007).

Berghel, H., and J. Uecker. "WiFi Attack Vectors." *Communications of the ACM*, Vol. 48, No. 8. (August 2005).

Center for Public Policy and Private Enterprise. "CSI/FBI Computer Crime and Security Survey." 2005. **cpppe. umd. edu/Bookstore/Documents/2005CSISurvey.pdf** (accessed January 2007).

CompTIA. "Organizations Ignoring Main Culprit in Information Security Breaches, New CompTIA Research Reveals." April 11, 2006. **morerfid.com/details.php? subdetail=Report&action=details&report_id=1560& display=RFID** (accessed April 2007).

Comscore.com (accessed January 2007).

CVE. **cve.mitre.org** (accessed January 2007).

DOJ. "Disgruntled UBS PaineWebber Employee Charged with Allegedly Unleashing 'Logic Bomb' on Company Computers." December 17, 2002. **usdoj.gov/criminal/ cybercrime/duronioIndict.htm** (accessed January 2007).

Emigh, J. "The Eyes Have It." *Security Solutions*, March 1, 2003. **securitysolutions.com/mag/security_eyes/** (accessed February 2007).

Ewing, J., G. Kral, and K. Young. "Protecting Reputational Risk Through Data Privacy Compliance." *The Metropolitan Corporate Counsel*, January 2006.

FBI. "What's the Current State of Computer Network Security?" July 25, 2005. **fbi.gov/page2/july05/cyber072505. htm** (accessed January 2007).

Fisher, D. "MyDoom E-Mail Worm Spreading Quickly." *eWeek*, January 26, 2004. **eweek.com/article2/0,1759, 1460809,00.asp** (accessed February 2007).

FTC. "FTC Consumer Fraud and Identity Theft Complaint Data." **consumer.gov/sentinel/pubs/Top10Fraud2005.pdf** (accessed December 2006).

Gage, D. "Bank of America Seeks Anti-Fraud Anodyne." *Baseline*, May 15, 2006. **baselinemag.com/article2/ 0,1540,1962470,00.asp** (accessed January 2007).

Gaudin, S. "Nightmare on Wall Street: Prosecution Witness Describes 'Chaos' in UBS PaineWebber Attack." *Information Week*, June 6, 2006. **informationweek.com/story/showArticle.jhtml? articleID=188702216** (accessed January 2007).

Hearing of the Senate Armed Services Committee on Worldwide Threats to U.S. National Security. Washington, D.C. Federal News Service. February 28, 2006.

Honeynet. *Know Your Enemy: Learning About Security Threats*, 2nd ed. Boston, MA: Addison-Wesley, 2004.

Honeynet.org (accessed February 2007).

Jepson, K. "Bewear. Bware. Beware. The Typosquatters." Credit Union Journal, Vol. 10, No. 27 (July 31, 2006).

LeClaire, J. "Social Networking Sites in the Crosshairs?" *TechNewsWorld*, January 3, 2007. **technewsworld.com/ story/54932.html** (accessed January 2007).

Legal Information Institute of the Cornell Law School. **www4.law.cornell.edu/uscode/html/uscode18/usc_sec_ 18_00001030——000-.html** (accessed February 2007).

Net-security.org (accessed January 2007).

Prince, B. " 'Storm' Worm Continues Surge Around Globe." *eWeek*, January 22, 2007. **eweek.com/article2/0,1895,**

2086374,00.asp?kc=EWWHNEMNL012507EOAD (accessed January 2007).

Roberts, P. F. "Webroot Uncovers Thousands of Stolen Identities." *InfoWorld*, May 8, 2006. **infoworld.com/ article/06/05/09/78139_HNTrojanrebery_1.html** (accessed January 2007).

RSAsecurity.com (accessed January 2007).

SANS. "SANS Top-20 Internet Security Attack Targets, 2006 Annual Update." 2006. **sans.org/top20** (accessed January 2007).

"Seventh Annual Online Fraud Report, 2006 Edition." **cybersource.com/resources/collateral/Resource_ Center/whitepapers_and_reports/CYBS_2006_Fraud_ Report.pdf** (accessed December 2006).

Sophos. "Sophos Reveals 'Dirty Dozen' Spam Relaying Countries." July 24, 2006. **sophos.com/pressoffice/ news/articles/2006/07/dirtydozjul06.html** (accessed February 2007).

TSSI. "Biometrics Gains UK Approval." *IT Reseller Magazine,* December 19, 2006. **itrportal.com/ absolutenm/templates/article-biometrics.aspx? articleid=3614&zoneid=50** (accessed February 2007).

Van Riper, T. "Biggest E-Shopping Day in History." *Forbes,* November 29, 2006. **forbes.com/2006/11/29/ cyber-monday-shopping-record-biz-cx_ tvr_1129shop.html** (accessed December 2006).

Venes, R. "A Closer Look at Biometrics." *Computeractive*, June 24, 2004. **infomaticsonline.co.uk/computeractive/ features/2014022/closer-look-biometrics** (accessed February 2007).

Whitman, J "UBS Wants to Bar Public at Tech 'Bomb' Trial." *New York Post*, June 6, 2006. **nypost.com/ business/69615.htm**.

Wolfe, D. "SecurityWatch." *American Banker*, June 2, 2006.

ELECTRONIC PAYMENT SYSTEMS

Content

Learning Objectives

Upon completion of this chapter, you will be able to:

1. Understand the shifts that are occurring with regard to noncash and online payments.

2. Discuss the players and processes involved in using credit cards online.

3. Discuss the different categories and potential uses of smart cards.

4. Discuss various online alternatives to credit card payments and identify under what circumstances they are best used.

5. Describe the processes and parties involved in e-checking.

6. Describe payment methods in B2B EC, including payments for global trade.

7. Discuss electronic bill and invoice presentment and payment.

8. Understand the sales tax implications of e-payments.

PAY-PER-VIEW PAGES: THE NEXT ITUNES

The Problem

Since 2004, the search engine companies Google, MSN, and Yahoo! have scanned and digitized the collections of some of the largest libraries in the world. MSN has been scanning the collections of the British, University of Toronto, and the University of California libraries. Yahoo! is also working with these same universities. However, the most comprehensive of these projects is certainly the Google Book Search Library Project. It is a partnership between Google and 12 major institutions like Harvard, Oxford, the University of Michigan, the Universidad Complutense of Madrid, and the New York Public Library. In Google's words, the aim of the Library Project is to "make it easier for people to find relevant books—specifically books they wouldn't find any other way such as those that are out of print—while carefully respecting authors' and publishers' copyrights. Our ultimate goal is to work with publishers and libraries to create a comprehensive, searchable, virtual card catalog."

The Google project is also the most controversial. Unlike MSN and Yahoo!, Google is digitizing and making available for search not only books with expired copyrights but those that have copyrights still in effect. If the copyright is still in effect, then a search on Google will only produce a "snippet" of text rather than providing access to the whole text. If a publisher objects to Google's use of the copyrighted material, then Google wants the publisher to tell Google not to scan it, requiring the publisher to opt out rather than opt in. Because of this, the Authors Guild (*authorsguild.org*) has filed suit against Google to block Google's scanning of books still under copyright. There is another reason why the publishers are upset. Although Google has positioned the project as an altruistic endeavor, Google stands to make additional advertising revenues by offering these search capabilities. So far, Google has shown no interest in sharing any of the advertising royalties generated from the searches.

Unwilling to wait for the courts to determine the fate of Google's Library Project and to let Google, Yahoo!, and MSN determine the digital destiny of published works, Amazon.com and Random House announced separately in 2005 plans to allow consumers to read books and pages of books online. Selling books online—either hardcopy or electronic—is straightforward. Selling pages online is another story. In the online world, the vast majority of consumers use credit cards to make purchases. The financial institutions issuing credit cards charge a fixed percentage for each credit card purchase, as well as a fixed fee. At something like $0.05 a page, which is what Random House has suggested, a consumer would have to purchase 100 pages or more for the vendor to come close to breaking even. It is the same problem faced by merchants in the offline world. Fortunately for both the online and offline world, the credit card companies, as well as electronic payment companies like PayPal, are well aware of the issues associated with small value purchases and have begun to address the problem.

The Solution

Purchases under $5 are also called micropayments. In the offline world, "cash has been king of these small sales, because credit card companies charge merchants too much in fees to make the transactions profitable." Cash doesn't work in the online world. In the online world, virtually every attempt to "disintermediate" cash and credit cards has failed. Yet, there is ample evidence that consumers are willing to use their credit cards for micropayments. In 2004, American consumers spent a total of $1.3 trillion on purchases under $5, and $35 billion of this was made by credit cards. Gartner Inc. predicts that by 2015 Americans will average more than 20 micropayments on a credit or debit card per month (LeClaire 2004).

In the online world, Apple iTunes has clearly been a success. The iTunes store sells songs for $0.99 a piece. In 2006, they had their billionth download. In a race to become the iTunes of the publishing world, Amazon.com and Random House are both developing systems to allow consumers to purchase access to any page of a book. Amazon.com's system is called Amazon Pages. "The idea is to do for books what Apple has done

for music, enabling readers to buy and download parts of individual books for their own" (Wyatt 2005). The way in which Apple has overcome the costs associated with credit and debit card fees is by having consumers set up accounts. The purchases of single items are then summed or aggregated until the total amount makes it cost effective to submit to the credit or debit card issuer. This is the same principle used by other e-payment vendors like Peppercoin whose systems enable payments to be batched together and submitted after a certain time period has passed or a certain dollar value is reached.

The credit and debit card companies, as well as e-payment vendors like PayPal, are well aware of the difficulties associated with using cards for online micropayments. In response they have lowered their fees in an effort to entice online (and offline) vendors to permit credit and debit card micropayments. Even with these newer fees, purchases under $2 are still very cost prohibitive for the average merchant. They are much less prohibitive for larger vendors whose volume of card purchases enable them to negotiate with the card issuers for even smaller fees.

The Results

Even though Amazon.com and Random House announced their pay-per-page plans at the end of 2005, their systems are still in development. As a consequence, it is too early to tell whether they will be successful or not. Clearly, Amazon.com is in a position to negotiate for smaller credit card fees. Like iTunes, they also have the ability to aggregate purchases for individual buyers. On the other hand, Random House will not sell directly to the public. Instead, they will rely on other vendors, such as Amazon.com, to do the selling for them. Even with a viable micropayment system, there is no guarantee that pay-per-page will interest consumers, especially given the restrictions placed on the purchase.

Consider, for a moment, a few of the restrictions underlying the Random House program (Quint 2005):

- Books will be available for full indexing, search, and display.
- No downloading, printing, or copying will be permitted.
- Encryption and security measures must be applied to ensure protection of the digital content and compliance with the prescribed usage rules and territorial limitations.

In essence, the only thing the purchaser can do is view the page online. This is much more onerous than the restrictions placed on music or video downloads, which at least permit the purchaser to copy the content to their PCs or multimedia players. Unless these restrictions are loosened or eliminated, they will likely lead to the long-run failure of the Random House effort and other similar efforts.

Sources: D'Agostino (2006), Kelly (2006), LeClaire (2004), Quint (2005), and Wyatt (2005).

WHAT WE CAN LEARN . . .

The overwhelming majority of B2C purchases are paid for by credit card. For merchants, the costs of servicing card payments are high. Transaction costs, potential chargeback fees for fraudulent transactions, and the costs of creating and administering a secure EC site for handling card payments are steep. Over the years, a number of less costly e-payment alternatives to credit cards have been proposed. Digital Cash, PayMe.com, Bank One's eMoneyMail, Flooz, Beenz, Wells Fargo's and eBay's Billpoint, and Yahoo!'s PayDirect are examples of alternatives that failed to gain a critical mass of users and subsequently folded. For a variety of reasons, PayPal is one of the few alternatives to credit cards that has succeeded against significant odds (see Online File W12.1 for a description of PayPal and its use by a smaller online merchant). The same can be said for the world of B2B e-payments. Although a number of diverse payment methods have been proposed, few have survived.

This chapter discusses various e-payment methods for B2C and B2B and the underlying reasons why some have been adopted and others have not. It also examines related issues such as tax payments.

12.1   THE PAYMENT REVOLUTION

According to Sapsford (2004), "A currency can be anything that all members of a society agree it should be." Prior to the tenth century BC, shells often were used in trade and barter. Metal coins appeared in Greece and India somewhere between the tenth and sixth centuries BC and dominated trade for 2,000 years. In the Middle Ages, Italian merchants introduced checks. In the United States, paper money was first issued in Massachusetts in 1690. In 1950, Diners Club introduced credit cards in the United States. Until recently, cash was king, at least for in-store payments; checks were the dominant form of noncash payment.

Today, we are in the midst of a payment revolution, with cards and electronic payments taking the place of cash and checks. In 2003, the combined use of credit and debit cards for in-store payments for the first time exceeded the combined use of cash and checks (Gerdes et al. 2005). By 2005, debit and credit cards accounted for 55 percent of in-store payments, with cash and checks making up the rest. The growth in the use of plastic is attributable to the substantial growth in the use of debit cards and the decline in the use of cash. For example, from 1999 to 2005, debit card in-store payments went from 21 percent to 33 percent, while cash dropped from 39 percent to 33 percent (Dove Consulting 2006).

Similar trends are occurring in noncash payments of recurring bills. In 2001, 78 percent of all recurring bills were paid by paper-based methods (e.g., paper checks), while 22 percent of these payments were made electronically. By 2005, the percent of electronic payments of recurring bills had grown to 45 percent (Dove Consulting 2006). This change in the mix of payment methods is likely to continue.

For decades people have been talking about the cashless society. Although the demise of cash and checks is certainly not imminent, many individuals can live without checks and nearly without cash. In the online B2C world, they already do. In North America, for example, 90 percent of all online consumer purchases are made with general-purpose credit cards (Dove Consulting 2006). The same is true for the overwhelming majority of online purchases in the United Kingdom, France, and Spain. Although Visa and MasterCard are certainly worldwide brands, many consumers outside these countries prefer other online payment methods. For instance, consumers in Germany, the Netherlands, and Japan prefer to pay with either direct debit or bank cards.

For online B2C merchants, the implications of these trends are straightforward. In the United States and Western Europe, it is hard to run an online business without supporting credit card payments, despite the costs. It also is becoming increasingly important to support payments by debit card. Under current growth patterns, the volume of debit card payments will soon surpass credit card payments both online and off-line. For merchants who are interested in international markets, there is a need to support a variety of e-payment mechanisms, including bank transfers, COD, electronic checks, private label cards, gift cards, instant credit, and other noncard payment types, such as PayPal. Merchants who offer multiple payment types have lower shopping cart abandonment rates and up to 20 percent higher order conversion on the average, resulting in increased revenues (CyberSource 2005).

As the opening case study suggests, the short history of e-payments is littered with the remains of companies that have attempted to introduce nontraditional payment systems. It takes years for any payment system to gain widespread acceptance. For example, credit cards were introduced in the 1950s but did not reach widespread use until the 1980s. A crucial element in the success of any e-payment method is the "chicken-and-egg" problem: How do you get sellers to adopt a method when there are few buyers using it? And, how do you get buyers to adopt a method when there are few sellers using it? A number of factors come into play in determining whether a particular method of e-payment achieves critical mass. Some of the crucial factors include the following (Evans and Schmalensee 2005).

Independence. Some forms of e-payment require specialized software or hardware to make the payment. Almost all forms of e-payment require the seller or merchant to install specialized software to receive and authorize a payment. Those e-payment methods that require the payer to install specialized components are less likely to succeed.

Interoperability and Portability. All forms of EC run on specialized systems that are interlinked with other enterprise systems and applications. An e-payment method must mesh with these existing systems and applications and be supported by standard computing platforms.

Security. How safe is the transfer? What are the consequences of the transfer's being compromised? Again, if the risk for the payer is higher than the risk for the payee, then the payer is not likely to accept the method.

Anonymity. Unlike credit cards and checks, if a buyer uses cash, there is no way to trace the cash back to the buyer. Some buyers want their identities and purchase patterns to remain anonymous. To succeed, special payment methods, such as e-cash, have to maintain anonymity.

Divisibility. Most sellers accept credit cards only for purchases within a minimum and maximum range. If the cost of the item is too small—only a few dollars—a credit card will not do. In addition, a credit card will not work if an item or set of items costs too much (e.g., an airline company purchasing a new airplane). Any method that can address the lower or higher end of the price continuum or that can span one of the extremes and the middle has a chance of being widely accepted.

Ease of Use. For B2C e-payments, credit cards are the standard due to their ease of use. For B2B payments, the question is whether the online e-payment methods can supplant the existing off-line methods of procurement.

Transaction Fees. When a credit card is used for payment, the merchant pays a transaction fee of up to 3 percent of the item's purchase price (above a minimum fixed fee). These fees make it prohibitive to support smaller purchases with credit cards, which leaves room for alternative forms of payment.

Regulations. A number of international, federal, and state regulations govern all payment methods. Even when an existing institution or association (e.g., Visa) introduces a new payment method, it faces a number of stringent regulatory hurdles. PayPal, for instance, had to contend with a number of lawsuits brought by state attorneys general that claimed that PayPal was violating state banking regulations.

Section 12.1 ▶ REVIEW QUESTIONS

1. Describe the trends that are occurring in cash and noncash payments in the United States.
2. What types of e-payments should B2C merchants support?
3. What is the "chicken-and-egg" problem in e-payments?
4. Describe the factors that are critical for an e-payment method to achieve critical mass.

12.2 USING PAYMENT CARDS ONLINE

Payment cards are electronic cards that contain information that can be used for payment purposes. They come in three forms:

▶ **Credit cards.** A credit card provides the holder with credit to make purchases up to a limit fixed by the card issuer. Credit cards rarely have an annual fee. Instead, holders are charged high interest—the annual percentage rate—on their average daily unpaid balances. Visa, MasterCard, and EuroPay are the predominant credit cards.

▶ **Charge cards.** The balance on a charge card is supposed to be paid in full upon receipt of the monthly statement. Technically, holders of a charge card receive a loan for 30 to 45 days equal to the balance of their statement. Such cards usually have annual fees. American Express's Green Card is the leading charge card, followed by the Diner's Club card.

▶ **Debit cards.** With a debit card, the money for a purchased item comes directly out of the holder's checking account (called a demand-deposit account). The actual transfer of funds from the holder's account to the merchant's takes place within one to two days. MasterCard, Visa, and EuroPay are the predominant debit cards.

payment card
Electronic card that contains information that can be used for payment purposes.

PROCESSING CARDS ONLINE

The processing of card payments has two major phases: authorization and settlement. **Authorization** determines whether a buyer's card is active and whether the customer has sufficient available credit line or funds. **Settlement** involves the transfer of money from the buyer's to the merchant's account. The way in which these phases actually are performed varies somewhat depending on the type of payment card. It also varies by the configuration of the system used by the merchant to process payments.

There are three basic configurations for processing online payments. The EC merchant may:

▶ **Own the payment software.** A merchant can purchase a payment-processing module and integrate it with its other EC software. This module communicates with a payment gateway run by an acquiring bank or another third party.

▶ **Use a point of sale system (POS) operated by an acquirer.** Merchants can redirect cardholders to a POS run by an acquirer. The POS handles the complete payment process and directs the cardholder back to the merchant site once payment is complete. In this case, the merchant system only deals with order information. In this configuration, it is important to find an acquirer that handles multiple cards and payment instruments. If not, the merchant will need to connect with a multitude of acquirers.

▶ **Use a POS operated by a payment service provider.** Merchants can rely on servers operated by third parties known as **payment service providers (PSPs)**. In this case, the PSP connects with the appropriate acquirers. PSPs must be registered with the various card associations they support.

authorization
Determines whether a buyer's card is active and whether the customer has sufficient funds.

settlement
Transferring money from the buyer's to the merchant's account.

payment service provider (PSP)
A third-party service connecting a merchant's EC systems to the appropriate acquirers. PSPs must be registered with the various card associations they support.

EXHIBIT 12.1 Credit Card Purchases: Online Versus Off-Line

Online Purchase	Off-Line Purchase
1. The *customer* decides to purchase a CD on the Web, adding it to the electronic shopping cart and going to the checkout page to enter his or her credit card information.	1. The *customer* selects a CD to purchase, takes it to the checkout counter, and hands his or her credit card to the sales clerk.
2. The *merchant* site receives the customer's information and sends the transaction information to its *payment processing service (PPS)*.	2. The *sales clerk* swipes the card and transfers transaction information to a *point-of-sale (POS)* terminal.
3. The PPS routes information to the *processor* (a large data center for processing transactions and settling funds to the merchant).	3. The POS terminal routes information to the *processor* via a dial-up connection.
4. The processor sends information to the *issuing bank* of the customer's credit card.	4. The processor sends information to the *issuing bank* of customer's credit card.
5. The issuing bank sends the transaction to the processor, either authorizing the payment or not.	5. The issuing bank sends the transaction to the processor, either authorizing the payment or not.
6. The processor routes the transaction result to the PPS.	6. The processor routes the transaction result to the POS.
7. The PPS passes the results to merchant.	7. The POS shows the merchant whether the transaction has been approved or declined.
8. The merchant accepts or rejects transaction.	8. The merchant tells the customer the outcome of the transaction.

Source: VeriSign (2004). Used with permission of VeriSign, Inc.

For a given type of payment card and processing system, the processes and participants are essentially the same for off-line (card present) and online (card not present) purchases. Exhibit 12.1 compares, for instance, the steps involved in making a credit card purchase both online and off-line. As the exhibit demonstrates, there is very little difference between the two.

Based on the processes outlined in Exhibit 12.1, the key participants in processing card payments online include the following:

▶ **Acquiring bank.** Offers a special account called an *Internet Merchant Account* that enables card authorization and payment processing.
▶ **Credit card association.** The financial institution providing card services to banks (e.g., Visa and MasterCard).
▶ **Customer.** The individual possessing the card.
▶ **Issuing bank.** The financial institution that provides the customer with a card.
▶ **Merchant.** A company that sells products or services.
▶ **Payment processing service.** The service provides connectivity among merchants, customers, and financial networks that enables authorization and payments. Usually operated by companies such as CyberSource (cybersource.com) and VeriSign (verisign.com).
▶ **Processor.** The data center that processes card transactions and settles funds to merchants.

FRAUDULENT CARD TRANSACTIONS

Although the processes used for authorizing and settling card payments off-line and online are very similar, there is one substantial difference between the two. In the online world, merchants are held liable for fraudulent transactions. In addition to the lost merchandise and shipping charges, merchants who accept fraudulent transactions can incur additional fees and penalties imposed by the card associations. However, these are not the only costs. There also are the costs associated with combating fraudulent transactions. These include the costs of tools and systems to review orders, the costs of manually reviewing orders, and the revenue that is lost from rejecting orders that are valid. Recent surveys by CyberSource indicate that fraudulent card transactions are a growing problem for online merchants in spite of their increasing efforts to combat fraud.

For the past eight years, CyberSource has sponsored a survey to address the detection, prevention, and management of fraud perpetrated against online merchants. CyberSource's 2006 survey of 404 merchants documented the following trends (CyberSource 2007):

▶ Although the percentage of revenue loss per merchant was relatively flat, the total dollars lost to fraud increased substantially from $1.9 billion in 2003 to $3.0 billion in 2006. The rise was attributable to the increase in the amount of business that was being done online, which grew by 20 percent or more annually over the same time period.

▶ In 2006, merchants estimated that an average of 1.1 percent of their orders were fraudulent. This represented a slight decline from the previous year. The fraudulent orders resulted in merchants' crediting the real cardholder's account or a chargeback. The median value of these fraudulent orders was $150, or 50 percent above the average value of valid orders.

▶ Sixty-one percent of the merchants surveyed accepted international orders outside the United States and Canada. These orders represented 17 percent of the sales for these merchants. The fraud rate for these orders was approximately 2.7 percent, or more than two times higher than the fraud rate for domestic orders.

▶ Certain merchants were more susceptible to fraud than others. This was due to a number of factors: the merchant's visibility on the Web, the steps the merchant had taken to combat fraud, the ease with which the merchant's products could be sold on the open market, and the merchant's size. Larger firms were less susceptible to fraud than smaller firms.

▶ Because of the expected increase in online sales, close to half of the merchants surveyed indicated that they expected online payment fraud to increase in the coming year. The primary reason given for this expectation is the increasing sophistication and improved methods of the fraudsters.

In addition to tracking cyberfraud trends, the CyberSource surveys also have monitored the steps taken by merchants to combat fraud (CyberSource 2005). In 2006, merchants used more tools than in the past to combat fraud. The median number of tools was five in 2006 compared with three in 2003. Merchants also were spending more to combat fraud. The median amount was 0.5 percent of online revenues. Most of the money was spent on review staff (46 percent), followed by third-party tools and services (28 percent) and internally developed tools (26 percent). The key tools used in combating fraud were:

▶ **Address Verification System (AVS).** Seventy-nine percent of all merchants use this method, which compares the address entered on a Web page with the address information on file with the cardholder's issuing bank. This method results in a number of false positives, meaning that the merchant rejects a valid order. Cardholders often have new addresses or simply make mistakes in inputting numeric street addresses or zip codes. AVS is only available in the United States and Canada.

▶ **Manual review.** Seventy-three percent of all merchants use this method, which relies on staff to manually review suspicious orders. For small merchants with a small volume of orders, this is a reasonable method. For larger merchants, this method does not scale well, is expensive, and impacts customer satisfaction. In spite of these limitations, the percentage of merchants using this method is increasing along with the percentage of items being reviewed. In 2005, the number of orders being reviewed was one in three versus one in four in 2003.

Address Verification System (AVS)
Detects fraud by comparing the address entered on a Web page with the address information on file with the cardholder's issuing bank.

▶ **Fraud screens and automated decision models.** Seventy percent of all merchants use these methods, which are based on various automated rules that determine whether a transaction should be accepted, rejected, or suspended. A key element of this method is the ability of the merchant to easily change the rules to reflect changing trends in the fraud being perpetrated against the company.

▶ **Card verification number (CVN).** Sixty-nine percent of all merchants use this method, which relies on comparing the verification number printed on the signature strip on the back of the card with the information on file with the cardholder's issuing bank. However, if a fraudster possesses a stolen card, the number is in plain view.

▶ **Card association payer authentication services.** In the last couple of years, the card associations have developed a new set of payer identification services (e.g., Verified by Visa and MasterCard SecureCode). These services require cardholders to register with the systems and merchants to adopt and support both the existing systems and the new systems. These services are described in Case 12.1. In 2004, it was estimated that over 55 percent of merchants would be using this method by 2005. In reality, only 29 percent of the merchants in the 2006 survey indicated that they had adopted this method.

▶ **Negative files.** Thirty-four percent of all merchants use this method, which is a file of the customer's information (IP address, name, shipping/billing address, contact numbers, etc.) and the status of that customer. A customer's transaction is matched against this file and flagged if the customer is a known problem.

The overall impact of these tools is that merchants are rejecting a significant number of orders due to suspicion of fraud. In 2003, merchants rejected three orders for every fraudulent order accepted. In 2006, the average number of rejected orders was four for every fraudulent order accepted. In 2006, this represented a rejection rate of 4 percent of the orders. The problem with these rejection rates is that a number of the rejected orders are valid, resulting in lost revenue.

The trends in tool use uncovered by the CyberSource surveys are supported by a series of annual surveys conducted by the Merchant Risk Council (MRC) (merchantriskcouncil.org). The MRC was formed in 2002 when the Merchant Fraud Squad headed by American Express, ClearCommerce, and Expedia merged with the Internet Fraud Roundtable headed by HP and ClearCommerce. Both voluntary organizations were focused on encouraging best practices in fraud prevention. Today, MRC's membership consists of 7,500 merchants, vendors, financial institutions, and law enforcement agencies. Since 2003, the MRC has surveyed its merchant members to identify and quantify their spending on fraud prevention. The 2005 results (Merchant Risk Council 2006) indicated online fraud rates are similar to the fraud rates for brick-and-mortar stores; fraudsters are using more sophisticated schemes than in the past; merchants are using more tools to combat fraud than they did in 2003; and the most commonly used fraud prevention tools were AVS (74 percent) and CVN (65 percent).

VIRTUAL CREDIT CARDS

Although the volume and dollar amount of online purchases are growing significantly, a number of consumers still are leery of using their credit card numbers online. Virtual credit cards were designed to address these concerns. With a **virtual credit card**, the online buyer is provided by the card company at the time of purchase with a randomly generated card number that is tied to the buyer's actual card number. The buyer enters this number rather than the actual number to complete a purchase. Generally, the number can only be used once. This is why virtual credit cards also are known as *single-use card numbers*.

Although single-use numbers combat certain types of fraud, they have their drawbacks. Purchases made with single-use numbers cannot be confirmed at a later date. For example, if a person makes an airline or hotel reservation online and needs the card number to confirm it at a later date, there is no way to obtain the number for this purpose. Similarly, if a person prepurchases an item, there is no way to confirm the card number later, because the number will have expired. Finally, there is no way to pay recurring bills or subscriptions with a single-use number.

Virtual credit cards have had mixed success. American Express, for instance, had a special service called *Private Payments*. Early in 2004, it discontinued this service. In contrast, Citi, MBNA, and Discover Card continue to offer this alternative to their cardholders. For

CASE 12.1
EC Application

COMPUSA RELIES ON MASTERCARD SECURECODE

CompUSA is a well-known retailer of electronic products and services. They have over 200 retail stores and sell a large inventory of items on their Web site (*compusa.com*). Like other retailers they are concerned with online credit card fraud. First, it is difficult to verify the identity of an online buyer. Second, because there is no signed receipt, it is difficult to dispute a buyer's claim that he or she did not authorize the purchase. These problems also arise in the off-line world; however, with online shopping, the merchant bears responsibility for the following risks:

▶ **Stolen cards.** If someone steals a card and the valid cardholder contests the charges made by the thief, the issuer will credit the cardholder's account and charge back the merchant.

▶ **Reneging by the customer.** A customer can authorize a payment and later deny it. If the denial is believable to the issuer, the merchant will bear the loss.

In general e-commerce charge-back rates are six times higher than off-line rates. CompUSA's charge-back rate was 7.41 percent.

In the past, CompUSA has relied on a combination of methods to combat the charge-back problem. Any online purchase made by a card required a check against internal and external databases of known fraudsters, problem customers, as well as lists of good customers. CompUSA also employed a fraud scoring system based on several factors to determine the likelihood of fraud. Those purchases flagged as potentially fraudulent required a great deal of manual inspection. Not only was this a time-consuming and expensive process, but it often resulted in "false positives." A false positive is a good purchase order that is flagged as fraudulent. For the merchant, a false positive represents lost revenue.

In an effort to overcome these problems, CompUSA decided to adopt MasterCard's SecureCode. SecureCode is based on 3-Domain (3-D) Secure payment authentication. 3-D Secure is also the basis of Verified by Visa and JCB J/Secure. It relies on SSL encryption and a merchant server plug-in to pass information between the merchant's site and the hosted service, to query participants to authenticate the cardholder during online purchase, and to protect card information as it is transmitted via the Internet. The three domains in 3-D Secure are (Visa 2006):

▶ **Issuer domain.** The issuer is responsible for managing the enrollment of its cardholders in the service, including verifying the identity of each cardholder who enrolls and authenticating cardholders during online purchases.

▶ **Acquirer domain.** The acquirer is responsible for defining the procedures to ensure that merchants participating in

Internet transactions are operating under a merchant agreement with the acquirer and providing the transaction processing for authenticated transactions.

▶ **Interoperability domain.** This domain facilitates the transaction exchange between the other two domains with a common protocol and shared services.

MasterCard SecureCode, Verified by Visa, and JCB J/Secure support 3-D Secure authentication.

It is relatively easy to implement MasterCard SecureCode, as well as the other alternatives. Cardholders enroll in the program with their issuing bank. At that time, they select a password to use with their online purchases. Merchants enroll in the program through their acquiring bank or a third-party supplier, such as CardinalCommerce. To support 3-D authentication, the merchant or its PSP adds a plug-in to the company's payment system. When cardholders make online purchases and enter their card numbers, the numbers are checked against the card association's database to determine if they are enrolled. If they are, the plug-in pops up a window asking for the password. The password is then verified, and the transaction is completed or rejected.

The major benefit of 3-D Secure for merchants is the reduction in disputed transactions, handling expenses, and revenue loss. One estimate suggests that this system could eliminate 80 percent or more of these costs and losses. For example, CompUSA does not bear the operational or charge-back costs for transactions conducted via MasterCard SecureCode. Today, CompUSA's online chargeback costs are virtually zero.

Unlike other payment and authentication schemes, the 3-D secure will eventually gain critical mass. For instance, MasterCard's International Operations Committee (IOC) mandated issuers to implement support for MasterCard SecureCode by November 2004. For other ways to combat the chargeback problem, see Online File W12.2.

Sources: Condensed from MasterCard (2005) and Visa (2006).

Questions

1. What type of fraud was CompUSA trying to control?
2. What are the three domains in 3-D Secure payment authentication?
3. How do merchants deploy 3-D Secure?
4. What are the benefits of MasterCard SecureCode?

example, Discover Financial Services offers its customers a single-use card service called *Discover Deskshop* (discovercard.com/deskshop). Discover customers who register with the service download a small piece of software called the Deskshop. Anytime the user encounters a checkout form, the software pops up and asks the user whether he or she wants the software to automatically complete the form and enter a single-use number. Unlike earlier counterparts, the number generated by Deskshop has the same expiration date as the actual card, which means that it can be used for recurring bills but only for the site for which the number was generated.

Section 12.2 ❱ REVIEW QUESTIONS

1. Describe the three types of payment cards.
2. What options does a merchant have in setting up an e-payment system?
3. List the major participants in processing cards online.
4. What costs does an online merchant incur if it submits a fraudulent card transaction?
5. Describe the major trends in fraudulent orders perpetrated against online merchants.
6. What steps are often taken by online merchants to combat fraudulent orders?
7. How does a virtual credit card work?

12.3 SMART CARDS

Outside North America, smart cards often are used in place of or in addition to traditional credit and debit cards. They also are used widely to support nonretail and nonfinancial applications. A **smart card** looks like a plastic payment card, but it is distinguished by the presence of an embedded microchip (see Exhibit 12.2). The embedded chip may be a microprocessor combined with a memory chip or just a memory chip with nonprogrammable logic. Information on a microprocessor card can be added, deleted, or otherwise manipulated; a memory-chip card is usually a "read-only" card, similar to a credit card. Although the microprocessor is capable of running programs like a computer does, it is not a stand-alone computer. The programs and data must be downloaded from and activated by some other device (such as an ATM machine).

TYPES OF SMART CARDS

There are two distinct types of smart cards. The first type is a **contact card**, which is activated when it is inserted into a smart card reader. The second type of card is a **contactless (proximity) card**, meaning that the card only has to be within a certain proximity of a smart card reader to process a transaction. *Hybrid cards* combine both types of cards into one.

smart card
An electronic card containing an embedded microchip that enables predefined operations or the addition, deletion, or manipulation of information on the card.

contact card
A smart card containing a small gold plate on the face that when inserted in a smart card reader makes contact and passes data to and from the embedded microchip.

contactless (proximity) card
A smart card with an embedded antenna, by means of which data and applications are passed to and from a card reader unit or other device without contact between the card and the card reader.

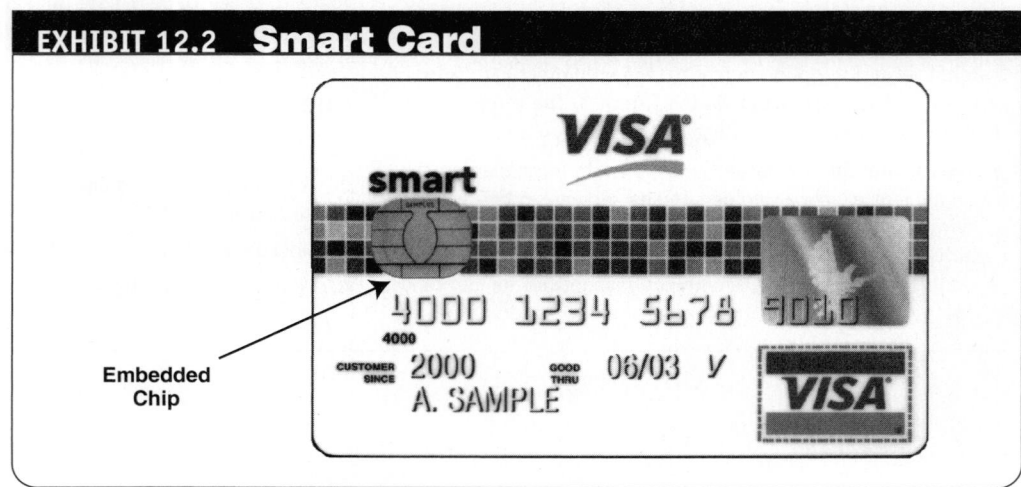

EXHIBIT 12.2 Smart Card

Embedded Chip

Source: Courtesy of Visa International Service Association.

Contact smart cards have a small gold plate about one-half inch in diameter on the front. When the card is inserted into the smart card reader, the plate makes electronic contact and data are passed to and from the chip. Contact cards can have electronically programmable, read-only memory (EPROM) or electronically erasable, programmable, read-only memory (EEPROM). EPROM cards can never be erased. Instead, data are written to the available space on the card. When the card is full, it is discarded. EEPROM cards are erasable and modifiable. They can be used until they wear out or malfunction. Most contact cards are EEPROM.

In addition to the chip, a contactless card has an embedded antenna. Data and applications are passed to and from the card through the card's antenna to another antenna attached to a smart card reader or other device. Contactless cards are used for those applications in which the data must be processed very quickly (e.g., mass-transit applications, such as paying bus or train fares) or when contact is difficult (e.g., security-entering mechanisms to buildings). Proximity cards usually work at short range, just a few inches. For some applications, such as payments at highway toll booths, the cards can operate at considerable distances.

With *hybrid* and *dual-interface* smart cards, the two types of card interfaces are merged into one. A hybrid smart card has two separate chips embedded in the card: contact and contactless. In contrast, a dual-interface, or combi, smart card has a single chip that supports both types of interfaces. The benefit of either card is that it eliminates the need to carry multiple cards to support the various smart card readers and applications.

With both types of cards, smart card readers are crucial to the operation of the system. Technically speaking, a smart card reader is actually a read/write device. The primary purpose of the **smart card reader** is to act as a mediator between the card and the host system that stores application data and processes transactions. Just as there are two basic types of cards, there are two types of smart card readers—*contact* and *proximity*—which match the particular type of card. Smart card readers can be transparent, requiring a host device to operate, or stand alone, functioning independently. Smart card readers are a key element in determining the overall cost of a smart card application. Although the cost of a single reader is usually low, the cost can be quite high when hundreds or thousands are needed to service a large population of users (e.g., all the passengers traveling on a metropolitan mass transit system).

smart card reader
Activates and reads the contents of the chip on a smart card, usually passing the information on to a host system.

Widespread use of smart cards for multiple applications requires standardization and interoperability among the various card and card reader technologies. Without them, end users would have to carry separate cards for every type of reader and application. Global Platform (globalplatform.org) is an international, nonprofit smart card association whose main goal is to create and advance interoperable technical specifications for smart cards, acceptance devices, and systems infrastructure. Many of the technical standards governing smart cards are set by the International Standards Organization (ISO; iso.org). ISO/IEC 7816 and ISO/IEC 14443 are the main standards pertaining to contact and contactless cards, respectively. These standards form the basis of a number of other smart card standards. For example, in 1995 Europay International, MasterCard, and Visa (EMV) established a set of standards for the interoperability and security of smart credit and debit cards. EMV, whose current specification is EMV Version 4.1, was built on ISO/IEC 7816. In 2002, Europay was absorbed by MasterCard. Today, EMV is managed by the EMV Corporation (emvco.com), whose members include MasterCard, Visa, and JCB Company.

Like computers, smart cards have an underlying operating system. A **smart card operating system** handles file management, security, input/output (I/O), and command execution and provides an application programming interface (API). Originally, smart card operating systems were designed to run on the specific chip embedded in the card. Today, smart cards are moving toward multiple and open application operating systems such as MULTOS (multos.com) and Java Card (java.sun.com/products/javacard). These operating systems enable new applications to be added during the life of the card.

smart card operating system
Special system that handles file management, security, input/output (I/O), and command execution and provides an application programming interface (API) for a smart card.

APPLICATIONS OF SMART CARDS

The use of smart cards is growing rapidly both outside and inside the United States. Globally, an estimated 3 billion smart cards were shipped in 2005. In North America, the number of shipments was estimated to be over 200 million, although the number of shipments is growing 27 percent annually (Frost and Sullivan 2005). The growth in smart card usage is being driven by its applications. A general discussion of these applications can be found at the GlobalPlatform Web site (globalplatform.org/showpage.asp?code=implementations). The following are some of the more important applications.

Retail Purchases

The credit card associations and financial institutions are transitioning their traditional credit and debit cards to multiapplication smart cards. For example, MasterCard announced in November 2004 that it had issued more than 200 million MasterCard, Maestro, and Cirrus smart cards worldwide (MasterCard International 2004). Close to half of these support the EMV card standard. These cards are accepted at over 1.5 million EMV terminals worldwide. From MasterCard's perspective, as well as that of the other card associations and card companies, smart cards have reached mass-market adoption rates in Europe, Latin America, and APMEA (Asia/Pacific, the Middle East, and Africa). Compared to 2005, MasterCard experienced more than a 470 percent increase in the number of contactless payment cards and other payment devices issued in the APMEA region in the third quarter of 2006 (Smart Card Alliance 2006).

In most cases smart cards are more secure than credit cards and can be extended with other payment services. In the retail arena, many of these services are aimed at those establishments where payments are usually made in cash and speed and convenience are important. This includes convenience stores, gas stations, fast-food or quick-service restaurants, and cinemas. Contactless payments exemplify this sort of value-added service.

Over the past few years, the card associations have been piloting a number of contactless payment systems that are aimed at retail operations where speed and convenience are crucial. Mastercard's *PayPass* (mastercard.com/aboutourcards/paypass.html), American Express's *ExpressPay* (americanexpress.com/expresspay), and Visa's *Wave* fit into this category. All these systems utilize the existing POS and magnetic strip payment infrastructure used with traditional credit and debit cards. The only difference is that a special contactless smart card reader is required. To make a purchase, a cardholder simply waves his or her card near the terminal, and the terminal reads the financial information on the card.

In 2003, MasterCard introduced PayPass in a market trial conducted in Orlando, Florida, with JPMorgan Chase & Co., Citibank, and MBNA. The trial involved more than 16,000 cardholders and more than 60 retailers. The introduction of PayPass served as a catalyst to increase card usage and loyalty in the Orlando area. During the trial, MasterCard experienced an 18 percent active rate for previously inactive accounts. MasterCard also saw a 23 percent increase in transaction value, a 28 percent increase in total weekly spending, and a 12 percent month-over-month increase in transaction volumes at participating merchants.

Following the trial in 2005, MasterCard began rolling out PayPass to selected markets in the United States, United Kingdom, Turkey, and the Philippines. That same year, American Express introduced ExpressPay. ExpressPay replaced the smart chip on the American Express Blue card. Currently, ExpressPay is accepted at a number of merchants and fast food restaurants including 7-Eleven, CVS pharmacy, Walgreen's pharmacy, AMC theaters, United Artists theaters, Arby's, McDonald's, Jack in the Box, and Meijer's supermarkets. Following a pilot study in 2004, Visa began rolling out their Visa Wave card in Malaysia in February 2005. The card, which is based on the global EMV standard, was offered to 500,000 cardholders in Malaysia and accepted at 4,000 Malaysian merchants including convenience stores, fast-food restaurants, theaters, gas stations, and supermarkets. In 2005, Visa also launched with Chinatrust Commercial Bank a second pilot program in Taiwan. The card was offered to 25,000 cardholders and is accepted at more than 150 merchants including gas stations, DVD shops, Taiwan Railways, bus services, parking lots, laundries, cafes, and restaurants.

Transit Fares

In major U.S. cities, commuters often have to drive to a parking lot, board a train, and then change to one or more subways or buses to arrive at work. If the whole trip requires a combination of cash and multiple types of tickets, this can be a major hassle. For those commuters who have a choice, the inconvenience plays a role in discouraging the use of public transportation. To eliminate the inconvenience, most major transit operators in the United States are implementing smart card fare-ticketing systems. The U.S. federal government also is providing incentives to employers to subsidize the use of public transportation by their employees. The transit systems in Washington, D.C., San Francisco, Los Angeles, Boston, Minneapolis, Atlanta, San Diego, Orlando, and Chicago have all either instituted smart card payment systems or are currently running pilot systems (American Public Transportation Association 2006).

Metropolitan transit operators are moving away from multiple, nonintegrated fare systems to systems that require only a single contactless card regardless of how many modes of transportation or how many transportation agencies or companies are involved. The SmarTrip program run by the Washington Metropolitan Area Transit Authority (WMATA) in the District of Columbia exemplifies this movement (wmata.com/riding/smartrip.cfm). WMATA was the first transportation system in the United States to employ smart cards. The program started in 1999. SmarTrip is a permanent, contactless, rechargeable fare card that can hold up to $300 in fare value. The card can be used with 17 different transit systems, including Metro-operated parking lots, the Metrorail, Metrobuses, and other regional rail services. SmarTrip handles the complexities associated with the various systems, including zone-based and time-based fares, volume discounts, and bus-to-train and bus-to-bus transfers. To date, close to a half million SmarTrip cards have been issued and well over one-third of Metrorail riders use the cards regularly.

The U.S. smart card transit programs are modeled after the transit systems in Asia. Case 12.2 describes one of these—the TaiwanMoney Card—and Online File W12.3 discusses another of the Asian projects. Like their Asian counterparts, some U.S. transit operators are looking to partner with retailers and financial institutions to combine their transit cards with payment cards to purchase goods and services such as snacks, bridge tolls, parking fees, or food in restaurants or grocery stores located near the transit stations.

In addition to handling transit fares, smart cards and other e-payment systems are being used for other transportation applications. For instance, Philadelphia has retooled all its 14,500 parking meters to accept payment from prepaid smart cards issued by the Philadelphia Parking Authority (philapark.org). Similarly, many of the major toll roads in the United States and elsewhere accept electronic payments rendered by devices called transponders that operate much like contactless smart cards.

E-Identification

Because they have the capability to store personal information, including pictures, biometric identifiers, digital signatures, and private security keys, smart cards are being used in a variety of identification, access control, and authentication applications. As an example, several are in the planning or pilot stages of launching national identification smart card programs. By far, the largest e-ID program is in China. In March 2004, China began issuing smart card IDs to all citizens over the age of 16 who live in the cities of Beijing, Itanjin, Shanghai, Shenzhen, and Changsha. The cards are designed to reduce the widespread forging of ID papers and will enable China's citizens to move more freely within the country. The ID cards are the size of standard bank cards and use contactless chips. Only Chinese vendors are allowed to supply the cards. The overall goal is to issue ID cards to 1 billion citizens by 2008.

Malaysia is another Asian country that has instituted an electronic identification program (Berney 2006). They have issued 18 million MyKad ID contact smart cards to every one of their 23 million residents over the age of 12. Unlike, China's e-ID cards, the Malaysian cards are multipurpose. They contain fingerprint biometrics and health data. They can also be used as a payment card and to digitally sign electronic documents.

In Europe, Belgium was the first country to adopt a standardized (e-ID) card (Smart Card Alliance 2004). By the end of 2009, Belgium's 10 million citizens will be required to carry an e-ID card. The cards will be valid for five years and will contain the citizen's date of birth, family tree, civil status, current and past addresses, and military situation. The card also will contain the holder's digital signature.

Because of privacy concerns, the United States is not likely to implement a national ID program anytime soon. However, many federal agencies are in the process of implementing smart card IDs for employee identification and access control. In 2003, the U.S. Office of Management and Budget (OMB) issued a memorandum detailing the e-government initiative

CASE 12.2
EC Application
TAIWANMONEY CARD

In October 2005, the Kaohsiung City Government (KCG) in Taiwan began, as part of its e-City initiative, the Smart Transport Card Project. Similar to other municipalities in Asia, KCG was interested in utilizing smart card technology to enable contactless payments throughout its transport system. Unlike other municipalities, however, KCG was not interested in introducing a specialized transport card. Typically, transport cards are purchased from a transport authority, and their primary function is to pay transport fares. Occasionally, they can be used at other venues. For example, the Hong Kong metro card known as the Octopus Card can be used at fast-food restaurants and convenience stores. Instead, KCG decided to partner with MasterCard to produce a single money card that could be used for both retail and transport payments. In this way, KCG could avoid many of the problems associated with issuing the cards, managing the overall payment systems, and instituting specialized legislation dictating how the cards could be used.

The card produced by MasterCard for KCG is called the TaiwanMoney Card. Technically the card was MasterCard's first OneSMART PayPass Chip Combi Card. The card complies with the EMV standard, making it the first EMV-based card to support transport payments. While KCG is the owner of the Smart Transport Card Project, the cards are marketed, issued, and serviced by Cathay United Bank, E. Sun Bank, and Bank of Kaohsiung.

The KCG system, which is operated by Mondex Taiwan, supports two types of cards. There are *Standalone Cards* for children, nonlocal and nonbanked customers that are used for single trips. The second card is *Payment Plus*. This type of card is for existing MasterCard holders and new account customers. It is a dual-branded MasterCard credit card or debit card that can be used for both transportation and shopping.

In order for the transportation system to support the cards, contactless TaiwanMoney Card readers had to be installed on all buses. In order for retailers to support the cards, their POS terminals had to be upgraded to accept the TaiwanMoney or MasterCard PayPass contactless cards.

By the end of 2005, there were approximately 100,000 cardholders using the TaiwanMoney Cards to pay fares on buses running in Kaohsiung and six other cities in southern Taiwan. They were also using the cards to make purchases at 5,000 convenience stores, supermarkets, and other retail outlets in the region.

While the cards enjoy widespread use throughout southern Taiwan, they still have a major drawback. It takes about .6 to .7 seconds to complete a transaction. This is fine for retail outlets and buses, but it will not work with the metro (subway) system. The metro system requires a transaction speed of .4 seconds or faster. The project's systems integrator, Acer of Taiwan, is working with the chip and card manufacturers to meet this service level requirement. Once this is accomplished, MasterCard plans to expand the program to Taipei and to the Chinese market.

Sources: Card Technology (2006) and Multos (2006).

Questions

1. What is the TaiwanMoney Card?
2. Why did KCG decide to use a smart money card for their transportation system rather than a specialized transportation card?
3. Why can't the TaiwanMoney Card be used with KCG's metro system?

on authentication and identity management. In 2004, the Federal Identity Credentialing Committee (FICC) issued policy guidance on the use of smart cards in identification and credentialing systems. Its aim was to help agencies establish and implement credentialing and identification systems for government employees and their agents. That same year a U.S. presidential directive mandated the promulgation of a federal standard for a secure form of identification to protect federal facilities against access and attacks by terrorists. While this directive did not specify the form, it certainly encouraged the implementation of e-identification.

Currently, the U.S. government is sponsoring 24 smart card projects (Government Accounting Office 2004). Of these, half are large-scale projects aimed at providing an entire agency's employees or some other large group with smart card identification. The Department of Defense (DOD) *Common Access Card* (CAC) program is a good example of these projects. For the most part, the cards allow employees and contractors to gain physical access to buildings and logical access to computers and to digitally sign and encrypt electronic transactions. By August 2006, CAC cards were being issued at a rate of 10,000 per day. As of that date, approximately 11.2 million CAC cards had been issued. The cards have been distributed at over 1,400 sites in 27 countries (CR80News 2006).

Like other smart card projects, many of these federal projects are combining e-identification with other functions, such as asset management and stored value for e-payments. For instance, the Marine Corps is using the DOD CACs to track weapons issued by its armories. For a complete description of these and the other U.S. federal government smart card programs, see Hunt and Holcombe (2004) and Government Accounting Office (2004).

Health Care

In general, smart cards are used to store data, identify and authenticate the cardholder, and permit or limit access to physical facilities or information sources. In health care, this translates to a variety of functional possibilities, including:

- Storing vital medical information in case of emergencies
- Preventing patients from obtaining multiple prescriptions from different physicians
- Verifying a patient's identity and insurance coverage
- Speeding up the hospital or emergency room admissions process
- Providing medical practitioners with secure access to a patient's complete medical history
- Speeding up the payment and claims process
- Enabling patients to access their medical records over the Internet

For example, these are the functions envisioned for the electronic health card system in Germany. The German system is the largest in the world. After running a series of pilot projects, Germany began distributing the electronische Gesundheitkarte (eGK) or electronic health card to its 71 million citizens in January 2006. There are two types of cards in the system. First, there are the cards used by patients. These cards contain patient applications and the cardholder's prescriptions. Second, there are the cards used by health-care professionals. These provide secure access to the system and enable physicians and others to digitally sign medical documents and prescriptions. Over time, these cards will be employed in a variety of ways including:

- Insurance cards—containing patient IDs and policy information
- Emergency medical cards—containing medical and contact information tailored to the needs of emergency medical personnel
- Hospital admission cards—containing comprehensive insurance and demographic information
- Follow-up cards—storing medical data tailored for specialties such as cardiology, diabetes, dialysis, maternity, pharmacy, and oncology
- Universal health cards—containing insurance ID information, key demographic data, and links to the patient's medical record

Smart card programs for health care are starting or are underway in a number of European and Asian countries, including Austria, Belgium, Czech Republic, Finland, France, Italy, Korea, Malaysia, the Netherlands, Norway, Romania, Slovenia, Spain, Sweden, Taiwan, and the United Kingdom (HBS Consulting 2004). In all these countries, health care is state funded or state run. For this reason, many of the countries that have implemented or are in the process of implementing multiapplication ID smart cards are considering adding health-care functions to these cards. Malaysia's ID card already contains health-care information. Romania, Thailand, and Belgium are considering adding health-care functions to their ID cards in the next few years. Because of concerns about privacy and civil liberties, people are hesitant about having their personal health data mixed with other data on the same card. Most people would rather carry separate cards despite the fact that smart card operating systems can ensure the secure separation of one application from another. This is why Italy is considering launching a separate health-care card even though it originally planned to put health-care functions on its new e-ID cards.

Although health-care smart cards have been promoted for their data storage capabilities (e.g., storing vital medical information), in practice they are used most often to verify entitlement for health-care services. For example, starting in 2004 the European Commission mandated that existing E111 forms, which provide access to emergency health-care services to

Europeans traveling throughout the European Union, would be supplanted by the European Health Insurance Card (EHIC). There are 29 European countries participating in the EHIC program. The estimate is that close to 170 million cards will be issued by 2006 when the mandate goes into effect (E-Health Insider 2004). Because the EHIC card is a smart card, this will expand the use of smart cards in Europe substantially.

SECURING SMART CARDS

Smart cards store or provide access to either valuable assets (e.g., e-cash) or to sensitive information (e.g., medical records). Because of this, they must be secured against theft, fraud, or misuse. In general, smart cards are more secure than conventional payment cards. If someone steals a payment card, the number on the card is clearly visible, as is the owner's signature. Although it may be hard to forge the signature, in many situations only the number is required to make a purchase. The only protection cardholders have is that there usually are limits on how much they will be held liable for (e.g., in the United States it is $50). If someone steals a stored-value card (or the owner loses it), the original owner is out of luck.

On the other hand, if someone steals a smart card, the thief is usually out of luck. The major exception is a "wave and go" card such as the Visa Wave card used for retail purchases. Some smart cards show account numbers but others do not. Before the card can be used, the holder may be required to enter a PIN that is matched with the card. Theoretically, it is possible to "hack" into a smart card. Most cards, however, now store information in encrypted form. The smart cards can also encrypt and decrypt data that is downloaded or read from the card. Because of these factors, the possibility of hacking into a smart card is classified as a "class 3" attack, which means that the cost of compromising the card far exceeds the benefits.

Because of the highly confidential nature of medical information, PKI and other cryptographic techniques are being used to secure access to health-care data. In this instance, smart cards contain not only the encrypted keys that are required by health-care practitioners to access patient data but also pointers to data that may be housed in different databases on different networks. In France, the next generation of electronic social security cards (i.e., the *Vitale* card), which is used for health-care reimbursements, is incorporating cryptographic mechanisms based on PKI. Since 2001, Vitale cards have been issued to all individuals over the age of 16 who are entitled to social security coverage (Smart Card Alliance 2006). To date, approximately 50 million cards have been issued. In 2006, the Vitale cards were upgraded to include the enhanced security feature. This was done to ensure that the cards were in compliance with France's new identification, authentication, and signature standards for the fields of health and welfare.

Section 12.3 ▶ REVIEW QUESTIONS

1. What is a smart card? Contact card? Contactless card?
2. What is a smart card operating system?
3. Describe the use of smart cards in metropolitan transportation systems.
4. Describe the smart card ID programs in China.
5. What is the DOD CAC program?
6. What are some of the potential uses of smart cards in health care?

12.4   STORED-VALUE CARDS

stored-value card
A card that has monetary value loaded onto it and that is usually rechargeable.

What looks like a credit or debit card, acts like a credit or debit card, but isn't a credit or debit card? The answer is a **stored-value card**. As the name implies, the monetary value of a stored-value card is preloaded on the card. From a physical and technical standpoint, a stored-value card is indistinguishable from a regular credit or debit card. It is plastic and has a magnetic strip on the back although it may not have the cardholder's name printed on it. The magnetic strip stores the monetary value of the card. This distinguishes a stored-value card from a smart card. With smart cards, the chip stores the value. Consumers can use stored-value cards to make purchases, off-line or online, in the same way that they use credit and debit cards—relying on the same networks, encrypted communications, and electronic banking protocols. What is different about a stored-value card is that anyone can obtain one without regard to prior financial standing or having an existing bank account as collateral.

Stored-value cards come in two varieties: *closed loop* and *open loop*. Closed-loop, or single-purpose, cards are issued by a specific merchant or merchant group (e.g., a shopping mall) and can only be used to make purchases from that merchant or merchant group. Mall cards, store cards, gift cards, and prepaid telephone cards are all examples of closed-loop cards. Gift cards represent a strong growth area, especially in the United States. According to an annual survey conducted by Stored Value Systems (Ceridian 2005), over 70 percent of the population over 18 years of age said they purchased gift cards in 2005. The average value of the cards was $40, which is about the same as the figure from the 2004 survey. However, the average number of cards purchased was 6.5, which is an increase from 4.5 in 2004. Among those who said they received gift cards, approximately 75 percent use their cards up completely.

In contrast, an open-loop, or multipurpose, card can be used to make debit transactions at a variety of retailers. Open-loop cards also can be used for other purposes, such as receiving direct deposits or withdrawing cash from ATM machines. Financial institutions with card association branding, such as Visa or MasterCard, issue some open-loop cards. They can be used anywhere that the branded cards are accepted. Payroll cards, government benefit cards, and prepaid debit cards are all examples of open-loop cards.

Stored-value cards may be acquired in a variety of ways. Employers or government agencies may issue them as payroll cards or benefit cards in lieu of checks or direct deposits. Merchants or merchant groups sell and load gift cards. Various financial institutions and nonfinancial outlets sell preloaded cards by telephone, online, or in person. Cash, bank wire transfers, money orders, cashiers' checks, other credit cards, or direct payroll or government deposits fund preloaded cards.

The stored-value card market is growing rapidly. Market analysts estimate that there are over 2,000 stored value programs with over 7 million Visa and MasterCard branded cards in use today (Mercator 2006). In 2005, the total spent on both closed and open cards was $165 billion. By 2009, the total spent is expected to reach $236 billion, a compound annual growth rate (CAGR) of over 9 percent. While the spending on closed cards in 2009 will far exceed the spending on open cards ($192 billion versus $43 billion), the spending on open cards is growing much more rapidly than the spending on closed cards (32 percent versus 9 percent). Gift cards are the fastest growing market followed by employer and consumer incentives, open campus, and state unemployment cards.

Stored-value cards are being marketed heavily to the "unbanked" and "overextended." Approximately 50 million adults in the United States do not have credit cards, and 20 million do not have bank accounts—people with low incomes, young adults, seniors, immigrants, minorities, and others (Milligan 2004). Among those with credit cards, 40 percent are running close to their credit limits. The expectation is that these groups will be major users of prepaid cards in the future. For example, individuals in the United States transferred over $12 billion to individuals in Mexico. Instead of sending money orders or cash, programs like the EasySend card from Branch Banking and Trust (BB&T) provide a secure alternative to transferring money to relatives and friends. With the EasySend program, an individual establishes a banking account, deposits money in the account, and mails the EasySend card to a relative or friend, who can then withdraw the cash from an ATM machine. When it was introduced in 2004, EasySend was focused primarily on the Hispanic community. Today, it is used by immigrant populations all over the world (Branch Banking and Trust 2006).

In a slightly different vein, the MasterCard MYPlash and Visa Buxx cards, which are described in detail in Case 12.3, provide younger populations with a prepaid preloaded card alternative to credit cards or cash. Among other things, these alternatives provide a relatively risk-free way to teach kids fiscal responsibility. In addition, employers who are using payroll cards as an extension of their direct deposit programs are driving the growth of the prepaid preloaded card market. Like direct deposit, payroll cards can reduce administrative overhead substantially. Payroll cards are especially useful to companies in the health-care, retail, and other industries where the workforce is part time or transient and less likely to have bank accounts.

EC Application

STORED-VALUE CARDS: TAPPING THE TEEN AND PRETEEN MARKETS

"We're living on a plastic planet, where even vending machines, parking meters and Starbucks branches are now accepting credit and debit cards for everyday transactions. Small wonder that high schoolers—who were expected to spend $195 billion in 2006, according to a study by the Harrison Group—hanker for their own charge cards" (Campbell 2006). According to a 2006 study by the Jump$tart Coalition for Financial Literacy, almost 50 percent of high school seniors in the United States have a credit card. Close to half of the students have a card in their own names, while the other half use their parents' cards. In order to serve the market of kids under the age of 18, MasterCard and Visa have introduced a number of preloaded, open loop stored-value cards. These prepaid cards look like a regular plastic credit card, but the cardholder has no line of credit. Instead, they are more like debit cards where the cardholder can only spend up to the amount loaded on the card. The cards are accepted anywhere a MasterCard credit card or Visa credit card are accepted—at stores, online, and at ATM machines.

For the under-18 market, MasterCard offers the affinity-based MYPlash card, which features images of rock stars and athletes on the cards, as well as the Allow Card (short for allowance card) and PAYjr card. While the upper age for MYPlash and the Allow Card is 18, the PAYjr card is for kids 12 and under. The MYPlash and PAYjr card works on the allowance principle. The cardholder's parents deposit their allowance onto the cards. With PAYjr, the payment of the allowance can be tied to completion of a certain list of chores. With both cards, the cardholder and parents can monitor card usage online. Additionally, parents can block spending at certain types of merchants.

Not to be outdone, Visa offers a variety of cards that cater to the under-18 market. One of these is the RushCard, developed in conjunction with hip-hop mogul Russell Simmons. Besides working anywhere a Visa card is accepted, the card also works with mobile phones and provides discounts on clothing from Simmons' Phat Farm and Baby Phat. Another is the Visa UPside card, which teaches responsible spending. Towards this end, Visa has developed a number of financial literacy programs for teachers and schools (see *spendresponsibly.com*).

Probably the best known of the Visa offerings aimed at the under-18 market is the Visa Buxx card (pronounced "bucks"). The Visa Buxx program was started in the fall of 1999 by WildCard Systems. WildCard created the system in order to tap into the teen market. In the United States, there are more than 30 million teens between 13 and 18 years of age, and they spend more than $160 billion annually. Most of their spending involves cash provided by their parents.

WildCard was looking for a way to provide a turnkey payment system that would meet the needs of both parents and teens by offering a card that would provide:

▶ A parent-controlled reloadable payment card that would be accepted anywhere that Visa was accepted, including online and ATM cash machines.

▶ Stored-value functionality so that teens can only spend up to the amount established by their parents and loaded onto the card.

▶ A Web site where parents and teens could enroll for the card; add value through checking accounts, savings accounts, credit cards, or debit cards; set up recurring allowance schedules; shop online; and check balances and transaction history.

▶ Parental-control features so parents could maintain control over the account through the Web site.

▶ An educational component on the Web site so that teens could learn about financial responsibility and budgeting.

WildCard licensed the Visa Buxx product to Visa. Five Visa card issuers, including Bank of America, Capital One, National City, U.S. Bank, and Wachovia Bank, launched the system in 2000. Today, the card is offered by a wide range of banks throughout the United States. For issuing banks, the card helps build stronger relationships with existing customers (parents) and establishes relationships with new customers (the teens). In 2005, eFunds (*efunds.com/wildcardsystems*) acquired WildCard.

While there are benefits to these prepaid cards, there is also a big downside. Excluding the actual use of the card, card issuers charge users fees for virtually every action. Most card issuers collect fees for enrolling in the program, reloading or replacing the card, and for making inquiries about the balance remaining on the card. Some issuers charge the cardholder if the card isn't used for a few weeks or months.

Sources: Adapted from WildCard Systems (2004), Campbell (2006), and Jump$tart Coalition for Financial Literacy (2006).

Questions

1. What is the market for the MasterCard MYPlash card and Visa RushCard?

2. What key characteristics underlie WildCard's Visa Buxx system?

3. What is the major downside of prepaid, preloaded cards for the under-18 market?

Section 12.4 ▌ REVIEW QUESTIONS

1. What is a closed-loop stored-value card? What is an open-loop card?
2. What are the major markets for stored-value cards?

12.5 E-MICROPAYMENTS

Consider the following online shopping scenarios:

▸ A customer goes to an online music store and purchases a single song that costs $0.99.

▸ A person goes online to a leading newspaper or news journal (such as *Forbes* or *Business Week*) and purchases (downloads) a copy of an archived news article for $1.50.

▸ A person goes to an online gaming company, selects a game, and plays it for 30 minutes. The person owes the company $3 for the playing time.

▸ A person goes to a Web site selling digital images and clip art. The person purchases a couple of images at a cost of $0.80.

These are all examples of **e-micropayments**, which are small online payments, usually under $5. From the viewpoint of many vendors, credit and debit cards do not work well for such small payments. Vendors who accept credit cards typically must pay a minimum transaction fee that ranges from $0.25 to $0.35, plus 2 to 3 percent of the purchase price. The same is true for debit cards where the fixed transaction fees are larger even though there are no percentage charges. These fees are relatively insignificant for card purchases over $5, but can be cost-prohibitive for smaller transactions. Even if the transaction costs were less onerous, a substantial percentage of micropayment purchases are made by individuals younger than 18, many of whom do not have credit or debit cards.

Regardless of the vendor's point of view, there is substantial evidence, at least in the offline world, that consumers are willing to use their credit or debit cards for purchases under $5. A random sample telephone survey conducted in 2006 by Ipsos Insight and Peppercoin examined consumers' spending habits for low-priced items (Ipsos Insight 2006). Based on the survey, more than 67 million Americans had used their credit cards in the 30 days prior to the survey to purchase items priced at $5 or less. For the most part, these purchases were made at convenience stores, at quick service restaurants, to buy coffee, or for subway or other transportation tolls. In the online world, there is evidence that consumers are interested in making smaller valued purchases, but the tie to credit or debit card payments is less direct. For example, in February of 2006 Apple's iTunes music store celebrated their billionth download. A substantial percentage of these were downloads of single songs at $0.99 a piece. While most of iTunes' customers paid for these downloads with a credit or debit card, the payment was not on a per transaction basis. Instead, iTunes customers set up accounts. The account is paid for with a credit or debit card, not the individual download. Other areas where consumers have shown a willingness to purchase items under $5 are cellular ringtones and online games. Figures from Jupiter Research indicate that in the United States alone the cellular ringtone market eclipsed $217 million in 2004 and will grow to $724 million by 2009 (CNET 2005). The download of ringtones is charged to the consumer's cellular bill. Similarly, Jupiter estimated that the mobile game market in the United States will grow to $430 million by 2009. Like the download of songs, the download of a game is usually charged to the consumer's account, which is, in turn, paid by credit or debit card.

As far back as 2000, a number of companies had attempted to address the perceived market opportunity by providing e-micropayment solutions that circumvent the fees associated with credit and debit cards. For the most part, the history of these companies is one of unfulfilled promises and outright failure. Digicash, First Virtual, Cybercoin, Millicent, and Internet Dollar are some of the e-micropayment companies that went bankrupt during the dot-com crash. A number of factors played a role in their demise, including the fact that early users of the Internet thought that digital content should be free. More recently, Bitpass declared on January 2007 that they were going out of business. As late as fall 2006, Bitpass launched a digital wallet service that enabled consumers to store online downloads of digital content and the payment method used to fund their accounts (i.e., credit cards, PayPal, or automated clearing house debits). Bitpass succeeded in partnering with a large number of

e-micropayments
Small online payments, typically under $10.

smaller vendors, as well as a number of larger companies, such as Disney Online and ABC Inc. However, they purposely focused on the sale of digital content rather than branching out into other markets. Their narrow focus was probably a major factor in their demise.

Currently, there are five basic micropayment models that do not depend solely or directly on credit or debit cards and that have enjoyed some amount of success. Some of them are better suited for offline payments than online payments, although there is nothing that precludes the application of any of the models to the online world. The models include (D'Agostino 2006):

- **Aggregation.** Payments from a single consumer are batched together and processed only after a certain time period has expired (20 business days) or a certain monetary threshold (e.g., $10) is reached. This is the model used by Apple's iTunes. The e-commerce payment offerings from Peppercoin (peppercoin.com) also support it. This model is well suited for vendors with a lot of repeat business.
- **Direct Payment.** Micropayments are added to a monthly bill for existing services, such as a phone bill. This is the model used by the cellular companies for ringtone downloads. The payment service provider PaymentOne (paymentone.com) provides a network and e-commerce platform that enable consumers to add purchases of any size to their phone bills.
- **Stored Value.** Upfront payments are made to a debit account from which purchases are deducted as they are made. Offline vendors (e.g., Starbucks) often use this model, and music download services use variants of this model.
- **Subscriptions.** Single payment covers access to content for a defined period of time. Online gaming companies often use this model, and a number of online newspapers and journals (e.g., *Wall Street Journal*) also use it.
- **Á la Carte.** Vendors process purchases as they occur and rely on the volume of purchases to negotiate lower credit and debit card processing fees. Golden Tee Golf video game uses this model, and quick service restaurants (QSRs) like McDonald's and Wendy's also use it.

In the past couple of years, micropayments have come to represent a growth opportunity for the credit card companies because credit cards are being used increasingly as a substitute for cash. In response, both Visa and MasterCard have lowered their fees, especially for vendors like McDonald's with high transaction volumes. In August 2005, PayPal also entered the micropayment market when they announced a new alternative fee structure of 5 percent plus $0.05 per transaction. This is in contrast to their standard fees of 1.9 to 2.9 percent plus $0.30 per transaction. If a PayPal vendor is being charged at a rate of 1.9 percent plus $0.30, then the alternative fee of 5 percent plus $0.05 will be cheaper for any item that costs $7 or less (you can do the math). It is $12 or less for 2.9 percent plus the $0.30 rate. Overall, the movement of the credit card companies and PayPal into the micropayment market does not bode well for those companies that provide specialized software and services for e-micropayments. In the long run, the credit card companies and PayPal will dominate this market.

Section 12.5 ❯ REVIEW QUESTIONS

1. What is a micropayment?
2. List some of the situations where e-micropayments can be used.
3. Outside of using credit or debit cards, what are some of the alternative ways that an online merchant can handle micropayments.

12.6 E-CHECKING

As noted in Section 12.1, in the United States paper checks are the only payment instrument that is being used less frequently now than five years ago (Gerdes et al. 2005). In 2003, checks represented 45 percent of all noncash payments, down from 57 percent in 2000. In contrast, e-check usage is growing rapidly. In 2004, the use of online e-checks grew by 40 percent over the previous year, reaching 968 million transactions. Based on a CyberSource survey (2005) of Web merchants, this percentage will continue to grow. Web merchants hope that e-checks will raise sales by reaching consumers who do not have credit cards or who are unwilling to provide credit card numbers online. According to CyberSource, online merchants that implement e-checks experience a 3 percent to 8 percent increase in sales on the average.

An **e-check** is the electronic version or representation of a paper check. E-checks contain the same information as a paper check, can be used wherever paper checks are used, and are based on the same legal framework. E-checks work essentially the same way a paper check works but in pure electronic form with fewer manual steps. With an online e-check purchase, the buyer simply provides the merchant with his or her account number, the nine-digit bank ABA routing number, the bank account type, the name on the bank account, and the transaction amount. The account number and routing number are found at the bottom of the check in the *magnetic ink character recognition (MICR)* numbers and characters.

E-checks rely on current business and banking practices and can be used by any business that has a checking account, including small and midsize businesses that may not able to afford other forms of electronic payments (e.g., credit and debit cards). E-checks or their equivalents also can be used with in-person purchases. In this case, the merchant takes a paper check from the buyer at the point of purchase, uses the MICR information and the check number to complete the transaction, and then voids and returns the check to the buyer (see Case 12.4 for a complete description of the process).

Most businesses rely on third-party software to handle e-check payments. CheckFree (checkfreecorp.com), Telecheck (telecheck.com), AmeriNet (debit-it.com), Chase Paymentech (paymentech.com), and Authorize.Net (authorize.net) are some of the major vendors of software and systems that enable an online merchant to accept and process electronic checks directly from a Web site. For the most part, these software offerings work in the same way regardless of the vendor.

The system shown in Exhibit 12.3 is based on Authorize.Net and is typical of the underlying processes used to support e-checks. Basically, it is a seven-step process. First, the merchant receives written or electronic authorization from a customer to charge his or her bank account (step 1). Next, the merchant securely transmits the transaction information to the Authorize.Net Payment Gateway server (step 2). The transaction is accepted or rejected based on criteria defined by the Payment Gateway. If accepted, Authorize.Net formats the transaction information and sends it as an Automated Clearing House (ACH) transaction to

e-check
A legally valid electronic version or representation of a paper check.

EXHIBIT 12.3 Processing E-Checks with Authorize.Net

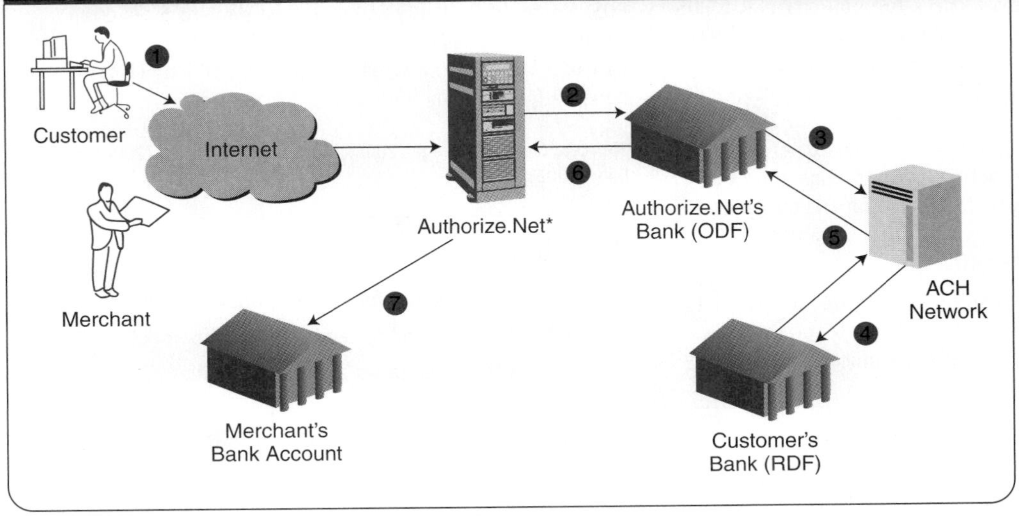

Source: Authorize.Net®. "eCheck.Net® Operating Procedures and Users Guide," October 28, 2004. *Authorize.net/files/echecknetuserguide.pdf.* Copyright 2004. Authorize.Net and eCheck.Net are registered trademarks of Lightbridge, Inc.

TO POP OR BOC: DIGITAL CHECKS IN THE OFFLINE WORLD

The use of e-checks is growing in the online world. Paradoxically, the same is true in the offline world, although it is occurring at a slower rate. In the near future, the rate of adoption in the offline world is likely to hasten. First, there is evidence that the use of a special NACHA system known as Purchase Order Processing (POP) is on the uptake. Second, another NACHA system called Back-Office Order Conversion (BOC) will become effective March 2007. With both systems, merchants convert checks written by consumers into the equivalent of e-checks and process them as ACH debits. The difference between the two systems is whether the check is converted at the POS by a cashier or converted after the sale by other staff in the back office.

The traditional processes used in handling paper checks written by consumers to make purchases in a store involve a number of steps and intermediaries (as many as 28). At a minimum, the checks taken by cashiers are collected periodically throughout the day. After collection, back office personnel process them. Once this is done, an armored car usually takes them from the store and delivers them to the store's bank. The store's bank processes them and sends them to a clearing house. From the clearing house, they move to the customer's bank. Not only is this time consuming, but it is also costly. Statistics show that it costs companies $1.25 to $1.55 to handle a paper check. This is in comparison to the administrative costs for an e-check which can be as low as $0.10 per transaction. Based on these figures, any sized company stands to save a substantial amount of money by streamlining these traditional processes. This is where POP and BOC come into play.

The Gap, Wal-Mart, Old Navy, and KB Toys are some of the companies that have instituted POP. With POP consumer checks are converted to ACH transactions at the time of the sale. When a customer writes a check for a purchase at a POS device, an MICR reader scans the check to capture the check details. The reader either keys or inserts the payment amount and the payee name at the time of purchase. At this point, the customer signs a written authorization. The casher then voids the check and returns it to the customer with a signed receipt. Eligible transactions pass through the ACH system, and a record of payment appears on the customer's bank statement.

POP has a number of benefits:

▶ Back-office and check-handling costs are substantially reduced.
▶ Consumer payments are received more quickly.

▶ Availability of funds is improved.
▶ Notification of insufficient funds happens sooner.

Although POP saves money, it also has a number of costs. According to Hughes and Edwards (2006), critics of POP have suggested:

▶ It requires specialized readers for each checkout counter.
▶ Cashiers need special training to convert the checks to ACH transactions at the POS.
▶ The authorization process can be cumbersome and confusing to consumers.
▶ It slows down the purchase process.

For these reasons, these critics have indicated that BOC is a better alternative for the average merchant.

With BOC, the customer experience is similar to the traditional process (Daly 2006). The customer writes a check for a purchase. The clerk either accepts or rejects the check after the merchant's verification service or guarantee provider verifies it. This does not require explicit customer authorization to convert the check to an electronic form. Once the checks are collected and moved to the back office, they are scanned into an ACH file and processed electronically. In this way, a merchant only needs one or two scanners and a few personnel to handle the process.

Best Buy is one of the better known retailers piloting BOC. The pilot is based on a "digital payment processing" solution called PayBack from FIS Risk Management and Analytics (Chain Store Age 2006). The solution eliminates all manual-based check deposits. PayBack provides the facilities required to convert a check to a form of electronic settlement, create and maintain images of the check, generate an electronic deposit file, and submit it to a financial institute. None of these processes require specialized equipment at the POS. No doubt Best Buy will move the pilot to production when BOC becomes official in 2007 because the project is part of a larger risk management process, which FIS has handled for Best Buy for the past 18 years.

Sources: Chain Store Age (2006), Hughes and Edwards (2006), and Daly (2006).

Questions

1. What does POC stand for and how does it work?
2. What does BOC stand for and how does it work?
3. What are the advantages and disadvantages of POC?

its bank (called the Originating Depository Financial Institution, or ODFI) with the rest of the transactions received that day (step 3). The ODFI receives transaction information and passes it to the ACH Network for settlement. The ACH Network uses the bank account information provided with the transaction to determine the bank that holds the customer's account (which is known as the Receiving Depository Financial Institution, or RDFI) (step 4). The ACH Network instructs the RDFI to charge or refund the customer's account (the customer is the receiver). The RDFI passes funds from the customer's account to the ACH Network (step 5). The ACH Network relays the funds to the ODFI (Authorize.Net's bank). The ODFI passes any returns to Authorize.Net (step 6). After the funds' holding period, Authorize.Net initiates a separate ACH transaction to deposit the e-check proceeds into the merchant's bank account (step 7).

As Exhibit 12.3 illustrates, the processing of e-checks in the United States relies quite heavily on the **Automated Clearing House (ACH) Network.** The ACH Network is a nationwide batch-oriented electronic funds transfer (EFT) system that provides for the interbank clearing of electronic payments for participating financial institutions. The Federal Reserve and Electronic Payments Network act as ACH operators, which transmit and receive ACH payment entries. ACH entries are of two sorts: credit and debit. An ACH credit entry credits a receiver's account. For example, when a consumer pays a bill sent by a company, the company is the receiver whose account is credited. On the other hand, a debit entry debits a receiver's account. For instance, if a consumer preauthorizes a payment to a company, then the consumer is the receiver whose account is debited. In 2005, the ACH Network handled an estimated 13 billion transactions worth \$21 trillion (Automated Clearing House 2005). The vast majority of these were direct payment and deposit entries (e.g., direct deposit payroll). Only 1.3 billion of these entries were Web-based, although this represented a 40 percent increase from 2004 to 2005.

> **Automated Clearing House (ACH) Network**
> A nationwide batch-oriented electronic funds transfer system that provides for the interbank clearing of electronic payments for participating financial institutions.

E-check processing provides a number of benefits:

- It reduces the merchant's administrative costs by providing faster and less paper-intensive collection of funds.
- It improves the efficiency of the deposit process for merchants and financial institutions.
- It speeds the checkout process for consumers.
- It provides consumers with more information about their purchases on their account statements.
- It reduces the float period and the number of checks that bounce because of insufficient funds (NSFs).

Section 12.6 ▶ REVIEW QUESTIONS

1. What is an e-check?
2. Briefly describe how third-party e-check payment systems work.
3. What is the ACH?
4. List the benefits of e-checking.

12.7 ELECTRONIC BILL PRESENTMENT AND PAYMENT

One area where e-checks and the ACH play a prominent role is in the area of e-billing; that is, paying recurring bills via the Internet. E-billing also is known as **electronic bill presentment and payment (EBPP).** *Presentment* involves taking the information that is typically printed on a bill and hosting it on a bill-presentment Web server. (See Exhibit 12.4 for an example.) Once the bill is available on the Web server, a customer can access the bill with a browser, review it, and pay it electronically. After the payment is received, it must be posted against the biller's accounts receivable system. Payments generally are transferred from the customer's checking account through ACH. In e-billing, the customers may be individuals or companies.

> **electronic bill presentment and payment (EBPP)**
> Presenting and enabling payment of a bill online. Usually refers to a B2C transaction.

EXHIBIT 12.4 E-Bill Presentment

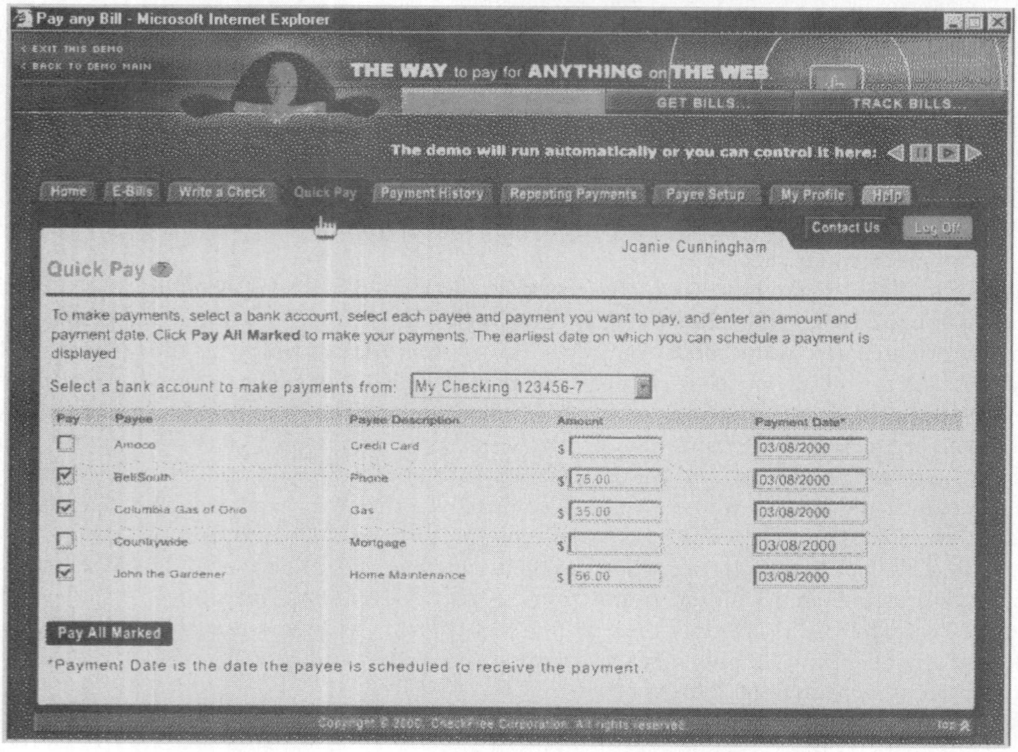

TYPES OF E-BILLING

There are three ways to pay bills over the Internet:

▶ **Online banking.** The consumer signs up for a bank's online bill-pay service and makes all his or her payments from a single Web site. Some banks offer the service for free with a checking account; others offer it if the account holder maintains a minimum balance. Others charge a monthly fee of $5 to $7.

▶ **Biller direct.** The consumer makes payments at each biller's Web site either with a credit card or by giving the biller enough information to complete an electronic withdrawal directly from the consumer's account. Exhibit 12.5 shows the general steps in the EBPP process of a single biller. The biller makes the billing information available to the customer (presentment) on its Web site or the site of a billing hosting service (step 1). Once the customer views the bill (step 2), he or she authorizes and initiates payment at the site (step 3). The payment can be made with a credit or debit card or an ACH debit. The biller then initiates a payment transaction (step 4) that moves funds through the payment system (payment), crediting the biller and debiting the customer (step 5).

▶ **Bill consolidator.** Exhibit 12.6 shows the steps in the process used by bill consolidators. The customer enrolls to receive and pay bills for multiple billers (service initiation). The customer's enrollment information is forwarded to every biller that the customer wishes to activate (service initiation). For each billing cycle, the biller sends a bill summary or bill detail to the consolidator (presentment). The bill summary, which links to the bill detail stored with the biller or consolidator, is forwarded to the aggregator and made available to the customer (presentment). The customer views the bill and initiates payment instructions (payment). The customer service provider (CSP) or aggregator

EXHIBIT 12.5 E-Billing Process for Single Biller

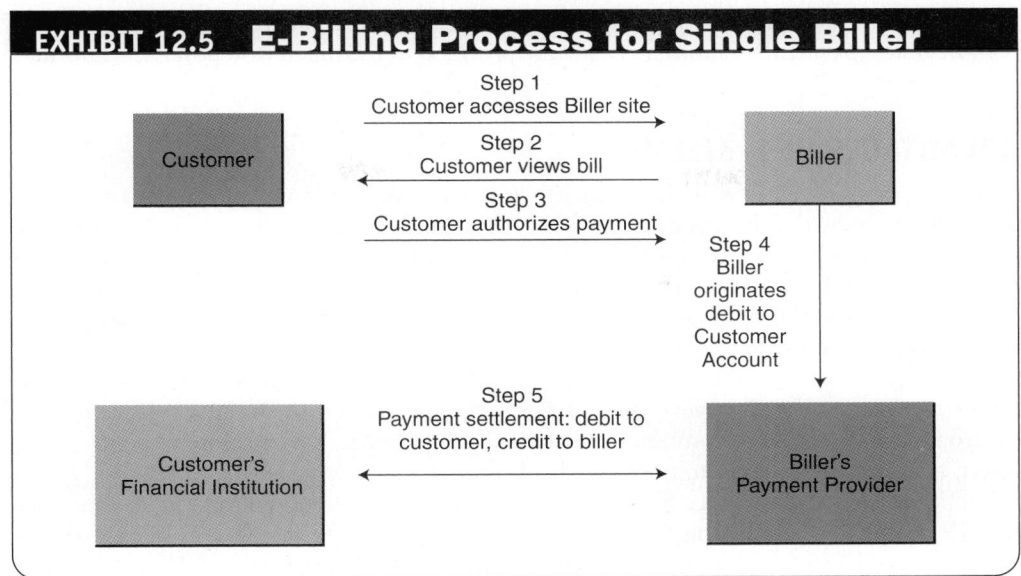

Customer
Step 1
Customer accesses Biller site
Step 2
Customer views bill
Step 3
Customer authorizes payment
Biller
Step 4
Biller originates debit to Customer Account
Step 5
Payment settlement: debit to customer, credit to biller
Customer's Financial Institution
Biller's Payment Provider

Source: ebilling.org. Courtesy of NACHA–The Electronic Payments Association, Council for Electronic Billing and Payment.

EXHIBIT 12.6 E-Billing Processes for Bill Consolidator

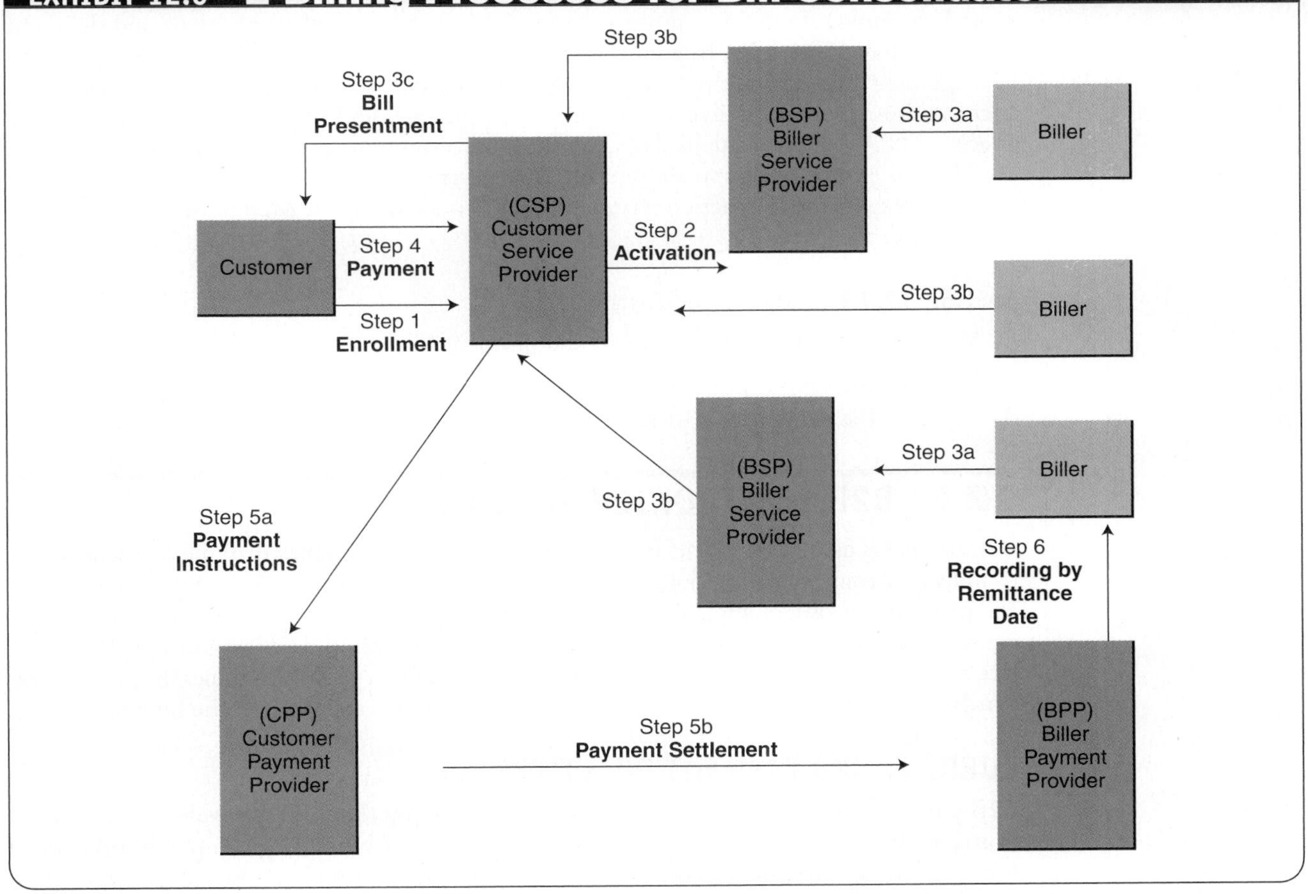

Step 3b
Step 3c
Bill Presentment
(BSP) Biller Service Provider
Step 3a
Biller
Customer
Step 4
Payment
(CSP) Customer Service Provider
Step 2
Activation
Step 1
Enrollment
Step 3b
Biller
(BSP) Biller Service Provider
Step 3a
Biller
Step 3b
Step 5a
Payment Instructions
Step 6
Recording by Remittance Date
(CPP) Customer Payment Provider
Step 5b
Payment Settlement
(BPP) Biller Payment Provider

Source: ebilling.org. Courtesy of NACHA–The Electronic Payments Association, Council for Electronic Billing and Payment.

initiates a credit payment transaction that moves funds through the payment system to the biller (payment). Remittance data are provided to the biller, who posts this information to its own accounts receivable system (posting).

ADVANTAGES OF E-BILLING

From the perspective of the billing firm, e-billing has several advantages. The most obvious benefit is the reduction in expenses related to billing and processing payments. The estimate is that paper bills cost between $0.75 and $2.70 per bill. E-billing costs between $0.25 and $0.30 per bill. E-billing also enables better customer service. Not only can customer service representatives see the same presentment that the customer is seeing, but the presentment also can provide access to frequently asked questions and help boxes.

Another advantage relates to advertising. A paper bill can include advertising and marketing inserts. Usually, every customer gets the same ads or materials. With e-billing, electronic inserts can be customized to the individual customer. If a customer responds to the insert, then it is much easier to trace which ads or materials are successful.

There also are advantages from the customer's perspective. E-billing reduces the customer's expenses by eliminating the cost of checks, postage, and envelopes. E-billing simplifies and centralizes payment processing and facilitates better record keeping. Customers can review and pay bills at virtually any time. In this way, the customer has direct control over the timing of the payment.

By far, CheckFree (checkfree.com) is the leading third-party e-billing vendor. CheckFree was founded in 1981 and is currently headquartered in Atlanta, Georgia. CheckFree is a consolidator, aggregating all a customer's bills into a single presentment. It can also set up payments with companies that do not offer electronic billing. CheckFree serves about 6 million consumers in over 1,000 businesses and over 350 financial institutions (including most U.S. banks). In 2006, it processed over 1.1 billion payment transactions and delivered approximately 185 e-bills. In addition to these services, CheckFree also provides portfolio management, reconciliation products and services, check conversion, e-billing and payment and e-statement delivery, consumer e-commerce, and for years has been a leading processor of ACH payments. Today, CheckFree processes more than two-thirds of the nation's ACH payments. CheckFree alerts users if there is a problem with any of the payments. Users can export the transaction records to Quicken or Microsoft Money. See checkfree.com for a demo.

Section 12.7 ▶ REVIEW QUESTIONS

1. What is electronic bill presentment and payment (EBPP)?
2. Describe the three types of EBPP.
3. Describe the benefits of EBPP.

12.8   B2B ELECTRONIC PAYMENTS

B2B payments usually are much larger and significantly more complex than the payments made by individual consumers. The dollar values often are in the hundreds of thousands, the purchases and payments involve multiple items and shipments, and the exchanges are much more likely to engender disputes that require significant work to resolve. Simple e-billing or EBPP systems lack the rigor and security to handle these B2B situations. This section examines the processes by which companies present invoices and make payments to one another over the Internet.

CURRENT B2B PAYMENT PRACTICES

B2B payments are part of a much larger financial supply chain that includes procurement, contract administration, fulfillment, financing, insurance, credit ratings, shipment validation, order matching, payment authorization, remittance matching, and general ledger accounting. From a buyer's perspective, the chain encompasses the procurement-to-payment process. From the seller's perspective, the chain involves the order-to-cash cycle. Regardless of the perspective, in financial supply chain management the goal is to optimize accounts payable

(A/P) and accounts receivable (A/R), cash management, working capital, transaction costs, financial risks, and financial administration.

Unlike the larger (physical) supply chain, inefficiencies still characterize the financial supply chains of most companies. A number of factors create these inefficiencies, including (Barnhart 2004):

- The time required to create, transfer, and process paper documentation
- The cost and errors associated with manual creation and reconciliation of documentation
- The lack of transparency in inventory and cash positions when goods are in the supply chain
- Disputes arising from inaccurate or missing data
- Fragmented point solutions that do not address the complete end-to-end processes of the trade cycle

These inefficiencies are evident especially with A/P and A/R processes where payments are still made with paper.

Based on a survey of 304 members of the Association for Financial Professionals (2004), little has changed in the world of B2B payments since the Association conducted a similar survey four years ago in 2000. The vast majority of B2B payments are still made by check, and the barriers to electronic payments remain essentially the same. The major change is that more organizations indicated a willingness to migrate from checks to electronic payments in the future. Some of the findings of the survey are as follows:

- **Current payment practices.** Fifty-one percent of those surveyed indicated that checks make up more than 80 percent of their disbursements, whereas only 43 percent indicated that they receive more than 80 percent of their collections by check. Those companies with revenues over $1 billion make and receive significantly fewer payments by check.
- **Electronic payments.** Electronic payments are used more widely for disbursements and collections when the businesses are major suppliers or customers. However, regardless of the trading relationship between the businesses, ACH credits are the most widely used form of electronic payment, followed by wire transfers. Purchasing cards and ACH debits are used rarely.
- **Role of EDI.** There has been virtually no change in the use of EDI to send or receive remittance information associated with an electronic payment. Approximately 25 percent of the organizations use EDI to send information, and 35 percent receive information in this format. Most remittance information is sent and received through banks and comes in the form of faxes or mail.
- **Integration of electronic payment and accounting systems.** Forty-five percent of the organizations have integrated their electronic payment systems with either their A/P systems, A/R systems, or both. In most cases, the integration has been achieved through ERP systems or via proprietary software. Those companies that have integrated their systems have done so to achieve internal operating efficiencies or to reduce costs and staff.
- **Barriers to electronic payment.** Most companies can cite a long list of barriers inhibiting the move to electronic payments. The four major barriers include: a shortage of IT staff, a lack of integration of payment and accounting systems, a lack of a standard format for remittance information, and the inability of trading partners to send or receive electronic payments with sufficient remittance information.
- **Prospects for electronic payments.** Twenty-eight percent indicated that their organizations plan to convert the majority of their B2B payments from check to electronic payments over the next three years. In support of this move, a number of companies are planning to centralize their payment controls, use purchasing cards for capital goods and higher value items, integrate their payment and accounting systems, and image the checks they send and receive to banks for clearance and settlement.

ENTERPRISE INVOICE PRESENTMENT AND PAYMENT

The process by which companies present invoices and make payments to one another through the Internet is known as **enterprise invoice presentment and payment (EIPP)**. For

enterprise invoice presentment and payment (EIPP)
Presenting and paying B2B invoices online.

many firms, presentment and payment are costly and time consuming. It can cost up to $15 to generate a paper invoice and between $25 and $50 to resolve a disputed invoice. On the payment side, it takes three to five days for a check to arrive by mail. This means that millions of dollars of B2B payments are tied up in floats. This reduces the recipients' cash flow and increases the amount they must borrow to cover the float. In the same vein, manual billing and remittance can result in errors, which in turn can result in disputes that hold up payments. Given that most firms handle thousands of invoices and payments yearly, any reduction in time, cost, or errors can result in millions of dollars of savings. According to a survey by Credit Research Foundation, the major reasons companies turn to EIPP solutions are improved cash flow, customer service for billing and remittance, and improved data that can lower invoice processing costs (Lucas 2005).

EIPP Models

EIPP automates the workflow surrounding presentment and payment. Like EBPP, there are three EIPP models: seller direct, buyer direct, and consolidator.

Seller Direct. This solution links one seller to many buyers for invoice presentment. Buyers navigate to the seller's Web site to enroll in the seller's EIPP program. The seller generates invoices on the system and informs the appropriate buyers that they are ready for viewing. The buyers log into the seller's Web site to review and analyze the invoices. The buyers may authorize invoice payment or communicate any disputes. Based on predetermined rules, disputes may be accepted, rejected, or reviewed automatically. Once payment is authorized and made, the seller's financial institution processes the payment transaction.

This model typically is used when there are preestablished relationships between the seller and its buyers. If a seller issues a large number of invoices or the invoices have a high value, then there can be a substantial payoff from implementing an EIPP. For this reason, firms in the manufacturing, telecommunication, utilities, health-care, and financial services industries use this model often.

Buyer Direct. In this model, there is one buyer for many sellers. Sellers enroll in the buyer's EIPP system at the buyer's Web site. Sellers post invoices to the buyer's EIPP, using the buyer's format. Once an invoice is posted, the buyer's staff will be notified. The buyer reviews and analyzes the invoices on the system. The buyer communicates any disputes to the appropriate seller. Based on predetermined rules, disputes may be accepted, rejected, or reviewed automatically. Once an invoice is approved, the buyer will authorize payment, which the buyer's financial institution will process.

This is an emerging model based on the buyer's dominant position in B2B transactions. Again, it is used when the buyer's purchases result in a high volume of invoices. Companies such as Wal-Mart are in a strong position to institute buyer-direct EIPPs.

Consolidator. This is a many-to-many model with the consolidator acting as an intermediary, collecting or aggregating invoices from multiple sellers and payments from multiple buyers. Consolidators are generally third parties who not only provide EIPP services but also offer other financial services (e.g., insurance, escrow). In this model, the sellers and buyers register with the consolidator's EIPP system. The sellers generate and transfer invoice information to the EIPP system. The consolidator notifies the appropriate buyer organization that the invoice is ready. The buyer reviews and analyzes the invoice. Disputes are communicated through the consolidator EIPP. Based on predetermined rules, disputes may be accepted, rejected, or reviewed automatically. Once the buyer authorizes the invoice payment, the consolidator initiates the payment. Either the buyer's or the seller's financial institution processes the payment.

The consolidator model eliminates the hassles associated with implementing and running an EIPP. The model has gained ground in those industries where multiple buyers rely on the same suppliers. The Xign Payment Services Network (XPSN; xign.com) and the Global eXchange Services (GXS) Trading Grid (gxs.com) are both third-party consolidators linking thousands of suppliers and buyers. XPSN had more than 42,000 active suppliers in its network, generating over $35 billion in transactions. GSX's Trading Grid supports online trading among 40,000 customers in over 60 countries, exchanging over 1 billion electronic transactions representing $1 trillion in goods and services. Each of these networks eliminates the need for point-to-point connections between suppliers and buyers; automates core functions of the A/P process, including invoice receipt, validation, routing, dispute management, approval, and payment; and complements and integrates with the suppliers' and buyers' existing purchasing and procurement systems.

EIPP Options

A variety of online options are available for making payments in an EIPP system. They differ in terms of cost, speed, auditability, accessibility, and control. The selection of a particular mechanism depends on the requirements of the buyers and sellers. Some frequently used B2B payment options follow.

ACH Network. The ACH Network is the same network that underlies the processing of e-checks (described in Section 12.6). The difference is that there are three types of B2B payments, which vary by the amount of remittance information that accompanies the payments. The remittance information enables a buyer or seller to examine the details of a particular invoice or payment. The three types of ACH entries for B2B transactions are: Cash Concentration or Disbursement (CCD), which is a simple payment, usually for a single invoice, that has no accompanying remittance data and is typically initiated by the buyer who credits the seller's account; Cash Concentration or Disbursement with Addenda (CCD+), which is the same as a CCD payment except that it has a small amount of remittance data (up to 80 characters); and Corporate Trade Exchange (CTX), which generally is used to pay multiple invoices and has a large amount of accompanying remittance data (up to a maximum of 9,999 records of 80 characters each).

The ACH Network does not require any special hardware. The cost of the software needed to initiate ACH transactions depends on the volume of CTX transactions. High volumes of CTX transactions require a much larger investment. In addition to hardware and software costs, the buyer's and the seller's financial institutions also charge file, maintenance, transaction, and exception handling fees for ACH transactions.

Purchasing Cards. Although credit cards are the instrument of choice for B2C payments, this is not the case in the B2B marketplace. In the B2B marketplace, the major credit card companies and associations have encouraged businesses and government agencies to rely on *purchasing cards* instead of checks for repetitive, low-value transactions. **Purchasing cards (p-cards)** are special-purpose payment cards issued to a company's employees. They are used solely for the purpose of paying for nonstrategic materials and services (e.g., stationery, office supplies, computer supplies, repair and maintenance services, courier services, and temporary labor services) up to a limit (usually $1,000 to $2,000). These purchases often represent the majority of a company's payments but only a small percentage of the dollars spent. Purchasing cards operate essentially the same as any other charge card and are used for both off-line and online purchases. The major difference between a credit card and a purchase card is that the latter is a nonrevolving account, meaning that it needs to be paid in full each month, usually within five days of the end of the billing period. Exhibit 12.7 shows how a purchasing card is used.

Purchasing cards enable a company or government agency to consolidate the purchases of multiple cardholders into a single account and, thus, issue a single invoice that can be paid through EDI, EFT, or an e-check. This has the benefit of freeing the purchasing department from day-to-day procurement activities and from the need to deal with the reconciliation of individual invoices. With a single invoice, accounts can be settled more quickly, enabling a company or agency to take advantage of discounts associated with faster payment. A single invoice also enables a company or agency to more easily analyze the spending behavior of the cardholders. Finally, the spending limits make it easier to control unplanned purchases. Some estimates suggest that efficiencies resulting from the use of purchasing cards can reduce transaction costs from 50 percent to 90 percent. To learn more about purchasing cards, see the National Association of Purchasing Card Professionals (napcp.org).

Fedwire or Wire Transfer. Among the forms of online B2B payments, Fedwire is second only to ACH in terms of frequency of use. Fedwire, also known as wire transfer, is a funds transfer system developed and maintained by the U.S. Federal Reserve system. It typically is used with larger dollar payments where time is the critical element. The settlement of real estate transactions, the purchase of securities, and the repayment of loans are all examples of situations where Fedwire is likely to be used. When Fedwire is used, a designated Federal

purchasing cards (p-cards)
Special-purpose payment cards issued to a company's employees to be used solely for purchasing nonstrategic materials and services up to a preset dollar limit.

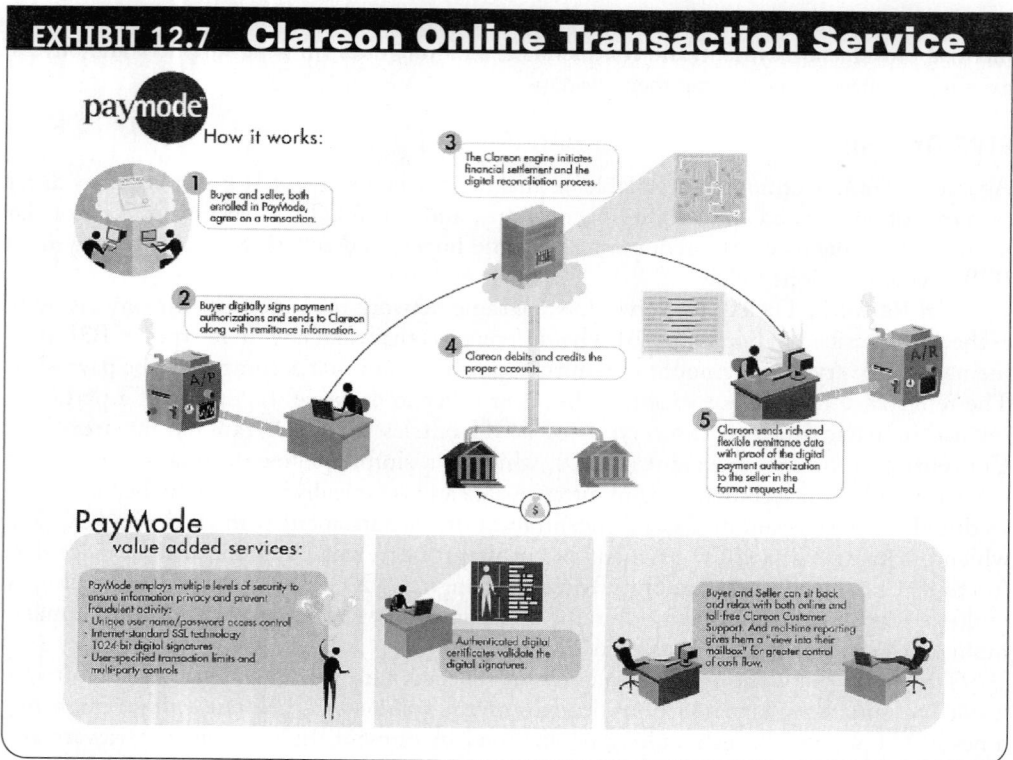

EXHIBIT 12.7   Clareon Online Transaction Service

Source: Used with permission of Clareon, a division of FleetBoston.

Reserve Bank debits the buyer's bank account and sends a transfer order to the seller's Federal Reserve Bank, which credits the seller's account. All Fedwire payments are immediate and irrevocable.

letter of credit (LC)
A written agreement by a bank to pay the seller, on account of the buyer, a sum of money upon presentation of certain documents.

Letters of Credit for Global Payments. Letters of credit often are used when global B2B payments need to be made, especially when there is substantial risk associated with the payment. A **letter of credit (L/C)**, also called a documentary credit, is issued by a bank on behalf of a buyer (importer). It guarantees a seller (exporter) that payment for goods or services will be made, provided the terms of the L/C are met. Before the credit is issued, the buyer and seller agree on all terms and conditions in a purchase and sale contract. The buying company then instructs its bank to issue a documentary credit in accordance with the contract. A credit can be payable at sight or at term. *At sight* means that payment is due upon presentation of documents after shipment of the goods or after a service is provided. Alternatively, if the seller allows the buyer an additional period, after presentation of documents, to pay the credit (30, 60, 90 days, etc.), then the credit is payable *at term*. L/C arrangements usually involve a series of steps that can be conducted much faster online than off-line. The Real-World Case at the end of the chapter and Online File W12.4 describe the benefits of replacing L/Cs with online payments.

For sellers the main benefit of an L/C is reduced risk—the bank assures the creditworthiness of the buyer. For those global situations where the buyer is a resident in a country with political or financial instability, the risk can be reduced if the L/C is confirmed by a bank in the seller's country. Reduced risk also is of benefit to buyers who may use this fact to negotiate lower prices.

Section 12.8 ▶ REVIEW QUESTIONS

1. Describe the financial supply chain.
2. Describe the current state of B2B e-payments.
3. What is electronic invoice presentment and payment (EIPP)?

4. Describe the three models of EIPP.

5. Describe the basic EIPP options.

6. What is a purchasing card?

12.9 THE SALES TAX ISSUE

Suppose you buy a laptop computer online from Amazon.com. How much sales tax will you owe? Most likely, you will not owe sales tax on the purchase. What if you buy a laptop computer online from CompUSA? How much sales tax will you owe in this case? The answer is, it depends, primarily on the tax laws where you have the laptop shipped. The reason why the Amazon.com purchase is likely to be sales-tax free is because of a 1992 ruling by the U.S. Supreme Court. In that ruling, the Court held that a state cannot force out-of-state businesses to collect sales taxes unless the business has a physical presence—a store, factory, or distribution center—in the state. The court reasoned that the various sales tax systems were too complex for retailers to keep track. This ruling is still in effect. In a number of states, when a consumer makes a purchase from a business without a physical presence in the state, the consumer is required to pay a "use tax." In practice few consumers pay the use tax, and most states ignore the tax unless a high-value item is purchased (e.g., expensive jewelry). Amazon.com does not have retail stores, but CompUSA does. This means that CompUSA is required to charge sales tax in those states where it has a physical presence. The amount varies from one state to the next.

In the United States, there are over 11,000 taxing jurisdictions. Some states have consistent sales tax rates for all items in all localities. Other states charge different rates for different items. For instance, food and clothing often are exempt from sales tax. Also, in many states there is a statewide sales tax plus local (city, county, or both) sales taxes that range dramatically from one jurisdiction to another. For example, sales taxes in the Denver area vary from under 4 percent to over 8 percent. When a buyer purchases an item in person, the store charges the same sales tax for the item regardless of where the buyer resides. When the same item is purchased online, the merchant has to know the tax laws in the state and locale where the item is being shipped. As the 1992 Supreme Court ruling suggests, this can be a very complicated task especially because sales tax laws change quite frequently. Overall, there are approximately 44,000 tax rates in effect across the United States. There are approximately 600 to 800 changes made to these rates every year.

Researchers at the University of Tennessee estimate that in the United States state and local governments have lost $15.5 billion in sales taxes because of online sales (Chang 2003). They project that the loss will grow to $21.5 billion by 2008 as EC continues to grow. To combat the loss, a number of states joined together a few years ago to simplify their sales tax laws, making it easier for online retailers to collect sales taxes and use taxes. Thirty-five states have signed on to a program called the Streamlined Sales Tax Project (SSTP; streamlinedsalestax.org). In 2003, state legislatures began the process of introducing legislation aimed at conforming their state sales and use taxes to the SSTP. To date, 30 states and the District of Columbia have passed the conforming legislation. However, under the legislation, collection of sales taxes and use taxes by online merchants remains voluntary until the U.S. Congress or the Supreme Court makes it mandatory.

Because of the complexities, many online businesses (B2C and B2B) rely on specialized third-party software and services to calculate the taxes associated with a sale. The software and services handle the detailed computations and keep abreast of tax law changes. Some of the better known companies providing this type of software and services are:

▶ **Salestax.com.** This company is part of CCH Tax and Accounting (tax.cchgroup.com). It licenses a wide range of software products that automatically verify shipping addresses and calculate sales and use taxes. These products come in the form of Web services that are incorporated into the merchants' existing EC systems. The software is updated monthly to accommodate changes in the tax laws.

▶ **Sales Tax Clearinghouse.** The Sales Tax Clearinghouse (STC; thestc.com) provides a variety of tools for online merchants to calculate both sales and use taxes. Merchants can utilize STC's manual online calculator; subscribe to STC's raw sales tax data, which can be incorporated in their EC systems; or license STC's TaxCalc software, which links the merchants' systems with STC tax calculation servers. For those merchants who incorporate the raw sales tax data into their systems, updates are made monthly or quarterly, depending on the merchant's preferences.

▶ **Cybersource.** The Cybersource Tax Calculation Service provides real-time tax calculation capabilities for orders based on where they originate. Tax calculations are made on an item-by-item basis rather than being applied to the total amount of the purchases in an order. The service covers the 44,000 tax jurisdictions in the United States and Canada, as well as the 100 value added tax (VAT) systems outside the United States and Canada.

Section 12.9 ▶ REVIEW QUESTIONS

1. Describe the EC tax calculation problem.
2. Describe possible solutions to the tax-collection problem.

MANAGERIAL ISSUES

Some managerial issues related to this chapter are as follows.

1. **What B2C payment methods should we use?** Companies that only accept credit cards rule out a number of potential segments of buyers. Teenagers, non–U.S. customers, and customers who cannot or do not want to use credit cards online are examples of market segments that are unable or unwilling to use credit cards to make online purchases. E-checks, virtual credit cards, stored-value cards, and PayPal are some possible alternatives to credit cards. Also, when the purchase price is less than $10, credit cards are not a viable solution. In this case various e-micropayment systems can be used. Online merchants and other sellers need to be aware of the volatility and true costs of many of these alternatives. Because many of the various alternatives do not yet enjoy widespread use, it is always possible that they will not exist tomorrow.

2. **What B2B payment methods should we use?** Keep an open mind about online alternatives. When it comes to paying suppliers or accepting payments from partners, most large businesses have opted to stick with the tried-and-true methods of EFT or checks over other methods of electronic payment. For MROs, consider using purchasing cards. For global trade, electronic letters of credit are popular. The use of e-checks is another area where cost savings can accrue. Finally, innovative methods such as TradeCard can be very effective. With all these methods, a key factor is determining how well they work with existing accounting and ordering systems and with business partners.

3. **Should we use an in-house payment mechanism or outsource it?** It takes time, skill, money, software, and hardware to integrate the payment systems of all the parties involved in processing any sort of e-payment. For this reason, even a business that runs its own EC site should consider outsourcing the e-payment component. Many third-party vendors provide payment gateways designed to handle the interactions among the various financial institutions that operate in the background of an e-payment system. Also, if a Web site is hosted by a third party (e.g., Yahoo! Store), an e-payment service will be provided.

4. **How secure are e-payments?** Security and fraud continue to be a major issue in making and accepting e-payments of all kinds. This is especially true for online credit cards where fraud continues to grow. B2C merchants are employing a wide variety of tools (e.g., address verification and other authentication services) to combat fraudulent orders. These and other measures that are employed to ensure the security of e-payments have to be part of a broader security scheme that weighs risks against issues such as the ease of use and the fit within the overall business context.

RESEARCH TOPICS

Here are some suggested topics related to this chapter. For details, references, and additional topics, refer to the Online Appendix A "Current EC Research."

1. **The Payment Revolution**
   - The history of money and payments in the twentieth and twenty-first centuries
   - Patterns and trends in cash, check, and noncash payments

2. **Magnitude, Methods of Perpetration, and Preventive Measures Regarding Fraudulent Payments**
   - Patterns and trends in fraudulent payments
   - Merchant liabilities concerned with fraudulent payments
   - Categories of online orders with high fraud potential
   - Methods and tools for preventing fraudulent payments
   - Decision models and automated rules for detecting and preventing fraudulent payments
   - Role of PKI and digital signatures in preventing fraudulent payments

3. **The History and Future of Electronic Payments**
   - Economic, technological, and institutional forces shaping the credit card industry
   - History and reasons for the rapid growth and success of PayPal
   - Algorithms for producing and implementing e-payment systems
   - Global patterns and trends in the use of e-payment alternatives
   - Demographic patterns and trends in the use of e-payment alternatives
   - Cryptographic and encryption techniques underlying electronic cash and e-micropayments

   - Role of e-micropayments in the online content industry (e.g., music, video, and games)

4. **The Increasingly Important Role of Trade Networks in B2B**
   - Role of EDI in intercompany online payments
   - XML standards proposed and used for collaborative business processes and trading relationships
   - Forces determining the success or failure of online trading in various industries (e.g., auto parts)
   - Integration of e-payment systems with accounting and ERP systems
   - Issues of trust and dispute resolution in B2B e-payments
   - Network architecture in the operation of trading exchanges

5. **Smart Card Applications**
   - Components and operation of contact and contactless smart card systems
   - Operating systems and programming languages for smart cards
   - Privacy issues in e-identification and health-care applications of smart cards
   - Differences in the use and acceptance of smart cards in Europe, Asia, and North America
   - Markets for stored-value cards
   - Role of PKI and biometrics in smart card security
   - Role of smart cards in biometric security systems
   - Integration of smart cards into nationwide transportation systems

SUMMARY

In this chapter, you learned about the following EC issues as they relate to the learning objectives.

1. **Payment Revolution.** Cash and checks are no longer kings. Debit and credit cards now rule—both online and off-line. This means that online B2C businesses need to support debit and credit card purchases. In international markets outside of Western Europe, buyers often favor other forms of e-payment (e.g., bank transfers). With the exception of PayPal, virtually all the alternatives to charge cards have failed. None have gained enough traction to overcome the

"chicken-and-egg" problem. Their failure to gain critical mass has resulted from the confluence of a variety of factors. (e.g., they required specialized hardware or setup or they failed to mesh with existing systems).

2. **Using Payment Cards Online.** The processing of online card payments is essentially the same as it is for bricks-and-mortar stores and involves essentially

the same players and the same systems—banks, card associations, payment processing services, and the like. This is one of the reasons why payment cards predominate in the online world. The major difference is that the rate of fraudulent orders is much higher online. Surveys, such as those conducted annually by CyberSource, indicate that merchants have adopted over the past few years a wide variety of methods to combat fraudulent orders, including address verification, manual review, fraud screens and decision models, card verification numbers, card association authentication services, and negative files. In the same vein, some consumers have turned to virtual or single-use credit cards to avoid using their actual credit card numbers online.

3. **Smart Cards.** Smart cards look like credit cards but contain embedded chips for manipulating data and have large memory capacity. Cards that contain microprocessor chips can be programmed to handle a wide variety of tasks. Other cards have memory chips to which data can be written and from which data can be read. Most - memory cards are disposable, but others—smart cards— can hold large amounts of data and are rechargeable. Smart cards have been and will be used for a number of purposes, including contactless retail payments, paying for mass transit services, identifying cardholders for government services, securing physical and network access, and storing health-care data and verifying eligibility for health-care and other government services. Given the sensitive nature of much of the data on smart cards, PKI and other cryptographic techniques are used to secure their contents.

4. **Stored-Value Cards.** A stored-value card is similar in appearance to a credit or debit card. The monetary value of a stored value card is housed in a magnetic strip on the back of the card. Closed-loop stored-value cards are issued for a single purpose by a specific merchant (e.g., a Starbucks gift card). In contrast, open-loop stored-value cards are more like standard credit or debit cards and can be used for multiple purposes (e.g., a payroll card). Those segments of the population without credit cards or bank accounts—people with low incomes, young adults, seniors, and minorities—are spurring the substantial growth of stored-value cards. Specialized cards, like EasySend, make it simple for immigrant populations to transfer funds to family members in other countries. Similarly, specialized cards, such as MasterCard's MYPlash, provide teens and preteens with prepaid debit cards that function like standard credit or debit cards while helping parents monitor and maintain control over spending patterns.

5. **E-Micropayments.** When an item or service being sold online costs less than $5, credit cards are too costly for sellers. A number of other e-payment systems have been introduced to handle these micropayment situations. For the most part, they have failed. Yet, there is ample evidence indicating that consumers are interested in using their credit and debit cards for small-valued online purchases (e.g., iTunes, online game, and ringtone sales). In response, a number of newer micropayment models, such as aggregated purchases, have been developed to reduce the fees associated with credit and debit cards.

6. **E-Checking.** E-checks are the electronic equivalent of paper checks. They are handled in much the same way as paper checks and rely quite heavily on the Automated Clearing House (ACH) Network. E-checks offer a number of benefits, including speedier processing, reduced administrative costs, more efficient deposits, reduced float period, and fewer "bounced" checks. These factors have resulted in the rapid growth of e-check usage. The rapid growth is also being spurred by the use of e-checks for in-store purchases. Purchase Order Processing (POP) and Back-Office Order Conversion (BOC) are two systems, established by NACHA, that enable retailers to convert paper checks used for in-store purchases to ACH debits (i.e., e-checks) without the need to process the checks using traditional procedures.

7. **Electronic bill presentment and payment.** Although most consumers still pay their bills with paper checks, the percentage paying their bills online is growing at a rapid rate. Bills can be paid one at a time (through an online banking service or directly at the biller's Web site) or several can be paid at once (through a bill consolidator). Electronic bill presentment and payment (EBPP) reduces both the billers' and customers' costs and makes it easier for customers to track and review their payment records. The leading vendor of third-party EBPP is CheckFree. CheckFree services about 6 million consumers, currently processes over 1 billion payment transactions annually, and handles about two-thirds of the nation's ACH payments.

8. **B2B Electronic Payments.** B2B payments are part of a much larger financial supply chain that encompasses the range of processes from procurement to payment and order to cash. Today, the vast majority of B2B payments are still made by check, although many organizations are moving to enterprise invoice presentment and payment (EIPP). Like EBPP, there are three models of EIPP: seller direct (buyers go to the seller's Web site), buyer direct (sellers post invoices at the buyer's Web site), and consolidator (many buyers and many sellers are linked through the consolidator's Web site). Two of the largest consolidators are Xign Payment Services and GSX Trading Grid. In addition to these models, there are several EIPP payment options, including the ACH Network, purchasing

cards, wire transfers, and letters of credit (L/C). The move to EIPP is being inhibited by the shortage of IT staff, the lack of integration of payment and account systems, the lack of standard formats for remittance information, and the inability of trading partners to send or receive electronic payments with sufficient remittance information.

9. **Tax Issues.** The issues of sales and use taxes computation and collection for online purchases are complex. First, for any given buyer, it is difficult to determine whether sales or use taxes should be charged. Second, if taxes are charged, it is difficult to calculate how

much should be charged because the tax rate varies from one tax jurisdiction to the next and within a jurisdiction from one item to the next. The problem is that there are thousands of taxing jurisdictions in the United States and Canada and over 100 VAT jurisdictions in the rest of the world. Because of a 1992 Supreme Court ruling, it is also difficult to determine which online merchants are required to collect sales taxes. Because of the complexities, most online B2C and B2B businesses rely on outside companies to calculate sales and use taxes.

KEY TERMS

QUESTIONS FOR DISCUSSION

1. Suppose a company wanted to introduce a new e-micropayment method on the Web. What factors should it consider to increase the chance of success?

2. A textbook publisher is interested in selling individual book chapters on the Web. Should they let students use credit or debit cards to purchase the individual chapters? Why or why not? If credit or debit cards are permitted, then what other e-payment methods would you recommend to the publisher?

3. Recently, a merchant who accepts online credit card payments has experienced a wave of fraudulent orders. What steps should the merchant take to combat the fraud?

4. A retail clothing manufacturer is considering e-payments for both its suppliers and its buyers. What sort of e-payment method should it use to pay for office supplies?

How should it pay suppliers of raw materials? How should its customers—both domestic and international clothing retailers—pay?

5. A recent immigrant to the United States would like to send funds to a relative living in Mexico. What e-payment alternatives are available?

6. A metropolitan area wants to provide riders of its public transportation system with the ability to pay transit fares, as well as make retail purchases, using a single contactless smart card. What sorts of problems will they encounter in setting up the system, and what types of problems will the riders encounter in using the cards?

7. If you buy a CD from Apple's iTunes store, will you owe sales taxes on the purchase? Explain. What if you buy the same CD from Amazon.com?

INTERNET EXERCISES

1. This chapter listed the names of e-payment companies that failed to gain critical mass (e.g., Digital Cash, Flooz, etc.). Select two of these companies. Using information gathered from the Web, explain why you think they failed.

2. Go to **checkfree.com**. What sorts of EBPP services does CheckFree provide? Would you use the service? Why or why not?

3. Go to **peppercoin.com**. Explain in detail how its e-micropayment system works. What are the key benefits and limitations of the system?

4. Select a major B2C merchant and detail the e-payment options offered. Based on CyberSource's *The Insider's Guide to E-Commerce Payment*, Second Edition, what other types of e-payment systems should it offer?

5. Enter **tradecard.com**. Run the procure-to-pay demo. Summarize the processes and benefits of the service to a small exporter.

6. Go to **cybersource.com**. Identify the services it provides for B2B e-payments. Describe the features of CyberSource's major products that provide these merchant services.

7. Run the demo of Deskshop at the Discover Card Deskshop Web site **discovercard.com/deskshop**. Write a brief report describing the functions, benefits, and limitations of Discover Card's Deskshop service.

8. Download *Payment Card Industry Futures* report from **market platforms.com**. Who are the primary authors of the report? Among other things the report details the current status and future use of credit and debit cards by Generations X and Y. Who is included in Generation X and in Generation Y? What are some of the key facts and predictions about the use of cards by these two groups?

9. Download *Transit and Contactless Financial Payments* (October 2006) from **smartcardalliance.org//pages/publications-transit-financial**. Based on the report, what type of payment system is New York City Transit (NYCT) piloting? Who are NYCT's partners in the pilot? What factors helped determine the type of system to be piloted? How does the pilot work?

10. Enter **xign.com**. What types of companies are serviced by Xign Payment Services Network? What types of products and services does Xign provide?

11. Go to **nacha.org**. What is NACHA? What is its role? What is the ACH? Who are the key participants in an ACH e-payment? Describe the "pilot" projects currently underway at ACH.

TEAM ASSIGNMENTS AND ROLE PLAYING

1. Select some B2C sites that cater to teens and some that cater to older consumers. Have team members visit these sites. What types of e-payment methods do they provide? Are there any differences among the methods used on different types of sites? What other types of e-payment would you recommend for the various sites and why?

2. Write a report comparing smart card applications in two or more European and/or Asian countries. In the report, discuss whether those applications would succeed in North America.

3. Have one team represent MasterCard *PayPass* and another represent American *ExpressPay*. The task of each team is to convince a company that its product is superior.

4. Have each team member interview three to five people who have made a purchase or sold an item at auction over the Internet. Find out how they paid. What security and privacy concerns did they have regarding the payment? Is there an ideal payment method?

Real-World Case

ELIMINATING LETTERS OF CREDIT: RITE AID DEPLOYS THE TRADECARD SOLUTION

Rite Aid Corporation (*riteaid.com*) is one of the leading drugstore chains in the United States. The company began in 1962 as Thrif D Discount Center in Scranton, Pennsylvania. Over the years it has grown by acquisition. Today, Rite Aid has over 3,300 stores in 27 states and employs approximately 70,000 full- and part-time associates. At the end of 2006, their total sales were over $17 billion. The typical Rite Aid store handles a large number of items, although pharmaceuticals account for the majority of the sales. Like other major drugstore chains, Rite Aid's import supplier base, which includes over 300 vendors located throughout the world, provide a number of the items carried in their stores.

As far back as 2002, Rite Aid established a fairly strict set of supply chain guidelines and policies for their warehouse vendors. The guidelines cover the following areas:

▶ **Merchandise Information and Technology**—provides requirements for accurate item information, source tagging guidelines, purchase orders, unsalable merchandise, and EDI.

▶ **Shipment and Routing**—outlines requirements for distribution and transportation of merchandise.

▶ **Accounts Payable**—provides requirements for accurate vendor information and invoice processing.

▶ **Key Performance Indicators (KPIs)**—details the KPIs that have been selected to monitor the compliance or performance of warehouse vendors.

▶ **Expense Offsets**—identifies noncompliance areas and penalties.

▶ **Import Information**—outlines requirements for import vendors.

Prior to 2004, Rite Aid encountered substantial difficulties in dealing with their import vendors even with the detailed guidelines. One area of major concern revolved around the use of letters of credit (LC). In the past, virtually all Rite Aid's orders to their import vendors required an LC. This is general practice in the world of global procurement. An LC requires the retailer to commit their money early in the purchase process. The money lies in wait until all the required documents have been filed. Not only does this leave the money in a nonproductive state for the retailer and vendor but it can also result in cash-flow issues. The only one that benefits from this impasse is the financial institution that holds the money and collects fees from both the retailer and vendor.

In 2004, Rite Aid decided to implement a Web-based financial platform for transacting payments to their import vendors. The platform was based on a solution from TradeCard (*tradecard.com*). TradeCard is a New York City-based provider of technology and services designed to automate the financial processes of a global supply chain. TradeCard's solution handles the major areas of trading partner management (e.g., purchase-order management), accounts payable management (e.g., electronic invoicing), and financial management (e.g., LC replacement). TradeCard has an open network of partners—supplier and buyers—that facilitates services such as credit protection and trade finance in many countries.

The solution provided by TradeCard handles all the steps from purchase order to settlement and receipt of goods. The steps include:

1. Rite Aid initiates purchase orders and sends them electronically to TradeCard.

2. TradeCard will notify sellers of all new purchase orders, and ask the sellers to approve them online.

3. Sellers create and approve invoices on TradeCard as goods are readied for shipment.

4. Sellers send the goods and documents to the logistics service provider (LSP).

5. The logistics service provider will issue a hard-copy forwarder's cargo receipt to the seller once goods have been received and all document requirements have been met. The LSP will then transmit proof of delivery (POD) data to TradeCard.

6. TradeCard's automated compliance check will compare the shipment documents (invoice and POD) to the procurement documents (purchase order, including any amendments).

7. After TradeCard completes the compliance check, it will alert Rite Aid to review any discrepancies and approve or negotiate the payment authorization document. Once finalized, TradeCard will determine payment based on the terms of the transactions.

8. Rite Aid wires payment to TradeCard's payment service provider, JPMorgan Chase, who then remits payment to seller's account at the bank seller designates.

Because the new workflow provided by the TradeCard solution eliminated LCs, Rite Aid and TradeCard were concerned about the response from their import vendors. Rite Aid and TradeCard held a face-to-face meeting with the vendors to describe and discuss the new system. Based on the meeting, Rite Aid decided to rollout the system in two phases corresponding to the Christmas holiday and back-to-school seasons. In

January 2005, Rite Aid started using the system for online transactions. The processes and workflow have become part of their written supply chain guidelines and policies. Today, the system handles virtually all global payments.

In addition to eliminating the fees and cash flow problems associated with LCs, Rite Aid has documented a variety of benefits provided by their system. These include:

▶ Electronic delivery of purchase orders
▶ Automated creation of a commercial invoice based on purchase order information
▶ Automated document compliance checking
▶ Real-time visibility and reporting to all parties
▶ Improved communication among all parties
▶ Improved data quality across shipping documents
▶ Improved planning and reporting capabilities
▶ Payment assurance, if desired, for 100 percent of the value of an order
▶ Access to a variety of export financing options.

Sources: Gentry (2006) and Rite Aid (2006).

Questions

1. Go to Rite Aid's portal (*raportal.riteaid.com/RA/RAPORTAL/RAMN0001.aspx*). Click on the Vendor Management Section and download the Vendor Supplier Guide. In the Guide go to the section on Imports. Based on this section, what policies must an import vendor follow in order to do business with Rite Aid? Which of the major tasks in the order-settlement process are handled by Rite Aid, by TradeCard, and by the vendor?

2. One of the key benefits of the TradeCard system is that it provides a merchant with real-time visibility into complete financial supply chain. Based on the Rite Aid TradeCard Workflow diagram displayed in the Guide, which steps of the order-settlement supply chain can Rite Aid and their vendors track with the system?

3. Do a Google search for electronic letters of credit. Based on the results of this search, who are some of the other companies that Rite Aid might have used to implement their order-settlement system? Describe some of the functions provided by these vendors. Do the capabilities of these companies match those provided by TradeCard?

REFERENCES

American Public Transportation Association (APTA). "Smart Cards and U.S. Public Transportation." June 2006. **apta.com/research/info/briefings/briefing_6.cfm** (accessed February 2007).

Association for Financial Professionals (AFP). "2004 Electronic Payments Survey." 2004. **afponline.org/pub/pdf/2004_10_research_epay_report.pdf** (accessed February 2007).

Authorize.Net. "ECheck.Net Operating Procedures and Users Guide." October 28, 2004. **authorize.net/files/echecknetuserguide.pdf** (accessed February 2007).

Automated Clearing House (ACH). "Understanding the ACH Network: An ACH Primer." 2005. **nacha.org/OtherResources/Buyers2005/BuyersGuide2005_UnderACH.pdf** (accessed February 2007).

Barnhart, T. "The Financial Supply Chain: Could This Be the Next Corporate Paradigm after ERP?" April 1, 2004. **dso-news.info/The-Financial-Supply-Chain-Could-this-be-the-next-corporate-paradigm-after-ERP-_a1469.html** (accessed February 2007).

Berney, L. "Global National ID Survey: Smart Cards Advance, but Slowly." *CardTechnology News Bulletin*, October 2006. **cardtechnology.com/article.html?id=200610020IZ4I66J** (accessed February 2007).

Branch Banking and Trust (BB&T). "BB&T Makes EasySend Money Transfer Free." June 2006. **paymentsnews.com/2006/06/bbt_makes_easys. html** (accessed February 2007).

Campbell, C. "Educating Teens About Credit." 2006. **bankrate.com/cnn/news/cc/20070109_teen_credit_debit_card_a1.asp** (accessed February 2007).

Card Technology. "The TaiwanMoney Card Is Still Too Slow for Subways." 2006. **cardtechnology.com/article.html?id=20060317366M1LIB** (accessed February 2007).

Ceridian. "Annual Survey Shows Gift Card Spending Level to Increase this Holiday Season." Ceridian press release, October 13, 2005. **ceridian.com/corp/article/1,2868,12452–59852,00.htm** (accessed February 2007).

Chain Store Age. "Checks in a Digital World." June 2006. *Chain Store Age*.

Chang, R. "Internet Sales Tax Looms." *PCWorld*, October 1, 2003. **pcworld.com/news/article/0,aid,112723,00.asp** (accessed February 2007).

CNET. "Study: Ring Tones, Mobile Games to SkyRocket." *CNET News*, March 15, 2005. **news.com.com/Study+Ring+tones,+mobile+games+to+skyrocket/2100–1039_3-5618320.html** (accessed February 2007).

CR80News. "Department of Defense Common Access Card Gets a FIPS 201 Facelift." November 2006. **cr80news.com/library/2006/11/30/department-of-defense-common-access-card-gets-a-fips-201-facelift** (accessed February 2007).

CyberSource. "Eighth Annual Online Fraud Report." 2007. **cybersource.com/resources/collateral/Resource_Center/whitepapers_and_reports/CYBS_2007_Fraud_Report.pdf** (accessed February 2007).

CyberSource. "Insiders Guide to E-Commerce Payment: 20 Tools Successful Merchants Are Using to Unlock Hidden Profit: Second Edition." 2005. **cybersource.com/resources/collateral/Resource_Center/whitepapers_and_reports/insiders_guide.pdf** (accessed February 2007).

D'Agostino, D. "Pennies from Heaven." *CIO Insight*, January 2006.

Daly, J. "Will Those Who Won't POP Do BOC Instead?" October 2006. **digitaltransactions.net/files/1006Networks.doc** (accessed February 2007).

Dove Consulting. "Consumer Payment Preferences: Understanding Choice." 2006. **aciworldwide.com/pdfs/consumer_payment_preferences_trend.pdf** (accessed February 2007).

eBilling.org. "Building the EBPP Business Case." 2002. **ebilling.org/ebpp/default.htm** (accessed February 2007).

E-Health Insider. "Health Insurance Smart Card Scheme Starts in EU." June 2004. **e-health-insider.com/news/item.cfm?ID=754** (accessed February 2007).

Evans, D., and R. Schmalensee. *Paying with Plastic: The Digital Revolution in Buying and Borrowing*, 2nd ed. Cambridge, MA: MIT Press, 2005.

Frost and Sullivan. "America's Smart Card Market." August 2005. **smartcardalliance.org/resources/pdf/SCA_Executive_Summary_Final_092605.pdf** (accessed February 2007).

Gentry, C. "Moving Money." *Chain Store Age*. February 2006. **tradecard.com/languages/EN/news/articles/chainStoreAge_Feb2006.pdf** (accessed February 2007).

Gerdes, G., J. Walton, M. X. Liu, and D. W. Parke. "Trends in the Use of Payment Instruments in the United States." Spring 2005. **federalreserve.gov/pubs/bulletin/2005/spring05_payment.pdf** (accessed February 2007).

Government Accounting Office (GAO). "Electronic Government: Federal Agencies Continue to Invest in Smart Card Technology." Report to the Subcommittee on Technology, Information Policy, Intergovernmental Relations, and the Census, Committee on Government Reform, House of Representatives. September 2004. **gao.gov/highlights/d04948high.pdf** (accessed February 2007).

HBS Consulting. "Smart Cards—Current Trends, Developments, and Future Prospects in the Healthcare Industry." January 2004.

Hughes, S., and N. Edwards. "Best Practices for a Successful POP Implementation." May 9, 2006. **pop.epson.com/checks/pdfs/walmartpres.ppt** (accessed February 2007).

Hunt, J., and B. Holcombe. *Government Smart Card Handbook*. Washington, D.C.: U.S. General Services Administration, 2004. **smart.gov/information/smartcard** handbook.pdf (accessed February 2007).

Ipsos Insight. "More than 67 Million Americans Have Used Credit or Debit Cards for Purchases of Less Than $5 in the Past 30 Days." June 2006. **ipsosinsight.com/pressrelease.aspx"id=3284** (accessed February 2007).

Jump$tart Coalition for Financial Literacy. "2006 Jump$tart Questionnaire with Answers." 2006. **jump$tart.org** (accessed February 2007).

Kelly, K. "Scan this Book!" May 14, 2006. *New York Times*, May 14, 2006. **nytimes.com/2006/05/14/magazine/14publishing.html?ei=5090&en=c07443d368771bb8&ex=1305259200&adxnnl=1&adxnnlx= 171852200-KMPhOGBlav8LFn/Vt95ugw** (accessed February 2007).

LeClaire, J. "Micro-Commerce Presents Mega-Opportunities." *E-Commerce Times*. December 10, 2004. **ecommercetimes.com/story/Microcommerce-Presents-Mega-Opportunities-38734.html** (accessed April 2007).

Lucas, P. "Taming the Paper Tiger." *Collectionsworld.com*, February 2005. **collectionsworld.com/cgi-bin/readtory2.pl?story=20040601CCRV263.xml** (accessed February 2007).

MasterCard. "MasterCard SecureCode Case Study: CompUSA." 2005. **mastercard.com/us/wce/PDF/12351_Final_SecureCode_Case_Study_CompUSA.pdf** (accessed February 2007).

MasterCard International. "MasterCard International Surpasses 200 Million Smart Card Milestone." November 4, 2004. **mastercardintl.com/cgi-bin/news-room.cgi?id=950&category=date&date=2004** (accessed February 2007).

Mercator. "Mercator Announces Survey of Prepaid Market." *Payment News*, September 2006. **paymentsnews.com/2006/09/mercator_announ.html** (accessed February 2007).

Merchant Risk Council. "Online Fraud Rates Approaching Fraud Rates at Card-Present Retail According to 5th Annual Survey by Merchant Risk Council." November 22, 2004. **merchantriskcouncil.org/files/press_pdf/ 24_041805.pdf** (accessed February 2007).

Milligan, J. "Future Threat?" *BAI Banking Strategies*, May–June 2004. **bai.org/bankingstrategies/2004-may-jun/future** (accessed February 2007).

Multos. "TaiwanMoney Card." 2006. **multos.com/downloads/marketing/CaseStudy_Taiwan_Money.pdf** (accessed February 2007).

Quint, B. "Books Online: The Fee versus Free Battle Begins." November 21, 2005. **infotoday.com/newsbreak/nb051121–2.shtml** (accessed February 2007).

Rite Aid. "Vendor Supply Chain Guide." September 2006. **riteaidediservices.com/SupplyChain/RiteAid_Vendor_Supply_Chain_Guide.pdf** (accessed February 2007).

Sapsford, J. "The Power of Plastic." *Wall Street Journal*. November 2004. **wsjclassroomedition.com/archive/ 04nov/econ_plasticnation.htm** (accessed February 2007).

Smart Card Alliance. "SCM Microsystems Delivers Smart Card Readers for Belgium's National e-ID Program." *Smart Card Alliance Industry News,* October 26, 2004. **martcardalliance.org/articles/2004/10/26/scm-microsy stems-delivers-smart-card-readers-for-belgiums- national-e-id-program** (accessed February 2007).

Smart Card Alliance. "Sesam Vitale." October 2006, **smartcardalliance.org/resources/pdf/Sesam_Vitale.pdf** (accessed February 2007).

VeriSign. "Business Guide to Online Payment Processing." 2004. **paypal.teamingup.net/pdf/OPPBusinessGuide. pdf** (accessed February 2007).

Visa. "Verified by Visa." December 30, 2006. **partnernetwork. visa.com/pf/3dsec/download/3ds_intro.pdf** (accessed February 2007).

WildCard Systems. "Visa Buxx: Case Study." 2004. **corporate.wildcardsystems.com/index.cfm?pageid=p09** (accessed February 2007).

Wyatt, E. "Want 'War and Peace' Online? How about 20 Pages at a Time." *New York Times*, November 5, 2005. **nytimes.com/2005/11/04/technology/04publish.html? ei=5088&en=f3a77910153398a4&ex=1288760400&ad xnnl=1&partner=rssnyt&emc=rss&pagewanted= print&adxnnlx=1171758489-jV/wkJh QDPbc1v5G1PRVBQ** (accessed February 2007).

CHAPTER 13

ORDER FULFILLMENT, eCRM, AND OTHER SUPPORT SERVICES

Content

Learning Objectives

Upon completion of this chapter, you will be able to:

1. Describe the role of support services in EC.
2. Define *EC order fulfillment* and describe the EC order fulfillment process.
3. Describe the major problems of EC order fulfillment.
4. Describe various solutions to EC order fulfillment problems.
5. Describe CRM, its methods, and its relationship with EC.
6. Describe eCRM implementation and tools.
7. Describe other EC support services.
8. Discuss the drivers of outsourcing support services.

HOW AMAZON.COM FULFILLS ORDERS

The Problem

With traditional retailing, customers go to a physical store and purchase items that they then take home. With e-tailing, customers want the goods quickly and have them shipped to their homes; therefore, maintaining an inventory of items becomes critical. Maintaining inventory and shipping products costs money and takes time, which may negate the advantages of e-tailing. Let's see how Amazon.com, the "king" of e-tailing, handles the situation.

When Amazon.com launched in 1995, the business model called for virtual retailing—no warehouses, no inventory, no shipments. The idea was to take orders and receive payments electronically and then let others fill the orders. It soon became clear that this model, although appropriate for a small company, would not work for a giant e-tailer.

The Solution

Amazon.com decided to change its business model and handle its own inventory. The company spent close to $2 billion to build warehouses around the country and became a world-class leader in warehouse management, warehouse automation, packaging, and inventory management. Amazon.com outsourced the actual shipment of products to UPS and the U.S. Postal Service (USPS).

How is Amazon.com able to efficiently fulfill millions of orders?

- **Step 1.** When a customer places an order online, a computer program checks the location of the item. It identifies the Amazon.com distribution center that will fulfill the order. Alternatively, it may identify the vendor that will fulfill the order in those cases where Amazon.com acts as an intermediary only. The program transmits the order automatically and electronically to the appropriate distribution center or vendor. Here, we describe what happens in Amazon.com's distribution centers, such as the 800,000-square-foot facility in Fernley, Nevada.

- **Step 2.** A "flowmeister" (see exhibit above, right) at the distribution center receives all orders and assigns them electronically to specified employees.

- **Step 3.** The items (books, games, CDs, etc.) are stocked in bins. Each bin has a red light and a button (see exhibit on facing page). When an order for an item is assigned, the red light turns on automatically. Pickers move along the rows of bins and pick an item from the bins with red lights; they press the button to reset the light. If the light returns, they pick another unit until the light goes off.

- **Step 4.** The picked items are placed into a crate moving on a conveyor belt, which is part of a winding belts system that is more than 10 miles long in each warehouse. Each crate can reach many destinations; bar code readers (operated automatically or manually) identify items in the crate at 15 different points in the conveyor maze. This tracks the location of an item at any given time and reduces errors to zero.

- **Step 5.** All crates arrive at a central location where bar codes are matched with order numbers. Items are

moved from the crates to chutes where they slide into cardboard boxes. Sophisticated technology allows items picked by several people in different parts of the warehouse to arrive in the same chute and packed in one box.

- **Step 6.** If gift wrapping was selected, this is done by hand.

- **Step 7.** Boxes are packed, taped, weighed, labeled, and routed to one of 40 truck bays in the warehouse. From there, they go to UPS or the USPS. The items are scanned continuously.

Amazon.com rents space in its warehouse and provides logistic services to other companies. It takes orders for them too. How does it work?

1. Label, pack, and ship your items to Amazon.com.

2. When Amazon.com receives your items, they store them until an order is placed.

3. When an order is placed, Amazon.com will pick, pack, and ship the item, and may combine it with other items in the same order.

4. Amazon.com manages postorder customer service and handles returns as needed.

The Results

Each warehouse can deliver 200,000 or more pieces a day. All five warehouses must handle more than 3 million pieces a day during the busiest part of the holiday season. However, in 2004, the warehouses were able to deliver only 1 million pieces a day, creating some delays during peak periods. Amazon.com leases space to other retailers with online businesses (e.g., such as Target and Toys "R" Us) as well as companies overseas.

The system gives Amazon.com the ability to offer lower prices and stay competitive, especially because the company is becoming a huge online marketplace that sells thousands of items. As of 2007, profitability is increasing steadily.

To increase efficiency, Amazon.com combines items into one shipment if they are small enough. Shipping warehouses do not handle returns of unwanted merchandise—the Altrec.com warehouse in Auburn, Washington, handles returns.

Sources: Compiled from news items at Heizer and Render (2004), Kopytoff (2004), and LaMonica (2006).

WHAT WE CAN LEARN . . .

The Amazon.com case illustrates the complexity of order fulfillment by a large e-tailer and some of the solutions employed. Order fulfillment is a major EC support service, and it is the topic of this chapter. This chapter examines other support services, primarily customer services and CRM.

13.1 ORDER FULFILLMENT AND LOGISTICS—AN OVERVIEW

The implementation of most EC applications requires the use of support services. The most obvious support services are security (Chapter 11), payments (Chapter 12), infrastructure and technology (Online Chapter 19), and order fulfillment and logistics (this chapter). Most of the services are relevant for both B2C and B2B. Exhibit 13.1 summarizes the major services described in these chapters, which organizes services into the following categories, as suggested by the Delphi Group (delphigroup.com): e-infrastructure, e-process, e-markets, e-content, e-communities, and e-services. The exhibit shows representative topics in each category. This section of the chapter gives an overview of order fulfillment and logistics.

Taking orders over the Internet could well be the easy part of B2C. Fulfillment and delivery to customers' doors are the tricky parts (e.g., see Vitasek and Manrodt, 2006). Many e-tailers have experienced fulfillment problems, especially during the 1990s. Amazon.com,

EXHIBIT 13.1 E-Commerce Services

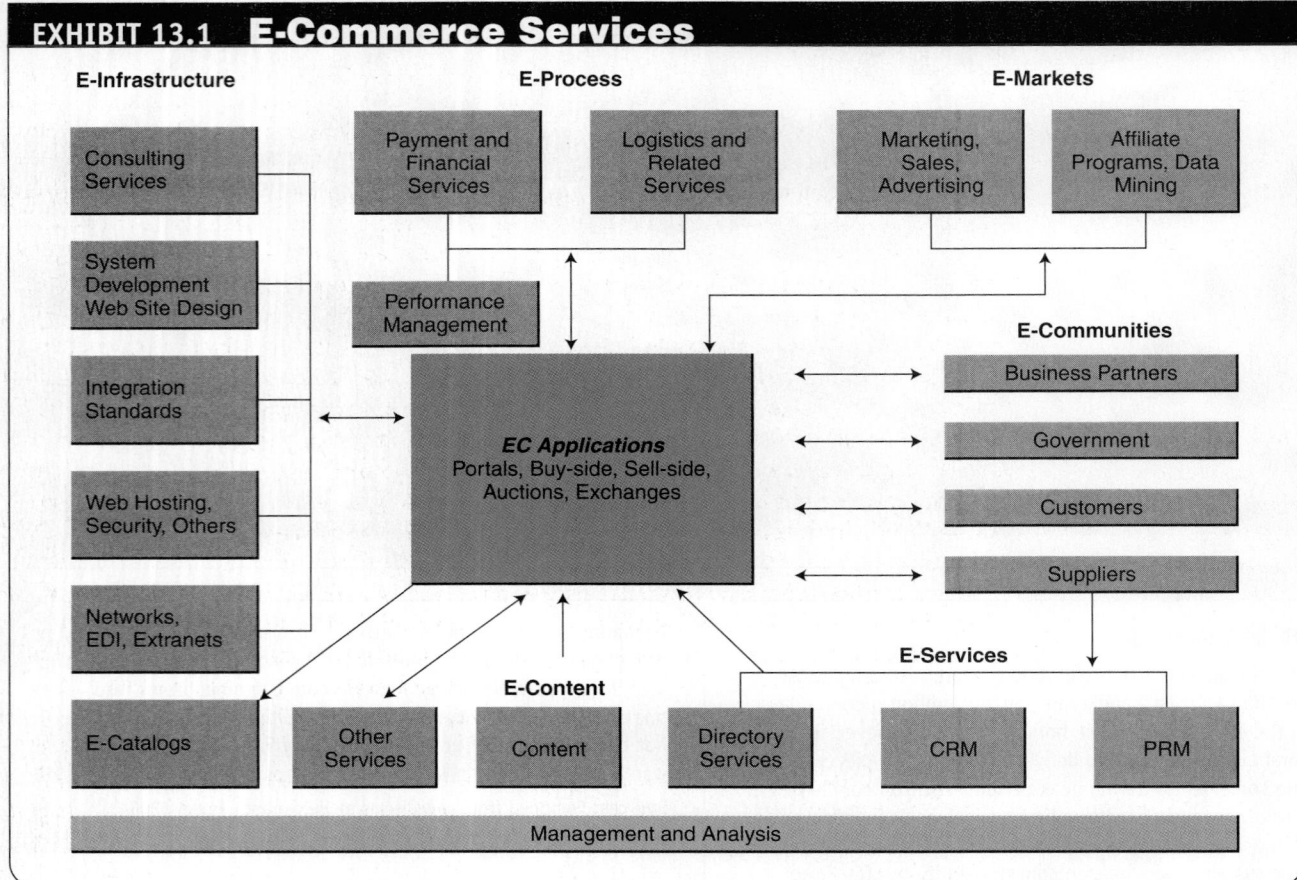

Sources: Adapted from Chio (1997), p. 18, from Murphy (2004), and from Natural Fusion (naturalfusion.com).

for example, which initially operated as a totally virtual company, added physical warehouses with thousands of employees in order to expedite deliveries and reduce order fulfillment costs.

Deliveries may be delayed for several reasons. These range from an inability to accurately forecast demand to ineffective e-tailing supply chains. Many of the same problems affect off-line businesses. One issue typical to EC is that EC is based on the concept of "pull" operations that begin with an order, frequently a customized one. This is in contrast with traditional retailing, which usually begins with a production to inventory that is then "pushed" to customers (see Exhibit 2A.1 on page 88). In the EC pull case, it is more difficult to forecast demand because of lack of experience and changing consumer tastes. Another reason for delays is that in a B2C pull model, many small orders need to be delivered to the customers' doors, whereas in brick-and-mortar retailing, the goods are shipped in large quantities to retail stores where customers pick them up.

Before we analyze the order fulfillment problems and describe some solutions, we need to introduce some basic order fulfillment and logistics concepts.

OVERVIEW OF ORDER FULFILLMENT

Order fulfillment refers not only to providing customers with what they have ordered and doing so on time but also to providing all related customer services. For example, a customer must receive assembly and operation instructions with a new appliance. This can be done by including a paper document with the product or by providing the instructions on the Web. (A nice example of this is available at livemanuals.com.) In addition, if the customer is not happy with a product, an exchange or return must be arranged.

Order fulfillment involves **back-office operations**, which are the activities that support the fulfillment of orders, such as packing, delivery, accounting, inventory management, and

order fulfillment
All the activities needed to provide customers with their ordered goods and services, including related customer services.

back-office operations
The activities that support fulfillment of orders, such as packing, delivery, accounting, and logistics.

shipping. It also is strongly related to the **front-office operations**, or *customer-facing activities*, which are activities, such as advertising and order taking, that are visible to customers.

OVERVIEW OF LOGISTICS

The Council of Supply Chain Management Professionals defines **logistics** as "the process of planning, implementing, and controlling the efficient and effective flow and storage of goods, services, and related information from point of origin to point of consumption for the purpose of conforming to customer requirements" (Council of Supply Chain Management Professionals 2007). Note that this definition includes inbound, outbound, internal, and external movement and the return of materials and goods. It also includes *order fulfillment*. However, the distinction between logistics and order fulfillment is not always clear, and the terms are sometimes used interchangeably, as we do in this text.

The key aspects of order fulfillment are delivery of materials or services at the right time, to the right place, and at the right cost.

THE EC ORDER FULFILLMENT PROCESS

In order to understand why there are problems in order fulfillment, it is beneficial to look at a typical EC fulfillment process, as shown in Exhibit 13.2. The process starts on the left, when an order is received and after verification that it is a real order. Several activities take place, some of which can be done simultaneously; others must be done in sequence. These activities include the following steps:

▶ **Activity 1: Making sure the customer will pay.** Depending on the payment method and prior arrangements, the validity of each payment must be determined. In B2B, the

front-office operations
The business processes, such as sales and advertising, that are visible to customers.

logistics
The operations involved in the efficient and effective flow and storage of goods, services, and related information from point of origin to point of consumption.

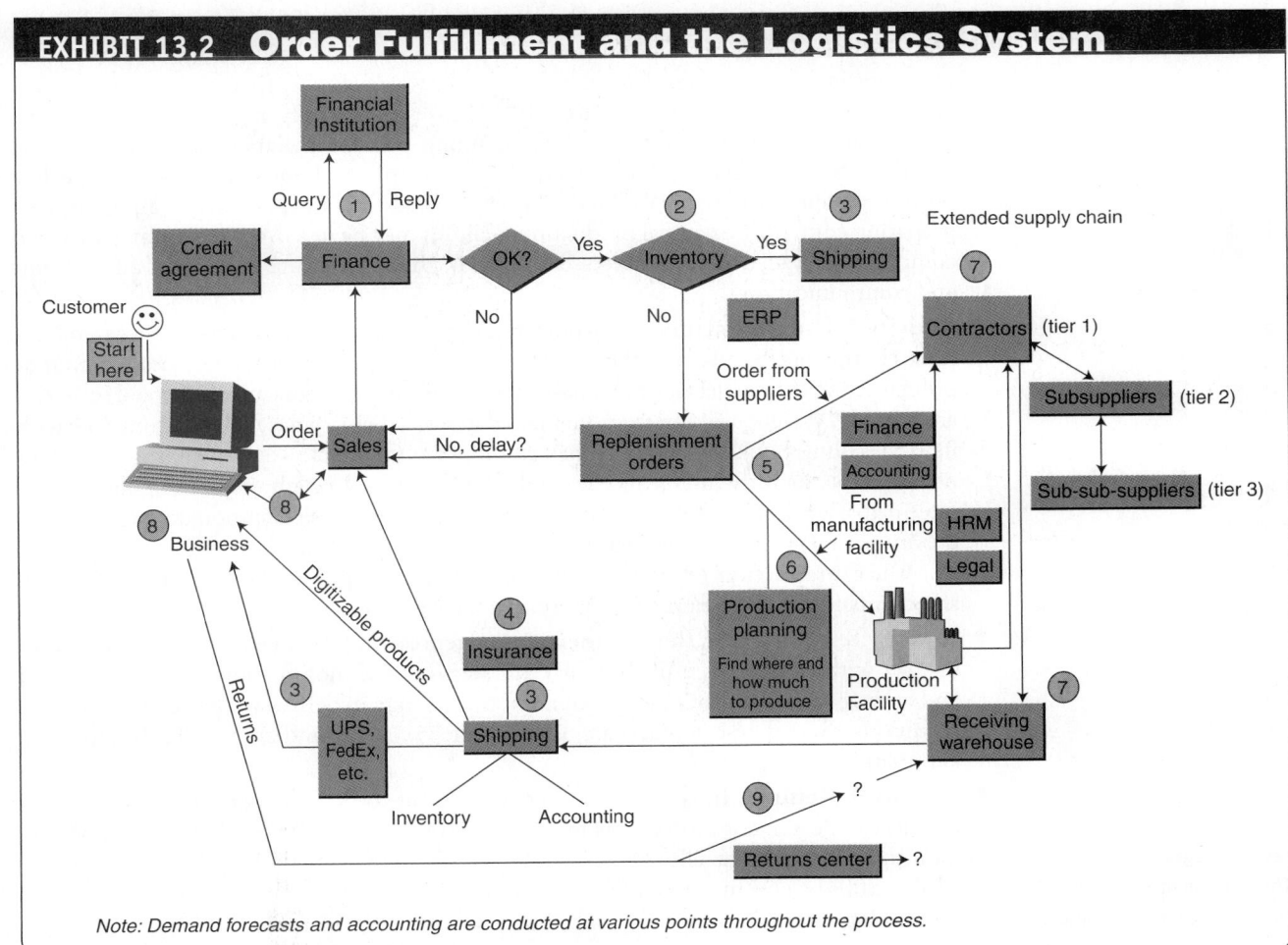

EXHIBIT 13.2   Order Fulfillment and the Logistics System

Note: Demand forecasts and accounting are conducted at various points throughout the process.

company's finance department or financial institution (i.e., a bank or a credit card issuer, such as Visa) may do this. Any holdup may cause a shipment to be delayed, resulting in a loss of goodwill or a customer. In B2C, the customers usually prepay, frequently by credit card.

▶ **Activity 2: Checking for in-stock availability.** Regardless of whether the seller is a manufacturer or a retailer, as soon as an order is received, an inquiry needs to be made regarding stock availability. Several scenarios are possible here that may involve the material management and production departments, as well as outside suppliers and warehouse facilities. In this step, the order information needs to be connected to the information about in-stock inventory availability.

▶ **Activity 3: Arranging shipments.** If the product is available, it can be shipped to the customer right away (otherwise, go to step 5). Products can be digital or physical. If the item is physical and it is readily available, packaging and shipment arrangements need to be made. It may involve both the packaging or shipping department and internal shippers or outside transporters. Digital items are usually available because their "inventory" is not depleted. However, a digital product, such as software, may be under revision, and unavailable for delivery at certain times. In either case, information needs to flow among several partners.

▶ **Activity 4: Insurance.** Sometimes the contents of a shipment need to be insured. This could involve both the finance department and an insurance company, and again, information needs to flow, not only inside the company, but also to and from the customer and insurance agent.

▶ **Activity 5: Replenishment.** Customized orders will always trigger a need for some manufacturing or assembly operation. Similarly, if standard items are out of stock, they need to be produced or procured. Production can be done in-house or by contractors. The suppliers involved may have their own suppliers (subsuppliers or tier-2 suppliers).

▶ **Activity 6: In-house production.** In-house production needs to be planned. Production planning involves people, materials, components, machines, financial resources, and possibly suppliers and subcontractors. In the case of assembly, manufacturing, or both several, plant services may be needed, including possible collaboration with business partners. Services may include scheduling of people and equipment, shifting other products' plans, working with engineering on modifications, getting equipment, and preparing content. The actual production facilities may be in a different country than the company's headquarters or retailers. This may further complicate the flow of information and communication.

▶ **Activity 7: Use contractors.** A manufacturer may opt to buy products or subassemblies from contractors. Similarly, if the seller is a retailer, such as in the case of amazon.com or walmart.com, the retailer must purchase products from its manufacturers. Several scenarios are possible. Warehouses can stock purchased items, which is what Amazon.com does with its best-selling books, toys, and other commodity items. However, Amazon.com does not stock books for which it receives only a few orders. In such cases, the publishers or intermediaries must make the special deliveries. In either case, appropriate receiving and quality assurance of incoming materials and products must take place.

Once production (step 6) or purchasing from suppliers (step 7) is completed, shipments to the customers (step 3) are arranged.

▶ **Activity 8: Contacts with customers.** Sales representatives need to keep in constant contact with customers, especially in B2B, starting with notification of orders received and ending with notification of a shipment or a change in delivery date (see Insights and Additions 13.1). These contacts are usually done via e-mail and are frequently generated automatically.

▶ **Activity 9: Returns.** In some cases, customers want to exchange or return items. Such returns can be a major problem, as more than $100 billion in North American goods are returned each year (Kuzeljevich 2004). Returns cost UK retailers EU$720 million a year (Boles 2004). The movement of returns from customers back to vendors is called **reverse logistics**.

reverse logistics
The movement of returns from customers to vendors.

Insights and Additions 13.1 What Services Do Customers Need?

Bayles (2001) and Kelsall (2006) provide the following insights on online customer services, which are based on Forrester Research studies (1999–2001):

▶ **Customer preferences.** Customers tend not to do much self-service in terms of getting information from companies (e.g., only 19 percent use FAQs), so they require attention. As more companies offer online self-service, though, this situation is changing. When contacting companies for information, customers use e-mail more than the telephone (71 percent versus 51 percent).

▶ **Types of service.** Four types of service exist, based on where the customer is in the purchase experience: *during shopping* (search products, compare, find product attributes); *during buying* (questions on warranties, billing, receipt, payment); *after placing the order* (checking status in processing and in shipment); and *after receiving the item* (checking return procedures, how to use the item).

▶ **Problem resolution.** Customers expect quick resolutions to problems, and to their satisfaction. Easy returns and order tracking are desirable.

▶ **Shipping options.** Several shipping options are needed.

▶ **Fraud protection.** Customers need to make sure that sellers or others are not going to cheat them.

▶ **Order status and updates.** Customers want to have some way to check on the status of their order, either by phone or online. These services are highly desired, including order notification and a clear return policy.

▶ **Developing customer relationships.** This includes building trust, providing security, and ensuring privacy protection (see Chapters 4, 11, and 17).

▶ **Agent profiling.** The process of matching customer service agents directly with the needs and personalities of customers is a win-win situation for businesses, customers, and employees.

Order fulfillment processes may vary, depending on the product and the vendor. The order fulfillment process also differs between B2B and B2C activities, between the delivery of goods and of services, and between small and large products. Furthermore, certain circumstances, such as in the case of perishable materials or foods, require additional steps.

Such a complex process may have problems (Section 13.2); automating the various steps can minimize or eliminate several of these problems.

The Administrative Activities of Order Taking and Fulfillment

The administrative activities of order taking and fulfillment involve (according to Wikipedia, 2006) the following:

▶ **Product Inquiry**—Initial inquiry about offerings, visit to the Web site, catalog request
▶ **Sales Quote**—Budgetary or availability quote
▶ **Order Configuration**—Where ordered items need a selection of options or order lines need to be compatible with each other
▶ **Order Booking**—The formal order placement or closing of the deal
▶ **Order Acknowledgment or Confirmation**—Confirmation that the order is booked or received
▶ **Order Sourcing or Planning**—Determining the source or location of item(s) to be shipped
▶ **Order Changes**—Changes to orders, if needed
▶ **Shipment Release**—Process step where the warehouse/inventory stocking point starts the shipping process. May be comprised of picking, packing, and staging for shipment
▶ **Shipment**—The shipment and transportation of the goods
▶ **Delivery**—The delivery of the goods to the consignee or customer
▶ **Invoicing and Billing**—The presentment of the commercial invoice or bill to the customer
▶ **Settlement**—The payment of the charges for goods, services, and delivery
▶ **Returns**—In case the goods are unacceptable or not required

EXHIBIT 13.3 How E-Logistics Differs from Traditional Logistics

Characteristic	Traditional Logistics	EC Logistics
Type, quantity	Bulk, large volume	Small, parcels
Destinations	Few	Large number, highly dispersed
Demand type	Push	Pull
Value of shipment	Very large, usually more than $1,000	Very small, frequently less than $50
Nature of demand	Stable, consistent	Seasonal (holiday season), fragmented
Customers	Business partners (in B2B), usually repeat customers (B2C), not many	Usually unknown in B2C, many
Inventory order flow	Usually unidirectional, from manufacturers	Usually bidirectional
Accountability	One link	Through the entire supply chain
Transporter	Frequently the company, sometimes outsourced	Usually outsourced, sometimes the company
Warehouse	Common	Only very large shippers (e.g., *amazon.com*) operate their own

Order Fulfillment and the Supply Chain

The nine-step order fulfillment process previously described, as well as order taking, are integral parts of the *supply chain*. The flows of orders, payments, information, materials, and parts need to be coordinated among all the company's internal participants, as well as with and among external partners (see Kelsall 2006). The principles of SCM (Online Tutorial T2) must be considered when planning and managing the order fulfillment process.

Traditional versus EC Logistics

e-logistics

The logistics of EC systems, typically involving small parcels sent to many customers' homes (in B2C).

EC logistics, or **e-logistics**, refers to the logistics of EC systems mainly in B2C. The major difference between e-logistics and traditional logistics is that the latter deals with the movement of large amounts of materials to a few destinations (e.g., to retail stores). E-logistics shipments typically are small parcels sent to many customers' homes. Other differences are shown in Exhibit 13.3.

Section 13.1 ▶ REVIEW QUESTIONS

1. Define *order fulfillment* and *logistics*.
2. List the nine steps of the order fulfillment process.
3. Compare logistics with reverse logistics.
4. Compare traditional logistics with e-logistics.

13.2 PROBLEMS IN ORDER FULFILLMENT

During the 1999 holiday season, logistics problems plagued the B2C e-tailers, especially those that sold toys. Price wars boosted demand, and neither the e-tailers nor the manufacturers were ready for it. As a result, supplies were late in coming from manufacturers. Toys "R" Us, for example, had to stop taking orders around December 14. The manufacturers, warehouses, and distribution channels were not in sync with the e-tailers. As a result, many customers did not get their holiday gifts on time. (For more on the order fulfillment troubles experienced by Toys "R" Us, see Online File W13.1 at the book's Web site.)

TYPICAL SUPPLY CHAIN PROBLEMS

The inability to deliver products on time is a typical problem in both off-line and online commerce. Several other problems have been observed along the supply chain: Some companies grapple with high inventory costs; quality problems exist due to misunderstandings; shipments of wrong products, materials, and parts occur frequently; and the cost to expedite operations or shipments is high. The chance that such problems will occur in EC is even higher due to the lack of appropriate infrastructure and e-tailing experience, as well as the special characteristics of EC. For example, most manufacturers' and distributors' warehouses are designed to ship large quantities to several stores; they cannot optimally pack and ship many small packages to many customers' doors. Improper inventory levels are typical in EC, as are poor delivery scheduling and mixed-up shipments.

Another major activity related to the supply chain problem is the difficulties in *demand forecasting*. In the case of standard or commodity items, such as toys, a demand forecast must be done in order to determine appropriate inventories of finished goods at various points in the supply chain. Such a forecast is difficult in the fast-growing field of ordering online. In the case of customized products, it is necessary to forecast the demand for the components and materials required for fulfilling customized orders. Demand forecasting must be done with business partners along the supply chain, as described in Chapter 7. Supply chain problems jeopardize order fulfillment.

WHY SUPPLY CHAIN PROBLEMS EXIST

Many problems along the EC supply chain stem from *uncertainties* and from the need to *coordinate* several activities, internal units, and business partners.

A major source of the uncertainties in EC, as noted earlier, is the demand forecast. Factors such as consumer behavior, economic conditions, competition, prices, weather conditions, technological developments, and consumer taste and confidence influence demand. Any one of these factors may change quickly. The demand forecast should be conducted frequently, in conjunction with collaborating business partners along the supply chain in order to correctly gauge demand and make plans to meet it. As shown in Chapter 7, companies attempt to achieve accurate demand forecasts by methods such as information sharing in collaborative commerce.

Other uncertainties that lead to supply chain and order fulfillment problems are variable delivery times, which depend on many factors ranging from machine failures to road conditions, and quality problems of materials and parts, which may create production time delays. RFID can improve this area. RFID helps locate shipments in real time to minimize delays and enhance customer service.

Pure EC companies are likely to have more problems because they do not have a logistics infrastructure already in place and are forced to use external logistics services rather than in-house departments for these functions. These external logistics services often are called **third-party logistics suppliers (3PL)**, or *logistics service providers*. Outsourcing such services can be expensive, and it requires more coordination and dependence on outsiders who may not be reliable. For this reason, large virtual retailers such as Amazon.com have or are developing their own physical warehouses and logistics systems. Other virtual retailers are creating strategic alliances with logistics companies or with experienced mail-order companies that have their own logistics systems.

third-party logistics suppliers (3PL)
External, rather than in-house, providers of logistics services.

In addition to uncertainties, lack of coordination and an inability or refusal to share information among business partners also create EC supply chain fulfillment problems. One of the most persistent order fulfillment problems is the bullwhip effect (see Chapter 7 and Online Tutorial T2).

EC (and IT) can provide solutions to these order fulfillment problems, as the next section will show.

Section 13.2 ▶ REVIEW QUESTIONS

1. List some problems along the EC supply chain.
2. Explain how uncertainties create order fulfillment problems. List some of these problems.
3. Describe the role of 3PLs.

13.3 SOLUTIONS TO ORDER FULFILLMENT PROBLEMS

Many EC logistics problems are generic; they can be found in the non-Internet world as well. Therefore, many of the solutions that have been developed for these problems in brick-and-mortar companies also work for e-tailers. IT and by EC technologies, as shown in Chapter 7, facilitate most of these solutions. In this section, we will discuss some of the specific solutions to the EC order fulfillment problems (Hett and Davis, 2006).

IMPROVEMENTS IN THE ORDER-TAKING PROCESS

One way to improve order fulfillment is to improve the order-taking process and its links to fulfillment and logistics. Order taking can be done via EDI, EDI/Internet, the Internet, or an extranet, and it may be fully automated. For example, in B2B, orders can be generated and transmitted automatically to suppliers when inventory levels fall below a certain threshold. The result is a fast, inexpensive, and more accurate (no need to rekey data) order-taking process. In B2C, Web-based ordering using electronic forms expedites the process, makes the process more accurate (e.g., intelligent agents can check the input data and provide instant feedback), and reduces processing costs for sellers. When EC order taking can interface or integrate with a company's back-office system, it shortens cycle times and eliminates errors.

Order-taking improvements also can take place *within* an organization, for example, when a manufacturer orders parts from its own warehouse. Whenever delivery of such parts runs smoothly, it minimizes disruptions to the manufacturing process, reducing losses from downtime. For example, as detailed in the Online File W13.2, Dell has improved the flow of parts in its PC repair operations, resulting in greater efficiency and cost savings.

Implementing linkages between order-taking and payment systems also can be helpful in improving order fulfillment. Electronic payments can expedite both the order fulfillment cycle and the payment delivery period. With such systems, payment processing can be significantly less expensive, and fraud can be better controlled.

WAREHOUSING AND INVENTORY MANAGEMENT IMPROVEMENTS

warehouse management system (WMS)
A software system that helps in managing warehouses.

A popular EC inventory management solution is a **warehouse management system (WMS)**. WMS refers to a software system that helps in managing warehouses. It has several components. For example, in the case of Amazon.com, the system supports item pickers as well as packaging. Amazon.com's B2C WMS can handle hundreds of millions of packages. In Case 13.1, we describe a B2B WMS at Schurman Inc., which demonstrates several applications.

Other Inventory Management Improvements

WMS is useful in reducing inventory and decreasing the incidence of out-of-stocks. Such systems also are useful in maintaining an inventory of repair items so repairs can be expedited (e.g., Dell, see Online File W13.2); picking items out of inventory in the warehouse (e.g., Amazon.com and Schurman); communicating (e.g., Schurman); managing product inventory (e.g., Schurman); receiving items at the warehouse (e.g., Schurman); and automating the warehouse (e.g., Amazon.com). For example, introducing a make-to-order (pull) production process and providing fast and accurate demand information to suppliers can minimize inventories. Allowing business partners to electronically track and monitor inventory levels and production activities can improve inventory management and inventory levels, as well as minimize the administrative expenses of inventory management. In some instances, the ultimate inventory improvement is to have no inventory at all; for products that can be digitized (e.g., software), order fulfillment can be instantaneous and can eliminate the need for inventory. Two methods of inventory improvements are VMI and the use of RFID (Chapter 7). Next are some other methods.

Automated Warehouses

Large-volume EC fulfillment requires automated warehouses. Regular warehouses are built to deliver large quantities to a small number of stores and plants. In B2C, however, businesses need to send small quantities to a very large number of individuals. Automated warehouses can minimize the order fulfillment problems that arise from this need.

CASE 13.1
EC Application

HOW WMS HELPS SCHURMAN IMPROVE ITS INTERNAL AND EXTERNAL ORDER FULFILLMENT SYSTEM

Schurman Fine Paper (*schurman.com*) is a manufacturer and retailer of greeting cards and related products. It sells through its own 170 specialty stores (Papyrus), as well as through 30,000 independent retail outlets.

Using RedPrairie (*redprairie.com*) integrated logistics software solutions, Schurman improved its demand forecast and minimized both out-of-stocks and overstocking. The system also allows physical inventory counts to be conducted without the need to shut down the two central warehouses for a week three times a year.

The central warehouses receive shipments from about 200 suppliers worldwide (500 to 1,000 orders per day). Until 2003, all inventory and logistics management was done manually. One problem solved by the software is picking products from multiple stock-keeping unit (SKU) locations. Picking is faster now, with a minimum of errors.

Customers' orders go directly from the EDI to shipping, which ignites the fulfillment and shipment process. This system automatically generates an advanced shipping notice (replacing the lengthy process of manual scanning). The new system also automates the task of assessing the length, width, height, and weight of each item before it goes into a box (to determine which item goes into what box). The system also improved inventory replenishment allocations. In the past, the list of items to be picked up included items not available in the primary location. Pickers wasted time looking for these items, and unfound items had to be picked up later from the reserve storage center,

resulting in delays. The WMS simultaneously created two lists, expediting fulfillment. This tripled the number of orders fulfilled per picker per day. The system also generates automatic replenishment orders for items falling below a minimum level at any storage location.

In addition, special software provides Schurman's customer service department with *real-time* access to inventory and distribution processes, allowing the department to track the status of all orders. The WMS also tracks the status of all orders and sends alerts when an order problem occurs (e.g., delay in downloading). An e-mail goes to all necessary parties in the company so they can fix the problem. Finally, information collected about problems can be analyzed so remedies can be made quickly. All this helps to reduce both overstocks and out-of-stocks.

Sources: Compiled from Parks (2004), *schurman.com* (accessed January 2007), Maloney (2006), and *redprairie.com* (accessed January 2007).

Questions

1. Identify what the WMS automates, both in receiving and shipping.

2. In the future, RFID tags could replace the bar codes that are currently used. What would be the advantages of using RFID? Where can it be used?

3. How has inventory management been improved?

Automated warehouses may include robots and other devices that expedite the pick-up of products. An example of a company that uses such warehouses is Amazon.com (see the opening case).

The largest EC/mail-order warehouse in the United States was operated by a mail-order company, Fingerhut. This company handled its own order fulfillment process for mail orders and online orders, as well as orders for Wal-Mart, Macy's, KbKids, and many others. Other companies (e.g., fosdickfulfillment.com and efulfillmentservices.com) provide similar order fulfillment services. The keys to successful inventory management, in terms of order fulfillment, are efficiency and speed, which wireless devices can facilitate.

Using Wireless Technologies

Wireless technologies have been used in warehouses for over a decade (see Chapter 9). Case 13.2 provides an example of how wireless supports WMS.

Using RFID to Improve WMS. In Chapter 7, we introduced the potential uses of RFID in the supply chain. We provided an example of how RFID can track items as they move from the manufacturer's to the customer's warehouses. Once inside the customer's warehouse, RFID can track the whereabouts of the items (see Case 13.1, question 2). This can facilitate inventory counts as well as save pickers' trips.

CASE 13.2
EC Application

PEACOCKS USES WIRELESS WMS TO SMOOTH ITS SUPPLY CHAIN

Peacocks of Wales (*peacocks.co.uk*) operates approximately 250 retail stores, selling clothes and home furniture in Wales and southern England. The company had a problem with its internal supply chain: Its paper-based system of managing product distribution was prone to problems, such as incorrectly completed pick-lists, wrongly picked items, transcription errors, delays in generating and receiving data, and much more. These interfered with the company's growth strategy and reduced its profit.

In 1997, Peacocks consolidated its six warehouses into a single distribution center (100,000 square feet, three stories). Stores were ordering more than 4,000 SKUs each day. These needed to be picked and shipped to stores effectively and efficiently. Using one place instead of six solved some of Peacocks' problems; however, the paper-based communication system was still ineffective. With the paper-based pick system, it was easy to run out of products at a specific location. When this occurred, the picker had to either wait for more products to arrive or return to his or her original location. The paper-based pick system had delays built into it, and stock problems were difficult to predict.

In 1998, the company began to replace its paper-based system with a wireless system (from Symbol Technologies, a division of Motorola). The fully automated distribution center now is equipped with a hands-free, real-time put-away and picking system. It is based on a combination of 28 wearable computers and 6 truck-mounted terminals supported by a wireless LAN. The system provides real-time control. Whether an item moves by hand or by truck, Peacocks knows precisely where it is. If at any point in the process someone is at the wrong location, handling the wrong product, or trying to send it to the wrong place, the system simply sends out an alert and prevents the action. When Peacocks receives a delivery from a manufacturer, the consignment is checked and the individual cartons from each delivery are given an identifying bar code label and scanned to report receipt. In this way, every item can be tracked through the distribution center from the minute it arrives. The system immediately knows if there is a requirement at a pick location.

Once individual cartons are labeled, Peacock uses an automated conveyor system to send cartons to either the pick face or to the pallet store, as directed by the wireless WMS.

Each member of the picking team wears a wrist-mounted terminal that receives picking instructions from Peacocks' host system via the wireless LAN. As empty trolleys arrive in the pick area, the picker scans a bar code on the empty trolley, and the terminal's LCD screen tells the picker which aisle to go to, which location to pick from, and which items to pick. When a picker arrives at the pick face, the picker scans the bar code mounted at the end of the aisle. This verifies that the picker is in the correct aisle (see the photo) The picker then scans another bar code at

Source: Symbol Technologies, "Peacocks Case Study." *symbol.com/category.php?filename=cs-27_peacocks.xml* (accessed February 2007).

the product location to verify that the location is correct. Finally, the picker scans each item as it is placed into the trolley.

Once each pick is complete, the conveyor system takes each trolley to the dispatch area to be loaded into crates for delivery to a Peacocks store.

Because the data are sent to the host in real time as the picking operation proceeds, the system knows when pick-face stocks are approaching the replenishment level set by Peacocks. When an item needs to be replenished, the system sends an alert to a truck-mounted terminal in the pallet store. As with the wrist-mounted terminals, an LCD screen on the truck terminal directs the driver to a precise location in the pallet racking. On arrival at the location, the driver uses a handheld scanner to scan the location bar code. This confirms that the truck driver is at the right location and selecting the right product.

The hands-free arrangement saves time and minimizes damage to the devices. The system also is user-friendly, so training is minimal.

Sources: Compiled from Symbol Technologies (2005), *symbol.com* (2006), and Peacocks Case Study (2007).

Questions

1. Describe Peacocks' internal order fulfillment process.
2. Identify all segments of Peacocks' supply chain that are improved by the system and describe the improvements.
3. How has the new system corrected the previous problems?
4. What are the advantages of wireless tools?
5. Investigate how RFID may improve this system in the future.

SPEEDING DELIVERIES

In 1973, an innovative, then tiny company initiated the concept of "next-day delivery." It was a revolution in door-to-door logistics. A few years later, that company, FedEx, introduced its "next-morning delivery" service. Today, FedEx moves over 6 million packages a day, all over the globe, using several hundred airplanes and several thousand vans. Incidentally, by one report (Pickering 2000), 70 percent of these packages are the result of EC.

Same Day, Even Same Hour, Delivery

In the digital age, however, even the next morning may not be fast enough. Today, we talk about *same-day delivery*, and even delivery within an hour. Deliveries of urgent materials to and from hospitals are an example of such a service. Two of the newcomers to this area are eFullfillment Service (efulfillmentservice.com) and One World (owd.com). These companies have created networks for the rapid distribution of products, mostly EC-related ones. They offer national distribution systems across the United States in collaboration with shipping companies, such as FedEx and UPS.

Delivering groceries is another area where speed is important, as discussed in Chapter 3. Quick pizza deliveries have been available for a long time (e.g., Domino's Pizza). Today, many pizza orders can be placed online. Also, many restaurants deliver food to customers who order online, a service called "dine online." Examples of this service can be found at dineonline.com, gourmetdinnerservice.com.au, and letsdineonline.com. Some companies even offer aggregating supply services, processing orders from several restaurants and then making deliveries (e.g., dialadinner.com.hk in Hong Kong).

Supermarket Deliveries

Supermarket deliveries are done same day or next day. Arranging and making such deliveries may be difficult, especially when fresh food is to be transported, as discussed in Chapter 3. Buyers may need to be home at certain times to accept the deliveries. Therefore, the distribution systems for such enterprises are critical. For an example of an effective distribution system, see Online File W13.3 about Woolworths of Australia at the book's Web site.

One of the most comprehensive delivery systems is that of GroceryWorks (now a subsidiary of Safeway USA). Online File W13.4 illustrates this system. Note that the delivery trucks can pick up other items (such as rented videos and dry cleaning).

A Speedier Superstore Using a Drive-In Model

AutoCart (autocrat.biz) allows you to pick up orders of groceries, dry cleaning, prescription medicine, DVD rentals, and more without leaving your car. Here is how it works. Customers make their selection online, by phone, or on site using a touch screen Tablet PC. Each driver is assigned to a pick-up station. The orders show up on screen inside a 130,000 square foot specialized warehouse where a computer directs employees to products via headset. After items are picked, they are placed on a high-speed conveyor belt and travel to the consolidation zone where purchases are placed into bags. Shoppers waiting at the pick up station can watch TV while receiving the audio on their car radio. A shopping card icon at each parking station indicates the progress of the driver's order. Approximately 15 minutes after the order is placed (on average), it is ready for delivery via a conveyor belt to the customer. The customer pays with credit card, cash, or check and picks up the goods. There are other delivery models (see autocrat.biz).

Failed Delivery Companies

As described in Chapters 1 and 3, one of the most publicized dot-com failures was Webvan, an express-delivery company that lost $1.2 billion (the largest of any failed dot-com loss). Another well-publicized failure was that of Kozmo.com, described Case 13.3.

CASE 13.3
EC Application
THE RISE AND FALL OF KOZMO.COM

The idea sounded logical: Create an express delivery system for online orders and deliver within an hour. The idea is not new. Domino's Pizza built its fortune on this idea, and today many companies deliver pizzas, door-to-door, in less than an hour in thousands of cities worldwide.

Kozmo.com's business model was based on this idea. But instead of pizzas, Kozmo.com envisioned the delivery of food items, rented videos, electronic games, and convenience products. Also, the model targeted only large cities, especially New York and Boston, where people use public transportation that may not be in operation at certain times. Items were delivered by "Kozmonauts"—employees with vans, bikes, or scooters. Orders were placed on the Internet, but telephone and fax orders also were accepted. The products were delivered from Kozmo.com's distribution centers.

The first logistics problem faced by Kozmo.com was the *return* of the rented videos. It was uneconomical to send the Kozmonauts to collect them. So Kozmo.com built drop boxes (like the FedEx boxes), initially in New York. Many of these boxes were vandalized. In an attempt to solve the problem, Kozmo.com partnered with Starbucks and moved the boxes to Starbucks cafés, some of which are open 24 hours a day. In exchange, Starbucks became an investor in Kozmo.com. Kozmo.com started to deliver coffee products to Starbucks' customers, and Starbucks printed Kozmo.com's logo on its coffee cups.

With a venture capital investment of over $250 million, the company expanded rapidly to 10 cities. During the initial period, delivery was free, and no minimum dollar amount of order was required. This strategy attracted many customers but resulted in heavy losses, especially on small-value items. The company's growth was rapid: By the end of 2000, it had 1,100 employees, and it launched an IPO.

Soon after, more problems started to surface. As with other B2C dot-coms, the more Kozmo.com sold, the larger the losses grew. In response, Kozmo.com closed operations in San Diego and Houston, imposed minimum charges, and added more expensive items (such as rented DVD players) to its offerings. This helped to generate profits in New York and San Francisco. However, with hundreds of dot-coms going out of business in late 2000 and early 2001, a major financial backer withdrew its support. Kozmo.com eventually ran out of cash and as a result had to close its doors on April 11, 2001.

Sources: Compiled from *kozmo.com* (2002) (note: site no longer available) and Blair (2000, 2001).

Questions

1. Draw the supply chains for food and rented items at Kozmo.com. What logistics problems did these supply chains present?

2. Compare Kozmo.com with Domino's Pizza. Why did Domino's do so well while Kozmo.com failed? Analyze the situation from an order fulfillment point of view.

3. The partnership with Starbucks was said to be extremely innovative, but Kozmo.com cancelled it when its financial problems began. (Kozmo.com had paid money to Starbucks for the permission to place the drop boxes.) Analyze this partnership.

4. Later in this chapter, you will learn about returns. After you have read that discussion, come back to this case and answer the following question: What advice could you have given Kozmo.com regarding the return of rented items? Also, recall the Netflix model in Chapter 4.

PARTNERING EFFORTS AND OUTSOURCING LOGISTICS

An effective way to solve order fulfillment problems is for an organization to partner with other companies. For example, several EC companies partner with UPS or FedEx, which may own part of the EC company.

Logistics-related partnerships can take many forms. For example, another partnering example is marketplaces managed by forwarders.com and aacb.com that help companies with goods find "forwarders"—the intermediaries that prepare goods for shipping. The company also helps forwarders find the best prices on air carriers, and the carriers bid to fill the space with forwarders' goods that need to be shipped.

SkyMall (skymall.com), now a subsidiary of Gem-Star TV Guide International, is a retailer that sells from catalogs on airplanes, over the Internet, and by mail order. It relies on its catalog partners to fill the orders. For small vendors that do not handle their own shipments and for international shipments, SkyMall contracts distribution centers owned by fulfillment outsourcer Sykes Enterprise. As orders come in, SkyMall conveys the data to the appropriate vendor or to a Sykes distribution center. A report is then sent to SkyMall.

Comprehensive Logistics Services

Major shippers, notably UPS and FedEx, offer comprehensive logistic services. These services are for B2C, B2B, G2B, and other types of EC. See Insights and Additions 13.2 for a description of the broad EC services UPS offers.

Insights and Additions 13.2 UPS Provides Broad EC Services

UPS is not only a leading transporter of goods sold on the Internet, but it also is a provider of expertise, infrastructure, and technology for managing global commerce—synchronizing the flow of goods, information, and funds for its customers.

UPS has a massive infrastructure to support these efforts. For example, it has an over 120-terabyte (10^{12}-byte) database (in 2003) that contains customer information and shipping records. More than 100,000 UPS customers have incorporated UPS Online Tools into their own Web sites to strengthen their customer services. In addition, UPS offers the following EC applications:

▶ Electronic supply chain services for corporate customers, by industry. This includes a portal page with industry-related information and statistics.

▶ Calculators for computing shipping fees.

▶ Helping customers manage their electronic supply chains (e.g., expediting billing and speeding up accounts receivable).

▶ Improved inventory management, warehousing, and delivery.

▶ A shipping management system that integrates tracking systems, address validation, service selection, and time-in-transit tools with Oracle's ERP application suite (similar integration with SAP exists).

▶ Notification of customers by e-mail about the status and expected arrival time of incoming packages.

Representative Tools

UPS's online tools—a set of seven transportation and logistics applications—lets customers do everything from tracking packages to analyzing their shipping history using customized criteria to calculating exact time-in-transit for shipments between any two postal codes in the continental United States.

The tools, which customers can download to their Web sites, let customers query UPS's system to get proof that specific packages were delivered on schedule. For example, if a company is buying supplies online and wants them delivered on a certain day, a UPS customer can use an optimal-routing feature to ensure delivery on that day, as well as to automatically record proof of the delivery in its accounting system.

UPS offers logistics services tailored for certain industries. For example, UPS Logistics Group provides supply chain reengineering, transportation network management, and service parts logistics to vehicle manufacturers, suppliers, and parts distributors in the auto industry worldwide. UPS Autogistics improves automakers' vehicle delivery networks. For example, Ford reduced the time to deliver vehicles from plants to dealers in North America from an average of 14 days to about 6. UPS Logistics Group offers similar supply chain and delivery tracking services to other kinds of manufacturers.

UPS also is expanding into another area important to e-business—delivery of digital documents. The company was the first conventional package shipper to enter this market in 1998 when it launched UPS Document Exchange. This service monitors delivery of digitally delivered documents and provides instant receipt notification, encryption, and password-only access.

UPS offers many other EC-related services. These include the ability to enter the UPS system from wireless devices; helping customers configure and customize services; and providing for electronic bill presentation and payment (for B2B), EFT, and processing of COD payments.

Sources: Compiled from Violino (2000), Farber (2003), and UPS (2007).

Questions

1. Why would a shipper, such as UPS, expand to other logistic services?

2. Why would shippers want to handle payments?

3. Why does UPS provide software tools to customers?

4. What B2B services does UPS provide? (*Note:* Check *ups.com* to make sure that your answers are up-to-date.)

Outsourcing Logistics

Instead of a joint venture or equity ownership with partners, most companies simply outsource logistics (see Bayles 2001). One advantage of this is that it is easy to change the logistics provider, as can be seen in the case of National Semiconductor Corporation described in Online File W13.5. Outsourcing is especially appealing to a small company such as BikeWorld, as illustrated in Online File W13.6.

INTEGRATED GLOBAL LOGISTICS SYSTEMS

An increase in global trading created a need for an effective global logistic system. Order fulfillment problems described earlier tend to be even larger in longer supply chains that cross country borders. The number of partners in such situations is larger (e.g., custom brokers, global carriers), and so is the need for coordination, communication, and collaboration. Furthermore, such systems require a high level of security, especially when the Internet is the centric technology platform.

HANDLING RETURNS (REVERSE LOGISTICS)

Allowing for the return of unwanted merchandise and providing for product exchanges are necessary to maintain customers' trust and loyalty. The Boston Consulting Group (2001) found that the "absence of a good return mechanism" was the number two reason shoppers cited for refusing to buy on the Web frequently. According to Ellis (2006), a good return policy is a must in EC.

Dealing with returns is a major logistics problem for EC merchants. Several options for handling returns exist:

▶ **Return the item to the place of purchase.** This is easy to do with a purchase from a brick-and-mortar store but not a virtual one. To return a product to a virtual store, a customer needs to get authorization, pack everything up, pay to ship it back, insure it, and wait up to two billing cycles for a credit to show up on his or her statement. The buyer is not happy and neither is the seller, who must unpack, check the paperwork, and resell the item, usually at a loss. This solution is workable only if the number of returns is small or the merchandise is expensive (e.g., at Blue Nile, Chapter 2).

▶ **Separate the logistics of returns from the logistics of delivery.** With this option, returns are shipped to an independent returns unit and are handled separately. This solution may be more efficient from the seller's point of view, but it does not ease the returns process for the buyer.

▶ **Completely outsource returns.** Several outsourcers, including UPS and FedEx, provide logistics services for returns (as described in Bayles 2001). The services deal not only with delivery and returns but also with the entire logistics process. FedEx, for example, offers several options for returning goods (see fedex.com).

▶ **Allow the customer to physically drop the returned item at a collection station.** Offer customers locations (such as a convenience store or the UPS Store) where they can drop off returns. In Asia and Australia, returns are accepted in convenience stores and at gas stations. For example, BP Australia Ltd. (gasoline service stations) teamed up with wishlist.com.au, and Caltex Australia is accepting returns at the convenience stores connected to its gasoline stations. The accepting stores may offer in-store computers for ordering and may also offer payment options, as at Japanese 7-Eleven's (7dream.com). And in Taiwan, you can pay, pick up books and other item orders, and return unwanted items at a 7-Eleven store. Click-and-mortar stores usually allow customers to return merchandise that was ordered from the online outlet to their physical stores (e.g., amazon.com, walmart.com, and eddiebauer.com).

▶ **Auction the returned items.** This option can go hand-in-hand with any of the previous solutions.

For strategy and guidelines on returns, see Parry (2006), and Ellis (2006). Reverse Logistics Executive Council (rlec.org) is a major portal on reverse logistics.

ORDER FULFILLMENT IN B2B

Most of the discussion in this section has centered on B2C order fulfillment. Some of the discussion pertains to B2B fulfillment as well. Exhibit 13.4 shows the B2B fulfillment options. The exhibit shows how the buy options (brown lines) relate to the shipping options (blue lines). For another overview of B2B fulfillment, see Supplychainer.com (2006).

B2B fulfillment may be more complex than that of B2C because it has at least six dimensions of complexity (versus two in B2C): shipment size, multiple distribution channels, more variety of shipment frequency, uneven breadth of carrier services, fewer carrier EC offerings, and complex EC transaction paths.

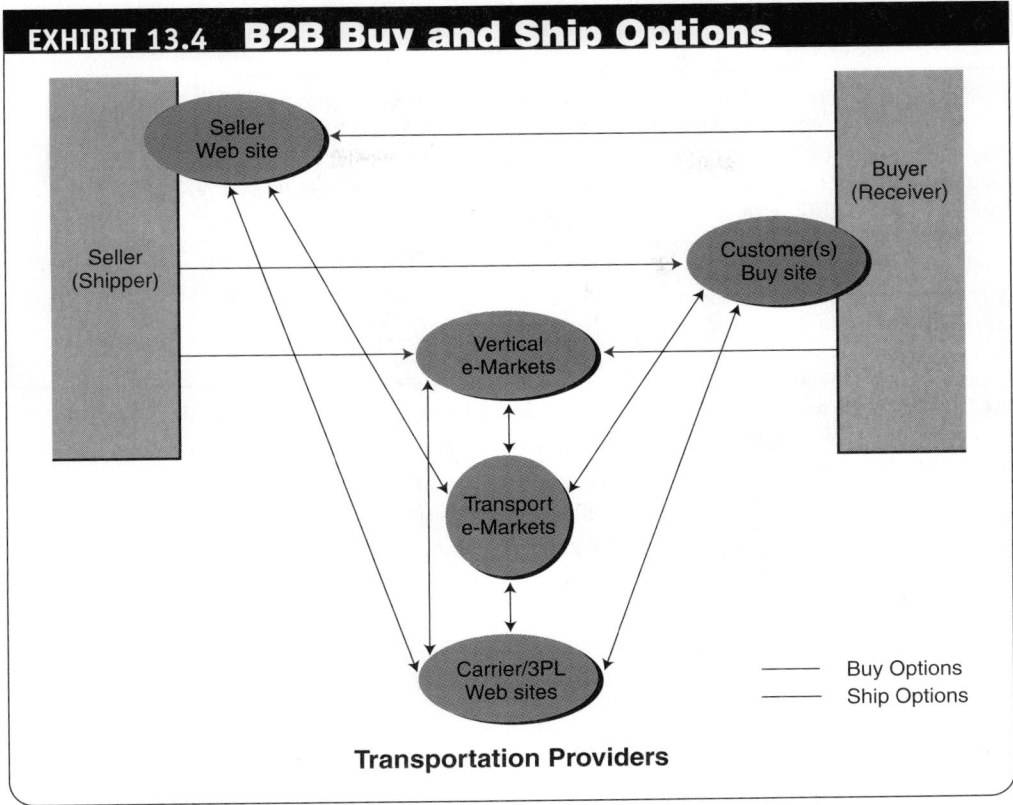

EXHIBIT 13.4 B2B Buy and Ship Options

Transportation Providers

— Buy Options
— Ship Options

Source: Courtesy of Norbridge Inc., © 2003.

Using BPM to Improve Order Fulfillment

B2B order fulfillment commonly uses business processes management (BPM) software to automate various steps in the process as done by Daisy Brand (Case 13.4). The case also demonstrates how customers pressure suppliers, such as Daisy Brand, to improve the order fulfillment process.

CASE 13.4
EC Application
HOW DAISY BRAND FULFILLS B2B ORDERS

Daisy Brand is a large U.S. producer of sour cream products known for its quality products. Its major customers are supermarkets that operate in a very competitive environment. Many customers require that suppliers provide certain services that will improve the efficiency of their operations—for example, vendor-managed inventory (VMI in Chapter 7), collaborative planning, and forecasting (Chapter 7). Most large Daisy Brand's customers did the same. The customers pressured Daisy Brand to improve its services along the supply chain; the order processing became a prime target for improvement.

The Daisy Brand IS team sought technology that would improve the efficiency of its existing order fulfillment process. Customers submit orders electronically. Every order that Daisy Brand handles travels through three applications:

Customers submit orders through an electronic data interchange (EDI) transaction. From there, orders flow to an Invensys Protean enterprise resource planning (ERP) system and various other systems for fulfillment and ultimately to shipping. The company sought to implement a workflow solution that could integrate and automate this order-to-delivery process.

Using TIBCO's business integration and business process management solution (see *tibco.com*), the IS team designed, developed, tested, and deployed a workflow in only three weeks. The workflow manages the order process from inception all the way to the point of delivery to ensure that orders move forward within the set timeframe. The company can also send notifications about shipping activity back to the customer.

(continued)

CASE 13.4   (continued)

If an order is to ship out within a certain number of hours and hasn't shipped, TIBCO's solution can trace that order that does not meet this criterion and get it moving faster. TIBCO's solution also helps stop problems before they start by auditing customer order information before it enters the ERP system.

In addition to improving the efficiency of order processing at Daisy Brand, TIBCO's solution also enables the company to more flexibly accommodate customer needs. For example, a retail customer might change an order after the order is sent to the warehouse—perhaps to request that the order ship on a different day or with a different amount. In these cases, the TIBCO-based system sends an alert to the logistics management workbench to immediately notify the warehouse that the order has been modified. Thus, the logistics team can quickly implement the change, ensuring minimum impact on the order cycle time.

The workflow software is part of TIBCO's BPM software suite, which includes other applications for control of business processes and to improve agility. Future projects

include automation of new customer entry; integration of plant control systems; support for collaborative planning, forecasting, and replenishment (CPFR) and vendor-managed inventory (VMI); and implementation of a real-time order-arrival board.

Sources: Compiled from Tibco.com (2006) and Staffware.com (2006). **Note:** A video supporting this case is available at *tibco.com*.

Questions

1. Describe the steps in order fulfillment at Daisy Brand.
2. How is the automation of order fulfillment done?
3. How can supermarkets benefit from introducing electronic processing by Daisy Brand?
4. Enter *tibco.com* and find information about their BPM and workflow products. How can they support order fulfillment?
5. How can Daisy Brand improve its agility?

 Online File W13.7 lists some representative B2B fulfillment players and challenges.

Using E-Marketplaces and Exchanges to Ease Order Fulfillment Problems in B2B

In Chapters 5 and 6, we introduced a variety of e-marketplaces and exchanges. One of the major objectives of these entities is to improve the operation of the B2B supply chain. Let's see how this works with different business models.

▶ A company-centric marketplace can solve several supply chain problems. For example, CSX Technology developed an extranet-based EC system for tracking cross-country train shipments as part of its supply chain initiative and was able to effectively identify bottlenecks and more accurately forecast demand.

▶ Using an extranet, Toshiba America provides an ordering system for its dealers to buy replacement parts for Toshiba's products. The system smoothes the supply chain and delivers better customer service.

▶ A vertical exchange connects many suppliers with buyers. Many of them deal with both buying and selling. The direct contact between buyers and sellers in such exchanges reduces communication and search problems in the supply chain and helps with order fulfillment.

▶ Supplychainer.com (2006) suggested taking into consideration the following seven elements (per High Jump Software) for optimal order fulfillment:

1. Integrate your systems.
2. Automate your pickings.
3. Incorporate automated shipment planning (ASP).
4. Automate shipment verification.
5. Reduce or eliminate paper work.
6. Source orders based on facility workloads.
7. Incorporate sales and marketing into the process.

For additional discussion on how fulfillment is done in B2B, see fedex.com, ups.com, and supplychainer.com.

Order Fulfillment in Services

Thus far, we have concentrated on order fulfillment with physical products. Fulfilling service orders (e.g., buy or sell stocks, process insurance claims) may involve more information processing, which requires more sophisticated EC systems. The Real-World Case at the end of this chapter (CIGNA Corp.) describes one such system. Case 13.5 describes another system.

INNOVATIVE E-FULFILLMENT STRATEGIES

Bowman (2006) and Vitasek and Manrodt (2006) propose several innovative e-fulfillment strategies. They call one of these innovations *logistics postponement*. Supply chain partners can move information flows and hold off shipping actual physical goods until a point at which they can make more-direct shipments. Two examples of logistics postponement are (1) merge-in-transit and (2) rolling warehouses.

Merge-in-transit is a model in which components for a product may come from two different physical locations (Croxton et al. 2003). For example, in shipping a PC, the monitor may come from the East Coast of the United States and the CPU from the West Coast. Instead of shipping the components to a central location and then shipping both together to the customer, the components are shipped directly to the customer and merged into one shipment by the local deliverer (so the customer gets all the parts in one delivery), reducing unnecessary transportation.

With a **rolling warehouse**, products on the delivery truck are not preassigned to a destination, but the decision about the quantity to unload at each destination is made at the time of unloading (Knaack 2001). Thus, the latest order information can be taken into account, assisting in inventory control and lowering logistics costs (by avoiding repeat delivery trips). The rolling warehouse method also works in the ocean shipping industry, where it is called a *floating warehouse*.

merge-in-transit
Logistics model in which components for a product may come from two (or more) different physical locations and are shipped directly to the customer's location.

rolling warehouse
Logistics method in which products on the delivery truck are not preassigned to a destination, but the decision about the quantity to unload at each destination is made at the time of unloading.

CASE 13.5
EC Application
HOW SUNDOWNER MOTOR INNS FULFILLS ITS ONLINE RESERVATIONS

Based in Shepparton Victoria, Australia, Sundowner Motor Inns owns and franchises 24 large motels throughout rural Australia. In 2003, Sundowner Motor Inns initiated a *customer supply chain system* to automate the management of room inventory. Software was developed to enable two existing systems to "talk" to each other: (1) the online booking systems and (2) the offline property management system (PMS). The system has worked successfully since then and is continuously improved.

Here is how the system fulfills orders:

1. Customers make a reservation inquiry at the company's Web site (*sundownermotorinns.com.au*) or at online reservation portals (e.g., *wotif.com, expedia.com*).
2. Customers are connected automatically to a Web server, and the PMS provides graphic files, pricing, and room availability information.
3. In real time, the customer reviews room details.
4. The customer confirms the reservation by submitting their credit card details via the secure Web page.
5. Upon confirmation of the reservation, the PMS is updated automatically for availability.
6. The company sends an automatic e-mail confirmation to the customer.

A significant internal process change was the shifting of a large network of rural motel managers from manually interacting with customers over the Internet to allowing an automated system to do it for them. Sundowner Motor Inns plan to continually deliver more customer value using the Web site as a central transaction platform. "Packaged" online deals will be available, offering a whole range of customized offers.

Sources: Compiled from Multimedia Victoria (2004) and from *sundownermotorinns.com.au* (2007).

Questions

1. Once you automate the order fulfillment and your data are online, you can generate additional revenue. How?
2. What are the criteria for a good order fulfillment in online hotel reservations?
3. Why is it advantageous to integrate the front-end and back-end systems?

Another example of innovative e-fulfillment strategies proposed by Lee and Whang (2001) is *leveraged shipments*. By this, they mean planning shipments based on a combination of size (or value) of the order and the geographic location. The size of the orders shipped by most e-tailers is small. The cost of delivery is justified only if there is a high concentration of orders from customers located in close proximity or if the value of the order is large enough. *Delivery-value density* is a decision support tool that helps determine whether it is economical to deliver goods to a neighborhood area in one trip. (The density is computed by dividing average total dollar volume of the shipment per trip by the average travel distance per trip.) The larger the density value, the better. One example of leveraging shipments is to deliver to specific geographic areas on specific days of the week and to install delivery receptacles at the destination so drivers do not have to return to or wait at the site for a customer to arrive. A second example of leveraging shipments is when a 3PL hires "dealers" that are familiar with the physical region of the delivery. The 3PL provides the dealers with the products, and the dealers deliver to the final destination.

A World Class B2C and B2B System Works at Dell

One of the most sophisticated order fulfillment systems is at Dell Computer. On one hand, Dell needs to fulfill both orders from individual customers and from businesses. On the other hand, Dell's suppliers need to fulfill Dell's orders. Here is how it is done.

Dell has completely automated its ability to take thousands of orders, translate them into millions of component requirements, and work directly with its suppliers to build and deliver products to meet customer requirements. More than 90 percent of Dell's component purchases now are handled online: Suppliers use an Internet portal to view Dell's requirements and changes to forecasts based on marketable activity and to confirm their ability to meet Dell's delivery requirements. Then, as Dell factories receive orders and schedule assemblies, a "pull" signal to the supplier triggers the shipment of only the materials required to build current orders, and suppliers deliver the materials directly to the appropriate Dell assembly lines.

Using Web service, Dell now schedules every line in every factory around the world every two hours, and only brings two hours' worth of materials into the factory. This has decreased the cycle time at Dell's assembly factories and reduced warehouse space—space that has been replaced by more manufacturing lines.

The project has produced more than just enhanced supply chain efficiencies and accelerated, highly reliable order fulfillment. At any given time, there is less than four days of inventory in the entire Dell operation, whereas many competitors routinely carry 30 days or more. In addition, automation has helped Dell react more quickly to correct potentially out-of-balance situations, made it much easier to prevent components from becoming obsolete, and improved response times across the supply chain by providing a global view of supply and demand at any specific Dell location at any time.

For another example, see Online File W13.8 about Ingram Micro.

Section 13.3 ▶ REVIEW QUESTIONS

1. List the various order-taking solutions.
2. List solutions for improved delivery.
3. Describe same-day shipments.
4. Describe some innovative e-strategies for order fulfillment.
5. Describe how to effectively manage the return of items.
6. Describe issues in B2B fulfillment.

13.4 CRM AND ITS RELATIONSHIP WITH EC

Customer relationship management (CRM) recognizes that customers are the core of a business and that a company's success depends on effectively managing its relationships with them (see Seybold 2006, and Payne 2005). CRM focuses on building long-term and sustainable customer relationships that add value both for the customer and the selling company. (See also crm-forum.com and crmassist.com.)

Just like their off-line counterparts, online companies also must deliver *customer services*. Customer services are an integral part of CRM.

WHAT IS CRM: DEFINITIONS, TYPES, AND CLASSIFICATIONS

In Chapter 1, we provided some definitions of CRM. Greenberg (2004) provides more than 10 definitions, several made by CEOs of CRM providers or users. Scott and Lee (2005) and Payne (2005) provide several additional definitions. Why are there so many definitions? The reason is that CRM is relatively new and still evolving. Also, it is an interdisciplinary field so each discipline (e.g., marketing, MIS, management) defines CRM differently. We will repeat part of the definition from Chapter 1 here.

> **Customer relationship management (CRM)** *is a business strategy to select and manage customers to optimize long-term value. CRM requires a customer-centric business philosophy and culture to support effective marketing, sales, and service processes.* (CRMguru.com 2007)

customer relationship management (CRM)
A customer service approach that focuses on building long-term and sustainable customer relationships that add value both for the customer and the selling company.

Types and Classification of CRM

In Chapter 1, we distinguished three types of CRM activities: operational, analytical, and collaborative. Operational CRM related to typical business functions involving customer services, order management, invoice or billing, or sales and marketing automation and management. Analytical CRM involves activities that capture, store, extract, process, analyze, interpret, and report customer data to a user who then analyzes them as needed. Collaborative CRM deals with all the necessary communication, coordination, and collaboration between vendors and customers. For details see mariosalexandrou.com/definition/crm.asp.

Tan et al. (2002) and Payne (2005) distinguish the following classifications of CRM programs:

- **Loyalty programs.** These programs try to increase customer loyalty. An example is the frequent-flyer points given by airlines.
- **Prospecting.** These promotion programs try to win new, first-time customers (see Chapter 4).
- **Save or win back.** These are programs that try to convince customers not to leave or, if they have left, to rejoin. When one of the authors of this book left AOL, for example, the company's representative offered many incentives to return.
- **Cross-sell or up-sell.** By offering complementary products (cross-sell) or enhanced products (up-sell) that customers would like, companies make customers happy and increase their own revenue.

Another classification of CRM programs divides them by the service or product they offer (e.g., self-configuration, account tracking, call centers). Section 13.5 presents these programs.

eCRM

Managing customer relationships is a business activity that corporations have practiced for generations. As evidenced by the many successful businesses that existed before the computer, companies were not required to manage one's customers well. However, since the mid-1990s, competition intensified, and CRM has enhanced various types of information technologies. CRM technology is an evolutionary response to environmental changes, making use of new IT devices and tools. The term **eCRM** was coined in the mid-1990s when customers started using Web browsers, the Internet, and other electronic touch points (e-mail, POS terminals, call centers, and direct sales). eCRM also includes online process applications, such as segmentation and personalization. The use of the Internet, intranets, and extranets made customer services, as well as services to partners (see PRM in Chapter 6), much more effective and efficient than before the Internet.

eCRM
Customer relationship management conducted electronically.

Through Internet technologies, data generated about customers can easily be fed into marketing, sales, and customer service databases for analysis. The success or failure of CRM efforts can now be measured and modified in real time, further elevating customer expectations. In the Internet-connected world, eCRM has become frequently a requirement for survival, not just a competitive advantage. eCRM covers a broad range of topics, tools, and methods, ranging from the proper design of digital products and services to pricing and loyalty programs (e.g., see e-sj.org, the *Journal of Service Research,* jsr.sagepub.com, and ecrmguide.com).

Note that eCRM is sometimes referred to as *e-service*. However, the term *e-service* has several other meanings. For example, some define e-service as EC in service industries, such as banking, hospitals, and government, whereas others confine its use to e–self-service. To avoid confusion, we prefer to use the term *eCRM* rather than *e-service*. Note that people use the terms *eCRM* and *CRM* interchangeably. Most vendors use just *CRM,* and the accounting-profession literature uses that term most often.

THE SCOPE OF CRM

For online transactions, CRM often provides help features. In addition, if a product is purchased off-line, customer service may be offered online. For example, if a consumer purchases a product off-line and needs expert advice on how to use it, he or she may find detailed instructions online (e.g., livemanuals.com).

According to Voss (2000), there are three levels of CRM:

1. **Foundation services.** This includes the *minimum necessary* services, such as site responsiveness (e.g., how quickly and accurately the service is provided), site effectiveness, and order fulfillment.
2. **Customer-centered services.** These services include order tracing, configuration and customization, and security/trust. These are the services that *matter the most* to customers.
3. **Value-added services.** These are *extra services,* such as dynamic brokering, online auctions, and online training and education.

The Extent of Service

Customer service should be provided throughout the entire product life cycle. Four parts compose the value chain for CRM (Plant 2000):

1. **Customer acquisition (prepurchase support).** A service strategy that reflects and reinforces the company's brand and provides information to potential customers to encourage them to buy.
2. **Customer support during purchase.** This service strategy provides a shopping environment that the consumer sees as efficient, informative, and productive.
3. **Customer fulfillment (purchase dispatch).** This involves timely delivery, including keeping the customer informed about the fulfillment process, especially if there are any delays.
4. **Customer continuance support (postpurchase).** Information and support help maintain the customer relationship between purchases.

Case 13.6 provides several examples of how companies use eCRM, and the Real-World Case at the end of this chapter provides an additional example.

BENEFITS AND LIMITATIONS OF CRM

The major benefit of CRM is the provision of superior customer care through the use of the Internet and IT technologies. In other words, CRM makes customers happy by providing choices of products and services, fast problem resolution and response, easy and quick access to information, and much more (see Seybold 2006 and Section 13.5). Companies try to gain competitive advantage over their competitors by providing better CRM.

The major limitation of CRM is that it requires integration with a company's other information systems, which may not be an easy task. In addition, as will be discussed later in this section, justifying the expense of CRM is not easy. Also, it is difficult to support mobile employees with some CRM applications. It is only in the last few years that m-commerce has encouraged the creation of exciting CRM applications.

CRM IMPLEMENTATION ISSUES

According to a *CIO Insight* study (2004) and Petersen (2006), culture, commitment of top management, and communication lead to CRM success—not technology. Bohling, et al. (2006), Holland and Abrell (2005), and Seybold (2006) highlight some important steps

CASE 13.6
EC Application
HOW COMPANIES USE eCRM

Almost all large companies have a formal CRM program (Agarwal et al. 2004). However, CRM programs may be implemented in a variety of different ways due to the large number of tools available (Section 13.5). Here are a few examples of how companies have implemented CRM:

- Continental Airlines monitors telephone calls to its data center, using software from Witness Systems (*witness.com*), which uses software agents to analyze recorded conversations. The analysis tells Continental Airlines what customers really want. It also helps the company craft marketing plans and business strategy. Results serve customers better and resolve problems immediately, saving the company $1 million annually. To increase efficiency, Continental Airlines uses Call-Miner, a labor-saving Witness Systems program that automatically transcribes conversations into digitized text.
- Micrel Inc., a leading manufacturer of integrated circuit solutions for enterprise, consumer, industrial, mobile, telecommunications, automotive, and computer markets has become known for being "fast on its feet" in responding to customer needs. To improve response time and relevancy of information delivered to customers online, the company uses a sophisticated self-service search and navigation engine that directs customers to the right information at the right time to help them reach buying decisions. As a result, Web site traffic grew by 300 percent; the retention rate for new site visitors increased by 25 percent; saved $40,000 a year; and customer satisfaction increased significantly (see IBM 2006 for details).
- Employees at more than 200 Sheraton Hotels owned by Starwood Hotels and Resorts are using a new eCRM system to coordinate fast responses to guests' complaints and unmet needs. When an employee does not respond to a request or complaint within a time frame predetermined by hotel management, the color of a computerized notice changes from green to yellow and possibly to red. Red triggers management to quickly intervene and perhaps include special compensation for the guest. Starwood has reported significantly better operating results since it implemented the system. For details, see Babcock (2004).
- Online-only bank NetBank Inc. uses CRM to leverage customer contacts via the Web and call centers by analyzing

customers' profiles in real time and presenting the employee interacting with each customer with potential for cross-sell and up-sell offers. The bank now can do more targeted marketing campaigns that better address its customers' needs (see Chapter 18 for the full story).
- Boots the Chemists, a UK retailer of over 1,400 health and beauty stores, uses business intelligence and data mining (eCRM analytics) to learn about customers in its e-loyalty programs. The retailer uses data mining to acquire insights into customer behavior. Customer service agents can analyze, predict, and maximize the value of each customer relationship. This enables better one-to-one marketing efforts and reduces customer dissatisfaction.
- In a similar manner, outdoor product retailer REI brings customer data into a single location and analyzes and manages it in real time. The results are used for various CRM initiatives. See Amato-McCoy (2003) for details.
- Harrah's Entertainment Inc. treats its customers differently: The more a customer spends in a casino—the more rewards the customer gets. The company assigns a value to each customer by using data mining.
- FedEx's CRM system enables the company to provide superb service to millions of customers using 56 call centers. Each of its 4,000 call center employees has instant access to a customer's profile. The profile tells the employee how valuable the customer is and the details of the current transaction. The more an agent knows about the customer, the better the service provided. Customers use one phone number regardless of where the company is or the destination of the package. The CRM reduced calls for help, increased customer satisfaction, and enabled better advertising and marketing strategy. For details, see Guzman (2004).

Questions

1. Identify common elements of CRM in these examples.
2. In addition to customer service, CRM systems provide managerial benefits. Identify and discuss these benefits.
3. Why is data mining becoming so important in CRM?

in building an EC strategy that is centered on the customer. These steps include a focus on the end customer; systems and business processes that are designed for ease of use and from the end customer's point of view; and efforts to foster customer loyalty (a key to profitability in EC). To successfully make these steps, businesses must take the following actions:

- Deliver personalized services (e.g., dowjones.com)
- Target the right customers (e.g., aa.com, national.com)
- Help customers do their jobs (e.g., boeing.com)
- Let customers help themselves (e.g., iprint.com)
- Streamline business processes that impact customers (e.g., ups.com, amazon.com)

▶ "Own" the customer's total experience by providing every possible customer contact (e.g., amazon.com, hertz.com).

▶ Provide a 360-degree view of the customer relationship (e.g., wellsfargo.com, verizon.com)

Many of these steps are valid both for B2C and for B2B EC. In B2B, CRM is known as PRM (see Chapter 6).

Large-scale CRM implementation is neither easy nor cheap. Tan et al. (2002) suggest five factors that are required to implement a CRM program effectively:

1. **Customer-centric strategy.** A customer-centric strategy should be established first at the corporate level. The strategy must be based on and consistent with the overall corporate strategy and must be communicated across the whole organization.

2. **Commitments from people.** The more commitments from people across the corporation to the transformation of the business strategy, the more likely the CRM implementation will succeed. Employees should be willing to learn the necessary technological skills.

3. **Improved or redesigned processes.** It is inherently difficult to identify the processes that need to be involved and frequently redesigned when implementing CRM.

4. **Software technology.** CRM software can record business transactions, create operations-focused databases, facilitate data warehousing and data mining, and provide decision-making support and marketing campaign management tools. Companies should select the appropriate CRM packages to meet specific corporate CRM needs as well as to enable integration with legacy enterprise applications, such as the ERP system. Major CRM vendors are Siebel, Oracle, SAP, IBM, and Nortel/Clarify. Smaller players are Vignettee, BroadVision, Onyx, Microstrategy, E.piphany, Roundarch, and KANA. Major CRM consultants are KMPG Consultants, Deloitte Consultants, and the Patricia Seybold Groups (see Greenberg 2004).

5. **Infrastructure.** Effective CRM implementation requires a suitable corporate infrastructure. This infrastructure includes network setup, storage, data backup, computing platforms, and Web servers. However, only effective corporate infrastructure *integration* can provide solid support for CRM implementation.

Agarwal et al. (2004) and Bohling et al. (2006) claim that many CRM projects are disappointing at the beginning and require remediation because companies do not manage them properly. They offer an extensive methodology on how to implement CRM. See Compton (2004), CIO.com (2006), and Hagen (2006) for additional tips on CRM implementation.

INTEGRATING CRM INTO THE ENTERPRISE

Some CRM applications are independent of enterprise systems. However, many CRM applications must be integrated with other information systems. To understand why, let us examine Exhibit 3.3 (p. 99 in Chapter 3).

As the exhibit shows, CRM lies primarily between the customers and the enterprise. The communication between the two is done via the Internet, regular telephone, snail mail, and so on. However, to answer customer queries, it is necessary to access files and databases. In medium and large corporations, these are usually part of a legacy system and/or ERP system. Companies may check data relevant to a customer order with their manufacturing plants, transportation vendors, suppliers, or other business partners. Therefore, CRM needs to interface with the supply chain, and do so easily, inexpensively, and quickly. In addition, CRM must be integrated with the data warehouse because, as Online File W4.3 showed, it is easier to build applications using data in the warehouse than using data residing in several internal and external databases. Finally, CRM itself collects customer and product data, including click stream data. These need to be prepared for data mining and other types of analysis.

The integration of ERP and CRM must include low-level data synchronization as well as business process integration so that the integrity of business roles can be maintained across systems and workflow tasks can pass between the systems. Such integration also ensures that organizations can perform *business intelligence* across systems.

JUSTIFYING CUSTOMER SERVICE AND CRM PROGRAMS

Two major problems arise when companies try to justify expenditures for customer service and CRM programs. The first problem is the fact that most of the benefits of CRM are intangible, and the second is that substantial benefits can usually be reaped only from loyal customers over the long run. This is true for both off-line and online organizations. In a 1990 study published in *Harvard Business Review* titled "Zero Defections: Quality Comes to Services" (see details at Reichheld and Schefter 2000), researchers demonstrated that the high cost of acquiring customers renders many customer relationship programs unprofitable during their early years. Only in later years, when the cost of retaining loyal customers falls and the volume of their purchases rises, do CRMs generate big returns. Therefore, companies are very careful about determining how much customer service to provide (see *CIO Insight* 2004 and Smith 2006). For approaches for CRM justification, see Chapter 15, CIO.com (2006) and Bonde (2004).

Metrics in Customer Service and CRM

One way to determine how much service to provide is to compare a company against a set of standards known as **metrics**. Metrics are either quantitative or qualitative. (See Jagannathan et al. 2001 and Sterne 2002.) Here are some Web-related metrics a company can use to determine the appropriate level of customer support:

metrics
Performance standards; may be quantitative or qualitative.

- **Response time.** Many companies have a target response time of 24 to 48 hours. If a company uses intelligent agents, a response can be made in real time or the system can provide an acknowledgment that the customer's message has been received and a response will be forthcoming.
- **Site availability.** Customers should be able to reach the company's Web site at any time (24 hours a day). This means that downtime should be as close to zero as possible.
- **Download time.** Users usually will not tolerate downloads that last more than 10 to 20 seconds.
- **Timeliness.** Information on the company site must be up-to-date. The company sets an interval (e.g., every month) at which information must be revised. If a set interval is not used, companies may have new products in stores but not on the Web or vice versa. In either case, it may lose potential sales.
- **Security and privacy.** Web sites must provide sufficient privacy statements and an explanation of security measures. (This metric is measurable as "yes" or "no"—either the statement and explanation are there or they are not.)
- **On-time order fulfillment.** Order fulfillment must be fast and comply with promised delivery dates. For example, a company can measure the time it takes to fulfill orders, and it can count the number of times it fails to meet its fulfillment promises.
- **Return policy.** In the United States and several other countries, return policies are a standard service. Having a return policy increases customer trust and loyalty. The ease by which customers can make returns is important to customer satisfaction.
- **Navigability.** A Web site must be easy to navigate. To gauge navigability, companies might measure the number of customers who get partway into an order and then "bail out."

eCRM Analytics

Analytic CRM refers to the use of business analytics techniques and business intelligence such as data mining and online analytic processing (see Turban et al., 2007) to CRM applications. Exhibit 13.5 illustrates the basic concept. On the left side we see the many sources of customer data including real-time Web movement activities and real-time customer interaction and activities in POS and even while playing slot machines in the casinos. The large amount of data is processed and stored in a data warehouse (Section 13.5) and/or in a data mart or just in databases. Several types of analytical tools can be applied to create, for example, customer profiles (Chapter 4) used for planning advertising and marketing campaigns.

analytic CRM
Applying business analytics techniques and business intelligence such as data mining and online analytic processing to CRM applications.

EXHIBIT 13.5 CRM Analytics

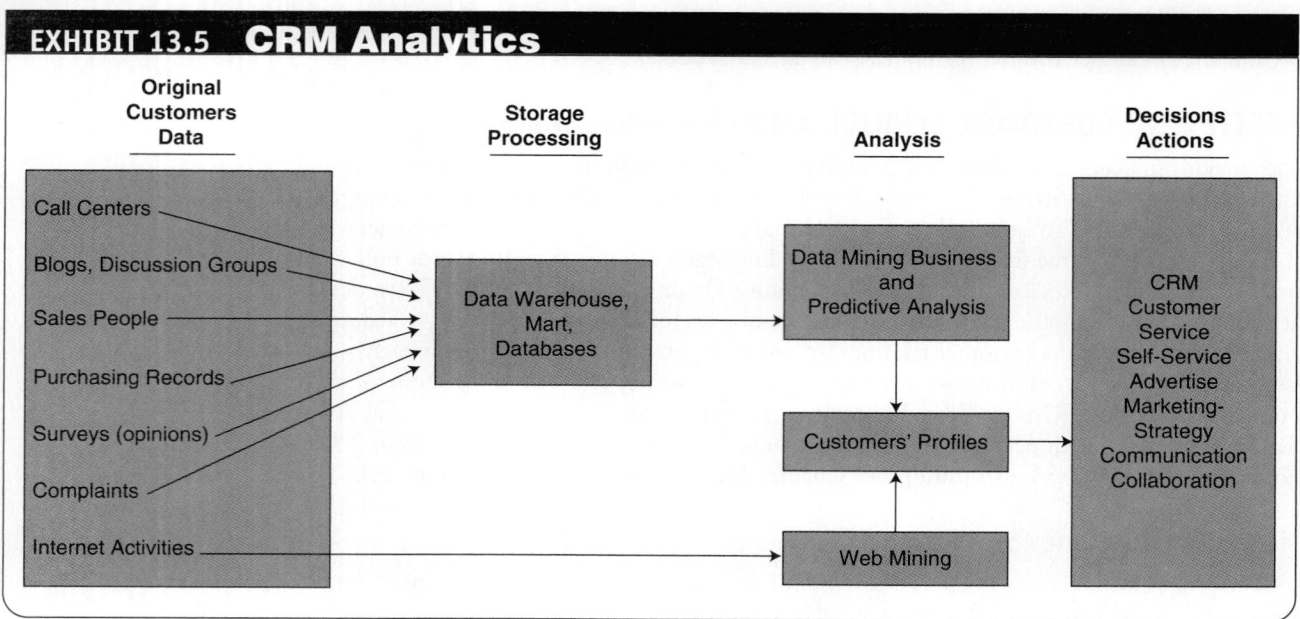

As Web sites have added a new and often faster way to interact with customers, the opportunity and the need to turn data collected about customers into useful information has become apparent. As a result, a number of software companies have developed products that do customer data analysis (e.g., SAP's Business One CRM, Microsoft's Dynamics CRM 3.0).

Analytics can provide customer segmentation groupings (for example, dividing customers into those most and least likely to repurchase a product); profitability analysis (which customers lead to the most profit over time); personalization (the ability to market to individual customers based on the data collected about them); event monitoring (for example, when a customer reaches a certain dollar volume of purchases); what-if scenarios (how likely is a customer or customer category that bought one product to buy a similar one); and predictive modeling (for example, comparing various product development plans in terms of likely future success given the customer knowledge base).

Benefits of CRM analytics lead not only to better and more productive customer relations in terms of sales and service but also to improvement in advertisement planning and analysis, marketing strategies, and supply chain management (lower inventory and speedier delivery) and, thus, lower costs and more competitive pricing.

To derive the most benefits from eCRM, it is necessary to properly collect and analyze relevant customer data. Nemati et al. (2004) provide results of a study on the integration of data in eCRM analytics. Analytics can analyze and document online customer or visitor patterns to acquire and retain users. Using data mining properly provides companies with valuable information on how to serve customers online. According to a 2004 CRM study (*CIO Insight* 2004), 75 percent of all large CRM users are using or will soon use CRM with data mining and analytics.

FUTURE DIRECTIONS OF CRM

Greenberg (2006) points to the following CRM future directions:

▶ The customer experience with products, services, and the company providing them will be the foundation for CRM's going forward and increasingly will be a consideration for corporate strategies. Metrics will be developed to measure the success of the customer experience, and the idea that value resides with the customer will be critical in the future. CRM, as we know it, will disappear by the end of 2008.

▶ "CRM on Demand" will become preeminent, and though on-premise vendors will continue to survive, most companies considering IT investments and system investments will choose on-demand products for the enterprise and as a platform. For advantages see

CIO.com (2006). However, the on-demand functionality will still not be as complete as on-premise by year's end, though that won't matter. Also see IBM (2006).

▶ The open source movement and companies like SugarCRM will become a credible competition to the on-demand market. (Open source CRM established itself as a solid alternative in 2006.)

▶ CRM will be integrated increasingly with strategies for social networking and at the application level, with social networking tools like podcasting, blogs, and wikis, in addition to the harder core social networking applications, such as LinkedIn.

A large number of tools and applications can provide CRM, as Section 13.5 will illustrate.

Section 13.4 ▶ REVIEW QUESTIONS

1. Define *CRM*.
2. Describe the benefits and limitations of CRM.
3. List the major types of CRM.
4. Define *eCRM*.
5. Describe some implementation issues relating to CRM, including integration with the enterprise.
6. Discuss the issue of justifying CRM service.
7. Describe metrics related to CRM and customer service.

13.5 DELIVERING CUSTOMER SERVICE IN CYBERSPACE: CRM APPLICATIONS AND TOOLS

CRM applications are customer service tools designed to enhance customer satisfaction (the feeling that a product or service has met the customer's expectations). CRM applications improve on traditional customer service by means of easier communications and speedier resolution of customer problems, starting with automatic responses to questions, customer self-service, or allowing the customer to request a telephone call from a customer service employee. Today, in order to satisfy increased customer expectations, EC marketers must respond by providing the best, most powerful, and innovative CRM systems. They must create customer-centric EC systems.

Customer service (or support) is the final link in the chain between providers and customers. It adds value to products and services and is an integral part of a successful business. Almost all medium and large companies today use the Web as a customer support channel. CRM applications on the Web can take many forms, ranging from providing search and comparison capabilities (Chapter 3) to allowing customers to track the status of their orders.

The first step to building customer relationships is to give customers good reasons to visit and return to the Web site. In other words, the organization should create a site that is rich in information, hopefully with more content than a visitor can absorb in a single visit. The site should include not just product information but also have value-added content from which visitors can get valuable information and services for free. Exhibit 16.9 (p. 759) lists some ways in which online businesses can build customer relationships through content.

CLASSIFICATIONS OF CRM APPLICATIONS

The Patricia Seybold Group (2002) distinguishes among *customer-facing, customer-touching*, and *customer-centric intelligence* CRM applications. Exhibit 13.6 shows these three categories of applications. The exhibit also shows how customers interact with these applications.

▶ **Customer-facing applications.** These include all the areas where customers interact with the company: call centers, including help desks; sales force automation; and field service automation. Such CRM applications basically automate information flow or support employees in these areas.

mobile devices can increase customer service. Field service automation applications support the customer service efforts of field service reps and service managers. These applications manage customer service requests, service orders, service contracts, service schedules, and service calls. They provide planning, scheduling, dispatching, and reporting features to field service representatives. Examples are wireless devices, such as provided in SFA. Some of these are *wearable devices* (see Chapter 9).

CUSTOMER-TOUCHING APPLICATIONS

Customer-touching applications are those where customers use interactive computer programs rather than interacting with people. The following are popular customer-touching applications.

Personalized Web Pages

Many companies provide customers with tools to create their own individual Web pages (e.g., MyYahoo!). Companies can efficiently deliver customized information, such as product information and warranty information, when the customer logs on to the personalized page. Not only can a customer pull information from the vendor's site, but the vendor can also push information to the consumer. In addition, these Web pages can record customer purchases and preferences. Typical personalized Web pages include those for bank accounts, stock portfolio accounts, credit card accounts, and so on. On such sites, users can see their balances, records of all current and historical transactions, and more.

American Airlines is an example of one company that uses personalized Web sites to help increase the bottom line, as shown in Case 13.8.

E-Commerce Applications

As described in Chapter 1, e-commerce applications implement marketing, sales, and service functions through online touch points, most typically the Web. These applications let customers shop for products through a virtual-shopping-cart metaphor and purchase the products in their shopping carts through a virtual-check-out metaphor. Customers may also

---

CASE 13.8
EC Application

AMERICAN AIRLINES OFFERS PERSONALIZED WEB SITES

In late 1998, American Airlines (AA) unveiled a number of features on its Web site (*aa.com*) that some thought made the site the most advanced (at that time) for personalized, one-to-one interactions and transactions on the Web. The site's most innovative feature was its ability to generate personalized Web pages for each of more than 1 million registered, travel-planning customers. How was AA able to handle such a large amount of information and provide real-time customized Web pages for each customer? The answer—intelligent agents.

BroadVision (*broadvision.com*), a major developer of one-to-one marketing applications, developed the AA site using a complex software called One-to-One Application. One of the core components needed to generate personalized Web pages is intelligent agents, which dynamically match customer profiles (built on information supplied by the customer, observed by the system, or derived from existing customer databases) to the database of contents. The output of the matching process triggers the creation of a real-time customized Web page, which for AA can contain information on the consumer's home airport and preferred destinations.

By using intelligent agent technology, AA built a considerable edge over its competitors. Personalizing Web pages offered the potential to increase customer loyalty and cement relationships with customers. The Web site also fostered the community of AA frequent flyers.

In May 2002, AA launched the new and improved Web site using the flexibility of Art Technology Group's (ATG) Relationship Management platform. The new site offers more value and convenience and greater personalization with its platform upgrade, new booking engine, and improved navigation. Today, most competitors have similar systems.

Sources: Compiled from *aa.com* (accessed January 2007), *broadvision.com* (accessed January 2007), and Yoon (2002).

Questions

1. What are the benefits of the personalized pages to AA?
2. What role do intelligent agents play in the personalization process?

perform self-service support tasks such as checking order status, history inquiry, returns processing, and customer information management. This provides convenience to many customers and also saves them money, thus, increasing their satisfaction. Chapter 3 provides details on such EC applications.

Web Self-Service

The Web environment provides an opportunity for customers to serve themselves. Known as **Web self-service**, this strategy provides tools for users to execute activities previously done by corporate customer service personnel. Personalized Web pages, for example, are one tool that may support Web self-service. Self-service applications can be used with customers (e.g., to support CRM; see rightnow.com) and with employees, suppliers, and any other business partners.

A well-known example is FedEx's *self-tracking* system. Previously, if customers wanted information about the whereabouts of a package, they had to call a representative, give the information about their shipment, and wait for an answer. Today, customers go to fedex.com, insert their airbill number, and view the status of their package shipment. Many other examples exist, ranging from checking the arrival time of an airplane to finding the balance of a checking account. Initially, self-service was done in voice-based customer response systems (known as voice-activated response [VAR]; e.g., netbytel.com). Today, these systems are integrated and complementary to Web-based systems.

Some self-service applications are done only online. Examples are using FAQs at a Web site and self-diagnosis of computers online. On the other hand, updating an address with a personnel department can be done online or via VAR.

The benefits of Web self-service for customers are quick response time, consistent and sometimes more accurate replies or data, the possibility of getting more details, and less frustration and more satisfaction. The benefits for organizations are lower expenses of providing service (up to 95 percent savings), the ability to scale service without adding more staff, strengthening business partnerships, and improved quality of service.

It is not easy to implement large-scale self-service systems. They require a complex blend of work processes and technology. Also, only well-defined and repeatable procedures are well-suited for such systems. For further details and implementation tips, see IBM (2006).

Of the various self-service tools available, three are of special interest: self-tracking, FAQs, and self-configuration.

Self-Tracking. Self-tracking refers to systems, like that of FedEx, where customers can find the status of an order or service in real (or close to real) time. Most large delivery services provide such services as do direct marketers such as Dell, Amazon.com, and Staples. Some auto manufacturers (e.g., Ford) allow customers to track the progress of the production of a customized car. Some employers, universities, and public agencies will let job applicants track the status of their job application.

Customer Self-Service Through FAQs. Every Web site needs an "frequently asked questions", FAQ page that helps customers help themselves. An **FAQ page** lists questions that are frequently asked by customers and the answers to those questions. By making an FAQ page available, customers can quickly and easily find answers to their questions, saving time and effort for both the Web site owner and the customer. An effective FAQ page has the characteristics shown in Online File W13.10.

Self-Configuration and Customization. Many build-to-order vendors, from Dell to Mattel, provide customers with tools to self-configure products or services. One of the best ways to satisfy customers is to provide them with the ability to customize products and services (see Chapters 1 and 2). Holweg and Pil (2001) assert that in order to have an effective build-to-order system, companies and their suppliers must first understand what customers want. This can be done by finding the customers' requirements (e.g., via self-configuration) and then linking the configured order directly to production so that production decisions are based on real customer demand (see the Dell case in Chapter 1). In addition, customers should be linked interactively to the company and *if necessary* to product designers at the company (see Chapter 7). According to Berry (2001), the superior "new retailer" provides for customization, offers superb customer services, and saves the customer time.

Web self-service
Activities conducted by users on the Web to find answers to their questions (e.g., tracking) or for product configuration.

FAQ page
A Web page that lists questions that are frequently asked by customers and the answers to those questions.

CUSTOMER-CENTRIC APPLICATIONS

Customer-centric applications support customer data collection, processing, and analysis. The major applications are as follows.

Data Reporting and Warehousing

CRM data need to be collected, processed, and stored. Online File W4.3 describes the general business intelligence process. Here, we present two elements of the process: reports and data warehouses.

Data Reports. Data reporting presents raw or processed CRM-related information, which managers and analysts can view and analyze. Reports provide a range of tabular and graphical presentation formats. Analysts can interact with the report presentation, changing its visual format, "drilling up" into summary information or "drilling down" into additional detail.

Data Warehouse. Medium and large corporations organize and store data in a central repository called a **data warehouse** so that it will be easy to analyze later on, when needed. Online File W4.3 describes this process. Data warehouses contain both CRM and non-CRM data. According to the Patricia Seybold Group (2002), data warehouses can be effective CRM tools if they contain the following information: customer information used by all operational CRM applications and by possible analytic applications (such as customer value scores); information about the company's products and services and the channels through which it offers them; information about the company's marketing, sales, and services initiatives and customers' responses to them; information about customer requests and the company's responses; and information about customer transactions. For more information see Dutta and Roy (2006).

> **data warehouse**
> A single, server-based data repository that allows centralized analysis, security, and control over the data.

Data Analysis and Mining

Analytic applications automate the processing and analysis of CRM data. Many statistical, management science, and decision support tools can be used for this purpose (e.g., see Turban et al. 2007 and Seybold 2006). Analytic applications process a warehouse's data, whereas reports merely present that information. Analytic applications are tools that analyze the performance, efficiency, and effectiveness of an operation's CRM applications. Their output should enable a company to improve the operational applications that deliver customer experience in order to achieve the CRM objectives of customer acquisition and retention. For example, analytic applications may be designed to provide insight into customer behavior, requests, and transactions, as well as into customer responses to the corporation's marketing, sales, and service initiatives. Analytic applications also create statistical models of customer behavior, values of customer relationships over time, and forecasts of customer acquisition, retention, and desertion. See SAS (2007) for additional information and examples.

Data mining is another analytic activity that involves sifting through an immense amount of data to discover previously unknown patterns. In some cases, the data are consolidated in a data warehouse and data marts; in others, they are kept on the Internet and in intranet servers. For more on data analysis and data mining, see Online File W4.3 and Nisbet (2006).

An example of analytic CRM is provided in Case 13.9.

ONLINE NETWORKING AND OTHER APPLICATIONS

Online networking and other applications support communication and collaboration among customers, business partners, and company employees. Representative technologies are discussed here.

Online Networking

Representative online networking tools and methods include the following:

- ▶ **Forums.** Available from Internet portals, such as Yahoo! and AOL, forums offer users the opportunity to participate in discussions as well as to lead forums on a "niche" topic.
- ▶ **Chat rooms.** Found on a variety of Web sites, they offer one-to-one or many-to-many real-time conversations.

CASE 13.9
EC Application

HOW HSBC MEXICO ATTRACTS NEW BUSINESS AND MAXIMIZES EXISTING RELATIONSHIPS WITH CRM

The retail banking environment is very competitive and is operating in a rapidly fluctuating business environment (currency exchange changes, interest rate fluctuations, deregulations, online banking). With 1,900 branches, over 17,000 employees, and over 6 million customers, this bank faces both opportunities and stiff competition. Using CRM, HSBC Mexico was able to become one of the fastest growing financial services firms in Mexico. This is how they did it.

The bank's executives decided to use EC to target customers with intelligent offers that can increase profitability. This is done by using CRM solutions that provide the right product or service, at the right time, and through the right channel.

In the competitive environment, it was necessary to keep the existing customers and develop more profitable relationships with them. The CRM targeted the most valuable customers (including the ones that have a potential to become so). The company needed to find such customers and then reach out to them with excellent services and one-to-one intelligent offers—give them what they really need or want.

Using analytic CRM (mainly data mining, due to the large number of customers and data about each) and campaign management software (both from *infor.com*, a global software company for enterprise solutions), HSBC Mexico was able to improve its interactions with customers, support the cross selling of services and identify and retain the most valuable (and profitable) customers. The solution also works in real time, so when an employee talks to a customer, or answers an e-mail, the employee can find the customer's profile online in a second.

A major portion of the project was to integrate the CRM with other information systems as well as align it with the corporate business goals. Using the software, HSBC is able to plan, develop, execute, manage, and analyze the results of multichannel marketing campaigns. The channels are: e-mail, Web portal, ATMs, and face-to-face conversations. The bank also pushes special offers and uses relationship building programs (e.g., preferred relationship-based pricing). The information collected also helps to improve asset allocation strategies to the branches.

In its first year, the bank's CRM offers generated 23,000 new accounts, and its CRM-based campaigns brought in 22 percent of all credit card accounts, 12 percent of all personal loans, and 8 percent of all car loans. The retention rate of profitable customers increased from 77 percent to 90 percent.

The bank is planning even more one-to-one offerings. Also, by coordinating offers in real time across its network of ATMs, call centers, online banking sites, and retail branches, the company continues to increase its offers' acceptance rates.

Finally, HSBC Mexico captured Gartner's prestigious CRM Excellence Award for Large Enterprises.

Sources: Compiled from Infor (2006) and Lager (2006).

Questions

1. Why was it necessary to define the business goals?
2. Why does the bank want to raise the retention rate?
3. Enter *infor.com* and check their SSA Outbound and Inbound Marketing Products. Which one was used here? Why?
4. What CRM tools are being used here?
5. Many banks offer gifts to anyone that opens an account. Are CRM-based decisions to go to one-to-one incentives really superior?

- ◗ **Usenet groups.** These are collections of online discussions grouped into communities. (See usenet2.org for details.)
- ◗ **Blogs and Wikis.** Blogs and wikis are becoming the major online networking tools (see Chapter 8 and 17). Blogs enable companies to approach focused segments of customers. In addition to Stonyfield Farm (Chapter 8), airlines, cruise companies, banks, and similar businesses sponsor blogs for their customers. Companies can learn from the blogs and try to improve their operations to make customers happier. For example, monitoring their blog, U.S. Cellular learned that many teenagers were unhappy due to the limited time on their cell phones. The company then started offering unlimited "call me" minutes to attract the teenagers. Note that wikis can be considered collaborative whiteboards because everyone can participate.
- ◗ **E-mail newsletters.** These newsletters usually offer the opportunity for readers to write in, particularly in "Let us hear from you" sections. Users can find newsletters of interest by browsing a topic in a search engine. Many newsletter services (e.g., emarketer.com) invite you to sign in. Others (e.g., aberdeen.com) only allow access to articles to users who register. Usually registration is an opt-in option (i.e., a person can remove his or her name from the list at any time).

▶ **Discussion lists.** A discussion list is a redistribution tool through which an e-mail is sent to one address and then is automatically forwarded to all the people who subscribe to the list.

The following text discusses these last two networking tools in more detail.

E-Mail Newsletters

The goal of an e-mail newsletter, according to Kinnard (2002), is to build a relationship with the subscribers. The best beginning is to focus on service by providing valuable information about an industry, which may range from tips ("tip of the day") to a full-blown newsletter consisting of extensive text and graphics.

Because of the current bulk of e-mail advertising and marketing, customers may initially be distrustful of e-mail marketing. Therefore, newsletter articles, commentary, special offers, tips, quotes, and other pieces of information e-mailed to people must be presented in a professional and attractive manner. As customers find that they can trust the information provided, they will supply a company with more demographic and personal information that the company can add to its customer database.

Sample resources for information on e-mail newsletters are list-universe.com and new-list.com.

Discussion Lists

Discussion lists automatically forward an e-mail to all the people who subscribe to the list so that they can react to it. Discussion lists are distributed *post-by-post* (each recipient gets each e-mail from other members individually) or as *digests* (all e-mails are compiled and sent out according to a schedule—for example, once per day).

The three main reasons a company may use such lists are (1) to learn more about customers in a particular industry (assuming customers will react to the e-mail), (2) to market the company's products and services, and (3) to gather and share information with a community of individuals with similar interests. If a company hosts a discussion list, it can define the subject matter to be discussed, determine the frequency of the publication, and even make it a revenue-gathering tool. Sources for more information on discussion lists are title.net and everythingemail.net/email_discussion.html.

The Creative Enterprises Network at creativethought.com, About.com's chat site at chatting.miningco.com, and Usenet 2 at usenet2.org provide additional information about networking online.

Mobile CRM

mobile CRM
The delivery of CRM applications to any user, whenever and wherever needed, by use of the wireless infrastructure and mobile devices.

Mobile CRM refers to the delivery of CRM applications to any user, whenever and wherever needed, by use of the wireless infrastructure and mobile devices.

Many wireless and mobile m-commerce tools can provide customer service. As described in Chapter 9, services such as finding your bank balance, stock trading, and checking airline arrival times are available with wireless devices. The major objective is to provide customer service faster and more conveniently. Furthermore, companies can use a "push" rather than a "pull" approach to giving customers needed information (e.g., by sending SMSs). As shown in the 511 case in Online File W1.3, the government also is going wireless with some of its public services. Finally, many employees' and partners' services are provided in a wireless environment. The advantages of mobile CRM over traditional CRM are shown in Exhibit 13.9.

Mobile video, which became commercial in 2007, became a platform for fostering communication with customers.

Voice Communication and Understanding by Machines

The most natural way of communicating is by voice. Given the opportunity to do so, many customers prefer to connect to the Internet via voice. During the 1990s, VAR systems became popular. Today, Web-based voice systems are taking their place. Companies such as bevocal.com and TellMe (tellme.com) provide one solution for accessing the Internet by voice. It involves converting voice to text, processing and transmitting the text message,

EXHIBIT 13.9 Traditional versus Mobile CRM

Traditional CRM Information Gap

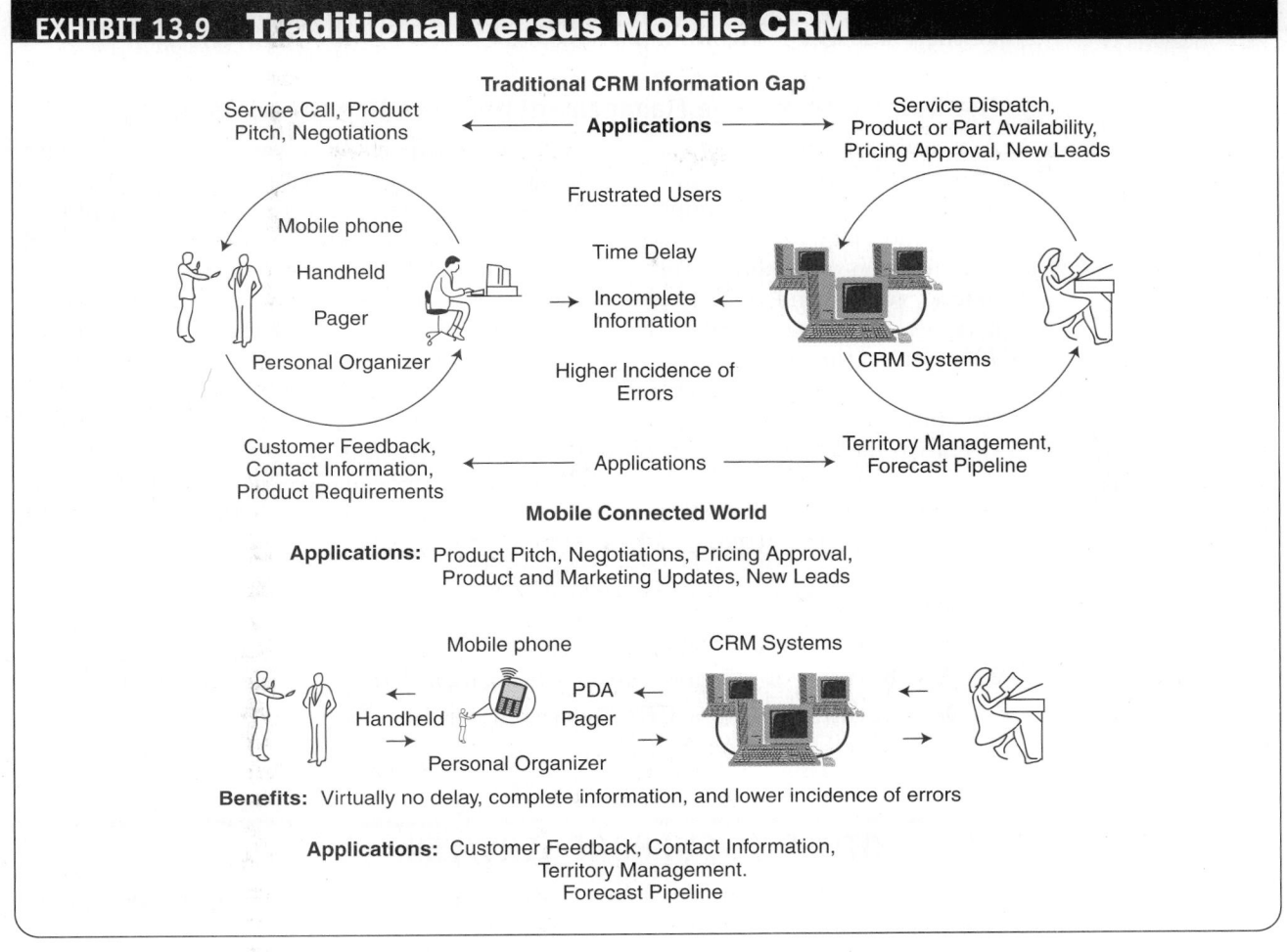

Service Call, Product Pitch, Negotiations ← Applications → Service Dispatch, Product or Part Availability, Pricing Approval, New Leads

Mobile phone / Handheld / Pager / Personal Organizer

Frustrated Users
Time Delay
Incomplete Information
Higher Incidence of Errors

CRM Systems

Customer Feedback, Contact Information, Product Requirements ← Applications → Territory Management, Forecast Pipeline

Mobile Connected World

Applications: Product Pitch, Negotiations, Pricing Approval, Product and Marketing Updates, New Leads

Mobile phone / Handheld / PDA / Pager / Personal Organizer — CRM Systems

Benefits: Virtually no delay, complete information, and lower incidence of errors

Applications: Customer Feedback, Contact Information, Territory Management. Forecast Pipeline

and then converting text found on the Web to voice. Even more advanced systems will be available in the near future.

Imagine the following scenario: A traveler gets stuck in traffic on the way to the airport. She calls the airport on her cell phone and hears. "All agents are busy. You are important to us; please stay on the line." With Visual Text to Speech technology from AT&T, she can click on "talk to agent" on her Internet-enabled smartphone. The smiling face of a virtual agent appears on the phone screen. The traveler tells the agent her problem and asks to reschedule her flight. A voice confirmation is provided in seconds, and action is taken within a short time.

Most people are more comfortable talking with a person, even a virtual one, than they are interacting with machines. The smile and the clear pronunciation of the agent's voice increases shoppers' confidence and trust. For details, see Lohr et al. (2002).

Speech Analytics, a device that monitors word usage, analyzes voices of callers to call centers, recognizing words such as "need assistance" and "problems" for example. Another device is *emotion detector,* which can track voice volume and pitch to alert managers to angry callers.

Speech recognition by computers is critical to the operation of efficient call centers because it cuts costs considerably and enables real-time responses. The use of voice portals such as tellme.com is increasing rapidly. While not perfect, speech recognition is critical for self-service. For an overview, applications, and resources, see D'Agostino (2005). Related to speech recognition is language translation by computers.

Language Translation

Some people prefer customer service to be in their native or selected language. Web site translation is most helpful in serving tourists. A device called InfoScope (from IBM) can read signs, restaurant menus, and other text written in one language and translate them into several other languages. See Wisegeek (2006). Currently, these translators are available only for short messages. For more on this topic, see Chapter 14.

The Role of Knowledge Management and Intelligent Agents in CRM

Automating inquiry routing and answering queries requires *knowledge,* which can be generated from historical data and from human expertise and stored in knowledge bases for use whenever needed. Examples would be the answers to FAQs or the detailed product information requested by customers. Companies need to automate the provision of such knowledge in order to contain costs. *Intelligent agents* support the mechanics of inquiry routing, autoresponders, and so on. Some autoresponders, for example, use agents that use keyword recognition to guess what the query is about. The answer may be correct in only 80 percent of the cases.

Kwok et al. (2001) developed a much more intelligent system that can answer less-structured and nonroutine questions. This is done via intelligent information retrieval systems, using a technology called *natural language processing.*

For more on intelligent agents in CRM, see Chapter 4 and Online Appendix C. Online File W13.11 provides a summary of some of the applications presented in this chapter, as well as some additional applications.

Section 13.5 ▶ REVIEW QUESTIONS

1. Discuss key customer-facing CRM applications.
2. Describe customer-touching CRM applications, including Web self-service.
3. Describe customer-centric CRM applications.
4. List online networking CRM applications.

13.6 OTHER EC SUPPORT SERVICES

Depending on the magnitude of its EC initiatives, a company may require several other support services.

CONSULTING SERVICES

How does a firm learn how to do something that it has never done before? Many firms, both startups and established companies, are turning to consultants that have established themselves as experts in guiding their clients through the maze of legal, technical, strategic, and operational problems and decisions that must be addressed in order to ensure success in this new business environment. Some of these firms have established a reputation in one area of expertise, whereas others are generalists. Some consultants even take equity (ownership) positions in the firms they advise. Some consultants will build, test, and deliver a working Web site and may even host it and maintain it for their clients. There are three broad categories of consulting firms.

The first type of consulting firm includes those that provide expertise in the area of EC but not in traditional business. Some of the consultants that provide general EC expertise are Agency.com, Virtusa.com, Sun.com, Inforte, Sapient, Autonomy.com, and WebTrends.

See Online File W13.12 for an overview of the EC consulting services offered by one firm, Sapient.

The second type of consulting firm is a traditional consulting company that maintains divisions that focus on EC. These include the so-called Big Four U.S. accounting firms and the large established U.S. national consulting firms. These firms leverage their existing relationships with their corporate clients and offer EC value-added services. Representative companies are Accenture, Computer Service Corp., Cambridge Technology Partners, Boston Consulting Group, Booz-Allen & Hamilton, Deloitte & Touche, Ernst and Young, EDS, KPMG, McKinsey, and PricewaterhouseCoopers. Also, most large technology companies have extensive management-oriented consulting services (e.g., IBM, Microsoft, Sun Microsystems, Oracle, SAP, and Intel).

EXHIBIT 13.10 Other B2B Services

Category	Description	Examples
Marketplace concentrator (aggregator)	Aggregates information about products and services from multiple providers at one central point. Purchasers can search, compare, shop, and sometimes complete the sales transaction.	InternetMall, DealerNet, Insweb.com, Industrial Marketplace
Information brokers (infomediaries)	Provide product, pricing, and availability information. Some facilitate transactions, but their main value is the information they provide.	PartNet, Travelocity, Auto-by-Tel
Transaction brokers	Buyers can view rates and terms, but the primary business activity is to complete the transaction.	E*TRADE, Ameritrade
Digital product delivery	Sells and delivers software, multimedia, and other digital products over the Internet.	Regards.com, PhotoDisc, SonicNet
Content provider	Creates revenue by providing content. The customer may pay to access the content, or revenue may be generated by selling advertising space or by having advertisers pay for placement in an organized listing in a searchable database.	*Wall Street Journal* Interactive, Tripod
Online service provider	Provides service and support for hardware and software users.	CyberMedia, TuneUp.com
Specialized directories	Provide leads to a variety of B2B services categories.	Business.com Knowledgestorm.com Searchedu.com

Client Matching. TechRepublic (techrepublic.com) matches business clients with firms that provide a wide variety of IT services. It works like a matchmaking service. Clients define what they want, and TechRepublic performs the searching and screening, checking against some general parameters and criteria. This reduces the risk of clients' making bad choices. Buyers also save time and have greater exposure to a larger number of IT service providers.

E-Business Rating Sites. A number of services are available for businesses to research rankings of potential partners and suppliers. Bizrate.com, forrester.com, gomez.com, and consumersearch.com all provide business ratings.

Security and Encryption Sites. VeriSign (verisign.com) provides valuable encryption tools for all types of EC organizations. It provides domain site registration and several security mechanisms.

Web Research Services. A number of Web research providers help companies learn more about technologies, trends, and potential business partners and suppliers. Some of these are WebTrack (webtrack.net), IDC (idc.com), ZDNet (zdnet.com), and Forrester (forrester.com).

Coupon-Generating Sites. A number of vendors help companies generate online coupons. Some of these are Q-pon.com (q-pon.com), CentsOff.com (centsoff.com), and TheFreeSite.com (thefreesite.com).

Exhibit 13.10 presents additional services available for B2B operations.

Section 13.6 ▶ REVIEW QUESTIONS

1. Describe the role of EC consultants and list their major types.
2. Describe the value offered by directory services. Provide three examples of what value they add.
3. Explain why specialized search engines are needed.
4. List some other EC support services.

13.7 OUTSOURCING EC SUPPORT SERVICES

Most companies do not maintain in-house support services. Instead, they outsource many of these services.

WHY OUTSOURCE EC SERVICES?

Historically, early businesses were vertically integrated—they owned or controlled their own sources of materials, manufactured components, performed final assembly, and managed the distribution and sale of their products to consumers. Later, nearly all firms began to contract with other firms to execute various activities along the supply chain, from manufacturing to distribution and sale, in order to concentrate their activities in their *core competency*. This contracting practice is known as *outsourcing*.

When EC emerged, it became obvious that it would be necessary to outsource some of the support services involved in its deployment. The major reasons why many companies prefer to do this include the following:

▶ A desire to concentrate on the core business
▶ The need to have services up and running rapidly
▶ Lack of expertise (experience and resources) for many of the required support services
▶ The inability to have the economy of scale enjoyed by outsourcers, which often results in high costs for in-house options
▶ Inability to keep up with rapidly fluctuating demands if an in-house option is used
▶ The number of required services, which usually are simply too many for one company to handle

To show the importance of outsourcing, we will look at the typical process of developing and managing EC applications (the e-infrastructure), a topic we address in detail in Online Chapter 19. The process includes the following major steps:

1. EC strategy formulation
2. Application design
3. Building (or buying) the systems
4. Hosting, operating, and maintaining the EC site

Each of these steps may include several activities, as shown in Exhibit 13.11. A firm may execute all the activities of this process internally, or it may outsource some or all of them. In addition to design and maintenance of technical systems, many other system design issues and business functions related to using a Web site also must be addressed. For example, a firm doing EC must design and operate its order fulfillment system and outbound logistics (delivery) functions; it must provide dynamic content on the site; and it must also provide services to its customers and partners.

IT OUTSOURCING AND APPLICATION SERVICE PROVIDERS

IT is the most frequently outsourced business activity. Most enterprises engaged in EC practice a very large degree of IT outsourcing. While concentrating on core competencies, they develop strategic alliances with partner firms in order to provide activities such as payment processing, order fulfillment, outbound logistics, Web site hosting, and customer service.

Outside contractors best serve SMEs with few IT staff and smaller budgets. Outside contractors also have proven to be a good choice for large companies wanting to experiment with EC without a great deal of up-front investment. In addition, outsourcing allows them to protect their own internal networks or to rely on experts to establish sites over which they will later assume control. Some of the best-known B2C sites on the Web (e.g., eddiebauer.com and 1800flowers.com) are run by third-party vendors.

Several types of providers offer services for creating and operating electronic storefronts as shown in Online File W13.13.

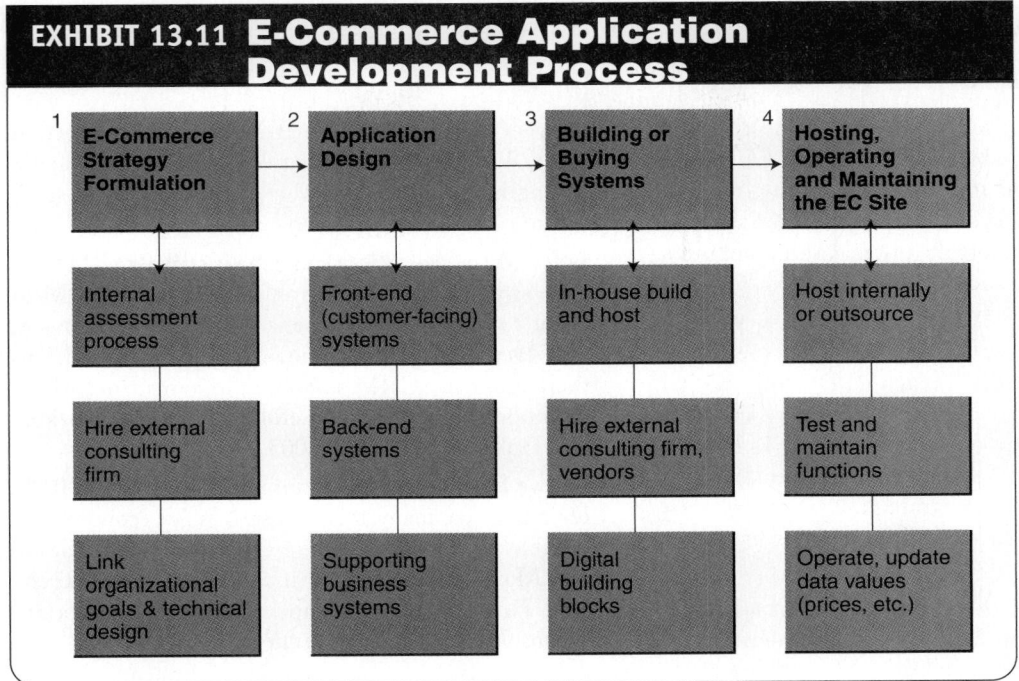

EXHIBIT 13.11 **E-Commerce Application Development Process**

1. **E-Commerce Strategy Formulation**
   - Internal assessment process
   - Hire external consulting firm
   - Link organizational goals & technical design

2. **Application Design**
   - Front-end (customer-facing) systems
   - Back-end systems
   - Supporting business systems

3. **Building or Buying Systems**
   - In-house build and host
   - Hire external consulting firm, vendors
   - Digital building blocks

4. **Hosting, Operating and Maintaining the EC Site**
   - Host internally or outsource
   - Test and maintain functions
   - Operate, update data values (prices, etc.)

One of the most interesting types of EC outsourcing is the use of application service providers. An **application service provider (ASP)** is an agent or vendor who assembles the functions needed by enterprises and packages them with outsourced development, operation, maintenance, and other services (see Online Chapter 19 for details).

On-Demand CRM

Like several other enterprise systems, CRM can be delivered in two models *on-premise* and *on-demand*. The traditional way to deliver such systems was on-premise—meaning users purchased the system and installed it on premise. This was very expensive with a large up-front payment. Many small and medium companies could not justify it, especially because most of the CRM benefits are intangible (Chapter 15).

The solution to the situation, which appears in several similar variations and names, is to lease the software. Initially, this was done by ASPs for SMEs. Later, Salesforce.com pioneered the concept for their several CRM products (including supporting sales people), under the name of *On-Demand CRM*, offering the software over the Internet. The concept of on-demand is known also as utility computing, and it is discussed in detail in Online Chapter 19. **On-demand CRM** is basically CRM *hosted* by an ASP or other vendor on the vendor's premise; in contrast to the traditional practice of buying the software and using it *on-premise*. According to Overby (2006), the hype surrounding hosted, on-demand CRM must be weighted against the following implementation problems: Many ASPs went belly-up, leaving customers without service. It is difficult, or even impossible to modify hosted software. Upgrading could have become a problem, and relinquishing strategic data to a hosting vendor could become a risk. Finally, integration with existing software may be difficult.

The benefits are: improved cash flow due to savings in front-up purchase, no need for corporate software experts, ease of use, fast time-to-market, and use of vendors' expertise.

application service provider (ASP)
An agent or vendor who assembles the functions needed by enterprises and packages them with outsourced development, operation, maintenance, and other services.

on-demand CRM
CRM *hosted* by an ASP or other vendor on the vendor's premise; in contrast to the traditional practice of buying the software and using it *on-premise*.

Section 13.7 ▶ REVIEW QUESTIONS

1. List the major reasons why companies outsource EC support services.
2. Which types of services are outsourced the most?
3. Define *ASPs*.

MANAGERIAL ISSUES

Some managerial issues related to this chapter are as follows.

1. **Have we planned for order fulfillment?** Order fulfillment is a critical task, especially for virtual EC vendors. Even for brick-and-mortar retailers with physical warehouses, delivery to customers' doors is not always easy. The problem is not just the physical shipment but also the efficient execution of the entire order fulfillment process, which may be complex along a long supply chain.

2. **How should we handle returns?** Dealing with returns can be a complex issue. A company should estimate its percentage of returns and design and plan a process for receiving and handling them. Some companies completely separate the logistics of returns from that of order fulfillment and outsource its execution.

3. **Do we want alliances in order fulfillment?** Partnerships and alliances can improve logistics and alleviate supply chain problems. Many possibilities and models exist. Some are along the supply chain, whereas others are not related to it.

4. **What EC logistics applications would be useful?** One should think not only about how to create logistical systems for EC, but how to use EC applications to improve the supply chain.

5. **How is our response time?** Acceptable standards or metrics for response in customer service must be set. For example, customers want acknowledgment of their query within 24 hours. Many companies seek to provide this response time and do so at a minimum cost.

6. **How do we measure and improve customer service?** The Internet provides an excellent platform for delivery of superb customer service via a variety of tools. The problem is that the returns are mostly intangible and may only be realized in the distant future.

7. **Is CRM for real? How can it be justified?** CRM is a necessity; most companies must have some CRM in order to survive. The issue is how much to provide. However, it is difficult to financially justify CRM, and there are many CRM software programs from which to choose. Therefore, a careful analysis must be done (see Holland and Arbell, 2005, and Chapter 15).

8. **Do we have to use electronically supported CRM?** For a large company, it is a must. It is not economically feasible to provide effective CRM otherwise. Some eCRM programs, such as e-mail response, are inexpensive. However, large computerized call centers are expensive to install and operate.

9. **EC consultants are expensive. Should we use them?** It depends. If the company lacks expertise or time, consultants may be the best solution. However, first consider using publicly available information on the Internet. Some publicly available information is quite valuable.

10. **Should we outsource EC services?** Outsourcing is a viable option that must be considered. Even large IT companies outsource. Again, if a company lacks time or expertise, selective outsourcing may be the best course of action.

11. **Can we integrate CRM?** The ability to integrate CRM with existence technology is a CSF for e-CRM analytics (van Dyke, et al., 2006, and Moore et al., 2006).

RESEARCH TOPICS

Here are some suggested topics related to this chapter. For details, references, and additional topics, refer to the Online Appendix A "Current EC Research."

1. **Order Fulfillment and Logistics**
   - Optimal delivery strategy and routing in the demand chain environment
   - The performance of third-party logistics with regard to the geographic topology between suppliers and buyers
   - Business models of logistic partnerships and their performance
   - Delivery time reduction by using a third-party deliverer's hub warehouse
   - Comparative country and industry studies of culture and power related to bearing the delivery cost and its influence in delivery cost reduction (e.g., United States, Japan, Korea, and China)

> Consumer behavior regarding the charge of delivery cost—independent or included models—and its impact on the diffusion of e-commerce

> Delivery cost comparison of portal sites and application of the XRML approach

2. **Applications of RFID in Logistics**
    > POS management with RFID
    > Optimal dynamic routing control in the RFID environment
    > Cross-docking management with RFID in an in-demand chain situation
    > Process monitoring and control with RFID

3. **Content Management**
    > Standardization efforts and adoption by the big players
    > Reconciliation of multiple perspectives of contents categorization

> Aggregating external content online and organizing it from the user's point of view

4. **CRM**
    > How to justify CRM
    > The business value of complete information for CRM
    > Metrics in CRM
    > Intelligent agents in CRM
    > Integrating CRM with knowledge management
    > CRM implementation issues
    > The value of FAQs as a CRM tool and their validation
    > Natural language processing and autoresponders
    > Data mining and CRM
    > How to improve machine translation

SUMMARY

In this chapter, you learned about the following EC issues as they relate to the learning objectives.

1. **The role of support services in EC.** Support services are essential to the success of EC. They range from order fulfillment to providing customer service. They can be done by the companies or they can be outsourced.

2. **The order fulfillment process.** Large numbers of support services are needed for EC implementation. Most important are payment mechanisms and order fulfillment. On-time delivery of products to customers may be a difficult task, especially in B2C. Fulfilling an order requires several activities ranging from credit and inventory checks to shipments. Most of these activities are part of back-office operations and are related to logistics. The order fulfillment process varies from business to business and also depends on the product. Generally speaking, however, the following steps are recognized: payment verification, inventory checking, shipping arrangement, insurance, production (or assembly), plant services, purchasing, customer contacts, and return of products.

3. **Problems in order fulfillment.** It is difficult to fulfill B2C orders due to uncertainties in demand and potential delays in supply and deliveries. Problems also result from lack of coordination and information sharing among business partners.

4. **Solutions to order fulfillment problems.** Automating order taking (e.g., by using forms over the Internet) and smoothing the supply chain are two ways to solve order fulfillment problems. Several other innovative solutions exist, most of which are supported by software that facilitates correct inventories, coordination along the supply chain, and appropriate planning and decision making.

5. **CRM, its technologies, and EC connection.** CRM is becoming a necessity for doing business, and IT facilitates it. Its major categories are customer-facing applications, customer-touching applications, and customer-centric intelligent applications. Using CRM methods, customers can order online more easily, check their orders and accounts, and communicate and collaborate with the company better.

6. **Implementing customer service online.** Retaining customers by satisfying their needs is the core of customer service. Customer service on the Web is provided by e-mail, on the corporate Web site, at customer interaction (call) centers, by automated responses, in personalized Web pages, by the use of data warehousing and data mining, by online networking, and by intelligent agents. Online customer service is media rich, effective, and usually less expensive than off-line services.

7. **Other support services.** EC support services include consulting services, directory services, infrastructure providers, and many more. One cannot practice EC without some of them. These support services need to be coordinated and integrated. Some of them can be done in-house; others must be outsourced.

8. **Outsourcing EC services.** Selective outsourcing of EC services usually is a must. Lack of time and expertise forces companies to outsource, despite the risks of doing so. Using ASPs is a viable alternative, but they are neither inexpensive nor risk-free. (See Online Chapter 19.)

KEY TERMS

QUESTIONS FOR DISCUSSION

1. Discuss the problem of reverse logistics in EC. What types of companies may suffer the most?

2. Explain why UPS defines itself as a "technology company with trucks" rather than as a "trucking company with technology."

3. Chart the supply chain portion of returns to a virtual store. Check with an e-tailer to see how it handles returns. Prepare a report based on your findings.

4. Under what situations might the outsourcing of EC services not be desirable?

5. Why does it make sense to use a consultant to develop an e-strategy?

6. UPS and other logistic companies also provide financial services. Discuss the logic behind this.

7. Differentiate order fulfillment in B2C from that of B2B.

8. Discuss the pros and cons of using ASPs.

9. How do the CRM techniques discussed in Section 13.5 add value for the customer and the company?

10. Many question the short-term return on investment of CRM tools. Explain why.

11. How would you convince a CEO to invest in Web self-services? With what issues could the CEO counter your advice?

12. Discuss how CRM can increase the profitability of a business.

13. Discuss when on-demand CRM is more beneficial than CRM (see Patton and Wailgum, 2006, and Overby, 2006).

14. Discuss the benefits of analytical CRM to customers and to the selling company.

15. Compare AutoCart with Kozmo and Webvan. What are the advantages of AutoCart? (See Flight [2005] and other sources.) Will this company fail or not? Why?

16. Discuss the motivation of suppliers to improve the supply chain to customers.

INTERNET EXERCISES

1. The U.S. Postal Service also is in the EC logistics field. Examine its services and tracking systems at **usps.com/shipping**. What are the potential advantages of these systems for EC shippers?

2. Enter **redprairie.com** and find their order fulfillment-related products and services. Prepare a list. Also, review the RFID products that can be used for order fulfillment.

3. Visit **ups.com** and find its recent EC initiatives. Compare them with those of **fedex.com**. Then go to **onlinestore.ups.com** and simulate a purchase. Report your experiences.

4. Visit **freightquote.com** and the sites of one or two other online freight companies. Compare the features offered by these companies for online delivery.

5. Enter **efulfillmentservice.com**. Review the products you find there. How does the company organize the network? How is it related to companies such as FedEx? How does this company make money?

6. Enter **categoric.com** and find information about products that can facilitate order fulfillment. Write a report.

7. Enter **kewill.com**. Find the innovations offered there that facilitate order fulfillment. Compare it with **shipsmo.com**. Write a report.

8. Enter **rikai.com**. Find any Japanese Web site that deals with a topic of your choice and try to get the English translation. Report your results.

9. Enter **b2byellowpages.com** and **a2zofb2b.com**. Compare the information provided on each site. What features do both sites share? How do the sites differ?

10. Visit **b2btoday.com**. Go to the B2B Communities area and identify the major vendors there. Then select three vendors and examine the services they provide to the B2B community. Also enter **sharedinsights.com** and examine the information provided and the usefulness of joining the site.

11. Enter **ahls.com** and find out what services it offers. Comment on the uniqueness of the services.

12. Enter **dell.com** and examine all the available options. What CRM services are provided?

13. Enter **support.dell.com** and examine all the services available. Examine the tracking services Dell provides to its customers. Finally, examine Dell's association with **bizrate.com**. Write a report about customer service at Dell.

14. Enter **oracle.com/siebel** and **rmondemand.com**. Find what it offers in its CRM OnDemand product. Why does Siebel collaborate with IBM's OnDemand program?

15. Review Insights and Additions 13.2 and enter **ups.com** and answer the following questions:
    a. Why would a shipper such as UPS expand to other logistic services?
    b. Why would shippers want to handle payments?
    c. Why does UPS provide software tools to customers?
    d. What B2B services does UPS provide?

16. Enter **rlec.org** and summarize the differences between reverse and forward logistics. Also include returns management.

17. Enter **autocrat.biz** and review the different classifications (options) available. Write a summary report.

TEAM ASSIGNMENTS AND ROLE PLAYING

1. Each team should investigate the order fulfillment process offered at an e-tailer's site, such as **amazon.com**, **staples.com**, or **landsend.com**. Contact the company, if necessary, and examine any related business partnerships. Based on the content of this chapter, prepare a report with suggestions for how the company can improve its order fulfillment process. Each group's findings will be discussed in class. Based on the class's findings, draw some conclusions about how companies can improve order fulfillment.

2. FedEx, UPS, the U.S. Postal Service, DHL, and others are competing in the EC logistics market. Each team should examine one such company and investigate the services it provides. Contact the company, if necessary, and aggregate the team's findings into a report that

will convince classmates or readers that the company in question is the best. (What are its best features? What are its weaknesses?)

3. Each team should select an overnight delivery service company (FedEx, DHL, UPS, U.S. Postal Service, and so on). The team will then identify all the online customer service features offered by the company.

Each team then will try to convince the class that its company provides the best customer service.

4. Each team is assigned a CRM software company (e.g., Siebel, Salesforce, NetSuite, Accpac, or E.piphany). Find the company's leading products and prepare a presentation of their capabilities. All teams should consult Caton (2004).

Real-World Case

HOW CIGNA FULFILLS SERVICE ORDERS AND IMPROVES CRM

The Problem

CIGNA (*cigna.com*) is the fourth-largest insurance company in the United States. Increased competition in the insurance industry contributed to a $500 million net loss for CIGNA in 2002 and a 40 percent decrease in the company's stock price. CIGNA was under other business environment pressure as well.

First, thousands of doctors nationwide who were furious about delays in payment for patient care sued the company, along with other national insurers, such as Aetna and Humana. The doctors accused the insurers of deliberately delaying payments and improperly rejecting claims in order to save money.

Second, CIGNA's sales team, in order to win large employer accounts in an increasingly competitive environment, had promised that CIGNA would implement new EC systems to provide improved customer service. However, the systems had not yet been developed.

Third, CIGNA's management was under pressure to cut costs after posting disappointing earnings. Executives were anxious for the new system's promised cost reductions and productivity gains.

The Solution

CIGNA developed an ambitious plan to consolidate and upgrade its antiquated IT systems, some of which dated back to 1982, to a Web-based EC system. The idea was to have an integrated system for enrollment, eligibility, and claims processing so that customers would receive one bill, medical claims could be processed faster and more efficiently, and customer service representatives would have a single, unified view of customers (called "members").

To accomplish these goals, CIGNA would have had to consolidate its old systems for claims processing and billing and integrate them with new EC applications. CIGNA developed and integrated two systems: one for claims eligibility for use by customers and another for billing. CIGNA's IT group had to build an entire information infrastructure from scratch that

could support the two main systems. To do all this, the IT group had to completely reengineer its legacy back-end systems.

CIGNA hired Cap Gemini Ernst & Young (CGEY) to help implement the change management and business processes involved. CIGNA also worked with CGEY to develop and implement the new EC customer-facing applications that would allow members to enroll, check the status of their claims and benefits, and choose from different health-plan offerings—all online. Those applications also give customer service representatives a single unified view of members' accounts so that when a member called with problems or questions the representatives would have a full history of the member's interactions with the company.

The Results

In January 2002, CIGNA's $1 billion IT overhaul and CRM initiative went live in a big way, with 3.5 million members moved from 15 legacy systems to the two new platforms in a matter of minutes. The migration to the new systems did not go smoothly—there were glitches in customer service.

After six months of hard work, CIGNA succeeded in fixing the problems with the new systems. The company also launched myCIGNA.com, an online portal where CIGNA members can look up their benefits, choose from an array of health plans, check on the status of their claims, retrieve health-related information, and talk to nurses online.

The CRM strategy seems to be paying off. According to Woehr (May 2006), 6 million of CIGNA's 9 million members are now using online services, and of those, 3 million have registered to use the online e-business portals, up from only 50,000 when the first revamped portal was launched in 2002. Moreover, CIGNA's online transactions have increased from 3,000 transactions per month in 2002 to the current 2.5 million transactions per month. Plus, the carrier has saved money by making it easier for users to conduct online transactions on its system.

CIGNA is also using technology to drive consumerism into its distribution channels. Through its broker portal, CIGNA's direct sales force, consultants, and third-party administrators can direct an employer to a benefit plan that fits the organization. The portal also includes CIGNA's Custom Benefit Builder, which gives the employee options to create a customized plan specific to the individual's situation—allowing an employee to select from a standard set of health plans such as a PPO or an HMO—and also lets the employee choose the size of a deductible for the plan.

Sources: Compiled from Bass (2003) and Woehr (2006).

Questions

1. Why is it sometimes necessary to restructure and automate the customer-facing systems and the back-end systems?
2. Identify the CRM activities implemented by CIGNA.
3. How do the CRM activities relate to "order fulfillment" in services? Identify who is placing orders and who fulfills them.
4. How has the system improved the order fulfillment process?
5. Relate the broker portal to CRM.

REFERENCES

Agarwal, A., D. P. Harding, and J. R. Schumacher. "Organizing for CRM." *McKinsey Quarterly, member edition* (August 2004).

Amato-McCoy, D. M. "REI Conquers Mountains of Customer Data." *Stores*, September 2003.

aa.com (accessed January 2007).

Babcock, C. "Five-Star Application Service." *Information Week*, March 22, 2004. **informationweek.com/story/showarticle.jhtml?articleid=18400885** (no longer available online).

Bass, A. "CIGNA's Self-Inflicted Wounds." *CIO Magazine*, March 15, 2003.

Bayles, D. L. *E-Commerce Logistics and Fulfillment*. Upper Saddle River, NJ: Prentice Hall, 2001.

Berry, L. L. "The Old Pillars of New Retailing." *Harvard Business Review* (April 2001).

Blair, J. "Behind Kozmo's Demise." *New York Times*, April 13, 2001.

Blair, J. "Online Delivery Sites Finding that Manhattan Can Be a Hard Place to Make It." *New York Times*, October 2000.

Bohling, T., D. Bowman, S. LaValle, V. Mittal, D. Narayandas, G. Ramani, and R. Varadarajan. "CRM Implementation: Effectiveness Issues and Insights." *Journal of Service Research*, Vol. 9, No. 2 (2006).

Boles, T. "Returned Goods Clog British Roads." *Knight Ridder Tribune Business News*, October 24, 2004.

Bonde, A. "The Big Payoff from Self-Service." *ROI Insider*, November 24, 2004.

Boston Consulting Group. "Winning the Online Consumer: The Challenge of Raised Expectations." 2001. **bcg.com/publications/files/022101_Winning_online_consumer_report_summary.pdf** (accessed April 2007).

Bowman, R. J. "The Greening of the Supply Chain." *Global Logistics and Supply Chain Strategies*, November 2006. **glscs.com/archives/11.06.green.htm?adcode=75** (accessed December 2006).

BroadVision. **broadvision.com** (accessed January 2007).

Caton, M. "Hosted CRM Systems Mature." *eWeek*, May 31, 2004.

Chio, S. Y., et al. *The Economics of Electronic Commerce*. Indianapolis, IN: Macmillan Technical Publishing, 1997.

CIO.com. "The ABCs of CRM." November 2, 2006. **cio.com/research/crm/edit/crmabc.html** (accessed January 2007).

CIO Insight. "A CRM 2004 Survey." *CIO Insight*, August 1, 2004.

Compton, J. "How to…Select a CRM Implementation Partner." *Customer Relationship Management*, Vol. 8, No. 11 (2004).

Council of Supply Chain Management Professionals. cscmp.org (accessed January 2007).

CRMGuru. **crmguru.com** (accessed January 2007).

Croxton, K. L., B. Gendron, T. L. Magnanti. "Models and Methods for Merge-in-Transit Operations." *Transportation Science*, Vol. 37, No. 1 (2003).

D'Agostino, D. "First Responders," *CIO Insight*, February 2006.

D'Agostino, D. "Host in Translation," *CIO Insight*, December 2005.

Diorio, S. *Beyond "e."* New York: McGraw-Hill, 2002.

Dutta, A., and R. Roy. "Managing Customer Service Levels and Sustainable Growth: A Model for Decision Support." Proceedings of the 39th Annual Hawaiian International Conference on Systems Sciences, Kauai, Hawaii, January 4–7, 2006.

Ellis, D. "Seven Ways to Improve Returns Processing." *Multichannelmerchant.com*, January 4, 2006. **multichannelmerchant.com/opsandfulfillment/returns/improve_returns_processing_01042006** (accessed December 2006).

Entrepreneur.com. "Where Do I Find One?" *Entrepreuner.com*, June 1999. **entrepreneur.com/mag/article/0,1539,23036–3–,00.html** (no longer available online).

Farber, D. "UPS Takes Wireless to the Next Level." *ZDNet.com*, April 25, 2003. **techupdate.zdnet.com/techupdate/stories/main/0,14179,2913461,00.html** (accessed January 2007).

Flight, G. "A Speedier Super Store." *Business 2.0*, December 1, 2005. **money.cnn.com/magazines/business2/business2_archive/2005/12/01/8364582/index.htm** (accessed January 2007).

Ganapathy, S., C. Ranganathan, and B. Sankaranaryannan. "Visualization Strategies and Tools for Enhancing CRM." *Communications of the ACM* (November 2004).

Gateau, B., D. Khadraoui, O. Boissier, and E. Dubois. "Contract Model for Agent Mediated Electronic Commerce." *Proceedings of the Third International Joint Conference on Autonomous Agents and Multiagent Systems*, New York, July 19–23, 2004.

Greenberg, P. *CRM at the Speed of Light: Capturing and Keeping Customers in Internet Real Time*, 3rd ed. New York: McGraw-Hill, 2004.

Greenberg, P. "Say Goodbye to CRM as We Once Knew It." Searchcrm.com, January 4, 2006. **searchcrm.techtarget.com/originalContent/0,289142,sid11_gci1155499,00.html** (accessed December 2006).

GTNexus. "The Global Supply Chain." 2003. **gtnexus.com/download.php?doc=brochures/gtnexus_overview.pdf** (accessed January 2007).

Guzman, Y. "FedEx Delivers CRM." SearchCRM.com, April 14, 2004. **searchcrm.techtarget.com/originalcontent/0,289142,sid11_gci958859,00.htm** (no longer available online).

Hagen, P. "Creating the Relationship-Centric Organization: Nonprofit CRM." *Idealware.org*, June 2006. **idealware.org/articles/relationship_centric_org_CRM.php** (accessed December 2006).

Heizer, J., and B. Render. *Operations Management*, 7th ed. Upper Saddle River, NJ: Prentice Hall, 2004.

Hett, S., and S. Davis. "System for Order Allocation Among Warehouses." *Issues in Information Systems*, Vol. 7, No. 2 (2006).

Holland, M., and T. Abrell. "Customer Relationship Management Strategies" (a four-part article), *Technology Evaluation.com*, February 14, 2005. **technology-evaluation.com/login.asp?l=/tec.asp&name=article&article=MI_CR_XMH_02_17_05_1.asp&category=Crm&path=/Research/ResearchHighlights/Crm/2005/02/research_notes/MI_CR_XMH_02_17_05_1.asp** (accessed January 2007).

Holweg, M., and F. Pil. "Successful Build-to-Order Strategies." *MIT Sloan Management Review* (Fall 2001).

IBM. **ibm.com** (accessed January 2007).

IBM. "Micrel Triples Web Site Traffic with IBM Self-Service Module for OmniFind Discovery Edition." June 9, 2006. **ftp.software.ibm.com/common/ssi/rep_sp/6/GC380736/GC380736.PDF** (accessed December 2006).

Infor. "HSBC Mexico." November 1, 2006. **wp.bitpipe.com/resource/org_1161875403_261/InforCRM_HSBC_3wp_edp.pdf?site_cd=bw** (accessed January 2007).

Jagannathan, S., et al. *Internet Commerce Metrics*. Upper Saddle River, NJ: Prentice Hall, 2001.

Kelsall, A. "Matching Customer Service Agents to Your Customers' Needs." *Multichannelmerchant.com*, July 25, 2006. **multichannelmerchant.com/opsandfulfillment/contact_center_advisor/customeragents_need** (accessed December 2006).

Khosrow-Pour, M. (ed.), *Encyclopedia of E-Commerce, E-Government, and Mobile Commerce*, Hershey, PA: Idea Group Reference, 2006.

Kinnard, S. *Marketing with E-Mail*. Gulf Breeze, FL: Maximum Press, 2002.

Knaack, M. "Rolling Warehouse." *Reeves Journal*, Vol. 81, No. 10 (2001).

Kopytoff, V. "Amazon Perfects New Process of Packaging Multiple Orders." *San Francisco Chronicle*, December 21, 2004. **sfgate.com/cgi-bin/article.cgi?file=/chronicle/archive/2004/12/21/BUG01AETCM1.DTL&type=tech** (accessed January 2007).

Kuzeljevich, J. "Targeting Reverse Logistics." *Canadian Transportation Logistics*, Vol. 107, No. 9 (2004).

Kwok, C., O. Etzioni, and D. S. Weld. "Scaling Question Answering to the Web." *ACM Transactions on Information Systems*, Vol. 19, No. 3 (2001).

Lager, M. "Financial Success, Successful Finance Through CRM." *DestinationCRM.com*, September 19, 2006. **destinationcrm.com/articles/default.asp?ArticleID=6352** (accessed January 2007).

LaMonica, M. "Amazon: Utility Computing Power Broker." *CNET News*, November 16, 2006. **news.com.com/Amazon+Utility+computing+powe+broker/2100-7345_3-6135977.html** (accessed December 2006).

Lee, H. L., and S. Whang. "Winning the Last Mile of E-Commerce." *MIT Sloan Management Review* (Summer 2001).

Lohr, S., et al. "The Future in Gear." *PC Magazine*, September 3, 2002.

Maloney, D. "More than Paper Savings." *DC Velocity*, January 2006. **dcvelocity.com/articles/20060101/pdfs/06_01techreview.pdf** (accessed December 2006).

Moore, R. S., M. Warkentin, and M. Moore. "Information Integration for Relationship Management," in Khosrow-Pour (2006).

Multimedia Victoria. "Sundowner Motor Inns." *eCommerce Case Studies*. Victoria Government, Australia, 2004. **mmv.vic.gov.au/uploads/downloads/ICT_Projects/eCommerce/SundownerMotorInns.pdf** (accessed January 2007).

Nemati, R., C. D. Barko, and A. Moosa. "e-CRM Analytics: The Role of Data Integration." *PCAI*, March 2004.

Nisbet, R. A. "Data Mining Tools: Which One Is Best for CRM? Part 3." *DM Review*, March 21, 2006.

Overby, S. "The Truth About On-Demand CRM," *CIO Magazine*, January 15, 2006.

Parks, L. "Schurman Fine Papers Rack Up Labor Savings." *Stores*, February 2004.

Parry, T. "Study: Simpler Online Returns Make Happier Customers." *Multichannelmerchant.com*, January 11, 2006. **multichannelmerchant.com/opsandfulfillment/returns/onlinereturn_customer** (accessed December 2006).

Patricia Seybold Group. *An Executive's Guide to CRM*. Boston, MA: Patricia Seybold Group, 2002. **e-learning.dmst.aueb.gr/mis/Cases/Chemconnect/Case/Training_Files/An_Executive's_Guide_To_CRM.pdf** (accessed January 2007).

Patton, S., and T. Wailgum. "The ABCs of CRM." *CIO Magazine*, November 2, 2006. **cio.com/research/crm/edit/crmabc.html?page=2** (accessed January 2007).

Payne, A. *Handbook of CRM: Achieving Excellence Through Customer Management*, Amsterdam: Elsevier/Butterworth-Heineman, 2005

"Peacocks Case Study." **symbol.com/category.php?filename=cs-27_peacocks.xml** (accessed January 2007).

Petersen, G. S. "Positioning Your CEO in CRM Implementation." November 23, 2006.

Pickering, C. "New Power Centers—FedEx Hub." *Business 2.0*, January 2000.

Plant, R. T. *E-Commerce: Foundation of Strategy*. Upper Saddle River, NJ: Prentice Hall, 2000.

redprairie.com (accessed January 2007).

Reichheld, F. F., and P. Schefter. "E-Loyalty: Your Secret Weapon on the Web." *Harvard Business Review*, Vol. 78, No. 4 (2000).

SAS. **sas.com** (accessed January 2007).

schurman.com (accessed January 2007).

Scott, J., and D. Lee. *Microsoft CRM 3 for Dummies*. New York: For Dummies/Wiley, 2006.

Seybold, P. *Outside Innovation: How Your Customers Will Co-Design Your Company's Future*. Boston, MA: Seybold Group, 2006.

Smith, A. "CRM and Customer Service: Strategic Asset or Corporate Overhead?" *Handbook of Business Strategy*, Vol. 7, No. 1 (2006).

Staffware.com. "Daisy Brand Uses BPM to Improve Agility," **staffware.com/resources/customers/successstory_daisybrand.pdf** (accessed January 2007).

Sterne, J. *Web Metrics: Proven Methods for Measuring Web Site Success*. New York: Wiley, 2002.

sundownermotorinns.com.au. "Sundowner Motels: About Us." 2007. **sundownermotorinns.com.au/Sundowner MotelsAboutUs/sundowner_investor_information.aspx** (accessed January 2007).

Supplychainer.com. "Seven Ways to Immediately Increase Fulfillment Speed." June 22, 2006. **supplychainer.com/50226711/seven_ways_to_immediately_increase_order_fulfillment_speed.php** (accessed December 2006).

Symbol Technologies. "Case Study: Peacocks Distribution Centre." 2005. **symbol.com/category.php?filename=cs-27_peacocks.xml** (accessed January 2007).

symbol.com (accessed January 2007).

Tan, X., D. C. Yen, and X. Fang. "Internet Integrated Customer Relationship Management." *Journal of Computer Information Systems*, Spring 2002.

Tibco.com. "Daisy Brand Uses TIBCO's Solution to Deliver Fresh Services." 2006. **tibco.com/resources/customers/successstory_daisybrand** (accessed January 2007).

Turban, E., et al. *Decision Support and Business Intelligent Systems*, 8th ed. Upper Saddle River, NJ: Prentice Hall, 2007.

UPS. **e-logistics.ups.com** (accessed January 2007).

van Dyke, T. P., H. R. Nemati, and C. D. Barko. "Leveraging Customer Data Integration for Effective E-CRM Analytics," in Khosrow-Pour, (2006).

Violino, B. "Supply Chain Management and E-Commerce." *InternetWeek*, May 4, 2000.

Vitasek, K., and K. Manrodt. "Perfecting the Perfect Order." *Multichannelmerchant.com*, May 10, 2006. **multichannelmerchant.com/opsandfulfillment/advisor/perfect_order** (accessed December 2006).

Voss, C. "Developing an eService Strategy." *Business Strategy Review*, Vol. 11, No. 11 (2000).

Wikipedia. "Order Fulfillment." 2006. **en.wikipedia.org/wiki/Order_fulfillment** (accessed December 2006).

Wisegeek. "What is an Infoscope?" 2006. **wisegeek.com/what-is-an-infoscope.htm** (accessed December 2006).

Woehr, M. "Give 'Em What They Want." *Bank Systems and Technology*, May 3, 2006. **banktech.com/showArticle.jhtml;jsessionid=PQEKUE4S2QLQOQSNDLRCKH0CJUNN2JVN?articleID=187003272** (accessed December 2006).

Yoon, S. "Brand Names Are at the Virtual Mall." *Wall Street Journal Europe*, June 13, 2002.

E-COMMERCE STRATEGY AND GLOBAL EC

Learning Objectives

Upon completion of this chapter, you will be able to:

1. Describe the strategic planning process.

2. Describe the purpose and content of a business plan.

3. Understand how e-commerce impacts the strategic planning process.

4. Understand how to formulate, justify, and prioritize EC applications.

5. Describe strategy implementation and assessment, including the use of metrics.

6. Evaluate the issues involved in global EC.

7. Analyze the impact of EC on small and medium-sized businesses.

Content

The Success of Travelocity E-Strategy

Managerial Issues

Real-World Case: Pierre Lang Expands into Eastern Europe

THE SUCCESS OF TRAVELOCITY E-STRATEGY

The Problem

Travelocity (*travelocity.com*) was the first online travel company (owned by American Airlines and Sabre). Its initial strategy was to concentrate on airline ticketing and some hotel booking and to sell advertisements on its Web site. This business model worked very well initially making the company the leading online travel service. However, this business model became ineffective when the airlines reduced and then eliminated the commission to the travel agents and when competitors entered the market successfully.

Expedia became the market leader, and by 2002 it pulled in nearly five times more revenue than Travelocity. The losses in market share resulted in mounting financial losses.

The Solution

Guided by rigorous study of customer behavior, the company developed new strategy and business and revenue models. Specifically, instead of focusing on airline tickets, Travelocity moved to selling customized packages including more hotel rooms and car rentals. Instead of being a commission-based intermediary, it started to buy blocks of airline tickets and hotel rooms (discounted wholesale) and sold them to individual customers in customized "merchant travel" packages. Another strategy was to create a fast and effective search engine for finding the lowest prices for its customers.

To better understand customer behavior and to set performance standards for its e-strategy, the company used business analysis done by the operations research department of Sabre Holding, Travelocity's parent company.

The study pointed out a need for better customer service. This became a top priority strategy. For example, data mining,

Web mining, and data warehouses execute searches for flight possibilities 30 percent faster and easier. When there are airfare price discounts, customers on the mailing lists receive e-mail alerts.

Improving the performance of the overall system meant setting performance goals for each of the subsystems and then improving them by using several software packages.

Quantitative targets and goals form the basis for the whole system. Once these are set, the planning focuses on how to achieve them. The performance standard was related to a mathematical model of how customers choose between travel options, based on the utility of each option (utility is a function of criteria such as price, departure time, trip time, and airline name). Different customers prioritize the criteria differently, and Travelocity is trying to provide their needs. For example, cost-conscious travelers receive e-mails about price drops of more than 20 percent (from or to favorite destinations). This program, known as "Good Day to Buy," is a major CRM contributor.

The Results

By the first quarter of 2006, revenue grew to almost half of Expedia's (versus 20 percent in 2002), about 300 percent of its performance in 2002. The acquisition of Lastminute.com, a strategic acquisition completed in 2005, contributed to part of this growth.

Using three performance metrics, Travelocity made the following progress.

- *Brand impact index:* The image people have of the company. From sixth place in 2004 to third in 2005.
- *Conversion impact index:* Conversion from browsing sites to shopper. Fifty-five percent improvement, which placed

Travelocity in first place in the industry in 2005 versus second place in 2004.

- *Customer satisfaction from the Web site.* Second place in 2005 versus fourth in 2004. (Only 6 percent said they could not find the lowest fares in 2005 versus 18 percent in 2004.)

Overall, Travelocity is turning itself around from a loser to a winner. It trimmed losses from $100 million in 2003 to 2.8 million in 2005.

Sources: Compiled from Carr (2006) and Gagnon et al. (2002).

WHAT WE CAN LEARN . . .

Proper strategy can help companies survive and excel. For pure play companies, it may be even more important to change strategies quickly. Strategies are based on *performance indexes,* which are used as targets as well as measures of success. Once performance targets are set, including quantitative measures, improvement plans can be initiated; then the strategy can be implemented. Later progress can be assessed. These are the basic steps in EC strategy, which is the main subject of this chapter. The chapter also presents the related topics of global EC and EC in small and medium-sized enterprises (SMEs).

14.1 ORGANIZATIONAL STRATEGY: CONCEPTS AND OVERVIEW

strategy
A broad-based formula for how a business is going to accomplish its mission, what its goals should be, and what plans and policies will be needed to carry out those goals.

An organizational **strategy** is a broad-based formula for how a business is going to accomplish its mission, what its goals should be, and what plans and policies it will need to accomplish these goals. An organization's strategy addresses fundamental questions about the current position of a company and its future directions, such as (Jelassi and Enders 2005):

- What is the long-term direction of our organization?
- What is the overall plan for deploying our organization's resources?
- What trade-offs are necessary? What resources will it need to share?
- What is our unique positioning vis-à-vis competitors?
- How do we achieve sustainable competitive advantage over rivals in order to ensure lasting profitability?

STRATEGY AND THE WEB ENVIRONMENT

Strategy is more than deciding what a company should do next. Strategy also is about making tough decisions about what *not* to do. Strategic positioning is about making decisions about trade-offs, recognizing that a company must abandon or not pursue some products, services, and activities in order to excel at others. How are these trade-offs determined? Not merely with a focus on growth and increases in revenue but also on profitability and increases in shareholder value over the long run. How is this profitability and economic value determined? By establishing a unique *value proposition* and the configuration of a tailored *value chain* that enables a company to offer unique value to its customers. Therefore, strategy has been, and remains, focused on questions about organizational fit, trade-offs, profitability, and value (Porter 2001).

Any contemporary strategy-setting process must include the Internet. Strategy guru Michael Porter (2001) argues that a coherent organizational strategy that includes the Internet is more important than ever before: "Many have argued that the Internet renders strategy obsolete. In reality, the opposite is true . . . it is more important than ever for companies to distinguish themselves through strategy. The winners will be those that view the Internet as a complement to, not a cannibal of, traditional ways of competing" (p. 63).

To illustrate this point, Porter (2001) has identified several ways that the Internet impacts each of the five forces of competitiveness—bargaining power of consumers and suppliers, threats from substitutes and new entrants, and rivalry among existing competitors—that were originally described in one of his seminal works on strategy (Porter 1980). These five forces and associated Internet impacts are shown in Exhibit 2.8 (p. 70). The majority of impacts are negative, reflecting Porter's view that "The great paradox of the Internet is that its very benefits—making information widely available; reducing the difficulty of purchasing, marketing, and distribution; allowing buyers and sellers to find and transact business with one another more easily—also make it more difficult for companies to capture those benefits as profits" (Porter 2001, p. 66).

e-commerce strategy (e-strategy)
The formulation and execution of a vision of how a new or existing company intends to do business electronically.

Exhibit 2.8 (p. 70) is a generalization, and the impact of the Internet on strategic competitiveness and long-term profitability will differ from industry to industry. Accordingly, many businesses are taking a focused look at the impact of the Internet and EC on their future. For these firms, an **e-commerce strategy**, or **e-strategy**, is the formulation and execution of a vision of how a new or existing company intends to do business electronically. (See Wang and Forgionne 2006.) The process of building an e-strategy is explained in detail later in this chapter. First, though, we continue our overview of organizational strategy and IT strategy, of which e-commerce strategy is a component.

strategic information systems planning (SISP)
A process for developing a strategy and plans for aligning information systems (including e-commerce applications) with the business strategies of an organization.

Strategic Information Systems Planning

Strategic information systems planning (SISP) refers to a process for developing a strategy and plans for aligning information systems (including e-commerce applications) with the business strategies of an organization. Researchers have suggested that more extensive SISP

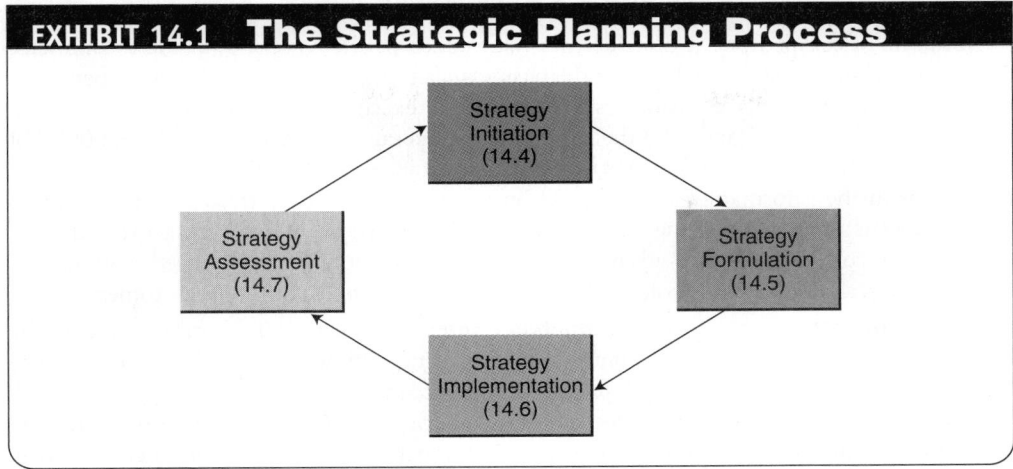

EXHIBIT 14.1   The Strategic Planning Process

in an uncertain environment produces greater planning success. Managers must decide whether, and if so when, to perform such SISP. For further details, see bizplan.com/sisp.html.

THE STRATEGIC PLANNING PROCESS

A strategy is important, but the *process* of developing a strategy maybe is even more important. (See Online File W14.1 on the book's Web site for what some famous people have said about the planning process.) No matter how large or how small the organization, the strategic planning process forces corporate executives, a company's general manager, or a small business owner to assess the current position of the firm, where it should be, and how to get from here to there. The process also involves primary stakeholders, including the board of directors, employees, and strategic partners. This involvement ensures that stakeholders buy into the strategy and reinforces stakeholder commitment to the future of the organization.

Strategy development will differ depending on the type of strategy, the implementation method, the size of the firm, and the approach that is taken. Nevertheless, any strategic planning process has four major phases, as shown in Exhibit 14.1. (Note that the phases in Exhibit 14.1 correspond to section numbers in this chapter.) The major phases of the strategic planning process, and some identifiable activities and outcomes associated with each phase, are discussed briefly in the following text. The phases are then discussed more extensively as part of the e-commerce strategic planning process in Sections 14.4 through 14.7. Note that the process is cyclical and continuous. For a proposed methodology, see Clegg and Tan (2006).

Strategy Initiation

In the **strategy initiation** phase, the organization examines itself and its environment. The principal activities include setting the organization's mission and goals, examining organizational strengths and weaknesses, assessing environmental factors impacting the business, and conducting a competitor analysis. As emphasized throughout this chapter, this includes an examination of the potential contribution that the Internet and other emerging technologies can make to the business.

Specific outcomes from this phase include:

◗ **Company analysis and value proposition.** The company analysis includes the vision, mission, value proposition, goals, capabilities, constraints, strengths, and weaknesses of the company. Questions typically asked in a company analysis are: What business are we really in? Who are our future customers? Do our mission statement and our goals adequately describe our intended future? What opportunities, and threats, do our business and our industry face? One key outcome from this analysis should be a clear statement of the company's **value proposition**—the benefit that a company's products or services provide to a company and its customers. Value proposition is actually a statement that summarizes the

strategy initiation
The initial phase of strategic planning in which the organization examines itself and its environment.

value proposition
The benefit that a company's products or services provide to a company and its customers.

customer segment, competitor target, and the core differentiation of one's product from the offering of competitors. It describes the value added by the company (or the e-commerce projects), and usually is included in the business plan. It is only by knowing what benefits a business is providing to customers that chief-level executives can truly understand "what business they are in" and who their potential competitors are (Clegg and Tan 2006). For example, Amazon.com recognizes that it is not just in the book-selling business but that it also is in the information-about-books business. Amazon.com's strategists know this is where customers find value in shopping at Amazon.com and where a great deal of Amazon.com's competitive advantage lies. So Amazon.com has introduced new services such as "search inside the book" to deliver on that value proposition to its customers.

- **Core competencies.** A core competency refers to the unique combination of the resources and experiences of a particular firm. It takes time to build these core competencies, and they can be difficult to imitate. For example, Google's core competency is its expertise in information search technology, and eBay's core competency is in conducting online auctions. A company is using its core competency to deliver a product or service. Google's products are adWords and adSense, and Intel produces chips.

- **Forecasts.** Forecasting means identifying business, technological, political, economic, and other relevant trends that are currently affecting the business or that have the potential to do so in the future.

- **Competitor (industry) analysis.** Competitor analysis involves scanning the business environment to collect and interpret relevant information about direct competitors, indirect competitors, and potential competitors. Several methodologies are available to conduct such an analysis, including a strengths, weaknesses, opportunities, and threats (SWOT) analysis and competitor analysis grid.

Strategy Formulation

strategy formulation
The development of strategies to exploit opportunities and manage threats in the business environment in light of corporate strengths and weaknesses.

Strategy formulation is the development of strategies to exploit opportunities and manage threats in the business environment in light of corporate strengths and weaknesses. In an EC strategy, the end result is likely to be a list of EC applications or projects to be implemented. Specific activities and outcomes from this phase include:

- **Business opportunities.** If the strategy initiation has been done well, a number of scenarios for future development of the business will be obvious. How well these scenarios fit with the future direction of the company are assessed. Similarly, the first phase may also have identified some current activities that are no longer relevant to the company's future and are candidates for divestiture, outsourcing, or elimination.

- **Cost-benefit analysis.** Each proposed opportunity must be assessed in terms of the potential costs and benefits to the company in light of its mission and goals. These costs and benefits may be financial or nonfinancial, tangible or intangible, or short-term or long-term. More information about conducting a cost-benefit analysis is included in Chapter 15.

- **Risk analysis, assessment, and management.** The risks of each proposed EC initiative (project) must be analyzed and assessed. If a significant risk is evident, then a risk management plan is required. Of particular importance in an EC strategy are business risk factors such as transition risk and partner risk, which are discussed in Section 14.5.

- **Business plan.** Many of the outcomes from these first two phases—goals, competitor analysis, strategic opportunities, risk analysis, and more—come together in a business plan. As described in Section 14.2, every business—large or small, new or old, successful or not—needs a business plan to acquire funding and to ensure that a realistic approach is being taken to implement the business strategy. According to Access eCommerce (2006), a business plan for EC is likely to include these activities: introduction, technology audit, check out the competition, set goals, identify the audience, build a team, create a budget, locate resources, use a Web site planning checklist, try a Web site promotion checklist, send a press release, evaluate the plan, prepare appendices to the plan, and identify related resources. The value proposition part of a business plan includes, these four phases: (1) value definition, (2) value development, (3) value measurement, and (4) value communication (see en.wikipedia.org/wiki/Value_proposition for details).

Strategy Implementation

In this phase, the emphasis shifts from "what do we do?" to "how do we do it?" In the **strategy implementation** phase, detailed, short-term plans are developed for carrying out the projects agreed on in strategy formulation. Specifically, decision makers evaluate options, establish specific milestones, allocate resources, and manage the projects.

Specific activities and outcomes from this phase include:

▶ **Project planning.** Inevitably, strategy implementation is executed through an EC project or a series of projects. Project planning includes setting specific project objectives, creating a project schedule with milestones, and setting measurable performance targets. Normally, a project plan would be set for each project and application.

▶ **Resource allocation.** Organizational resources are those owned, available to, or controlled by a company. They can be human, financial, technological, managerial, or knowledge based. This phase includes business process outsourcing (BPO) consideration and use.

▶ **Project management.** This is the process of making the selected applications and projects a reality—hiring staff; purchasing equipment; licensing, purchasing, or writing software; contracting vendors; and so on.

strategy implementation
The development of detailed, short-term plans for carrying out the projects agreed on in strategy formulation.

Strategy Assessment

Just as soon as implementation is complete, assessment begins. **Strategy assessment** is the continuous evaluation of progress toward the organization's strategic goals, resulting in corrective action and, if necessary, strategy reformulation. In strategy assessment, specific measures called *metrics* (discussed in Section 14.7) assess the progress of the strategy. In some cases, data gathered in the first phase can be used as baseline data to assess the strategy's effectiveness. If not, this information will have to be gathered. For large EC projects, business performance management tools can be employed (see hyperion.com).

What happens with the results from strategy assessment? As shown in Exhibit 14.1 the strategic planning process starts over again, immediately. Note that a cyclical approach is required—a strategic planning process that requires constant reassessment of today's strategy while preparing a new strategy for tomorrow.

A major organizational restructuring and transformation was the reason for the development of a new strategic plan for InternetNZ, as Case 14.1 describes.

strategy assessment
The continuous evaluation of progress toward the organization's strategic goals, resulting in corrective action and, if necessary, strategy reformulation.

STRATEGIC PLANNING TOOLS

Strategists have devised a number of strategic planning tools and techniques that can be used in strategic planning. Exhibit 14.2 (p. 645) shows a representative list of these tools. This section briefly describes a few of the most popular tools. A strategic management textbook or handbook can provide more information about these and other strategic planning tools.

SWOT analysis
A methodology that surveys external opportunities and threats and relates them to internal strengths and weaknesses.

Representative Strategic Planning Tools

The following are useful tools:

SWOT analysis is a methodology that surveys the opportunities (O) and threats (T) in the external environment and relates them to the organization's internal strengths (S) and weaknesses (W).

A **competitor analysis grid** is a strategic planning tool that highlights points of differentiation between competitors and the target firm. The grid is a table with the company's most significant competitors entered in the columns and the key factors for comparison entered in the rows. Factors might include mission statements, strategic partners, sources of competitive advantage (e.g., cost leadership, global reach), customer relationship strategies, and financial resources. An additional column includes the company's data on each factor so that significant similarities and differences (i.e., points of differentiation) will be obvious. A competitor analysis grid template is available in Online Tutorial T1 (An E-Business Plan Tutorial) on the book's Web site.

competitor analysis grid
A strategic planning tool that highlights points of differentiation between competitors and the target firm.

Scenario planning offers an alternative to traditional planning approaches that rely on straight-line projections of current trends. These approaches fail when low-probability events occur that radically alter current trends. The aim of scenario planning is to generate

scenario planning
A strategic planning methodology that generates plausible alternative futures to help decision makers identify actions that can be taken today to ensure success in the future.

CASE 14.1
EC Application
STRATEGIC PLANNING AT INTERNETNZ

InternetNZ is not only an Internet-based business; its business is the Internet. An incorporated, nonprofit organization, InternetNZ describes itself as "the guardian of the Internet for New Zealand," and its primary business activity is management of the .nz ccTLD (Country Code Top-Level Domain).

After a somewhat turbulent transition from its predecessor organization, the Internet Society of New Zealand, in early 2004 InternetNZ embarked on a comprehensive strategic planning exercise. The result of that exercise, *InternetNZ Strategic Plan: 2004–2007,* is a model of content that should be in every strategic plan.

Environment Analysis. In addition to describing trends that affect the global Internet and the Internet in New Zealand, a PEST analysis lists factors in the political, economic, and social environment that affect the conduct of InternetNZ's business. For example: "No large pro-censorship lobby in NZ" (political), "Increasing dependence on the Internet for information" (social), and "The Internet bridges NZ's geographical disadvantage" (economic).

Vision Statement. Sixteen visionary goals (e.g., "Benefits of the Internet have been extended to all New Zealanders") follow a vision statement for 2007 ("The Internet, open and uncapturable, offering high performance and unfettered access for all").

Mission Statement. "To protect and promote the Internet in New Zealand" captures many of the characteristics—visionary, realistic, easily understood, short and concise—of a good mission statement.

SWOT Analysis. A SWOT analysis lists 13 strengths (e.g., "Committed, involved, clever volunteers," "Has created a best practice model for .nz ccTLD"), 13 weaknesses (e.g., "Perception of InternetNZ as mainly 'geeks' or 'techies,'" "Lack of internal resources to respond to rapidly changing environment"), 14 opportunities (e.g., "A leader in the fight against spam," "Help insure widespread broadband access"), and 11 threats (e.g., "Unnecessary government intervention or regulation," "Low level of membership, hence, providing little funding and vulnerable to take over").

Core Values. Six core values—openness, transparency, ethical behavior, neutrality, supportive, commitment—are identified and described briefly.

Goal Statements. Eight strategies (e.g., management of .nz ccTLD, advocacy and representation to government, promote the Internet, support Internet innovation and technical leadership) are listed. For each strategy, one to eight goals are listed, and it clearly identifies the InternetNZ committee held accountable for achievement of the strategy. The 2004–2007 InternetNZ business plan identifies a goal statement of purpose, projected outcomes, and specific examples for execution of the goal for each goal.

Business Plan. Separate from, but an integral part of the *InternetNZ Strategic Plan: 2004–2007,* is the *InternetNZ Business Plan: 2004–2007*. This document lists, describes, and prioritizes the specific activities that are necessary to achieve the goals, with associated income and expenses, also available in the 2006–2009 plan.

The InternetNZ Council adopted the strategic plan and the business plan at its April 2004 meeting, and both plans are in the process of being implemented.

Finally, Davidson, who was appointed as executive director of the company in 2005 said that the continued fulfillment of InternetNZ's Strategic Plan is his major focus in his new role. This plan outlines steps for InternetNZ's management of the .nz ccTLD advocacy to the government, support for industry best practice and self-regulation, protection and promotion of the Internet, as well as NZ representation globally.

Sources: Compiled from InternetNZ (2004), InternetNZ (2006), and Auckland (2005).

Questions

1. Why would a nonprofit organization, such as InternetNZ, need a strategic plan or a business plan?
2. What is the difference between a vision statement and a mission statement?

several plausible alternative futures, giving decision makers the opportunity to identify actions that can be taken today to ensure success under varying future conditions (see en.wikipedia.org/wiki/Scenario_planning).

The basic method in scenario planning is that a group of analysts generates simulation games for policy makers (see en.wikipedia.org/wiki/Scenario_planning). The games combine projected factors about the future, such as *demographics, geography, military, political,* and *industrial information,* with plausible alternative social, technical, economic, and political (STEP) trends, which are key driving forces.

Scenario planning can include *anticipatory thinking (futures)* elements that are difficult to formalize, such as subjective interpretations of facts, shifts in values, new regulations, or inventions.

EXHIBIT 14.2 Strategic Planning Tools

Tools Used in Strategy Initiation

SWOT analysis	Analyze external opportunities and threats and relate them to internal strengths and weaknesses
Competitor analysis grid	Seek points of differentiation between competitors and the target firm
Strategy canvas	Plot a strategic profile based on competition factors (see Kim and Mauborgne 2002).
PEST analysis	Assess political, environmental, sociocultural, and technological (PEST) factors for their impact on the organization (see Online File W14.2).

Tools Used in Strategy Formulation

Scenario planning	Generate, and prepare for, several plausible alternative futures
Return on investment (ROI)	A quantitative financial measure of costs and benefits
BCG growth-share matrix	Compare projects on potential market growth and market share to determine the best projects to adopt, sell, redesign, or abandon (discussed in Section 14.5).

Tools Used in Strategy Implementation

Project management	A planned effort to accomplish a specific effort of defined scope, resources, and duration (see LeBrosse 2006).
Business process reengineering (BPR)	Redesign an enterprise's processes to accommodate a new application (discussed in Section 14.6 and in Chapter 16).

Tools Used in Strategy Assessment

Balanced scorecard	A tool that measures organizational performance in finance, customer assessment, business processes, and other areas
Web analytics	Tracking Web site visitor behavior to discover interactions between a site's content and design and visitors' activities (discussed in Section 14.7).

Balanced scorecard is a tool that assesses organizational progress toward strategic goals by measuring performance in a number of different areas. Originally proposed by Kaplan and Norton (1996) as an alternative to narrowly focused financial assessments, the balanced scorecard seeks more balance by measuring organizational performance in four areas: finance, customers' assessments, internal business processes, and learning and growth. For more information about the balanced scorecard, see Niven (2005), Chapter 15, and Section 14.6. For additional tools and methodology, see Clegg and Tan (2006).

balanced scorecard
A management tool that assesses organizational progress toward strategic goals by measuring performance in a number of different areas.

Section 14.1 ▶ REVIEW QUESTIONS

1. What is strategy?
2. Describe the strategic planning process.
3. Describe the four phases of strategic planning.
4. Why is a cyclic approach to strategic planning required?
5. Describe four tools that can be used for strategic planning.

14.2 BUSINESS PLANNING IN E-COMMERCE

One almost inevitable outcome of strategy setting is a business plan. A **business plan** is a written document that identifies the company's goals and outlines how the company intends to achieve the goals. Exhibit 14.3 shows a typical, nondetailed outline of a business

business plan
A written document that identifies the company's goals and outlines how the company intends to achieve those goals.

EXHIBIT 14.3   Outline of a Business Plan

Executive Summary: The executive summary is a synopsis of the key points of the entire business plan. Its purpose is to explain the fundamentals of the business in a way that both informs and excites the reader.

Business Description: The business description describes the nature and purpose of the business and includes the firm's mission statement, goals, value proposition, and a description of the products and services it provides. The purpose of the business description is to objectively explain and justify the business idea in a positive and enthusiastic manner.

Operations Plan: The operations section of the business plan describes the inputs, processes, procedures, and activities required to create what products the business will sell or what services it will deliver.

Financial Plan: The financial plan estimates the monetary resources and flows that will be required to carry out the business plan. The financial plan also indicates when and by how much the business intends to be profitable. Finally, the financial statements (e.g., balance sheet, cash-flow statement) tell a lot about the entrepreneur in terms of business commitment and financial wherewithal to make the business a profitable success.

Marketing Plan: The central part of the marketing plan is the market analysis, which defines the firm's target markets and analyzes how the organization will position its products or services to arouse and fulfill the needs of the target markets in order to maximize sales. Other aspects of the marketing plan include pricing strategy, promotion plan, distribution plan, and a demand forecast.

Competitor Analysis: The competitor analysis (a) outlines the competitive strengths and weaknesses of rivals in the industry and (b) reveals the firm's competitive position in the marketspace.

plan. This outline follows the Online Tutorial T1 (An E-Business Plan Tutorial) at the book's Web site, where detailed information about each section of the outline is available.

BUSINESS PLAN FUNDAMENTALS

Business plans are written for a variety of purposes. The customary reason why a business needs a business plan is to acquire funding. Entrepreneurs in start-up companies use business plans to get funding from investors, such as a *venture capitalist* or a bank. An existing company may write a business plan to get funding from a bank, the financial markets, or a prospective business partner.

A second reason to write a business plan is to acquire nonfinancial resources. A prospective landlord, equipment supplier, or ASP may want to see a viable business plan before entering into a contract. Similarly, a business plan can be useful for recruiting senior management. Any person truly capable of leading a medium-sized or large business will want to see an organization's business plan before accepting the position.

Another purpose for writing a business plan is to obtain a realistic approach to the business. The process of writing the plan forces the business owner to think ahead, set achievable goals, seek out and analyze competitors, figure out how to reach target markets, anticipate problems, and compare projected revenue streams against realistic expense statements. As with strategy setting, the process, not the plan itself, increases the likelihood that the business will be a success.

A realistic approach also means that sometimes the most successful outcome of writing a business plan is a decision not to proceed. Researching and writing a plan can reveal the realities of tough competition, a too-small target market, or an income and expense statement that is awash in red ink. Many owners of failed start-ups would have saved considerable time, money, and heartbreak if a proper business plan had been done.

When to do a business plan? The most obvious time is when a new business is seeking start-up funds and other resources. However, a business plan may also be required if an existing company is planning to create a separate division, reengineer or restructure the existing company, or launch the company in a new direction. A plan also is required when the existing plan is reaching its use-by date. If the original plan set forth a three-year plan and the business just celebrated its second birthday, it is time to write a new plan.

Several software packages are available for the creation of business plans (e.g., see bplans.com and planware.org). Insights and Additions 14.1 highlights the differences between a traditional business plan and an e-business plan.

BUSINESS CASE

A distinctive type of business plan is the *business case*. As described in the previous section, a business plan often is used when launching a new business. A **business case** is a business plan for a new initiative or large, new project *inside an existing organization*. Its purpose is the same as with a business plan—to justify a specific investment of funds—but the audience is the company's board of directors and senior management, not an external funding agency. The business case helps clarify how the organization will use its resources by identifying the strategic justification ("Where are we going?"), technical justification ("How will we get there?"), operational justification ("When will we get there?"), and financial justification ("Why will we win?") (Dell Public 2005). Examples of EC initiatives that may require a business case include the launch or major revision of a Web site, implementation of an e-procurement project, or deploying a CRM system.

As a special case of a business plan, the content of a business case is similar to that of a business plan. One difference is that the business plan concentrates on the viability of

business case
A business plan for a new initiative or large, new project inside an existing organization.

Insights and Additions 14.1 Putting the "E" in E-Business Planning

How is an e-business plan different from any other business plan? First, it must be said that there are far more similarities than differences. A business is a business and a plan is a plan, so most of what one would expect to see in a business plan also will be in an e-business plan. Beyond adding an *e* to the title, what are some of the differences that make writing an e-business plan different from writing a business plan?

▶ The Internet is unlike any other sales channel (Walsh 2004). The Internet allows companies to distribute information at the speed of light and at almost zero cost, reach out to customers with both reach and range, introduce new and innovative business models, and reduce costs and generate savings. There are many, many more differences, as discussed elsewhere in this book. On the other hand, the Internet also creates more bargaining power for the customer, creates a more perfect information market to the customer's benefit, and makes it easier for competitors to invade a company's marketplace, as also discussed in this textbook. So the first, and biggest, difference in e-business planning is the need for the entrepreneur to recognize the different and unique capabilities of the Internet and to begin to think differently, and creatively, about the opportunities and problems the Internet presents.

▶ The Internet is global. Being on the Web means a business will be visible to an international audience. This introduces complexity for payment options (e.g., show prices in U.S.

dollars or local currency?), distribution channels, Web site design, and the logistics of product returns.

▶ Web storefronts never close. Being on the Web means a store will be open 24/7. The e-business plan must account for this difference in Web hosting and customer service requirements.

▶ E-commerce is conducted at Internet speed. This means Web site deployment must be planned in months, or even weeks, not years. Companies will lose first-mover advantage if they are unable to move at Internet speed, and e-business plan readers know that. Also, changes must be done quickly.

▶ The Web allows greater opportunities for personalization of content, one-to-one marketing, and customer self-service. A company must incorporate these into its e-commerce strategy because its serious competitors certainly will.

▶ The Internet facilitates serious customer relationship management. Business has always been about "getting close to the customer," but that was in a world without the potential of personalization, one-on-one marketing, data mining, concurrent reach and range, and customer relationship management. The Internet, and the customer-oriented applications that the Internet makes possible, means that every e-business must totally focus on the customer.

In all these ways, and more, writing a business plan for an e-business is different, new, exciting, and difficult (see Online Tutorial T1).

a company, whereas a business case assesses both viability of the project and the fit of the initiative with the firm's mission and goals. A business case also will almost certainly have more operational detail and a justification that it is the best way for the organization to use its resources to accomplish the desired strategy. The Online Tutorial T1 on the book's Web site highlights other differences between a business plan and a business case.

With a firm foundation of organizational strategy and business planning in place, we now turn our attention to e-commerce strategy.

Section 14.2 ▶ REVIEW QUESTIONS

1. What is a business plan?
2. List three situations that require a business plan.
3. How is an e-business plan different from a traditional business plan?
4. What is a business case? How is it different from a business plan?

14.3 E-COMMERCE STRATEGY: CONCEPTS AND OVERVIEW

What is the role of the Internet in organizational strategy? According to Ward and Peppard (2002), strategy setting begins with the business strategy—determining an organization's vision, mission statement, and overall goals (see Exhibit 14.4). Then the information systems (IS) strategy is set, primarily by determining *what* information and associated information systems are required to carry out the business strategy. The information and communications technology (ICT) strategy is decided based on *how* to deliver the information and information systems via technology. The EC strategy is a derivative of both the IS strategy and the ICT strategy. The solid downward pointing arrows in Exhibit 14.4 depict the top-down portion of the process. The broken line indicates possible bottom-up activities, which means that lower-level strategies cause adjustments in higher-level strategies (see Joyce and Winch 2005).

The Internet impacts all levels of organizational strategy setting, as shown by the shaded boxes in Exhibit 14.4. Business strategists need to consider the Internet's role in creating or innovating products, in product and service delivery, in supplier and customer relationships, and its impact on competition in the marketplace. Generally, strategic planners need to view

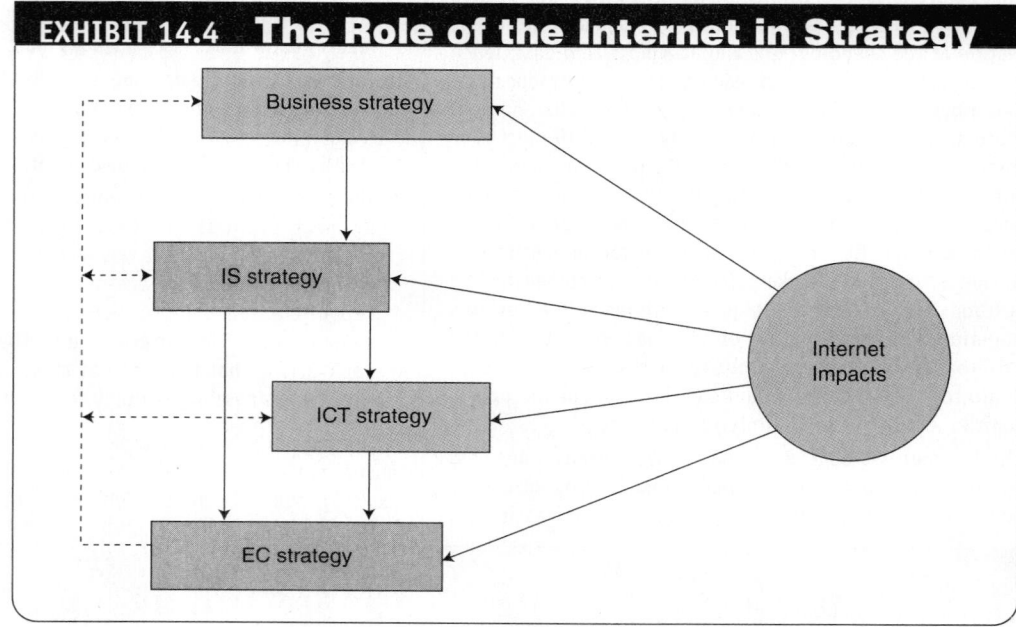

EXHIBIT 14.4 The Role of the Internet in Strategy

the Internet as a complement to traditional ways of competing, not as a source of competitive advantage in and of itself (Porter 2001). IS strategists need to consider the Internet as a tool for collecting information and distributing it to where it is required. ICT planners will need to plan the integration of the Internet-based technologies into the existing ICT infrastructure. Thinking about and planning for the Internet should be subsumed into each of the four strategy levels (McKay and Marshall 2004).

Using the above process, businesses continue to evolve their own e-commerce strategies, defined as the formulation and execution of a vision of how a new or existing company intends to do business electronically. The following sections explain in detail the process of building an e-strategy.

Section 14.3 ▶ REVIEW QUESTIONS

1. Describe the process of deriving an EC strategy.
2. Describe the role of the Internet in setting EC strategy.
3. How should business strategic planners consider the Internet and EC? IS strategists? ICT planners?

14.4 E-STRATEGY INITIATION

In the *strategy initiation* phase, the organization prepares the initial steps needed for starting the cycle, such as collecting information about itself, its competitors, and its environment. Information that describes the contribution that EC can make to the business is of special importance here. The steps in strategy initiation are to review the organization's vision and mission; to analyze its industry, company, and competitive position; and to consider various initiation issues.

ISSUES IN E-STRATEGY INITIATION

With company, competitor, and trend data in hand, the company faces a number of questions about its approach to and operation of its EC strategy that need to be explored prior to strategy formulation. These include the following.

Be a First Mover or a Follower?

Is there a real advantage to being the first mover in an industry or market segment? In e-commerce, does "the early bird get the worm?" Or does the old saying about pioneers— "they are the ones with arrows in their backs"—apply to EC? The answers to these questions are far from clear.

The business, IT, and e-commerce worlds all have examples of companies that succeeded with first-mover advantage, companies that failed despite first-mover advantage, and late movers that are now success stories. Generally, the advantages of being first include an opportunity to make a first and lasting impression on customers, to establish strong brand recognition, to lock in strategic partners, and to create switching costs for customers. The risks of being a first mover include the high cost of pioneering EC initiatives, making mistakes, the chance that a second wave of competitors will eliminate a first mover's lead through lower cost and innovation, and the risk that the move will be too early (before the market is ready, e.g., home banking systems in the early 1990s). Although the importance of a speedy market entry cannot be dismissed, some research suggests that over the long run first movers are substantially less profitable than followers (Kalamas et al. 2006).

So what determines whether a first mover succeeds or fails? In their examination of "the first-mover advantage misconception," Rangan and Adner (2001) suggest that the following factors are important determinants of EC marketplace success: (1) the size of the opportunity (i.e., the first-mover company must be big enough for the opportunity, and the opportunity must be big enough for just one company); (2) the nature of the product (i.e., first-mover advantage is easier to maintain in commodity products in which later entrants have a hard time differentiating their product); and (3) whether the company can be the best in the market. Insights and Additions 14.2 emphasizes this last point. Time and time again, a company has lost first-mover advantage because it failed to capitalize on its first-mover position or, more precisely, a late mover offered a better and more innovative product or service. Usually it is *best*-mover advantage, not necessarily first-mover advantage that will determine the market leader.

Born-on-the-Net or Move-to-the-Net?

Another key distinction in EC strategy at the initiation phase is whether the company is a *born-on-the-Net* or a *move-to-the-Net* business (also called *brick-and-click* or *click-and-mortar*). Born-on-the-Net and move-to-the-Net firms both start with substantial assets and liabilities that influence their ability to formulate and execute an e-commerce strategy (see Exhibit 14.5). However, the difference between success and failure is rarely the assets and liabilities on the company's strategy balance sheet but in the company's ability to utilize its strengths effectively. For example, the customer, product, and market knowledge in the move-to-the-Net firm is worthless unless processes and systems are in place to acquire, store, and distribute this knowledge to where it is needed, and innovative management direction is required to

Insights and Additions 14.2 First-Mover and Best-Mover Success Stories

Companies that "got there first" and leveraged their first-mover advantage for success	
eBay	eBay was a first mover into the online auction market. Listening to customers and constantly adding new features and services has kept eBay on top.
Blogger	*Blogger.com* was the first Web site to provide Weblog (blog) hosting services to blog authors; it is still the dominant provider.
Yahoo!	The world's first Internet directory remains the world's most popular Internet directory. Innovations such as MyYahoo! (*my.yahoo.com*), Yahoo! Groups (*groups.yahoo.com*), and Web-page hosting (*geocities.yahoo.com*) have helped Yahoo! morph into a profitable Internet portal.
Apple Computer	Being first with a Windows Desktop, mouse, hard floppy disk, floppyless laptops, and wireless technology has given Apple a frontier-pushing reputation that keeps it in the personal computer operating system market, while others (e.g., IBM's OS/2) have floundered in the face of the Microsoft Windows juggernaut.
Companies that had first-mover advantage but lost the marketplace battle to late movers	
Citibank	The company that invented automatic teller machines (ATMs) has lost the ATM protocol race to Cirrus.
Sony	Being first and having the technically superior Betamax videotape format did not prevent Sony from being beaten by Matsushiata's VHS format.
Chemdex	The original B2B digital exchange closed down when revenue growth slowed, and the owners decided to change to a different business model.
Netscape	The world's first Internet browser company saw its dominance of the browser market diminish as Microsoft bundled Internet Explorer into the Windows operating system.
Companies that were late movers but gained success over first movers by being best movers	
Intel	Intel did not invent the microchip, but its alliance with Microsoft ("Wintel") and its world-best research and development efforts have made Intel the world's leading microchip manufacturer.
America Online	Innovative marketing (e.g., mass distribution of free installation disks) and provision of online information people could use moved AOL to the top of the ISP market, whereas first movers (e.g., CompuServe, Prodigy) failed.
Google	While other search engines battled for supremacy in the "keyword ranking" battleground, Google invented "link popularity" and soared to the top of the search engine market.

EXHIBIT 14.5   An EC Strategy Balance Sheet for Born-on-the-Net and Move-to-the-Net Firms

Assets of the Born-on-the-Net Firm	Liabilities of the Born-on-the-Net Firm
• Executive management tends to be young and entrepreneurial and is willing to take risks and make commitments for the long-term. • Some funding is available to start the project. • The organizational structure is flat and flexible, with wide spans of control, so the organization can respond rapidly to change. • Information systems are new, allowing rapid implementation of fast, Web-based services that customers demand. • The company as a whole is agile, flexible, hungry for success, and looking to topple the market leader from its perch. • An innovative idea(s) exists, possibly patented.	• Executive management tends to be focused on the short-term, looking after satisfactory next quarter results and going IPO rather than the long-term viability of the company. • Product knowledge, logistics channels, and value chain partnerships must be built from scratch. • The lack of a brand, reputation, and physical presence raises issues of quality uncertainty among customers. Assets such as brand and reputation must be built, at considerable cost. • The born-on-the-Net business must be built from scratch, using limited venture capital funds or bank loans. If results, and revenues, do not appear fast, the company will go under. • The initiators frequently lack managerial experience or capabilities; yet, they hold the CEO position.

Assets of the Move-to-the-Net Firm	Liabilities of the Move-to-the-Net Firm
• A customer base and decades of knowledge about customers and their requirements is available. This knowledge base can be mined to anticipate customer needs and demands. • The firm is willing and able to take risk. • The firm has the knowledge and personnel to undertake (or outsource) the project. • Years of experience in the product marketplace are available to the company, which knows what its customers buy, how they buy, and why they buy. • An established brand, a marketplace reputation, and a physical presence gives customers reassurance in terms of trust, long-term viability, and convenience (e.g., for returns). • The initiation of an EC application or project can be funded from existing or redirected resources. A long-term commitment to funding an EC application is possible.	• The customer base on day one is zero, and each new customer must be acquired from an existing firm within a competitive marketplace. Need to spend big money on customer acquisition. • The organizational infrastructure is old and lethargic, with layers of management that make responding to change difficult. • Legacy information systems make implementation of strategic EC applications difficult. • The company as a whole is rigid, satisfied with the established way of doing things and, if it is an industry leader, complacent in its market prominence. • Resistance to change from the existing parts may slow down or even "kill" the move to the Internet.

Sources: Compiled from Plant (2000), pp. 13, 38, 78–79, and from Bergendahl (2002).

recognize its use for competitive advantage in the marketplace. Similarly, whereas the lack of a logistics channel and value chain partnerships is a born-on-the-Net liability, it is frequently easier to build a brand-new Web-based value chain than to change an established one with flawed practices and processes.

Lonely Planet is a move-to-the-Net firm that is using its strengths—a superb reputation, a community of independent travelers, an immense database of maps and travel information—to find new opportunities on the Internet (see Online File W14.3 on the book's Web site). Wal-Mart online is attempting to leverage its physical presence and iconic brand name into a powerful move-to-the-Net strategy, as described in Chapter 3. Sears is trying to do it too, but with less success than Wal-Mart (see Online File W14.4).

Determining Scope

Inevitably, most e-strategy efforts are intended to grow the business. This can be done in a variety of ways, primarily by expanding the firm's appeal to a new set of customers, by increasing the size or scale of the business, or by broadening the scope through a wider range of products and services. Chapter 4 discusses expanding the customer base, and Chapter 15 discusses economies of scale. This section offers a few comments on the proper determination of scope.

When determining scope, the organization considers the number of products or services it sells. The most efficient way to expand an organization's scope is to introduce new products or services into new or existing markets without increasing production facilities or staff. This way revenues and profits grow while production costs increase only slightly. This strategy is usually most effective when the expanded scope is consistent with the firm's existing core competencies and value proposition to its customers. For example, almost all of Google's expanding scope is based on its core competency in search technology (see opening case in Chapter 1).

Expanding scope as an e-strategy usually is less effective when it requires a large investment and when it threatens the existing value proposition. Sears discovered this when it expanded from a retail store into financial services and real estate. Neither strategy was profitable, and Sears eventually withdrew from these markets (see Online File W14.4). In summary, the critical question that businesses contemplating an EC strategy that involves expanding products and services should ask is: What else do our customers want to buy in addition to the products and services we currently offer (Jelassi and Enders 2005)?

Have a Separate Online Company?

Separating a company's online operations into a new company makes sense when: (1) the volume of anticipated e-business is large, (2) a new business model needs to be developed apart from the constraints of current operations, (3) the subsidiary can be created without dependence on current operations and legacy systems, and (4) the online company is given the freedom to form new alliances, attract new talent, set its own prices, and raise additional funding. Barnes & Noble, Halifax in the United Kingdom (online banking), and the ASB Bank in New Zealand (see Online File W14.5) are a few examples of companies that have established separate companies or subsidiaries for online operations. Some of these cancelled the separate online companies later on.

The advantages of creating a separate company include reduction or elimination of internal conflicts; more freedom for the online company's management in pricing, advertising, and other decisions; the ability to create a new brand quickly (see next section); the opportunity to build new, efficient information systems that are not burdened by the legacy systems of the old company; and an influx of outside funding if the market likes the e-business idea and buys the company's stock. The disadvantages of creating an independent division are that it may be very costly, risky, or both; and the new company will not benefit from the expertise and spare capacity in the business functions (marketing, finance, distribution) unless it gets superb collaboration from the parent company.

Creating a separate company is not the only approach that is available to a click-and-mortar firm looking to enhance its EC future. Strategic partnerships (e.g., Rite Aid bought an equity stake in Drugstore.com) and joint ventures (e.g., KB Toys joined forces with BrainPlay.com to create Kbkids.com) can also be used. These options, and other permutations, enable an aspiring click-and-mortar company to strike an effective balance between the freedom and flexibility that come with separation and the marketing leverage and access to organizational knowledge that is inherent with in-house development (Power Home Biz 2006).

Have a Separate Online Brand?

A company faces a similar decision when deciding whether to create a separate brand for its online offerings. Generally, companies with strong, mature, international brands will want to retain and promote those brands online. As noted in the Real World Case on Google in Chapter 1 and Section 18.2, Google has chosen extensions or variations of its strong brand name—Google Desktop, Google Print, GMail, Froogle—in introducing new products and services.

However, existing firms with a weak brand or a brand that does not reflect the intent of the online effort may decide to create a new brand. An analysis from an e-commerce strategic planning effort identified an opportunity to deliver an integrated e-commerce solution in the marketplace (see Case 14.2). To capitalize on this opportunity and retain its reputation, the company created a new division and launched a new brand, Quality Direct, to distinguish this effort within the parent company.

CASE 14.2
EC Application
MEASURING PROFIT ON THE WEB

Axon Computertime (*axon.co.nz*) is an IT solutions company with locations in New Zealand's four largest cities. Axon's goal is "to be New Zealand's most recommended IT Services Company."

In 2002, as part of an examination of the success of its Quality Direct service, Axon issued a white paper that examined business profitability on the Web. Specifically the white paper listed four areas of potential profits from Web activities and metrics that Axon used to assess the impact of the Web on business profit. This EC Application Case provides a real example of a small business that is profiting from its Web-based delivery of services and has collected some quantitative data to demonstrate its EC success.

Metrics were applied in four areas. Each of the four areas are described briefly below, followed by some of the metrics (a partial list) Axon used to assess goal achievement.

Cost Avoidance and Reduction
Web technologies can enhance profitability by reducing or eliminating transaction costs (e.g., product purchase) or interaction costs (e.g., a meeting, a phone call). Cost avoidance and reduction happens through activities such as improved access to information, customer self-help, and error reduction.

The following metrics demonstrated cost avoidance and reduction by Axon:

▶ Selling costs were reduced by 40 percent for each dollar of margin generated.
▶ Call volume to sales support increased at less than 50 percent of the traditional rate.
▶ Warehouse space was reduced by 40 percent, while volume increased by 40 percent.
▶ Obsolete stock write-offs as percentage of revenue were reduced by 93 percent.

Customer Service Enhancements
Delivering information to customers on all aspects of their transactions helps make the product or service more visible. Increased visibility generates increased value from a customer's perspective.

The following metrics demonstrated customer service enhancements by Axon:

▶ Average days to delivery were reduced by 20 percent over 2 years.
▶ Satisfaction with the delivery process is consistently greater than 80 percent.

New Market Opportunities
New market opportunities include new services to existing clients, changing the value proposition for existing clients, and targeting new markets.

The following metrics demonstrated new market opportunities by Axon:

▶ Product revenue increased over 40 percent in the first 12 months of full operation.
▶ New customers were added at twice the rate that previously was being achieved.

New Media Options
"New media" includes improved communication, advertising, and marketing efforts through lower collateral costs, improved target marketing, subscriber lists, and sold advertising space.

The following metrics demonstrated the use of new media options by Axon:

▶ Cost per item for e-mail is less than 1 percent of the cost per item for postal mail.
▶ Response rate to e-mail is five times the response rate to postal mail.
▶ Expenditures on brochure design and production were reduced by 45 percent.

IT Best Investment Opportunities for 2005 and Beyond
The following are areas related to e-commerce:

▶ Application management and access to applications
▶ Desktop and server management
▶ Information collaboration
▶ Mobile and convergence technologies
▶ Server and storage consolidation
▶ Service optimization

Sources: Compiled from Green (2002) and from *axon.co.nz* (accessed January 2007).

Questions

1. List four areas in which Axon is demonstrating increased profitability through the use of the Web.
2. Describe the characteristics of the metrics listed here (e.g., financial, customer service, quantitative, time based).
3. What other metrics might apply? (Hint: Consult Chapter 15.)

Section 14.4 ▶ REVIEW QUESTIONS

1. Describe the advantages, risks, and success factors that first movers face.
2. What are the advantages and disadvantages of creating a separate online company?
3. Why would an existing company want to create a new brand for its e-commerce initiative?

14.5 E-STRATEGY FORMULATION

The outcome of the strategy initiation phase should be a number of potential EC initiatives that exploit opportunities and manage threats in the business environment in light of corporate strengths and weaknesses. In the strategy formulation phase, the firm must decide which initiatives to implement and in what order. *Strategy formulation* activities include evaluating specific EC opportunities and conducting cost-benefit and risk analyses associated with those opportunities. Specific outcomes include a list of approved EC projects or applications, risk management plans, pricing strategies, and a business plan that will be used in the next phase of strategy implementation.

SELECTING EC OPPORTUNITIES

As with many other business decisions, there are correct approaches to EC strategy selection and incorrect ones. According to Tjan (2001), incorrect approaches include (1) indiscriminately funding many projects and hoping for a few winners (this wastes scare resources); and (2) betting it all in a single, high-stakes initiative; and (3) "trend-surfing," which means following the crowd to the newest and most fashionable idea.

More productive strategy selection approaches can be used when compelling internal or external forces drive the strategy selection process. A *problem-driven strategy* may be best when an organization has a specific problem that an EC application can solve. For example, disposing of excess equipment was the motivation behind the implementation of forward e-auctions at General Motors. A *technology-driven strategy* can occur when a company owns technology that it needs to use. A *market-driven strategy* can occur when a company waits to see what competitors in the industry do. As noted earlier, this late-mover strategy can be effective if the company can use its brand, technology, superior customer service, or innovative products and strategies to overcome any lost first-mover advantage (e.g., Wal-Mart online).

Consulting company PricewaterhouseCoopers (PWC) has developed, with Carnegie Mellon University, an *e-business maturity model* (known by the acronym emm@). The model evaluates online initiatives within the context of established business criteria. Described as both a diagnostic and a prescriptive tool for assessing a company's e-business capability, the model helps companies think of what's necessary to implement an e-business.

Most times, however, a systematic methodology that determines which initiatives to pursue and when best serves businesses. The next section describes such an approach.

DETERMINING AN APPROPRIATE EC APPLICATION PORTFOLIO MIX

For years, companies have tried to find the most appropriate portfolio (group) of projects among which an organization should share its limited resources. The classic portfolio strategy attempts to balance investments with different characteristics. For example, the company would combine long-term speculative investments in new, potentially high-growth businesses with short-term investments in existing, profit-making businesses.

The BCG Model

One well-known framework of this strategy is the Boston Consulting Group's (BCG) *growth-share matrix* with its star, cash cow, wild card, and dog opportunities.

In the 1970s, the BCG created the popular "growth-share" matrix to assist corporations in deciding how to allocate cash among their business units and projects. The matrix has two dimensions: "Market growth rate," which can be low or high, and relative "market share," which

EXHIBIT 14.6 The Internet Portfolio Map

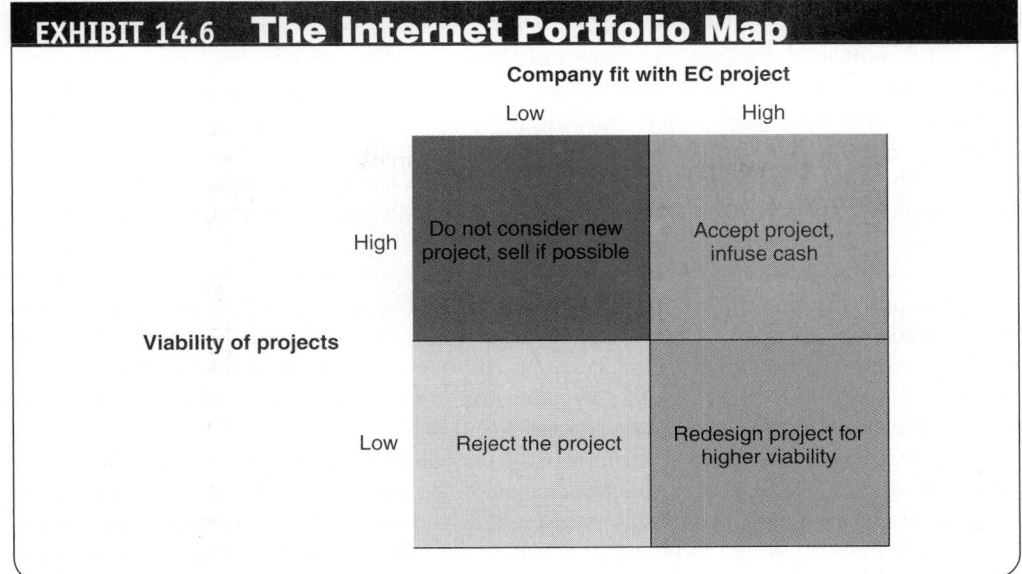

Sources: Compiled from Tjan, A. K. "Finally, a Way to Put Your Internet Portfolio in Order." *Harvard Business Review* (February 2001); Sons, J. "Resolving the Complexity Dilemma in E-Commerce Firms through Objective Organization." *Logistics Information Management* (January 2001); and authors' experience.

can be low or high. This results in four cells: *stars* (high growth, high share), *cash cows* (high share, low growth), *question marks* (high growth, low share), and *dogs* (low growth, low share). The corporation would then categorize its business units (or projects) as stars, cash cows, question marks, and dogs, and allocate budgets accordingly, moving money from cash cows to stars and to question marks that had higher market growth rates, and hence higher upside potential (see en.wikipedia.org/wiki/Boston_Consulting_Group#BCG_growth-share_matrix for details.)

An Internet Portfolio Map for Selecting Applications

Tjan (2001) adapted the BCG approach to create what he calls an "Internet portfolio map." Instead of evaluating market potential and market share, the Internet portfolio map is based on *company fit* and *project viability*, both of which can be either low or high. Various criteria such as market value potential, time to positive cash flow, time to implementation, and funding requirements can assess *viability*. Similarly, metrics such as alignment with core capabilities, alignment with other company initiatives, fit with organizational structure, and ease of technical implementation can evaluate *fit*. Together, these create an *Internet portfolio map* (see Exhibit 14.6).

Each company will want to determine for itself the criteria used to assess viability and fit. Senior managers and outside experts evaluate each proposed EC initiative (e.g., a B2B procurement site, a B2C store, an enterprise portal) on each of these criteria, typically on a quantitative (e.g., 1 to 100) or qualitative (e.g., high, medium, low) scale. If some criteria are more important than others, these can be weighted appropriately. The scores are combined, and average fit and viability scores are calculated for each initiative. Initiatives in which there is high agreement on rankings can be considered with more confidence.

The various initiatives are then mapped onto the Internet portfolio map. If both viability and fit are low, the project is *rejected*. If both are high, the project is *adopted*. If fit is high but viability is low, the project is *redesigned* (to get higher viability). Finally, if the fit is low but the viability is high, the project is not adopted, or *sold*. (An example of this process is shown in Online File W14.6 on the book's Web site.) Senior management must also consider factors such as cost-benefit (discussed in Chapter 15) and risk (discussed next) in making the final decision about what initiatives get funded and in what order. However, the Internet portfolio map can be an invaluable guide for navigating an e-commerce strategy through uncharted waters.

RISK ANALYSIS AND MANAGEMENT

Risk is inherent in all business activities and especially when organizations are moving into new territory, as an e-commerce strategy inevitably implies. Managing that risk is a process of analyzing the risk factors and then taking the steps necessary to reduce the threat to the business from that risk. **E-commerce (EC) risk** is the likelihood that a negative outcome will occur in the course of developing and operating an e-commerce initiative. Risk on the Internet and in EC environments has special characteristics (Muncaster 2006), one of which is Internet security threats and vulnerabilities.

e-commerce (EC) risk
The likelihood that a negative outcome will occur in the course of developing and operating an electronic commerce strategy.

Mention e-commerce risk and most business professionals think of information security—the threat posed by hackers and negligent loss of data. This is the most obvious, but not the most threatening, aspect of EC risk. *The most dangerous risk to a company engaged in e-commerce is business risk*—the possibility that developing and operating an e-commerce strategy could negatively impact the well-being of the organization itself. Chapter 11 focuses on information security; the emphasis here is on business risk.

The first step in any risk assessment is risk analysis—identifying and evaluating the sources of risk. Deise et al. (2000), for example, list 15 sources of e-business risk: dependence on partners, competitive environment, operations, human resources, legal and regulatory, reputation, strategic direction, technology, security, culture, project management, governance, business process controls, tax, and currency (i.e., *company risks* How can an organization manage customer relations in an online world that is different from the traditional marketplace?); and *business partner risk* (i.e., How can organizations manage increasing dependence on business partnerships?).

Once sources of risk have been identified, the next step is risk assessment, namely to assess the potential damage. If it is large enough, we move to *risk management*—to put in place a plan that reduces the threat posed by the risk. Risk management involves taking steps to reduce the probability that the threat will occur, minimizing the consequences if it occurs anyway, or both. Many risk management strategies in the off-line world of business apply to e-commerce risk management. For example, commonly used control systems can mitigate risk factors in e-commerce sourcing (Saeed and Leitch 2003). In other risk areas, new and innovative risk management strategies are necessary. For example, putting trust-generating policies and procedures in place can minimize customer-induced risk.

Various methods can be used to conduct risk assessment (e.g., see Wheelen and Hunger 2003). A number of sources offer specific advice about analyzing and managing e-commerce risk (e.g., Minsky 2006 and Suh and Han 2003).

Security Issues

According to Tennant Risk Services (2004), the following security issues need to be addressed in an EC strategy:

- Fraudulent and malicious acts committed by either employees or third parties against the insured's computer systems
- Computer virus attacks that hinder or even close down the operations of the insured
- Accidental alteration or destruction to electronic information and records
- Loss of intellectual property when trade secrets are copied or recorded
- Extortion
- Business interruption and extra expense caused by a computer virus or other malicious acts
- Accidental or malicious destruction of electronic information
- Costs to mitigate a covered loss
- Multimedia liability such as libel, slander, invasion of privacy, infringement of copyright, plagiarism, and false advertising
- Liability for damage to a third party's computer system

ISSUES IN STRATEGY FORMULATION

A variety of issues exist in strategy formulation, depending on the company, industry, nature of the applications, and so forth. This section discusses some representative issues.

How to Handle Channel Conflict

As discussed in Chapters 2 and 3, channel conflict may arise when an existing company creates an additional distribution channel online. Several options exist for handling channel conflict. These include the following:

- Let the established distributors handle e-business fulfillment, as the auto industry is doing. Buyers can order online, or they can provide directions to distributors online.

- Provide online services to intermediaries (e.g., by building portals for them) and encourage them to reintermediate themselves in other ways.

- Sell some products only online, such as LEGO (lego.com) is doing. Other products may be advertised online but sold exclusively off-line.

- Avoid channel conflict entirely by not selling online. In such a case, a company could still have an EC presence by offering promotion and customer service online, as BMW (bmw.com) is doing.

How to Handle Conflict Between the Off-Line and Online Businesses

In a click-and-mortar business, the allocation of resources between off-line and online activities can create difficulties. Especially in sell-side projects, the two activities can be viewed as competitors. In this case, personnel in charge of off-line and online activities may behave as competitors. This conflict may cause problems when the off-line side needs to handle the logistics of the online side or when prices need to be determined. As noted in Online File W14.4, Sears lessened this conflict by offering a sales commission to its retail stores on all online sales based on the zip code of the online customers.

Corporate culture, the ability of top management to introduce change properly, and the use of innovative processes that support collaboration will all determine the degree of collaboration between off-line and online activities in a business. Clear support by top management for both the off-line and online operations and a clear strategy of "what and how" each unit will operate are essential.

Pricing Strategy

Traditional methods for determining price are the cost-plus and competitor models. *Cost-plus* means adding up all the costs involved—material, labor, rent, overhead, and so forth—and adding a percentage mark-up as profit. The *competitor model* determines price based on what competitors are charging for similar products in the marketplace.

Pricing products and services for online sales changes these pricing strategies in subtle ways:

- **Price comparison is easier.** In traditional markets, either the buyer or, more often, the seller has more information than the other party, and this situation is exploited in determining a product's price. By facilitating price comparison, the Internet helps create what economists call a *perfect market*—one in which both the buyer and the seller have ubiquitous and equal access to information, usually in the buyer's favor. On the Internet, search engines, price comparison sites (e.g., mysimon.com, comparenet.com), infomediaries, and intelligent agents make it easy for customers to find who offers the product at the best price.

- **Buyers sometimes set the price.** Name-your-own-price models such as Priceline.com and auction sites mean that buyers do not necessarily just take the price; sometimes they *make* the price.

- **Online and off-line goods are priced differently.** Pricing strategy may be especially difficult for a click-and-mortar company. Setting prices lower than those offered by the off-line business may lead to internal conflict, whereas setting prices at the same level will hurt competitiveness.

- **Differentiated pricing can be a pricing strategy.** For decades, airline companies have maximized revenues with yield management—charging different prices for the same product. In the B2C EC marketplace, one-on-one marketing can extend yield management from a class of customer (e.g., buying an airline seat early or later) to individual

EXHIBIT 14.7 Three Strategies for Smarter Pricing on the Internet

Pricing Strategy	Source of Value from the Internet	B2C Examples	B2B Examples
Precision: Determine the highest price that has little or no impact on purchase decisions (i.e., price at the top of the zone of price indifference).	Prices can be tested continually in real time, leading to better understanding of the zone of price indifference.	Commodity products, such as toys, books, and CDs.	Maintenance, repair, and operation (MRO) products.
Adaptability: Change prices frequently in response to market conditions, inventory levels, or competitor pricing.	Prices can be changed fast and frequently and in response to Internet-monitored conditions.	Consumer goods with short product life cycles (e.g., electronics); goods with fluctuating demand (e.g., luxury cars).	Perishable goods (e.g., chemicals) or goods with fluctuating demand and availability (e.g., raw materials).
Segmentation: Divide customers into different classes and offer different prices based on customer segments.	Easily identify which segment a buyer belongs to and create barriers between segments.	Products in which customer profitability varies widely (e.g., credit cards, mortgages) or goods purchased in response to special offers (e.g., automobiles).	"Fill-in" customers (purchasing in emergency) will pay more than regular customers (e.g., industrial components, business, consulting fees).

Source: Three Strategies for Smarter Pricing on the Internet from "Price Smarter on the Net" by Baker, et al., *Harvard Business Review,* 2001 ©Copyright 2001. Reprinted by permission.

versioning
Selling the same good, but with different selection and delivery characteristics.

customers. In the B2B EC marketplace, extranets with customized pricing pages present different prices to different customers based on purchasing contracts, the customer's buying history, and other factors. **Versioning**, which is selling the same good but with different selection and delivery characteristics (Bockstedt et al. 2005), is especially effective in selling digitized goods. For example, time-critical information such as stock market prices can be sold at a higher price if delivered in real time rather than with a 20-minute delay. As with all forms of differentiated pricing, versioning information is based on the fact that some buyers are willing to pay more to receive some additional advantage.

The overall impact of these changes is good news for the consumer. Internet technologies tend to provide consumers with easier access to pricing information, which increases their bargaining power. To remain competitive and profitable, sellers will have to adopt smarter pricing strategies. Specifically, businesses will have to look at ways of using the Internet to optimize prices, primarily through greater precision in setting prices, more adaptability in changing prices, and new ways of customer segmentation for differentiated pricing (see Exhibit 14.7).

Examples of E-Strategies

▶ On March 2, 2006, China Southern Airlines announced their plan to improve their in-house e-ticketing system and cooperate with more online travel agencies and meta-search companies (per Zhuhai Flight Training Center 2006).

▶ On October 26, 2006, Nike Inc. created a position of vice president, global e-commerce, reporting directly to the company's president and CEO. The vice president will be responsible for driving an integrated global e-commerce strategy for the Nike brand and Nike Inc. subsidiaries including Converse and Cole Haan. According to a press release (PRNewswire 2006), the e-commerce sites represent an incredible opportunity, a way to build deeper consumer connections and support the overall growth of the Nike Inc. brand portfolio. The vice president will accelerate the company's efforts to create an integrated global e-commerce strategy across the company portfolio and deliver consistent and compelling brand experiences for consumers. Nike has been a leader in creating unique personalized shopping experiences for consumers through innovative sites such as Nike iD, which gives consumers the opportunity to design their own Nike product. Nike also relaunched its global nikestore.com e-commerce site with new leading-edge technology. The changes in the store are designed to introduce deeper product storytelling, faster functionality, and enhanced customer service; they encompass the first major renovation of Nike's online store since its launch in 1999. The result is a new, more dynamic online shopping experience, in which the common conventions of e-commerce are adapted to the unique character of the Nike brand. The site offers more than 30,000 products.

Section 14.5 ▶ REVIEW QUESTIONS

1. Describe how a company should *not* select EC applications.
2. Explain Tjan's Internet portfolio map.
3. List four sources of business risk in EC. What questions exemplify each source of risk?
4. Discuss three strategies for smarter pricing online.
5. How can a company handle channel conflict?

14.6 E-STRATEGY IMPLEMENTATION

The execution of the strategic plan takes place in the *strategy implementation* phase, in which detailed, short-term plans are developed for carrying out the projects agreed on in strategy formulation. Decision makers evaluate options, establish specific milestones, allocate resources, and manage the projects.

Typically, the first step in strategy implementation is to establish a Web team, which then initiates and manages the execution of the plan. As EC implementation continues, the team is likely to introduce changes in the organization. Thus, during the implementation phase, it also becomes necessary to develop an effective change management program, including the possibility of business process management.

In this section, we deal with some of the topics related to this implementation process. Chapter 16 continues the implementation discussion with an overview of many of the practical considerations involved in launching an online business. For more information, see Papazoglou and Ribbers (2006).

Create a Web Team

In creating a Web (project) team, the organization should carefully define the roles and responsibilities of the team leader, team members, Web master, and technical staff. The purpose of the Web team is to align business goals and technology goals, and to implement a sound EC plan with available resources.

Every Web project, and every Web team, also requires a project champion. In his study of EC strategy in 43 companies, Plant (2000) found, "In every successful e-commerce project studied, a strong project champion was present in the form of a senior executive or someone in a position to demonstrate to a senior executive the potential added value such a project could bring to the organization" (pp. 34–35). Similarly, "top management championship" was identified as a critical factor for organizational assimilation of Web technologies (Chatterjee et al. 2002). The **project champion** is the person who ensures that the project gets the time, attention, and resources required and defends the project from detractors at all times. The project champion may be the Web team leader or a senior executive.

project champion
The person who ensures the EC project gets the time, attention, and resources required and defends the project from detractors at all times.

Start with a Pilot Project

Implementing EC often requires significant investments in infrastructure. Therefore, a good way to start is to undertake one or a few small EC pilot projects. Pilot projects help uncover problems early, when the plan can easily be modified before significant investments are made.

General Motors' pilot program (GM BuyPower) is an example of the successful use of a pilot project. On its Web site, gmbuypower.com, shoppers can choose car options, check local dealer inventory, schedule test drives, arrange financing, and get best-price quotes by e-mail or telephone. GM BuyPower started as a pilot project in four western U.S. states before expanding to all states. Similarly, when Home Depot decided to go online in 2000, it started in six stores in Las Vegas, then moved to four other cities in the western United States, and eventually went nationwide.

Allocate Resources

The resources required for EC projects depend on the information requirements and the capabilities of each project. Some resources—software, computers, warehouse capacity, staff—will be new and unique to the EC project. Even more critical for the project's success is effective allocation of infrastructure resources that many applications share, such as databases, the intranet, and possibly an extranet.

Manage the Project

A variety of tools can assist in resource allocation. Project management tools, such as Microsoft Project, assist with determining project tasks, milestones, and resource requirements. Standard system design tools (e.g., data flow diagrams) can help in executing the resource-requirement plan.

STRATEGY IMPLEMENTATION ISSUES

There are many strategy implementation issues, depending on the circumstances. Here we describe some common ones.

Application Development

Implementation of an EC application requires access to the construction of the Web site and integration of the site with the existing corporate information systems (e.g., front end for order taking, back end for order processing). At this point, a number of decisions of whether to build, buy, or outsource various construction aspects of the application implementation process face the company. Some of these decisions include the following:

- Should site development be done internally, externally, or by a combination of internal and external development?
- Should the software application be built or will commercially available software be satisfactory?
- If a commercial package will suit, should it be purchased from the vendor or rented from an ASP? Should it be modified?
- Will the company or an external ISP host the Web site?
- If hosted externally, who will be responsible for monitoring and maintaining the information and system?

Each option has its strengths and weaknesses, and the correct decisions will depend on factors such as the strategic nature of the application, the skills of the company's technology group, and the need to move fast or not. Chapter 16 and especially Online Chapter 19 discuss in more detail many of these options—build or buy, in-house or outsource, host externally or internally.

Partners' Strategy

Another important issue is that many EC application developments involve business partners—ASPs, ERP vendors and consultants, and ISPs—with different organizational cultures and their own EC strategies and profit motives. A key criterion in choosing an EC partner is finding one whose strategy aligns with or complements the company's own.

When negotiating a partnership, the partner's goal is to make a profit, and it is the negotiator's responsibility to make sure that is not being done at the expense of the company's bottom line. One popular EC partner strategy is **outsourcing**, which is the use of an external

outsourcing
The use of an external vendor to provide all or part of the products and services that could be provided internally.

vendor to provide all or part of the products and services that could be provided internally. For example, many firms in the United States have found it advantageous to outsource call center functions offshore.

The bottom line here is that partnerships can be an effective way to develop and implement an EC strategy, but they require a realistic evaluation of the potential risks and rewards.

Business Alliances and Virtual Corporations

At a higher level of cooperation and trust than a regular partnership is a business alliance. Specifically, the EC strategic planning process may identify a strategic opportunity that is larger than the organization itself. It may be a large-scale EC application, an initiative that is too difficult or complex for one company to undertake alone, an idea that works best across the industry rather than within a single firm, or a strategy that requires a variety of competencies to implement. In these cases, an alliance may be formed with other businesses, perhaps even competitors.

One type of business alliance is a B2B e-marketplace. As noted in Online File 14.4, Sears was one of the founding members of GlobalNetXchange (GNX). The purpose of GNX was to reduce procurement costs and product prices for its members while making the purchase process more efficient. Eventually Sears, Carrefour (a global retailer), Kroger (United States), Metro AG (Europe), Coles Myer (Australia), and others joined GNX (Ranganathan et al. 2003). GNX later was expanded under the name Agent Rick (Chapter 6).

Another form of business alliance is a **virtual corporation (VC)**, an organization composed of several business partners sharing costs and resources for the production or utilization of a product or service. A virtual corporation typically includes several companies, each creating a portion of the product or service in an area in which it has a superior core competency (e.g., product development, manufacturing, marketing) or special advantage (e.g., exclusive license, low cost). VCs may be *permanent* (designed to create or assemble a broad range of productive resources on an ongoing basis) or *temporary* (created for a specific purpose and existing for only a short time).

virtual corporation (VC)
An organization composed of several business partners sharing costs and resources for the production or utilization of a product or service.

A particularly interesting type of business alliance is co-opetition. **Co-opetition** is a combination of the words *cooperate* and *competition*. It describes when two or more companies cooperate on some activities for mutual benefit, even while competing against each other in the marketplace. A global airline alliance, such as OneWorld or Star Alliance, is an example of co-opetition. Individually, the airlines compete against each other for passengers. However, when flights can be combined to save costs without compromising customer service, the airlines cooperate through the alliance. The most visible aspect of this is code-share flights, in which passengers who bought tickets from a number of different airlines fly together on the same flight. Through co-opetition, the airlines are reducing inefficiencies in their competing supply chains, and the result is an excellent example of strategic supply chain alignment.

co-opetition
Two or more companies cooperate together on some activities for their mutual benefit, even while competing against each other in the marketplace.

There are several other types of business alliances, such as resource-sharing partnerships, permanent supplier-company relationships, and joint research efforts. Ernest et al. (2001) examined the viability of e-alliances in light of the dot-com failures of 2000–2001. Their conclusion is that e-alliances are more essential now than ever because EC implementation requires a diversity of support services, which a single organization can seldom provide by itself. An e-alliance provides synergy when companies bring complementary contributions.

Working with partners may not be a simple task; partnerships can be risky and difficult to manage. Shenkar and Reuer (2005) and BeeAgile (2007) offer guidelines on how to make strategic alliances work; Xie and Johnston (2004) offer a typology of e-business alliances.

Redesigning Business Processes

An internal issue many firms face at the implementation stage is the need to change business processes to accommodate the changes an EC strategy brings. Sometimes these changes are incremental and can be managed as part of the project implementation process. Sometimes the changes are so dramatic that they affect the manner in which the organization operates. In this instance, BPM is usually necessary.

business process reengineering (BPR)
A methodology for conducting a comprehensive redesign of an enterprise's processes.

Business process reengineering (BPR) is a methodology for conducting a one-time comprehensive redesign of an enterprise's processes. BPR may be needed for the following reasons:

▶ To fix poorly designed processes (e.g., processes are not flexible or scalable)

▶ To change processes so that they will fit commercially available software (e.g., ERP, e-procurement)

▶ To produce a fit between systems and processes of different companies that are partnering in e-commerce (e.g., e-marketplaces, ASPs)

▶ To align procedures and processes with e-services such as logistics, payments, or security

On its way to becoming an e-business, IBM instituted a comprehensive BPR initiative for several of the reasons cited previously. The results were dramatic improvements in IBM's global operations, as described in Online File W14.7.

BPR may be very complex and expensive, especially when it involves many business partners. A major tool used in conjunction with redesign is workflow technology (see Chapter 7). For more on BRP, see Kim and Ramkaran (2004) for details.

Business Process Management

business process management (BPM)
Method for business restructuring that combines workflow systems and redesign methods; covers three process categories—people-to-people, systems-to-systems, and systems-to-people interactions.

The term **business process management (BPM)** refers to activities performed by businesses to improve their processes. While such improvements are hardly new, software tools called business process management systems have made such activities faster and cheaper. BPM systems monitor the execution of the business processes so that managers can analyze and change processes in response to analysis rather than just a hunch. BPM differs from BPR in that it deals not just with one-time change to the organization but long-term consequences and repetitive actions. The activities that constitute business process management can be grouped into three categories: design, execution, and monitoring. For details see en.wikipedia.org/wiki/business_process_management.

Section 14.6 ▶ REVIEW QUESTIONS

1. Describe a Web (project) team and its purpose.
2. What is the role of a project champion?
3. What is the purpose of a pilot project?
4. Discuss the major strategy implementation issues of application development, partners' strategy, business alliances, and BPR.
5. Describe BPM and the need for it in EC development.

14.7 E-STRATEGY AND PROJECT ASSESSMENT

The last phase of e-strategy begins as soon as the implementation of the EC application or project is complete. *Strategy assessment* includes both the continual assessment of EC metrics and the periodic formal evaluation of progress toward the organization's strategic goals. Based on the results, corrective actions are taken and, if necessary, the strategy is reformulated.

THE OBJECTIVES OF ASSESSMENT

Strategic assessment has several objectives. The most important ones are:

▶ Measure the extent to which the EC strategy and ensuing projects are delivering what they were supposed to deliver. If they are not delivering, apply corrective actions to ensure that the projects are able to meet their objectives.

▶ Determine if the EC strategy and projects are still viable in the current environment.

▶ Reassess the initial strategy in order to learn from mistakes and improve future planning.

▶ Identify failing projects as soon as possible and determine why they failed to avoid the same problems on subsequent projects.

Web applications often grow in unexpected ways, expanding beyond their initial plan. For example, Genentec Inc., a biotechnology giant, wanted merely to replace a homegrown bulletin-board system. It started the project with a small budget but soon found that the intranet had grown rapidly and had become very popular in a short span of time, encompassing many applications. Another example is Lockheed Martin, which initially planned to put its corporate phone directory and information about training programs on the intranet. Within a short time, it placed many of its human resources documents on the intranet as well, and soon thereafter, the use of the Web for internal information expanded from administrative purposes to collaborative commerce and PRM applications.

MEASURING RESULTS AND USING METRICS

Each company measures success or failure by a different set of standards. Some companies may find that their goals were unrealistic, that their Web servers were inadequate to handle demand, or that expected cost savings were not realized. Others may experience so much success that they have to respond to numerous application requests from various functional areas in the company.

Assessing EC is difficult because of the many configurations and impact variables involved and the sometimes intangible nature of what is being measured. However, a review of the requirements and design documents should help answer many of the questions raised during the assessment. It is important that the Web team develop a thorough checklist to address both the evaluation of project performance and the assessment of a changing environment. One way to measure a project's performance is to use metrics.

EC Metrics

A **metric** is a specific, measurable standard against which actual performance is compared. Metrics assist managers in assessing progress toward goals, communicating the strategy to the workforce through performance targets (Rayport and Jaworski 2004), and identifying where corrective action is required. Exhibit 15.3 (p. 690) lists a number of tangible and intangible metrics for various EC users, and a number of financial metrics are suggested by Maxwell (2006). An example of a company that has implemented a comprehensive EC metrics approach is Axon Computertime, as shown in Case 14.2 (p. 653).

metric
A specific, measurable standard against which actual performance is compared.

Corporate (Business) Performance Management and Balance Scorecards

Corporate (business) performance management (CPM, BPM) is a closed loop process that links strategy to execution in order to optimize business performance. The major steps of the process are:

1. Setting goals and objectives
2. Establishing initiatives and plans to achieve those goals
3. Monitoring actual performance against the goals and objectives
4. Taking corrective action

corporate (business) performance management (CPM, BPM)
Advanced performance measuring and analysis approach that embraces planning and strategy.

It is a real-time system that alerts managers to potential opportunities, impending problems and threats, and then empowers them to react through models and collaboration.

Strategic planning in CPM includes the following eight steps:

1. Conduct a current situation analysis
2. Determine the planning horizon
3. Conduct an environment scan
4. Identify critical success factors
5. Complete a gap analysis (performance versus goals)
6. Create a strategic vision
7. Develop a business strategy
8. Identify strategic objectives and goals

This provides an answer to the question: "Where do we want to go?" Then the CPM tells us "how to get there." Then we monitor performance, usually using the balanced scorecard. This answers the question "how are we doing?" Finally, by comparing actual performance to the

EXHIBIT 14.8   Blueprint of the Performance Dashboard

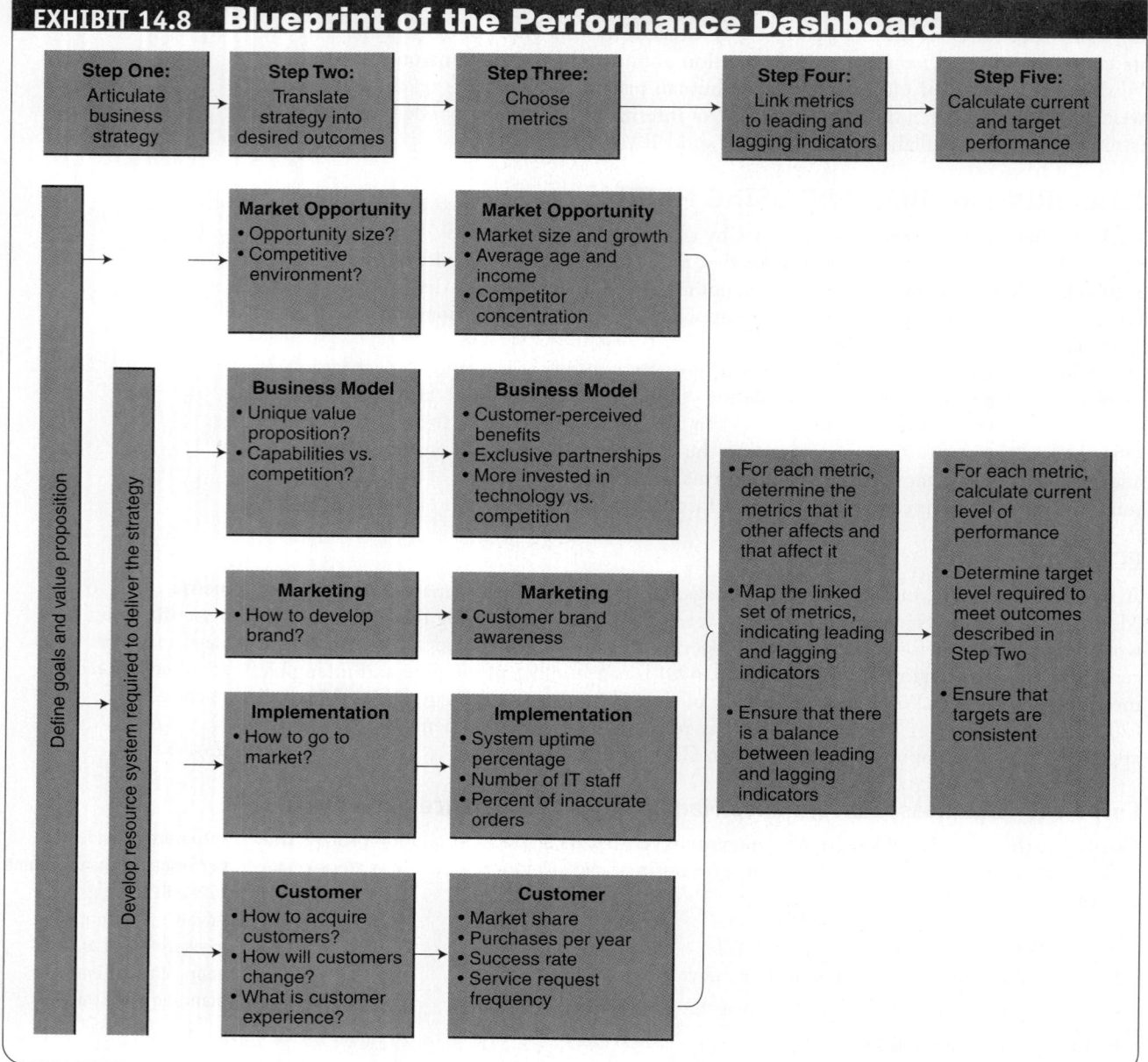

Source: Rayport, J., and B. J. Jaworski. *Introduction to E-Commerce*, 2d ed. Boston: McGraw-Hill, 2004. Copyright © McGraw-Hill Companies, Inc.

strategy and goal, the company can decide "what needs to be done differently," and then act and adjust plans and execution.

The *balanced scorecard* approach is a popular strategy assessment methodology (see details in Lawson, et al. 2006) that encourages measuring organizational performance in a number of areas. Taking a balanced scorecard approach, Plant (2000) suggests seven areas for assessment of an e-commerce strategy: financial impact, competitive leadership, brand, service, market, technology, and internal site metrics. Similarly, Zhu and Kraemer (2002) suggest four metric areas—information, transaction, interaction and customization, and supplier connection—that manufacturing firms should use for assessing performance of their e-commerce strategy. Finally, Rayport and Jaworski (2004) propose five categories of financial and nonfinancial metrics to assess strategy in a five-step process they call the *performance dashboard* (see Exhibit 14.8).

For an extensive discussion on metrics and management, see Straub et al. (2002) and Jackson (2005).

Web Analytics

One large and growing area of EC strategy assessment is **Web analytics**, the analysis of click-stream data to understand visitor behavior on a Web site. (See Chapter 4 for details.) Web analytics begins by identifying data that can assess the effectiveness of the site's goals and objectives (e.g., frequent visits to a site map may indicate site navigation problems). Next, analytics data are collected, such as where site visitors are coming from, what pages they look at and for how long while visiting the site, and how they interact with the site's information. The data can reveal the impact of search engine optimization or an advertising campaign, the effectiveness of Web site design and navigation, and most important, visitor conversion. Because the goal of most EC Web sites is to sell product, the most valuable Web analytics are those related to step-by-step conversion of a visitor to a customer down the so-called *purchase funnel* (Burby 2004).

Information about Web analytics is available from Burby (2006), emetrics.org, and jimnovo.com. Two of many Web analytics tools include WebTrends (webtrends.com) and ClickTracks (clicktracks.com).

Web analytics
The analysis of click-stream data to understand visitor behavior on a Web site.

Section 14.7 ▶ REVIEW QUESTIONS

1. Describe the need for assessment.
2. Define *metrics* and their contribution to strategic planning.
3. Describe the corporate performance management approach to strategy assessment.
4. Define *Web analytics*.

14.8 GLOBAL E-COMMERCE

Global electronic activities have existed for more than 25 years, mainly EFT and EDI in support of B2B and other repetitive, standardized financial transactions. However, these activities required expensive and inflexible private telecommunications lines and, therefore, were limited mostly to large corporations. The emergence of the Internet and technologies such as extranets and XML has resulted in an inexpensive and flexible infrastructure that can greatly facilitate global trade. For global marketing considerations, see Egea and Mendez (2006).

A global electronic marketplace is an attractive thrust for an EC strategy. "Going global" means access to larger markets, mobility (e.g., to minimize taxes), and flexibility to employ workers anywhere. However, going global is a complex and strategic decision process due to a multiplicity of issues. Geographic distance is the most obvious dimension of conducting business globally, but frequently, it is not the most important dimension. Instead cultural, legal, administrative, and economic dimensions are equally likely to threaten a firm's international ambitions (Kraemer 2006). This section briefly examines the opportunities, problems, and solutions for companies using e-commerce to go global.

BENEFITS AND EXTENT OF OPERATIONS

The major advantage of EC is the ability to do business at any time, from anywhere, and at a reasonable cost. These are the drivers behind global EC, and there have been some incredible success stories in this area. For example:

▶ One can use E*TRADE or boom.com to buy and sell stocks online in several countries.

▶ Exchanges such as ChemConnect have members in dozens of countries.

▶ Amazon.com sells books and hundreds of other items to individuals and organizations in over 190 countries.

▶ Small companies, such as ZD Wines (zdwines.com), sell to hundreds of customers worldwide. Hothothot (hothothot.com) reported its first international trade only after it went online; within two years global sales accounted for 25 percent of its total sales. By 2007, the company had over 10,000 hits per day (up from 500 in 1997), and its annual growth rate is over 125 percent, selling to customers in 45 countries.

▶ Major corporations, such as GE and Boeing, have reported an increasing number of out-of-the-country vendors participating in their electronic RFQs. These electronic bids have resulted in a 10 to 15 percent cost reduction and an over 50 percent reduction in cycle time.

▶ Many international corporations considerably increased their success in recruiting employees for foreign locations when they used online recruiting (see xing.com).

▶ Several global trading exchanges have been created in the past few years (see Chapter 6).

BARRIERS TO GLOBAL EC

Despite the benefits and opportunities offered by globalization, there are many barriers to global EC. Some of these barriers face any EC venture but become more difficult when international impacts are considered. These barriers include authentication of buyers and sellers (Chapter 11), generating and retaining trust (Chapters 4 and 7), order fulfillment and delivery (Chapter 13), security (Chapter 11), and domain names (Chapter 16). Others are unique to global EC. We will use the culture, administration, geography, economics (CAGE) distance framework proposed by Ghemawat (2001) to identify areas in which natural or man-made barriers hinder global EC. Each of the four factors represents a different type of distance (difference) between two companies.

Cultural Issues

The Internet is a multifaceted marketplace made up of users from many cultures. The multi-cultural nature of global EC is important because cultural attributes determine how people interact with companies, agencies, and each other based on social norms, local standards, religious beliefs, and language (Thanasankit 2003). Doing business globally requires *cultural marketing*, a strategy for meeting the needs of a culturally diverse population.

Cultural and related differences include language (e.g., English versus other languages), spelling differences (e.g., American versus British spelling), information formatting (e.g., dates can be mm/dd/yy or dd/mm/yy), graphics and icons (e.g., mailbox shapes differ from country to country), measurement standards (e.g., metric versus imperial system), the use of color (e.g., white is a funeral color in some countries), protection of intellectual property (e.g., Chinese tolerance of copyright infringement has Confucian roots), time standards (e.g., local time zones versus Greenwich Mean Time), and information requests (e.g., requiring a zip code in an order form can lead to abandoned shopping carts in countries without postal codes). Even the way individuals access the Web—at home, work, or an Internet café—varies by country, with implications for the use of graphics and personalization strategies.

Culture and Language Translation

Solutions for overcoming cultural barriers begin with an awareness of the cultural identities and differences in the target markets. Different sites may need to be created for different cultural groups, taking into account site design elements, pricing and payment infrastructures, currency conversion, customer support, and language translation. Language translation is one of the most obvious and most important aspects of maintaining global Web sites. The primary problems with language translation are speed and cost. It may take a human translator a week to translate a medium-sized Web site into another language. For large sites, the cost can be up to $500,000, depending on the complexity of the site and languages of translation, and it may take a long time. A good translator needs to pay attention to cultural issues. Some companies address the cost and time problems by translating their Web pages into different languages through so-called *machine translators* (a list of these translator programs is available in Online File W14.8 on the book's Web site). However, machine translation is only about 75 percent accurate (*CNN.com* 2006), which is why many companies use native-language, in-country translators to review and revise the results from machine translation software (see He 2006). For an organization that is successfully using machine translation, see Case 14.3.

CASE 14.3
EC Application

WEB PAGE TRANSLATION AT THE DENVER METRO CONVENTION AND VISITORS BUREAU

Denver, Colorado is one of America's fastest growing cities. Situated in the Rocky Mountains, the Mile High City entertains over 8.8 million visitors a year with people coming to enjoy the city's outstanding cultural attractions, museums, shopping, dining, and nightlife.

Denver Metro Convention and Visitors Bureau (DMCVB) (*denver.org*) is a marketing organization responsible for promoting the Denver metropolitan area and the rest of Colorado. Local, national, and international travelers, conventioneers, and meeting planners use the site. Many of the international visitors attracted to Denver come from non-English speaking parts of the world, including Germany, Latin and South America, Japan, and Korea.

The Problem

DMCVB knew its Web site was an economical means to get information to potential international visitors considering Denver as a destination. After seeking a foreign language solution for about two years, the organization chose WorldLingo's Instant Website translator. The solution made it possible for international visitors to get current information about Denver in their own language instantly.

The Solution

The *Instant Website Translator* is a Web-based solution that is extremely simple to implement and easy to install. Installation is a simple cut and paste of the code into existing Web pages. Updates to translations happen dynamically whenever modifications are made to the Web site's contents, making the site easy to maintain. The implementation provides an accurate machine translation service that translates the original English into ten languages; French; German; Italian; Spanish; Portuguese (Brazilian); Dutch; Korean; Chinese; Japanese; and Greek. Flag identifiers on the Web site's home page make it simple for visitors to select the language that they require with a click of the mouse. Visitor tracking devices are also available garnering valuable demographic tracking that monitors and reports the languages used at the site.

Results

Denver's Visitor Information Centers, in particular, have overcome the language barrier and offer a better service by referring multilingual visitors to Web pages in their own language. The organization also refers international phone and mail enquiries to the Web site for better service. Numerous translations are now requested as traffic to the site continues to increase. The multilingual capability has given the Web site an edge that many other official visitor sites lack.

Sources: Compiled from Wordlingo.com (2006a) and Wordlingo.com (2006b).

Questions

1. What drove the need for translation?
2. What is translated and how?
3. Enter *wordlingo.com* and review their products and services. Prepare a report.

Transclick (transclick.com) provides real-time machine translation of e-mails, SMS, text messages, and instant messaging over computers, smart phones, and mobile PDAs in 16 different languages. For more on machine translation, see en.wikipedia.org/wiki/Machine_Translation.

Administrative Issues

One of the most contentious areas of global EC is the resolution of international legal issues. A number of national governments and international organizations are working together to find ways to avoid uncoordinated actions and encourage uniform legal standards.

An ambitious effort to reduce differences in international law governing EC is the United Nations Commission on International Trade Law (UNCITRAL) Model Law on Electronic Commerce. Its purpose is to "offer national legislators a set of internationally acceptable rules which detail how a number of legal obstacles to the development of e-commerce may be removed, and how a more secure legal environment may be created" (*e-Business World* 2000). The Model Law has been adopted in some form in many countries and legal jurisdictions, including Singapore, Australia, Canada, Hong Kong, and some American states (e.g., California, Colorado, Iowa, and Kentucky).

International trade organizations, such as the World Trade Organization (WTO) and the Asia-Pacific Economic Cooperation (APEC) forum, have working groups that are attempting to reduce EC trade barriers in areas such as pricing regulations, customs, import/export restrictions, tax issues, and product specification regulations.

Geographic Issues and Localization

The geographic issues of shipping goods and services across international borders are well known. Barriers posed by geography differ based on the transportation infrastructure between and within countries and the type of product or service being delivered. For example, geographic distance is almost irrelevant with online software sales.

Example. The Nutralogic Laboratories Inc. provides its global customers with an advanced multilanguage e-commerce site (nutralogixlabs.com). Revenues from Europe and Asia increased significantly since the introduction of the native languages.

Companies launching a worldwide EC strategy need to evaluate bandwidth requirements and availability in the main target countries. A country's market-access infrastructure is key to accommodating all users and all types of data. Monitoring and complying with technical standards will also minimize the possibility of incompatible technologies between the company and the international user.

Localization. Many companies use different names, colors, sizes, and packaging for their overseas products and services. This practice is referred to as *localization*. In order to maximize the benefits of global information systems, the localization approach should also be used in the design and operation of the supporting information systems. For example, many Web sites offer different language or currency options, as well as special content. Europcar (europcar.com), for example, offers portals in 118 countries, each with an option for 1 of 10 languages. For more on localization, see Rigby and Vishwanath (2006).

Economic Issues

Economic and financial issues encompassing global EC include government tariffs, customs, and taxation. In areas subject to government regulation, tax and regulatory agencies have attempted to apply the rules used in traditional commerce to electronic commerce, with considerable success. Exceptions include areas such as international tariff duties and taxation. Software shipped in a box would be taxed for duties and tariffs when it arrives in the country. However, software downloaded online relies on self-reporting and voluntary payment of tax by the purchaser, something that does not happen very often.

The key financial barrier to global EC is electronic payment systems. To sell effectively online, EC firms must have flexible payment methods that match the ways different groups of people pay for their online purchases. Although credit cards are used widely in the United States, many European and Asian customers prefer to complete online transactions with off-line payments. Even within the category of off-line payments, companies must offer different options depending on the country. For example, French consumers prefer to pay with a check, Swiss consumers expect an invoice by mail, Germans commonly pay for products only upon delivery, and Swedes are accustomed to paying online with debit cards.

Pricing is another economic issue. A vendor may want to price the same product at different prices in different countries in consideration of local prices and competition. However, if a company has one Web site, differential pricing will be difficult or impossible. Similarly, what currency will be used for pricing? What currency will be used for payment?

BREAKING DOWN THE BARRIERS TO GLOBAL EC

A number of international organizations (e.g., OECD 2001) and experts (e.g., Stone 2005; Sheldon and Strader 2002) have offered suggestions on how to break down the barriers to global EC. Some of these suggestions include the following:

▶ **Be strategic.** Identify a starting point and lay out a globalization strategy. Remember that Web globalization is a business-building process. Consider what languages and countries it makes sense for the company to target and how the company will support the site for each target audience.

▶ **Know your audience.** Carefully consider the target audience. Be fully informed of the cultural preferences and legal issues that matter to customers in a particular part of the world.

▶ **Localize.** As much as practical and necessary, offer Web sites in national languages; offer different sites in different countries (e.g., "Yahoo! Japan" is at yahoo.co.jp); price products in local currencies; and base terms, conditions, and business practices on local laws and cultural practices. Chapter 4 included a brief discussion of localization in advertising.

▶ **Think globally, act consistently.** An international company with country Web sites managed by local offices must make sure that areas such as brand management, pricing, corporate information, and content management are consistent with company strategy (Cagni 2004).

▶ **Value the human touch.** Trust the translation of the Web site content only to human translators, not machine translation programs (Dubie 2003). Involve language and technical editors in the quality assurance process. One slight mistranslation or one out-of-place graphic may turn off customers forever.

▶ **Clarify, document, explain.** Pricing, privacy policies, shipping restrictions, contact information, and business practices should be well documented and located on the Web site and visible to the customer. To help protect against foreign litigation, identify the company's location and the jurisdiction for all contract or sales disputes.

▶ **Offer services that reduce barriers.** It is not feasible to offer prices and payments in all currencies, so link to a currency exchange service (e.g., xe.com) for the customer's convenience. (See Yunker 2006.) In B2B e-commerce, be prepared to integrate the EC transaction with the accounting/finance internal information system of the buyer.

We close our discussion of global e-commerce with a reference to the Pierre Lang Europe Real-World Case that concludes this chapter. Briefly, Pierre Lang Europe is a jewelry design and manufacturing company with a strong customer base in Western Europe. When Pierre Lang became interested in expanding into Eastern Europe, the firm realized it would have to change its information systems. Like other companies expanding internationally, it needed to be able to handle the multiple legal and language requirements of doing business in many different countries. The Real-World Case details the challenges Pierre Lang faced in "going global," and how it met those challenges.

Section 14.8 ▶ REVIEW QUESTIONS

1. Describe globalization in EC and the advantages it presents.
2. Describe the major barriers to global EC in each dimension of the CAGE framework.
3. What can companies do to overcome the barriers to global EC?

14.9 E-COMMERCE IN SMALL AND MEDIUM-SIZED ENTERPRISES

Some of the first companies to take advantage of Web-based electronic commerce were SMEs. While larger, established, tradition-bound companies hesitated, SMEs moved onto the Web because they realized there were opportunities in marketing, business expansion, business launches, cost cutting, and tighter partner alliances. Some examples are virtualvine.com, hothothot.com, and philaprintshop.com.

SMEs consider the Internet to be a valuable business tool. According to a 2004 survey by Interland (*eMarketer* 2004), 28 percent of small businesses expect more than three-quarters of their annual sales to come from the Internet. And it isn't only online sales that are being used to measure success. Although one-third of respondents measure site success by sales, almost half (47 percent) measure site success based on measures such as customer comments about the site and the volume of site traffic. For further discussion, see Tatnall and Burgess (2006).

EXHIBIT 14.9 Advantages and Disadvantages of EC for Small and Medium-Sized Businesses

Advantages/Benefits	Disadvantages/Risks
• Inexpensive sources of information. A Scandinavian study found that over 90 percent of SMEs use the Internet for information search (OECD 2001). • Inexpensive ways of advertising and conducting market research. Banner exchanges, newsletters, chat rooms, and so on are nearly zero-cost ways to reach customers. • Competitor analysis is easier. The Scandinavian study found that Finnish firms rated competitor analysis third in their use of the Internet, after information search and marketing. • Inexpensive ways to build (or rent) a storefront. Creating and maintaining a Web site is relatively easy and cheap (see Chapter 16). • SMEs are less locked into legacy technologies and existing relationships with traditional retail channels. • Image and public recognition can be generated quickly. A Web presence makes it easier for a small business to compete against larger firms. • An opportunity to reach worldwide customers. No other medium is as efficient at global marketing, sales, and customer support. • Other advantages for SMEs include increased speed of customer payments, closer ties with business partners, reduced errors in information transfer, lower operating costs, and other benefits that apply to all businesses.	• Lack of financial resources to fully exploit the Web. A transactional Web site may entail relatively high up-front, fixed costs in terms of cash flow for an SME. • Lack of technical staff or insufficient expertise in legal issues, advertising, etc. These human resources may be unavailable or prohibitively expensive to an SME. • Less risk tolerance than a large company. If initial sales are low or the unexpected happens, the typical SME does not have a large reserve of resources to fall back on. • When the product is not suitable or is difficult for online sales (e.g., experiential products such as clothes or beauty products; perishable products, such as certain foods) the Web opportunity is not as great. • Reduced personal contact with customers represents the dilution of what is normally a strong point for a small business. • Inability to afford entry to or purchase enough volume to take advantage of digital exchanges.

However, many SMEs have found it difficult to formulate or implement an EC strategy, mainly because of low use of EC and IT by customers and suppliers, lack of knowledge or IT expertise in the SME, and limited awareness of the opportunities and risks (OECD 2001). Exhibit 14.9 provides a more complete list of major advantages and disadvantages of EC for SMEs.

When analyzing e-commerce for SMEs when integration or use of RFID or XML may be necessary, one should distinguish between B2C, which may be simple, and B2B, which may be complex when the SME is a supplier to a large company (e.g., see Lawson-Body and Illia 2006).

CRITICAL SUCCESS FACTORS FOR SMES

EC success for small businesses is not a just matter of chance. Considerable research identifies the critical success factors that help determine whether a small business will succeed in EC. Many of the small businesses that have succeeded on the Internet, either as click-and-mortar or pure online businesses, have the following strategies in common:

▶ **Product is critical.** The most effective product (service) strategy for SMEs has been niche or specialty items. It is difficult to compete against online bookstores, such as Amazon.com, unless one specializes, as lindsaybks.com does in the technical book market. Other strategies are to sell a wide variety of low-volume products that regular stores do not stock (e.g., dogtoys.com), international products not readily available in neighborhood stores (e.g., russianfoods.com), goods that appeal to hobbyists or a community's special interests (e.g., diecastmodelcars.com), regional products (e.g., newyorkartworld.com), or local information (e.g., baliadventuretours.com).

▶ **Payment methods must be flexible.** Some customers prefer to mail or fax in a form or talk to a person rather than transmit a credit card number over the Internet.

▶ **Electronic payments must be secure.** Fortunately, ISPs and banks can easily provide this security.

▶ **Capital investment should be kept to a minimum.** Doing so enables companies to keep their overhead and risk low. For example, SMEs typically outsource from Web hosting.

▶ **Inventory control is crucial.** Carrying too much stock ties up valuable capital. Too little stock on hand results in unfilled orders and disappointed customers. Contingency plans for scaling up inventory fast are recommended.

▶ **Logistics services must be quick and reliable.** Many small businesses have successfully subcontracted out their logistical services to shipping firms such as UPS, FedEx, or DHL.

▶ **Owner support.** The higher the owner's level of familiarity with the Internet, the more likely the firm will adopt the Internet and its applications (Karakaya and Khalil 2004).

▶ **High visibility on the Internet.** The Web site should be submitted to directories such as Yahoo! and search engines such as Google, MSN Search, and Lycos and optimized for prominent search engine placement, as described in Chapter 16.

▶ **Join an online community.** The company may want to become a member of an online service or mall, such as AOL or ViaWeb's Viamall. Other partnership strategies that bring in customers include affiliate programs (see affiliatematch.com) and Web rings (see webring.com).

▶ **A Web site should provide all the services needed by consumers.** In addition, the Web site should look professional enough to compete with larger competitors and be updated on a continual basis to maintain consumer interest. Chapter 16 covers this topic in more detail. Wan (2006) describes the use of comparison shopping agents by SMEs. For more on EC barriers for SMEs, see Sharma (2006).

For a successful implementation of e-commerce strategy in a company see Case 14.4. For another success story, see Case 16.3, Anglesea Online.

SUPPORTING SMES

SMEs have a variety of support options. Almost every developed country in the world has a government agency devoted to helping SMEs become more aware of and able to participate in electronic commerce (e.g., sba.gov, business.gov.au).

Vendors realized the opportunity represented by thousands of businesses going online, and many have set up a variety of service centers that typically offer a combination of free information and fee-based support. Examples are IBM's Small Business Center (ibm.com/businesscenter) and Microsoft's Small Business Center (microsoft.com/smallbusiness). Professional associations, Web resource services (e.g., smallbusiness.yahoo.com, workz.com), and small businesses that are in the business of helping other small businesses go online sponsor other small business support centers. For more on e-commerce barriers for SMEs, see Sharma (2006).

Section 14.9 ▶ REVIEW QUESTIONS

1. What are the advantages or benefits of EC for small businesses?
2. What are the disadvantages or risks of EC for small businesses?
3. What are the CSFs for small businesses online?

CASE 14.4
EC Application
NETWORX EVENTS USES E-COMMERCE

Networx Events (*networxevents.com.au*) is a relatively new, small business (two full-time and one part-time staff member) that arranges professional events in Melbourne and Sydney, Australia. Networx's founder, Kimberly Palmer, started by sending e-mail invitations to 20 of her friends and colleagues. The mailing list grew rapidly and orders for tickets exploded. This required a sophisticated and secure transaction-enabled ticketing system. By 2004, sales over the Internet reached AU$140,850, for a gross profit of $100,350. The system also saved $3,240 on reduced postage, telephone calls, etc. The initial investment was only $13,100 and the operating expenses $4,040. Thus, the system net profit was $86,450, an amazing return on the investment (see calculations in Chapter 15). The system also provides CRM and payment arrangement.

Here is how the ticket-purchasing process works:

1. Prospect "opts-in" to receive e-mail invitations to future events (permission e-mail, Chapter 4).
2. Personalized invitation is e-mailed to opt-in database of recipients
3. If accepting, the recipient fills out an online form to register for the event
4. Once booking details are confirmed, the recipient fills in credit card details (if it is not stored already)
5. The recipient pays using credit card and Secure Socket Layer payment system (Chapter 12)
6. Upon successful transmission, the e-ticket and receipt are automatically returned to the recipient via e-mail.

For a small business, a logical approach to provide the technology was outsourcing. Invitee and member contact details are stored in a third-party database. E-mails are delivered via an ASP on a cost per e-mail basis. The Eventix (*eventix.com.au*) ticketing system provides the ticketing, e-mail, and payment component, and in addition to the establishment cost, Networx pays a percentage of its ticket price to the operator.

The ASP model reduces upfront costs. Networx has avoided much of the negative publicity surrounding spam due to careful adherence to its privacy policy. Networx has always sought permission to send e-mails and, therefore, was not obligated to make any major change once the Australian Government's Spam Act was introduced in April 2004.

However, Networx has always promoted the notion of "forwarding" invitations to other friends and colleagues, (viral marketing, Chapter 4) which does not contravene the current Spam Act requirements.

Networx Events plans to expand in both territory and range. It is about to launch its first franchise in Queensland—a move set to be replicated in other territories while expanding from marketing into entrepreneurship and other vertical professions. Both of these plans will continue to be underpinned by opt-in e-mail, electronic customer relationship management, and online ticketing infrastructures.

Sources: Compiled from *networxevents.com.au* (accessed January 2007), Vic.gov.au (2007), and Aptstrategies.com (2007).

Questions

1. What were the drivers of e-commerce in this case?
2. Discuss the strategy of dealing with technological issues.
3. Discuss the strategies of permission and viral marketing.
4. Would you recommend a Web site for order fulfillment (such as the Starwood hotel chain, Chapter 13)? Why or why not?
5. Does the planned expansion make sense?

MANAGERIAL ISSUES

Some managerial issues related to this chapter are as follows.

1. **What is the strategic value of EC to the organization?** Management needs to understand how EC can improve marketing and promotions, customer service, and sales. More significantly, the greatest potential of EC is realized when management views EC from a strategic perspective, not merely as a technological advancement.

2. **Who determines EC strategy?** Strategy is ultimately the responsibility of senior management. But participation in setting an e-commerce strategy is something that should happen at all levels and in all areas of the organization. It frequently is said that "soon all business will be e-business." If this is true, then planning this evolutionary process must include marketing, operations, information technology, and all other areas of the business.

3. **What are the benefits and risks of EC?** Strategic moves have to be carefully weighed against potential risks. Identifying CSFs for EC and doing a cost-benefit analysis should not be neglected. Benefits often are hard to quantify, especially because gains tend to be strategic. In such an analysis, risks should be addressed with contingency planning (deciding what to do if problems arise).

4. **Why do we need a plan?** A strategic plan is both a document and a process. Dwight D. Eisenhower, former U.S. army general and U.S. president, once said "Plans are nothing, planning is everything." A planning process that includes management, employees, business partners, and other stakeholders not only produces a planning document that will guide the business into the future but also achieves buy-in among the participants about where the company is going and how it intends to get there. The same can be said for business planning—the process is as important as the plan itself.

5. **What metrics should we use?** The use of metrics is very popular, but the problem is that one must compare "apples with apples." Companies first must choose appropriate metrics for the situation and then exercise caution in deriving conclusions whenever gaps between the metrics and actual performance exist.

6. **What staffing is required?** Forming a Web team is critical for EC project success. The team's leadership, the balance between technical and business staff, getting the best staff representation on the team, and having a project champion are essential for success.

7. **How can we go global?** Going global is a very appealing proposition, but it may be difficult to do, especially on a large scale. In B2B, one may create collaborative projects with partners in other countries.

8. **Should the dot-com activities be spun off as a separate company?** This is a debatable issue. Sometimes it is useful to do it to eliminate conflicts of prices and strategy. Also, using the spin-off as an IPO can be rewarding. In other cases, it can create problems and administrative expenses. (See Thomas et al. 2005.)

9. **Can we learn to love smallness?** Small can be beautiful to some; to others it may be ugly. Competing on commodity-type products with the big guys is very difficult, and even more so in cyberspace. Finding a niche market is advisable, but it will usually be limited in scope. More opportunity exists in providing specialized support services than in selling goods and services.

10. **Is e-business always beneficial?** According to Coltman et al. (2002), e-business may not fit some businesses. It may be too expensive to justify the benefits or it may result in internal conflicts. Many businesses simply do not need e-business or need only limited e-business capabilities. Therefore, businesses must conduct a careful analysis of fitness.

RESEARCH TOPICS

Here are some suggested topics related to this chapter. For details, references, and additional topics, refer to the Online Appendix A "Current EC Research."

1. **Critical Success Factors for EC within the EC Life Cycle**
   ◗ The CSFs for EC from corporate, industry, and country perspectives
   ◗ CSFs in the development of B2B EC strategy (see also Chapter 5)
   ◗ CSFs in the development of e-tailing strategy (see also Chapter 3)
   ◗ The relationship between CSFs and the balanced scorecard approach
   ◗ Predict the future of EC with a Delphi study

2. **Strategies for E-Business Transformation**
   ◗ Alignment of a corporation's business strategy with its e-business strategy
   ◗ Framework of market mix models in EC
   ◗ Challenges for EC strategies
   ◗ Strategic readiness for EC by company, industry, and country

   ◗ B2C and Web marketing strategies (see Chapter 3)
   ◗ Strategies for B2B EC (see Chapter 5)
   ◗ Strategies for transforming traditional businesses to e-businesses, including synergistic combination and substitution of strategies
   ◗ Strategy for expanding a pure e-business into a click-and-brick business
   ◗ Relationship of project champions to e-business project success

3. **Performance Assessment of EC Using the Balanced Scorecard and Business Performance Management**
   ◗ Impact of EC on business performance
   ◗ Performance measures for the planning and control of EC strategies
   ◗ Association of balanced scorecard with the functional areas of e-business (e.g., marketing, CRM, procurement, SCM, and e-commerce)

▶ How to design the balanced scorecard—top-down and bottom-up approaches

4. **The Dynamics of EC Technology Adoption**

▶ Reconciliation of the cost-benefit model with the technology-acceptance model (TAM)

▶ What makes people believe that EC can be adopted easily

▶ Dynamic changes in EC adoption

▶ Industry and case studies of the various circumstances of EC adoption

5. **Localization in Global EC**

▶ Challenges of global EC: culture, laws, and languages

▶ Comparative country study of international policies for global EC

▶ Transformation of international trade brokers in EC

▶ The role of brands in international EC

▶ Implementation of the letter of credit in the EC global context

▶ Procedures to handle sales tax for cross-border or interstate B2C and B2B transactions

6. **SMEs in EC**

▶ Readiness of SMEs for EC at industry and country levels

▶ Role of buyers in the readiness of SMEs

▶ Benefit to SMEs of accommodating the buying organization's standards

▶ How to harmonize the heterogeneous protocols of multiple buying organizations

▶ Survival strategy of SMEs in Internet marketing and e-tailing

▶ Adoption of ASPs by SMEs to implement e-business—executive perception and organization learning

▶ Reconciliation of MIS strategy with e-business strategy in SMEs

7. **Others**

▶ Structure of virtual organization

▶ Content distribution in virtual organization

▶ Value management in e-commerce

SUMMARY

In this chapter, you learned about the following EC issues as they relate to the learning objectives.

1. **The strategic planning process.** Four major phases compose this cyclical process: initiation, formulation, implementation, and assessment. A variety of tools are available to carry out this process.

2. **Writing a business plan.** A business plan is an essential outcome of a strategic planning process. Writing the business plan may produce more significant outcomes than the plan itself. The purpose of the plan is to describe the operation of the business, and its content includes revenue sources, business partners, and trading procedures.

3. **The EC strategic process.** Considering e-commerce in strategy development does not radically change the process, but it does impact the outcome. Move-to-the-Net firms must approach the process differently than born-on-the-Net firms, but both types of firms must recognize the way electronic technologies, such as the Internet, make an e-difference. Because of the comprehensiveness of EC, formal strategic planning is a must.

4. **E-strategy initiation and formulation.** The strategy initiation phase involves understanding the company, the industry, and the competition. Companies must consider questions such as "Should we be a first mover?" "Should we go global?" "Should we create a separate company or brand?" In strategy formulation, specific opportunities are selected for implementation based on project viability, company fit, cost-benefit, risk, and pricing.

5. **E-strategy implementation and assessment.** Creating an effective Web team and ensuring that sufficient resources are available initiate the implementation phase. Other important implementation issues are whether to outsource various aspects of development and the need to redesign existing business processes. Immediately after implementation, assessment begins. Metrics provide feedback, and management acts by taking corrective action and reformulating strategy, if necessary.

6. **Issues in global EC.** Going global with EC can be done quickly and with a relatively small investment. However, businesses must deal with a number of different issues in the cultural, administrative, geographic, legal, and economic dimensions of global trading.

7. **Small businesses and EC.** Depending on the circumstances, innovative small companies have a

tremendous opportunity to adopt EC with little cost and to expand rapidly. Being in a niche market provides the best chance for small business success, and a variety of Web-based resources are available that small business owners can use to help ensure success.

KEY TERMS

QUESTIONS FOR DISCUSSION

1. How would you identify competitors for a small business that wants to launch an EC project?

2. How would you apply Porter's five forces and Internet impacts in Exhibit 2.8 to the Internet search engine industry?

3. Why must e-businesses consider strategic planning to be a cyclical process?

4. How would you apply the SWOT approach to a small, local bank that is evaluating its e-banking services?

5. Discuss how writing an e-business plan differs from writing a traditional business plan.

6. Offer some practical suggestions as to how a company can include the impact of the Internet in all levels of planning.

7. Explain the logic of Tjan's Internet portfolio map.

8. Amazon.com decided not to open physical stores, whereas First Network Security Bank (FNSB), which was the first online bank, opened its first physical bank in 1999. Compare and discuss the two strategies.

9. Discuss the pros and cons of going global with a physical product.

10. For each part of the CAGE framework, briefly discuss one barrier that may negatively impact e-commerce companies doing business globally.

11. Find some SME EC success stories and identify the common elements in them.

INTERNET EXERCISES

1. Survey several online travel agencies (e.g., **travelocity.com**, **orbitz.com**, **cheaptickets.com**, **priceline.com**, **expedia.com**, **bestfares.com**, and so on) and compare their business strategies. How do they compete against physical travel agencies? (See Chapter 18.)

2. Enter **digitalenterprise.org** and go to Web analytics. Read the material on Web analytics and prepare a report on the use of Web analytics for measuring advertising success.

3. Check the music CD companies on the Internet (e.g., **cduniverse.com**, **musica.co.uk**). Do any companies focus on specialized niche markets as a strategy? What is the uniqueness of **venusrecords.com**)?

4. Enter **ibm.com/procurement** and go to the e-procurement section. Prepare a report on how IBM's Supplier Integration Strategy can assist companies in implementing an EC strategy.

5. Compare the following search engines: **google.com**, **search.yahoo.com**, **search.ask.com**, and **mooter.com**. Conduct a comparative search (i.e., search for the same term at each site), learn more about how each search engine works (e.g., click on "about us" or similar link), and look for comparative articles at Web sites such as **searchenginewatch.com**. Consider the strengths and weaknesses of each site, when one would be more useful than another, and what special features distinguish it in the search engine marketplace. Prepare a report based on your findings.

6. One of the most global companies is Amazon.com (**amazon.com**). Find stories about its global strategies and activities (try **google.com** and **forbes.com**). What are the most important lessons you learned?

7. Visit **abcsmallbiz.com** and find some of the EC opportunities available to small businesses. Also, visit the Web site of the Small Business Administration (SBA) office in your area. Summarize recent EC-related topics for SMEs.

8. Enter **alloy.com** and **bolt.com**. Compare the sites on functionality, ease of use, message boards, homepage layout, and so on. Prepare a report based on your findings.

9. Find out how Web sites such as **tradecard.com** facilitate the conduct of international trade over the Internet. Prepare a report based on your findings.

10. Use a currency conversion table (e.g., **xe.com/ucc**) to find out the exchange rate of US$100 with the currencies of Brazil, Canada, China, India, Sweden, the European Union, and South Africa.

11. Conduct research on small businesses and their use of the Internet for EC. Visit sites such as **microsoft.com/smallbusiness/hub.mspx** and **uschamber.org**. Also, enter **google.com** or **yahoo.com** and type "small businesses + electronic commerce." Use your findings to write a report on current small business EC issues.

12. Enter **businesscase.com** and review their products. What are the benefits of CaseBuilder to people conducting e-commerce strategy development?

13. Enter **advisorzones.com/adv/e-commerceAdvisor**. Find the services provided for areas related to this chapter. Write a summary.

14. Enter **languageweaver.com** and find the product they have for language translation for multinational corporations. Write a report.

TEAM ASSIGNMENTS AND ROLE PLAYING

1. Have three teams represent the following units of one click-and-mortar company: (1) an off-line division, (2) an online division, and (3) top management. Each team member represents a different functional area within the division. The teams will develop a strategy in a specific industry (a group of three teams will represent a company in one industry). Teams will present their strategies to the class.

2. The relationship between manufacturers and their distributors regarding sales on the Web can be very strained. Direct sales may cut into the distributors' business. Review some of the strategies available to handle such channel conflicts. Each team member should be assigned to a company in a different industry. Study the strategies, compare and contrast them, and derive a proposed generic strategy.

3. Each team must find the latest information on one global EC issue (e.g., cultural, administrative, geographic, economic). Each team will offer a report based on their findings.

4. Survey **google.com** and **isworld.org** to find out about EC efforts in different countries. Assign a country or two to each team. Relate the developments to each

country's level of economic development and to its culture.

5. Enter **stassmann.com** and find 10 entries related to e-strategy (including videos). Prepare summaries of them relating to this chapter.

6. Compare the services provided by Yahoo!, Microsoft, and Website Pros Inc. to SMEs in the e-commerce area. Each team should take one company and make a presentation.

Real-World Case

PIERRE LANG EXPANDS INTO EASTERN EUROPE

Pierre Lang Europe (*pierrelang.com*) sells designer jewelry throughout Western Europe. Its traditional business model was to sell earrings, pendants, necklaces, and other jewelry through the firm's 5,500 sales representatives. When Pierre Lang decided to expand into Eastern Europe, the firm decided it needed to change this business model and the underlying information systems and business processes.

The company knew it was losing business because it was unable to keep track of customers and it did not have direct contact with them. If sales representatives left the company for any reason, they would take their customers with them. Pierre Lang Europe wanted more than sales from its customers, it wanted customer relationships for follow-on sales and customer support.

Like many companies expanding globally, Pierre Lang also anticipated that this expansion could double its revenues and order volume. The company needed better information about its finances, improved control of its order process, and a system that could handle the multiple legal and language requirements of doing business in many different countries.

Pierre Lang selected mySAP after evaluating several competing solutions. Installation began in July 2003; early rollout projects were in place by November; and financial and controlling capabilities went live in all company locations in January 2004.

Today, Pierre Lang uses country-specific versions of mySAP to handle invoicing, tax, language, and fiscal issues. France, for example, has unique requirements for tracking the import and export of gold and silver. "Lots of small things like that have to be considered because they're vital for Pierre Lang. It has to work perfectly in every country, so they have to know whom they will charge what, and do that automatically," says Rudolf Windisch, one of Pierre Lang's consulting partners on this project. "They also have to deal with all the tax issues,

which vary considerably from one country to another. There are no homogeneous tax systems in Europe."

Pierre Lang expects to increase the accuracy of its information and eliminate the need for manual transfers of tax data to develop reports. Executives also anticipate decreased inventory costs through improved material disposition as well as better information about sales efforts and costs that will lead to improved forecasting and planning.

As noted in this chapter, expanding regionally or globally can have a dramatic impact on a company's bottom line but only if it is prepared to deal with the heterogeneous legal and financial systems in different countries. Pierre Lang knew this and met the challenge.

To safeguard its multinational enterprise network, the company uses an integrated network security platform (from *fortinet.com*). The system protects both the headquarters in Vienna and 65 sales offices throughout Europe. The centrally managed system protects every remote user. The system is updated in real time.

Sources: SAP AG (2004), *sap.com* (accessed December 2006), and from Fortinet.com (2005).

Questions

1. Why was it necessary for Pierre Lang to look at fundamental changes in its business model and information systems?

2. Relate the facts of this case to the CAGE framework discussed in Section 14.8.

3. What have been the results of implementing mySAP at Pierre Lang?

4. Why is security so important to the company and how is it protected?

5. Enter *fortinet.com* and examine the capabilities of their FortiGate products.

REFERENCES

Access eCommerce. "Developing Your Internet Business Plan." 2006. **access-ecom.info/section.cfm?sid=bp& xid=MN** (accessed November 2006).

Aptstrategies.com. "Networx Case Study." **aptstrategies. com.au/case_studies/Networx** (accessed February 2007).

Auckland, J. S. "Davidson Appointed InternetNZ Executive Director." *Computerworld*, May 31, 2005. **computerworld.co.nz/news.nsf/0/C77829204EE519 15CC257011006C7F51?OpenDocument&pub= Computerworld** (accessed November 2006).

Baker, W., M. V. Marn, and C. Zawada. "Price Smarter on the Net." *Harvard Business Review* (February 2001).

BeeAgile. "Creating Effective Partnerships." 2006. **beeagile. com/Creating_Effective_Service_Partnerships.pdf** (accessed December 2006).

Bockstedt, J. C., R. J. Kauffman, and F. J. Riggins. "The Move to Artist-Led Online Music Distribution: Explaining Structural Changes in the Digital Music Market." *Proceedings of the 38th Annual Hawaiian International Conference on Systems Sciences*, Big Island, Hawaii, January 3–6, 2005.

Burby, J. "Meaningful Metrics: Collect What Counts." *ClickZ Experts*, May 25, 2004. **clickz.com/showPage. html?page=3358121** (accessed February 2007).

Burby, J. "Web Analytics: The Results of Tabbed Browsing," *CliczNetwork*, August 29, 2006. **clickz.com/ showPage.html?page=3623280** (accessed December 2006).

Cagni, P. "Think Globally, Act European." *Strategy and Business*, August 30, 2004. **strategy-business.com/ enewsarticle/enews083004?pg=all** (accessed December 2006).

Carr, D. F. "Changing Course amid Turbulence." *Baseline Magazine*, September 2006.

Chatterjee, D., R. Grewal, and V. Sambamurthy. "Shaping Up for E-Commerce: Institutional Enablers for the Organizational Assimilation of Web Technologies." *MIS Quarterly* (June 2002).

Clegg, B., and B. Tan. "E-Business Planning and Analysis Framework," in Khosrow-Pour (2006).

CNN.com. "DARPA Challenge: Build the Ultimate Speech Translation Machine." November 6, 2006. **cnn.com/2006/TECH/11/06/darpa.translation.ap/ index.html** (accessed December 2006).

Coltman, T., T. M. Devinney, A. S. Latukefu, and D. F. Midgley. "Keeping E-Business in Perspective." *Communications of the ACM,* (August 2002).

Deise, M. V., et al. *Executive's Guide to E-Business—From Tactics to Strategy*. New York: Wiley, 2000.

Dell Public. "Building a Business Case for a Technology Investment." August 2005. **dell4slg.com/resource_ detail.php?ri=664&si=60** (accessed November 2006).

Dubie, D. "Going Global." *eBusinessIQ*, March 13, 2003. **findarticles.com/p/articles/mi_zd4149/is_200410/ai_ n9476589** (accessed February 2007).

e-Business World. "Global Imperative . . . and the Pitfalls of Regionalism." *e-Business World*, January–February 2000.

Egea, J. M. O., and M. Recio. "Menéndez Global Marketing on the Internet," in Khosrow-Pour (2006).

eMarketer. "Small Businesses Expecting E-Sales." *eMarketer*, December 14, 2004. **emarketer.com/ article.aspx?1003177** (no longer available online).

Ernest, D., T. Halevy, J. Monier, and H. Sarrazin. "A Future for E-Alliances." *The McKinsey Quarterly* (April–June 2001).

Fortinet.com. "Pierre Lang Jewelers Safeguards Multi-National Enterprise Network," March 30, 2005. **fortinet.com/news/pr/2005/pr033005.html** (accessed February 2007).

Gagnon, D., S. Lee, F. Ramirez, S. Ravikumar, and J. Santiago. "Consumer Power and the Internet." MIT Sloan School of Management, June 11, 2002. **mitsloan. mit.edu/50th/pdf/consumerpowerpaper.pdf** (accessed February 2007).

Ghemawat, P. "Distance Still Matters: The Hard Reality of Global Expansion." *Harvard Business Review* (September 2001).

Green, S. *Profit on the Web*. Auckland, New Zealand: Axon Computertime, 2002.

He, S. "Multilingual Web Sites in Global Electronic Commerce," in Khosrow-Pour (2006).

InternetNZ. *InternetNZ Strategic Plan: 2004–2007*. April 2004. **internetnz.net.nz/pubs/plans/2004/planning 040424adoption.html** (accessed February 2007).

InternetNZ. *InternetNZ Strategic Plan: 2006*. February 23, 2006. **internetnz.net.nz/pubs/plans/2006/2006–03–04- strategicplan** (accessed February 2007).

Jackson, S. "How Key Performance Indicators Can Improve E-Commerce Strategy." Part I (June 12, 2005), Part II (August 24, 2005). *Seotoday.com*. **seotoday.com/browse.php/category/articles/id/500/ index.php** (accessed February 2007).

Jelassi, I., and A. Enders. *Strategies for e-Business*. Harlow, England: FT Prentice Hall, 2005.

Joyce, P. and G. W. Winch. "An E-Business Design and Evaluation Framework Based on Entrepreneurial, Technical and Operational Considerations." *International Journal of Electronic Business*, Vol. 3, No. 2 (2005). **ideas.repec.org/p/hhb/gunwba/2002_389.html# provider** (accessed November 2006).

Kalamas, M., M. Cleveland, M. Laroche, and R. Laufer. "The Critical Role of Congruency in Prototypical Brand Extensions." *Journal of Strategic Marketing*, Vol. 14, No. 3 (2006).

Kaplan, R. S., and D. P. Norton. *The Balanced Scorecard: Translating Strategy into Action*. Boston: Harvard Business School Press, 1996.

Karakaya, F., and O. Khalil. "Determinants of Internet Adoption in Small and Medium-sized Enterprises." *International Journal of Internet and Enterprise Management*, Vol. 2, No. 4 (2004).

Khosrow-Pour, M. (ed.), *Encyclopedia of E-Commerce, E-Government, and Mobile Commerce.* Hershey, PA: Idea Group Reference, 2006.

Kim, H., and R. Ramkaran. "Best Practices in e-Business Process Management: Extending a Reengineering Framework." *Business Process Management Journal,* Vol. 10, No. 1 (2004).

Kim, W. C., and R. Mauborgne. "Charting Your Company's Future." *Harvard Business Review* (June 2002).

Kraemer, K. *Global E-Commerce: Impacts of National Environment and Policy.* Cambridge, MA: Cambridge University Press, 2006.

Lawson, R., W. Stratton, and T. Hatch. "Scorecarding Goes Global." *Strategic Finance,* March 2006.

Lawson-Body, A., and A. Illia. "SME's Perceptions of B2B E-Commerce," in Khosrow-Pour (2006).

Maxwell, S. "Show Me the Metrics!" *Posts from an Expansion Stage Venture Capitalist.* January 30, 2006. **scottmaxwell. wordpress.com/2006/01/30/show-me-the-metrics** (accessed December 2006).

McKay, J., and P. Marshall. *Strategic Management of eBusiness.* Milton, Australia: John Wiley & Sons, 2004.

Minsky, S. "The Power of Expert Opinion: A Lesson in Risk Management." *eBizQ.net,* October 17, 2006. **ebizq.net/ blogs/chief_risk_officer/2006/10/the_power_of_expert_ opinion_a.php** (accessed December 2006).

Muncaster, P. "Risk policy needs rethink." *IT Week,* June 30, 2006. **itweek.co.uk/itweek/news/2159522/risk-policy- needs-rethink** (accessed December 2006).

Niven, P. *Balanced Scorecard Diagnostics.* Hoboken, NJ: John Wiley and Sons, 2005.

OECD (Organization for Economic Cooperation and Development). *Enhancing SME Competitiveness: The OECD Bologna, Italy, Ministerial Conference.* 2001.

Papazoglou, M., and P. Ribbers. *Building B2B Relationships— Technical and Tactical Implementation of an e-Business Strategy.* Hoboken, NJ: John Wiley and Sons, 2006.

Plant, R. T. *E-Commerce: Formulation of Strategy.* Upper Saddle River, NJ: Prentice Hall, 2000.

Porter, M. E. *Competitive Strategy: Techniques for Analyzing Industries and Competitors.* New York: The Free Press, 1980.

Porter, M. E. "Strategy and the Internet." *Harvard Business Review* (March 2001).

Power Home Biz. "Partnership Formula: Winning E-Commerce." 2006. **powerhomebiz.com/vol56/ partnership.htm** (accessed November 2006).

PRNewswire. "Nike, Inc., Elevates Global E-Commerce Strategy." October 24, 2006. **moqvo.com/en/nike_inc_ elevates_global_ecommerce_strategy_pr_newswire_ 3957322.html** (accessed February 2007).

Rangan, S., and R. Adner. "Profits and the Internet: Seven Misconceptions." *Sloan Management Review* (Summer 2001).

Ranganathan, C., et al. "E-Business Transformation at the Crossroads: Sears' Dilemma." *Proceedings of the 24th International Conference on Information Systems,* Seattle, Washington, December 14–17, 2003.

Rayport, J., and B. J. Jaworski. *Introduction to E-Commerce,* 2nd ed. Boston: McGraw-Hill, 2004.

Rigby, D. K, and V. Vishwanath. "Localization: The Revolution in Consumer Markets." *Harvard Business Review* (April 2006).

Saeed, K. A., and R. A. Leitch. "Controlling Sourcing Risk in Electronic Marketplaces." *Electronic Markets,* (June 2003).

SAP AG. "Pierre Lang Europe." **sap.com/solutions/ business-suite/erp/pdf/cs_pierre_lang.pdf** (accessed February 2007).

Sharma, S. K. "E-Commerce in a Digital Economy," in Khosrow-Pour (2006).

Sheldon, L. A., and T. J. Strader. "Managerial Issues for Expanding into International Web-Based Electronic Commerce." *SAM Advanced Management Journal* (Summer 2002).

Shenkar O., and J. J. Reuer. "The Alliance Puzzle: Known Terrain, Black Boxes, and the Road Ahead," in *Handbook of Strategic Alliances*, O. Shenkar and J. J. Reuer (eds.). Newburry Park, CA: Sage Publications, 2005.

Stone, A. "Breaking Down Language Barriers." *Forbes.com,* October 19, 2005. **forbes.com/enterprisetech/2005/10/ 19/language-translation-cell-cz_as_1019language.html** (accessed December 2006).

Straub, D. W., et al. "Toward New Metrics for Net-Enhanced Organizations." *Information Systems Research* (September 2002b).

Suh, B., and I. Han. "The IS Risk Analysis Based on a Business Model." *Information and Management,* (December 2003).

Tatnall, A., and S. Burgess. "Innovation Translation and E-Commerce in SMEs," in Khosrow-Pour (2006).

Tennant Risk Services. "Technology and Cyber-Risk Insurance." 2004. **tennant.com/p-cyber.php#ecom** (accessed December 2006).

Thanasankit, T. (ed.). *E-Commerce and Cultural Values.* Hershey, PA: Idea Group Publishing, 2003.

Thomas, D., C. Ranganathan C., and K. Desouza. "Race to Dot.com and Back: Lessons on E-Business Spin-Offs and Reintegration." *Information Systems Management*, Summer 2005.

Tjan, A. K. "Finally, a Way to Put Your Internet Portfolio in Order." *Harvard Business Review* (February 2001).

Vic.gov.au. "Network Events." **mmv.vic.gov.au/uploads/ downloads/ICT_projects/eCommerce/NetworxEvets. pdf** (accessed February 2007).

Walsh, B. "Building a Business Plan for An E-Commerce Project." 2004. **networkcomputing.com/917/917f2. html;jsessionid=AHPLYA1KSHEPEQSNDBCS KHSCJUMEKJVN** (accessed February 2007).

Wang, F, and G. Forgionne. "BSC-Based Framework for E-Business Strategy," in Khosrow-Pour (2006).

Ward, J., and J. Peppard. *Strategic Planning for Information Systems*, 3rd ed. Chichester, UK: John Wiley & Sons, 2002.

Wheelen, T., and J. Hunger. *Cases in Strategic Management and Business Policy*, 9th ed. Upper Saddle River, NJ: Prentice Hall, 2003.

Wordlingo.com, "Case Study: DMCV." *Wordlingo.com*, 2006. **worldlingo.com/en/company/wl_case_study001.html** (accessed November 2006).

Wordlingo.com, "Instant Website Translator," *Wordlingo.com*, 2006. **worldlingo.com/en/products/instant_website_translator.html** (accessed November 2006).

Xie, F. T., and W. J. Johnston. "Strategic Alliances: Incorporating the Impact of e-Business Technological Innovations." *Journal of Business and Industrial Marketing,* (March 2004).

Yunker, J. "Lowering the Currency Exchange Barrier." *Global by Design*, March 3, 2006. **globalbydesign.com/2006/03/03/lowering-the-currency-exchange-barrier** (accessed December 2006).

Zhu, K., and K. Kraemer. "E-Commerce Metrics for Net-Enhanced Organizations: Assessing the Value of E-Commerce to Firm Performance in the Manufacturing Sector." *Information Systems Research* (September 2002).

Zhuhai Flight Training Center. "Southern China Planning Aggressive E-Commerce Strategy. March 2, 2006. **zhftc.com/news_detailEN.asp?id=86** (accessed February 2007).

ECONOMICS AND JUSTIFICATION OF ELECTRONIC COMMERCE

Content

Learning Objectives

Upon completion of this chapter, you will be able to:

1. Describe the need for justifying EC investments, how it is done, and how metrics are used to determine justification.

2. Understand the difficulties in measuring and justifying EC investments.

3. Recognize the difficulties in establishing intangible metrics and describe how to overcome them.

4. List and briefly describe traditional and advanced methods of justifying IT investments.

5. Understand how e-CRM, e-learning, and other EC projects are justified.

6. Describe some economic principles of EC.

7. Understand how product, industry, seller, and buyer characteristics impact the economics of EC.

8. Recognize key factors in the success of EC projects and the major reasons for failures.

JUSTIFYING INVESTMENT IN IT AND EC AT CALIFORNIA STATE AUTOMOBILE ASSOCIATION

The Problem

California State Automobile Association (CSAA) is a 7,000 employee, not-for-profit organization serving residents across northern California, Nevada, and Utah. Focusing on membership, travel, and insurance, CSAA provides services for more than 5 million members and annually processes 3 billion documents and scans 1.6 million images.

To support its members and employees, CSAA had a major IT infrastructure based on 600 servers. However, these servers were 4.5 years old; vendors were no longer supporting their operating systems; there were security patches and outages; and disk failures and crashes were common. In short, the existing infrastructure was nearing its end of life. This created numerous problems not to mention the inability to launch or improve e-commerce projects, such as automated members self-service capabilities and enterprise-level customer service.

The Solution

To support existing and future EC and IT applications, it was necessary to replace the 600 servers. The upgrading would reduce the number of servers to 136 for less maintenance and better utilization. Also, the solution would ensure CSAA received the latest security patches and antivirus updates for its 8,500 PCs. The solution also calls for innovations such as Web farms (or Web servers), which increase the capabilities of the individual servers.

CSAA developed a business case for the solution and its outsourcing. EDS, a large outsourcer won the bid. The projected cost of the project was $5 million for hardware and $2.5 million for EDS services. A five-year rate-of-investment (ROI) projection justified the project (see the spreadsheet calculations below). This was part of the business case submitted to top management.

Projected Costs and Benefits for the CSAA Infrastructure Proposal

Project Costs	Year 1	Year 2	Year 3	Year 4	Year 5	Total
Hardware	$5,000,000	$0	$0	$0	$0	$5,000,000
EDS Charge	$2,500,000	$0	$0	$0	$0	$2,500,000
Total Project Costs	$7,500,000	$0	$0	$0	$0	$7,500,000

Benefits	Year 1	Year 2	Year 3	Year 4	Year 5	Total
Productivity	$270,000	$270,000	$270,000	$270,000	$270,000	$1,350,000
Cost Avoidance	$1,680,000	$1,680,000	$1,680,000	$1,680,000	$1,680,000	$8,400,000
Hardware Savings	$3,644,800	$3,644,800	$3,644,800	$3,644,800	$3,644,800	$18,224,000
Support Improvement	$1,795,200	$1,795,200	$1,795,200	$1,795,200	$1,795,200	$8,976,000
Total Benefits	$7,390,000	$7,390,000	$7,390,000	$7,390,000	$7,390,000	$36,950,000

Financial Analysis	Year 1	Year 2	Year 3	Year 4	Year 5
Net Value	($110,000)	$7,390,000	$7,390,000	$7,390,000	$7,390,000
Cumulative Net Value	($110,000)	$7,280,000	$14,670,000	$22,060,000	$29,450,000
Net Present Value	$21,863,789				

The Results

The results of the spreadsheet analysis indicate extremely positive return on the investment. The required investment of $7.5 million would be paid back in just over 12 months. The total accumulated tangible realized net benefits of almost $29.5 million translates into almost $22 million NPV (based on a 9 percent interest rate). The computed ROI of 493 percent is extremely high, and it convinced management to approve the project. In addition to the financial results, CSAA can deliver

better and faster customer service; reduce the total cost of ownership of its IT infrastructure; support the company's growth; and offer EC services, such as automated self-service capabilities. Finally, security and privacy protection improved dramatically, all of which makes the 5 million members and the 7,000 employees much happier.

Sources: Compiled from EDS.com (2006a), EDS.com (2006b), and *scaa.com* (accessed January 2007).

WHAT WE CAN LEARN . . .

The case illustrates a situation in which an organization needed to decide on upgrading and restructuring its infrastructure used for several EC and IT applications. Once the goals and the technical solution were specified, CSAA prepared a business case that was used both for conducting a bid among competing vendors and for getting the approval from top management. To justify the investment, CSAA used a five-year projection utilizing three traditional tools to assess the ROI, NPV, and payback period. While the justification included only measurable tangible benefits, the analysis recognized significant intangible benefits, such as improved customer service.

In this case there was no need to quantify the intangible benefits because the return of the tangible benefits was more than sufficient to justify the investment. Furthermore, several quantifiable results, such as total cost of operation (TCO), and increased response time, were excluded from the financial spreadsheet for the same reason. Finally, CSAA decided to outsource the upgrading project and concentrate on its core competency.

The previous concepts are the main topics described in this chapter. Other topics described are more advanced tools that can be used for more complex justification situations and for handling the intangible benefits and costs. The chapter also presents the topics of the economics of EC and the conditions necessary to ensure its success.

15.1 WHY JUSTIFY E-COMMERCE INVESTMENTS; HOW CAN THEY BE JUSTIFIED?

Companies need to justify their EC investments for a number of different reasons.

INCREASED DEMAND FOR FINANCIAL JUSTIFICATION

Once upon a time, or so the story goes, the beggars of New York City decided to conduct a competition as to who could collect the most money in one day. Many innovative ideas were employed, and several beggars collected almost $1,000 each. The winner, however, collected $5 million. When asked how he did it, the beggar replied: "I made a sign that said 'EC experts need funding for an innovative electronic marketplace' and put the sign in front of the New York Stock Exchange."

This story symbolizes what happened from 1995 through 2000, when EC projects and start-up companies were funded with little analysis of their business viability or finances. The result of the rush to invest was the 2001–2003 "dot-com bust," when hundreds of EC start-ups went out of business and the stock market crashed. Some companies and individual investors lost over 90 to 100 percent of their investments! Furthermore, many companies, even large ones such as Disney, Merrill Lynch, and Sears terminated EC projects after losing considerable amounts of money and realizing few benefits from huge investments. The positive result of the crash was the "back-to-basics" movement, namely, a return to carefully checking and scrutinizing any request for EC funding.

Today, companies are holding the line on IT and EC budgets. According to Pisello (2004), IT executives feel the demand for financial justification and planning from executives (see Peppard and Ward 2005), but most face an uphill battle to address this new accountability, as demonstrated by the following statistics:

- Sixty-five percent of companies lack the knowledge or tools to do ROI calculations.
- Seventy-five percent have no formal processes or budgets in place for measuring ROI.
- Sixty-eight percent do not measure how projects coincide with promised benefits six months after completion.

At the same time, demand for expanding or initiating e-business projects remains strong. In order to achieve the optimal level of investment, CIOs will need to effectively communicate the value of proposed EC projects in order to gain approval.

OTHER REASONS WHY EC JUSTIFICATION IS NEEDED

The following are some additional reasons for conducting EC justification:

- Companies now realize that EC is not necessarily the solution to all problems. Therefore, EC projects must *compete for funding and resources* with other internal and external projects, as described in Chapter 14. Analysis is needed to determine when funding of an EC project is appropriate.
- Some large companies, and many public organizations, mandate a formal evaluation of requests for funding.
- Companies need to assess the success of EC projects after completion, and later on a periodic basis (see Chapter 14).
- The success of EC projects may be assessed in order to pay bonuses to those involved with the project.

Reasons for IT and EC justification reported by *CIO Insight* (2004) are: pressure from top management, internal competition for funding, the large amount of money involved, and weak business conditions. The same study found that justification forces EC and IT into better alignment with the corporate business strategy. Finally, justification increases the credibility of EC projects.

EC INVESTMENT CATEGORIES AND BENEFITS

Before we look at how to justify EC investments, let's examine the nature of such investments. One basic way to categorize different EC investments is to distinguish between investment in infrastructure and investment in specific EC applications.

The *IT infrastructure* provides the foundation for EC applications in the enterprise. The IT infrastructure includes intranets, extranets, data centers, data warehouses, and knowledge bases, and many applications throughout the enterprise share the infrastructure (see Broadbent and Weill 1997). Infrastructure investments are made for the long-term.

EC applications are specific systems and programs for achieving certain objectives; for example, taking a customer order online or providing eCRM. The number of EC applications can be large. They may be in one functional department or several departments may share them, which makes evaluation of their costs and benefits more complex.

Ross and Beath (2002) propose another way to look at EC and investment categories. They base their categories on the *purpose of the investment*. They also suggest a cost justification (funding) approach as well as the probable owner of each application (e.g., specific department or corporate ownership). Devaraj and Kohli (2002) offer other investment categories—dividing EC investments into operational, managerial, and strategic types—along with Martin (2006). The variety of EC investment categories demonstrates the complex nature of EC investments.

The basic reasons that companies invest in IT and EC are to: improve business processes, lower costs, increase productivity, increase customer satisfaction and retention, increase revenue, reduce time-to-market, and increase market share.

Specific Benefits

According to a *CIO Insight* (2004) survey, companies want to get the following benefits from an IT (including EC) investment: cost reduction (84 percent); productivity improvement (77 percent); improved customer satisfaction (66 percent); improved staffing levels

(57 percent); higher revenues (45 percent); higher earnings (43 percent); better customer retention (42 percent); more return of equity (33 percent); and faster time-to-market (31 percent). (Note that separate data for EC are not available.)

HOW IS AN EC INVESTMENT JUSTIFIED?

Justifying an EC investment means comparing the costs of each project against its benefits in what is known as a **cost-benefit analysis**. To conduct such an analysis, it is necessary to define and measure the relevant EC benefits and costs. Cost-benefit analysis is frequently assessed by *return on investment (ROI),* which is also the name of a specific method for evaluating investments (see Paton and Troppito 2004).

A number of different methods measure the *business value* of EC and IT investments. Traditional methods that support such analyses are net present value (NPV) and ROI (see Online File W15.1). More advanced methods also can be used to justify these investments. Section 15.3 discusses traditional and more advanced justification methods.

cost-benefit analysis
A comparison of the costs of a project against the benefits.

Business Justification and Business Case

In Chapter 14 we presented the topic of *business case,* which is the formal document for justifying investments in internal IT or EC projects (recall the CSAA case). The cost-benefit analysis and the business value are part of the business case.

Several vendors provide templates, tools, guidelines, and more for preparing the business case for specific areas. For example, businessedge.com provides an SOA Business Case Resource Kit (The templates are in Microsoft Word). ROI is calculated with Excel's templates (see businessedge.com/commerce/?c=419).

WHAT NEEDS TO BE JUSTIFIED? WHEN SHOULD JUSTIFICATION TAKE PLACE?

Not all EC investments need to be formally justified. In some cases, a simple one-page qualitative justification will do. The following are cases where formal evaluation may not be needed:

▶ When the value of the investment is relatively small for the organization
▶ When the relevant data are not available, are inaccurate, or are too volatile
▶ When the EC project is mandated—it must be done regardless of the costs and benefits involved

However, even when formal analysis is not required, an organization should have at least some qualitative analysis to explain the logic of investing in the EC project. For more details, see Martin (2006) and Sawhney (2002a).

USING METRICS IN EC JUSTIFICATION

A **metric** is a specific, measurable standard against which actual performance is compared. Metrics are used to describe costs, benefits, or the ratio between them. They are used not only for justification but also for other economic activities (e.g., to compare employee performance in order to reward specific employees). Metrics can produce very positive results in organizations by driving behavior in a number of ways. According to Rayport and Jaworski (2004), metrics can:

metric
A specific, measurable standard against which actual performance is compared.

▶ Define the value proposition of business models
▶ Communicate a business strategy to the workforce through performance targets
▶ Increase accountability when metrics are linked with performance-appraisal programs
▶ Align the objectives of individuals, departments, and divisions to the enterprise's strategic objectives
▶ Track the performance of EC systems, including usage, types of visitors, page visits, conversion rate, etc.
▶ Assess the health of companies by using tools such as balanced scorecards and performance dashboards

An example of IT metrics implementation can be found in a white paper on the impact of a new online service on the profitability of Axon Computertime, a small computer services business in New Zealand (Green 2002 and Chapter 14). Axon used the following metrics: *revenue growth*, *cost reduction*, *cost avoidance*, *customer fulfillment*, *customer service*, and *customer communications*. The last few metrics in this list highlight the importance of including nonfinancial measures in the measurement of organizational performance.

In many cases, such measures involve intangible benefits, a topic we will discuss later. Also, note that metrics require the definition of particular measures.

Metrics, Measurements, and Key Performance Indicators

Metrics need to be defined properly with a clear way to measure them. For example, *revenue growth* can be measured in total dollars, in percentage change over time, or in percentage growth as compared to the entire industry. *Cost avoidance,* for example, can be achieved in many ways, one of which may be "decrease obsolete stock write-offs as percentage of revenue." Defining the specific measures is critical; otherwise, what the metrics actually measure may be open to interpretation.

The *balanced scorecard method* (introduced in Chapter 14 and discussed later in this chapter) uses customer metrics, financial metrics, internal business processes metrics, and learning and growth metrics. Metrics are related to the goals, objectives, vision, and plans of the organization. **key performance indicators (KPI)**, which are the quantitative expression of critically important metrics (known as *critical success factors*), frequently measure metrics that deal directly with performance (e.g., sales, profits). Frequently, one metric has several KPIs.

Any organization, private or public, can use metrics. Let's look at an example. In Australia, the government of Victoria (vic.gov.au) is one of the leaders in exploiting the Internet to provide a one-stop service center called "Do It Online." In the United States, MyCalifornia (my.ca.gov) offers many services for the citizens of California. In either case, the metric of "travel and wait time" for the citizens who would otherwise have to visit a physical office justifies offering the service of renewing driver's licenses.

We limit our discussion here mostly to individual EC projects or initiatives. EC projects deal mostly with the automation of business processes, and as such, they can be viewed as *capital investment* decisions. Chapter 16 discusses investment in a start-up company.

Now that we understand the need for conducting EC justification and the use of metrics, let's see why EC justification is so difficult to accomplish.

key performance indicators (KPI)
The quantitative expression of critically important metrics.

Section 15.1 ▶ REVIEW QUESTIONS

1. List some of the reasons for justifying an EC investment.
2. Describe the risks of not conducting an EC justification study.
3. Describe how an EC investment is justified.
4. List the major EC investment categories.
5. When is justification of EC investments unnecessary?
6. What are metrics? What benefits do they offer?

15.2 DIFFICULTIES IN MEASURING AND JUSTIFYING E-COMMERCE INVESTMENTS

Justifying EC (and IT) projects can be a complex and, therefore, difficult process. Let's see why.

THE EC JUSTIFICATION PROCESS

The EC justification process varies depending on the situation and the methods used. However, in its extreme, it can be very complex, as shown by Gunasekaren et al. (2001), Misra (2006), and Tillquist and Rodgers (2005). They identified five areas that must be considered in the justification of IT projects, as shown in Exhibit 15.1. In this section, we

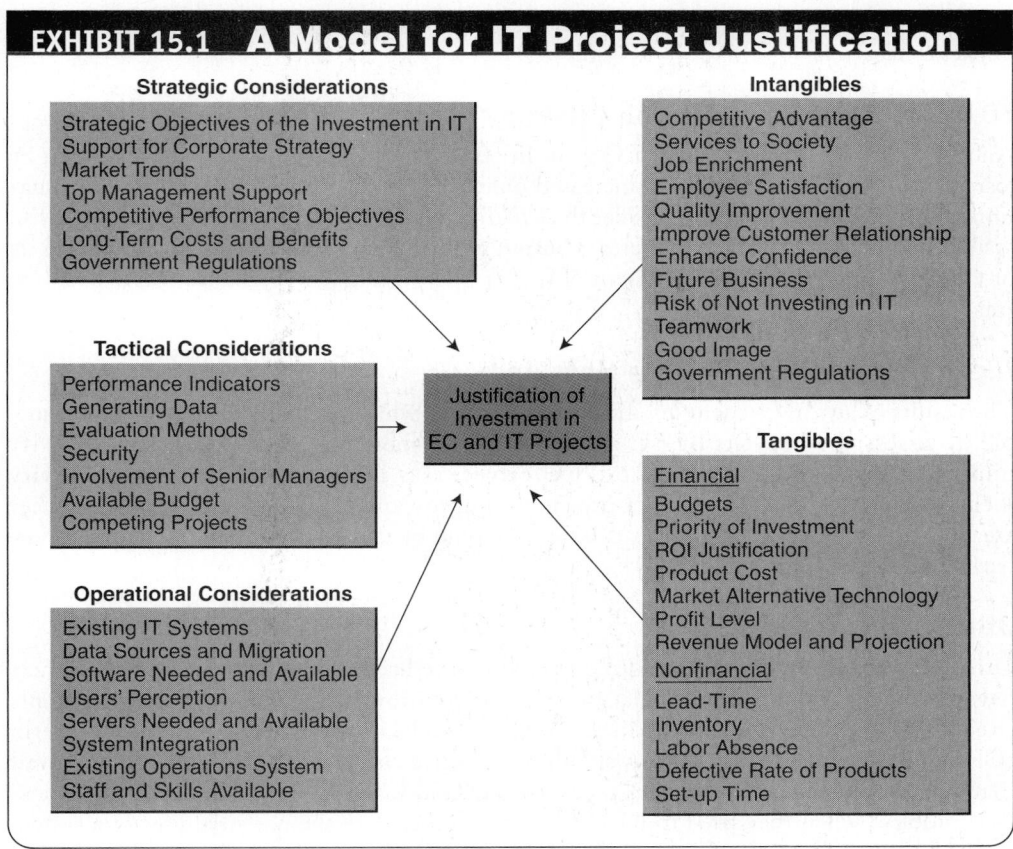

EXHIBIT 15.1   A Model for IT Project Justification

Strategic Considerations

Strategic Objectives of the Investment in IT
Support for Corporate Strategy
Market Trends
Top Management Support
Competitive Performance Objectives
Long-Term Costs and Benefits
Government Regulations

Tactical Considerations

Performance Indicators
Generating Data
Evaluation Methods
Security
Involvement of Senior Managers
Available Budget
Competing Projects

Operational Considerations

Existing IT Systems
Data Sources and Migration
Software Needed and Available
Users' Perception
Servers Needed and Available
System Integration
Existing Operations System
Staff and Skills Available

Justification of
Investment in
EC and IT Projects

Intangibles

Competitive Advantage
Services to Society
Job Enrichment
Employee Satisfaction
Quality Improvement
Improve Customer Relationship
Enhance Confidence
Future Business
Risk of Not Investing in IT
Teamwork
Good Image
Government Regulations

Tangibles

Financial
Budgets
Priority of Investment
ROI Justification
Product Cost
Market Alternative Technology
Profit Level
Revenue Model and Projection
Nonfinancial

Lead-Time
Inventory
Labor Absence
Defective Rate of Products
Set-up Time

Sources: Compiled from Gunasekaran, A., et al. "A Model for Investment Justification in Information Technology Projects." *International Journal of Information Management* (October 2001), copyright (2001), with permission from Elsevier, and Misra, R. "Evolution of the Philosophy of Investments in IT Projects," *Issues in Informing Sciences and Information Technology,* Vol. 3, 2006.

also discuss intangibles and tangibles. In Chapter 14, we discussed some strategic and tactical considerations.

We will see later in this section that one major difficulty with EC justification is measuring intangible benefits and costs. Next, we provide other difficulties in conducting justifications.

DIFFICULTIES IN MEASURING PRODUCTIVITY AND PERFORMANCE GAINS

One of the major benefits of using EC is increased productivity. However, productivity increases may be difficult to measure for a number of different reasons.

Data and Analysis Issues

Data, or the analysis of the data, may hide productivity gains. Why is this so? For manufacturing, it is fairly easy to measure outputs and inputs. For example, General Motors produces motor vehicles—a relatively well-defined product—that show gradual quality changes over time. It is not difficult to identify the inputs used to produce these vehicles with reasonable accuracy. However, in service industries, such as finance or health-care delivery, it is more difficult to define what the products are, how they change in quality, and how they may be related to corresponding benefits and costs.

For example, banks now use EC to handle a large portion of deposits and withdrawal transactions through ATMs. The ability to withdraw cash from ATMs 24/7 is a substantial benefit for customers compared with the limited hours of the physical branch. But, what is the value of this to the bank in comparison with the associated costs? If the incremental value exceeds the incremental costs, then it represents a productivity gain; otherwise the productivity impact is negative.

EC Productivity Gains May Be Offset by Losses in Other Areas

Another possible difficulty is that EC gains in certain areas of the company may be offset by losses in other areas. For example, increased online sales may decrease off-line sales, a situation known as *cannibalism*. Or consider the situation where an organization installs a new EC system that makes it possible to increase output per employee; if the organization reduces its production staff but has to increase its IT staff, the productivity gains from EC could be small, or even negative.

Incorrectly Defining What Is Measured

The results of any investment justification depend on what is actually measured. For example, to assess the benefits of EC investment, one should usually look at productivity improvement in the area where the EC project was installed. However, productivity increase may not necessarily be a profitable improvement (e.g., due to losses in other areas). The problem of definitions can be overcome by using appropriate metrics and key performance indicators.

Other Difficulties

Other performance measurement difficulties also have been noted. A number of researchers have pointed out, for example, that time lags may throw off productivity measurements (Reichheld and Schefter 2000; Misra 2006). Many EC investments, especially those in eCRM, take five to six years to show significant positive results, but many studies do not wait that long to measure productivity changes. Devaraj and Kohli (2003) suggested another possible problem when they tried to relate the actual rather than the potential uses of a system with IT expenditures. For a list of other factors that impact performance, see Devaraj and Kohli (2002).

RELATING IT EXPENDITURES TO ORGANIZATIONAL PERFORMANCE

Exhibit 15.2 shows some of the difficulties in finding the relationship between EC investment and organizational performance. The exhibit shows that the relationship between investment and performance is indirect; factors such as shared IT assets and how they are used can impact organizational performance and make it difficult to assess the value of an IT (or EC) investment.

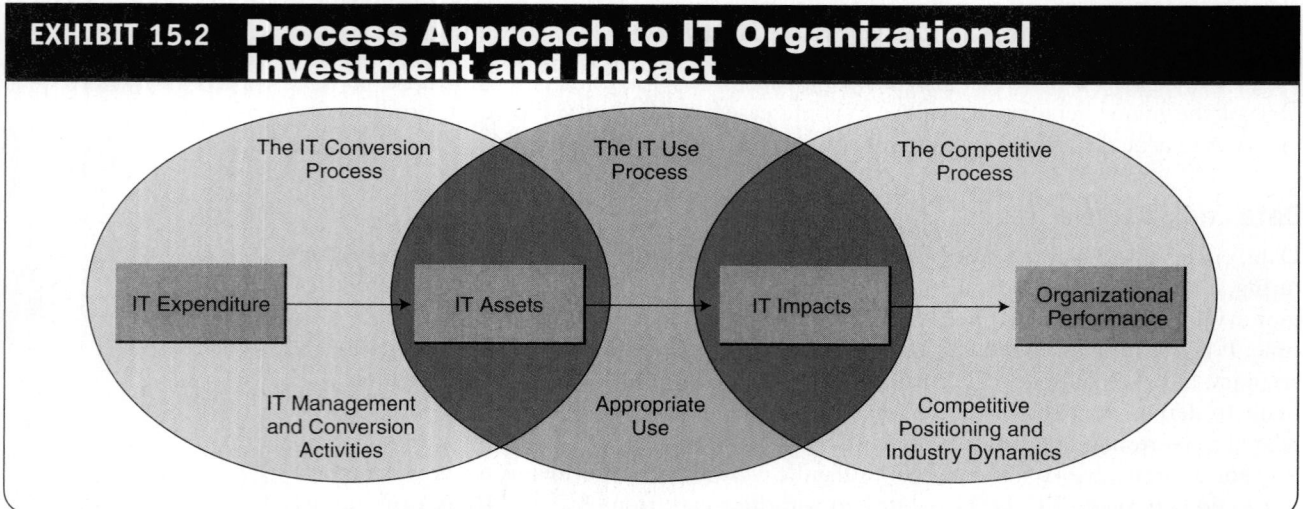

EXHIBIT 15.2 Process Approach to IT Organizational Investment and Impact

Source: Soh, C., and L. M. Markus, "How IT Creates Business Value: A Process Theory Synthesis," *Proceedings of the 16th International Conference on Information Systems,* Amsterdam, Netherlands, December 1995. Used with permission of the authors.

Furthermore, changes in organizational performance may occur years after installing an EC application. Thus, proper evaluation must be done over the entire life cycle of the system. This requires forecasting, which may be difficult. In EC, it is even more difficult because investors often require that risky and fast-changing EC systems pay for themselves within three years. For further discussion, see Keystone Strategy (2006).

DIFFICULTIES IN MEASURING INTANGIBLE COSTS AND BENEFITS

Broadly speaking, EC costs and benefits can be classified into two categories: tangible and intangible. *Tangible* costs and benefits are easier to measure once metrics, such as the cost of software (cost) and the amount of labor saved (benefit), are determined. *Intangible* costs and benefits are usually more difficult to measure.

Tangible Costs and Benefits

Tangible costs are those that are easy to measure and quantify and that relate directly to a specific investment. The costs involved in purchasing hardware, software, consulting, and support services usually are tangible, as are the costs of telecommunication services, maintenance, and labor. These costs can be measured through accounting information (e.g., from the general ledger). Similarly, tangible benefits, including increased profitability, improved productivity, and greater market share, can be measured with relative ease.

Intangible Costs and Benefits

When it comes to *intangible* costs and benefits, organizations must develop innovative metrics to track them as accurately as possible. Intangible costs may include the learning curve of the firm's customer service employees to incorporate an EC system to respond to customer inquiries. Another intangible cost may involve having to change or adapt other business processes or information systems, such as processing items returned by customers or building and operating an inventory tracking system. An additional difficulty is separating EC costs from the costs of routine maintenance of inventory and other relevant IT systems.

In many cases, EC projects generate intangible benefits, such as faster time-to-market, increased employee and customer satisfaction, easier distribution, greater organizational agility, and improved control. These are very desirable benefits, but it is difficult to place an accurate monetary value on them. For example, many people would agree that e-mail improves communications, but it is not at all clear how to measure the value of this improvement. Managers are very conscious of the bottom line, but no manager can prove that e-mail is responsible for so many cents per share of the organization's total profits.

Let's consider the case of Web-based portals that consolidate information across the organization so that employees and customers can quickly access information and services from a single point. A large part of the ROI of a portal lies in the efficiency gained by internal users. Portals enable employees, for example, to access customer information quickly, accurately, and efficiently in order to better respond to the customer's needs. Such benefits are intangible.

One specific EC application may generate multiple intangible benefits, some of which will materialize only after a year or two.

Intangible benefits can be complex, yet substantial. For example, according to Arno Penzias, a Nobel Laureate in physics, the New York Metropolitan Transit Authority (MTA) had not found the need to open another airport for almost two decades, even though air traffic had tripled. According to Penzias's study, the existing airports were able to meet increased air traffic needs due to productivity gains derived from improved IT systems (quoted by Devaraj and Kohli 2002). IT systems added by the MTA played critical roles in ticket reservations, passenger and luggage check-in, crew assignment and scheduling, runway maintenance and management, and gate assignments. These improvements enabled the MTA to cope with increased traffic without adding new facilities, saving hundreds of millions of dollars. Many similar examples of increased capacity exist. Intangible benefits are especially common in service and government applications (see Steyaert 2004).

One class of intangible benefits, according to Ryan and Gates (2004), is *social subsystem issues* that include comfort to employees, impact on the physical environment, changes to the power distribution in an organization, and preventing invasion of the privacy of employees and customers.

An analyst could ignore intangible benefits, but doing so implies that their value is zero, which may lead the organization to reject EC investments that could substantially increase revenues and profitability. Therefore, it is necessary to consider intangible benefits in a way that reflects their potential impact. The question is how to do it. For further discussion, see Borenstein et al. (2005).

Handling Intangible Benefits

The first step in dealing with intangible benefits is to define them and specify how they are going to be measured by attaching metrics to them. Exhibit 15.3 provides an example of intangible and tangible metrics as they relate to EC users.

The most straightforward solution to the problem of evaluating intangible benefits in cost-benefit analysis is to make *rough estimates* of the monetary values of all the intangible

EXHIBIT 15.3 Sample EC Metrics for Various Entities of Users

EC User	Tangible Metrics	Intangible Metrics
Buyer (B2C)	• Cost/price of the product • Time in executing the transaction • Number of available alternatives	• Ease of use of EC • Convenience in purchasing • Information availability • Reliability of the transaction • Privacy of personal data
Seller (B2C)	• Profit per customer • Conversion rate of visitors • Customer retention rate • Inventory costs • Profit per item sold • Market share	• Customer satisfaction • Customer loyalty • Transaction security
Net-enhanced organization (B2B)	• From design-to-market (time) • Cash-to-cash cycle • Percentage of orders delivered on time or early • Profit per item sold	• Flexibility in changing purchase orders • Agility to sustain unplanned production increase • Risk reduction • Improved quality of products/services
Government (G2C)	• Reduction in cost of transactions • Reduction in licensing fees • Increase in participation in government programs • Lower tax rates	• Citizen satisfaction • Reelection of candidates • Choice of interacting with elected officials • Promoting democratic principles • Disseminating more information quickly

Additional Examples of Measurements Made Using Metrics

- More than one-third of consumers use the same password for online banking as they do for other online activities.
- More than 50 brands were targeted by phishing scams in November 2004.
- More than half of consumers say they are less likely to respond to an e-mail from their bank because of phishing threats.
- Experts say that 80 percent of the infrastructures of large industries are likely to be hit by cyber attacks.
- Some consumers of financial products say phishing has turned them away from Web transactions.
- Consumers are slightly more likely to receive permission-based e-mails from online merchants than other retail businesses.
- Two-thirds of computers have spyware on them.
- Spam messages are considerably shorter than legitimate e-mails.
- eBay tops the list of online destinations on Black Friday (the day after Thanksgiving).
- Spam takes up volume, but not bandwidth.

Sources: Compiled from *cio.com/metrics/index.cfm* (accessed December 2004–January 2005), Borenstein et al. (2005), and Sardar et al. (2006).

benefits and then conduct an ROI or similar financial analysis. The simplicity of this approach is attractive, but in many cases the assumptions used in these estimates are debatable. If an organization acquires the EC technology because decision makers assigned too high a value to intangible benefits, the organization could find that it has wasted some valuable resources. On the other hand, if the valuation of intangible benefits is too low, the organization may reject the EC investment and later find itself losing market share to competitors who did implement the technology. See Plumtree Corp. (now a part of BEA Corp.) for a study on translating intangible benefits to dollar amounts.

Intangible costs and benefits may be approached in a number of different ways (e.g., see Sawhney 2002a). Several of the methods presented in Section 15.3 also can be used to evaluate intangible benefits. For more on intangible costs and benefits, see Online File W15.2.

The problems of measuring intangible costs and benefits become more complex as companies try to justify large investments in EC because of the special characteristics of EC. Intuitively, we know that EC provides significant benefits of flexibility, ease of use, and low transaction costs. However, how can management quantify these intangible benefits? Nucleus Research (2002) suggests that ROI justification metrics should provide management with a consistent, reliable, and repeatable process that can compare the relative impact of investment opportunities on the company's bottom line.

Handling Uncertainties

Return on EC projects are far from being certain. Lucas (2005) provides examples of IT and EC projects and provides their probability of success. The problem is that success can be in a broad range, even 0 to 1. Lucas suggests using the most likely value and multiplying it by the anticipated value of the benefits.

THE PROCESS OF JUSTIFYING EC AND IT PROJECTS

Justifying large-scale investments is not only about selecting a method; it is also about how to execute it. The appropriate process is not simple. The major steps of this process according to Alinean.com (2006) and *Baseline* (2006) are:

- Lay an appropriate foundation for analysis with your vendor, and then conduct your ROI.
- Conduct a good research on metrics (including internal and external metrics) and validate them.
- Justify and document the cost and benefit assumptions.
- Document and verify all figures used in the calculation. Clarify all assumptions.
- Do not leave out strategic benefits, including long-term ones. Is the project really bolstering the company's competitive and strategic advantage?
- Be careful not to underestimate cost and overestimate benefits (a tendency of many managers).
- Make figures as realistic as possible and include risk analysis.
- Commit all partners, including vendors and top management.

These difficulties cause many companies not to measure the value of IT and EC projects (Alter 2006). This can be a risky approach. For those companies that like to try a formal justification, we present a number of methods in Sections 15.3 and 15.4.

Section 15.2 ▶ REVIEW QUESTIONS

1. How do organizations measure performance and productivity? What are the difficulties in measuring performance and productivity?
2. Why is it difficult to relate EC (IT) investments to organizational performance? List the major reasons.
3. Define *tangible costs and benefits*.
4. Define *intangible costs and benefits* and explain why they must be considered when justifying an IT investment.
5. Why is it difficult to measure the value of intangible benefits?

6. Describe a simple approach to the intangibles problem.

7. How should management handle the uncertainties of benefits?

15.3 METHODS AND TOOLS FOR EVALUATING AND JUSTIFYING E-COMMERCE INVESTMENTS

Now that we have an understanding of the difficulties of EC justification and how organizations evaluate EC investments, let's examine the methods and tools used for such evaluation and justification. Companies use commercially available tools or develop in-house tools through the use of spreadsheets (e.g., Excel spreadsheets). And as with the economic justification of non-EC investments, a number of different methods can be applied to EC investments.

Devaraj and Kohli (2002) discuss a number of different justification methods, such as *cost-benefit analysis, break-even point, NPV, economic value added,* and *real options* for traditional IT investment. At their core, all economic justification approaches attempt to account for the costs and benefits of investments. They differ in their ability to account for the tangible and intangible and the present and future costs and benefits of EC, particularly when compared to other corporate investments. Borenstein et al. (2005) proposed a multicriteria model.

OPPORTUNITIES AND REVENUE GENERATED BY EC INVESTMENT

A major difficulty in assessing the EC value is the *measurement* of possible benefits (tangible and intangible) that drive EC investment (see Peppard and Ward 2005 and Tillquist and Rogers 2005). Furthermore, some of these are opportunities that may or may not materialize, so there is only a certain probability for return on the EC investment. Lucas (2005) refers to these investments as the *opportunity matrix*.

In preparing the business case for EC investment, as we will describe later, one should examine the potential *additional revenues* that are expressed in the *revenue models.* Chapter 1 presented the typical revenue models generated by EC and the Web. In addition, many other opportunities exist (e.g., see Straub 2004). Examples are:

▶ Companies that allow people to play games for a fee or watch a sports competition in real time for a fee (e.g., see espn.com).

▶ Increased revenues via products or services from a larger global market because of more effective product marketing on the Web.

▶ Increased margins attained by using processes with lower internal cost (e.g., using lower-cost thin client terminals, which are low-cost, centrally-managed computers without CD-ROM players, diskette drives, and expansion slots limiting the capabilities of these computers to only essential applications, usually using software as a service [SaaS]) and from higher prices because of value—added services to the customer (e.g., information attached to product).

▶ Increased revenues as a consequence of becoming an online portal.

▶ Increased value-added content from selling searches, access to data, and electronic documents.

METHODOLOGICAL ASPECTS OF JUSTIFYING EC INVESTMENTS

Before presenting the specific methods for EC justification, let's examine the methodological issues that are common to most of these methods.

Types of Costs

Although costs may appear to be the simple side of a cost-benefit analysis, they may not be so simple. Here are a few things to consider:

▶ **Distinguish between initial (up-front) costs and operating costs.** The initial costs may be a one-time investment or they may spread over several months or a year. In addition, system operating cost needs to be considered.

❿ **Direct and indirect share costs.** *Direct costs* can be related directly to a specific project. *Indirect costs* usually are infrastructure-related costs. In addition, the costs may be related to several EC and IT projects. Therefore, one needs to *allocate* these costs to the specific projects. Such allocation may not be easy to perform; a number of approaches to cost allocation are available (consult an accountant).

❿ **In-kind costs.** Although it is easy to track monetary payments, costs also may be *in kind*; for example, contributions of a manager, machine time, and so on. These frequently are indirect *shared* costs (e.g., overhead), which complicates their calculation.

TRADITIONAL METHODS FOR EVALUATING EC INVESTMENTS

The following are the most popular methods for evaluating IT and EC investments. For details see Pisello (2006) and Wattemann (2007).

ROI Method

The ROI method uses a formula that divides the total net benefits (revenues less costs, for each year) by the initial cost. The result is a ratio that measures the ROI for each year or for an entire period. Online File W15.1 provides the ROI formula and an example. In calculating ROI, one should consider the following.

Payback Period

With the payback-period method, the company calculates how long it will take for the net benefits to pay back the entire initial investment. Online File W15.1 also provides the details of this method.

NPV

Organizations often use NPV calculations for cost-benefit analyses. In an NPV analysis, analysts convert future values of benefits to their present-value equivalents by discounting them at the organization's cost of funds. This requires that analysts determine a discount rate, which can be the average or the marginal interest rate paid by a company to obtain loans. Then the analyst can compare the present value of the future benefits with the present value of the costs required to achieve those benefits, to determine whether the benefits exceed the costs. A project with estimated NPV greater than zero may be a candidate for acceptance. One with an estimated NPV less than zero would probably be rejected. One needs to consider the intangible benefits. For more specific guidelines and decision criteria on how NPV analysis works, consult a financial management textbook and Online File W15.1.

Business ROI

When conducting cost-benefit analyses, it is advisable to distinguish between *business ROI* and *technology ROI* (see alinean.com/P_ROIcalculator.asp).

Business ROI relates to the EC investment benefits incurred for the improvement of the business and its operations, such as:

❿ Improved user ability to access all the resources to deliver key business processes
❿ Streamlined and lower costs of business processes both inside and outside the organization
❿ Collaboration by people across locations to gain operational efficiencies
❿ Embedded training within the EC application to ensure organizational compliance
❿ Increased satisfaction among users as well as partners
❿ Transformation of the organization by streamlining access to information and automating processes such as online filing of expense statements, ordering office supplies, and making travel arrangements

Here is a simple example of computing business ROI.

Example: ROI for Coffeehouse and Restaurants Wi-Fi. Between 2004 and 2006 a large number of coffeehouses and restaurants installed Wi-Fi hotpoints for their customers.

Notable were Starbucks and McDonald's (Chapter 9). Does it really pay off (especially when it is provided for free)? Spark (2004) cites the following two examples:

Schlotzsky's Inc., owner of 600 deli restaurants, installed free hotspots in 30 of their restaurants in 2004. For those 30 restaurants, the company figures that 6 percent of customers come for the free access and free computers. As a result, Schlotzsky's estimates that in-store computing generates 15,000 additional customer visits a year. With customers spending an average of $7 per visit, that's more than $1 million in revenue per store per year.

Dan Welch, who owns three World Cup Coffee shops in Portland, Oregon, estimates that his free Wi-Fi network has added 10 percent to his overall revenue. Welch credits Wi-Fi consumers with spending three times as much on food compared with the average consumer. (Note: To find these free Wi-Fi places, enter jiwire.com.)

Technology ROI

Technology ROI relates to the EC investment benefits incurred by improvements in the integration of technology and its deployment, such as:

- Architecture that supports continued growth and proliferation of an EC project throughout the organization
- Simplified purchase, use, and deployment of technology
- Establishment of an open development environment to ensure seamless integration and access to information
- Embedded collaboration across all of an organization's applications
- Reduced complexity of managing content, applications, infrastructure, and stand-alone tools

Usually, several EC and IT projects share technology ROI so it is difficult to allocate costs to specific EC projects. Technology ROI is often ignored in traditional ROI analysis, where the focus generally is only on the business ROI. Although the business case and ROI must drive the decision-making process, the technology ROI constitutes the evaluation of soft costs, which, if ignored, can bias the business ROI. Without the rigor of analysis offered by ad-hoc ROI calculators, EC projects may not live up to the scrutiny of financial experts.

ROI Calculators

ROI calculator
Calculator that uses metrics and formulas to compute ROI.

Vendors and consulting companies have accumulated quite a bit of experience in developing metrics and tools called **ROI calculators** to evaluate investments. Recently, companies specializing in ROI also have developed ROI calculators, some of which are in the public domain.

The Offering from *Baseline* Magazine. One of the major sources of simple calculators is *Baseline* (baselinemag.com). They offer several dozen Excel-based calculators (for free). An example of calculators they offer include:

- How to calculate ROI (*Baseline* 2006)
- Figuring the ROI of RFID
- Comparing smart phones and laptops
- The ROI of Application Performance Management
- Figuring out your true total cost of ownership (TCO)
- The ROI of VoIP
- The cost of videoconferencing solutions

In addition, *Baseline* offers tutorials, guides, statistical data, and more related to these calculators.

Other Calculators. Nucleus Research Inc. (NRI; nucleusresearch.com), a research and advisory company, uses several ROI calculators in helping businesses evaluate IT investments. NRI argues that if a company must make frequent justifications for EC and has unique intangible costs and benefits, it may be necessary to custom build an ROI evaluation tool. For more on NRI see *CIO* (2006).

ROI calculators for e-services are also available. For instance, Streaming Media Inc. (streamingmedia.com) provides an ROI calculator to measure the costs and benefits of telecommunication bandwidth for videoconferencing, streaming video, and video file servers.

Few organizations have attempted to assess the ROI on e-learning, perhaps because it is so difficult to calculate and justify. However, Learnativity.com (learnativity.com) provides resources such as ROI calculators, methodologies, a bibliography, and online communities to support the assessment of e-learning (see learnativity.com/roi-learning.html).

ROI calculators also are available from various other companies, such as Phoenix Technologies (phoenix.com), Citrix (acecostanalyzer.com), and Alinean Inc. (alinean.com). Covalentworks.com specializes in B2B calculators. For more examples of ROI calculators, see roi-calc.com, gantrygroup.com, and phormion.com.

Internal Rate of Return (IRR)

For an investment that requires and produces a number of cash flows over time, people use the internal rate of return (IRR) method. The IRR is the discount rate that makes the NPV of those cash flows equal to zero. Some companies set a minimum acceptable IRR (or hurdle rate) based on their own cost of capital and the minimum percentage return they'd like to see from their investments.

Break-Even Analyses

A *break-even point* is the point at which the benefits of a project are equal to the costs. Firms use this type of analysis to determine the point at which the EC investment starts to pay for itself.

The Total Cost and Benefits of Ownership

The costs of an IT system may accumulate over many years. An interesting approach for IT cost evaluation is the *total cost of ownership*. **Total cost of ownership (TCO)** is a formula for calculating the cost of owning, operating, and controlling an IT system, even one as simple as a PC. The cost includes acquisition costs (hardware and software), operations costs (maintenance, training, operations, evaluation, technical support, installation, downtime, auditing, virus damage, and power consumption), and control costs (standardization, security, central services). The TCO may be 100 percent higher than the cost of the hardware, especially for PCs.

total cost of ownership (TCO)
A formula for calculating the cost of owning, operating, and controlling an IT system.

By identifying these various costs, organizations can make more accurate cost-benefit analyses. David et al. (2002) offer a methodology for calculating TCO. They also provide a detailed example of the items to include in TCO calculations. For further discussion, see Bothama (2006). For a comprehensive study of TCO, see Ferrin and Plank (2002). For calculations in open source environment, see Spector (2006).

A similar concept is **total benefits of ownership (TBO)**. This calculation includes both tangible and intangible benefits. By calculating and comparing TCO and TBO, one can compute the payoff of an IT investment (i.e., *Payoff = TBO − TCO*).

total benefits of ownership (TBO)
Benefits of ownership that include both tangible and intangible benefits.

Economic Value Added

Economic value added (EVA) attempts to quantify the net value added by an investment. It is the return on invested capital (i.e., after-tax cash flow) generated by a company minus the cost of the capital used in creating the cash flow. For example, if the earnings per share are 10 percent and the cost of capital is 12 percent per share, the investment reduces rather than adds economic value.

For a comparison of some of these methods, see Exhibit 15.4 and Pisello (2006).

Using Several Traditional Methods

As you may recall from the opening case, CSAA used the ROI, NPV, and payback period to justify the investment. Each of these measures, as well as the other traditional ones, provides us with a different dimension of the analysis.

EXHIBIT 15.4   Evaluating EC and IT Traditional Investments Methods

Method	Advantages	Disadvantages
Internal rate of return (IRR)	Brings all projects to common footing. Conceptually familiar.	Assumes reinvestment at same rate. Can have multiple roots. No assumed discount rate.
Net present value (NPV) or net worth (NW)	Very common. Maximizes value for unconstrained project selection	Difficult to compare projects of unequal lives or sizes.
Payback period	May be discounted or nondiscounted. Measure of exposure.	Ignores flows after payback is reached. Assumes standard project cash flow profile.
Benefit-to-cost analysis or ratio	Conceptually familiar. Brings all projects to common footing.	May be difficult to classify outlays as expenses or investments.
Economic value added	Measures net value created for the stakeholder.	The true benefits can be difficult to measure.

The ROI is measured over three years (five in the CSAA due to infrastructure nature). It is expressed as a percentage and helps assess the net benefits of a project relative to initial investment. The NPV indicates the magnitude of the project and whether it generated a profit. It is expressed in terms of a currency (e.g., dollars, pounds, yuan). The payback provides information about the risk. The longer the projected period, the longer the risk of obsolescence. It also measures the positive cumulative cash flow. The IRR is frequently used to decide whether to commit to an investment. In many cases, an investment is accepted when the IRR is greater than the opportunity cost.

ADVANCED METHODS FOR EVALUATING IT AND EC INVESTMENTS

According to Sidana (2006), traditional methods based only on tangible financial factors may not be sufficient for most IT and EC justification. Therefore, the traditional methods evolved with time and now include intangible factors such as customer satisfaction. These changes may supplement the ROI traditional methods or replace them.

Renkema (2000) presents a comprehensive list of over 60 different appraisal and justification methods for IT investments. For details of some of these and other methods, see McKay and Marshall (2004). Most justification methods can be categorized into the following four types:

▶ **Financial approaches.** These appraisal methods consider only those impacts that can be valued monetarily. They focus on incoming and outgoing cash flows as a result of the investment made. NPV and ROI are examples of financial-approach methods.

▶ **Multicriteria approaches.** These appraisal methods consider both financial impacts and nonfinancial impacts that cannot be (or cannot easily be) expressed in monetary terms. These methods employ quantitative and qualitative decision-making techniques. Examples include information economics, balanced scorecard, and value analysis (see Online File W15.3). For further description see Borenstein et al. (2005).

▶ **Ratio approaches.** These methods use several ratios to assist in EC investment evaluation (e.g., EC expenditures versus total turnover). The metrics used usually are financial in nature, but other types of metrics can be used as well. An example of this would be EC expenditures divided by annual sales or EC expenditures as a percentage of the operating budget.

▶ **Portfolio approaches.** These methods apply portfolios (or grids) to plot several investment proposals against decision-making criteria. Portfolio methods are more informative than multicriteria methods and generally use fewer evaluation criteria. These are very complex; for more information see Hovenden et al. (2005).

EXHIBIT 15.5   Advanced Methods for EC Justification Evaluation

- **Value analysis.** With the value analysis method, the organization evaluates intangible benefits using a low-cost, trial EC system before deciding whether to commit a larger investment in a complete system.
- **Information economics.** Using the idea of critical success factors, this method focuses on key organizational objectives and the potential impacts of the proposed EC project on each of them.
- **Scoring methodology.** This method assigns weights and scores to various aspects of the evaluated project (e.g., weights to each metric) and then calculates a total score. Information economics methods are used to determine the aspects to include in the scoring.
- **Benchmarks.** This method is appropriate for evaluating EC infrastructure. Using industry standards, for example, the organization can determine what the industry is spending on e-CRM. Then the organization can decide how much it should spend. Benchmarks may be industry metrics or best practices recommended by professional associations or consultants.
- **Management by maxim.** An organization may use this method to determine how much it should invest in large EC (and IT) infrastructures. It is basically a combination of brainstorming and consensus-reaching methodologies.
- **Real-options valuation.** This is a fairly complex assessment method, and it is used only infrequently. It can be fairly accurate in certain situations. The idea behind this method is to look at future opportunities that may result from the EC investment and then place monetary values on them.
- **Balanced scorecard.** This method evaluates the health or performance of the organization by looking at a broad set of factors, not just financial ones. It is becoming a popular tool for assessing EC projects. (See Beasley et al. 2006, and Pearlson and Sounders 2006)
- **Performance dashboard.** This is a variant of the balanced scorecard that is used widely in e-business situations. A dashboard is a single view that provides the status of multiple metrics. (See Pearlson and Sounders 2006.)
- **Activity-based costing and justification.** This managerial accounting concept was adapted for assessing EC investments in recent years and has been proven to be fairly successful. See Peacock and Tanniru (2005).

Exhibit 15.5 summarizes the representative advanced methods useful in evaluating EC investments.

Online File W15.3 provides more information on the EC justification methods. Turban et al. (2008) describe the last three methods.

Unfortunately, none of these methods is perfect or universal. Therefore, one needs to look at the advantages and disadvantages of each. Exhibit 15.6 shows the popularity (or use) of the major methods.

EXHIBIT 15.6   Popularity of the Various Justification Methods

Technique	Percentage Who Use It (2004)	Percentage Who Use It (2006)
ROI	44	52
Internal ROI	40	47
Activity-based costing	37	32
Company-specific measure	36	57
Net present value	35	33
Economic value added	29	31
Balanced scorecard	24	NA
Return on assets	24	35
Return on equity	18	19
Portfolio management	16	NA
Applied information economics	9	9
Real options	6	NA
Time to payback	NA	60

Sources: Compiled *CIO Insight* (2005 and Alter (2006).

NA = Not available

Section 15.3 ▶ REVIEW QUESTIONS

Section 15.3 ▶ REVIEW QUESTIONS

1. List the items that constitute the business ROI and the technical ROI for an EC portal application.
2. What are the components of the balanced scorecard?
3. What are ROI calculators?
4. Differentiate between business and technology ROI.
5. Describe the TCO and TBO.

15.4 EXAMPLES OF E-COMMERCE PROJECT JUSTIFICATION

The methods and tools described in the previous section can be used alone, in combination, or with modifications to justify different EC projects. Here, we provide a few examples of how these methods and tools can be used to justify different types of EC projects.

E-PROCUREMENT

E-procurement (see Chapter 5) is not limited to just buying and selling; it also encompasses the various processes involved in buying and selling: selecting suppliers, submitting formal requests for goods and services to suppliers, getting approval from buyers, processing purchase orders, fulfilling orders, delivering and receiving items, and processing payments.

Given the diversity of activities involved in e-procurement, the metrics used to measure the value of e-procurement must reflect how well each process is accomplished. However, the focus on the metrics used will differ for buyers and sellers. For example, *buyers* will be interested in metrics such as how quickly they can locate a seller; *sellers* will be most interested in click-to-release time (i.e., the time that elapsed from when the customer clicked to buy an item online until the warehouse staff had a ticket to pick and pack the order). For examples of e-procurement metrics, see Insights and Additions 15.1. Setting metrics for e-procurement is especially difficult when procurement is done in exchanges (see Online File W15.4). One solution to ease such problems is the use of Web Services (see Online File W15.5).

Insights and Additions 15.1 E-Procurement Metrics

Measuring the success of e-procurement is in many ways similar to measuring the success of the purchasing department. Some direct measures involve the company's ability to secure quality, cost-effective materials and supplies that are delivered on time. The following metrics indicate progress in e-procurement:

▶ Increased order fulfillment rate
▶ Increased on-time deliveries
▶ Decreased number of rejects received from suppliers
▶ Decreased purchase order processing time
▶ Decreased prices due to increased supplier visibility and order aggregation
▶ Decreased ratio of freight costs to purchases

Indirect metrics include minimized costs, including:

▶ Reduced inventory costs
▶ Reduced raw material costs
▶ Reduced rework costs
▶ Reduced operating costs
▶ Reduced freight costs

E-procurement can directly or indirectly affect these metrics. Measuring and monitoring e-procurement activities is crucial to identifying both problematic and successful areas. It provides insight into what an organization is doing right and wrong so that it can pinpoint which activities it needs to investigate and adjust.

The University of Pennsylvania measures e-procurement performance through several metrics, as shown here.

(continued)

Insights and Additions 15.1 *(continued)*

E-Procurement Performance Metrics and KPIs at the University of Pennsylvania

Performance Metric	Description	Sample Metrics
Customer satisfaction	Customer satisfaction and performance surveys	• Ease of ordering • Ability to find items
Spend management	Utilization of university-authorized buying methods	• Dollars spent • Percent of purchases
Strategic contracting	Specific and group purchasing contracting activity	• Total purchasing contracts
Contract utilization	Preferred contract supplier purchase activity	• Percent of total purchase order dollars with preferred contract suppliers
Group purchasing	Group purchasing organization supplier	• Total group purchase order dollars purchase activity
E-procurement enablement	Penn Marketplace supplier purchase activity	• Total number of marketplace-participating suppliers
Diversity inclusion	Diversity and local community supplier purchase activity	• Number of diversity suppliers
Electronic invoicing	EDI purchase order invoice transaction activity	• Percent of invoices processed via EDI
Cost savings	Formal cost containment activity	• Total cost containment program savings • Year-to-date savings
Electronic sourcing	Online formal competitive bidding initiatives	• Annual savings by major product category
Supplier rationalization	Strategic supplier rationalization activities	• Number of deactivated suppliers and dollar amounts
Transaction audits	Purchasing card utilization audits for e-procurement suppliers	• Transaction leakage (amount purchased from participating suppliers outside of e-procurement)
Electronic marketing	Showcase electronic marketing activity	• Number of visitors

Table Source: Modified from a table on the University of Pennsylvania Web site (*purchasing.upenn.edu/about/performance.php*).

Sources: Compiled from Minahan (2004) and Cisco Systems (2005).

CUSTOMER SERVICE AND ECRM

Customer service and eCRM (Chapter 13) can be provided in a number of different ways. For example, Lowe's seeks to improve customer service on its Web site (lowes.com) by providing a "do it yourself" information portal (e.g., offering information about how to install a ceiling fan or fix paint problems). Such information may already be available online, and the company uses it to train service personnel. EC-based banking sites often add customer value by lowering risks and providing information relating to the last successful log on and the number of unsuccessful log-on attempts. Online prescription drug companies, such as Medco Health Solutions (medcohealth.com), proactively provide information via e-mail on prescription refills and warn consumers of drug recalls.

Recent surveys of eCRM applications have continued to show mixed payoffs. Only a fraction of companies have demonstrated a significantly positive ROI for their eCRM investments. What can we learn from those companies that have successfully deployed eCRM and have extracted significant business value? For answers, look at Online File W15.6.

CASE 15.1
EC Application

AMERICAN EXPRESS USES PROJECT MANAGEMENT SOFTWARE TO INCREASE ROI

American Express (Amex) controls investments with smart software. Amex allocates a large amount of money among many projects in its 10 divisions every year. In the past, it financed projects based not on how they contribute to the company's overall goals but on the project's individual merit and who made "the most noise" (politics). At least 35,000 Excel worksheets kept track of the worldwide investments. Each division (unit) used its own system to calculate return on investment using different discount rates. There was little control and no standards. Strategic investments were done in a poor manner.

Introducing the Web-based Investment Optimization System (IOS) enabled the company to automate the process of requesting and allocating investment project money. With IOS, the spreadsheets were uploaded to the SQL server where business analytics software read and analyzed them. The improved analysis led to the reallocation of millions of dollars for more optimal investments.

With a return on investment of 2,736.1 percent, the first generation of IOS was the grand-prize winner of the *Baseline* 2005 ROI Leadership Awards (see Bennet 2005). The second generation is a Web-based product built into

Microsoft.NET by software maker Solver (*solver.com*). By 2006, over 800 employees in four business units entered budget requests, forecasting, and other financial data into an online form. IOS calculates the information and assigns a risk level to each project. The request passes through a chain of approvers until a final decision is made.

Another generation of IOS was introduced in 2006. Bigger benefits came when Amex's project-tracking system, which consolidates project results and actual return on investments, was integrated with IOS.

Sources: Compiled from Dignan et al. (2005) and from *solver.com* (accessed January 2007).

Questions

1. Can other companies use this approach to evaluate EC investments?
2. What is the benefit of the project tracking system?
3. Discuss the importance of standards and controls in the system.

ADVANCED ANALYTICS AND COMBINING METHODS

When large sums of money are involved, or when many projects need to be evaluated, organizations develop their own method that may be composed of several of the above methods. One example is Iowa ROI, the real case at the end of this chapter. Another example is that of American Express (Case 15.1). Note that most of the projects evaluated are not EC or even IT, but the method used by American Express works for all.

A report from a survey of SMEs conducted by the Yankee Group, an IT consulting company, also echoes the issues in assessing the ROI of eCRM. The Yankee Group found that CRM-based EC applications are effective only when they are part of a company's overall business plan and not just an EC investment (Kingston 2004). The Yankee Group report outlines key eCRM metrics in three areas: sales, marketing, and service, as shown in Exhibit 15.7. These CRM success metrics can also be viewed as tangible, intangible, and risk-related measures. For instance, revenue per salesperson represents financial tangible metrics; marketing dollars and efficiency metrics are captured in the average time to close and average response time. Intangible metrics are captured as customer satisfaction and call quality. Although financial and efficiency measures are also classified as risk measures, risk metrics in the Yankee Group report are captured through the first-call resolution rate and the accuracy of the data entered (listed under the "Service" column of Exhibit 15.7). These metrics constitute what is of value to the EC sellers and buyers.

An example of an ROI study for a call center, which is part of CRM, is available from HeartMath (2004).

JUSTIFYING A PORTAL

In making the case for investing in a Web portal, Bisconti (2004) suggests that the fundamental business case should be made from the internal and external perspectives of the

EXHIBIT 15.7   Key Metrics for Measuring CRM Success

Sales	Marketing	Service
Revenue per sales person; cost per sale made	Marketing dollars as a percentage of revenue	First-call resolution rate
Average sale cycle; average deal size	Average return on marketing	Call quality (as measured by quality monitoring)
Sales representative turnover rate	Total leads generated	Voice service level (by type of call)
New rep ramp time	Average response rate	E-mail service level (by type of e-mail)
Average administrative time/rep	Lead qualification rate	Average speed of answer
Percentage of representatives that achieve quota	Lead close rate	Abandon rate
Average time to close	Percent of marketing collateral used by sales representatives	Average handle time
Average price discount	Change in market penetration	Cost per contact (calls, e-mail)
Percentage of accurate forecasted opportunities	Improved time-to-market; percentage of customer retention	Average call value
Average number of calls to close deal	Number of feedback points	Average close rate
Average number of presentations necessary to close deal	Marketing execution time	Agent turnover
Average number of proposals needed to close the deal	Message close rate	Customer satisfaction
Average win rate	Marketing dollars as a percentage of revenue	Accuracy of data entered (e.g., trouble tickets)

Sources: Compiled from Kingstone (2004), Exhibit, p. 7; Alter (2006); and *teradata.com* (accessed February 2007).

business. The internal payoff must result in productivity improvements, whereas revenue generation determines the external value. Although several commercial portal development environments are available, large companies may consider building theirs in-house. Bisconti argues that metrics and ROI analysis can serve as a prerequisite to the build-versus-buy decision.

Large companies often have an array of intranet and other information systems; the integration of these systems becomes key to the success of the portal. Thus, the compatibility and flexibility of the portal technology becomes paramount. Bisconti asserts that justification for a portal must focus on *business ROI* as well as *technology ROI*. White (2003) discusses the difficulty of building a business case for a portal due to the intangible benefits. For examples of ROI of portals, see *Baseline* (2006) and Sullivan (2004).

JUSTIFYING E-TRAINING PROJECTS

The pervasive use of EC means that knowledge of and the ability to use EC is essential, no matter what kind of work is being done. Whether in a government agency or a multinational corporation, inadequate employee EC and IT skills will undermine the day-to-day functioning of any organization.

End-user training that helps employees acquire or improve their EC and IT skills plays a key role in ensuring the smooth operation of organizations in the information economy. However, such training and retraining can be expensive, slow, and ineffective. Therefore, a large number of organizations are considering e-training (Chapter 8) to supplement or substitute traditional classroom training.

When comparing e-training and traditional training methods, several factors, most of which are intangible, must be evaluated. Mahaptra and Lai (2005) developed a framework for evaluating end-user training. Exhibit 15.8 shows some of the metrics that may be included in such an evaluation. In executing such a justification, the organization also needs to consider the financial factors of e-training versus traditional training methods.

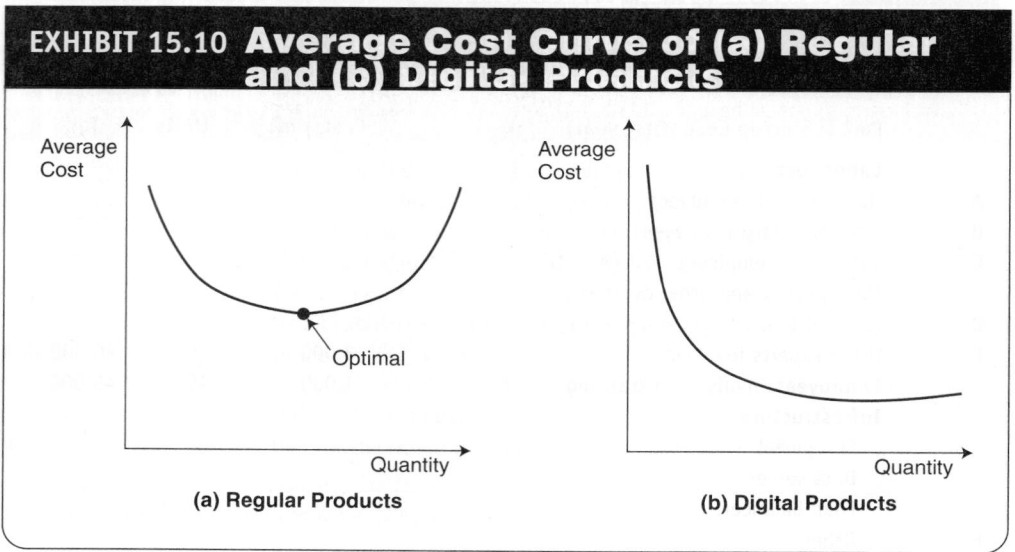

EXHIBIT 15.10 Average Cost Curve of (a) Regular and (b) Digital Products

Average Cost

Optimal

Quantity

(a) Regular Products

Average Cost

Quantity

(b) Digital Products

delivering digital content to individual customers, or of processing transactions are very low, and therefore, the market for EC is large and growing rapidly.

The economic environment of e-commerce is broad and diversified. In this section, we present only representative topics that relate to the traditional economic microeconomic theory and formula such as:

Profit = Revenues – Production – Transaction costs

E-commerce helps to decrease costs and increase revenues, resulting in increased profits.

REDUCING PRODUCTION COSTS

Production costs are the costs to produce the product or service a company is selling. E-commerce makes a major contribution to lower production costs. For example, e-procurement may result in cost reductions. Much of intrabusiness EC deals with cost reductions. The following economic principles express these reductions.

Product Cost Curves

average-cost curve (AVC)
Behavior of average costs as quantity changes; generally, as quantity increases, average costs decline.

The **average-cost curve (AVC)** represents the behavior of average costs as quantity changes. The AVC of many physical products and services is U shaped (see Exhibit 15.10). This curve indicates that, at first, as quantity increases, the average cost declines. As quantity increases still more, the cost goes back up due to increasing variable costs (especially marketing costs) and fixed costs (more management is needed) in the short run. However, the variable cost per unit of digital products is very low (in most cases) and almost fixed (once the initial investment is recovered), regardless of the quantity. Therefore, as Exhibit 15.10 shows, with digital products the average cost per unit declines as quantity increases because the fixed costs are spread (prorated) over more units. This relationship results in increasing returns with increased sales.

Production Function

production function
An equation indicating that for the same quantity of production, *Q*, companies either can use a certain amount of labor or invest in more automation.

The **production function**, shown in Exhibit 15.11, represents a mathematical formula that indicates that for the same quantity of production, Q, companies either can use a certain amount of labor or invest in more automation (e.g., they can substitute IT capital for labor). For example, for a quantity $Q = 1,000$, the lower the amount of labor needed the higher the required IT investment (capital costs). When EC enters the picture, it *shifts* the function inward (from L_1 to L_2), lowering the amount of labor and/or capital needed to produce the same $Q = 1,000$.

Kleist (2003) points to the importance of production function outcomes in evaluating whether EC really leads to greater production output or if results are simply increased page views and "eyeballs," as has been the case with many Web-based technologies. Hahn and Kauffman (2005) applied the production function to EC by treating the functionalities of a Web site as

EXHIBIT 15.11 **The Economic Effects of EC: The Production Function and Agency Costs**

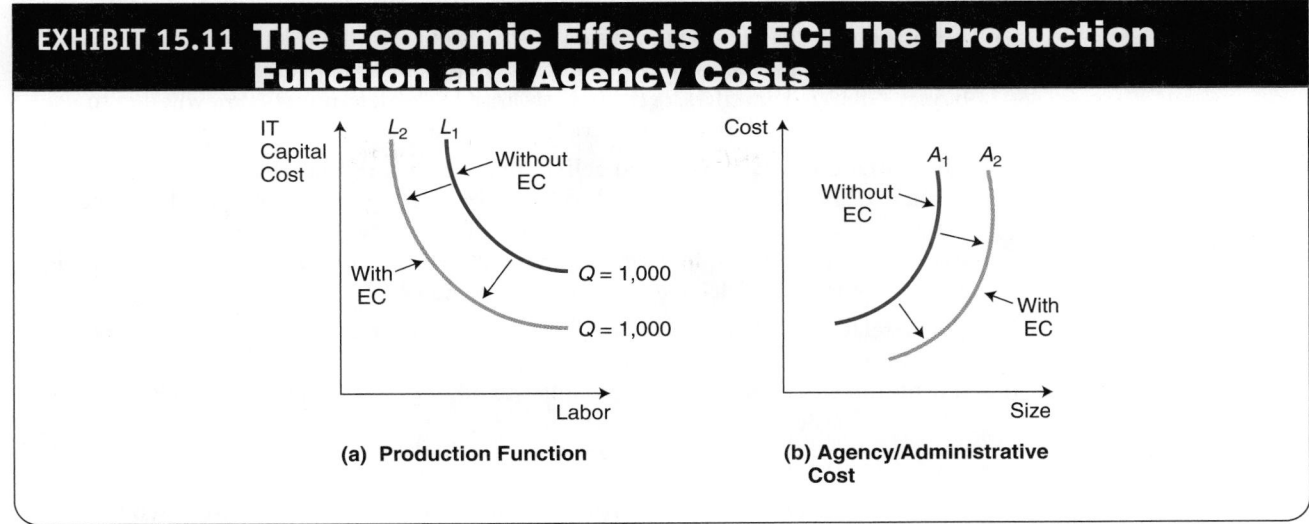

(a) **Production Function**

(b) **Agency/Administrative Cost**

inputs and the completed Web transactions as the outputs to arrive at the effectiveness of EC applications. Such a value-driven approach is a simple, as well as goal-oriented way, to measure the effectiveness of EC investments.

Agency Costs

Exhibit 15.11 shows the economics of the firm's **agency costs** (or *administrative costs*). These are the costs incurred in ensuring that certain support and administrative tasks related to production are performed as intended (e.g., by an agent). In the "old economy," agency costs (A_1) grew with the size (and complexity) of the firm, reaching a high level of cost quickly and frequently preventing companies from growing to a very large size. In the digital economy, the agency costs curve shifts outward, to A_2. This means that as a result of EC, companies can significantly expand their business without too much of an increase in administrative costs before reaching a high level of cost.

A balance between EC investments and administrative and other infrastructure costs must be achieved. Kleist (2003) cautions that returns on EC investments may peak at a certain point, and upon reaching that point businesses may not see many additional benefits, especially when compared with other types of investments, such as those in warehouses, machinery, and the sales force. The key, according to Kleist, is that businesses should identify a mix of optimal EC administrative and infrastructure investments to maximize production from total investments. When computing agency cost, companies should consider only production-related costs and should ignore transaction costs.

Transaction Costs

Transaction costs cover a wide range of costs that are associated with the distribution (sale) and/or exchange of products and services. Most economists (e.g., Chen 2005) divide these costs into the following six categories:

1. **Search costs.** Buyers and sellers incur costs in locating each other and in locating specific products and services.
2. **Information costs.** For buyers, this includes costs related to learning about the products and services of sellers and the basis for their cost, profit margins, and quality. For sellers, this includes costs related to learning about the legitimacy, financial condition, and needs of the buyer, which may lead to a higher or lower price.
3. **Negotiation costs.** Buyers and sellers need to agree on the terms of the sale (e.g., quantity, quality, shipments, financing, etc.) Negotiation costs result from meetings, communication-related expenses, exchanges of technical data or brochures, entertainment, and legal costs.

agency costs
Costs incurred in ensuring that the agent performs tasks as expected (also called *administrative costs*).

transaction costs
Costs that are associated with the distribution (sale) or exchange of products and services including the cost of searching for buyers and sellers, gathering information, negotiating, decision making, monitoring the exchange of goods, and legal fees.

4. **Decision costs.** For buyers, decision costs result from the evaluation of sellers and their internal processes, such as purchasing approval, to ensure that they meet the buyers' policies. For sellers, decision costs arise in the determination of whether to sell to one buyer instead of another buyer, or not at all.

5. **Monitoring costs.** Buyers and sellers need to ensure that the goods or services purchased translate into the goods or services exchanged. In addition, they need to make sure that the exchange proceeds according to the terms under which the sale was made. This may require transaction monitoring, inspection of goods, and negotiations over late or inadequate deliveries or payments.

6. **Legal-related costs.** Buyers and sellers need to ensure that they remedy unsatisfied terms. Legal-related costs include costs that arise from fixing defects and providing substitutions and agreeing on discounts and other penalties. They also include litigation costs in the event of a legal dispute.

As we have seen throughout the book, e-commerce can reduce all these costs. For example, search engines and comparison bots can reduce search costs and information costs. EC also can drastically reduce the costs of monitoring, collaborating, and negotiating.

Exhibit 15.12 reflects one aspect of transaction costs. As seen in the exhibit, there is a trade-off between transaction cost and size (volume) of business. Traditionally, in order to reduce transaction costs, firms had to grow in size (as depicted in curve T_1). In the digital economy, the transaction cost curve shifts downward to position T_2. This means that EC makes it possible to have low transaction costs even with smaller firm size and to enjoy much lower transaction costs as firm size increases.

INCREASED REVENUES

Throughout the text, we have demonstrated how an organization can use EC to increase revenues through online storefronts, auctions, cross-selling opportunities, multichannel distribution arrangements, and so on. EC can also be used to improve reach and richness.

Reach versus Richness

Another economic impact of EC is the trade-off between the number of customers a company can reach (called *reach*) and the amount of interactions and information services it can provide to them (*richness*). According to Evans and Wurster (2000), for a given level of cost (resources), there is a trade-off between reach and richness. The more customers a company wants to reach, the fewer services it can provide to them. Exhibit 15.13 depicts this economic relationship. With EC, the curve can shift outward. This means increased revenues.

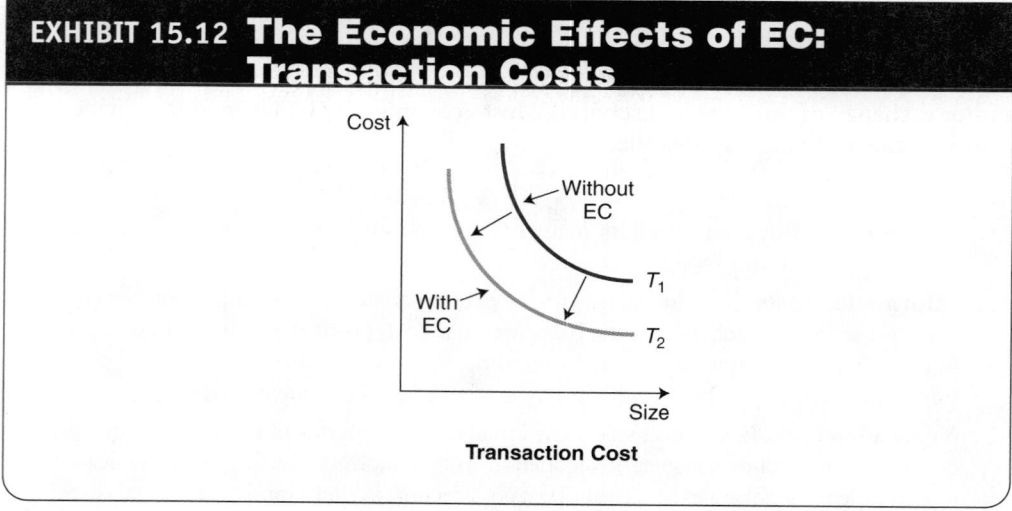

EXHIBIT 15.12 The Economic Effects of EC: Transaction Costs

EXHIBIT 15.13 Reach Versus Richness

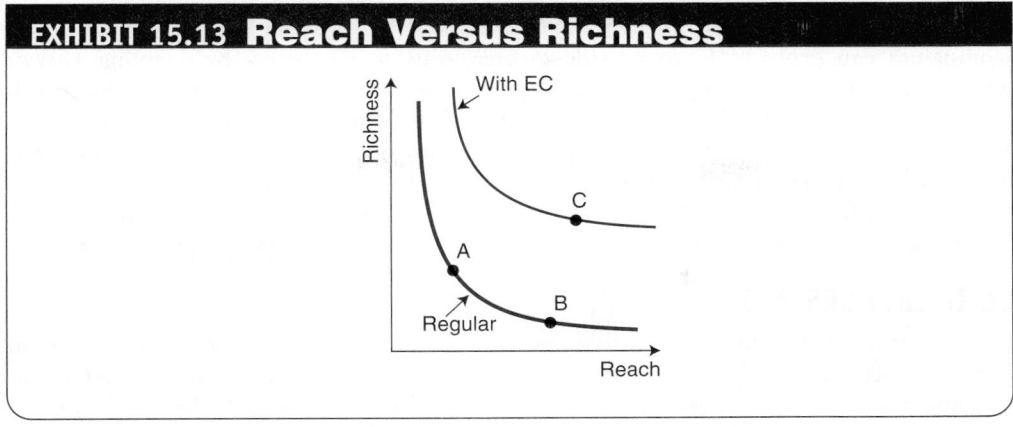

The case of stock broker Charles Schwab illustrates the implementation of the reach versus richness trade-off. Initially, Schwab attempted to increase its reach. To do so, the company went downward along the curve, reducing its richness. However, with its Web site (schwab.com), Schwab was able to drastically increase its reach (moving from point A to B) and at the same time provide more richness in terms of customer service and financial information to customers, moving from point B to point C. For example, Schwab's *Mutual Fund Screener* allows customers to design their own investment portfolios by selecting from an array of mutual funds. Providing such services (richness) allows Schwab to increase the number of customers (reach), as well as charge higher fees than competitors that provide few value-added services. In summary, the Internet pushes the curve outward toward the upper right-hand corner of the chart, allowing more reach with the same cost. For additional details, see Jelassi and Enders (2005).

Other Ways to Increase Revenues

Straub (2004) suggests other ways that EC can be used to increase revenues:

- Increased revenues via products or services from a larger global market because of more effective product marketing on the Web
- Increased margins attained by using processes with lower internal cost (e.g., using lower-cost computers) and from higher prices because of value-added services to the customer (e.g., information attached to product)
- Increased revenues as a consequence of becoming an online portal
- Value-added content sold from selling searches, access to data, and electronic documents

The remainder of this section deals with some other issues related to the economics of EC.

REDUCING TRANSACTION FRICTION OR RISK

EC can reduce risk for companies by providing them with timely information. Kambil (2001) suggests that organizations can increase the value of their products or services by using the unique capabilities of EC to reduce risks to consumers, such as those involving psychological relationships, quality concerns, delays, and financial transactions.

Allowing the customer to utilize an EC-based calculator and avoid potentially embarrassing situations can reduce psychological risks. For example, online tracking tools reduce psychological risk by allowing customers to check the status of a package. By publishing specifications and providing product comparison engines, EC can help reduce a customer's risk of purchasing an unwanted product or one of poor quality. EC also has been instrumental in providing customers with an accurate picture of product availability, helping them to avoid the risk of unexpected delays. EC also can mitigate customer concerns over the security of EC transactions. Finally, linking the transaction to third-party security providers, such as the Better Business Bureau or VeriSign, can address customer concerns over privacy and security. In this way, EC can provide value by lowering the transaction friction or risk and providing the customer with *economic value*. For more on risk analysis see Beasley et al. (2006).

FACILITATING PRODUCT DIFFERENTIATION

Companies can exploit EC to provide greater value to customers by enabling *product differentiation*. Organizations can use EC to provide **product differentiation**—products with special features. For example, McAfee allows users of its VirusScan virus-detection software to automatically update the latest security patches online, differentiating itself from those that require manual upgrades. Differentiation does not necessarily require a physical product; services also can be differentiated. EC can provide differentiation through better product information, informing users on how to use the product, how to replenish it, and how to supply feedback.

EC INCREASES AGILITY

EC can provide firms with the **agility** to monitor, report, and quickly respond to changes in the marketplace and the business environment. Companies with agile systems can respond to customer requests quickly, improving customer service. FedEx, UPS, and other delivery companies can provide location information because they use EC to connect with customers and make available package tracking information. EC systems enable companies to learn more about customers and understand their buying habits. This enables a company to better predict trends for better planning and quickly introducing changes when needed. Similarly, e-procurement has given firms the ability to quickly locate sellers and place orders. Sellers, in turn, use e-fulfillment to quickly locate products in their warehouses and fill customer orders.

MARKETS VERSUS E-MARKETS

As described in Chapter 2, a *market* is a medium for the exchange of goods, services, and information between many potential buyers and many potential sellers. Electronic markets are markets in which the exchanges are conducted electronically among buyers, sellers, market employees, and support services, (e.g., financial institutions) in an *efficient* and *effective* manner (see Malone et al. 1989). E-markets are more efficient because they increase the amount of information, the speed at which it is sent, and its accuracy. At the same time, they may reduce the flow of physical goods. For example, as described in Online File W6.3, in a B2B flower exchange, it is not necessary to bring the flowers to the auction place. The flowers can go directly from a seller to a buyer. The same is true for many other goods, such as used cars.

Even if the flow of physical goods does not decrease, the information provided in e-markets better informs participants and, therefore, allows them to make better decisions. This helps in reducing market friction, which benefits the entire economy by making it more efficient. This is the primary reason why many governments provide incentives for e-commerce (see Davis and Benamati 2003).

VALUATION OF EC COMPANIES

Valuation is the process of trying to determine the value or worth of a company. It is done for the purpose of selling a company or determining its value for a proposed merger. In the EC context, valuation often is conducted to determine a reasonable IPO price when a company goes public (see Malik 2005.)

Many valuation methods exist. The three most common ones, according to Rayport and Jaworski (2004), are the comparable method, the financial performance method, and the venture capital method:

▶ **The comparable method.** With this method, analysts compare the company with similar companies on as many factors as possible (e.g., size, industry, customer base, products, growth rate, book value, debt, sales, financial performance). In addition, they may look at performance trends, management teams, and other features. A major difficulty with this method is finding such information for privately held companies.

▶ **The financial performance method.** This method uses projections of future earnings (usually five years), cash flows, and so on to find the NPV of a company. With this method, the analyst needs to discount future cash flows using a discount or interest rate. The major problem with this method is in determining the discount rate, which is based on future interest rates. Analysts may use pro forma income statements, free cash flow values, and the company's terminal value (the value of the company, if sold, three to five years in the future) to generate a valuation.

▶ **The venture capital method.** Venture capital (VC) firms (Chapter 16) invest in start-ups and usually take them through to their IPOs. They may use combinations of the first two methods, concentrating on terminal value. The VC firm then discounts the terminal value of the company, using a very high discount rate (e.g., 30 percent to 70 percent). When companies pay using their stocks, they have high valuation so they can afford to buy a high-valuation EC company. An example is IAC/Interactive Corp. that purchased AskJeeves in March 2005 in an all-stock acquisition. This compensates them for the high risk they assume.

Let's look at one of the most successful IPOs of an EC company—Google. Google floated its IPO in fall 2004, targeting it at $85 per share. Within a few weeks, the share price more than doubled reaching over $450 in late 2005, and $500 in 2006, giving Google a market capitalization of $140 billion a year.

The increase in share price indicated that investors were willing to pay huge premiums for anticipated future performance and valuation. Many acquisitions and mergers from 1996 through 2001 involved unrealistically high valuations, and so did the acquisition of social networks from 2005 to 2006. For example, Google paid $1.65 billion for YouTube.com in 2006. Note that when EC companies acquire other EC companies, they frequently pay in the form of stock, not cash, so such high valuations are more appropriate. Google uses this same strategy to acquire other companies.

According to Malik (2005), the too high valuation that caused the dot-com failures between 2000 and 2003 are back for highly trafficked Web sites. Malik calculates the validation at that period in terms of price per monthly unique visitor, which reached several hundred dollars (e.g., $385 for Lycos, $384 for Excite). Today, the price is still low (e.g., $36 for MySpace, $44 for Ask Jeeves). But since 2003 it is increasing. News Corp. paid $580 million for MySpace; Interactive Group paid $1.9 billion for Ask Jeeves; and Google paid $1.65 billion for YouTube. IAC/InterActive paid almost $2 billion for a relatively small search engine company, Ask.com. Although this seems like too much of an investment, it allows IAC/InterActive to use Ask.com to integrate a $20 billion Web portfolio of companies. IAC/InterActive based the high valuation on the expectation of online ads, which went from $8.2 billion in 2001 to $6 billion in 2002. However, by 2006 the spending reached $15 billion. Malik estimates the valuation of popular blogs and social networks to be very high (e.g., Facebook at $127 million).

In summary, the economics of EC enable companies to be more competitive and more profitable. It also enables them to grow faster, collaborate better, provide superb customer service, and innovate more quickly. As in any economic environment, here, too, those that capitalize on these opportunities will excel; the rest are doomed to mediocrity or failure.

OTHER ISSUES

Several other issues relate EC and economics. For example, Hopkins and Kehoe (2006) suggested an economics-based approach to evaluate e-marketplaces when companies are about to choose which one to join. A relationship matrix that includes customer requirements on one side and functionalities on the other side are the basis for the assessment. Then, importance ratings are added for each requirement and feature. This is used to evaluate different marketplaces.

Section 15.5 ▶ REVIEW QUESTIONS

1. How can EC enhance increasing returns in a business? (Hint: Consult roi-calc.com.)
2. How does EC impact the production cost curve?
3. Define *transaction costs*. List some examples and explain how EC can reduce such costs.
4. How can EC increase revenues?
5. What are the benefits of increasing reach? How can EC help?
6. How can organizations reduce psychological risk?
7. Explain the impact of EC on product differentiation and agility.
8. Define *valuation*. Why is it so high for some EC start-ups?
9. How can a company decide which e-marketplace to join?

15.6 FACTORS THAT DETERMINE E-COMMERCE SUCCESS

The economic capabilities of EC described in Section 15.5 influence some industries more than others (Chapter 18). The success factors of EC depend on the industry, the sellers and buyers, and the products sold. Furthermore, the ability of sellers to create economic value for consumers will determine the EC success. When deciding to sell online, looking at the major factors that determine the impact of EC can evaluate the potential for success.

CATEGORIES OF EC SUCCESS

Strader and Shaw (1997) have identified four categories of e-market success factors: product, industry, seller, and consumer characteristics.

Product Characteristics

Digitized products, such as software, documents, music, and videos, are particularly well suited for e-markets because they can be distributed to customers electronically, resulting in instant delivery and very low distribution costs. Digitization also decreases the amount of time involved in the order-taking cycle because automation can be introduced to help customers search for, select, and pay for a product, anyplace and anytime, without the intervention of a sales or technical person. Finally, product updates can be communicated to customers rapidly.

A product's *price* may also be an important determinant of its success. The higher the product price, the greater the level of risk involved in the market transaction between buyers and sellers who are geographically separated and who may have never dealt with each other before. Therefore, some of the most common items currently sold through e-markets are low-priced items such as CDs and books. Riquelme (2001) found that the price of low-price products depends on the customer's benefits of information search in the e-marketplace (i.e., Riquelme [2001] found that for more expensive products, such as fine wines, diamonds, and perfumes, or service-based products, such as hotel and vacation bookings, customers often rely on the e-marketplace's *reputation* or information availability rather than just on price). In either case, EC can play a significant role in facilitating business.

Another product characteristic is the cost and speed of *product customization*. Millions of consumers configure computers, cars, toys, clothes, and services to their liking, and if sellers can fulfill such requests at a reasonable cost and in a short amount of time, they can assure success (e.g., Dell). Finally, computers, electronic products, consumer products, and even cars can be sold online because consumers know exactly what they are buying. The more product information that is available, the easier it is to sell. The use of multimedia and product tutorials (e.g., see bluenile.com) can dramatically facilitate product description.

Another aspect of a product's characteristics is *cross-selling* and *up-selling*. EC enables efficient and effective cross-selling and up-selling of many (but not all) products and services.

Industry Characteristics

Electronic markets are most useful when they are able to match buyers and sellers directly. However, some industries require transaction brokers. E-markets affect these industries less than those that do not require brokers. Stockbrokers, insurance agents, and travel agents may provide needed services, but in some cases, software may reduce the need for these brokers. This is particularly true as intelligent systems become more available to assist consumers.

Zhu (2001) supports these findings and argues that in B2B it is desirable to make a vast amount of data about prices and costs available on the Internet, which makes e-marketplace information more transparent.

Other important industry characteristics include the following: Who are the major players (corporations) in the industry? How many companies in the industry are well managed? How strong is the competition, including foreign companies?

Seller Characteristics

Electronic markets reduce *search costs*, allowing consumers to find sellers that offer lower prices, better service, or both. As in the case of the motion picture industry, this may reduce profit margins for sellers that compete in e-markets, but it may increase the number of transactions that take place (i.e., people watching more movies). However, if sellers are unwilling to participate in this environment, it may reduce the impact of e-markets. In highly competitive industries with low *barriers to entry*, sellers may not have a choice but to join in; if they do not, online customers' searches will lead them to an online competitor's distribution channel.

Consumer Characteristics

Consumers can be classified as impulse, patient, or analytical. Electronic markets may have little impact on industries in which impulse buyers make a sizable percentage of purchases. Because e-markets require a certain degree of effort and preparation on the part of the consumer, e-markets are more conducive to consumers who do some comparisons before buying (i.e., the patient and analytical buyers). Mobile devices are changing this situation because real-time information is available now while shoppers are in physical stores.

Analytical buyers can use the Internet to evaluate a wide range of information before deciding where to buy. On the other hand, *m-commerce* and especially *l-commerce*, which provides and even customizes services based on a customer's location, are banking on impulse buyers—on the customer's being in the right place at the right time. However, m-commerce also offers indirect benefits to consumers through improved location services. Team Assignment 2 presents a case where you can identify costs and benefits of a mobile computing system.

THE LEVELS OF EC MEASUREMENT

An issue related to establishing EC metrics is the *level of measurement* at which the EC value is calculated. Metrics vary based on whether the level of measurement is an individual EC customer, an EC firm, an EC-enabled process, or the EC value chain. For an individual, EC metrics will include product variety, price savings, and satisfaction. For an EC firm, the metrics of interest will be converting site visitors to customers, inventory turns, and cross-selling. At the process level, firms may be interested in the speed of the order-taking process or in a change in the routing of a product. The EC value chain involves firms and their suppliers and customers on either side of a transaction. EC value chain metrics may involve cost reductions in acquiring raw materials, producing the product, and delivering it to the customer.

Ultimately, the level of measurement relates to *what is of value* to the various constituents at each level. Value manifests itself in various forms. In Chapter 2, we examine how to extract the real value of EC by exploiting product characteristics with an EC strategy. This value of EC may be economic (e.g., cost savings), or it may be from reduced transaction friction or risk, product differentiation, or increased agility. For further discussion, see Rayport and Jaworski (2004).

Section 15.6 ▶ REVIEW QUESTIONS

1. Describe product characteristics in EC.
2. Describe pricing issues in EC.
3. What are industry characteristics in EC?
4. What are seller characteristics in EC?
5. What are consumer characteristics in EC?
6. List the four levels of metric measurement.

15.7 OPPORTUNITIES FOR SUCCESS IN E-COMMERCE AND AVOIDING FAILURE

Now that EC has been around for several years, it is possible to observe certain patterns that contribute to its success or failure. By examining EC patterns, one can find indications of the opportunities that lie ahead and avoid pitfalls along the way. This section examines EC failures, the key factors to EC success, how EC is creating digital options, and the complementary investments that are needed to enable EC success.

E-COMMERCE FAILURES

By examining the economic history of previous innovations, the failure of EC initiatives and EC companies (see discussions in Chapters 1 through 3 and 6) should come as no surprise. Three economic phenomena suggest why this is the case:

1. At a macroeconomic level, technological revolutions, such as the railroad and the automobile industries, have had a boom–bust–consolidation cycle. For example, between 1904 and 1908, more than 240 companies entered the then-new automobile manufacturing business in the United States. In 1910, the shakeout began. Today, there are only three U.S. automakers, but the size of the auto industry has grown several hundred times.

   Arthur (1996) compared the Internet revolution with the railroad revolution and found that both followed a similar pattern. First, there was the excitement over the emerging technology, then irrational euphoria followed by inflated market values of anything related to the new technology, and then the bust. However, Arthur notes that following the bust, the railroads saw their golden period, in which railroad activities in England grew tenfold. Why was this the case? Arthur believes that the real benefits of a technology come when organizations structure their activities around the cluster of technologies (e.g., after railroads emerged, steel rails, track safety systems, traffic control systems, and so on were needed). Similarly, businesses relocated to where the cost and availability of raw materials were favorable along the railroad lines.

   Similar to the railroads, we are now seeing a reemergence in EC activity. For example, early B2B online businesses involved simple transactions; today, B2B involves electronic integration and synchronization with supply chain partners.

2. At a mid-economic level, the bursting of the dot-com bubble from 2000 through 2003 is consistent with periodic economic downturns that have occurred in real estate, precious metals, currency, and stock markets.

3. At a microeconomic level, the "Web rush" reflected an overallocation of scarce resources—venture capital and technical personnel—and too many advertising-driven business models. This is analogous to the influx of people and resources to specific places during a "gold rush."

Chapters 3 and 14 provide some of the specific reasons for failure in B2C EC: lack of profitability, excessive risk exposure, the high cost of customer acquisition, poor performance, and static Web site design. Two additional financial reasons are lack of funding and incorrect revenue models (discussed in Chapter 2).

With EC, B2B businesses have been trying to improve interfirm operations and customer service by allowing customers and partners to interact directly with the Web sites to do self-service. However, Schultze and Orlikowski (2004) found that in click-and-mortar EC applications, the use of the self-serve technology made it more difficult for sales representatives to build and maintain customer relationships. The use of IT altered the nature and quality of information shared by the participants, undermined the ability of sales representatives to provide consulting services to customers, reduced the frequency of their interaction, and prompted sales representatives to expend social capital to promote the customers' technology adoption. These changes produced intended and unintended shifts in the network relations and raised serious challenges to the viability of their business model.

In both the B2C and B2B markets, other anecdotal reasons for failure include misdirected energies; a lack of understanding of market needs; poor business planning; greed; and a mismatch of innovative youth, inexperience, and overeager sponsors (Yap 2002). The reasons for past failures are important in that they provide insight for avoiding such failures in the future.

E-COMMERCE SUCCESSES

Despite the failure of hundreds of start-ups and thousands of EC projects, EC is alive and well and continues to grow rapidly after a short pause from 2001 through 2002, as discussed throughout the text.

EXHIBIT 15.14 Critical Success Factors: Old Economy and EC

Old Economy CSFs	EC CSFs
Vertically integrate or do it yourself	Create new partnerships and alliances, stay with core competency
Deliver high-value products	Deliver high-value service offerings that encompass products
Build market share to establish economies of scale	Optimize natural scale and scope of business, look at mass customization
Analyze carefully to avoid missteps	Approach with urgency to avoid being locked out; use proactive strategies
Leverage physical assets	Leverage intangible assets, capabilities, and relationships—unleash dormant assets
Compete to sell product	Compete to control access and relationships with customers; compete with Web sites

EC success stories abound, primarily in specialty and niche markets. One example is puritan.com, a successful vitamin and natural health-care product store. Another is Campusfood.com, which allows college students to order take-out food online (Chapter 1). Also doing very well are employment sites, such as monster.com. Alloy.com is a successful shopping and entertainment portal for young adults. As pointed out in Chapter 3, online services such as stock trading, travel reservations, online banking, and more are commanding a major part of the business in their industries. For a comparison of how these and other thriving online businesses have translated CSFs from the old economy into EC success, see Exhibit 15.14.

The following are some of the reasons for EC success and suggestions from EC experts and consultants on how to succeed in EC.

Strategies for EC Success

Thousands of brick-and-mortar companies are adding online channels with great success. Examples are uniglobe.com, staples.com, homedepot.com, walmart.com, clearcommerce.com, 800flowers.com, and Southwest Airlines (iflyswa.com). Weill and Vitale (2001) suggest that existing firms can use organizational knowledge, brand, infrastructure, and other "morphing strategies" to migrate from the off-line marketplace to the online marketspace (see also Chapter 16). Weill and Vitale (2001) predicted that in the post-dot-com-bust EC world, a few dot-coms will exist in each major business sector; most will evolve with a combination of online and physical business models, and traditional businesses will need to make substantial investments in EC to succeed. Other experts and researchers have blended a variety of factors into their own recipes for EC success. The following is a representative list of these strategies and critical success factors that aid the achievement of these strategies.

- Kauffman et al. (2006) assert strategies that include moving to higher-quality customers, changing products or services in their existing market, and establishing an off-line presence (e.g., moving from pure-play dot-com to click-and-mortar). The authors provide guidelines for understanding successful e-business strategy.
- Pavlou and Gefen (2004) found that institutional-based trust, which is derived from buyers' perceptions that effective third-party institutional mechanisms are in place, is critical to EC success. These mechanisms include (1) feedback mechanisms, (2) third-party escrow services, and (3) credit card guarantees. This helps explain why, despite the inherent uncertainty that arises when buyers and sellers are separated in time and in space, online marketplaces are proliferating.
- Brown (2006) was looking at improving customer experience, claiming that usability is not a sufficient measure of customer acceptance. (See also Wikipedia 2007).

▶ A group of Asian CEOs recommend the following EC CSFs: select robust business models, anticipate the dot-com future, foster e-innovation, carefully evaluate a spin-off strategy, co-brand, employ ex-dot-com staffers, and focus on the e-generation, as alloy.com and bolt.com have done (Phillips 2000).

▶ Huff and Wade (2000) suggest the following EC CSFs: add value, focus on a niche and then extend that niche, maintain flexibility, get the technology right, manage critical perceptions, provide excellent customer service, create effective connectedness, and understand Internet culture.

▶ Barua et al. (2001) provide a systematic approach for driving EC excellence, including guidelines for selecting appropriate business models and assuring sufficient ROI.

▶ Kambil and van Heck (2002) found that for an EC exchange to be successful, it has to create value for *all* participants, not just the sellers, the market maker, or the buyers. The issue of value in an online exchange is the subject of debate among the many suppliers in the electronic marketplace. In Team Assignment 3, you will learn more about electronic hubs and have the opportunity to participate in identifying collaborative opportunities. These authors also recommend that for EC to be successful it should support and enrich human interactions through technologies such as virtual reality (i.e., increase richness).

▶ Pricing in EC has continued to be a challenge for sellers because of handling and shipping costs. Often the seller and market maker will see the potential for profits and ignore the fact that the buyers will subscribe to EC only if they see the benefit in price or product variety. For example, in January 2005, Amazon.com decided to absorb such costs for orders above a certain level (e.g., $25).

▶ New technologies can boost the success of EC. For example, RFID has great potential for improving the supply chain (Chapter 7); however, it will take a large investment in EC infrastructure and applications to realize its full potential (see Section 15.4).

▶ Wikipedia (2007) provides guidelines for success in the following areas:
  ▶ Technical and organizational aspects of good management
  ▶ Customer-oriented approach
  ▶ Handling problems properly and quickly
  ▶ Product suitability for online sale (especially digital products)
  ▶ Consumer acceptance of electronic shopping

▶ Peters (2006) offered 15 steps to EC success at WebsiteCM.com. Peters supports several of Wikipedia's guidelines.

▶ Veneeva (2006) suggests that the current improvements in the Internet services and their inherent characteristics like improved security, reliability, user friendliness, two-way communication, low costs, accessibility and customizability, have been the driving forces for e-commerce.

A number of experts and consultants (e.g., Sponder 2006; Yap 2002) have proposed many more keys to success.

Additional Guidelines for EC Success. A research study of 30 organizations identified the following factors that contributed to the successful implementation of B2C and B2B EC projects (Esichaikul and Chavananon 2001):

▶ The top three factors for successful B2C e-commerce were effective marketing management, an attractive Web site, and building strong connections with the customers.

▶ The top three factors for successful B2B e-commerce were the readiness of trading partners, information integration inside the company and in the supply chain, and the completeness of the EC system.

▶ The top three factors for the overall success of an e-business were a proper business model, readiness of the firm to become an e-business, and internal enterprise integration.

At this still-early stage of the EC revolution, success cannot be assured, and failure rates will remain high. However, if companies learn from the mistakes of the past and follow the guidelines offered by experts and researchers, their chances for success are greatly enhanced.

In the remaining parts of this section, we will discuss important strategies and factors that should be considered to assure EC success. The first one is the creation of digital options.

CREATING DIGITAL OPTIONS

Firms have welcomed the EC project evaluation process, including the tools of economic justification (Section 15.3), because it allows them to justify an EC investment, compare it with other potential investments, and evaluate the potential risk or payoff. However, EC and information technologies play an innate role in supporting business projects that may not be well suited for the types of economic justification that work well for other types of investments. Researchers and practitioners are rethinking the extent to which ROI and related financial measures should play a role in the decision to invest in EC.

Sawhney (2002a) argues that increased focus on ROI in evaluating e-business initiatives can lead to the bias of looking inward only and forcing out initiatives with little immediate and tangible ROI but with significant long-term value to the company. He suggests that firms should think broadly and follow the unanticipated benefits of EC projects, as in the example of Eli Lilly & Co., which created a Web site called InnoCentive (innocentive.com) to attract scientists to solve chemistry problems in exchange for financial rewards. In doing so, Eli Lilly has established contact with over 8,000 scientists that the human resources department can tap into for future hiring and consulting needs.

Sambamurthy et al. (2003) refer to such opportunities from EC applications as **digital options**, a set of IT-enabled capabilities in the form of digitized enterprise work processes and knowledge systems. They refer to these capabilities as *options* because, as in the case of Eli Lilly, the firm has an option to exploit the project for other purposes. They suggest that exploiting such options increases agility. Had Eli Lilly only used the ROI justification approach, it might not have invested in the EC-based Web site. However, the "value" it provides in identifying and establishing contact with over 8,000 scientists may be significant and last for the long term.

Case 15.2 describes how GE Aircraft Engines has created digital options from a data collection system created to improve manufacturing operations.

digital options
A set of IT-enabled capabilities in the form of digitized enterprise work processes and knowledge systems.

COMPLEMENTARY INVESTMENTS

The returns from EC investments can be maximized to make **complementary investments**. Complementary investments are cases in which a smaller project is added that requires different capabilities; then, the projects are funded jointly. Ignoring complementary investments can lead to less-than-optimal payoffs and even contribute to failure. Zhu (2004) found that complementary investment in information technology infrastructure can play a critical role in the use of EC for improved performance. He found that when organizations make the complementary investments in infrastructure, such as personal computers or LANs, they realize improved firm performance through increased returns on assets, sales per employee, costs of goods sold per employee, and reduced inventory turnover.

Sherer et al. (2003) studied Cisco's upgrade of the operating system on 34,000 employee PCs and found that the firm's complementary investment in change management led to a smooth transition, which was reflected in the higher client satisfaction ratings. Other complementary investments include training programs for customers, linking of internal systems, creating customer support teams, and establishing links with suppliers and service providers.

complementary investments
Additional investments, such as training, made to maximize the returns from EC investments.

CULTURAL DIFFERENCES AND EC

Chapter 1 mentioned culture as a possible barrier to the use of EC. In Chapter 14, we discussed the need to understand cultural issues such as differences in social norms, measurement standards, and nomenclature. Here, we raise the issue of cultural differences so that appropriate metrics can be developed.

One of the strengths of EC is the ease with which its adopters can reach a global population of consumers. However, EC-driven businesses must consider the cultural differences in this diverse global consumer base because without the broad acceptance of the EC channel, consumers may choose not to participate in online transactions. Critical elements that can affect the value of EC across cultures are perceived trust, consumer loyalty, regulation, and political influences. Even the content of online ads can mean different things in different

CASE 15.2

CASE 15.2
EC Application

GE AIRCRAFT ENGINES' DIGITAL OPTIONS

Over 25 years ago, GE Aircraft Engines (GEAE) created a system that enables the remote monitoring of aircraft engines. Each aircraft engine has hundreds of sensors that relay information to an onboard computer while the aircraft is in flight. The data are then transmitted via a satellite to a ground-based computer system. Over the years, this data collection system has blossomed into an entire operations system for engine control. GEAE has used this information technology to create *digital options*.

GEAE uses the collected information to inform and educate its engineers and maintenance workers. This enables the company to continually improve its engines, and thereby improve customer service. GEAE created a revenue-generating digital option by selling some of the information it collected back to the airlines. It sells information such as guidelines on how and when to service engines, which engines perform better under what flying conditions, and the costs of maintaining fleets in-house versus outsourcing their the maintenance.

The system, called OnPoint Solutions provides customers with comprehensive solutions to meet their diverse operational, financial, and technical demands. With an improved, simplified product portfolio that includes maintenance, material, and asset management services, GE provides the flexibility to develop an OnPoint Solution to meet the customer's specific need. To achieve this, it established a flexible process to ensure customer satisfaction.

Compared with traditional aircraft engine maintenance service options, OnPoint enables GE to provide more significant benefits to customers. From flexible cash-flow timing, to optimized and guaranteed cost of ownership, to shared financial risk, GE remains committed to working with customers to find the appropriate solution for every service need.

Further, GEAE has improved customer relationships through its ability to predict and identify when an engine part needs replacement, notifying customers so that parts are ready and available when the plane lands. This has enabled the airlines to minimize maintenance time and keep their airplanes in the air. Thus, GEAE's digital option has led to improved product designs, improved customer service, and additional revenue.

Sources: Compiled from Sviokla and Wong (2003), and from GEAE.com (2007).

Questions

1. What digital option did GEAE create?
2. List some other options that GEAE might be able to create.
3. What metrics can GEAE use to calculate ROI of the EC project (the electronic feedback information system)?
4. Why is this considered e-commerce?

---

cultures. Due to these differences, the transaction costs, including coordination costs, may vary among the consumer base.

A 2005 research study by Sung (2005) found that security, privacy, and technical expertise are the most explanatory EC CSFs in South Korea; in contrast, ease of use is the most important success factor in the United States. Firms must address EC issues arising from cultural differences. For instance, to deal with issues such as transactional trust, in which consumers may not trust foreign firms, EC sellers can partner with respectable local firms, banks, or chambers of commerce and build trust among their prospective clientele. Further, online testimonials from local customers can positively influence transactional trust. EC metrics from other countries should not be applied automatically.

EC IN DEVELOPING ECONOMIES

Similar to cultural differences, developed and developing economies vary in how EC is used and whether the economics favor this channel of commerce. Developing economies struggle with various issues taken for granted in developed economies, such as the United States or Singapore.

Developing economies often face power blackouts, unreliable telecommunications infrastructure, undependable delivery mechanisms, and the fact that only a few customers own computers and credit cards. Such limitations make it difficult for firms to predict whether EC investments will pay off, and when. However, developing economies, such as China and India, represent a significant opportunity for EC to connect businesses to customers, as well as other businesses. The potential volume of transactions in developed countries can make EC investments more attractive for established firms. This is because much of the cost of EC systems development would have already been recovered because EC initiatives frequently can use existing IT infrastructures.

The traditional EC assumption is that every computer user has the investment capacity to own a computer and maintain a dedicated Internet connection, as is the case in developed economies. In developing economies, the assumption will have to be revised to incorporate low-cost access, pay for use only, a community of users, and mass coverage. The payoffs from EC use in developing countries are likely to go beyond financial returns. Enabling people to take advantage of EC technology without disrupting their traditions may be the most valuable, yet intangible, return. Case 15.3 presents an example of such a situation.

Section 15.7 ▶ REVIEW QUESTIONS

1. List three reasons why EC failure should not come as a surprise.

2. What are some reasons for EC success?

3. Define *digital options*.

4. What are complementary investments?

5. What are digital options?

6. Relate EC to cultural differences.

CASE 15.3
EC Application
THE SUCCESS STORY OF E-CHOUPAL

In the remote villages of southern India, most farmers are illiterate and have never used a computer. They grow soybeans, wheat, and coffee on small plots of land. After the farmers harvest their crops, it generally takes them up to two days to transport the crops to the local auction. Due to a lack of information, they have been unaware of current market prices.

ITC, one of India's leading agribusiness companies, set up an e-market called *e-choupal* (*echoupal.com*), the Hindi word for "gathering place." Run by a *sanchalak* (an operator, usually a male) and accessed by a PC at the operator's home, Internet cafés, or kiosks in public places, e-choupals act as community meeting places as well as e-commerce hubs.

The e-choupal model required ITC to make relatively large investments in creating and maintaining its own IT network in rural India. It also had to identify and train local farmers to manage each e-choupal. The e-choupal computer or kiosk links to the Internet via phone lines or, increasingly, by a VSAT connection. Each e-choupal serves an average of 600 farmers in 10 surrounding villages within a 5 kilometer radius. Each e-choupal costs between US$3,000 and US$6,000 to set up and about US$100 per year to maintain. The farmers can use the system to obtain information for free. A public oath obligates the sanchalak to serve the entire community; the sanchalak benefits from increased prestige and a commission paid for each e-choupal transaction.

Farmers benefit from more accurate pricing information, improvements in the product-weighing process, faster processing time, prompt payment, and access to a wide range of information, including accurate market prices and market trends, which help them decide when, where, and at what price to sell. Also, farmers are able to access information on soils and planting improvements, crop planning, and building relationships that ensure the flow of supplies. Farmers use the e-choupal system to purchase seed and fertilizer, order soil-testing kits, share best practices, and check grain prices, including those at the Chicago Board of Trade.

The e-choupal system has had a measurable impact on what the farmers choose to plant and where they sell their products. In areas covered by e-choupals, the percentage of farmers planting soy, for example, has increased dramatically, from 50 percent to 90 percent in some regions. The volume of soy marketed through "mandis" (open-air markets) has dropped by as much as half.

Further, by selling through the e-choupal, farmers take their crops directly to ITC collection points, saving on the cost of packing and transportation that would be involved in going to the auction market. By reintermediation (as discussed in Chapter 2), instead of disintermediation, ITC saves $5 per ton as well.

The e-choupal system has decreased ITC's net procurement costs by about 2.5 percent (it saves on commission fees and on transportation costs it would otherwise pay to traders who serve as its buying agents at the mandi), and it has more direct control over the quality of what it buys. The company reports that it recovered its equipment costs in the first year of operation and that the venture as a whole is profitable. By 2004, the e-choupal system had grown to 1,000 kiosks. The farmers have been able to save money without changing their lifestyle.

Sources: Compiled from Sawhney (2002b), Hammond and Prahalad (2004), Digital Dividend (2005), and Anupindi and Silvakumar (2005).

Questions

1. List the metrics that can measure the EC success of the e-choupal system.

2. How does e-choupal differ from a regular electronic meeting place?

MANAGERIAL ISSUES

Some managerial issues related to this chapter are as follows:

1. **How do we measure the value of EC investment?** EC investments must be measured against their contribution to business objectives. Such investments will involve direct and indirect costs as well as benefits. The impact of EC on integrating existing processes and systems must not be ignored. Furthermore, EC must create value for all participants, support or improve existing processes, and supplement rather than replace the human element of transactions. The measurement of EC value should occur against the backdrop of metrics that define business performance and success.

2. **What complementary investments will be needed?** Companies should expect to make complementary investments in other functional areas to ensure EC success. Procurement is done differently in many organizations; introducing models such as forward auctions and affiliate programs may have a major impact on marketing and sales.

3. **Is a shift from tangible to intangible benefits necessary?** Few opportunities remain for automation projects that simply replace manual labor with IT on a one-for-one basis. Therefore, the economic justification of EC applications will increasingly depend on intangible benefits, such as increased quality or improved customer service. It is much more difficult to accurately estimate the value of intangible benefits prior to the actual implementation. Managers need to understand and use tools that bring intangible benefits into the decision-making processes for IT investments.

4. **Who should conduct a justification?** For small projects, the finance department can do the analysis. For a large or complex project, an outside consultant may be advisable.

5. **Should we use the ROI calculator provided by a vendor who wants to sell us an EC system?** It is always safer to use a calculator from an unbiased source. However, some vendors may provide calculators that better fit with your application.

6. **How does one know if the valuation of EC companies is justifiable?** Only time can tell. The price paid for MySpace seems to be a bargain, but Ask.com was probably sold for too much.

7. **Is it possible to predict EC success?** The more analysis we do, the more accurate will be the justification of the EC project and its chance for success. A back-to-basics approach is needed. Yet the EC business environment is very volatile so failures will occur.

RESEARCH TOPICS

Here are some suggested topics related to this chapter. For details, references, and additional topics, refer to the Online Appendix A "Current EC Research."

1. **Technology-Level Economic Analysis**
   - Internet access pricing
   - Impact of the technical transparency of software agents in Internet markets
   - Cost-effectiveness of the Internet for buyers and sellers
   - Impact of XML standards in expanding the network externality

2. **Product-Level Economic Analysis**
   - Pricing of digital products and services
   - Identifying CSF for products or services
   - Ability to search for a product on the Internet and its impact on product purchase
   - Value of digital–physical bundles
   - Effect of network externality on EC

3. **Business-Process-Level Economic Analysis**
   - Governance theories for the EC business environment
   - Value propositions of governance for buyers and suppliers, large and small firms
   - Optimal selection of buyers by suppliers as well as the optimal selection of sellers by buyers
   - Finding CSF for EC projects
   - Effect of EC on a firm's internal structure
   - Benefits and risks of virtual alliances in EC
   - EC business models that can offer sustainable competitive advantage
   - EC competitive advantage versus competitive necessity

4. **Market-Level Economic Analysis**
   - Theories that explain the boundary conditions for effective digital intermediation or explain the dynamics of disintermediation in the presence of software agents
   - Theories that characterize efficiency problems in electronic markets
   - Understanding how multi-item and multiunit auctions operate on the Internet
   - The human decision-making processes in EC, such as in Internet-based auctions
   - New models to determine what constitutes value of Internet-related network effects from the user or customer perspective
   - Understanding the value and performance of B2B e-markets
   - Normative models for the adoption of B2B market services

   - New theories and empirical results on the efficacy of trust mechanisms for Internet commerce

5. **Macroeconomic-Level Economic Analysis**
   - Measurement of the digital economy
   - Analysis of industry competition
   - EC proliferation in developing nations
   - Design of optimal EC taxation and assessment of the performance of the design
   - Economic antecedents of EC
   - Social effects of EC in the international setting

6. **Other Research Topics**
   - Compare the effectiveness of justification methods
   - Develop specific metrics for generic EC projects
   - Compare various EC calculators
   - EC and economic theories—further investigation
   - Is cost-benefit analysis really effective?
   - How much to invest in cost-benefit analysis?

SUMMARY

In this chapter, you learned about the following EC issues as they relate to the learning objectives.

1. **The need for EC justification.** Like any other investment, EC investment (unless it is small) needs to be justified. Many start-up EC companies have crashed because of no or incorrect justification. In its simplest form, justification looks at revenue minus all relevant costs. Analysis is done by defining metrics related to organizational goals.

2. **The difficulties in justifying EC investment.** The nature of EC makes it difficult to justify due to the presence of many intangible costs and benefits. In addition, the relationship between investment and results may be complex, extending over several years. Also, several projects may share both costs and benefits, several areas may feel the impacts (sometimes negative).

3. **Difficulties in established intangible metrics.** Intangible metrics may be difficult to define. Some of these benefits change rapidly; others have different values to different people or organizational units. Intangible metrics have qualitative measures that are difficult to compare. One solution is to quantify the qualitative measures. Scoring methodology, value analysis, and other advanced methods, as described in Online File W15.3, can do this.

4. **Traditional methods for evaluating EC investments.** Evaluating EC involves a financial analysis, usually an ROI analysis, as well as an assessment of the technology and its architecture. Future costs and benefits need to be discounted, using the NPV method, especially if the costs and benefits will extend over several years. A payback period describes how long it will take to recover the initial investment. However, financial ROI alone can lead to an incomplete and misleading evaluation. Tools to integrate the various ROI aspects of EC investment include the balanced scorecard (BSC), which also focuses on the internal business processes and learning and growth perspective of the business. EC ROI should take into account the risk of reducing possible failures or adverse events that can drain the financial ROI. Other advanced methods (e.g., real options, value analysis, benchmarks, and management by maxim) look at future benefits. No method is universal or perfect, so selecting a method (or a mix of methods) is critical.

5. **Understand how to justify specific EC projects.** All EC projects include intangible and tangible benefits and costs that must be identified. Then, a method(s) must be selected to match the particular characteristics of the EC application.

6. **EC investment evaluation.** Economic fundamentals must be kept in mind when evaluating an EC investment. With nondigital products, the cost curve shows that average per unit costs decline as quantity increases. However, with digital products, the variable cost per unit usually is low, and thus, the evaluation will differ. Similar differences are evident in EC's ability to lower transaction costs, agency costs,

and transaction risks. EC can also enable the firm to be agile in responding faster to changing market conditions and ensure increasing returns to scale regardless of the volume involved. Finally, EC enables increased reach with multimedia richness at a reasonable cost.

7. **E-marketplace economics.** Products, industry, seller, and consumer characteristics require different metrics of EC value. With the growing worldwide connectivity to the Internet, EC economics will play a major role in supporting buyers and sellers. As compared with traditional commerce, EC can quickly succeed due to its ability to create network effects, lock-in effects, and disintermediation, especially in case of digital products.

8. **Reasons for EC success and failure.** Like other innovations, EC is expected to go through the cycle of enormous success, followed by speculation, and then disaster before the reality of the new situation sets in. Some EC failures were the result of problematic Web site design, lack of sustained funding, and weak revenue models. Success in EC has come through automating and enhancing familiar strategies, such as branding, morphing, trust building, and creating value for all trading partners by enriching the human experience with integrated and timely information. EC investments can go beyond the traditional business models by creating digital options. To ensure success, complementary investments must be made in managing change and responding to cultural differences among EC users.

KEY TERMS

QUESTIONS FOR DISCUSSION

1. A mail-order catalog company that is adding online selling has hired you. Develop EC success metrics for the company. Develop a set of metrics for the company's customers.

2. Your state government is considering an online vehicle registration system. Develop a set of EC metrics and discuss how these metrics differ from those of an online catalog company (see the previous question).

3. Consider the various economic justification methods. Are there conditions under which one may be more useful than the others?

4. Discuss the advantage of using several methods (e.g., ROI, payback period) to justify investments.

5. How has Amazon.com caused disintermediation? Name two industries where EC has resulted in disintermediation.

6. Enter businesscase.com and find material on ROI analysis. Discuss how ROI is related to a business case.

7. A craftsperson operates a small business making wooden musical instruments in a small U.S. town. The business owner is considering using EC to increase the business's reach to the nation and the world. How can the business owner use EC to increase richness to make the products more attractive to consumers?

8. You are considering moving your bank account to an online bank. What features and services can the bank provide to reduce your psychological risk in making EC transactions?

9. How does EC facilitate the creation of digital options?

10. The BSC approach can be adapted for various applications. Develop a BSC and a set of metrics for your college bookstore.

11. A company is planning a wireless-based CRM system. Almost all the benefits are intangible. How can you justify the project to top management?

12. The valuation of Google is more than twice that of GM even though its profits are about 10 percent of GM's. This means that people are willing to pay 20 times more for a share of Google. Given people's experiences in the dot-com bust, is there any logic to this behavior? Discuss.

13. Discuss the value of TCO and TBO concepts for EC investment evaluation.

INTERNET EXERCISES

1. Enter **alinean.com/AlineanPress_ROITWhitepaper.asp** and other sources in the site and find information that explains Alinean's approach to measuring return on IT. You can download two free e-books from the site that relate to this chapter. Summarize your findings in a report.

2. Enter **doubleclick.com**. Go to "Knowledge Central" and then "Research" and "Advertising." Examine research on the value of consumer responses to online advertising. Summarize the issues considered by researchers.

3. Enter **nucleusresearch.com**. Go to "Research," "Latest Research," and then click "View ROI Scorecards." Open the PDF file titled "Market Scorecard: Hosted CRM" for a review of hosted CRM vendors. Summarize your findings in a report. (Note: use Google to find this information.)

4. Enter **schwab.com**. Examine the list of online services available for Planning and Retirement, and Advised Investment Services. Relate them to richness and reach.

5. Go to **google.com** and search for articles dealing with the ROI of RFID. List the key issues in measuring the ROI of RFID.

6. Enter **acerostanalyzer.com**, **shark finesse.com**, and **covalentwork.com**. Review their calculators, Write a report.

7. Go to **acecostanalyzer.com** and register. Review the ACE Demo Training Video. Find the capabilities of the calculators. Calculate the ROI of a project of your choice as well as the TCO.

8. Enter **sas.com**, **corvu.com**, **balancedscorecard.com**, and **cio.com**. Find demos and examples of how to use the various tools and methods to evaluate EC projects. Write a report.

9. Enter **solutionmatrix.com** and find information about ROI, metrics, and cost-benefit tools. Write a report based on your findings.

10. Enter **roi-calc.com**. View the demos. What investment analysis services does the company provide?

11. Enter **zebra.com** and find their ROI calculators (go to resource library). What analysis do the calculators provide?

12. Enter **google.com** and **baselinemag.com**. Find information related to EC investment evaluation. Summarize your findings in a report.

TEAM ASSIGNMENTS AND ROLE PLAYING

1. Download the ROI case study "Venda Xerox Document Supplies (Case Study E11)" from the Nucleus Research (**nucleusresearch.com**) Web site. Read the Venda Xerox case study. While you are connected to the Internet, click "ROI Help Tutorial" in the NR_Standard_ROI_Tool.xls file and read modules 1 through 4. Enter your assumptions of costs and benefits into the calculator and examine how they impact the overall ROI, payback period, NPV, and average yearly cost of ownership (under the Summary tab).

   Answer the following questions based on the Venda Xerox Document Supplies ROI case study.

   a. What were the key reasons why Xerox developed an EC system?

   b. What were the areas in which Xerox could benefit from EC?

   c. How did Xerox calculate the ROI of the EC system?

2. In this activity, you will measure the business value of a mobile computing system for the field service representatives at Alliance Insurance Company (AIC), a fictitious company name based on some actual companies. See Online File W15.8 for details.

3. Explore the business value of EC. Each member enters a different site (e.g., **nicholasgcarr.com**, Tom Pisello at **techtarget.com**, **baselinemag.com**, Paul Strassmann (**strassmann.com**, etc.). Prepare a presentation on issues, value, and directions.

JUSTIFYING EC AND IT INVESTMENT IN THE STATE OF IOWA

The Problem

For years, there was little planning or justification for EC and IT projects by the government of the state of Iowa. Any state agency that needed money for an EC or IT project slipped it into its budget request. State agencies requested many projects, knowing that only a few would be funded. Bargaining, political favors, pressures, and other outside influences determined which agencies' requests were. As a result, some important projects were not funded, and unimportant ones were. In addition, there was very little incentive to save money. This was the situation in Iowa until 1999, and it still exists in many other states, countries, cities, and other public institutions. However, in Iowa, everything changed in 1999 when a request for $22.5 million to resolve the Y2K problem was made.

The Solution

Iowa's solution to its IT planning and spending program, the Iowa Return on Investment Program (ROI Program), is an *IT value model*. The basic idea is to promote **performance-based government**, an approach that measures the results of government programs. The state of Iowa developed the ROI Program to justify investment in the Y2K solution. The basic principles of the model follow.

performance-based government

An approach that measures the results of government programs.

First, a pot of money called the Pooled Technology Account, which is appropriated by the legislature and controlled by the state's IT department, primarily funds new investments. Pooling of funds makes budget oversight easier and prevents duplications. Second, agencies submit requests for funding future EC and IT projects from the pooled account. To support their requests, agency managers must document the expected costs and benefits of the project based on a set of factors. The maximum score for each factor ranges from 5 to 15 points, for a maximum total score of 100 points. In addition, they must specify metrics related to those factors in order to determine the project's success. The scores are based on 10 criteria that are used to determine value (for details on these criteria, see Varon 2003).

The ROI Program requires agencies to detail their technology requirements and functional needs. This enforces standards, and it also helps officials identify duplicate projects and expenditures. For example, in 2001 several agencies proposed building pieces of an ERP system that would handle e-procurement and human resources management. The IT department suggested

that the state deploy a single, more cost-effective ERP system that several agencies could share. The project, which had an estimated cost of $9.6 million, could easily have cost many times that amount if agencies were allowed to go it alone. Once a project is funded, the state saves money by scrutinizing expenses. Agencies must submit their purchase orders and invoices to the Enterprise Quality Assurance Office for approval before they can be reimbursed. This IT value model is universal and fits EC projects as well. The IT department reimburses agencies for expenses from the Pooled Technology Account only after verifying that the expenses were necessary. If an agency's expenditures are not in line with the project schedule, it presents a red flag for auditors that the project could be in trouble.

The Results

Iowa's ROI Program became a national model for documenting value and prioritizing IT and EC investments in the public sector. In 2002, the National Association of State Chief Information Officers (NASCIO) named the program the "Best State IT Management Initiative." It saved taxpayers more than $5 million in less than four years (about 16 percent of the spending on new IT projects).

The process also changed users' behavior. For example, during fiscal year 2003, 17 EC and IT projects were requested through the budget approval process, and only 6 were approved. For the year 2004, 4 projects were requested, and all were approved. Also, there is considerable collaboration and use of cross-functional teams to write applications. State agencies are now thinking through their IT and EC investments more carefully. Another improvement is collaboration among agencies that submit joint proposals, thereby eliminating duplicate projects. Finally, the methodology minimizes political pressure. The success of Iowa's ROI Program led to the Iowa Accountable Government Act of 2001, which requires establishing a similar methodology for all state investments, not just EC or IT projects.

Sources: Compiled from Varon (2003) and State of Iowa (2007).

Questions

1. List the major deficiencies of the old method of project funding.
2. How are projects justified under the new method?
3. List the advantages of the new program.
4. What are the limitations of the method?

REFERENCES

Alinean.com. "CIOs to IT Vendors—"Get Real on ROI." 2006. **alinean.com/ROIselling_CIOtoITvendors.asp** (accessed November 2006).

Alter, A. "The Bitter Truth about ROI." *CIO Insight*, July 2006.

Anupindi, R., and S. Sivakumar. "ITC's E-Choupal: A Platform Strategy for Rural Transformation." *Conference on Global Poverty: Business Solutions and Approaches*, Cambridge, MA, December 1–3, 2005.

Arthur, W. B. "Increasing Returns and the New World of Business." *Harvard Business Review*, Vol. 74, No. 4 (1996).

Barua, A., et al. "Driving E-Business Excellence." *MIT Sloan Management Review*, Vol. 43, No. 1 (2001).

Baseline. "How to Calculate ROI." September 6, 2006. **baselinemag.com/article2/0,1540,2012723,00.asp** (accessed November 2006).

Beasley, M., A. Chen, K. Nunez, and L. Wright. "Balanced Scorecard and Enterprise Risk Management." *Strategic Finance*, March 2006.

Bennet, E. "Baseline 2005 ROI Leadership Awards." *Baseline*, July 8, 2005. **baselinemag.com/article2/0,1540,1836622,00.asp** (accessed February 2007).

Bisconti, K. "Determining the Value and ROI of an Enterprise Portal, Part 2." *Enterprise Systems*, November 16, 2004. **esj.com/enterprise/article.aspx?EditorialsID=1197** (accessed January 2007).

Borenstein, D., P. Betencourt, and R. Baptista. "A Multi-Criteria Model for the Justification of IT Investments." *INFOR*, February 2005.

Bothama, H. "State of the Art in TCO," *Sap.com* white paper with ASUG, January 2006.

Broadbent, M., and P. Weill. "Management by Maxim: How Business and IT Managers Can Create IT Infrastructures." *Sloan Management Review* (Spring 1997).

Brown, B. "Improving Customer Experience: Usability Testing Is Not Enough." *Ecommercetimes.com*, January 19, 2006. **ecommercetimes.com/rsstory/48318.html** (accessed November 2006).

Chen, S. *Strategic Management of E-Business*, 2nd ed. West Sussex, England: John Wiley & Sons, Ltd., 2005.

CIO.com. **cio.com/metrics/index.cfm** (accessed December 2004–January 2007).

CIO Insight. "Top Trends for 2005." *CIO Insight*, December 2004.

Cisco Systems. "What You Need to Implement an E-Procurement Solution." *Cisco.com*. **whitepapers.techrepublic.com.com/whitepaper.aspx?&docid=79748&promo=100511** (accessed February 2007).

David, J. S., D. Schuff, and R. St. Louis. "Managing Your IT Total Cost of Ownership." *Communications of the ACM*, Vol. 45, No. 1 (2002).

Davis, W. S., and J. Benamati. *E-Commerce Basics*. Boston: Addison Wesley, 2003.

Devaraj, S., and R. Kohli. "Information Technology Payoff Paradox and System Use: Is Actual Usage the Missing Link?" *Management Science*, Vol. 49, No. 3 (2003).

Devaraj, S., and R. Kohli. *The IT Payoff: Measuring Business Value of Information Technology Investment*. Upper Saddle River, NJ: Financial Times Prentice-Hall, 2002.

Digital Dividend. "What Works: ITC's E-Choupal and Profitable Rural Transformation." December 1, 2005. **digitaldividend.org/case/case_echoupal.htm** (accessed January 2007).

Dignan, L., M. Duvall, and E. Bennett. "Triumphs and Trip-Ups in 2005." *Baseline*, December 2005.

EDS.com. "Case Study: California State Automobile Association." 2006. **eds.com/services/casestudies/downloads/csaa_roi** (accessed February 2007).

EDS.com. "EDS Exceeds Expectation for CSAA." EDS press release, August 14, 2006. **eds.com/news/features/3145** (accessed February 2007).

Esichaikul, V., and S. Chavananon. "Electronic Commerce and Electronic Business Implementation Success Factors." *Proceedings of the 14th Bled Electronic Commerce Conference*, Bled, Slovenia, June 25–26, 2001.

Evans, P., and T. S. Wurster. *Blown to Bits: How the New Economics of Information Transforms Strategy*. Boston, MA: Harvard Business School Press, 2000.

Ferrin, B. G., and R. E. Plank. "Total Cost of Ownership Models: An Exploratory Study." *Journal of Supply Chain Management* (Summer 2002).

GEAE.com. "The Next Level of Service: OnPoint Solutions." **geae.com/services/onpoing_nextlevel.html** (accessed February 2007).

Green, S. *Profit on the Web*. Auckland, New Zealand: Axon Computertime, 2002. **axon.co.nz/info/About.htm** (accessed February 2007).

Gunasekaran, A., P. Love, F. Rahimi, and R. Miele. "A Model for Investment Justification in Information Technology Projects." *International Journal of Information Management* (October 2001).

Hahn, J., and R. Kauffman. "A Methodology for Business Value-Driven Web Site Evaluation: A Data Envelopment Analysis Approach." University of Minnesota, Minneapolis, MN Working Paper March 31, 2005. **misrc.umn.edu/workingpapers/fullpapers/2005/0509_033105.pdf** (accessed January 2007).

Hammond, A. L., and C. K. Prahalad. "Selling to the Poor." *Foreign Policy*, 142 (2004).

HeartMath. "A Fortune 50 High Tech Call Center: An ROI Study." HeartMath LLC, **heartmath.com/corporate/roi_analysis** (accessed February 2007).

Hopkins, J. L., and D. F. Kehoe. "The Theory and Development of a Relationship Matrix-Based Approach to Evaluating E-Marketplaces." *Electronic Markets*, Vol. 16, No. 3, 2006.

Hovenden, D., D. St. Clair, and M. Potter. "From Projects to Portfolios: A Strategic Approach to IT Investment." *ATKearney Executive Agenda*, Vol. 6, No. 1, March 2005. **atkforum.cn/index.php?option=com_docman&task=doc_download&gid=204** (accessed February 2007).

Huff, S., and M. Wade. *Critical Success Factors for Electronic Commerce.* New York: Irwin/McGraw-Hill, 2000.

Jelassi, T., and A. Enders. *Strategies for E-Business.* Harlow, England: FT/Prentice Hall, 2005.

Kambil, A. "Reduce Customer Risks with eCommerce." Accenture, 2001. **accenture.com/Global/Research_and_Insights/Institute_For_High_Performance_Business/By_Subject/Customer_Relationship_Management/ReduceECommerce.htm** (accessed January 2007).

Kambil, A., and E. van Heck. *Making Markets: How Firms Can Design and Profit from Online Auctions and Exchanges.* Boston, MA: Harvard Business School Press, 2002.

Kauffman, R. J., T. Miller, and B. Wang. "When Internet Companies Morph: Understanding Organizational Strategy Changes in the 'New' New Economy." *Special Issue: Commercial Applications of the Internet*, July 2006.

Keepmedia.com. "Tool: The Return on Stopping Viruses." Keepmedia.com, February 7, 2005. **keepmedia.com/pubs/baseline/2005/02/07/721943** (no longer available online).

Keystone Strategy Inc. Enterprise IT Capabilities and Business Performance Study. March 16, 2006.

Kingstone, S. "The Financial Realities of CRM: A Guide to Best Practices, TCO, and ROI." The Yankee Group, 2004.

Kleist, V. F. "An Approach to Evaluating E-Business Information Systems Projects." *Information Systems Frontiers* Vol. 5, No. 3 (2003).

Lucas, H. C., Jr. *Information Technology: Strategic Decision Making for Managers.* Hoboken, NJ: John Wiley & Sons, 2005.

MacDonald, D. "Foundations for Anytime, Anywhere Computing." *Montgomery Research, Inc.* May 23, 2003.

Mahapatra, R., and V. S. Lai. "Evaluating End-User Training Programs." *Communications of the ACM* (January 2005).

Malik, O., "The Return of Monetized Eyeballs," *Business 2.0*, December 2005.

Malone, T. W., et al. "The Logic of Electronic Markets." *Harvard Business Review*, Vol. 67, No. 3 (1989).

Martin, O. "Configuration Management: A CA IT Service Management Process Map." *Computer Associates* white paper, June 2006. **wp.bitpipe.com/resource/org_1103740304_372/30265_In_Network.pdf?site_cd=bp&asrc=ORG_OSE_GOOGUS** (accessed November 2006).

McKay, J., and P. Marshall. *Strategic Management of E-Business.* Milton, Australia: Wiley, 2004.

Minahan, T. "The E-procurement Benchmark Report: Less Hype, More Results." Aberdeen Group, September 29, 2004. **ketera.com/pdf/Aberdeen%20Whitepaper%20on%20eProcurement%20Benchmark%20Reports.pdf** (accessed January 2007).

Misra, R. "Evolution of the Philosophy of Investments in IT Projects." *Issues in Informing Sciences and Information Technology*, Vol. 3 (2006).

Nucleus Research. "Manifesto: Separating ROI Fact from Fiction." *Research Note C51*, 2002. **nucleusresearch.com/research/c51.pdf** (accessed March 2005).

Paton, D., and D. Troppito. "Eye on ROI: ROI Review." *DM Review*, March 25, 2004. **dmreview.com/article_sub.cfm?articleId=1000671** (accessed February 2007).

Pavlou, P. A., and D. Gefen. "Building Effective Online Marketplaces with Institution-Based Trust." *Information Systems Research*, Vol. 15, No. 1 (2004).

Pearlson, K. E., and C. S. Sounders. *Managing and Using Information Systems.* Hoboken NJ: John Wiley & Sons, 2006.

Peppard, J., and J. Ward, "Unlocking Sustained Business Value from IT Investments," *California Management Review* (Fall 2005).

Peters, J. "15 Steps to E-Commerce Success." *WebsiteCM.com*, August 1, 2006. **websitecm.com/news/26/15-Steps-to-ECommerce-Success-Part-1-of-3.html** (accessed February 2007).

Phillips, M. "Seven Steps to Your New E-Business." *Business Online*, August 2000.

Pisello, T. "CRM ROI: Fact or Fiction?" *Alinean.com*, April 27, 2004. **searchcrm.techtarget.com/tip/0,289483,sid11_gci952037,00.html** (accessed February 2007).

Pisello, T. "Metrics: ROI, IRR, NPV, Payback, Discounted Payback." *Techtarget*, September 15, 2006a. **searchcrm.techtarget.com/expert/KnowledgebaseAnswer/ 0,289625,sid11_gci1216028,00.html** (accessed November 2006).

Pisello, T. "The ROI of RFID in the Supply Chain." *RFID Journal* (August 21, 2006b). **rfidjournal.com/article/articleview/2602/1/2/** (accessed November 2006).

Rayport, J., and B. J. Jaworski. *Introduction to E-Commerce*, 2nd ed. New York: McGraw-Hill, 2004.

Reichheld, F., and P. Schefter. "E-Loyalty—Your Secret Weapon on the Web." *Harvard Business Review* (July–August 2000).

Renkema, T. J. W. *The IT Value Quest: How to Capture the Business Value of IT-Based Infrastructure.* Chichester (UK) and New York: John Wiley & Sons, 2000.

Riquelme, H. "An Empirical Review of Price Behaviour on the Internet." *Electronic Markets*, Vol. 11, No. 4 (2001).

Ross, J. W., and C. M. Beath. "Beyond the Business Case: New Approaches to IT Investment." *MIT Sloan Management Review* (Winter 2002).

Ross, S. S. "Computer Security: The First Step." *Baseline*, February 1, 2005. **baselinemag.com/article2/0,1540,1764732,00.asp** (accessed April 2005).

Ryan, S. D., and M. S. Gates. "Inclusion of Social Subsystem Issues in IT Investment Decisions: An Empirical Assessment." *Information Resources Management Journal* (January–March 2004).

Sambamurthy, V., A. Bharadwaj, and V. Grover. "Shaping Agility Through Digital Options: Reconceptualizing the Role of Information Technology in Contemporary Firms." *MIS Quarterly*, Vol. 27, No. 2 (2003).

Sawhney, M. "Damn the ROI, Full Speed Ahead: 'Show Me the Money' May Not Be Right Demand for E-Business Projects." *CIO Magazine*, 2002a.

Sawhney, M. "Fields of Online Dreams: E-Commerce Can Flourish Anywhere if You Build the Right Business Model." *CIO Magazine*, 2002b.

Schultze, U., and W. J. Orlikowski. "A Practice Perspective on Technology-Mediated Network Relations: The Use of Internet-Based Self-Serve Technologies." *Information Systems Research*, Vol. 15, No. 1 (2004).

Sherer, S. A., R. Kohli, and A. Baron. "Complementary Investment in Change Management and IT Investment Payoff." *Information Systems Frontiers*, Vol. 5, No. 3 (2003).

Sidana, N. "The ROI on IT Investment." *Network Magazine*, December 2006. **networkmagazineindia.com/200612/ analyst'scorner01.shtml** (accessed February 2007).

Soh, C., and L. M. Markus. "How IT Creates Business Value: A Process Theory Synthesis." *Proceedings of the 16th International Conference on Information Systems*, Amsterdam, Netherlands, December 1995.

Spector, D. H. M. "Calculating TCO and ROI in Open Source Platforms." *TechRepublic*, April 6, 2006. **articles.techrepublic.com.com/5100–10877–6058525. html** (accessed November 2006).

Sponder, M. "The MindValley Way to Ecommerce Success–Part 1." *Webmetricsguru.com*, July 4, 2006. **webmetricsguru.com/2006/07/the_mindvalley_way_ to_ecommerc.html** (accessed November 2006).

State of Iowa. "ROI Program." **state.ia.us/itd//roi/ roi_program.html** (accessed February 2007).

Steyaert, J. C. "Measuring the Performance of Electronic Government Services." *Information and Management* (January–February 2004).

Strader, T. J., and M. J. Shaw. "Characteristics of Electronic Markets." *Decision Support Systems*, Vol. 21, No. 3 (1997).

Straub, D. *Foundations of Net-Enhanced Organizations*. Hoboken, NJ: Wiley, 2004.

Sullivan, D. *Proven Portals: Best Practices for Planning, Designing, and Developing Enterprise*. Boston, MA: Addison Wesley Professional, 2004.

Sung, T. K. "E-Commerce Critical Success Factors: East Versus West." *Technological Forecasting and Social Change* (forthcoming 2005).

Sviokla, J., and A. Wong. "CRM Is Not for Micromanagers: Get Value from CRM, Use IT to Empower People— Not Keep Tabs on Them." *CIO Magazine*, 2003. **cio.com/archive/040103/reality.html** (accessed January 2007).

Tillquist, J., and W. Rodgers. "Measuring the Value of IT," *Communication of the ACM*, January 2005.

Turban, E., et al. *Business Intelligence: A Managerial Approach*. Upper Saddle River, NJ: Prentice Hall, 2008.

University of Pennsylvania. "Procure to Pay Performance Metrics." **purchasing.upenn.edu/about/performance. php** (accessed January 2007).

Varon, E. "R. O. Iowa: By Centralizing Its State IT Budget Process, Establishing a Scoring Method and Instituting Value Metrics, Iowa Has Become a National Model for Gauging Project ROI." *CIO Magazine*, 2003.

Veneeva, V. "E-Business: Success or Failure?" *Ezinearticles.com*, June 29, 2006. **ezinearticles.com/?E-Business:-Success- of-Failure?&id=232635** (accessed November 2006).

Wattemann, R. "ROI 101: Making the Business Case for Technology Investment." *CIO.com*, *Analyst Report #1344* (by Nucleus Research). **cio.com/analyst/ report1344.html** (accessed January 2007).

Weill, P., and M. Vitale. *Place to Space: Migrating to E-Business Models*. Boston, MA: Harvard Business School Press, 2001.

White, C. "Determining Enterprise Portal ROI." *DM Review*, April 2003.

Wikipedia. "Electronic Commerce." 2007. **en.wikipedia. org/wiki/Electronic_commerce** (accessed February 2007).

Yap, E. "Seven Keys to Successful e-Business." *MIS Asia*, March 1, 2002.

Zhu, K. "Information Transparency in Electronic Marketplaces: Why Data Transparency May Hinder the Adoption of B2B Exchanges." *Electronic Markets*, Vol. 12, No. 2 (2001).

Zhu, K. "The Complementarity of Information Technology Infrastructure and E-Commerce Capability: A Resource-Based Assessment of Their Business Value." *Journal of Management Information Systems*, Vol. 21, No. 1 (2004).

LAUNCHING A SUCCESSFUL ONLINE BUSINESS AND EC PROJECTS

Learning Objectives

Upon completion of this chapter, you will be able to:

1. Understand the fundamental requirements for initiating an online business.
2. Describe the process of initiating and funding a start-up e-business or large e-project.
3. Understand the process of adding EC initiatives to an existing business.
4. Describe the issues and methods of transforming an organization into an e-business.
5. Describe the process of acquiring Web sites and evaluating building versus hosting options.
6. Understand the importance of providing and managing content and describe how to accomplish this.
7. Evaluate Web sites on design criteria, such as appearance, navigation, consistency, and performance.
8. Understand how search engine optimization may help a Web site obtain high placement in search engines.
9. Understand how to provide some major support e-services.
10. Understand the process of building an online storefront.
11. Be able to build an online storefront with templates.

Content

OBO Sets Its Goals for Success

OBO SETS ITS GOALS FOR SUCCESS

The Problem

OBO of New Zealand sells protective gear for field hockey goalkeepers. The leg guards, helmets, gloves, and other products protect goalies from the hard hockey ball without inhibiting the goalie's need to move quickly and easily. OBO's protective foam has a tighter and more consistent cell structure than competitors' products to provide maximum, long-wearing protection, and OBO's unique three-dimensional thermo-bonding manufacturing process produces equipment that reflects the way the body moves. By manufacturing a quality product and listening to its customers, OBO has become the market leader in most of the 20 countries in which its products are sold. In the 2000 Olympics, all the medal-winning teams wore OBO gear.

OBO is based in Palmerston North, a small provincial town in New Zealand that is a very long way from its principal markets in Europe and the Americas. OBO sells a niche product that it sells best through agents or stores to ensure a proper fit. How does OBO use its Web site to market an experiential product to a global market from New Zealand?

The Solution

The goals of the *obo.co.nz* Web site are community building, product sales, and research and development. As the "About OBO" page proudly boasts, "OBO loves the Web because it lets us have contact with the people we exist to serve."

Community building happens through online discussion forums, sponsored players, and an image gallery. OBO's company director Simon Barnett says: "We sponsor goalkeepers. We e-mail out to 900–1,000 people biweekly and give them the opportunity to ask an expert about the game and the equipment, join a database, link to other hockey sites, and seek readers' opinions. We try to get people involved by having their photo on the Web site. If we can get people involved, they'll love the brand name and the image and the feelings that go with it" (New Zealand Ministry of Economic Development [MED] 2000, p. 12).

OBO also sells goalie equipment through the Web site. However, the main marketing and sales goal of the Web site is to convince the visitor of the value of the product and direct the customer to a store or agent to make the purchase. Barnett calls the Web site "a support mechanism for the brand and the sale of equipment through the agents, and we will pick up the odd sale here and there" (New Zealand MED 2000, p. 12).

OBO meets its research and development goal through online surveys, solicitation of players' opinions of the products, and focus groups. According to Barnett: "We use the Web site for research and development through focus groups. We give a topic such as goalkeeping shoes—Is there a need for them? What features should they have? What pricing? The focus group is carefully selected off the database, given the brief (the purpose of the questions), and asked to respond by the end of the week with their opinions" (New Zealand MED 2000, p. 12).

The Results

The OBO Web site is most successful at community building. In 2000, over 100,000 people visited the Web site, many of them first-time OBO equipment buyers who must register their product warranty online. Many become registered "team players" and contribute to discussion forums as well as create their own "favorites" section and online address book. The site also builds community by promoting a goalie-friendly approach to OBO's customers. Simon Barnett signs his introduction letter as "Team Captain" and says, "The most special thing about OBO are its people. The people who bring you the OBO product are dedicated, honest, and earnest about our work" (OBO 2005).

Online product sales are modest and growing slowly. This is in line with the company's expectation that the Web site should support, not compete with, OBO's agent network. For example, prices at the Web site are slightly higher than in retail stores. However, online sales are expected to grow because OBO has introduced a new line of clothes designed specifically for goalies that is sold exclusively through the Web site.

The focus groups deliver high-value feedback at almost no cost, and the discussion forums contribute to both community building and a constant stream of feedback about OBO's product in the marketplace.

Sources: Compiled from New Zealand Ministry of Economic Development (2000) and from *obo.co.nz* (accessed February 2007).

WHAT WE CAN LEARN . . .

OBO's use of the Web matches many of the expectations that online business owners have for their own Web sites. A small company with a great product is using its Web site to reach its target markets in distant countries. Like many successful online businesses, OBO uses its site to support business goals and to meet the needs and expectations of its target audience. The Web site is simple and well designed: It includes "attractors" that encourage customer interaction and keep customers coming back, it contains content that promotes cross-selling, and it effectively promotes sustainable customer relationships. OBO is one of tens of thousands of small businesses successfully using the Web for e-commerce. The purpose of this chapter is to describe the requirements for creating and maintaining a successful e-business or EC initiative. This chapter builds on the conceptual material offered in previous chapters to provide a practical understanding of what it takes to be successful in the competitive world of electronic commerce. Finally, it teaches you how to build a storefront quickly.

16.1 GETTING INTO E-COMMERCE

According to Maier (2005), it is a terrific time to be an entrepreneur. The availability of cheap computer hardware, free software, and high-speed Internet access has created a powerful base from which to launch new business and expand or transform existing ones. Maier provides 14 tips of how you can build the next Google. This chapter describes some of these tips.

Now that you are familiar with EC and its potential, you may want to know how to get into EC yourself. You can start an e-commerce venture in any number of ways; your only limit is your imagination. In this chapter, we will discuss some of the most common ways of starting an e-business. Specifically, this chapter presents the following topics:

▶ Starting a new online business (a *start-up*; see Section 16.2)
▶ Adding e-commerce initiative(s) to an existing business (i.e., becoming a click-and-mortar organization; see Section 16.3)
▶ Transforming to an e-business (Section 16.3)
▶ Opening a storefront on the Web (Section 16.9)

Almost any e-commerce initiative will require support activities and services, as well as plans for attracting visitors to a Web site (see Kavassalis et al. 2004). This chapter presents the following with regards to these types of activities:

▶ Developing a Web site (Section 16.4)
▶ Hosting the Web site and selecting and registering a domain name (Section 16.5)
▶ Developing, updating, and managing the content of a Web site (Section 16.6)
▶ Designing a Web site for maximum usability (Section 16.7)
▶ Providing support services (Section 16.8)

16.2 STARTING A NEW ONLINE BUSINESS

Success in the online marketplace is never an assured outcome. As in the brick-and-mortar marketplace, the failure rate for online companies is high (Kauffman et al. 2002). Why do so few online companies succeed while many others fail? What does the *entrepreneur* need to know to launch a profitable online business (see Schonfeld 2006)?

Online businesses may be *pure play* companies (online only) or *click-and-mortar* companies that add online projects, such as e-procurement or selling online, as additional marketing channels.

AN E-START-UP IS A START-UP

Before we start our discussion, we need to emphasize that an e-start-up is basically a start-up and, as such, must consider all the issues faced by a physical start up. Many books, magazines, and articles are dedicated to starting a new business. Magazines such as *Entrepreneur* are fully dedicated to start-ups. *Business 2.0* (June 2006 issue) concentrates on innovation and idea generation in start-ups. Copeland and Malik (2006) provide a 16-step process and guidelines for building a bulletproof start-up. They also provide a list of "things to avoid," "tools you need," "tips for success," and more. The Internet is contributing to what Hise is calling "America's love affair with entrepreneurship." In 2005, 672,000 new companies were developed versus 642,000 in 2004. However, not all are e-businesses. Also, note that 544,800 small businesses closed in 2005 (Hise 2007).

In this chapter, we concentrate on online start-ups and their specific issues. An aspiring entrepreneur must consider the generic steps of start-ups, which are not cited in this chapter, as well.

Many physical start-ups are click-and-mortars, or they are using the Web for support services. For example, Sloan (2006) describes how entrepreneurs are using the Web to build a large customer base before they even have the ability to deliver what they plan to sell.

One of the major steps in any start-up is to find a viable product (service). This may take a long time because the concept comes first, followed by a prototype, and then a market test (see Winnick 2006). For a case of an e-start-up that is failing after two years see Craig (2006). Also, finding the correct business model is critical (Chapter 1, Fan 2006, and Online Tutorial T1).

Umesh et al., (2005) provides some interesting guidelines to avoid dot-com failures. Specifically, they suggest looking at: (1) the growth rate of the market you plan to enter, (2) the timing of your market entry, (3) the revenue flow, and (4) what cycle a market is in. This can help create successful entrepreneurial ventures in EC. Maier (2005) suggests that starting small with two founders is the best option, although as many as four founders can work.

CREATING A NEW COMPANY OR ADDING AN ONLINE PROJECT

Most new businesses—brick-and-mortar, pure play, or click-and-mortar—begin in a similar manner. The following three steps describe the process:

- **Step 1: Identify a consumer or business need in the marketplace.** Many businesses simply begin with a good idea. A magazine article, a personal observation, an unsolved problem, a small irritation, or a friend's suggestion may trigger an idea, and the prospective business owner sees a gap between what people want and what is available. For example, see Case 16.1. Note that the key here is innovation. For many examples see various issues of *Business 2.0*, Holden (2006), and Williams (2006).

- **Step 2: Investigate the opportunity.** Just because a person perceives that an opportunity exists does not mean that it is real. Perhaps the potential number of individuals interested in purchasing the product or service is too small. Perhaps the cost of manufacturing, marketing, and distributing the product or providing the service is too large. The revenue model may be wrong, others may have tried already and failed, satisfactory substitute products may be available, and so on. For example, online grocery shopping would seem like a wonderful opportunity—relieving busy professionals of the time-consuming and tiresome task of regular visits to a grocery store. Many have tried to provide large- and small-scale online grocery ventures (e.g., NetGrocer, Peapod, HomeGrocer, Webvan), but most have failed or continue to lose money because they misjudged the logistical problems associated with grocery warehousing and delivery (Kurnia et al. 2005). This is why it is so important to develop a business plan. One of the purposes of a *business plan* is to determine the feasibility and viability of a business opportunity in the marketplace.

- **Step 3: Determine the business owner's ability to meet the need.** Assuming that a realistic business opportunity exists, does the prospective business owner have the ability to convert the opportunity into success? Some personal qualities are important: Is the business in an industry the prospective business owner knows well? Is it something the entrepreneur loves doing? Are family and friends supportive? Business skills in staff

INNOVATION AND CREATIVITY AT AMAZON.COM

Call it fate or call it the right person having the right idea at the right time. Whatever you call it, the idea behind Amazon.com and its founder, Jeff Bezos, seemed destined for each other.

Bezos was born in January 1964 in Albuquerque, New Mexico. Even as a boy, his cleverness, intelligence, and entrepreneurial skills were obvious. At the age of 12, Bezos built a motorized mirrored Infinity Cube because he couldn't afford the $20 to buy one. A few years later, he graduated as valedictorian of his Florida high school. As a young entrepreneur, he created a summer camp for middle-school students and promoted it by saying that it "emphasizes the use of new ways of thinking in old areas," which was in many ways a prediction of his future success.

Bezos graduated from Princeton University with a degree in computer science, and his first employment was in electronic commerce, building an EDI network for settling cross-border equity transactions. A few jobs later, he was a senior vice president at the hedge fund firm D. E. Shaw, responsible for exploring new business opportunities on the Internet. It was then that his intelligence, entrepreneurial talents, computing education, and e-commerce experience all came together in a brilliant idea: The most logical thing to sell over the Internet was books. Several years later he added dozens of other products.

Why books? Behind the thousands of brick-and-mortar bookstores are just two large book distributors, with an extensive list of books already online in the distributors' databases. Bezos was willing to bet that book buyers would be willing to give up the cozy, coffee-shop, browsing environment of the local bookstore if he could offer them the "earth's biggest bookstore," fantastic customer service, and features that no physical bookstore could match—customer book reviews, author interviews, personalized book recommendations, and more.

The other driving force behind his idea was what Bezos calls his "regret-minimization framework." "When I am 80," he asked himself, "am I going to regret leaving Wall Street? No. Will I regret missing a chance to be there at the start of the Internet? Yes" (Bayers 1999).

The rest of the story is the stuff of legend. Bezos left his six-figure Wall Street salary and wrote the Amazon.com business plan during a cross-country move to Seattle, Washington. The Amazon.com (Chapter 3) Web site was built in a cramped, poorly insulated garage. When Amazon.com launched in July 1995, a bell would ring every time the server recorded a sale. Within a few weeks the constant bell ringing became unbearable, and

they turned it off. Today, on a busy day, Amazon.com sells hundreds of products to about 3 million customers.

In the late 1990s and early 2000s, Amazon.com invested $2 billion in physical warehouses (see the opening case to Chapter 13) and expansion opportunities. This was in line with Bezos's vision for Amazon.com as "broader than books and music." After years of large losses, Amazon.com announced its first small profit in the fourth quarter of 2001. By 2005, the company had become more profitable. It all began with a smart entrepreneur whose life experiences gave him a brilliant idea that led to the founding of a legendary e-tailing company.

During its first decade of operation, Amazon.com changed its business model several times, adding innovative ideas. It also acquired other companies or stakes in companies in several countries (e.g., *joyo.com*—the largest e-tailer of books, music, and videos in China). Amazon Services, Inc., a subsidiary of Amazon.com, has projects with a number of different partners (e.g., American Express). Amazon Theater offers film viewing from its Web site as well as many more innovations. However, Bezos's most original idea is his vision of Blue Origin, a futuristic center for suborbital spaceships (Klotz 2005). Perhaps it will only be a matter of time before customers can purchase tickets for space trips from Amazon.com.

Bezos is indeed an innovator. In the last few years, he has worked on commercializing space trips. Bezos's Blue Origin commercial space venture is developing a vehicle to take occupants on a 10-minute ride to the edge of space, nearly 60 miles (96 km) above the earth and back.

In 2006, Amazon.com showed how innovative it could be by creating a special Web site called *endless.com*. Rather than selling from its brand name Amazon.com site, the company is trying to break in with a special upscale online boutique for handbags, footwear, and accessories.

Sources: Compiled from Spector (2000), Business Wire (2004a and 2004b), and Klotz (2005).

Questions

1. What were the opportunities and needs in the consumer market that inspired Bezos to create Amazon.com?

2. What factors, at both personal and business levels, led Bezos to his brilliant idea?

recruitment, management, negotiation, marketing, and financial management are required, as well as entrepreneurial attitudes such as innovation, risk taking, and being proactive. Many good ideas and realistic initiatives have failed in the execution stage because the owners or principals of the business lacked sufficient business skills to make it a reality. Boo.com, for example, seemingly had a great concept (retailing ultramodern, designer clothing) and superior software, but it failed because of the inability of management to organize the business and manage the projects necessary to bring Boo.com online before it burned through $120 million of start-up capital (Cukier 2000).

The process for developing EC projects in existing companies is similar, except that step 3 changes to: "Determine the organization's ability to meet the need."

Winnick (2006) provides the following five "secrets" to help you come up with the next big thing:

1. **Do Your Homework.** Research what's really happening in the world. Simple innovations are not understated. They have to be tangibly more effective than anything already on the market. For example, attend ExpoMart, where the annual Innovation New Product Exposition (INPEX), takes place (see Williams 2006).

2. **Aim for Excitement.** Make your customers say "wow" or "finally," such as Bezos's taking future customers to space.

3. **Whittle, Shape, Iterate, Repeat.** Test and improve the ideas and prototypes several times. Your designers and developers can do this.

4. **Get Real.** Build physical prototypes to get feedback from friends, suppliers, and customers (see Copeland and Malik 2006).

5. **Avoid Creating a Gizmo.** Beware of creating a product (service) with obvious faults, even if it looks like a brilliant design. Even though a product (service) must be attractive to customers, it must also work.

For further guidelines see *Business 2.0* (2006) and Williams (2006).

Beyond these general platitudes about what it takes to start a prosperous business, the owner of an online business must consider some requirements that reflect the online nature of the business. The first of these is the need to understand Internet culture. Activities such as spam, extensive use of graphics, forced visitor registration, and intrusive pop-up browser windows are counter to the accepted norms of behavior on the Internet (Huff et al. 2001). Similarly, business owners new to the Net need to realize that, contrary to expectations, textual exchanges of information are "media rich" (Crosbie 2006, Petrecca 2006, and Stam 2005); customers are active in how they absorb and use information; and the Internet is a personal, helping, and sharing place for most users. Businesses that ignore the cultural and behavioral norms of the Internet do so at their peril.

A second requirement that the owner of an online business must consider is the nature of appropriate products and services. Although virtually anything is available for sale on the Internet, the degree of sales success is somewhat dependent on the type of item or service being offered. For example, digitized products (e.g., information, music, software) sell well and are delivered easily. Similarly, services (e.g., stock brokering, travel ticket sales), and commodities (e.g., books, CDs) also have been quite successful. In contrast, experiential products, such as expensive clothes, do not sell well. However, one of the greatest opportunities the Internet offers is in niche marketing. Rare and quirky sales ideas, such as antique Coke bottles (antiquebottles.com), gadgets for left-handed individuals (anythingleft-handed.co.uk), Swedish gourmet food (wikstromsgourmet.com), toys for cats and dogs (cattoys.com), and gift items from Belize (belizenet.com), would rarely succeed in a physical storefront, but the Internet offers the owners of these sites an opportunity to pursue their business idea and be successful. According to Maier (2005), it is better to handle the sales yourself rather than hiring an expensive salesforce. The Internet's worldwide reach makes it easy for people with a common interest to find each other and conduct business together.

ONLINE BUSINESS PLANNING

Every new online business needs at least an informal business plan. As defined in Chapter 14, a **business plan** is a written document that identifies a company's goals and outlines how the company intends to achieve those goals and at what cost. A business plan includes both *strategic* elements (e.g., mission statement, business model, value proposition, and competitive positioning statement) and *operational* elements (e.g., operations plan, financial statements) of how a new business intends to do business. Medium and large businesses, or those seeking external funding, must have a formal business plan. Paloalto.com (paloalto.com) offers *Business Plan Pro 2007* that includes more than 500 sample plans. See microsoft.com/smallbusiness/hub.mspx.

business plan
A written document that identifies a company's goals and outlines how the company intends to achieve the goals and at what cost.

The primary reason an entrepreneur writes a business plan is to acquire funding from a bank, an angel investor, a venture capitalist, or the financial markets. Similarly, in an existing business a *business case* needs to be written for any new large EC project, so management can decide whether to fund it (see the opening case and the Real-World Case in Chapter 15). A business plan also is important for a new venture as a tool to recruit senior management and to convince business partners to make a commitment to the business. A business plan helps ensure a thriving business by encouraging an entrepreneur to set goals, anticipate problems, set measures for success, and keep the business on track after starting it. A business plan forces the entrepreneur to be realistic about the business's prospects. Sometimes the most successful outcome of a business plan is a decision not to proceed. For all aspects of business plans for start-up companies see hjventures.com. For a sample of business plan software see planware.org, planmagic.com, abs-usa.com, and paloalto.com.

Online Tutorial T1 on the book's Web site explores this topic in further depth and offers a detailed explanation of how to prepare a business plan.

The Business Case

business case

A document that justifies the investment of internal, organizational resources in a specific application or project.

An existing brick-and-mortar business looking to move online (either to add EC projects or to transform itself to an e-business) also needs a **business case**—a document that is used to justify the investment of internal, organizational resources in a specific application or project (see Chapters 14 and 15). A business case for a large, resource-intensive EC project resembles a business plan. Online Tutorial T1 on the book's Web site includes the similarities and differences in writing such a business case. For a small or medium-size project, the business case can be much simpler. Insights and Additions 16.1 presents a business case high-level template that you can use to justify new online applications, such as a new e-procurement, e-learning, an extranet, or participation in a digital exchange.

FUNDING A NEW ONLINE BUSINESS

Launching an online business can be expensive. The brave entrepreneur is usually willing to invest personal funds from savings, personal lines of credit, or a house mortgage, but these sources of "bootstrap funding" are unlikely to be enough. According to Maier (2005) you should "bootstrap" it as long as possible, but don't wait too long to tap into the venture community. The new venture involves significant risk, so some traditional sources of debt financing, such as a bank loan, are difficult or impossible to get. What are other sources of funding for a start-up business? (See Pearlson and Sounders 2006). For an introduction to sources of e-business funding, see businesspartners.com.

First Round of Initial Funding: Angel Investors and Incubators

angel investor

A wealthy individual who contributes personal funds and possibly expertise at the earliest stage of business development.

When the entrepreneur's personal funds are insufficient, the entrepreneur will go to friends, family members, or to angel investors. An **angel investor** is a wealthy individual who contributes personal funds and possibly expertise at the earliest stage of business development. Angel investors can be found through organizations like the Angel Capital Association (angelcapitalassociation.org) (Maier 2005).

A typical angel investor scenario begins with, for example, a young software developer who has identified a niche in the market for a new software application and has used his own money to get started but has insufficient funding to continue. An angel investor may provide the developer with an office, hardware, software, salary, and access to the human and financial resources required to write the software application. In most cases, the angel investor also provides guidance or access to management expertise. In addition to sometimes-altruistic goals, the angel investor is looking for a reasonable return on the investment. In other words, the angel investor is almost always a pre-VC funding source and may be paid later from the infusion of venture capital funds. An angel investor is an excellent source of funding for the entrepreneur; however, angel funding is scarce and difficult to find.

incubator

A company, university, or nonprofit organization that supports businesses in their initial stages of development.

Another important source of support, if not direct funding, for pre-VC firms is an incubator. An **incubator** is a company, university, or nonprofit organization that supports promising businesses in their initial stages of development. Although some incubators offer start-up funding, the primary purpose of most incubators is to offer a variety of support services—office space, accounting services, group purchasing schemes, reception services, coaching, and

Insights and Additions 16.1 A High-Level Business Case Template

This template shows the justification for the expenditure of resources on a specific online project or initiative in an existing business. If the business is considering a number of different initiatives, you should prepare a separate business plan or case for each one. If the initiative is for a new business, it will require a more comprehensive business plan.

▶ **Goals.** Begin with a specific description of what the business intends to achieve through the initiative—increased sales, reinforcement of the brand or corporate image, improved customer support, reduction in communications and marketing costs, and so forth. A useful approach is to define the problem, propose a solution, and describe the expected outcomes or impacts. Conclude this section with *goals*—one or more statements that succinctly describe a desired future condition toward which the business will direct its efforts. Here, it will be advantageous to use a business model (Fan 2006).

▶ **Cost savings.** If one or more goals include reduction of existing expenditures, then calculate the following: (1) an itemized and quantified list of existing costs that the project will affect and (2) the estimated levels of savings that the project will generate (e.g., reduce long-distance telephone costs by 45 percent). Multiply the costs by the saving levels to find the expected reduction of expenditures. You should estimate these savings for a short-term time frame, perhaps the first three years of the project's operation.

▶ **New revenue.** If one or more of the goals suggests an increased revenue stream, then calculate: (1) an itemized and quantified list of existing net income (revenue from sales minus cost of sales) the application or project will affect and (2) the estimated levels of new sales that you expect (e.g., increase product sales by 12 percent). When you multiply the net income by the increased sales levels, you get the expected amount of increased revenue. Do this for the same multiyear time frame as used in the cost-savings calculation.

▶ **Extra benefits.** List and, if possible, quantify any additional fiscal benefits that are associated with the project (e.g., improved staff productivity, faster collection of outstanding debts). If these are difficult to estimate accurately, it is best to list them but neither quantify them nor add them to the benefits identified previously. This approach will produce an overall more conservative estimate of benefits, building in an extra cushion for project success in the event that the business does not realize all quantified benefits.

▶ **Cost of the solution.** This is an itemized and quantified list of costs associated with the online project. You should estimate both direct costs (e.g., amortized costs of Web site development and Web site hosting) and indirect costs (e.g., staff training) for the period.

▶ **Net benefits.** Add together all benefits (i.e., cost savings, new revenue, extra benefits) and subtract the costs. The result should be a specific amount of expected monetary gains (or losses) resulting from successful implementation of the project in each year of the period being examined.

▶ **Recommendation.** Summarize the decision that is being recommended in light of the foregoing analysis. If the net benefit result is strongly positive, then a decision to proceed is likely, and you can start the next steps (e.g., a risk analysis, customer survey, staff hiring). If the results are slightly positive or negative in one or all years of operation, you can still justify the decision to proceed on the basis of seeing the online initiative as a long-term strategy, a competitive imperative, or simply the cost of staying in business. If the bottom line is strongly negative, then the most likely outcome will be a decision that there is no justification for the project, saving the business a lot of time and money. Even that can be viewed as a positive outcome of a business case.

For details of this high-level template see Online Tutorial T1.

---

information technology consulting—at little or no cost. In return, the incubator receives a modest fee, start-up equity in the company, or both (Phan et al. 2005, Conway 2004).

Second Round Financing: Venture Capital

One major source of funding during the dot-com boom was venture capital. **Venture capital (VC)** is money invested in a business by an individual, a group of individuals (venture capitalists), or a funding company in exchange for equity in the business. Venture capitalists tend to invest in companies that have identified what seems to be an outstanding business opportunity, have taken some action to make the opportunity happen (e.g., written a new software application, secured a patent, built an interesting Web site that attracts many visitors, conducted some promising experiments, and recruited key personnel), and need an infusion of funds and management expertise to expand and launch the business. Some venture capitalists may have connections with CEOs who would be good strategic guides for your business,

venture capital (VC)
Money invested in a business by an individual, a group of individuals (venture capitalists), or a funding company in exchange for equity in the business.

others may be more market specific (e.g., experts on software development). It is therefore important to match your VC with your business (Maier 2005). Venture capitalists usually invest large sums of money and expect, in return, some management control and a profit on their investment within three to five years when the successful start-up goes public (an IPO) or a larger company merges with it or acquires it. The start-up company receives the funds and experienced management guidance it needs during its launch and expansion stages.

The downside for the start-up business to acquire VC is minimal; it loses some control over the business in return for funds it is unlikely to acquire from any other source. The more difficult problem is *finding* VC. Due to the many dot-com failures in 2000 and onward, many VC sources have disappeared, and competition for venture capital is fierce.

The downside for the venture capitalist is that if the business fails, or even if it is a mediocre success, then the promised return on equity from going public, merging, or being bought out does not happen. This occurrence is common, and venture capitalists plan on one wildly successful investment to make up the losses from several less-than-successful ventures. For factors that venture capitalists consider see Solvik (2005). For what a venture capitalist wants to see in you, see *Business 2.0* (2006).

Some well-known VC companies are vFinance Capital (vfinance.com), the Capital Network (thecapitalnetwork.com), and Garage Technology Ventures (garage.com) founded by personal-computing guru Guy Kawasaki. Venture capitalists may be start-ups. Most of them lost large amounts of money for their investors during the dot-com bust. Rayport and Jaworski (2004) offer a more comprehensive discussion of VC markets and other sources of equity financing, such as holding companies and corporate ventures. For more information, see the National Venture Capital Association (nvca.org), the Venture Capital Marketplace (v-capital.com.au), Mobius Venture Capital (mobiusvc.com), and Vcapital (vcapital.com).

Additional Funding: A Large Partner

As part of a VC investment or after the depletion of VC money, one or more large companies may step into the process. For example, Yahoo!, IBM, Microsoft, Motorola, Google (Time Warner News Corp.), and Oracle have invested in hundreds of EC start-up companies. Eventually, they may acquire the start-up completely. Such investments are frequently done in complementary or competing areas. For example, Yahoo! is a major investor in Google and in Baidu in China; News Corp., acquired the start up MySpace.com; and Google invested in dozens of companies related to advertisement, including the purchase of YouTube in 2006. Google and other EC companies are buying companies before they try to get the VC support.

The IPO

Once the company is well known and successful, it will go to a stock exchange to raise money via an *initial public offer* (IPO). In such offerings, investors will pay a much larger amount of money per share than that paid by the initial and secondary funding source, sometimes 5 or 10 times more per share.

Section 16.2 ▶ REVIEW QUESTIONS

1. Describe the formation process of a typical online business.
2. What special requirements must an online business consider in its formation? In e-business planning?
3. What is a business case and how does it contribute to business success?
4. Describe initial, secondary, and IPO funding options available to a start-up.
5. Describe innovation and idea generation for online ventures.

16.3 ADDING E-COMMERCE INITIATIVES OR TRANSFORMING TO AN E-BUSINESS

Creating an e-business start-up certainly is exciting, but it also is very risky. As with any other business, the failure rate is very high. However, in cyberspace the risks and uncertainties, plus lack of experience, result in an even higher rate of failure. Nevertheless, thousands of new online businesses have been created since 1995, mostly small ones (see Section 16.9 and Chapter 14). A much more common option is adding one or several EC initiatives to an existing business.

ADDING EC INITIATIVES TO AN EXISTING BUSINESS

Almost all medium-to-large organizations have added or plan to add EC initiatives to the existing business. The most common additions are:

▶ **A storefront.** Adding an online sales channel is common in both B2C (e.g., godiva.com, walmart.com) and B2B (e.g., ibm.com). The required investment is fairly low because storefront hosting is available from many vendors (see Sections 16.5 and 16.9). Customers like the option of buying online, and gradually more of them will use the storefront. You can build a storefront fairly quickly, and the damage in case of failure may not be too large. Because the required investment is not large, it may not be necessary to expend the time and money in developing a formal business case. This is a practical strategy for an SME (Chapter 14). For a large-scale storefront, a company will need to follow the steps suggested in Section 16.2, especially the preparation of a business case, in order to secure internal funding and the blessing of top management. For further details on developing storefronts, see Online Chapter 19 and the "Getting Started Guide" at smallbusiness.yahoo.com. A major issue in developing a storefront is deciding what support services to offer and how to provide them. Note that some well-known companies may create a special subsidiary for online activities using external funding. Such a strategy often results in an IPO.

▶ **A portal.** As discussed in Chapter 7, there are several types of corporate portals. Almost all companies today have one or several portals that they use for external and/or internal collaboration and communication. A storefront for employees or for external customers may be a part of a portal. Adding a portal (or several portals) may be a necessity, and it may not be preceded by a formal business case. Issues of content and design, as well as security, are of utmost importance. Because many vendors offer portal-building services, vendor selection may be an important issue (see Online Chapter 19).

▶ **E-procurement.** This EC initiative is popular with large companies, as described in Chapter 5. Online Chapter 19 describes the development of an e-procurement initiative. E-procurement usually requires significant investment; therefore, a business case is needed. E-procurement also requires extensive integration (both internally and externally), so an EC architecture must be in place.

▶ **Auctions and reverse auctions.** Large corporations need to consider building their own auction or reverse auction (for e-procurement) sites. Although forward auctions can be added to a storefront at a reasonable cost, a reverse auction usually requires more integration with business partners and, consequently, a larger investment and a business case.

▶ **Other initiatives.** Organizations may consider many other EC initiatives, following the business models presented in Chapter 1. For example, Qantas Airways (qantas.com.au) sells tickets online directly from its Web site and from a B2B exchange; it buys supplies and services from its e-procurement site as well as from several exchanges; it provides e-training for its employees; operates several corporate portals; offers online banking services to its employees; provides eCRM and ePRM; manages its frequent-flyer program; supports a wireless notification system to customers; and so on. Large companies such as GE and IBM have hundreds of active EC projects.

TRANSFORMATION TO AN E-BUSINESS

As the brick-and-mortar organization implements more EC projects, it becomes a click-and-mortar organization and eventually an e-business. Being an e-business does not imply that the organization is a pure online company, it just means that it conducts as many processes as possible online (see Ranganathan et al. 2004 and the Siemans case in Online File W16.1). A rapid or large-scale change from brick-and-mortar to e-business involves organizational transformation.

What Is Organizational Transformation?

Organizational transformation is a comprehensive concept that implies a major organizational change. According to McKay and Marshall (2004), a *transformation* is not only a major change but also a sharp break from the past. The key points in understanding organizational transformation are as follows:

▶ The organization's ways of thinking and vision will fundamentally change.

▶ There will be revolutionary changes to the process and context involved in creating a new organizational vision and rethinking business models and business strategy.

▶ The change must involve a substantial break from previous ways of acting. It will likely involve discovering and developing new opportunities and new ways of doing things.

▶ The change must permeate through and impact on the behavior of a majority of organizational members.

▶ The change will involve creating new systems, procedures, and structures that not only enable and dictate how new processes function but will also impact on the deeply embedded business models and understandings that drive the organization.

According to Hendon (2003), an e-business transformation is not solely about technology. Technologies must be integrated with possible changes in business strategy, processes, organizational culture, and infrastructure.

How an Organization Can Be Transformed into an E-Business

Transforming an organization, especially a large company, into an e-business can be a very complex endeavor. For an organization to transform itself into an e-business, it must transform several major processes, such as procurement, sales, CRM, and manufacturing, as well as deal with *change management*.

Such a transformation involves several strategic issues. Lasry (2002) raised several of these issues in an investigation of the rate at which brick-and-mortar retail firms adopt the Web as an additional sales channel. He examined organizational strategies, such as internal restructuring, the formation of joint ventures, and outsourcing. He concluded that implementing EC requires a disruptive and potentially hazardous change in core features. He suggests that companies spin off EC activities as part of the transformation process (see the discussion in Chapter 14).

Ginige, et al. (2001) and Muller-Lankenau, et al. (2006) provide a comprehensive description of the transformation to e-business, describing both the internal and external processes supported by IT, as shown in Exhibit 16.1. They then show the support of IT at each stage. Finally, they describe the necessary *change management* activities.

Baseline magazine offers a calculator to measure business transformation. For details see Strassmann (2007).

Business Process Reengineering

Several other studies have examined transformation to e-business. For example, Chen and Ching (2002) explored the relationship of BPR and e-business and investigated the change process both for individuals and organizations. They proposed a process of redesigning an organization for e-business, providing several research propositions. Bosilj-Vuksic et al. (2002) explored the use of simulation modeling for enabling transformation to e-business. They examined the process of BPR and suggested using simulation and process maps to support the process. Turban, et al. (2008a) described the use of business intelligence. Finally, Jackson and Harris (2003) explored organizational change issues in transformation to e-business.

Business Process Management

business process management (BPM)
Method for business restructuring that combines workflow systems and redesign methods; covers three process categories—people-to-people, systems-to-systems, and systems-to-people interactions.

Lately, *business process management* has been used to facilitate organizational transformation.

The term **business process management (BPM)** refers to activities performed by business to improve their processes. While such improvements are hardly new, software tools

EXHIBIT 16.1   Roadmap to Becoming an E-Business

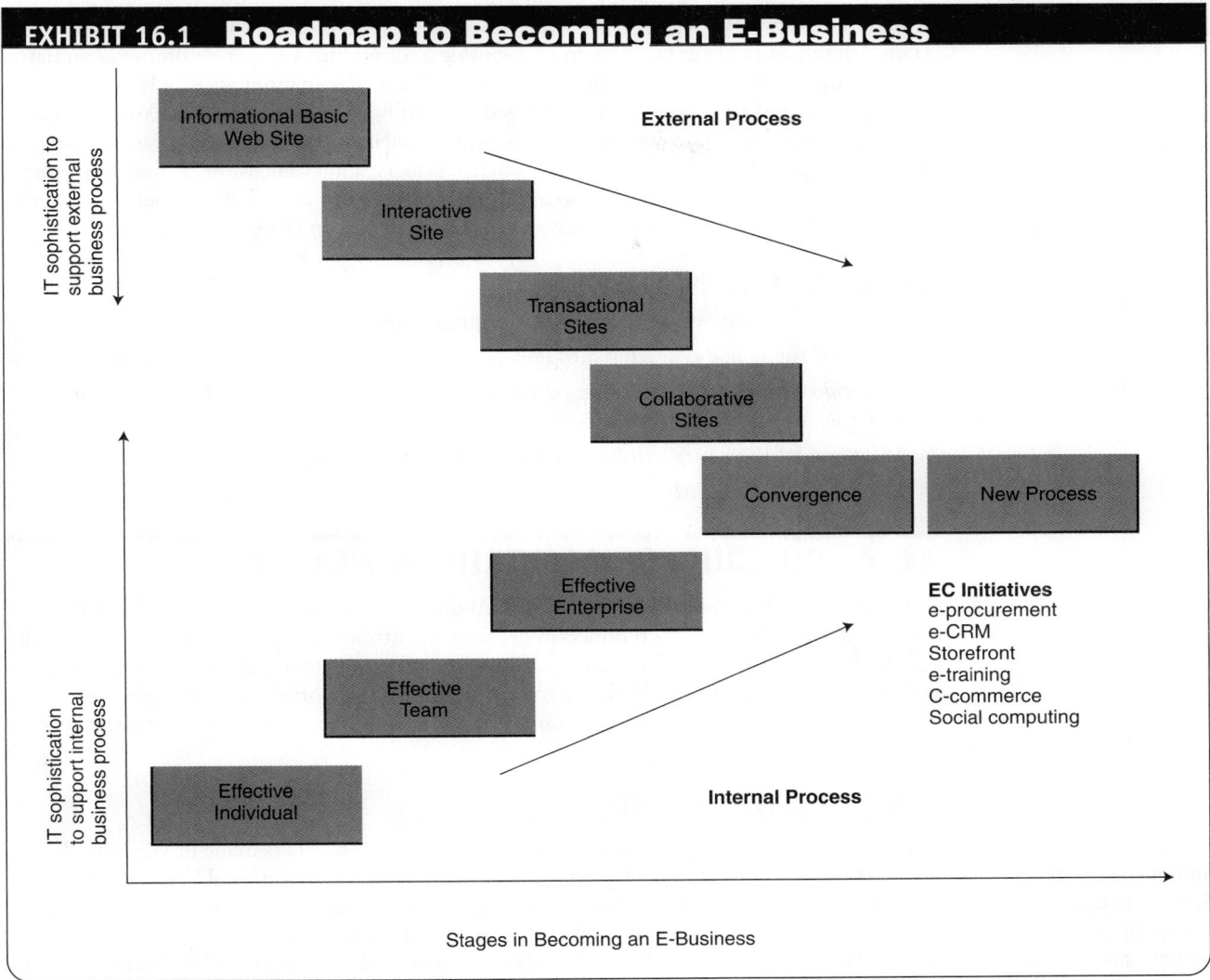

Source: Ginige, A., et al. "A Road Map for Successfully Transforming SMEs into E-Business." *Cutter IT Journal*, May 2001. Used with permission of the author.

called business process management systems have made such activities faster and cheaper. BPM systems monitor the execution of the business processes so that managers can analyze and change processes in response to data, rather than on just a hunch. BPM differs from BPR in that it deals not just with one time changes to the organization, which is what BPR does, but with long-term consequences. The major activities of BPM are process design, process execution, and process monitoring. For details see en.wikipedia.org/wiki/Business_process_management, Smith (2006), and Jeston and Nelis (2006).

Software Tools for Facilitating Transformation to E-Business

Several vendors offer methodologies and tools to facilitate transformation to e-business (e.g., see IBM 2006 and Ould 2003). A methodology developed by Integic Corp. (integic.com/solutions/methodology.cfm) includes a framework for e-strategy, solution development and deployment, a guide for organizational change, a framework for project management, and a systematic approach to quality management. Using this methodology, organizations in the public sector, such as the Federal Aviation Administration, the Office of the Comptroller in New York City, as well as public utilities, have achieved dramatic cost and cycle time reductions (see "Case Studies" at integic.com).

Change Management

Transforming an existing business to an e-business, or adding a major e-commerce initiative means a manager must change business processes and the manner in which people work, communicate, and are promoted and managed. According to Ash and Burn (2006), this requires systematic attention to learning processes, organizational culture, technology infrastructure, people's thinking, and systems. Employees, business partners, and even customers may resist such a change. Ash and Burn developed a model of e-business change as well as a model for managing e-business change that Chapter 18 provides in the discussion on change management.

Section 16.3 ▶ REVIEW QUESTIONS

1. Which EC initiatives are brick-and-mortar organizations most likely to add?
2. Describe the major characteristics (key points) of organizational transformation.
3. Describe the stages in becoming an e-business (per Ginige et al. 2001) and the major activities involved in the process.
4. List some of the issues involved in transforming to an e-business.
5. Define *BPR* and *BPM*.

16.4 BUILDING OR ACQUIRING A WEB SITE

Every online business needs a Web site. A Web site is the primary way any firm doing business on the Internet advertises its products or services and attracts customers. Many Web sites also sell products and services, and businesses with digital products usually deliver their products via the Web site as well. The Web site may be a storefront, a portal, an auction site, and so on. How can an organization build or acquire such a site? First, let's examine the different types of Web sites that exist.

CLASSIFICATION OF WEB SITES

informational Web site
A Web site that does little more than provide information about the business and its products and services.

interactive Web site
A Web site that provides opportunities for the customers and the business to communicate and share information.

attractors
Web site features that attract and interact with visitors in the target stakeholder group.

transactional Web site
A Web site that sells products and services.

Web sites come in all shapes and sizes. One of the major distinctions made in Web site classification is the level of functionality inherent in the site. An **informational Web site** does little more than provide information about the business and its products and services. For many brick-and-mortar businesses, such as a New England weathervane shop (vtweatherworks.com), a Cook Islands beach house (varas.co.ck), or an informational "brochureware" Web site is perfectly satisfactory. The major purpose is to have a *presence* on the Web.

An **interactive Web site** provides opportunities for the customers and the business to communicate and share information. An interactive site will contain all the information about products and services that an informational site does, but it also will deliver informational features intended to encourage interaction between the business and customers or among customers, such as an e-newsletter, product demonstrations, blogs, and customer discussion forums. An interactive Web site will strongly encourage feedback by including contact e-mail addresses, providing feedback forms, and encouraging completion of online surveys. Features such as the ability to search the site, a well-designed site map, and mouseovers (clickable buttons that change shape or color when a visitor passes a mouse cursor over the button) make navigation more interactive. Value-added tools such as currency converters, price comparisons, calendars, and various types of calculators (e.g., a mortgage calculator on a bank's Web site) can enhance interactivity.

At a higher level of interactivity are **attractors**—Web site features that attract and interact with site visitors. Attractors such as games, puzzles, prize giveaways, contests, and electronic postcards encourage customers to find the Web site, visit again, and recommend the site to their friends. For example, Ragu's Web site does not sell spaghetti sauce or other Ragu products, but the recipes, customer interaction ("talk to mama"), unforgettable domain name (eat.com), and other features make this an attractor-loaded site that increases brand awareness and sells Ragu's products in the customer's next trip to the grocery store.

A **transactional Web site** sells products and services. These Web sites typically include information and interactivity features but also have sell-side features, such as a shopping cart, a product catalog, customer-personalized account, a shipping calculator, and the ability to accept credit cards to complete the sale.

A **collaborative Web site** is a site that allows business partners to collaborate (i.e., it includes many supportive tools; see Chapters 6, 7, and 13). B2B exchanges may also provide collaboration capabilities.

collaborative Web site
A site that allows business partners to collaborate

BUILDING A WEB SITE

Assuming that a business has completed the preparatory work of business formation, writing a business plan, and acquiring initial funding, as outlined in Section 16.2, the process of building a Web site is as follows:

▶ **Step 1—Select a Web host.** One of the first decisions that an online business will face is where to locate the Web site on the Internet. The Web site may be included in a virtual shopping mall, such as activeplaza.com, or hosted in a collection of independent storefronts, as at Yahoo! (smallbusiness.yahoo.com) or ebay.com (even if you do not do auctions). However, many medium-size and large businesses will build a stand-alone Web site either with an independent hosting service or through self-hosting arrangements.

▶ **Step 2—Register a domain name.** Nearly concurrent with the selection of a Web host will be the domain name decision. In a mall or Web storefront, the business's name may be an extension of the host's name (e.g., smallbusiness.yahoo.com/mybusiness). A stand-alone Web site will have a stand-alone domain name (e.g., mybusiness.com), and decisions will have to be made about which top-level domain name to use and whether the domain name includes the business name or some aspect of branding.

▶ **Step 3—Create and manage content.** The Web site also needs content—the text, images, sound, and video that deliver the information that site visitors need and expect. Content can come from a variety of sources, but getting the right content in place, making it easy for viewers to find, delivering it effectively, and managing content so it remains accurate and up-to-date are crucial to the success of the online business (see discussion in Section 16.6). Hosting services may provide templates that show where content is to be placed and some suggestions on how to organize content. Exhibit 16.2 lists the primary criteria Web site visitors use to evaluate the content of a Web site.

▶ **Step 4—Design the Web site.** This is the critically important and creative part of the process that determines what the site will look like (e.g., color schemes, graphics, typography) and how visitors will use it (e.g., information architecture, navigation design). Mall or storefront businesses may have limited options, but the design choices for the stand-alone Web site are nearly unlimited. Exhibit 16.2 also lists the primary criteria that Web site visitors use to evaluate the design of a Web site. Section 16.7 and the Online Technical Appendix B provide details.

▶ **Step 5—Construct the Web site and test.** Businesses must also decide whether to design and construct the Web site internally, contract it out to a Web design firm, or some combination of both. When the business owners are satisfied with the Web site, it is transferred to the Web site host. At this point, the Web site is open for business, but it requires final testing to ensure that all the links work and that the processes function as expected (e.g., acceptance of credit cards). For details, see Section 16.8 and Online Chapter 19.

▶ **Step 6—Market and promote the Web site.** At this stage, the business promotes the location, or URL, of the Web site widely on products, business cards, letters, and promotional materials. A business can use any of the advertising strategies discussed in Chapter 4—banner exchanges, e-mail, chat rooms, viral marketing, or other methods. Another key strategy for attracting customers is increased visibility via search engine optimization, which Section 16.8 discusses.

EXHIBIT 16.2 Web Site Evaluation Criteria

How Web Site Visitors Evaluate Content

Criteria (and related "subcriteria")	Explanation
Relevance (applicable, related, clear)	Concerned with issues such as relevancy, clearness, and "goodness" of the information.
Timeliness (current, continuously updated)	Concerned with the currentness of the information.
Reliability (believable, accurate, consistent)	Concerned with the degree of accuracy, dependability, and consistency of the information.
Personality	Delivery of content the way you like it.
Scope (sufficient, complete, covers a wide range, detailed)	Evaluates the extent of information, range of information, and level of detail provided by the Web site.
Perceived usefulness (informative, valuable, instrumental)	Visitors' assessment of the likelihood that the information will enhance their purchasing decision.

How Web Site Visitors Evaluate Web Site Design

Criteria (and related "subcriteria")	Explanation
Access (responsive, loads quickly) (see w3.org/WAI)	Refers to the speed of access and the availability of the Web site at all times.
Usability (simple layout, easy to use, well organized, visually attractive, fun, clear design)	Concerned with the extent to which the Web site is visually appealing, consistent, fun, and easy to use.
Navigation	Evaluates the links to needed information.
Interactivity (customized product; search engine; ability to create list of items, change list of items, and find related items)	Evaluates the search engine and the personal features (e.g., shopping cart) of the Web site.
Attractiveness, Appearance	Proper use of multimedia, colors.

Sources: Compiled from McKinney et al. (2002); Drostdesigns (2006); and from Nielsen (2005).

The following sections discuss each of these steps and processes

Section 16.4 ▶ REVIEW QUESTIONS

1. Distinguish between informational, interactive, transactional, and collaborative Web sites.
2. List the six steps in building a Web site.
3. Describe five criteria that Web site visitors use to evaluate Web site content.
4. Describe four criteria that visitors use to evaluate Web site design.
5. Describe business process management.

16.5 WEB SITE HOSTING AND OBTAINING A DOMAIN NAME

Every brick-and-mortar business has a storefront from which it sells goods and services. The business either owns or rents the storefront in a mall or independent location. Every online business usually has a storefront. The decisions about whether to own (self-host) or rent, where to host the Web site (store builder service, ISP, pure Web hosting service, or self-hosting), and the site's domain name are some of the first important decisions an online business owner has to make. This section discusses the considerations in making these decisions.

WEB HOSTING OPTIONS

The following are the major Web hosting options.

storebuilder service
A hosting service that provides disk space and services to help small and microbusinesses build a Web site quickly and cheaply.

Storebuilder Service

A **storebuilder service** (also called a design-and-host service) provides Web hosting as well as storage space, templates, and other services to help small businesses build a Web site quickly and cheaply.

An example of a company that offers comprehensive storebuilding hosting services and software is Yahoo! Web Hosting. Yahoo!'s base service offers Web hosting as well as customized templates and other support for $11.95 per month; the next plan up, which is offered for $19.95 a month, offers additional services; a package for professionals that includes security features is available for $39.95 a month. All levels of Yahoo! Web Hosting include access to template-based software, SiteBuilder, which offers more than 330 customizable templates. The software can build a storefront quickly and easily (see Section 16.9 and Team Assignment 6). Yahoo!'s Web Hosting package also provides marketing tools, domain name selection assistance, a payment gate, storage (disk) space, and shipment services. The package also works with the Yahoo! Merchant Solutions, which Section 16.9 describes. Yahoo! Web Hosting usually offers a Web site address (e.g., a URL such as smallbusiness.yahoo.com/mybusiness), management tools, security features, and Internet connection maintenance. Yahoo! combines Web hosting and store building, but other vendors may separate the two functions, as shown later in this section.

The advantage of a storebuilder service is that it is a quick, easy, and inexpensive way to build a Web site. The disadvantages are the lack of a strong online identity, limited functionality (e.g., accepting credit cards may not be possible), dependence on the service for proper management of connectivity to the site, and some lack of differentiation (the Web site tends to look like other sites because everyone is using the same set of templates). Despite the disadvantages, storebuilder services are the prime choice of small and sometimes medium-size businesses (see Case 16.2).

eBay offers similar storefront software tools called webtools4less.com ranging from $3.99 per month to $89.00. The advantage of going with storebuilders is that hosting at Yahoo! Store or e-Bay exposes the sellers to a large number of potential buyers who visit these sites (e.g., see Elms 2006). Storebuilders are a special case of a pure hosting service. Maier (2005) suggests that open source free software programs help keep infrastructure costs down.

A Pure Hosting Service

A **Web hosting service** is a dedicated Web site hosting company that offers a wide range of hosting services and functionality to businesses of all sizes. Companies such as Hostway (hostway.com) and 1and1 (1and1.com) offer more and better services than an ISP because Web site hosting is their core business. Almost all Web hosting companies have internal Web design departments to assure the cooperation between the designer and the host. Also, functionality such as database integration, shipping and tax calculators, sufficient bandwidth to support multimedia files, shopping carts, site search engines, and comprehensive site statistics are likely to be readily available.

A Web hosting service can be the best option for an online business that needs one or more mirror sites. A **mirror site** is an exact duplicate of the original Web site, but it is physically located on a Web server on another continent or country. A business may decide that it needs a mirror site when large numbers of customers are a far distance from the original site. A mirror site reduces telecommunications costs and improves the speed of customer access because the site reduces the distance between the Web server and the customer's browser. Typically, customers do not know, or care, that they are accessing a mirror site.

A variation of the Web hosting service is **co-location**. In this arrangement, a business places a Web server owned and maintained by the business in a Web hosting service that manages the server's connection to the Internet. This allows the business maximum control over site content and functionality, as with self-hosting (described next) but without the need for specialized staff or other requirements for 24/7 network management. For more on the previous options and how to choose one, see Spangler (2005).

ISP Hosting

The same company that delivers e-mail and Web access to a business probably can host the company's Web site. An **ISP hosting service** provides an independent, stand-alone Web site

Web hosting service
A dedicated Web site hosting company that offers a wide range of hosting services and functionality to businesses of all sizes.

mirror site
An exact duplicate of an original Web site that is physically located on a Web server on another continent or in another country.

co-location
A Web server owned and maintained by the business is given to a Web hosting service that manages the server's connection to the Internet.

ISP hosting service
A hosting service that provides an independent, stand-alone Web site for small and medium-sized businesses.

CASE 16.2
EC Application

HOW SMALL COMPANIES USE A STOREBUILDER

The following are illustrative examples of how small companies build e-stores using storebuilding services.

▶ Laura Modrell was looking for the best price for the Thomas the Tank Engine character her son adored. Searching the Web, she discovered that people were buying these toy trains and reselling them online at a huge profit. So she built a simple storefront in 1999 using free templates and selling unique educational toys including Thomas the Tank Engine and Friends. The business grew rapidly, and in 2000 she switched to Yahoo! Store. She needed not only the professional look but also the support services. By using Yahoo! Store, Modrell has complete control over her site (*trains4tots.com*) with regards to product descriptions, prices, orders, and so on at a minimal cost and with limited computer knowledge. Revenues grew from $100,000 in 2000 to about $2,000,000 in 2005.

▶ Kristine Wylie started writing ads and Web content in 2002. As a freelance writer, she needed to promote her writing and copyediting services. She selected Yahoo!'s Web Hosting and its e-mail service. Using SiteBuilder, she constructed a site (*mswrite.com*) in 2003, and within a year, she obtained clients in several countries around the world. Income tripled in a year, enabling Wylie to hire helpers and expand the business further.

▶ Ken and Pat Gates retired in 2001. While surfing the Internet, they discovered how easy it was to go into e-commerce. The couple decided to sell online products related to their favorite collegiate sports teams. Using Yahoo!'s Web Hosting service and templates, in 2003 they built their store, College Sports Stuff (*collegesportsstuff.com*), and generated $35,000 in sales. By 2005, they covered 62 teams, including noncollege ones, tripling their sales. Their store ships customers' orders within an hour.

▶ Using Yahoo!'s SiteBuilder software, Springwater Woodcraft, an established Canadian furniture manufacturer, was able to add a new sales channel (*springwaterwoodcraft.com*). The software helped not only with sales but also with accounting. It also led the company into the international market.

▶ TailorMade-adidas Golf (TMaG) is the world's leading manufacturer of metal and wood golf clubs. When they launched the revolutionary r7 Quad, they had to make sure that their customers (golf retailers) would understand the new product and its benefits in order to transform those benefits into customer sales. To do that, they created courses that they offered online to educate the golf retailers. Using Yahoo! Merchant Solutions, it rapidly launched the e-training B2B project (*tmagconnection.com*). Participation in the course was high, and when the store opened online, it attracted 15 percent of all TMaG customers who placed $600,000 in orders in the first three months. The company created several other storefronts (e.g., one for selling its products to employees of TMaG's parent company).

Source: Compiled from Yahoo! (2006).

Questions

1. What benefits did the owners of these businesses derive from using Yahoo!'s services?
2. Identify the common elements in all these cases.
3. Why would a large company, such as TMaG, use templates to create a B2B site?

for small and medium-sized businesses. The ISP will probably provide additional hosting services (e.g., more storage space, simple site statistics, credit card gateway software) at the same or slightly higher cost than the storebuilder services. The List of ISPs (thelist.com) provides lists of ISPs and providers of commercial Internet access.

The major difference between a storebuilder and an ISP hosting service is that with the ISP service, the time-consuming and sometimes expensive task of designing and constructing the Web site becomes the responsibility of the business. The business owners, usually with the help of a contracted Web designer, must use a Web site construction tool to create the Web site (e.g., Ibuilt at ibuilt.net) or a Web page editor (e.g., Dreamweaver at macromedia.com or FrontPage at microsoft.com). This is not necessarily a bad thing. Compared with a storebuilder template, the combination of an ISP hosting service and a Web designer or builder offers the business increased flexibility as to what it can do with the site, so the site can be distinctive and stand out from the competition. Sites hosted by an ISP also will have a branded domain name. However, one disadvantage of using an ISP is that most providers have limited functionality (e.g., an ISP may be unwilling to host a back-end database). Another consideration is the commitment of the ISP to maintaining quality service and keeping its hosting services up-to-date. In many cases, the main business of an ISP is providing Internet access, not hosting Web sites.

Self-Hosting

With **self-hosting**, the business acquires the hardware, software, staff, and dedicated telecommunications services necessary to set up and manage its own Web site. Self-hosting is beneficial when a business has special requirements, such as maximum data security, protection of intellectual property, or most likely, when the business intends to have a large and complex site.

The disadvantages of self-hosting are the cost and the speed of construction. The other Web-hosting options allow the hosting company to amortize the costs of site hosting across hundreds or thousands of customers. A business that hosts its own Web site will have to bear these costs alone, not to mention concerns about security and full-time Web site management. These costs must be weighed against the benefits of better control over site performance and increased flexibility in site design, improvement, and functionalities.

REGISTERING A DOMAIN NAME

Selecting a domain name is an important marketing and branding consideration for any business. The domain name will be the business's online address, and it provides an opportunity to create an identity for the business.

A **domain name** is a name-based address that identifies an Internet-connected server. Usually, it is designated by the portion of the address that comes to the left of .com or .org and including the .com or .org. The domain name should be an easy-to-remember name (e.g., congress.gov) that the *domain name system (DNS)* maps to a corresponding IP address (e.g., 140.147.248.209). Each domain name must include a *top-level domain (TLD)*. This is either a general top-level domain (e.g., .com or .biz for commercial businesses, .org for nonprofit organizations, .name for individuals), or it is a country-code Top-Level Domain (ccTLD) (e.g., .au for Australia, .jp for Japan). Most ccTLDs also have a *second-level domain name* that indicates the type of organization (e.g., redcross.org.au, yahoo.co.jp). At the left side of the domain name is the organization's name (e.g., dell.com), a brand name (e.g., coke.com for Coca-Cola), or a generic name (e.g., plumber.com). For legal issues related to domain names, see Chapter 17.

Domain name assignment is under the authority of the Internet Corporation for Assigned Names and Numbers (ICANN; icann.org). ICANN has delegated responsibility for domain name registration procedures and database administration in the general TLDs to top-level domain administrators such as Afilias (for .info), Public Interest Registry (for .org), and VeriSign Global Registry Services (for .com and .net). Similarly, regional Internet registries administer the ccTLDs (e.g., Nominet for the .uk domain, Japan Registry Service for .jp).

Hundreds of ICANN-accredited registrars carry out the actual registration of domain names. These are located in various countries, but most are in the United States. A list of these registrars is available at icann.org/registrars/accredited-list.html. A **domain name registrar** is a business that assists prospective Web site owners with finding and registering a domain name of their choice.

The first step for a prospective Web site owner is to visit a domain name registrar such as AllDomains (alldomains.com) or directNIC (directnic.com). Typically, the owner will use the domain name lookup service at the registrar's Web site to determine if the desired domain name is available. If it is, the visitor is invited to register it through the registrar for a small fee. The registrar submits the domain name and the owner's details to the appropriate domain name database, and the name then becomes unavailable to anyone else. If the domain name is not available, most registrars automatically offer a list of available alternatives.

If the desired domain name has been taken, it sometimes can be purchased from the current owner. The Better Whois database of registered domain names (betterwhois. com) contains the name, postal address, e-mail address, and telephone number of the domain name owner. A business with an established Web site will be reluctant to give up a domain name, but if the domain name is reserved but not in use, the owner may be willing to sell it for a negotiated price (e.g., check buydomains.com).

Some investors and speculators made a fortune from buying domain names and then selling them. Sloan (2006) provides an overview of how this is done, including money the domain owner collects from advertisers. Some domain name owners have over 5,000 names.

---

self-hosting
When a business acquires the hardware, software, staff, and dedicated telecommunications services necessary to set up and manage its own Web site.

domain name
A name-based address that identifies an Internet-connected server. Usually, it refers to the portion of the address to the left of .com and .org, etc.

domain name registrar
A business that assists prospective Web site owners with finding and registering the domain name of their choice.

Once you register the name with a registrar, the registrar can hold it until the hosting service is in place. Then management of the domain name can transfer from the registrar or previous owner to the host for establishment of the Web site.

Online File W16.2 provides some suggestions for selecting a good domain name.

A useful resource for learning more about domain names and the registration process is About Domains (aboutdomains.com), which offers "guides and resources for successful Internet presence," including a domain name glossary, a registration FAQ file, and "horror stories" from domain name owners who have had bad experiences with registrars. Also, look at 2CreateaWebsite.com (2006).

Section 16.5 ▶ REVIEW QUESTIONS

1. What are the advantages and disadvantages of the different Web hosting options?
2. What is a mirror site? Why would a company use a mirror site?
3. What criteria should an online business consider in choosing a Web hosting service?
4. What is a domain name? Why is selecting a domain name an important step for going online?
5. How are domain names controlled in order to avoid duplication?

16.6 CONTENT CREATION, DELIVERY, AND MANAGEMENT

content
The text, images, sound, and video that make up a Web page.

Content is the text, images, sound, and video that make up a Web page. Creating and managing content is critical to Web site success because content is what a visitor is looking for at a Web site, and content is what the Web site owners use to sell the site, the product or service, and the company that stands behind the site. A successful Internet presence has always been about effective delivery of the information the visitor wants—"Content is king!" (Agarwal and Venkatesh 2002). This section describes the role content plays in successful online business operations and the key aspects of creating, delivering, and managing Web site content.

CATEGORIES AND TYPES OF CONTENT

Providing content to EC sites may be a complex job because of the variety and quantity of sources from which to acquire content and the fact that the content must frequently be updated (see Vassil, et al. 2004). Also, B2B content, especially in online catalogs, may include pictures, diagrams, and even sound.

The major content categories are information about the company, products, services, customers, investor relations, press releases, and so on; detailed product information provided in electronic catalogs, which companies sometimes personalize for major customers; customers' personalized Web pages; and information provided to the B2B community, such as industry news. One of the difficulties in Web content management is that some content needs to be kept up-to-the-minute (e.g., news, stock prices, weather). This is referred to as **dynamic Web content**, as distinguished from *static Web content*, which is updated infrequently.

dynamic Web content
Content that must be kept up-to-date.

For each type of content, companies may use a different approach for content creation and delivery. Exhibit 16.3 shows the content life cycle. As shown in the exhibit, once content is created, it may appear in different formats (e.g., text, video, music). Then, it moves to a content syndicator. A syndicator (to be described later in this section) moves the content to a portal or news site. From there, a hosting service moves the content, possibly via an optimizer (such as akamai.com). The optimizer delivers the content to the final consumer. We will discuss this process and its elements in more detail a bit later.

Content may be in the public domain, or it may be proprietary in nature (e.g., information about the company and its products and services). The sites that offer content may be general-purpose consumer portals, such as Yahoo! or Lycos, or they may be specialized portals designed to appeal to a specific audience, such as espn.com or ski.com.

Up-to-the-minute dynamic content is what attracts new and returning customers ("eyeballs") and makes them stay longer ("stickiness"). Therefore, dynamic content contributes to customer loyalty.

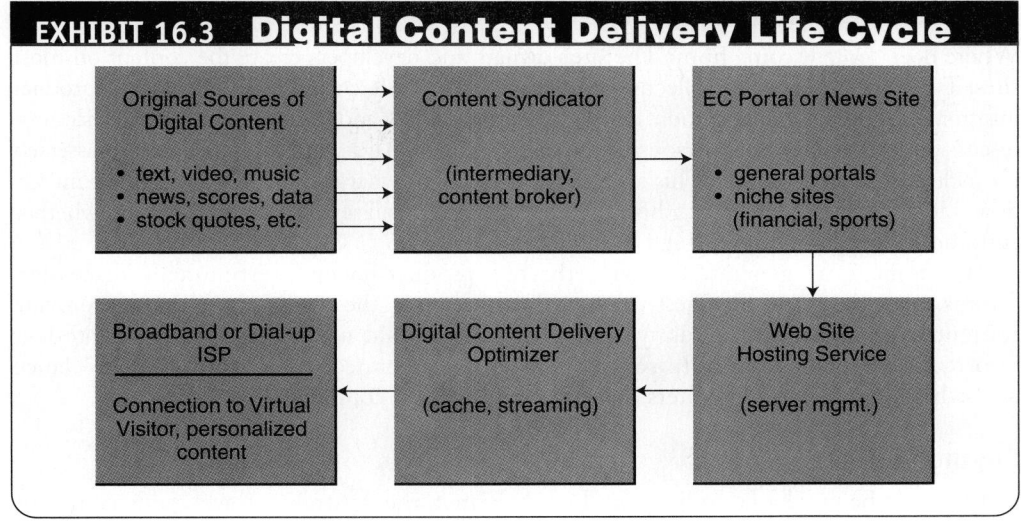

EXHIBIT 16.3   Digital Content Delivery Life Cycle

Although every Web site has content, Web sites differ according to the criticality of the content to the company's business goals. Some sites offer **commodity content**, which is information that is widely available and generally free (McGovern 2005b). Portals, such as MSN.com, and content aggregators, such as Nua Internet Surveys (nua.ie), collect information published elsewhere on the Net and make it available to visitors. The value added is the *aggregation* of the content.

commodity content
Information that is widely available and generally free to access on the Web.

Primary and Secondary Content

Content pages should contain more than information about the product itself (the *primary content*). A Web site also should include *secondary content* that offers marketing opportunities, such as the following:

- **Cross-selling.** Using content for **cross-selling** means offering similar or complementary products and services to increase sales. In the off-line world, the McDonald's question, "Would you like fries with that?" exemplifies cross-selling. In the online world, Amazon.com offers book buyers options such as "customers who bought this book also bought . . ." and "look for similar books by subject." Accessories, add-on products, extended warranties, and gift wrapping are other examples of cross-selling opportunities that companies can offer to buyers on the product pages or in the purchase process. Another example is that if you buy a car online, you may need insurance and financing.

  cross-selling
  Offering similar or complementary products and services to increase sales.

- **Up-selling.** Creating content for **up-selling** means offering an upgraded version of the product in order to boost sales and profit. McDonald's practices up-selling every time a sales clerk asks a combo-meal buyer, "Would you like to super-size that?" Amazon.com offers "great buy" book combinations (buy two complementary books for slightly more than the price of one). (It also practices *down-selling* by offering visitors cheaper, used copies of a book directly under the new book price.) Up-selling activities usually include offering products with a different design, color, fabric, or size.

  up-selling
  Offering an upgraded version of the product in order to boost sales and profit.

- **Promotion.** A coupon, rebate, discount, or special service is secondary content that can increase sales or improve customer service. Amazon.com frequently offers reduced or free shipping charges, and it promotes this offer on each product page.

- **Comment.** Reviews, testimonials, expert advice, or further explanation about the product can be offered after introducing the product. Amazon.com book pages always have editorial and customer reviews of the book, and the "look inside this book" feature sometimes allows Web site visitors to preview book contents online.

Creating effective content also means fulfilling the information needs and experiential expectations of the visitor.

CREATION OR ACQUISITION

Where does content come from? The site's owners and developers create the content on most sites. Typically, it begins by collecting all the content that is currently available (e.g., product information, company information, logos). Then the value of additional content—e-newsletters, discussion forums, customer personalization features, FAQ pages, and external links—is assessed for inclusion in the Web site. This assessment determines what is critical, important, or merely desirable by carefully considering how each bit of content will serve the site's goals and whether customers will want it or expect it.

Customers can generate content—through product reviews, testimonials, discussion forums, and other ways. Business partners downstream in the supply chain also can provide content (e.g., a chemical industry digital exchange would not need to duplicate product information but could simply source it from the chemical manufacturers). Freelance researchers, compilers, and writers also can create original content.

Buying Content

Content can be purchased or licensed. Lonely Planet, the Australian travel guide company, and the popular Mobile Travel Guide both sell travel information to Web sites such as Travelocity. *Content syndicators* such as Content Outfitter (contentoutfitter.com), NewsEdge (dialog.com/newsedge), and Content Finder (electroniccontent.com/conFinder.cfm) serve as intermediaries that link content creators with businesses interested in acquiring content. Finally, some individuals and businesses, such as Mike Valentine's WebSite 101 (website101.com/freecontent.html), provide free content and ask only for proper attribution in return.

Content that is acquired from outside sources should be supplemental content, not primary content. If primary content is purchased that does not add any additional value, visitors will go to the originating site and not return. A major source for secondary content is a syndicator.

Buying from a Syndicator

syndication

The sale of the same good (e.g., digital content) to many customers, who then integrate it with other offerings and resell it or give it away free.

Web syndication

A form of syndication in which a section of a Web site is made available for other sites to use.

According to Werbach (2000), **syndication** involves the sale of the same good to many customers, who then integrate it with other offerings and resell it or give it away for free. Syndication has been extremely popular in the world of entertainment and publishing but was rare elsewhere until the arrival of the Internet. The digitization of products and services, and the resulting ease with which information can flow, makes syndication a popular business model (e.g., see yellowbrix.com). Let's look at a few examples.

Web syndication is a form of syndication in which a section of a Web site is available for other sites to use (see en.wikipedia.org/wiki/Web_syndication). Simply licensing the content so that other people can use it can accomplish this; however, in general, *Web syndication* refers to making Web feeds available from a site in order to provide other people with a summary of the Web site's recently added content (such as the latest news or forum posts). This originated with news and blog sites but is increasingly used to syndicate other types of information. Millions of online publishers including newspapers, commercial Web sites, and blogs now publish their latest news headlines, product offers, or blog postings in standard format news feed.

Virtual stockbrokers, such as E*TRADE, offer considerable information on their portals (e.g., financial news, stock quotes, research, etc.). Yahoo! and other portals offer other types of information. These brokers and portals buy the information from information creators or originators, such as Reuters, who sell *the same information* to many other portals or users. Customers may buy directly from the information creators, but in many cases creators use a supply chain of syndicators and distributors, as shown on Exhibit 16.4, to move news and information to the end consumers. Content creators, such as Inktomi and Reuters, make their money by selling the same information to many syndicators or distributors (e.g., yellowbrix.com). The information distributors, such as E*TRADE, then distribute free information to the public (customers).

Example. An example of syndication and creation of a news feed is that of a joint venture of contact creator Associated Press and game producer Nintendo for Nintendo's Wii and other users.

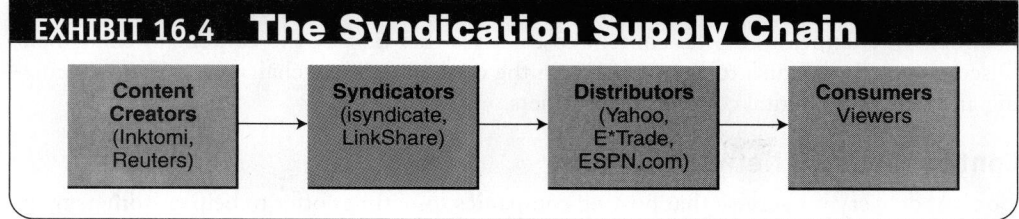

EXHIBIT 16.4   The Syndication Supply Chain

Content Creators (Inktomi, Reuters) → Syndicators (isyndicate, LinkShare) → Distributors (Yahoo, E*Trade, ESPN.com) → Consumers Viewers

There are currently (2007) eight news sections: National News, Regional News, International News, Sports, Arts and Entertainment, Business, Science and Health, and Technology. Users can view the headlines per topic, or spin a virtual globe to see all news by city or region. Different icons show whether the user can view the news story by region and whether it has photos attached.

An updated version of the News Channel is available in Europe, which shows "more extensive" European news for free.

The Wii News Channel was launched officially in the United States on January 27, 2007.

RSS and Podcasting. RSS (short for "rich site summary," "RDF site summary," or Really Simple Syndication) is an XML format for syndicating Web content (the XML fill is added to the RSS feed). A Web site that wants to allow other sites to publish some of its content creates an RSS document and registers the document with an RSS publisher. It is used especially to publish frequently updated digital content, such as blogs, news, or podcasts. A user that can read RSS-distributed content can use the content on a different site. This enables the sharing of Web content. Users can view it as a distributable "What's New" on a site, and it is popular with bloggers. Major sites such as CNET, BBC, CNN, Disney, TechTarget, ZDNet, Red Herring, and Wired use RSS to share content among themselves. As a user, there are a number of key benefits of RSS:

RSS
An XML format for syndicating and sharing Web content.

▶ Timeliness—Automatically receive updates from your favorite Web site when new content becomes available instead of going to the news Web site.

▶ Efficiency—Quickly scan over headlines and summaries and only read the content that interests you.

▶ Coverage—Receive updates from multiple Web sites into one location—your RSS reader or aggregator.

This technology solves problems such as long traffic delays caused by increased site traffic and expediting the gathering and distributing of news. For a tutorial, see mnot.net/rss/tutorial. According to eMarketer (2005), RSS is listed as one of the "top 10 E-Business trends for 2005." Mozilla's Firefox Web browser includes RSS, making it very popular. Several advertisers have begun to use it as a platform for targeted advertisements. For details see en.wikipedia.org/wiki/RSS_(file_format).

Podcasting. A **podcast** is a media file that is distributed by subscription (paid or unpaid) over the Internet using syndication feeds (such as RSS news feeds) for playback on mobile devices and personal computers. Like "radio," it can mean both the content and the method of syndication. It is a collection of audio files in MP3 format, represented by an RSS 2.0 news feed. The host or author of a podcast is often called a *podcaster*, who can offer direct download or streaming of its content. A podcast distinguishes itself from other digital audio formats by its ability to download automatically using software capable of reading feed formats such as RSS.

podcast
A media file distributed over the Internet using syndication feeds. A collection of audio files in MP3 format.

Podcasting is emerging as an e-commerce tool (see Lewin 2005). For example, podcasts create a new channel for Web sites to communicate with customers. Because podcasts are audio-based, it enables companies to deliver audio-specific content, including music, speeches, radio-style presentations, and more (see en.wikipedia.org/wiki/Podcasting).

Representative Content-Related Vendors

A large number of vendors support content creation and management that facilitates the sharing of an organization's digital assets. Online File W16.3 describes representative vendors.

Thus far, we have discussed the role of intermediaries and other third-party B2B providers in channeling digital content to the sites that display the content to consumers. Discussion will now turn to the next step in the content delivery chain, the task of optimizing and delivering digital content to customers.

Content Delivery Networks

Content delivery is a service that hosting companies sometimes offer to help customers manage their content. Using *content delivery networks (CDNs)*, companies can update content, improve the quality of the site, increase consistency, control content, and decrease the time needed to create or maintain a site. Mediasurface (mediasurface.com) and Akamai (akamai.com) provide CDNs. Later in this section, we will discuss the case of Akamai.

In B2B, the information contained in electronic catalogs is of extreme importance. Companies can create and maintain the content in-house, or they can outsource such tasks.

Personalizing Content

personalized content
Web content that matches the needs and expectations of the individual visitor.

Personalized content is Web content that is prepared to match the needs and expectations of the individual visitor. Such content enables visitors to find the information they need faster than at traditional sites, resulting in more visitors coming to the site.

The process begins by tracking the visitor's behavior on the Web site via cookies. This information is provided to server software that generates dynamic Web pages that contain content the visitor can use. Amazon.com's Web site is the king of personalized content, offering content such as recommendations for products based on previous purchases, recently viewed items, and even a personalized "Welcome Back" message for repeat visitors. The downside of personalization is that it is expensive and can slow performance.

Delivering Content By E-Newsletter

e-newsletter
A collection of short, informative articles sent at regular intervals by e-mail to individuals who have an interest in the newsletter's topic.

One of the most effective strategies for delivering content of interest to potential customers is an e-mail newsletter. An **e-newsletter** is a collection of short, informative content sent at regular intervals via e-mail to individuals who have an interest in the newsletter's topic. Examples are *E-Marketer Daily* and *Commerce Minutes*. An e-newsletter can support the business and the product. For details see Online File W16.4.

Writing Effective Content

Delivering effective content involves not only what is said, but how it is said. Online File W16.5 provides some of the rules Web wordsmiths use when creating Web content.

CONTENT MANAGEMENT AND MAINTENANCE

content management
The process of adding, revising, and removing content from a Web site to keep content fresh, accurate, compelling, and credible.

Content management is the process of collecting, publishing, revising, and removing content from a Web site to keep content fresh, accurate, compelling, and credible. Almost all sites begin with a high level of relevant content, but over time material becomes dated, irrelevant, or incorrect. Content management makes sure a site remains relevant and accurate long after the initial push to launch the site is over. Content management applies quality assurance processes and content development to promote the reliability and integrity of the site (Awad 2002). *Web content* management differs from *Web site* management, which focuses on ease of navigation, availability, performance, scalability, and security. Web content management makes sure that a site eliminates clutter and does not waste visitors' time. For an overview of Web content management, see McGovern (2005b); for a list of content management vendors, see CMS Watch (2006).

Content Testing and Updating

An obvious task in content management is testing the content. Web managers need to make extensive and frequent checks of material for accuracy, clarity, typos, poor punctuation, misspelled words, and inconsistencies. Employees knowledgeable about the content should read site material to test it for accuracy; customer focus groups and professional editors should read it to check for clarity; and everyone should read new content to find mistakes. For ongoing testing, new employees may be asked to read the Web site content to learn about the company and to look for improvements with a "fresh eye." Content testing leads to updating. For content testing, see kefra.com, offermatice.com, ringcentral.com, and optimost.com.

Measuring Content Quality

How does a company know if the content on its Web site is meeting its e-commerce goals? How does a company know if it is delivering what its customers need? According to Barnes (2001), companies need metrics to control the quality of their online content. In addition, content must meet privacy requirements, copyright and other legal requirements, language translation needs, and much more. You may use guidelines for knowledge management as well. Metrics are available from W3C (w3c.org/PICS) and periodically in *Baseline* magazine. Measuring the quality of content also requires appropriate Web traffic measurement tools (see Online Chapter 19). For specific suggestions on how to effectively use metrics to measure content quality, see Norguet et al. (2006) and McGovern (2005a). For a comprehensive discussion of data quality in e-business systems, see Kim et al. (2005).

Pitfalls of Content Management

According to Byrne (2002), companies face various content management pitfalls. Online File W16.6 presents the top six content management pitfalls and the best practices for avoiding them.

Content Removal

An important task within content management is removing old, out-of-date pages from the Web server. Even if all references to the page in the Web site have been removed, the page is still visible to search engines, searches on the site itself, and links from other Web pages. Delete or remove expired pages to an off-line location that can serve as an archive.

Content Management Software

Content management software allows nontechnical staff to create, edit, and delete content on the company's Web site. The driving forces behind *content management software (CMS)* include the desire for companies to empower content owners to manage their own content and the inability of the computing services staff to keep up with demands for new or changed content on the Web site.

Content management systems generally include workflow systems for monitoring content creation, review, approval, distribution, posting, and evaluation processes. Most contain tools that allow nontechnical personnel to publish content without specialized training. Other features include content expiration schedules, backup and archive management, security features, and enterprise application integration functions.

Even a small EC site may be content extensive, and in such a case software can help, as in the case of Anglesea Online (Case 16.3).

Companies embarking on a CMS purchase should do the following (Arnold 2003):

▶ Conduct a thorough needs analysis.

▶ Document requirements and discuss them with at least two other companies that have purchased a CMS.

▶ Start small and with CMS that has a trial version or low-entry cost.

▶ Assess the system after 30 days to determine what is right, wrong, needed, and unnecessary.

▶ Repeat the assessment process regularly, increasing functionality as requirements and resources permit.

For information about and a comparison of the most popular CMS packages, see Rapoza (2004).

The Real-World Case about Telecom New Zealand at the end of this chapter gives an example of a comprehensive content management case. For CMS, see emc.com and vignette.com.

CASE 16.3
EC Application

ANGLESEA ONLINE USES CONTENT MANAGEMENT SOFTWARE FOR SUCCESS

Anglesea Online is a really small business of one employee (owner), Nicholas Soames. It is an online community and business directory in rural Australia (*anglesea-online.com.au*). Launched in December 2002, the online directory became popular, providing information about the community, its life, community news, etc. Business advertisers, who can use rich media ads, support the site. The owner and three casual contributors create most of the content. The site grew rapidly, reaching over 2,000 pages by 2005. Anglesea is located on Victoria's western surf coast, and it is blessed with tourists who also use the site. The surge in popularity increased dramatically after the demise of Anglesea's local newspaper. Soames soon realized that he could no longer manage the rapid growth of the Web site without some technological improvement. As a result, he developed a *content management system* (using a Microsoft Access database) to streamline the management of the more dynamic sections of the site such as the business directories, gig guides, events listings, and classifieds.

How Does the Technology Work?

The content management system takes items such as classified listings and publishes them in a standard format within Web page templates. The following steps are carried out to amend sections of the Web site listings and to add, move, or delete listings.

1. Soames accesses the content management system databases, keying the elements into the prescribed template fields.
2. The CMS then identifies each element by which field it is entered into and places it into the required format, depending on the section of the site.

3. The CMS then publishes this content to the site in the appropriate section, which can then be reviewed and either saved or amended.
4. Once the content is correct and approved, it is published on the live site.

The content management system gave Soames more time to write content and pursue advertising revenue from the community.

For such a small company, cost is important. Computer hardware and software amounted to a one-time expenditure of $12,000 and operational expenses of $2,300 per year, whereas annual revenue from the EC business were $29,000 in 2003 (estimated to be $35,000 in 2006).

Sources: Compiled from Anglesea Online, Case Study 1: *Vic.gov.au* (2007) and *anglesea-online.com.au* (accessed January 2007).

Questions

1. List the improvements to content management generated by the software.
2. Discuss the social and cultural aspects of the site.
3. Soames used a self-developed content management system, and it worked well. Why do most companies buy or lease systems from vendors such as Vignette?
4. Soames said that his site is no longer a hobby but a revenue-generating business. Comment on his statement.
5. Online photograph sales and online advertising have become major revenue sources. Relate this to content management.

CATALOG CONTENT AND ITS MANAGEMENT

Much of the content in B2B and B2C sites is catalog based. Chapter 2 discussed the benefits of electronic catalogs. Although there are many positive aspects of electronic catalogs, poorly organized ones may deter buyers. Companies need to make sure that their catalog content is well managed.

For B2B buyers who aggregate suppliers' catalogs on their own Web sites, content management begins with engaging suppliers and then collecting, standardizing, classifying, hosting, and continually updating their catalog data. That is no small task, considering that most large buying organizations have hundreds or even thousands of suppliers, each using different data formats and nomenclature to describe their catalog items. The management of catalog content has some unique aspects and options, as shown in Online File W16.7.

CONTENT MAXIMIZATION AND STREAMING SERVICES

Many companies provide media-rich content, such as video clips, music, or Flash media, in an effort to reach their target audience with an appealing marketing message. For example, automakers want to provide a virtual driving experience as seen from the car's interior; realtors want to provide 360-degree views of their properties; and music sellers want to provide easily downloadable samples of their songs. Public portals and others are using considerable amounts of media-rich information as well. Finally, B2B e-catalogs may include thousands of photos.

These and other content providers are concerned about the download time from the user's perspective. Impatient or fickle Web surfers may click "Stop" before the multimedia has had a chance to fully download. Remember that B2C and B2B customers not only want their news stories, music, video clips, reference information, financial information, and sports scores delivered to them over the Web, but they also want them delivered quickly and effortlessly. Therefore, it is important that content providers and marketers use technical delivery solutions that will not cause "traffic jams" during downloading. Several technical solutions are available from vendors who are referred to as *content maximizers* or *streaming services*. They use what is called "content delivery networks" (see Pallis and Vakali 2006). The leading vendor is Akamai, described in Case 16.4. To manage content that includes multimedia, one can use products such as those offered by Kontiki.com (kontiki.com).

Section 16.6 ▶ REVIEW QUESTIONS

1. What is content? Commodity content? Premium content? Dynamic content? Personalized content?
2. How can a business use content for cross-selling? For up-selling? For promotion?
3. Where does content come from? Identify four sources of Web site content. What is content creation?
4. What is syndication? How does it relate to content?
5. Describe RSS and podcasting.
6. What e-newsletter content does a subscriber value most? (Hint: see Online File W16.4.)
7. What is the purpose of content management?
8. Describe content maximization.

16.7 WEB SITE DESIGN

The goal of any Web site is to deliver quality content to its intended audience and to do so with an elegant design (Nielsen 2005; Wiedman 2007). With the Web site's content in hand, the Web site owner's next task is Web site design, including information architecture, navigation design, colors and graphics, and maximizing site performance. The purpose of this section is to enable you to contribute to the design of a Web site when working with professionals.

Successful Web site design is about meeting customer expectations. Design starts with identifying customer needs, expectations, and problems. Then a site is designed to meet those needs and expectations or to solve the customers' problems. Exhibit 16.5 (p. 753) shows a list of important Web site design criteria, with relevant questions. This and other chapters discuss some of these criteria, such as interactivity, scalability, and security. The focus of this section is on the fundamental design criteria of navigation, consistency, performance, appearance, and quality assurance.

INFORMATION ARCHITECTURE

A Web site's **information architecture** determines how a site organizes, labels, and navigates its Web pages to support browsing and searching (Rosenfeld and Morville 2002). Information architecture begins with designing the site's structure. The most common site structure is hierarchical. Exhibit 16.6 (p. 753) shows a typical hierarchical structure for an online store. Most hierarchical Web sites are built wide and shallow, putting 3 to 10 sections in the second level and limiting most sections to two or three levels. If the hierarchy is narrow (few second-level sections) and deep (many levels), visitors become frustrated by being forced to click through numerous levels to find the information they need.

information architecture
How the site and its Web pages are organized, labeled, and navigated to support browsing and searching throughout the Web site.

CASE 16.4
EC Application
AKAMAI TECHNOLOGIES

An Internet company decided to name itself after a Hawaiian word that means "intelligent, clever, or cool"—*Akamai* (AH-kuh-my). And indeed, the company has created a clever product. Let's explain.

As user interest in high-speed Internet connections has grown, demand for bandwidth-heavy applications and media also has begun to surge. Paul Kagen Associates estimated that revenues from streaming media services will total $1.5 billion by 2002 and $21 billion by 2008 (as reported at Three Squared Inc. 2000). Finally, Accustream iMedia Research reported that the streaming video market grew to over $25 billion in 2006 (reported by Internet Marketing Newswatch 2007).

However, user connection speeds are only part of the streaming media picture. How will the networks handle the influx of bandwidth-chewing material? With a growing number of users and an abundance of rich media, the Internet is becoming extremely congested. Network traffic control is needed. Akamai and its competitors (Digital Island, Ibeam, and Mirror Image) are stepping in to manage Internet traffic.

Akamai products act as Internet traffic cops by using complicated mathematical algorithms to speed Web pages from the closest Akamai-owned server to a customer's location, thereby passing through fewer router hops. This process also helps to eliminate Internet gridlock. Today, caching and content distribution are the only practical ways to reduce network delay.

How does it work? To provide the service, Akamai maintains a global network of over 20,000 servers in 71 countries (in 2007) and leases space on them to giant portals, such as Yahoo! and CNN. These sites use the servers to store graphic-rich information closer to Internet users' computers in order to circumvent Web traffic jams and enable faster page loads; therefore, reducing delivery time to the users by 20 percent to 30 percent. If a company's Web server is in Germany and a user in the United States visits the Web site, the multimedia content of the site has to be transmitted halfway around the globe. Akamai's FreeFlow technology speeds the delivery of images, multimedia, and other Web content by placing that content on servers worldwide. Using the FreeFlow Launcher, Web site designers "Akamaize" their sites by marking content for delivery using the Akamai network. FreeFlow takes this

content and stores it on Akamai Web servers around the world. When a user visits a Web site that has been "Akamaized," the images and multimedia content are downloaded from an Akamai server near the user for faster content delivery. Akamai allows customer data to move to and from big Web sites through its global network for a fee. (In 2004, the fee was $2,500 for setup and $5,500 per month per data center.)

Unfortunately, the service is not 100 percent reliable. The speed for the end user depends on how many people are using the user's LAN at any given point in time and also on the speed of the server downloading any given Web site. A number of competing technologies are trying to provide the same solutions, and only a limited number of large companies that use lots of rich media are willing to pay for the service.

In 2001, Akamai started to diversify, offering a comprehensive suite of content delivery, streaming audio and video, traffic management, and other services, such as dynamic page view, bundled in a package called EdgeAdvantage. Akamai and its competitors were losing money in early 2001, but their revenues were increasing rapidly. By January 2005, the company had 14,000 servers in 65 countries, storing data for its worldwide clientele (Junnarkar 2003; Akamai 2006).

One advantage of using Akamai or a similar service is the added security. For example, on June 15, 2004, a cyber-criminal attacked some of Akamai's major clients including Microsoft, Google, and Apple using a DoS attack (see Chapter 11). Within minutes, Akamai deleted the attacks and solved the problem (Fogarty 2005). According to Pallis and Vakali, Akamai controls 80 percent of the content delivery networks.

Sources: Compiled from Mulqueen (2001), Pallis and Vakali (2006), Akamai (2006), and *akamai.com/html/technology/index.html* (accessed January 2007).

Questions

1. What services does Akamai provide?
2. What is the company's revenue model?
3. What are the services' limitations?

Other, less frequently used structures are circular and linear ones. A circular structure is useful when presenting training materials. A linear structure is useful when telling a story or presenting a tutorial. For example, Online File W16.8 presents an abbreviated version of the linear structure of the E-Business Plan in Online Tutorial T1.

A Web site typically includes a *home page* that welcomes a visitor and introduces the site; *help* pages that assist the visitor to use or navigate through the site; *company* pages that inform the visitor about the online business; *transaction* pages that lead the customer through the purchase process; and *content* pages that deliver information about products and services at all stages of the purchase process, from information search to postpurchase service and evaluation.

EXHIBIT 16.5 Web Site Design Criteria

Navigation	Is it easy for visitors to find their way around the site?
	Does the site comply with the three-click rule?
Consistency	Are design elements, especially look and feel, consistent across all pages?
	Will the Web site and contents appear the same on all visitors' screens?
Response Time	How long does it take for the page to appear?
	Does the site comply with the 12-second rule? With the 4-second rule?
Appearance	Is the site aesthetically pleasing?
	Are the colors pleasant to the eye?
	Do the site's look and feel express the company's desired image?
	Is the site easy to read, easy to navigate, and easy to understand?
Quality assurance	Do the site's calculators, navigation links, visitor registration processes, search tools, etc., work properly?
Availability	Are all dead links fixed promptly?
	Is the site available for full service 24 hours a day, 7 days a week?
Interactivity	Does the site encourage the visitor to play an active role in learning about the business's products or services?
	Are all appropriate contact details available on the Web site so that visitors can submit feedback and ask questions?
Content	How much multimedia? How timely and relevant is the content? Is it easy to read? Informative?
Usability	How easy it is to use to site? How easy it is to learn the site? To make errors and to avoid them?
Security	Is customer information protected?
	Does the customer feel safe in actions such as submitting credit card information?
Scalability	Does the site design provide a seamless path for enhancements or upgrades in the future?
	Will site growth and increased usage protect the initial investment in site construction?

Sources: Adapted from Awad (2002), pp. 145–146; Nielsen (2005); and from Firstgov.gov (2006).

EXHIBIT 16.6 A Simple Hierarchical Web Site Structure

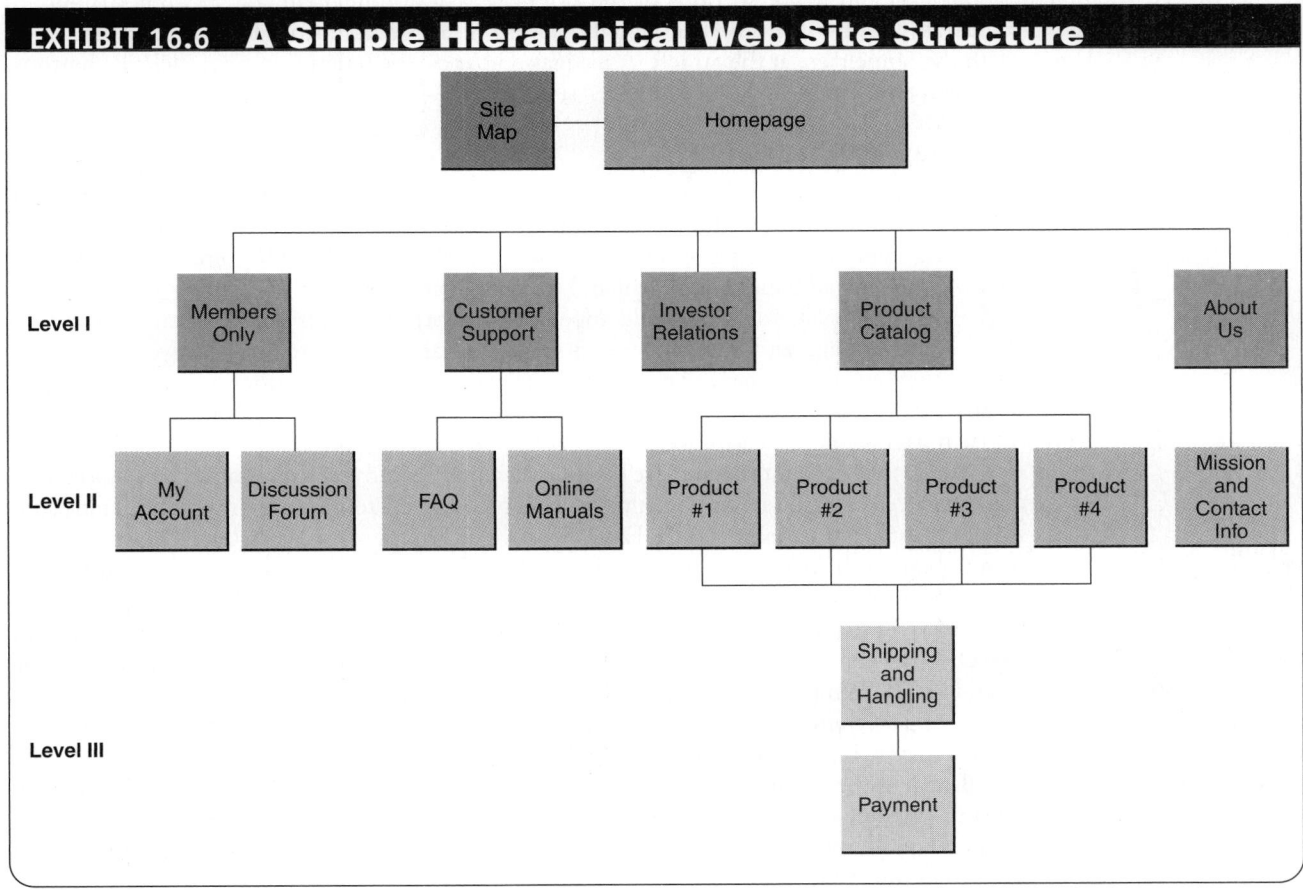

EXHIBIT 16.7   A Typical Navigation Bar

| Home | Products | Support | Community | Guided Tour | About Us |

Online File W16.9 provides some suggestions for organizing and labeling the site and its Web pages to support browsing and searching.

SITE NAVIGATION

The purpose of **site navigation** is to help visitors quickly and easily find the information they need on a Web site. Among the questions considered in site navigation are: How will visitors enter a site? How will visitors use the site? How will they find what is available at the site? How will they get from one page to another and from one section to another? How will visitors find what they are looking for? Site navigation has to help visitors find information quickly because visitors do not want to take the time to figure out how to move around on a site. Site navigation has to be easy; visitors want moving around the site to be predictable, consistent, and intuitive enough that they do not have to think about it (Cheung and Lee 2005; Yahoo.com 2006).

Web designers execute successful site navigation through consistency (described later) and through navigation aids such as a navigation bar, a navigation column, a site map, and search tools.

The simplest navigation aid is a *navigation bar* (see example in Exhibit 16.7). A navigation bar provides the visitor an opportunity to link to likely destinations (e.g., home page, "about us") and major sections of the Web site (e.g., product catalog, customer support). Generally, the items in the bar should decrease in importance from left to right, beginning with the home page at the far left. A navigation bar can be built using text, clickable buttons, or menu tabs.

Site Map and Navigation

A navigation bar almost always appears at the top of the page where it will load first in the browser window and be visible "above the fold." However, if the page contains banner ads, then the navigation bar should be placed prominently below the ads. Why? Frequent Web users develop "banner ad blindness" in which they ignore banner ads and everything above them.

A second navigation bar should appear at the bottom of every page. Then, visitors who have read the page and have not found what they are looking for can easily be guided to where they need to go next. An effective navigation scheme is to offer a simple, attractive, graphical navigation bar at the top of the page and a longer, text navigation bar at the bottom of each page.

If the site's contents need more options than what can fit on a navigation bar, subsections can be placed in each section of the navigation bar (e.g., customer support might include subsections such as customer service FAQ, product information, order status). The subsections can appear on the navigation bar via a pull-down menu or a mouseover (when a visitor passes a mouse cursor over the button, a submenu will pop up).

A Web site that has a lot to offer needs a navigation column on the left side of the browser window. This concept arose with the introduction of browser frames in the mid-1990s. A **frame** is an HTML element that divides the browser window into two or more separate windows. For the most part, frames are no longer used, but the idea of a navigation column as a site's "table of contents" remains as a familiar, comfortable, and easy navigation aid.

Large and medium-size sites should include a *site map* page so that the visitor who is unsure of where to go can see all the available options. The site map should be easily accessible, reflect the information structure of the Web site, and be presented simply with easy-to-understand text links.

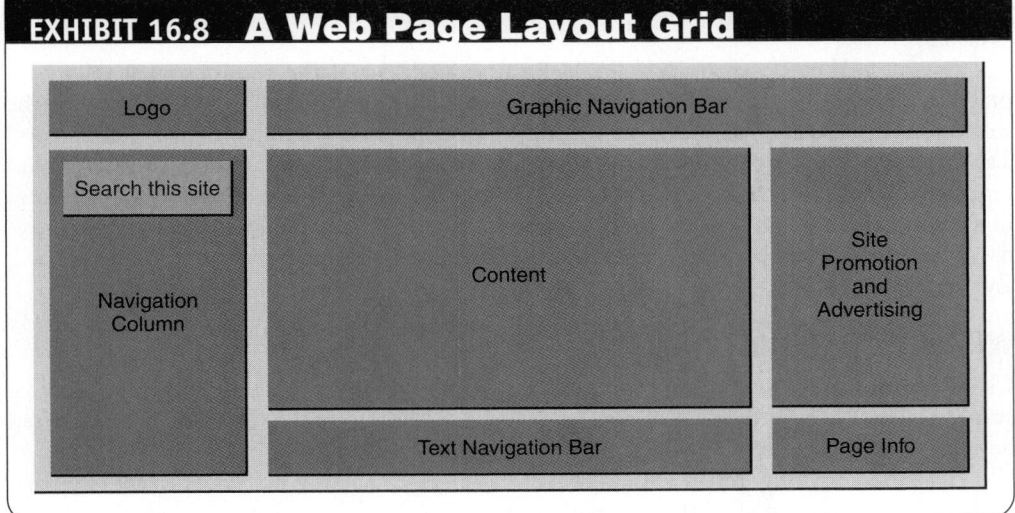

EXHIBIT 16.8   A Web Page Layout Grid

Exhibit 16.8 illustrates many of the information architecture and navigation concepts discussed here.

Online File W16.10 provides other suggestions for designing successful Web site navigation.

PERFORMANCE

Speed ranks at or near the top of every list of essential design considerations, for good reason. Visitors who have to wait more than a few seconds for a Web page to load are likely to hit the "stop" or "back" button and go somewhere else.

A number of factors affect the speed at which the page transfers from the Web server to the client's browser. Factors out of the control of the Web designer and site owner are the visitor's modem speed, the bandwidth available at the customer's ISP, and to some degree, the current bandwidth available at the Web host's location. The critical factor that is under the control of the Web designer is the content and design of the page. A competent Web designer will know what can be done to improve a page's download speed or at least give it the appearance of loading fast.

The most widely recognized cause of long download times is a large graphic or a large number of small graphics on a single page. Create graphics at the lowest possible resolution so that the visitor can clearly see the picture, art, or icon so that the graphic file is only a few kilobytes in size. If a large, high-resolution graphic image is important, thumbnail images can be put on the page and linked to full-size, higher-resolution images available at the visitor's discretion.

Other design traps that affect a page's loading time are page personalization features that require information from a back-end database for dynamic page creation, Java applets, sound files, animated banner ads, and complex table structures, especially the page-in-a-table that requires the entire table or page to load before any of it displays. To decrease page download time, avoid these features or use them sparingly.

COLORS AND GRAPHICS

The Web is a colorful and graphic world, and colors, pictures, artwork, and video can be used effectively if used correctly.

The key to effective use of color and graphics is to design the site to match the expectations of the target audience. Financial services sites tend to use formal colors (e.g., green, blue) with simple charts to illustrate the text but not many pictures. Sites directed at a female audience tend to feature lighter colors, usually pastels, with many pictures and an open design featuring lots of white space. Game sites are one type of site that can get away with in-your-face colors, Flash effects, and highly animated graphics.

Online File W16.11 provides other rules that guide the use of color and graphics on Web sites.

Are these Web design rules followed in practice? To test the application of theory on practice, usability gurus Jakob Nielsen and Marie Tahir tested home pages from 50 of the world's most popular Web sites, such as eBay, Microsoft, and Victoria's Secret (Nielsen and Tahir 2002). Their analysis of compliance with design and navigation standards was reported as the good, the bad, and the ugly feature. A similar study that tested 62 Web sites in the United Kingdom on 12 design tests found that most companies are committing fundamental errors when presenting themselves online (BBC Training and Development 2002; Zviran 2006).

WEB SITE USABILITY

usability (of Web site)
The quality of the user's experience when interacting with the Web site.

Usability measures the quality of a user's experience when interacting with a product or system—whether a Web site, software application, mobile technology, or any user-operated device.

In general, usability refers to how well users can learn and use a product to achieve their goals as well as how satisfied they are with that process. Usability means that people who use the Web site can do so quickly and easily to accomplish their tasks and may also consider such factors as cost-effectiveness and usefulness.

According to Nielsen (2005) and usability.gov, the following factors measure usability:

- **Ease of learning**—How fast can a user who has never seen the user interface before learn it sufficiently well to accomplish basic tasks? How easy and intuitive is it to learn to use the Web site?
- **Efficiency of use**—Once an experienced user has learned to use the system, how fast can he or she accomplish tasks?
- **Memorability**—If a user has used the system before, can he or she remember enough to use it effectively the next time, or does the user have to start over again learning everything?
- **Error frequency and severity**—How often do users make errors while using the system, how serious are these errors, and how can users recover from these errors?
- **Subjective satisfaction**—How much does the user *like* using the system? How pleasant is it to use the Web site design?

On the Web, usability is a necessary condition for survival. If a Web site is difficult to use, people *leave*. This results in negative financial performance.

Proper design ensures usability. Online File W16.12 discusses the 10 design mistakes made most often. For further details see usability.gov and useit.com/alertbox.

Section 16.7 ▶ REVIEW QUESTIONS

1. Describe eight criteria used to judge Web site design.
2. Describe four site navigation aids.
3. Why is performance a key design criterion? What causes slow performance? What can decrease download time?

4. Describe some issues for proper use of color and graphics on a Web site. (Hint: See Online File W16.11.)
5. Define *Web site usability*. List the major criteria used to measure usability.

16.8 PROVIDING E-COMMERCE SUPPORT SERVICES

Creating content and designing the Web site are the creative aspects of building a Web site. Determining how the Web site actually will be built and by whom are the business parts of Web site construction. Web site construction is usually about three options—internal development, outsourcing, and partnering—spread over two time periods—start-up construction and ongoing maintenance (see Online Chapter 19).

WHO BUILDS THE WEB SITE?

Early in the Web site development process, the online business owner has to decide whether to build the Web site with internal staff, an outside contractor, or a combination of these two options. This involves managerial considerations such as control, speed, and desired organizational competencies, as generally described in information technology textbooks (e.g., Turban et al. 2008b; especially McNurlin and Sprague 2005). For managerial considerations see Online File W16.13 and Online Appendix B.

PAYMENTS: ACCEPTING CREDIT CARDS

Another important service is payments (see Chapter 12). You can't do business if you can't get paid. This truism means that every online business has to face decisions about electronic payment systems. The dominant form of B2C payment is accepting credit cards over the Internet.

Chapter 12 described the process for accepting credit card payments. As noted there, processing credit card payments on the Internet differs only slightly from the process in traditional, face-to-face transactions. What are these differences from a merchant's perspective? What are the basic requirements for an online business to be able to accept credit cards for payment?

First, in the online process, the credit card reader in the store is replaced with credit card processing software (a credit card gateway) that is capable of accepting input from a Web page and submitting it into the credit card system (the merchant's bank, the customer's bank, and the credit card interchange, such as Visa or MasterCard).

Second, with online transactions, a signature and verification of the signature by the merchant is not required, resulting in what is known as a **card-not-present (CNP) transaction**. This situation removes a considerable amount of certainty and security from the process. In response to this increased risk, banks are more selective about who gets an online merchant account, and they require that the entire process be as secure as possible (e.g., checking that the shipping address provided by the customer matches the billing address on file at the customer's bank). In addition, banks charge higher transaction fees for CNP transactions to offset the increased risks.

card-not-present (CNP) transaction
A credit card transaction in which the merchant does not verify the customer's signature.

An online business that wants to accept credit cards for payment generally has to do the following:

- ▶ **Open a merchant account.** It is likely that the business's current bank will be happy to extend banking privileges for the business to accept credit cards online. However, some small, regional banks may not offer this service; other banks may establish thresholds that are too high for the business to qualify (i.e., banks are more selective about CNP merchant accounts). Opening a merchant account means acquiring bank approval, making an application, signing a contract with one or more credit card companies, and paying the bank and card companies a set-up fee. Ongoing costs for a merchant account include a percentage-based transaction fee and additional charges for other services, such as when a customer credit is issued.

- ▶ **Purchase credit card processing software.** Credit card gateway companies such as authorize.net, cybersource.com, and charge.com provide credit card processing software and services that accept credit card numbers and manage their transfer into and back from the credit card system. Factors to consider in deciding which gateway company to use include companies that the site developer has worked with before and what software the organization hosting the Web site will accept. A business typically pays the credit card gateway a set-up fee and a per-transaction fee.

- ▶ **Integrate the credit card processing software into the transaction system.** To work effectively, the software must be able to manage the flow of data between the transaction and customer databases and the credit card systems. The site developer writes scripts that enable the different components in the credit card transaction to share data they require.

For best practices regarding merchants' protection against fraud, see Chapter 17 and Merchantrates.com (2005).

WEB SITE PROMOTION

Every successful online business needs a highly visible Web site (see Kavassalis et al. 2004). Chapter 4 discussed external Web site promotion through advertising (e.g., banner ads, pop-up ads) and marketing strategies (e.g., banner swapping, chat room sponsorship). This section focuses on internal Web site promotion (selling the Web site on the site) and search engine optimization (getting the Web site to the top of the search engine listings).

Internal Web Site Promotion

Internal Web site promotion begins by including content that establishes the site as a useful site for customers so that they remember the site and return and make a purchase. To do this, the Web site should become not only a place to buy something, but also an indispensable resource with compelling content, useful links to other Web sites, and features that will make customers want to return.

Promoting the Web site internally often includes a page of testimonials from satisfied customers. If the site or the business has received any awards, draw the visitor's attention to them. If the business owner's background or credentials relate to the business, then list any degrees, professional affiliations, and awards that relate to the online business.

Site promotion continues with a marketing plan that includes the URL on every product, business card, letterhead, package, and e-mail message that leaves the business. A **signature file** is a simple text message that an e-mail program adds automatically to outgoing messages. A typical signature file includes the person's name, title, contact details, and name and URL of the business. A promotional signature file also includes something that encourages the reader to visit the Web site. For example, a diet center includes this teaser on all outgoing messages: "Are you the right weight for your shape? The answer might surprise you. Take our body shape quiz and find out for yourself."

signature file
A simple text message an e-mail program automatically adds to outgoing messages.

Search Engine Optimization

How is a Web site found in the vast world of cyberspace? How does a new online business get noticed ahead of its more well-established competitors? In addition to promotional and advertising strategies discussed in this and other chapters, perhaps the most important and cost-effective way to attract new customers is search engine optimization. **Search engine optimization (SEO)** is the application of strategies intended to position a Web site at the top of Web search engines such as Google, AllTheWeb, and Teoma. Search engines are the primary way many Web users find relevant Web sites; an online business cannot ignore SEO strategies.

The strategies to maximize a Web site's ranking in search engines should be part of content creation, Web site design, and site construction. Optimizing search engine rankings through keyword placement and link building is much easier, less time consuming, and less expensive if it is integrated into the Web site development process. Online File W16.14 provides a comprehensive guide to SEO.

search engine optimization (SEO)
The application of strategies intended to position a Web site at the top of Web search engines.

Several SEO services (e.g., webposition.com, searchsummit.com) are available that will supervise the entire SEO process for a Web site. However, SEO requires constant monitoring to be effective, and decisions such as which companies are acceptable linking partners are management decisions that should not be left to neutral parties. SEO services can assist, but successful SEO requires supervision and involvement by the site owner.

CUSTOMER RELATIONSHIP MANAGEMENT

As defined in Chapter 13, *customer relationship management (CRM)* is a customer service approach that focuses on building long-term and sustainable customer relationships that add value for the customer and the company. This section focuses on what every start-up online business needs to know in order to initiate an effective CRM program. After getting these fundamentals right, successful online firms will be ready to move into more advanced CRM techniques, such as contact management, data mining, and personalization.

EXHIBIT 16.9 Building CRM Through Content

Content Strategy	Description	CRM Benefits
Provide membership	Offer registration at the site to gain access to premium content and services	Community building, targeted marketing, paid subscription opportunity
Personalize the user experience	Present content that the site visitor has indicated an interest in through previous browsing or member profiles	Community building, targeted commerce offers, customer and site loyalty
Attract visitors	Provide free games, shows, and blogs	Customer loyalty, revisits, tell friends
Support users	Provide responsive and convenient customer service	Community building, customer and site loyalty, repeat purchases
Communicate via the community	Allow visitors to communicate with each other and the publisher through the site	Community building, customer and site loyalty
Reward visitors	Provide visitors with rewards for visiting and using the Web site	Customer and site loyalty, promotional product up-sell and cross-sell opportunities
Consumer education	Educate consumer on important topics (e.g., medical, diets)	Community building
Market effectively	Promote the site's content and products without alienating current and potential customers	Customer and site loyalty, promotional product up-sell and cross-sell opportunity
Set up smart affiliate relationships	Establish affiliate relationships with both private (consumer) and commercial Web publishers	Customer and site loyalty, new revenue stream

Sources: Tomsen (2000); author's experience; and from Ariguzo et al. (2006).

Using Content to Build Customer Relationships

The first step to building customer relationships is to give customers good reasons to visit and return to the Web site. In other words, the site should be rich in information and have more content than a visitor can absorb in a single visit. The site should include not just product information but also value-added content from which visitors can get valuable information and services for free. Exhibit 16.9 lists some ways in which online businesses can build customer relationships through content.

Online File W16.15 and Chapter 13 cover other steps and activities.

Section 16.8 ▶ REVIEW QUESTIONS

1. Define the three options for Web site construction.
2. What factors favor internal development of a Web site? What factors favor external development?
3. How is site construction best managed?
4. Describe the process required for an online business to accept credit cards over the Internet.
5. List four types of Web site content that can promote the Web site internally.
6. What is search engine optimization? Why is it important?
7. List ways Web sites can use content to manage customer relationships.
8. Describe three electronic discussion groups, with an emphasis on their similarities and differences.

16.9 OPENING A WEB STOREFRONT

The most common EC project on the Internet is the *storefront*. Millions of storefronts exist on the Internet, mostly those of small businesses. However, large corporations, as well as many individuals, including students and even children, have storefronts as well. As we have seen throughout the book, most online entrepreneurs, such as the initiators of campusfood.com, amazon.com, cattoys.com, and thaigem.com, started with a storefront. Storefronts appear in all different shapes, and their construction and operating expenses vary greatly. Storefronts primarily sell products or services (see en.wikipedia.org/wiki/Electronic_commerce), yet their functionalities differ considerably (for a list of functionalities, see Online Chapter 19).

OPTIONS FOR ACQUIRING STOREFRONTS

Storefronts can be acquired in several ways:

- **Build them from scratch.** Pioneering storefronts, such as hothothot.com, wine.com, and amazon.com, built their stores from scratch. Specifically, they designed them and then hired programmers to program all the necessary software. The major advantage of this approach is that the site owner can customize the site to his or her liking. The disadvantages are that the process is slow, expensive, and error prone and requires constant maintenance. Consequently, only large corporations build their storefronts from scratch today. See Online Chapter 19 for more on how to build a storefront from scratch. Most companies today use other alternatives (see Bracken 2006).

- **Build them from components.** This option is faster and less expensive than the first one. The site owner purchases off-the-shelf components (or sometimes obtains them for free), such as a shopping cart, an e-catalog, and a payment gate, and then assembles them. The site owner can replace the components if they become obsolete; therefore, the site owner can save on maintenance. The downside is that the resulting site may not fit the online business owner's needs very well. See Online Chapter 19 for information on how to build a site from components. This approach allows for adapting the application design to the specific needs of the business and for differentiating the storefront from those of the competitors. An example of this type of solution is Microsoft's Site Server Commerce Edition, which has a built-in wizard that helps users model their own online business processes graphically. This approach, however, is usually more costly than building from templates and may take longer. In addition, it usually requires some in-house technical expertise for installation of the required hardware and software as well as for continued operation and maintenance. Monsterecommerce.com/shopping_cart_features_new.asp provides many such components.

- **Build with templates (storebuilders).** As described earlier in the chapter, using storebuilders is one of the most viable options for starting an online business. Several vendors provide storebuilding templates. Some provide them free, free for 30 days, or for a nominal monthly fee that includes hosting the site on their servers. Using this approach is especially attractive to small businesses because the cost is relatively low (usually $10 to $99 per month), the business can construct the store in one or a few days, and it does not require extensive programming skills. The site owner basically fills out forms and attaches pictures. Another major benefit of this approach is that hosting is usually provided, as well as support services, such as payment collection, shipments, and security. Furthermore, the vendor will take care of all software maintenance. Many vendors also offer store and inventory management as well as other features, as described later in this section. Finally, and perhaps most important, if the site owner uses a vendor such as Yahoo!, the site will be included in Yahoo!'s e-marketplace, which provides a great deal of exposure. The downside of this approach is that it limits the site owner to the available templates and tools. However, some vendors provide a professional version that allows customization. Representative vendors that provide templates are:
  - Yahoo! Small Business (see next section) and Yahoo Merchant
  - eBay (Prostores) (see Elms 2006)
  - Bigstep (bigstep.com)
  - GoEmerchant.com
  - StoreFront (storefront.net)
  - 1and1.com and shopping.com

- ShoppingCartsPlus.com (shoppingcartsplus.com)
- MonsterCommerce (monstercommerce.com)

For a comparison and evaluation of these vendors and others, see ecommerce-software-review.toptenreviews.com.

- **Use someone else's storefront.** Another option is to place products on someone else's storefront. The most notable examples of this are amazon.com and ebay.com. People can even sell used items on such sites. The easiest things to sell are items that are already in Amazon.com's catalog (e.g., items that a person purchased at Amazon.com in the past that are no longer needed). Amazon.com even tells sellers how much they can expect to receive for the items. To sell an item that is not in Amazon.com's catalog, a seller can add it to the catalog by adding a product detail page using the Pro Merchant feature (available only to those with a seller account). Amazon.com also provides payment and shipping services.

Selecting a Development Option

Before choosing the appropriate development option, you need to consider a number of issues in order to generate a list of requirements and capabilities (Online Chapter 19). The following is a list of representative questions that need to be addressed when defining requirements:

- **Customers.** Who are the target customers? What are their needs? What kind of marketing tactics should a business use to promote the store and attract customers? How can a business enhance customer loyalty?
- **Merchandising.** What kinds of products or services will the business sell online? Are soft (digitized) goods or hard goods sold? Are soft goods downloadable?
- **Sales service.** Can customers order online? How? Can they pay online? Can they check the status of their order online? How are customer inquiries handled? Are warranties, service agreements, and guarantees available for the products? What are the refund procedures?
- **Promotion.** How are the products and services promoted? How will the site attract customers? Are coupons, manufacturer's rebates, or quantity discounts offered? Is cross-selling possible?
- **Transaction processing.** Is transaction processing in real time? How are taxes, shipping and handling fees, and payments processed? Are all items taxable? What kinds of shipping methods will the site offer? What kinds of payment methods, such as checks, credit cards, or cybercash, will the site accept? How will the site handle order fulfillment?
- **Marketing data and analysis.** What information, such as sales, customer data, and advertising trends, will the site collect? How would the site use such information for future marketing?
- **Branding.** What image should the storefront reinforce? How is the storefront different from those of the competition?

The initial list of requirements should be as comprehensive as possible. It is preferable to validate the identified requirements through focus-group discussions or surveys with potential customers. The business can then prioritize the requirements based on the customers' preferences. The final list of prioritized requirements serves as the basis for selecting and customizing the appropriate package or designing a storefront from scratch.

In the remainder of this section, we will introduce the Yahoo! Store package.

YAHOO! SMALL BUSINESS

Yahoo! offers one of the most popular storefront packages at smallbusiness.yahoo.com. It offers three levels of merchant solutions: *starter, standard,* and *professional.* The capabilities and fees of each plan are available on Yahoo!'s Web site. Yahoo! offers an 11-step guide that explains how Yahoo! Merchant Solutions works and how you can use it to build, manage, and market an online business. Read on to gain valuable tips and guidance that will help you succeed in developing your own online storefront.

Getting Started

Read the E-Commerce Basics Guide. Online File W16.16 provides a summary of the 11-step guide (as of January 2007), and you can download a copy at smallbusiness.yahoo.com/merchant/gstart.php.

Take a Tour

To see all the features that come with Yahoo! Merchant Solutions, take a tour (click "Tour"). Once welcomed, you will see a slideshow that lists all its capabilities. Notable features include the following: Web hosting and domain name registration; e-mail; EC tools (shopping cart, payment processing, inventory management); business tools and services (site design, marketing, site management); order processing tools; site development tools (site editor, templates, uploading content, for example, with Yahoo! SiteBuilder); finding and keeping customers (per Chapter 4; from e-mail campaigns to cross-selling suggestions); payment acceptance tools; tax calculators; order notification and confirmations; and performance-tracking tools (statistics, drill-downs, measuring the effectiveness of marketing campaigns).

Using the Templates

You can build your store in several ways. Your primary tool is an easy-to-use online Store Editor. You can create a front page, and you can set up various store sections and add to them. You can upload content developed in Microsoft FrontPage, Macromedia Dreamweaver, or Yahoo! SiteBuilder (discussed in Section 16.5). See Online File W16.17 for how to create "sections" and "items" with the editor.

Section 16.9 ▶ REVIEW QUESTIONS

1. List the various options for acquiring a storefront.
2. What are the advantages of building with templates? What are the disadvantages?
3. List the typical features of a storefront.
4. What are some of the selection criteria for a software option?

MANAGERIAL ISSUES

Some managerial issues related to this chapter are as follows.

1. **What does it take to create a successful online business?** The ability of a business to survive, and thrive, in the marketplace depends on the strength of the business concept, the capabilities of the entrepreneur, and successful execution of the business plan. Creativity, entrepreneurial attitudes, and management skills represent a human capital investment that every potentially successful business needs. For further discussion, see Chapter 14 and Umesh et al. (2005).

2. **Is creating a Web site a technical task or a management task?** It is both. Although somewhat expensive, the technical skills required to build a Web site are readily available in the marketplace. The prerequisite managerial skills are somewhat more difficult to find. Online business owners need to possess traditional business skills as well as understand the technical aspects of building a Web site in order to be able to hire and work with information architects, Web designers, and Web site hosting services.

3. **How do we attract visitors to the Web site?** Search engine optimization is important, but the key to attracting visitors, getting them to return, and encouraging them to tell others about the site is to offer credible content that fulfills a value exchange proposition. That is, both the site owner and the customer must receive value from the visit. What the site says (content) is important, but so is *how* it says it. Web design delivers content in a compelling manner that enhances the readability of the content and the quality of the customer experience.

4. **How do we turn visitors into buyers?** Getting people to come to the Web site is only half the battle. Visitors become buyers when a Web site offers products and services that customers need, with promotions and a price that entice visitors to buy there rather than go somewhere else, in an environment that promotes trust.

5. Are best practices useful? For an inexperienced EC person or company, the best practices of others can be extremely useful (see Maguire 2005). The experiences of vendors, companies, academicians, and others are most useful. E-Business Advisor and E-Commerce Advisor (at **advisorzones.com**) provide many resources, and you can get advice for a fee. Free advice is available from many sources (e.g., **ecommercepartners.net**).

6. How much of my new business should we give to funders? It all depends. The important thing is to maintain control by keeping at least 51 percent of the shares (at least up to the IPO).

7. How do we save on Web hosting expenses? If you use templates and a storebuilder, you will pay very little for hosting. If you need a more complicated site, you can use a tendering system with an RFQ (see the example in Online File W16.18).

RESEARCH TOPICS

Here are some suggested topics related to this chapter. For details, references, and additional topics, refer to the Online Appendix A "Current EC Research."

1. **Common Web Site Design Features**
   - Important design features
   - How to optimize and manage content
   - Benchmarking design features
   - Opportunities for enhancing a commercial Web site
   - Factors that require a specific configuration for a Web site

2. **Factors That Influence Web Site Design**
   - Curiosity as a design factor
   - Cultural differences in perceptions of Web site design characteristics
   - Models for small-scale Web sites
   - Effects of country, industry, and market on Web site design

3. **Web Site Implementation**
   - Selection of development options
   - Web site implementation by small businesses
   - The determinants of success of Web site development and how they vary in different countries
   - The effect of consumer shopping orientation on the creation of a retail Web site
   - Development of Web sites for impaired users
   - Empirical studies on the key elements of B2C and B2B Web sites

4. **Factors for Web Site Evaluation**
   - Criteria for Web site evaluation, including business function, corporate credibility, content reliability, Web site attractiveness, systematic structure, and navigation
   - Usability measurements and evaluation
   - Factors associated with Web site success for EC (e.g., information and service quality, system use, playfulness, and system design quality)
   - Factors such as download delay, navigation, content, interactivity, and responsiveness on the success of Web sites
   - Dimensions of Web quality, including content, content quality, appearance, and technical adequacy
   - Ability to and methods of attracting and informing visitors about Web sites
   - Special-interest content versus general-interest content in generating Web site traffic

5. **Web Site Evaluation Methods and Tools**
   - Industry-specific Web site evaluation methods and tools
   - The use of benchmarking in the evaluation of Web sites
   - Tools that assess Web-based EC applications
   - Tools that measure a site's ease of use and effectiveness

6. **Adoption and Value of Web Sites**
   - Consumer preferences on commercial Web sites
   - Impact of Web site value and advertising on the firm's performance in the context of EC
   - Effect of cultural differences in adopting Web sites

- Motivations and reasons why users choose to use particular Web sites
- Effect of Web sites on the flow of human interaction
- How Web sites have evolved and changed over time

7. **Factors That Influence Users' Attitudes Toward Web Sites**
   - Users expectations and the ranking of quality factors

- Domain name and site hosting preferences
- Effects of adaptive Web sites
- Effects of personalization on the use of Web sites
- Effects of culture and context on perception and interaction with multilingual EC Web sites

SUMMARY

In this chapter, you learned about the following EC issues as they relate to the learning objectives.

1. **Fundamental requirements for initiating an online business.** A good idea becomes a successful online business when owners with the required skills, attitudes, and understanding of Internet culture execute a powerful business plan.

2. **Funding options for a start-up online business.** Incubators usually provide support services, whereas angel investors and venture capitalists provide funds for a prospective online business. The business and business owners usually benefit greatly from these arrangements, but the funding sources are scarce and competition for funds is stiff.

3. **Adding e-initiatives.** Adding e-initiatives (or projects) is common. A large project requires a business case. Additions are made gradually that eventually make the business a click-and-mortar one. Common projects are e-procurement, eCRM, and a storefront.

4. **Transformation to e-business.** In an e-business, all possible processes are conducted online. Achieving such a state in a large organization is a complex process involving change management.

5. **Web site hosting options for an online business.** Storebuilder services, ISPs, dedicated Web site hosting services, and self-hosting give online business owners a range of options in deciding how and where to host the Web site. A well-chosen domain name is an "address for success," a way of making the site easy to find and remember. Choosing a domain name is an important step in setting up the hosting site.

6. **Web site construction options for an online business.** Internal development, external contracting, and partnerships give business owners a range of options in deciding who builds the Web site.

7. **Provide content that attracts and keeps Web site visitors.** Content is king. Content can be created, purchased, or acquired for free and used for site promotion, sales, and building customer relationships. Successful Web sites offer content that the site's target audience wants and expects.

8. **Design a visitor-friendly site.** Although text is content rich and inexpensive, a text-only site is a barren and unmemorable site. Select graphics and colors with the site's business goals and visitors' needs in mind. Web site owners and designers should never overestimate the attention span of the site visitor, so it is best to include small graphics that are few in number so that the end result is an attractive page but one that also will load fast. The key to visitor-friendly navigation is to project a visitor's mental map on the Web site: where they are, where they were, where they should go next, and how to get to where they want to be.

9. **High placement in search engines is key.** Keyword occurrence and placement on a merchants' site and promoting link popularity are the fundamental strategies for search engine optimization. High placement on search engine keyword searches will guarantee visitors, the essential first step toward online business success.

KEY TERMS

QUESTIONS FOR DISCUSSION

1. Compare and contrast setting up a traditional, brick-and-mortar business and an online business. Consider factors such as entrepreneurial skills, facilities and equipment, and business processes.

2. Compare and contrast the creation of a new online business and the establishment of an online initiative in an existing company. Consider factors such as resource acquisition, start-up processes, and competitor analysis.

3. How is an e-business plan different from a traditional business plan?

4. Discuss the logic of adding an e-storefront versus making all sales off-line.

5. Define *organizational transformation* and discuss some of the difficulties involved.

6. Discuss the logic of outsourcing the combined Web hosting and site construction. What are some of the disadvantages?

7. How would you decide which Web site hosting option an online business should use? List and briefly explain factors to consider in your decision.

8. What are the trade-offs in giving the customer everything possible (e.g., personalized content, high-resolution graphics, a feature-full site) and the fundamental rules of Web design?

9. Who should be on a Web site development team for a small business? For a large business?

10. Should a small business build its own Web site? Why or why not? Should a large business build its own Web site? Why or why not?

11. Should a small business maintain its own Web site? Why or why not? Should a large business maintain its own Web site? Why or why not?

12. Several times in this chapter we advise online business owners to gather competitive intelligence from competitors (e.g., in SEO, what sites link to competitor sites). Is this ethical? Why or why not?

13. Why is a store such as **cattoys.com** not economically feasible off-line?

14. What are the advantages and disadvantages of using templates to build a storefront?

15. Yahoo! provides many services, including Web site hosting, storebuilding tools, and an online mall. List the benefits of these services. What are the drawbacks, if any?

16. Discuss the relationship of RSS to podcasting.

17. How is usability related to Web site design?

INTERNET EXERCISES

1. Go to the vFinance Capital (**vfinance.com**) and the National Venture Capital Association (**nvca.com**) Web sites and identify any trends or opportunities in acquiring start-up funding.

2. Go to a Yahoo! category, such as tourist agencies or insurance companies, and pick 10 sites. Classify them as informational, interactive, or transactional Web sites. Make a list of any informational, interactive, or transactional features.

3. Many individuals try to make a living simply by buying and selling goods on eBay. Visit **ebay.com** and make a list of the ways in which these entrepreneurs use cross-selling and up-selling in their sales activities.

4. Visit the Webmaster Forums (**webmaster-forums.net**). Register (for free) and visit the Web site critique area. Compare the design rules offered in this chapter with some of the Web sites offered for critique at the site. Offer at least one design suggestion to a Webmaster who is soliciting feedback.

5. Explore the Web to find five dedicated Web site hosting services. Compare them using the criteria listed in this chapter. Write a report based on your findings.

6. Select five firms from an industry, such as banking, stock trading, or ISPs. Go to **google.com** and enter *link:URL* for each of the five firms where URL is the firm's home page. Which firms have higher numbers of incoming links? Examine their Web sites and try to determine why this is so.

7. Go to **integic.com** and examine its services and methodology. In what way can it help in the transformation of a brick-and-mortar bank, hospital, or toy manufacturer?

8. Enter **monstercommerce.com**. View the shopping cart demo. What features impress you the most and why? What related services does it provide? Compare it to **storefront.net** and **nexternal.com**.

9. Compare the shopping malls of Yahoo!, **amazon.com**, and **internetmall.com**.

10. Go to **godaddy.com**. Examine their Traffic Blazer. How can it help you with an online business.

11. Enter **1and1.com**. Examine their hosting, development, and other tools. Take the Test Drive. Compare it with services offered by **jstreettech.com**. Write a report.

12. Enter **bontragerconnection.com**. View its tutorials and comment on its usefulness to EC site builders.

13. Enter **1and1.com** and find the services it provides to an online start-up company. List all the services.

14. Enter **websidestory.com**. How does it help with site optimization? What other services does it provide?

15. Go to **checkout.google.com** and find the services offered to buyers. Why is shopping here faster than in Amazon.com or Yahoo!?

16. Enter **documentum.com** and find its enterprise content management products. Write a report.

TEAM ASSIGNMENTS AND ROLE PLAYING

1. Pretend your team has been asked to make a 20-minute presentation to a local business group about how to launch an online business. Prepare the presentation by highlighting the most important considerations you learned in this chapter.

2. Write an RFQ for a fictitious company following the example provided in Online File W16.18. Submit the RFQ to several local ISPs. (Be honest and tell them this is a student assignment; most ISPs will be happy to assist if you volunteer to send them a copy of your report.) Write a report that compares the responses, selects a winning ISP, and justifies your decision.

3. The students should form teams. Assume that a commercial or nonprofit organization in your community has asked for your assistance in selecting and registering a domain name. Write a report that identifies several appropriate available domain names, explain the pros and cons of each name, make a recommendation, and justify your recommendation.

4. Form two teams, a client team and a Web design team. After suitable preparation, both teams meet for their first Web site planning meeting. Afterward, both teams critique their own and the other team's performance in the meeting.

5. Form two debating teams. One team supports the proposition that using a number of images and colors on a Web site is okay because "soon everyone will have a high-speed connection to the Internet." The other team disagrees with this statement and its justification.

6. Enter **sitebuilder.yahoo.com/ps/sb** and download the SiteBuilder. As a team, build a storefront for your dream business. You can try it for free for 30 days. Use the design features available. Have visitors check out the site. The instructor and class will review the sites for design and usability. Awards will be given to the best stores. Alternatively, you may use the equivalent tools from eBay, or **1and1.com**.

Real-World Case

HOW TELECOM NEW ZEALAND (TNZ) EXCELS WITH CONTENT MANAGEMENT

Telecom New Zealand (TNZ) is a major telecommunication and online provider offering a full range of advanced services to most of the population in New Zealand. The company wants its customers to use its Web site (*telecom.co.nz*) not only for customer service but as the primary marketing and sales channel for both standard and complex products and services. To do so, TNZ is using a comprehensive solution called Enterprise Content Management from Vignette (*vignette.com*) that supports Web site creation, management, process automation, publishing, and analysis. Vignette provides a suite of products that help TNZ control, manage, and share content; optimize business processes; integrate the site content with existing enterprise applications; and deliver the entire inventory of content in a personalized fashion to TNZ's choice of devices.

The solution also enables TNZ to run segment-focused marketing campaigns, save time and money in site development to support marketing campaigns, and develop one-to-one relationships with customers by delivering relevant and tailored content. The solution enables TNZ to continuously increase the sophistication of their marketing campaigns by supporting appropriate result-based analysis.

To attract customers, the company needed to provide site content related to products and services, which are provided both to individuals and organizations (B2B), in such a way that the content is current, comprehensive, and easy to find and understand—all of which needed to be done in a cost-effective manner.

Working with IT software and service provider Sybase (including wireless technologies), TNZ implemented Vignette's products in 2000. By 2007, TNZ developed several applications that make Web site content delivery faster and more manageable. Improvements were registered in:

▶ Manageability of all content
▶ Easier online publishing (using templates to automate the process)
▶ Faster training of employees in online publishing

▶ Creating efficiency of online publishing (reduction from days to hours)
▶ More staff are publishing online
▶ Creating consistency in style and design of pages by different employees (template-based content is also more accurate)
▶ Easier self-service by customers. For example, customers can enter their phone number to find if broadband Internet access is available in their areas, as well as the waiting time and cost.
▶ Site visits increased 25 percent in six months, and online sales grew by 150 percent in a one-year period
▶ The online call center operates much more efficiently and effectively

To ensure that users were gaining maximum benefits from the Web site, TNZ conducted a content audit. The audit indicated that customers wanted more personalization, so using the software, TNZ provided it. Also, the 3,000 different pieces of content are now presented in about 6,000 different ways. Now content can be presented in the right context with the right look and feel to please each customer.

Using integration with back-end customer information (e.g., billing), TNZ offers very detailed and personalized service regarding its usage and accounts. Finally, the data collected on content usage (click stream analysis) were analyzed to provide TNZ information about customer behavior and behavioral changes due to marketing campaigns.

To assure that the company is working together as one entity, the entire content of the intranet (35,000 pages on 220 disparate sites) was moved to a content management system. This aligned with TNZ's business objectives.

In early 2007, TNZ joined forces with Yahoo! to provide an enhanced suite of online content and application services to New Zealanders.

Sources: Compiled from CRM Advocate (2002), Vignette.com, and from Myle (2004).

Questions

1. What are the benefits to TNZ from offering the advanced services and how does better content management help achieve these benefits?

2. Enter *vignette.com/us/products* and look at the product categories. List each category and explain how it supported TNZ's needs.

3. How does better content increase sales of TNZ products and services?

4. How can better content provide better service to TNZ's customers?

5. How can the system improve marketing campaigns?

6. What were the objectives of moving the entire intranet to a content management system?

REFERENCES

2createawebsite.com. "How to Register a Domain Name." 2006. **2createawebsite.com/prebuild/register_domain. html** (accessed November 2006).

Agarwal, R., and V. Venkatesh. "Assessing a Firm's Web Presence: A Heuristic Evaluation Procedure for the Measurement of Usability." *Information Systems Research*, Vol. 13, No. 2 (2002).

Akamai. "Akamai Launches Suite of Solutions Designed to Accelerate and Scale Dynamic Web Sites Built on Web 2.0 Technologies." June 12, 2006. **akamai.com/html/ about/press/releases/2006/press_061206.html** (accessed November 2006).

Ariguzo, G. C., E. G. Mallach, and D. S. White. "The First Decade of E-Commerce."*International Journal of Business Information Systems*, Vol. 1, No. 3, 2006.

Arnold, S. E. "Content Management's New Realities." *OnLine Magazine*, Vol. 27, No. 1 (2003). **infotoday.com/ online/jan03/arnold.shtml** (accessed February 2007).

Ash, C. G., and J. M. Burn. "Managing E-Business Change," in Khosrow-Pour (2006).

Awad, E. M. *Electronic Commerce: From Vision to Fulfillment*. Upper Saddle River, NJ: Prentice Hall, 2002.

Barnes, H. "Three Steps to Effective Web Content Measurement." *e-Business Advisor*, June 2001.

Bayers, C. "The Inner Bezos." *Wired*, Vol. 7, No. 3 (1999).

BBC Training and Development. *The 12 Deadly Sins of Site Design*. October 2002. (Note: no longer available online.)

Bosilj-Vuksic, V., M. Indihar Stemberger, J. Jaklic, and A. Kovacic. "Assessment of E-Business Transformation Using Simulation Modeling." *Simulation*, December 2002.

Bracken, B. *The eCommerce Solution Guide—Easy UK eCommerce on a Budget*. September 14. 2006. **ebyro.com/ read-article/the-ecommerce-solution-guide-easy-uk- ecommerce-on-a-budget/912** (accessed February 2007).

Business 2.0. "How to Build a Bulletproof Startup." June 2006. **money.cnn.com/magazines/business2/startups/ index.html** (accessed February 2007).

Business Wire. "Amazon Services to Provide American Express Merchants with Special Offer for Selling Through Amazon.com." July 24, 2004a. **accessmylibrary.com/ coms2/summary_0286–1279385_ITM** (accessed January 2007).

Business Wire. "Amazon.com to Acquire Joyo.com Limited." August 19, 2004b. **findarticles.com/p/ articles/mi_m0EIN/is_2004_August_19/ai_n6161725** (accessed January 2007).

Byrne, T. "Top Six Content Management Pitfalls." *PC Magazine*, September 17, 2002.

Chen, J. S., and R. K. H. Ching. "A Proposed Framework for Transition to an e-Business Model." *Quarterly Journal of E-Commerce* (October–December 2002).

Cheung, C. M. K., and M. K. O. Lee. "The Asymmetric Impact of Web Site Attribute Performance on User Satisfaction: An Empirical Study." *Proceedings of the Hawaii International Conference on System Sciences*, Big Island, Hawaii, January 3–6, 2005.

CMS Watch. "Web Content Management Vendor List." 2006. **cmswatch.com/CMS/Vendors/** (accessed November 2006).

Conway, C. "Incubators and Hatcheries." *International Journal of Entrepreneurship and Innovation*, Vol. 5, No. 4 (2004).

Copeland, M. V. and O. Malik. "How to Build a Bulletproof Startup?" *Business 2.0*, June 2006.

Craig, R., "Developing a Viable Product for an Emerging Market," in Khosrow-Pour (2006).

CRM Advocate. "Case Study: Telecom New Zealand Improves Content Management, Online Marketing and Delivers Personalized Content with Vignette," April 2002. **crmadvocate.com/casestudy/vignette/ telecomnz_70.pdf** (accessed February 2007).

Crosbie, V. "Bugmenot.com Lets Consumers Circumvent Forced Registration." Poynteronline, January 29, 2004. **poynter.org/column.asp?id=31&aid=60149** (accessed November 2006).

Cukier, K. N. "Boo's Blues." *Red Herring*, May 4, 2000. **redherring.com/vc/2000/0504/vc-boo050400.html** (no longer available online).

Drostdesigns.com. "Web Site Evaluation Criteria Discussion." 2006. **drostdesigns.com/web-siteevaluation-criteria** (accessed November 2006).

Elms, J. "Good Things in (eBay) Store." *Entrepreneur*, April 2006.

eMarketer. "Top Ten E-Business Trends for 2005." *eMarketer.com*, January 5, 2005. **emarketer.com/article.aspx?1003202** (no longer available online).

Fan, Y. H. "Structure and Components of E-Commerce Business Model," in Khosrow-Pour (2006).

Firstgov.gov. "Web Managers Best Practice Awards—2006." **firstgov.gov/webcontent/improving/marketing/awards/best_practice_awards.shtml** (accessed November 2006).

Fogarty, K. "Your Money or Your Network." *Baseline*, February 2005.

Ginige, A., et al. "A Road Map for Successfully Transforming SMEs into E-Business." *Cutter IT Journal* (May 2001).

Hendon, I. M. "E-Business: Think Big, Start Small, Act Quickly." *Aviation Now*, December 18, 2003.

Hise, P. "Everyone Wants to Start a Business." *Fortune Small Business*, January 23, 2007. **money.cnn.com/2007/01/22/magazines/fsb/entrepreneurship.boom.fsb** (accessed February 2007).

Holden, G., "Fast Forward (How 10 Entrepreneurs Tapped into the Power of eBay and Made Millions)," *Entrepreneur*, May 2006.

Huff, S., et al. *Cases in Electronic Commerce*, 2nd ed. Boston: Irwin McGraw-Hill, 2001.

IBM. "Web Cast: Leveraging Information for Business Transformation." April 4, 2006.

Internet Marketing Newswatch. "Streaming Media Growth and Content Category share: 2006–2010." March 8, 2007. **imnewswatch.com/archives/2007/03/streaming_media.html?visitFrom=1** (accessed April 2007).

Jackson, P., and L. Harris. "E-business and Organizational Change: Reconciling Traditional Values with Business Transformation." *Journal of Organizational Change Management*, Vol. 16, No. 5 (2003).

Jeston, J., and Nelis, J., *Business Process Management: Practical Guides to Successful Implementation*. Burlington, MA: Butterworth-Heinemann, 2006.

Junnarkar, S. "Akamai Ends Al-Jazeera Server Support." *CNET News*, April 4, 2003. **news.com/1200–1035–995546.html** (accessed February 2007).

Kauffman, R. J., T. Miller, and B. Wang. "When Internet Companies Morph: Understanding Organizational Strategy Changes in the 'New' New Economy." *First Monday*, July 2002. **firstmonday.org/issues/issue7_7/kauffman** (accessed February).

Kavassalis, P., S. Lelis, M. Rafea, and S. Haridi. "What Makes a Web Site Popular?" *Communications of the ACM*, February 2004.

Khosrow-Pour M. (Ed.) *Encyclopedia of E-Commerce, E-Government, and Mobile Commerce*. Hershey, PA: Idea Group Reference, 2006.

Kim, Y. J., R. Kishore, and G. L. Sanders. "From DQ to EQ: Understanding Data Quality in the Context of E-Business Systems." *Communications of the ACM*, October 2005.

Klotz, I. "Space Race 2: Bezos and Life Beyond Amazon." *Washington Times*, January 18, 2005.

Kurnia, S., U. Leimstoll, and P. Schubert. "An Evaluation of Australian on Swiss E-Shops in the Grocery Sector." *Proceedings of the 38th Hawaii International Conference on System Sciences*, Big Island, Hawaii, January 3–6, 2005.

Lasry, E. M. "Inertia.com: Rates and Processes of Organizational Transformation in the Retail Industry." *Quarterly Journal of E-Commerce* (July–September 2002).

Lewin, J. "Podcasting Emerges as an eBusiness Tool," *ITWorld.com*, E-Commerce in Action, May 31, 2005. **itworld.com/Tech/2403/nls_ecommercepod050601/pfindex.html** (accessed February 2007).

Maguire, J. "E-Commerce Best Practices: Ten Rules of the Road." *Ecommercepartners.net*, January 11, 2005. **ecommerce-guide.com/solutions/advertising/article.php/3457431** (accessed February 2007).

Maier, M. "Building the Next Google." *Business 2.0*, November 2005.

McGovern, G. "How to Measure the Value of Your Web Content." *New Thinking*, January 24, 2005.

McGovern, G. "Web Content Management Is Not Data Management." *New Thinking*, May 23, 2005. **gerrymcgovern.com/nt/2005/nt_2005_05_23-web-content-management.htm** (accessed November 2006).

McKay, J., and P. Marshall. *Strategic Management of e-Business*. Milton, Australia: John Wiley and Sons, 2004.

McKinney, V., K. Yoon, and F. M. Zahedi. "The Measurement of Web-Customer Satisfaction: An Expectation and Disconfirmation Approach." *Information Systems Research*, Vol. 13, No. 3 (2002).

McNurlin, B. C., and P. Sprague. *Information Systems: Management in Practice*, 6th ed. Upper Saddle River, NJ: Prentice Hall, 2005.

Merchantrates.com. "ECommerce Best Practices and Fraud Control Programs." 2005. **merchantrates.com/MOTO/default.asp** (accessed January 2007).

Müller-Lankenau, K., K. Wehmeyer, and S. Klein. Strategic Channel Alignment: An Analysis of the Configuration of Physical and Virtual Marketing Channels." *Information Systems and E-Business Management*, April 2006.

Mulqueen, J. T. "Fast 50: #1 Akamai." *Eweek.com*, July 9, 2001. **findarticles.com/p/articles/mi_zdewk/is_200107/ai_ziff7287** (accessed February 2007).

Myle, S. "Content Management Helps Us to Work Smarter at Telecom New Zealand," *The Electronic Library*, Vol. 22, No. 6 (2004).

New Zealand Ministry of Economic Development (MED). *E-Commerce: A Guide for New Zealand Business*. Wellington, New Zealand: New Zealand Ministry of Economic Development, 2000.

Nielsen, J., and M. Tahir. *Homepage Usability: 50 Web Sites Deconstructed*. Indianapolis, IN: New Riders Publishing, 2002.

Nielsen, J. "Top Ten Mistakes in Web Design," 2005. **useit.com/alertbox/9605.html** (accessed January 2007).

Norguet, J.-P., E. Zimányi, and R. Steinberger. "Improving Web Sites with Web Usage Mining, Web Content Mining, and Semantic Analysis." *Proceedings of the 32nd Conference on Current Trends in Theory and Practice of Computer Science*, Merín, Czech Republic, January 21–27, 2006.

OBO. **obo.co.nz** (accessed January 2007).

Ould, M. A. *Business Process*. Chichester, UK: John Wiley & Sons, 2003.

Pallis, G., and A. Vakali. "Insights and Perspectives for Content Delivery Networks." *Communications of the ACM*, January 2006.

Pearlson, K. E., and C. S. Sounders. *Managing and Using Information Systems*, 3rd ed. Hoboken, NJ: John Wiley & Sons, 2006.

Petrecca, P. "Product Placement—You Can't Escape It." *USA Today*, October 10, 2006. **usatoday.com/money/advertising/2006–10–10-ad-nauseum-usat_x.htm** (accessed November 2006).

Phan, P. H., D. S. Siegel, and M. Wright. "Science Parks and Incubators: Observations, Synthesis, and Future Research." *Journal of Business Venturing*, Vol. 20, No. 2 (2005).

Ranganathan, C., A. Shetty, and G. Muthukumaran. "E-Business Transformation at a Crossroads: Sears' Dilemma." *Journal of Information Technology*, Vol. 19, No. 2 (2004).

Rapoza, J. "Web Content Management Face-Off." *eWeek*, August 7, 2004.

Rayport, J., and B. J. Jaworski. *Introduction to E-Commerce*, 2nd ed. Boston: McGraw-Hill, 2003.

Rosenfeld, L., and P. Morville. *Information Architecture for the World Wide Web*, 2nd ed. Cambridge, MA: O'Reilly, 2002.

Saunders, C. "Study: Streaming Media Marketing to Rake in $3.1 Billion in 2005." *Internetnews.com*, June 18, 2001. **internetnews.com/iar/article.php/12_786611** (no longer available online).

Schonfeld, E. "5 Ways to Start a Company." *Business 2.0*, May 2006.

Sloan, P. "The Startup Façade." *Business 2.0*, October 2006.

Smith, R. F. *Business Process Management and the Balanced Scorecard*. Hoboken, NJ: Wiley, 2006.

Solvik, P. "Something Ventured." *CIO Insight*, November 2005.

Spangler, T. "Choosing Host That Isn't Toast." *Baseline*, January 2005.

Spector, R. *Amazon.com—Get Big Fast: Inside the Revolutionary Business Model That Changed the World*. New York: HarperBusiness, 2000.

Stam, N. "Media Here, Media There, Media Everywhere!" *PC Magazine*, January 2005. **findarticles.com/p/articles/mi_zdpcm/is_200501/ai_n8671118** (accessed January 2007).

Sterne, J. *Web Metrics*. New York: John Wiley & Sons, 2002.

Strassmann, P. A. "Calculator: Measuring Business Transformation." *Baseline*, January 25, 2007.

Three Squared Inc. "Three Squared First to Market as One-Stop-Shop for Streaming Media Services." Three Squared Press Release, April 2000. **threesquared.com/download/market.pdf** (no longer available online).

Tomsen, M. *Killer Content: Strategies for Web Content and E-Commerce*. Boston: Addison-Wesley, 2000.

Turban, E., et al. *Business Intelligence: A Managerial Approach*. Upper Saddle River, NJ: Prentice Hall, 2008a.

Turban, E., et al. *Information Technology for Management*, 6th ed. New York: John Wiley & Sons, 2008b.

Umesh, U. N., M. Huynh, and L. Jessup. "Creating Successful Entrepreneurial Ventures in IT." *Communications of the ACM*, June 2005.

Vassil, G., C. Stolz, R. Neuneier, M. Skubacz, and D. Seipel. "Matching Web Site Structure and Content." *Proceedings of the 13th International World Wide Web Conference*, New York, May 17–22, 2004.

Vignette.com. "Telecom New Zealand Customer Story." 2006. **vignette.com/dafiles/docs/Downloads/CS0605_TelecomNZ.pdf** (accessed February 2007).

Werbach, K. "Syndication—The Emerging Model for Business in the Internet Era." *Harvard Business Review* (May–June 2000).

Wiedemann, J. *Web Design: E-Commerce*. London: Taschen UK, 2007.

Williams, G. "Mother of Invention." *Entrepreneur*, May 2006.

Winnick, M. "5 Secrets to a Successful Launch." *Business 2.0*, October 2, 2006. **money.cnn.com/magazines/business2/business2_archive/2006/09/01/8384346/index.htm** (accessed February 2007).

Vic.gov.au. "Web Site Development." **mmv.vic.gov.au/uploads/downloads/ICT_Projects/eCommerce/WebsiteDevelopment.pdf** (accessed January 2007).

Yahoo!. "6 Tips for Easy Web Site Navigation." 2006. **smallbusiness.yahoo.com/r-article-a-70123-m-6-sc-37–6_tips_for_easy_web_site_navigation-i** (accessed November 2006).

Zviran, M., et al. "Does Color in E-Mail Make a Difference?" *Communication of the ACM*, April 2006.

CHAPTER 17

LEGAL, ETHICAL, AND COMPLIANCE ISSUES IN EC

Content

Learning Objectives

Upon completion of this chapter, you will be able to:

1. Understand the foundations for legal and ethical issues in EC.

2. Describe civil, intellectual property, and common law.

3. Understand legal and ethical challenges and how to contain them.

4. Explain privacy, free speech, and defamation and their challenges.

5. Discuss the challenges caused by spam, splogs, and pop-ups.

6. Describe types of fraud on the Internet and how to protect against it.

SPLOGS AND SEARCH ENGINE SPAM TO CAPTURE CUSTOMER TRAFFIC

The Problem

For many online businesses, a majority of their customer traffic comes from search engines. Various surveys indicate that up to 75 percent of Internet shoppers use search engines to find products and services. "Getting found" among the millions of competing Web sites is what businesses want. There are several ethical marketing methods such as **search engine marketing (SEM)** to increase the ranking of a Web site in the search results. One SEM method, **search engine optimization (SEO)**, takes into consideration how search engines work (e.g., logical deep-linking or strategic keyword) to maximize the number of qualified visitors to a site. Because SEO improves sales, (see success cases at *reprisemedia.com/clients.aspx*), a dark side quickly emerged—one that uses spam-based practices to get a high ranking or to divert traffic away from intended Web sites.

With antispam software and ISP spam filters defeating traditional e-mail spam, spamming tactics have mutated. Those mutations seek to ensure—*by any means*—a good shopper delivery rate. To capture customers, unsolicited junk advertisements are sent to all types of messaging media, including blogs, instant messages (IM), and cellular telephones. Spammers flood these media with so-called **comment spam** promoting their gambling sites, prescription drugs, get-rich schemes, and the like. (There are also those who use the Internet for crime, e.g., identity theft, money laundering, auction fraud, as discussed in Chapter 11.)

While content spam impacts media users, the greater concern to ethical e-commerce sites is **search engine spam**, which Yahoo! defines as "pages created deliberately to trick the search engine into offering inappropriate, redundant, or poor-quality search results" (Hunt 2005). Those pages, called **spam sites**, use techniques that deliberately subvert a search engine's algorithms to artificially inflate the page's rankings. A similar tactic involves the use of **splogs** (short for *spam blog sites*), which are blogs created solely for marketing purposes. Spammers create hundreds of splogs that they link to the spammer's site to increase that site's search engine ranking. This method makes use of the fact that the number of links influence a page's rank, as in Google's PageRank system, which calculates a page's position in search results by weighing the links to that page. These deceptive practices are collectively referred to as **search engine spamming**. For information on search engine algorithms and page rankings, see *google.com/technology* and Slegg (2006).

search engine marketing (SEM)
Marketing methods to increase the ranking of a Web site in the search results.

search engine optimization (SEO)
Technique takes into consideration how search engines work (e.g., logical deep linking or strategic keyword) to maximize the number of qualified visitors to a site.

comment spam
Spam sent to all types of messaging media, including blogs, IM, and cellular telephones to promote products or services.

search engine spam
Pages created deliberately to trick the search engine into offering inappropriate, redundant, or poor-quality search results.

The Solution

Both legal and technological defenses are used to prevent or punish search engine and other forms of commercial spam. In one case, Verizon Wireless filed a lawsuit against the Florida-based travel agency Passport Holidays for violating federal and state laws by sending 98,000 unsolicited text messages to Verizon Wireless customers. Passport's messages encouraged recipients to call a toll-free number to claim a cruise to the Bahamas. In February 2006, a federal court judge granted Verizon Wireless's request for an injunction barring Passport Holidays from sending text message spam. Passport Holidays agreed to pay $10,000 to compensate Verizon Wireless.

Sending spam that disguises a sales pitch to look like a personal e-mail to bypass filters violates the U.S. Controlling the Assault of NonSolicited Pornography and Marketing (CAN-SPAM) Act of 2003. However, many spammers hide their identity to escape detection by using hijacked PCs, or spam zombies, to send spam, as discussed in Chapter 11.

Filtering achieves more immediate solutions. Bloggers plagued by comment spam can get help from sites such as SplogSpot *splogspot.com* or Splog Reporter *splogreporter.com*, which collect information on such content to help network administrators filter it out. Search engines constantly test and implement new algorithms with stronger filters to keep Web site rankings honest and objective.

spam site
Page that uses techniques that deliberately subvert a search engine's algorithms to artificially inflate the page's rankings.

splog
Short for *spam blog*. A site created solely for marketing purposes.

search engine spamming
Collective term referring to deceptive online advertising practices.

The Results

The motivator for splogs, fraud, and other online scams is quick profit. Online scams create millionaires—even in remote areas like Lagos (Lawal 2006). Not only are they the fastest path to wealth for criminals of any age, they are near-instant businesses with no deterrent factor. Sploggers and spammers know the risk of detection and prosecution is low.

Evidence shows that unethical and illegal business tactics that exploit or mimic e-commerce operations will not stop. To defend themselves, Google (*google.com/contact/spamreport.html*), MSN Search (*feedback.search.msn.com/default.aspx*), and Yahoo! (*add.yahoo.com/fast/help/us/ysearch/cgi_reportsearchspam*) have turned to aggressive measures. They have implemented spam site reporting systems, built algorithms that check for and penalize deceptive rank-boosting practices, and banned violators' sites outright. In 2006, Google temporarily banned BMW and Ricoh's German Web sites from its search index for using JavaScript redirect, or doorway pages that presented visitors with different content than they had displayed to the search engine.

Google has warned that it is expanding its efforts to clampdown on unethical tricks and tactics. As abuses become known or intolerable, additional laws will be passed with varying degrees of effectiveness.

Sources: Harwood (2006), Hunt (2005), Spring (2006), *CIO.com* (2006), and Verizon Wireless News Center (2005).

WHAT WE CAN LEARN . . .

Although its origins go back to the 1960s, consumer and commercial use of the World Wide Web really began in the mid-1990s. Those uses continue to reshape business, marketing, and communications in diverse ways, including unethical or illegal ones. The Internet has empowered widespread and immediate dissemination of information more than any technological development since the printing press in the fifteenth century. Some predict that it could be the most important technological advance in five hundred years. It is also an environment where companies are pushing legal and ethical limits to the maximum and beyond. See Online File 11.3 for the customers' reactions to unethical tactics.

This raises a crucial question: Why should EC companies comply with ethical and legal practices? The answer centers on trust. Customers need to trust the online marketplace and its businesses. Unethical business practices have long-lasting negative business consequences that cannot be repaired. Violators expose themselves to harsh penalties from various government agencies and victimized customers, as well as bloggers and consumer interest groups (e.g., privacy groups). The integrity of EC, as well as national economies, depends on people's knowing and obeying the letter and spirit of laws that apply to business and online transactions.

New tactics to maximize competitive advantage or attract customers raise a number of questions about what constitutes illegal, unethical, intrusive, or undesirable behavior. In the world of commerce, copyright, trademark, and patent infringement, freedom of thought and speech, theft of property, and fraud are not new issues. However, EC has added to the scope and scale of these issues.

This chapter provides an introduction to legislation and court decisions to help you understand the risks and liability exposure arising from attempts to manipulate EC operations or defraud customers. This overview of the legal system provides a foundation for assessing whether current and controversial proposals for government regulations, such as Internet neutrality, are good for e-business. A full analysis of the legal and ethical issues is far beyond the scope of one chapter.

17.1 FUNDAMENTAL LEGAL, ETHICAL, AND REGULATORY ISSUES

Ethics characterize how individuals choose to interact with one another. In philosophy, ethics define what is good for the individual and society and the nature of duties that people owe themselves and one another. One duty is to not intrude on a person's **privacy**, which stems from the right to be left alone and free of unreasonable personal intrusions.

Law (that is, public law) embodies ethical principals, but they are not the same. Acts that are generally considered unethical may not be illegal. Lying to a friend may be unethical, but it is not illegal. Conversely, the law is not simply the coding of ethical norms, nor are all ethical codes incorporated into public law.

A common agreement in a society as to what is right and wrong determines ethics, but they are not subject to legal sanctions except when they overlap with activities that also are illegal. Online File W17.1 at the book's Web site shows a framework for ethical issues.

Regulation in cyberspace does not consist only of laws that government issues and enforces. Private parties (e.g., individuals, special interest groups, a cluster of consumer

ethics
The branch of philosophy that deals with what is considered to be right and wrong.

privacy
The right to be left alone and free of unreasonable personal intrusions.

groups, organizations), use online interactive technology to regulate—or attempt to regulate—what is communicated or done on the Internet. Private regulation may have positive impacts (Google filtering out search engine spam) or it might potentially lead to abusive behavior or illegal acts—and interfere with free speech, privacy, or intellectual property. **Intellectual property** is a creation of the mind, such as inventions, literary and artistic works, and symbols, names, images, and designs, used in commerce.

LAWS ARE SUBJECT TO INTERPRETATION

Keep in mind that most laws and regulations are *broadly written* and, therefore, only provide outlines to guide public policy. Even physical crime laws that sound specific (e.g., killing a human being is illegal) do not apply in all situations, such as in self-defense.

Specific disputes (such as the legality of spam) cannot be resolved by simply referring to relevant laws for two reasons. First, the scope of a law (i.e., whether it applies to a specific situation) needs to be interpreted by looking at the intent of the lawmakers. Second, laws may conflict with each other. For example, how companies use information collected from customers via their Web sites are subject to privacy laws. One privacy law may prohibit a company from sharing customers' social security numbers with business partners, whereas a homeland security law may require revealing the identity of customers. (Banks with CRM programs often encounter these legal conflicts). Another example of legal conflict is the debate between free speech and protection of children from offensive content.

Free Speech Online versus Child Protection Debate

A fierce debate occurred over whether it was legal for public libraries to filter out offensive online content. The conflict over free speech versus child protection erupted after the **Children's Internet Protection Act (CIPA)** was signed into law in December 2000. CIPA mandated the use of filtering technologies in schools and libraries that received certain types of U.S. federal funding. CIPA was immediately challenged in court, so it did not go into effect at that time.

Opponents of the law relied on earlier court cases (that is, a legal precedent) saying that government-imposed limitations on the public's right to freely read and learn at public libraries violated the free speech protections of the First Amendment. A **legal precedent** is a judicial decision that may be used as a standard in subsequent similar cases. For details of the debate, see ACLU (2006). It was a major victory for proponents of free speech online in May 2002 when a District Court declared the CIPA as unconstitutional. The District Court judges ruled that CIPA was overbroad and would violate the First Amendment rights of library patrons, both adults and minors. That court ordered that CIPA not be enforced. The conflict did not end there. The District Court's decision was appealed to the Supreme Court. In June 2003, the Supreme Court Judges declared that the CIPA was constitutional. Their review represented the third time justices had heard arguments pitting free speech against attempts to protect children from offensive online content. CIPA went into effect in 2004, and efforts to defeat it continued.

For another example of the courts resolving novel conflicts such as whether a company can link to a Web site without permission, see the story of *Ticketmaster v. Microsoft* provided in Online File W17.2.

Political Spam Versus Dependence on Political Fund-Raising

Another legal complication arises when determining the scope of a law, particularly when it involves ethical issues. Consider the use of unsolicited bulk e-mails to reach voters by candidates for political office—and the difficulty in determining its legality and possible ethical impacts. Commonly known as *political spam*, this campaign tactic offers an inexpensive alternative to television, radio, and print ads. Those who favor the use of political spam believe that campaigning via the Internet reduces candidates' dependence on wealthy fundraisers, which reduces political favoritism and other paybacks that are not in the public's best interest. Critics believe that political spam is no different from other types of spam. All spam is a nuisance, clogs mail servers, and creates security risks. See Exhibit 17.1 for a list of the fiercely debated questions that this situation has triggered.

intellectual property
Creations of the mind, such as inventions, literary and artistic works, and symbols, names, images, and designs, used in commerce.

Children's Internet Protection Act (CIPA)
Law that mandates the use of filtering technologies in schools and libraries that received certain types of U.S. federal funding.

legal precedent
A judicial decision that may be used as a standard in subsequent similar cases.

EXHIBIT 17.1   Controversial Issues Regarding Political Spam

Political E-Mail: Protected Speech or Unwelcome Spam?

- Is political spam legal given that communication over the Internet (including e-mail) is a form of speech protected by the Constitution?
- What distinguishes political spam from other forms of speech, from regulated political speech, and from advertising spam?
- Does political spam diminish candidates' dependence on wealthy special interest groups (SIG)?
- If political spam does diminish candidates' dependence on wealthty SIGs, can it actually improve the integrity of elected officials? To what extent?

California gubernatorial candidate Bill Jones was at the center of many complaints about political spam when his staff sent e-mail to over a million people—and to many who never should have received the e-mail. One of the biggest criticisms was the inaccuracy of his mailing list (McCurry and Purpuro, 2002). Intending to mail only California residents, the campaign staff sent the e-mail to people with the suffix ".ca," which is a Canadian domain. They wrongly thought they were using the abbreviation for California, which is CA. Their mistake was one that is easily correctable with a more sophisticated e-mailing program—or with more qualified staff. The circumstances of this spam case at that time were not enough to outlaw political e-mail altogether. However, it could have raised issues of negligence on the part of the campaign staff for not understanding what they were doing. For details on the legal issues and precedents, see *Duke Law and Technology Review* (2003).

In March 2007, a 74-second video of political satire was anonymously posted on YouTube. The video, called "Hillary 1984," raised ethical questions about the power of the Internet in the political process—and the opportunities for subterfuge (Helmore 2007). The video depicted Hillary Clinton, a candidate for the Democratic nomination for U.S. president, as a politically correct and totalitarian Big Sister, and her supporters as compliant automatons. The "Hillary 1984" video had been created by Phil de Vellis, a technician who worked for the firm that designed Barack Obama's Web site, a rival presidential candidate, but it was released without Obama's endorsement. Within two weeks after being posted on YouTube, the video had been viewed several million times. This attack highlights how the author of a viral political video can damage the person being ridiculed as well as his unwitting sponsor, in this case Barack Obama.

This overview gives you a better understanding of the complexity and conflicts surrounding legal, ethical, and regulatory issues, particularly those involving online conduct. Fundamentally, laws protect the rights and guarantees described in a nation's constitution. That sounds simple enough. But as you've learned, getting agreement on whose rights and which rights are being protected and whose are being violated may not be possible. You will see other examples of such dilemmas throughout the chapter.

LAW: A SYSTEM FOR SOCIAL CONTROL

Law provides a *system* for social control. As with all systems, the formation of laws is a dynamic process that responds to ever-changing conditions. The nature of law is dynamic, in part, because it must be responsive to new threats or abuses that violate a nation's constitution. That is why significant changes in the nature of business or crimes lead to new laws.

Without knowledge of the basics of the legal system, nature of law, and due process, those involved in EC risk fines, prison times, or other penalties (see Chapter 11). **Due process** is essentially a guarantee of basic fairness and fair procedures. In a legal system, the government produces a set of rules and regulations and has the power to enforce them, as shown in the legal framework in Exhibit 17.2. These rules and regulations create both rights and duties. A **right** is a legal claim that others not interfere with an individual's or organization's protected interest. In broad terms, **protected interests** are interests, such as *life*, *liberty*, and *property*, that are protected by national constitutions

due process
A guarantee of basic fairness and fair procedures in legal action.

right
Legal claim that others not interfere with an individual's or organization's protected interest.

protected interests
Interests, such as life, liberty, and property, that a national constitution protects.

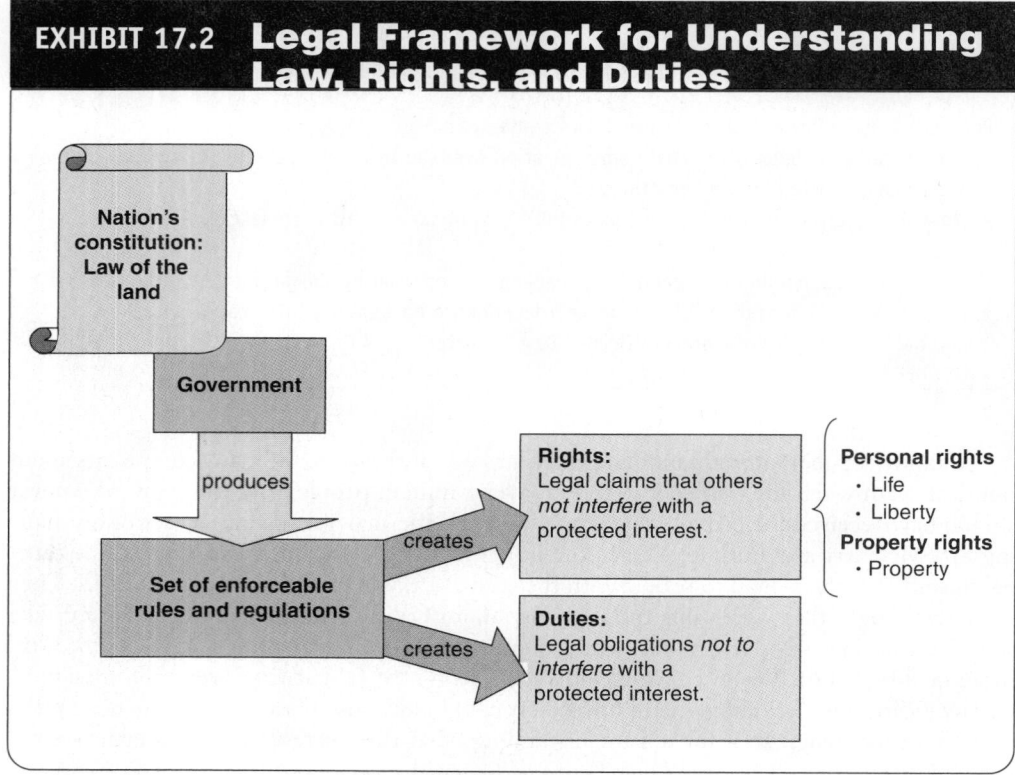

EXHIBIT 17.2   Legal Framework for Understanding Law, Rights, and Duties

Nation's constitution: Law of the land

Government

produces

Set of enforceable rules and regulations

creates

Rights: Legal claims that others *not interfere* with a protected interest.

creates

Duties: Legal obligations *not to interfere* with a protected interest.

Personal rights
- Life
- Liberty

Property rights
- Property

---

duty
Legal obligation imposed on individuals and organizations that prevents them from interfering with another's protected interest or right.

civil litigation
An adversarial proceeding in which a party (the plaintiff) sues another party (the defendant) to get compensation for a wrong committed by the defendant.

Privacy, intellectual property, and free speech are examples of protected interests. Those interests are not absolute. For example, a person convicted of a felony crime is going to jail—and cannot claim that being confined to jail violates his or her right to liberty. To learn more about protected interests, see FindLaw (2007). A **duty** is a legal obligation imposed on individuals and organizations that prevents them from interfering with another's protected interest or right. See World Intellectual Property Organization (WIPO) (2007) for a global perspective on these rights and duties.

PERSONAL AND PROPERTY RIGHTS

Rights are divided into two categories: personal rights and property rights. Generally, the interests of *life* and *liberty* fall into the personal rights category. *Property* interests are in the category of property rights. Internet business Web sites, proprietary systems, and customer lists are examples of property. Exhibit 17.3 lists property rights relevant to EC and Web sites.

Referring to both Exhibits 17.2 and 17.3, it is clear that an online business has the legal right to prevent spammers or other businesses from interfering with or harming the benefits (profits) from its EC site—and can file lawsuits against them. Lawsuits are one type of **civil litigation**, which is an adversarial proceeding in which a party (the plaintiff)

EXHIBIT 17.3   Property Rights Relevant to Electronic Commerce

Owners of property, including intellectual property, are entitled to:
1. Control of the use of the property
2. The right to any benefit from the property
3. The right to transfer or sell the property
4. The right to exclude others from the property

sues another party (the defendant) to get compensation for a wrong committed by the defendant. For example, the entertainment industry has the right to its intellectual property (IP) and can file lawsuits (civil charges) against online businesses, such as YouTube and MySpace, for any interference with the ability to profit from its IP or for profiting from the recording industry's property without authorization and compensation. In contrast, law enforcement or a public official brings criminal litigation. The next section discusses criminal and civil laws further. You will also learn the terminology needed to understand legal issues.

CRIMINAL LAW AND CIVIL LAW

Laws are passed to protect the public as well as their interests. The term *public* refers to one or more individuals, groups, or organizations. An example is the **Controlling the Assault of Non-Solicited Pornography and Marketing Act**, or **CAN-SPAM Act**, which was signed into U.S. law on December 16, 2003. CAN-SPAM went into effect on January 1, 2004. You can find the text of the bill at spamlaws.com/federal/can-spam.shtml. The CAN-SPAM law makes it a crime to send commercial e-mail messages with false or misleading message headers or misleading subject lines. Other provisions of the law include:

CAN-SPAM Act
Law that makes it a crime to send commercial e-mail messages with false or misleading message headers or misleading subject lines.

- Requires marketers to identify their physical location by including their postal address in the text of the e-mail messages.
- Requires an opt-out link in each message, which must also give recipients the option of telling senders to stop all segments of their marketing campaigns.
- Allows for suits to be brought by ISPs, state attorneys general, and the federal government.
- Carries penalties of up to $250 per spammed e-mail message, with a cap of $2 million, which can be tripled for aggravated violations. There is no cap on penalties for e-mail sent with false or deceptive headers.
- Those found guilty of violating the law may face up to five years in prison.

Characteristics of Criminal and Civil Laws

There are several important legal concepts to understand. First, a **crime** is an offensive act against society that violates a law and is punishable by the government. Second, in order for an act to be a crime, the act must violate at least one criminal law. Third, an act can violate both criminal and civil law. For example, spammers who violate CAN-SPAM can be charged with a crime and punished under criminal law, and they also can be sued under civil law if the spam causes an identifiable loss to an online business.

crime
Offensive act against society that violates a law and is punishable by the government.

Criminal laws are laws to protect the public, human life, or private property. Rules called **statutes** define criminal laws. In contrast, **civil laws** are laws that enable a party (individual or organization) that has suffered harm or a loss to bring a lawsuit against whomever is responsible for the harm or loss (e.g., spammers).

criminal laws
Laws to protect the public, human life, or private property.

An offensive act or omission, such as failing to take reasonable care to prevent the loss of personal data typically violates both criminal law and civil law. Exhibit 17.4 presents a comparison of key characteristics of criminal and civil laws.

statutes
Rules that define criminal laws.

civil laws
Laws that enable a party (individual or organization) that has suffered harm or a loss to bring a lawsuit against whomever is responsible for the harm or loss.

Computer Fraud and Abuse Act (CFAA)

Laws that relate to computer crimes and or Internet abuse, in particular, are amended when changes are warranted. An example is the major computer crime law, the **Computer Fraud and Abuse Act (CFAA)**, which was passed in 1984 and amended several times.

Initially, the scope and intent of CFAA was to protect government computers and financial industry computers from criminal theft by outsiders. In 1986, the CFAA was amended to include stiffer penalties for violations, but it still only protected computers used by the federal government or financial institutions. Then, as the Internet expanded in scope, so did the CFAA. In 1994, there was a significant revision of CFAA that added a civil law component and civil charges to this criminal law. You will learn about the areas of civil law used most extensively by EC companies in the next section.

Computer Fraud and Abuse Act (CFAA)
Major computer crime law to protect government computers and other Internet-connected computers.

EXHIBIT 17.4   Differences Between Criminal and Civil Laws

Characteristics	Criminal Law	Civil Law
Objective	To protect society's interests by defining offenses against the public	To provide an injured private party the opportunity to bring a lawsuit for the injury
Purpose	To deter crime and punish criminals	To deter injuries and compensate the injured party
Wrongful act	It violates a statute	It causes harm or loss to an individual, group of people, or legal entity (e.g., organization)
Who brings charges against an offender	A local, state, or federal government body	A private party, which may be a person, company, or group of people, as in a class-action lawsuit
Deals with	Criminal violations	Noncriminal harm or loss
Burden of proof	Beyond a reasonable doubt	Preponderance of the evidence
Principal types of penalties or punishment	Capital punishment, fines, or imprisonment	Monetary damages paid to victims or some equitable relief

Section 17.1 ▶ REVIEW QUESTIONS

1. Define *ethics, criminal law, civil law,* and *common (case) law.*
2. Give an example of each of an online violation of ethics, criminal law, civil law, and common law.
3. List major EC ethical issues (consult Online File W17.1).
4. Explain why amendments to the CFAA were needed.

17.2 CIVIL LAW, INTELLECTUAL PROPERTY LAW, AND COMMON LAW

The legal system is faced with the task of maintaining a delicate balance between preserving social order and protecting individual rights. Keep in mind that the term *individual* when used in law is broadly defined to mean a person, group of people, or other legal entity such as an organization. In this section, we explain the various types of laws.

CIVIL LAW

Civil law deals with noncriminal injuries. Civil law gives an injured party the opportunity to bring a lawsuit (a civil charge) against a violator to get compensated for the injury or harm caused by the violator. Certain conditions must be met for a lawsuit to proceed. For example, to sue for breach of contract, there must be proof that the party failed to perform any term of the contract without a legitimate legal excuse. Lawsuits also serve to warn and deter others from similar violations, particularly violations of intellectual property law.

INTELLECTUAL PROPERTY LAW

Intellectual property law is the area of the law that includes patent law, copyright law, trademark law and trade secret law and other branches of the law, such as licensing and unfair competition.

Another perspective is that intellectual property law is concerned with the legal regulation of mental products, including creativity. It affects such diverse subjects as the visual and performing arts, electronic databases, advertising, and video games. Creativity is an integral part of the entire business world, as is the protection of innovation. Visit Online File W17.3 for intellectual property Web sites.

EXHIBIT 17.5 Intellectual Property Laws and Their Protections

Laws	Protection Provided by the Law
Intellectual property law	Protects creations of the human mind.
Patent law	Protects inventions and discoveries.
Copyright law	Protects original works of authorship, such as music and literary works, and computer programs.
Trademark law	Protects brand names and other symbols that indicate the source of goods and services.
Trade secret law	Protects confidential business information.
Law of licensing	Enables owners of patents, trademarks, copyrights, and trade secrets to share them with others on a mutually agreed upon basis.
Law of unfair competition dealing with counterfeiting and piracy	Protects against those who try to take a free ride on the efforts and achievements of creative people.

There are various intellectual property law specialties, as shown in Exhibit 17.5. Those specialty laws are related and may even overlap.

Copyright

Numerous high-profile lawsuits have been filed for copyright infringement. A **copyright** is an exclusive right of the author or creator of a book, movie, musical composition, or other artistic property to print, copy, sell, license, distribute, transform to another medium, translate, record, perform, or otherwise use. In the United States, as soon as a work is created and in a tangible form such as through writing or recording, the work automatically has federal copyright protection. A copyright does not last forever; it is good for a fixed number of years after the death of the author or creator (e.g., 50 in the United Kingdom). In the United States, copyright was extended to 70 years after the death of the author by the *1998 Sonny Bono Copyright Extension Act*. After the copyright expires, the work reverts to the public domain. The legal term for the use of the work without permission or contracting for payment of a royalty is **infringement**.

To protect its interests, the Recording Industry Association of America (RIAA), the recording industry's trade group, uses lawsuits to stamp out rampant music piracy on university campuses. RIAA launched a lawsuit-settlement Web site, p2plawsuits.com and sent a mass mailing to college and university presidents across the United States asking for their cooperation in its ongoing war against file sharing. RIAA sought compensation from university students for losses that it alleged were caused by copyright infringement. In February 2007, RIAA announced that it would give 400 college students at 13 universities suspected of illegally pirating music online the option to reach discounted settlements before being sued for greater damages for copyright infringement. According to Mitch Bainwol, RIAA chairman and CEO, "theft of music remains unacceptably high and undermines the industry's ability to invest in new music" (Veiga 2007). Judges' decisions on legal cases, such as this one, can have an immediate and long-lasting impact because they become common law.

Universal Music Group, the world's largest music company, filed a lawsuit against MySpace for copyright infringement of thousands of artists' work (Reuters 2007). French media-giant Vivendi owns Universal. It filed the lawsuit at the U.S. District Court of California. Universal estimated maximum damages for each copyrighted work at $150,000. YouTube avoided a similar lawsuit by reaching a licensing agreement with Universal Music.

The entertainment industry, led primarily by the Motion Picture Association of America (MPAA) and the RIAA, is also attempting technical solutions via the legal system to protect its interests. It is actively pursuing digital rights management policy initiatives through federal legislation and the courts.

copyright
An exclusive right of the author or creator of a book, movie, musical composition or other artistic property to print, copy, sell, license, distribute, transform to another medium, translate, record, perform, or otherwise use.

infringement
Use of the work without permission or contracting for payment of a royalty.

Digital Rights Management (DRM)

digital rights management (DRM)
An umbrella term for any of several arrangements that allow a vendor of content in electronic form to control the material and restrict its usage.

Digital rights management (DRM) is an umbrella term for any of several arrangements that allow a vendor of content in electronic form to control the material and restrict its usage. These arrangements are really technology-based protection measures. Typically, the content is a copyrighted digital work to which the vendor holds rights.

In the past, when content was analog in nature, it was easier to buy a new copy of a copyrighted work on a physical medium (e.g., paper, film, tape) than to produce such a copy independently. The quality of most copies often was inferior. Digital technologies make it possible to produce a high-quality duplicate of any digital recording with minimal effort. The Internet virtually has eliminated the need for a physical medium to transfer a work, which has led to the use of DRM systems for protection.

fair use
The legal use of copyrighted material for noncommercial purposes without paying royalties or getting permission.

However, DRM systems may restrict the *fair use* of material by individuals. In law, **fair use** refers to the use of copyrighted material for noncommercial purposes. Several DRM technologies were developed without regard for privacy protection. Many systems require the user to reveal his or her identity and rights to access protected content. Upon authentication of identity and rights to the content, the user can access the content (see epic.org/privacy/drm).

Patents

patent
A document that grants the holder exclusive rights to an invention for a fixed number of years.

A **patent** is a document that grants the holder exclusive rights to an invention for a fixed number of years (e.g., 17 years in the United States and 20 years in the United Kingdom). Patents serve to protect tangible technological inventions, especially in traditional industrial areas. They are not designed to protect artistic or literary creativity. Patents confer monopoly rights to an idea or an invention, regardless of how it may be expressed. An invention may be in the form of a physical device or a method or process for making a physical device. Similar to a patent is a **trademark**, which is a symbol businesses use to identify their goods and services; government registration of the trademark confers exclusive legal right to its use.

trademark
A symbol used by businesses to identify their goods and services; government registration of the trademark confers exclusive legal right to its use.

Certain patents granted in the United States deviate from established practices in Europe. For example, Amazon.com successfully obtained a U.S. patent on its *1-Click* ordering procedure. Using this patent, Amazon.com sued Barnes & Noble in 1999 and in 2000, alleging that its rival had copied its patented technology. Barnes & Noble was enjoined by the courts from using the procedure. Similarly, in 1999, Priceline.com filed a suit against Expedia.com alleging that Expedia was using Priceline's patented reverse-auction business model. The suit was settled in 2001 when Expedia.com agreed to pay Priceline.com royalties for use of the model. However, in Europe and many Asian, African, and South American countries, it is almost impossible to obtain patents on business methods or computer processes.

COMMON LAW

Despite what seems like an endless number of criminal and civil laws, statutes do not cover all situations. When statutes do not cover certain situations, judges create laws through their court decisions. Judges' court decisions set precedents and become **common law** or **case law**. Even though common laws do not have a statutory basis, when judges create laws through written opinions, they become binding on future decisions of lower courts—that is, until new common laws or precedents are set.

common law (case law)
Law created by judges in court decisions.

Laws primarily relating to property, contracts, and torts typically are part of the common law. A **tort** is a civil wrong that can be grounds for a lawsuit. The main types of torts are negligence, nuisance, and defamation. Exhibit 17.6 explains these three types of torts, and examples are listed below.

tort
Civil wrong that can be grounds for a lawsuit.

Example of the three types of torts are:

▶ **Negligence**. ChoicePoint was charged with multiple counts of negligence for failing to follow *reasonable* information security practices that resulted in the compromise of the personal and financial information of 145,000 individuals.

▶ **Nuisance**. Universal Tube & Rollform Equipment, a company with the domain name *uTube.com* since 1996, filed a lawsuit against YouTube Inc. for illegal acts that resulted in the direction of millions of nuisance Internet visitors to the *uTube* Web site. According to the lawsuit, due to confusion in the minds of consumers, the spillover of nuisance

EXHIBIT 17.6 Common Types of Torts in E-Commerce

Torts	Definitions	Examples
Negligence	The failure to exercise reasonable care toward others, or taking action that results in an accident that causes physical or property damage. Not practicing the standard of due care can be considered negligence.	ChoicePoint was charged with multiple counts of negligence for failing to follow *reasonable* information security practices that resulted in the compromise of the personal and financial information of 145,000 individuals.
Nuisance	The unreasonable, unwarranted, or unlawful use of property that causes inconvenience or damage to others, either to individuals or the general public.	Universal Tube and Rollform Equipment, a company with the domain name *uTube* since 1996, filed a lawsuit against YouTube Inc. for illegal acts that resulted in the direction of millions of nuisance internet visitors to the *uTube* Web site. According to the lawsuit, due to confusion in the minds of consumers, the spillover of nuisance traffic to *utube.com* has destroyed the value of their trademark and Internet property, repeatedly caused the shutdown of their Web site, increased Internet costs by thousands of dollars a month, and damaged the company's good reputation. The full text of the complaint is available at *pub.bna.com/eclr/062628.pdf*
Defamation	Making an untrue statement (expressly stated or implied to be factual) about a person, company, or product that damages their reputation. If the defamatory statement is printed or broadcast over the media, it is **libel**, If the statement is oral (or transitory), it is **slander**.	The first British internet libel case, *Keith-Smith v. Williams* (2006) resulted in the successful prosecution of an individual poster in a chat room. The case involved an ex-teacher, Tracy Williams, who had falsely accused Michael Keith Smith of being a sexual offender and racist bigot. The court ordered her to pay £10,000 plus costs. The accusations were made in a Yahoo! discussion group with about 100 members, but damages were awarded based on the remarks being available through out the world. For further reading, see *lv19.org/article.htm*.

traffic to *uTube.com* has destroyed the value of their trademark and Internet property, repeatedly caused the shut down of their Web site, increased Internet costs by thousands of dollars a month, and damaged the company's good reputation. The full text of the complaint is available at pub.bna.com/eclr/062628.pdf.

▶ **Defamation.** The first British Internet libel case, *Keith-Smith v. Williams* (2006) resulted in the successful prosecution of an individual poster in a chat room. The case involved an ex-teacher, Tracy Williams, who had falsely accused Michael Keith Smith of being a sexual offender and racist bigot. The court ordered her to pay £10,000 plus costs. The accusations were made in a Yahoo! discussion group with about 100 members, but damages were awarded based on the remarks' being available worldwide. For further reading, see lvl9.org/article.htm.

libel
Defamatory statement that is printed or broadcast over the media that causes damage.

slander
Oral or spoken defamatory statement that causes damage.

Section 17.2 ▶ REVIEW QUESTIONS
1. What are the purposes of a lawsuit?
2. What is common law? How does it differ from criminal and civil law?
3. Define *DRM*. Describe one potential impact on privacy.

4. What is meant by *fair use*?

5. List the legal rights of a copyright owner.

6. Define *tort* and explain three types of torts.

17.3 LEGAL AND ETHICAL CHALLENGES AND GUIDELINES

Business ethics defines how a company integrates the core values of honesty, trust, respect, and fairness into its policies and practices—and complies with legal standards and regulations. The scope of business ethics has expanded to encompass a company's actions with regard not only to how it treats employees and obeys laws but to the nature and quality of the relationships with shareholders, customers, business partners, suppliers, the community, environment, and future generations. European companies especially have embraced this expanded definition of ethics. Under recent clarifications of the U.S. Federal Sentencing Guidelines (ussc.gov/guidelin.htm), companies with credible ethics programs, as opposed to merely *paper* programs such as that of Enron, may reduce penalties or avoid prosecution for crimes committed by managers or employees.

Because of the worldwide scope and universal accessibility of the Internet, there are serious questions as to which ethical rules and laws apply. These questions involve an appreciation of the law that is constantly changing. Lawsuits and criminal charges are very disruptive, expensive, and may damage customer relations. The best strategy is to avoid behaviors that expose the company to these types of risk.

Business people engaging in e-commerce need guidelines as to what behaviors are reasonable and what risks are foreseeable under a given set of circumstances. Based on what you have read, it is clear that the two major risks are a criminal charge or lawsuit (civil charge). Exhibit 17.7 lists examples of safeguards to minimize exposure to those risks.

EC ETHICAL ISSUES

There are many EC- and Internet-related ethical issues (Palmer 2005; Kracher and Corritore 2004; Petrovic-Lazarevic and Sohal 2004). Examples of ethical issues discussed elsewhere in this book are channel conflict (Chapter 3), pricing conflict (Chapter 3), disintermediation (Chapters 2, 3, and 7), and trust (Chapter 4). Two additional EC-related ethical issues are non–work-related use of the Internet and codes of ethics.

Non–Work-Related Use of the Internet

A majority of employees use e-mail and the Web for non–work-related purposes. The use of company property for e-mail and Internet use creates risk. The degree of risk depends on the extent to which the company has implemented policies and procedure to prevent

EXHIBIT 17.7   Safeguards to Minimize Exposure to Risk of Criminal or Civil Charges

1. Does the Web site clearly post shipment policies and guarantees? Can the company fulfill those policies and guarantees? Does the Web site explain what happens in case of a missed deadline? Does it comply with Federal Trade Commission (FTC) rules?

2. Does the Web site clearly articulate procedures for customers to follow when returning gifts or seeking a refund for services not received?

3. Has the company checked backgrounds before entering agreements with third-party vendors and supply chain partners? Do those agreements with vendors and partners indemnify (i.e., protect) the company against their failure to deliver goods or process transactions on time and correctly?

4. If a third-party ISP or Web-hosting service is used, are there safeguards if the site crashes, is infected by malware, or if bandwidth is insufficient to meet all of your customers' needs?

5. Is there sufficient customer support staff, and are they knowledgeable and adequately trained to process inquiries from customers?

and detect illegal uses. For example, companies may be held liable for their employees' use of e-mail to harass another employee, participate in illegal gambling, or distribute child pornography.

Some employees may use the company e-mail to advertise their own businesses. Using other corporate computing facilities for private purposes may be a problem, too. For example, in some universities 50 percent to 70 percent of Internet use is for entertainment, clogging the systems at times. Last, but not least, is the amount of time employees waste surfing non–work-related Web sites during working hours.

Codes of Ethics

A practical and necessary approach to limiting non–work-related Internet surfing is an Internet acceptable use policy (AUP) that all employees must agree to (Volonino and Robinson 2004). Without a formal AUP, it is much more difficult to enforce acceptable and eliminate unacceptable behaviors and punish violators. Whenever a user signs on to the corporate network, the user should see a reminder of the AUP and be notified that online activities are monitored. Such notification should be a part of a code of ethics.

Corporate *codes of ethics* state the rules and expected behavior and action. Typically, the ethics code should address offensive content and graphics, as well as proprietary information. It should encourage employees to think about who should and who should not have access to information before they post it on the Web site. The code should specify whether the company allows employees to set up their own Web pages on the company intranet and state policies regarding private e-mail usage and non–work-related surfing during working hours. A company should formulate a general idea of the role it wants Web sites to play in the workplace. This should guide the company in developing an AUP and provide employees with a rationale for that policy. Finally, do not be surprised if the code of ethics looks a lot like simple rules of etiquette; it should. Exhibit 17.8 lists several useful guidelines for a corporate Web policy. For a list of Web site quality guidelines, see Online File W17.4 at the book's Web site.

Section 17.3 ▶ REVIEW QUESTIONS

1. What does business ethics define?
2. Give an example of an EC activity that is unethical but not illegal.
3. Identify an employee activity that exposes a company to legal risk.
4. List the major issues a code of ethics should include.

EXHIBIT 17.8   Corporate Web Policy Guidelines

- Issue written AUP guidelines about employee use of the Internet and communication systems including e-mail and instant messaging.
- Make it clear to employees that they cannot use copyrighted or trademarked material without permission.
- Post disclaimers concerning content, such as sample code, that the company does not support.
- Post disclaimers of responsibility concerning content of online forums and chat sessions.
- Make sure that Web content and activity comply with the laws in other countries, such as those governing contests and privacy.
- Make sure that the company's Web content policy is consistent with other company policies.
- Appoint someone to monitor Internet legal and liability issues and have that person report to a senior executive or legal counsel.
- Have attorneys with cyber law expertise review Web content to make sure that there is nothing unethical or illegal on the company's Web site and that all required statements and disclaimers are properly included.

17.4 PRIVACY, FREE SPEECH, AND DEFAMATION

The explosion in communications technologies has created complex new ethical dilemmas for businesses. As transaction costs for processing, storing, and transmitting data dropped dramatically and sophisticated tracking and monitoring software became widespread, concerns rose around online consumer privacy, free speech, and defamation. There is increasing risk of personal privacy invasion from compromising photos that digital cameras or cell phones digitally capture, particularly when they are posted on the Internet (Puentes 2007).

ORIGIN OF PRIVACY RIGHTS AND THE EVOLUTION OF ITS MEANING

Privacy rights also have their roots in common law dating back to 1890 when Samuel Warren and Louis D. Brandeis published the influential *Harvard Law Review* (1890–1891) article, "The Right to Privacy." These legal scholars explained that the scope of the legal *right to life* had broadened to include the right to be left alone; and the term *property* has grown to comprise every form of possession—both intangible and tangible. The article is available at the Louis D. Brandeis School of Law Library (2004) louisville.edu/library/law/brandeis/privacy.html.

Privacy means different things to different people. In general, privacy is the right to be left alone and the right to be free of unreasonable personal intrusions. (For other definitions of privacy, see Privacy Rights Clearinghouse.) Privacy has long been a legal, ethical, and social issue in most countries.

Section 5 of the FTC Act, which prohibits unfair or deceptive practices and gives the FTC (a regulatory agency) authority to take action against companies whose lax security practices could expose the personal financial information of customers to theft or loss, protects privacy. For explanation of the Act, see ftc.gov/privacy/privacyinitiatives/promises.html. Those practices extend to privacy, free speech, and defamation if the company does not fulfill its duty to protect the rights of others.

Today, virtually all U.S. states and the federal government, either by statute or by common law, recognize the right to privacy. The definition of privacy can be interpreted quite broadly. However, the following two rules have been followed fairly closely in past U.S. court decisions: (1) The right of privacy is not absolute. Privacy must be balanced against the needs of society. (2) The public's right to know is superior to the individual's right of privacy. These two rules show why it is sometimes difficult to determine and enforce privacy regulations.

To some extent privacy concerns have been overshadowed by post-September 11 terrorism efforts, but consumers still expect and demand that companies behave as responsible custodians of their personal data. One way to manage this issue is opt-in and opt-out information practices. **Opt out** is a businesses practice that gives consumers the opportunity to refuse to share information about themselves. Offering opt out is good customer service, but it is difficult to opt out in some industries either because consumer demand for opt out is low or the value of the customer information is high. In contrast, **opt in** is based on the principle that information-sharing should not occur unless customers affirmatively allow it or request it.

opt out
Business practice that gives consumers the opportunity to refuse sharing information about themselves.

opt in
Agreement that requires computer users to take specific steps to allow the collection of personal information.

FREE SPEECH

Rights to privacy and free speech have an increasingly important role in an information society and to EC. As with all rights, the right of free speech is not unlimited. Free speech does not mean any speech. Some of the traditional restrictions on what may be freely said or published are defamation laws (see Exhibit 17.6), contempt of court, and national security. For example, it is illegal to scream "fire" in a crowded theatre or make bomb threats in an airport. Laws against libel (making of defamatory statements in a fixed medium such as blogs or Web sites) may be out-of-date now that victims of defamation have the ability to respond via the Internet.

THE PRICE OF PROTECTION

In the past, the complexity of collecting, sorting, filing, and accessing information manually from several different government agencies was a built-in protection against misuse of private information. It was simply too expensive, cumbersome, and complex to invade a person's privacy. The Internet, in combination with large-scale databases, eliminated those barriers.

The inherent power in systems that can access vast amounts of data can be used for the good of society. For example, by matching records with the aid of a computer, it is possible to eliminate or reduce fraud, crime, government mismanagement, tax evasion, welfare fraud, family support thieves employment of illegal aliens, and so on. The question is: What price must every individual pay in terms of loss of privacy so that the government can better apprehend these types of criminals? Case 17.1 illustrates the conflict between protection and privacy.

CASE 17.1
EC Application
PROTECTION PITTED AGAINST PRIVACY

In February 2007, Republican Congressman Lamar Smith introduced the bill called *Stopping Adults Facilitating the Exploitation of Today's Youth Act* (SAFETY). As the name implies, the purpose of the law would be to combat the exploitation of children (child pornography). SAFETY would require ISPs to monitor and retain information about users' identities and their online activities. At a minimum, SAFETY would require retention of the name and address of the subscriber or registered user to whom an IP address, user identification, or telephone number was assigned. The law would also require Web labeling by owners of sexually explicit Web sites, which would have to post warning labels on their pages or face imprisonment.

Because there is no limit on how broad the rules can be (recall the discussion of interpretation of laws), U.S. Attorney General Gonzales would be able to force ISPs to keep logs of Web browsing, instant message exchanges, and e-mail conversations indefinitely. SAFETY's broad wording also would permit private litigants to obtain records in civil cases, such as divorces and employment disputes. That raises additional privacy concerns, civil libertarians say.

Privacy advocates and Internet industry groups oppose the law. They cite numerous data breaches, concerns about government surveillance, and monitoring of employees in the workplace as reasons against the law. Employees of any ISP who failed to store that information would face fines and prison terms of up to one year, the bill says. The U.S. Justice Department could order the companies to store those records forever.

Supporters of the proposal focus on protection. They state that it is necessary to help track criminals because if police cannot respond immediately to reports of illegal activity, Internet providers could delete relevant logs. They cite cases of child molestation. To rebut, industry representatives said there was no evidence that ISPs had dragged their feet when responding to subpoenas from law enforcement.

Typically, ISPs discard log files that are no longer required for business reasons, such as network monitoring,

fraud prevention, or customer billing disputes. But when contacted by law enforcement, ISPs preserve the data. Currently the *Electronic Communication Transactional Records Act of 1996* regulates data preservation. It requires ISPs to retain any record in their possession for 90 days "upon the request of a governmental entity."

ISPs must comply with a federal law to report child pornography sightings to the *National Center for Missing and Exploited Children*, which forwards that report to the appropriate police agency.

When adopting its data retention rules, the European Parliament approved the requirement that communications providers in its 25 member countries, even those that had already enacted their own data retention laws, retain customer data for a minimum of six months and a maximum of two years. This Europe-wide requirement, which may take effect in 2008, applies to a broad range of *traffic* and *location* data, including the identities of the customers' correspondents; the date, time, and duration of phone calls, VoIP calls, or e-mail messages; and the location of the device used for the communications. The content of these communications is not supposed to be retained.

Two obstacles to these laws requiring massive data retention practices are identity theft and the cost of implementing and securing such systems.

Sources: Compiled from the Legal Information Institute (2007), Library of Congress (2007), Lemos (2007), and McCullagh (2007).

Questions

1. What are some of the ways in which the SAFETY Act might infringe on an individual's privacy rights?

2. What are some of the key elements in SAFETY?

3. Use a search engine to find recent issues relating to the status of SAFETY.

EXHIBIT 17.9 How to Use the Internet to Find Information

- By reading an individual's blogs or newsgroup postings
- By looking up an individual's name and identity in an Internet directory
- By reading an individual's e-mail, IM, or text messages
- By monitoring and conducting surveillance on employees
- By wiretapping wire-line and wireless communication lines
- By asking an individual to complete a registration form on a Web site
- By recording an individual's actions as they navigate the Web with a browser, usually using cookies
- By using spyware, keystroke loggers, and similar methods

The Internet offers a number of opportunities to collect private information about individuals. Exhibit 17.9 lists several ways that the Internet can be used to find information about an individual.

Of the ways in Exhibit 17.9, the last three are the most common ways of gathering information on the Internet.

Web Site Registration

A joint study by TNS and TRUSTe (2004) found that Internet users were skeptical of the necessity of giving personal information to online businesses. Among the 1,068 participants, 71 percent dislike registering at Web sites they visit, 15 percent refuse to register at all, and 43 percent do not trust companies not to share their personal information.

Virtually all B2C, marketing Web sites, and social networks ask visitors to fill out registration forms. During the process, individuals voluntarily provide their names, addresses, phone numbers, e-mail addresses, hobbies and likes or dislikes, and other personal information to participate, win a lottery, or for some other item of exchange. There are few restraints on the ways in which the site can use this information. The site might use it to improve customer service. Or the site could just as easily sell the information to another company, which could use it in an inappropriate or intrusive manner.

Cookies

Another way that a Web site can gather information about an individual is by using cookies. As described in Chapter 4, a *cookie* contains data that are passed back and forth between a Web site and an end user's browser as the user navigates the site. Cookies enable sites to keep track of users without having to constantly ask the users to identify themselves. Web bugs and spyware, described in Section 4.4, are similar to cookies.

Originally, cookies were designed to help with personalization and market research, as described in Chapter 4. However, cookies also can invade an individual's privacy. Cookies allow Web sites to collect detailed information about a user's preferences, interests, and surfing patterns. The personal profiles created by cookies often are more accurate than self-registration because users have a tendency to falsify information in a registration form.

Although the ethics of the use of cookies are still being debated, concerns about cookies reached a pinnacle in 1997 at the U.S. FTC hearings on online privacy. Following those hearings, Netscape and Microsoft introduced options enabling users to block cookies. Since that time, the uproar has subsided because most users accept cookies rather than fight them. The problem with deleting or disabling cookies is that the user will have to keep reentering information and, in some instances, may be blocked from viewing particular pages.

Spyware and Similar Methods

In Chapter 11 and Online File W11.4, we discussed spyware as a tool that some merchants use to spy on users without their knowledge. Spyware infections are the number one threat to intellectual property, according to 62 percent of corporate IT security professionals according to the "Survey on the Corporate Response to Spyware," a study conducted by the Ponemon Institute (ponemon.org) and sponsored by Mi5 Networks (mi5networks.com) (Burns 2006). Spyware, also referred to as crimeware, is defined in the study as "all unwanted software programs designed to steal proprietary information or that target data stores housing confidential information."

Spyware may enter the user's computer as a virus or as a result of the user's clicking an option in a deceptive pop-up window. Sometimes when users download and install legitimate programs, they get spyware as well. Spyware is very effective in tracking users' Web surfing habits. It can scan computer hard drives for sensitive files and send the results to hackers or spammers. Spyware is clearly a violation of the computer user's privacy. It can also slow down computer performance. Spyware writers are getting more innovative and are trying to avoid detection. For example, *Keystroke Logger* runs in the background of the user's computer and records every keystroke the user makes. A hacker can then steal the user's social security number, bank account number, and password!

Antivirus software and Internet firewalls cannot "see" spyware; special protection is needed. Many free and low-cost antispyware software packages are on the market. Representative free programs are Ad-Aware, Spybot, SpyKiller, and PestPatrol. For-fee programs include SpySubtract, Spy Sweeper, Ad-Aware Plus, and SpyWasher.

The danger of spyware has resulted in quick legislation in the United States. The U.S. House of Representatives passed the Spy Act (H.R. 2929) in October 2004 with 399 votes in favor and 1 opposed. The Act prohibits outside entities from installing or modifying any software or disabling antivirus software without the user's permission or authorization. The California Anti-Spyware Bill (September 2004) bans the unauthorized installation of spyware and allows consumers to sue spyware developers for damages (SB 1436). A major objective of the federal and state legislation is to combat identity theft (see the discussion later in the chapter).

RFID's Threat to Privacy

As mentioned in earlier chapters, privacy advocates fear that the information stored on RFID tags or collected with them may be used to violate an individual's privacy. To protect the individual, RSA Security and others are developing locking technologies that will protect consumers from being tracked after buying products with RFID tags. Several states (e.g., California) are considering legislation to protect customers from a loss of privacy due to the tags.

Privacy of Employees

In addition to customers' privacy, there is the issue of employees' privacy. Many employers monitor their employees' e-mail and Web activities. In addition to wasting time online, employees may disclose trade secrets and possibly make employers liable for defamation based on what they do on the corporate Web site. In response to these concerns, most companies monitor their employees' communications.

Another privacy concern stems from the "underground Internet" consisting of private online communities called **darknets** that are only open to those who belong to the private network. See Online File W17.5 for examples of darknets.

darknets
Private online community that is only open to those who belong to it.

PRIVACY PROTECTION

The ethical principles commonly applied to the collection and use of personal information also apply to information collected in e-commerce. These principles include the following:

▶ **Notice or awareness.** Consumers must be given notice of an entity's information practices prior to the collection of personal information. Consumers must be able to make informed decisions about the type and extent of their disclosures based on the intentions of the party collecting the information.

▶ **Choice or consent.** Consumers must be made aware of their options as to how their personal information may be used, as well as any potential secondary uses of the information. Consent may be granted through opt-out clauses.

CASE 17.2
EC Application

PROPERTY RIGHTS EXTENDED TO DOMAIN NAMES AND DIGITAL PROPERTY

In 2005, Mexican authorities arrested Stephen Cohen when he tried to renew his Mexican work visa and handed him over to U.S. marshals. After a $65 million ruling against him in a California federal court, Cohen, a con man, had hidden outside the United States for six years. Cohen had stolen what was considered the most valuable domain name in the world, sex.com.

After a five-year court battle, Judge James Ware found Cohen guilty of hijacking the sex.com domain name from plaintiff Gary Kremen, the founder of Match.com. Kremen had registered Sex.com in 1994. In 1995, Cohen stole the domain name by defrauding the domain registrar, VeriSign/Network Solutions, Inc. (NSI).

In a separate court case, Kremen filed a lawsuit against NSI for transferring ownership of the Sex.com domain name—property that belonged to Kremen—to Cohen. This unauthorized transfer was obtained using forged letters. NSI had switched domain name registry records without bothering to check the veracity of these documents. In a hearing before a federal appeals court panel in San Francisco, lawyers representing Sex.com argued that NSI, which runs the central database for the dot-com addresses, committed a breach of contract when it failed to verify a forged request to transfer the domain with its owner.

A Ninth Circuit Court of Appeals judge ruled that Gary Kremen had a property right to the stolen domain and that NSI was potentially liable for giving it away without proper authorization.

Internet activists praised the appeal court's ruling in the case, which set an important legal precedent. The court's Sex.com decision provides Internet domain registrants with protection from inappropriate domain name seizures. NSI paid Kremen an out-of-court settlement thought to be worth up to $20 million.

The Sex.com decision is likely to influence legal developments in the handling of intangible (digital) property. The Ninth Circuit's decision is an important step in applying settled principles to this new realm of digital property rights. Some believe that Sex.Com single-handedly caused the courts to define domain names as property and, thus, changed the laws governing the World Wide Web.

Sources: Compiled from Boyle (2005), McCarthy (2005), and Posner (2004).

Questions

1. Why is a domain name considered property?
2. What is the difference between tangible property and intangible property?
3. What precedent was set by the Ninth Circuit Court of Appeals's decision?

▸ **Access or participation.** Consumers must be able to access their personal information and challenge the validity of the data.

▸ **Integrity or security.** Consumers must be assured that their personal data are secure and accurate. It is necessary for those collecting the data to take whatever precautions are required to ensure that they protect data from loss, unauthorized access or alteration, destruction, and fraudulent use, and to take reasonable steps to gain information from reputable and reliable sources. This principle has been extended to digital property, as described in Case 17.2.

▸ **Enforcement or redress.** A method of enforcement and remedy must be available. Otherwise, there is no real deterrent or enforceability for privacy issues.

In the United States, the broadest law in scope is the Communications Privacy and Consumer Empowerment Act (1997), which requires, among other things, that the FTC enforce online privacy rights in EC, including the collection and use of personal data. For existing U.S. federal privacy legislation, see Online File W17.6. For the status of pending legislation in the United States, visit the Center for Democracy and Technology at cdt.org.

THE USA PATRIOT ACT

The USA PATRIOT Act (officially, Uniting and Strengthening America by Providing Appropriate Tools to Intercept and Obstruct Terrorism) was passed in October 2001, in the aftermath of the September 11 terrorist attacks. Its intent is to give law enforcement agencies broader range in their efforts to protect the public. The American Civil Liberties Union

(ACLU), the Electronic Freedom Foundation (EFF), and other organizations have grave concerns, including (1) expanded surveillance with reduced checks and balances, (2) overbreadth with a lack of focus on terrorism, and (3) rules that would allow U.S. foreign intelligence agencies to more easily spy on Americans.

On March 9, 2007, the U.S. Department of Justice (DOJ) said that the FBI had improperly used provisions of the USA Patriot Act to obtain thousands of telephone, business, and financial records without prior judicial approval (Johnson and Lipton 2007). The report is available on the DOJ's Web site at justice.gov/oig/new.htm. The result of this report may restrain some of the parts of the Act that allowed expanded surveillance in the following areas:

- E-mail and Internet searches
- Nationwide roving wiretaps
- Requirement that ISPs hand over more user information
- Expanded scope of surveillance based on new definitions of terrorism
- Government spying on suspected computer trespassers with no need for court order
- Wiretaps for suspected violations of the Computer Fraud and Abuse Act
- Dramatic increases in the scope and penalties of the Computer Fraud and Abuse Act
- General expansion of Foreign Intelligence Surveillance Act (FISA) authority
- Increased information sharing between domestic law enforcement and intelligence
- FISA detours around federal domestic surveillance limitations; domestic surveillance detours around FISA limitations

PRIVACY PROTECTION IN OTHER COUNTRIES

In 1998, the European Union passed a privacy directive (EU Data Protection Directive) reaffirming the principles of personal data protection in the Internet age. Member countries are required to put this directive into effect by introducing new laws or modifying existing laws in their respective countries. The directive aims to regulate the activities of any person or company that controls the collection, storage, processing, or use of personal data on the Internet.

In many countries, the debate continues about the rights of the individual versus the rights of society.

Section 17.4 ▶ REVIEW QUESTIONS

1. Define *privacy*.
2. List some of the ways that the Internet can collect information about individuals.
3. What are cookies and what do they have to do with online privacy?
4. List four common ethical principles related to the gathering of personal information.
5. How has the USA PATRIOT Act expanded the government's reach?

17.5 SPAM, SPLOGS, AND POP-UPS

A blog—a Web site or Web page that displays journal-like entries—often contains genuine (nondeceitful) links to other pages, images, music, or videos. Hosted on Web sites such as MySpace, they offer a way for users to keep in touch with each other and share and watch music and videos. In contrast, a splog is a blog-style site consisting of nonsense words or content.

Spam, splogs, and other scams damage online businesses. Dubious businesses promote their Web sites by using tactics to improve their search engine rankings. Referring to these problems, David Sifry, chief executive of Technorati, a search engine that indexes blogs, warned: "The first thing to recognise is that every healthy ecosystem has its parasites" (Rigby 2006).

SPAM AND SPLOGS

Just as with e-mail spam, unsolicited advertising (splogs) affects blogs. The growth of splogs parallels the growth of blogs—both are now too numerous to count. These bogus blog sites contain nothing but gibberish and advertisements. However, that gibberish is full of keywords carefully selected to capture users of search engines. In effect, it is an unethical (possibly illegal) application of SEM, which was discussed in this chapter's opening scenario.

Sploggers work on the principle that once Web surfers arrive at their site, a few will click on one of the linked advertisements. Each of these clicks earns a few cents for the splogger. And because any one splogger can run thousands of splogs, the scam can be very profitable. One splog partnership claimed $71,136.89 in earnings in the three months from August to October 2005 (*Wilson Quarterly* 2006).

Trackback

trackback
An acknowledgment or signal from an originating site to a receiving site.

Abusive tactics include the misuse of trackbacks. A **trackback** is simply an acknowledgment or signal from an originating site to a receiving site. For example, when an advertisement link is clicked on another's Web page, the advertiser receives a signal of that click. The trackback feature is abused when spammers insert their links without authority on legitimate blogs. Spammers do this to make money when visitors to the blog unwittingly click the link. This is similar to comment spam (a type of blog spam), except that it avoids some of the safeguards designed to stop that practice. For an illustration of how trackback works, see cruftbox.com/cruft/docs/trackback.html. While many blogs allow readers to comment on their entries, unscrupulous individuals can use software to generate comments automatically.

As a defense against abusive trackback tactics, trackback spam filters (similar to those fighting against comment spam) have been implemented in blog publishing systems. Because filtering may be ineffective, many blogs have stopped using trackbacks because dealing with spam is too burdensome. The persistent problem with spam-blocking software is that spammers find ways to circumvent the programs.

Automated Spam

Captcha tool
Completely Automated Public Turing test to tell Computers and Humans Apart, which uses a verification test on comment pages to stop scripts from posting automatically.

Bloggers have found hundreds of automatically generated comments with links to herbal Viagra and gambling vendors on their pages. Software bots that trawl the Internet looking for suitable forms to fill in automatically generate the majority of blog spam. Blog owners can use tools to ensure that humans—and not an automated system—enter comments on their blogs. Blog owners can also use a **Captcha tool** (Completely Automated Public Turing test to tell Computers and Humans Apart), which uses a verification test on comment pages to stop scripts from posting automatically. These tests may require the person to enter sequences of random characters, which automated systems (software scripts) cannot read.

Another potential effective measure against blog spam and other undesirable content is to only allow comments posted on the blog to be made public after they have been checked. But like the fight against e-mail spam, it is a constant battle in which the spammers seem to have the advantage. Sometimes the only solution to comment spam is for users to turn off their comments function. For more information, see the CAUCE's Web site (cauce.org). Exhibit 17.10 shows an example of how a spam blocker works.

Even with tools such as Captcha turned on, it is risky to simply allow comments to go unchecked. Blog owners may be held responsible for anything illegal or defamatory posted on their blogs. As you've learned, owners could be sued for damages or face criminal charges in court for libel.

PROTECTING AGAINST POP-UP ADS

As discussed in Chapter 4, use of pop-ups and similar advertising programs is exploding. Sometimes it is even difficult to close these ads when they appear on the screen. Some of these ads may be part of a consumer's permission marketing agreement, but most are unsolicited. What can a user do about unsolicited pop-up ads? The following tools help stop pop-ups.

Tools for Stopping Pop-Ups

One way to avoid the potential danger lurking behind pop-up ads is to install software that will block pop-up ads and prevent them from appearing in the first place. Several software packages offer pop-up stoppers. Some are free (e.g., panicware.com and adscleaner.com);

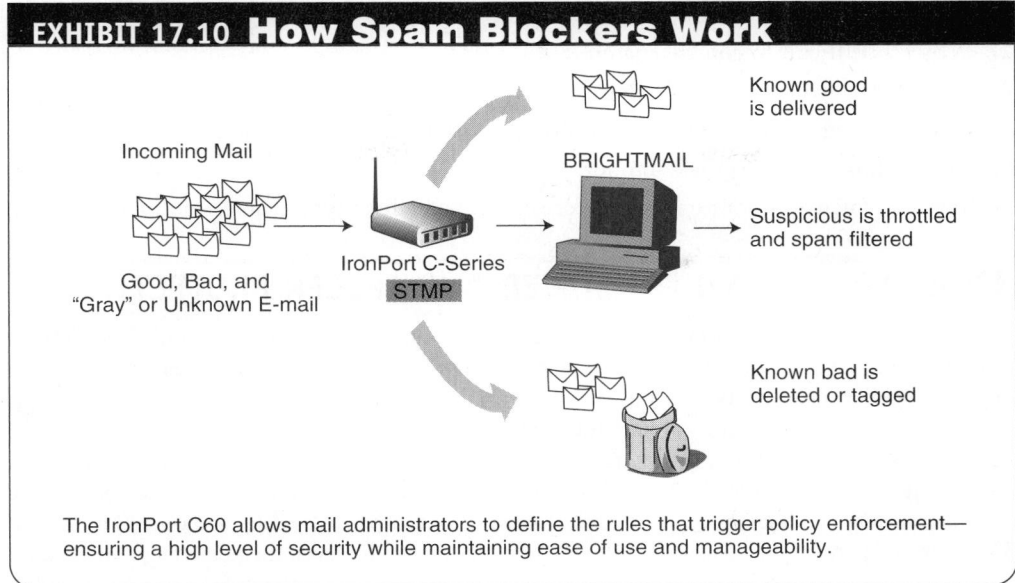

EXHIBIT 17.10 How Spam Blockers Work

The IronPort C60 allows mail administrators to define the rules that trigger policy enforcement—ensuring a high level of security while maintaining ease of use and manageability.

Source: Ironport.com. "Charter Get Hooked: Ironport Understands ISPs." Ironport.com 2004. **ronport.com/pdf/ironport_charter_communications_case_study.pdf** (accessed January 2005).

others are available for a fee. For a list of pop-up blocking software, visit snapfiles.com/ Freeware/misctools/fwpopblock.html and netsecurity.about.com/od/popupadblocking/a/ aafreepopup.htm.

Many ISPs offer tools to stop pop-ups from appearing. The Mozilla and Firefox Web browsers do not allow pop-ups. Even the Google Toolbar will block pop-up ads. Microsoft added pop-up blocking to its Internet Explorer browser with Windows XP Service Pack 2.

However, adware or software that gets bundled with other popular applications like Kazaa, is able to deliver the pop-up ads because they originate from the desktop, not the browser, and blocking tools do not govern them.

Like spam, pop-ups have mutated to in-pages ads, called overlays or floater ads. These ads float over a Web page to catch people's attention before reading requested content. Visitors typically cannot manipulate the ads like they can a pop-up by minimizing the window or clicking the exit button. Floating ads may remain on the page until they disappear or until the visitor leaves the page. Pop-up blockers like Google's or Yahoo!'s cannot prevent them because they use a different command.

FAN AND HATE SITES

Fan and hate Web sites are part of the Internet self-publishing phenomenon that includes blogging (see Chapters 8 and 18). Fan sites may violate intellectual property rights. For example, some people get advanced copies of new movies or TV programs or create sites that compete with the formal sites of the movie or TV producer. Although the producers can get a court order to close such sites, new sites can appear the next day. Although the intention of the fans may be good, they may cause damage to the creators of the intellectual property.

Hate Web sites can cause problems for corporations as well. Many hate sites are directed against large corporations (e.g., Wal-Mart, Microsoft, Nike). Associated with hate sites is the idea of **cyberbashing**, which is the registration of a domain name that criticizes an organization or person (e.g., paypalsucks.com, kbhomessucks.com, walmart-blows.com, or even ms-eradication.org). As long as these Web sites contain legitimate complaints that aren't libelous, defaming in character, sponsored by competitors, or infringing upon trademark rights by confusing consumers, they probably fall within the protections of the First Amendment.

Material published on fan sites, hate sites, and newsgroups may violate the copyrights of the creators or distributors of intellectual property. This issue is another example of the conflict between protection of intellectual property and free speech, as discussed in Section 17.4.

cyberbashing
Domain name that criticizes an organization or person.

Section 17.5 ▶ REVIEW QUESTIONS

1. Why is it difficult to control spamming?
2. Why is it difficult to control splogs?
3. How can blog owners protect themselves against automatically generated comments?
4. Explain how sploggers make money.
5. Identify which types of pop-ups you can block and which types you cannot. Explain why.

17.6 FRAUD AND CONSUMER AND SELLER PROTECTION

An environment where buyers and sellers cannot see each other breeds fraud. Recall from Chapter 11 that fraud is any business activity that uses deceitful practices or devices to deprive another of property or other rights.

Fraud is still a problem for online retailers. Even though actual losses are rising, the rate of those losses is flattening out. In other words, the threat actually may be lessening—somewhat. According to the "Eighth Annual Online Fraud Report," released by CyberSource (cybersource.com), losses from online fraud in the United States and Canada in 2006 totaled $3 billion, a 7 percent increase over 2005 (eMarketer 2007). However, the percentage of revenues lost to fraud dropped to 1.4 percent in 2006, down from 1.6 percent the year before. Since 2004, the percentage rate of revenue loss has declined. Since e-commerce sales continue to grow by about 20 percent a year, the overall dollar-loss amount showed a rise.

Online merchants reject roughly 4 percent of incoming orders because of suspicion of fraud. An estimated 1 percent of accepted orders turn out to be fraudulent. Among online merchants that accepted orders from outside the United States and Canada in 2006, those orders made up 17 percent of their total order volume. Of those, 2.7 percent of the orders were fraudulent. That rate is 2.5 times higher than the rate associated with orders from the United States and Canada.

Tools enable online merchants to estimate the risk of orders based on information gathered from the screen. For example, CyberSource's Internet Fraud Screen (IFS) enables merchants to set the level of risk (threshold) that they are willing to accept in an order. IFS assigns a risk score to each transaction. Transactions whose scores fall below the risk threshold are declined.

During the first few years of EC, many types of crime came to light, ranging from the online manipulation of stock prices to the creation of a virtual bank that disappeared together with the investors' deposits. This section is divided into the following parts: Internet fraud, consumer protection (including automatic authentication), and seller protection.

FRAUD ON THE INTERNET

Internet fraud has grown even faster than the Internet itself. Insights and Additions 17.1 presents some examples of fraud. The following examples demonstrate the scope of the problem. Also visit the Open Directory Project at dmoz.org/Society/Issues/Fraud/Internet/ for a comprehensive set of fraud resources.

Insights and Additions 17.1 Typical Fraud Schemes

The following are typical online fraud attempts:

▶ When one of the authors advertised online that he had a house to rent, several "doctors" and "nurses" from the United Kingdom and South America applied. They agreed to pay a premium for a short-term lease and said they would pay with a cashier's check. They asked if the author would accept checks for $6,000 to $10,000 and send them back the balance of $4,000 to $8,000. When advised that this would be fine, but that the difference would be returned only after the checks had cleared, none of the would-be renters followed up.

(continued)

Insights and Additions 17.1 (*continued*)

▶ Phishing uses spam e-mails or pop-up messages to deceive victims into disclosing credit card numbers, bank account information, Social Security numbers, passwords, or other sensitive information. Typically, the e-mail or pop-up message claims to be from a business or organization that the recipient may deal with; for example, an ISP, bank, online payment service, or even a government agency.

▶ Extortion rings in the United Kingdom and Russia pried hundreds of thousands of dollars from online sports betting Web sites. Any site refusing to pay protection fees was threatened with Zombie computers using DoS attacks (see Chapter 11).

▶ Fake escrow sites take advantage of the inherent trust of escrow sites, stealing buyers' deposits. Dozens of fake escrow sites on the Internet have convincing names like Honest-Escrow.net and use ads such as: "Worried about getting scammed in an Internet auction? Just use an escrow service like us."

▶ Click fraud is a common concern for advertisers and search vendors alike. **Click fraud** scams and deceptions inflate advertising bills for thousands of companies of all sizes. The spreading scourge poses the single biggest threat to online advertising. It is perpetrated in both automated and human ways. The most common method is the use of online robots, or bots, programmed to click on advertisers' links that are displayed on Web sites or listed in search queries. Because advertisers pay fees based on number of clicks, bogus clicks inflate those fees. Google claims to be well-equipped to handle the dilemma. They state, "Our Click Quality team investigates every inquiry we receive from advertisers who believe they may have been affected by undetected click fraud. Many of these cases are misunderstandings, but in most cases where malicious activity is found, the clicks have already been filtered out (and not charged for) by our real-time filters" (Reprise Media 2007).

Other Financial Fraud

Stock fraud, as discussed in Case 17.3, is only one of many areas where swindlers are active. Other areas include the sale of bogus investments, phantom business opportunities, and other schemes. In addition, foreign-currency-trading scams are increasing on the Internet because most online currency-exchange shops are not licensed.

click fraud
Scams and deceptions that inflate advertising bills.

OTHER LEGAL ISSUES

Exhibit 17.11 (p. 795) summarizes some of these EC legal issues. We will discuss a few of them here.

Electronic Contracts

A legally binding contract requires a few basic elements: an offer, acceptance, and consideration. However, these requirements are difficult to establish when the human element in the processing of the transaction is removed and the contracting is performed electronically. For example, Web site development agreements can be very complex. For software-supported B2B trading contracts, see Chapter 5.

Electronic (Digital) Signatures

One method to help distinguish between legitimate and fraud transactions is electronic signatures. Electronic signature legislation is designed to accomplish two goals: (1) to remove barriers to e-commerce and (2) to enable and promote the desirable public policy goal of e-commerce by helping to build trust and predictability needed by parties doing business online.

Electronic signature is a generic, technology-neutral term that refers to the various methods by which one can "sign" an electronic record. Although all electronic signatures are represented digitally (i.e., as a series of ones and zeroes), many different technologies can create them. Examples of electronic signatures include: a name typed at the end of an e-mail message by the sender; a digitized image of a handwritten signature attached to an electronic document; a secret code or PIN to identify the sender to the recipient; a code or "handle" that the sender of a message uses to identify himself; a unique biometrics-based identifier, such as a fingerprint or a retinal scan; and a digital signature created through the use of public key cryptography (see Chapter 11).

electronic signature
A generic, technology-neutral term that refers to the various methods by which one can "sign" an electronic record.

CASE 17.3
EC Application
INTERNET STOCK FRAUD

There are two reasons spam won't go away: It works and it's profitable. A 2006 study by Purdue University assistant professor of finance Laura Frieder and law professor Jonathan Zittrain from Oxford University's Internet Institute concluded that stock spam moves markets. The researchers found that the average investor who buys a stock during a spam promotion (campaign) and then sells after the campaign ends loses about 5.5 percent of their investment. In contrast, the spammer who buys stock *before* the spam campaign and sells during the campaign makes a 5.79 percent return.

The federal government made headlines on March 8, 2007, by cracking down on dozens of penny stocks whose prices spam e-mailers had manipulated. The success of the Securities and Exchange Commission's (SEC) *Operation Spamalot* still will not end spam. Despite increased enforcement, warnings, and federal laws, spam is not only continuing but flourishing. And there's no reason to think the SEC will be able to do anything to stop it.

Stock spam has gotten much worse in the last few years. Stock spam messages rose 120 percent during the six-month period ending March 2007 (Lerer 2007). In total, stock-related messages make up about 20 percent of all e-mail spam. The SEC estimates that 100 million stock spam messages are sent each week.

Technology has increased spammers' ability to send junk e-mail. Spammers used to have to send all their messages from one computer, making them easily blocked by spam filters. Today, spammers send their messages through botnets (linked networks of computers) that they control. With the extra bandwidth, they are sending billions of messages with promotional text embedded in image files—called *image spam*. Image spam looks identical to normal spam but sneaks by antispam programs that look only at text, not pictures or photos.

During 2006, global spam volume had tripled. During a six week period, Secure Computing Research had seen an increase of 50 percent in spam. Spam now accounts for nearly 90 percent of all e-mail. In that same time, there has also been a tripling in the amount of spam that is image spam, which today accounts for 30 percent of all spam.

Sources: Compiled from Lerer (2007) and *SecureComputing.com* (2007).

Questions

1. Speculate why people might buy the penny stocks promoted in an e-mail message from an unknown source?

2. Use the Internet to find what can be done to filter image spam.

---

digital signature
Term for a technology-specific type of electronic signature. It involves the use of public key cryptography to "sign" a message.

Digital signature is a term for a technology-specific type of electronic signature. It involves the use of public key cryptography to "sign" a message. Digital signatures have generated the most business and technical efforts, as well as legislative responses.

A signature, whether electronic or on paper, is a symbol that signifies intent to be bound to the terms of the contract or transaction. Thus, the definition of *signed* in the Uniform Commercial Code includes "any symbol" so long as it is "executed or adopted by a party with present intention to authenticate a writing."

Other Type of EC Fraud

Many nonfinancial types of fraud also exist on the Internet. For example, customers may receive poor-quality products and services, may not get products in time, may be asked to pay for things they assume sellers will pay for, and much more. For typical schemes, see ftc.gov.

Buyers can protect against EC fraud in several ways. We describe the major methods next.

CONSUMER PROTECTION

Consumer protection is critical to the success of any commerce, especially electronic, where buyers do not see sellers. The FTC enforces consumer protection laws in the United States (see ftc.gov). The FTC provides a list of 10 scams that are most likely to arrive by bulk e-mail (see onguardonline.gov/spam.html). In addition, the European Union and the United States are attempting to develop joint consumer protection policies. For details, see the TransAtlantic Consumer Dialogue Web site at tacd.org/about/about.htm.

Tips for safe electronic shopping include the following:

⏵ Users should make sure that they enter the real Web site of well-known companies, such as Wal-Mart, Disney, and Amazon.com, by going directly to the site, rather than through a link, and should shop for reliable brand names at those sites.

EXHIBIT 17.11 Summary of Important EC Legal Issues

Issue	Description
E-filings in court	Litigation means a large quantity of paper. Some courts allow electronic filing of such documents.
Evidence, electronic evidence (e-evidence)	Some electronic documents can be used as evidence in court. The State of New York, for example, allows e-mails to be used as evidence. For an overview of electronic evidence, see Volonino et al (2007).
Jurisdiction	Ability to sue in other states or countries: Whose jurisdiction prevails when litigants are in different states or countries? Who can sue for Internet postings done in other countries?
Liability	The use of multiple networks and trading partners makes the documentation of responsibility difficult. How can liability for errors, malfunctions, or fraudulent use of data be determined?
Defamation	Is the ISP liable for material published on the Internet because of services they provide or support? (Usually not.) Who else is liable for defamation? What if the publisher is in another country?
Identity fraud	The Identity, Theft, and Assumption Deterrence Act of 1998 makes identity fraud a federal felony carrying a 3- to 25-year prison sentence.
Computer crime	The Information Infrastructure Protection Act (IIP Act, 1996) protects information in all computers.
Digital signature	Digital signatures are recognized as legal in the United States and some other countries, but not in all countries (see Chapter 11).
Regulation of consumer databases	The United States allows the compilation and sale of customer databases; the European Union Directive on Data Protection prohibits this practice.
Encryption technology	Export of U.S. encryption technology was made legal in 1999. (Countries still restricted from export are Iran, Syria, Sudan, North Korea, and Cuba.)
Time and place	An electronic document signed in Japan on January 5 may have the date January 4 in Los Angeles. Which date is considered legal if disputes arise?
Location of files and data	Much of the law hinges on the physical location of files and data. With distributed and replicated databases, it is difficult to say exactly where data are stored at any given time.
Electronic contracts	If all the elements to establish a contract are present, an electronic contract is valid and enforceable.
E-communications privacy	The Electronic Communications Privacy Act (ECPA) of 1986 makes it illegal to access stored e-mail or e-mail in transmission.
IPOs online	Web sites with the necessary information on securities offerings are considered a legal channel for selling stock in a corporation.
Antitrust	*U.S. DOJ v. Microsoft* found that (1) Microsoft used predatory and anticompetitive conduct to illegally maintain the monopoly in Windows OS; (2) Microsoft illegally attempted to monopolize the market for Internet browsing software; and (3) Microsoft illegally bundled its Web browser with Windows OS, engaging in a tying arrangement in violation of the Sherman Act.
Taxation	Taxation of sales transactions by states is on hold in the United States and some (not all) countries, but the issue will be revived.
Money laundering	How can money laundering be prevented when the value of the money is in the form of a smart card?

Sources: Compiled from Cheeseman (2004), *FTC.gov*, Volonino et al (2007), and Volonino and Robinson (2004).

▶ Check any unfamiliar site for an address and telephone and fax numbers. Call and quiz a salesperson about the seller.

▶ Check out the seller with the local chamber of commerce, Better Business Bureau (bbbonline.org), or TRUSTe.

▶ Investigate how secure the seller's site is and how well it is organized.

▶ Examine the money-back guarantees, warranties, and service agreements before making a purchase.

Insights and Additions 17.2 Resources for Further Information

The following are useful sources of information on the rights of Internet shoppers:

▶ The FTC (*ftc.gov*): abusive e-mail should be forwarded to *uce@ftc.gov; ftc.gov/bcp/menu-internet.htm* provides tips for online shopping and Internet auctions.

▶ National Fraud Information Center (*fraud.org*)

▶ Consumer Information Center (*pueblo.gsa.gov*)

▶ U.S. Department of Justice (*usdoj.gov*)

▶ The FBI's Internet Fraud Complaint Center (*ifccfbi.gov*)

▶ The American Bar Association provides online shopping tips at *safeshopping.org*.

▶ The Better Business Bureau (*bbbonline.org*)

▶ The U.S. Food and Drug Administration (*fda.gov/oc/buyonline*)

▶ The Direct Marketing Association (*the-dma.org/*)

> *Disclaimer:* This is general information on consumer rights. It is not legal advice on how any particular individual should proceed. If you require specific legal advice, consult an attorney.

▶ Compare prices online with those in regular stores—too-low prices may be too good to be true.

▶ Ask friends what they know. Find testimonials and endorsements.

▶ Find out what redress is available in case of a dispute.

▶ Consult the National Fraud Information Center (fraud.org).

▶ Check the resources available at consumerworld.org.

In addition to these tips, consumers also have shopper's rights on the Internet, as described in Insights and Additions 17.2.

Third-Party Assurance Services

Several public organizations and private companies attempt to protect consumers. The following are just a few examples.

TRUSTe's "Trustmark." TRUSTe (truste.org) is a nonprofit group whose mission is to build users' trust and confidence in the Internet by promoting the policies of disclosure and informed consent. TRUSTe certifies and monitors Web site privacy, e-mail policies, and practices, and resolves thousands of consumer privacy problems every year (TRUSTEe 2007). Sellers who become members of TRUSTe can add value and increase consumer confidence in online transactions by displaying the TRUSTe Advertising Affiliate "Trustmark" (a seal of quality). This mark identifies sites that have agreed to comply with responsible information-gathering guidelines. In addition, the TRUSTe Web site provides its members with a "privacy policy wizard," which helps companies create their own privacy policies. The site offers seven types of seals: privacy, children, e-health, safe harbor, wireless, e-mail services, and international services (in January 2005).

The TRUSTe program is voluntary. The licensing fee for use of the Trustmark ranges from $500 to $5,000, depending on the size of the online organization and the sensitivity of the information it is collecting. More than 1,500 Web sites were certified as TRUSTe participants, including AT&T, CyberCash, Excite, IBM, Buena Vista Internet Group, CNET, GeoCities, Infoseek, Lycos, Netscape, the *New York Times*, and Yahoo!. However, there still seems to be a fear that signing with TRUSTe could expose firms to litigation from third parties if they fail to live up to the letter of the TRUSTe pact, and that fear is likely to deter some companies from signing up.

Better Business Bureau. The Better Business Bureau (BBB), a private nonprofit organization supported largely by membership, provides reports on businesses that consumers can review before making a purchase. The BBB responds to millions of inquiries each year. Its BBBOnLine program (bbbonline.com) is similar to TRUSTe's Trustmark. The goal of the program is to promote confidence on the Internet through two different seals. Companies that meet the BBBOnLine standards for the Reliability Seal are members of the local BBB and have good truth-in-advertising and consumer service practices. Those that exhibit the BBBOnLine Privacy Seal on their Web sites have an online privacy protection policy and standards for handling consumers' personal information. In addition, consumers are able to click on the BBBOnLine seals and instantly get a BBB report on the participating company.

WHICHonline. Supported by the European Union, WHICHonline (which.net) gives consumers protection by ensuring that online traders under its Which?Web Trader Scheme abide by a code of proactive guidelines. These guidelines outline issues such as product information, advertising, ordering methods, prices, delivery of goods, consumer privacy, receipting, dispute resolution, and security.

Web Trust Seal and Others. The Web Trust seal program is similar to TRUSTe. The American Institute of Certified Public Accountants (cpawebtrust.org) sponsors it. Another program, Gomez (gomez.com), monitors customer complaints and provides merchant certification.

Online Privacy Alliance. The Online Privacy Alliance is a diverse group of corporations and associations that lead and support self-regulatory initiatives that create an environment of trust and foster the protection of individuals' privacy online. They have guidelines for privacy policies, enforcement of self-regulation, and children's online activities. Major members are AT&T, Bell Atlantic, Dell, IBM, Microsoft, NETCOM, AOL Time Warner, and Yahoo!. The Online Privacy Alliance supports third-party enforcement programs, such as the TRUSTe and BBB programs, because the symbol awarded by these programs signifies to consumers the use of a privacy policy that includes the elements articulated by the Online Privacy Alliance.

Evaluation by Consumers. A large number of sites include product and vendor evaluations offered by consumers. For example, Deja.com, now part of Google, is home to many communities of interest whose members trade comments about products at groups. google.com. In addition, epubliceye.com allows consumers to give feedback on reliability, privacy, and customer satisfaction. It makes available a company profile that measures a number of elements, including payment options.

Authentication and Biometric Controls

In cyberspace, buyers and sellers do not see each other. Even when videoconferencing is used, the authenticity of the person on the other end must be verified unless the person has been dealt with before. However, if one can assure the identity of the person on the other end of the line, one can imagine improved and new EC applications: Students will be able to take exams online from any place, at any time, without the need for proctors. Fraud among recipients of government entitlements and transfer payments will be reduced to a bare minimum. Buyers will be assured who the sellers are, and sellers will know who the buyers are, with a very high degree of confidence. Arrangements can be made so that only authorized people in companies can place (or receive) purchasing orders. Interviews for employment and other matching applications will be accurate because it will be almost impossible for imposters to represent other people. Overall, trust in online transactions and in EC in general will increase significantly.

As discussed in Chapter 11, the solution for such *authentication* is provided by information technologies known as *biometric controls*. Biometric controls provide access procedures that match every valid user with a *unique user identifier* (*UID*). They also provide an authentication method that verifies that users requesting access to the computer system are really who they claim to be. Authentication and biometric controls are valid for both consumer and merchant protection.

SELLER PROTECTION

The Internet makes fraud by customers or others easier because of the ease of anonymity. It must protect sellers against:

▶ Customers who deny that they placed an order

▶ Customers who download copyrighted software and/or knowledge and sell it to others

▶ Customers who give false payment (credit card or bad checks) information in payment for products and services provided

▶ Use of their name by others (e.g., imposter sellers)

▶ Use of their unique words and phrases, names, and slogans and their Web addresses by others (trademark protection)

What Can Sellers Do?

The Web site cardcops.com provides a database of credit card numbers that have had charge-back orders recorded against them. Sellers who have access to the database can use this information to decide whether to proceed with a sale. In the future, the credit card industry is planning to use biometrics to deal with electronic shoplifting. Also, sellers can use PKI and digital certificates, especially the SET protocol, to help prevent fraud (see Chapter 11).

Other possible solutions include the following:

▶ Use intelligent software to identify possibly questionable customers (or do this identification manually in small companies). One technique, for example, involves comparing credit card billing and requested shipping addresses.

▶ Identify warning signals—that is, red flags—for possible fraudulent transactions.

▶ Ask customers whose billing address is different from the shipping address to call their bank and have the alternate address added to their bank account. Retailers agree to ship the goods to the alternate address only if this is done.

For further discussion of what merchants can do to protect themselves from fraud, see OnGuard Online at onguardonline.gov/spam.html.

Section 17.6 ▶ REVIEW QUESTIONS

1. Why is there so much fraud on the Internet?

2. What types of fraud are most common?

3. Describe types of electronic signatures.

4. Describe consumer protection measures.

5. Describe assurance services.

6. What must a company do to protect itself against fraud? How can a company accomplish this?

MANAGERIAL ISSUES

Some managerial issues related to this chapter are as follows.

1. **What legal and ethical issues should be of major concern to an EC enterprise?** Key issues to consider include the following: (1) What type of proprietary information should we allow and disallow on our site? (2) Who will have access to information that visitors post to our site? (3) Do the content and activities on our site comply with laws in other countries? (4) What disclaimers do we need to post on our Web site? (5) Are we using trademarked or copyrighted materials without permission? Regardless of the specific issues, an attorney should periodically review the content on the site, and someone should be responsible for monitoring legal and liability issues.

2. **What are the most critical ethical issues?** Negative or defamatory articles published about people, companies, or products on Web sites or blogs can lead to charges of libel—and libel can stretch across countries. Issues of privacy, ethics, and legal exposure may seem tangential to running a business, but ignoring them puts the company at risk of fines, customer anger, and disruption of the operation of an organization. Privacy protection is a necessary investment.

3. **Should we obtain patents?** Some people claim that patents should not be awarded to business or computer

processes related to EC (as is the case in Europe). Therefore, investing large amounts of money in developing or buying patents may be financially unwise in cases where patents may not hold.

4. **What impacts on business is EC expected to make?** The impacts of EC and the Internet can be so strong

that the entire manner in which companies do business will change, with significant impacts on procedures, people, organizational structure, management, and business processes.

RESEARCH TOPICS

Here are some suggested topics related to this chapter. For details, references, and additional topics, refer to the Online Appendix A "Current EC Research."

1. **Fraud on the Internet**
   - Use of deceptive advertising tactics by legitimate businesses
   - Areas of significant potential for misleading and fraudulent practices
   - Consumers' perceptions of online credit card theft
   - Trusted e-mail
   - Tools to detect and deter fraud
   - Intelligent systems and data mining for fraud detection

2. **Intellectual Property Rights**
   - Reasons why regulation of digital media, including the Digital Millennium Copyright Act, are not successful
   - The promise and problems of the No Electronic Theft (NET) Act
   - Risks of digital rights management
   - Protection strategies for online software and digital content distribution
   - Watermarking of electronic text documents to prevent their illegal copy and redistribution
   - Influence of institutional prestige on the licensing of university inventions

3. **E-Taxation**
   - Pros and cons of taxing electronic commerce
   - Taxation systems of state and local governments in the United States
   - Issues of the neutral sales tax between online and traditional channels
   - Sales tax protocol for international taxation
   - Taxation policy and appropriate electronic payment methods
   - Tax jurisdiction for cross-border trades

   - Optimal methods to register foreign supplies in the countries where the B2C customers are located
   - IT architecture system design for the cross-border tax clearance

4. **Freedom of Speech**
   - The effect of the Child Online Protection Act on the civil liberties of Americans
   - Legal basis for monitoring pornography and sexual harassment online

5. **Anonymity**
   - Legal issues of anonymity and pseudonymity
   - Technical solutions for producing anonymous communication
   - Software for secure, consistent, and pseudonymous aliases for Web users

6. **Privacy**
   - Users' concerns, technologies, and implications of privacy on the Web for businesses and individuals
   - Antecedents and consequences of consumer privacy concerns
   - Typology of Internet users and online privacy concerns
   - Necessity of balancing privacy and digital rights management
   - Conflict between personalization and privacy
   - Tools for Internet privacy protection
   - Privacy seal programs
   - Framework of relationship marketing and social exchange theory to explain trust and privacy
   - Managing the cost of information privacy
   - The legal environment on direct marketers' use of public records
   - Privacy disclosures and consumer database information
   - Cross-cultural studies on privacy

SUMMARY

In this chapter, you learned about the following EC issues as they relate to the learning objectives.

1. **Understanding the foundation for legal and ethical issues.** Laws and regulations are broadly written and can only provide outlines to guide public policy. Ethics also are generally defined. Simply referring to relevant laws or philosophical principles cannot resolve specific legal disputes or ethical dilemmas. Law and ethics provide systems for social control and achieving the greater good. As with all systems, the formation of laws is a dynamic process that responds to ever-changing conditions. The nature of law is dynamic so that it can be responsive to new threats to individual rights or failures to perform one's duties. The Net not only offers freedom of speech but also widens opportunities for irresponsible activity. Despite laws and technical defenses, new types of spam have emerged to capture customer traffic. The legal framework for EC—both statutory and common law—continues to evolve. To date, the major legal issues in EC have involved rights of privacy, intellectual property, freedom of speech and censorship, and fraud. In the absence of legal constraints, ethical codes help to fill the gap. Differences in interpretations of what is legal or illegal often leads to rigorous and even contentious debates.

2. **Civil, intellectual property, and common law.** EC operations are subject to various types of laws—some of which judges create in landmark court cases. Civil law provides companies with ways to get compensated for damages or misuse of their property rights. Laws passed by Congress are being amended to better protect EC. These protections are needed because it is easy and inexpensive to copy or steal intellectual works on the Internet (e.g., music, photos, movies) and to distribute or sell them without the permission of the owners. These actions violate or infringe on copyrights, trademarks, and patents. Although the legal aspects seem fairly clear, monitoring and catching violators remains difficult.

3. **Understanding legal and ethical challenges and how to contain them.** The global scope and universal accessibility of the Internet creates serious questions as to which ethical rules and laws apply. Ignoring laws expose companies to lawsuits or criminal charges that are disruptive, expensive, and damaging to customer relations. The best strategy is to avoid behaviors that expose the company to these types of risk. Important safeguards are a corporate *codes of ethics* stating the rules and expected behavior and action and an Internet acceptable use policy.

4. **Privacy, free speech, and defamation and their challenges.** B2C companies depend on customer information to improve products and services and use CRM. Registration and cookies are two of the ways used to collect this information. The key privacy issues are who controls this information and how private it should remain. Strict privacy laws have been passed recently that carry harsh penalties for any negligence that exposes personal or confidential data.

   There is ongoing debate about censorship on the Internet. The proponents of censorship feel that it is up to the government and various ISPs and Web sites to control inappropriate or offensive content. Others oppose any form of censorship; they believe that control is up to the individual. In the United States, most legal attempts to censor content on the Internet have been found unconstitutional. The debate is not likely to be resolved.

5. **Challenges caused by spam, splogs, and pop-ups.** Spam, splogs, and other scams damage online businesses. They are also easy to deploy and profitable, so they continue to mutate for survival. That makes them impossible to control legally or technologically. A dangerous development is the use of deceptive marketing practices by legitimate companies trying to gain a competitive advantage.

6. **Fraud on the Internet and how to protect against it.** Protection is needed because there is no face-to-face contact, there is a great possibility for fraud, there are insufficient legal constraints, and new issues and scams appear constantly. Several organizations, private and public, attempt to provide the protection needed to build the trust that is essential for the success of widespread EC. Of special importance are electronic contracts (including digital signatures), the control of gambling, and what taxes should be paid to whom on interstate and international transactions. Although the trend is not to have a sales tax or a value-added tax, this may not be the case for too much longer.

KEY TERMS

QUESTIONS FOR DISCUSSION

1. Consider political activism on the Net and the use of political spam. Which political groups may political spam help?
2. How does legitimate search engine marketing and search engine optimization work? How can those methods be used unethically?
3. What are some of the things that EC Web sites can do to ensure the safeguarding of personal information?
4. Why would legitimate companies, such as BMW, use search engine spam, commercial spam, splogs, or other deceptive marketing practices?
5. Should spamming be illegal? Explain why or why not.
6. Privacy is the right to be left alone and free of unreasonable personal intrusions. What are some intrusions that you consider "unreasonable?"
7. Explain how private regulation could have positive impacts (Google filtering out search engine spam) or potentially lead to abusive behavior or illegal acts that would interfere with free speech, privacy, or intellectual property.
8. Who should control minors' access to "offensive" material on the Internet—parents, the government, or ISPs? Why?
9. Discuss the conflict between freedom of speech and the control of offensive Web sites.
10. How are rights, protected interests, and duties related?
11. Why is CAN-SPAM ineffective?
12. Discuss what the RIAA hopes to achieve by using lawsuits (civil law) against college students for copyright infringement.
13. Discuss the conditions that distinguish hostile speech from defamation.
14. Discuss the insufficient protection of opt-in and opt-out options. What would you be happy with?
15. The IRS buys demographic market research data from private companies. These data contain income statistics that could be compared with tax returns. Many U.S. citizens feel that their rights within the realm of the Electronic Communications Privacy Act (ECPA) are being violated; others say that this is an unethical behavior on the part of the government. Discuss.
16. Clerks at 7-Eleven stores enter data regarding customers (gender, approximate age, and so on) into the computer. These data are then processed for improved decision making. Customers are not informed about this, nor are they being asked for permission. (Names are not keyed in.) Are the clerks' actions ethical? Compare this with the case of cookies.
17. Many hospitals, health maintenance organizations, and federal agencies are converting, or plan to convert, all patient medical records from paper to electronic storage (using imaging technology). Once completed, electronic storage will enable quick access to most records. However, the availability of these records in a database and on networks or smart cards may allow people, some of whom are unauthorized, to view another person's private medical data. To protect privacy fully may cost too much money or may considerably slow the speed of access to the records. What policies could health-care administrators use to prevent unauthorized access? Discuss.

18. Why do many companies and professional organizations develop their own codes of ethics?

19. Cyber Promotions Inc. attempted to use the First Amendment in defense of its flooding of AOL subscribers with junk e-mail. AOL tried to block the junk e-mail. A federal judge agreed with AOL that unsolicited e-mail is annoying, a costly waste of Internet time, and often inappropriate and, therefore, should not be sent. Discuss some of the issues involved, such as freedom of speech, how to distinguish between junk and nonjunk e-mail, and the analogy with regular mail.

20. Digital Equipment paid over $3 million for the AltaVista name and Tom.com paid $8 million for its domain name. Why are companies willing to pay millions of dollars for domain names?

21. The Communications Decency Act, which was intended to protect children and others from pornography and other offensive material online, was approved by the U.S. Congress but then was ruled unconstitutional by the courts. Discuss the importance and implications of this incident.

22. Why does the government warn customers to be careful with their payments for EC products and services?

23. Some say that it is much easier to commit fraud online than off-line. Do you agree?

24. This book includes many innovative ideas. Why can't they be patented? How are the rights of the authors and publisher protected?

INTERNET EXERCISES

1. Whatever is published online may be there forever. Innumerable pages of Web text can be stored for extremely long times. Visit the Internet Archive Web site at **archive.org** to review the archives of Web sites. Discuss how this archive impacts the risk of being charged with defamation.

2. You want to set up an ethical blog. Using sites, such as the CyberJournalist.net: A Bloggers' Code of Ethics at **cyberjournalist.net/news/000215.php**, review the suggested guide to publishing on a blog. Make a list of the top ten ethical issues for blogging.

3. You want to set up a personal Web site. Using legal sites such as **cyberlaw.com**, prepare a report summarizing the types of materials you can and cannot use (e.g., logos, graphics, etc.) without breaking copyright law.

4. Use **google.com** to prepare a list of industry and trade organizations involved in various computer privacy initiatives. One of these groups is the World Wide Web Consortium (W3C). Describe its Privacy Preferences Project (**w3.org/tr/2001/wd-p3p-20010928**).

5. Enter **pgp.com**. Review the services offered. Use the free software to encrypt a message.

6. Enter **calastrology.com**. What kind of community is this? Check the revenue model. Then enter **astrocenter.com**. What kind of site is this? Compare and comment on the two sites.

7. Enter **nolo.com**. Try to find information about various EC legal issues. Find information about international EC issues. Then go to **legalcompliance.com** or **webtriallawyer.com**. Try to find information about international legal aspects of EC. Locate additional information on EC legal issues with a visit to **google.com** or a search on Yahoo!. Prepare a report on the international legal aspects of EC.

8. Find the status of the latest copyright legislation. Try **fairuse.stanford.edu**. Is there anything regarding the international aspects of copyright legislation?

9. Enter **ftc.gov** and identify some of the typical types of fraud and scams on the Internet.

10. Enter **usispa.org** and **ispa.org.uk**, two organizations that represent the ISP industry. Identify the various initiatives they have undertaken regarding topics discussed in this chapter.

11. Private companies such as **thepubliceye.com** and **investigator.com** can act as third parties to investigate the honesty of a business. What do these companies do? Why are the services of these companies necessary given the services of TRUSTe and BBBOnLine? (That is, are the services of TRUSTe and BBBOnLine somehow insufficient?)

12. Visit **consumers.com**. What protection can this group give that is not provided by BBBOnLine?

13. Download freeware from **junkbuster.com** and learn how to prohibit unsolicited e-mail. Describe how your privacy is protected.

14. Enter **scambusters.com** and identify and list its antifraud and antiscam activities.

15. Enter **ironport.com** and see how it protects e-mail. List all the product's capabilities.

TEAM ASSIGNMENTS AND ROLE PLAYING

1. The number of lawsuits in the United States and elsewhere involving EC has increased. Have each team prepare a list of five legal cases on each topic in this chapter (e.g., privacy, digital property, defamation, domain names). Prepare a summary of the issues of each case, the parties, the courts, and dates. What were the outcomes of these cases? What was (or might be) the impact of each decision?

2. Consider whether Web issues are unique. Have each team choose two other technologies or innovations, such as radio, telegraph, railroads, or electricity, and find out what ethical and legal issues and controversies arose about them. Compare and contrast the problems and issues to current problems and issues about the Web. How well do those solutions apply to the EC?

3. Form three teams. Have a debate on *free speech versus protection of children* between two teams. The third team acts as judges. One team is for complete freedom of speech on the Internet; the other team advocates protection of children by censoring offensive and pornographic material. After the debate, have the judges decide which team provided the most compelling legal arguments.

4. It is legal to monitor employees' Internet activity, e-mail, and instant messages. Why is that necessary? To what extent is it ethical? Are employees' rights being violated? Have two teams debate these issues.

5. Enter **whatis.techtarget.com** or similar resource sites. Read about spam and splogs. Find how spam and splog filters work (also see **ironport.com** and other vendors). Finally, take the self-assessment quiz at **searchcrm.techtarget.com** or **networkicom puting.com**. Prepare a report and class presentation.

Real-World Case

NET NEUTRALITY: GOOD FOR E-BUSINESS?

Internet neutrality (also *network neutrality*, *net neutrality*, or *NN*) is a hotly debated topic that will shape the future of the Internet. It became a high-profile topic when the telecommunications network operators (telcos) AT&T and Verizon stated that they should have the right to charge extra for premium placement on their network to recoup vast investments in their infrastructure. In response, numerous grassroots campaigns emerged to try to stop such a practice.

Basically, net neutrality would be new government regulation. The regulation would *prohibit* telcos from prioritizing any content or services that traveled across their networks. For example, without NN, a telco could charge the social network Web site YouTube extra fees to have its site delivered faster than the Web site of a company who could not afford the premium service fees.

It is a major issue as the United States considers new telecommunications laws. In May 2006, the U.S. House of Representatives passed telecom bill, H.R. 5252, without net neutrality protections. As of March 2007, the debate was in the Senate, where advocates were working to get strong net neutrality language in the bill, known as the Snowe-Dorgan legislation. It would bar network operators from blocking or degrading access to Internet content and services and from preventing consumers from connecting external devices to the network, with exceptions for security and other consumer protection purposes.

Supporters of Net Neutrality

Those in favor view net neutrality as a necessity to keep the Internet a level playing field. They argue that if net neutrality does not pass, there is no restriction on the telcos, which enables them to prioritize traffic according to the level of service (e.g., basic or premium) the customer bought. (An analogy is the airline industry offering different classes of service—first class, business class, and coach—at different prices.)

Internet giants, Google and Amazon.com, are strong supporters of net neutrality. In a prepared statement to the U.S. Senate Committee Hearing on *Network Neutrality* on February 7, 2006, Vinton G. Cerf, codeveloper of the Internet Protocol and Google's chief Internet evangelist stated:

> Allowing broadband carriers to control what people see and do online would fundamentally undermine the principles that have made the Internet such a success . . . A number of justifications have been created to support carrier control over consumer choices online; none stand up to scrutiny.

Opponents of Net Neutrality

Those opposed to net neutrality warn that it would eliminate incentives to invest and upgrade networks and next-generation network services. One of the primary

Internet inventors, Bob Kahn, criticizes net neutrality as a slogan that would halt experimentation and improvement in the Internet's core. Except for Vinton Cerf (employed by Google—a major proponent of NN), most senior internetworking engineers, agree with Kahn.

Some NN opponents believe NN is too important to be left to government regulators because of mistakes in past attempts to regulate Internet activities and technology. They cite the Can-Spam Act and Digital Millennium Copyright Act as examples of laws that did not achieve their intended objectives. As such, they fear that legislation with the stated purpose of preserving network neutrality would have precisely the opposite effect. Their contempt is evident in the following:

Legislators would sit in back rooms with representatives of big business and emerge with network neutrality laws that favor companies with revenues greater than $1 billion. The laws would

protect the Yahoo!s, Microsofts, and Googles of the world, while leaving innovative startups out in their cold garage (Wagner 2007).

Sources: Cerf (2006), Ford (2007), Wagner (2007), Timbl's Blog (2006), Google (2007), Hands Off the Internet (2007), and Wikipedia (2007).

Questions

1. Why is net neutrality a hotly debated issue?
2. How do proponents support their position? Do you agree with their position? Explain.
3. How do opponents support their position? Do you agree with their position? Explain.
4. What is the current state of net neutrality?

REFERENCES

ACLU. "Libraries, the Internet, and the Law: Adults Must Have Unfiltered Access." November 16, 2006 **aclu-wa.org/detail.cfm?id=556** (accessed March 2007).

Boyle, M. "Sex.com, Drugs, and a Rocky Road." *Fortune,* December 12, 2005. **money.cnn.com/magazines/fortune/fortune_archive/2005/12/12/8363122/index.htm** (accessed March 2007).

Brandeis, L., and Warren, S. "The Right to Privacy," *Harvard Law Review*, Vol. 4, No. 5 (1890–1891).

Burns, E. "Intellectual Property Threatened by Spyware," ClickZ Stats, November 14, 2006. **clickz.com/showPage.html?page=3623943** (accessed March 2007).

Cerf, V. "Prepared Statement to U.S. Senate Committee on Network Neutrality," February 7, 2006. **commerce.senate.gov/pdf/cerf-020706.pdf** (accessed 2007).

Cheeseman, H. R. *Business Law*, 5th ed. Upper Saddle River, NJ: Prentice Hall, 2004.

CIO.com. "Microsoft, Yahoo to Test IM Interoperability Plan," July 13, 2006. **cio.com/blog_view.html?CID=22943.**

CyberSource Corporation. "Eighth Annual Online Fraud Report." 2007.

Darknet. (2007) **Darknet.com** (accessed March 2007).

Duke Law and Technology Review. "Political E-Mail: Protected Speech or Unwelcome Spam?" January 14, 2003. **law.duke.edu/journals/dltr/articles/2003dltr0001.html** (accessed March 2007).

eMarketer. "Online Fraud Mounts," January 25, 2007. **enterpriseinnovator.com/index.php?articleID=9781&sectionID=25** (accessed March 2007).

FindLaw. "U.S. Constitution: Fourth Amendment: Annotations," 2007. **caselaw.lp.findlaw.com/data/constitution/amendment04/01.html** (accessed March 2007).

Ford, G. S., T. Koutsky, and L. Spiwak. "Network Neutrality and Foreclosing Market Exchange." *Phoenix Center Policy Paper Series,* March 2007. **phoenix-center.org/pcpp/PCPP28Final.pdf** (accessed March 2007).

Google. "A Guide to Net Neutrality for Google Users," 2007. **google.com/help/netneutrality.html** (accessed March 2007).

Green, H. "The Underground Internet." *Business Week,* September 15, 2003.

Hands Off the Internet. "A Reply to Mike @ Techdirt." March 9, 2007.**handsoff.org/blog** (accessed March 2007).

Harwood, S. "BMW Ban Sparks SEO Clampdown." *Revolution* (London), March 2006.

Helmore, E. "YouTube: The Hustings of the 21st Century?" *The Observer,* March 25, 2007. **politics.guardian.co.uk/media/story/0,,2042052,00.html** (accessed April 2007).

Hunt, B. "What, Exactly is Search Engine Spam." *SearchEngineWatch.com,* February 16, 2005. **searchenginewatch.com/showPage.html?page=3483601** (accessed February 2007).

Jackman, M. "Spies in the Server Closet." *CIO,* November 1, 2005. **cio.com/archive/110105/tl_filesharing.html** (accessed March 2007).

Johnson, D. and E. Lipton. "Justice Department Says F.B.I. Misused Patriot Act." *New York Times,* March 9,

2007. **nytimes.com/2007/03/09/washington/09cnd-fbi.html?hp** (accessed March 2007).

Kracher, B., and C. L. Corritore. "Is there a Special E-Commerce Ethics?" *Business Ethics Quarterly*, Vol. 14, No. 1 (2004).

Lawal, L. "Online Scams Create 'Yahoo! Millionaires.'" *Fortune*, May 22, 2006.

Legal Information Institute. *U.S. Code Collection*. Cornell Law School. **law.cornell.edu/uscode/html/uscode42/usc_sec_42_00013032----000-.html** (accessed March 2007).

Lemos, R. "Bill Would Require ISPs to Track Users." Security-Focus.com, February 19, 2007. **securityfocus.com/brief/439** (accessed March 2007).

Lerer, L. Why the SEC Can't Stop Spam." *Forbes*, March 8, 2007. **forbes.com/2007/03/08/sec-spam-stock-tech-security-cx_ll_0308spam.html?partner=daily_newsletter** (accessed March 2007).

Library of Congress. "Internet Stopping Adults Facilitating the Exploitation of Today's Youth Act (SAFETY) of 2007." February 6, 2007. **thomas.loc.gov/cgi-bin/query/z?c110:H.R.837:** (accessed March 2007).

McCarthy, K. "Sex.com Thief Arrested." *The Register* (UK). October 28, 2005. **theregister.co.uk/2005/10/28/sexdotcom_cohen_arrested** (accessed March 2007).

McCullagh, D. "GOP Revives ISP-Tracking Legislation." *CNET News.com*. February 6, 2007. **news.com.com/GOP+revives+ISP-tracking+legislation/2100-1028_3-6156948.html** (accessed March 2007).

McCurry, M., and Purpuro, L. "A Vote for Political Spam." *Boston Globe*, August 23, 2002.

Mulligan, D. K. "Digital Rights Management and Fair Use by Design." *Communications of the ACM*, Vol. 46, No. 4 (2003).

Palmer, D. E. "Pop-Ups, Cookies, and Spam: Toward a Deeper Analysis of the Ethical Significance of Internet Marketing Practices." *Journal of Business Ethics*, Dordrecht, Vol. 58, Nos. 1–3, May 2005.

Petrovic-Lazarevic, S., and A. S. Sohal. "Nature of E-Business Ethical Dilemmas." *Information Management and Computer Security*, Vol. 12, No. 2/3 (2004).

Posner, J. "Sex.com Settles Monumental Case Against VeriSign/Network Solutions." *CircleID*, April 20, 2004. **circleid.com/posts/sexcom_settles_monumental_case_against_verisign_network_solutions** (accessed March 2007).

Puente, M. "Hello to Less Privacy." *USA Today*, February 28, 2007. **usatoday.com/tech/news/2007-02-27-camera-phones-privacy_x.htm** (accessed March 2007).

Reprise Media. "Click Fraud . . . Is Google Finally Solving the Problem?" *SearchViews.com*, March 1, 2007. **searchviews.com/archives/2007/03/click_fraud_is.php** (accessed March 2007).

Reuters. "Universal Music Sues MySpace Over Copyrights," *The Financial Express*, January 8, 2007.

Rigby, R. "Splogging Clogging Blogging." *FT.com* (London), October 30, 2006.

SecureComputing.com. "How To Protect Your Company and Employees from Image Spam," **securecomputing.com/image_spam_WP.cfm** (accessed March 2007).

Slegg, J. "Analyzing the Google AdWords Landing Page Algorithm." *Searchenginewatch.com*, July 25, 2006. **searchenginewatch.com/showPage.html?page=3622950** (accessed March 2007).

Spring, T. "Spam Mutates." *PC World*, Vol. 24, Issue 4 (April 2006). **pcworld.com/article/id,124822-page,1/article.html** (accessed March 2007).

Timbl's Blog. "Blogging Is Great." November 3, 2006. **dig.csail.mit.edu/breadcrumbs/blog/4** (accessed March 2007).

TNS and TRUSTe. "Consumer Behaviors and Attitudes about Privacy." *TNS-TRUSTe Consumer Privacy Index Q4*, 2004.

TRUSTe. **truste.org/about/index.php** (accessed March 2007).

Veiga, A. "Music Industry Group Targets Students." *FindLaw.com*, February 28, 2007. **news.corporate.findlaw.com/ap/f/66/02-28-2007/2538000b9e255e43.html** (accessed March 2007).

Verizon Wireless News Center. "Wireless Spam Scheme Targeted by Verizon Wireless." November 23, 2005 **news.vzw.com/news/2005/11/pr2005-11-23.html** (accessed February 2007).

Volonino, L., and S. Robinson. *Principles and Practices of Information Security*. Upper Saddle River, NJ: Prentice Hall, 2004.

Volonino, L., R. Anzaldua, and J. Godwin. *Computer Forensics: Principles and Practices*. Upper Saddle River, NJ: Prentice Hall, 2007.

Wagner, M. "Net Neutrality Is Too Important to Leave to the Government." *InformationWeek*, March 8, 2007. **informationweek.com/blog/main/archives/2007/03/net_neutrality_4.html** (accessed March 2007).

Wikipedia. "Network Neutrality," 2007. **en.wikipedia.org/wiki/Network_neutrality** (accessed March 2007).

World Intellectual Property Organization (WIPO). "Splot Alert." *Wilson Quarterly*, Vol. 30, No. 4 (Autumn 2006). **wipo.int/portal/index.html.en** (accessed January 2007).

SOCIAL NETWORKS AND INDUSTRY DISRUPTORS IN THE WEB 2.0 ENVIRONMENT

Learning Objectives

Upon completion of this chapter, you will be able to:

1. Understand the Web 2.0 revolution, social and business networks and industry and market disruptors.

2. Describe Google and the search engine industry, the impact on advertisement, and the industry competition.

3. Understand the concept, structure, types, and issues of virtual communities.

4. Understand the social and business networks and describe MySpace, Flickr, Facebook, Cyworld, and other amazing sites.

5. Understand person-to-person video sharing and describe YouTube and its competitors.

6. Describe business networks.

7. Describe why the travel and hospitality industry is moving so rapidly to Web 2.0.

8. Describe P2P lending, ZOPA, and Prosper

9. Describe how the entertainment industry operates in the Web 2.0 environment.

10. Describe some of the enablers of the Web 2.0 revolution: blogging, wikis, mashups, etc.

11. Understand the financial viability that accompanies digital Web 2.0 implementation.

12. Describe the anticipated future of EC and the Web 3.0 concept.

Content

Wikipedia and Its Problems of Content Quality and Privacy Protection

Managerial Issues

Real-World Case: Web 2.0 at Eastern Mountain Sport

WIKIPEDIA AND ITS PROBLEMS OF CONTENT QUALITY AND PRIVACY PROTECTION

The Problem

Wikipedia is the largest free online pop culture collaborative encyclopedia that Web 2.0 communities have created. In 2007, it has over 5.3 million articles in over 230 languages, and it generates some 80 million hits per day. By comparison, Wikipedia is 42 times bigger than the *Encyclopedia Britannica,* which only contains 120,000 articles (reported by McNichol 2007). However, Wikipedia's greatest strength is also its biggest weakness. Its contents are user created; therefore, sometimes people with no special expertise on their chosen topics or people with malicious agendas post so-called "facts." For instance, there was once a contributor to a Pope Benedict article who substituted the Pontiff's photo with that of Emperor Palpatine from the Star Wars films. Another example was an accusation made by a contributor against distinguished journalist and long-time civil rights advocate John Seigenthaler that alleged Seigenthaler was involved in the assassinations of President John Kennedy and his brother Bobby Kennedy. The contributor practically fabricated the entire article. Seigenthaler pursued legal action against the anonymous Wikipedia contributor through a lawsuit using the poster's IP address and charged the unidentified accuser with defamation. For Seigenthaler, Wikipedia is "populated by volunteer vandals with poison-pen intellects," and should not be permitted to exist in its current form. According to Farrell (2007), Microsoft paid experts to write information about the company. This information was found to be inaccurate. (For more about the inaccuracy issue, see McNichol 2007.)

Another problem is invasion of privacy. Even if information about a certain individual or company is correct (i.e., no defamation), the individuals may not care for the information to become public. Because most contributors do not ask permission from those they are writing about, an invasion of privacy occurs.

Solution

In order to avoid false or misleading entries, the Wikimedia Foundation, which operates Wikipedia along with several other wiki initiatives (such as Wikibooks), is evaluating alternatives to improve the quality. The first step was the creation of a more formal advisory board. The second step was to empower system administrators to block access to the site to certain users who repeatedly vandalized entries. Next, the process of handling complaints has also been improved.

Ultimately, the owners plan to change the site to Wikipedia 2.0 and are considering the following three options:

1. The editing of mediocre Wikipedia articles by experts in the specific field; especially the use of quality art editors to improve Wikipedia's humanities coverage.

2. The creation of original articles from the ground up. According to Larry Sanger, one of the owners and creators, this could provide a more distinctive culture that will provide more pride in the articles. In this case, the name of the site would change to *citizendium.*

3. Making the users' policy more interactive. Wikipedia is asking readers to notify the company whenever they read inaccurate or incomplete content.

The Results

While the Seigenthaler issue was debated in fall 2005, early quality measures were instituted, and the site founder, Jimmy Wales appeared on CNN with Seigenthaler in December 2005, the traffic to Wikipedia nearly tripled (Martens 2006). Yet the problems still exist, with complaints against both content and privacy invasion online.

Sources: Compiled from Martens (2006), Cone (2007), Flynn (2006), and McNichol (2007).

WHAT WE CAN LEARN . . .

The Wikipedia case illustrates a *wiki implementation,* a collaborative online encyclopedia that volunteers primarily write. Murray-Buechner (2006) lists it as one of the 25 sites "we cannot live without" and labeled it as a "real Web wonder." It is a typical Web 2.0 application done for people by people. It illustrates both the benefits to society and the problems of content accuracy by volunteers. It also illustrates the potential of invasion of privacy, potential of litigation against the site, and the need for financial viability, especially when money is needed to check what people contribute for the online publishing.

In this chapter, we present several of the Web 2.0 applications (see the basics of Web 2.0 in Chapter 1) and their impact on the way we live and do business, relating it to the experience of Wikipedia and other companies. We also introduce some Web 2.0 newcomers, and particularly social networks, that may change markets or even whole industries. We also present specific companies, such as YouTube, Facebook, and Flickr that have already changed the lives of millions of people.

18.1 THE WEB 2.0 REVOLUTION, SOCIAL NETWORKS, INNOVATIONS, AND INDUSTRY DISRUPTORS

The closing chapter of the text deals with the newest areas of e-commerce—the so called Web 2.0 applications.

THE WEB 2.0 REVOLUTION

Time Magazine 2006 Person of the Year is "You," reflecting the Web's digital democracy (Grossman 2006/2007). Yes, ordinary and regular people like you and me now control, use, and are immersed in the information age. What makes this possible is the phenomenon known as Web 2.0 (defined and described briefly in Chapter 1). It has become the framework for bringing together the contributions of millions of people, no matter how small and inconsequential or huge and significant the systems are, and Web 2.0 applications to make everyone's work, thoughts, opinions, and essentially their identity, matter (Rheingold 2003). If Web 1.0 was organized around pages, software, technology, and corporations, Web 2.0 is organized around ordinary people and services. Ordinary people created Web 2.0: hobbyists, diarists, armchair pundits, people just sharing their two cents' worth through blogs, wikis, social networks, and videos using the Web's greatly evolving conversation for the sheer joy of it. By 2007, no one had more power to influence society than Web 2.0 communities. For a description, see Gillin (2007a). Yet does this influence truly benefit us, or will we suffer because of it (Anderson 2006; *Business 2.0* Staff 2007)?

According to *The Economist* (2007), Tim Berners-Lee, the creator of the Web, regards Web 2.0 as a movement that encompasses a range of technologies such as blogs, wikis, and podcasts—representing the Web adolescence. It has all the hallmarks of youthful rebellion against the conventional social order and is making many traditional media companies tremble.

You can view Web 2.0 as a large-scale and global social experiment, and like any other experiment that is worth undertaking, it needs to be evaluated in the future, and it may fail. Why? As seen in the Wikipedia case, there are serious concerns regarding the quality and integrity of user-created content on the Web as, well as security problems. Although it harnesses the wisdom of a large percentage of its users, it may harness the stupidity and ignorance of many others. For example, what are the impacts of blogging and free-for-all user-created references like Wikipedia on traditional journalism, students, and scholarship?

WHAT IS IN WEB 2.0?

Web 2.0
The popular term for advanced Internet technology and applications including blogs, wikis, RSS, and social bookmarking. One of the most significant differences between Web 2.0 and the traditional World Wide Web is greater collaboration among Internet users and other users, content providers, and enterprises.

Web 2.0 is the popular term for advanced Internet technology and applications including blogs, wikis, RSS, and social bookmarking. One of the most significant differences between Web 2.0 and the traditional World Wide Web is greater collaboration among Internet users and other users, content providers, and enterprises. As an umbrella term for an emerging core of technologies, trends, and principles, Web 2.0 is not only changing what's on the Web but also how it works. Many believe that companies that understand these new applications and technologies—and apply the benefits early on—stand to greatly improve internal business processes. Among the biggest advantages is better collaboration with customers, partners, and suppliers, as well as among internal users (see the Real World Case at the end of this chapter).

In addition to Wikipedia, there are several other Web 2.0 products of the Wikimedia Foundation such as *Wikibooks*, a collection of free textbooks that the readers can edit; *Wiktionary*, a collaborative project to produce a free, multilingual dictionary (389 languages in February 2007) including definitions, etymologies, pronunciations, and similar information and *Wikinews*, a free-content news source wiki focusing on collaborative news creation. As you may recall from Chapter 1, O'Reilly (2006) included in Web 2.0, in addition to wikis, Google AdSense (Chapter 4), Flickr (Section 18.4), blogging (Chapter 8 and Section 18.10), Web Services (Chapter 19), RSS and podcasting (Chapter 16), search engines (Section 18.2), and Napster (P2P, Chapter 8 and Section 18.8). *Innovations* (2006) adds social networks (Section 18.4), service-oriented architecture (Online Chapter 19), software as a service (Online Chapter 19), and mashups (Section 18.10). And there are more products available.

According to *Innovations* (2006), 12 percent of all U.S. consumers already use RSS, and 12 million U.S. households will regularly subscribe to podcasts by 2010.

Here are some key Web 2.0 statistics as of January 2007:

- There are more than 53 million blogs.
- There are 150,000 blogs created every day, or an average of two blogs per second.
- The "blogosphere" doubles in size every five to seven months.
- Forty percent of those who start a blog are still posting on it three months later.
- Users upload 70,000 new videos to the YouTube site every day.
- YouTube Web users watch 100 million videos every day.

Web 2.0 is a story about a community and the collaboration of that community on a scale we have never seen before. It is about the cosmic compendium of knowledge like Wikipedia, the million-channel people's networks like YouTube, and the online metropolis like MySpace. Web 2.0 gives ordinary people like us an opportunity to create a new form of person-to-person, citizen-to-citizen relationships. You and I have not only changed the world but have also changed the way the world changes. We absolutely deserve to be the People of the Year.

FOUNDATION OF WEB 2.0

Proponents of the Web 2.0 approach believe that Web usage has been increasingly moving toward interaction and rudimentary social networking, which can serve content that exploits the network effect with or without creating a visual, interactive Web page. Web 2.0 sites sometimes act more as user-dependent Web portals than as traditional Web sites. Access to consumer-generated content facilitated by Web 2.0 brings the Web closer to the concept of the Web as a democratic, personal, and do-it-yourself medium of communications. For details see Rheingold (2003).

REPRESENTATIVE CHARACTERISTICS OF WEB 2.0

Web 2.0 is about everyday people (you and me) using the Web for communication, collaboration, and creation. The following are representative characteristics (O'Reilly 2006):

- The ability to tap into the collective intelligence of users. The more users contribute, the more popular and valuable a Web 2.0 site becomes.
- Making data available in new or never-intended ways. Web 2.0 data can be remixed or "mashed up," often through Web-service interfaces, much the way a dance-club DJ mixes music.
- The presence of lightweight programming techniques and tools lets nearly anyone act as a developer.
- The virtual elimination of software-upgrade cycles makes everything a perpetual beta or work in progress and allows rapid prototyping using the Web as a platform.

  Other characteristics are:

- Networks as platforms, delivering and allowing users to use applications entirely through a browser.
- Users own the data on the site and exercise control over that data.
- An architecture of participation and digital democracy encourages users to add value to the application as they use it.
- New business models are created (Chesbrough 2006).
- A major emphasis on social networks.
- A rich interactive, user-friendly interface based on Ajax or similar frameworks. Ajax, (Asynchronous JavaScript and XML), is a Web development technique for creating interactive Web applications. The intent is to make Web pages feel more responsive by exchanging small amounts of data with the server behind the scenes so that the entire Web page does not have to be reloaded each time the user makes a change. This is meant to increase the Web page's interactivity, speed, and usability. (See Online Chapter 19 for details.)

Web 2.0 Companies

O'Reilly (2006) explained what Web 2.0 is and listed some typical companies such as Google. Later on, dozens of companies emerged as providers of infrastructure and services to social networks. In addition, many companies provide the technology for Web activities (see list in Section 18.10). A large number of startups appeared in 2005–2007. Here are some examples: Sloan (2007a) provides a guide to the 25 hottest Web 2.0 companies and the powerful trends that are driving them. (Others are described in Gillin (2007a). The 25 include:

- *In social media*: StumbleUpon (stumbleupon.com), Slide (slide.com), Bebo (bebo.com), Meebo (meebo.com), and Wikia (wikia.com).
- *In video*: Joost (joost.com), Metacafe (metacafe.com), Dabble (dabble.com), Revision3 (revision3.com), and Blip TV (blip.tv).
- *In the mobile area*: Mobio (mobio.com), Soonr (soonr.com), TinyPicture (tinypicture.com), Fon (fon.com), and Loopt (loopt.com). (For 20 companies in this area, see Longino 2006.)
- *In advertising*: Adify (adify.com), Admob (admob.com), Turn (turn.com), Spotrunner (spotrunner.com), and Vitrue (vitrue.com).
- *In enterprise*: SuccessFactors (successfactors.com), Janrain (janrain.com), Logowork (logowork.com), Simulscribe (simulscribe.com), and ReardenCommerce (reardencommerce.com).

Several of these companies are described in this chapter.

Web 2.0 Going Global

Schonfeld (2006a) believes a major characteristic of Web 2.0 is the global spreading of innovative Web sites. As soon as a successful idea is deployed as a Web site in one country, other sites appear around the globe. He presents 23 Web 2.0 type sites in 10 countries. This section presents some of these sites. Others appear in different sections of this chapter. Another excellent source for material on Web 2.0 is Search CIO's *Executive Guide: Web 2.0* (see searchcio.techtarget.com/general/0,295582,sid19_gci1244339,00.html#glossary).

SOCIAL MEDIA

social media

The online platforms and tools that people use to share opinions and experiences, including photos, videos, music, insights, and perceptions with each other.

One of the major phenomena of Web 2.0 is the emergence and rise of mass social media. **Social media** refers to the online platforms and tools that people use to share opinions and experiences including photos, videos, music, insights, and perceptions with each other. Social media can take many different forms including text, images, audio, or video clips. Section 18.9 describes popular social media. The key is that people *control* and use them rather than the organizations. Furthermore, people can use these media with ease at little or no cost. It is a powerful democratization force; the network structure enables communication and collaboration on a massive scale. For details see Hinchcliffe (2007). Exhibit 18.1 shows the emergence and rise of mass social media.

Notice that traditional media content goes from the technology to the people, whereas in social media, people create and control the content. Hinchcliffe defines the following ground rules of social media:

1. **Communication in the form of conversation, not monologue.** This implies that social media must facilitate two-way discussion, discourse, and debate with little or no moderation or censorship. In other words, the increasingly ubiquitous comments section of your local blog or media sharing site is NOT optional and must be open to everyone.

2. **Participants in social media are people, not organizations.** A third-person voice is discouraged. The source of ideas and participation is clearly identified and associated with the individuals that contributed them. Anonymity is also discouraged but permissible in some very limited situations.

3. **Honesty and transparency are core values.** Spinning, controlling, manipulating, and even spamming the conversation are thoroughly discouraged. Social media are often

EXHIBIT 18.1 The Emergence and Rise of Mass Social Media

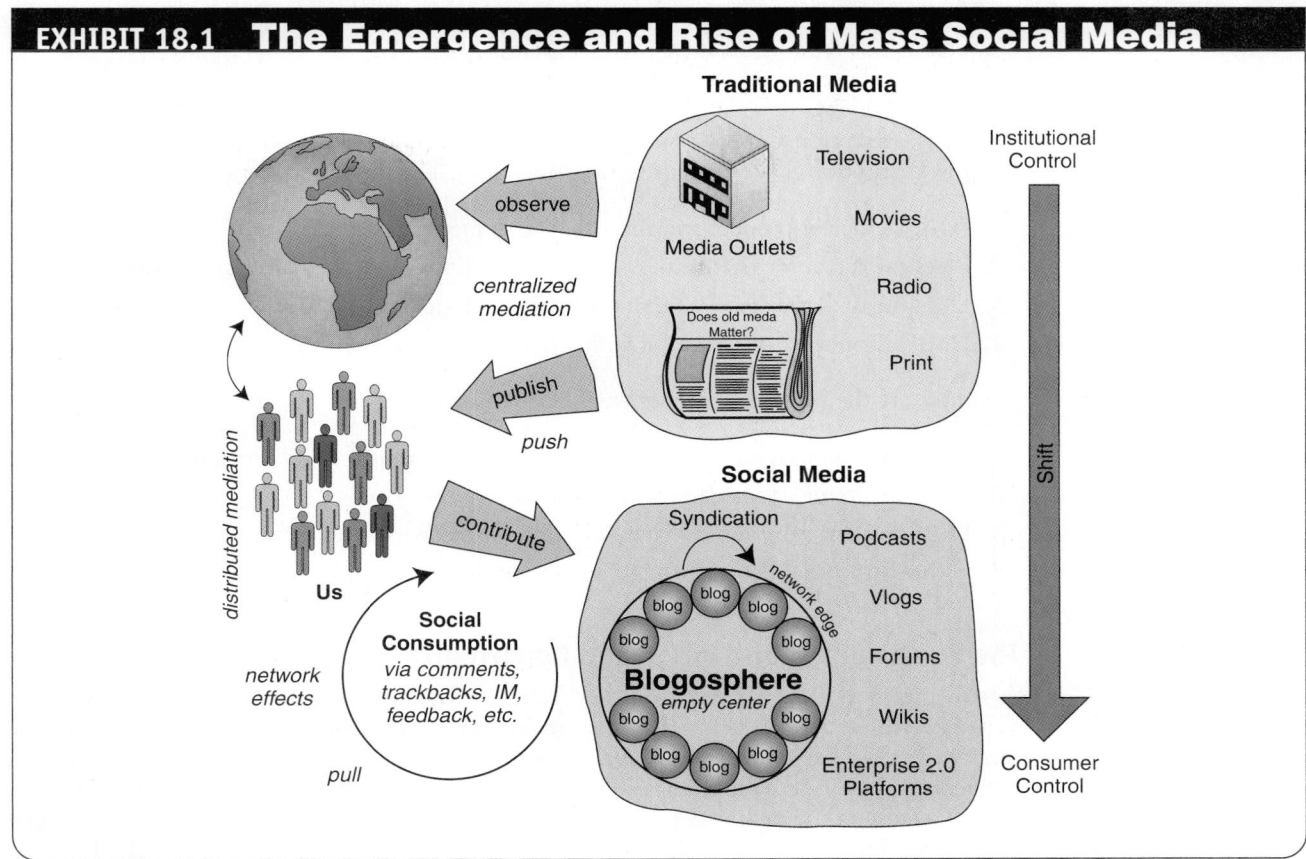

Source: Hinchcliffe, D. *Web 2.0 Blog. web2.wsj2.com.*

painfully candid forums, and traditional organizations—which aren't part of the conversation other than through their people—will often have a hard time adjusting to this.

4. **It's all about pull, not push.** Brown and Hagel (2005) observed that *push-based systems,* of which one-way marketing and advertising and command-and-control management are typical examples, are nowhere near as efficient as *pull systems.* Pull systems let people bring to them the content and relationships that they want, instead of having an external entity force it upon them. Far from being a management theory, much of what we see in Web 2.0 shows the power of pull-based systems with extremely large audiences. One of the core techniques of shaping a social media community is understanding how to embrace pull instead of push. In social media, people are in control of their conversations, not the pushers.

5. **Distribution instead of centralization.** One often overlooked aspect of social media is the fact that the interlocutors are many and varied. Gone are the biases that inevitably creep into information when only a few organizations control the creation and its distribution. Social media are highly distributed and made up of tens of millions of voices making it far more textured, rich, and heterogeneous than old media could ever be (or want to be). Encouraging conversations on the vast edges of our networks, rather than in the middle, is what it is all about.

INDUSTRY AND MARKET DISRUPTORS

In this book, we described several cases of companies that introduced innovations that could disrupt and reorder markets or even entire industries due to their activities in e-commerce. They introduce a major change in the way companies do business (see Schonfeld and Borzo 2006). An example is Blue Nile (Chapter 2), which displaced hundreds of jewelers and is changing the jewelry retail industry. *Business 2.0* refers to such companies as **disruptors**.

disruptors
Companies that introduce a significant change in their industries, thus, causing disruption in business operations.

Disruptors are companies, such as ZOPA, that facilitate person-to-person lending; thus, they may change the lending business (Section 18.8).

Business 2.0 created *The Disruption Group* with its blog (e.g., see Urlocker (2006) and Schonfeld (2006b).

The Disruption Group developed a checklist of questions to help identify disruptors (see the Disruption Scorecard at ondisruption.com). The top four questions are:

1. Is the service or product simpler, cheaper, or more accessible?
2. Does the disruptor change the basis of competition with the current suppliers?
3. Does the disruptor have a different business model?
4. Does the product or service fit with what customers value and pay for?

And here are the top four killers of would-be-disruptors:

1. Is the disruptor trying to be beat the mainstream supplier at its own game?
2. Is the disruptor choosing growth ahead of profits?
3. Does the disruptor need to change consumer behavior or to "educate" the customer?
4. Is the disruptor saddled with old business processes or an outdated business model?

The Potential for Disruption and Opportunity

According to Hinchcliffe (2007), the Web is a fundamentally different platform from any platform we've seen before. Unlike previous general-purpose IT platforms, the Web is fundamentally *communications-oriented* instead of *computing-oriented*. Sure, computing still happens, but what the Web does that is so important is its ability to connect information and people together. The *hyperlink* is the intrinsic unit of thought on the Web. The basic difference is that links connect information instead of programs operating on data. All of us can now be directly and continuously connected to the products and services we need. The very best companies in the future are likely to be the ones that will create innovative new ways to facilitate collaboration by the hundreds of millions of us who can be reached and embraced by effective architectures of participation. The big winners will enable us and encourage us to take control, contribute, shape, and direct the designs of the products and services that we, in turn, consume.

The good news is: Only a few industry leaders and early adopters fully appreciate the significance of these trends or even how to fully exploit and monetize them. There is still enormous opportunity. For existing businesses with large investments in existing business models, creating a new business model before someone else does will be the order of the day. This will prove very difficult for most to do successfully, and therein lies the potential for significant industry disruption in the next five years as new players with core competency in Product Development 2.0 push older, slow-to-adapt businesses off the stage.

Exhibit 18.2 illustrates how consumer-generated content swamping is disrupting traditional media.

Example: Will Online Wedding Services Disrupt the Traditional Industry?

Wedding services is a big industry. However, more online competition is coming because people use technology to disintermediate traditional vendors, such as live bands, DJs, and invitation printers (see Insights and Additions 18.1).

Another example of disruption in the real estate brokerage industry is made by companies such as Zillow (zillow.com) and Homegain (homegain.com), which provide more services and information than Web 1.0 companies such as realtor.com, realtytrack.com, and similar sites provide. According to O'Brien (2007), you can enter zillow.com and go to zestimate to get an approximation of your home's market value with a map of your neighborhood. Then you add all the extra features of your house. Then a comparison of the new estimate can be made with your neighbors' home (see Team Exercise #1 at the end of this chapter). Users can list their homes for free after calculating the actual selling price in the neighborhood. The service

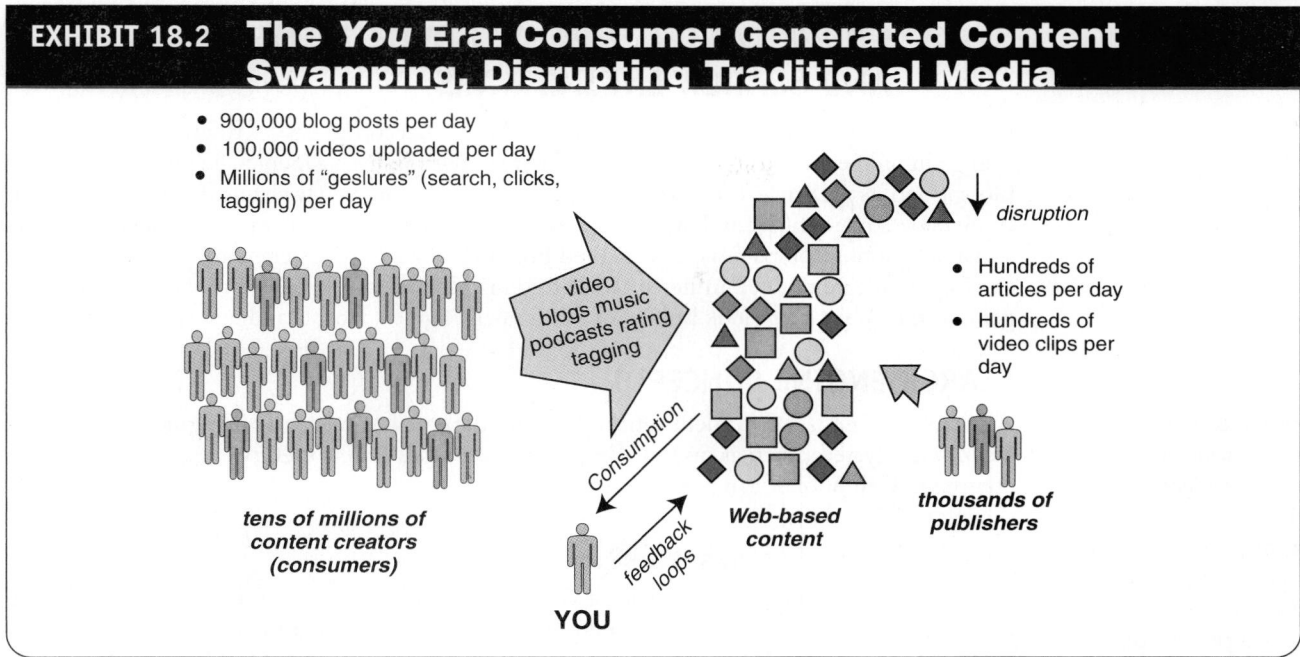

EXHIBIT 18.2 **The *You* Era: Consumer Generated Content Swamping, Disrupting Traditional Media**

- 900,000 blog posts per day
- 100,000 videos uploaded per day
- Millions of "geslures" (search, clicks, tagging) per day

video blogs music podcasts rating tagging

Consumption

tens of millions of content creators (consumers)

feedback loops

YOU

Web-based content

disruption

- Hundreds of articles per day
- Hundreds of video clips per day

thousands of publishers

Source: Hinchcliffe, D. *Web 2.0 Blog. web2.wsj2.com.*

is good not only for sellers. Buyers can use Zillow to buy a house that is not even on the market—without open houses, bidding wars, or buyer's remorse—and get it cheaper by passing over the 6 percent commission. Will real estate agents be made extinct? Some will. More likely the 6 percent commission in the U.S. will lower closer to the 1 percent commission common in other countries.

Section 18.1 ▶ REVIEW QUESTIONS

1. Define *Web 2.0*.
2. List the major characteristics of Web 2.0.
3. List the Web 2.0 technologies.
4. Define *social media*.
5. List the major rules of social media.
6. Define *industry and market disruptors*.

Insights and Additions 18.1 Weddings Are Going W2.0 High Tech

Technology in the United States and some other countries has shaken up the traditional wedding. Today, many couples create their own wedding sites to keep their guests informed about the wedding plans. Many couples use the Internet for bridal registries. Guests can buy the most preferred gifts online from major department stores. Wedding Webcasts are becoming popular too: couples can broadcast the wedding ceremony on the Web for people who are not able to attend, as well as post wedding videos on YouTube and pictures on Flickr. Friends can start a blog or a wiki too.

Next is the use of digital music. Couples create their own playlists on their iPods and use them for both wedding ceremony and reception music, especially for small, intimate weddings. This is noninteractive, but it is original and less costly. Couples also save money by using the Internet to compare items they need to buy (e.g., see *knot.com*). Finally, couples can design and buy their wedding rings online (e.g., see *bluenile.com*). All in all, there is more competition among vendors to serve 2.4 million weddings annually in the United States.

18.2 GOOGLE AND COMPANY: ADVERTISEMENT AND SEARCH ENGINE WARS

One of the major changes from Web 1.0 to Web 2.0 according to O'Reilly (2005) was the change in online advertisement from collaborative filtering (e.g., DoubleClick in Chapter 4) to Google and its AdSense technology (Chapter 4). Google completely changed online advertising by giving it a major boost and driving the creation of many Web 2.0 companies, including many social networking companies that benefited from the new advertisement concepts. However, the success of Google resulted in fierce competition in search-engine–based companies. Before we get into this subject, let's look briefly into the search engine concepts and industry.

SEARCH ENGINE CONCEPTS

search engine
A document retrieval system designed to help find information stored on a computer system, such as on the Web, inside corporate proprietary files, or in a personal computer.

A **search engine** is a document retrieval system designed to help find information stored on a computer system, such as on the Web, inside corporate or proprietary files, or in a personal computer. Cell phones can perform searches as well.

How Do Search Engines Work?

A search engine allows one to request content that meets specific criteria (typically those containing a given word or phrase), and retrieves a list of items that match those criteria. This list is often sorted with respect to some measure of relevance of the results. Search engines use regularly updated indexes to operate quickly and efficiently. There are differences in the ways various search engines work. But they all perform three basic tasks:

1. They keep an index of words they find, and where they find them.
2. They allow users to look for words or combinations of words found in that index.
3. They search the Internet based on keywords.

Types of Search Engines

There are hundreds of search engines in dozens of categories. Wikipedia provides examples of 28 categories (see en.wikipedia.org/wiki/Search_engines). Exhibit 18.3 provides representative examples.

SEARCH WARS: GOOGLE VERSUS YAHOO! AND OTHERS

One of the most spirited arenas of Internet competition is that of Web search engines, and never more so than in 2004. Historically, Excite, Lycos, AltaVista, Inktomi, and others had held the title of "top search engine." These search engines mostly relied on *keyword analysis*—counting the frequency and placement of keywords in the Web page—and few ever made a profit.

The Web search world changed in 1998 when Google introduced *link popularity*—counting the number of links and importance of those links—in its search algorithm (see *The Economist* [2004] for an explanation of this search algorithm). Soon, Google became the top search engine; now it is part of our everyday language (e.g., *to google* is now a verb and *google bombing* is a page-ranking strategy). Google also is the Internet's first highly profitable search engine, earning substantial profits from sponsored ads and achieving a highly successful IPO launch in mid-2004. The Real World Case in Chapter 1 describes some of the essentials of Google. Many consider Google the best company to work for (Lashinsky 2007b).

Google's success has not gone unnoticed. Nothing attracts competition like success, and in 2004 other companies, large and small, began to enter this competitive arena. The biggest battles in the search wars are between Google and some of the search engine giants of electronic commerce—notably Yahoo!. The search war is about the Internet advertising dollars.

In February 2004, Yahoo!, an innovative and profitable company that had changed itself from a Web directory into an Internet portal, launched Yahoo! Search. It is based on Yahoo!'s 2002 and 2003 acquisitions of search engine technology from Inktomi, AltaVista, and AllTheWeb, all of which were significant search engines in their own right (Sullivan 2004).

EXHIBIT 18.3 Search Engine Categories

Category	Examples
1. General search engines	Google, Windows Live, Yahoo! search
2. Open source search engines	DataParkSearch, Namazu, Xapian
3. Metasearch engines	Dogpile, Excite, Hotbot, Mamma, Sidestep
4. Regional search engines	Baidu (China), Naver (Korea), Rediff (India)
5. People search engines	Chacha, Zoominfo
6. E-mail-based search engines	TEK
7. Visual search engines	Kartoo, Grokker
8. Answer-based search engines	Answers.com, Lycos IQ, Yahoo! Answers
9. Google-based search engines	AOL Search, Netscape
10. Yahoo!-based search engines	Alta Vista, GoodSearch
11. Windows-Live-based search engines	A9.com (Amazon), Lycos, Alexa Internet
12. Job search engines	Hotjobs, Monster, Craigslist, Eluta.ca
13. Blog search engines	Bloglines, IceRocket, Pubsub.com
14. News search engines	Google News, Yahoo! News, Topix.net
15. Multimedia search engines	Podscope, Picsearch
16. Code search engines	Krugle, Koders
17. Bit Torrent search engines	Bit Torrent, Mininova
18. Accountancy search engines	IFACnet
19. Medical search engines	WebMD, Entrez
20. Property search engines	Zillow, Home.co.uk
21. Business search engines	Thomasnet, Business.com
22. Comparison-shopping search engines	Froogle, MySimon, PriceGrabber, Shopzilla
23. Geographic search engines	Google Maps, MapQuest, Yahoo! Maps
24. Social search engines	Google Co-op, Rollyo, Wink
25. Desktop search engines	Ask.com, Google Desktop, Copernic, Hotbot, XI Enterprise
26. Video search engine	Mamma.com

In September 2004, Amazon.com introduced A9 (a9.com), a "search engine with memory." A9 allows users to store and edit bookmarks, revisit links clicked on previous visits, and make personal notes on Web pages for later viewing. Commentators describe Amazon.com's competitive advantage as follows: "The ability to search through your own history of Web searches is insanely powerful," and "It's not just about search, it's about managing your information" (Markoff 2004a).

In November 2004, Microsoft released its test version of MSN Search (now Windows Live), its primary artillery in the search wars. MSN Search seeks to fulfill the battle cry its CEO Bill Gates issued earlier in 2004: "We took an approach [ignoring the Web search market] that I now realize was wrong, [but] we will catch them" (Markoff 2004c). Perhaps more significantly, Microsoft includes comprehensive Web and desktop search capabilities in Vista, its Windows operating system.

Google also is facing competition from smaller companies that are trying to create the next "great leap forward" in Web search technology (Roush 2004). For example:

▶ Mooter (mooter.com) makes searches more personal by recording which links get clicked and adjusting the ranking of Web sites in subsequent searches based on these preferences.

▶ Clusty (clusty.com) organizes search results into folders, or "clusters," by grouping similar items together based on textual and linguistic similarity. For example, a search on "George Bush" produces clusters such as "White House," "election," "quotes," and "Iraq," and each cluster contains a number of search results.

▶ Snap (snap.com) uses click-stream information (e.g., what sites Web users visit, how long they stay) to rank Web search results as well as sorting the results based on various criteria.

Why is there such intense interest in Web search technology and winning the search wars? All these companies want to be the next Google, obtaining the profits and fame that Google has acquired. However, winning in this arena also is about power. Brewster Kahle, the founder of the Internet Archive, notes that 20 percent of all Web traffic goes to only 10 Web sites, and search engines dominate that list. He observes: "The level of mind space that provides is enormous. If you want to control the world, it's essential that you be there" (Markoff 2004b).

How Does Google Compete?

Google is meeting the competitive challenges it faces head on. Google offers an expanding repertoire of tools in line with its core competency in search technology. The major tools are:

- ▶ Froogle (froogle.google.com) is a product-comparison search engine for online shopping. A similar search tool is Google Catalogs (catalogs.google.com), which searches a database of mail-order catalogs.
- ▶ Google News (news.google.com) searches news-oriented Web sites and displays stories according to a computer algorithm that rates stories based on how many news sites are publishing the stories, how recently the articles were published, and for searches, keyword occurrence.
- ▶ Google Earth (earth.google.com) is a collection of zoomable aerial and satellite 3D photos of the earth that enables you to find information linked to geographic location.
- ▶ Google Maps (maps.google.com) and Google Maps for Mobile (google.com/gmm) present countless maps of cities and streets around the globe. They enable you to get driving instructions from one location to another.
- ▶ Google Scholar (scholar.google.com) searches the scholarly literature, including peer-reviewed papers, theses, books, preprints, abstracts, and technical reports. Many hits are abstracts or citations, not full articles, and some are "cloaked" behind subscription-only journal subscriptions.
- ▶ Google also has introduced Google Wireless (google.com/mobile) and Google Groups (groups.google.com).

Strategically, Google is leveraging its widely recognized brand name and search technology expertise into areas beyond Web searching. Sometimes these projects bring Google into direct competition with the EC giants mentioned earlier.

- ▶ Google Print (books.google.com) is similar to Amazon.com's "search inside the book" feature. Users can search by keyword (e.g., "books about Nelson Mandela") and then search for keywords or phrases within the books.
- ▶ GMail (gmail.google.com) is Google's offering in the huge Web-based e-mail market that is currently dominated by Microsoft's Hotmail and Yahoo! Mail. In beta testing and only available by invitation as of late 2006, GMail offers new services such as grouping related messages together and keyword searching through e-mail messages.
- ▶ Google Mini (google.com/mini) is a cost effective appliance businesses use to deploy corporate searches that mimic the main Google Web search engine.
- ▶ Google Desktop (desktop.google.com) searches the contents of computer files, e-mail messages, books, and even recently viewed Web pages. This is a dramatic improvement on the Windows "Find" feature, which only searches computer files and then mostly by file name. Google Desktop preempts technology that Microsoft is intending to put into Longhorn. The strategic moves Google is making are all in line with its mission statement: "to organize the world's information and make it universally useful and accessible."
- ▶ Orkut (orkut.com) is a social-networking service that competes in one of the fastest-growing Internet markets—Web sites that connect people through networks of friends or business contacts to find new friends or contacts. In order to sign in at Orkut, you must have a Google account (see Section 18.4).

Financially, Google also is proving to be very successful, reporting revenues of almost $2.7 billion in the third quarter of 2006. As of February 2007, its market capitalization is

$146 billion, about the same as IBM, and more than Ford and General Motors combined (Goldberg 2006).

What is ahead for Google? Financial observers have noted that while its roots are in search engine technology, its revenues and profits are in sponsored advertising, the same as portals such as MSN and Yahoo! (Munarriz 2004). Will further expansion by Google into new territory dilute its search engine reputation, brand name, and profits? Or are these moves necessary to assist in its inevitable evolution into a portal? What business is Google really in? The answers to these questions will determine Google's next moves in the Internet marketspace.

According to NetRatings Inc., the market share of the major search engines (advertising revenue) was: Google 53.7 percent, Yahoo! 2.7 percent, MSN 8.9 percent, AOL 5.4 percent, and Ask.com 1.8 percent. Both Google and Yahoo! are slowly increasing their share at the expense of others (Nielsen NetRatings 2007).

Here are some facts about the two main rivals:

1. Google is a crawler-based search engine; Yahoo! is a human-powered directory.
2. Google dominates search; Yahoo! dominates content.
3. Google sells AdSense; Yahoo! sells Content Match.
4. Google works on pay per click, which is useful for SMBs; Yahoo! works on sell per impression, which is great for large companies but not so much for small publishers.
5. Google works with a technical, systematic approach; Yahoo! works with a people-oriented approach.
6. Google is viewed as an Internet search company; Yahoo! is viewed as an Internet media company.
7. In April 2007, Google purchased DoubleClick, an online ad pioneer (Chapter 4), for $3.1 billion. This may strengthen Google's position considerably (Story and Helft 2007).
8. In 2007, Google partnered with Echostar to launch a new, automated system for buying, selling, delivering, and measuring ads over the 125-channel Dish Network (Hefflinger 2007).

In November 2006, Yahoo Inc. signed a revenue-sharing deal with 176 newspapers to sell ads, share content, and deliver Internet searches, graphics, and classified advertising to customers (Walsh 2006). This agreement provides a competitive edge to Yahoo!, but Google is making similar agreements with other newspapers (Story 2006).

For more details on Google see Carr (2006b). In 2007, Yahoo! instituted an improved ad system (code name Panama) that may provide it with an advantage over Google (see Chmielewski 2007). Also, the acquisition of Flickr (Section 18.4) may help Yahoo! with its struggle against Google (see Schonfeld 2005).

ANSWER-BASED SEARCH ENGINES

Some of the interesting types of search engines are those that provide answers to questions. Insights and Additions 18.2 provides an example. Google discontinued its answer-based search in November 2006.

DISRUPTORS OF GOOGLE: WILL THEY SUCCEED?

Many companies want to displace or to become as successful as Google. Here are two examples.

Intelligent Search Engine—Will It Work?

The various search engine models are based on keywords, which may result in poor or incorrect answers. So people can improve a search by adding one or two keywords (which most people do not do) for an advanced search. Powerset.com, a new start-up company, wants to use natural language queries instead of keywords as a model. So Powerset cut a deal with Xerox's PARC labs, a top research company on natural language understanding. Major unknowns are the quality of the natural language processing and whether searchers will be willing to key in the long natural language queries instead of simple short keywords.

Insights and Additions 18.2 Amazon.com's Askville Service

Amazon.com recently launched an interesting service called Askville. According to Garrett (2007), this is a Web 2.0 product. The online service lets users ask questions and get a response from other users in lieu of posting query after query to one of the Web's many search engines.

Amazon.com bills Askville as a place where users can "ask, answer, meet, and play." If you'd like to know about food safety or the proper care of hedgehogs, just leave your question on one of Askville's forums, where other users are free to respond. Users get "Quest Coins" and "Experience Points" for their activity, which they can redeem at Questville, a Web site that Amazon.com manages.

Unlike Google's defunct service, Askville's users can jazz up their answers with self-made movies from YouTube, Bolt.com, and yes, even Google Video. They can also integrate Google Maps into their answers if their subject deals with geography.

Sites like these—sites where users become authors, providing the site with its head count of writers and more than copious content—are part of Web 2.0.

If we use the common exemplars, the blogging phenomenon, wikis, the rise of Wikipedia, it's very much about community content.

The major traditional-style competitors are Yahoo! Answers and Answers.com (see Chapter 16).

However, if successful, this concept may disrupt the search engine industry and intensify the industry wars.

According to Sloan (2007b), Web advertisers are moving beyond search by using powerful science to figure out what people want—sometimes before the searchers even know.

Wikia.com and Collaborative Innovation

Wikia.com is a for-profit Web site related to Wikipedia Foundation (which is a not-for-profit organization). Wikia is growing very rapidly; 30,000 contributors created 500,000 Wikia articles in 45 languages in a 2–year period (see McNichol 2007). One of its projects uses the people's community brain to build a better search engine than Google. The idea is to tap into the enthusiasm of users (see McNichol 2007 for details).

Conclusion

The moves Google is making are consistent with its core competencies in search technology and the value proposition it offers to its customers, as stated in its mission statement "to organize the world's information."

Google was not a first mover in Web search engines, but it has been a best mover by innovating the Web search technology market and becoming phenomenally successful.

An interesting area in the search engine war is the global market. For example, in China, Google is only number two (baidu.com is number one). Baidu chose a poetic Chinese name because it wanted the users to remember its heritage. As a native speaker of the Chinese language, Baidu focuses on what it knows best—Chinese language search. Applying avant-garde technology to the world's most ancient and complex language is as challenging as it is exciting. For example, there are at least 38 ways of saying "I" in Chinese. However, Google is gaining ground, probably because its search results are more attractive to advertisers.

In summary, Google's innovative approach to its strategic placement in the marketplace exemplifies many of the key points about EC strategy made in Chapter 14.

Section 18.2 ▶ REVIEW QUESTIONS

1. Define *search engines*.
2. List the major types of search engines.
3. Compare Yahoo! to Google.
4. Review Google's competitive strategy.
5. Describe answer-based search engines.

18.3 VIRTUAL COMMUNITIES

A *community* is a group of people with some interest in common who interact with one another. A **virtual (Internet) community** is one in which the interaction takes place by using the Internet. Virtual communities parallel typical physical communities, such as neighborhoods, clubs, or associations, but people do not meet face-to-face. Instead, they meet online. Virtual communities offer several ways for members to interact, collaborate, and trade (see Exhibit 18.4 and Blanchard and Markus 2004). Similar to the click-and-mortar model, many *physical communities* have a Web site for Internet-related activities.

virtual (Internet) community
A group of people with similar interests who interact with one another using the Internet.

CHARACTERISTICS OF COMMUNITIES AND CLASSIFICATION

Pure-play Internet communities may have thousands or even millions of members. This is one major difference with purely physical communities, which usually are smaller. Another difference is that offline communities frequently are confined to one geographic location, whereas only a few online communities are geographically confined.

Many thousands of communities exist on the Internet. Several communities are independent and are growing rapidly. For instance, GeoCities grew to 10 million members in less than two years and had over 50 million members in 2004 (Geocities 2007). MySpace (see Case 1.4) grew to 100 million members in about a year. GeoCities members can set up personal home pages on the site, and advertisers buy ad space targeted to community members. Insights and Additions 18.3 present a number of examples of online communities. Sections 18.4 through 18.9 present social networking types of communities.

Virtual communities can be classified in several ways. One possibility is to classify members as *traders*, *players*, *just friends*, *enthusiasts*, or *friends in need*. A more common classification is the one proposed by Hagel and Armstrong (1997). This classification recognizes the five types of Internet communities shown in Exhibit 18.5 (p. 821). For a different, more complete classification, see the classification proposed by Schubert and Ginsburg (2000).

Cashel (2004) proposed another classification of communities, identifying 10 specific niches within the online community space that are bucking the trend and demonstrating strong revenues. These 10 important trends include: (1) search communities, (2) trading communities, (3) education communities, (4) scheduled events communities, (5) subscriber-based communities, (6) community

EXHIBIT 18.4	**Elements of Interaction in a Virtual Community**
Category	**Element**
Communication	Bulletin boards (discussion groups)
	Chat rooms or threaded discussions (string Q&A)
	E-mail, instant messaging, and wireless messages
	Private mailboxes
	Newsletters, "netzines" (electronic magazines)
	Blogging, wikis, and mashups
	Web postings
	Voting
Information	Directories and yellow pages
	Search engine
	Member-generated content
	Links to information sources
	Expert advice
EC Element	Electronic catalogs and shopping carts
	Advertisements
	Auctions of all types
	Classified ads
	Bartering online

Insights and Additions 18.3 Examples of Communities

The following are examples of online communities.

▶ **Associations.** Many associations have a Web presence. These range from Parent–Teacher Associations (PTAs) to professional associations. An example of this type of community is the Australian Record Industry Association (*aria.com.au*).

▶ **Ethnic communities.** Many communities are country or language specific. An example of such a site is *elsitio.com*, which provides content for the Spanish- and Portuguese-speaking audiences mainly in Latin America and the United States. A number of sites, including *china.com*, *hongkong.com*, *sina.com*, and *sohu.com*, cater to the world's large Chinese-speaking community.

▶ **Gender communities.** *Women.com* and *ivillage.com*, the two largest female-oriented community sites, merged in 2001 in an effort to cut losses and become profitable.

▶ **Affinity portals.** These are communities organized by interest, such as hobbies, vocations, political parties, unions (e.g., *workingfamilies.com*), and many more. Many communities are organized around a technical topic (e.g., a database), a product (e.g., Lotus Notes), or a company (e.g., Oracle Technology news at *oracle.com/technology*). A major subcategory here is medical and health related. According to Johnson and Ambrose (2006), almost 30 percent of the 90 million members who participated in communities in 2005 were in this category.

▶ **Catering to young people (teens and people in their early twenties).** Many companies see unusual opportunities here. Three community sites of particular interest are *alloy.com*, *bolt.com*, and *blueskyfrog.com*. Alloy.com is based in the United Kingdom and claims to have over 10 million members. Bolt.com claims to have 4.5 million members and operates from the United States. Blueskyfrog.com operates from Australia, concentrating on cell phone users, and claims to have more than 2.5 million devoted members.

▶ **Megacommunities.** Megacommunities combine numerous smaller communities under one "umbrella" (under one name). GeoCities is one example of a megacommunity with many subcommunities. Owned by Yahoo!, it is by far the largest online community.

▶ **B2B online communities.** Chapter 6 introduced many-to-many B2B exchanges. These are referred to as *communities*. B2B exchanges support community programs such as technical discussion forums, blogs, interactive Webcasts, user-created product reviews, virtual conferences and meetings, experts' seminars, and user-managed profile pages. Classified ads can help members to find jobs or employers to find employees. Many also include industry news, directories, links to government and professional associations, and more.

▶ **Social networks.** These are megacommunities, such as MySpace and YouTube, in which millions of unrelated members can express themselves, find friends, exchange photos, view video tapes, and more (Section 18.4).

---

consulting firms, (7) e-mail-based communities, (8) advocacy communities, (9) CRM communities, and (10) mergers and acquisitions activities. See Cashel (2004) for details.

COMMERCIAL ASPECTS OF COMMUNITIES

A logical step as a community site grows in members and influence may be to turn it into a commercial or revenue-generating site. Examples of such community-commercial sites include ivillage.com and wikia.com. The following are suggestions on how to make the transformation from a community site to a commercial one:

▶ Understand a particular niche industry, its information needs, and the step-by-step process by which it does the research needed to do business, and try to match the industry with a potential or existing community.

▶ Build a site that provides that information, either through partnerships with existing information providers or by gathering it independently, or identify a community that can be sponsored.

▶ Set up the site to mirror the steps a user goes through in the information-gathering and decision-making process (e.g., how a chip designer whittles down the list of possible chips that will fit a particular product).

▶ Build a community that relies on the site for decision support (or modify an existing one).

▶ Start selling products and services that fit into the decision-support process (such as selling sample chips to engineers who are members of the community).

EXHIBIT 18.5   Types of Virtual Communities

Community Type	Description
Transaction and other business	Facilitates buying and selling (e.g., *ausfish.com.au*). Combines information portal with infrastructure for trading. Members are buyers, sellers, intermediaries, etc., focused on a specific commercial area (e.g., fishing).
Purpose or interest	No trading, just an exchange of information on a topic of mutual interest. Examples: Investors consult the Motley Fool (*fool.com*) for investment advice; rugby fans congregate at the Fans Room at *nrl.com.au*; music lovers go to *mp3.com*; *geocities.yahoo.com* is a collection of several areas of interest in one place.
Relations or practice	Members are organized around certain life experiences. Examples: *ivillage.com* caters to women, and *seniornet.com* to senior citizens. Professional communities also belong to this category. Examples: *isworld.org* for information systems faculty, students, and professionals.
Fantasy	Members share imaginary environments. Examples: Sport fantasy teams at *espn.com*; GeoCities members can pretend to be medieval barons at *dir.yahoo.com/Recreation/games/role_playing_games/titles*. See *games.yahoo.com* for many more fantasy communities.
Social networks	Members communicate, collaborate, create, share, form smaller groups, entertain, and more. MySpace is the leader.

Sources: Compiled from Hagel and Armstrong (1997) and from Rheingold (2000).

Electronic communities can create value in several ways. Members input useful information to the community in the form of comments and feedback, elaborating on their attitudes, beliefs, and information needs. This information can then be retrieved and used by other members or by marketers. The community organizers may also supply their own content to communities, as AOL does.

Rheingold (2000 and 2003) thinks that the Web is being transformed from just a communication and information-transfer tool into a social Web of communities. He thinks that every Web site should incorporate a place for people to chat. A community site should be an interesting place to visit, a kind of virtual community center. He believes that it should be a place where discussions may range over many controversial topics.

KEY STRATEGIES FOR SUCCESSFUL ONLINE COMMUNITIES

The model of self-financing communities (i.e., those without a sponsor) has not worked very well. Several communities that were organized for profit sustained heavy losses. Examples include ivillage.com, china.com, and elsitio.com. Several other communities ceased operations in 2000 and 2001 (e.g., esociety.com and renren.com). The trend toward mergers and acquisitions among communities, started in 2001, is expected to improve the financial viability of some communities. For financial viability of social networks see Section 18.11.

The management consulting company Accenture outlined the following eight critical factors for community success (see details in Duffy 1999):

1. Increase traffic and participation in the community.
2. Focus on the needs of the members; use facilitators and coordinators.
3. Encourage free sharing of opinions and information—no controls.
4. Obtain financial sponsorship. This factor is a must. Significant investment is required.
5. Consider the cultural environment.
6. Provide several tools and activities for member use; communities are not just discussion groups.
7. Involve community members in activities and recruiting.
8. Guide discussions, provoke controversy, and raise sticky issues. This keeps interest high.

Leimeister and Krcmar (2004) add the following top six success factors based on their own 2004 survey:

1. Handle member data sensitively.
2. Maintain stability of the Web site with respect to the consistency of content, services, and types of information offered.
3. Provide fast reaction time of the Web site.
4. Offer up-to-date content.
5. Offer continuous community control with regard to member satisfaction.
6. Establish codes of behavior (netiquette or guidelines) to contain conflict potential.

Examples of some communities that use one or more of these principles of success include the following: earthweb.com, icollector.com, webmd.com, terra.es, slcafe.com, ivillage.com, icq.com, letsbuyit.com, paltalk.com, radiolinja.fi, and projectconnections.com. For more details and discussion of communities, see Dholakia et al. (2004) and Porter (2004).

The virtual communities described here evolved in 2005 to one of the major phenomena of e-commerce, the *social networks*, as described in Section 18.4.

Section 18.3 ▶ REVIEW QUESTIONS

1. Define *virtual (Internet) communities* and describe their characteristics.
2. List the major categories of virtual communities.
3. Describe the commercial aspects of virtual communities.
4. Describe the CSFs for virtual communities.

18.4   ONLINE SOCIAL NETWORKS

social network

A special structure made of individuals (or organizations). It includes the ways in which individuals are connected through various social familiarities.

As you may recall, we defined a **social network** as a place where people create their own space, or home page, on which they write blogs (web logs), post pictures, videos or music, share ideas, and link to other Web locations they find interesting. Social networkers *tag* the content they post with keywords they choose themselves, which makes their content searchable. In effect, they create online communities of people with similar interests.

CONCEPTS AND DEFINITIONS

A *social network* is a social structure made of nodes that are generally individuals or organizations. It indicates the ways in which individuals are connected through various social familiarities ranging from casual acquaintance to close familial bonds.

Social network theory views social relationships in terms of *nodes* and *ties*. Nodes are the individual actors within the networks, and ties are the relationships between the actors. There can be many kinds of ties between the nodes. In its most simple form, a social network is a map of all the relevant ties between the nodes being studied. The network can also determine the social assets of individuals. Often, a social network diagram displays these concepts, where nodes are the points and ties are the lines.

The shape of the social network helps determine a network's usefulness to its individuals. Smaller, tighter networks can be less useful to their members. This is one reason for the large size of the networks.

Social networking also refers to a category of Internet applications to help connect friends, business partners, or other individuals together using a variety of tools. These applications, known as online social networks are becoming increasingly popular (e.g., see Read/Write Web 2006; and en.wikipedia.org/wiki/Social_marketplace). The companies that provide these services are known as social networking services.

Social Network Analysis

Social network analysis (SNA) (related to *network theory*) has emerged as a key technique in modern sociology, anthropology, geography, social psychology, information science, and organizational studies, as well as a popular topic of speculation and study. Research in a number of academic fields has demonstrated that social networks operate on many levels, from families up to the level of nations, and may play a critical role in determining the way problems are solved, organizations are run, and the degree to which individuals succeed in achieving their goals. For an example of the benefits of communities in health care, see Johnson and Ambrose (2006).

Social network analysis (SNA) is the mapping and measuring of relationships and flows between people, groups, organizations, animals, computers or other information or knowledge processing entities. The nodes in the network are the people and groups, whereas the links show relationships or flows between the nodes. SNA provides both a visual and a mathematical analysis of relationships.

Social Networking Services

Social networking services are Web sites that allow anyone to build a home page for free. People can list personal information, communicate with others, upload files, communicate via IM, or blog. Social networks can contain links to user-generated content. Although blogs and wikis are influential social tools, social software also includes IM, RSS, and Internet forums.

We describe some of these tools in Section 18.10. Chapters 7 and 16 describe others.

REPRESENTATIVE SOCIAL NETWORKS: FROM FACEBOOK TO CLASSMATES.COM

There are thousands of social networks online with many added each week. (For a list of the major communities including user count see en.wikipedia.org/wiki/List_of_social_networking_websites).

Here, we provide a small list of major Web sites with minimal details (details are changing frequently). The Wikipedia Web site (wikipedia.org), where content is constantly updated, describes all these companies.

Representative Social Networking Web Sites

Here are some popular sites.

Flickr. Flickr (flickr.com) is a photo sharing Web site, Web services suite, and an online community platform.

In addition to being a popular Web site for users to share personal photographs, the service is widely used by bloggers as a photo repository. Its innovative online community tools that allow photos to be tagged and browsed by folksonomic means have fueled Flickr's popularity.

Flickr provides a search engine (based on keywords). It has limits on contacts (3,000) and tags (75) for photos. Yahoo! owns it, and the service is free. It has two main stated goals:

1. To help people make their photos available to the people who matter to them.
2. To enable new ways to organizing photos.

Facebook. Facebook (facebook.com) is a social networking Web site, popular among college students. It was originally developed for university students, faculty, and staff but has since expanded to include everyone, including high school, corporate, and geographic communities.

As of December 2005, the Web site had the largest number of registered users among college-focused sites (at over 17 million college students worldwide). It is the number one site for photos, ahead of sites such as Flickr, with 2.3 million photos uploaded daily (see en.wikipedia.org/wiki/Facebook).

There have been concerns expressed regarding the use of Facebook as a means of surveillance and data mining for possible invasion of privacy. For other concerns, see Wikipedia.org and Chapter 17.

Classmates Online. Classmates Online (classmates.com) helps members find, connect, and keep in touch with friends and acquaintances from throughout their lives—including kindergarten, primary school, high school, college, work, and the U.S. military. Classmates Online has more than 40 million active members in the United States and Canada.

It is free for people to register as a Basic member of Classmates Online in order to list themselves to be found and to search the entire database for friends. Members may also post

social network analysis (SNA)
The mapping and measuring of relationships and flows between people, groups, organizations, animals, computers or other information or knowledge processing entities. The nodes in the network are the people and groups, whereas the links show relationships or flows between the nodes. SNA provides both a visual and a mathematical analysis of relationships.

photographs, announcements, biographies, read community message boards, and be informed of upcoming reunions. Gold members, who pay a fee, can also initiate sending e-mail to any member, use Web site tools for planning reunions and events, and form private groups and use My Network to communicate with friends.

Owned by United Online, the company itself owns social networking companies in Germany and Sweden. The site is profitable.

Friendster. Friendster (friendster.com) is based on the Circle of Friends technique for networking individuals in virtual communities and demonstrates the small-world phenomenon.

Friendster was considered the top online social network service until around April 2004, when it was overtaken by MySpace. Friendster has also received competition from all-in-one sites (sites that offer a diversity of services), such as Windows Live Spaces, Yahoo! 360, and Facebook. Generally speaking, the members of Friendster's service are young adults in Europe, North America, and Asia about 21 to 30 years old.

Orkut. Orkut (orkut.com) is an Internet social network service run by Google. It claims to be designed to help users meet new friends and maintain existing relationships. Similar to Friendster and MySpace, Orkut goes a step further by permitting the creation of easy-to-set-up simple forums (called "communities") of users. Until October 2006, Orkut was an invitation-only site, but it now permits users to create accounts without an invitation.

Orkut's use as a social tool is complex because various people frequently try to add strangers to their own pool of friends, often just to increase the number indicating their number of friends next to their name in their profile. Many "add-me" communities exist solely for this purpose. A large number of bogus, cloned, fake, invisible and "orphaned" profiles also exist.

Users can rate their friends, and profile information is available to all. It is popular mostly in Brazil (almost 60 percent of about 45 million members), and Portuguese is the first default language.

Xanga. Xanga (xanga.com) is a Web site that hosts Weblogs, photoblogs, and social networking profiles. It is operated by Xanga.com, Inc. Users of Xanga are referred to as "Xangans." Xanga's origins can be traced back to 1998, when it began as a site for sharing book and music reviews. It has since then evolved into one of the most popular blogging and networking services on the Web, with an estimated 27 million users worldwide (see en.wikipedia.org/wiki/Xanga).

A blogring connects a circle of Weblogs with a common focus or theme. All Xanga users are given the ability to create a new blogring or join an existing one. Blogrings are searchable by topic. A list of blogrings that the user is associated with appears in a module typically on the left side of the Web site. Each user is allowed a maximum of eight blogrings.

Digg. Digg (digg.com) is a community-based popularity Web site with an emphasis on technology and science articles see en.wikipedia.org/wiki/Digg. The site has recently expanded to provide a variety of other categories such as politics and videos. It combines social bookmarking, blogging, and syndication with a form of nonhierarchical, democratic editorial control. Users submit news stories and Web sites, and then a user-controlled ranking system promotes these stories and sites to the front page. This differs from the hierarchical editorial system that many other news sites employ. When you read many news items, you can see an option "digg it" or "digg that."

Readers can view all the stories that fellow users have submitted in the "digg/All/Upcoming" section of the site. Once a story has received enough "diggs," it appears on Digg's front page. Should the story not receive enough diggs, or if enough users report a problem with the submission, the story will remain in the "digg all" area, where it may eventually be removed. For further details, see en.wikipedia.org/wiki/Digg and Heilemann (2006b).

Cyworld. Cyworld (cyworld.com) is a South Korean Web community site operated by SK Telecom. Literally translated, "Cyworld" can mean "cyberworld," but it's also a play on the Korean word for relationship, so it could also mean "relationship world." It takes the concept of personal, "virtual rooms" similar to MySpace and CokeMusic to promote their products.

Members cultivate on- and off-line relationships by forming *Ilchon* buddy relationships with each other through a service called "minihompy," which encompasses a photo gallery, message board, guestbook, and personal bulletin board (see en.wikipedia.org/wiki/Cyworld). A user can link his or her minihompy to another user's minihompy to form a buddy relationship. It is similar to U.S.–based Facebook and MySpace Web sites. Reports show that as many as 90 percent of South

Koreans in their twenties and 25 percent of the total population of South Korea are registered users of Cyworld, and as of September 2005, daily unique visitors numbered about 20 million.

Today, Cyworld operates its site in the United States, China, Japan, Taiwan, Vietnam, and South Korea. For analysis, see Schonfeld (2006a).

Some Other Social Network Sites. The following sites are interesting:

Bebo.com—popular in the United Kingdom, Ireland, and New Zealand; it is similar to MySpace.

Piczo.com—popular in Canada and the United Kingdom; it is a teen-friendly site designed to deter perverts.

His.com—most popular in Mexico and Spain; it is a major competitor of MySpace.

Reunion.com—connects alumni of schools and organizes reunions; it owns several related Web sites.

friendsreunited.co.uk—similar to Reunion.com; it is the U.K. version where users can also find dating and job-search sites.

iwiw.net—a Hungarian social network with a multilingual interface.

Migente.com—focuses on the America Latino community.

Blackplanet.com—focuses on African American issues and people.

Grono.net—a Poland-based social network.

Section 18.4 ▶ REVIEW QUESTIONS

1. Define *social network*.
2. Define *social network analysis and services*.
3. Describe Flickr, Facebook, Classmates, and Friendster.
4. Describe Digg.
5. What is Cyworld?

18.5 YOUTUBE AND COMPANY—A WHOLE NEW WORLD

Free video-sharing Web sites (where users can upload, view, and share video clips) became very popular after the inception of YouTube in February 2005. Many companies try to compete with YouTube, which was named by *Time* magazine as the "Invention of the Year 2006." In this section, we will present the company and some of its competitors.

YOUTUBE: THE ESSENTIALS

YouTube is a consumer media company where people can watch and share original videos worldwide through a Web experience.

Everyone can watch videos on YouTube—both on YouTube.com and across the Internet. People can see firsthand accounts of current events, find videos about their hobbies and interests, and discover the quirky and unusual. As more people capture special moments on video, YouTube is empowering them to become the broadcasters of tomorrow. Users can rate videos; the site shows the average rating and the number of times users have watched a video.

What Is YouTube?

YouTube is a place for people to engage in new ways by sharing videos and commenting on them. YouTube originally started as a personal video-sharing service and has grown into an entertainment destination where people have watched about 100 million videos on the site daily (by the end of 2006). It is a prime example of a *social network*. With YouTube, people can:

▶ Upload, tag, and share videos worldwide
▶ Browse millions of original videos uploaded by community members
▶ Find, join, and create video groups to connect with people who have similar interests
▶ Customize the experience by subscribing to member videos, saving favorites, and creating play lists

▶ Integrate YouTube videos on Web sites using video embeds or APIs

▶ Make videos public or private—users can elect to broadcast their videos publicly or share them privately with specified friends and family upon upload

YouTube is building a community that is highly motivated to watch and share videos. The service is free for everyone. The company always encourages users to contact YouTube with thoughts, suggestions, feedback, or otherwise random ramblings. The site advises users to check out YouTube's blog in order to keep up to date on all the latest developments.

BRIEF HISTORY AND TECHNOLOGY

YouTube's video playback technology is based on Macromedia's (an Adobe company) Flash Player7 and uses the Sorenson Spark H.263 video codec. This technology allows users to display videos (including movies, TV clips, music videos, videoblogging, etc.) with quality comparable to more established video playback technologies that generally require their user to download and install a small piece of software called a browser plug-in in order to watch video. Flash itself requires a plug-in, but the Flash 7 (or newer) plug-in is generally considered to be present on approximately 90 percent of Internet-connected computers. Alternatively, users can use a number of Web sites to download the videos to their own computers. The use of Flash video was most likely a key component of YouTube's success, allowing viewers to watch video instantly without installing software or dealing with a common problem experienced with other Web video technologies—incompatible or varying versions of video players.

YouTube was one of the fastest-growing Web sites on the Internet during the summer of 2006 and was ranked as the fifth most popular Web site on Alexa (a popular rating company, see Section 18.10), far outpacing even MySpace's growth rate. YouTube's preeminence in the online video market is staggering. By July 2006, 100 million clips were viewed daily on YouTube, with an additional 65,000 new videos uploaded each day (en.wikipedia.org/wiki/YouTube). The site has about 20,000,000 visitors per month.

Google purchased YouTube for US$1.65 billion in stock on October 9, 2006. The purchase agreement between Google and YouTube came after YouTube presented three agreements with media companies in an attempt to escape the threat of copyright-infringement lawsuits (Chapter 17). YouTube continues to operate independently.

Like many start-ups, YouTube began as an angel-funded enterprise in a small office in San Mateo, California. Later on, Sequoia Capital, a venture capital firm, invested more money (see the process in Chapter 16). It is interesting to note that much of the early publicity for the site has come from the frequent demands to remove material from the site. Also, NBC, which initially demanded the removal of copyrighted material, created a strategic alliance with YouTube. An official NBC channel on YouTube now showcases promotional clips of its videos.

Social Impact of YouTube—The Celebrities

YouTube's popularity has led to the creation of many *YouTube Internet celebrities*, popular individuals who have attracted significant publicity in their home countries through their videos. The most subscribed YouTube member, as of August 16, 2006, is Geriatric 1927, an 80-year-old pensioner from England who gained widespread recognition within a week of making his debut on the site. For these users, Internet fame has had various unexpected effects. As an example, a YouTube user and former receptionist, Brooke Brodack, from Massachusetts has been signed by NBC's Carson Daly for an 18-month development contract. Another example is the blogger known as lonely girl, 15, who ended up being the fictitious character created by New Zealand actress Jessia Rose and some film directors. In 2007, a Dutch vocalist and songwriter named Esmée Denters announced that she would be traveling to the United States for professional recording sessions on the strength of her YouTube appearances. For a representative list of others who became Internet phenomena, see en.wikipedia.org/wiki/YouTube.

Band and Music Promotion. YouTube has also become a means of promoting bands and their music. One such example is OK Go that received a huge radio hit and an MTV Video Music Awards performance out of the treadmill video for "Here It Goes Again." In the same light, a video broadcasting the Free Hugs Campaign with accompanying music by the Sick

Puppies led to instant fame for both the band and the campaign. The main character of the video, Juan Mann who also achieved fame, is now being interviewed on Australian news programs and even has appeared on *The Oprah Winfrey Show*.

THE BUSINESS AND REVENUE MODELS

Before being bought by Google, YouTube had an advertising-based business model. Some industry commentators speculated that YouTube's running costs—specifically the bandwidth required—might be as high as US$1 million per month, thereby fueling criticisms that, like many Internet start-ups, it did not have a viably implemented business model (see en.wikipedia.org/wiki/YouTube).

The site launched advertisements in March 2006. In April 2006, YouTube started using Google AdSense. Given its traffic levels, video streams, and page views, some have calculated YouTube's potential revenues could be in the millions per month.

Strategic Advantages of the Business Model

The growth of YouTube has been extremely rapid, depending largely on referrals from users who alert their friends and family to a favorite video. Many of the viewers who discovered the site and then decided to share their own videos is a factor that continually expands YouTube's pool of content. A steady increase in high-speed Internet connections at home has propelled YouTube's success, making the distribution and consumption of online video more effective. Online File W18.1 and Case 18.1 show typical applications of YouTube.

IMPLEMENTATION DIFFICULTIES: THE COPYRIGHT PROBLEM

YouTube policy does not allow content to be uploaded by anyone not permitted by U.S. copyright law to do so, and the company frequently removes uploaded infringing content. Nonetheless, a large amount of copyrighted videos continues to be uploaded. Generally, YouTube only discovers these videos via indications within its community through self-policing. The service offers a flagging feature, intended as a means for reporting questionable content, including that which might constitute copyright infringement. However, the feature can be susceptible to abuse; for a time, some users were flagging other users' original content for copyright violations purely out of spite. It proceeded to remove copyright infringement from the list of offenses flagable by members. The primary way in which a user identifies the content of a video is through the search terms that uploaders associate with clips. However, some users have created alternative words as search terms when uploading copyrighted types of files. This makes it difficult to find them.

TV journalist Robert Tur filed the first lawsuit against YouTube in summer 2006, alleging copyright infringement for hosting a number of famous news clips without permission. As of January 2007, the case was not resolved.

The Brazilian Court Case

In Chapter 17, we discussed the legal problems of social networks and YouTube. Here is an example of how complex the issue can be. In early January 2007, a Brazilian court ordered (for the second time) YouTube to block footage of super-model Daniela Cicarelli and her boyfriend in intimate scenes along a beach in Spain. YouTube removed the clip in September 2006, but the clip still appears periodically on YouTube under different titles. The judge said YouTube must find a way to use filters so the clip stops popping up in Brazil on the Web site. Lawyer Rubens Decousseau Tilkian, who represents Cicarelli's boyfriend, said YouTube had not gone *far enough* to prevent access to the clip because people succeeded in posting it using different names for the video. Can YouTube comply with the court order? And at what cost? The Brazilian court has the authority to fine YouTube about $120,000 for each day the video is viewable.

Content owners are not just targeting YouTube for copyright infringements on the site, but they are also targeting third-party Web sites that link to infringing content on YouTube and other video-sharing sites.

CASE 18.1
EC Application

HOW YOUTUBE CAPITALIZES ON MAJOR EVENTS AND COMMERCIAL VIDEOS

Here are some examples of how YouTube collaborates with both advertisers and media companies:

▶ The Sundance Channel announced a strategic alliance with YouTube on January 17, 2007, (YouTube 2007) for coverage of the 2007 Sundance Film Festival, including a video blog on YouTube. YouTube will show special clips from the festival throughout 2007 (see *youtube.com/sundancechannel*). Also, it will show profiles of competing filmmakers, clips from past festivals, and in-depth daily coverage by YouTube users Arin Crumley and Susan Buice. The partnership also provides advertising for YouTube partners including Sundance.

The Sundance Channel syndicated a video blog created by Crumley and Buice exclusively for YouTube. Crumley and Buice served as Sundance Channel correspondents during the 2007 Sundance Film Festival and documented their daily experiences from a festival-attendee and independent filmmaker perspective. They pioneered new strategies for independent film distribution through digital technology including podcasts, custom Google maps, and a 2007 screening of their film *Second Life* in the virtual world.

The Sundance Channel's Festival's minisite includes all content available on YouTube, plus exclusive photos and a blog hosted by Peter Bowen, senior Editor of *Filmmaker* Magazine, who follows the buzz around films and acquisitions. Sundance pays fees for the advertisements on YouTube.

▶ YouTube and Coca-Cola introduced video cards for the 2007 holiday season (YouTube 2006a). People were able to send their own personal videos as a holiday greeting card online. Visitors were also able to share their holiday spirit by uploading their own videos, customizing video greetings created by popular YouTube personalities including Geriatric 1927, Boh3m3, TerraNaomi, Renetto, TheWineKone, and LisaNova. Holiday-themed videos were also available to share from Coca-Cola including clips from vintage Coke advertisements. Selected video greetings that users chose to share with the world were featured as part of a video play list on Coca-Cola.com called the Holiday WishCast and were seen by people around the world.

The Coca-Cola Holiday WishCast gave friends and families a new way to communicate during the 2006 holiday season. WishCast was a unique way for people to connect, whether it was helping loved ones keep in touch, creating a last-minute holiday card, or allowing bands to send personalized greetings to their fans. It was the latest evolution in the development of Coca-Cola.com following the relaunch of the site in July 2006 that included user-generated content and the addition of digital music downloads in August 2006.

The partnership with Coca-Cola gave the YouTube community the ability to send holiday wishes in a way that truly harnesses the creativity of the users. To send a holiday video greeting, people visited either *youtube.com/wishcast* or *coca-cola.com/wishcast*.

▶ According to YouTube (2006b), the YouTube Community and Warner Music Group (WMG) artists created "Special New Year's Messages to Share with the World" (sponsored by Chevrolet). The first-ever YouTube New Year's Eve Countdown celebrated New Year's as it happened around the world with new videos featured every hour from dozens of locations worldwide. For details, see Online File W18.2.

▶ Starting January 31, 2007, Plaxo, RockYou.com, Technorati, and three other small companies are putting their versions of Superbowl-style ads on the Web. The companies have bundled their ads together in a YouTube channel called SuperDotComAdsXLI; they hope to use their various social networks and corporate blogs to generate audiences for all the commercials.

The various start-ups involved began kicking the idea around January 15, 2007. Plaxo is home to some budding filmmakers, so McCrea (vice president of marketing at Plaxo) let a small team of employees put something together. He was so impressed with the results that he decided to use the spot to launch Plaxo's new logo and tagline. Now he's considering doing even more video ads solely for the online medium. Because these ads are inexpensive to produce it makes sense that Web-based companies use that platform to promote themselves.

Sources: YouTube (2007), YouTube (2006a), and YouTube (2006b).

Questions

1. What are the benefits to Sundance? Why is this a Web 2.0 application?

2. Describe how a video card works? What are the benefits to Coca-Cola?

3. Read Online File W18.2 and identify the reasons why the New Year's Eve Countdown is a true Web 2.0 application.

4. YouTube collects money from its partners in all four of the applications mentioned previously. Why are the partners willing to pay?

In 2007, big media, such as Viacom, NBC, and News Corp., have all taken shots at YouTube (see La Monica 2007 and Chapter 17).

THE COMPETITION

The success of YouTube drove a large number of companies to compete with it. On one hand, there were several start-ups completely dedicated to video sharing. On the other hand, several social networks (e.g., MySpace) added video sharing as one of their offerings. Online File W18.3 provides a comparison of the following 10 companies: eyespot, Google Video, Grouper, Jumpcut, Ourmedia, Rever, Video Egg, Vimeo, vSocial and YouTube. Details are available at dvguru.com (posting by Bilsborrow-Koo 2006). Other competitors are: blip.tv, veoh, videojug, Flurl.com, and Yahoo! Video, and Meetcafe. Meetcafe meetcafe.com, a rival of YouTube, launched a new forum of online video content by putting amateur contributors together with professional film makers in 2007. Known as Café Confidential, the new channel is an attempt to introduce higher standards to the often chaotic user-generated content. Meetcafe also rewards amateurs that use this channel. According to Media Metrix market news on September 26, 2006, MySpace already accounts for 20 percent of the 7.2 billion video streams across the Web (comScore 2006). So MySpace may be the major competitor of YouTube. Five major media companies joined MySpace in 2007 (see Lashinsky 2007a) who offer free legitimate videos to "kill" YouTube.

To counter the competition, YouTube is offering innovative applications such as video awards to most creative and popular original videos (youtube.com/YTAwards).

Section 18.5 ▶ REVIEW QUESTIONS

1. Define *video sharing* and describe how it is done at YouTube.
2. What can people do on YouTube?
3. How can YouTube create Internet celebrities?
4. How can YouTube promote music and artists?
5. What are YouTube's revenue sources? How are these revenue models related to Google?

18.6   BUSINESS AND ENTREPRENEURIAL NETWORKS

In Chapter 1 we introduced a business network named Xing.com. Here, we describe some other such networks.

BUSINESS NETWORKS

A **business network** is defined as a group of people that have some kind of commercial or business relationship—for example, the relationships between sellers and buyers, buyers among themselves, buyers and suppliers, and colleagues and other colleagues. Business networking functions best when individuals offer to help others to find connections rather than "cold-calling" on prospects themselves (see en.wikipedia.org/wiki/Business_network). Business networking can take place outside of traditional business physical environments. For example, public places such as airports or golf courses provide opportunities to make new business contacts if an individual has good social skills. The Internet is also proving to be a good place to network.

business network
A group of people that have some kind of commercial relationship. For example, the relationships between sellers and buyers, buyers among themselves, buyers and suppliers, and colleagues and other colleagues.

Example: LinkedIn

The main purpose of LinkedIn is to allow registered users to maintain a list of contact details of people they know and trust in business (see en.wikipedia.org/wiki/LinkedIn). The people in the list are called *connections*. Users can invite anyone, whether they are a LinkedIn user or not, to become a connection.

Here is how the site works:

- A contact network is built up consisting of their direct connections, each of their connections' connections (called second degree connections) and also the connections of second degree connections (called third degree connections). This can be used, for example, to gain an introduction to someone you wish to know through a mutual, trusted contact. LinkedIn's officials are members and have hundreds of connections each (see Copeland 2006).
- It can then be used to find jobs, people, and business opportunities recommended by anyone in your contact network.
- Employers can list jobs and search for potential candidates.
- Job seekers can review the profile of hiring managers and discover which of their existing contacts can introduce them.

The "gated-access approach," where contact with any professional requires either a preexisting relationship or the intervention of a contact of theirs, is intended to build trust among the service's users. LinkedIn participates in the EU Safe Harbor Privacy Framework.

The newest (as of January 2007) LinkedIn feature is "LinkedIn Answers." As the name suggests, the service is similar to Answers.com or Yahoo! Answers. The service allows LinkedIn users to ask questions for the community to answer. "LinkedIn Answers" is free, and the questions are potentially more business-oriented.

For more on LinkedIn and its capabilities and success see Copeland (2006).

Entrepreneurial Network

In business, *entrepreneurial networks* are social organizations offering different types of resources to start or improve entrepreneurial projects or start-ups. Combined with leadership, the entrepreneurial network is an indispensable kind of social network not only necessary to properly run the business or project but also to differentiate the business from similar ones.

The goal of most entrepreneurial networks is to bring together a broad selection of professionals and resources that complement each others' endeavors (see en.wikipedia.org/wiki/Entrepreneurial_network). Initially a key priority is to aid successful business launches. Subsequently, the networks provide motivation, direction, and increased access to opportunities and other skill sets. Promotion of each member's talents and services both within the network and out in the broader market increases opportunities for all participants.

One of the key needs of any start-up is capital, and often entrepreneurial networks focus on help in obtaining financial resources particularly tailored to their membership demographic.

Entrepreneurial networks may also become online communities involved in endorsing reforms, legislation, or other municipal drives that accommodate their organization's goals.

Examples of entrepreneurial networks are:

- Ecademy.com (ecademy.com) is a global social network for business people. There you can: build trust with business professionals; share contacts, knowledge, and support; find jobs, prospects and clients; attend networking events; and trade across the globe.
- European young professionals (eyplondon.org) promotes links between European business professionals.

Note: Both organizations conduct physical activities as well.

SOCIAL MARKETPLACE

social marketplace
The term *social marketplace* is derived from the combination of social networking and marketplaces, such that a social marketplace acts like an online community harnessing the power of one's social networks for the introduction, buying, and selling of products, services, and resources, including people's own creations. A social marketplace can also be referred to as a structure that resembles a social network but has a focus on its individual members.

The term **social marketplace** is derived from the combination of social networking and marketplaces, such that a social marketplace acts like an online community harnessing the power of one's social networks for introducing, buying, and selling of products, services, and resources, including people's own creations. A social marketplace can also be referred to as a structure that resembles a social network but has a focus on its individual members.

Ideally, a social marketplace should enable members' own creations as much as they blog, link, and post. Section 18.9 describes a market for musicians, filmmakers, authors, designers, and other creative individuals.

Examples of social marketplaces include (per en.wikipedia.org/wiki/Social_marketplace):

- **Windows Live Expo.** Windows Live Expo is an online social marketplace similar to Craigslist in that it provides online classifieds. A major focus of the site is that users choose listings they want to search sorted either by friends and contacts or by geographic proximity.
- **Fotolia.** Fotolia is a social marketplace for royalty-free stock images, a huge community of creative people who enjoy sharing, learning, and expressing themselves through forums and blogs, allowing other individuals and professionals to legally buy and share stock images and illustrations.
- **Flipsy.** Anyone can use Flipsy to list, buy, and sell books, music, movies, and games. It was created to fill the need for a free and trustworthy media marketplace. Flipsy sells products by identification using bar codes. It does not charge commissions in order to foster increased trading, with payment processing is handled by a third party, such as PayPal.

Section 18.6 ▶ REVIEW QUESTIONS

1. Define *business network*.
2. Describe LinkedIn and its capabilities.
3. Define *entrepreneurial network*.
4. Define *social marketplace*.

18.7 TRAVEL AND TOURISM—THE EC REVOLUTION IS HERE

Travel and tourism is a rapidly growing industry, and in some countries, it is the largest or the fastest growing sector in the economy. It has a large international dimension, and as we saw in Chapters 3 and 6, it has a very high level of Web adaptation. In this section, we will mainly look at the intense competition on the Web.

THE MAJOR PLAYERS

The major players in the industry are:

- **The service providers.** These include airlines, hotels, car rental companies, and similar travel-related businesses. These can be divided into two categories:
  1. Click-and-mortar companies, which are basically the norm in the industry today. For example, airlines have physical offices, but they also sell tickets online.
  2. Brick-and-mortar companies do business only in the physical world. This category is disappearing.
- **The travel agents and other intermediaries.** Here again we have click-and-mortar and brick-and-mortar categories, as well as the pure online companies. They can serve the retail market, be wholesalers, or serve businesses only (B2B). Some companies specialize in tours (e.g., Trafalgar). Many of the pure online companies concentrate on discounts in industry segments (e.g. cheap airline tickets). Travel agents use different models such as "name-your-own-price" used by Priceline (Chapter 10). Yahoo!, Amazon.com, and thousands of other e-tailers offer online travel.
- **Aggregators and comparison price provider.** These companies are intermediaries that provide information to travelers, including price comparisons, and are sometimes affiliated with travel agents or providers, receiving a commission for referrals.
- **Traveler service providers.** This includes travel guide issuers (e.g., Lonely Planet, see Chapter 14), travel insurance providers, computerized reservation system providers, event monitoring, city guide publishers, and the like.
- **Social networks.** As we will see later, some social networks are dedicated to travel (e.g. WAYN.com).

Many of these players support blogs and special social networks (which we will discuss later). The roles played by these participants vary and at times overlap. All these accelerate the competition in the industry (Chapter 2).

THE IMPACTS OF THE WEB

The traditional tourism industry is changing. Special tourism products such as sports, cruises, MICE (meetings, incentives, congresses, and exhibitions) tourism, and market segments, such as ecotourism, youth, or senior tourism, are expanding rapidly. Therefore, intercultural awareness and personal friendships fostered through tourism are a powerful force for improving international understanding. International tourism becomes the world's largest export earner and an important factor in the economy of many nations.

Representative Impacts

The Internet has the potential to change the roles and the balance of power among the industry players and the travelers (e.g., see Werthner and Ricci 2004). Some may experience an increase in power and profitability; others may experience the opposite; and still others may even find that they have been bypassed and lost their market share. For example, in the case of air travel, airlines have a motive to bypass travel agencies. The airlines could handle ticket sales directly online because they can target customers with the information they obtain through sources such as frequent-flyer programs.

Tourism can be viewed as an information business. Tourists leave their daily environment and move elsewhere to consume the product. Thus, the product itself cannot be tested and controlled in advance, but information about it can be useful. Thus, information is the backbone that supports tourism, and it must be timely and accurate relevant to the consumer's needs. Within the fiercely competitive global tourism environment, prospective travelers are faced continuously with more information and options. The combination of these forces and the need for professionalism in handling information supplied to the consumer necessitates the use of IT to gather, manage, distribute, and communicate information.

The Web has the potential to eliminate expensive intermediary systems in working toward a network system and e-marketplaces. IT is now evidenced in the entire supply and value chains of the industry's players. The Internet is also a possible instrument to close the gap between local suppliers and the demand side. It also offers the small, local players a chance for direct customer contact and the opportunity to sell their products on the global market.

Here are some impacts of the Web: Direct sale of airline tickets over the Web constitutes more than 50 percent of all airline ticket sales in the United States and is increasing because it is less expensive to do. Airline booking via cell phones is becoming a reality. Self check-in is available in many airports, and printing of boarding passes at home is common. Soon we will see check-in kiosks that can process multiple airlines. All these provide more convenience to travelers and save money for the airlines.

Finally, the Web is changing, not only for the providers but also for the travelers who actually act as their own "travel agents" building a personalized travel package (see Werthner and Ricci 2004).

Online Collaboration

The Web offers travel companies the ability to collaborate online.

Example. Ctrip is the largest Chinese online travel company preparing for the many tourists who will arrive for the 2008 Olympic Games. At the same time, on the other side of the Taiwan Straits, a smaller company, ezTravel, is collaborating with Ctrip to book lodging, transportation, and events for travelers attending the Olympics. Also, with an increase in Chinese tourists coming to Taiwan, ezTravel makes the arrangement for those Chinese tourists who are using Ctrip.

TRAVELERS AND SOCIAL NETWORKS

Starting in 2005, online leisure travelers' use of social computing technologies, such as blogs, RSS, wikis, and user reviews, for researching travel has skyrocketed. Travel e-businesses, marketing executives, and managers realized that social computing was increasingly playing a larger role in corporate online strategy, even if all a company does is monitor what travelers say about a certain company in third-party forums. Those companies implementing social computing technologies on their own Web sites probably need to view it primarily as supporting business goals, such as improving customer communication or increasing engagement of customers, and less as a sales or customer service tool.

As travelers forge connections and share information with like-minded travelers online, their needs and expectations change. They want more relevance and more correct information. Social computing has shifted online travel from passive selling to active customer engagement, which affects each part of the way travel companies and agents distribute and market their products (Epps et al. 2007). Several social networks have travel channels that cater to travelers. One such network is Wikia.com. In a special report, Harteveldt (2006) provided guidelines for travel e-commerce and marketing executives and managers on how travelers embrace social computing technologies. Let's now look at an example of a social network.

WAYN: A Social Network for Travelers

WAYN (standing for *Where Are You Now?*) is a social networking Web site (wayn.com) with a goal of uniting travelers from around the world. WAYN was launched in London in May 2003. It grew from 45,000 to about 7 million members by 2007 (about 2 million members in the United Kingdom). It is also strong in the United States, Canada, Australia, New Zealand, and other countries in Western Europe. It is growing by 20,000 members daily.

As with many other social networking services, WAYN enables its users to create a personal profile, upload photos, and store photos. Users can then search for others with similar profiles and link them to their profiles as friends. It is also possible to send and receive messages using discussion forums. Because it is designed for travelers, members are able to search for contacts based on a particular location. Using a world map, it enables a user to visually locate where each of their contacts are situated around the world. The service is intended to be used for its members to keep friends informed of where they are while traveling and locating their friends.

In addition, users can send SMSs to any of their contacts worldwide; chat online using WAYN's Instant Messenger; plan trips and notify their friends about them. Using WAYN, users can create discussion groups, ask for recommendations, and send smiley icons to all. Finally, chat bots (avatars) are dynamic and fully active, representing one of the best ways of meeting people in the WAYN community.

WAYN is one of the very few sites that didn't lose the impact of new subscriptions after introducing fees for taking advantage of the premier membership service, making it one of the few social networking communities that has managed to quickly become profitable.

WAYN has grown popular in over 220 countries becoming a global brand. It is most popular within the 18 to 25 age group but also seems to have a strong position among the 35 to 45-plus age group. Members can find out who will be traveling to their next intended destination, at the same time as they are.

For further information, see wayn.com, en.wikipedia.org/wiki/WYAN, and PRWeb.com (2003).

Travel Recommendation

One of the characteristics of Web 2.0 is *personalization*. For an example of how it is being done in the travel industry, see Case 18.2.

Corporate Social Network

In Chapter 1, we cited the case of Carnival Cruise Line with its social network at carnivalconnection.com. The major objective is to find things that need fixing (e.g., services that need to be addressed to provide better customer service) and also participate in free viral marketing. Section 18.11 discusses soliciting customer comments.

Providers' Networks

Travel service providers are jumping on the Web 2.0 wagon as well. For example, American Express Business Travel and Rearden Commerce (a Web-based travel management service start up) are developing Web 2.0 applications for corporate customers. The applications are based on service-oriented architecture (see Online Chapter 19), which is frequently used in Web 2.0 applications.

CASE 18.2
EC Application
CONTENT-BASED FILTERING AT EUROVACATIONS.COM

Increasingly, travel and tourism Web sites are using recommendation systems to help travelers make more informed decisions for their vacations in less time. EuroVacations.com (*eurovacations.com*), one of the most successful travel counseling Web sites, uses TripleHop Technologies's TripMatcher to provide customized recommendations on destinations and travel products, according to the site visitors' stated or implied preferences.

The software, called Destination Wizard on EuroVacations.com, primarily takes a content-based approach in generating recommendations. The site asks users to indicate their needs and constraints (e.g., activities interests, budget, duration) by selecting the options available under a list of questions. The system then compares the user inputs with the attributes of a list of available travel products and destinations in the database.

To reduce user effort, the system simultaneously builds an attribute-based behavioral profile of the user as he or she interacts with the system each time he or she visits the Web site, and from this, implicit information about the users' interests can be extracted. The system then predicts the user's preference by combining statistics on his or her past queries and a weighted average of importance of different attributes assigned by similar users. Hence, users need to answer only a limited number of questions to obtain personalized recommendations targeted to their interests. The system presents the output to users in order of relevance. By exploiting content-based recommendation technology, it is possible for EuroVacations.com to achieve a higher browser-to-buyer conversion rate.

Sources: Compiled from Eyefortravel.com (2007) and *eurovacations.com* (accessed March 2007).

Questions

1. Explain how the system makes recommendations.
2. In your opinion, what are the limitations of such a system?
3. Can you use any other Web 2.0 technologies to improve this system?

Section 18.7 ▶ REVIEW QUESTIONS

1. List the major players in the tourism industry.
2. How do online activities impact the industry?
3. How do social networks change the industry operations?
4. What services can a social network provide?

18.8 ZOPA, PROSPER, AND P2P LENDING: WILL THEY DISRUPT BANKING?

Any industry making a huge profit margin off its customers is a good candidate for disruption. Banking is a classic case—just think of the 19 percent interest you pay on credit cards and the 2 percent you earn on your savings account.

In this section, we will introduce two Web 2.0 companies that are trying to disrupt the banking industry—ZOPA in the United Kingdom and Prosper in the United States.

THE INNOVATION: PERSON-TO-PERSON LENDING

person-to person lending
Lending done between individuals circumventing the bank traditional role in this process.

Individuals who want to borrow money may be required to pay 10 to 20 percent interest if they use their revolving credit cards. At the same time, they receive 2 percent to 5.5 percent interest on their savings. The banks take the difference, but they also take the risk from the lenders. Now assume that an individual lender can negotiate directly with an individual borrower. It is likely that each can be better off than with the bank. Suppose they agree on 8 percent interest. The lender will get much more. The borrower will pay much less. The problem is how they find each other and negotiate and secure loans. This is where innovative sites such as ZOPA enter the picture. The basic idea is that of **person-to-person lending**, meaning you lend money directly to a consumer rather than "selling" your money to the bank, and the banks then loan their money to consumers.

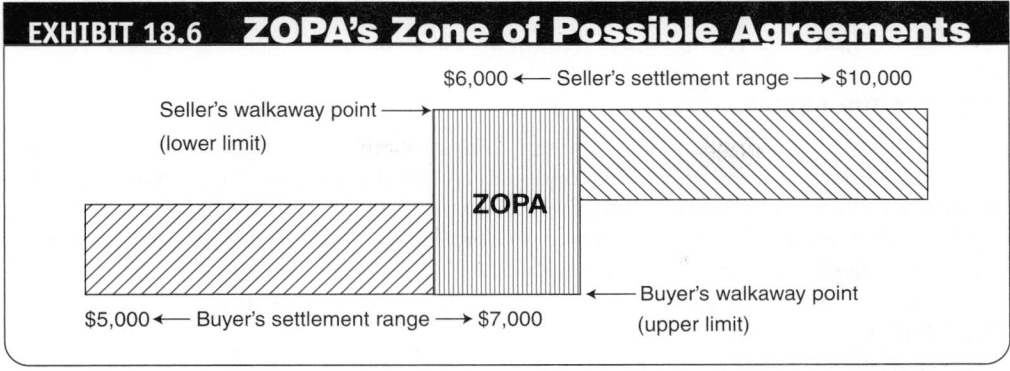

EXHIBIT 18.6   ZOPA's Zone of Possible Agreements

The Zone of Possible Agreements in Negotiation

Exhibit 18.6 illustrates a typical negotiation situation. Suppose you want to sell your used car. Usually, you have some range of expectation within which you are willing to settle. You know that you will never get more than $10,000 for your car, but in the worst case, you will accept $6,000 (these numbers may be changed with the time and the experience of offers). The buyer also has a settlement range, for example, $5,000 to $7,000.

Notice that in such a case there is an overlap between the ranges, which means that a deal is possible. The seller will start with $10,000 and reduce the price slowly, and the buyer will start with $5,000 increasing it slowly. If the ranges do not overlap, there will be no deal. Otherwise, you will sell your car with a price in the overlapping zone. This overlapping range is called the "Zone of Possible Agreements" (ZOPA), and this is also the name of the pioneering company. Agreement in this zone must also be more beneficial to both sides than what they can get in the bank. Note that ZOPA has a lower limit, which signifies the seller's walkaway position ($6,000 in our example). If an offer is less than $6,000, the seller will not entertain it. Similarly, the buyer's walkaway point is $7,000; therefore, he or she will not consider any higher price.

The same idea applies to lending. However, this time you need intermediation, and this is where ZOPA and Prosper enter the picture. These (and similar companies) are using the Web to allow personal lending on a massive scale. ZOPA was the first company to introduce such peer-to-peer lending. What Skype did to telecoms and Amazon.com did to retailers is being done here to traditional banks, namely—disintermediation.

ZOPA LTD.

ZOPA was founded in London in March 2005, and by January 2007 it had 40 employees and 105,000 registered member users (lenders and borrowers). ZOPA arranges for more than $100,000 loans every day.

Securing the Loans

ZOPA tries to check the background of the borrowers in the following ways:

▶ Conducting a credit rating investigation at Experion, Equifax, or a similar company
▶ Checking people's eBay rating (if available)
▶ Checking the borrower's profile (if available online)
▶ Only one account is permitted for each borrower
▶ Checking the possibility of identity theft by a borrower by asking questions about past borrowing, demographics, etc.

In addition, ZOPA advises lenders to spread out the risk by lending from one individual to several borrowers. In addition, if you like to sleep better, you can get insurance (for a fee) on the amount you lend. The risk, however, is not large; the actual bad debt rate is less than 0.05 percent. A possible explanation of the low default rate is that borrowers are more likely to pay back real people than a faceless bank. The unlucky lenders can use a collection agency as in any other unpaid debt.

Finally, ZOPA covers any damage from fraud done to your ZOPA account by intruders provided you have kept your personal account details secure.

The Revenue Model

ZOPA takes 0.5 percent of the loan amount from both the lender and the borrower. There are no hidden fees, and the only other (optional) cost to the lender is the insurance (plus the fees that ZOPA takes for arranging the insurance). At the moment there is no advertisement on the site. But it is likely that in the future vendors will try to sell related products or services to either the lenders or the buyers.

The Lending Process

Step 1. Let's say that a lender has $20,000. She transferred it to her ZOPA account stating her willingness to get a 7.5 percent interest rate from borrowers of top credit rating, for two years.

Step 2. ZOPA organizes a pool of, for example, 40 borrowers with a similar credit worthiness of top rating, one that meets the lender's requirement. Each will get $20,000 divided by 40 = $500.

Step 3. The lender can read the profile of the prospective borrowers and the intended use of the money. The borrowers can read the lender's profile as well. This fosters a personal relationship between borrowers and lenders and helps in reducing default(s).

Step 4. ZOPA arranges the contracts.

Step 5. ZOPA collects interest payments and mails the lender a monthly check.

Step 6. ZOPA arranges repayment of the loan after two years.

PROSPER

Prosper (prosper.com) is the first U.S. P2P lender. Started in February 2006, it was created to make consumer lending more financially and socially rewarding for everybody. In January 2007, Prosper reported 130,000 members and outstanding loans of $30 million. It operates somewhat similar to ZOPA, but its revenue model is different. Prosper collects a 1–2 percent fee of the funded loan from the borrowers. In addition, lenders pay .5 percent annual loan servicing fees. Because of the higher fees, the company can assume more risk. Thus, they check only credit scores and borrowers' group affiliation.

The way Prosper works is intuitive to people who have used eBay. However, instead of listing (by sellers) and bidding (by buyers) on items, lenders here bid and borrowers list needs using Prosper's online auction platform. For details see Steiner (2007). Here are the major steps of the process:

1. Borrowers create a loan listing on Prosper, specifying amount needed, the purpose of the loan, and the interest rate they are willing to pay.
2. Prosper displays borrower credit grade (from AA to higher risk).
3. Borrowers provide photos of themselves, their children, and even of their pets. They also provide the purpose of the required money and how they plan to pay it back.
4. Lenders review loan listings and bid to fund only the ones they choose using a bidding process.
5. Group leaders manage borrower groups and use their reputation to get great rates for borrowers.
6. When a match is found, Prosper arranges for the money transfer and then manages the loan.

Groups on Prosper are formed to bring people together for the common goal of borrowing at better rates. Groups earn reputations according to their members' repayment records. Borrowers that organize groups earn rewards.

COMPETITION

P2P lending competes both with traditional banks and with online banking. Online banking is especially attractive to small investors, with some banks offering online savings accounts of 5 percent to 6 percent in 2006 through 2007.

Section 18.8 ▶ REVIEW QUESTIONS

1. Define *P2P lending*.
2. Define the *zone of possible agreements*.
3. Describe how ZOPA arranges loans.
4. Describe security measures for lenders.
5. Describe Prosper.

18.9 ENTERTAINMENT WEB 2.0 STYLE: FROM COMMUNITIES TO ENTERTAINMENT MARKETPLACES

The rich media of Web 2.0 technologies, the involvement of millions of young people who are interested in online entertainment, the availability of innovative tools, and the creative and collaborative nature of Web 2.0 all facilitate entertainment. Also, Web 2.0 tools facilitate the proliferation of entertainment on demand (Tynan 2006). In this section, we describe entertainment-centered communities as well as other issues related to Web 2.0 entertainment.

ENTERTAINMENT AND BUSINESS COMMUNITIES

A large number of social networks and communities are fully or partially dedicated to entertainment. Here are a few examples:

Last.FM

Last.FM (last.fm) is an Internet radio station and music *recommendation* system that merged with sister site Audioscrobbler in August 2005. In May 2007, CBS purchased Last.FM in order to extend its reach online (*The New York Times* 2007). The system builds a detailed profile of each user's musical taste, also recommending artists similar to members' favorites, showing their favorite artists and songs on a customizable profile Web page comprising the songs played on its stations selected via a collaborative filter, or optionally, recorded by a Last.FM plug-in installed into its users' music playing application.

A Last.fm user can build a musical profile using two methods: by listening to their personal music collection on a music player application with an Audioscrobbler plug-in or by listening to the Last.FM Internet radio service. Songs played are added to a log from which personal top artist or track bar charts and musical recommendations are calculated. They call this automatic track logging scrobbling. The user's page also displays recently played tracks, which are available via Web services, allowing users to display them on blogs or as forum signatures.

Regular membership is free, whereas premium membership is $3 per month. Owned by Last.FM Ltd. (United Kingdom), the site won Best Community Music Site at the BT Digital Music Awards in October 2006, and in January 2007 it was nominated for Best Web site in the NME Awards. The site operates in 10 major languages.

Mixi

Mixi, Inc. (mixi.co.jp) is an invitation-only social networking service site in Japan. The focus of mixi is "community entertainment," that is, meeting new people by way of common interests. Users can send and receive messages, write in a diary, read and comment on others' diaries, organize and join communities, and invite their friends to join. There were more than 5.7 million members and 490,000 communities of friends and interests as of November 2006 (see en.wikipedia.org/wiki/Mixi). The word *mixi* is a combination of *mix* and *I*, referring to the idea that the user, "I," "mixes" with other users through the service.

Mixi Station, a client program that detects songs being played in iTunes and Windows Media Player, uploads them automatically to a communally accessible list in the "Music" section, was implemented late in June 2006. By July 2006, support for the multimedia player Winamp was implemented via a Winamp plug-in and was made official by Mixi.

Second Life

In 2003, a three-dimensional world called Second Life was opened to the public. The world is entirely built and owned by its residents. In 2003, the virtual world consisted of 64 acres.

It has since grown to 65,000 acres and is inhabited by 8,558,745 residents from around planet (see secondlife.com). The virtual world consists of a huge digital continent, people, entertainment, experiences, and opportunity.

Thousands of new residents join each day, creating an avatar through which they travel around the Second Life world; meeting people, having fun, and buying virtual land where they can open a business or build a personal space limited only by their imaginations and their ability to use the Virtual 3D applications.

Second Life is dedicated to creativity, and everything in Second Life is resident-created. Residents retain the rights to their digital creations and can buy, sell, and trade with other residents at various in-world venues. Businesses succeed by the ingenuity, artistic ability, entrepreneurial acumen, and the owners' reputation.

Real-world businesses use the virtual world too. IBM uses it as a location for meetings, training and recruitment (Reuters 2006). American Apparel is the first major retailer to set up shop in Second Life (Jana 2006). Starwood Hotels uses Second Life as a relatively low-cost market research experiment in which avatars visit Starwood's virtual Aloft hotel. While the endeavor has created publicity for the company, feedback on the design of the hotel is solicited from visiting avatars and will be reflected in brick-and-mortar when the first real-world Aloft hotels open in 2008 (Carr 2007).

ADVERTISING MOVIES AND EVENTS IN COMMUNITIES

Communities are a natural place to advertise events such as movies. Here is an example.

Clerks II was released in August 2006 by Kevin Smith, the producer. Smith used MySpace to promote the film in a true "Indy Guerilla style." The movie characters (e.g., Dante Hicks, Randall Graves) have their own pages at MySpace linked to the movie's hub pages as biographies.

Each week, starting in May 2006 and running until the release of *Clerks II* on August 18, 2006, users went into the "Our Friends" list and picked out fellow MySpacers at random participating in a contest. Those who have the *Clerks II* MySpace page in their top 8 won a prize shipped directly from the View Askew offices in Red Bank, New Jersey (Smith 2006).

By word-of-mouth, the information about the contest and the movie was spreading at MySpace, enabling Smith to stay within a low budget, yet grossing millions from the movie.

ONLINE MARKETPLACE FOR MOVIES

InDplay Inc. (indplay.com) is a start-up with a mission to connect films with professional buyers through an online marketplace. It can be viewed as occupying the middle ground between the user-generated videos on YouTube and the select world of theatrical distribution. It uses databases such as those from IMD6 Inc.

In the marketplace, owners of any video can register as sellers and upload preview clips and any other information. Buyers representing theaters, DVD, TV, cable, Internet sites, and other outlets, register and make e-mail offers to the sellers. Purchases and payments are made via PayPal or wire transfer. InDplay gets an 8 percent standard commission. According to Woyke (2006), there are more than 10 million films and TV programs around the world available for sale (or license), and more than 100,000 professional buyers.

The site includes community features such as ratings and reviews (similar to eBay), and connects people at all stages of a film project via wikis and blogs. For more on movie downloading, see the Netflix Opening Case in Chapter 4.

Start-ups such as Audio, Lulu, Pump, and Zatto offer similar online markets for music, TV shows, and books.

THE HYPE MACHINE

The Hype Machine is a new invention (Heilemann 2006a). Here is how it works: (1) A server scans music blogs for posting with links to MP3 files. (2) When a file is found, it gets indexed, and the file is added to a database. The title is posted on the Hype Machine directory. (3) Users can listen to tracks through the site's built-in player or buy music through links to Amazon.com or iTunes. The users can also search the database for their favorite bands.

INTERNET SERIES

Similar to soap operas on TV, there is an increasing number of Internet series; some are already on DVDs. Examples are: *Broken Series* (24 episodes by October 2006), *Soup of the Day* (34 episodes), and *Floaters* (15 episodes). For details see Arnold (2006).

MOBILE WEB 2.0 DEVICES FOR ENTERTAINMENT AND WORK

Several mobile devices were designed with blogs, wikis, and other P2P services in mind. Here are some examples.

iPhone

The iPhone (from apple.com) is an *all-in-one* smartphone introduced in 2007. It is considered a disruptor in the cell phone market. Soon after iPhone's release, Samsung announced a competitor phone.

On one hand the iPhone has the functionalities of BlackBerry (Chapter 9). On the other hand, as a personal media player, the iPhone offers all the capabilities of an iPod, with music and video playback, plus the benefits of a high-resolution widescreen display for showing movies and video. It is a touch screen smartphone with full-blown Internet communications capabilities, quad-band, EDGE-capable mobile phone, and it has a brain (i.e., PAD capabilities) making it simple and easy to use. It also has a camera, a headset jack, and a built-in speaker.

Here are some more features: There is a sleep/wake button; a proximity sensor turns off the screen when users hold the phone to their heads; and automatic orientation adjustment switches on the fly between portrait and landscape modes. The iPhone boasts virtually no dedicated controls; instead, everything is driven using a new (patented) multitouch touch screen, claimed to be far more accurate than previous touch-sensitive displays. For further details, see apple.com/iphone, Murphy and Malykhina (2007), and Metz (2007).

The iPhone would let companies such as Apple and Google "merge without merging" by delivering Google services through Apple hardware. Also, Yahoo! is offering free "push" e-mail capabilities to Yahoo! Mail users. When you get a message, it'll push it right out to the phone for you, as in Yahoo! Go.

Yahoo! Go

Yahoo! Go is optimized for the "small screen" of a mobile phone, which truly makes it easy and fun to access the Internet. Everything about the Yahoo! Go interface is designed to be both visually striking and give you what you want with the fewest clicks possible. All your e-mail, news, photos, and more are "pushed" to your phone. It includes Yahoo! oneSearch, a new mobile search that gives you answers on the spot.

At its core is the *carousel*, used to navigate intuitively among the various Yahoo! Go *widgets*: your own personal channels for e-mail, local information and maps, news, sports, finance, entertainment, weather, Flickr photos, and search. The carousel is used to scroll over the widget you want. Because Yahoo! Go uses advanced caching and background loading technology, your widget content is automatically and continuously "pushed" to your phone. For details see mobile.yahoo.com/go.

Nokia's N800 Internet Tablet

Nokia's N800 Internet Tablet, which is about the size of a paperback mystery novel, lets you surf the Internet, send and receive e-mail and instant messages, download audio and video, and get RSS feeds. The new model adds a Webcam for videoconferencing and a microphone for Internet phone calls.

As a media player, the N800 handles MP3 and Windows Media files and other common formats, displaying images on a 4.1-inch color screen and playing audio through built-in stereo speakers or a headphone jack. It uses Wi-Fi networking when available but can also connect to a compatible Nokia phone via Bluetooth and be used as a wireless modem.

The Tablet, available from retailers and nokiausa.com, has an on-screen keyboard that automatically adjusts its key size and spacing for finger or stylus operation. It recognizes text written on the screen with a stylus as illustrated in the above photo.

Section 18.9 ▶ REVIEW QUESTIONS

1. Define *entertainment communities* and provide an example.
2. Describe Second Life and its capabilities.
3. Describe online marketplaces for music.
4. What is an entertainment series?
5. Describe the iPhone.
6. What is unique to the Nokia N800 Internet Tablet?

18.10 TECHNOLOGY SUPPORT: FROM BLOGGER.COM TO INFRASTRUCTURE SERVICES

A large number of software tools is used to facilitate the various Web 2.0 activities. Here are some representative examples.

EXHIBIT 18.7   Social Software Tools

Tools for online communication

- Instant messaging
- VoIP and Skype
- Text chat
- Internet forums
- Blogs or Weblogs
- Wikis
- Collaborative real-time editor
- Prediction markets

Types of services

- Social network services
- Social network search engines
- Social guides
- Social bookmarking
- Social citations
- Social libraries
- Virtual worlds and Massively Multiplayer Online Games (MMOGs)
- Other specialized social applications
- Politics and journalism
- Content management tools

Emerging technologies

- Peer-to-peer social networks
- Virtual presence
- Mobile tools for Web 2.0

Tools for individuals

- Personalization
- Customization
- Search
- RSS
- File-sharing tools

Web 2.0 development tools

- Mashups
- Web services (Online Chapter 19)

Sources: Complied from *en.wikipedia.org/wiki/Social_software,* Hinchcliffe (2007), and Weblogsinc.com (2007).

WEB 2.0 AND SOCIAL SOFTWARE

Social software enables people to rendezvous, connect, or collaborate through computer-mediated communication. Many advocates of these tools believe that they help create actual community with its structures.

The more specific term *collaborative software* applies to cooperative work systems and is usually narrowly applied to software that enables work functions (see Chapters 7 and 13). Distinctions between the usage of the terms *social* and *collaborative* are in the applications, not the tools, although there are some tools that are only rarely used for work collaboration. Exhibit 18.7 shows the major categories of tools.

Here, we describe some of these tools. A complete list of free tools is available in the May 2006 issue of *PCWorld* (see find.pcworld.com/52516) and Gillin (2007b).

TOOLS FOR BLOGGING AND WIKIS

Many tools are available for bloggers and wiki writers.

Tools for Blogging

Problogger (problogger.net) lists dozens of blog tools in the following categories: statistical packages, blog editors, news aggregators, e-mail subscriptions and newsletter services, blog poll tools, and others. For details, see Rowse (2006).

Notable tools are:

- Blogger.com (offered free from Google) is a Weblog publishing system. For details, see blogger.com and en.wikipedia.org/wiki/Blogger).
- Digg.com (digg.com) and Del.icio.us (del.icio.us) are social bookmarking tools for sourcing stories and linking to get traffic.

Wiki Tools

Representative tools are: EditMe (editme.com), SeedWiki (seedwiki.com), Socialtext Workspace (socialtext.com), Swiki (swiki.net), TeamFlux (teamflux.com), OpenWiki (openwiki.com), and GooWiki (goowiki.com). For more on the use of these tools, see Tapscott and Williams (2006), Online File W18.4, and Hinchcliffe (2007).

Tools for RSS and Podcasting

RSS and podcasting were introduced in Chapter 8. These Web 2.0 tools are now entering use in enterprises (see Real World Case at the end of this chapter and Gibson (2007). Representative companies in this area are NewsGator.com and KnowNow.com, which boast integration with Microsoft's Exchange e-mail platform and Microsoft's Outlook.

Wikis, Blogs, and RSS Are Replacing E-mail

E-mail has proven itself to be an indispensable form of communication, but it has limits as a collaborative tool. Enterprise content management systems are important for codifying and organizing important corporate data, but they can be expensive and inflexible.

The point-to-point nature of e-mail limits its use as a collaborative tool. Furthermore, the CC and BCC fields in an e-mail can be dangerous. Often the wrong person gets a copy of the message. And many people ignore a message with a wide distribution. Or the one person who might have a key insight on the issue may be left off the list. Poor decisions are often made regarding to whom the e-mail should be forwarded. In theory, a blog or wiki can be seen by everyone, as are the reader responses and edits. No one is left out of the loop. Blogs and wikis can fill in the collaborative gap.

E-mail was never designed to be a news source. Therefore, according to Gibson (2007), an increasing number of companies are providing RSS-based tools to their employees in order to manage news feeds that they pick from the outside and distribute inside the enterprise. For benefits and corporate applications see Gibson (2007).

Enterprise Wiki and Blog Tools

Companies such as Traction (tractionsoftware.com) and Socialtext (socialtext.com) make enterprise versions of wiki and blog software that include security controls, archiving, and identity management tools. Many companies with grassroots adoption of wikis and blogs use open source versions of the technology, but CIOs may prefer deploying tools developed specifically for the enterprise. For a detailed case, see McGillicuddy (2006b).

Blogging for Business

According to Sloan and Kaihla (2006), enterprises are now experimenting with blogs, so team members can publish items that were formerly sent as e-mail and copied to "My whole Division." Newsreader clients can capture these feeds using RSS or ATOM, two simple text formats published by many Web sites, blogging tools, and wikis. Users subscribe to the feeds and receive results in a common Web browser or customized reader application. Feed subscribers can be more selective about what they receive than users of traditional e-mail. For example, rather than download entire articles, they can first see headlines and summaries only. (For a discussion of blog marketing see Wright 2006).

For SAP, blogging has been a change for the better. Until 2006, SAP would pay a clipping service to collect relevant news stories and then e-mail the article to large groups. Now, the Six Apart's Movable Type Weblog system is used to send news articles to field staff. SAP's blog also acts as a central source for competitive data with field personnel contributing content. Their comments, tags, and data create a virtual conversation around the way the team works. It is much better than a stream of "FYI" e-mailed articles. And because the blog is field-generated, the content is highly relevant. The blog's value is not so much saving money but improving the depth of competitive news. Many companies are using wikis and blogs to facilitate online training (see Weinstein 2006 and Wright 2006 for details).

MASHUPS

Mashups are tools that combine data from two (or more) Web sites to create new applications. An example is housingmaps.com. The site plots Craigslist's apartments for rent and homes for sale on Google Map and allows you to preview a listing by simply clicking on one of the pushpins. A similar service is available at bidnearby.com, where you can search and locate classifieds from Craigslist as well as local physical auctions.

mashups
Tools that combine data from two (or more) Web sites to create new applications.

For a list of thousands of mashups, their traffic and rating, see programmableweb.com. Also, see several articles and blogs by R. D. Hof at *Business Week Online* (e.g., July 25, 2005, and February 17, 2006).

Here are some more applications:

- Pubwalk.com combines bar listings in your community with reviews from City Search with Google Map. Each pushpin has a pop-up window with bar (or restaurant) information, including rating and pictures. Finally, you can plot and print the driving directions to get to a desired one!
- Google.com/transit lets you plan public transportation trips in dozens of cities. After you provide the addresses *from and to,* the planner gives you directions, combining walking, buses, and trains, and approximates travel times and fares. Finally, you can compare, and have an alternative to, the cost of driving.

PERSONALIZATION TOOLS: FROM MY YAHOO! TO NETVIBES

Users can create highly personalized pages that are constantly updated with information like news and stock prices as well as view photos, use a calculator, or perform similar actions, all in one page. Users can also post necessary tools shown as modules, which appear as small square or rectangular objects, with the content or functionality inside. You can arrange these as you like. Users produce a wide variety of modules, and they upload them on My Yahoo! and similar software and make them available for free. The personalization can be done as Web pages when you are online, or you can arrange pages offline.

One such tool is My Yahoo!, which allows you to combine page segments featuring Yahoo!'s own news and information with segments containing RSS feeds. Microsoft's My MSN is another tool (both sites were revised in 2007).

On the desktop, the best known miniapplication system is Apple's Dashboard, which allows Macintosh users to install tiny programs called Widgets that perform searches, display photo slideshows, track stocks, play music, and more. Microsoft's Windows Vista operating system has a comparable system called Sidebar.

Netvibes.com offers the best features of My Yahoo! and Dashboard. Modules can be added easily and are arranged in a menu (for details see Mossberg 2007).

For graphically rich content, one can use Pageflakes (pageflakes.com).

DEVELOPMENT TOOLS

To implement Web 2.0 applications, you may need a development framework for building rich media Internet applications—Web-based programs that run like they're on a desktop, refreshing page views without resetting the page through the server.

These frameworks come in different styles, including Flash, a multimedia development platform; and JavaScript, a Web-developed language. These are helping organizations to build Web applications faster and cheaper than before. Several other tools exist.

Example

The American Cancer Society redesigned its online bookstore using Adobe Systems' Flex 2, a development environment based on Flash that lets visitors read book descriptions and drag selections into a shopping cart without waiting for a server to refresh the page.

Before using Flex, the society's Web presence—built on HTTP—was not efficient because it was necessary to call back to the server each time a user clicked a different link. The process was too cumbersome. The new solution is really flashy, catches attention, and makes an emotional impression as well as an educational one for the user. For details see Watson (2007a).

Social Bookmarking

Social bookmarking is a Web service for sharing Internet bookmarks. The sites are a popular way to store, classify, share, and search links through the practice of folksonomy techniques on the Internet and intranets. Examples of such sites are Reddit, Digg, and Del.icio.us. For details see en/wikipedia.org/wiki/Social_bookmarking and Hammond et al. (2005).

Intel's Web 2.0 Software Suite

Intel has put together a collaboration software suite for small and medium-size businesses via its resellers. Called SuiteTwo, the package includes software from Six Apart (free blogging service that lets you decide who gets to see what—if anything—of your blog), Socialtext (enterprise wiki systems), NewsGator (RSS platform and readers), and SimpleFeed (feed parsing using RSS to allow customers to subscribe to topics of interest). These are small software companies that provide applications for blogs, RSS feeds, wikis, and social networking. All these so-called Web 2.0 applications are more commonly associated with and used by consumers. But corporations are increasingly using blogs, wikis, and social networking applications.

By partnering with these software providers, Intel hopes to have Intel-optimized programs in the emerging Web 2.0 area. Intel envisions other software bundles in the future.

TOOLS THAT SUPPORT APPLICATIONS

A large amount of tools support Web 2.0 applications. Here are a few examples:

File Sharing Tools

According to Schonfeld (2006b), several new services let people exchange large digital files (some for free, some for a fee). A few examples follow:

▶ AllPeers (allpeers.com) allows you to transfer files to your buddies
▶ Glide Presenter from TransMedia (transmediacorp.com) stores and shares digital media
▶ MediaMax (mediamax.com) stores digital photos and movies on the Web
▶ Myfabrik (myfabrik.com) sends links to shared files stored on the Web
▶ Pando (pando.com) bypasses e-mail attachment limits for P2P transfers
▶ YouSendit (yousendit.com) sends links to uploaded files
▶ Zapr (zapr.net) turns any file on your PC into a shareable Web link

For details see Schonfeld (2006b).

Alexa: Web Traffic Information Provider

Alexa Internet (alexa.com) is a Web site owned by Amazon.com that provides information on Web traffic to other Web sites. Alexa collects information from users who have installed an "Alexa Toolbar," allowing them to provide statistics on Web site traffic, as well as lists of related links. Alexa ranks sites based on visits from users of its Alexa Toolbar for Internet Explorer and from integrated sidebars in Mozilla and Netscape.

There is some controversy over how representative Alexa's user base is of typical Internet behavior (see en.wikipedia.org/wiki/Alexa_Internet). If Alexa's user base is a fair statistical sample of the Internet user population (e.g., a random sample of sufficient size), Alexa's ranking should be quite accurate. In reality, not much is known about the sample, and it may or may not have many sources of sampling bias. Another concern is whether Alexa ratings are easily manipulated. Some Webmasters claim that they can significantly improve the Alexa ranking of less popular sites by making them the default page, by exchanging Web traffic with other Webmasters, and by requiring their users to install the Alexa toolbar; however, such claims are often anecdotal and are offered without statistics or other evidence.

Competitors in the Internet market research space include Complete Inc., ComScore, Hitwise, Nielsen/NetRatings, and Netcraft.

Mobile Phones and Social Networks

Mobile phones are heavily used by members of social networks. Thus, e-commerce opportunities are enormous. Examples include:

- In 2007 mobile phone company Vodafone disclosed a deal that will allow its customers to access the popular online video service YouTube. The launch focuses on the United Kingdom initially and involves YouTube's providing a daily selection of videos. Vodafone said customers will also be able to forward links of their favorite clips and upload their own content from the phones.
- Vodafone also said it would roll out a service with MySpace. That deal will allow its customers to access the social network via cell phones.
- Vodaphone became the latest operator to offer online auction site eBay on mobile phones.
- Verizon made a deal with YouTube to bring popular videos from YouTube to cell phones using Verizon's V-cast service.

INFRASTRUCTURE SUPPORT

With millions of members, and in the case of MySpace, close to 200 million members, the heavy traffic demands put a constant stress on the social networks' computing infrastructure. The problem is getting even more serious as sites add more functionalities becoming all-in-one communities. In addition, many companies are adding Web 2.0 tools, so the demand on their infrastructure increases. In the Real-World Case at the end of this chapter, we see how one company added blogs and wikis. This is a modest start. Carr (2007) provides the following examples of Web 2.0 technologies in a toy manufacturer:

- **Ratings.** Consumers create profiles and rate and comment on the company's products.
- **Forums.** Consumers create their own topic areas and build communities around shared interests.
- **Blogs.** Staff editors lead company-formatted essays and discussions that allow (but do not drive) customer comments.
- **E-Newsletters.** Available on an opt-in basis; flow information to customers, partners, and employees.
- **Streaming Video.** Many videos, some created by consumers about their family, showing the use of toys and some from the company TV commercials about new toys, are all available for view.
- **Contests.** Sweepstakes, do-it-yourself challenges, incentives, and other initiatives involve customers from product development to marketing campaigns.
- **Search Engine.** Using search engines (e.g., Google AdWords and Google Desktop) attract even more customers and traffic.

To get the most of what is going on in these and other Web 2.0 applications, companies need to continuously analyze the data that add more demand on information infrastructure and processing.

The heavy traffic may create other problems. For example, Universal Tube (Toledo, Ohio) filed a lawsuit against YouTube, claiming that the company had to shut down its Web site, utube.com because millions of people mistook it for youtube.com. Utube received 68 million hits in August 2006.

Luckily, social network growth is slow enough to enable appropriate infrastructure. Carr (2007) described how the MySpace owners had to adopt new technologies in each of the following stages of growth (in millions of users: 0, .5, 1, 2, 3, 10, 17, 26). MySpace has managed to scale its Web site infrastructure to meet booming demand by using a mix of time-proven and leading-edge information technologies. By 2007, MySpace was able to support 140 million accounts and more than 38 billion page views a month.

The Need for Very Rich Media

MySpace was successful with its infrastructure because the site is not rich media. Consider this: CondéNet Inc. launched Flip.com a rich media, social network for teens. The new style may make MySpace two dimensional static pages obsolete. Instead, we see Flash-heavy slideshows. A start-up, VUVOX.com, makes special authoring tools that enable users to turn every amateur Web page creator into an Adobe Photoshop expert. How MySpace and others will deal with this development is yet to be seen (*Fortune* Technology Staff 2007).

Other Tools

Gillin (2007b) provides examples of infrastructure support tools such as:

▶ Services that monitor online chatting and give subscribers reports on topics such as opinions, preferences, issues, and coming trends that are being discussed. These include Nielsen BuzzMetrics—BrandPulse) (nielsenbuzzmetrics.com), Cymfony—Orchestra (cymphony.com), Nstein—NtelligentEnterpriseSearch (nstein.com), and Factiva's several tracking products (factiva.com).

▶ Monitoring what the media has to say about any topic. Free service is provided by Google Alerts.

▶ Advanced search features. For example, the linkdomain and allinanchor commands at Yahoo! provide useful information, as does Amazon's AG search engine. The above can be customized.

▶ Popular RSS-based search engines include Technorati (technorati.com), IceRocket (icerocket.com), Feedster (feedster.com), and BlogPulse (blogpulse.com). These can be used to search blogs as well (e.g., Technorati's Top 100 blogs monitor the links from these for other bloggers). Monitoring over two million blogs is not an easy task.

▶ Podcasts are difficult to search because the content is hard to index. Some interesting search engines are Podscope (podscope.com) and Podzinger (podzinger.com).

▶ Tracking comments on blogs assess information about their popularity. Several companies provide such services, (e.g., BuzzMetrics—BrandPulse by Nielsen).

▶ Aggregation engines analyze link blogs, topical blogs, and community news sites. Sites such as BoingBoing.Net (boingboing.net), Metafilter (metafilter.com), Waxy.org (waxy.org), and ScienceBlogs (scienceblogs.com) are all link blogs and are major influencers in social media.

For details on the above, see Gillin (2007a).

WHERE IS WEB 2.0 SOFTWARE GOING?

By 2007, there were several hundred Web 2.0 products on the market, with little agreement on standards (Watson 2007b). However, it looks as if many of them will disappear, and others will be purchased by large companies (such as the purchases of Groove by Microsoft and Blogger.com by Google).

Large companies like to see Web 2.0 tools in their existing collaboration products (See Raman 2006). And IBM is adding such tools to their Lotus/Domino Collaboration Suite (Taft 2007; Hoover 2007).

For example, IBM Lotus is adding the following products to make it easier for people to work more closely with each other: Lotus Connection (social networking software for the enterprise including Activities, Communities, Dogear for social bookmarking and Profiles and Blog), Lotus Quickr, Lotus Sametime, and IBM WebSphere have been redesigned to support collaboration. (See Taft 2007 for details.) Another example is Intel's Web 2.0 software suite. Even Acrobat 8.0 (from Adobe Systems) added collaboration capabilities in its professional version.

Section 18.10 ▶ REVIEW QUESTIONS

1. Describe some tools for blogging and wikis.
2. Define *mashups* and explain their use via an example.
3. Define *social software* and list some examples.
4. Define *social bookmarking*.

5. Describe suites of Web 2.0 tools and the integration of tools.

6. Describe the need for IT infrastructure in regard to the Web 2.0 revolution.

7. Describe the future direction Web 2.0 software.

18.11 WEB 2.0, SOCIAL NETWORKS, AND E-COMMERCE

Implementing Web 2.0 sites, especially social networks and similar communities, attracts a large number of visitors. This opens the door to several e-commerce initiatives.

Virtual communities are closely related to EC. For example, Zetlin and Pfleging (2002) describe online, consumer-driven markets in which most of the consumers' needs, ranging from finding a mortgage to job hunting, are arranged from a community Web site. This gathering of needs in one place enables vendors to sell more and community members to get discounts. Internet communities will eventually have a massive impact on almost every company that produces consumer goods or services, and they could change the nature of corporate advertising and community sponsorship strategies and the manner in which business is done. Although this process of change is slow, we can see some of the initial commercial development changes.

Also, some communities charge members content fees for downloading certain articles, music, or pictures, thus producing sales revenue for the site. Finally, because many community members create their own home pages, it is easy to learn about them and reach them with targeted advertising and marketing. For more on this topic, see Lee et al. (2003).

WHY IS THERE AN INTEREST?

Web 2.0 applications and especially social networks attract a huge number of visitors. Furthermore, they are spreading rapidly, and many of them cater to a specific segment of the population (e.g., music lovers, travelers, game lovers, cars fans, etc.). Finally, a large proportion of the visitors is young—but in the future will grow up and will have more money to spend (see Regan 2006 for a discussion). For these reasons, many believe that social networks, blogging, and other Web 2.0 activities will play a major role in the future of e-commerce. In the following sections, we will cover a few areas where success is already evidenced.

Retailers stand to benefit from online communities in several important ways:

▶ Consumers can be a source of feedback (similar to a focus group) on product design and features, marketing and advertising campaigns, and how well customer service and support are performing, which can lead to innovation for a retailer.

▶ Word-of-mouth (i.e., viral marketing) is free advertising and increases the visibility of niche retailers and products.

▶ Increased Web site traffic, a common effect of viral marketing, inevitably brings with it more ad dollars.

▶ Increased sales can come from harnessing techniques based on personal preferences such as collaborative filtering; at a more advanced level, retailers strive for a higher degree of relevance in matching the knowledge of one person to someone of like interests who has a need to know (the "twinsumer" concept).

Case 18.3 demonstrates some of the potential of EC social networks.

ADVERTISING

Several advertisers are already placing ads on MySpace and YouTube or are using Google AdSense with user searches in community sites. The following areas are developing.

Viral Marketing

Young adults are especially good at viral marketing. What they like can spread very quickly, sometimes to millions of people at a minimal cost to companies. One example is YouTube. The company conducted almost no advertising in the first months of its inception, but millions joined. Similarly, if members like some product or service, word-of-mouth advertising works rapidly. Note that SpiralFrog.com (spiralfrog.com) provides free downloads of songs; instead of paying money for Apple's iTunes, you watch ads to obtain the free songs. The company aims at mobile phones only.

CASE 18.3

EC Application CASE

REVENUE SOURCES AT YOUTUBE

Some people think that Google paid too much for YouTube, especially in light of their legal problems. The opposite may be true. Consider these examples:

1. **Two minute YouTube clips were just the start.** As television comes to the Internet, dozens of companies are gunning to become the networks of tomorrow. Where the ants go, advertisers are expected to follow. YouTube's ad-revenue potential in 2007 alone has been pegged at $200 million by Citigroup. And wherever there's video programming, viewers will be seeing more video ads. One forecast from research firm eMarketer calls for overall video advertising on the Web (including video ads replacing banners on regular Web pages) to hit $2.9 billion in 2010, a sevenfold leap from the 2006 tally of $410 million (Schonfeld 2007).

2. **Brand-created entertainment content.** In 2005, Nike produced a pseudo home digital video of soccer star Ronaldinho, practicing while wearing his new Nike Gold shoes. The clip was downloaded 3.5 million times on YouTube in one week and provided Nike with tremendous exposure to its core mostly young male audience. As the young generation moves away from traditional TV, it dedicates its time to watching the likes of YouTube.

3. **User-driven product advertising.** User-generated videos could be leveraged in a similar fashion to product placement on TV. Although not intentional, the use of Logitech's Webcam features on a short clip by a 17-year-old girl talking about the breakup with her boyfriend was viewed by YouTube users and greatly contributed to the awareness of Logitech's offering. The product placement trend is also

expanding across the blogosphere with Nokia, for example, promoting its N90 phone through the 50 most influential bloggers in Belgium and establishing a blogger relationship blog.

4. **Multichannel word-of-mouth campaign.** When Chevrolet decided to combine its *Apprentice* Tahoe Campaign with an online consumer generated media (CGM) campaign, it did not anticipate the additional viral impact of YouTube. On the Chevrolet site, users could create their own customized video commercial, complete with text and background music. Environmentalists took the opportunity to produce spoof videos and published them on YouTube. However, the word-of-mouth advertising Chevrolet got on YouTube was ultimately beneficial to Chevrolet and contributed to the 4 million page views, 400,000 unique visitors, and 22,000 ad submissions on their site. This has been one of the most creative and successful promotions.

Note: YouTube announced that they will share revenue with the users who helped generate the revenue.

Sources: Sandoval (2006), and Sandoval (2006) and Schonfield (2007).

Questions

1. List the different advertising models on YouTube.
2. List the success factors from these cases.
3. What are the benefits for the advertisers?

The MyPickList.com (mypicklist.com) viral marketing program seems to utilize the usual loyalty program mechanisms without the real worries of discounting perception or loyalty erosion. Here is how it is done: MyPicList.com helps consumers make purchase decisions by creating a social commerce network Web site that drives word-of-mouth commerce by leveraging the community aspects of a social network. The effort integrates a user profile and favorite product recommendations (hence, the name "pick list") into a networked community. Once a user creates a pick list, the user can share it with family, friends, or the public at large. When creating a pick list, a user goes through the following steps:

1. Pick a product category. Categories include: books, movies, music, electronics, computers, photo and imaging, games and toys, women's apparel, men's apparel, shoes, sports and outdoors items, jewelry and accessories, and gifts.

2. Choose a preferred merchant for product sale direct from the pick list.

3. Add the product to the pick list.

4. Write a short product review.

5. Tag the "pick."

Any product from a retailer or the Internet can be added to the pick list, but only products that are sold through a retailer in their network are eligible for a commission when someone purchases an item off a member's pick list. The members can request payment of their commission once they have accumulated $25 or more in their account. All payments are made via PayPal; therefore, members must have a PayPal account set up. Once a user creates the pick list, there are several primary ways to get a pick list viewed or distributed. For details see *Revenue News* (2006).

According to Megna (2007) and Goldsmith (2006), many retailers are capitalizing on the word-of-mouth marketing of bloggers. This brings up an interesting question; can bloggers be bought? According to Wagnar (2006), companies pay bloggers to endorse products via an intermediary called PayPerPost.

Example. PayPerPost (payperpost.com) runs a marketplace where advertisers can find bloggers, video bloggers, online photographers, and podcasters willing to endorse their products.

This is how it works: A company with a product or service to advertise registers with PayPerPost and describes what it wants. A sneaker company, for example, might post a request for people willing to write a 50-word blog entry about their sneakers or upload a video of themselves playing basketball in the sneakers. The company also says what it's willing to pay for the posting.

Bloggers and other content creators sign up with PayPerPost and shop for opportunities they like. They create the blog post (or whatever content is requested), and inform PayPerPost, which checks to see that the content matches what the advertiser asked for, and PayPerPost arranges payment. The criticism is that bloggers are not required to disclose that they're being paid for the endorsements (see Wagner 2006).

Classifieds and Job Listing

MySpace has provided classifieds and job listings since fall 2005 competing with Craigslist and CareerBuilder. According to O'Malley (2006), MySpace is already a force in e-commerce: It sends more traffic to shopping and classifieds sites than MSN and is fast closing on Yahoo!. MySpace accounted for 2.53 percent of all visits to EC sites for the last week of August 2006—up from 1.28 percent the last week of February 2006.

Google partnered in 2006 with eBay to roll out "click-to-call" advertising across Google and eBay sites—a deal that is expanding to MySpace's giant network.

Mobile Advertising

Mobile advertising is a rapidly developing area (Sharma 2007). The competition for ad revenue is intensifying; especially with the increasing use of the cell phones for access to the Internet, online advertising will also swell.

SHOPPING

Shopping is a natural area for social networks to be active, and although by 2007 it was only beginning to grow, it has enormous potential. Here are some examples:

▶ According to Kafka (2007), Many of MySpace's most popular pages came from e-tailers who stock the site with low-cost come-on cosmetics, other Web site ads, and the like. The value is $140 million or more per year.

▶ MySpace lets brand owners create profile pages such as the Burger King mascot, "The King."

▶ MySpace is planning its own behavioral targeting, which is similar to collaborative filtering (Chapter 4). Based on the members' voluntary information on what they like and what they don't, MySpace will serve up its users to relevant advertisers. For example, DaimlerChrysler's Jeep already has its own MySpace page. In the future, it can conduct sales campaigns to targeted individuals.

▶ MySpace's music-download service, detailed by the company in September 2006, allows the site's independent and signed musicians to sell their work directly from their profile pages. Snocap, a copyright-services company cofounded by Napster creator Shawn Fanning, supports the relationship. MySpace and Snocap get a cut of every track sold. By allowing users to self-publish, MySpace has become a launching pad for about 3 million musicians from garage bands to big names.

> ◗ In 2006, Google signed an agreement to pay more than $900 million over five years in ad revenue to MySpace for the right to serve searches inside MySpace. The deal includes exposure of Google's checkout payment service (pay once for several vendors) to MySpace.

FEEDBACK FROM CUSTOMERS

Companies are starting to utilize Web 2.0 tools to get feedback from customers.

Conversational Marketing

Web 2.0 opens the feedback loop. In Chapter 4, we described customer feedback via questionnaires, focus groups, and other sources. However, Web 2.0 brings in feedback via blogs, wikis, online forums, chat rooms, and social networking sites. Companies are finding these "conversational marketing" outlets not only generate faster and cheaper results than traditional focus groups but also foster closer relationships with customers. For example, Macy's quickly removed a metal toothbrush holder from its product line after receiving several complaints about it online (see Gogoi 2007). Companies like Dell are also learning that conversational marketing is less expensive and yields quicker results than focus groups. The computer maker recently launched a feedback site called IdeaStorm, where it allows customers to suggest and vote on improvements in its offerings (see Scable and Israel 2006).

Known also as *enterprise feedback management*, companies are interested not only in collecting information but also in interaction between customers and company employees and properly distributing customer feedback throughout the organization.

According to Gogoi (2007), retailers are taking a page from MySpace. They know that customers, especially the younger and more Net-savvy, want to be heard, and they also want to hear what others like them think. So, increasingly, retailers are opening up their Web sites to customers, letting them post product reviews, ratings, and in some cases photos and videos. The result is that customer reviews are emerging as a prime place to visit for online shoppers.

Marketing companies have longed for years to have a window on how consumers use their products in order to develop product innovations and improve marketing. Customer reviews have long been part of cutting-edge sites like Amazon.com and Netflix, but by the end of 2006, 43 percent of EC sits offered customer reviews and ratings. As much as 50 percent of customers 18 to 34 years old have posted a comment or review on products they bought or used. A large part of the reason for this achievement is the confluence of social computing and the success of sites like MySpace, FaceBook, and YouTube.

Example: PETCO. PETCO operates 800 pet supply stores nationally. The site launched customer reviews in October 2005 and within a week noticed that customers who clicked on the highest customer-rated products were 49 percent more likely to buy something.

PETCO also noticed that top customer-rated pet toys and items draw customers, even if the customers weren't necessarily planning on buying them; people trust someone else's opinion that is independent of the manufacturer or retailer.

PETCO's experience is not unique. According to an eVoc Insights study, 47 percent of consumers consult reviews before making an online purchase, and 63 percent of shoppers are more likely to purchase from a site if it has ratings and reviews. Negative reviews not only help the retailer address a defect or poorly manufactured item, they also help decrease the number of returns. People are less likely to return an item due to personal expectation because reviews give realistic views of a product and its characteristics. (See Gorgoi 2007 for details.)

Risks

There are some risks involved in opening up your marketing and advertising to the less-controlled social networks. For example, according to Regan (2006), aligning a product or company with such sites where *content* is user-generated and often not edited or filtered has its downsides. A company needs to be willing to have negative reviews and feedback. If your company has really positive customer relationships and strong feedback, and you are willing to have customers share the good, the bad, and the ugly, you are a good candidate. If you worry about what your customers would say if they were alone in a room with your prospects—your product or business might not be ready to use Web 2.0.

Another thing to consider is the 20–80 rule. Namely that a minority of individuals contributes most of the content material in some Web 2.0 blogs, wikis, and similar sites. For example, about 1,000 of the millions of contributors write most of the Wikipedia. According to *Business 2.0* Staff (2007), in an analysis of thousands of submissions over a three-week period on audience voting sites like Digg and Reddit, the *Wall Street Journal* reported that one-third of the stories that made it to Digg's home page were submitted by 30 users (out of 900,000 registered), and that one single person on Netscape, who goes by the online handle "Stoner," was responsible for 13 percent of the top posts on that site.

Any social media site that relies on the contributions of its users will find a similar distribution curve, with a relatively small number of top contributors representing the bulk of submissions. For instance, user-submitted stock photography site iStockphoto has more than 35,000 contributing photographers, but only about 100 have sold more than 100,000 images (at about $1 to $5 a pop). The difference is that with iStockphoto, users submit work in hopes of getting paid. Companies such as BuzzzMetrics offer many services that tell companies what their customers are saying on the Internet and what it means to their brands and markets. For details, see *Taipei Times* (2006). The financial incentives are clear and upfront because it is an EC site.

Finally, according to *Innovations* (2006), 74 percent of al CIOs surveyed said that Web 2.0 applications will significantly increase their security risk over the next three years. For more on security and other Web 2.0 implementation issues, see Ricadela (2006) and D'Agostino (2006).

OTHER REVENUE-GENERATION STRATEGIES IN SOCIAL NETWORKS

The following are some interesting ways social networks generate revenues:

- Offer premium service for a monthly or per service fee
- Organizations partner with the social networks, paying them a monthly service fee
- Some social networks have a network of thousands of local physical venues where members can meet (e.g., meetup.com). These venues, like coffee shops, may choose to pay a fee to be affiliated with the social network.

According to Millard (2004), Tickle Inc. implemented an integrated advertising campaign with Fox TV studio's program *North Shore*. The site created social networking profiles for some of the key characters on the show and promoted them on the site as "featured members." To learn how a blog can bring in big money, see Sloan and Kaihla (2006) and Wright (2006).

Hinchcliffe (2007) provides Exhibit 18.8, which illustrates revenue generation from Web 2.0 applications.

Hinchcliffe (2007) also provides the following strategies for making the most of Web 2.0 applications:

1. There are three direct ways to monetize Web 2.0: advertising, subscriptions, and commissions.

2. Some indirect ways that lead to *revenue growth*, *user growth*, and *increased resistance to competition*, which in turn lead to increased *subscriptions*, *advertising*, and *commission* revenue, are:

   - **Strategic acquisition:** Identifying and acquiring Web 2.0 companies on the exponential growth curve before the rest of the market realizes what it's worth.
   - **Maintaining control of hard to recreate data sources.** Let users access everything, but do not let them keep it, such as Google's providing access to their search index only over the Web.
   - **Building attention trust.** By being patently fair with customer data and leveraging users' loyalty, you can get them to share more information about themselves, which in turns leads to much better products and services tailored to them.
   - **Turning applications into platforms:** One single use of an application is simply a waste of software. Online platforms are actually easy to monetize, *but having compelling content or services first* is a prerequisite.
   - **Fully automated online customer self-service.** Let users get what they want, when they want it, without help.

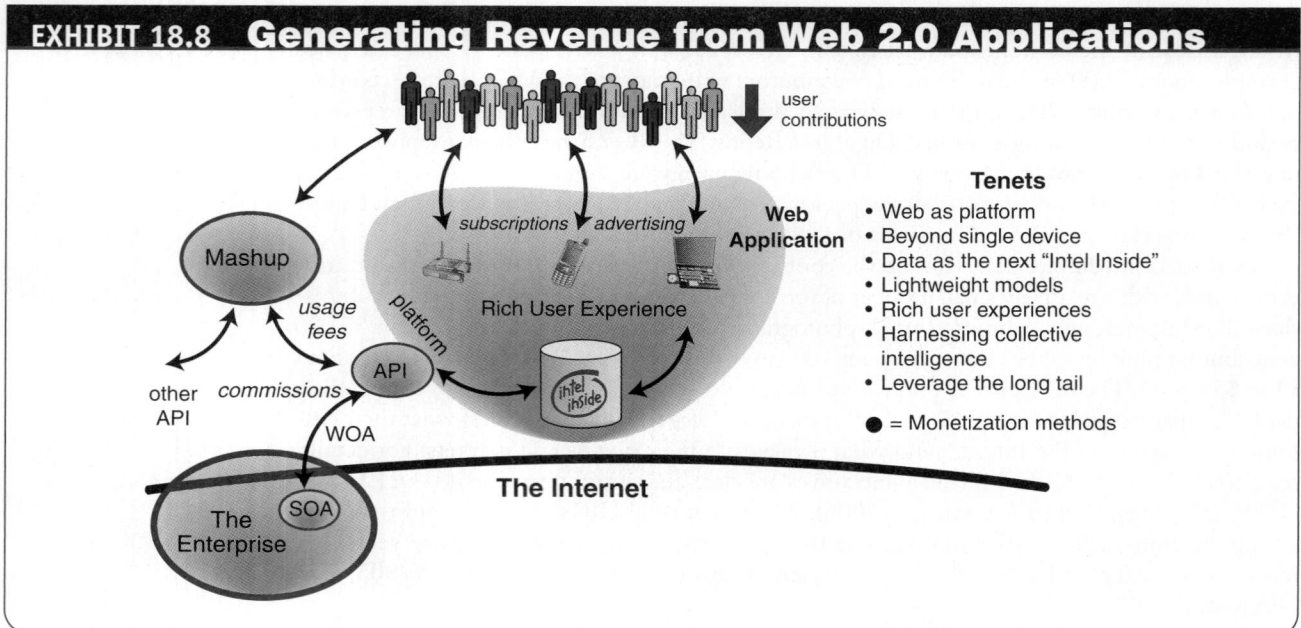

EXHIBIT 18.8 Generating Revenue from Web 2.0 Applications

Source: D. Hinchcliffe. *Web 2.0 Blog. web2.wsj2.com.*

WEB 2.0 COMMERCE ACTIVITIES INSIDE THE ENTERPRISE

Whereas many companies use Web 2.0 technology for supporting B2C and B2B e-commerce by building up their brand online, advertising and selling, other companies use these technologies inside the enterprise. McGillicuddy (2006a) describes the following guidelines:

▶ Allow employees to collaborate and communicate in an employee-driven system (e.g., see Real World Case at the end of this chapter).

▶ Promote the use of enterprise wikis via demonstrations.

▶ Set up internal blogs and incorporate them into internal directories so users can see who has a blog.

▶ Set up enterprise social bookmarking systems so users can see what sort of content their colleagues are tagging.

▶ CIOs should be involved from the beginning to make sure the right infrastructure and tools are in place.

For an example of how T. Rowe Price Group Inc. is using internal Web 2.0 technology, see McGilicuddy (2006). For tutorials see Hinchcliffe, (2007) and Web 2.0 central.com.

Section 18.11 ▶ REVIEW QUESTIONS

1. Why is there so much interest in EC via social communities?
2. How can a social network facilitate viral marketing?
3. Why is there so much interest in classifieds?
4. How can social networks support shopping?
5. How is customer feedback solicited in social networks?

18.12 THE FUTURE OF EC AND WEB 3.0

Generally speaking, the consensus is that the future of EC is bright. EC will become an increasingly important method of reaching customers, providing services, and improving operations of organizations. Also, EC facilitates collaboration and people-to-people interactions. Analysts differ in their predictions about the anticipated growth rate of EC and how long it will take for it to become a substantial portion of the economy, as well as in the identification of industry segments that will grow the fastest. However, based on nontechnological success factors (see Online File W18.5) and technological factors and trends (see Online File W18.6), there is general optimism about the future of EC. For a discussion, see Stafford (2006).

WEB 3.0: WHAT'S NEXT?

Web 3.0 will not be just about shopping, entertainment, and search. It's also going to deliver a new generation of business applications that will see business and social computing converge on the same fundamental on-demand architecture as consumer applications. So this is not something that's of merely passing interest to those who work in enterprise IT. The Web 3.0 era will radically change individuals' career paths as well as the organizations where they work (see Rouch 2006).

According to Stafford (2006), the next-generation Internet won't just be more portable and personal, it will also harness the power of people, making it even easier to zero in on precisely what you're looking for. To do it we already see:

- Faster, far-flung connectivity
- New Web Services that work entirely within a browser window
- More powerful search engines
- More clout for everyday people

Web 3.0 Technologies

The topology of Web 3.0 can be divided into four distinct layers: API services, aggregation services, application services, and serviced clients.

Application Program Interface (API) Services. API services are the hosted services that have powered Web 2.0 and will become the engines of Web 3.0. Google's search and AdWords APIs, Amazon.com's affiliate APIs, a large number of RSS feeds, a multitude of functional services, such as those included in the StrikeIron Web Services Marketplace (strikeiron.com) (Wainewright 2005), are just some examples. One of the most significant characteristics of this foundation layer is that it is a commodity layer. As Web 3.0 matures, an almost perfect market will emerge and squeeze out virtually all the profit margin from the highest-volume services.

Aggregation Services. These services are the intermediaries that take some of the hassle out of locating all those raw API services by bundling them together in useful ways. Representative examples are the various RSS aggregators and emerging Web services marketplaces like the StrikeIron service.

Application Services. This layer is where the biggest, most durable profits should be found. These services will not be like the established enterprise application categories, such as CRM or ERP, but a new class of composite applications that bring together functionality from multiple services to help users achieve their objectives in a flexible, intuitive way. An example of an area that is expected to grow is **voice commerce (v-commerce)**, which is an umbrella term for the use of speech recognition to allow voice activated services including Internet browsing and e-mail retrieval.

Serviced Clients. There is a role for client-side logic in the Web 3.0 landscape, but users will expect it to be maintained and managed for them.

From the billions of documents that form the Web and the links that weave them together, computer scientists and a growing number of start-up companies are finding new ways to mine human intelligence. Their goal is to add a layer of meaning on top of the existing Web that will make it less of a catalog and more of a guide—and even provide the foundation for systems that can reason in a human fashion. That level of artificial intelligence, with machines doing the thinking instead of simply following commands, has eluded researchers for more than half a century.

Referred to as *Web 3.0*, the effort is in its infancy, and the very idea has given rise to skeptics who have called it an unobtainable vision. But the underlying technologies are rapidly gaining adherents, at big companies like IBM and Google as well as small ones. Their projects often center on simple, practical uses, from producing vacation recommendations to predicting the next hit song. For details see Markoff (2006).

voice commerce (v-commerce)
An umbrella term for the use of speech recognition to allow voice activated services including Internet browsing and e-mail retrieval.

INTEGRATING THE MARKETPLACE WITH THE MARKET SPACE

Throughout this book, we have commented on the relationship between the physical marketplace and the market space. We have pointed out conflicts in certain areas, as well as successful applications and cooperation. The fact is that from the point of view of the consumer, as well as of most organizations, these two entities exist, and will continue to exist, together.

Probably the most noticeable integration of the two concepts is in the click-and-mortar organization. For the foreseeable future, the click-and-mortar organization will be the most prevalent model (e.g., see Wal Mart and Walmart.com), though it may take different shapes and formats. Some organizations will use EC as just another selling channel, as most large retailers do today. Others will use EC for only some products and services while they sell other products and services the conventional way (e.g., LEGO and GM). As experience is gained on how to excel at such a strategy, more organizations, private and public, will move to this dual mode of operation.

A major problem with the click-and-mortar approach is how the two outlets can cooperate in planning, advertising, logistics, resource allocation, and so on, and how the strategic plans of the market space and marketplace can align. Another major issue is the potential conflict with existing distribution channels (i.e., wholesalers, retailers).

Another area of coexistence is in many B2C ordering systems, where customers have the option to order the new way or the old way. For example, consumers can bank both online and off-line. People can trade stocks via the computer, by placing a call to their broker, or just by walking into a brokerage firm and talking to a trader. In the areas of B2B and G2B, the option to choose the old way or the new way may not be available much longer; some organizations may discontinue the old-economy option as the number of off-line users declines below a certain threshold. However, in most B2C activities, the option will remain, at least for the foreseeable future.

In conclusion, many people believe that the impact of EC on our lives will be as much as, and possibly more profound than, that of the Industrial Revolution. No other phenomenon since the Industrial Revolution has been classified in this category. It is our hope that this book will help you move successfully into this exciting and challenging digital revolution.

Web 3.0 and the Semantic Web

One potential area for Web 3.0 is the increased use of the *Semantic Web* (see Wikipedia). According to *The Economist* (2007), a Semantic-Web browser will be available soon in which people will be able to display the data, draw graphs, and so on. An example would be "friend-of-a-friend" networks, where individuals in online communities provide data in the form of links between themselves and friends. The Semantic Web could help to visualize such complex networks and organize them to allow deeper understanding of the communities' structures.

Semantic Web
An evolving extension of the Web in which Web content can be expressed not only in natural language but also in a form that can be understood, interpreted, and used by intelligent computer software agents, permitting them to find, share, and integrate information more easily.

The **Semantic Web** is an evolving extension of the Web in which Web content can be expressed not only in natural language but also in a form that can be understood, interpreted, and used by intelligent computer software agents, permitting them to find, share, and integrate information more easily (see en.wikipedia.org/wiki/semantic_web). The technology is derived from W3C director Tim Berners-Lee's vision of the Web as a universal medium for data, information, and knowledge exchange. At its core, the Semantic Web comprises a philosophy, a set of design principles, collaborative working groups, and a variety of enabling technologies.

A similar view about the role of the Semantic Web is expressed by Borland (2007), according to which the role of it in Web 3.0 is certain, and coming soon. Borland believes that the Web 3.0 new tools (some of which are already helping developers 'stitch' together complex applications), improve and automate database searches, help people choose vacation destinations, and sort through complicated financial data more efficiently. For more on Web 3.0 and the Semantic Web see Markoff (2006).

MOBILE SOCIAL NETWORKS

An explosive growth of mobile social networks is predicted by ABI Research (see Mello 2006), tripling the 50 million members in 2006 to 174 million in 2011. The explosion of wireless Web 2.0 services and companies (see Longino 2006) enables many social communities to be based on the mobile phone and other portable wireless devices. This extends the reach of social interaction to millions of people who don't have regular or easy access to computers. For example, MySpace can be accessed via Cingular's mobile system. At minimum, existing members who use PCs will supplement their activities with wireless devices.

Future Threats

According to Stafford (2006) the following four trends may slow EC and Web 2.0 and even cripple the Internet:

▶ **Security concern.** Both shoppers and users of e-banking and other services worry about online security. The Web needs to be made safer.

▶ **Lack of Net neutrality.** If the big telecom companies are allowed to charge companies for a guarantee of faster access, critics fear that small innovative Web companies could be crowded out by the Microsofts and Googles that can afford to pay more.

▶ **Copyright complaints.** The legal problems of YouTube, Wikipedia, and others may result in a loss of vital outlets of public opinion, creativity, and discourse.

▶ **Choppy connectivity.** Upstream bandwidths are still constricted, making uploading of video files a time-consuming task. Usable mobile bandwidth still costs a lot, and some carriers impose limitations on how Web access can be employed.

Section 18.12 ▶ REVIEW QUESTIONS

1. Describe nontechnological EC trends. (Hint: see Online File W18.5).
2. Describe technological trends for EC. (Hint: see Online File W18.6).
3. What is Web 3.0, and how will it differ from Web 2.0?
4. Discuss the integration of marketplaces and market spaces.
5. Describe the future of mobile social networks.
6. List the major potential inhibitors of e-commerce and Web 2.0.

MANAGERIAL ISSUES

Some managerial issues related to this chapter are as follows.

1. **What impacts on business is EC expected to make?** The impacts of EC and the Internet can be so strong that the entire manner in which companies do business will be changed, with significant impacts on procedures, people, organizational structure, management, and business processes. (Read "The Economic and Social Impact of Electronic Commerce" at oecd.org/subject/e_commerce.)

2. **What are the impacts of the Web 2.0 boom?** With the push toward Web 2.0 technologies, *Time* magazine (Grossman 2006/2007) named "you" as the person of the year for 2006. In the new information age, no one has more power to influence society than Web 2.0 communities. Yet does this influence truly benefit us, or will we suffer because of it?

3. **Should we explore Web 2.0 collaboration?** Consider whether your corporate culture is ready to experiment with public collaboration (Web 2.0) tools. Work with your corporate-learning or organization-development department to find areas likely for experimentation.

4. **How shall we start?** Start small: Determine whether a collaborative tool would benefit a team or group working on a specific project. Marketing groups are often good first targets for information sharing with others because they're usually the ones tasked with sharing corporate information. Try establishing a wiki for a team's collaborative project. Some wikis are hosted on an internal server while others are available as open source or via a hosted service.

5. **Do we need a community?** Although sponsoring a community may sound like a good idea, it may not be simple to execute. Community members need services, which cost money to provide. The most difficult task is to find a community that matches your business.

6. **How should we deal with Web 2.0 risks?** There are several possible risks depending on the applications. Consult your internal security experts and get some outside legal advice. Use a consultant for large projects to examine the risks.

RESEARCH TOPICS

Here are some suggested topics related to this chapter. For details, references, and additional topics, refer to the Online Appendix A "Current EC Research."

1. **The growth and impact of Web 2.0 applications**
   - The impacts of Web 2.0 innovations on e-commerce
   - Person-to-person computing like blogging
   - Threats and opportunities of commercial blogs
   - Rules and policies of blogging

2. **Web 2.0 Tools**
   - What are the benefits of AJAX?
   - What preparations are necessary for Web 2.0 training?

3. **Financial viability of communities**
   - Explore various revenue models for communities

   - How to measure the intangible benefits of communities
   - Contributions of communities on CRM

4. **Advertisement and social networks**
   - Viral marketing
   - Search engines in communities

5. **Social networks**
   - Creation and sustainability of the networks
   - Collaboration among members
   - Collaboration among communities
   - Security and privacy issues

SUMMARY

In this chapter you learned about the following EC issues as they relate to the learning objectives.

1. **Web 2.0 and person-to-person computing application.** Web 2.0 is about innovative application of existing technologies. Web 2.0 has brought together the contributions of millions of people and made their work, opinions, and identity matter. The consequences of the rapid growth of person-to-person computing like blogging are currently hard to understand and difficult to estimate.

2. **Google and the search engine industry.** Google invented an effective methodology for advertising based on the search engine to become a leader in the field. Several hundreds of tools in two dozen categories help in special searches. There is fierce competition for adverting dollars. The major competitors are Google, Yahoo!, and MSN (Microsoft). The success of social networks is mainly their ability to attract advertisers.

3. **The role of virtual communities.** Virtual communities create new types of business opportunities—people with similar interests that congregate at one Web site are a natural target for advertisers and marketers. Using chat rooms, members can exchange opinions about certain products and services. Of special interest are communities of transactions, whose interest is the promotion of commercial buying and selling. Virtual com-

munities can foster customer loyalty—increase sales of related vendors that sponsor communities and facilitate customer feedback for improved service and business.

4. **Online social networks.** These are very large Internet communities that allow the sharing of content, including videos, photos, and virtual socialization and interaction. Hundreds of networks are popping up around the world, some of which are global, competing for advertising money.

5. **YouTube and others.** Sharing videos, movies, and TV shows is becoming a major activity of social networks including YouTube and about a dozen of its competitors. Facing much litigation, these companies are still growing rapidly, along with other social networks (e.g., My Space is offering video sharing).

6. **Business networks.** These are communities concentrating on business issues both in one country and around the world (e.g., recruiting, finding business partners). Social marketplaces meld social networks and some aspects of business.

7. **Online travel industry.** The online travel industry is growing rapidly and adopting Web 2.0 applications, such as travel-oriented social communities, blogs, and mashups.

8. **P2P lending and ZOPA.** P2P lending can lead to benefits for both lenders and borrowers, and intermediaries such as ZOPA and Prosper facilitate them. While the volume of these loans is insignificant, such services may disrupt retail banking.

9. **Web 2.0 and entertainment.** The entertainment industry is embracing Web 2.0 tools. Many communities provide entertainment, and others are fully dedicated to it. Wonderful innovations bring user-created entertainment to others. Videos and movies are at the forefront of this area, as well as mobile entertainment.

10. **Web 2.0 enablers.** Blogs, wikis, and mashups are popular tools. Web services and open sources are used in the infrastructure as well as rich media and sharing tools.

11. **Social networks and e-commerce.** The major areas of interface are online shopping, online advertising, online market research, and innovative revenue models. The major attraction is the volume of social networks and the hope that the young people in the communities will be online buyers in the future.

12. **The future of EC.** EC will continue to expand fairly rapidly for a number of reasons. To begin with, its infrastructure is becoming better and less expensive with time. Consumers will become more experienced and will try different products and services and tell their friends about them. Security, privacy protection, and trust will be much higher, and more support services will simplify the transaction process. Legal issues will be formally legislated and clarified, and more products and services will be online at reduced prices. The fastest growing area is B2B EC. Company-centric systems (especially e-procurement) and auctions will also continue to spread rapidly. The development of exchanges and other many-to-many e-marketplaces will be much slower. Wireless technologies (especially Wi-Fi) will facilitate EC. Finally, and most importantly, is the increased rate of innovation with new business models and applications appearing constantly.

KEY TERMS

Business network	829	Semantic Web	854	Social network analysis (SNA)	823
Disruptors	811	Social bookmarking	844	Virtual (Internet) community	819
Mashups	843	Social marketplace	830	Voice commerce (v-commerce)	853
Person-to-person lending	834	Social media	810	Web 2.0	808
Search engine	814	Social network	822		

QUESTIONS FOR DISCUSSION

1. Discuss the differences between a desktop search and an Internet search. (Hint: check Wikipedia for desktop search.)
2. Discuss the relationship between virtual communities and doing business on the Internet.
3. Discuss the relationship between Google and social networks.
4. What criteria would you use to evaluate the usefulness of a search engine?
5. Discuss why Cyworld may take over members from other sites.
6. Discuss why a social marketplace is a Web 2.0 instrument.
7. In what ways is Second Life a Web 2.0 application?
8. Discuss the commercial aspects of Second Life (visit the site).
9. Discuss how the money works at Second Life (visit the site).
10. Discuss the difference between Web computing and traditional computing.
11. Discuss the advantages and disadvantages of social bookmarking. (Hint: go to Wikipedia.)
12. Discuss the Web 2.0 requirements for infrastructure.
13. What are the benefits of conversational marketing?

INTERNET EXERCISES

1. Enter desktop.google.com/enterprise and xi.com/enterprise, take the tours, and compare the products' capabilities. Write a report.

2. In August 2006, Google and MySpace signed a deal in which MySpace users can conduct a search on Google without leaving the MySpace site. Find information about the deal (try GoogleNews) and summarize the benefits to both companies.

3. Enter the Web site of an Internet community (e.g., myspace.com or geocities.yahoo.com). Build a home page free of charge. Add a chat room and a message board to your site using the free tools provided. Describe the other capabilities available.

4. Investigate the community services provided by Yahoo! to its members (groups.yahoo.com). List all the services available and assess their potential commercial benefits to Yahoo!.

5. Enter calastrology.com. What kind of community is this? Check the revenue model. Then enter astrocenter.com. What kind of site is this? Compare and comment on the two sites.

6. Enter answers.com, answers. yahoo.com and askville.amazon. com. Post the same question in all places. Comment on the sites' capabilities based on the answers you receive.

7. Enter e-discovery.com and describe its functionalities. (See also Carr 2006a.) Write a report.

8. Enter classmates.com, myspace.com, and linkedin.com and find their sources of revenue.

9. Enter xing.com and linkedin.com and compare their functionalities. Write a report.

10. Enter ps3seeker.com/wii. Find the nearest place to buy a Nintendo Wii. Find a local eBay auction and other applications. Then enter coverpop.com/wheeloffood and enter your zip code and favorite type of food. Write a report on your experience.

11. Enter mapper.com. Learn its capabilities, try it, and report your experience. What Web 2.0 tool is this?

12. Enter flip.com and compare its rich media with that of MySpace.com and Cyworld.com. Prepare a report.

13. Enter clickstar.com. Why is it an online entertainment service? What are the benefits to viewers? Compare this site to starz.com.

14. Enter joost.com and find similarities with skype.com.

15. Enter zopa.com and prosper.com. Compare their operations.

16. Enter gnomz.com. What does this site help you accomplish?

17. Enter advertising.com. Find what innovative/scientific methods they use. Relate to Web 2.0 and search.

18. Enter the paulgillin.com blog and find information related to enterprise applications of Web 2.0 technologies. Write a report.

19. Enter pandora.com. Check how you can create and share music with friends. Why is this a Web 2.0 application?

20. Enter realtytrack.com and match.com. What is similar in these two sites?

21. Enter zepheira.com. What are the capabilities of the site? Relate it to Semantic Web.

22. Enter webkinz.com and compare its activities to that of facebook.com. Enter netratings.com and find the average stay time in both social network sites.

23. Enter smartmobs.com. Go to blogroll. Find three blogs related to Web 2.0 and summarize their major points.

24. Enter oreilly.com and find their latest conferences on Web 2.0. Look for topics not covered in this chapter. Write a summary. Find their RSS and Atom products. Discuss their capabilities.

TEAM ASSIGNMENTS AND ROLE PLAYING

1. Each group member selects a single family house where he(she) lives, or where a friend lives. Next, enter **zillow.com** and find the value of a house in the neighborhood. Then, add all improvements and reprice the house. Find out how to list the house for sale on Zillow and other sites (e.g., **craigslist.com**). Write a summary. Compare each members' experiences.

2. Assign each team member a different type of community, per Exhibit 18.5. Identify the services offered by that type of community. Have each team compare the services offered by each type of community. Prepare a report.

3. Have each team investigate the acquisitions made by Yahoo!, Google, Microsoft, and similar companies in areas related to search and advertisement. Summarize the findings.

4. Enter **web2.wsj2.com, web2.0central.com**, and other sites for Web 2.0. Each team member selects one area of

Web 2.0 (e.g., social media, development tools, strategies, etc.). Prepare a class presentation on the major topics of the Web. (Hint: Explore the links on the left side.)

5. Read some news items on e-commerce (e.g., at CNN, Yahoo!). Find some that include "Digg This." Click on some of them. Describe your experience with several different items.

6. Each member registers at Second Life (it is free), and creates an avatar. Get free land offered by the site and have your avatar interact with four other avatars (two from your own group and two others). Write a report about all these activities. Find a forum and describe what is going on there. Finally, describe ways the site facilitates creativity.

7. Debate the issue of paying bloggers to endorse products or services without disclosure (it is up to the bloggers to tell about it).

Real-World Case

WEB 2.0 AT EASTERN MOUNTAIN SPORT

Eastern Mountain Sport (EMS) (*ems.com*) is a medium-sized specialty retailer (annual sales $200 million) selling via over 80 physical stores, a mail order catalog, and online. Operating in a very competitive environment, the company uses leading-edge IT technologies and now is introducing a complementary set of Web 2.0 tools in order to increase collaboration, information sharing, and communication among stores and their employees, suppliers, and customers. Let's see how this works.

The Business Intelligence Strategy and System

During the last few years, the company implemented a business intelligence (BI) system that includes business performance management and dashboards. A BI system collects raw data from multiple sources, processes them into a data warehouse (or data mart), and conducts analyses that include comparing performance to operational metrics in order to assess the health of the business (see details in Turban, et al. 2008).

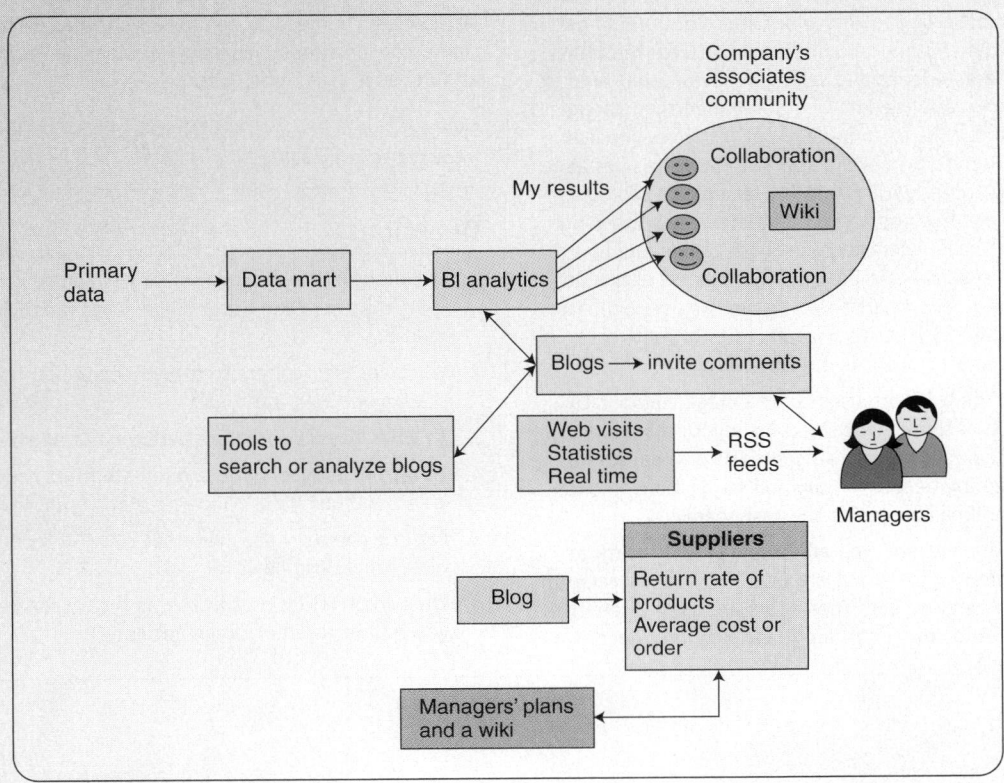

The following exhibit illustrates how the system works. Point-of-sale information and other relevant data, which are available on an IBM AS/400 computer, is loaded into Microsoft's SQL Server and into a data mart. The data are then analyzed with Information Builders' WebFOCUS 7.12 platform. The results are presented via a series of dashboards that users can view via their Web browsers. This way users can access a unified, high-level view of key performance indicators (Chapter 15) such as sales, inventory, and margin levels, and drill down to granular details that analyze specific transactions.

The Web 2.0 Collaboration, Sharing, and Communication System

The company created a multifunction employee workbench called E-Basecamp. It contains all the information relevant to corporate goals integrated with productivity tools (e.g., Excel) and role-based content, customized to each individual user. Then, it added a set of Web 2.0 tools (see the exhibit). The system facilitates collaboration among internal and external stakeholders. EMS is using 20 operation metrics (e.g., inventory levels and turns). These also include e-tailing where e-commerce managers monitor hour-by-hour Web traffic and conversion rates (Chapter 4). The dashboard shows deviations from targets with a color code. It uses the following Web 2.0 tools:

▶ **RSS feeds.** These are embedded into the dashboards to drive more focused inquiries. These feeds are the base for information sharing and online conversations. For example, by showing which items are selling better than others, users can collectively analyze the transaction characteristics and selling behaviors that produce the high sales. The knowledge acquired then cascades throughout the organization. For instance, one manager observed an upward spike in footwear sales at store X. Investigating "why" revealed that store X employees had perfected a multistep sales technique that included recommending (both online and in stores) special socks designed for specific uses along with an inner sole. The information was disseminated using the RSS feed. As a result, sales of footwear increased 57 percent in a year.

▶ **Wikis.** The wikis are used to encourage collaborative interaction throughout the company. Dashboard users are encouraged to post a hypothesis or requests for help and invite commentary and suggestions, almost like a notepad alongside the dashboard.

▶ **Blogs.** Blogs were created around specific data or a key metric. The blogs are used to post information and invite comment. Then tools are used to archive, search, and categorize blogs for easy reference.

For example, store managers post an inquiry or explanation regarding sale deviations (anomalies). Keeping comments on blogs lets readers observe patterns they might have overlooked using data analysis alone.

Going to Business Partners Externally

In the next phase, which that started in late 2006, suppliers have been added. For example, suppliers can monitor the return rate of their product on the dashboard and invite store managers to provide explanations and suggestions using wikis or blogs. Assuming proper security of data is installed, suppliers can get almost real-time data about how well their products sell, preparing a better production plan.

The objectives are to build a tighter bond with the business partners. For example, by attaching a blog to the suppliers' dashboards, the suppliers view current sale information and post comments to the blogs. Product managers use a wiki to post challenges for the next season, such as a proposed percentage increase in sales, and then ask vendors to suggest innovative ways to achieve these goals. Several of the customers and other business partners subscribe to RSS feed.

Called Extreme Deals (big discounts for a limited time), blogs are also embedded into the EMS product-management lifecycle (PLM) tool. This allows vendors to have virtual conversations with the product development managers.

The major impact of the Web 2.0 collaboration tools is that instead of having conversations occur in the hallway (where you need to be in the right place at the right time), conversations take place on blogs and wikis where all interested parties can participate.

Sources: Compiled from Nerille (2007) and from *ems.com* (accessed February 2007).

Questions

1. Why not just have regular meetings and send e-mails rather than using blogs, wikis, and RSS feeds?

2. What are the benefits to EMS of combining its BI system and Web 2.0 tools?

3. In what ways is corporate performance bolstered?

4. How can customers of the retail stores utilize the Web 2.0 tools?

5. Can the company use any other Web 2.0 technologies? What, and how?

6. What information on *ems.com* is typical for what you find in Internet communities?

REFERENCES

Anderson, C. *The Long Tail: How Endless Choice Is Creating Unlimited Demand.* New York: Random House Business Books, 2006.

Bilsborrow-Koo, R. "Ten Video Sharing Services Compared." *Dvguru.com,* April 7, 2006. **dvguru.com/2006/04/07/ten-video-sharing-services-compared** (accessed February 2007).

Blanchard, A. L., and M. L. Markus. "The Experienced 'Sense' of a Virtual Community: Characteristics and Processes." *The DATA BASE for Advances in Information Systems,* Vol. 35, No. 4 (2004).

Borland, J. "A Smarter Web." *Technology Review,* March/April 2007.

Brown, J. S., and J. Hagel. "Push Pull: The Next Frontier of Innovation." *McKinsey Quarterly,* No. 3 (2005).

Business 2.0 Staff. "The Next Net 25." (Web 2.0 Companies) *Business 2.0,* February 22, 2007.

Carr, D. F., "E-Discovery." *Baseline,* November 2006a.

Carr, D. F. "How Google Works." *Baseline,* June 6, 2006b.

Carr, D. F. "Inside MySpace." *Baseline,* January 2007.

Carr, D. F. "Tapping into Virtual Markets." *Baseline Magazine,* March 1, 2007. **baselinemag.com/article2/0,1540,2098846,00.asp** (accessed August 2007).

Cashel, J. "Top Ten Trends for Online Communities." *Online Community Report.* **onlinecommunityreport.com/features/10** (accessed October 2004).

Chesbrough, H. W. *Open Business Models.* Boston, MA: Harvard Business School Press, 2006.

Chmielewski, D. C. "Yahoo!'s Ad System is Almost Ready." *LA Times,* January 24, 2007.

comScore. "MySpace Leads in Number of U.S. Video Streams Viewed Online, Capturing 20 Percent Market Share; Yahoo! Ranks #1 in Number of People Streaming." September 27, 2006. **comscore.com/press/release.asp?press=1015** (accessed February 2007).

Cone, E. "Comment: Put a Fork in the Plan to Fork." *Blog.eweek.com,* January 22, 2007.

Copeland, M. V. "The Missing Link." *Business 2.0,* September 2006.

Dholakia, U. M., R. Bagozzi, and L. K. Pearo. "A Social Influence Model of Consumer Participation in Network- and Small-Group-Based Virtual Communities." *International Journal of Research in Marketing,* Vol. 21, No. 3 (2004).

D'Agostino, D. "Security in the World of Web 2.0." *Innovations,* Winter 2006.

Duffy, D. "It Takes an E-Village." *CIO Magazine,* October 25, 1999.

The Economist. "How Google Works." September 16, 2004.

The Economist. "Watching the Web Grow Up." *Technology Quarterly,* March 10, 2007.

Epps, S. R., H. H. Harteveldt, and B. McGowan. "How Social Computing Changes the Way You Sell Travel."

Forrester Research, April 30, 2007. **forrester.com/Research/Document/Excerpt/0,7211,42100,00.html** (accessed May 2007).

Eyefortravel.com. "TripleHop Recommendation Engine Makes Tailored Service Available to More Than 30 Million Leisure Travelers Through EuroVacations.com Software Facilitates Decision Process." April 26, 2001. **eyefortravel.com/index.asp?news=15008** (accessed March 2007).

Farrell, N. "Microsoft Rambled over Wikipedia Edits." **theinquirer.net/print.aspx?article=37170** (accessed January 2007).

Flynn, N. *Blog Rules: A Business Guide to Managing Policy, Public Relations, and Legal Issues.* Saranac Lake, NY: AMACOM, 2006.

Fortune Technology Staff. "The Browser: Analyzing the Tech Biz." February 7, 2007. **money.cnn.com/blogs/browser/index.html** (accessed March 2007).

Garrett, D. "Who Needs Google? We've Got Amazon." *NewsFactor Network,* January 4, 2007. **newsfactor.com/story.xhtml?story_id=0110010E57Q6** (accessed March 2007).

Geocities. **geocities.yahoo.com** (accessed January 2007).

Gibson, S. "RSS in the Enterprise." *eWeek,* January 15, 2007.

Gillin, P. *The New Influencers.* Sanger, CA: Quill Driver Books, March, 2007a.

Gillin, P. "Web 2.0 Tools of the Trade." *SearchSMB.com,* March 22, 2007b.

Gogoi, P. "Retailers Take a Tip from MySpace." *Business Week Online,* February 13, 2007. **businessweek.mobi/detail.jsp?key=6158&rc=sb&p=4&pv=1** (accessed March 2007).

Goldberg, M. "Market Wrap Up." *Financial Sense Online,* December 13, 2006. **financialsense.com/Market/goldberg/2006/1214.html** (accessed February 2007).

Goldsmith, R. "Electronic Word-of-Mouth." In Khosrow-Pour, 2006.

Grossman, L. "Time Person of the Year—YOU." "Power to People." *Time,* December 25, 2006–January 1, 2007.

Hagel, J., and A. Armstrong. *Net Gain.* Boston: Harvard Business School Press, 1997.

Hammond, T., T. Hannay, B. Lund, and J. Scott. "Social Bookmarking Tools I." *D-Lib Magazine,* April 2005. **dlib.org/dlib/april05/hammond/04hammond.html** (accessed March 2007).

Harteveldt, H. H. "Travelers Embrace Social Computing Technologies." *Forrester Research Report,* October 23, 2006. **forrester.com/Research/Document/Excerpt/0,7211,39928,00.html** (accessed February 2007).

Hefflinger, M. "Google, Echostar Partner on Satellite TV Ad Sales System." *DigitalMediaWire,* April 3, 2007.

dmwmedia.com/news/2007/04/03/google-echostar-partner-on-satellite-tv-ad-sales-system (accessed April 2007).

Heilemann, J. "Capturing the Buzz." *Business 2.0*, October 2006a.

Heilemann, J. "Digging Up News." *Business 2.0*, April 2006b.

Hinchcliffe, D. "Profitably Running an Online Business in the Web 2.0 Era." *SOA Web Services Journal* (November 29, 2006). **web2.wsj2.com** (accessed March 2007).

Hoover, N. J. "Lotus' Leap." *InformationWeek*, January 29, 2007.

Innovations. "Going Beyond Networking." *Innovation* (Winter 2006).

Jana, R. "American Apparel's Virtual Clothes." *Business Week* June 27, *2006.* **businessweek.com/innovate/content/jun2006/id20060627_217800.htm** (accessed August 2007).

Kafka, P. "Blue Sky." *Forbes*, February 12, 2006.

Khosrow-Pour, M. *Encyclopedia of E-Commerce, E-Government, and Mobile Commerce.* Hershey, PA: Idea Group Reference, 2006.

La Monica, P. R. "Big Media Beats Up on YouTube." *CNNMoney.com*, February 9, 2007.

Lashinsky, A. "Catching Google's YouTube Won't Be Easy." *Fortune*, March 26, 2007a **zines/fortune/lashinsky_pluggedin_nbcu.fortune/index.htm** (accessed April 2007).

Lashinsky, A. "Google is Number 1: Search and Enjoy." *CNNMoney.com*, January 10, 2007b. **money.cnn.com/2007/01/05/magazines/fortune/Search_and_enjoy.fortune/index.htm** (accessed February 2007).

Lee, M., D. Vogel, and L. Moez. "Virtual Communities Informatics: A Review and Research Agenda." *Information Technology Theory and Applications*, Vol. 5, No. 1 (2003).

Leimeister, J. M., and H. Krcmar. "Success Factors of Virtual Communities from the Perspective of Members and Operators: An Empirical Study." *Proceedings of the 37th Annual HICCS Conference*, Kauai, Hawaii, January 4–7, 2004.

Longino, C. "Your Wireless Future." *Business 2.0*, May 2006.

Magna, M. "Bust or Boom? Calculate Blog ROI." *E-Commerce Guide*, February 8, 2007. **ecommerce-guide.com/news/news/article.php/3658776** (accessed February 2007).

Markoff, J. "Amazon to Take Searches on Web to a New Depth." *New York Times*, September 15, 2004a. **nytimes.com/2004/09/15/technology/15search.html?ex=1252900800&en=63edc8f5d6ce2fc6&ei=5090&partner=rssuserland** (accessed March 2007).

Markoff, J. "Microsoft Unveils Its Internet Search Engine, Quietly." *New York Times*, November 11, 2004b. **nytimes.com/2004/11/11/technology/11search.html?ex=1257915600&en=bd174957c62c5cfd&ei=5090&partner=rssuserland** (accessed March 2007).

Markoff, J. "The Coming Search Wars." *New York Times*, February 2, 2004c. **nytimes.com/2004/02/01/business/yourmoney/01goog.html?ex=1390971600&en=4290df4187bde817&ei=5007&partner=USERLAND** (accessed March 2007).

Markoff, J. "Entrepreneurs See a Web Guided by Common Sense," *New York Times",* November 12, 2006.

Martens, C. "Wikipedia to Strive for Higher Quality Content." *PC World,* August 4, 2006.

McGillicuddy, S. "IT Executives Eager to Exploit 2.0 Wave." *SMB News*, October 24, 2006a. **searchsmb.techtarget.com/originalContent/0,289142,sid44_gci1226154,00.html** (accessed April 2007).

McGillicuddy, S. "Wikis and Blogs Transforming Workflow." *CIO News,* April 25, 2006b. **searchcio.techtarget.com/originalContent/0,289142,sid19_gci1184607,00.html** (accessed March 2007).

McNichol, T., "Building a Wiki World." (Wikia vs. Wikipedia), *Business 2.0*, March 2007.

Mello, J. P. "Explosive Growth Predicted for Mobile Social Networks." *Ecommerce Times*, December 12, 2006.

Metz, C. "First Look: iPhone Truly Is a Revelation." *PCMAG.com*, January 12, 2007.

Millard, E. "Online Social Networks and the Profit Motive." *E-Commerce Times*, June 12, 2004. **ecommercetimes.com/story/34422.html** (accessed March 2007).

Mossberg, W. "Netvibes Brings Personalized Web Pages to Another Level." *Honolulu Advisor*, February 6, 2007.

Munarriz, R. A. "What's Google's Growth Strategy?" *The Motley Fool Take*, August 31, 2004. **fool.com/news/take/2004/take040831.htm** (accessed March 2007).

Murphy, C., and E. Malykhina. "iPhone Calling." *Information Week,* January 15, 2007.

Murray-Buechner, M. "25 Sites We Can't Live Without." *Time*, August 3, 2006.

Nerille, J. "X-treme Web 2.0." *Optimize Magazine*, January 2007.

The New York Times. "CBS Buys Last.FM Online Radio Site." May 31, 2007 **nytimes. com/2007/05/31/business/media/31radios.html?ex=1338264000&en=32fe4d40014e63c1&ei=5088& partner=rssnyt&emc=rss** (accessed July 2007).

Nielsen NetRatings. "Nielsen/Netratings Announces January U.S. Search Share Rankings." February 28, 2007. **nielsen-netratings.com/pr/pr_070228.pdf** (accessed February 2007).

O'Brien, J. M. "What's Your House Really Worth?" *Fortune*, February 29, 2007.

O'Malley, G. "MySpace vs. eBay? Site Leaps into E-Commerce." *Advertising Age*, September 11, 2006.

O'Reilly, T. "What is Web 2.0?" *OReillynet.com*, September 30, 2006.**oreillynet.com/pub/a/oreilly/**

tim/news/2005/09/30/what-is-web-20.html (accessed September 2006).

Porter, C. E. "A Typology of Virtual Communities: A Multi-Disciplinary Foundation for Future Research." *Journal of Computer-Mediated Communication,* Vol. 10, No. 1 (2004).

PRWeb.com. "A New Way of Keeping in Touch." 2003. prweb.com/releases/2003/8/prweb77491.htm (accessed February 2007).

Raman, M. "Wiki Technologies as 'Free' Collaborative Tools within an Organization." *Information Systems Management* (Fall 2006).

Read/Write Web. "Latest NSN Numbers, MySpace Streaks Ahead." January 9, 2006. readwriteweb.com/archives/latest_sns_numb.php (accessed February 2007).

Regan, K. "Plugging In: Can E-Commerce Leverage Social Networks?" *E-Commerce Times,* November 2, 2006.

Reuters, A. "IBM Eyes Move into Second Life 'V-Business'." *Second Life News Center,* October 24, 2006. secondlife.reuters.com/stories/2006/10/24/ibm-eyes-move-into-second-life-v-business (accessed August 2007).

Revenue News. "MyPickList Tackles Social Networking and Word-of-Mouth Advertising." May 25, 2006.

Rheingold, H. *Smart Mobs: The Next Social Revolution,* New York: Basic Books, 2003.

Rheingold, H. *The Virtual Community: Homesteading on the Electronic Frontier,* rev. ed. Boston: MIT press, 2000.

Ricadela, A. "Under Construction." *InformationWeek,* November 6, 2006.

Roush, W. "Search beyond Google." *Technology Review,* March 1, 2004. technologyreview.com/Infotech/13505 (accessed March 2007).

Rouch, W. "Social Networking 3.0." *Technology Review* from MIT's Emerging Technologies Conference, September 27–29, 2006. technologyreview.com/read_article.aspx?id=15908&ch=infotech.

Rowse, D. "Blog Tools." *problogger.net,* April 15, 2006. problogger.net/archives/2006/04/15/blog-tools (accessed July 2007).

Sandoval, G. "Teen Filmaker Attracts Logitech's Focus." ZDNET News, March 28, 2006. news.zdnet.com/2100-1040_22-6054602.html (accessed August 2007).

Scable, R., and S. Israel. *Naked Conversations: How Blogs Are Changing the Way Businesses Talk with Customers.* New York: Hungry Minds/Wiley, 2006.

Schonfeld, E. "Cyworld Attacks!" *Business 2.0,* August 2006a.

Schonfeld, E. "The Disruptors Get Rowdy." *The.Next.Net,* October 27, 2006b. blogs.business2.com/business2blog/2006/10/the_disruptors.html (accessed February 2007).

Schonfeld, E. "The Flickrization of Yahoo!" *Business 2.0,* December 2005.

Schonfeld, E. "Make Way for Must Stream TV." *Business 2.0,* March 2007.

Schonfeld, E. "Web TV's Top-Rated Acts." *Business 2.0,* February 23, 2007.

Schonfeld, E., and J. Borzo. "The Next Disruptors." *Business 2.0,* October 2006.

Schubert, P., and M. Ginsburg. "Virtual Communities of Transaction: The Role of Personalization in E-Commerce." *Electronic Markets,* Vol. 10, No. 1 (2000).

Sharma, A. "Banner Year: Companies Compete for Ad Revenue on Mobile Internet." *Wall Street Journal,* January 18, 2007.

Sloan P. "The Next Net 25 (Web 2.0 Companies)." *Business 2.0,* March 2007a.

Sloan P. "The Quest for the Perfect Online Ad." *Business 2.0,* March 2007b.

Sloan, P., and P. Kaihla. "Blogging for Dollars." *Business 2.0,* September 2006.

Smith, D. "Discovering Where Web Evolution Is Taking Us." *The Observer* (Silicon Valley, California); reprinted in the *Taipei Times,* December 1, 2006.

Stafford, A. "The Future of the Web." *PC World,* November 2006.

Steiner, C. "The eBay of Loans." *Forbes,* March 12, 2007.

Story, L. "Google Navigates an Offline Course." *Taipei Times,* November 23, 2006.

Story, L., and M. Helft. "Google Buys an Online Ad Firm for $3.1 Billion." *The New York Times,* April 14, 2007.

Sullivan, D. "Search Wars: Battle of the Superpowers." April 29, 2004. searchenginewatch.com/showPage.html?page=3347181 (accessed March 2007).

Taft, D. K. "IBM Enters Social Scene." *eWeek,* January 29, 2007.

Taipei Times. "Trawling the Net for Your Innermost Desires." December 17, 2006.

Tapscott, D., and A. D. Williams, *Wikinomics: How Mass Collaboration Changes Everything.* Woodlands, TX: Portfolio (December 28, 2006).

Turban, E., et al. *Business Intelligence: A Managerial Approach.* Upper Saddle River, NJ: Prentice Hall, 2008.

Tynan, D. "Entertainment on Demand." *PC World,* November 2006.

Urlocker, M. "Urlocker on Disruption." The Disruption Group." September 20, 2006. ondisruption.com/my_weblog/2006/09/business_20_top.html (accessed February 2007).

Wagner, M. "Can Bloggers Be Bought?" *Information Week,* October 16, 2006.

Wainewright, P. "What to Expect from Web 3.0." *ZDNet.com,* November 29, 2005. blogs.zdnet.com/SAAS/?p=68 (accessed March 2007).

Walsh, M. "Yahoo!, Newspapers Form Major Alliance." *MediaPost Publications,* November 21, 2006. publications.mediapost.com/index.cfm?fuseaction=Articles.showArticle&art_aid=51432 (accessed March 2007).

Watson, B. P. "Web 2.0: Business Tools That Save Time, Money." *Baseline*, February 2, 2007a.

Watson, B. "Web 2.0: The Internet Refreshed." *Baseline*, January 2007b.

Websloginc.com. "The Social Software Weblog." 2007. **socialsoftware.Weblogsinc.com** (accessed February 2007).

Weinstein, M. "On Demand Is in Demand." *Training*, October 2006.

Werthner, H., and F. Ricci. "E-Commerce and Tourism." *Communications of the ACM* (December 2004).

Woyke, E. "The eBay Model Goes to the Movies." *Business Week*, December 11, 2006.

Wright, J. *Blog Marketing*. New York: McGraw Hill, 2006.

YouTube. "Sundance Channel Video Clips Available on YouTube in 2007." January 17, 2007. **youtube.com/press_room_entry?entry=pmcIOsL7s98** (accessed February 2007).

YouTube. "YouTube and Coca Cola Introduce Video Greeting Cards for the Holidays." December 8, 2006a. **youtube.com/press_room_entry?entry=3qfzQhQXryg** (accessed February 2007).

YouTube. "YouTube, Chevrolet and Warner Music Group Present New Year's Eve Countdown Around the World." December 29, 2006b. **youtube.com/press_room_entry?entry=JrYI-yzd3Q0** (accessed February 2007).

Zetlin, M., and B. Pfleging. "The Cult of Community." *Smart Business*, June 2002.

CHAPTER 19

BUILDING E-COMMERCE APPLICATIONS AND INFRASTRUCTURE

Content

Helping Customers Navigate the Web Site and Increase Sales at Campmor

Learning Objectives

Upon completion of this chapter, you will be able to:

1. Discuss the major steps in developing an EC application.

2. Describe the major EC applications and list their major functionalities.

3. List the major EC application development options along with their benefits and limitations.

4. Discuss various EC application outsourcing options, including application service providers (ASPs), software as a service (SaaS), and utility computing.

5. Discuss the major EC software packages and EC application suites.

6. Describe various methods for connecting an EC application to back-end systems and databases.

7. Discuss the value and technical foundation of Web Services and their evolution into second-generation tools in EC applications.

8. Understand service-oriented architecture (SOA) and virtualization and their relationship to EC application development.

9. Describe the criteria used in selecting an outsourcing vendor and package.

10. Understand the value and uses of EC application log files.

11. Discuss the importance of usage analysis and site management.

A complete version of this chapter is available on the textbook's Web site.

GLOSSARY

1G The first generation of wireless technology, which was analog based.

2.5G An interim wireless technology that can accommodate voice, text, and limited graphics.

2G The second generation of digital wireless technology; accommodates voice and text.

3G The third generation of digital wireless technology; supports rich media such as video.

3.5G This generation was inserted into the ranks of cellphone generations; it refers to the packet-switched technologies used to achieve higher transmission speeds.

4G The expected next generation of wireless technology that will provide faster display of multimedia.

802.11a This Wi-Fi standard is faster than 802.11b but has a smaller range.

802.11b The most popular Wi-Fi standard; it is inexpensive and offers sufficient speed for most devices; however, interference can be a problem.

802.11g This fast but expensive Wi-Fi standard is mostly used in businesses.

acceptable use policy (AUP) Policy that informs users of their responsibilities when using company networks, wireless devices, customer data, etc.

acceptance testing Determining whether a Web site meets the original business objectives and vision.

access control Mechanism that determines who can legitimately use a network resource.

access log A record kept by a Web server that shows when a user accesses the server; kept in a common log file format, each line of this text file details an individual access.

active token Small, stand-alone electronic device that generates one-time passwords used in a two-factor authentication system.

ad management Methodology and software that enable organizations to perform a variety of activities involved in Web advertising (e.g., tracking viewers, rotating ads).

ad views The number of times users call up a page that has a banner on it during a specific period; known as *impressions* or *page views*.

Address Verification System (AVS) Detects fraud by comparing the address entered on a Web page with the address information on file with the cardholder's issuing bank.

admediaries Third-party vendors that conduct promotions, especially large-scale ones.

advanced planning and scheduling (APS) systems Programs that use algorithms to identify optimal solutions to complex planning problems that are bound by constraints.

advergaming The practice of using computer games to advertise a product, an organization, or a viewpoint.

advertising networks Specialized firms that offer customized Web advertising, such as brokering ads and targeting ads to select groups of consumers.

advertorial An advertisement "disguised" to look like editorial content or general information.

affiliate marketing An arrangement whereby a marketing partner (a business, an organization, or even an individual) refers consumers to the selling company's Web site.

agency costs Costs incurred in ensuring that the agent performs tasks as expected (also called *administrative costs*).

agility An EC firm's ability to capture, report, and quickly respond to changes happening in the marketplace and business environment.

Ajax A Web development technique for creating interactive Web applications.

analytic CRM Applying business analytics techniques and business intelligence such as data mining and online analytic processing to CRM applications.

angel investor A wealthy individual who contributes personal funds and possibly expertise at the earliest stage of business development.

application firewalls Specialized tools designed to increase the security of Web applications.

application service provider (ASP) An agent or vendor who assembles the functions needed by enterprises and packages them with outsourced development, operation, maintenance, and other services.

application-level proxy A firewall that permits requests for Web pages to move from the public Internet to the private network.

associated ad display (text links) An advertising strategy that displays a banner ad related to a key term entered in a search engine.

attractors Web site features that attract and interact with visitors in the target stakeholder group.

auction A competitive process in which a seller solicits consecutive bids from buyers (forward auctions) or a buyer solicits bids from sellers (backward auctions). Prices are determined dynamically by the bids.

auction aggregators Companies that use software agents to visit Web auction sites, find information, summarize it, and deliver it to users.

auction vortals Another name for a vertical auction vertical portal.

auditing Process of recording information about what Web site, data, file, or network was accessed, when, and by whom or what.

authentication Process to verify (assure) the real identity of an individual, computer, computer program, or EC Web site.

authorization Process of determining what the authenticated entity is allowed to access and what operations it is allowed to perform.

Automated Clearing House (ACH) Network A nationwide batch-oriented electronic funds transfer system that provides for the interbank clearing of electronic payments for participating financial institutions.

automatic crash notification (ACN) Device that automatically sends the police the location of a vehicle that has been involved in a crash.

autoresponders Automated e-mail reply systems (text files returned via e-mail) that provide answers to commonly asked questions.

availability Assurance that access to data, the Web site, or other EC data service is timely, available, reliable, and restricted to authorized users.

avatars Animated computer characters that exhibit human-like movements and behaviors.

average-cost curve (AVC) Behavior of average costs as quantity changes; generally, as quantity increases, average costs decline.

B2B portals Information portals for businesses.

back end The activities that support online order fulfillment, inventory management, purchasing from suppliers, payment processing, packaging, and delivery.

back-office operations The activities that support fulfillment of orders, such as packing, delivery, accounting, and logistics.

balanced scorecard A management tool that assesses organizational progress toward strategic goals by measuring performance in a number of different areas.

bandwidth The speed at which content can be delivered across a network; it is rated in bits per second (bps).

banner On a Web page, a graphic advertising display linked to the advertiser's Web page.

banking Trojan A trojan that comes to life when computer owners visit one of a number of online banking or e-commerce sites.

banner exchanges Markets in which companies can trade or exchange placement of banner ads on each other's Web sites.

banner swapping An agreement between two companies to each display the other's banner ad on its Web site.

bartering The *exchange* of goods and services.

bartering exchange An intermediary that links parties in a barter; a company submits its surplus to the exchange and receives points of credit, which can be used to buy the items that the company needs from other exchange participants.

bastion gateway A special hardware server that utilizes application-level proxy software to limit the types of requests that can be passed to an organization's internal networks from the public Internet.

bid shielding Having phantom bidders bid at a very high price when an auction begins; they pull out at the last minute, and the real bidder who bid a much lower price wins.

biometric An individual's unique physical or behavioral characteristics that can be used to identify an individual precisely (e.g., fingerprints).

biometric systems Authentication systems that identify a person by measurement of a biological characteristic, such as fingerprints, iris (eye) patterns, facial features, or voice.

Blackberry A handheld device principally used for e-mail.

blog A personal Web site that is open to the public to read and to interact with; dedicated to specific topics or issues.

Bluetooth A set of telecommunications standards that enables wireless devices to communicate with each other over short distances.

botnet A huge number (e.g., hundreds of thousands) of hijacked Internet computers that have been set up to forward traffic, including spam and viruses, to other computers on the Internet.

brick-and-mortar (old-economy) organizations Old-economy organizations (corporations) that perform their primary business off-line, selling physical products by means of physical agents.

brick-and-mortar retailers Retailers who do business in the non-Internet, physical world in traditional brick-and-mortar stores.

build-to-order (pull system) A manufacturing process that starts with an order (usually customized). Once the order is paid for, the vendor starts to fulfill it.

bullwhip effect Erratic shifts in orders up and down supply chains.

bundle trading The selling of several related products and/or services together.

business case A document that justifies the investment of internal, organizational resources in a specific application or project.

business impact analysis (BIA) An exercise that determines the impact of losing the support of an EC resource to an organization and establishes the escalation of that loss over time, identifies the minimum resources needed to recover, and prioritizes the recovery of processes and supporting systems.

business model A method of doing business by which a company can generate revenue to sustain itself.

business network A group of people that have some kind of commercial relationship. For example, the relationships between sellers and buyers, buyers among themselves, buyers and suppliers, and colleagues and other colleagues.

business plan A written document that identifies a company's goals and outlines how the company intends to achieve the goals and at what cost.

business process management (BPM) Method for business restructuring that combines workflow systems and redesign methods; covers three process categories—people-to-people, systems-to-systems, and systems-to-people interactions.

business process reengineering (BPR) A methodology for conducting a comprehensive redesign of an enterprise's processes.

business-to-business (B2B) E-commerce model in which all of the participants are businesses or other organizations.

business-to-business e-commerce (B2B EC) Transactions between businesses conducted electronically over the Internet, extranets, intranets, or private networks; also known as *eB2B* (*electronic B2B*) or just *B2B*.

business-to-business-to-consumer (B2B2C) E-commerce model in which a business provides some product or service to a client business that maintains its own customers.

business-to-consumer (B2C) E-commerce model in which businesses sell to individual shoppers.

business-to-employees (B2E) E-commerce model in which an organization delivers services, information, or products to its individual employees.

button A button is a small banner that is linked to a Web site. It may contain downloadable software.

buy-side e-marketplace A corporate-based acquisition site that uses reverse auctions, negotiations, group purchasing, or any other e-procurement method.

CAN-SPAM Act Law that makes it a crime to send commercial e-mail messages with false or misleading message headers or misleading subject lines.

Captcha tool Completely Automated Public Turing test to tell Computers and Humans Apart, which uses a verification test on comment pages to stop scripts from posting automatically.

card-not-present (CNP) transaction A credit card transaction in which the merchant does not verify the customer's signature.

card verification number (CVN) Detects fraud by comparing the verification number printed on the signature strip on the back of the card with the information on file with the cardholder's issuing bank.

Cascading Style Sheets (CSS) A standard that uses text files to specify formatting characteristics (styles) for various elements in an HTML document, allowing styles to be controlled and changed easily.

certificate authorities (CAs) Third parties that issue digital certificates.

channel conflict Situation in which an online marketing channel upsets the traditional channels due to real or perceived damage from competition.

chatterbots Animation characters that can talk (chat).

Children's Internet Protection Act (CIPA) Law that mandates the use of filtering technologies in schools and libraries that received certain types of U.S. federal funding.

CIA security triad (CIA triad) Three security concepts important to information on the Internet: confidentiality, integrity, and availability.

ciphertext A plaintext message after it has been encrypted into a machine-readable form.

civil laws Laws that enable a party (individual or organization) that has suffered harm or a loss to bring a lawsuit against whoever is responsible for the harm or loss.

civil litigation An adversarial proceeding in which a party (the plaintiff) sues another party (the defendant) to get compensation for a wrong committed by the defendant.

click (click-through or ad click) A count made each time a visitor clicks on an advertising banner to access the advertiser's Web site.

click-and-mortar (click-and-brick) organizations Organizations that conduct some e-commerce activities, usually as an additional marketing channel.

click-and-mortar retailers Brick-and-mortar retailers that offer a transactional Web site from which to conduct business.

click fraud Scams and deceptions that inflate advertising bills.

clickstream behavior Customer movements on the Internet.

clickstream data Data that occur inside the Web environment; they provide a trail of the user's activities (the user's clickstream behavior) in the Web site.

click-through ratio The ratio between the number of clicks on a banner ad and the number of times it is seen by viewers; measures the success of a banner in attracting visitors to click on the ad.

codecs The compression algorithms that are used to encode audio and video streams; short for *compression and decompression*.

collaboration hub The central point of control for an e-market. A single c-hub, representing one e-market owner, can host multiple collaboration spaces (c-spaces) in which trading partners use c-enablers to exchange data with the c-hub.

collaborative commerce (c-commerce) The use of digital technologies that enable companies to collaboratively plan, design, develop, manage, and research products, services, and innovative EC applications.

collaborative filtering A market research and personalization method that uses customer data to predict, based on formulas derived from behavioral sciences, what other products or services a customer may enjoy; predictions can be extended to other customers with similar profiles.

collaborative planning, forecasting, and replenishment (CPFR) Project in which suppliers and retailers collaborate in their planning and demand forecasting to optimize flow of materials along the supply chain.

collaborative portals Portals that allow collaboration.

collaborative Web site A site that allows business partners to collaborate

co-location A Web server owned and maintained by the business is given to a Web hosting service that manages the server's connection to the Internet.

comment spam Spam sent to all types of messaging media, including blogs, IM, and cellular telephones to promote products or services.

commodity content Information that is widely available and generally free to access on the Web.

common (security) vulnerabilities and exposures (CVE) Publicly known computer security risks, which are collected, listed, and shared by a board of security-related organizations (cve.mitre.org).

common law (case law) Law created by judges in court decisions.

Compact Hypertext Markup Language (cHTML) A scripting language used to create content in i-mode.

company-centric EC E-commerce that focuses on a single company's buying needs (many-to-one, or buy-side) or selling needs (one-to-many, or sell-side).

competitive forces model Model devised by Porter that says that five major forces of competition determine industry structure and how economic value is divided among the industry players in an industry; analysis of these forces helps companies develop their competitive strategy.

competitor analysis grid A strategic planning tool that highlights points of differentiation between competitors and the target firm.

complementary investments Additional investments, such as training, made to maximize the returns from EC investments.

Computer Fraud and Abuse Act (CFAA) Major computer crime law to protect government computers and other Internet-connected computers.

Computing Technology Industry Association (CompTIA) Nonprofit trade group providing information security research and best practices.

confidentiality Assurance of data privacy and accuracy. Keeping private or sensitive information from being disclosed to unauthorized individuals, entities, or processes.

consortium trading exchange (CTE) An exchange formed and operated by a group of major companies in an industry to provide industrywide transaction services.

consumer-to-business (C2B) E-commerce model in which individuals use the Internet to sell products or services to organizations or individuals seek sellers to bid on products or services they need.

consumer-to-consumer (C2C) E-commerce model in which consumers sell directly to other consumers.

contact card A smart card containing a small gold plate on the face that when inserted in a smart card reader makes contact and passes data to and from the embedded microchip.

contactless (proximity) card A smart card with an embedded antenna, by means of which data and applications are passed to and from a card reader unit or other device without contact between the card and the card reader.

content The text, images, sound, and video that make up a Web page.

content management The process of adding, revising, and removing content from a Web site to keep content fresh, accurate, compelling, and credible.

contextual computing The enhancement of a user's interactions by understanding the user, the context, and the applications and information required.

conversion rate The percentage of clickers who actually make a purchase.

cookie A data file that is placed on a user's hard drive by a remote Web server, frequently without disclosure or the user's consent, that collects information about the user's activities at a site.

co-opetition Two or more companies cooperate together on some activities for their mutual benefit, even while competing against each other in the marketplace.

copyright An exclusive right of the author or creator of a book, movie, musical composition or other artistic property to print, copy, sell, license, distribute, transform to another medium, translate, record, perform, or otherwise use.

corporate (business) performance management (CPM, BPM) Advanced performance measuring and analysis approach that embraces planning and strategy.

corporate (enterprise) portal A gateway for entering a corporate Web site, enabling communication, collaboration, and access to company information.

corporate portal A major gateway through which employees, business partners, and the public can enter a corporate Web site.

cost-benefit analysis A comparison of the costs of a project against the benefits.

CPM (cost per thousand impressions) The fee an advertiser pays for each 1,000 times a page with a banner ad is shown.

crime Offensive act against society that violates a law and is punishable by the government.

crimeware Software designed to infect a computer and take personal information that can be used to steal from the computer user.

criminal laws Laws to protect the public, human life, or private property.

cross-selling Offering similar or complimentary products and services to increase sales.

CSI/FBI Computer Crime and Security Survey Annual security survey of U.S. corporations, government agencies, financial and medical institutions, and universities conducted jointly by the FBI and the Computer Security Institute.

customer interaction center (CIC) A comprehensive service entity in which EC vendors address customer-service issues communicated through various contact channels.

customer relationship management (CRM) A customer service approach that focuses on building long-term and sustainable customer relationships that add value both for the customer and the selling company.

customer-to-customer (C2C) E-commerce model in which consumers sell directly to other consumers.

customization Creation of a product or service according to the buyer's specifications.

cyberbashing Domain name that criticizes an organization or person.

cybermediation (electronic intermediation) The use of software (intelligent) agents to facilitate intermediation.

darknet Private online community that is only open to those who belong to it.

data conferencing Virtual meeting in which geographically dispersed groups work on documents together and exchange computer files during videoconferences.

Data Encryption Standard (DES) The standard symmetric encryption algorithm supported by the NIST and used by U.S. government agencies until October 2000.

data warehouse A single, server-based data repository that allows centralized analysis, security, and control over the data.

demilitarized zone (DMZ) Network area that sits between an organization's internal network and an external network (Internet), providing physical isolation between the two networks that is controlled by rules enforced by a firewall.

denial of service (DOS) attack An attack on a Web site in which an attacker uses specialized software to send a flood of data packets to the target computer with the aim of overloading its resources.

desktop purchasing Direct purchasing from internal marketplaces without the approval of supervisors and without the intervention of a procurement department.

desktop search Search tools that search the contents of a user's or organization's computer files rather than searching the Internet. The emphasis is on finding all the information that is available on the user's PC, including Web browser histories, e-mail archives, and word-processor documents, as well as in all internal files and databases.

detection measures Ways to determine whether intruders attempted to break into the EC system; whether they were successful; and what they may have done.

differentiation Providing a product or service that is unique.

digital economy An economy that is based on digital technologies, including digital communication networks, computers, software, and other related information technologies; also called the Internet economy, the new economy, or the Web economy.

digital enterprise A new business model that uses IT in a fundamental way to accomplish one or more of three basic objectives: reach and engage customers more effectively, boost employee productivity, and improve operating efficiency. It uses converged communication and computing technology in a way that improves business processes.

digital envelope The combination of the encrypted original message and the digital signature, using the recipient's public key.

digital options A set of IT-enabled capabilities in the form of digitized enterprise work processes and knowledge systems.

digital products Goods that can be transformed to digital format and delivered over the Internet.

digital rights management (DRM) An umbrella term for any of several arrangements that allow a vendor of content in electronic form to control the material and restrict its usage.

digital signature Validates the sender and time stamp of a transaction so it cannot be later claimed that the transaction was unauthorized or invalid.

direct marketing Broadly, marketing that takes place without intermediaries between manufacturers and buyers; in the context of this book, marketing done online between any seller and buyer.

direct materials Materials used in the production of a product (e.g., steel in a car or paper in a book).

disintermediation The removal of organizations or business process layers responsible for certain intermediary steps in a given supply chain.

disruptors Companies that introduce a significant change in their industries, thus causing disruption in business operations.

distance learning Formal education that takes place off campus, usually, but not always, through online resources.

document type definition (DTD) In XML, a file that defines the tags that are allowed and the manner in which they can be used; basically, a set of grammar rules for the tags in a particular document.

domain name A name-based address that identifies an Internet-connected server. Usually, it refers to the portion of the address to the left of .com and .org, etc.

domain name registrar A business that assists prospective Web site owners with finding and registering the domain name of their choice.

domain name system (DNS) Translates (converts) domain names to their numeric IP addresses.

dotted-quad addressing The format in which Internet addresses are written as four sets of numbers separated by periods.

double auction Auction in which multiple buyers and sellers may be making bids and offers simultaneously; buyers and their bidding prices and sellers and their asking prices are matched, considering the quantities on both sides.

due process A guarantee of basic fairness and fair procedures in legal action.

duty Legal obligation imposed on individuals and organizations that prevents them from interfering with another's protected interest or right.

dynamic pricing A rapid movement of prices over time, and possibly across customers, as a result of supply and demand matching.

dynamic trading Trading that occurs in situations when prices are changing continuously, being determined by supply and demand (e.g., in auctions).

dynamic Web content Content that must be kept up-to-date.

e-bartering (electronic bartering) Bartering conducted online, usually in a bartering exchange.

e-book A book in digital form that can be read on a computer screen or on a special device.

e-business A broader definition of EC that includes not just the buying and selling of goods and services but also servicing customers, collaborating with business partners, and conducting electronic transactions within an organization.

EC architecture A plan for organizing the underlying infrastructure and applications of a site.

EC security programs All the policies, procedures, documents, standards, hardware, software, training, and personnel that work together to protect information, the ability to conduct business, and other assets.

EC security strategy A strategy that views EC security as the process of preventing and detecting unauthorized use of the organization's brand, identity, Web site, e-mail, information, or other asset and attempts to defraud the organization, its customers, and employees.

EC suite A type of merchant server software that consists of an integrated collection of a large number of EC tools and components that work together for EC applications development.

e-check A legally valid electronic version or representation of a paper check.

e-commerce (EC) risk The likelihood that a negative outcome will occur in the course of developing and operating an electronic commerce strategy.

e-commerce strategy (e-strategy) The formulation and execution of a vision of how a new or existing company intends to do business electronically.

e-co-ops Another name for online group purchasing organizations.

eCRM Customer relationship management conducted electronically.

e-distributor An e-commerce intermediary that connects manufacturers with business buyers (customers) by aggregating the catalogs of many manufacturers in one place—the intermediary's Web site.

edutainment The combination of education and entertainment, often through games.

e-government E-commerce model in which a government entity buys or provides goods, services, or information to businesses or individual citizens.

e-grocer A grocer that takes orders online and provides deliveries on a daily or other regular schedule or within a very short period of time.

elasticity The measure of the incremental spending (demand) by buyers as a result of price changing.

e-learning The online delivery of information for purposes of education, training, or knowledge management.

electronic auction (e-auction) Auction conducted online.

electronic banking (e-banking) Various banking activities conducted from home or the road using an Internet connection; also known as cyberbanking, virtual banking, online banking, and home banking.

electronic bartering (e-bartering) Bartering conducted online, usually by a bartering exchange.

electronic bill presentment and payment (EBPP) Presenting and enabling payment of a bill online. Usually refers to a B2C transaction.

electronic catalog The virtual-world equivalent of a traditional paper catalog of products; contains product descriptions and photos, along with information about various promotions, discounts, payment methods, and methods of delivery.

electronic commerce (EC) The process of buying, selling, or exchanging products, services, or information via computer networks.

electronic data interchange (EDI) The electronic transfer of specially formatted standard business documents, such as bills, orders, and confirmations, sent between business partners.

electronic market (e-marketplace) An online marketplace where buyers and sellers meet to exchange goods, services, money, or information.

Electronic Product Code (EPC) An RFID code that identifies the manufacturer, producer, version, and serial number of individual consumer products.

electronic retailing (e-tailing) Retailing conducted online, over the Internet.

electronic shopping cart An order-processing technology that allows customers to accumulate items they wish to buy while they continue to shop.

electronic signature A generic, technology-neutral term that refers to the various methods by which one can "sign" an electronic record.

electronic voting Voting process that involves many steps ranging from registering, preparing, voting, and counting (voting and counting are all done electronically).

e-logistics The logistics of EC systems, typically involving small parcels sent to many customers' homes (in B2C).

e-loyalty Customer loyalty to an e-tailer or loyalty programs delivered online or supported electronically.

e-mall (online mall) An online shopping center where many online stores are located.

e-marketplace An online market, usually B2B, in which buyers and sellers exchange goods or services; the three types of e-marketplaces are private, public, and consortia.

e-micropayments Small online payments, typically under $10.

emulation A software emulator allows computer programs to run on a platform (computer architecture and/or operating system) other than the one for which they were originally written.

encryption The process of scrambling (encrypting) a message in such a way that it is difficult, expensive, or time-consuming for an unauthorized person to unscramble (decrypt) it.

encryption algorithm The mathematical formula used to encrypt the plaintext into the ciphertext, and vice versa.

e-newsletter A collection of short, informative articles sent at regular intervals by e-mail to individuals who have an interest in the newsletter's topic.

Enhanced Messaging Service (EMS) An extension of SMS that can send simple animation, tiny pictures, sounds, and formatted text.

enterprise application integration (EAI) Class of software that integrates large systems.

enterprise invoice presentment and payment (EIPP) Presenting and paying B2B invoices online.

e-procurement The use of Web-based technology to support the key procurement processes, including requisitioning, sourcing, contracting, ordering, and payment. E-procurement supports the purchase of both direct and indirect materials and employs several Web-based functions such as online catalogs, contracts, purchase orders, and shipping notices.

e-sourcing The process and tools that electronically enable any activity in the sourcing process, such as quotation/tender submittance and response, e-auctions, online negotiations, and spending analyses.

e-supply chain A supply chain that is managed electronically, usually with Web technologies.

e-supply chain management (e-SCM) The collaborative use of technology to improve the operations of supply chain activities as well as the management of supply chains.

e-tailers Retailers who sell over the Internet.

e-tailing Online retailing, usually B2C.

ethics The branch of philosophy that deals with what is considered to be right and wrong.

exchange A public electronic market with many buyers and sellers.

exchanges See public e-marketplaces.

exchanges (trading communities or trading exchanges) Many-to-many e-marketplaces, usually owned and run by a third party or a consortium, in which many buyers and many sellers meet electronically to trade with each other.

exchange-to-exchange (E2E) E-commerce model in which electronic exchanges formally connect to one another for the purpose of exchanging information.

expert location systems Interactive computerized systems that help employees find and connect with colleagues who have expertise required for specific problems—whether they are across the country or across the room—in order to solve specific, critical business problems in seconds.

exposure The estimated cost, loss, or damage that can result if a threat exploits a vulnerability.

Extensible Hypertext Markup Language (xHTML) A general scripting language; compatible with HTML; a standard set by W3 Consortium.

eXtensible Markup Language (XML) An open standard for defining data elements. Like HTML, it uses a set of tags along with content (or values), but unlike HTML, the tags are defined by the Web designer (i.e., there are no fixed tags).

eXtensible Style Language Transformations (XSLT) A special type of style sheet defines how the contents of an XML document are to be displayed.

extranet A network that uses a virtual private network (VPN) to link intranets in different locations over the Internet; an "extended intranet."

e-zines Electronic magazine or newsletter delivered over the Internet via e-mail.

fair use The legal use of copyrighted material for noncommercial purposes without paying royalties or getting permission.

FAQ page A Web page that lists questions that are frequently asked by customers and the answers to those questions.

firewall A single point between two or more networks where all traffic must pass (choke point); the device authenticates, controls, and logs all traffic.

forward auction An auction in which a seller entertains bids from buyers. Bidders increase price sequentially.

frame An HTML element that divides the browser window into two or more separate windows.

fraud Any business activity that uses deceitful practices or devices to deprive another of property or other rights.

front end The portion of an e-seller's business processes through which customers interact, including the seller's portal, electronic catalogs, a shopping cart, a search engine, and a payment gateway.

front-office operations The business processes, such as sales and advertising, that are visible to customers.

geographical information system (GIS) A computer system capable of integrating, storing, editing, analyzing, sharing, and displaying geographically referenced (spatial) information.

global positioning system (GPS) A worldwide satellite-based tracking system that enables users to determine their position anywhere on the earth.

Global System for Mobile Communications (GSM) An open, nonproprietary standard for mobile voice and data communications.

government-to-business (G2B) E-government category that includes interactions between governments and businesses (government selling to businesses and providing them with services and businesses selling products and services to government).

government-to-citizens (G2C) E-government category that includes all the interactions between a government and its citizens.

government-to-employees (G2E) E-government category that includes activities and services between government units and their employees.

government-to-government (G2G) E-government category that includes activities within government units and those between governments.

grid computing A form of distributed computing that involves coordinating and sharing computing, application, data, storage, or network resources across dynamic and geographically dispersed organizations.

group decision support system (GDSS) An interactive computer-based system that facilitates the solution of semistructured and unstructured problems by a group of decision makers.

group purchasing The aggregation of orders from several buyers into volume purchases so that better prices can be negotiated.

groupware Software products that use networks to support collaboration among groups of people who share a common task or goal.

hash A mathematical computation that is applied to a message, using a private key, to encrypt the message.

hit A request for data from a Web page or file.

honeynet A network of honeypots.

honeypot Production system (e.g., firewalls, routers, Web servers, database servers) that looks like it does real work, but which acts as a decoy and is watched to study how network intrusions occur.

horizontal exchange An exchange that handles materials used by companies in different industries.

horizontal marketplaces Markets that concentrate on a service, materials, or a product that is used in all types of industries (e.g., office supplies, PCs).

hotfix Microsoft's name for a patch. Microsoft bundles hotfixes into service packs for easier installation.

hotspot An area or point where a wireless device can make a connection to a wireless local area network (using Wi-Fi).

human firewalls Methods that filter or limit people's access to critical business documents.

hypermediation Extensive use of both human and electronic intermediation to provide assistance in all phases of an e-commerce venture.

Hypertext Markup Language (HTML) The language used to create Web pages.

Hypertext Transport Protocol (HTTP) A lightweight communication protocol that enables Web browsers and Web servers to converse with one another; of its seven commands, GET and POST make up the majority of requests issued by browsers.

incubator A company, university, or nonprofit organization that supports businesses in their initial stages of development.

indirect materials Materials used to support production (e.g., office supplies or light bulbs).

infomediaries Electronic intermediaries that provide and/or control information flow in cyberspace, often aggregating information and selling it to others.

information architecture How the site and its Web pages are organized, labeled, and navigated to support browsing and searching throughout the Web site.

Information assurance (IA) The protection of information systems against unauthorized access to or modification of information whether in storage, processing or transit, and against the denial of service to authorized users, including those measures necessary to detect, document, and counter such threats.

information intelligence Information, data, knowledge, and semantic infrastructure that enable organizations to create more business applications.

information portal A single point of access through a Web browser to business information inside and/or outside an organization.

informational Web site A Web site that does little more than provide information about the business and its products and services.

infringement Use of the work without permission or contracting for payment of a royalty.

insourcing In-house development of applications.

integration testing Testing the combination of application modules acting in concert.

integrity Assurance that stored data have not been modified without authorization and that a message that was sent is the same message that was received.

intellectual property Creations of the mind, such as inventions, literary and artistic works, and symbols, names, images, and designs, used in commerce.

interactive marketing Online marketing, facilitated by the Internet, by which marketers and advertisers can interact directly with customers and consumers can interact with advertisers/vendors.

interactive voice response (IVR) A voice system that enables users to request and receive information and to enter and change data through a telephone to a computerized system.

interactive Web site A Web site that provides opportunities for the customers and the business to communicate and share information.

intermediary A third party that operates between sellers and buyers.

internal procurement marketplace The aggregated catalogs of all approved suppliers combined into a single *internal* electronic catalog.

Internet A public, global communications network that provides direct connectivity to anyone over a LAN via an ISP.

Internet2 The next generation of the Internet; it will create a network for the national research community, enable revolutionary Internet applications, and ensure the rapid transfer of new network services and applications to the broader Internet community.

Internet-based (Web) EDI EDI that runs on the Internet and is widely accessible to most companies, including SMEs.

Internet Corporation for Assigned Names and Numbers (ICANN) Nonprofit organization that manages various technical and policy issues relating to the Internet that require central coordination; it has no regulatory or statutory power.

Internet ecosystem The business model of the Internet economy.

Internet radio A Web site that provides music, talk, and other entertainment, both live and stored, from a variety of radio stations.

Internet service providers (ISPs) Companies that provide Internet delivery subnetworks at the local and regional level.

interoperability Connecting people, data, and diverse systems. The term can be defined in a technical way or in a broad way, taking into account social, political, and organizational factors.

interorganizational information systems (IOSs) Communications systems that allows routine transaction processing and information flow between two or more organizations.

interstitial An initial Web page or a portion of it that is used to capture the user's attention for a short time while other content is loading.

intrabusiness EC E-commerce category that includes all internal organizational activities that involve the exchange of goods, services, or information among various units and individuals in an organization.

intranet A secure internal corporate or government network that uses Internet tools, such as Web browsers, and Internet protocols.

intraorganizational information systems Communication systems that enable e-commerce activities to go on within individual organizations.

intrusion detection systems (IDSs) A special category of software that can monitor activity across a network or on a host computer, watch for suspicious activity, and take automated action based on what it sees.

IP address An address that uniquely identifies each computer connected to a network or the Internet.

IP version 4 (IPv4) The current version of Internet Protocol, under which Internet addresses are 32 bits long and written as four sets of numbers separated by periods.

IP version 6 (IPv6) Version of the Internet Protocol, still in the planning stage, that will replace IPv4 and improve network management.

ISP hosting service A hosting service that provides an independent, stand-alone Web site for small and medium-sized businesses.

Key (key value) The secret code used to encrypt and decrypt a message.

key performance indicators (KPI) The quantitative expression of critically important metrics.

key space The large number of possible key values (keys) created by the algorithm to use when transforming the message.

keyword banners Banner ads that appear when a predetermined word is queried from a search engine.

knowledge management (KM) The process of capturing or creating knowledge, storing it, updating it constantly, interpreting it, and using it whenever necessary.

knowledge portal A single point of access software system intended to provide timely access to information and to support communities of knowledge workers.

latency The time required to complete an operation, such as downloading a Web page.

learning agents Software agents that have the capacity to adapt or modify their behavior (to learn).

legal precedent A judicial decision that may be used as a standard in subsequent similar cases.

letter of credit (LC) A written agreement by a bank to pay the seller, on account of the buyer, a sum of money upon presentation of certain documents.

libel Defamatory statement that is printed or broadcast over the media that causes damage.

localization The process of converting media products developed in one environment (e.g., country) to a form culturally and linguistically acceptable in countries outside the original target market.

location-based commerce (l-commerce) An m-commerce application targeted to a customer whose location, preferences, and needs are known in real time.

location-based m-commerce Delivery of m-commerce transactions to individuals in a specific location, at a specific time.

logistics The operations involved in the efficient and effective flow and storage of goods, services, and related information from point of origin to point of consumption.

macro virus (macro worm) A virus or worm that executes when the application object that contains the macro is opened or a particular procedure is executed.

malware A generic term for malicious software.

market liquidity The degree to which something can be bought or sold in a marketplace without significantly affecting its price. It is determined by the number of buyers and sellers in the market and the transaction volume.

market maker The third party that operates an exchange (and in many cases, also owns the exchange).

market segmentation The process of dividing a consumer market into logical groups for conducting marketing research and analyzing personal information.

marketspace A marketplace in which sellers and buyers exchange goods and services for money (or for other goods and services), but do so electronically.

mash-up Combination of two or more Web sites into a single Web site that provides the content of both sites (whole or partial) to deliver a novel product to consumers.

maverick buying Unplanned purchases of items needed quickly, often at non-prenegotiated higher prices.

m-business The broadest definition of m-commerce, in which e-business is conducted in a wireless environment.

merchant brokering Deciding from whom (from what merchant) to buy a product.

merchant server software Software for selling over the Internet that enables companies to establish selling sites relatively easily and inexpensively.

merge-in-transit Logistics model in which components for a product may come from two (or more) different physical locations and are shipped directly to customer's location.

message digest (MD) A summary of a message, converted into a string of digits, after the hash has been applied.

metric A specific, measurable standard against which actual performance is compared.

microbrowser Wireless Web browser designed to operate with small screens and limited bandwidth and memory requirements.

micropayments Electronic payments for small-purchase amounts (generally less than $10).

middleware Separate products that serve as the glue between two applications; sometimes called *plumbing*, because it connects two sides of an application and passes data between them.

mirror site An exact duplicate of an original Web site that is physically located on a Web server on another continent or in another country.

mobile agents Software agents that can transport themselves across different system architectures and platforms in order to perform their tasks.

mobile commerce (m-commerce, m-business) Any business activity conducted over a wireless telecommunications network, or from mobile devices.

mobile computing Use of portable devices, including smart cell phones, usually in a wireless environment. It permits real-time access to information, applications, and tools that, until recently, were accessible only from a desktop computer.

mobile CRM The delivery of CRM applications to any user, whenever and wherever needed, by use of the wireless infrastructure and mobile devices.

mobile portal A customer interaction channel that aggregates content and services for mobile users.

mobility The degree to which the agents themselves travel through the network.

MRO (maintenance, repair, and operation) Indirect materials used in activities that support production.

multi-agent systems (MASs) Computer systems in which there is no single designer who stands behind all the agents; each agent in the system can be working toward different, even contradictory, goals.

multichannel business model A business model where a company sells in multiple marketing channels simultaneously (e.g., both physical and online stores).

Multimedia Messaging Service (MMS) The emerging generation of wireless messaging; MMS is able to deliver rich media.

multitiered application architecture EC architecture consisting of four tiers: Web browsers, Web servers, application servers, and database servers.

m-wallet (mobile wallet) Technologies that enable cardholders to make purchases with a single click from their wireless device.

name-your-own-price model Auction model in which a would-be buyer specifies the price (and other terms) he or she is willing to pay to any willing and able seller. It is a C2B model that was pioneered by Priceline.com.

native virtualization Leverages hardware-assisted capabilities available in the latest processors to provide near-native performance.

Netizen A citizen surfing the Internet.

network access point (NAP) An intermediate network exchange point that connects ISPs to NSPs.

network service providers (NSPs) Major telecommunications companies, such as MCI and Sprint, that maintain and service the Internet's high-speed backbones.

nonrepudiation Assurance that an online customer or trading partner cannot falsely deny (repudiate) their purchase or transaction.

nontechnical attack An attack that uses chicanery to trick people into revealing sensitive information or performing actions that compromise the security of a network.

on-demand CRM CRM *hosted* by an ASP or other vendor on the vendor's premise; in contrast to the traditional practice of buying the software and using it *on-premise*.

on-demand delivery service Express delivery made fairly quickly after an online order is received.

one-to-one marketing Marketing that treats each customer in a unique way.

online banking See *electronic banking (e-banking)*.

online intermediary An online third party that brokers a transaction online between a buyer and a seller; may be virtual or click-and-mortar.

online negotiation A back-and-forth electronic process of bargaining until the buyer and seller reach a mutually agreeable price; sometimes supported by software (intelligent) agents.

online publishing The electronic delivery of newspapers, magazines, books, news, music, videos, and other digitizable information over the Internet.

ontology A collection of related statements that together specify a variety of relationships among data elements and ways of making logical inferences among them.

Open Profiling Standard (OPS) Standard that provides Internet site developers with a uniform architecture for using Personal Profile information to match personal preferences with tailored content, goods, and services while protecting users' privacy.

opt in Agreement that requires computer users to take specific steps to allow the collection of personal information.

opt out Business practice that gives consumers the opportunity to refuse sharing information about themselves.

order fulfillment All the activities needed to provide customers with their ordered goods and services, including related customer services.

organizational knowledge base The repository for an enterprise's accumulated knowledge.

outsourcing The use of an external vendor to provide all or part of the products and services that could be provided internally.

P2P distributed computation Computer architecture that uses P2P resource sharing to combine idle computer resources over a network, forming a *virtual computer* across which large computational jobs can be distributed.

packet-filtering routers Firewalls that filter data and requests moving from the public Internet to a private network based on the network addresses of the computer sending or receiving the request.

packet filters Rules that can accept or reject incoming packets based on source and destination addresses and the other identifying information.

packets Small segments of messages sent over the Internet; each packet contains both data from and the addresses of the sending and receiving computers.

page A page is an HTML (Hypertext Markup Language) document that may contain text, images, and other online elements, such as Java applets and multimedia files. It may be generated statically or dynamically.

partner relationship management (PRM) Business strategy that focuses on providing comprehensive quality service to business partners.

passive token Storage device (e.g., magnetic strip) that contains a secret code used in a two-factor authentication system.

patch Program that makes needed changes to software that is already installed on a computer. Software companies issue patches to fix bugs in their programs, to address security problems, or to add functionality.

patent A document that grants the holder exclusive rights to an invention for a fixed number of years.

payment card Electronic card that contains information that can be used for payment purposes.

payment service provider (PSP) A third-party service connecting a merchant's EC systems to the appropriate acquirers. PSPs must be registered with the various card associations they support.

peer-to-peer (P2P) Applications that use *direct* communications between computers (peers) to share resources rather than relying on a centralized server as the conduit between client devices.

performance-based government An approach that measures the results of government programs.

permission advertising (permission marketing) Advertising (marketing) strategy in which customers agree to accept advertising and marketing materials (known as "opt-in").

person-to-person lending Lending done between individuals circumventing the bank's traditional role in this process.

personal area network (PAN) A wireless telecommunications network for device-to-device connections within a very short range.

personal digital assistant (PDA) A handheld computer principally used for personal information management.

personal firewall A network node designed to protect an individual user's desktop system from the public network by monitoring all the traffic that passes through the computer's network interface card.

personalization The matching of services, products, and advertising content with individual consumers and their preferences.

personalized content Web content that matches the needs and expectations of the individual visitor.

pervasive computing Invisible, everywhere computing that is embedded in the objects around us.

phishing A crimeware technique to steal the identity of a target company to get the identities of its customers.

plaintext An unencrypted message in human-readable form.

podcast A media file that is distributed over the Internet using syndication feeds for playback on mobile devices and personal computers. As with the term *radio*, it can mean both the content and the method of syndication.

podcaster The host or author of a podcast.

policy of least privilege (POLP) Policy of blocking access to network resources unless access is required to conduct business.

policy-based resource-management tools Automate and standardize all types of IT management best practices, from initial configuration to ongoing fault management and asset tracking.

policy-based service-level-management tools Coordinate, monitor, and report on the ways in which multiple infrastructure components come together to deliver a business service.

pop-under ad An ad that appears underneath the current browser window, so when the user closes the active window the ad is still on the screen.

pop-up ad An ad that appears in a separate window before, after, or during Internet surfing or when reading e-mail.

pretexting Impersonating someone else to gain access to information that is restricted.

prevention measures Ways to help stop unauthorized users (also known as "intruders") from accessing any part of the EC system.

privacy The right to be left alone and free of unreasonable personal intrusions.

private e-marketplaces Markets in which the individual sell-side or buy-side company has complete control over participation in the selling or buying transaction.

private key Encryption code that is known only to its owner.

private marketplaces E-marketplaces that are owned and operated by one company. Also known as *company-centric marketplaces.*

procurement The process made up of a range of activities by which an organization obtains or gains access to the resources (materials, skills, capabilities, facilities) they require to undertake their core business activities.

procurement management The planning, organizing, and coordination of all the activities relating to purchasing goods and services needed to accomplish the mission of an organization.

product brokering Deciding what product to buy.

product differentiation Special features available in products that make them distinguishable from other products. This property attracts customers that appreciate what they consider an added value.

product lifecycle management (PLM) Business strategy that enables manufacturers to control and share product-related data as part of product design and development efforts.

production function An equation indicating that for the same quantity of production, Q, companies either can use a certain amount of labor or invest in more automation.

project champion The person who ensures the EC project gets the time, attention, and resources required and defends the project from detractors at all times.

protected interests Interests, such as life, liberty, and property, that a constitution protects.

protocol A set of rules that determine how two computers communicate with one another over a network.

protocol tunneling Method used to ensure confidentiality and integrity of data transmitted over the Internet, by encrypting data packets, sending them in packets across the Internet, and decrypting them at the destination address.

proxies Special software programs that run on the gateway server and pass repackaged packets from one network to the other.

proxy bidding Use of a software system to place bids on behalf of buyers; when another bidder places a bid, the software (the proxy) will automatically raise the bid to the next level until it reaches the predetermined maximum price.

public (asymmetric) key encryption Method of encryption that uses a pair of matched keys—a public key to encrypt a message and a private key to decrypt it, or vice versa.

public e-marketplace (exchange) A many-to-many e-marketplace. Trading venues open to all interested parties (sellers and buyers); usually run by third parties. Some are also known as *trading exchanges.*

public key Encryption code that is publicly available to anyone.

public key infrastructure (PKI) A scheme for securing e-payments using public key encryption and various technical components.

purchasing cards (p-cards) Special-purpose payment cards issued to a company's employees to be used solely for purchasing nonstrategic materials and services up to a preset dollar limit.

radio frequency identification (RFID) Tags that can be attached to or embedded in objects, animals, or humans and use radio waves to communicate with a reader for the purpose of uniquely identifying the object or transmitting data and/or storing information about the object.

random banners Banner ads that appear at random, not as the result of the user's action.

Really Simple Syndication (RSS) A family of Web-feed formats used to publish frequently updated digital content.

Real-Time Protocol (RTP) Streaming protocol that adds header information to the UDP packets, thus enabling the synchronized timing, sequencing, and decoding of the packets at the destination.

Real-Time Streaming Protocol (RTSP) Streaming protocol that adds controls for stopping, pausing, rewinding, and fast-forwarding the media stream; it also provides security and enables usage measurement and rights management.

recommendation systems Intelligent agents that provide recommendation services.

reintermediation The process whereby intermediaries (either new ones or those that had been disintermediated) take on new intermediary roles.

Representational State Transfer (REST) Refers to a collection of *architectural* principles.

request for proposal (RFP) Notice sent to potential vendors inviting them to submit a proposal describing their software package and how it would meet the company's needs.

request for quote (RFQ) The "invitation" to participate in a tendering (bidding) system.

resident agents Software agents that stay in the computer or system and perform their tasks there.

reusability The likelihood a segment of source code can be used again to add new functionalities with slight or no modification.

revenue model Description of how the company or an EC project will earn revenue.

reverse auction (bidding or tendering system) Auction in which the buyer places an item for bid (*tender*) on a request for quote (RFQ) system, potential suppliers bid on the job, with the price reducing sequentially, and the lowest bid wins; primarily a B2B or G2B mechanism.

reverse logistics The movement of returns from customers to vendors.

right Legal claim that others not interfere with an individual's or organization's protected interest.

Rijndael An Advanced Encryption Standard (AES) used to secure U.S. government communications since October 2, 2000.

risk The probability that a vulnerability will be known and used.

ROI calculator Calculator that uses metrics and formulas to compute ROI.

rolling warehouse Logistics method in which products on the delivery truck are not preassigned to a destination, but the decision about the quantity to unload at each destination is made at the time of unloading.

rootkit A special Trojan horse program that modifies existing operating system software so that an intruder can hide the presence of the Trojan program.

routers Special computers that determine the paths traversed by data packets across the Internet.

RSA The most common public key encryption algorithm; uses keys ranging in length from 512 bits to 1,024 bits.

RSS An XML format for syndicating news and other Web content, such as blogs and wikis.

RSS Reader Client software that enables an end user to subscribe to various syndicated Web, blog, or wiki sites and to organize the presentation of the feeds coming from those sites.

RuBee Bidirectional, on-demand, peer-to-peer radiating transceiver protocol under development by Institute of Electrical and Electronics Engineers.

sales force automation (SFA) Software that automates the tasks performed by salespeople in the field, such as data collection and its transmission.

sales force mobilization The process of equipping sales force employees with wireless Internet-enabled computing devices.

scalability How big a system can grow in various dimensions to provide more service; measured by total number of users, number of simultaneous users, or transaction volume.

scenario planning A strategic planning methodology that generates plausible alternative futures to help decision makers identify actions that can be taken today to ensure success in the future.

screen-sharing software Software that enables group members, even in different locations, to work on the same document, which is shown on the PC screen of each participant.

sealed-bid auction Auction in which each bidder bids only once; a silent auction, in which bidders do not know who is placing bids or what the bid prices are.

search engine A document retrieval system designed to help find information stored on a computer system, such as on the Web, inside corporate proprietary files, or in a personal computer.

search engine optimization (SEO) The application of strategies intended to position a Web site at the top of Web search engines.

search engine marketing (SEM) Marketing methods to increase the ranking of a Web site in the search results.

search engine spam Pages created deliberately to trick the search engine into offering inappropriate, redundant, or poor-quality search results.

search engine spamming Collective term referring to deceptive online advertising practices.

Secure Socket Layer (SSL) Protocol that utilizes standard certificates for authentication and data encryption to ensure privacy or confidentiality.

security protocol A communication protocol that encrypts and decrypts a message for online transmission; security protocols generally provide authentication.

self-hosting When a business acquires the hardware, software, staff, and dedicated telecommunications services necessary to set up and manage its own Web site.

sell-side e-marketplace A Web-based marketplace in which one company sells to many business buyers from e-catalogs or auctions, frequently over an extranet.

semantic Web An evolving extension of the web in which web content can be expressed not only in natural language but also in a form that can be understood, interpreted, and used by intelligent computer software agents, permitting them to find, share, and integrate information more easily.

semantic Web Services A combination of semantic Web and Web Services.

sensor network A series of interconnected sensors that monitor the environment in which they are placed.

service pack The means by which product updates are distributed. Service packs may contain updates for system reliability, program compatibility, security, and more.

service-level agreement (SLA) A formal agreement regarding the division of work between a company and a vendor.

service-oriented architecture (SOA) An application architecture in which executable components, such as Web Services, can be invoked and executed by client programs based on business rules.

settlement Transferring money from the buyer's to the merchant's account.

shilling Placing fake bids on auction items to artificially jack up the bidding price.

shopping portals Gateways to e-storefronts and e-malls; may be comprehensive or niche oriented.

shopping robots (shopping agents or shopbots) Tools that scout the Web on behalf of consumers who specify search criteria.

Short Message Service (SMS) A service that supports the sending and receiving of short text messages on mobile phones.

signature file A simple text message an e-mail program automatically adds to outgoing messages.

simple agents Software agents that work within the context of a single application and focus on a single set of tasks with a circumscribed set of outcomes.

Simple Object Access Protocol (SOAP) Protocol or message framework for exchanging XML data across the Internet.

simulation Attempts to gather a great deal of runtime information as well as reproducing a program's behavior.

single auction Auction in which at least one side of the market consists of a single entity (a single buyer or a single seller).

site navigation Aids that help visitors find the information they need quickly and easily.

slander Oral or spoken defamatory statement that causes damage.

smart card An electronic card containing an embedded microchip that enables predefined operations or the addition, deletion, or manipulation of information on the card.

smart card operating system Special system that handles file management, security, input/output (I/O), and command execution and provides an application programming interface (API) for a smart card.

smart card reader Activates and reads the contents of the chip on a smart card, usually passing the information on to a host system.

smartphone Internet-enabled cell phone that can support mobile applications.

SMEs Small-to-medium enterprises.

sniping Entering a bid during the very last seconds of an auction and outbidding the highest bidder (in the case of selling items).

social bookmarking Web service for sharing Internet bookmarks. The sites are a popular way to store, classify, share, and search links through the practice of folksonomy techniques on the Internet and intranets.

social computing An approach aimed at making the human–computer interface more natural.

social engineering A type of nontechnical attack that uses some ruse to trick users into revealing information or performing an action that compromises a computer or network.

social marketplace The term *social marketplace* is derived from the combination of social networking and marketplaces, such that a social marketplace acts like an online community harnessing the power of one's social networks for the introduction, buying, and selling of products, services, and resources, including people's own creations. A social marketplace can also be referred to as a structure that resembles a social network but has a focus on its individual members.

social media The online platforms and tools that people use to share opinions and experiences, including photos, videos, music, insights, and perceptions with each other.

social network A social network is a category of Internet applications that help connect friends, business partners, or other individuals with specified interests by providing free services such as photos presentation, e-mail, blogging, etc., using a variety of tools.

social networking analysis (SNA) The mapping and measuring of relationships and flows between people, groups, organizations, animals, computers or other information or knowledge processing entities. The nodes in the network are the people and groups, whereas the links show relationships or flows between the nodes. SNA provides both a visual and a mathematical analysis of human relationships.

software (intelligent) agents Software programs that continuously perform three functions: they perceive dynamic conditions in the environment; they take action to affect conditions in the environment; and they use reasoning to interpret perceptions, solve problems, draw inferences, and determine actions.

software as a service (SaaS) A model of *software delivery* where the software company provides maintenance, daily technical operation, and support for the software provided to their client. SaaS is a model of software delivery rather than a market segment.

spam site Page that uses techniques that deliberately subvert a search engine's algorithms to artificially inflate the page's rankings.

spamming Using e-mail to send unwanted ads (sometimes floods of ads).

splog Short for *spam blog*. A site created solely for marketing purposes.

spot buying The purchase of goods and services as they are needed, usually at prevailing market prices.

spy-phishing A blended threat that uses the phishing technique with spyware programs to target online banks and other password-driven sites.

spyware Software that gathers user information over an Internet connection without the user's knowledge.

SpywareGuide A public reference site for spyware.

standard of due care Care that a company is reasonably expected to take based on the risks affecting its EC business and online transactions.

statutes Rules that define criminal laws.

stickiness Characteristic that influences the average length of time a visitor stays in a site.

storebuilder service A hosting service that provides disk space and services to help small and microbusinesses build a Web site quickly and cheaply.

stored-value card A card that has monetary value loaded onto it and that is usually rechargeable.

storefront A single company's Web site where products or services are sold.

strategic (systematic) sourcing Purchases involving long-term contracts that usually are based on private negotiations between sellers and buyers.

strategic information systems planning (SISP) A process for developing a strategy and plans for aligning information systems (including e-commerce applications) with the business strategies of an organization.

strategy A broad-based formula for how a business is going to accomplish its mission, what its goals should be, and what plans and policies will be needed to carry out those goals.

strategy assessment The continuous evaluation of progress toward the organization's strategic goals, resulting in corrective action and, if necessary, strategy reformulation.

strategy formulation The development of strategies to exploit opportunities and manage threats in the business environment in light of corporate strengths and weaknesses.

strategy implementation The development of detailed, short-term plans for carrying out the projects agreed on in strategy formulation.

strategy initiation The initial phase of strategic planning in which the organization examines itself and its environment.

streaming The delivery of content in real time; consists of two types, *on demand* (HTTP streaming) and *live* (true streaming).

subscriber identification module (SIM) card An extractable storage card used for identification, customer location information, transaction processing, secure communications, and the like.

supplier relationship management (SRM) A comprehensive approach to managing an enterprise's interactions with the organizations that supply the goods and services it uses.

supply chain The flow of materials, information, money, and services from raw material suppliers through factories and warehouses to the end customers.

supply chain management (SCM) A complex process that requires the coordination of many activities so that the shipment of goods and services from supplier right through to customer is done efficiently and effectively for all parties concerned. SCM aims to minimize inventory levels, optimize production and increase throughput,

decrease manufacturing time, optimize logistics and distribution, streamline order fulfillment, and overall reduce the costs associated with these activities.

SWOT analysis A methodology that surveys external opportunities and threats and relates them to internal strengths and weaknesses.

symmetric (private) key system An encryption system that uses the same key to encrypt and decrypt the message.

synchronization The exchange of updated information with other computing devices.

syndication The sale of the same good (e.g., digital content) to many customers, who then integrate it with other offerings and resell it or give it away free.

technical attack An attack perpetrated using software and systems knowledge or expertise.

teleconferencing The use of electronic communication that allows two or more people at different locations to have a simultaneous conference.

telematics The integration of computers and wireless communications to improve information flow using the principles of telemetry.

telewebs Call centers that combine Web channels with portal-like self-service.

tendering (bidding) system Model in which a buyer requests would-be sellers to submit bids; the lowest bidder wins.

third-party logistics suppliers (3PL) External, rather than in-house, providers of logistics services.

throughput The number of operations completed in a given period of time; indicates the number of users that a system can handle.

time-to-exploitation The elapsed time between when a vulnerability is discovered and the time it is exploited.

tort Civil wrong that can be grounds for a lawsuit.

total benefits of ownership (TBO) Benefits of ownership that include both tangible and the intangible benefits.

total cost of ownership (TCO) A formula for calculating the cost of owning, operating, and controlling an IT system.

trackback An acknowledgment or signal from an originating site to a receiving site.

trademark A symbol used by businesses to identify their goods and services; government registration of the trademark confers exclusive legal right to its use.

transaction costs Costs that are associated with the distribution (sale) or exchange of products and services including the cost of searching for buyers and sellers, gathering information, negotiating, decision making, monitoring the exchange of goods, and legal fees.

transaction log A record of user activities at a company's Web site.

transactional Web site A Web site that sells products and services.

Transmission Control Protocol/Internet Protocol (TCP/IP) Two combined protocols that together solve the problem of global internetworking by ensuring that two computers can communicate with each other reliably; each TCP communication must be acknowledged as received, or the sending computer will retransmit the message.

Transport Layer Security (TLS) As of 1996, another name for the SSL protocol.

Trojan horse A program that appears to have a useful function but that contains a hidden function that presents a security risk.

Trojan-Phisher-Rebery A new variant of a Trojan program that stole tens of thousands of identities from 125 countries that the victims believed were collected by a legitimate company.

trust The psychological status of willingness to depend on another person or organization.

turnkey approach *Ready* to use without further *assembly* or *test*ing; *supplied* in a *state* that is ready to *turn on* and *operate*.

Uniform Resource Locator (URL) The addressing scheme used to locate documents on the Web.

unique visits A count of the number of visitors entering a site, regardless of how many pages are viewed per visit.

unit testing Testing application software modules one at a time.

Universal Description, Discovery, and Integration (UDDI) An XML framework for businesses to publish and find Web Services online.

universal man-in-the-middle phishing kit A tool used by phishers to set up a URL that can interact in real-time with the content of a legitimate Web site, such as a bank or EC site, to intercept data entered by customers at log-in or check out Web pages.

up-selling Offering an upgraded version of the product in order to boost sales and profit.

usability (of Web site) The quality of the user's experience when interacting with the Web site.

usability testing Testing the quality of the user's experience when interacting with a Web site.

User Datagram Protocol (UDP) Transport protocol used in place of TCP by streaming servers.

user profile The requirements, preferences, behaviors, and demographic traits of a particular customer.

utility (on-demand) computing Unlimited computing power and storage capacity that can be used and reallocated for any application—and billed on a pay-per-use basis.

valuation The fair market value of a business or the price at which a property would change hands between a willing buyer and a willing seller who are both informed and under no compulsion to act. For a publicly traded company, the value can be readily obtained by multiplying the selling price of the stock by the number of available shares.

value proposition The benefit that a company's products or services provide to a company and its customers.

value-added networks (VANs) Private, third-party-managed networks that add communications services and security to existing common carriers; used to implement traditional EDI systems.

vendor-managed inventory (VMI) The practice of retailers making suppliers responsible for determining when to order and how much to order.

venture capital (VC) Money invested in a business by an individual, a group of individuals (venture capitalists), or a funding company in exchange for equity in the business.

versioning Selling the same good, but with different selection and delivery characteristics.

vertical auction Auction that takes place between sellers and buyers in one industry or for one commodity.

vertical exchange An exchange whose members are in one industry or industry segment. It trades only in materials/services unique for that industry.

vertical marketplaces Markets that deal with one industry or industry segment (e.g., steel, chemicals).

Vickrey auction Auction in which the highest bidder wins but pays only the second-highest bid.

video teleconference Virtual meeting in which participants in one location can see participants at other locations on a large screen or a desktop computer.

viral marketing Word-of-mouth marketing by which customers promote a product or service by telling others about it.

viral video Video clip that gains widespread popularity through the process of Internet sharing, typically through e-mail or IM messages, blogs, and other media-sharing Web sites.

virtual (Internet) community A group of people with similar interests who interact with one another using the Internet.

virtual corporation (VC) An organization composed of several business partners sharing costs and resources for the production or utilization of a product or service.

virtual credit card An e-payment system in which a credit card issuer gives a special transaction number that can be used online in place of regular credit card numbers.

virtual (pure-play) e-tailers Firms that sell directly to consumers over the Internet without maintaining a physical sales channel.

virtual meetings Online meetings whose members are in different locations, even in different countries.

virtual (pure-play) organizations Organizations that conduct their business activities solely online.

virtual private network (VPN) A network that creates tunnels of secured data flows, using cryptography and authorization algorithms, to provide secure transport of private communications over the public Internet.

virtual university An online university from which students take classes from home or other off-site locations, usually via the Internet.

virtualization A technique for hiding the physical characteristics of computing resources from the way in which other systems, applications, or end users interact with those resources.

virus A piece of software code that inserts itself into a host, including the operating systems, in order to propagate; it requires that its host program be run to activate it.

visit A series of requests during one navigation of a Web site; a pause of a certain length of time ends a visit.

voice commerce (v-commerce) An umbrella term for the use of speech recognition to allow voice activated services including Internet browsing and e-mail retrieval.

voice portal A Web site with an audio interface that can be accessed through a telephone call.

voice XML (VXML) An extension of XML designed to accommodate voice.

Voice-over-IP (VoIP) Communication systems that transmit voice calls over Internet Protocol–based networks.

vortals B2B portals that focus on a single industry or industry segment; "vertical portals."

vulnerability Weakness in software or other mechanism that threatens the confidentiality, integrity, or availability of an asset (recall the CIA model). It can be directly used by a hacker to gain access to a system or network.

warehouse management system (WMS) A software system that helps in managing warehouses.

wearable devices Mobile wireless computing devices, attached to various parts of employees, for employees who work on buildings and other climbable workplaces.

Web 2.0 The second-generation of Internet-based services that let people collaborate and create information online in perceived new ways—such as social networking sites, wikis, communication tools, and folksonomies.

Web analytics The analysis of click-stream data to understand visitor behavior on a Web site.

Web bugs Tiny graphics files embedded in e-mail messages and in Web sites that transmit information about users and their movements to a Web server.

Web hosting service A dedicated Web site hosting company that offers a wide range of hosting services and functionality to businesses of all sizes.

Web mining Data mining techniques for discovering and extracting information from Web documents. Web mining explores both *Web content* and *Web usage*.

Web self-service Activities conducted by users on the Web to find answers to their questions (e.g., tracking) or for product configuration.

Web Services An architecture enabling assembly of distributed applications from software services and tying them together.

Web Services Description Language (WSDL) An XML document that defines the programmatic interface—operations, methods, and parameters—for Web Services.

Web syndication A form of syndication in which a section of a Web site is made available for other sites to use.

Webcasting A free Internet news service that broadcasts personalized news and information, including seminars, in categories selected by the user.

Webinars Seminars on the Web (Web-based seminars).

Weblogging (blogging) Technology for personal publishing on the Internet.

Web-oriented architecture (WOA) A set of Web protocols (e.g., HTTP and plain XML) as the most dynamic, scalable, and interoperable Web Service approach.

Wi-Fi (wireless fidelity) The common name used to describe the IEEE 802.11 standard used on most WLANs.

wiki A Web site that enables visitors to add, remove, edit, and change content without the need for registration.

wikilog (wikiblog or wiki) A blog that allows everyone to participate as a peer; anyone may add, delete, or change content.

WiMax A wireless standard (IEEE 802.16) for making broadband network connections over a medium-sized area such as a city.

wireless 911 (e-911) In the United States, emergency response system that processes calls from cellular phones.

wireless access point An antenna that connects a mobile device to a wired LAN.

Wireless Application Protocol (WAP) A suite of network protocols designed to enable different kinds of wireless devices to access WAP-readable files on an Internet-connected Web server.

wireless local area network (WLAN) A telecommunications network that enables users to make short-range wireless connections to the Internet or another network.

Wireless Markup Language (WML) A scripting language used to create content in the WAP environment; based on XML, minus unnecessary content to increase speed.

wireless metropolitan area network (WMAN) A telecommunications network that enables users to make medium-range wireless connections to the Internet or another network.

wireless mobile computing (mobile computing)
Computing that connects a mobile device to a network or another computing device, anytime, anywhere.

wireless wide area network (WWAN) A telecommunications network that offers wireless coverage over a large geographical area, typically over a cellular phone network.

workflow The movement of information as it flows through the sequence of steps that make up an organization's work procedures.

workflow management The automation of workflows so that documents, information, and tasks are passed from one participant to the next in the steps of an organization's business process.

workflow systems Business process automation tools that place system controls in the hands of user departments to automate information-processing tasks.

worm A software program that runs independently, consuming the resources of its host in order to maintain itself, that is capable of propagating a complete working version of itself onto another machine.

XBRL A version of XML for capturing financial information throughout a business' information processes. XBRL makes it possible to format reports that need to be distributed to shareholders, SOX regulators, banks, and other parties. The goal of XBRL is to make the analysis and exchange of corporate information more reliable (trustworthy) and easier to facilitate.

XML (eXtensible Markup Language) Standard (and its variants) used to improve compatibility between the disparate systems of business partners by defining the meaning of data in business documents.

zero-day incidents Attacks through previously unknown weaknesses in computer networks.

zombies Computers infected with malware that are under the control of a spammer, hacker, or other criminal.

Index

Bounty, 52
BountyQuest, 52
Bowen, Peter, 828
BP Australia Ltd., 602
Brand Advocacy Insights, 175
Brandeis, Louis D., 784
Brand images, establishing, 73
Branding, 138, 185
Break-even analysis, 695
Brick-and-mortar company, 5, 102–103
   defined, 102
   vs. digital enterprise, 30, 30E1.11
Bristol-Myers Squibb, 242, 313
British Airways (BA), 2, 106, 107, 185, 529
British Bankers' Association, 120
British Telecommunications, 904
Broadband (cable and DSL) services, 458
BroadVision, 57, 195, 618
Brochureware sites, 139
Broker, 52
BrownCo, 117
B2bcommunities.com, 179
B2bmarketingtrends.com, 180
B2BToday.com, 625
B2Business.net, 625
Buena Vista Internet Group, 796
Buffett, Warren, 60
Build-to-market concept, 87
Build-to-order production (pull system)
   defined, 77–78, 87
   vs. push systems, 87, 88E2A.1
Build-your-own (BYO) decision book, 388
Bullwhip effect, 313
Bundle trading, 486
Burger King, 87
Burton, 444
Business case, 647–648, 732
   template, 733
Business environment, 16–17
   impact model, 17, 17E1.5
   organizational response strategies, 18
      innovative, 18, 19E1.8
   pressures of, major, 18, 18E1.6
Business impact analysis (BIA), 521
Business intelligence, 178
Business law, 12
Business models, 18–19
   atomic, 19–20
   vs. business plans, 19
   competition between, 69
   comprehensive, elements of, 20
   defined, 18
   for e-tailing, 99
      classification by distribution channel, 99–103
      special, in B2C, 103–105, 104E3.4
   functions of, 22
   structures of, 19–20
   types of, major, 22–24
   value proposition and, 20, 21–22
Business networks
   defined, 829
   entrepreneurial networks, 830
   LinkedIn, 829–830
Business-oriented networks, 27, 29
   revenue models of, 29
   Xing.com, 29
Business plan
   business case, 647–648
   defined, 645–646, 731
   fundamentals of, 646–647
   outline of, 646E14.3

Business Plan Archive, 12
Business Plan Pro 2007, 732
Business pressures
   magnitude of, evaluating, 34
   major, 18, 18E1.6
Business process management (BPM), 736–737
Business process reengineering (BPR), 662
Business rating sites, 133
Business Review Weekly of Australia, 288
Business-to-business (B2B), 2, 6, 8, 34
   attractive nature of, reasons for, 34
   defined, 8
   e-auctions in, 59–61, 80, 475
      forward auctions, 230–232
      reverse, 61
   electronic payment systems in, 572–576, 576E12.7
   integration of, research topics on, 81
   many-to-many models of, comparing, 280E6.9
   m-commerce and supply chain management, 443
   online transactions in, 6
   orderfulfillment in, 602–605, 603E13.4
   P2P networks in, 404–405
   see also Internet marketing in B2B
Business-to-business electronic exchanges
   advantages of, 266
   ChemConnect and, 261–262
   classification of, 263–264, 263E6.2
   directory services and search engines in, 270, 271E6.5
   dynamic pricing in, 264–265
   dynamic trading in, 279
   in e-marketplaces, building, 282
   functions of, 265
   gains and risks in, 267E6.4
   governance and organization of, 266
   iMarketKorea (iMK), 298–299, 299E6.12
   implementation issues, 285
      in disintermediation and reintermediation, 290
      private marketplaces *vs.* public exchanges, 288–289
      in software agents, 288–290
   information in, flow and access to, 263E6.1
   integration issues and solutions, 282–283
   limitations of, 266
   managing, 291
      B2B marketplaces, new directions for, 292–294
      centralized, 291
      evaluation, 291
      issues in, 294–295
      success factors, critical, 291–292, 293
   networks, implementing, 283–284
      company-centered (private), 284
      public industrywide (vertical), 284, 286–287
      transindustry and global, 284–285, 285E6.11
   overview of, 262
   ownership of, 265–266
   partner relationship management (PRM) in e-communities, 280–281
      e-communities, 281–282
   revenue model of, 266–268

   services in, 267E6.3
   supplier relationship management (SRM) in, 281, 281E6.10
   third wave of, 292–294
   see also Consortium trading exchanges (CTEs); Third party exchanges
Business-to-business (B2B) e-marketplaces and services, 217, 254
   benefits and limitations of, 224
   B2B2C, 221
   characteristics of, 221–222, 223
   concepts of, basic, 219
   direct sales, 226–230
   General Motors' initiative, 218
   generations of, 220E5.1
   infrastructure for, 248–249
   integration of systems involved in, 249–250
      with business partners, 249–250
      competing approaches to, 250
      internal, 249, 250
      standards in, role of, 250–251
   market size and content of, 219
   new directions for, 292–294
   sell-side models and activities, 225–226, 225E5.3
   software agents in, role of, 251
   supply chain relationships in, 222–223
   trade, direction of, 222
   traded materials, types of, 222
   transactions and activities, basic types of, 219, 220E5.1–2, 222
   types of, 219, 220E5.2, 221
   virtual service industries in, 223–224
   Whirlpool B2B trading portal, 228
Business-to-business portals
   Alibaba.com, 269–270
   defined, 268
   Thomas Global, 269
Business-to-business (B2B) tasks, automating, 246
   contract management and, 246
   e-procurement management and, 248
   Ozro Negotiate and, 247
   sourcing management and negotiation, 246–247
   spend management and, 246
Business-to-business-to-consumer (B2B2C), 8, 9, 221
Business-to-consumer (B2C), 2, 6, 8, 12, 13
   electronic retailing in, size and growth of, 93–94
   in Japan (mobile), 97
   P2P networks in, 405
   special services, representative, 103–104, 104E3.4
   trends in, 97
Business-to-employees (B2E), 9, 13
Business-to-exchange (B2X), 284
Business-to-mobile employees (B2ME), 9
BusinessTown, 181
Business 2.0, 811–812, 851
Butterfields, 500
Button, 183
Buy4Now.com, 128
Buy.com, 5, 47, 68
Buyer aggregation model, 272, 273, 274E6.7
Buyer-concentrated markets, 274
Buyers, in e-marketplace, 51
Buyersbag.com, 83
Buyers' cart ("b-cart"), 58

U

X

Y